UK Wholesalers of Beers, Wines and Spirits

Profiles of the leading 4500 companies

John D Blackburn

Editor

dp

First Edition

Spring 2019

ISBN-13: 978-1-912736-15-7

ISBN-10: 1-912736-15-2

All rights reserved. No part of this publication may be reproduced, distributed, or transmitted in any form or by any means, including photocopying, recording, or other electronic or mechanical methods, without our prior written permission, except in the case of brief quotations embodied in critical reviews and certain other non-commercial uses permitted by copyright law. For permission requests, please write to us.

Copyright © 2019 Dellam Publishing Limited

Printed in 8pt Nimbus Sans L

Designed by URW++ Design and Development GmbH

Dellam Publishing Limited

2 Heath Drive, Sutton, Surrey, SM2 5RP

Fax: 020 8770 7478   email: enquiries@dellam.com

SAN: 0177881   EAN/GLN: 5030670177882

Table of Contents

1 Acknowledgements iv

2 Introduction v

3 Total Assets League Table 1
- As a measure of size, total assets is preferable to turnover which is influenced by profit margins and whether companies are capital or labour intensive.

4 Age of Companies 25
- Each company is ranked by its date of incorporation. Newcomers are defined as those registered since 2017.

5 Geographic Distribution 49
- Each company is classed by county.

6 Company Profiles 73
- Full company name, date incorporated, net worth, total assets, registered office, activities, shareholders and parent company, directors (with date of birth, nationality and occupation) and number of employees (if available).

7 Index of Directorships 351
- Alphabetical list of directors showing their directorships. If several directors have identical names then their date of birth is shown.

8 Standard Industrial Classification 447
- These codes are used to classify businesses by the type of economic activity in which they are engaged.

9 *finis* 464

Acknowledgements

This is a long and detailed publication containing thousands of facts and figures. It is only to be expected, despite continuous and repeated editing and checking, that errors may occur. In such cases, once we are aware of any, we publish a correction on our website.

Readers are encouraged to check regularly at www.dellam.com/books for any corrections and updates.

Although we take extreme care to ensure accuracy and being up-to-date, we cannot accept responsibility for any errors or omissions.

Contains public sector information licensed under Open Government Licence v3.0. from The Charity Commission (England and Wales) and The Charity Commission for Northern Ireland. © Crown Copyright and database right (2018).

Contains information from the Scottish Charity Register supplied by the Office of the Scottish Charity Regulator and licensed under the Open Government Licence v.2.0. © Crown Copyright and database right (2018).

Contains OS data © Crown copyright and database right (2018)

Contains Royal Mail data © Royal Mail copyright and database right (2018)

Contains National Statistics data © Crown copyright and database right (2018)

Contains Office for National Statistics © Crown copyright and database right (2018)

Maps based on those produced by the Office for National Statistics Geography GIS & Mapping Unit (2012 and 2018).

Contains HM Land Registry data © Crown copyright and database right (2018).

Contains Parliamentary information licensed under the Open Parliament Licence v3.0.

House of Commons Library Briefing Papers licensed under the Open Parliament Licence v3.0.

Contains Food Standards Agency data © Crown copyright and database right (2018).

Contains Eurostat data, 1995-2018, copyright European Commission by the Decision of 12 December 2011.

Maps based on produced by ONS Geography GIS & Mapping Unit.

Contains Companies House data supplied under section 47 and 50 of the Copyright, Designs and Patents Act 1988 and Schedule 1 of the Database Regulations (SI 1997/3032).

We appreciate your interest in our publications, and your comments and suggestions are always welcome. Please contact us at enquiries@dellam.com.

Introduction

This study looks at all companies registered in the United Kingdom where they identify themselves as wholesalers of wine, beer, spirits and other alcoholic beverages.

This study includes companies that are dormant or non-trading some of which might be latent while others may operate under their owners' names but are incorporated to protect the business name. In addition, all newly incorporated companies are included. The study will exclude those companies that do not specifically identify themselves as wholesalers of wine, beer, spirits and other alcoholic beverages.

The aim of this study is to provide an overview of the key movers and shakers in the UK wholesale market in wine, beer, spirits and other alcoholic beverages. Only key data has been isolated, particularly the company's net worth and total assets, but also its full name, date incorporated, registered office, other activities, shareholders, directors (with date of birth, occupation and nationality) and number of employees.

In the years 2016, 2017 and 2018, new company incorporations in the alcohol wholesale sector were 353, 583 and 1,069 respectively.

Two indicators of size are used: net worth and total assets. These are preferable to turnover which is influenced by profit margins and whether the companies are capital or labour intensive.

In Great Britain, 57% of those aged 16 years and over in 2017 drank alcohol (29 million people of the population) while 20% did not drink alcohol at all.

Breakdown of beverages in the UK is as follows: soft drinks (28%), beer (27%), whisky (25%), cider (7%), gin (3%), mineral water (3%) and others (2%).

The top two wholesalers, Matthew Clark and Diageo's distribution arm, account for 11% of the market. Distributors and wholesalers can be alcohol-focused specialists, such as Matthew Clark, which focuses on pubs; or general suppliers, such as Palmer & Harvey PLC, which collapsed in November 2017, that serve supermarkets.

The Federation of Wholesale Distributors (FWD) is the trade association for food and drink wholesalers in the UK. According to the FWD, the sector spent a total of £24 billion on their suppliers with alcoholic drinks accounting for £1.9 billion and non-alcoholic drinks £2.2 billion. With an annual turnover of £30 billion and 60,000 employees, the sector supports over 400,000 retail and catering businesses.

The sector suppies 81,000+ outlets in retail, travel and leisure worth £3 billion; 165,000+ hotels, pubs and restaurants worth £5 billion; 116,000+ outlets in the contract sector worth £4 billion. The sector generated £830 million in taxes in 2016. This included £300 million in value added tax, £170 million in employers' NI contributions, £150 million in business rates and £70 million in corporation tax.

More than 11,000 pubs have closed in the UK in the last decade, a fall of almost a quarter (23%). The number of UK pubs has fallen from around 50,000 in 2008 to some 39,000 in 2018.

Standard cataloguing guidelines for company names in the profile section have been used, but there will be occurrences when the name may not be strictly alphabetical. A certain licence was adopted where it was felt that strictly alphabetical could lead to improper cataloguing. Some company names have been shortened in the league tables for aesthetic reasons.

John D Blackburn
Editor

This page is intentionally left blank

Total Assets League Table

Company	Revenue	Company	Revenue
Diageo Great Britain Limited	£3,436,999,936	Cider of Sweden Ltd	£48,552,928
Justerini & Brooks, Limited	£1,432,017,024	Concha y Toro UK Limited	£45,458,360
Molson Coors Brewing Company (UK) Limited	£878,267,008	Signatory Vintage Scotch Whisky Company Limited	£44,839,152
Pernod Ricard UK Limited	£576,435,968	Marston's Acquisitions Limited	£44,600,000
John Dewar and Sons Limited	£537,265,024	Speymalt Whisky Distributors Limited	£43,225,660
Highland Distillers Limited	£374,300,000	Farr Vintners Limited	£40,755,556
Shepherd Neame Limited	£334,227,008	Corney and Barrow Group Limited	£40,117,000
Glen Turner Company Limited	£302,870,016	Corney and Barrow Limited	£39,744,000
Matthew Clark Bibendum Limited	£302,287,008	Hydes' Brewery Limited	£38,585,184
Tennent Caledonian Breweries UK Limited	£263,192,000	Diageo Northern Ireland Limited	£38,528,000
International Procurement and Logistics Limited	£260,690,000	HT Drinks Ltd	£37,335,000
BB & R Limited	£254,874,000	Diageo Global Supply IBC Limited	£35,549,000
Majestic Wine PLC	£251,967,008	Lanchester Wine Cellars Limited	£34,806,348
William Grant & Sons Brands Limited	£251,652,000	Sazerac UK Limited	£33,908,028
Loch Lomond Distillers Limited	£217,186,000	Liberty Wines Limited	£31,104,502
Hall & Woodhouse Limited	£206,032,992	Amathus Drinks PLC	£30,882,864
S.A.Brain & Company, Limited	£192,684,992	Berkmann Wine Cellars Limited	£30,443,210
Dhamecha Foods Limited	£188,968,992	Fine & Rare Wines Limited	£29,503,260
St.Austell Brewery Company Limited	£188,327,008	Greencroft Bottling Company Limited	£29,484,372
Distell International Limited	£171,064,992	Berkmann Family Holdings Limited	£28,857,532
Angus Dundee Distillers PLC	£164,446,112	Mast-Jaegermeister UK Limited	£28,586,000
Loch Lomond Distillery Company Limited	£154,226,000	Drinks Inc. Ltd	£28,128,664
Glen Scotia Distillery Company Limited	£154,226,000	In Vino Bidco Limited	£27,959,740
Wadworth and Company Limited	£152,864,992	Imperial Cash & Carry Limited	£27,892,548
William Grant & Sons UK Limited	£146,531,008	Bibendum PLB Group Limited	£27,291,000
Ian MacLeod Distillers Limited	£145,944,992	John E.Fells & Sons Limited	£27,073,200
Charles Wells, Limited	£141,250,000	Philip Russell Limited	£26,927,764
Majestic Wine Warehouses Limited	£138,679,008	Wallaces Express Limited	£26,347,828
Edrington-Beam Suntory UK Distribution Limited	£134,907,008	Aspall Cyder Limited	£25,999,500
Quality Spirits International Limited	£116,992,000	United Wholesale Grocers Limited	£25,720,696
Bacardi-Martini Limited	£114,699,000	William Morton Limited	£25,315,952
Everards Brewery Limited	£111,340,000	H.B.Clark & Co.(Successors) Limited	£24,827,042
The Littlemill Distillery Company Limited	£110,479,000	Spar (UK) Limited	£24,605,934
Asahi UK Ltd	£109,625,000	Venus Wine & Spirit Merchants PLC	£24,123,172
W.H. Brakspear & Sons Limited	£106,872,000	Mentzendorff & Company Limited	£23,962,904
Moet Hennessy U.K. Limited	£102,096,768	Hammonds of Knutsford PLC	£22,859,692
Enotria Winecellars Limited	£91,997,264	Freixenet Copestick Limited	£22,577,178
Boutinot Limited	£82,608,976	Blue Tree Limited	£19,974,350
World Brands Duty Free Limited	£82,534,000	Thomas Ridley and Son, Limited	£19,910,284
Kingsland Drinks Limited	£79,140,000	All Market Europe Limited	£19,229,848
In Vino Limited	£74,332,672	Global Foods Limited	£19,162,588
CADV Limited	£73,567,000	Davy & Company Limited	£19,024,476
LWC Drinks Limited	£72,563,552	Lanson International UK Limited	£18,322,000
Arkell's Brewery Limited	£70,877,672	Distell International Holdings Limited	£18,152,844
Kingsland Drinks Group Limited	£68,237,000	Atom Supplies Limited	£18,093,900
James E. McCabe Limited	£65,369,696	Goedhuis & Company Limited	£17,668,416
Charles Wells Brewery Limited	£65,067,000	Hallgarten Wines, Limited	£17,434,252
Adnams PLC	£64,708,000	Cellar Trends Limited	£17,051,138
Kitwave Limited	£63,259,264	United Wine Merchants Limited	£16,961,920
Tennent Caledonian Breweries Wholesale Limited	£62,979,348	Wise Trading Limited	£16,904,696
South Downs Real Estate Limited	£62,515,272	M.& M.Value Limited	£16,719,293
Millennium Cash & Carry Limited	£53,710,732	Lay & Wheeler Limited	£16,707,000
Speciality Drinks Limited	£49,235,136	Row & Company Limited	£16,136,183
Bl Wines and Spirits Limited	£48,678,520	Remy Cointreau UK Distribution Limited	£15,852,757

UK Wholesalers of Beers, Wines and Spirits — dellam

Company	Amount	Company	Amount
Wemyss Vintage Malts Limited	£15,660,336	Nectar Imports Limited	£7,579,812
Duncan Taylor Scotch Whisky Limited	£15,140,837	Tanners Wines Limited	£7,556,743
J.G. Distillers Limited	£14,977,495	Compass Supply Solutions Limited	£7,536,151
Lamba Trading Co. Limited	£14,359,649	E I Wines Limited	£7,530,545
Cobra Beer Partnership Limited	£14,096,065	Vinum Fine Wines Limited	£7,417,750
Casa Julia Limited	£13,883,850	Empire Star Limited	£7,355,451
Wilkinson Vintners Limited	£13,420,092	Maisons Marques et Domaines Limited	£7,306,545
Naked Wines Prepayments Trustee Company Ltd	£13,361,000	Mangrove Global Limited	£7,298,294
Landmark Wholesale Limited	£13,090,641	Allson Sparkle Limited	£7,289,341
Armit Holding Limited	£13,029,346	O.W.Loeb & Co Limited	£7,223,783
Negociants UK Limited	£12,991,000	Delegat Europe Limited	£6,925,916
Les Caves de Pyrene Limited	£12,672,123	Manchester Drinks Company Ltd	£6,903,282
Speyside Distillers Company Limited	£12,144,597	Mast-Jaegermeister UK Holding Limited	£6,805,000
Today's Wholesale Services Limited	£12,075,000	Franciacorta Limited	£6,786,359
Coe of Ilford Limited	£12,040,525	Kwik-Keg Limited	£6,776,864
Alliance Wine Company Limited	£12,006,068	Ely & Sidney Limited	£6,741,256
C Carnevale Limited	£11,901,745	House of Townend Limited	£6,687,892
Blends Wine Estates UK Ltd	£11,817,875	Marussia Beverages UK Limited	£6,667,441
Douglas Laing & Company Limited.	£11,683,044	Maison Maurice Limited	£6,645,845
Armit Wines Limited	£11,612,215	Tolchards Limited	£6,623,436
Casella Family Brands (Europe) Limited	£11,399,190	Alivini Company Limited	£6,575,749
Tanners (Shrewsbury) Limited	£10,743,567	Edrington European Travel Retail Limited	£6,514,611
Good Food Wines Limited	£10,668,573	Liv-Ex Limited	£6,500,368
Narang Wholesalers Limited	£10,358,287	Seckford Wines Limited	£6,382,622
Origin Wine Limited	£10,213,517	Lea & Sandeman Group of Companies Limited	£6,227,559
Temple Wines (Cash & Carry) Limited	£9,808,691	Toorank UK Limited	£6,155,354
Ellis of Richmond (Holdings) Limited	£9,633,510	Anthony Byrne Fine Wines Limited	£6,094,454
Broom House Investments Limited	£9,620,780	Naked Fine Wine Bonds PLC	£6,093,000
Hi-Spirits Ltd	£9,584,388	Chateau de Sours Estates Limited	£6,012,162
The Three Stills Company Limited	£9,540,301	Barrique Vintners Limited	£5,804,571
Quintessential Brands Spirit Solutions Limited	£9,515,000	C & D Wines Limited	£5,799,325
Hills Prospect Holdings Ltd	£9,307,573	David Berryman Limited	£5,656,133
Dillon Bass Limited	£9,290,578	Drumstick Products Company Limited	£5,636,975
Glenforest Limited	£9,290,394	Bottle Green Limited	£5,610,000
Marc Fine Wines Limited	£9,258,172	Chilli Marketing Brand Management Ltd	£5,563,390
Hills Prospect PLC	£9,251,692	Main Rum Company Limited (The)	£5,558,230
Deckers Restaurants Limited	£9,034,201	Quintessential Brands Premium Brands Limited	£5,544,000
H.T.White & Company,Limited	£8,944,191	Louis Latour Limited	£5,521,704
Tom MacFarlane and Company Limited	£8,903,972	Purity Brewing Company Limited	£5,428,463
T. & J.T. Barton (Bottlers) Limited	£8,811,326	Lacons Brewery Limited	£5,394,371
RWM Holdings Limited	£8,782,118	Eurochoice Limited	£5,293,382
Vintage & Fine Wine International Limited	£8,774,116	Pieroth Limited	£5,232,441
Laurent-Perrier (UK) Limited	£8,502,846	Hi - Line Wines Limited	£5,220,125
Freixenet UK Ltd	£8,232,514	Alliance Foods Limited	£5,176,621
Gleeson N.I. Limited	£8,152,965	ASCO Foods Limited	£5,103,317
Gonzalez Byass UK Limited	£8,145,926	The Offie Limited	£5,089,589
Ellis of Richmond Limited	£8,047,245	Nickolls & Perks Limited	£5,081,055
Aceo Limited	£7,907,415	KIC Inventories Limited	£5,077,631
Asahi Premium Brands Ltd	£7,887,753	The Vintage Malt Whisky Company Limited	£5,031,725
Champers (Wholesale) Limited	£7,854,751	Vintage Capital II PLC	£5,029,026
Uisce Ard Ltd	£7,833,778	Champagne Warehouse Ltd	£4,992,298
Laytons Wine Services Limited	£7,711,524	A.F.T. (Liquor Stores) Limited	£4,953,725
J.W.G. PLC	£7,685,623	Vranken Pommery UK Ltd.	£4,929,697
Greenwood Spirits Limited	£7,645,300	Eurowines Limited	£4,884,157

Barrel Booze Limited	£4,874,818	Winning Invest & Trade Ltd	£3,470,543
Zonin UK Limited	£4,857,743	Eastcoast Supplies Ltd.	£3,441,785
G & G Gallo Enterprises Limited	£4,811,061	Spirits Development & Management Company (SDMC)	£3,439,762
Inter Trading Leicester Limited	£4,810,791	The Vinorium Limited	£3,392,663
Alchemy Inns Limited	£4,784,856	Baby Bottles (Wholesale) Limited	£3,392,245
Bordeaux Wine Investments Limited	£4,766,934	North South Wines Limited	£3,382,827
Brookfield Beverages Limited	£4,741,928	Levin Wines Limited	£3,382,464
William Cadenhead Limited	£4,739,575	Martin Miller's Gin Limited	£3,377,683
Golden Harvest Wholesale Limited	£4,719,372	Ty Nant Spring Water Limited	£3,366,041
L.A. Drinks Company Limited	£4,665,195	RDM Wines Limited	£3,350,739
Monolith (UK) Ltd	£4,647,557	A. S. D. Wholesale Limited	£3,350,733
Chetan Wholesalers Limited	£4,643,368	Elliston Fine Wines Limited	£3,315,766
The Hurns Beer Co. Limited	£4,630,683	Chateau Musar (U.K.) Limited	£3,310,544
Kamros Cash and Carry Limited	£4,624,249	Kal Wine Source UK Ltd	£3,302,196
CRVC UK Limited	£4,620,381	RD Wines Limited	£3,260,000
Brookfield Drinks Limited	£4,574,059	Speciality Brands Ltd	£3,195,152
Brockmans Gin Limited	£4,508,086	Wine-Invest Ltd	£3,189,529
Cellar & Co Limited	£4,420,926	Primo Drinks Ltd	£3,183,989
Kestrel Brewing Company Limited	£4,419,432	Hurns Mineral Water Co. Limited	£3,167,253
Myliko International (Wines) Ltd.	£4,399,963	Levenridge Limited	£3,135,767
Flint Wines Limited	£4,387,308	Libra Drinks Wholesale Limited	£3,107,849
Eurovenus Limited	£4,372,716	East West Ales Limited	£3,091,366
Fortmount Trading Limited	£4,307,544	Nene Charter Company Limited	£3,063,589
Kanlaon Limited	£4,288,873	Mondial Wine Limited	£3,054,799
Bon Coeur Fine Wines Limited	£4,226,339	Ratcliffe & Brown Wines and Spirits Limited	£3,042,079
Morgenrot Group PLC	£4,192,147	Jascots Wine Merchants Limited	£3,023,350
The Wine Enterprise Investment Scheme Limited	£4,181,794	Gandhi Wine Suppliers Limited	£3,017,932
Springbank Distillers Limited	£4,160,030	G.W. Fields & Sons (Great Yarmouth) Limited	£3,016,408
World of Patria International Limited	£4,085,428	Jackson Nugent Vintners Limited	£2,999,574
Grants-EU Limited	£4,054,572	Colombier Vins Fins Limited	£2,993,441
DGB Europe Limited	£4,039,832	The Last Drop Distillers Limited	£2,955,156
E.W.G.A. Limited	£4,036,547	Atlas Fine Wines Limited	£2,950,437
Heidi Beers Limited	£4,032,332	Gordons (Bolton) Limited	£2,927,824
Steamin' Billy (Property) Limited	£4,027,760	Direct Booze Limited	£2,924,597
Annessa Imports Limited	£3,934,850	Town Centre Inns Limited	£2,899,131
Poulter Group UK Limited	£3,915,320	Orsa Major Ltd	£2,895,828
Robb Brothers Wine Merchants Ltd	£3,913,172	Connollys' Liquor Wholesale Limited	£2,890,990
Hops and Barley Limited	£3,913,148	Hayward Bros (Wines) Limited	£2,846,043
Branded Drinks Ltd	£3,886,575	Hochfeld International Ltd	£2,844,874
Clarke Wholesale Limited	£3,840,743	A & B Vintners Limited	£2,836,696
Indie Brands Ltd.	£3,829,331	Di Vine Importers Limited	£2,828,842
Tate-Smith Limited	£3,811,111	Maidenhead Wine Company Limited	£2,823,087
Raisin Social Limited	£3,772,493	Crouch Vale Brewery Limited	£2,822,445
Falcon Vintners Limited	£3,764,429	Emporia Brands Limited	£2,805,689
Thorman Hunt & Co Limited	£3,703,488	Popaball Limited	£2,755,478
Bancroft Wines Limited	£3,688,703	Southern England Wines (UK) Ltd	£2,754,968
Kedem Europe Limited	£3,672,280	Rafine Limited	£2,737,212
Kingfisher Beer Europe Limited	£3,646,017	Swallow (Soft Drinks, Beer and Cider Wholesalers) Ltd	£2,730,827
James Nicholson Wine Limited	£3,623,122	Raeburn Fine Wines Ltd.	£2,719,305
Middleton Associates Limited	£3,593,650	Approved Products Ltd	£2,664,400
Amish Wholesalers Limited	£3,572,830	Branda Ltd	£2,653,156
21 Whiskies Limited	£3,571,489	Vito International Ltd	£2,628,447
Edwards Beers and Wine Supplies Ltd	£3,517,661	MSD Wholesale Limited	£2,604,655
United Breweries International (U.K.) Limited	£3,493,883	Supermalt UK Limited	£2,572,578

UK Wholesalers of Beers, Wines and Spirits — dellam

Company	Value	Company	Value
Lilley's Cider Limited	£2,567,968	Hutton & Mitchell Licensed Traders Limited	£1,931,190
Tanner Brodin Limited	£2,564,310	Coombe Castle Fine Wines Limited	£1,929,379
Champagnes and Chateaux Ltd.	£2,560,485	Premium Vineyard Company UK Limited	£1,928,770
Euro Wines (C & C) Limited	£2,556,135	Oeno Limited	£1,925,795
Chilli Brands Limited	£2,554,847	The Drinks Club Ltd	£1,908,987
Wine World Producers Limited	£2,516,579	Key Brands International Ltd	£1,898,084
N. McLoone & Co. Ltd	£2,466,941	New Generation Wines Limited	£1,894,149
Small Beer Limited	£2,453,937	General Wine and Liquor Company Limited	£1,885,791
Hollandwest Limited	£2,453,779	Venus 14 Limited	£1,873,599
Jassim Limited	£2,438,942	Edrington International Brands Limited	£1,871,262
Seckford Agencies Limited	£2,404,807	Anjo Wines Limited	£1,864,565
Hennings Wine Merchants Limited	£2,359,742	Vine Trail Limited	£1,852,899
Glamorgan Brewing Company Limited	£2,357,248	JF Kegs (Scotland) Limited	£1,852,500
Campbell Inns Limited	£2,353,097	Donatel Freres Limited	£1,851,869
Vintage Roots Limited	£2,340,761	Frazier's Wine Merchants Ltd.	£1,851,550
Merchant Vintners Company Limited (The)	£2,298,168	Vinimpo (U.K.) Limited	£1,834,266
The Creative Whisky Company Limited	£2,279,288	Watermark Fine Wine Limited	£1,831,386
Little Rock Wine Company Limited	£2,272,073	ABA Eaglesham Ltd	£1,821,470
247 Enterprises UK Ltd	£2,266,958	Proof Drinks Limited	£1,817,175
Kallwin Limited	£2,264,425	Rarus Ltd	£1,815,626
Georges Barbier of London Limited	£2,239,135	Wold Toppers Limited	£1,794,538
Village Selections Limited	£2,212,201	IKP Trading Limited	£1,784,731
Alchemy Drinks Ltd.	£2,202,683	Hameed Investments Limited	£1,781,003
Horizon Soft Drinks Limited	£2,201,561	Andrews Beer & Mineral Company Limited	£1,780,222
Belfast Distillery Company Limited	£2,192,911	Duvel Moortgat UK Limited	£1,777,542
Direct Wine Factory Ltd	£2,174,676	The Beer Belly Company Incorporated Limited	£1,775,833
Pinglestone Estate Limited	£2,147,771	Manchester Trading Limited	£1,764,238
Ditton Wine Traders Ltd	£2,137,418	Marshall McGregor Limited	£1,762,976
Adrian Mecklenburgh Limited	£2,129,189	Appellations Limited	£1,751,699
DBS Isherwood Limited	£2,116,006	Khosla Wines Ltd	£1,750,464
Bibendum Wine Limited	£2,109,000	Distell Europe Ltd.	£1,746,009
Humble Group Ltd	£2,103,920	Oliver's Beer and Wine Limited	£1,730,247
The Society of Vintners Limited	£2,089,065	The Bombay Spirits Company Limited	£1,699,000
Manzi Developments Limited	£2,085,243	Barmaster (Independant Wholesalers) Limited	£1,698,951
Demball Limited	£2,080,221	First Whisky Limited	£1,696,990
Wigan Beer Company Limited	£2,080,144	J & A Drinks Limited	£1,686,432
Lyndon Drinks Limited	£2,080,058	Wineservice Limited	£1,668,640
Marlico Limited	£2,078,893	The Beer Company Limited	£1,662,319
Michel Couvreur (Scotch Whiskies) Limited	£2,077,092	Real Ale Limited	£1,656,962
The Vintner London Ltd	£2,076,235	WLG Limited	£1,649,945
Connoisseur Estates Limited	£2,071,432	Millesima Limited	£1,649,820
The Gala Drinks Company Limited	£2,048,900	Christopher Piper Wines Limited	£1,647,033
International Diplomatic Supplies Limited	£2,040,367	W. Hall & Son (Holywell) Limited	£1,642,509
Cambridge Wine Merchants Ltd	£2,004,327	Morecambe Bay Wines Limited	£1,638,859
Spirit Traders Ltd	£2,000,001	Occidental & Oriental Cellars Limited	£1,638,564
Intertrade Wholesale Limited	£1,972,373	Codorniu UK Limited	£1,621,925
Old St.Andrews Limited	£1,968,533	Chelsea Vintners London Limited	£1,614,420
Wine Importers (Edinburgh) Limited	£1,966,941	Astrum Wine Cellars Limited	£1,610,967
The Wright Wine Company Limited	£1,964,576	Ooberstock Limited	£1,592,134
Kato Enterprises Limited	£1,954,357	The Wine Fusion Limited	£1,592,013
Yapp Brothers Limited	£1,948,024	Vinum Limited	£1,591,607
American Fizz (UK) Limited	£1,947,009	Kirklee Scotch Whisky Limited	£1,580,819
Charles Taylor Wines Limited	£1,945,855	J. Chandler & Company, Limited	£1,580,660
Beer Express Limited	£1,937,517	LDC Scotland Limited	£1,550,313

Company	Amount	Company	Amount
Edwards Beers and Minerals Limited	£1,541,994	N D John Wine Merchants Limited	£1,178,240
Marathon Food Limited	£1,501,561	Reid Wines (1992) Limited	£1,177,055
Claret-E Limited	£1,494,315	United Supplies Limited	£1,173,117
North of Scotland Distilling Company Limited	£1,481,745	Eythrope Wine Limited	£1,167,722
C. & O. Wines Limited	£1,480,254	Jack Sullivan Limited	£1,164,695
J W Wines Ltd	£1,475,867	Glasgow Distillers Limited	£1,160,452
Frank Stainton Wines Limited	£1,475,790	Raer Scotch Whisky Ltd	£1,141,138
Le Soula Limited	£1,472,643	David Berryman Holdings Limited	£1,133,224
Whiskybroker Limited	£1,463,636	Decorum Vintners Limited	£1,132,594
Brunswick Fine Wines and Spirits Limited	£1,443,417	William Riddell & Sons Limited	£1,132,326
Swara Trading International Limited	£1,436,683	J M & D Limited	£1,122,880
Shree Sai Trading Ltd	£1,426,703	Worldwine UK Ltd	£1,121,270
Laytons Wine Merchants Limited	£1,424,482	Soho Wine Supply Limited (The)	£1,119,884
Expression du Terroir Limited	£1,391,073	Indigo Wine Limited	£1,118,623
Grape Passions Limited	£1,381,747	Peter Graham Wines Limited	£1,114,312
GCBW Catrine Ltd	£1,375,964	Portavadie Distillery Limited	£1,110,483
CKW Trading Limited	£1,373,444	Hay Hampers Limited	£1,104,457
Friarwood Fine Wines Limited	£1,355,171	Albion Wine Shippers Limited	£1,101,207
Premier UK Trading Limited	£1,353,211	Spencers (Bromsgrove) Limited	£1,087,337
Southwick Court Fine Wines (2012) Ltd	£1,350,018	Les Producteurs et Vignerons de France Limited	£1,083,751
Beatville Limited	£1,337,569	Alivini (North) Limited	£1,077,817
In Vino Veritas Ltd	£1,305,784	Hazewater Food Services Ltd	£1,075,189
Las Bodegas Limited	£1,302,005	Pivovar Ltd	£1,074,325
Atlasaim International Limited	£1,288,761	Barton, Brownsdon & Sadler Limited	£1,073,883
Le Bon Vin Limited	£1,284,345	Billecart - Salmon (UK) Limited	£1,071,725
Blackadder International Limited	£1,280,294	Viscount Agencies Limited	£1,067,907
Quintessential Brands UK Limited	£1,266,546	VDS UK Limited	£1,067,140
Harrow & Hope Limited	£1,254,141	Clark Foyster Wines Limited	£1,061,456
MK Wine Art Ltd	£1,248,979	Triple AAA Limited	£1,055,789
Allied Ship Supplies (Ireland) Limited	£1,248,146	Chalie Richards & Company Limited	£1,051,000
A. Dewar Rattray Limited	£1,241,716	Sheridan Cooper's Limited	£1,044,434
Jenkins and Beckers Fine Wine Limited	£1,241,363	Norvic Ltd	£1,039,063
Young's Beers Wines & Spirits Ltd	£1,238,026	Coral Management Limited	£1,038,267
The Beer Warehouse (Maidenhead) Limited	£1,236,490	Vinissimo Limited	£1,031,826
Taste Merchants Ltd	£1,234,247	Barrys Discount Ltd.	£1,025,938
C. & T. Licata & Son Limited	£1,233,339	The Beer Company Consolidations Limited	£1,022,201
10 International Limited	£1,233,272	Continental Cash & Carry Limited	£1,015,835
The Champagne Company (UK) Limited	£1,223,505	Expressmode Limited	£1,009,969
David J. Watt (Fine Wines) Limited	£1,222,138	Celtic Wines Limited	£1,001,423
Gift Creation and Design Limited	£1,221,853	Pigs Ears Beers Limited	£999,197
Digby Wine Ltd	£1,219,494	Euro Beer Distribution Ltd	£998,000
Digby Fine English Ltd	£1,218,131	Budge Brands Ltd	£994,208
W.& J.Cruickshank and Company Limited	£1,214,700	Barcode Traders Limited	£993,804
Euroboozer Limited	£1,213,187	Primo Drinks (Merseyside) Ltd	£986,116
Warwickshire Drinks Plus Limited	£1,211,173	Kater Four (Cash & Carry) Limited	£984,235
Lithuanian Beer Limited	£1,208,640	Fox Fitzgerald Whisky Trading Company Limited	£983,193
Amphora Portfolio Management Limited	£1,204,884	Murcotts Ltd.	£980,838
Thames Distillers Limited	£1,204,068	Harp Wines & Spirits Ltd	£973,779
Liquid Vision Enterprise Limited	£1,202,885	Edwards Beers and Wines (Holdings) Ltd	£968,966
Dourthe UK Limited	£1,196,609	Heath Trading Limited	£960,763
The Mullwood Wine Company Limited	£1,190,697	Robert Rolls & Co. Limited	£955,388
Worldewide Limited	£1,188,543	The Brewers Wholesale Limited	£952,342
Duncairn Wines Limited	£1,188,302	Sommeliers Choice Limited	£949,527
Dedicated Wines Ltd	£1,180,842	C C & C Limited	£948,594

Connolly's (Wine Merchants) Limited	£944,898	Cascriva Ltd	£744,811
Agro Investment Ltd	£943,864	Swig Wines Limited	£744,403
Michel Roux Limited	£941,924	Weavers (Nottingham) Limited	£743,664
More Beer Wholesale Limited	£938,416	City Wine Collection Limited	£741,908
Europemarca Limited	£938,276	Frontier Trading International Limited	£739,750
LGVA Solutions Limited	£936,895	Field and Fawcett Wine Merchants and Delicatessen Ltd	£735,254
Slurp Wine Company Limited	£935,089	BM Wines Limited	£733,929
Italicus Ltd	£924,740	Klostergut Limited	£732,496
Cascade Drinks Limited	£924,119	Yorkshire Vintners Limited	£725,154
Castle Eden Brewery Ltd	£922,028	Jean Juviniere Limited	£724,432
Chardon Wines Limited	£921,578	The Wine Treasury Limited	£723,456
Moreno Wine Importers Company Limited	£916,970	Eebria Limited	£722,881
South Eastern Beers & Minerals Limited	£916,374	Caves de Pierre Limited	£722,790
Morgan Classic Wines Limited	£914,429	Harlequin (Stockport) Limited	£721,713
H2vin Limited	£913,483	Identity Drinks Brands Limited	£720,984
European Brand Trading Limited	£906,357	A.I.M.S. (Refreshments) Limited	£719,223
Wimbledon Wine Cellar Limited	£901,411	Hard To Find Wines Limited	£718,629
S H Jones Wines Ltd	£898,359	Medoc Wines Limited	£714,367
New Wave (Scotland) Limited	£896,696	Kingsbury Wine & Spirits Co. Ltd.	£711,068
Laurence Smith & Son (Edinburgh) Limited	£887,021	Alfie Fiandaca Limited	£705,667
Starstock Ltd	£885,973	Condor Wines Ltd	£704,088
DEF Investments Limited	£885,686	Middlesex Wines Limited	£702,272
Windfall Logistics Limited	£877,970	Calibre Brands Limited	£699,253
Paul Roberts Wines Limited	£877,245	De Burgh Fine Wine Limited	£697,403
Thameside Wines Limited	£875,597	Rippingale Promotions Limited	£694,587
Gin Fizz Ltd	£869,640	Sandham Wine Merchants Ltd	£693,696
Joseph Keegan & Sons Limited	£868,490	La Diva Drinks & Food Ltd	£690,577
Beer52 Limited	£865,624	Vintage 1947 Limited	£687,989
Primo Drinks (North East) Ltd	£860,570	Waters (1802) Limited	£684,422
Primo Drinks (Lancashire) Ltd	£859,005	Xuyang International Ltd	£672,420
Liquid Measure Limited	£853,996	G Point 7 Ltd	£664,538
Capacha Limited	£851,588	Graftyset Limited	£661,876
London & Scottish International Limited	£836,843	Templeton Beer Wine & Spirit Co Ltd	£657,601
Classic Malts Limited	£835,537	Hatton & Edwards Fine Wine Merchants Limited	£656,041
Poltom Limited	£835,534	Superior Import/Export Limited	£653,431
MBM Resource Trading International Limited	£833,833	Jaitly Trading Co Ltd	£651,497
Free Trade Beers and Minerals Limited	£832,558	Savage Selection Limited	£651,355
Squarewalk Limited	£829,701	Best Price Retail and Wholesale Limited	£648,228
Rok Drinks Limited	£827,765	Smouse & Marchand Limited	£646,991
Cathay Importers (London) Limited	£827,408	Mercanti Imports Limited	£646,703
V.C. Vintners Limited	£826,967	Winetraders (UK) Limited	£643,969
Gordano Wines Limited	£825,243	Eden Fine Wines Limited	£640,298
Kaleboard Limited	£811,531	HG Wine Limited	£639,970
Wm.Addison (Newport) Limited	£811,503	LHK Fine Wines Limited	£638,997
Lindisfarne Limited	£811,398	Stedman Bros. (Events) Limited	£637,713
W.J.Armstrong Limited	£798,807	The Malt Whisky Company Limited	£635,943
Barn Direct Limited	£797,389	Praban Na Linne Limited	£635,317
Primo Drinks (Yorkshire) Ltd	£787,971	Bacchus-Les-Vignobles de France Limited	£634,694
Drinks Direct Limited	£787,686	Vintage Wines Limited	£629,429
Wilks & Company Wine Merchants Limited	£783,659	Europlus Trading Limited	£626,419
Del Professore Limited	£764,753	Citrosoft Drinks Limited	£622,717
Vineyard Belfast Limited	£761,643	Regency Wines Limited	£619,567
Coral MGT Limited	£754,854	Magenta Wine Investors Limited	£618,649
Lanark House Investments Limited	£746,812	Quartz Group Scotland Ltd	£615,716

G M Drinks Limited	£600,103	Primo Drinks (Staffordshire) Ltd	£487,937
PMWine Trade Limited	£599,781	Crystle Limited	£484,463
Stewart Wines Limited	£596,969	Ultracomida Trading Co. Limited	£483,179
More or Less Drinks Company Limited	£595,876	TFC Wholesale Ltd	£479,969
Drinkrite Limited	£595,304	Prime Cash & Carry Limited	£479,785
Viserra Limited	£594,758	UK Vintners (of London) PLC	£479,256
Colemans ABC Ltd	£590,202	The Glenallachie Distillers Co Limited	£476,095
Cellar Supplies Cheltenham Limited	£587,819	Steevenson Wines Limited	£474,692
Sunnyside Incorporated Limited	£586,723	Chalgrove Wines Limited	£472,357
Alexander Wines Ltd.	£582,193	Signature Brew Ltd	£471,671
Birrificio Del Ducato London Limited	£581,836	D'Arcy Wine Merchants Limited	£464,565
Red Squirrel Brewery Limited	£574,906	Alice Wholesale Trading Limited	£461,258
S and S Wines Limited	£574,373	Canal Cellars Ltd	£461,177
First Bar Supplies Limited	£568,781	Graysons Freight Services Limited	£459,955
MCAL Merchant Limited	£566,623	Churchill Graham Limited	£458,734
City Beer Limited	£566,142	Broadoak Cider Company Limited	£457,775
Oliver Burridge & Company Limited	£565,828	Ellustria Limited	£455,710
Greenfield Bacon Limited	£565,797	Hamptons Wine Ltd	£454,477
Whitebridge Wines Limited	£564,395	S & F Drinks Limited	£453,804
RDV Spirits Ltd	£564,104	Rosemount Pub Co. Limited	£453,595
Felix Solis Avantis UK Ltd	£556,349	Swallow Dispensed Drinks Solutions Limited	£453,365
Norman Price Wines Limited	£555,659	The Perfect Cellar Ltd	£453,022
Wine & Spirit International Limited	£551,883	I I Wine Limited	£452,415
Keltek Cornish Brewery Limited	£550,492	West End Drinks Limited	£451,839
Bhanbore Trading Company PVT Ltd	£550,337	Celebration Drinks Limited	£451,798
Ask Drinks Ltd	£549,691	USSR Limited	£450,417
Island Ales Limited	£546,994	Number One Drinks Company Limited	£450,252
Yates low Brewery Limited	£545,559	Red Squirrel Wine Ltd.	£449,814
Jake Mason Ltd	£540,582	Kicking Horse Ltd.	£449,312
R & B Drinks Ltd	£539,978	Thomson & Scott Limited	£448,107
Carson & Carnevale Limited	£539,350	Crush Wines Ltd	£446,438
Amis Trading Limited	£531,106	Cumbrae Supply Company Limited	£445,215
Pandemonio Limited	£524,620	Wholly Grape Limited	£444,273
Twaites and Jones Limited	£523,910	Bridge Vintners Limited	£439,692
Morosini Mills Limited	£523,037	Superyacht Supplies Limited	£439,175
Park Royal Wholesale Limited	£519,414	Franchiserv Limited	£439,040
Henry C. Collison and Sons Limited	£518,826	Provenance Fine Wines Ltd	£437,805
Mitchell's Vintners Limited	£518,717	A.H.Rackham Limited	£437,254
The Winemakers Club 2000 Limited	£518,368	Drinks21 Ltd	£434,875
Eurovines Limited	£516,898	Goldbeach Trading Limited	£431,136
Triberg Limited	£516,563	Biercraft Ltd	£431,032
Cellar Twelve Limited	£516,459	Holdsworth Spirits & Company Limited	£430,575
Express Drinks Ltd	£514,914	D K International (UK) Limited	£428,507
Bijou Bottles Limited	£514,690	Snow Leopard Vodka Limited	£426,693
Festina Drinks Ltd	£510,538	Flying Firkin Distribution Limited	£426,482
The Fine Wine (Old World) Trading Company Limited	£508,827	180 East Limited	£422,677
Fine Products Exporters Limited	£508,415	Mundus Wines Limited	£421,576
Elicite Ltd	£508,250	Pimlico Dozen Limited	£421,306
Vinceremos Wines & Spirits Limited	£503,628	Hunny Pot Pub Co. Limited	£420,770
Gelston Castle Fine Wines Limited	£502,935	Stokes Fine Wines Limited	£418,610
Broughton Ales Limited	£502,688	Whittalls Wines Limited	£418,278
MWH Wine Merchants Limited	£498,196	Rackham Investments Limited	£417,811
Sunset Wines Limited	£492,294	All Drinks Cash & Carry Limited	£416,958
Bohemia Beer House Limited	£491,943	Central Pubs (UK) Limited	£416,704

Company	Amount	Company	Amount
County Catering (Midlands) Limited	£416,102	Sagittarius Royaume-Uni Limited	£349,547
Loughborough Student Services Limited	£414,904	L H Cellar Supplies Limited	£347,843
Balman Import & Export Limited	£413,936	Raymond Reynolds Limited	£347,211
Brighton Soft Drinks Limited	£413,205	Tec-Sol Limited	£347,016
Boutique Brands Limited	£413,115	The Bajan Trading Company Limited	£344,674
Foxstead Limited	£410,626	Tenby Drinks (UK) Limited	£344,409
Trilogy Beverage Brands Ltd	£407,707	Konigsberg Seven Bridges Breweries Ltd	£342,764
Theatre of Wine Limited	£407,638	Bengal Foods Limited	£338,487
Noreast Beers (N.I.) Ltd	£407,015	Templar Wines Ltd	£337,936
Europa Drinks Limited	£404,998	Frizzenti Limited	£337,435
Storesrealm Limited	£404,033	Just Miniatures Limited	£336,914
Lebanese Fine Wines Limited	£401,347	Tower International Limited	£336,076
Lancashire Beer Company Limited	£397,390	CSS On-Trade Limited	£335,220
Great Western Wine Company Limited (The)	£395,251	Dennhofer Wines Limited	£335,021
Newcomer Wines Limited	£394,616	Tudor Drinks Ltd	£334,737
Ellis Wharton Wines Ltd	£391,998	JF Tobias Limited	£334,456
Bloomsbury Drinks Ltd	£391,988	Craft Locals Limited	£334,021
DWS Wholesale Limited	£390,246	Exigo (UK) Limited	£330,617
Momentum Wines Limited	£387,972	Mythop Gardens Limited	£330,039
Latin Spirits & Beers (UK) Ltd	£387,787	Burridges of Arlington St Ltd	£329,074
Winefantastic Limited	£387,084	Southern Wines Limited	£328,975
Uncharted Wine Company Ltd.	£386,290	Kudos Drinks Ltd	£328,645
Axiom Brands Limited	£384,760	Gurkha Beer Ltd	£327,881
Glug Limited	£383,225	GS Wholesalers Ltd	£327,235
G. Bravo & Son Limited	£380,978	Ffarm Vintners Limited	£326,870
Orso Wine Agencies Limited	£379,709	Genesis Wines Limited	£326,713
Museum Wines Limited	£376,197	London Cash & Carry Ltd	£325,943
Bear Smyth Limited	£373,714	Liquid Projects International Limited	£325,768
James Fine Wines Limited	£373,611	Global Wine Distributors Limited	£325,144
Phoenix Premium Drinks Limited	£371,713	The Knotted Vine Limited	£324,852
Il Palagio Ltd	£371,554	Cubic Brands Limited	£320,257
J. & G. Barclay and Company Limited	£370,663	Daniel Lambert Wines Limited	£320,114
R S Wines Limited	£370,297	Cellar Link Limited	£319,776
Charter Brands Limited	£370,131	Yeastie Boys UK Ltd	£319,667
Noble Merchants Limited	£369,660	Rasputin Leisure Ltd	£319,093
For The Love of Wine Limited	£367,028	Beer Barrels & Minerals (Wales) Limited	£319,029
K. Colombier Limited	£366,959	The Brewgooder Foundation	£318,083
Leomar Limited	£365,410	Pulse Products Limited	£317,469
Portal Dingwall & Norris Limited	£365,232	Malpas Stallard Limited	£316,801
Gergovie Wines Limited	£362,686	Brewgooder Limited	£316,047
N & M Wholesale Ltd	£361,001	Sell My Wine Ltd	£315,432
Erin Vintners Ltd	£359,890	Shindigger Craft Beer Ltd	£315,103
Wineways (Harrogate) Limited	£357,956	R.L.G. Trading Limited	£313,696
Rodney Fletcher Vintners Ltd	£357,884	Winepro Limited	£312,193
Neill & Company Wine Importers Ltd	£357,565	R & B Wines Ltd	£311,760
Worldwide Drinks Limited	£356,987	Knight Trade (Oakham) Limited	£310,833
K & S Hosking Ltd	£356,598	T J Wines Ltd	£310,170
Spiced Wine Company Limited	£355,702	Michael Woolley Limited	£308,670
Wine de Vine Ltd	£355,235	Beer Paradise (York) Limited	£307,477
Creswick Inns & Leisure Ltd	£354,225	Cocktail Express Ltd	£306,012
Earle Wines Ltd.	£353,346	Quantock Abbey Wine Cellars Limited	£305,776
The Wine Barn Limited	£351,738	Winegrowers Direct Limited	£305,624
One Point Supplies Limited	£349,919	Scavelli's Limited	£305,151
Talking Wines Limited	£349,610	Grands Vins de France Limited	£305,139

Rawson Trading (Doncaster) Limited	£304,023	East Street Wine Company Limited	£263,444
Balthazar Limited	£303,821	Associated Church Clubs Limited	£262,038
Durrants Fine Wines Limited	£303,396	Pierhead Drinks Limited	£261,856
The Taunton Cider Company Limited	£303,318	Molvino Fine Wine & Spirits Company Ltd	£259,011
DLRF Limited	£302,231	Noble Green Wines Limited	£258,597
Henry Mitchell & Sons Limited	£302,124	Ormos Trades Limited	£255,924
Boxford Wine Company Limited (The)	£302,021	Charles Mitchell Wines Limited	£255,540
Lant Street Wine Company Limited	£301,842	Latitude Wine Limited	£253,070
J & W Nicholson & Co Ltd	£301,009	Chiltern Trading Ltd	£251,926
Russetglow Limited	£301,001	Bubbles & Wines Limited	£251,393
Barwell & Jones Limited	£299,874	Celex Foods Limited	£250,615
Mayfair Brands Limited	£297,724	Ghost Drinks Ltd	£249,428
Crudo Limited	£295,469	Dhesis Wholesale Ltd	£249,404
Devine Distillates Group Limited	£294,420	Speyside Trading Company Limited	£248,919
Beermaster Derby Ltd	£294,002	Kegs R Us Ltd	£246,361
Drayman Drinks Ltd	£292,009	Ossau Vins & Spiritueux Ltd	£245,778
The Antipodean Sommelier Limited	£290,927	Imported Brands International Limited	£244,730
Vin-X Enterprise Investment Scheme Ltd	£288,937	Boondales Limited	£243,804
Line Point Global UK Limited	£288,860	World Beers Limited	£242,761
Black Forest Beers Limited	£288,751	Tutto Wines Limited	£242,289
Indigo Drinks Limited	£288,428	Docklands Trading Company Limited	£241,090
GW Wines Limited	£287,195	Greens Beers Limited	£240,948
Drinks Global Ltd	£286,091	Kingdom Foods & Drinks Limited	£240,439
Smartprice (NE) Ltd	£286,070	Gusto Wines Ltd	£239,936
Provenance Marketing Ltd	£285,688	SP (DPH) Exports Limited	£239,841
East London Brewing Company Limited	£284,896	Intercellar Distribution Limited	£239,592
DH Global Wine Ltd	£283,207	Belvoir Brewery Limited	£238,945
Continental Wines Limited	£282,974	Firth and Co Wine Merchants Limited	£238,065
Select Whisky Limited	£282,970	The Single Cask Ltd	£238,030
UK Lesiure Ltd	£282,582	D.J. Limbrey Distilling Co. Limited	£237,767
Geo Hill (Grocers) Limited	£281,414	Artisan Wine Storage Ltd	£237,330
The Great Newsome Brewery Limited	£279,828	London Drinks Limited	£237,089
Trywines Expertise Limited	£279,181	White's Cellar Supplies (UK) Limited	£236,451
Tipple Brands Ltd	£278,487	Mayfair Delivers Limited	£236,199
Crown Cash & Carry Ltd	£278,015	Earny Limited	£236,197
VIP Bottles Ltd	£277,325	Be My Wine Ltd.	£235,710
Beef and Burgundy Limited	£276,964	CS Wines Limited	£235,567
The Craft Drink Co Ltd	£276,837	Sefton Beer Company Limited	£234,681
Santat Wines Limited	£276,256	London Wholesale Ltd	£234,661
London Wine Agencies Limited	£276,242	SDC Wine Importers Ltd	£233,822
Valley Vineyards Limited	£274,558	Corkers Wine Limited	£233,225
HNB Trade Ltd	£273,735	Clapham Wine Company Limited	£233,097
OM Beers & Minerals Ltd	£272,556	GDK Drinks Ltd	£232,870
Jonesborough Wholesale Ltd	£271,009	S & N Products Ltd	£232,587
C & R Wines Limited	£270,373	Carte Blanche Wines Limited	£230,725
N.Double and Company Limited	£267,561	Tengu Sake Limited	£229,906
BL011 Limited	£266,790	Vinals Wine & Food Limited	£229,764
De Paolis Limited	£266,613	Special Cases Limited	£229,264
The Westbourne Drinks Company Limited	£266,091	Worsley Wines Limited	£228,447
Flagship Brands Ltd	£264,669	Martin Enterprises Limited	£227,679
Fine Wine Company Limited	£264,603	Bermondsey Gin Limited	£225,051
Wrights Lion Brewery Limited	£264,481	Yorke Vines Ltd	£223,394
Verre Anglais Limited	£263,719	Lincoln West End Limited	£222,606
The Carob Tree Limited	£263,642	Excess UK Limited	£222,559

Sardinia Wine Ltd	£222,346	Barry Drinks Ltd	£188,645
Goldcrest Drinks Limited	£222,213	Four Corners Wine Company Limited	£188,168
Korzinka Taste of Europe Limited	£221,870	Vin Est... Ltd	£188,148
Winkleigh Cider Company Limited	£220,834	Psychopomp Ltd	£187,351
Battlefield Beers Limited	£220,294	Myrlex Southend Limited	£186,872
LC Wine Brokers Limited	£219,712	Collins Wines Limited	£186,637
Southbourne Brewing Limited	£219,633	Brayston Leisure Ltd.	£186,552
Sibell Trading Limited	£219,299	Real Ale Direct Limited	£186,360
Bringmevino (UK) Limited	£218,885	Matteo Lupi Wines Ltd	£185,815
Point Beer UK Limited	£215,331	Yorkshire Beers Limited	£185,037
Star Value Limited	£214,828	Experience Wine Limited	£184,729
Francis Fine Wines Ltd	£214,774	Premium Brands Distribution Limited	£184,462
Signorellis Deli Ltd	£214,119	Mongoose Brewing Company Limited	£184,260
Monopole Wine Portfolio Management Ltd	£213,753	Railway Bar & Grill Ltd	£183,724
Champers Wines Limited	£213,525	The Real Al Company Limited	£183,278
Vinfinity Limited	£213,392	Enjoydrinks Limited	£182,900
Fine Drinks Cooperative Limited	£212,994	Star Beers Ltd	£182,742
Under The Bonnet Wines Limited	£211,653	LVB Limited	£182,668
Veravinea Ltd	£211,170	Le Vignoble Ltd	£182,526
Premier Pubco Limited	£209,606	Prosecco 1754 Limited	£181,161
The Kitchen Table Wine Co. Ltd	£208,129	Terrae Vinariae Limited	£180,177
Bohemian Brands Limited	£208,123	Lora Trading (Europe) Ltd	£179,773
Carson Wines Ltd	£207,734	Time & Tide Brewing Limited	£178,562
Ireland Craft Beers Ltd	£207,406	Miraj Beers & Wines Limited	£178,217
Cumberland Bargin Booze Limited	£207,133	Malthouse Inns PLC	£178,213
The Tirion Trading Company Limited	£207,062	Harvey's Wholesale Limited	£178,200
Top Spirits Ltd	£206,821	Giovanni Food & Wine Limited	£177,652
Whittaker Wines Limited	£206,756	Windermere Wine Stores Limited	£177,601
MC Drinks Limited	£206,340	Dudley Craig Wines Limited	£176,539
Cellar 28 Ltd	£205,571	Quintessential Spirits UK Limited	£176,535
Alcohol By Volume Limited	£205,551	Blue Diamond (UK) Ltd	£175,951
North Star Spirits Ltd.	£202,105	Sterling Wine Agencies Limited	£175,008
Battys Discount Drinks Store Limited	£201,729	Melius Drinks Ltd.	£174,948
Hannah Whisky Merchant's Ltd	£200,839	B.D. (S/W) Ltd	£174,659
Sandbar German Beer Ltd	£200,022	R Spirit Ltd	£174,583
Global Beer Company Ltd	£199,145	Ashanti Drinks Limited	£174,576
Wickedsoup Ltd.	£199,057	Chateau Wines Ltd.	£174,314
Sixpenny Wines Limited	£198,939	Richard Harvey Wines Limited	£173,369
Pirate's Grog Rum Ltd	£195,202	Whitmore and White Limited	£172,988
Aotearoa Distribution Ltd	£194,538	Wine Poole Limited	£169,965
Mywinelabel Limited	£194,020	Highfern Limited	£169,909
Premier Inc. Ltd	£193,238	Green Island (UK) Limited	£169,539
AMK Wholesale Ltd	£193,212	Premier Cru Fine Wine Ltd.	£168,238
Nothing But The Grape Limited	£193,132	Sarah Marsh Ltd	£167,614
Cavoda Limited	£192,998	Pub Pool (711) Limited	£167,336
Gravity Drinks Ltd	£192,069	The Circle Wine Company Limited	£167,198
Lamberton Whisky & Spirits Limited	£191,576	Euro-Trade and Finance Limited	£165,092
Globus Wines (UK) Ltd	£191,132	Gleann Mor Spirits Company Limited	£163,812
HP Enterprises Limited	£191,095	SK Trading (N.I.) Ltd	£163,359
The Wine Portfolio UK Limited	£190,148	The Hitchin Wine Company Limited	£163,327
Atom Brewing Co Limited	£190,136	Wildflower Wines Limited	£163,233
Viader Vintners Limited	£190,043	Blue Star Inns Limited	£163,039
G Sake Company Limited	£189,907	Bondi Brands Limited	£163,006
Languedoc Imports Ltd	£189,497	Battlefield Brewery Limited	£162,528

Blast Vintners Ltd	£162,028	Simply 1st Wine Company Limited	£137,412
ADP Wines Ltd	£161,030	Far Out Wines Limited	£135,806
Heroes Drinks Company C.I.C.	£160,603	First Class Beverages Ltd	£135,722
Wyfold Vineyard Limited	£160,521	Event Wine Solutions Limited	£135,693
Canopy Beer Company Ltd	£159,858	Perkins Independent Wine Traders Limited	£135,180
Viking Enterprises Limited	£159,180	GDD Chapuy Limited	£134,966
LA International Trading Ltd	£157,658	France Domaines Limited	£134,795
Inro Drinks (Abtec) Limited	£157,215	Tractor Shed Brewing Limited	£134,127
SMCA Enterprises Ltd.	£157,107	Quick-Keg Limited	£134,102
Crescent Fine Foods Ltd	£157,052	Ebenezer Leisure Limited	£133,766
F & B Premium Brands Limited	£156,788	Frenchbubbles Limited	£133,556
Dodotraders UK Limited	£155,933	John Villar Wines Limited	£133,468
PSR Distribution Limited	£155,334	Hobo Beer & Co. Ltd.	£133,004
Independent Drinks Supplies Limited	£154,958	Hofmeister Enterprises Ltd	£132,914
Modern Vintage Wines Ltd	£153,820	Bespoke Wines Ltd	£132,264
Everyday Wholesale Ltd	£153,484	Extravision Security Systems Limited	£131,680
Nottage Bar Supplier Limited	£153,464	CMT (Wines) Limited	£131,511
Harrisons Fine Wines Limited	£153,451	The Hop Shed Limited	£131,130
Cava Spiliadis UK Limited	£153,038	Easier Sales Limited	£131,128
Warwick Banks and Jenkins Limited	£152,641	Keeling Andrew & Co Limited	£129,934
General Bilimoria Wines Limited	£152,257	Keg Delivery Service Ltd	£129,647
Gunson Fine Wines Limited	£152,238	Prohibition Limited	£128,808
Mille Gusti Limited	£152,171	3 Tigers Limited	£128,341
Nick Dobson Ltd	£151,484	CRA Ltd	£128,309
Master Spirits Limited	£151,069	K R Wines & Beers Ltd	£128,289
The Beer and Gas Man Limited	£150,710	Ester Wines Limited	£127,600
New Zealand Beer Collective Ltd	£150,630	Empress Ale Ltd	£127,073
Nexus Wine Trading Ltd	£150,089	Wine2trade Limited	£126,735
Ales. R. Russ Limited	£149,730	Tolsta Brands Limited	£126,624
Crafty Devil Brewing Ltd	£149,411	3 Big Dogs Limited	£126,482
KD Wholesale Ltd	£149,391	Innvino Ltd	£126,454
The Beer Boutique Ltd	£148,845	Staid London Limited	£126,278
Southern Wine Roads Limited	£148,809	Lightbox Brands Limited	£126,227
Buon Vino Ltd	£148,789	AMK Distribution Ltd	£126,099
M & T Wholesale Ltd	£147,750	European Beverages Ltd	£125,805
London Wine Eis Limited	£147,513	Global Ethics Liquor Co Limited	£125,804
Tortuga Brands Limited	£147,489	Somborne Valley Vineyard Limited	£125,200
The Leamington Wine Company Limited	£147,415	World Sake Imports UK Ltd	£125,186
Cribbar Limited	£145,647	Exeter Drinks Ltd	£124,821
RHM Retail Ltd	£145,322	Waud Wines Limited	£124,698
AGS Vintners Limited	£145,297	Tasteturkey Limited	£124,606
Warwickshire Cash & Carry Limited	£144,498	Weiser Taverns Beers & Minerals Ltd	£123,459
Mega Kegs Limited	£144,328	Bonfire Hill Limited	£123,254
MSB Wholesale Services Limited	£143,097	Tequilas of Mexico Limited	£123,147
The Wineman Limited	£142,958	The Bloomsbury Distillery Ltd	£123,031
Northwest Drinks Ltd	£142,050	Gill Cash & Carry Limited	£122,982
The Dorset Wine Company Limited	£141,997	The Bottle Bank Limited	£122,445
MSM Foods Limited	£141,893	Cochin Heritage Ltd	£122,397
Ann et Vin Limited	£140,925	C N Drinks Limited	£122,059
Dago Wines Ltd	£140,752	Italy Abroad Network Limited	£121,498
Kentish Pip Ltd	£139,648	Aussie Rules Ltd	£120,974
Isle of Wight Brewery Limited	£139,346	Top Deal Services Ltd	£120,857
Divergent Drinks Ltd	£138,772	A.P. Claxton Ltd	£120,753
Roblex Ltd	£137,954	Iberiandrinks UK Ltd	£120,745

Meadrising Limited	£120,316	The Keg Company (N.I.) Ltd	£106,340
Six Rivers Limited	£120,166	PS Drinks Ltd	£106,210
North East Drinks Supplies Ltd	£119,429	Ayr Brewing Company Limited	£105,871
Toast Ale Ltd	£119,400	Dionysius Importers Ltd	£105,835
Made in Little France Import Limited	£118,612	Golden Everest Limited	£105,799
Connolly Wines Ltd	£118,584	White Pearl Ltd	£105,756
La Peira Limited	£118,372	Vinitaly Limited	£104,602
London Wine Shippers Limited	£118,139	Itedomum (UK) Ltd	£104,497
Forty Acres Ltd	£118,114	Bent Distribution Ltd	£104,484
Soar Valley Bar Supplies Ltd	£117,846	Spalco Ltd	£103,979
Mother Kelly's Distribution Limited	£117,705	C.P.A.'s Wine Limited	£102,799
Charente Enterprises Limited	£117,661	Cameron Cavendish Fine Wines Limited	£102,784
Radleigh Wines Limited	£117,643	International Business Solutions Ltd	£102,784
KB Agencies Ltd	£117,488	Just A Splash Limited	£102,767
Beer Gonzo Ltd	£117,416	Regent Wines Limited	£102,608
The Verrillo Partnership Limited	£117,415	Dragonwood Limited	£102,485
Thirstee Business Limited	£116,767	Cazcabel Drinks Limited	£102,478
Fine Wine Works Limited	£115,922	Magnetic Brands Limited	£102,269
The Responsible Trading Company Limited	£115,867	Isake International Limited	£102,146
Veda UK Limited	£115,706	Archangel Wines Limited	£101,992
Vin Neuf Limited	£115,685	The Bath Gin Company Limited	£101,798
Stargold Wholesale Ltd	£114,287	O'Donnell Moonshine Limited	£101,787
Laurus Brands Limited	£114,203	Lamjen Limited	£101,757
Regency Event Solutions Ltd	£113,841	Chalk & Charcoal Limited	£101,676
Withers Agencies Limited	£113,726	R & M Chateau Wines Ltd	£101,445
IGW Brokers Limited	£113,619	Morgan Jupe Limited	£100,793
J.W. Filshill International Limited	£113,066	Tayler Beers Limited	£100,471
Hix & Buck Ltd	£113,007	Magik Drinks Limited	£100,361
SJO Supplies Limited	£112,970	T.M.B Wine Trading Ltd	£99,934
Au Vodka Ltd	£112,136	Doran Family Vintners Limited	£99,787
WinesOnline Ltd	£112,107	Silverlite Cash & Carry Ltd	£99,471
Two Heads Beer Co Limited	£111,576	The Porterage Co Ltd	£99,303
Rondel Trading Ltd	£111,415	Litmus Wine Agencies Limited	£99,063
Marlborough International (UK) Limited	£111,398	Scrumpy Wasp Limited	£97,664
Avant Garde Drinks Ltd	£111,273	Triage Wines Limited	£97,523
Babco UK Ltd.	£111,163	Astir Cigars & Wine Ltd	£97,036
Lloyds Wines Limited	£110,176	SSL Leisure Limited	£96,946
Wine Story Limited	£109,905	Global24-7 (UK) Ltd	£96,864
Valentino Platinum Ltd	£109,780	C G Supplies Limited	£96,415
Astonburgh Limited	£109,433	Old Butcher's Wine Cellar Limited	£96,199
Openwine Limited	£109,071	Ralph's Wines Ltd	£96,170
Cattier UK Limited	£109,070	Xeco Wines Limited	£95,740
AKM Trading Services Ltd	£109,015	Blux UK Import Ltd	£95,611
Simply Cask Ltd	£108,975	St James's Fine Wine Limited	£94,743
Wholesale Beer Supplies Ltd	£108,286	Ravensbourne Wine Company Limited	£94,410
Ausavenues Limited	£108,156	TFWF Ltd	£94,309
Eastlin Alba Limited	£107,874	Imbibros Ltd	£94,171
Red Rose Drinks Limited	£107,830	Norwich Dry Gin Company Ltd	£94,035
Organica Food & Wine Ltd	£107,758	GM Catering Supplies Ltd	£93,753
Lytham Brewery Limited	£107,621	Mumbles Brewery Ltd	£93,326
Eventus Global Ltd	£107,092	Kol App Ltd	£93,020
Ultravino Limited	£106,897	Gourvid Limited	£92,098
Welford Retail Limited	£106,850	Fishers Gin Ltd	£92,035
Kash & Karry Supplies Ltd	£106,382	Cornish Point Wines UK Ltd	£91,864

Grape and Grain Management Limited	£91,690	Ginvino Ltd	£77,222
Philip von Nell Wines Limited	£91,378	Seven Cellars Ltd.	£77,143
Fourteen Drops Ltd	£91,269	Croatian Fine Wines Limited	£77,018
SJZP Limited	£90,751	Finebatch Limited	£76,777
Dramfool Ltd	£90,729	Triumph Foodservice Limited	£76,650
Finedon Convenience Store Limited	£90,579	Forest Road Brewing Co Ltd	£76,406
B & D Clarke Limited	£90,316	Blue Marble Consultants Limited	£76,202
Signature Wines Ltd	£89,881	The Whisky Palate Limited	£76,051
F.L. Dickins Limited	£89,707	Ionica Wine Cellars Ltd	£75,942
Yaad Rum Ltd	£89,509	Morrish & Banham Ltd	£75,699
TJC Corporate Events Limited	£89,197	Street Wines Limited	£75,667
Old Red Lion Theatre Pub Limited	£89,025	Mieland Limited	£75,448
Colosseum Wines Limited	£88,487	Epicure Wines Ltd	£75,355
Victoria Garry Group Ltd	£88,430	Wiltshire Liqueur Company Limited	£74,776
J. & J. Hunter Limited	£88,109	CRC Delta Ltd	£74,535
Raks Suppliers Limited	£88,004	Algodon Europe Limited	£74,517
Essex Catering Supplies Limited	£87,387	Eminent Life Limited	£74,392
Blackedge Brewing Company Ltd	£87,173	SAPM Commercial Ltd	£74,254
Bon Vin Inc. Limited	£86,813	Trevor Hughes Wines Limited	£73,967
Iceaction Limited	£86,496	Cool Apple Limited	£73,556
Brewed 4 U Ltd	£86,478	Konik's Tail Limited	£73,119
New Claire Wine Ltd	£86,090	Inn Control Management Services Ltd	£72,990
MDF Wholesale Ltd	£86,037	Quantum Vintners Limited	£72,940
Liquid Indulgence Ltd	£85,762	Orion Cash & Carry Limited	£72,900
MJLM Limited	£85,050	The Cocktail Pickers Club Ltd	£72,814
Richard Banks & Co Ltd	£84,610	Maha Cash & Carry Ltd	£72,802
Hillcrest Wines Limited	£84,398	Freshfield Fine Wines Limited	£72,730
C.O.D. Beers Limited	£83,906	Mark Jefferson Wines Limited	£72,451
AFC Direct Ltd	£83,765	Discover Wine Limited	£72,441
Rockin Robin Brewery Ltd	£83,159	Yorkshire Vino Ltd	£72,066
Urban Warehousing Limited	£82,965	Binning Trading Company Limited	£71,794
Winery Classic Limited	£82,842	Aben Wines Limited	£71,250
JD's Sports Bar Ltd	£82,774	Vino Vero Ltd	£71,077
Epic Beers Limited	£82,604	Meadow Trading Company Limited	£71,010
Gold Max Distribution Limited	£82,512	JDS Trading Limited	£70,771
Diamonds & Pearl Trading Limited	£82,428	Copper Still Company Limited	£70,700
The Langwith Brewing Company Limited	£81,617	Frontier Trading Limited	£70,635
Sindherfoods Limited	£81,374	Wine Divine Ltd	£70,521
Orbit Wines Limited	£81,246	Quest Leisure Limited	£70,494
Dowbridge Distributors Ltd	£80,814	NYSA International Ltd	£70,000
MCAL Sweet Retail Limited	£80,722	Oldschool Wines Limited	£69,835
Harrydev Limited	£80,523	Cangiani UK Ltd	£69,637
Evernex Ltd	£80,324	Preston Wines Ltd	£69,593
J.Braham Everett Imports Ltd	£80,083	Jetchill Ltd	£69,547
D & V Wines Ltd	£80,048	More Sake Limited	£68,957
The Special Cider Company Limited	£79,727	The Bottle Drinks Company Ltd	£68,468
Highball Brands Limited	£79,685	Westgarth Wines Limited	£68,275
Passion Wine International Limited	£79,227	Donaldson Reeves Limited	£68,005
Portuguese Story Ltd	£79,129	Spitfire Heritage Distillers Limited	£67,961
Professional Wine Services Limited	£78,263	West Coast Wines & Spirits Ltd.	£67,600
Wyld Rose Ltd	£78,176	Italian Appellations Limited	£67,433
Quiqui Mezcal Ltd	£78,069	Red & White Wines Limited	£66,854
The Wine Explorer Limited	£77,764	Vinnaturo Ltd	£66,409
The Wine Library Limited	£77,615	Co Stars London Ltd	£66,075

Company	Amount	Company	Amount
Ray Jules Limited	£66,035	Hamer & Perks Limited	£57,598
Alexander Muir & Son Limited	£65,903	Glacon Limited	£57,519
Fairway Foods Limited	£65,878	Underground Spirits Limited	£57,393
Cana Import Limited	£65,756	Frenchvines Limited	£57,333
Haslemere Wine Merchants Limited	£65,470	Aizia Ltd	£57,159
Diabolus Limited	£65,385	Carmelita Limited	£56,972
Edward James Limited	£65,238	Coles Trading Limited	£56,485
Smiley Rhyme Limited	£65,126	Domaine des Jeanne Limited	£56,445
Let There Be Beer Ltd	£65,080	The Brompton Wine Company Limited	£56,432
Moore's Enterprises Limited	£64,977	O'Neill Fine Wines Limited	£56,376
Marta Vine Limited	£64,946	Les Vignerons de Saint Georges Limited	£56,136
Waveney Ales and Ciders Limited	£64,827	Bristol Fine Wine Limited	£56,074
Ufton Travel Retail Limited	£64,648	Four Seasons Hastings Ltd	£55,947
Freerun Consulting Limited	£64,555	Valinch & Mallet Limited	£55,616
Traditional Beer Company Ltd	£64,508	The Bottle Shop (Penarth) Limited	£55,377
Smart Save Distribution Limited	£63,909	Woody Nook Wines (UK) Limited	£55,008
Peter Osborne Fine Wines Ltd	£63,725	Safeway Distribution Limited	£54,693
Olivers Wine Agency Limited	£63,686	Potocki Spirits (Europe) Limited	£54,651
Castle Eden Beer Company Limited	£63,656	Direct2door Food & Beverage Ltd.	£54,610
Bekel Limited	£63,427	Billings & Briggs Ltd	£54,567
The Salto Cachaca Company Limited	£63,412	Watson Food & Beverages Ltd	£54,532
Russell Mellor and Company Limited	£63,183	Brooks & Whitaker Limited	£54,297
Lynch Associates Ltd	£63,078	Vincisive Wines Limited	£54,045
Gianni. B. Limited	£63,070	Abyss Brewing Ltd	£53,799
Hardywood Park Craft Brewery Ltd.	£63,024	Inverarity Vaults Limited	£53,660
Broad Street Brands Limited	£62,949	Olive Wines Limited	£53,653
Wiland Wines Limited	£62,519	The Great Whisky Company Ltd	£53,229
The Broadway Drinks Company Ltd	£62,438	Decanter Wines Limited	£53,185
JR First Choice Cash & Carry Ltd	£62,142	Champagne Duval-Leroy (UK) Limited	£52,913
Sfuso Wine Limited	£61,820	The French Wine Project Limited	£52,851
Kold Group Limited	£61,807	Silly Point Wines Limited	£52,790
AK Cash & Carry Ltd	£61,778	Red Dragon Brewery Ltd.	£52,740
Italimport (Wessex) Limited	£61,609	Grape Drinks (UK) Limited	£52,651
First Crew Ltd	£61,575	Albion Fine Wines Ltd	£52,583
Vine Wine Limited	£61,468	Smashing Wines Limited	£52,454
CPC Business Limited	£61,297	Midhurst Wine Shippers Limited	£52,436
Mayfly Wine Company Ltd.	£61,160	Shellys Drinks Limited	£52,397
The Boutique Spirit Company Limited	£61,111	Old Town Blending Company Ltd	£52,228
Denby Dale Wines Limited	£60,626	Wanderlust Wine Limited	£52,198
Roland Wines Ltd	£60,574	Provence Impex Limited	£52,141
Iron Pier Brewery Limited	£60,568	Banini UK Ltd	£52,101
Chevalier de Mentaubert Limited	£60,107	Meanwhile Drinks Ltd.	£51,920
Inside Trax Limited	£60,072	Metropolitan Spirits (U.K.) Limited	£51,907
Boot Liquor Wholesale Limited	£60,040	Cocksure Brewing Company Limited	£51,883
Dark Revolution Ltd	£60,015	Kraft Beer UK Ltd	£51,731
Kese International Ltd	£60,000	The First & Last Brewery Ltd	£51,729
3F Leisure Limited	£59,771	Richway Cash and Carry Ltd	£51,545
The Wine Cellar Midlands Limited	£59,721	Sandhu IT Services Ltd	£51,440
Hallamshire Wine Shipping Co. Limited	£59,319	Spot Wines Limited	£51,408
Hanging Ditch Wine Merchants Ltd	£58,811	Humo International Limited	£51,332
Rip Mountain Brewery Ltd.	£58,528	Benjamin & Blum Limited	£51,247
Mephisto Wine Merchants Limited	£58,404	Oliver & Bird Limited	£51,165
JJ Wholesalers Ltd	£58,138	The Bottlers Limited	£50,982
Lancaster Wines Limited	£58,043	Harlington Wine Limited	£50,938

Vinovest Limited	£50,563	Wines of The Americas Limited	£45,502
Beer Belly's Ltd	£50,515	Leo Global Limited	£45,485
Fairview Wines Limited	£50,506	Liptons Food & Wine Limited	£45,434
Bordeaux Undiscovered Limited	£50,305	Richmond Distillers (Zurich) Limited	£45,195
Sedgemoor Drinks Limited	£50,002	Enopoli Limited	£45,150
Lunzer Wine Group Limited	£49,915	Worthington Wine and Spirits UK Limited	£45,061
Cleveland Bar Supplies Limited	£49,839	Dima's Vodka UK Ltd	£45,001
Greatvine Ltd	£49,807	Pearl Leisure Limited	£44,964
Single Malts Limited	£49,701	D D S Food Imports Ltd	£44,892
Winecorp Limited	£49,438	Casa Ambar Limited	£44,837
Guilty Libations Limited	£49,384	M D (Cash & Carry) Limited	£44,579
Midlands Drinks Limited	£49,265	Seth Ventures Limited	£44,480
Marta's Vinyard Limited	£49,260	Tom I'Anson Wines Ltd	£44,388
Specialist Cellars Ltd	£49,004	Thirsty Brands Ltd	£44,283
Icknield Stores Ltd	£48,967	Rurkee Trading Company Limited	£44,236
Wintrad Ltd	£48,892	Haycock's No.9 UK Ltd	£44,096
Yaved Ltd	£48,884	Babicka Vodka (International) Limited	£44,092
Peruvian Enterprises Limited	£48,638	Beveridge Wines Ltd	£44,033
Aston Jones Limited	£48,514	Sylvestre Limited	£43,864
Bourgognes Only Limited	£48,394	J.R.G. Investments Limited	£43,823
Ewer Limited	£48,092	Kegs of Camberley Limited	£43,688
Jack Sullivan (Properties) Limited	£48,042	Jays Beverages Limited	£43,562
James MacArthur & Co Limited	£47,982	Vitam Dare Limited	£43,478
Englishman Supplies Limited	£47,859	Bacchus Wine Auctions Limited	£43,459
Cooper Hill Brewery Ltd	£47,760	Tayst Ltd	£43,253
Andes Trading Limited	£47,639	Chez Antoine Ltd	£43,041
Brand Central (UK) Limited	£47,541	Mr. Alba International Trading Company Limited	£42,888
Liquid Solutions Distribution (N.I.) Limited	£47,462	Country Life Brewery Ltd	£42,879
Allum Limited	£47,452	PFG Marketing Ltd	£42,705
Impulse Global Ltd	£47,254	Marani Wines Limited	£42,603
Draft Link Limited	£47,244	D'Urberville Vineyard Limited	£42,492
Halifax Wine Company Ltd	£47,194	Ragarfield International Limited	£42,477
Hyde & Sons Limited	£47,157	Casa Leal Ltd	£42,408
United Phoenix Limited	£47,097	McKenzie Fine Wines Limited	£42,176
55 Above Ltd	£46,887	Whitetail Spirits Limited	£42,150
Prostimo Ltd	£46,733	Rutherglen Scotch Whisky Co. Ltd.	£41,912
Sporting Benefits Limited	£46,461	Dion Wines & Food Limited	£41,908
Waistcoat Wines Ltd	£46,445	Big Mouth Wine Limited	£41,827
Prime Wines Limited	£46,260	Fegan Wholesale Ltd	£41,827
100cl Limited	£46,156	Malvern Ltd	£41,527
Label Bouchon Limited	£46,150	Fine Cider Limited	£41,422
DN Pacifica Ltd	£46,124	Xisto Wines Limited	£41,343
Collective Trading Limited	£46,063	Family of Hounds Limited	£41,226
Epicurean Food and Drink Corporation Limited	£46,041	Leyland Home Brew Limited	£41,205
Mahal Enterprises Limited	£46,032	Bath Sixteen Limited	£41,083
Young in Spirit Ltd	£46,004	Different Wines Limited	£41,045
Fameface Import Limited	£46,000	Rutherford, Shirlaw and Denholm Limited	£41,012
Mercury Spirits Ltd	£45,984	Maison Liedberg Limited	£41,001
The Wineman (UK) Ltd	£45,825	Staibano Ltd	£41,001
Michael Jobling Wines Ltd	£45,757	LDW Wines Limited	£40,750
The Independent Vintner Ltd	£45,635	Westvine International Ltd	£40,563
Libertine Spirits Ltd	£45,629	Woodwinters Agencies Limited	£40,392
The Indian Runner Drinks Company Limited	£45,524	Lupton Wine Limited	£40,358
The Red Bottle Company Limited	£45,524	Anglo Drinks Limited	£40,098

Mike Hothersall Wines Limited	£40,068	Moke Fine Wines Limited	£34,964
The Wine Agency Ltd	£39,880	Spirimix Limited	£34,937
Australian Vintage (Europe) Limited	£39,710	Blakes Fine Wine Ltd	£34,904
Afrogrocers Ltd	£39,652	Utku Emre Ltd	£34,798
Lucky Drinks 4 U Ltd	£39,644	Woburn Wine Company Limited	£34,697
Pale Fox Wines Limited	£39,639	Grandi Vini Limited	£34,528
Wine Consultants Limited	£39,437	Fair Fayre Food & Wines Limited	£34,443
Otros Vinos Limited	£39,171	Aleksic & Mortimer Ltd	£34,415
Main Sail Trading Company Limited	£39,151	Drinkscraft Limited	£34,295
Varmont Ltd	£39,061	Original Wooden Case Limited	£34,211
Eurorock Trading Limited	£38,860	El Toro Wines Limited	£33,917
The Haycock's Drinks Company Ltd	£38,660	Moonshine Traders Ltd	£33,603
Deskbeers Limited	£38,619	The Wine Prophets Limited	£33,557
Soul Spirits Ltd	£38,601	Georges de la Chapelle Limited	£33,475
JSF Services Limited	£38,522	Jelly Bowl Ltd	£33,447
Ran Ales Ltd	£38,453	BD Wines Limited	£33,407
Cartwright Brothers Vintners Limited	£38,256	Belloni Limited	£33,291
Sagittarius World Limited	£38,132	Amwell Springs Brewery Company Limited	£33,156
Monaghan Marketing Limited	£37,997	Fizz Guru Limited	£33,093
Vickbar Limited	£37,990	Better Buy Ltd	£32,979
Supermarket Solutions Limited	£37,961	Bridgnorth Brewing Co. Ltd.	£32,938
Galette Wines Limited	£37,937	414 Alcohols Limited	£32,698
Gain Brands International (UK) Ltd	£37,933	Grace Wines (UK) Limited	£32,641
Drop The Anchor Brewery Ltd	£37,729	Spirits International Management Limited	£32,605
Organic Wine Company Limited (The)	£37,700	Alcohology Ltd	£32,597
Quintrox Limited	£37,629	Golden Decanters Limited	£32,534
DFG Distribution Ltd	£37,614	Paramount Vintners Ltd	£32,500
Elements Eight Rum Company Limited	£37,581	Favourite Beers Limited	£32,448
Markets It Ltd.	£37,442	Gudfish Limited	£32,143
Gabby & Bello Enterprises Ltd	£37,436	Hillbridge Estates Limited	£32,039
Conroy-Hood Limited	£37,325	H & W Wines Limited	£31,998
Peatreekers Limited	£37,267	Sloane Home Ltd	£31,948
Transylvania Wine Ltd	£37,166	Abercrombie Fine Wines Limited	£31,898
Kan Trading Limited	£37,008	MK Sales Training Limited	£31,896
North West Spirits Limited	£36,980	McNicoll and Cairnie Limited	£31,848
Deliverance Dot Com Limited	£36,864	Simavin Limited	£31,816
Stableyard Wines Limited	£36,671	Karma Beverages Ltd	£31,807
Personalised Care Solutions Ltd	£36,494	Brian Traders Ltd	£31,519
Giesen Wines UK Limited	£36,219	Test Tube Products Limited	£31,491
Vino Italiano Importers Limited	£36,123	Roohop Ltd	£31,416
Clarkes Drinks Direct Limited	£36,086	Gunners Cocktails Limited	£31,414
Maison du Vin Ltd	£35,822	Cold Formd Ltd	£31,230
Evokesomm Limited	£35,821	La Vigneronne Fine Wines Limited	£31,218
Etna Food & Wine Ltd	£35,758	London Calling Sweden Ltd	£31,101
Skull X Ltd	£35,710	Amirante Empire Limited	£31,022
Pembrokeshire Drinks Limited	£35,575	J.W.L Wholesale Drinks Ltd	£30,992
Paso-Primero UK Ltd.	£35,507	Lobins Limited	£30,965
BFA Holdings Limited	£35,361	Buzwine Limited	£30,778
Planet Wine Trading and Consulting Limited	£35,297	Anglium Ltd	£30,590
Retaliate Limited	£35,207	Jam Consultants Global Limited	£30,507
Aquitania Ltd	£35,178	Piaff Trading UK Limited	£30,503
Siderea Consulting Limited	£35,173	Walker & Wodehouse Wines Limited	£30,326
Prestige Vintners Limited	£35,134	Parmar Drinks & Wines Ltd	£30,253
Thorne Wines Limited	£35,071	Manor Park Drinks Ltd.	£30,102

Ftspot Limited	£30,029	Chateau de la Combe Ltd	£25,322
Groupe Prestige Ltd	£30,000	Burdett Wines Ltd	£24,946
Bedminster Beer Company Limited	£29,970	The Original Bier Company Limited	£24,702
Black Dog Wine Agency Limited	£29,918	Panton Ventures Limited	£24,604
The Beer People Limited	£29,801	Bibere Ltd.	£24,552
Beviqua Ltd	£29,773	Taste of Georgia Limited	£24,421
Malt Whisky Agency Ltd	£29,602	Cayenes Ltd	£24,172
Bone Machine Brewing Company Limited	£29,508	Zing Vodk Limited	£23,873
Jimmy's Beer & Gas (Wirral) Limited	£29,446	4 Star (Leicester) Limited	£23,855
Allied Wholesale Ltd	£29,398	Black Cat Brewery Limited	£23,795
Avalon Wholesale and Brewing Limited	£29,296	New School Wines Limited	£23,599
Force Brewery Limited	£29,262	3ABC Ltd	£23,568
Tristan James Ltd	£29,204	Pacta Connect UK Limited	£23,554
Talbot & Barr Limited	£28,966	Hot Corks Limited	£23,548
George Sinclair & Sons Limited	£28,960	Taste Buds Wines Limited	£23,384
W.G. Paterson & Son Limited	£28,790	Village Cottages (Cornwall) Limited	£23,370
Pollen Cider Ltd	£28,787	Champagne One Ltd	£23,108
Ishka Wines and Spirits UK Limited	£28,722	The Keg & Bottle Ltd	£23,097
Scrawny Al Ltd	£28,432	TL Step By Step Limited	£23,096
Jack Brooksbank Limited	£28,276	Hingston & Co. Ltd	£23,046
Ascott Invest Limited	£28,256	Trade Network Supplies Limited	£22,934
Polat International Ltd	£28,180	Iron & Rose Ltd	£22,893
D K Beers Ltd.	£28,132	Best of Hungary Ltd	£22,887
Northgate Wines Limited	£28,121	Woori Trade Ltd	£22,853
Discover Wine (UK) Ltd	£28,119	Chaps Group Limited	£22,742
Deholjob Limited	£28,020	Crazy Gin Ltd	£22,638
Taste Italia Limited	£27,923	Lisbon Wines Limited	£22,343
Olley (NE) Limited	£27,752	Thru The Glass Limited	£22,297
Burbage Wines Limited	£27,605	The Poshmakers Ltd	£22,287
Barkin Bars Ltd	£27,581	The Wine Carafe Limited	£22,122
Drinks 4 Less (UK) Limited	£27,446	Go Brazil Wines & Spirits (UK) Ltd	£21,895
A1 Resources Limited	£27,120	Fortunae Limited	£21,730
Simply Beers Limited	£27,084	All Food Supplies Ltd	£21,710
N G K Wholesale Limited	£27,083	Spirits for Good CIC	£21,646
Scotland Grindlay Limited	£27,009	H & G Corporation Ltd	£21,437
Infinity Wines Limited	£26,993	Distilled Brands Limited	£21,402
Montann Limited	£26,774	Largesse Corporate Gifts (2007) Limited	£21,274
V G International Trading Limited	£26,710	Zefino Family Limited	£21,233
Dr Dougan (Enterprises) Limited	£26,569	Natural Bay Limited	£20,990
Okowita Vodka Limited	£26,480	Chillwines Limited	£20,955
Lonerider UK Ltd	£26,429	Sarpanch Food & Wine Distributors Ltd	£20,926
Old Sport Limited	£26,371	Hooton Management Limited	£20,709
Padstow Brewing Company (2013) Ltd	£26,362	The Antique Wine Co (Holdings) Limited	£20,707
Italy on Tap Ltd	£26,298	Jays Trading Ltd	£20,685
Park Place Drinks Limited	£26,259	Cadestin International Wines Limited	£20,644
Cold Black Label Limited	£26,164	Arda Rohat Limited	£20,632
ASG Wines Limited	£26,078	Opus Cellars Limited	£20,604
Real Ales AT Limited	£25,981	MyNaturalCompany Limited	£20,512
Kolson Energy Limited	£25,939	Nowselect Limited	£20,420
Tikka Beer Limited	£25,906	Europebro Wholesalers Ltd	£20,414
Polskie Wodki Ltd	£25,658	Foxhole Spirits Limited	£20,333
Woodland Wine Store Limited	£25,614	Andina Trade Ltd	£20,277
Amy's Wine House Limited	£25,570	Cut Rum Limited	£20,211
Aurora Ales Limited	£25,500	ANA Distribution Limited	£20,204

Blue Island Limited	£20,134	Inverroche Ireland Ltd	£16,761
Villa Sofia Limited	£20,103	Valley Wines, Beer & Spirits Limited	£16,590
Up Front Brewing Limited	£19,927	Burton Rd Brewing Co Limited	£16,576
Noble Wines (UK) Limited	£19,850	Harmonicande Vintners Ltd	£16,475
DT1 Ltd	£19,723	Malts of Scotland Ltd	£16,373
Direct Beers Limited	£19,715	DSC Imports Limited	£16,349
Champagne G.H. Martel & Co. (U.K.) Ltd	£19,671	Wineguise Limited	£16,154
Friends of Wine Ltd	£19,533	Deeti Wholesale Limited	£16,136
Bottle Butler Limited	£19,495	Du Terroir A La Table Limited	£16,101
JH Wine Agencies Ltd	£19,490	Kilo Wines Ltd	£16,032
The Idle Hour Spirit Company Ltd	£19,462	Ledbury Wine Limited	£15,976
Coombe Farm Wines Limited	£19,306	Three Swallows Ltd	£15,916
Be Organiq Limited	£19,275	F & M Cressi Limited	£15,802
Emporium Import Ltd	£19,208	Enovino Organic Ltd	£15,801
Sam-Gel Global Ventures Limited	£19,208	Highlands Whisky Company Ltd	£15,763
Applethwaite Wines Ltd	£19,208	Lionel Export Agency Ltd	£15,718
Call-a-Keg Beverages Ltd	£19,169	Highly Spirited Ltd	£15,682
23 High Path Ltd	£19,039	Il Tastevin Ltd	£15,621
Strongwells Limited	£18,994	Skyfall Distribution Limited	£15,617
Deniz & Ada Limited	£18,984	Beer and Spirit Agencies International Limited	£15,528
The Drinks Agency Ltd	£18,975	Gemeaux Limited	£15,516
AB Care Connect Limited	£18,865	Tour de Force Wines Limited	£15,510
Skinny Booze Limited	£18,846	ASA Ventures Limited	£15,484
G Life Limited	£18,764	Separateflow Limited	£15,477
888 Global Trade Ltd	£18,591	I.G.T. Management Ltd	£15,368
Henry de Vaugency Ltd	£18,537	Liqueurs de France Limited	£15,358
Pan Euro Foods Limited	£18,448	The Original Herbale Brewing Company Ltd	£15,302
Mastiha World Ltd	£18,440	The Champagne Collection Limited	£15,266
Botella Imports Ltd	£18,403	Terra Wines Limited	£15,215
Bobby Beer Company Limited	£18,354	Decanter Trading Company Limited	£15,115
GreatWineDirect Limited	£18,165	Carter Importing Ltd	£15,033
Salonica Limited	£18,050	Horsetown Beers Limited	£15,022
Grapebee Ltd	£17,958	Dragon Drinks Limited	£15,016
Japan Gourmet (UK) Limited	£17,928	Bodega Uncielo (UK) Limited	£14,883
Full Logistic Ltd	£17,848	Hydraun Limited	£14,851
Whisky 78 Ltd	£17,832	Willoughbys Limited	£14,821
Southover Drinks Limited	£17,807	Dew Hill Blending Company (Glasgow) Limited	£14,662
Con Gusto Wines Limited	£17,763	Universal Drinks Ltd	£14,594
Whiteleys of Halifax Limited	£17,691	Caribbean Trade Ltd	£14,560
Kairos Solutions Ltd	£17,630	Call-a-Keg (Scotland) Limited	£14,358
Saints Row Brewing Co. Ltd.	£17,490	Scot Bottle Limited	£14,339
Invino Vitalis Ltd	£17,424	Kramjar Limited	£14,264
No.9 Leisure Limited	£17,419	Aberdrinks Scotland Limited	£14,162
Maverick Ventures UK Ltd	£17,328	HG & S Ltd	£14,161
Magic Spells Brewery Limited	£17,236	O & P Investments Limited	£14,157
Delivering Happiness Limited	£17,188	Fifty One Forty Limited	£14,092
The Quarter Cafe Bar Limited	£17,136	UK Wine & Food Supplies Ltd	£14,014
Premium Bulgarian Wine Ltd	£17,109	Beacon Wines Limited	£13,865
Vats Wine Co. Limited	£17,070	Play Limited	£13,843
Vertigo Beers Limited	£17,056	Pellegrino Wine and Food Distribution Ltd	£13,835
Jabru Bevco Ltd	£17,036	Giuseppe's Wines Limited	£13,808
Uokka Limited	£16,894	Drinks Depot Ltd	£13,756
KLR & RCR Distribution Ltd	£16,892	Viniguide Limited	£13,700
Distillers Direct Ltd	£16,862	The Drinks Guild Ltd	£13,683

Drinkintime Ltd.	£13,651	Simpsons Wine Imports Limited	£11,098
The Mixed Case Limited	£13,631	Beer Rocks Brewery Ltd	£11,064
Rafti Ltd.	£13,608	Atlantis Iberica Ltd	£10,966
Xpress Bootleg Limited	£13,562	Hoptimism Limited	£10,915
Provino Limited	£13,561	Bosman Wines UK Ltd	£10,850
The Three Graces Liverpool Ltd	£13,454	GWB Associates Limited	£10,817
Quick Liquids Limited	£13,443	NJA Marketing Ltd	£10,759
Jackson & Seddon Ltd	£13,338	Teqcoola Limited	£10,690
The Wine Keg Company Limited	£13,335	Kinkell Brewery Ltd	£10,684
The Portuguese Fine Wine Company Limited	£13,280	Adaka Group Ltd	£10,525
Gin Corporation Limited	£13,109	Leinburn Limited	£10,509
Chacalli-De Decker Ltd.	£13,085	Windward Trading Company Ltd	£10,507
Needhams Wines Limited	£13,073	Library Design Studio Ltd.	£10,388
Dumenil Champagne Limited	£12,977	Edward Tatham Champagne Limited	£10,376
Above Brand Limited	£12,966	Lucky Spirits Ltd	£10,367
Samuels Brewing Company Ltd	£12,933	Crafted Beverages Limited	£10,332
Camino Real Limited	£12,841	Sunny Group Limited	£10,312
Laurence Leisure Limited	£12,809	3 Lids Rum Ltd	£10,296
FVFC Limited	£12,808	Ora Brewing Company Ltd	£10,286
Dayboat Limited	£12,689	One Love Rum Company Limited	£10,218
Urban Wholesalers Limited	£12,582	Luxury Alcohols Limited	£10,180
M & B Distributions (UK) Ltd	£12,573	Cabezac Collections Limited	£10,096
Himalaya Wines Limited	£12,546	MA Wine and Spirit Imports Limited	£10,055
Burgundy Wines Limited	£12,531	The Madison Drinks Company Limited	£10,000
JWM Vintners Limited	£12,441	Authentic French Wines (Importers) Limited	£9,890
Healthy Wines Ltd	£12,365	Scott's of Quorn (Wine Bar & Vintners) Limited	£9,822
SJ Wines Ltd	£12,349	Aftersunset Ltd	£9,659
Tikves London Ltd	£12,193	D & K Capital Ltd	£9,591
Karla & Co. Spirits Limited	£12,166	Tokaj Merchants Ltd	£9,575
Profile Wines Limited	£12,119	Les Caves de Camille Ltd	£9,568
Hazelbank Limited	£12,116	Bemco International (UK) Limited	£9,473
Bordeaux and Beyond Ltd	£12,058	Vino Pronto UK Ltd	£9,431
The Ship & Mitre Brewing Company Limited	£12,051	Koha Distribution Limited	£9,421
Bablake Wines Limited	£12,000	MMC Sales and Marketing Limited	£9,366
La Vigna Vini Ltd	£12,000	Steel Coulson Ltd	£9,333
Evil Spirits Ltd	£11,979	Hannibal Brown Wine Services Limited	£9,299
Native Oracle Limited	£11,851	Neptune Rum Ltd	£9,292
London Drinks and Beers Ltd	£11,821	Drinksman Limited	£9,282
Clara Wines Limited	£11,780	Trust in Global Food Ltd	£9,260
The Opendoor Gin Company Ltd	£11,760	Helluva... Limited	£9,246
Oak Cask Distribution Ltd	£11,756	Amore G.N.A. Limited	£9,171
101 Reykjavik UK Ltd	£11,618	Ali Booze Company Limited	£9,169
Whitley Neill Limited	£11,612	RC Brands Ltd	£9,164
Schuler Wine St. Jakob's Cellars Limited	£11,600	The Plum Brandy Company Limited	£9,090
Buchanan Wines Ltd.	£11,553	Stag Brewery Ltd	£9,000
Vin D'Oc Limited	£11,544	The Cotswold Port Co. Ltd	£8,985
Half Cut Wines Limited	£11,539	Glenalan Limited	£8,850
The Art of Wine Ltd	£11,505	Scotch Whisky International Limited	£8,850
Novus BH Magister Ltd	£11,474	Love and Labour Ltd.	£8,837
World Cider Box Limited	£11,461	Intriguing Brands Limited	£8,820
Vinterest Limited	£11,351	Shonty Group Ltd	£8,783
Tenuta Tremollito Wines Ltd	£11,230	MGW World Ltd	£8,764
Gem Wines Ltd	£11,195	L'Altre VI Limited	£8,676
N R Wines Limited	£11,104	The Old Man Rum Company Limited	£8,568

Spowart Wines Limited	£8,557	Stow Brewery Limited	£6,762
The Rum Club Ltd	£8,515	D & M Nicholls Limited	£6,659
Chilli Marketing Promotions Limited	£8,500	Grainger Fine Wines Ltd	£6,652
Adam & Herv Limited	£8,480	Diwine Piemonte Limited	£6,391
Wine IT Limited	£8,423	Buke Limited	£6,386
Draught Services Ltd	£8,417	New Age Wines Ltd	£6,366
Da Vinci Traders Ltd	£8,398	Zinstream Wine Limited	£6,356
Grapes of Hungary Ltd	£8,355	Polaris Wines Ltd	£6,309
Enny Wines Ltd	£8,339	Da'mos Food & Beverages Limited	£6,230
Wester Spirit Co. Ltd	£8,331	Our Tino Ltd	£6,190
Vitkovitch Brothers Limited	£8,278	Whisky Global Ltd	£6,154
Trailblazing Wine Ltd	£8,255	The Drunk Maitre D Limited	£6,135
Nue Innovations Limited	£8,213	Domaine Watson Ltd	£6,096
Vitesse Vintners Limited	£8,212	Colchester Mann Limited	£6,091
Liquid Brand Marketing Limited	£8,177	The New Muscovy Company Limited	£6,072
Garmence Limited	£8,174	88 Connect Ltd	£6,053
Original Liqueur Co Ltd	£8,126	Present Tense Limited	£6,049
SO & T Consulting Limited	£8,099	Scimedex Limited	£6,002
Mathieu Poulain Limited	£8,047	Essenza Di Romagna Limited	£6,002
PSB Trading Limited	£7,994	The Wine Butler Limited	£6,000
Algebra Drinks Ltd	£7,979	Quero Enterprise Ltd	£5,956
Sharing The Best Limited	£7,972	Wineaux Ltd	£5,934
North East Hold Limited	£7,962	Wycombe Wine Company Limited	£5,927
RK Vodka Limited	£7,895	Basket Press Wines Ltd	£5,909
Wine Marketings Europe Ltd	£7,894	Sofibel Ltd	£5,870
Left Coast Distribution Limited	£7,873	Investmentwine Ltd	£5,811
Exmoor Wines Limited	£7,809	The Belgian Life Limited	£5,696
Tropical Ltd	£7,788	Milk Money Limited	£5,528
Premia Brands Trading Limited	£7,723	Booze Crew Leeds Ltd	£5,496
Zinea Global Services Limited	£7,704	Cenimex Ltd	£5,481
Lazy Lizard Beer Company Ltd	£7,700	Colorado Craft Spirits Ltd	£5,470
New World Trading Europe Ltd.	£7,694	Provenance Projects 2016 Ltd	£5,421
Infotonomy Ltd	£7,675	Samco Global Foods Ltd	£5,420
Mothership Beer Ltd	£7,661	Italian Wine Buyers Club Limited	£5,357
Oenofuture Limited	£7,651	Reids Gold Brewing Company Ltd	£5,305
Scotia Blending Company Limited	£7,620	Szicsek Palinka Ltd	£5,262
Nekter Wines Ltd	£7,619	Wokka Spirits Limited	£5,231
Winecraft Ltd	£7,578	Rhymney Brewery Western Ltd.	£5,216
Famille Clarke Limited	£7,571	Bondi Brewery Limited	£5,216
Mysomm.Com Ltd	£7,528	Altar Wines Limited	£5,131
Global Drinks (UK) Limited	£7,358	Iberian Wine Shippers Limited	£5,056
Manchester Merchant Wines Ltd	£7,341	Circle View Business Consultancy Ltd	£5,045
Neil Morrissey Real Ale Company Ltd	£7,330	Vickery Wines Limited	£5,029
Top Alco Ltd	£7,328	Angeli Del Vino Limited	£5,022
TTO Limited	£7,320	Cosmic Services Limited	£4,994
MM Drinks Ltd	£7,201	Sammartini Ltd	£4,938
JC Wine Events Ltd	£7,199	Continental Beer Services Ltd	£4,934
ANM Trading Limited	£7,142	Redvulette Ltd	£4,836
Pinewood Vyntners Limited	£7,131	Bouquet Limited	£4,816
Gvino Limited	£7,089	Rodney Tompkin Fine Wines Limited	£4,795
The Old Cellar Ltd	£7,075	LCW (Glasgow) Ltd	£4,762
The Dulwich Spirits Company Limited	£7,012	Victory Global Ltd	£4,485
Seabrook Wines Limited	£6,873	The Baijiu Beer Company Limited	£4,468
The Italian Wine Club Ltd	£6,763	Wine Associates Limited	£4,361

Vinotrans Ltd	£4,217	JJBrands Limited		£2,658
Big Fish Brewing Company Limited	£4,197	Andreev Services Ltd		£2,623
Delecta Limited	£4,122	Wein Forum - Fine Wines Limited		£2,514
Apley Hall Wines Limited	£4,096	The Atlantic Craft Soda Company Ltd		£2,472
Corkhaus Ltd	£4,068	The Ballance Group Limited		£2,431
Volfram Ltd	£4,063	Calduero Wine Importers Limited		£2,365
Lorelei Fine Wines Limited	£4,032	Saam Wine Company Limited		£2,340
Hoghton Brewery Limited	£4,000	Hurlingham Wine Merchants Limited		£2,255
C'est Nous UK Ltd	£3,967	YC Wines Limited		£2,220
Friendship Adventure Ltd.	£3,911	Paragon Brands Limited		£2,190
Jenuine Jamaican Products Limited	£3,858	Alexandria Partners Limited		£2,074
Sybarite Cellars Limited	£3,766	Hungarian Wine Ltd		£2,044
Vanilla Blue Limited	£3,674	De Christ Wines Ltd		£2,040
Alf Vini Limited	£3,632	Bodega Raffy UK Ltd		£2,038
Beaumont Beverages Ltd.	£3,615	Beerspotters Ltd		£2,037
Tiny Vessel Brewing Company Limited	£3,599	Highlands & Islands Scotch Whisky Company Limited		£2,014
Simon Mace Wine Broking Limited	£3,594	Seawoods Wine Ltd		£2,000
Greenmount Holdings Limited	£3,577	ACK Trading Ltd		£1,966
Pearly Queen Beer Company Ltd	£3,570	Cassago Imports Limited		£1,889
The Curious Wine Cellar Limited	£3,542	Keep Control Ltd		£1,882
CGAVL Imports Limited	£3,515	Guinexport Trade and Services Limited		£1,872
The Alternative Rum Company Limited	£3,512	Terra Toda Ltd.		£1,838
Blind Monkey Limited	£3,477	Londinio Liqueurs Ltd.		£1,795
Bad Joke Brew Co. Ltd.	£3,462	Splendid Corks Limited		£1,743
Banks & Company (Vintners) Ltd.	£3,432	Hindsight Collective Ltd		£1,711
David Alexander Wine Merchants Maidenhead Limited	£3,422	This Is Not A Party Limited		£1,667
Cru Prive Ltd	£3,328	The Jaded Group Limited		£1,607
Robb Trading Ltd	£3,309	Hurmiz UK Ltd		£1,561
The Rum Shop Limited	£3,255	Sisserou Marketing Limited		£1,548
Enmore Wine Limited	£3,225	PFS Business Services Limited		£1,546
Capion Trading Limited	£3,217	Wine Rascals Yorkshire Limited		£1,532
Europvin UK Limited	£3,196	A-Holding Ltd		£1,530
Meridian Centre Hospitality Ltd	£3,191	Medagio Limited		£1,521
Dedicated Wine Importers Limited	£3,177	Big D'Z Convenience and Winery Limited		£1,486
That Wineshop Limited	£3,174	Organic Country Drinks Ltd		£1,449
Union Brands Ltd	£3,123	Cellartrade Ltd		£1,449
Amlot Morgan Fine Wines Ltd	£3,100	Euro Link Beverages Ltd		£1,401
Lust Promotions Ltd	£3,062	79North Limited		£1,389
Mountcharge Limited	£3,012	The Drinks Link International Limited		£1,365
Xtraflow Limited	£3,007	The Glenlatterach Whisky Co Ltd		£1,360
Vett Limited	£3,006	Rebel Wine Ltd.		£1,357
Sherwood Outlaws Brewing Company Limited	£2,949	United Wine Estates Limited		£1,352
Pyvo UK Ltd	£2,945	Cadogan Wines Limited		£1,352
Ellismuir Limited	£2,938	Outstanding People Limited		£1,350
DC Imports UK Ltd	£2,937	Greenlink Enterprises Limited		£1,344
Eminent Wines Limited	£2,892	NDG (Hartlepool) Limited		£1,343
AKS Brands Limited	£2,860	Abloc UK Ltd		£1,338
The Global Wine Trading Company Limited	£2,848	Route des Vins Limited		£1,314
Saddleworth Real Ale Ltd	£2,825	Strategos Limited		£1,265
Danyal Ltd	£2,811	The Drinks Orchard Ltd		£1,262
Rive Gauche Wines (UK) Limited	£2,810	The Winesider UK Ltd		£1,261
Xorta Global Management Limited	£2,801	Mead Ho! Limited		£1,233
Altamira Management Services Limited	£2,769	Australian Wine Services Limited		£1,232
Little Gems Wine Ltd	£2,720	V & A Jobs UK Ltd		£1,230

UK Wholesalers of Beers, Wines and Spirits — dellam

Company	Amount	Company	Amount
Claribes Limited	£1,229	Anglo-African Trade Limited	£323
Vento Marino Ltd	£1,223	John Greenacre Limited	£296
Beer & Co Distribution and Sales Limited	£1,205	E J Bartholomew Limited	£295
Nightrep Limited	£1,197	Wise Imports Limited	£284
Spain Link Ltd	£1,184	Peachy Glow Limited	£245
Golden Crust & Co Limited	£1,144	The Little Grape Company Limited	£244
Craftibeer Limited	£1,142	Melen London Ltd.	£227
Oxus Gin Ltd.	£1,135	Inconcept Ltd	£221
Hoops and Champagne Ltd	£1,094	Highland Vintners Ltd	£200
Clos Vintners Limited	£1,047	Corktalk Limited	£193
Spirit of Glasgow Ltd	£1,036	UK Foods & Drinks Ltd	£178
Brighton Brew Co Ltd	£1,025	Sipping Liquor Ltd	£167
Lesont Ltd	£1,022	Vinovitaj Ltd	£159
Dita Grappolo Ltd	£1,004	Angus Wines Limited	£159
Beer Supply Limited	£1,001	Compasse Limited	£157
M & P Diffusion Limited	£1,000	Blue Magic Limited	£153
Redoor Limited	£1,000	Valenta Wine Limited	£131
Beercall Ltd	£1,000	Freight Brewing Co. Ltd	£130
Ubicumque International Ltd	£1,000	Trendbev Ltd.	£120
T & S Sales Limited	£920	Seb and Emma Ltd	£118
Cotrade Ltd	£898	The Spirit Beer Company Limited	£105
Vinexcel Limited	£897	Witney Wine Limited	£104
Spalathos Ltd.	£876	Places Trading (Suppliers) Limited	£100
Azizi Drinks Ltd	£873	KSS Drinks Limited	£100
Di.Wine Limited	£846	Logistic Park Ltd	£100
Natural Marketing Ltd	£828	Checkmate Premium Brands Ltd	£100
Premium Beverage Refreshments Ltd	£824	Kane Republik Ltd	£100
Afco Traders Ltd	£812	The Beer Company (Exports) Ltd	£100
My Global Ventures Limited	£807	The Drink Store Wholesale Limited	£100
Meless Group Limited	£780	Prestige Wine & Food (UK) Ltd	£100
Sonvino Ltd.	£741	PPbeer Ltd.	£100
Vinafrica Limited	£726	Cariel Spirits International Limited	£100
Life's A Bottle Limited	£709	Espana Imports Ltd	£100
Grey Cardinal Limited	£664	Briton Ferry Brewing Company Limited	£100
White Willows Beers, Wines and Spirits Limited	£657	Henderik & Co Limited	£100
Riedango Limited	£602	Rum Matters Limited	£100
Aims & Co Ltd	£594	MDS International Ltd.	£100
Party Drinks Company Limited	£585	Fast Moving Goods Ltd	£100
Acod S & C Ltd	£567	Lordsworth Limited	£100
London Creek Limited	£555	Blue Momentum Limited	£100
Italian Importers Ltd	£551	Swissgrapes Limited	£100
Sandhar & Kang (Birmingham) Limited	£548	Da Vinci Finest Italian Products Limited	£100
Prosit Wines Limited	£524	Copricom Ltd	£100
Franco Hetty Limited	£523	Crundale Wines Limited	£100
The Norfolk Vineyard Ltd	£464	London Spiced Dry Limited	£100
A and R Fine Wines Limited	£446	Heritiers Domec Ltd	£100
Pesodeocho Wines Ltd	£439	Attitude Spirits Ltd	£100
IMC Business Group Limited	£432	Asante Distributors Limited	£100
Vinoveritas (Europe) Limited	£423	Inverglen Scotch Whisky Co. Limited	£100
Jupiter Wholesale Limited	£408	Andrew R. Wilson Limited	£100
Shires Wine Services Limited	£405	The Shieling Scotch Whisky Co Ltd	£100
Casa Cocktails Limited	£372	Andrew Laing & Company Limited	£100
Monteadria (UK) Limited	£339	Hunter Douglas Scotch Whisky Limited	£100
Bielo Limited	£328	Raer Whisky Company Limited	£100

Philipshill Retirement Village Ltd	£100	Cantina Caputo Limited	£2		
Raer Whisky Limited	£100	United Spirit Brands Limited	£2		
Seriously Vodka Limited	£100	St.James Winery Ltd	£2		
Agave Union Limited	£100	Caribswede Ltd	£2		
Conic Brewing Limited	£100	Pull The Cork Limited	£2		
Traderhorn Limited	£99	The Drinks Emporium Limited	£2		
New Fine Wines Ltd	£91	Cador Limited	£2		
Port Ellen Distillery Company Limited	£90	Dankan Ltd	£2		
Port Ellen Distilling Limited	£90	The Bosun's Brewery Tap Ltd	£2		
Lord Krishna Trade Ltd	£64	The Oak Alliance Ltd.	£2		
Limbrey's Wine and Spirits Limited	£63	La Collina Biologica Ltd	£2		
Realsa Wines Import & Export Ltd	£58	Stack United Limited	£2		
Webdrinks Ltd	£56	Hilton & Rowley Ltd	£2		
Glenroy Spirits Limited	£35	Donnelly Wholesale Limited	£2		
Barcalima Wines Limited	£34	D.C Enterprises (Import/Export) Limited	£1		
Kerry Wines Limited	£32	Pimlico Cellars (Agencies) Limited	£1		
Sir Richard Blake & Associates Limited	£30	T.C.T.C. Services Ltd	£1		
Impala Transportation Ltd	£25	Lavinia UK Limited	£1		
Wallis Ventures Ltd	£25	Pemberton Central Limited	£1		
Coss Wines Ltd.	£18	Cosmopolitan Drinks Limited	£1		
Crucial Brands Holdings Limited	£14	ND John Wine Limited	£1		
Mill Distributors Limited	£13	B & B Drinks Ltd	£1		
Harvies of Edinburgh Limited	£11	Stewart Hill Walker UK Limited	£1		
Beer Land Ltd	£10	OM Wines Ltd	£1		
Wagner Spirits Ltd	£10	UK Beer & Soft Drinks Ltd	£1		
Highland Drinks Ltd	£10	Marlonn Food & Wine Ltd	£1		
Real Irish Whiskey Limited	£6	Amayan Terroir Selections Ltd	£1		
Muratina Limited	£5	Wine Pantry (Wholesale) Limited	£1		
Ourglass & Partners Ltd	£4	Indie Spirits Limited	£1		
The Little Big Wine Company Limited	£3	Oriental Drinks Limited	£1		
Bigg Market Brewery Company Ltd	£3	Indie Wines Limited	£1		
Bigg Market Beer Company Ltd	£3	C & E Transport Ltd	£1		
Cellarers (Wines) Limited	£2	The Cracking Little Wine Company Limited	£1		
Neu Brandenburger Beer Company Limited	£2	Leith Distillery Limited	£1		
Beyond The Ale (GB) Limited	£2	The Gin Room Scotland Ltd	£1		
Longview Wines Ltd	£2	Neat Drinks Limited	£1		

Age of Companies

1800s [8]
Adnams PLC
S.A.Brain & Co Ltd
W.H. Brakspear & Sons Limited
DEF Investments Limited
Hall & Woodhouse Limited
Marston's Acquisitions Limited
Molson Coors Brewing Co (UK) Ltd
Wadworth and Co Ltd

1900-1909
Cossart, Gordon and Co. Limited
Martinez Gassiot & Co Ltd
Justerini & Brooks, Limited

1910-1919 [8]
H.B.Clark & Co.(Successors) Ltd
Davy & Co Ltd
Hydes' Brewery Limited
Thomas Ridley and Son, Limited
Shepherd Neame Limited
St.Austell Brewery Co Ltd
Tanners (Shrewsbury) Limited
Charles Wells, Limited

1920-1929 [11]
Arkell's Brewery Limited
CADV Limited
Capper & Co Ltd
J. Chandler & Company, Ltd
John E.Fells & Sons Limited
James Hawker and Co Ltd
J. & J. Hunter Limited
Pulling & Co.Limited
George Sinclair & Sons Ltd
Waters (1802) Limited
H.T.White & Co Ltd

1930-1939 [15]
W.J.Armstrong Limited
Bacardi-Martini Limited
Oliver Burridge & Co Ltd
A. Dewar Rattray Limited
Everards Brewery Limited
Matthew Gloag & Son Limited
Gordons (Bolton) Limited
Geo Hill (Grocers) Limited
O.W.Loeb & Co Limited
Thomas Lowndes & Co. Limited
Henry Mitchell & Sons Limited
Row & Co Ltd
Stedman Bros. (Events) Limited
Wadworth & Company (Burford) Ltd
Weavers (Nottingham) Limited

1940-1949 [16]
BB & R Spirits Limited
Bruce Burlington and Co Ltd
F.L. Dickins Limited
Donatel Freres Limited
Ellis of Richmond Limited
GCBW Catrine Ltd
Hallgarten Wines, Limited
Joseph Keegan & Sons Limited
Douglas McGibbon & Co. Ltd
Russell Mellor and Co Ltd
Moet Hennessy U.K. Limited
N.Double and Co Ltd
Richmond Distillers (Zurich) Ltd
T.M. Robertson & Son Limited
Soho Wine Supply Limited
Michael Woolley Limited

1950-1959 [24]
ABA Eaglesham Ltd
Angus Dundee Distillers PLC
Bablake Wines Limited
Beefeater Distillery Limited
G. Bravo & Son Limited
Dew Hill Blending Company (Glasgow)
John Dewar and Sons Limited
Diageo Global Supply IBC Ltd
Diageo Great Britain Limited
Diageo Northern Ireland Ltd
Diageo United Kingdom Limited
Douglas Export Agency Limited
Emporia Brands Limited
Hayward Bros (Wines) Limited
Hyde & Sons Limited
Douglas Laing & Co Ltd.
Laing Shipping & Export Agency Ltd.
Ian MacLeod Distillers Ltd
Malpas Stallard Limited
A.H.Rackham Limited
Raleigh (Glasgow) Limited
Laurence Smith & Son (Edinburgh)
Spar (UK) Limited
Vintage Wines Limited

1960-1969 [35]
Wm.Addison (Newport) Limited
Berkmann Family Holdings Ltd
C & C 2011 (NI) Limited
Matthew Clark (Scotland) Ltd
Coe of Ilford Limited
Henry C. Collison and Sons Ltd
Corney and Barrow Group Ltd
Duncairn Wines Limited
Eurowines Limited
Freixenet UK Ltd
Hennings Wine Merchants Ltd
House of Townend Limited
Hurns Mineral Water Co. Ltd
If Eaglesham Ltd
J.R.G. Investments Limited
Lamba Trading Co. Limited
Landmark Wholesale Limited
M.& M.Value Limited
Ian MacLeod and Co Ltd
Mentzendorff & Co Ltd
Merchant Vintners Co Ltd
Nickolls & Perks Limited
Oldschool Wines Limited
Pieroth Limited
Rackham Investments Limited
Philip Russell Limited
Speymalt Whisky Distributors Ltd
Speyside Bonding Co Ltd
Springbank Distillers Limited
Tanners Cymru Limited
Tate-Smith Limited
Duncan Taylor Scotch Whisky Ltd
Traderhorn Limited
Vicomte Bernard de Romanet Ltd
Willoughbys Limited

1970-1979 [50]
A.F.T. (Liquor Stores) Limited
Bacchus-Les-Vignobles de France Ltd
T. & J.T. Barton (Bottlers) Ltd
Bedford Continental Wholesale Ltd
Sir Richard Blake & Associates Ltd
Broom House Investments Ltd
William Cadenhead Limited
Casa Julia Limited
Cascade Drinks Limited
Cathay Importers (London) Ltd
Cellarers (Wines) Limited
Collins Wines Limited
K. Colombier Limited
Colombier Vins Fins Limited
Connolly's (Wine Merchants) Ltd
W.& J.Cruickshank and Co Ltd
Dennhofer Wines Limited
Dhamecha Foods Limited
Dillon Bass Limited
Enotria Winecellars Limited
Epicurean Food and Drink Corporation
Farr Vintners Limited
Alfie Fiandaca Limited
G.W. Fields & Sons (Great Yarmouth)
Frazier's Wine Merchants Ltd.
Greenfield Bacon Limited
Thorman Hunt & Co Limited
Inverglen Scotch Whisky Co. Ltd
Jackson Nugent Vintners Ltd
S H Jones Wines Ltd
Kater Four (Cash & Carry) Ltd
Klostergut Limited
Laurent-Perrier (UK) Limited
Les Vignerons de Saint Georges Ltd
Lindisfarne Limited
Maison Maurice Limited
James E. McCabe Limited
Morgenrot Group PLC
Morosini Mills Limited
William Morton Limited
Praban Na Linne Limited
Quintessential Brands UK Ltd
Roberson Wine Merchant Limited
Society of Vintners Limited
Spirit Cartel Limited
Storesrealm Limited
Jack Sullivan Limited
Tanners Wines Limited
Village Cottages (Cornwall) Ltd
Wine Importers (Edinburgh) Ltd

1980-1989 [141]
Albion Wine Shippers Limited
David Alexander Wine Merchants Maidenhead
Alivini Co Ltd
Alliance Wine Co Ltd
Allson Sparkle Limited
Amathus Drinks PLC
Anjo Wines Limited
Armit Wines Limited
Aspall Cyder Limited
Baby Bottles (Wholesale) Ltd
Georges Barbier of London Ltd
Barton, Brownsdon & Sadler Ltd
Bekel Limited
Berkmann Wine Cellars Limited
David Berryman Limited
Bibendum Wine Limited
Boutinot Limited
Boxford Wine Co Ltd
Bridge Vintners Limited
Anthony Byrne Fine Wines Ltd
C & D Wines Limited
CRVC UK Limited
Champagnes and Chateaux Ltd.
Chateau Musar (U.K.) Limited
Chateau Musar International Ltd
Chetan Wholesalers Limited

UK Wholesalers of Beers, Wines and Spirits

Churchill Graham Limited
Churchill Vintners Limited
Citrosoft Drinks Limited
Continental Wines Limited
Coombe Castle Fine Wines Ltd
Corney and Barrow Limited
County Catering (Midlands) Ltd
Michel Couvreur (Scotch Whiskies)
Crouch Vale Brewery Limited
Deckers Restaurants Limited
Demball Limited
Distell International Limited
Edwards Beers and Minerals Ltd
Ely & Sidney Limited
Eurovenus Limited
France Domaines Limited
Gandhi Wine Suppliers Limited
Gelston Castle Fine Wines Ltd
General Wine and Liquor Co Ltd
Global Foods Limited
Goedhuis & Co Ltd
Good Food Wines Limited
William Grant & Sons UK Ltd
Graysons Freight Services Ltd
Great Western Wine Co Ltd
HT Drinks Ltd
Hanwood Limited
Horizon Soft Drinks Limited
Imperial Cash & Carry Limited
Imperial Distillers Co. Ltd
Imperial Wine Co Ltd
International Wine Forwarding Ltd
J.W.G. PLC
Michael Jobling Wines Ltd
Jean Juviniere Limited
Kingfisher Beer Europe Limited
Kitwave Limited
La Vigneronne Fine Wines Ltd
Lamjen Limited
Lanchester Wine Cellars Ltd
Les Producteurs et Vignerons de France
Liberty Liquors Ltd
Lombard Scotch Whisky Limited
Lorelei Fine Wines Limited
Lothbury Wine Shippers Limited
Loughborough Student Services Ltd
James MacArthur & Co Limited
Tom MacFarlane and Co Ltd
Main Rum Co Ltd
Maisons Marques et Domaines Ltd
Majestic Wine PLC
Majestic Wine Warehouses Ltd
Marathon Food Limited
Martin Enterprises Limited
Marussia Beverages UK Limited
Adrian Mecklenburgh Limited
Mieland Limited
Charles Mitchell Wines Ltd
Mondial Wine Limited
Moreno Wine Importers Co Ltd
Noreast Beers (N.I.) Ltd
Nowselect Limited
O'Neill Fine Wines Limited
Organic Wine Co Ltd
W.G. Paterson & Son Limited
Pernod Ricard UK Limited
Pimlico Dozen Limited
Christopher Piper Wines Ltd
Places Trading (Suppliers) Ltd
Prestige Vintners Limited
Quality Spirits International Ltd
Rafine Limited

Raisin Social Limited
Ravensbourne Wine Co Ltd
Quellyn Roberts (Wine Merchants)
Robert Rolls & Co. Limited
Michel Roux Limited
Russetglow Limited
Santat Wines Limited
Savage Selection Limited
Schuler Wine St. Jakob's Cellars Ltd
Seckford Wines Limited
Signatory Vintage Scotch Whisky Co Ltd
Squarewalk Limited
Stokes Fine Wines Limited
Tanner Brodin Limited
Charles Taylor Wines Limited
Tennent Caledonian Breweries Wholesale
Todd Vintners Limited
Glen Turner Co Ltd
Ty Nant Spring Water Limited
United Breweries International (U.K.)
United Supplies Limited
United Wholesale Grocers Ltd
United Wine Estates Limited
United Wine Merchants Limited
Vats Wine Co. Limited
Vickbar Limited
Vinexcel Limited
Vintage & Fine Wine International
Viscount Agencies Limited
David J. Watt (Fine Wines) Ltd
Whigham Fergusson Limited
Whitebridge Wines Limited
Whittaker Wines Limited
Andrew R. Wilson Limited
Windermere Wine Stores Limited
Windrush Holdings Ltd
Wine & Spirit International Ltd
Winecall Limited
Winelink Limited
Wise Trading Limited
World Wide Wines Limited
Wycombe Wine Co Ltd
Yapp Brothers Limited

1990-1994 [97]
A.I.M.S. (Refreshments) Ltd
Aben Wines Limited
Airways Bonded Warehouse Ltd
Alivini (North) Limited
Allum Limited
Annessa Imports Limited
Associated Church Clubs Ltd
Atlasaim International Limited
Australian Vintage (Europe) Ltd
J. & G. Barclay and Co Ltd
Baton Rouge Limited
Beatville Limited
Beer and Spirit Agencies International
Bottle Green Limited
C. & O. Wines Limited
C.P.A.'s Wine Limited
Cambridge Wine Merchants Ltd
Casella Family Brands (Europe) Ltd
Cattier UK Limited
Claribes Limited
Matthew Clark Bibendum Ltd
Colemans ABC Ltd
Dedicated Wine Importers Ltd
Drinklink Limited
East West Ales Limited
Ellis of Richmond (Holdings) Ltd
Euro-Trade and Finance Limited

Eurovines Limited
Ewer Limited
Fine & Rare Wines Limited
Finebatch Limited
Clark Foyster Wines Limited
Franchiserv Limited
Franciacorta Limited
Free Trade Beers and Minerals Ltd
G Sake Co Ltd
GSWD Catrine Ltd
GW Wines Limited
Glamorgan Brewing Co Ltd
Glenalan Limited
Hallamshire Wine Shipping Co. Ltd
Hay Hampers Limited
Walter Hicks Limited
Hops and Barley Limited
Hurns Beer Co. Limited
Imported Brands International Ltd
Inverarity Vaults Limited
Island Ales Limited
J.G. Distillers Limited
Kallwin Limited
Kedem Europe Limited
Kingsbury Wine & Spirits Co Ltd
Kingsland Drinks Limited
L H Cellar Supplies Limited
Lacons Brewery Limited
Louis Latour Limited
Levin Wines Limited
Lobins Limited
London & Scottish International Ltd
London & Scottish Spirits Ltd
Wm Maxwell (Scotch Whisky) Ltd
Marshall McGregor Limited
N. McLoone & Co. Ltd
Monteadria (UK) Limited
Alexander Muir & Son Limited
Myliko International (Wines) Ltd.
Nectar Imports Limited
Negociants UK Limited
Nene Charter Co Ltd
Neu Brandenburger Beer Co Ltd
Opus Wines Limited
Palmerston Fine Wines Ltd.
Premier Wines & Spirits Ltd
Prestonfield Whisky Co Ltd
Provenance Fine Wines Ltd
Quest Leisure Limited
Reid Wines (1992) Limited
Raymond Reynolds Limited
Chalie Richards & Co Ltd
Rivers Rum (UK) Limited
Sandhar & Kang (Birmingham) Ltd
Small Beer Limited
South Eastern Beers & Minerals Ltd
South WLC Limited
Supermalt UK Limited
Temple Wines (Cash & Carry) Ltd
Triberg Limited
Vinafrica Limited
Vinceremos Wines & Spirits Ltd
Vintage Malt Whisky Co Ltd
Wigan Beer Co Ltd
Wilkinson Vintners Limited
Wiltshire Liqueur Co Ltd
Wimbledon Wine Cellar Limited
Winery Classic Limited
Withers Agencies Limited
World Brands Duty Free Limited

1995 [28]
A. S. D. Wholesale Limited
Anglo-African Trade Limited
Beer Barrels & Minerals (Wales) Ltd
Belvoir Brewery Limited
Beyond The Ale (GB) Limited
Billecart - Salmon (UK) Ltd
Blackadder International Ltd
Broughton Ales Limited
Charente Enterprises Limited
F & M Cressi Limited
Falcon Vintners Limited
Flying Firkin Distribution Ltd
G & G Gallo Enterprises Ltd
Highland Distillers Limited
Iceaction Limited
L.A. Drinks Co Ltd
Les Caves de Pyrene Limited
Liptons Food & Wine Limited
Little Rock Wine Co Ltd
London Wine Shippers Limited
Middleton Associates Limited
Modern Vintage Wines Ltd
Narang Wholesalers Limited
North of Scotland Distilling Co Ltd
Scotch Whisky International Ltd
Scrawny Al Ltd
Swallow (Soft Drinks, Beer and Cider Wholesalers)
Whiteleys of Halifax Limited

1996 [26]
Antique Wine Co (Holdings) Ltd
Atom Supplies Limited
BI Wines and Spirits Limited
BM Wines Limited
Bengal Foods Limited
Bohemia Beer House Limited
Boondales Limited
Chacalli-De Decker Ltd.
Compass Supply Solutions Ltd
Inter Trading Leicester Ltd
Kato Enterprises Limited
Lanson International UK Ltd
Liberty Wines Limited
Life Science Limited
Madison Drinks Co Ltd
Northgate Wines Limited
Parverre Marketing Limited
Rutherglen Scotch Whisky Co Ltd
Seckford Agencies Limited
Simply Cask Ltd
Thames Distillers Limited
Vinimpo (U.K.) Limited
Vinissimo Limited
Vintage Roots Limited
Vranken Pommery UK Ltd.
Wintrad Ltd

1997 [27]
Astrum Wine Cellars Limited
Best of America Limited
Best of California Limited
Chateau de Sours Estates Ltd
D.C Enterprises (Import/Export) Ltd
Empire Star Limited
Frontier Trading Limited
Harlequin (Stockport) Limited
Richard Harvey Wines Limited
Highland Scotch Whisky Co Ltd
Highlands & Islands Scotch Whisky Co Ltd
Hillbridge Estates Limited
Interlink UK Exports Limited
Inverheath Limited
DBS Isherwood Limited
Keltek Cornish Brewery Limited
Laytons Wine Merchants Limited
Simon Mace Wine Broking Ltd
Midhurst Wine Shippers Limited
Molson Coors Brewing International
Pulse Products Limited
Sporting Benefits Limited
Star Value Limited
Jack Sullivan (Properties) Ltd
Sunnyside Incorporated Limited
Venus 14 Limited
Whittalls Wines Limited

1998 [35]
A & B Vintners Limited
Albion Fine Wines Ltd
Allied Ship Supplies (Ireland) Ltd
Beer Express Limited
Bombay Spirits Co Ltd
Bordeaux Wine Investments Ltd
CMT (Wines) Limited
Champagne Duval-Leroy (UK) Ltd
Champagne G.H. Martel & Co. (U.K.) Ltd
Delegat Europe Limited
Distell Europe Ltd.
Docklands Trading Co Ltd
Dram-a-Drinks Ltd.
Drinks Guild Ltd
Earle Wines Ltd.
Expressmode Limited
Far Out Wines Limited
Fronsacdirect Limited
Fronsacwines Limited
Hedges & Butler Limited
Highland Malt Whisky Co Ltd
Hurlingham Wine Merchants Ltd
Malthouse Inns PLC
Millesima Limited
New Muscovy Co Ltd
Pimlico Cellars (Agencies) Ltd
RD Wines Limited
Select Wine Co Ltd
Simply 1st Wine Co Ltd
Star Beers Ltd
Toorank UK Limited
Top Deal Services Ltd
Wincarnis Limited
Wine Barn Limited
Winetraders (UK) Limited

1999 [53]
Aceo Limited
Anglo Drinks Limited
Bancroft Wines Limited
Barmaster (Independent Wholesalers)
Barn Direct Limited
Barrel Booze Limited
Branded Drinks Ltd
C.O.D. Beers Limited
Cartwright Brothers Vintners Ltd
Cellar Trends Limited
Codorniu UK Limited
Cornish Point Wines UK Ltd
Crystle Limited
D S Food Imports Ltd
Decorum Vintners Limited
Di Vine Importers Limited
European Beverages Ltd
Europvin UK Limited
Fine Wine Trading Limited
Finest Wine & Delicatessen Brokers Ltd.
Fortmount Trading Limited
GWB Associates Limited
Hamer & Perks Limited
Hammonds of Knutsford PLC
Hunny Pot Pub Co. Limited
Innspired Taverns Limited
KSS Drinks Limited
Liv-Ex Limited
MBM Resource Trading International
MCAL Sweet Retail Limited
Mellasat Wines Limited
Millennium Cash & Carry Ltd
Martin Miller's Gin Limited
Mitchell's Vintners Limited
Morgan Classic Wines Limited
Mundus Wines Limited
Padstow Brewing Company (2013) Ltd
Planet Wine Trading and Consulting
Terry Platt Wine Merchants Ltd
R & B Wines Ltd
R S Wines Limited
Ratcliffe & Brown Wines and Spirits
Rosemount Pub Co. Limited
Sommeliers Choice Limited
Spencers (Bromsgrove) Limited
Speyside Distillers Co Ltd
Frank Stainton Wines Limited
Rodney Tompkin Fine Wines Ltd
Vickery Wines Limited
Wiland Wines Limited
Wine Library Limited
Wineman Limited
Worldewide Limited

2000 [42]
ASCO Foods Limited
Absolutely Organic Limited
Archangel Wines Limited
Babco UK Ltd.
Belloni Limited
Burgundy Wines Limited
Burn Stewart (U.S. Holdings) Ltd
Caves de Pierre Limited
Champagne Charlie (Midlands) Ltd
Champagne Warehouse Ltd
Claret-E Limited
Coddington Hepburn Limited
Concha y Toro UK Limited
Decanter Trading Co Ltd
Dourthe UK Limited
Edrington European Travel Retail Ltd
Edrington-Beam Suntory UK Distribution
Europemarca Limited
Europlus Trading Limited
Gleninver Limited
Peter Graham Wines Limited
Gunson Fine Wines Limited
N D John Wine Merchants Ltd
Le Bon Vin Limited
Marta's Vinyard Limited
Mickey Finn's Liquor Co Ltd.
Moore's Enterprises Limited
New Generation Wines Limited
Oeno Limited
Quartz Group Scotland Ltd
Rippingale Promotions Limited
Scavelli's Limited
Sunset Wines Limited

UK Wholesalers of Beers, Wines and Spirits

Thameside Wines Limited
Thirstee Business Limited
V.C. Vintners Limited
VDS UK Limited
WLG Limited
Winemakers Club 2000 Limited
Wokka Spirits Limited
Wold Toppers Limited
Wright Wine Co Ltd

2001 [37]

100 Pipers (Whisky) Limited
Alchemy Inns Limited
Allt A' Bhainne Distillery Ltd
Angove's (Europe) Limited
Balthazar Limited
Beer Warehouse (Maidenhead) Ltd
Blue Tree Limited
Bon Vin Inc. Limited
Calibre Brands Limited
Cameron Cavendish Fine Wines Ltd
Dalmunach Distillery Limited
Drinks Inc. Ltd
Euroboozer Limited
First Whisky Limited
Gordano Wines Limited
Grape Passions Limited
Hic-Cup Wines Limited
Hills Prospect PLC
I I Wine Limited
Isake International Limited
JWM Vintners Limited
Kerry Wines Limited
Maison Liedberg Limited
Marc Fine Wines Limited
Mullwood Wine Co Ltd
New World Trading Europe Ltd.
Potocki Spirits (Europe) Ltd
Premier Pubco Limited
R B M Leisure Limited
Scot Bottle Limited
Somborne Valley Vineyard Ltd
Superior Import/Export Limited
Vin Neuf Limited
Whisky Galore Limited
Wine Treasury Limited
Wine in Cornwall Limited
Winegrowers Direct Limited

2002 [68]

AMK Wholesale Ltd
Australian Wine Services Ltd
Battys Discount Drinks Store Ltd
Bemco International (UK) Ltd
Bottlers Limited
Burnfield Trading Co Ltd
Caribbean Trade Ltd
Cellar 28 Ltd
Champers Wines Limited
Childale Limited
Connoisseur Estates Limited
Cubic Brands Limited
De Wetshof International Ltd
Direct Booze Limited
Discover Wine Limited
Nick Dobson Ltd
Domaine Direct Limited
Essex Catering Supplies Ltd
Fairway Foods Limited
Fine Wine Co Ltd
Francis Fine Wines Ltd

Grants-EU Limited
H & W Wines Limited
HM47 Investment Projects Ltd
Hameed Investments Limited
Harvies of Edinburgh Limited
Hi-Spirits Ltd
Hoppl Wines Limited
In Vino Veritas Ltd
Intertrade Wholesale Limited
Kwik-Keg Limited
Laytons Wine Services Limited
Liqueurs de France Limited
Lithuanian Beer Limited
MJLM Limited
Maidenhead Wine Co Ltd
Main Sail Trading Co Ltd
Marlborough International (UK) Ltd
Mason & Mason Wines Limited
Meadow Trading Co Ltd
Meless Group Limited
Mountcharge Limited
N R Wines Limited
New Fine Wines Ltd
Park Royal Wholesale Limited
Portal Dingwall & Norris Ltd
Premier Cru Fine Wine Ltd.
Prostimo Ltd
RWM Holdings Limited
Red Rose Drinks Limited
Regency Event Solutions Ltd
Richmond Wine Agencies Limited
Paul Roberts Wines Limited
Sandbar German Beer Ltd
Sibell Trading Limited
Simpsons Wine Imports Limited
Sisserou Marketing Limited
Speciality Drinks Limited
T J Wines Ltd
Theatre of Wine Limited
Tikka Beer Limited
Town Centre Inns Limited
Vett Limited
Vine Trail Limited
Vineyard Belfast Limited-The
Wildflower Wines Limited
Wilks & Company Wine Merchants Ltd
Wine Explorer Limited

2003 [78]

Alcohol By Volume Limited
Ann et Vin Limited
B.D. (S/W) Ltd
Blue Island Limited
Bunnahabhain Distillery Co Ltd
C C & C Limited
Cellar Supplies Cheltenham Ltd
Celtic Wines Limited
Champagne Imports Limited
Chateau Wines Ltd.
Chilli Marketing Promotions Ltd
City Beer Limited
Cribbar Limited
Decanter Wines Limited
Deholjob Limited
Donaldson Reeves Limited
Drinkintime Ltd.
E.W.G.A. Limited
Elliston Fine Wines Limited
Exmoor Wines Limited
Genesis Wines Limited
Georges de la Chapelle Limited
Glasgow Distillers Limited

Graftyset Limited
Gordon Graham & Co Ltd
Greencroft Bottling Co Ltd
Harrow & Hope Limited
Hi - Line Wines Limited
Hollandwest Limited
Hot Corks Limited
Indigo Drinks Limited
Indigo Wine Limited
Inn Control Management Services Ltd
Inro Drinks (Abtec) Limited
Italian Wine Club Ltd
Italy Abroad Network Limited
J W Wines Ltd
Aston Jones Limited
Just Miniatures Limited
Daniel Lambert Wines Limited
Lang Brothers Limited
Levenridge Limited
C. & T. Licata & Son Limited
Lilley's Cider Limited
Liquid Measure Limited
M & T Wholesale Ltd
MCAL Merchant Limited
Manchester Merchant Wines Ltd
Marlico Limited
Natural Marketing Ltd
New Age Wines Ltd
OM Beers & Minerals Ltd
Offie Limited
Old St.Andrews Limited
Peter Osborne Fine Wines Ltd
Pivovar Ltd
Primo Drinks Ltd
Purity Brewing Co Ltd
Regency Wines Limited
Peter J Russell & Co Ltd.
S & F Drinks Limited
Sandham Wine Merchants Ltd
Sazerac UK Limited
Sheridan Cooper's Limited
Stableyard Wines Limited
Steevenson Wines Limited
Superyacht Supplies Limited
T.C.T.C. Services Ltd
Talking Wines Limited
Test Tube Products Limited
Trywines Expertise Limited
Unwined Limited
Vendange (European) Limited
Vin D'Oc Limited
Viniguide Limited
Wallaces Express Limited
Winefantastic Limited
Zonin UK Limited

2004 [64]

Alternative Rum Co Ltd
Asahi UK Ltd
Bermondsey Gin Limited
Blends Wine Estates UK Ltd
Bordeaux Undiscovered Limited
Cana Import Limited
Carob Tree Limited
Cellar Twelve Limited
Central Pubs (UK) Limited
Clarke Wholesale Limited
Cooper Hill Brewery Ltd
Creative Whisky Co Ltd
Ditton Wine Traders Ltd
Drinks Depot Ltd
Drinks Direct Limited

Ebenezer Leisure Limited
Englishman Supplies Limited
Enopoli Limited
Epicure Wines Ltd
Euro Beer Distribution Ltd
European Brand Trading Limited
Eurorock Trading Limited
Excess UK Limited
Fieldscot Ltd
Finedon Convenience Store Ltd
Gala Drinks Co Ltd
Gleeson N.I. Limited
Glug Limited
Gonzalez Byass UK Limited
Grape Escape Limited
Imbibros Ltd
International Procurement and Logistics
Mark Jefferson Wines Limited
Jelly Bowl Ltd
Kingsland Drinks Group Limited
Kirklee Scotch Whisky Limited
Las Bodegas Limited
Lavinia UK Limited
M & P Diffusion Limited
Magik Drinks Limited
Malt Whisky Co Ltd
Monaghan Marketing Limited
Monolith (UK) Ltd
Montrachet Limited
No.9 Leisure Limited
Noble Merchants Limited
Oliver & Bird Limited
Origin Wine Limited
Pembrokeshire Drinks Limited
Peruvian Enterprises Limited
Poltom Limited
Real Ale Limited
Route des Vins Limited
S and S Wines Limited
Sardinia Wine Ltd
Steamin' Billy (Property) Ltd
Taste Buds Wines Limited
Tower International Limited
UK Foods & Drinks Ltd
Universal Drinks Ltd
Whitley Neill Limited
Wickedsoup Ltd.
Wine Consultants Limited
Wine Story Limited

2005 [72]
Acacia Drinks Ltd
Astonburgh Limited
B & D Clarke Limited
BB & R Limited
Ballance Group Limited
Best of Beaujolais Limited
Best of Bordeaux Limited
Best of Burgundy Limited
Best of Loire Limited
Blue Star Inns Limited
Bon Coeur Fine Wines Limited
Boutique Brands Limited
Brighton Soft Drinks Limited
Budge Brands Ltd
Campbell Inns Limited
Casa Leal Ltd
Circle Wine Co Ltd
Coles Trading Limited
Spencer Collings & Co Limited
Coral Management Limited
Crush Wines Ltd

DGB Europe Limited
Dedicated Wines Ltd
Dhesis Wholesale Ltd
Direct Beers Limited
Drinks Link International Ltd
Du Terroir A La Table Limited
Durrants Fine Wines Limited
Edrington International Brands Ltd
Elements Eight Rum Co Ltd
Extravision Security Systems Ltd
Field and Fawcett Wine Merchants and Delicatessen
Flagship Brands Ltd
Foxstead Limited
Freixenet Copestick Limited
Frenchvines Limited
Green Island (UK) Limited
Harlington Wine Limited
Independent Drinks Supplies Ltd
International Diplomatic Supplies
Kitchen Table Wine Co. Ltd
Libra Drinks Wholesale Limited
Manchester Drinks Co Ltd
Sarah Marsh Ltd
Mille Gusti Limited
Momentum Wines Limited
Noble Green Wines Limited
Obadec Enterprises Limited
Oliver's Beer and Wine Limited
Organic Country Drinks Ltd
Orso Wine Agencies Limited
Pan Euro Foods Limited
Primo Drinks (Merseyside) Ltd
Queen of The Moorlands Whisky Co Ltd
Red & White Wines Limited
Rum Shop Limited
Rurkee Trading Co Ltd
Single Malts Limited
Snow Leopard Vodka Limited
South Downs Real Estate Ltd
Stewart Wines Limited
TFC Wholesale Ltd
USSR Limited
Universal Wines & Spirits Ltd
Vinorium Limited
Warwickshire Drinks Plus Ltd
Wemyss Vintage Malts Limited
West End Brands Ltd
Wine Divine Ltd
Wineaux Ltd
World of Patria International Ltd
Yates Iow Brewery Limited

2006 [75]
10 International Limited
247 Enterprises UK Ltd
3F Leisure Limited
4 Star (Leicester) Limited
Andrews Beer & Mineral Co Ltd
Anglium Ltd
BFA Holdings Limited
Balman Import & Export Limited
Barokes Limited
Battlefield Beers Limited
Black Forest Beers Limited
Bonfire Hill Limited
Bridgnorth Brewing Co Ltd
Brockmans Gin Limited
Brummells Gin Limited
Burbage Wines Limited
Chardon Wines Limited
Cider of Sweden Ltd

Colchester Mann Limited
Collective Trading Limited
Cumbrae Supply Co Ltd
D'Arcy Wine Merchants Limited
Denby Dale Wines Limited
Dorset Wine Co Ltd
Eden Fine Wines Limited
Eden Garden Trading Limited
Ellis Wharton Wines Ltd
Eminent Wines Limited
Flint Wines Limited
Freerun Consulting Limited
Friends of Wine Ltd
Pascal Garcia Consulting Ltd
Great Newsome Brewery Limited
Hard To Find Wines Limited
Harry's Road Fine Wine Limited
Harrydev Limited
Italy on Tap Ltd
Edward James Limited
Lay & Wheeler Limited
Leinburn Limited
Longview Wines Ltd
MWH Wine Merchants Limited
Maverick Ventures UK Ltd
Medoc Wines Limited
Mixed Case Limited
Duvel Moortgat UK Limited
Museum Wines Limited
James Nicholson Wine Limited
Norvic Ltd
Number One Drinks Co Ltd
Orion Cash & Carry Limited
Paragon Wines Limited
Norman Price Wines Limited
Provenance Marketing Ltd
Pub Pool (711) Limited
Quick-Keg Limited
Regent Wines Limited
Sin Shots (U.K.) Ltd.
Sterling Wine Agencies Limited
Swig Wines Limited
TJC Corporate Events Limited
Tiny Vessel Brewing Co Ltd
Tirion Trading Co Ltd
Triple AAA Limited
Venus Wine & Spirit Merchants PLC
Viader Vintners Limited
John Villar Wines Limited
Vitkovitch Brothers Limited
Warwick Banks and Jenkins Ltd
Weiser Taverns Beers & Minerals Ltd
Charles Wells Brewery Limited
Wine Rascals Yorkshire Limited
Wine World Producers Limited
Woody Nook Wines (UK) Limited
Worldwide Drinks Limited

2007 [70]
ADP Wines Ltd
AOC Distribution Ltd
Andes Trading Limited
Andreev Services Ltd
Approved Products Ltd
Bajan Trading Co Ltd
Bibendum PLB Group Limited
Blakes Fine Wine Ltd
Bordeaux and Beyond Ltd
Broadoak Cider Co Ltd
Brompton Wine Co Ltd
Andrew Bruce Fine Wines Ltd
Canal Cellars Ltd

UK Wholesalers of Beers, Wines and Spirits

Cayenes Ltd
City Wine Collection Limited
Colosseum Wines Limited
Connolly Wines Ltd
Coral MGT Limited
Corkers Wine Limited
DH Global Wine Ltd
Euro Wines (C & C) Limited
Exigo (UK) Limited
Experience Wine Limited
Fegan Wholesale Ltd
First Crew Ltd
G Life Limited
Giovanni Food & Wine Limited
Hanging Ditch Wine Merchants Ltd
Highlands Whisky Co Ltd
K & S Hosking Ltd
Hutton & Mitchell Licensed Traders
JF Kegs (Scotland) Limited
Keg & Bottle Ltd
LC Wine Brokers Limited
Largesse Corporate Gifts (2007) Ltd
Last Drop Distillers Limited
Les Caves de Camille Ltd
Lucky Drinks 4 U Ltd
Lytham Brewery Limited
McKenzie Fine Wines Limited
Mephisto Wine Merchants Ltd
N G K Wholesale Limited
Negociants Europe Limited
Portavadie Distillery Limited
Primo Drinks (Lancashire) Ltd
Provence Impex Limited
R.L.G. Trading Limited
Red Fox Wines Limited
Responsible Trading Co Ltd
Rhymney Brewery Western Ltd.
William Riddell & Sons Ltd
Saam Wine Co Ltd
Salonica Limited
Soar Valley Bar Supplies Ltd
Sophie's Choice Limited
Speciality Brands Ltd
Swara Trading International Ltd
Tasteturkey Limited
Templeton Beer Wine & Spirit Co Ltd
Thorn-Clarke Wines (UK) Ltd
Vento Marino Ltd
Vinitaly Limited
W S B C Limited
Wemyss Wines and Spirits Ltd
White Willows Beers, Wines and Spirits
White's Cellar Supplies (UK) Ltd
Windfall Logistics Limited
Winecorp Limited
Wineservice Limited
Wolf Leisure Limited

2008 [63]
Aleksic & Mortimer Ltd
Amish Wholesalers Limited
Armit Holding Limited
Barcode Traders Limited
Barwell & Jones Limited
Beer Co Ltd
Bespoke Wines Ltd
Bijou Bottles Limited
Brewed 4 U Ltd
Buon Vino Ltd
CPC Business Limited
CSS On-Trade Limited
Cantina Caputo Limited

C Carnevale Limited
Cellar Link Limited
Champagne Company (UK) Limited
Chilli Marketing Brand Management Ltd
Conroy-Hood Limited
Creswick Inns & Leisure Ltd
Drinks Global Ltd
Easy9 Limited
Eurochoice Limited
Euroworld Foods Limited
Frenchbubbles Limited
Frontier Trading International Ltd
Goldbeach Trading Limited
Golden Harvest Wholesale Ltd
Grands Vins de France Limited
HG Wine Limited
W. Hall & Son (Holywell) Ltd
Jaitly Trading Co Ltd
Jassim Limited
Key Brands International Ltd
LGVA Solutions Limited
La Diva Drinks & Food Ltd
Latin Spirits & Beers (UK) Ltd
Laurus Brands Limited
London and East India Drinks Co Ltd
MSM Foods Limited
Malts of Scotland Ltd
Jake Mason Ltd
Mayfair Delivers Limited
Naked Wines Prepayments Trustee Co Ltd
Neill & Company Wine Importers Ltd
Openwine Limited
Park Place Drinks Limited
Personalised Care Solutions Ltd
Primo Drinks (Staffordshire) Ltd
Proof Drinks Limited
RDM Wines Limited
Ragarfield International Ltd
Ralph's Wines Ltd
Templar Wines Ltd
Uisce Ard Ltd
United Spirit Brands Limited
Veda UK Limited
Vinum Limited
White Pearl Ltd
Wine Fusion Limited
Wine-Invest Ltd
Winehunters Ltd
World Sake Imports UK Ltd
Yorkshire Beers Limited

2009 [104]
AKM Trading Services Ltd
ASA Ventures Limited
Algodon Europe Limited
Alice Wholesale Trading Ltd
All Market Europe Limited
Amphora Portfolio Management Ltd
Ascott Invest Limited
Ashanti Drinks Limited
Ayr Brewing Co Ltd
Beef and Burgundy Limited
Beer Paradise (York) Limited
Beer Supply Limited
Beer and Gas Man Limited
Bellwether Wines Ltd
Best Price Retail and Wholesale Ltd
Beviqua Ltd
Blackedge Brewing Co Ltd
Bugle and Co Ltd
Call-a-Keg Beverages Ltd
Carte Blanche Wines Limited

Casa Ambar Limited
Castillon International Ltd
Cobra Beer Partnership Limited
Connollys' Liquor Wholesale Ltd
Cool Apple Limited
Craft Drink Co Ltd
Danyal Ltd
Deliverance Dot Com Limited
Discover Wine (UK) Ltd
Drinkrite Limited
E I Wines Limited
Edwards Beers and Wine Supplies Ltd
Edwards Wine Agencies Limited
Enjoydrinks Limited
Evernex Ltd
Fine Wines Direct UK Limited
Firth and Co Wine Merchants Ltd
Freshfield Fine Wines Limited
GDK Drinks Ltd
Gabby & Bello Enterprises Ltd
General Bilimoria Wines Ltd
Gianni. B. Limited
Gift Creation and Design Ltd
Global Village Wines Limited
Globus Wines (UK) Ltd
Gold Max Distribution Limited
Green Room Ales Limited
H2vin Limited
Harvey's Wholesale Limited
Heidi Beers Limited
Hix & Buck Ltd
Humble Group Ltd
Isle of Wight Brewery Limited
Italimport (Wessex) Limited
J M & D Limited
JJ Wholesalers Ltd
JSF Services Limited
Jetchill Ltd
Kan Trading Limited
Konik's Tail Limited
LHK Fine Wines Limited
Lea & Sandeman Group of Companies
Libertine Spirits Ltd
Litmus Wine Agencies Limited
London Wine Agencies Limited
Lust Promotions Ltd
Magenta Wine Investors Limited
Molvino Fine Wine & Spirits Co Ltd
Mongoose Brewing Co Ltd
Mythop Gardens Limited
Occidental & Oriental Cellars Ltd
Pacta Connect UK Limited
Pandemonio Limited
Perfect Cellar Ltd
Perkins Independent Wine Traders Ltd
Primo Drinks (Yorkshire) Ltd
Proper Wine Co Ltd
Quintrox Limited
Roblex Ltd
Royal Tokaji Wines of Hungary Ltd
Salto Cachaca Co Ltd
Sedgemoor Drinks Limited
Sheridan Wines Limited
Southern Wines Limited
Strategos Limited
Supermarket Solutions Limited
TTO Limited
Temperley Wines Limited
Tennent Caledonian Breweries UK Ltd
Tequilas of Mexico Limited
That Wineshop Limited
Tolchards Limited

Tractor Shed Brewing Limited
UK Lesiure Ltd
Ufton Travel Retail Limited
Valley Vineyards Limited
Vinos Latinos Ltd
Walker & Wodehouse Wines Ltd
Wine People Europe Ltd
Wine Portfolio UK Limited
Winesider UK Ltd
Xuyang International Ltd
Young's Beers Wines & Spirits Ltd
Philip von Nell Wines Limited

January-June 2010 [62]
All Food Supplies Ltd
Appellations Limited
Beer Gonzo Ltd
Beerfantastic Ltd
Brand Central (UK) Limited
Brewers Wholesale Limited
Bristol Fine Wine Limited
Bubbles & Wines Limited
CKW Trading Limited
Cabezac Collections Limited
Chalgrove Wines Limited
Coombe Farm Wines Limited
DCFT Investments Ltd.
Delecta Limited
Dowbridge Distributors Ltd
Edition Spirits Ltd.
Europa Drinks Limited
Favourite Beers Limited
Rodney Fletcher Vintners Ltd
Forth Wines Limited
Giesen Wines UK Limited
Global24-7 (UK) Ltd
Go Brazil Wines & Spirits (UK) Ltd
Hannibal Brown Wine Services Ltd
Harmonicande Vintners Ltd
Hatch Mansfield Cellars Ltd
Hazewater Food Services Ltd
Italian Appellations Limited
J.W.L Wholesale Drinks Ltd
Jays Beverages Limited
Jays Trading Ltd
Kamros Cash and Carry Limited
Khosla Wines Ltd
Latitude Wine Limited
Lebanese Fine Wines Limited
Lincoln West End Limited
Lynch Associates Ltd
MC Drinks Limited
Marta Vine Limited
Moke Fine Wines Limited
Montymac Vintners Ltd
New School Wines Limited
North East Drinks Supplies Ltd
Pemberton Central Limited
Poshmakers Ltd
Quero Enterprise Ltd
Radleigh Wines Limited
Scotia Blending Co Ltd
Spain Link Ltd
Sylvestre Limited
Trade Wines Ltd
Trading Import and Export Co Ltd
Twaites and Jones Limited
Ultracomida Trading Co. Ltd
United Phoenix Limited
V G International Trading Ltd
Vin Est... Ltd
Vintner London Ltd

Welford Retail Limited
Wineways (Harrogate) Limited
Winning Invest & Trade Ltd
Yorkshire Vintners Limited

July-December 2010 [53]
Ales. R. Russ Limited
Alf Vini Limited
Amis Trading Limited
Atlas Fine Wines Limited
Richard Banks & Co Ltd
Barrys Discount Ltd.
Beermaster Derby Ltd
Belfast Distillery Co Ltd
Bespoke London Wine Co Ltd
Carmelita Limited
Celebration Drinks Limited
Circle View Business Consultancy Ltd
Cold Black Label Limited
Cosmopolitan Drinks Limited
Country Life Brewery Ltd
Delivered Drinks Limited
Drinks Lover Ltd
Drinks21 Ltd
Edwards Beers and Wines (Holdings) Ltd
Enmore Wine Limited
F & B Premium Brands Limited
Flobegill Wines UK Ltd
Glenforest Limited
Global Drinks (UK) Limited
Grainger Fine Wines Ltd
John Greenacre Limited
Impala Transportation Ltd
Impulse Global Ltd
JC Wine Events Ltd
Kal Wine Source UK Ltd
Le Soula Limited
Ledbury Wine Limited
Limbrey's Wine and Spirits Ltd
Liquid Indulgence Ltd
Luxury Alcohols Limited
Mayfair Brands Limited
Metropolitan Spirits (U.K.) Ltd
Amlot Morgan Fine Wines Ltd
O & P Investments Limited
Ooberstock Limited
PMWine Trade Limited
Popaball Limited
Porterage Co Ltd
Red Squirrel Brewery Limited
Smartprice (NE) Ltd
Spiced Wine Co Ltd
Tec-Sol Limited
Three Swallows Ltd
Tikves London Ltd
Whiskies from Scotland Limited
Wine Carafe Limited
Winepro Limited
YC Wines Limited

January-June 2011 [66]
3 Barrel Co Ltd
Antipodean Sommelier Limited
Barcalima Wines Limited
Beer Boutique Ltd
Best of Champagne Limited
Best of France Limited
Best of Italy Limited
Best of New World Limited
Best of Portugal Limited
Best of Spain Limited

Black Dog Wine Agency Limited
Boutinot Wines Limited
Caribswede Ltd
Castle Eden Beer Co Ltd
Celex Foods Limited
Matthew Clark Limited
Matthew Clark Wholesale Bond Ltd
Matthew Clark and Sons Ltd
Clarkes Drinks Direct Limited
Classic Malts Limited
A.P. Claxton Ltd
Condor Wines Ltd
Croatian Fine Wines Limited
Donnelly Wholesale Limited
Drinks R Us Limited
East London Brewing Co Ltd
Everyday Wholesale Ltd
Ffarm Vintners Limited
Fine Wine House Ltd
G Point 7 Ltd
Gergovie Wines Limited
Goldcrest Drinks Limited
Golden Crust & Co Limited
Investmentwine Ltd
Kanlaon Limited
Keg Company (N.I.) Ltd
Kegs R Us Ltd
LWC Drinks Limited
Liquid Vision Enterprise Ltd
Little Big Wine Co Ltd
Mega Kegs Limited
Nielsen McKinsey Global Tourism & Hospitality Consulting
Nothing But The Grape Limited
Old Cellar Ltd
Olivers Wine Agency Limited
Premier UK Trading Limited
Quintessential Brands Spirit Solutions
R Spirit Ltd
Rive Gauche Wines (UK) Limited
Samco Global Foods Ltd
Sfuso Wine Limited
Shree Sai Trading Ltd
Simply Spirits Limited
Sky Wines Limited
St.James Winery Ltd
Themirtis Limited
Union Brands Ltd
Viserra Limited
Wholesale Beer Supplies Ltd
Windward Trading Co Ltd
Wine Agency Ltd
Wine Pantry Limited
Winkleigh Cider Co Ltd
Woburn Wine Co Ltd
Worsley Wines Limited
Zinstream Wine Limited

July-December 2011 [78]
88 Connect Ltd
AB Care Connect Limited
Alliance Foods Limited
American Fizz (UK) Limited
Aotearoa Distribution Ltd
Artisan Beer Import Co Ltd
Avant Garde Drinks Ltd
Babuji Ltd
Banks & Company (Vintners) Ltd.
Base Cachaca Import (UK) Ltd
Belgrave Distribution Ltd
Bestline Wholesale Ltd
Bodega Raffy UK Ltd

UK Wholesalers of Beers, Wines and Spirits

Broad Street Brands Limited
Brooks & Whitaker Limited
C G Supplies Limited
Cadogan Wines Limited
Call-a-Keg (Scotland) Limited
Charter Brands Limited
Doran Family Vintners Limited
Drinks 4 Less (UK) Limited
Drinkslynx Limited
Earny Limited
First Class Beverages Ltd
Greens Beers Limited
Groupe Prestige Ltd
H & G Corporation Ltd
HNB Trade Ltd
House of Sparkling Ltd
IGW Brokers Limited
Iberian Wine Shippers Limited
Indie Brands Ltd.
J & A Drinks Limited
J A Glass Limited
JJBrands Limited
Tristan James Ltd
ND John Wine Limited
Jonesborough Wholesale Ltd
Kegs of Camberley Limited
Knight Trade (Oakham) Limited
Logistic Park Ltd
London Drinks Limited
London Wholesale Ltd
Manzi Developments Limited
Mumbles Brewery Ltd
Origin Drinks Limited
PFG Marketing Ltd
PSB Trading Limited
Panton Ventures Limited
Parmar Drinks & Wines Ltd
Phoenix Premium Drinks Limited
Pigs Ears Beers Limited
Portuguese Story Ltd
Quantock Abbey Wine Cellars Ltd
Quintessential Spirits UK Ltd
Rarus Ltd
Rhuby Limited
SJO Supplies Limited
Scrumpy Wasp Limited
Seb and Emma Ltd
Signature Brew Ltd
Simply Beers Limited
Sindherfoods Limited
Street Wines Limited
Sunny Group Limited
Today's Wholesale Services Ltd
Tolsta Brands Limited
United Wines Ltd
Vincisive Wines Limited
Vinovitaj Ltd
Vitesse Vintners Limited
Volfram Ltd
Watson Food & Beverages Ltd
Whisky Global Ltd
Wine Enterprise Investment Scheme
Wine for Drinking Limited
Wineguise Limited
World Beers Limited

January-March 2012 [41]
Alexander Wines Ltd.
Beerspotters Ltd
Benjamin & Blum Limited
Burdett Wines Ltd
C N Drinks Limited

Castle Eden Brewery Ltd
Celtic Spirits Limited
Coss Wines Ltd.
Dragon Drinks Limited
Drinks Factory Limited
Enovino Organic Ltd
Force Brewery Limited
Galette Wines Limited
Great Whisky Co Ltd
Hitchin Wine Co Ltd
Hobo Beer & Co Ltd
JH Wine Agencies Ltd
Koha Distribution Limited
Kramjar Limited
Lamberton Whisky & Spirits Ltd
Le Vignoble Ltd
Life's A Bottle Limited
Lucky Spirits Ltd
MSD Wholesale Limited
Melen London Ltd.
Middlesex Wines Limited
Old Red Lion Theatre Pub Ltd
Passion Wine International Ltd
Primo Drinks (North East) Ltd
R & B Drinks Ltd
Rok Drinks Limited
SSL Leisure Limited
Seabrook Wines Limited
Smiley Rhyme Limited
Southover Drinks Limited
Top Spirits Ltd
Valentino Platinum Ltd
Varmont Ltd
Vice Enterprises Limited
Victory Global Ltd
Wineman (UK) Ltd

April-June 2012 [46]
ANA Distribution Limited
Alexandria Partners Limited
Atom Brewing Co Limited
BL011 Limited
Clapham Wine Co Ltd
DLRF Limited
Dago Wines Ltd
Digby Fine English Ltd
Digby Wine Ltd
Dionysius Importers Ltd
Dodotraders UK Limited
Greenlink Enterprises Limited
Hannah Whisky Merchant's Ltd
Helluva... Limited
Tom l'Anson Wines Ltd
Inside Trax Limited
Intriguing Brands Limited
Jam Consultants Global Limited
Keg Delivery Service Ltd
Knotted Vine Limited
Korzinka Taste of Europe Ltd
LDC Scotland Limited
Lanchester Wine Sales Limited
Malvern Ltd
Morgan Jupe Limited
New Claire Wine Ltd
Old Butcher's Wine Cellar Ltd
One Point Supplies Limited
Pierhead Drinks Limited
Pirate's Grog Rum Ltd
Premier Inc. Ltd
Quintessential Spirits Holdings Ltd
Quintessential Spirits Limited
Quintessential Wines Holdings Ltd

Quintessential Wines Limited
Raer Scotch Whisky Ltd
Rasputin Leisure Ltd
S & N Products Ltd
Sarpanch Food & Wine Distributors Ltd
Shires Wine Services Limited
Terra Wines Limited
Tokaj Merchants Ltd
UK Wine & Food Supplies Ltd
Waveney Ales and Ciders Ltd
West End Drinks Limited
Wine Cellar Midlands Limited

July-September 2012 [46]
Black Cat Brewery Limited
Bordeaux Index Limited
Bottle Butler Limited
Boutique Spirit Co Ltd
Brookfield Beverages Limited
Brookfield Drinks Limited
C & R Wines Limited
Champagne Collection Limited
Chelsea Vintners London Ltd
Chez Antoine Ltd
Cognac Growers' Collective Ltd
Euro Link Beverages Ltd
Fine Wine Works Limited
Glow Glow Ltd.
Grey Cardinal Limited
Gusto Wines Ltd
Heroes Drinks Company C.I.C.
Independent Vintner Ltd
KD Wholesale Ltd
Kestrel Brewing Co Ltd
Leo Global Limited
Lesont Ltd
Leyland Home Brew Limited
Lupton Wine Limited
More Sake Limited
NJA Marketing Ltd
Noble Wines (UK) Limited
Nottage Bar Supplier Limited
Original Liqueur Co Ltd
Ormos Trades Limited
Paramount Vintners Ltd
Point Beer UK Limited
Prime Cash & Carry Limited
Professional Wine Services Ltd
R & M Chateau Wines Ltd
Red Squirrel Wine Ltd.
Remy Cointreau UK Distribution Ltd
Seth Ventures Limited
Silly Point Wines Limited
Southwick Court Fine Wines (2012) Ltd
Staid London Limited
Starstock Ltd
Stratford's Wine Shippers and Merchants
Sunbird Wines UK Ltd
Whisky Trading Co Ltd
Woodland Wine Store Limited

October-December 2012 [36]
3 Tigers Limited
A and R Fine Wines Limited
Angus Wines Limited
Bargate Drinks Limited
Beer Rocks Brewery Ltd
Beveridge Wines Ltd
Bibere Ltd.
Biercraft Ltd
Crown Cash & Carry Ltd

De Burgh Fine Wine Limited
Distilled Brands Limited
Distilled Liquor Co Ltd
Distinction Armagnac Limited
Express Drinks Ltd
G M Drinks Limited
Gemeaux Limited
Grape and Grain Management Ltd
Iberiandrinks UK Ltd
Icknield Stores Ltd
Intelligent Trade Limited
Intercellar Distribution Ltd
Kash & Karry Supplies Ltd
London SCC Group Ltd
MWH Wine Agencies Ltd
Monopole Wine Portfolio Management Ltd
Premium Brands Distribution Ltd
Quantum Vintners Limited
Shindigger Craft Beer Ltd
Skinny Booze Limited
Sofibel Ltd
Tengu Sake Limited
Tudor Drinks Ltd
Usedsoft Ltd
Vines Wines Limited
Wine Associates Limited
Wine Poole Limited

January-March 2013 [46]
AK Cash & Carry Ltd
Alchemist Brewery Limited
Axiom Brands Limited
Battlefield Brewery Limited
Be My Wine Ltd.
Bloomsbury Drinks Ltd
Blue Diamond (UK) Ltd
CS Wines Limited
Cazcabel Drinks Limited
Cleveland Bar Supplies Limited
Cocktail Express Ltd
Cromfine Limited
Curious Wine Cellar Limited
Drayman Drinks Ltd
Eebria Limited
Event Wine Solutions Limited
For The Love of Wine Limited
Frizzenti Limited
Grape Drinks (UK) Limited
Import Brothers Limited
In Vino Bidco Limited
In Vino Limited
Jenuine Jamaican Products Ltd
Kold Group Limited
Laing Whisky Co Ltd
Mahal Enterprises Limited
More or Less Drinks Co Ltd
Morecambe Bay Wines Limited
Native Oracle Limited
Northwest Drinks Ltd
Oak Cask Distribution Ltd
Pull The Cork Limited
RCI Spirits Ltd
Real Irish Whiskey Limited
Redoor Limited
Special Cases Limited
Splendid Corks Limited
Three Stills Co Ltd
Traditional Beer Co Ltd
Vanilla Blue Limited
Villa Sofia Limited
Vino Vero Ltd
Westbourne Drinks Co Ltd

Wholly Grape Limited
Wine de Vine Ltd
Zing Vodk Limited

April-June 2013 [48]
A1 Resources Limited
Abercrombie Fine Wines Limited
Aberdrinks Scotland Limited
Aims & Co Ltd
B & B Drinks Ltd
Bath Gin Co Ltd
Bedminster Beer Co Ltd
Beer52 Limited
Boot Liquor Wholesale Limited
Bottle Drinks Co Ltd
J.Braham Everett Imports Ltd
CRC Delta Ltd
DWS Wholesale Limited
Dacastello Limited
Direct Wine Factory Ltd
Domaine des Jeanne Limited
Felix Solis Avantis UK Ltd
German Beer Co Limited
Hamptons Wine Ltd
Highly Spirited Ltd
Hoghton Brewery Limited
Trevor Hughes Wines Limited
I.G.T. Management Ltd
India Gold Limited
Indian Runner Drinks Co Ltd
Invest Inns Limited
Kaleboard Limited
Kudos Drinks Ltd
Lancaster Wines Limited
M & B Distributions (UK) Ltd
Midlands Drinks Limited
Moonshine Traders Ltd
More Beer Wholesale Limited
Mathieu Poulain Limited
RDV Spirits Ltd
Roust UK Ltd
SJZP Limited
Vernon Scott Limited
Simavin Limited
Trilogy Beverage Brands Ltd
Urban Wholesalers Limited
Veravinea Ltd
Vinnaturo Ltd
Wein Forum - Fine Wines Ltd
Westgarth Wines Limited
Wine Byre Limited
Worthington Wine and Spirits UK Ltd
Xtraflow Limited

July-September 2013 [48]
Babicka Vodka (International) Ltd
Bobby Beer Co Ltd
Bourgognes Only Limited
Branda Ltd
Bric Commerce Ltd
Checkmate Premium Brands Ltd
Cropol Luxury Products Ltd
Drinks Club Ltd
Emporium Import Ltd
Fine Drinks Cooperative Ltd
Funky Beer Co Ltd
Glen Scotia Distillery Co Ltd
Grape Opportunities Ltd
Harry Bromptons Ltd
Hatton & Edwards Fine Wine Merchants
Highfern Limited

IKP Trading Limited
Kicking Horse Ltd.
Left Coast Distribution Ltd
Line Point Global UK Limited
Little Gems Wine Ltd
Littlemill Distillery Co Ltd
Loch Lomond Distillers Limited
Loch Lomond Distillery Co Ltd
London Cash & Carry Ltd
London Wine Eis Limited
Lost Distillery Co Ltd
Mangrove Global Limited
Mast-Jaegermeister UK Holding Ltd
Mast-Jaegermeister UK Limited
Meadrising Limited
Naked Fine Wine Bonds PLC
Olley (NE) Limited
Prosecco 1754 Limited
Quiqui Mezcal Ltd
Signature Wines Ltd
Sixpenny Wines Limited
Southbourne Brewing Limited
Spowart Wines Limited
TL Step By Step Limited
Time & Tide Brewing Limited
Trust in Global Food Ltd
Viking Enterprises Limited
Village Selections Limited
Vin-X Enterprise Investment Scheme Ltd
Vintage 1947 Limited
Waverley Drinks Limited
Wine2trade Limited

October-December 2013 [48]
180 East Limited
Aquitania Ltd
Aussie Rules Ltd
BDDR Enterprises Limited
Barry Drinks Ltd
Bear Smyth Limited
Bottle Shop (Penarth) Limited
Calduero Wine Importers Ltd
Cavoda Limited
Cellarvino Limited
Champers (Wholesale) Limited
Corktalk Limited
Crackerjack Wines Limited
D K International (UK) Limited
Dion Wines & Food Limited
Fair Fayre Food & Wines Ltd
First Bar Supplies Limited
Fox Fitzgerald Whisky Trading Co Ltd
Gill Cash & Carry Limited
Global Wine Distributors Ltd
JF Tobias Limited
Just Perfect Wines Ltd
Kane Republik Ltd
Lord Krishna Trade Ltd
MDF Wholesale Ltd
Miraj Beers & Wines Limited
Mywinelabel Limited
Newcomer Wines Limited
Original & Distinctive Limited
Premium Beverage Refreshments Ltd
Prohibition Limited
Real Wine Cellar Limited
Recolte Wines Limited
Red Bottle Co Ltd
Rockin Robin Brewery Ltd
SP (DPH) Exports Limited
Saddleworth Real Ale Ltd
Sloane Home Ltd

UK Wholesalers of Beers, Wines and Spirits — dellam

Specialist Cellars Ltd
Spirits Development & Management Company (SDMC)
Spirits International Management Ltd
Thomson & Scott Limited
Triage Wines Limited
V & A Jobs UK Ltd
Vinemporium Limited
Whiskybroker Limited
Whitmore and White Limited
Wine Research Limited

January-March 2014 [57]

Afrogrocers Ltd
Aizia Ltd
Alchemy Drinks Ltd.
Artisan Wine Storage Ltd
Beer Belly Company Incorporated Ltd
Beerscellars (UK) Limited
Blast Vintners Ltd
Carson Wines Ltd
Carter Importing Ltd
Cascriva Ltd
Co Stars London Ltd
Coleburn Distillery Limited
Copper Still Co Ltd
Craft Distillers Scotland Ltd
Crudo Limited
Eastcoast Supplies Ltd.
Erin Vintners Ltd
Euro Speed Intl Ltd
FV Trading Europe Ltd
Grandi Vini Limited
William Grant & Sons Brands Ltd
Harp Wines & Spirits Ltd
Harris Filters Limited
Holdsworth Spirits & Co Ltd
Hooton Management Limited
Hops and Barley (Group) Ltd
Hops and Barley (UK) Limited
Hoptimism Limited
Il Palagio Ltd
JDS Trading Limited
Japan Gourmet (UK) Limited
Jascots Wine Merchants Limited
KIC Inventories Limited
Kraft Beer UK Ltd
LA International Trading Ltd
Lancashire Beer Co Ltd
D.J. Limbrey Distilling Co. Ltd
Melius Drinks Ltd.
Murray Brother's Whisky Ltd
National Drink Distributors Ltd
Norfolk Vineyard Ltd
North South Wines Limited
Original Wooden Case Limited
Pearl Leisure Limited
Polskie Wodki Ltd
Quintessential Brands Premium Brands
Railway Bar & Grill Ltd
Rip Mountain Brewery Ltd.
Sai Soft Drinks Ltd
Siderea Consulting Limited
Small Batch Bottlers Scotland Ltd
Soul Spirits Ltd
Stargold Wholesale Ltd
T.M.B Wine Trading Ltd
Tutto Wines Limited
Watermark Fine Wine Limited
Wyfold Vineyard Limited

April-June 2014 [66]

23 High Path Ltd
55 Above Ltd
Abbey Brands Limited
Amirante Empire Limited
Atlantis Iberica Ltd
Azizi Drinks Ltd
Beer Company Consolidations Ltd
Birrificio Del Ducato London Ltd
Bogart Spirits Limited
Cador Limited
Capacha Limited
Central Drinks Pub Co Ltd
Continental Cash & Carry Ltd
Cresco Import Exports Ltd
De Christ Wines Ltd
Diabolus Limited
Drinks Emporium Limited
Drumstick Products Co Ltd
Ester Wines Limited
European Wine Brokers Limited
J.W. Filshill International Ltd
Fine Cider Limited
Fine Products Exporters Ltd
Fizz Guru Limited
Forty Acres Ltd
GS Wholesalers Ltd
Georgian British Co Ltd
Grapes of Hungary Ltd
Haslemere Wine Merchants Ltd
Hungarian Wine Ltd
Innvino Ltd
Ionica Wine Cellars Ltd
JD's Sports Bar Ltd
Kingdom Foods & Drinks Limited
Lant Street Wine Co Ltd
Leomar Limited
Lyndon Drinks Limited
M D (Cash & Carry) Limited
Magnate Drinks Ltd
Stanley Marlow & Son Limited
Meridian Centre Hospitality Ltd
Neil Morrissey Real Ale Co Ltd
Ossau Vins & Spiritueux Ltd
Preston Wines Ltd
Prosit Wines Limited
Psychopomp Ltd
QNGC Limited
RDF Paper Ltd
Rawson Trading (Doncaster) Ltd
Riedango Limited
Robb Brothers Wine Merchants Ltd
Sam-Gel Global Ventures Ltd
Scott's of Quorn (Wine Bar & Vintners)
Sharing The Best Limited
Six Rivers Limited
Smouse & Marchand Limited
Spot Wines Limited
T & S Sales Limited
Trading Irmis Ltd
VIP Bottles Ltd
Vinterest Limited
Wine Butler Limited
Wine Keg Co Ltd
World Traveller Wines Limited
Xisto Wines Limited
Yorkshire Vino Ltd

July-September 2014 [53]

21 Whiskies Limited
ANM Trading Limited
Alcohology Ltd
Algebra Drinks Ltd
Aran Beers Limited
Aziken Ventures Limited
Beer Belly's Ltd
Beer Company (Exports) Ltd
Beer People Limited
Bier UK Limited
Black & Yellow Developments Ltd
Canopy Beer Co Ltd
Chateau de la Combe Ltd
Cochin Heritage Ltd
Compasse Limited
Crafty Devil Brewing Ltd
Dudley Craig Wines Limited
Crucial Brands Holdings Ltd
Deutsches Beer Limited
Deutsches Bier Limited
Diamond Stag Importers Ltd.
Direct2door Food & Beverage Ltd.
Draft Link Limited
Forest Road Brewing Co Ltd
Glenroy Spirits Limited
Global Ethics Liquor Co Ltd
Golden Everest Limited
Jerome Harlington Limited
Haycock's Drinks Co Ltd
Haycock's No.9 UK Ltd
Humo International Limited
KB Agencies Ltd
Konigsberg Seven Bridges Breweries Ltd
La Peira Limited
MK Wine Art Ltd
Manor Park Drinks Ltd.
Mastiha World Ltd
Needhams Wines Limited
North East Hold Limited
Old Town Blending Co Ltd
Original Beer Co Ltd
Original Bier Co Ltd
Phil Cellars Ltd
Raks Suppliers Limited
Ran Ales Ltd
Red Dragons Trading Limited
Safeway Distribution Limited
Southern Wine Roads Limited
Stewart Hill Walker UK Limited
Tipple Brands Ltd
Triumph Foodservice Limited
Vinals Wine & Food Limited
Webdrinks Ltd

October-December 2014 [44]

100cl Limited
Ask Drinks Ltd
Ausavenues Limited
Banini UK Ltd
E J Bartholomew Limited
Bhanbore Trading Company PVT Ltd
Blue Marble Consultants Ltd
Bubbles for Friends Ltd.
Chalk Farm Wines Ltd
Clos Vintners Limited
Deskbeers Limited
Di.Wine Limited
Diamonds & Pearl Trading Ltd
Diss Honest Brewing Co Ltd
Domaine Watson Ltd
Europebro Wholesalers Ltd
Eventus Global Ltd
Expression du Terroir Limited
Festina Drinks Ltd

Friarwood Fine Wines Limited
Gin Fizz Ltd
Grand Vin Wine Merchants Ltd
Guinexport Trade and Services Ltd
Ireland Craft Beers Ltd
Karma Beverages Ltd
Kese International Ltd
Kolson Energy Limited
Lightbox Brands Limited
Made in Little France Import Ltd
Mothership Beer Ltd
Orsa Major Ltd
Pesodeocho Wines Ltd
Polaris Wines Ltd
Pollen Cider Ltd
Premium Vineyard Company UK Ltd
Raeburn Fine Wines Ltd.
Realsa Wines Import & Export Ltd
St James's Fine Wine Limited
St Pierre Partners Limited
Tasting Barn Ltd
Tayler Beers Limited
Warwickshire Cash & Carry Ltd
Wine UK Direct Limited
WinesOnline Ltd

January 2015 [13]
AGS Vintners Limited
Bristol Cider Co Ltd
Buckingham Fine Wine Ltd
Cava Spiliadis UK Limited
Dark Revolution Ltd
Different Wines Limited
Gurkha Beer Ltd
JR First Choice Cash & Carry Ltd
Lock & Barrel Limited
MK Sales Training Limited
Otros Vinos Limited
Sagittarius Royaume-Uni Ltd
Trade Network Supplies Limited

February 2015 [17]
49 Wines Limited
Applethwaite Wines Ltd
Beer Bottle Co Ltd
Cadestin International Wines Ltd
Copper and Rye Limited
Global Beer Co Ltd
Himalaya Wines Limited
Identity Drinks Brands Limited
Litchquor UK Ltd
Maha Cash & Carry Ltd
Maison du Vin Ltd
Spirimix Limited
Taste Merchants Ltd
Tech-Beach UK Limited
Transylvania Wine Ltd
Under The Bonnet Wines Limited
Victoria Garry Group Ltd

March 2015 [27]
Au Vodka Ltd
Burgundy Tuscany Piedmont Ltd
Chalk & Charcoal Limited
Churnet Valley Drinks Limited
Deeti Wholesale Limited
Del Professore Limited
Direct Wine Importers Limited
Drink Store Wholesale Limited
Faridoon Wines Ltd
Gleann Mor Spirits Co Ltd

Golden Decanters Limited
Hunter Douglas Scotch Whisky Ltd
Andrew Laing & Co Ltd
Old Sport Limited
Scotland Grindlay Limited
Shieling Scotch Whisky Co Ltd
Swinkels Snackery and Backery Ltd
Thru The Glass Limited
Tour de Force Wines Limited
Trailblazing Wine Ltd
UK Vintners (of London) PLC
Up Front Brewing Limited
Utku Emre Ltd
Vino Italiano Importers Ltd
Wine Marketings Europe Ltd
Wine Outlet Ltd.
Worldwine UK Ltd

April 2015 [24]
Agro Investment Ltd
Azzurri Kitchen Ltd
Borders Distillers Limited
Chilli Brands Limited
Cocksure Brewing Co Ltd
Distribev Ltd.
Eminent Life Limited
Focus Beverages Ltd
Ghost Drinks Ltd
Global World Wide Beer Limited
Halifax Wine Co Ltd
IMC Business Group Limited
Itedomum (UK) Ltd
K R Wines & Beers Ltd
Let There Be Beer Ltd
M & M Community Development Initiatives
Old Man Rum Co Ltd
Olive Wines Limited
Premia Brands Trading Limited
Staibano Ltd
Edward Tatham Champagne Ltd
Taunton Cider Co Ltd
Waud Wines Limited
Yaved Ltd

May 2015 [32]
Anglocolombian Ltd
Art of Wine Ltd
Bdellium Trading Co Ltd
Be Organiq Limited
Better Buy Ltd
Big D'Z Convenience and Winery Ltd
Bondi Brands Limited
Bondi Brewery Limited
Chilli Brands (New Zealand) Ltd
Coca-Cola Amatil (UK) Limited
Cornucopia Wines Limited
Dankan Ltd
Distillers Direct Ltd
Dramfool Ltd
Empress Ale Ltd
Gain Brands International (UK) Ltd
GreatWineDirect Limited
Greenmount Holdings Limited
HP Enterprises Limited
Infinity Wines Limited
Jenkins and Beckers Fine Wine Ltd
La Pata Negra Ltd
Morrish & Banham Ltd
Organica Food & Wine Ltd
Rafti Ltd.
Roohop Ltd

Talbot & Barr Limited
Truman's Drink Solutions Ltd
Vine Wine Limited
Vitam Dare Limited
Wine IT Limited
Yeastie Boys UK Ltd

June 2015 [18]
Blux UK Import Ltd
Cask Whisky Ltd
Chaps Group Limited
Chevalier de Mentaubert Ltd
Continental Beer Services Ltd
Devine Distillates Group Ltd
French Wine Project Limited
Gudfish Limited
Kozuba & Sons Limited
Mead Ho! Limited
OM Wines Ltd
Oenofuture Limited
Sagittarius World Limited
Sammartini Ltd
Sonvino Ltd.
Stow Brewery Limited
TFWF Ltd
UK Beer & Soft Drinks Ltd

July 2015 [23]
Bent Distribution Ltd
Brocour Ltd.
Cangiani UK Ltd
Capital Languages Ltd
Diwine London Ltd
Drinksman Limited
Enny Wines Ltd
Fairview Wines Limited
Hoops and Champagne Ltd
Karla & Co. Spirits Limited
Langwith Brewing Co Ltd
London Creek Limited
Lunzer Wine Group Limited
Marlonn Food & Wine Ltd
Milk Money Limited
My Global Ventures Limited
Original Herbale Brewing Co Ltd
Paso-Primero UK Ltd.
Pearly Queen Beer Co Ltd
RK Vodka Limited
Tayst Ltd
Tenuta Tremollito Wines Ltd
Waistcoat Wines Ltd

August 2015 [17]
Ascona Retail (Leases) Limited
Casa Cocktails Limited
Chillwines Limited
Cross Brew Ltd
Exeter Drinks Ltd
Fifty One Forty Limited
Garmence Limited
LCW (Glasgow) Ltd
Liquid Solutions Distribution (N.I.)
London Drinks and Beers Ltd
Malt Whisky Agency Ltd
Peachy Glow Limited
Robb Trading Ltd
Tenby Drinks (UK) Limited
Verre Anglais Limited
Vinfinity Limited
West Coast Wines & Spirits Ltd.

September 2015 [28]
Beercall Ltd
Bevco Limited
Billings & Briggs Ltd
Bloomsbury Distillery Ltd
Brayston Leisure Ltd.
Da Vinci Traders Ltd
Fine Wine Trading Company (UK) Ltd
Ftspot Limited
G B Consortium Wholesale Ltd
Globe Logistics Limited
Greenwood Spirits Limited
Hillcrest Wines Limited
Hydraun Limited
Liquid Projects International Ltd
Manchester Trading Limited
Master Spirits Limited
Okowita Vodka Limited
Prima Import & Export Ltd
Real Grapes Ltd
Rum Club Ltd
SMCA Enterprises Ltd.
Thirsty Brands Ltd
Tropical Ltd
Valinch & Mallet Limited
Vinum Fine Wines Limited
Wanderlust Wine Limited
Winicious Limited
Woori Trade Ltd

October 2015 [22]
A Taste of The Caribbean Ltd
Barkin Bars Ltd
Bosun's Brewery Tap Ltd
Brighton Brew Co Ltd
Cru Prive Ltd
DT1 Ltd
G M Drinks of Hampshire Ltd
Hop Shed Limited
Ital Sardo Limited
Kay Distributions Ltd
Keep Control Ltd
Lora Trading (Europe) Ltd
Premier Distillers Ltd
Retaliate Limited
Silverlite Cash & Carry Ltd
Smart Save Distribution Ltd
Spirit Traders Ltd
Swallow Dispensed Drinks Solutions
Valley Wines, Beer & Spirits Ltd
Valvai Cash & Carry Ltd
Valvai Ltd
Wrights Lion Brewery Limited

November 2015 [18]
Authentic French Wines (Importers)
Avalon Wholesale and Brewing Ltd
Birdcage Gin Ltd.
Burton Rd Brewing Co Limited
Cenimex Ltd
DSC Imports Limited
Drink Warehouse Events Limited
Hills Prospect Holdings Ltd
Lazy Lizard Beer Co Ltd
Lloyds Wines Limited
Mother Kelly's Distribution Ltd
New Wave (Scotland) Limited
Oak Alliance Ltd.
Seven Cellars Ltd.
Strongwells Limited
TW Wine Solutions Ltd

Vito International Ltd
Warner Family Wines Limited

December 2015 [21]
Amayan Terroir Selections Ltd
Brewgooder Limited
Champagne One Ltd
GDD Chapuy Limited
Fishers Gin Ltd
Four Corners Wine Co Ltd
Four Seasons Hastings Ltd
Giuseppe's Wines Limited
Great Spirit Co Ltd
Half Cut Wines Limited
L'Altre VI Limited
Leamington Wine Co Ltd
Leith Distillery Limited
Port Ellen Distillery Co Ltd
Port Ellen Distilling Limited
RC Brands Ltd
Ray Jules Limited
Solitude Wines Limited
Spirit Still Ltd
Thorne Licence Wholesale Ltd
Toast Ale Ltd

January 2016 [22]
Astir Cigars & Wine Ltd
Bath Sixteen Limited
Beacon Wines Limited
Cellar & Co Limited
Champsonthego.co.uk Ltd
Cotswold Port Co. Ltd
Crazy Gin Ltd
Crescent Fine Foods Ltd
Cut Rum Limited
EFE Store Limited
Easier Sales Limited
LDW Wines Limited
New Zealand Beer Collective Ltd
Ora Brewing Co Ltd
Portuguese Fine Wine Co Ltd
Poulter Group UK Limited
Prestige Wine & Food (UK) Ltd
Pyvo UK Ltd
Rutherford, Shirlaw and Denholm Ltd
Sefton Beer Co Ltd
Smashing Wines Limited
Szicsek Palinka Ltd

February 2016 [28]
AMK Distribution Ltd
Brewgooder Foundation
Deceptive Wines Limited
Deluxe Wines Limited
Drinks Orchard Ltd
Drinkscraft Limited
Etna Food & Wine Ltd
Eythrope Wine Limited
Foxhole Spirits Limited
GM Catering Supplies Ltd
Healthy Wines Ltd
Highball Brands Limited
Iron & Rose Ltd
Italian Importers Ltd
Just A Splash Limited
MA Wine and Spirit Imports Ltd
Murcotts Ltd.
Myrlex Southend Limited
Nekter Wines Ltd
PPbeer Ltd.

Premium Bulgarian Wine Ltd
Ramstrad Trading Ltd
Real Ale Direct Limited
Henry de Vaugency Ltd
Vintage Capital II PLC
Winecraft Ltd
Witney Wine Limited
Xenon Wines & Spirits Limited

March 2016 [34]
79North Limited
Added Pressure Ltd
Altamira Management Services Ltd
Amy's Wine House Limited
Apley Hall Wines Limited
Artisan Lounge and Cellar Ltd
Atlantic Craft Soda Co Ltd
Botella Imports Ltd
Bringmevino (UK) Limited
Brunswick Fine Wines and Spirits Ltd
Cellar Supplies Limited
Chiltern Trading Ltd
D & K Capital Ltd
D K Beers Ltd.
Franco Hetty Limited
Idle Hour Spirit Co Ltd
Inconcept Ltd
KLR & RCR Distribution Ltd
Languedoc Imports Ltd
Lisbon Wines Limited
Muratina Limited
NDG (Hartlepool) Limited
North Star Spirits Ltd.
Norwich Dry Gin Co Ltd
Real Al Co Ltd
SAPM Commercial Ltd
Sandhu IT Services Ltd
Southern England Wines (UK) Ltd
Spalco Ltd
Spitfire Heritage Distillers Ltd
Terra Toda Ltd.
Urban Warehousing Limited
Viniexport Limited
Yorke Vines Ltd

April 2016 [18]
Adam & Herv Limited
Andina Trade Ltd
Booze Crew Leeds Ltd
Distell International Holdings Ltd
Fortunae Limited
Glacon Limited
Hofmeister Enterprises Ltd
Italian Wine Buyers Club Ltd
Party Drinks Co Ltd
Prime Wines Limited
Sandhu Wholesale & Events Ltd
Select Whisky Limited
Skyfall Distribution Limited
Speyside Trading Co Ltd
St. Max Wine Limited
Urban Beers and Wines Ltd
Vinoveritas (Europe) Limited
Zefino Family Limited

May 2016 [28]
AFC Direct Ltd
Acod S & C Ltd
Agave Thieves Ltd
Bottle Bank Limited
Cariel Spirits International Ltd
Cocktail Pickers Club Ltd
Cosmic Services Limited
D & V Wines Ltd
DFG Distribution Ltd
Euroofar Trading Limited
Greatvine Ltd
Italicus Ltd
James Fine Wines Limited
La Collina Biologica Ltd
Mediterranean Farm Finest Ltd
Myella Brands Ltd
Pinewood Vyntners Limited
Salmon Lady Limited
Same Day Beers Group Ltd
Sauvignon Wines UK Ltd
Scimedex Limited
Ship & Mitre Brewing Co Ltd
Signorellis Deli Ltd
Spirit of Glasgow Ltd
Sybarite Cellars Limited
Whisky Seller Limited
Wines of The Americas Limited
Xorta Global Management Ltd

June 2016 [28]
101 Reykjavik UK Ltd
BFV International Limited
Big Fish Brewing Co Ltd
Bosman Wines UK Ltd
CRA Ltd
Call-a-Keg Limited
Choice Drinks Limited
Deniz & Ada Limited
East Street Wine Co Ltd
Ellustria Limited
Espana Imports Ltd
Gourvid Limited
Infotonomy Ltd
Kentish Pip Ltd
Liquid Brand Marketing Limited
Loyalty Wines Limited
Meanwhile Drinks Ltd.
Medagio Limited
Miracle Drinks Limited
O'Vineyards Ltd
Orchard Wine Co Ltd
Oxus Gin Ltd.
Pick N Deliver Ltd
Provenance Projects 2016 Ltd
Rondel Trading Ltd
SJ Wines Ltd
Shonty Group Ltd
Young in Spirit Ltd

July 2016 [28]
All Drinks Cash & Carry Ltd
Amarri Prosecco Limited
Asiana Mart Limited
Bellwether Impex (UK) Limited
Bouquet Limited
Brian Traders Ltd
Briton Ferry Brewing Co Ltd
Cold Formd Ltd
Con Gusto Wines Limited
Crafted Beverages Limited

Essenza Di Romagna Limited
First & Last Brewery Ltd
Ginvino Ltd
Great Wine Group Limited
Gunners Cocktails Limited
Horsetown Beers Limited
Hurmiz UK Ltd
Inverroche Ireland Ltd
Kilo Wines Ltd
Label Bouchon Limited
Marani Wines Limited
Marlow Wine Co Ltd
J & W Nicholson & Co Ltd
Opendoor Gin Co Ltd
Opus Cellars Limited
Rebel Wine Ltd.
Stockholm Distillers and Vintners
West Country Wines Limited

August 2016 [38]
414 Alcohols Limited
Agua Piedra Mezcal & Co Ltd
Angeli Del Vino Limited
Arcari & Sons Ltd.
Arda Rohat Limited
Aurora Ales Limited
Bacchus Wine Auctions Limited
Big Red D Ltd
Jack Brooksbank Limited
Burridges of Arlington St Ltd
Corkhaus Ltd
Craftibeer Limited
Crafty Pint Limited
Dmomentum Ltd
Eastlin Alba Limited
Famille Clarke Limited
Flavour Foods & Drinks Ltd
Gin Room Scotland Ltd
Gravity Drinks Ltd
Guilty Libations Limited
Henderik & Co Limited
Heronsgate 7 Limited
Highland Vintners Ltd
Lonerider UK Ltd
M Wines Limited
MDS International Ltd.
MGW World Ltd
Mayfly Wine Co Ltd.
Montann Limited
Mr. Alba International Trading Co Ltd
Poleczka Limited
Project Wines UK Limited
Provino Limited
Rum Matters Limited
Saucy Drinks Co Ltd
Single Cask Ltd
Soltano Wines Ltd
Wellsh Brewers Cardiff Ltd

September 2016 [29]
Agrosale UK Limited
Amore G.N.A. Limited
David Berryman Holdings Ltd
Blue Magic Limited
Camino Real Limited
Carson & Carnevale Limited
Cibus Vitae Ltd.
Cumberland Bargin Booze Ltd
Da'mos Food & Beverages Ltd
De Paolis Limited
Diwine Piemonte Limited

Elicite Ltd
Hazelbank Limited
Mike Hothersall Wines Limited
International Business Solutions Ltd
Keeling Andrew & Co Limited
Mysomm.Com Ltd
Orale Ltd.
PFS Business Services Limited
Plum Brandy Co Ltd
Pug Vodka Ltd
Special Cider Co Ltd
Terrae Vinariae Limited
Uokka Limited
Valentino & Finch Ltd
Vino Pronto UK Ltd
Vitis-Terra Limited
Whitetail Spirits Limited
World Cider Box Limited

October 2016 [28]
AGT Professional Services Ltd
Abyss Brewing Ltd
Always Available Ltd
Baijiu Beer Co Ltd
Basket Press Wines Ltd
Bevimangia Limited
Champagnehub Limited
Cider Centrum Ltd
Cloud Wine Ltd
Dima's Vodka UK Ltd
Drum and Black Rum Co Ltd
Fast Moving Goods Ltd
Gem Wines Ltd
Magic Spells Brewery Limited
Natural Bay Limited
Nightcap Global Limited
Polat International Ltd
Quick Liquids Limited
R. St Barth Limited
Real Ales AT Limited
Ripped Earth Wines Limited
Spirit Beer Co Ltd
Spirits for Good CIC
Steel Coulson Ltd
TPA Trading Limited
Teqcoola Limited
Vinotrans Ltd
Wine Pantry (Wholesale) Ltd

November 2016 [42]
Anya Global Limited
Barrique Vintners Limited
Best of Hungary Ltd
Buchanan Wines Ltd.
C & D Exports Ltd
Cuvee Cavalier Limited
D'Urberville Vineyard Limited
Delivering Happiness Limited
Dr Dougan (Enterprises) Ltd
Draught Services Ltd
Drop The Anchor Brewery Ltd
Dumenil Champagne Limited
Evokesomm Limited
Family of Hounds Limited
Favela Cerveja Ltd
Full Logistic Ltd
Glennlay & Co Ltd
Grapebee Ltd
Greek Wineshop Ltd
Gvino Limited
Indie Spirits Limited

UK Wholesalers of Beers, Wines and Spirits — dellam

Jabru Bevco Ltd
Kinkell Brewery Ltd
La Vigna Vini Ltd
Lionel Export Agency Ltd
Liquid Market Limited
Mezcal Reina Limited
Neptune Rum Ltd
Novus BH Magister Ltd
O'Donnell Moonshine Limited
Philipshill Retirement Village Ltd
Play Limited
Raer Whisky Co Ltd
Saints Row Brewing Co Ltd
Savage Wines UK Limited
Sell My Wine Ltd
Separateflow Limited
Vino & Spirits Limited
Wenlen UK. Ltd
Whisky Biz Glasgow Ltd
Wisdom Whisky & Wine Limited
Zinea Global Services Limited

December 2016 [30]
Afco Traders Ltd
Arisaig Distillers Ltd
BD Wines Limited
Belgian Life Limited
Beverage Brothers Limited
Bohemian Brands Limited
Champagne House Ltd
Delta Western Distributions Ltd
Goldy Gin Limited
Indie Wines Limited
Ishka Wines and Spirits UK Ltd
Kol App Ltd
Kudu Food and Wine Ltd
MSB Wholesale Services Limited
Magnetic Brands Limited
Mercanti Imports Limited
Nightrep Limited
One Love Rum Co Ltd
Organic French Wines Limited
Oriental Drinks Limited
Oyster Import Export Limited
Pinglestone Estate Limited
Pink Gin Co Ltd
Present Tense Limited
Quaich Whisky Investments Ltd
Richway Cash and Carry Ltd
Value Focused Solutions Ltd
Wagner Spirits Ltd
Whisky Palate Limited
Xeco Wines Limited

January 2017 [51]
3 Big Dogs Limited
ASG Wines Limited
Beer Journey Ltd
Black Tartan Limited
Blue Momentum Limited
Bone Machine Brewing Co Ltd
Caps Off Ltd.
Craft Locals Limited
Crafty Cask Wholesale Ltd
DC Imports UK Ltd
Donnington Brewery Limited
Dragonwood Limited
Dulwich Spirits Co Ltd
Fiji Store Ltd
Freight Brewing Co. Ltd
Grace Wines (UK) Limited

HG & S Ltd
Hardywood Park Craft Brewery Ltd.
Hindsight Collective Ltd
Hingston & Co. Ltd
Hochfeld International Ltd
Il Tastevin Ltd
Invino Vitalis Ltd
Jimmy's Beer & Gas (Wirral) Ltd
Jin Bar Ltd
Jupiter Wholesale Limited
LVB Limited
Lanark House Investments Ltd
Lordsworth Limited
MMC Sales and Marketing Ltd
Matteo Lupi Wines Ltd
Mill Distributors Limited
Nitrogenics Ltd
Peatreekers Limited
Pellegrino Wine and Food Distribution
Profile Wines Limited
RHM Retail Ltd
Raer Whisky Limited
Reids Gold Brewing Co Ltd
River Widow Brewery Ltd
Roland Wines Ltd
Russbrit Ltd
Stag Brewery Ltd
Street Food & Beverages Co Ltd
UWD Limited
Underground Spirits Limited
Vinova Export Limited
Wester Spirit Co. Ltd
Whisky 78 Ltd
Wineworld Exchange UK Limited
Wisdom Whisky & Wine (Scotland) Ltd

February 2017 [37]
3ABC Ltd
A-Z Spirits Ltd
Above Brand Limited
Ace Incorporation Ltd
Altar Wines Limited
Asahi Premium Brands Ltd
Bielo Limited
Binning Trading Co Ltd
Brown Bear Tales Ltd
Campania Cucina Ltd
Colorado Craft Spirits Ltd
Dayboat Limited
Ellismuir Limited
Evil Spirits Ltd
Fameface Import Limited
Fines Master Spirit Co Ltd
Gordon & MacPhail Limited
I8 MGT Limited
Indian Ice Gola Co Ltd
International Wine Emporium Ltd.
Jaded Group Limited
Victor Lanson Brands Limited
Legacy Wines & Beverages UK Ltd
Liquid Ninja Limited
Loopland Brewing Co Ltd
Love and Labour Ltd.
Mayfield Distilling Co Ltd
Nexus Wine Trading Ltd
Seawoods Wine Ltd
Seriously Vodka Limited
Sherwood Outlaws Brewing Co Ltd
Tesh Beverages Limited
Top Alco Ltd
Traditional Italian Wine Co Ltd
Vertigo Beers Limited

Westvine International Ltd
Wise Imports Limited

March 2017 [47]
Absolute Wholesale Limited
Agave Union Limited
Albert Altima Trade House Ltd
Ali Booze Co Ltd
Allied Wholesale Ltd
Batarak Limited
Beaumont Beverages Ltd.
Beer & Co Distribution and Sales Ltd
Beverages Distribution Limited
Big Mouth Wine Limited
Bodega Uncielo (UK) Limited
Darley Abbey Wines Limited
Divergent Drinks Ltd
Evocative Wines Limited
Fine Wine (Old World) Trading Co Ltd
First Cape Vineyards Ltd
Glenallachie Distillers Co Ltd
Great Smattsby Limited
Hidden Gem - Urban Artisan Spirit Ltd
Iron Pier Brewery Limited
Jolly Good Beer Ltd
Kairos Solutions Ltd
Kegspertise Ltd
Leo's Cash & Carry Ltd
MM Drinks Ltd
D & M Nicholls Limited
Nue Innovations Limited
Orbit Wines Limited
PSR Distribution Limited
Portuguese Winery Limited
SK Trading (N.I.) Ltd
Sagitha Ltd
Sanghera Rum Co Ltd
Shack Drinks Limited
Sheffield Brewers Collective
Shellys Drinks Limited
Silenus Limited
Spalathos Ltd.
Swanbridge Fine Wines Ltd
Swissgrapes Limited
Taste Italia Limited
Telser & Pauli Ltd
Valenta Wine Limited
Verrillo Partnership Limited
Wine Prophets Limited
Winz International UK Ltd
Wyld Rose Ltd

April 2017 [47]
888 Global Trade Ltd
Adaka Group Ltd
Angola Beverages Holding Co Ltd
Bad Joke Brew Co Ltd
Bump Events U.K Limited
C & E Transport Ltd
Cassago Imports Limited
Cellartrade Ltd
Clara Wines Limited
Copricom Ltd
Crucial Drinks US Holdings Ltd
DLG Wholesale Ltd
Da Vinci Finest Italian Products Ltd
Dirty Drinks Collective Ltd
Drunk Maitre D Limited
El Toro Wines Limited
Epic Beers Limited
FVFC Limited

Firkin Whisky Co Ltd
Fourteen Drops Ltd
Goldy Limited
Illicit Spirit Co. Limited
J & De Limited
J & M Whisky Limited
Jezba Ltd
KT Global Ltd
Little Grape Co Ltd
Lost and Found Taprooms Ltd
Markets It Ltd.
McNicoll and Cairnie Limited
Neat Drinks Limited
Old Tullymet Whisky Co Ltd
Oris Black Ltd
Our Tino Ltd
Pale Fox Wines Limited
Piaff Trading UK Limited
Pingu & Co Ltd
Pulp Craft Cider Limited
Relaxandrinks Limited
Sipping Liquor Ltd
Slurp Wine Co Ltd
Stack United Limited
Teca Wines Limited
Tulaich Ltd
Ustuner Ltd
V Beverages Limited
Zachicado Ltd

May 2017 [43]
ANM Wholesale Limited
Aftersunset Ltd
Alky Limited
Appletree Cider Limited
C'est Nous UK Ltd
CGAVL Imports Limited
Chateau Miao Ltd
Dorys Shop Ltd
Family Choice Wholesale Ltd
Friendship Adventure Ltd.
Gin Corporation Limited
Glenlatterach Whisky Co Ltd
Global Wine Trading Co Ltd
Glugit Limited
Grande Marque Food & Beverage Ltd
Harrisons Fine Wines Limited
Impression Beverages Ltd
Kindred Spirit Partnership Ltd
Laurence Leisure Limited
NYSA International Ltd
Neon Brew Co Limited
Ourglass & Partners Ltd
Outstanding People Limited
PS Drinks Ltd
Paragon Brands Limited
Quicksip Ltd
Rando Global Alliance Limited
Red Dragon Brewery Ltd.
SO & T Consulting Limited
STM Traders & Services Ltd
Skull X Ltd
Stour Valley Events Limited
Bertrand Tailor Limited
Taste of Georgia Limited
Totally Awesome Wine Co Ltd
Trendbev Ltd.
Uncharted Wine Co Ltd.
Vinovest Limited
Woodwinters Agencies Limited
Worsley Gin Ltd
Xpress Bootleg Limited

Xpress Drinks Ltd
Yaad Rum Ltd

June 2017 [48]
3R'SB Limited
AB & R Import and Export Ltd
ABR Restaurant Group Ltd
Abloc UK Ltd
Abra Export UK Limited
Ale Trader Ltd
Ambal Fuel Ltd
Apex Dispense Limited
Brewland Ltd
Burgeon Allied Limited
Buzwine Limited
Citrone Limited
Compasses Gomshall Ltd
Conic Brewing Limited
Cotrade Ltd
Cubed A Ltd
DN Pacifica Ltd
Davenport Vineyards Limited
Delta World Trading Limited
Dita Grappolo Ltd
Drinks Agency Ltd
Fah Mai Holdings Limited
Ferintosh Distillery Limited
Fourteen Twelve Trading Ltd
Gargara Limited
Glen Monarch Distillery Ltd
Rachael Green Limited
JC Wholsale and Distribution Ltd
Little Vine Co Ltd
Maestral de Provence Ltd.
Monkey Shed Estate Brewing Co Ltd
Robin Navrozov Consulting Ltd
Nine Reigns Limited
Norlin Distribution Limited
Noy Brothers Enterprises Ltd
Quarter Cafe Bar Limited
Quintessential Decadence Ltd
Readywine UK Ltd
Retro Shotz Limited
Rockstar Spirits Limited
SDC Wine Importers Ltd
Samuels Brewing Co Ltd
Sol Regem Ltd.
Suwalki-UK Ltd
This Is Not A Party Limited
Turkish Kitchinn Wholesale Ltd
Ultravino Limited
Vitena Wines Ltd

July 2017 [49]
8 Drinks Ltd
Alfa Drinks Limited
Amwell Springs Brewery Co Ltd
B & M Produce Limited
BJ Drinks Ltd
Bigg Market Beer Co Ltd
Bigg Market Brewery Co Ltd
Bihl Ltd
Broadway Drinks Co Ltd
Buckingtons Ltd
Cape Secrets Limited
Carpet Bagger Limited
Celtavini.Com Limited
Chivalry Trading International Co. Ltd
Cibusrex Ltd
Cornish Rum Co Ltd
Cracking Little Wine Co Ltd

Crundale Wines Limited
Cullercoats Gin Co Ltd
Deco Spirits Limited
Rodney Densem Wines Limited
Fine Wine World Ltd
Heath Trading Limited
Heavenly Grapes Limited
Hidgate Ltd
Jackson & Seddon Ltd
Jervis Trading Limited
Kilted Drinks Limited
La Delizia UK Limited
Late Shop Ltd
Lazy Drinks Ltd.
London Calling Sweden Ltd
Luca Wine Limited
MV Distribution Ltd
Maxim & Co Limited
Mercury Spirits Ltd
MyNaturalCo Ltd
Native Wines Ltd
New Fairdeal Drinks Limited
Pomona Island Brew Co Ltd
RS Wholesale Limited
Redvulette Ltd
Rekhi Wholesale Ltd
Ricordo Ltd
Tan Dowr Limited
Tiger Vines Ltd
Tinkture Ltd
Ubicumque International Ltd
Wetherby Brew Co Limited

August 2017 [61]
106 Business Solutions Limited
ACK Trading Ltd
Artful Dodger Whisky Ltd
Beer Land Ltd
Birds of Arcadia Ltd
Blind Monkey Limited
Bourne & Co Solutions Ltd
Cape Wines Limited
Capion Trading Limited
Chesters Wine Merchants Ltd
Clements Harrison Limited
Clock Tower Distilleries Ltd
Costadoria Ltd
DC Wine Merchant Ltd
EL IP Rights Limited
Fairview Vineyard Ltd
Falcon Wholesaler Limited
J.T.Flanagan Trading Co Ltd
Ghost Laboratories Limited
Goldex International Ltd
Grape Wines Services Ltd
H R Drinks (Wholesale) Ltd
Healthier Products Limited
Hoppy Days Inn Ltd
KRD Distribution Co Ltd
Kimbland Distillery Ltd
Kukuruz Limited
Les Vins de Sylvain Ltd
Library Design Studio Ltd.
Lincolnshire Gin Ltd
Magic F & F Ltd
Maximus Wholesale Limited
McGin - The Glasgow Gin Ltd
Mercurial Brewing Limited
N & M Wholesale Ltd
Natural Wine Co Ltd
Nele Drinks Limited
North West Spirits Limited

UK Wholesalers of Beers, Wines and Spirits   dellam

OX Bespoke Logistics Ltd
Oxford Brewing Co Ltd
P & P Vino Limited
Panache Natural Flavour Infusions
Quint-Essential JQ Ltd
Rum Runna Ltd
Senor Agave Limited
Sunderland Gin Limited
Superba London Wines Ltd
Tamarind Drinks Limited
Taste of Alcohol Ltd
Tattoo Limited
Three Graces Liverpool Ltd
Two Heads Beer Co Limited
Vigneti Tardis UK Ltd
Vine & Cork Limited
Vine Street Wine Co Ltd
Wallis Ventures Ltd
Westend Cash and Carry Ltd
Wickersley Fine Wines Ltd
Wined Ltd
Yarm Gin Ltd
Yarm Spirits Co Ltd

September 2017 [58]
3 Lids Rum Ltd
AKS Brands Limited
All English Distribution Ltd.
Apna Distribution Ltd
Bang The Elephant Brewing Co Ltd
Bankside Brewing Limited
Bassrap Ltd
Bosworthcruises Ltd
Cape Wine Exporters (UK) Ltd
Colton Fox Trading Limited
Crafty Wolf (Drinks) Limited
Crafty Wolf Limited
Craftyard Events Limited
DC Cash and Carry Ltd
DTdist Ltd
Doctor Bird Rum Ltd
Domal Trading Limited
Drinks 2 You Limited
Expert Euro Exports Ltd
Fair City Spirits Limited
Fidra Fine Spirits Limited
Galldachd Na H-Alba Brewing Ltd
Gang of Five Ltd
Gente Di Mare Ltd
Glo-Rum Enterprise Limited
Interseel Ltd
Iturn Global Ltd
Jiggers Whistle Limited
L'Atypique Ltd
Laneberg Wine Ltd
MJM Hospitality Ltd
Maestrale Group Ltd
Mina Collection Ltd
Najpol Ltd
PatelCashAndCarry Limited
Pinckneys Gin Limited
Premier Beverages Limited
Quick Whisky Limited
RRK Supplies Limited
Rara Drinks Co Ltd
Refined Wine Club Ltd.
Sacred Spirits Holdings Ltd
Salt Rock Liquor Co Ltd
Sopwell Gin Co Ltd
Spirit Valley France Limited
Stockwell Beverages Ltd
T Warriors Brewery UK Limited

Team Spirit Beverage Ltd
Thorne Wines Limited
Tioluxe Europe Limited
Tortuga Brands Limited
Trebbiano Wines Ltd
Two Essentials Ltd.
Vinolex Ltd
Wedgbury Connections Ltd
White Wolf Brewery Ltd
Wine Art Co Ltd
Wine Raiders Limited

October 2017 [62]
23-7 Brewing Ltd
7 Day Cellar Limited
A-Holding Ltd
Anderson Beverages Ltd
B & P Beverages Ltd
Beets Incorporated Ltd
Bottles on Demand Limited
Brindle Distillery Limited
Brix & Porter Ltd.
Bullards Spirits Limited
Canapacampana Limited
Cassels and Sons Brewing Europe Ltd
Dallyla Ltd
Delicatezze Siciliane Limited
Desideria Ltd
Drink Link Grimsby Limited
Drinksology Limited
Field Bar Gin Limited
Gigglewater Productions Ltd
Gower Gin Co Ltd
Greatdrams Ventures Limited
Greater London Beer Exports Ltd
Greens Wholesale Ltd
HD Wine & Spirit Ltd
Heritiers Domec Ltd
Hilton & Rowley Ltd
Hitchin Brewery Ltd
House of Roo Ltd
IBL Wines Ltd
Jeffries Vintage Drinks Ltd
Kanpai (London) Food and Beverage Management Co.,
Knights Catering Impex Ltd
L'Atelier Terroir Limited
Langstone Beer Exports Ltd
Le Venue Wine Warehouse Ltd
Legends of Drinks Ltd
Little Horse Wines Limited
London Ale UK Ltd
London Spiced Dry Limited
Lush Wines Ltd
Marathon Beverages Ltd
Mode de Vie (Carbon) Limited
My Cocktail Club Limited
Nightingale Drinks Co Ltd
OAB Ventures Limited
PJ's Virtual Brewing Co Ltd
Pallet Price Wholesale Ltd
Panda Trading International Ltd
Penny Prize Limited
RSD Whisky International Ltd
Red Bonny Rum Limited
Ribox Quality Goods Ltd
Charles Samuel Imports & Exports Ltd
Sanwin Ltd
Silver Fox Wines Ltd
Siris Trading Ltd
Super Brit Bery Ltd
Triangle Wines Limited

Tribeology Limited
Vintage Wine Investments Ltd
W D L Wholesale Limited
Workshy Brewing Ltd

November 2017 [48]
3 Cities Brewing Co Ltd
Angel Wine & Spirit Group Co., Ltd.
Attitude Spirits Ltd
Bad Girls Brew Limited
Be Hop Ltd
Beer Seller Ltd
Boar Wine Ltd
Booze Bolton Limited
Camii Punch Ltd
Cartmel Spirit Co Ltd
Clubinn Together Limited
Creation Wines UK Limited
Demon Vodka Limited
Dionysus Premium Drinks Ltd
Drinkable Ltd
Drinks To Go Plus Ltd
H.B. Evelyo Ltd.
FFM Pasta Co Ltd
Frequency Enterprises Limited
GS Wines Ltd
Galloping Wine Nose Limited
Grafham Brewing Co Ltd
Highland Drinks Ltd
Horizons Enterprise Ltd
Human Brands PLC
Infinite Session Ltd
Jivana Spirits Ltd.
Koomor Brewing Co Ltd
Kristal Spirits UK Limited
Lion-Beer, Spirits & Wine (UK) Ltd
Liquid Lounge Drinks Co. Ltd
Liquor World Venture Ltd
Mo Madness Drinks Limited
Oak Wines Limited
Outlander Brands Limited
Pipehouse Gin Limited
Punchy Drinks Limited
Raven Spirits Limited
Redevined Wines Limited
Rodica Wine and Spirits Ltd
Silvertip Imports Limited
Sip Sip Wine Limited
Russell Smith F & B Limited
Star Direct Hospitality Ltd
TheTipsyTransit Ltd
Titanic Wines Limited
Vinny Labs Ltd
Wine Merchant Ltd

December 2017 [32]
A2Z Wines & Groceries Ltd
Alegri Trade Ltd.
B & W Distributors Limited
Bloody Drinks Limited
Borders Distilling Limited
Bruce Jack Wines Limited
Cambridge Champagne Co Ltd
Cincin Wines Ltd
Colne Confectionery Ltd
Euro Asia Distriubtion Limited
Explore British Drinks Limited
Fabijhon Wine Ltd
Gallachers Fine Wines Limited
Good Life Gin Co Ltd
Ian Hart Distilling Limited

JD Group Enterprises Ltd
K & A Eagle Limited
Kernow Rum Co Ltd
London Drinks Supplier Ltd
NCE Trading KFT Ltd
NM Lesuire Ltd
Old Wine House Ltd
Palms & Liquor Enterprises Ltd
Pop Cake Box Limited
Rico Rico Ltd
Savile Row Gin Limited
Solaris Wines Ltd
Somm in the Must Ltd
Stallion Spirits Limited
T & M Food Products Ltd
John Toma TDE Ltd
Zetas Ventures Ltd

January 2018 [74]
Afterthought Spirits Co Ltd
Apical Breweries UK Ltd
Articulate Drinks Co Ltd
Azienda Vitivinicola Stassi Ltd
Azurapada Worldwide Ltd
Benchmark Drinks Ltd
Blackstorm Rum Ltd
Blue Wine Ltd
Bosco-UK Limited
Brighton and Hove Wine Co Ltd
Bruist Trading Ltd
Bucks Spirits Ltd
Buke Limited
Bull Trading Worldwide Ltd
Bwinfusions Ltd
Calabria Family Wines (Europe) Ltd
Cask Industries Ltd
Cellar Select Ltd
Champagne Route Limited
Consulting & Food Ltd
Cyprian Services Limited
D & F Wines Ltd
Danish Snaps Co Ltd
Drinkologie Limited
Morgan Edwards Limited
Estelon Holdings Limited
For Goodness Sake Ltd
Garumbas Ltd
Gin Cooperative Ltd
Global Brands Trading Ltd
Grape Variety Ltd
HKK and Sons Ltd
Hurricane Rum Co Ltd
Isle of Bute Gin Co Ltd
Italy Service UK Ltd
Itasca Wines Limited
Jascera UK Ltd
Knightrate Wines Ltd
La Cerveceria Limited
Liquid Assets Group Ltd.
Loaded Spirits Ltd
McGrath's Brewing Limited
McLean's Gin Ltd
MegaTradingLtd Limited
Meless Consortium Ltd
Mexcal Ltd
N20winery Ltd
Navaladi Ltd
Northern Supplies (NE) Ltd
Nutricont Ltd
Oakmount Group Limited
Ocean Wines Limited
Othello Food and Wine Limited

Panemporium Ltd
Perscot Ltd
Pioneer Spirits Ltd
Ragul Ltd
Rarewood (London) Limited
Richdells Wine Merchants Holdings
Rum Fellows Limited
Silver Rocket Brewing Ltd
Srihari Haran Ltd
J & G Stewart Scotch Whisky Ltd
Thagam UK Limited
Tinnies Ltd
Tipo Loco Drinks Co. Limited
Valerieblue Ltd
Van Pur UK Ltd
Vektor Vodka UK Ltd
Voubearst Limited
Whisky Baron Ltd.
Whisky Point Limited
Wine House Warwick Limited
ZLCSolutions Ltd

February 2018 [82]
A & G Management Consultancy Ltd
A2Z Drinks Limited
Agave Partners Limited
Ambessa Goods Ltd
Appleton Estate Wines Ltd
Asante Distributors Limited
Asia-Pacific 11230699 Vitamin Beverage Co.,
At The Group Ltd
Bahamian Enterprise UK Limited
Bavarian Beer Co Ltd
Beer Traders UK Limited
Beerpol Ltd
Beverage Boys Ltd
Bridge Wine Limited
Burble Foods and Beverages Ltd
By His Grace Food Ltd
Can Man Ltd
Champions Cider Ltd
Circus Enjoy with Us Ltd
Clutha Distillery Co Ltd
Cornfield Foods and Beverages Ltd
Craftmaster Social Ltd
Crafty Warehouse Ltd
DBM Wines Limited
Deutschlond Brewery Limited
Diamond Aces Limited
Drinkss Cash and Carry Limited
Dromedary Trading & Resources Ltd
Edinburgh Cocktail Week Ltd
Evergreen Foods Limited
Forest Hill Brewing Co Ltd
Franko's Food Ltd
French Sommelier with a Wee Dog Ltd
Gin Dobry Gin Co Ltd
Ginkhana Limited
Gort Inn Ltd
Gremi Wine Trading (UK) Ltd
Highland Liquor Co Ltd
Hiline Wines Peterborough Ltd
Hobnobber Ltd
Il Tipico Italiano Ltd
Insignia Spirits Limited
Instabooze Limited
JB Champagne & Co Ltd
Janemac Ltd
Kindman Brewing Ltd
Laughing Ass Brewery Ltd
Londinio Liqueurs Ltd.
M M General Merchandise Ltd

MBW Traders Ltd
MCMCtrans Ltd
Maharaja & Sons Ltd
Mantra Trading Limited
Medicare Health & Energy Drinks Ltd
Molendinar Spirits Limited
Molotov Brand Limited
NMWLeisure Ltd
Novel Spirits Collection Ltd
Novel Spirits Limited
ONCC Import Limited
Octagon Industries Ltd
One Source Global Limited
Oso Brew Co Ltd
Perfect Pair Wines Ltd
Perth Distillery Co Ltd
Primos Group Ltd
Salford Rum Co Ltd
Signature Wine Gifts Ltd
Sinners Gin Ltd
Spirit Generation Limited
St George's Beer Co. of St Austell Ltd
St Ives Grog Co Ltd
Surprising Wines Ltd
Tump By Aj & Sonz Ltd
UK McLouis Liquor Co Ltd
Uncle Nearest Ltd.
Unfiltered Wines Limited
Vino Merchant Limited
Vins Ltd
WSB Investment and Consultancy Ltd
Wisca Beverages Limited
Zarb Distribution Ltd

March 2018 [94]
AMC Trading Co Ltd
Artizen Raw Ltd
Atom Brands Limited
Atom Cask Holdings Limited
Atom Drinks Limited
Atom Group Limited
Atom Scotland Limited
BL Drinks Ltd
BLSN Limited
Bacana Sangria UK Limited
Bearded Lion Drinks Co Ltd
Bournemouth Food Ltd
Buzz Booze Ltd
CMJ Pub Trade Ltd
Chateau Khornabuji Limited
Corfu SW Limited
Creative Juices Brewing Co Ltd
Crest Cyder Co Ltd
Dave and Dani Ltd
Deer & Badger Ltd
Deshi Bazar Ltd
Drink Connect Ltd
Drink Driver Ltd
Drinksbot Limited
Eclipse Drinks Limited
Eda Quality Foods North UK Ltd
FD Gin Co Ltd
Ferovinum Ltd
Fine Food & Wine Limited
Five Star Cash & Carry Ltd
Good Living Brew Co Limited
Greenwood Distillers Limited
Halton Turner Brewing Co Ltd
Harp & Crown Cider Co Ltd
R & J Harris Ltd
Headline Wines Ltd
I Caesar Limited

Impexpo Ltd
Innovative Cocktails Ltd
Island Drinks Limited
KB Suppliers Ltd
Kapaka Limited
Kayzar Ltd
Kosher Wines Limited
Lamson Wine Co Ltd
Lisaavo Ltd
Maison Sassy UK Limited
Malton Brewery Limited
Master of Malt Limited
Masters of Malt Limited
Maverick Brands Limited
Maverick Drinks Limited
Maverick Spirits Limited
Alistair McCoist & Jeff East (Vintners)
Mojito Bar Ltd
Nick Drinks Limited
Nisar Traders Ltd
Noahs Estate Ltd
Oracle Fine Wines Ltd.
Paisajes Trading Ltd
Parasol Wines Ltd
Peculiar Gin Co Ltd
Pot Still Drinks Ltd.
Raven Hill Brewery Limited
Rexon Group Festivals Limited
Riding Wine Co Ltd
SPP Wine Ltd
Sangiovesa Ltd
Sapling Spirits Ltd
Sco & Whisky Limited
Shocabo Ltd
Sky9 Ltd
Snickering Pig Drinks Co Ltd
Spirits Logistics Ltd
Stockwell Wholesalers Limited
Summerhall Distillery Asia Ltd
Grace Tilly Limited
Tipsy Events Ltd
Tolmid International Ltd
Tom's Tap and Brewhouse Ltd
Tops Food and Wine Limited
Truly Spirited Ltd
Ultimate Drinks Limited
Unicodrinks ESP Ltd
Union International Drinks Corporation
VDK Import Export Limited
Vicarage Spirit Limited
Vranac Stonecastle Limited
Alistair Walker Whisky Co Ltd
A J Walsh Consultant Limited
William of Orange Brands Ltd
Wineclub Online Limited
Wines Around Mediterranean Ltd
World of Drinks Limited

April 2018 [86]
Alko Vintages UK Ltd
Always 20 Limited
Arundo Limited
Bacchus Vin Ltd
Barge & Barrell Inns Ltd
Best Cask Ltd
Brewbarge Limited
Brexit Import and Export Co Ltd
CHX Distillers Ltd
Carousel Wines Limited
Cheti & Co Holdings Limited
Ciderfex Limited
Co.Bru Limited

Desi Wines Ltd
Divine Associates Ltd
Drill Wholesale Limited
El Brewery Limited
Ephemeris Solutions Ltd
Feni Global Limited
Free from Beer Co Ltd
Funemployed Agency Ltd
Funemployed Ltd
Glenreidh Liquor Co Ltd
Godin Tepe Limited
H & W Cash & Carry Ltd
HBN Ltd
Harmony Wines Limited
Head Thirst Ltd
Hidden Caveau Limited
House of Hops Limited
House of Wine Limited
Indra Beverages Limited
Irish Gin Co Ltd
JDT Drinks Co Ltd
JN Trading Limited
Jade General Merchants Ltd
Jia Bo Rui International Trade Ltd
Jordan Sky Ltd
Kingdom Distillers Limited
Kirker & Greer Whiskey Limited
LJW Wholesale Limited
Laurito Ltd
Limalimo UK Ltd
Lord Nelson Burnham Ltd
Lupe's Imports Limited
Message in a Bottle Ltd.
More Wine Ltd
Nice Brewing Co Ltd
Ourlocal Limited
P & P Distribution Limited
Paradigm Red Limited
Peace Bond Ltd
Plonq Wines Ltd
Port City Brewing UK Limited
Portsmouth Gin Co Ltd
Pruno Wines Ltd
Pryzm Cocktails Limited
Pure Organic Drinks Limited
RJR Fort Ltd
Re:Stalk Ltd
Reality Bio Wine Ltd
Red Door Gin Co Ltd
Rest Wine Ltd
Rich & Bad Ltd
Rock Beverages Limited
Rustic Tap Limited
SASC Enterprise Limited
Sailortown Brewing Limited
Shorty's Gins Ltd
Shy Simba Ltd
Snow Beer UK Ltd
Solent Off-License Ltd
Sotus Limited
JG Sousa Limited
Spiritory Ltd
TBpub Ltd
Teqbev Ltd
Toff Wine Ltd
Tomlinson Whisky Merchants Ltd
Urbeer Ltd
Vinvm Ltd
WLL Wholesale Ltd
Westworld Impex Limited
Whisky Merchants Trading Ltd
Whisky Rebellion Limited

Wine City Limited

May 2018 [95]
3Squires Wines Ltd
8000 Vintages Limited
Ababio Express Limited
Al Liver Management Limited
Alcohollect Ltd
Almaster Limited
B & F Enterprise UK Ltd
BF Wines UK Ltd
Bargain Food and Booze Limited
Beer & Wine (Northern) Limited
Belabon Drinks Ltd
Bellissimo Vino Edinburgh Ltd
Beverage Provider Limited
Biotanica Ltd
Bowsaw Bourbon Limited
Champagne Cellar Limited
Cheng International Co Limited
Clique Wine Limited
Cobblers Gin Limited
Cobev Limited
Comercio Ltd
Consolidated Wines Limited
Creative Juices Bar Limited
Delage & Haughton Limited
Delicious Drinks Limited
Delivery Offlicence Ltd
Destilado London Limited
Dionysus Boutique Wine Merchants Ltd
Drink Kind Ltd
Edgerton Holdings Limited
Ely's Cocktails Ltd
Emthea Ltd
FV Craft Beers Ltd
Global D & F Ltd
Glugged! Ltd
Goldy's Corner Shop Ltd
Good Spirits Ltd
Grandor Limited
High Jinks Limited
Imperial 21 Joya Ltd
J & D Wholesalers Ltd
Nicholas James Gin Ltd
KRW Leisure Limited
Kaur's Convenience Store Ltd
Koa Brewing Limited
La Guilde du Cognac Limited
Land'oc Wines Ltd
Liquid Brand Exports Limited
Lost Rivers Beer Co Ltd
Lpower Ltd
Luxury Gourmet Ltd
Magnus Wines Ltd
Manteo Trading Co Ltd
Mayday Island Limited
Mirfield Brewery Limited
Modest Merchant Limited
Mount Fetti Ltd
Neatly London Limited
Newhampton Wines Ltd
Now This Is It Ltd
Other World Wines Limited
Palmer Traders Ltd
Phoenix Spirits Ltd
Pradeeprjm Limited
Premium Bottles Limited
Publik Wine Limited
Punchline Ltd
Punjabi Ltd
Ragtag Wines Ltd

Reva Drinks Ltd
Robel Import Trading Ltd
Rude Mechanicals Limited
S.X Prosecco Party Limited
Sambatha Ltd
See Squared Ltd
Shropshire Beers Limited
Snowy Taverns Ltd
Solow Ltd
Solway Spirits Ltd
Source 360 Ltd
Stirling Whisky Co Ltd
Stoney Hospitality Limited
Symposia Wine Limited
Tilted Penguin Gin Ltd
UK McCullenvis Wine Group Ltd
Uist Distillery Ltd
Up Drinks Ltd
Veini Wine Co Ltd
Vineco Inco Ltd
Vino Italiano Ltd
Winelistphobia Ltd
Wineologia Ltd
World Wine Imports Limited
Xardins Wines and Cava Ltd
Yeast To West Ltd

June 2018 [87]
1879 Brand Ventures Ltd.
Albion Distillery Ltd
Albion Gin Ltd
Art Entertainment Ltd
Asta Barista Baby Ltd
Balcony Wines Ltd
Be Rude Not To Ltd
Bitter Lemons Gin Ltd
Bluetec Trading Services Ltd
Booze Cruz Ltd
Botanicals and Hops Limited
Brazen Rum Ltd
CBD Drinks Co Ltd
CDGH Pub Co Ltd
Chequers Distribution Ltd
Cider Is Wine Ltd
Corvin Import Export Ltd
Cru Classe Limited
Daves Drinks Ltd
Diffusion Food By Pina Co Ltd
Drink Artisan Ltd
Drink247 Ltd
Drinks Bay Limited
Duchy Beverages Ltd
Eastern Pantry Ltd
Ebony Drinks Limited
European Beer Exports Limited
GNR Distillery Limited
Gill's Drams Ltd.
Glam Drinks Ltd
Gold Tooth Limited
Heath London Limited
Hellenic Agora Limited
Hierarchy Brewing Co Ltd
Home2.0beer UK Ltd
Honkytonk Wine Library Limited
Hops and Dots Brewing Co Ltd
Imperial Capital D & G Ltd
Italia Wine and Food Ltd
Keeps Lager Co Ltd
Kermis Bier Ltd
Kibo Wines Ltd
Kuchh Hai Limited
La Madeleine Wines Limited

Lilo Beverages Ltd
Lizard Management Ltd
Loxwood Meadworks Ltd
Magna Juice Ltd
Mamajuana UK Ltd
Manoj Navaladi Ltd
Meridale Store Ltd
Middle Kingdom Ltd
Neilward Ltd
Nephtis Limited
Nifol Limited
Old Brenin Distillery Ltd
Panda Oriental Supermarket Ltd
Philsner Ltd
Pivo Beverages Ltd
Plymouth Rum Co Ltd
Pristine Trades Ltd
Prodolce Ltd
Quercus Wines Ltd
Rock and Roll Spirit Co Ltd
Sambath Trading Limited
Say It With Champers Ltd
Skyden Spirits Ltd
Snobby's Ltd
Swipe (Wine) Limited
TPSC Ltd
TVB Retail Limited
Tasmanian Liquor Distributors Ltd
Thrace Premium Drinks Ltd
Titanic Holdings Japan Ltd
Topmost Foods Distribution Ltd.
Toro Industries Ltd
Ttow Ltd
Vegan Wine Company London Ltd
Vine and Malt Ltd
Vino Unico Limited
Wilkies International Ltd
Wine Affairs Limited
Wine Castle Ltd
Wine Express Ltd
Wine Group Ltd
Witek Spirits Ltd
Ziv & Zivka Ltd

July 2018 [85]
Adventure Brands Ltd
Andris Holdings Limited
Angel Feathers Limited
Aztec Spirits Ltd
Bak Family Wines Limited
Bassen Ltd
Beer Me Now Ltd
Bitter End Limited
Black Kola UK Limited
Booze 2 U Ltd
Botan Grey Ltd
CKW (Europe) Limited
Daniel Carnio Ltd
Cathedral Wholesale and Events Ltd
Club Belmont Ltd
Concordia Wines Ltd
Connecting Italian Food UK Ltd
Corvinus Beverages International Ltd
Cotswolds Wine Co Ltd
Craftwater Brewing Co Ltd
DNG Group Ltd
DNG Trading Ltd
Daysh Beers Wines & Spirits Ltd
De Facto Spirits Limited
Dirt. Ltd
Drink Free Ltd
Empire Drinks Ltd

Ever-Tree Wholesale & Retail Ltd
Evolution Drinks Ltd
Foxbusiness Tobacco Ltd
Glenbrynth Limited
Golden Coin Trading Limited
Grizzly Endeavours Ltd
Hapusa Spirits UK Ltd
Harama Trading Ltd
H Harwood Ltd
Hayloft Ventures Ltd
Hop Drop Limited
Huddersfield Cash and Carry Ltd
Ineffable LDN Limited
Iridium Supplies Limited
Jocks and Peers Brewing Co Ltd
LM Spirits Ltd
Leppelmann & Nie Limited
Leverre Ltd
Liquor-Ish Ltd
Little White Dog Limited
Lounge Spirits Ltd
Medoff UK Ltd
Mercurion Ltd
Milk Vin Ltd
Murphy & Yeung Brewing Co Ltd
Mymexico Global Ltd
Naked Spirit Co Ltd
Novarto Drinks Ltd
Ohsake Ltd
Old Empire Events Ltd
Orchard-Lisle Wines Ltd
Oxford Beer House Limited
Ozpax Limited
PT Drinks Ltd
Palinka UK Ltd
Penryn Spirits Limited
Qtranly Ltd
RR Whisky Ltd
Rajpoot Traders Ltd
Rare Whisky Auctioneers Ltd
Ratherhavecava Ltd
Rebel Wine Club Ltd
Red Bay Brewing Co Ltd
Rovial Trans Ltd
S & B Impex Ltd
S & T Wines Limited
SSG Service Ltd
Southbrew Co Ltd
Spirito Limited
Tapp'd Ltd
Tata Trading Limited
Three Shires Distillery Ltd
Tipple Transport Limited
Trinity Drinks Limited
Unique Wine Safaris Limited
Viktor and Walker Ltd
Waterland Trading Limited
Way Outback Brewery Limited

August 2018 [92]
19th Beer Co Ltd
3Squires Ltd
After Eight Alcohol Concierge Ltd
Ana Express Ltd
Babyboyempire. Ltd
Bakewell Road Brewery Ltd
Barndiva Wine Co Ltd
Bazaar Store Ltd
Berkeley Cellars Limited
Blue Thorn Gin Limited
Boutinot USA Limited
Brew Boxes Ltd

UK Wholesalers of Beers, Wines and Spirits

dellam

Bristol Records Limited
Buveur Ltd
Candy Cotton Ltd
Cape Wine Merchants Ltd
Carpe Vinum Ltd
Cask and Craft Direct Ltd
Cheshire Gin Co Ltd
Choise Group Ltd
Corelli Wine Co Ltd
D & F Inns Ltd
Distant Lands Ltd
Estini Ltd
Evok3 Ltd
Exivi Limited
Fill Macan Limited
Flawless Spirits Ltd
Franc Wine Ltd
Good Wine Limited
Green Heart Wines Ltd
HSE of Drinks Ltd
Hayk Corporation Ltd
Holborn Gin Co Ltd
Honeybee Farm Ltd
Inkd Limited
William James & Sons Ltd
KC Brothers Ltd
KWM Supplies Ltd
Keepr's Ltd
Last Word Drinks Co Ltd
Late Night Liquor Ltd
Low-Key Essentials Ltd
MB Whisky Limited
Maha Wholesale Ltd
Maison Shane et Filles Ltd
Manley Wines UK Limited
Maw Berwick Ltd
Milae Vodka Limited
Mixed & Co By A Limited
Moody Spirit Co Ltd
Morley Way Limited
Near Beer Brewing Co. Ltd
NineTailsDistillery Ltd
Northpole Crush Ltd
Parkers Newsagents Ltd
Pau Drinks Limited
Petrelli Ltd
Phil Macan Limited
Python Controls Ltd
Rebel Pi Limited
Rendog Gin Ltd
Ross Earl Wine Co., Ltd.
Saj Holdings Ltd
Santa Code Limited
Sarpe L & C Ltd
Shamboozle Limited
Shandy Shack Ltd
Singolo Vino Limited
Slanj Whisky Ltd
Slightly Squiffy Limited
Slopemeister Brewing Co Ltd
SmsZee Limited
Stag Ales Ltd
Sun Exports Limited
Te Kano Estate Wines (UK) Ltd
Thameside Rum Co Ltd
Thiyagu Ltd
Titanic Distillers Belfast Ltd
Titanic Distillers Limited
Transylvania's Finest Ltd
Trinewine Ltd
Truekeg UK Ltd
Trusty Services Ltd

Urban Wine Co. Ltd
Uva Hitchin Ltd
Via Academia Vocatus Ltd
Victoria Island Beverage Co Ltd
Werfa Holdings Ltd
Wessex Wine Co Ltd
Wine & Spirits Club SA Ltd
Wine Freedom Limited

September 2018 [97]
A & S Drinks Ltd
Al & Lu (UK) Ltd
Alpha Whisky Ltd
Atkinson's Gin Ltd
Australian Cellar Ltd
Bacchus London Limited
Bittles Irish Whiskey Co Ltd
Blackcattaverns Ltd
Burton Drinks Limited
Busted Cow Ltd
C C and C London Ltd
Capsule Wine Ltd
Caribbean Collective Group Ltd
Cuba Trading Co Ltd
Distillery 96 Limited
Do Trading Limited
Drinks2u Ltd
Droylsden Craft Limited
Dunarea Albastra Ltd
Earth Elements Ltd
Eataly Food Distributors Ltd
Espir Baron & Solomon Limited
Eurotrade Supply Limited
Fine Wine Direct Limited
GBW Subscriptions Ltd
Gather 77 Limited
Gibraltar Gin Co Ltd
Goodeataly Ltd
Grassington Spirit Co Ltd
Great Orme Drinks Co. Ltd
Grwp Silwriad Cyf
HardyDistillery Ltd
Hips Drinks Ltd
Hobros Limited
Holy Grape Ltd
International Spirit Vault Ltd
J K Wholesales Ltd
JW Corporation Ltd
Just Incase Wines Ltd
Kingfisher Beer Ltd
Kinkladze Limited
Kylemore Trading Ltd
Laravita Ltd
Lemongrass and Cardamom Ltd
Lioness Paw UK Limited
Magma Liquid Ltd
Master of Sake Ltd
Medusa Wines Ltd
Moa Group Ltd
Mother of Wine Ltd
Mr Kegz Ltd
My Gin My Way Ltd
Mzansi UK Ltd
NTKS Ltd
Natural Beer Co Ltd
Nestle James & Co Ltd
O & E Food Ltd
Pago Wines Limited
Pandemonium Wines Ltd
Pastai di Serino Italian Food and Wine Excellence
Peoplegood Limited

Pongolo Ltd
Portugal Winelist Ltd
Presidente Wines Limited
Prestige Whisky Worldwide Ltd
Refresh 24 Group Limited
Renwick MacDonald Bars Ltd
Rome de Bellegarde Wines Ltd
Rosemille Ltd
Ruby & Claret Limited
Rumbaclaat Ltd
S.A.R.D.V.M Ltd
SW Group Spanish Wine Ltd
San Martino Limited
Satellite Brands Limited
Scozia Grappa Ltd
Sheikh Super Store Ltd
Sloshed Puppy Ltd
Smith & Harris Enterprises Ltd.
Stay Gold Beer Co Ltd
TPDirect Ltd
Tap HQ Ltd
Tasty Kameleon Ltd
Tewaina Ltd
Tipton Wines Limited
Toke Commodity Electro Limited
Trang Mai Exports Limited
Two Pal's Co Ltd
Vinandar Wines Limited
Vineus Limited
Vivir Drinks Ltd
Walking Back The Cat Limited
Walnut Tree Distillery Ltd
Wight & Wessex Wines Limited
Wine Bliss Ltd
Wine Tasting Angels Ltd
Wolf Wine Limited

October 2018 [104]
8 Barrels Club Ltd
AbruzzoWines Ltd
Ambassador Commodities Ltd
Atlas Food Wholesale Ltd
Auld Acquaintance Whisky Co Ltd
BV Group UK Limited
Bacchus Fine Wine & Food Ltd
Bacchus Merchantry Limited
Baijiu Evolution Ltd
Balkan Wines Ltd
Beeble Liquor Limited
Beverage Boutique Ltd
Bond Bar Ltd
Boutinot Canada Limited
Buzz Drinks Limited
Camden Drinks Co Ltd
Cascade Trade Services Ltd
Chandos Wines Ltd
Craddock Cocktails Ltd
Crazy Brew UK Limited
Czech Beer Alliance Limited
D & N Supplies Limited
Dega Trading Ltd
Dirty Drinks Ltd
Double Measure Club Ltd
Dracula Wine House Ltd
Drinkz Ltd
EJ Orendale Ltd
EW Bars Limited
Epiphany Bars Limited
F8t B8dgers Ltd
Falugamaro International Ltd
Free Spirits Group Ltd
Georgian Wine Co Ltd

Golden Whisky Limited
Happy Girl Beverage Co Ltd
Hatton Wholesale Ltd
Holcombe Gin Ltd
Hoversy Technologies Ltd
Jaguar Beverage Ltd
Jiangsu Wine Trading Co Ltd
Jub Club Top Bar Ltd
Lafferty & Sons Ltd
Laughing Pug Ltd
Le Petit Wine Cellar Ltd
Local Beer Delivered Ltd
Lucky Strike Pub Co Ltd
Lux Ex Dignitas Limited
MPS 64 Ltd
Mad Batchers Ltd
Majlen Ltd
Minarda General Trade Ltd
Mobay Drinks Ltd
Momento Vivere Holdings Ltd
Most Popular Limited
Newchesters Ltd
Night Out Entertainments Ltd
Nino and Blue Spruce Ltd
Nolo Drinks Co Ltd
Nordic Imports Ltd
Novus Drinks Ltd
Ocavia Wine & Spirits Ltd
Official Box Office UK Ltd
Ops Wines Ltd
Oui Vino Limited
Pant y Foel Gin Ltd
Parched Drinks Ltd
PimentoDrinks UK Ltd
Pioneer Gin Limited
Platinum Gin Ltd
Private Wine Shippers Ltd
Reformed Spirits Co Ltd
Revilo Group Limited
River Drinks Ltd
Russells and Wrangham Limited
Sageitude Ltd
Sativatech Ltd
Schnapp Lab Ltd
Second Eger Ltd
Selectia Wine Ltd
Simply Drinks Distribution Ltd
Smith & Humpston Ltd
Somerset Craft Distillery Ltd
Sourceror Ltd
Spainorama Ltd
Super Cooper Ltd
T.W.S Wines Ltd
TST Ventures Limited
Tender Vine Limited
Thames Cash & Carry (Birmingham) Ltd
Think Wine Group Ltd
Two Toes Ltd
Ultra Premium Drinks Limited
Union XV Gin Co Ltd
Uropa Group Ltd
Uva Wines Ltd
Vicar's Gin Ltd
Vieuxvino Investment Ltd
Vinature Ltd
Wee Vinoteca Ltd
West Spirits MCR Ltd
White Lion Gin Co Ltd
Wild Foragin Ltd
World of Drams Ltd

November 2018 [98]
11:11 Gin Ltd
A A Suppliers Ltd
A Little Bit of French Ltd
Alcos Trade Limited
Anna Wine & Food Ltd
Ariki Limited
Ark Inta Ltd
B Wines Limited
Beattie & Roberts Imports Ltd
Bespoke Fine Wines Limited
Black Dog Gin Co Ltd
Bonny Gin Ltd
Bonvoy Limited
Booze Village Limited
Browett & Fair Ltd
CPT Trading Ltd
Canny Class Ltd
Cask Trade Ltd
Cheti & Co Limited
Chic Fruit Ltd
Chosen Wine Limited
Crabtrees Craft Pubs and Bottle Merchants
Craft Beer Collaborative Ltd
Crafty Connoisseur Limited
Cuestion Tequila EMEA Ltd
Cuestion Tequila Limited
D.Rock Champagne Ltd
De-Laceys Tipples Limited
Delbrew Ltd
Delbroo Ltd
Double Hard Whiskey Co Ltd
Duple Social Club Sth Shore BPL . Ltd
Edmunds Cocktails Ltd
Eight Vodka Limited
Faking Bad Brewery Limited
Fcuk Ltd
Fightback Brewing Co Ltd
Foodiebusters Epic Food Authority Ltd
Forward Moving Limited
Global Trade & Consulting Ltd
Global Wine & Spirits Ltd
Goldfinch Whisky Merchants Ltd
Grape and Nectar Ltd
Hard Back Rum Limited
Hitchin Distillery Limited
I'll Ask The Boys Ltd
Icomex London Limited
In Wine & Spirit Solutions, Ltd
Incapico Inc Limited
Interactive Stage Ltd
KBB Components Ltd
Kasgo Limited
Kikijee Global Services Ltd
Labrat Brewing Limited
Lanty Slee Liquor Co Ltd
Lazy Hare Limited
Lexington Trading Limited
Lough Neagh Distillers - 1837 Ltd
MMGT Limited
Mahar Associates Ltd
Maiden Wines Limited
Manor Wholesale Ltd
Matheson Brewers Ltd
North West Industries Ltd
Northern Hospitality (MCR) Ltd
Ojo de Dios Ltd
One Stop East Limited
Plant Relief Ltd
Popjax Limited
Maurice Richard Ltd
Rosie & Gin Limited

Russian Doll Vodka Limited
Russian Investment II Limited
Scarlettes Ltd
Schoenlaub Limited
Shake's Ink Limited
Silence of The Drams Limited
Sladecs247 Ltd
Slainte Mhath Ltd
Southwell Trading Ltd
Spokesuk Ltd
Stida Beverages Ltd
Stockport Gin Ltd
Summerforever Ltd
Team Yebo Ltd
Tequila Shop Ltd
Tirg Limited
Triple Point Brewing Ltd
UK Blue Ribbon Group Beer Co., Ltd
VIP Services Scotland Ltd
Wine Cru Limited
Wine Place Limited
Winehood Ltd
Winery Jakubik UK Ltd
Winetage Ltd
Xpress Resolution Ltd
Yoka Family Limited
Young Malt Co Ltd

December 2018 [75]
4 Acre Brewing Co. Ltd
Alcofrolics Ltd
Aqua Vitae Vodka Limited
Art Beer Co Ltd
Atanas Distributors Ltd
Athila Roos Ltd
Bach & Co Solution Limited
Bar Joker Ltd
Beylerbeyi UK Ltd
Blush Gin Distrubutors UK Ltd
PNJ Bolton International Ltd
Brewis Beer Co Ltd
Buffet Restaurant Northampton Ltd
Burnobennie Distillery Limited
Cellar Capital Limited
Church Road Mini Market Ltd
Cornish Moonshine Co Ltd
Cremant Inc Ltd
Drinktonics Limited
Exul Limited
Fabulous Gin Ltd
Fairytale Gin Limited
Flava Foods Ltd
Flora Fine Wines Ltd
Florin Wholesaler Ltd
Frederick's Wine Co Ltd
From Cask To Bottle Limited
G & G International BCN Ltd
Gain & Coombs Ltd
Gleneagles Distillery Limited
Glenturret Limited
Grape Merchants Ltd
Samuel Gulliver & Co. Limited
HS13 Trading Ltd
Helver Wines Ltd
Home Farm Gin Limited
Ian MacBarrel & Spirits Ltd
Intercontinental Trade Solutions Ltd
It's A Gin Thing Ltd
Kanj Wholesale Ltd
Kohisar Limited
Laki & G Ltd
Les Vins de Latour Limited

UK Wholesalers of Beers, Wines and Spirits — dellam

Lewes Gin Limited
Liquor Box Ltd
Lusus Wines Ltd
Magazin Romanesc Ltd
Malthub Ltd
Marcin & Son Ltd
Mezzaro Ltd
Nat Trade SRL Ltd
Old and Rare Whisky Limited
Oxford Brewery Limited
Penzance Gin Ltd
Ramx Ltd
Real Ale (Export) Limited
Real Ale (Retail) Limited
Real Ale (Wholesale) Limited
Relais La Torre UK Ltd
Remfly Wines UK Limited
Reservedwines Ltd
SOS Whisky Limited
Sheila's Rum Punch Ltd
Square Wholesale Ltd
Square Wine Ltd
Swinging Vine Ltd
TBD Tipples Ltd
Tall Blond UK Ltd
Tims Tuga Ltd
Twilight Drinks Ltd
V I Wholsale Limited
Whiskey and Bourbon Club Ltd
Wine Online Ltd
Wine Shop Limited
Winnack and Hart Industries Ltd

January 2019 [102]
97 Catering Ltd
A Little Luxury Distillery Ltd
Adonko Bitters (UK) Ltd
Alinari Ltd
Antrobus Brothers Limited
Ballers Brands Ltd
Batch Cider Ltd
Bayede Wines UK Ltd
Beautiful Beers East Anglia (UK) Ltd
Beerco Limited
Belizaire Drinks Ltd
Brazen Beer Limited
Bubra Drinks Ltd
Bulgarsko Pivo Limited
Cabal Estates Limited
Cacheflow Ltd
Camis International Trading Co., Ltd.
Cashew Apple Co Ltd
Clarence Spirits Limited
Conti Coronini Ltd
Copper and Rye Leisure Ltd
Cotswold Wines Ltd
DT Wine Importers Ltd
DTB Distribution Ltd
DW Brands Ltd
Disley Gin Ltd
Drink Store Limited
Drinks Network Ltd
Dutch Courage Drinks Consultants Ltd
ERE Igga Ltd
Feewcha Services Ltd
Flower Miners Limited
Fortunella Spirits Ltd
Franklyn Road Brewing Ltd
Fyre Festival UK Ltd
GSYB Ltd
Group93 Ltd
Guest Wines & Co. Ltd

H & F Export Limited
Hop Hideout Limited
Hop To The Vine Limited
Hope Sisters Limited
Hopper House Brew Farm Ltd
Hotham's Spirits Ltd
Ironbridge Gorge Gin Co Ltd
JBD Booze Ltd
JPHA Ltd
Jackrabbit Brewing Co. Ltd
K & G Spirits Ltd
KBE Drinks Enterprises Limited
Kolden Ltd
La Aurora Ltd
Land's End Gin Limited
Levin Trading Limited
Melchior Limited
Mexican Spirits Carmen Del Rio Ltd
Mixology Collection Ltd
Moonberries Ltd
Nandha Murgesan Ltd
Noah Brothers Ltd
Noetic Wine Limited
Norfolk Rum Co Ltd
OX Wines Ltd
Oak Group One P.L.C.
Padlock Brewery Ltd.
Panache du Sud Ltd
Phone A Fix Ltd
Pink City Cider Ltd
Pioneering Spirits Limited
Prime Drinks Ltd
Project Urban Wines Ltd
Pure Techno Ltd
Quamina Quality Drinks Co Ltd
Rimpex-UK Limited
Ryder Partners Limited
Saltrock Brewing Co Ltd
Saravanan Traders (UK) Ltd
Savafrei Ltd
Sharpham Wine Limited
Shelsley Brewing Co Ltd
Shop Wine Limited
Sips 'n' Nibbles Ltd
Slim Gin Ltd
Sober Limited
Spirit of Bermondsey Ltd
St Davids Gin Limited
Sundown Vino & Liquor Ltd
Suntrack Ltd
TCG Winchester Limited
TH Nightlife Ltd
Taabs Investment UK Limited
Tapp'd Cocktails Ltd
Thames Wholesale Ltd
Tipple Spirits Co Ltd
UKAFDS Limited
Union Drinks Ltd
V B Cash & Carry Ltd
Vitosha Wine Ltd
Wave Wine Ltd
Whisky Work Play Ltd
Wine & People Limited
Xi-Spain Ltd

February 2019 [92]
4 Rabbits Ltd
A Di Maria & Sons Ltd
Agencia Ltd
Applecart Drinks Limited
Avazak Ltd
BCM Brewing Co Ltd

Best Bordeaux Wines Ltd
Best-One Local Ltd
Bianca Trading Wine Ltd
Blu-Dot Commodities Limited
Bopfags Services Ltd
Bucklebury Brewers Ltd
Bumble Mead Ltd
Burgundys Collection Limited
Cantium Spirit Ltd
Cask Hub Limited
Caspian Black Limited
Cazcabel Tequila Limited
Classic Cask Limited
Conscious Collaborative Ltd
Cow West Yorkshire Limited
Craft Wines Ltd
Csburrwine Ltd
DTA Drinks Ltd
Darlaston Drink Shop Limited
Desirable Drinks Ltd
Diverse Beers Limited
Dos Santos Bev Co UK Limited
Dragon Wines Limited
Drumgaw Holdings Ltd
East and West Foods Cash and Carry
Eight Brothers Corporation Ltd
Elixir Wine Ltd
Enzo's Food and Wine Ltd
Export and Import Trading Ltd
Fabre Brothers Ltd
Firewater Merchants Ltd
Fitlikey Brewery Ltd
Functional Drinks Co Limited
Green Cash & Carry Ltd
Green Leaf Liquids Limited
James Hocking Wine Limited
Imbibe Ltd
Imprint Wine Limited
Inception Drinks Limited
Infinitygroup1 Limited
Ishke Brands Ltd
JKVK International Import and Export Ltd
Anthony James Beverages Ltd
Junga Ltd
Kegs R Us (Leicester) Ltd
Law and Disorder Brew Co Ltd
Layered Cakes Ltd
Layered Ltd
London Barrelhouse Limited
London Long Drink Limited
Los Perros Sueltos Brewing Co Ltd
M & M Romanian Imports Ltd
MSSC (NW) Limited
Made To Measure Ltd
Mail-a-Wine Limited
Mamada Ltd
Maxwell's Trading Co Ltd
Melange Drinks Ltd
Modern Botanicals Limited
My Nan's Favourite Ltd
Paloma & Pablo Import & Export Ltd
Parthenon Import Co Ltd
Prasad Trading Co Ltd
RBW Fine Wines Limited
Rapid Fill Ltd
Rossendale Brew Co Ltd
Roydon Flavours Ltd
Ruffnek Beer Limited
Samphire Drinks Ltd
Seafire Brewing Co. Ltd
Southsea Gin Co Ltd
Spirit O' Clyde Drinks Co Ltd

Spirits of Borough Ltd
Steel City Exports Ltd
Swimming Pigs Ltd.
TBrands Distributor Ltd
TP Retail Ltd

Tipsy Tea Limited
Truk Limited
UBI Drinks Enterprises Limited
Vyce Ltd
Wall2wall Wines Limited

Wedding Wine Shop Ltd
West Lancs Drinks Ltd
Wild Life Botanicals Ltd
Wingwalker Vodka Limited

Geographic Distribution by County

Co Antrim [40]
Belfast Distillery Co Ltd
Beveridge Wines Ltd
Bowsaw Bourbon Limited
C & C 2011 (NI) Limited
Capital Languages Ltd
Connolly Wines Ltd
Connollys' Liquor Wholesale Ltd
Diageo Global Supply IBC Ltd
Diageo Northern Ireland Ltd
Dillon Bass Limited
Drinks Inc. Ltd
Drinksology Limited
Duncairn Wines Limited
Gleeson N.I. Limited
Greatvine Ltd
Harry's Road Fine Wine Limited
J. & J. Hunter Limited
Inverroche Ireland Ltd
Ireland Craft Beers Ltd
Mark Jefferson Wines Limited
Keg Company (N.I.) Ltd
Kirker & Greer Whiskey Limited
Liquid Solutions Distribution (N.I.)
Mayday Island Limited
McGrath's Brewing Limited
Mundus Wines Limited
Nele Drinks Limited
Norlin Distribution Limited
Original Liqueur Co Ltd
Phoenix Premium Drinks Limited
Red Bay Brewing Co Ltd
Red Bonny Rum Limited
Robb Trading Ltd
Philip Russell Limited
Sailortown Brewing Limited
Samuels Brewing Co Ltd
Titanic Distillers Limited
Titanic Holdings Japan Ltd
Vineyard Belfast Limited-The
Whisky Seller Limited

Co Armagh [12]
Beer Bottle Co Ltd
Drumgaw Holdings Ltd
Fegan Wholesale Ltd
Garumbas Ltd
L.A. Drinks Co Ltd
Little Rock Wine Co Ltd
Lough Neagh Distillers - 1837 Ltd
James E. McCabe Limited
New Age Wines Ltd
Nutricont Ltd
Robb Brothers Wine Merchants Ltd
United Wine Merchants Limited

Co Down [23]
A.F.T. (Liquor Stores) Limited
Anjo Wines Limited
Bittles Irish Whiskey Co Ltd
Clarke Wholesale Limited
Classic Malts Limited
Donnelly Wholesale Limited
GDK Drinks Ltd
Global Wine Distributors Ltd
DBS Isherwood Limited
JN Trading Limited
Jonesborough Wholesale Ltd
KWM Supplies Ltd
Loopland Brewing Co Ltd
Neill & Company Wine Importers Ltd

James Nicholson Wine Limited
Noreast Beers (N.I.) Ltd
Orchard Wine Co Ltd
PFG Marketing Ltd
Prohibition Limited
RHM Retail Ltd
Titanic Distillers Belfast Ltd
Titanic Wines Limited
Triberg Limited

Co Fermanagh
Blakes Fine Wine Ltd
Erin Vintners Ltd

Co Londonderry [6]
C & R Wines Limited
N. McLoone & Co. Ltd
SK Trading (N.I.) Ltd
Star Value Limited
Westvine International Ltd
Wine Byre Limited

Co Tyrone
Gort Inn Ltd
Irish Gin Co Ltd

Aberdeenshire [25]
Angus Wines Limited
Big Fish Brewing Co Ltd
Burnobennie Distillery Limited
Michel Couvreur (Scotch Whiskies)
De Facto Spirits Limited
Dion Wines & Food Limited
Expert Euro Exports Ltd
First Whisky Limited
Fitlikey Brewery Ltd
Gin Cooperative Ltd
Gin Room Scotland Ltd
Ginkhana Limited
Golden Whisky Limited
Kegspertise Ltd
Labrat Brewing Limited
Matheson Brewers Ltd
W.G. Paterson & Son Limited
Raven Spirits Limited
Reids Gold Brewing Co Ltd
Single Malts Limited
Duncan Taylor Scotch Whisky Ltd
Tipo Loco Drinks Co. Limited
Tipple Spirits Co Ltd
United Supplies Limited
Whisky Galore Limited

Angus [8]
Aberdrinks Scotland Limited
Call-a-Keg (Scotland) Limited
Call-a-Keg Beverages Ltd
Call-a-Keg Limited
JF Kegs (Scotland) Limited
McNicoll and Cairnie Limited
Sangiovesa Ltd
Wickedsoup Ltd.

Argyll
William Cadenhead Limited
Springbank Distillers Limited

Argyll & Bute
Portavadie Distillery Limited

Ayrshire [21]
A-Z Spirits Ltd
Alliance Wine Co Ltd
Ayr Brewing Co Ltd
Campbell Inns Limited
Copper and Rye Leisure Ltd
Crucial Brands Holdings Ltd
Crucial Drinks US Holdings Ltd
A. Dewar Rattray Limited
GCBW Catrine Ltd
GSWD Catrine Ltd
If Eaglesham Ltd
Inverglen Scotch Whisky Co. Ltd
LDC Scotland Limited
Lost Distillery Co Ltd
Old Tullymet Whisky Co Ltd
Rasputin Leisure Ltd
Roblex Ltd
Salt Rock Liquor Co Ltd
Tennent Caledonian Breweries Wholesale
Teqbev Ltd
Wallaces Express Limited

Banffshire
W.& J.Cruickshank and Co Ltd
Glenallachie Distillers Co Ltd

Clackmannanshire
Kindred Spirit Partnership Ltd
Lafferty & Sons Ltd
Park Place Drinks Limited

Dumfries & Galloway [6]
Creative Whisky Co Ltd
Galldachd Na H-Alba Brewing Ltd
Solway Spirits Ltd
Whisky Rebellion Limited
Whiskybroker Limited
Andrew R. Wilson Limited

Dunbartonshire [6]
Arisaig Distillers Ltd
Ferintosh Distillery Limited
North Star Spirits Ltd.
Pink Gin Co Ltd
Scotland Grindlay Limited
Wisdom Whisky & Wine (Scotland) Ltd

Fife [10]
414 Alcohols Limited
Allson Sparkle Limited
Greens Wholesale Ltd
Italian Appellations Limited
Kinkell Brewery Ltd
Land'oc Wines Ltd
Moonshine Traders Ltd
RR Whisky Ltd
Saltrock Brewing Co Ltd
Seafire Brewing Co. Ltd

Highland
Wingwalker Vodka Limited

Isle of Mull
Whitetail Spirits Limited

Isle of Skye
Praban Na Linne Limited
VIP Services Scotland Ltd

UK Wholesalers of Beers, Wines and Spirits

Kinross-shire
Craft Distillers Scotland Ltd
Siderea Consulting Limited
Small Batch Bottlers Scotland Ltd

Lanarkshire [138]
1879 Brand Ventures Ltd.
2l Whiskies Limited
ABA Eaglesham Ltd
AMC Trading Co Ltd
Agave Union Limited
Al Liver Management Limited
Amarri Prosecco Limited
Aussie Rules Ltd
J. & G. Barclay and Co Ltd
Bekel Limited
Sir Richard Blake & Associates Ltd
Bonny Gin Ltd
Brazen Rum Ltd
Brewgooder Limited
Bringmevino (UK) Limited
Broughton Ales Limited
Bruist Trading Ltd
Bunnahabhain Distillery Co Ltd
Burn Stewart (U.S. Holdings) Ltd
Burnfield Trading Co Ltd
C & D Exports Ltd
Matthew Clark (Scotland) Ltd
Conic Brewing Limited
Delicious Drinks Limited
Deliverance Dot Com Limited
Delivered Drinks Limited
Dew Hill Blending Company (Glasgow)
Distell International Limited
Distilled Brands Limited
Distilled Liquor Co Ltd
Douglas Export Agency Limited
Edinburgh Cocktail Week Ltd
Edition Spirits Ltd.
Edrington European Travel Retail Ltd
Edrington International Brands Ltd
Edrington-Beam Suntory UK Distribution
Ellismuir Limited
Fill Macan Limited
J.W. Filshill International Ltd
Forth Wines Limited
Gill's Drams Ltd.
Giuseppe's Wines Limited
Glam Drinks Ltd
Glasgow Distillers Limited
Glenbrynth Limited
Glenforest Limited
Glenreidh Liquor Co Ltd
Glenroy Spirits Limited
Glenturret Limited
Matthew Gloag & Son Limited
Goldfinch Whisky Merchants Ltd
Gordon Graham & Co Ltd
Grizzly Endeavours Ltd
Heidi Beers Limited
Highfern Limited
Highland Distillers Limited
Highland Malt Whisky Co Ltd
Highland Scotch Whisky Co Ltd
Highland Vintners Ltd
Highlands & Islands Scotch Whisky Co Ltd
Hope Sisters Limited
Hunter Douglas Scotch Whisky Ltd
Illicit Spirit Co. Limited
Imperial Distillers Co. Ltd
Inverarity Vaults Limited

Isle of Bute Gin Co Ltd
J A Glass Limited
J.G. Distillers Limited
JD's Sports Bar Ltd
KB Agencies Ltd
Kilted Drinks Limited
Kirklee Scotch Whisky Limited
Kwik-Keg Limited
LCW (Glasgow) Ltd
Andrew Laing & Co Ltd
Douglas Laing & Co Ltd.
Laing Shipping & Export Agency Ltd.
Laing Whisky Co Ltd
Levenridge Limited
James MacArthur & Co Limited
Tom MacFarlane and Co Ltd
Alistair McCoist & Jeff East (Vintners)
Douglas McGibbon & Co. Ltd
McGin - The Glasgow Gin Ltd
Marshall McGregor Limited
McLean's Gin Ltd
Mixed & Co By A Limited
Molendinar Spirits Limited
William Morton Limited
Mr. Alba International Trading Co Ltd
Alexander Muir & Son Limited
Myrlex Southend Limited
Native Oracle Limited
Natural Beer Co Ltd
Neat Drinks Limited
One Source Global Limited
Parthenon Import Co Ltd
Penny Prize Limited
Phil Macan Limited
Philipshill Retirement Village Ltd
Portuguese Winery Limited
Quartz Group Scotland Ltd
R.L.G. Trading Limited
Raer Whisky Co Ltd
Raer Whisky Limited
Raleigh (Glasgow) Limited
Re:Stalk Ltd
Regent Wines Limited
Relaxandrinks Limited
William Riddell & Sons Ltd
Rosemount Pub Co. Limited
Row & Co Ltd
Rutherglen Scotch Whisky Co Ltd
SSG Service Ltd
Seriously Vodka Limited
Shieling Scotch Whisky Co Ltd
Slanj Whisky Ltd
Speyside Bonding Co Ltd
Speyside Distillers Co Ltd
Speyside Trading Co Ltd
Spirit O' Clyde Drinks Co Ltd
Spirit of Glasgow Ltd
Stirling Whisky Co Ltd
Tennent Caledonian Breweries UK Ltd
Tolsta Brands Limited
Tropical Ltd
Tulaich Ltd
Union XV Gin Co Ltd
United Wholesale Grocers Ltd
Uokka Limited
Up Front Brewing Limited
Via Academia Vocatus Ltd
Vintage Malt Whisky Co Ltd
Wagner Spirits Ltd
Wester Spirit Co. Ltd
Westworld Impex Limited
Whiskies from Scotland Limited

Whisky Biz Glasgow Ltd

Moray [10]
Coleburn Distillery Limited
Glenlatterach Whisky Co Ltd
Gordon & MacPhail Limited
Highland Drinks Ltd
Ian MacBarrel & Spirits Ltd
Leinburn Limited
Nestle James & Co Ltd
Red Door Gin Co Ltd
Speymalt Whisky Distributors Ltd
Spirit Still Ltd

Perthshire [18]
888 Global Trade Ltd
Gleneagles Distillery Limited
Golden Decanters Limited
Grapes of Hungary Ltd
Harrisons Fine Wines Limited
Highlands Whisky Co Ltd
Inverheath Limited
KIC Inventories Limited
Malt Whisky Co Ltd
Nightrep Limited
Perscot Ltd
Perth Distillery Co Ltd
Port Ellen Distillery Co Ltd
Port Ellen Distilling Limited
Prestonfield Whisky Co Ltd
Radleigh Wines Limited
Signatory Vintage Scotch Whisky Co Ltd
Taste of Alcohol Ltd

Perth & Kinross
Fair City Spirits Limited

Renfrewshire [12]
100 Pipers (Whisky) Limited
Alexander Wines Ltd.
Allt A' Bhainne Distillery Ltd
CADV Limited
Clutha Distillery Co Ltd
Cumbrae Supply Co Ltd
Dalmunach Distillery Limited
Distinction Armagnac Limited
JC Wholsale and Distribution Ltd
Monaghan Marketing Limited
North of Scotland Distilling Co Ltd
Scotia Blending Co Ltd

Ross-shire
Celtic Spirits Limited
Highland Liquor Co Ltd

Roxburghshire
Borders Distillers Limited
Borders Distilling Limited
Lamberton Whisky & Spirits Ltd
Three Stills Co Ltd

Selkirkshire
Stow Brewery Limited

Shetland
J.W.G. PLC

South Uist
Uist Distillery Ltd

Stirlingshire [11]
Alchemy Drinks Ltd.
Alchemy Inns Limited
Malt Whisky Agency Ltd
Pago Wines Limited
Quick Whisky Limited
Scot Bottle Limited
Slopemeister Brewing Co Ltd
Super Cooper Ltd
Team Spirit Beverage Ltd
Alistair Walker Whisky Co Ltd
Woodwinters Agencies Limited

Sutherland
Ebenezer Leisure Limited

Anglesey
Birds of Arcadia Ltd
Joseph Keegan & Sons Limited

Bedfordshire [41]
19th Beer Co Ltd
Aqua Vitae Vodka Limited
Barrel Booze Limited
David Berryman Holdings Ltd
David Berryman Limited
Botan Grey Ltd
Brookfield Beverages Limited
Brookfield Drinks Limited
Cellarvino Limited
Claribes Limited
Conroy-Hood Limited
Continental Wines Limited
Csburrwine Ltd
Delivery Offlicence Ltd
Dhesis Wholesale Ltd
Easier Sales Limited
Edwards Beers and Minerals Ltd
Edwards Beers and Wine Supplies Ltd
Edwards Beers and Wines (Holdings) Ltd
Edwards Wine Agencies Limited
Exigo (UK) Limited
G Sake Co Ltd
Hallgarten Wines,Limited
Icknield Stores Ltd
International Wine Forwarding Ltd
J.R.G. Investments Limited
Kestrel Brewing Co Ltd
Jake Mason Ltd
Old Wine House Ltd
Opus Wines Limited
Other World Wines Limited
Pieroth Limited
Sky9 Ltd
Vickery Wines Limited
Vicomte Bernard de Romanet Ltd
Charles Wells Brewery Limited
Charles Wells,Limited
White Lion Gin Co Ltd
Wine Express Ltd
Winecorp Limited
Woburn Wine Co Ltd

Berkshire [74]
3R'SB Limited
AFC Direct Ltd
Artisan Wine Storage Ltd
Axiom Brands Limited
B & W Distributors Limited
Babuji Ltd

Bacana Sangria UK Limited
Beer Warehouse (Maidenhead) Ltd
Bluetec Trading Services Ltd
Bucklebury Brewers Ltd
Cape Wine Merchants Ltd
Cellar Link Limited
Cider Is Wine Ltd
Citrone Limited
Connoisseur Estates Limited
Corktalk Limited
Cotswolds Wine Co Ltd
Da'mos Food & Beverages Ltd
Drinks Factory Limited
Drinks21 Ltd
Dromedary Trading & Resources Ltd
Easy9 Limited
Ester Wines Limited
Excess UK Limited
Freixenet UK Ltd
Frizzenti Limited
Grape Merchants Ltd
Grape and Nectar Ltd
Hatch Mansfield Cellars Ltd
Headline Wines Ltd
Horizons Enterprise Ltd
Kegs of Camberley Limited
Kozuba & Sons Limited
Lupton Wine Limited
MWH Wine Agencies Ltd
MWH Wine Merchants Limited
Maidenhead Wine Co Ltd
Marlow Wine Co Ltd
Mercurial Brewing Limited
Most Popular Limited
Northgate Wines Limited
Ohsake Ltd
Old Butcher's Wine Cellar Ltd
Ooberstock Limited
Opendoor Gin Co Ltd
Origin Drinks Limited
Peter Osborne Fine Wines Ltd
Pipehouse Gin Limited
Polskie Wodki Ltd
RDV Spirits Ltd
Michel Roux Limited
SJ Wines Ltd
Saj Holdings Ltd
Select Wine Co Ltd
Singolo Vino Limited
Skyfall Distribution Limited
Sloshed Puppy Ltd
Sotus Limited
Tasting Barn Ltd
Thames Cash & Carry (Birmingham) Ltd
Thameside Rum Co Ltd
Trywines Expertise Limited
Unfiltered Wines Limited
V G International Trading Ltd
Vendange (European) Limited
Wedding Wine Shop Ltd
Westend Cash and Carry Ltd
Whisky Trading Co Ltd
Whitley Neill Limited
Wine Explorer Limited
Wineman Limited
Winetage Ltd
Woody Nook Wines (UK) Limited
ZLCSolutions Ltd

Buckinghamshire [47]
ADP Wines Ltd
ASCO Foods Limited

Ace Incorporation Ltd
Always Available Ltd
Amis Trading Limited
Bad Joke Brew Co Ltd
Bargate Drinks Limited
Beacon Wines Limited
C'est Nous UK Ltd
Collins Wines Limited
Craftyard Events Limited
Da Vinci Finest Italian Products Ltd
Delicatezze Siciliane Limited
Double Hard Whiskey Co Ltd
Eventus Global Ltd
Eythrope Wine Limited
Forty Acres Ltd
Franko's Food Ltd
Glennlay & Co Ltd
Godin Tepe Limited
Grace Wines (UK) Limited
Grands Vins de France Limited
Great Wine Group Limited
H & G Corporation Ltd
Harrow & Hope Limited
Hatton Wholesale Ltd
Humo International Limited
Kicking Horse Ltd.
Laurent-Perrier (UK) Limited
Lloyds Wines Limited
Lora Trading (Europe) Ltd
Mantra Trading Limited
Martin Enterprises Limited
Organic Wine Co Ltd
Oxus Gin Ltd.
Pinewood Vyntners Limited
R & M Chateau Wines Ltd
Rafine Limited
Remy Cointreau UK Distribution Ltd
S.X Prosecco Party Limited
Seabrook Wines Limited
Skull X Ltd
Tec-Sol Limited
Toorank UK Limited
Vivir Drinks Ltd
Wineman (UK) Ltd
Wycombe Wine Co Ltd

Cambridgeshire [41]
AGT Professional Services Ltd
Alchemist Brewery Limited
Antipodean Sommelier Limited
Bellwether Wines Ltd
Black Dog Gin Co Ltd
Blue Wine Ltd
Bugle and Co Ltd
Anthony Byrne Fine Wines Ltd
Cambridge Champagne Co Ltd
Cambridge Wine Merchants Ltd
Casella Family Brands (Europe) Ltd
Chateau Miao Ltd
Discover Wine Limited
Distant Lands Ltd
Drinkz Ltd
Enny Wines Ltd
Gargara Limited
Grafham Brewing Co Ltd
Guinexport Trade and Services Ltd
Hiline Wines Peterborough Ltd
J & De Limited
James Fine Wines Limited
Jenkins and Beckers Fine Wine Ltd
Jin Bar Ltd
Jolly Good Beer Ltd

UK Wholesalers of Beers, Wines and Spirits

Leverre Ltd
MBM Resource Trading International
Mixology Collection Ltd
Morley Way Limited
Mountcharge Limited
Nene Charter Co Ltd
Proper Wine Co Ltd
Recolte Wines Limited
Signorellis Deli Ltd
Simavin Limited
Solaris Wines Ltd
Strongwells Limited
T J Wines Ltd
Ustuner Ltd
White Wolf Brewery Ltd
Winegrowers Direct Limited

Cardiganshire

Italian Importers Ltd
Longview Wines Ltd
Ty Nant Spring Water Limited
Ultracomida Trading Co. Ltd

Carmarthenshire

J.W.L Wholesale Drinks Ltd
Lazy Hare Limited

Cheshire [86]

Agave Thieves Ltd
Angeli Del Vino Limited
Antrobus Brothers Limited
B & D Clarke Limited
Bianca Trading Wine Ltd
Black Dog Wine Agency Limited
Boutinot Canada Limited
Boutinot Limited
Boutinot USA Limited
Boutinot Wines Limited
Brayston Leisure Ltd.
C. & O. Wines Limited
Cantina Caputo Limited
Champagne Imports Limited
Cheshire Gin Co Ltd
Chiltern Trading Ltd
Croatian Fine Wines Limited
Crystle Limited
D & F Inns Ltd
Rodney Densem Wines Limited
Direct Wine Importers Limited
Disley Gin Ltd
Dr Dougan (Enterprises) Ltd
Morgan Edwards Limited
European Brand Trading Limited
F8t B8dgers Ltd
Fairview Vineyard Ltd
Flawless Spirits Ltd
GW Wines Limited
Grande Marque Food & Beverage Ltd
Greatdrams Ventures Limited
Rachael Green Limited
Greenmount Holdings Limited
Greens Beers Limited
HBN Ltd
Hammonds of Knutsford PLC
In Vino Bidco Limited
In Vino Limited
Jervis Trading Limited
Langwith Brewing Co Ltd
Late Shop Ltd
Lazy Drinks Ltd.
Lisaavo Ltd

Manchester Merchant Wines Ltd
Moreno Wine Importers Co Ltd
N R Wines Limited
North West Spirits Limited
Pandemonium Wines Ltd
Paragon Brands Limited
Piaff Trading UK Limited
Primo Drinks (Lancashire) Ltd
Primo Drinks (Merseyside) Ltd
Primo Drinks (North East) Ltd
Primo Drinks (Staffordshire) Ltd
Primo Drinks (Yorkshire) Ltd
Primo Drinks Ltd
Quero Enterprise Ltd
Quintessential Brands Premium Brands
Quintessential Brands Spirit Solutions
Quintessential Spirits Holdings Ltd
Quintessential Spirits Limited
Quintessential Spirits UK Ltd
Quintessential Wines Holdings Ltd
Quintessential Wines Limited
Quellyn Roberts (Wine Merchants)
Rossendale Brew Co Ltd
Rude Mechanicals Limited
SMCA Enterprises Ltd.
Same Day Beers Group Ltd
Sandbar German Beer Ltd
Sanwin Ltd
Signature Wine Gifts Ltd
Silence of The Drams Limited
Skinny Booze Limited
Snowy Taverns Ltd
Sporting Benefits Limited
Squarewalk Limited
Stockport Gin Ltd
Telser & Pauli Ltd
Three Shires Distillery Ltd
Tipsy Tea Limited
Tom's Tap and Brewhouse Ltd
United Phoenix Limited
Vito International Ltd
Whitmore and White Limited
Whittaker Wines Limited

Cleveland [18]

Andes Trading Limited
Botanicals and Hops Limited
Castle Eden Beer Co Ltd
Cleveland Bar Supplies Limited
El Toro Wines Limited
Fourteen Drops Ltd
Hameed Investments Limited
Hard Back Rum Limited
Helluva... Limited
Hierarchy Brewing Co Ltd
Hops and Dots Brewing Co Ltd
Michael Jobling Wines Ltd
My Gin My Way Ltd
NDG (Hartlepool) Limited
Olley (NE) Limited
Parkers Newsagents Ltd
Profile Wines Limited
Trendbev Ltd.

Clwyd [5]

Ffarm Vintners Limited
Great Orme Drinks Co. Ltd
Aston Jones Limited
Quick-Keg Limited
Wine Portfolio UK Limited

Co Derry

Allied Ship Supplies (Ireland) Ltd

Co Durham [25]

Absolute Wholesale Limited
B & P Beverages Ltd
Black & Yellow Developments Ltd
Caps Off Ltd.
Castle Eden Brewery Ltd
Cathedral Wholesale and Events Ltd
Connecting Italian Food UK Ltd
Cru Prive Ltd
DTA Drinks Ltd
Eden Fine Wines Limited
Europvin UK Limited
Greencroft Bottling Co Ltd
Harvies of Edinburgh Limited
Hopper House Brew Farm Ltd
Lanchester Wine Cellars Ltd
Lanchester Wine Sales Limited
MMC Sales and Marketing Ltd
Newchesters Ltd
Parverre Marketing Limited
Saints Row Brewing Co Ltd
Stag Ales Ltd
Universal Wines & Spirits Ltd
Wine Fusion Limited
Yarm Gin Ltd
Yarm Spirits Co Ltd

Cornwall [34]

Alcohology Ltd
Beets Incorporated Ltd
Blue Marble Consultants Ltd
Bottle Bank Limited
Burdett Wines Ltd
Cornish Moonshine Co Ltd
Cribbar Limited
Drinklink Limited
Drinkologie Limited
Drinktonics Limited
Duchy Beverages Ltd
Ellis Wharton Wines Ltd
Flower Miners Limited
Franchiserv Limited
Green Room Ales Limited
H Harwood Ltd
Walter Hicks Limited
Keltek Cornish Brewery Limited
Kernow Rum Co Ltd
Land's End Gin Limited
Liquid Lounge Drinks Co. Ltd
MV Distribution Ltd
Maverick Ventures UK Ltd
Oui Vino Limited
Penryn Spirits Limited
Penzance Gin Ltd
Samphire Drinks Ltd
Soul Spirits Ltd
St Ives Grog Co Ltd
St.Austell Brewery Co Ltd
Tan Dowr Limited
Tinkture Ltd
Village Cottages (Cornwall) Ltd
Wine in Cornwall Limited

Cumbria [14]
Applethwaite Wines Ltd
Battys Discount Drinks Store Ltd
Beer Express Limited
Bonvoy Limited
Brown Bear Tales Ltd
Cartmel Spirit Co Ltd
Crafty Pint Limited
Iridium Supplies Limited
Porterage Co Ltd
Frank Stainton Wines Limited
TPA Trading Limited
Tractor Shed Brewing Limited
Vinandar Wines Limited
Windermere Wine Stores Limited

Denbighshire
Barcalima Wines Limited
Pant y Foel Gin Ltd
W D L Wholesale Limited

Derbyshire [34]
A and R Fine Wines Limited
Alf Vini Limited
Aurora Ales Limited
Bakewell Road Brewery Ltd
Beermaster Derby Ltd
Classic Cask Limited
Colombier Vins Fins Limited
Continental Beer Services Ltd
Craft Beer Collaborative Ltd
D K International (UK) Limited
Direct Beers Limited
Diverse Beers Limited
Europa Drinks Limited
Flavour Foods & Drinks Ltd
Infinitygroup1 Limited
Inn Control Management Services Ltd
Intercellar Distribution Ltd
Jean Juviniere Limited
Kudos Drinks Ltd
Liquid Brand Exports Limited
Malthub Ltd
No.9 Leisure Limited
Ozpax Limited
Pallet Price Wholesale Ltd
Perkins Independent Wine Traders Ltd
Philsner Ltd
Renwick MacDonald Bars Ltd
Raymond Reynolds Limited
Scavelli's Limited
Shires Wine Services Limited
Snow Beer UK Ltd
Spiced Wine Co Ltd
Tomlinson Whisky Merchants Ltd
Unwined Limited

Devon [41]
Bermondsey Gin Limited
Beverage Brothers Limited
Bonfire Hill Limited
Booze Cruz Ltd
C N Drinks Limited
CMT (Wines) Limited
Country Life Brewery Ltd
Craftwater Brewing Co Ltd
H.B. Evelyo Ltd.
Exeter Drinks Ltd
Exmoor Wines Limited
HS13 Trading Ltd

Honkytonk Wine Library Limited
Mike Hothersall Wines Limited
Jaded Group Limited
Keg & Bottle Ltd
Kramjar Limited
LVB Limited
Le Vignoble Ltd
Luxury Alcohols Limited
Mad Batchers Ltd
Marlico Limited
Neatly London Limited
Oliver & Bird Limited
Party Drinks Co Ltd
Peace Bond Ltd
Christopher Piper Wines Ltd
Platinum Gin Ltd
Plymouth Rum Co Ltd
Norman Price Wines Limited
Regency Wines Limited
Retro Shotz Limited
Ripped Earth Wines Limited
Sedgemoor Drinks Limited
Sharpham Wine Limited
Steevenson Wines Limited
Tolchards Limited
UWD Limited
Whisky Global Ltd
Winkleigh Cider Co Ltd
Zarb Distribution Ltd

Dorset [28]
4 Rabbits Ltd
Acod S & C Ltd
American Fizz (UK) Limited
Anglocolombian Ltd
Atlantic Craft Soda Co Ltd
Dorset Wine Co Ltd
Drop The Anchor Brewery Ltd
Free from Beer Co Ltd
Freight Brewing Co. Ltd
Gvino Limited
Hall & Woodhouse Limited
Richard Harvey Wines Limited
K & S Hosking Ltd
Inception Drinks Limited
Instabooze Limited
Keepr's Ltd
Morrish & Banham Ltd
N.Double and Co Ltd
Nielsen McKinsey Global Tourism & Hospitality Consulting
Polaris Wines Ltd
Southover Drinks Limited
Templar Wines Ltd
Rodney Tompkin Fine Wines Ltd
Top Alco Ltd
Wessex Wine Co Ltd
Whiskey and Bourbon Club Ltd
Winepro Limited
Yorke Vines Ltd

Essex [176]
11:11 Gin Ltd
4 Acre Brewing Co. Ltd
55 Above Ltd
A2Z Drinks Limited
AB Care Connect Limited
ANM Wholesale Limited
Acacia Drinks Ltd
Albion Gin Ltd
Algodon Europe Limited

All Food Supplies Ltd
Anglo Drinks Limited
Authentic French Wines (Importers)
BFA Holdings Limited
Bavarian Beer Co Ltd
Bdellium Trading Co Ltd
Beer Me Now Ltd
Beerfantastic Ltd
Belgrave Distribution Ltd
Bent Distribution Ltd
Best-One Local Ltd
Bestline Wholesale Ltd
Bhanbore Trading Company PVT Ltd
Blue Diamond (UK) Ltd
Blux UK Import Ltd
Botella Imports Ltd
J.Braham Everett Imports Ltd
Brexit Import and Export Co Ltd
Bruce Burlington and Co Ltd
By His Grace Food Ltd
Casa Julia Limited
Celebration Drinks Limited
Cellar & Co Limited
Cellar Twelve Limited
Cellartrade Ltd
Charente Enterprises Limited
Chateau Wines Ltd.
Chetan Wholesalers Limited
Chillwines Limited
Circle View Business Consultancy Ltd
Collective Trading Limited
Crouch Vale Brewery Limited
Crown Cash & Carry Ltd
Cuba Trading Co Ltd
Dallyla Ltd
Demon Vodka Limited
Diamonds & Pearl Trading Ltd
Direct Booze Limited
Docklands Trading Co Ltd
Draft Link Limited
Draught Services Ltd
Drill Wholesale Limited
Drinks Lover Ltd
Empire Drinks Ltd
Essex Catering Supplies Ltd
European Beverages Ltd
Europlus Trading Limited
Export and Import Trading Ltd
Favela Cerveja Ltd
Five Star Cash & Carry Ltd
Free Trade Beers and Minerals Ltd
Frenchvines Limited
GNR Distillery Limited
GSYB Ltd
G & G Gallo Enterprises Ltd
Galloping Wine Nose Limited
Gandhi Wine Suppliers Limited
Gather 77 Limited
Gibraltar Gin Co Ltd
Goldcrest Drinks Limited
Golden Crust & Co Limited
Grants-EU Limited
Grape Passions Limited
Graysons Freight Services Ltd
H & W Cash & Carry Ltd
H R Drinks (Wholesale) Ltd
HD Wine & Spirit Ltd
Hamptons Wine Ltd
Hills Prospect Holdings Ltd
Hills Prospect PLC
Indra Beverages Limited
J K Wholesales Ltd

JPHA Ltd
JWM Vintners Limited
Jackrabbit Brewing Co. Ltd
William James & Sons Ltd
Edward James Limited
Just Miniatures Limited
Kamros Cash and Carry Limited
Kibo Wines Ltd
Kohisar Limited
Kolson Energy Limited
LDW Wines Limited
Limbrey's Wine and Spirits Ltd
Lithuanian Beer Limited
Logistic Park Ltd
Lost Rivers Beer Co Ltd
Lothbury Wine Shippers Limited
Lusus Wines Ltd
Lux Ex Dignitas Limited
M & M Community Development Initiatives
MBW Traders Ltd
MK Sales Training Limited
Magnetic Brands Limited
Mangrove Global Limited
Manor Wholesale Ltd
Manzi Developments Limited
Marathon Beverages Ltd
Mercurion Ltd
Mill Distributors Limited
Millennium Cash & Carry Ltd
Mixed Case Limited
Mojito Bar Ltd
Monolith (UK) Ltd
N & M Wholesale Ltd
N G K Wholesale Limited
Nolo Drinks Co Ltd
Occidental & Oriental Cellars Ltd
PFS Business Services Limited
PSB Trading Limited
PSR Distribution Limited
PT Drinks Ltd
Paragon Wines Limited
PatelCashAndCarry Limited
Pau Drinks Limited
Peoplegood Limited
Pirate's Grog Rum Ltd
Premium Vineyard Company UK Ltd
R. St Barth Limited
RDF Paper Ltd
Reservedwines Ltd
Ribox Quality Goods Ltd
Roydon Flavours Ltd
Rurkee Trading Co Ltd
SAPM Commercial Ltd
STM Traders & Services Ltd
Saam Wine Co Ltd
Sai Soft Drinks Ltd
Salonica Limited
Sanghera Rum Co Ltd
Seckford Agencies Limited
Sheikh Super Store Ltd
Shree Sai Trading Ltd
Silvertip Imports Limited
Siris Trading Ltd
Slim Gin Ltd
Spirimix Limited
Spirito Limited
Street Wines Limited
Sunbird Wines UK Ltd
Suwalki-UK Ltd
Taabs Investment UK Limited
Themirtis Limited
Tolmid International Ltd

Tortuga Brands Limited
Tower International Limited
Two Essentials Ltd.
USSR Limited
Universal Drinks Ltd
VDS UK Limited
Valentino Platinum Ltd
Valerieblue Ltd
Viking Enterprises Limited
Vino Vero Ltd
Vinovest Limited
Vinum Fine Wines Limited
Vranac Stonecastle Limited
Westgarth Wines Limited
Wilks & Company Wine Merchants Ltd
Windward Trading Co Ltd
Wine Affairs Limited
Wine Story Limited
Wine de Vine Ltd
Wine2trade Limited
Winefantastic Limited
Worsley Wines Limited
Xuyang International Ltd

Flintshire
Angel Feathers Limited

Glamorgan [55]
AK Cash & Carry Ltd
Au Vodka Ltd
Aztec Spirits Ltd
Beer Barrels & Minerals (Wales) Ltd
Beer Journey Ltd
Bespoke Wines Ltd
Bottle Shop (Penarth) Limited
S.A.Brain & Co Ltd
Briton Ferry Brewing Co Ltd
Buzz Booze Ltd
C.P.A.'s Wine Limited
Chaps Group Limited
Cold Black Label Limited
Crafty Devil Brewing Ltd
DWS Wholesale Limited
Delbrew Ltd
Fair Fayre Food & Wines Ltd
Family Choice Wholesale Ltd
Field Bar Gin Limited
Fine Wines Direct UK Limited
Fronsacdirect Limited
Fronsacwines Limited
GM Catering Supplies Ltd
Glamorgan Brewing Co Ltd
Global Foods Limited
Goldy's Corner Shop Ltd
Gower Gin Co Ltd
Grape and Grain Management Ltd
Hurns Beer Co. Limited
Hurns Mineral Water Co. Ltd
Jezba Ltd
ND John Wine Limited
N D John Wine Merchants Ltd
Kairos Solutions Ltd
Daniel Lambert Wines Limited
Langstone Beer Exports Ltd
Mumbles Brewery Ltd
NineTailsDistillery Ltd
Pellegrino Wine and Food Distribution
RDM Wines Limited
Sindherfoods Limited
Sloane Home Ltd
SmsZee Limited

Sol Regem Ltd.
Jack Sullivan (Properties) Ltd
Jack Sullivan Limited
Tayst Ltd
UK Wine & Food Supplies Ltd
Varmont Ltd
Viader Vintners Limited
Vitena Wines Ltd
Voubearst Limited
Wall2wall Wines Limited
Wellsh Brewers Cardiff Ltd
Worldwide Drinks Limited

Gloucestershire [48]
AOC Distribution Ltd
Aceo Limited
Asta Barista Baby Ltd
Beer Traders UK Limited
Branded Drinks Ltd
Cape Secrets Limited
Cellar Supplies Cheltenham Ltd
Cellar Supplies Limited
Cool Apple Limited
Coombe Farm Wines Limited
Cotswold Port Co. Ltd
Cotswold Wines Ltd
Craft Drink Co Ltd
Curious Wine Cellar Limited
D'Arcy Wine Merchants Limited
DLRF Limited
Donnington Brewery Limited
Drinks Agency Ltd
Eastern Pantry Ltd
FV Craft Beers Ltd
FVFC Limited
Favourite Beers Limited
Force Brewery Limited
Foxstead Limited
Tom I'Anson Wines Ltd
JC Wine Events Ltd
JJ Wholesalers Ltd
Just A Splash Limited
Ledbury Wine Limited
Life Science Limited
Moke Fine Wines Limited
Mother Kelly's Distribution Ltd
Neptune Rum Ltd
O'Vineyards Ltd
Oak Cask Distribution Ltd
Places Trading (Suppliers) Ltd
Prodolce Ltd
Real Wine Cellar Limited
S & F Drinks Limited
Savage Selection Limited
Talking Wines Limited
Tengu Sake Limited
Union Brands Ltd
Vin Est... Ltd
Vino Merchant Limited
Vinoveritas (Europe) Limited
Waistcoat Wines Ltd
Windrush Holdings Ltd

Gwent [7]
Caribswede Ltd
Carte Blanche Wines Limited
Decanter Trading Co Ltd
Dragon Wines Limited
Harvey's Wholesale Limited
Old Brenin Distillery Ltd
Red Dragon Brewery Ltd.

Hampshire [79]
79North Limited
David Alexander Wine Merchants Maidenhead
Alfa Drinks Limited
Apex Dispense Limited
Ariki Limited
Art Beer Co Ltd
Artisan Lounge and Cellar Ltd
BL Drinks Ltd
BL011 Limited
Bacardi-Martini Limited
Black Forest Beers Limited
Blue Momentum Limited
Bombay Spirits Co Ltd
Carter Importing Ltd
J. Chandler & Company, Ltd
Charter Brands Limited
Cincin Wines Ltd
Cloud Wine Ltd
Cubic Brands Limited
Cuvee Cavalier Limited
DN Pacifica Ltd
Deceptive Wines Limited
Deskbeers Limited
John Dewar and Sons Limited
Discover Wine (UK) Ltd
Drinks Guild Ltd
Drinksman Limited
Essenza Di Romagna Limited
Festina Drinks Ltd
Rodney Fletcher Vintners Ltd
For The Love of Wine Limited
Frederick's Wine Co Ltd
G M Drinks Limited
G M Drinks of Hampshire Ltd
Galette Wines Limited
William Grant & Sons UK Ltd
Hillcrest Wines Limited
Hobnobber Ltd
James Hocking Wine Limited
Hoppy Days Inn Ltd
Indian Runner Drinks Co Ltd
Italimport (Wessex) Limited
Itasca Wines Limited
J & A Drinks Limited
JDT Drinks Co Ltd
JF Tobias Limited
KRD Distribution Co Ltd
Key Brands International Ltd
Laurus Brands Limited
Liqueurs de France Limited
MM Drinks Ltd
Openwine Limited
Opus Cellars Limited
Portal Dingwall & Norris Ltd
Portsmouth Gin Co Ltd
Rebel Pi Limited
Rebel Wine Ltd.
Riedango Limited
Royal Tokaji Wines of Hungary Ltd
Rum Club Ltd
Shandy Shack Ltd
Solent Off-License Ltd
Somborne Valley Vineyard Ltd
South WLC Limited
Southbourne Brewing Limited
Southsea Gin Co Ltd
Staibano Ltd
TTO Limited
TheTipsyTransit Ltd
Tipsy Events Ltd

Vicarage Spirit Limited
Vinova Export Limited
Vitosha Wine Ltd
Way Outback Brewery Limited
Webdrinks Ltd
Wine Associates Limited
Wine Barn Limited
Wine Butler Limited
Wine Castle Ltd

Herefordshire [8]
Craftmaster Social Ltd
Fox Fitzgerald Whisky Trading Co Ltd
Lanark House Investments Ltd
Nothing But The Grape Limited
Shack Drinks Limited
John Villar Wines Limited
Vinature Ltd
Wild Foragin Ltd

Hertfordshire [90]
Aben Wines Limited
Annessa Imports Limited
E J Bartholomew Limited
Bevco Limited
Blue Tree Limited
Bohemia Beer House Limited
Boutique Brands Limited
Boutique Spirit Co Ltd
Jack Brooksbank Limited
Cava Spiliadis UK Limited
Celex Foods Limited
Chalk & Charcoal Limited
Ciderfex Limited
Clock Tower Distilleries Ltd
Coddington Hepburn Limited
Cornish Point Wines UK Ltd
Coss Wines Ltd.
Cossart,Gordon and Co.Limited
Craft Wines Ltd
Creative Juices Brewing Co Ltd
D D S Food Imports Ltd
F.L. Dickins Limited
Distribev Ltd.
Do Trading Limited
Dodotraders UK Limited
Drinks Link International Ltd
Earth Elements Ltd
Emporium Import Ltd
Enjoydrinks Limited
Euroboozer Limited
Ever-Tree Wholesale & Retail Ltd
John E.Fells & Sons Limited
Alfie Fiandaca Limited
Flava Foods Ltd
Gemeaux Limited
Globus Wines (UK) Ltd
Grandi Vini Limited
Grape Drinks (UK) Limited
Haslemere Wine Merchants Ltd
Hitchin Brewery Ltd
Hitchin Distillery Limited
Hitchin Wine Co Ltd
Hop To The Vine Limited
Infinity Wines Limited
Interlink UK Exports Limited
JDS Trading Limited
Kasgo Limited
Kimbland Distillery Ltd
Knightrate Wines Ltd
Languedoc Imports Ltd

Laravita Ltd
Lay & Wheeler Limited
Los Perros Sueltos Brewing Co Ltd
MC Drinks Limited
Maison Liedberg Limited
Majestic Wine PLC
Majestic Wine Warehouses Ltd
Marathon Food Limited
Moa Group Ltd
Muratina Limited
Naked Fine Wine Bonds PLC
Naked Wines Prepayments Trustee Co Ltd
Nue Innovations Limited
OX Wines Ltd
Poleczka Limited
Portuguese Fine Wine Co Ltd
Red Squirrel Brewery Limited
Ricordo Ltd
Scozia Grappa Ltd
Silenus Limited
Sladecs247 Ltd
Russell Smith F & B Limited
Sofibel Ltd
Sopwell Gin Co Ltd
Source 360 Ltd
Storesrealm Limited
Tenuta Tremollito Wines Ltd
Uisce Ard Ltd
Underground Spirits Limited
Urban Warehousing Limited
Uva Hitchin Ltd
Henry de Vaugency Ltd
Vine Street Wine Co Ltd
Vyce Ltd
Wee Vinoteca Ltd
Windfall Logistics Limited
Wine Research Limited
World Beers Limited
Worldwine UK Ltd
Zefino Family Limited

Humberside
Anglium Ltd
Beer Rocks Brewery Ltd

Isle of Wight [8]
Eurovines Limited
Island Ales Limited
Isle of Wight Brewery Limited
Laughing Pug Ltd
Spowart Wines Limited
TJC Corporate Events Limited
Wight & Wessex Wines Limited
Yates Iow Brewery Limited

Kent [169]
A1 Resources Limited
AKS Brands Limited
AMK Distribution Ltd
Agave Partners Limited
Alegri Trade Ltd.
Almaster Limited
Andrews Beer & Mineral Co Ltd
Ark Inta Ltd
Atkinson's Gin Ltd
Atom Brands Limited
Atom Cask Holdings Limited
Atom Drinks Limited
Atom Group Limited
Atom Supplies Limited
BD Wines Limited

UK Wholesalers of Beers, Wines and Spirits dellam

BM Wines Limited
Barcode Traders Limited
Beer Belly Company Incorporated Ltd
Beer Seller Ltd
Beviqua Ltd
Bihl Ltd
Bitter End Limited
Blue Magic Limited
Blush Gin Distrubutors UK Ltd
Bon Vin Inc. Limited
Bordeaux Wine Investments Ltd
Burgeon Allied Limited
Cadogan Wines Limited
Cantium Spirit Ltd
Cariel Spirits International Ltd
Carson & Carnevale Limited
Carson Wines Ltd
Cavoda Limited
Champers Wines Limited
Chevalier de Mentaubert Ltd
Childale Limited
Clapham Wine Co Ltd
Colorado Craft Spirits Ltd
Consolidated Wines Limited
Cumberland Bargin Booze Ltd
Da Vinci Traders Ltd
Dayboat Limited
Deholjob Limited
Deluxe Wines Limited
Di Vine Importers Limited
Domaine des Jeanne Limited
Dos Santos Bev Co UK Limited
Drayman Drinks Ltd
Drink Free Ltd
Drink Warehouse Events Limited
Durrants Fine Wines Limited
East West Ales Limited
Ebony Drinks Limited
Englishman Supplies Limited
Epicure Wines Ltd
Euro-Trade and Finance Limited
F & B Premium Brands Limited
Fah Mai Holdings Limited
Felix Solis Avantis UK Ltd
Firewater Merchants Ltd
First Bar Supplies Limited
Frenchbubbles Limited
Funemployed Agency Ltd
Funemployed Ltd
Georgian British Co Ltd
Gin Dobry Gin Co Ltd
Gold Max Distribution Limited
Good Food Wines Limited
Graftyset Limited
Grand Vin Wine Merchants Ltd
Hazelbank Limited
Heritiers Domec Ltd
High Jinks Limited
Hochfeld International Ltd
Hofmeister Enterprises Ltd
Holdsworth Spirits & Co Ltd
Hot Corks Limited
Hurlingham Wine Merchants Ltd
Identity Drinks Brands Limited
Imbibe Ltd
Impulse Global Ltd
Indie Brands Ltd.
Indie Spirits Limited
Indie Wines Limited
Iron Pier Brewery Limited
Italy on Tap Ltd
Jade General Merchants Ltd

Jaitly Trading Co Ltd
Anthony James Beverages Ltd
Jassim Limited
Jia Bo Rui International Trade Ltd
KBE Drinks Enterprises Limited
KSS Drinks Limited
Kentish Pip Ltd
Kingfisher Beer Europe Limited
Koomor Brewing Co Ltd
Lea & Sandeman Group of Companies
Let There Be Beer Ltd
Liptons Food & Wine Limited
Liquid Vision Enterprise Ltd
London Cash & Carry Ltd
London and East India Drinks Co Ltd
Lucky Spirits Ltd
MSD Wholesale Limited
Magik Drinks Limited
Main Sail Trading Co Ltd
Maison Maurice Limited
Marani Wines Limited
Marta's Vinyard Limited
Master of Malt Limited
Masters of Malt Limited
Maverick Brands Limited
Maverick Drinks Limited
Maverick Spirits Limited
Russell Mellor and Co Ltd
Mexcal Ltd
Moonberries Ltd
Needhams Wines Limited
OAB Ventures Limited
Old St.Andrews Limited
Organic Country Drinks Ltd
Original Wooden Case Limited
Ourlocal Limited
Pierhead Drinks Limited
Provenance Marketing Ltd
Quercus Wines Ltd
RRK Supplies Limited
Ragarfield International Ltd
Ramstrad Trading Ltd
Redoor Limited
Rekhi Wholesale Ltd
Rive Gauche Wines (UK) Limited
Rockin Robin Brewery Ltd
Roohop Ltd
Rumbaclaat Ltd
Sandhu IT Services Ltd
Shepherd Neame Limited
Silverlite Cash & Carry Ltd
Sommeliers Choice Limited
Sophie's Choice Limited
South Eastern Beers & Minerals Ltd
Southern Wine Roads Limited
Southern Wines Limited
Stag Brewery Ltd
Star Beers Ltd
Superior Import/Export Limited
TPDirect Ltd
TST Ventures Limited
Taste of Georgia Limited
Thameside Wines Limited
Time & Tide Brewing Limited
Todd Vintners Limited
Town Centre Inns Limited
Triumph Foodservice Limited
UBI Drinks Enterprises Limited
Ufton Travel Retail Limited
United Breweries International (U.K.)
Vanilla Blue Limited
Veda UK Limited

Vinorium Limited
Waud Wines Limited
Wholly Grape Limited
Wine Consultants Limited
Wintrad Ltd
Xi-Spain Ltd
Xtraflow Limited
YC Wines Limited
Yeastie Boys UK Ltd
Zinea Global Services Limited

Lancashire [175]
23-7 Brewing Ltd
247 Enterprises UK Ltd
A2Z Wines & Groceries Ltd
Abloc UK Ltd
Ask Drinks Ltd
At The Group Ltd
B & B Drinks Ltd
Babyboyempire. Ltd
Banini UK Ltd
T. & J.T. Barton (Bottlers) Ltd
Beer & Wine (Northern) Limited
Beerspotters Ltd
Belgian Life Limited
Belizaire Drinks Ltd
Bellwether Impex (UK) Limited
Blackedge Brewing Co Ltd
Booze Bolton Limited
Bottle Green Limited
Brindle Distillery Limited
Burton Rd Brewing Co Limited
CRA Ltd
Canal Cellars Ltd
Castillon International Ltd
Chilli Brands (New Zealand) Ltd
Chilli Brands Limited
Chilli Marketing Brand Management Ltd
Chilli Marketing Promotions Ltd
Choice Drinks Limited
Citrosoft Drinks Limited
Con Gusto Wines Limited
Crabtrees Craft Pubs and Bottle Merchants
Cracking Little Wine Co Ltd
Crafty Cask Wholesale Ltd
Cromfine Limited
Deckers Restaurants Limited
Deshi Bazar Ltd
Distillery 96 Limited
Dita Grappolo Ltd
Droylsden Craft Limited
Duple Social Club Sth Shore BPL . Ltd
E.W.G.A. Limited
EJ Orendale Ltd
Eastcoast Supplies Ltd.
El Brewery Limited
Etna Food & Wine Ltd
Evolution Drinks Ltd
First Class Beverages Ltd
Flagship Brands Ltd
Flying Firkin Distribution Ltd
Friends of Wine Ltd
Funky Beer Co Ltd
Gabby & Bello Enterprises Ltd
Gift Creation and Design Ltd
Gin Fizz Ltd
Glugged! Ltd
Gordons (Bolton) Limited
Grape Escape Limited
GreatWineDirect Limited
Hamer & Perks Limited
Hanging Ditch Wine Merchants Ltd

HardyDistillery Ltd
Harlequin (Stockport) Limited
Hidden Gem - Urban Artisan Spirit Ltd
Hindsight Collective Ltd
Holcombe Gin Ltd
Honeybee Farm Ltd
House of Hops Limited
Hurmiz UK Ltd
Hydes' Brewery Limited
Imperial 21 Joya Ltd
India Gold Limited
Infotonomy Ltd
It's A Gin Thing Ltd
Italia Wine and Food Ltd
J M & D Limited
Nicholas James Gin Ltd
Jays Beverages Limited
Jays Trading Ltd
Jiangsu Wine Trading Co Ltd
K R Wines & Beers Ltd
KC Brothers Ltd
Kaleboard Limited
Kanj Wholesale Ltd
Kash & Karry Supplies Ltd
Kingdom Foods & Drinks Limited
Kingsland Drinks Group Limited
Kingsland Drinks Limited
Kinkladze Limited
LJW Wholesale Limited
LWC Drinks Limited
Lancaster Wines Limited
Legacy Wines & Beverages UK Ltd
Leo's Cash & Carry Ltd
Leyland Home Brew Limited
London SCC Group Ltd
Luca Wine Limited
Lynch Associates Ltd
Lytham Brewery Limited
MA Wine and Spirit Imports Ltd
MMGT Limited
MSSC (NW) Limited
Malthouse Inns PLC
Manchester Drinks Co Ltd
Manchester Trading Limited
Marcin & Son Ltd
Middleton Associates Limited
Charles Mitchell Wines Ltd
Montann Limited
Moody Spirit Co Ltd
More Beer Wholesale Limited
Morecambe Bay Wines Limited
Morgenrot Group PLC
Mount Fetti Ltd
Mullwood Wine Co Ltd
My Cocktail Club Limited
Myliko International (Wines) Ltd.
Mythop Gardens Limited
NMWLeisure Ltd
Nisar Traders Ltd
Northern Hospitality (MCR) Ltd
Northwest Drinks Ltd
Oak Wines Limited
Ocean Wines Limited
Othello Food and Wine Limited
Padlock Brewery Ltd.
Panache Natural Flavour Infusions
Pearly Queen Beer Co Ltd
Pick N Deliver Ltd
Planet Wine Trading and Consulting
Provino Limited
Pub Pool (711) Limited
Rafti Ltd.

Rajpoot Traders Ltd
Rando Global Alliance Limited
Red Rose Drinks Limited
Rendog Gin Ltd
Rock Beverages Limited
Rockstar Spirits Limited
Rosie & Gin Limited
SSL Leisure Limited
Saddleworth Real Ale Ltd
Salford Rum Co Ltd
Samco Global Foods Ltd
Sammartini Ltd
Shellys Drinks Limited
Shindigger Craft Beer Ltd
Silver Fox Wines Ltd
JG Sousa Limited
Spalco Ltd
Spirit Valley France Limited
Spitfire Heritage Distillers Ltd
St George's Beer Co. of St Austell Ltd
Stratford's Wine Shippers and Merchants
Taste Italia Limited
Terrae Vinariae Limited
Traditional Italian Wine Co Ltd
Trilogy Beverage Brands Ltd
UK Foods & Drinks Ltd
UKAFDS Limited
Valley Wines, Beer & Spirits Ltd
Victory Global Ltd
Vinexcel Limited
Vinotrans Ltd
WLG Limited
Watson Food & Beverages Ltd
West Spirits MCR Ltd
H.T.White & Co Ltd
Wigan Beer Co Ltd
Willoughbys Limited
Wine Marketings Europe Ltd
Winicious Limited
World of Drams Ltd
Worsley Gin Ltd
Xpress Drinks Ltd
Young's Beers Wines & Spirits Ltd

Leicestershire [57]
3 Cities Brewing Co Ltd
4 Star (Leicester) Limited
Andina Trade Ltd
Belvoir Brewery Limited
Bengal Foods Limited
Burbage Wines Limited
Cellar Trends Limited
Distillers Direct Ltd
Drinks Orchard Ltd
EW Bars Limited
European Beer Exports Limited
Everards Brewery Limited
Francis Fine Wines Ltd
Gala Drinks Co Ltd
Globe Logistics Limited
John Greenacre Limited
H & W Wines Limited
Geo Hill (Grocers) Limited
Holborn Gin Co Ltd
Indigo Drinks Limited
Inter Trading Leicester Ltd
Jeffries Vintage Drinks Ltd
K & G Spirits Ltd
Kater Four (Cash & Carry) Ltd
Kegs R Us (Leicester) Ltd
Kegs R Us Ltd
Kilo Wines Ltd

Leo Global Limited
Loughborough Student Services Ltd
New School Wines Limited
Origin Wine Limited
P & P Vino Limited
Pastai di Serino Italian Food and Wine Excellence
Phoenix Spirits Ltd
Pure Organic Drinks Limited
R & B Drinks Ltd
Rarus Ltd
S and S Wines Limited
SO & T Consulting Limited
Sambatha Ltd
Scimedex Limited
Scott's of Quorn (Wine Bar & Vintners)
Sky Wines Limited
Soar Valley Bar Supplies Ltd
Stableyard Wines Limited
Steamin' Billy (Property) Ltd
Terra Wines Limited
Toke Commodity Electro Limited
Top Spirits Ltd
Truk Limited
Union Drinks Ltd
Utku Emre Ltd
VIP Bottles Ltd
Welford Retail Limited
Wiland Wines Limited
Wine City Limited
Winnack and Hart Industries Ltd

Lincolnshire [21]
3 Barrel Co Ltd
Alcos Trade Limited
Banks & Company (Vintners) Ltd.
Bedford Continental Wholesale Ltd
Bridge Vintners Limited
Cassago Imports Limited
Deco Spirits Limited
Drink Link Grimsby Limited
Golden Everest Limited
Hay Hampers Limited
Hoptimism Limited
JH Wine Agencies Ltd
Korzinka Taste of Europe Ltd
Library Design Studio Ltd.
Lincoln West End Limited
Lincolnshire Gin Ltd
Pesodeocho Wines Ltd
Salmon Lady Limited
Sandham Wine Merchants Ltd
Small Beer Limited
Swinkels Snackery and Backery Ltd

London [1227]
100cl Limited
106 Business Solutions Limited
180 East Limited
23 High Path Ltd
3ABC Ltd
88 Connect Ltd
A & B Vintners Limited
A & G Management Consultancy Ltd
A Little Luxury Distillery Ltd
ABR Restaurant Group Ltd
AKM Trading Services Ltd
AMK Wholesale Ltd
ASA Ventures Limited
ASG Wines Limited
Abbey Brands Limited

UK Wholesalers of Beers, Wines and Spirits

dellam

Abercrombie Fine Wines Limited
Abra Export UK Limited
AbruzzoWines Ltd
Adaka Group Ltd
After Eight Alcohol Concierge Ltd
Aftersunset Ltd
Agencia Ltd
Agro Investment Ltd
Agua Piedra Mezcal & Co Ltd
Aims & Co Ltd
Al & Lu (UK) Ltd
Albion Distillery Ltd
Albion Fine Wines Ltd
Albion Wine Shippers Limited
Alcofrolics Ltd
Aleksic & Mortimer Ltd
Alexandria Partners Limited
Algebra Drinks Ltd
Alice Wholesale Trading Ltd
Alinari Ltd
Alivini (North) Limited
Alivini Co Ltd
Alko Vintages UK Ltd
Alky Limited
All Market Europe Limited
Alliance Foods Limited
Allum Limited
Altamira Management Services Ltd
Always 20 Limited
Amathus Drinks PLC
Ambessa Goods Ltd
Amish Wholesalers Limited
Amphora Portfolio Management Ltd
Ana Express Ltd
Andris Holdings Limited
Angel Wine & Spirit Group Co., Ltd.
Angove's (Europe) Limited
Angus Dundee Distillers PLC
Anya Global Limited
Aotearoa Distribution Ltd
Apna Distribution Ltd
Appletree Cider Limited
Aran Beers Limited
Arcari & Sons Ltd.
Archangel Wines Limited
Arda Rohat Limited
Armit Holding Limited
Armit Wines Limited
Art Entertainment Ltd
Artful Dodger Whisky Ltd
Artisan Beer Import Co Ltd
Arundo Limited
Asia-Pacific 11230699 Vitamin Beverage Co.,
Astir Cigars & Wine Ltd
Astonburgh Limited
Atlantis Iberica Ltd
Attitude Spirits Ltd
Ausavenues Limited
Australian Cellar Ltd
Australian Wine Services Ltd
Avazak Ltd
Azienda Vitivinicola Stassi Ltd
Aziken Ventures Limited
Azizi Drinks Ltd
B & F Enterprise UK Ltd
B & M Produce Limited
B Wines Limited
BB & R Limited
BB & R Spirits Limited
BDDR Enterprises Limited
BF Wines UK Ltd
BI Wines and Spirits Limited

BV Group UK Limited
Bablake Wines Limited
Bacchus Fine Wine & Food Ltd
Bacchus London Limited
Bacchus Vin Ltd
Bacchus-Les-Vignobles de France Ltd
Bad Girls Brew Limited
Ballers Brands Ltd
Balman Import & Export Limited
Balthazar Limited
Bancroft Wines Limited
Georges Barbier of London Ltd
Barndiva Wine Co Ltd
Barokes Limited
Barrique Vintners Limited
Base Cachaca Import (UK) Ltd
Basket Press Wines Ltd
Batch Cider Ltd
Baton Rouge Limited
Be Hop Ltd
Be My Wine Ltd.
Be Organiq Limited
Bear Smyth Limited
Beattie & Roberts Imports Ltd
Beatville Limited
Beefeater Distillery Limited
Beer Boutique Ltd
Beer Land Ltd
Beercall Ltd
Beerpol Ltd
Belloni Limited
Bemco International (UK) Ltd
Benjamin & Blum Limited
Berkmann Family Holdings Ltd
Berkmann Wine Cellars Limited
Best Cask Ltd
Best Price Retail and Wholesale Ltd
Best of America Limited
Best of Beaujolais Limited
Best of Bordeaux Limited
Best of Burgundy Limited
Best of California Limited
Best of Champagne Limited
Best of France Limited
Best of Italy Limited
Best of Loire Limited
Best of New World Limited
Best of Portugal Limited
Best of Spain Limited
Beverage Provider Limited
Beylerbeyi UK Ltd
Bibere Ltd.
Bielo Limited
Biercraft Ltd
Big Mouth Wine Limited
Binning Trading Co Ltd
Biotanica Ltd
Birrificio Del Ducato London Ltd
Blackcattaverns Ltd
Blackstorm Rum Ltd
Blast Vintners Ltd
Blends Wine Estates UK Ltd
Bloody Drinks Limited
Bloomsbury Distillery Ltd
Bloomsbury Drinks Ltd
Blu-Dot Commodities Limited
Bodega Raffy UK Ltd
Bodega Uncielo (UK) Limited
Bohemian Brands Limited
PNJ Bolton International Ltd
Boot Liquor Wholesale Limited
Booze 2 U Ltd

Bopfags Services Ltd
Bordeaux Index Limited
Bosco-UK Limited
Bourgognes Only Limited
Bournemouth Food Ltd
Branda Ltd
Brewland Ltd
Brian Traders Ltd
Bric Commerce Ltd
Bridge Wine Limited
Broad Street Brands Limited
Broadway Drinks Co Ltd
Brockmans Gin Limited
Brocour Ltd.
Browett & Fair Ltd
Andrew Bruce Fine Wines Ltd
Bruce Jack Wines Limited
Brummells Gin Limited
Bubbles & Wines Limited
Bubra Drinks Ltd
Buckingham Fine Wine Ltd
Buke Limited
Bulgarsko Pivo Limited
Burble Foods and Beverages Ltd
Oliver Burridge & Co Ltd
Burridges of Arlington St Ltd
Busted Cow Ltd
Buveur Ltd
Buzwine Limited
C & D Wines Limited
CDGH Pub Co Ltd
CGAVL Imports Limited
CHX Distillers Ltd
CMJ Pub Trade Ltd
CRC Delta Ltd
CRVC UK Limited
CS Wines Limited
Cabal Estates Limited
Cacheflow Ltd
Cadestin International Wines Ltd
Calabria Family Wines (Europe) Ltd
Calibre Brands Limited
Camden Drinks Co Ltd
Camii Punch Ltd
Camino Real Limited
Camis International Trading Co., Ltd.
Canapacampana Limited
Candy Cotton Ltd
Cangiani UK Ltd
Canopy Beer Co Ltd
Capacha Limited
Cape Wine Exporters (UK) Ltd
Capion Trading Limited
Capsule Wine Ltd
Caribbean Collective Group Ltd
C Carnevale Limited
Daniel Carnio Ltd
Carob Tree Limited
Cartwright Brothers Vintners Ltd
Casa Ambar Limited
Casa Leal Ltd
Cascade Trade Services Ltd
Cascriva Ltd
Cashew Apple Co Ltd
Cask Hub Limited
Cask Industries Ltd
Cask Trade Ltd
Caspian Black Limited
Cathay Importers (London) Ltd
Cattier UK Limited
Caves de Pierre Limited
Cayenes Ltd

Cazcabel Drinks Limited
Cazcabel Tequila Limited
Cellar Capital Limited
Cellarers (Wines) Limited
Cenimex Ltd
Champagne Cellar Limited
Champagne Duval-Leroy (UK) Ltd
Champagne G.H. Martel & Co. (U.K.) Ltd
Champagne House Ltd
Champagne Route Limited
Champagnehub Limited
Champagnes and Chateaux Ltd.
Champsonthego.co.uk Ltd
GDD Chapuy Limited
Chateau Khornabuji Limited
Chateau de Sours Estates Ltd
Chateau de la Combe Ltd
Chelsea Vintners London Ltd
Cheti & Co Holdings Limited
Cheti & Co Limited
Chez Antoine Ltd
Chic Fruit Ltd
Chivalry Trading International Co. Ltd
Choise Group Ltd
Churchill Graham Limited
Churchill Vintners Limited
Cibus Vitae Ltd.
Cibusrex Ltd
Circle Wine Co Ltd
Circus Enjoy with Us Ltd
City Wine Collection Limited
Clara Wines Limited
Clements Harrison Limited
Club Belmont Ltd
Co.Bru Limited
Cobev Limited
Coca-Cola Amatil (UK) Limited
Cochin Heritage Ltd
Cocksure Brewing Co Ltd
Cocktail Express Ltd
Coe of Ilford Limited
Cold Formd Ltd
Spencer Collings & Co Limited
Colne Confectionery Ltd
K. Colombier Limited
Colosseum Wines Limited
Concordia Wines Ltd
Consulting & Food Ltd
Conti Coronini Ltd
Copper Still Co Ltd
Corney and Barrow Group Ltd
Corney and Barrow Limited
Cornfield Foods and Beverages Ltd
Cornucopia Wines Limited
Corvin Import Export Ltd
Corvinus Beverages International Ltd
Cosmic Services Limited
Cotrade Ltd
Craddock Cocktails Ltd
Craft Locals Limited
Crafted Beverages Limited
Craftibeer Limited
Dudley Craig Wines Limited
Crazy Brew UK Limited
Cremant Inc Ltd
Cropol Luxury Products Ltd
Cru Classe Limited
Crudo Limited
Crundale Wines Limited
Cut Rum Limited
Czech Beer Alliance Limited
D & N Supplies Limited

D & V Wines Ltd
D.Rock Champagne Ltd
DC Wine Merchant Ltd
DCFT Investments Ltd.
DEF Investments Limited
DFG Distribution Ltd
DLG Wholesale Ltd
DSC Imports Limited
DTdist Ltd
Dago Wines Ltd
Danish Snaps Co Ltd
Danyal Ltd
Dave and Dani Ltd
Daves Drinks Ltd
Davy & Co Ltd
De Christ Wines Ltd
Decorum Vintners Limited
Deeti Wholesale Limited
Dega Trading Ltd
Del Professore Limited
Delegat Europe Limited
Delivering Happiness Limited
Delta World Trading Limited
Demball Limited
Desi Wines Ltd
Desideria Ltd
Destilado London Limited
Deutschlond Brewery Limited
Di.Wine Limited
Diageo Great Britain Limited
Diageo United Kingdom Limited
Diamond Stag Importers Ltd.
Diffusion Food By Pina Co Ltd
Digby Wine Ltd
Dima's Vodka UK Ltd
Dionysius Importers Ltd
Dionysus Boutique Wine Merchants Ltd
Direct2door Food & Beverage Ltd.
Dirt. Ltd
Dirty Drinks Collective Ltd
Ditton Wine Traders Ltd
Divine Associates Ltd
Diwine London Ltd
Diwine Piemonte Limited
Dmomentum Ltd
Doctor Bird Rum Ltd
Domaine Direct Limited
Donatel Freres Limited
Dorys Shop Ltd
Dourthe UK Limited
Dracula Wine House Ltd
Dram-a-Drinks Ltd.
Drink Connect Ltd
Drink Store Limited
Drink247 Ltd
Drinkable Ltd
Drinks Bay Limited
Drinks Global Ltd
Drinkscraft Limited
Drinkss Cash and Carry Limited
Drum and Black Rum Co Ltd
Drumstick Products Co Ltd
Dulwich Spirits Co Ltd
E I Wines Limited
EFE Store Limited
EL IP Rights Limited
East London Brewing Co Ltd
East Street Wine Co Ltd
Eataly Food Distributors Ltd
Edgerton Holdings Limited
Eebria Limited
Eight Vodka Limited

Elements Eight Rum Co Ltd
Elicite Ltd
Ellustria Limited
Ely & Sidney Limited
Ely's Cocktails Ltd
Eminent Life Limited
Eminent Wines Limited
Emthea Ltd
Enopoli Limited
Enotria Winecellars Limited
Enovino Organic Ltd
Enzo's Food and Wine Ltd
Espir Baron & Solomon Limited
Estelon Holdings Limited
Estini Ltd
Euro Wines (C & C) Limited
European Wine Brokers Limited
Eurotrade Supply Limited
Eurovenus Limited
Eurowines Limited
Euroworld Foods Limited
Evergreen Foods Limited
Everyday Wholesale Ltd
Evok3 Ltd
Ewer Limited
Expression du Terroir Limited
FFM Pasta Co Ltd
FV Trading Europe Ltd
Fabre Brothers Ltd
Fairway Foods Limited
Falcon Wholesaler Limited
Falugamaro International Ltd
Fameface Import Limited
Far Out Wines Limited
Faridoon Wines Ltd
Farr Vintners Limited
Fcuk Ltd
Feewcha Services Ltd
Feni Global Limited
Ferovinum Ltd
Fine & Rare Wines Limited
Fine Cider Limited
Fine Wine (Old World) Trading Co Ltd
Fine Wine Direct Limited
Fine Wine House Ltd
Fine Wine Trading Company (UK) Ltd
First Cape Vineyards Ltd
Flint Wines Limited
Flobegill Wines UK Ltd
Flora Fine Wines Ltd
Foodiebusters Epic Food Authority Ltd
For Goodness Sake Ltd
Forest Hill Brewing Co Ltd
Forest Road Brewing Co Ltd
Fortmount Trading Limited
Fortunae Limited
Fortunella Spirits Ltd
Forward Moving Limited
Foxbusiness Tobacco Ltd
Clark Foyster Wines Limited
France Domaines Limited
Franciacorta Limited
Franklyn Road Brewing Ltd
Free Spirits Group Ltd
French Wine Project Limited
Friarwood Fine Wines Limited
Friendship Adventure Ltd.
Full Logistic Ltd
G & G International BCN Ltd
GS Wines Ltd
GWB Associates Limited
Pascal Garcia Consulting Ltd

UK Wholesalers of Beers, Wines and Spirits   dellam

Martinez Gassiot & Co Ltd
Gem Wines Ltd
General Bilimoria Wines Ltd
Genesis Wines Limited
Gente Di Mare Ltd
Georgian Wine Co Ltd
Gergovie Wines Limited
Gianni. B. Limited
Gigglewater Productions Ltd
Gill Cash & Carry Limited
Ginvino Ltd
Glen Monarch Distillery Ltd
Glen Scotia Distillery Co Ltd
Global Beer Co Ltd
Global Trade & Consulting Ltd
Global Wine Trading Co Ltd
Global World Wide Beer Limited
Glow Glow Ltd.
Glugit Limited
Goedhuis & Co Ltd
Gold Tooth Limited
Golden Coin Trading Limited
Goldex International Ltd
Goldy Gin Limited
Goldy Limited
Gonzalez Byass UK Limited
Good Spirits Ltd
Goodeataly Ltd
Grandor Limited
Grape Wines Services Ltd
Grapebee Ltd
Gravity Drinks Ltd
Great Smattsby Limited
Great Western Wine Co Ltd
Greater London Beer Exports Ltd
Green Heart Wines Ltd
Green Island (UK) Limited
Greenwood Distillers Limited
Greenwood Spirits Limited
Gremi Wine Trading (UK) Ltd
Grey Cardinal Limited
Group93 Ltd
Groupe Prestige Ltd
Gudfish Limited
Samuel Gulliver & Co. Limited
Gurkha Beer Ltd
HG & S Ltd
HG Wine Limited
HM47 Investment Projects Ltd
HNB Trade Ltd
HSE of Drinks Ltd
HT Drinks Ltd
Happy Girl Beverage Co Ltd
Harama Trading Ltd
Harmony Wines Limited
Harry Bromptons Ltd
Harrydev Limited
Ian Hart Distilling Limited
Hatton & Edwards Fine Wine Merchants
James Hawker and Co Ltd
Haycock's Drinks Co Ltd
Haycock's No.9 UK Ltd
Hayward Bros (Wines) Limited
Healthy Wines Ltd
Heath London Limited
Hellenic Agora Limited
Henderik & Co Limited
Heroes Drinks Company C.I.C.
Hidgate Ltd
Highball Brands Limited
Hillbridge Estates Limited
Hilton & Rowley Ltd

Hingston & Co. Ltd
Hix & Buck Ltd
Hobo Beer & Co Ltd
Hobros Limited
Hoghton Brewery Limited
Holy Grape Ltd
Home2.0beer UK Ltd
Hoops and Champagne Ltd
Hoversy Technologies Ltd
Human Brands PLC
Humble Group Ltd
Thorman Hunt & Co Limited
Hurricane Rum Co Ltd
I'll Ask The Boys Ltd
I.G.T. Management Ltd
I8 MGT Limited
IGW Brokers Limited
IMC Business Group Limited
Iberiandrinks UK Ltd
Icomex London Limited
Idle Hour Spirit Co Ltd
Il Palagio Ltd
Il Tastevin Ltd
Il Tipico Italiano Ltd
Imbibros Ltd
Imperial Cash & Carry Limited
Impexpo Ltd
Import Brothers Limited
Impression Beverages Ltd
In Wine & Spirit Solutions, Ltd
Inconcept Ltd
Indigo Wine Limited
Ineffable LDN Limited
Infinite Session Ltd
Inkd Limited
Innvino Ltd
Insignia Spirits Limited
Intelligent Trade Limited
International Business Solutions Ltd
International Spirit Vault Ltd
Interseel Ltd
Invino Vitalis Ltd
Isake International Limited
Ishka Wines and Spirits UK Ltd
Italian Wine Club Ltd
Italicus Ltd
Italy Service UK Ltd
Iturn Global Ltd
J & D Wholesalers Ltd
JB Champagne & Co Ltd
JKVK International Import and Export Ltd
JW Corporation Ltd
Jackson Nugent Vintners Ltd
Jaguar Beverage Ltd
Janemac Ltd
Japan Gourmet (UK) Limited
Jascots Wine Merchants Limited
Jelly Bowl Ltd
Jenuine Jamaican Products Ltd
Jivana Spirits Ltd.
Jocks and Peers Brewing Co Ltd
Jub Club Top Bar Ltd
Junga Ltd
Justerini & Brooks,Limited
KBB Components Ltd
KRW Leisure Limited
KT Global Ltd
Kal Wine Source UK Ltd
Kallwin Limited
Kane Republik Ltd
Kanpai (London) Food and Beverage Management Co.,

Karla & Co. Spirits Limited
Kayzar Ltd
Kedem Europe Limited
Keeling Andrew & Co Limited
Keep Control Ltd
Keeps Lager Co Ltd
Kese International Ltd
Kikijee Global Services Ltd
Kitchen Table Wine Co. Ltd
Knotted Vine Limited
Koa Brewing Limited
Koha Distribution Limited
Kol App Ltd
Kold Group Limited
Kolden Ltd
Konik's Tail Limited
Kosher Wines Limited
Kraft Beer UK Ltd
Kudu Food and Wine Ltd
Kukuruz Limited
Kylemore Trading Ltd
L'Atypique Ltd
LA International Trading Ltd
LC Wine Brokers Limited
LGVA Solutions Limited
LHK Fine Wines Limited
La Aurora Ltd
La Cerveceria Limited
La Collina Biologica Ltd
La Delizia UK Limited
La Diva Drinks & Food Ltd
La Madeleine Wines Limited
La Peira Limited
Laki & G Ltd
Lanson International UK Ltd
Lant Street Wine Co Ltd
Lanty Slee Liquor Co Ltd
Last Word Drinks Co Ltd
Late Night Liquor Ltd
Louis Latour Limited
Laurito Ltd
Lavinia UK Limited
Laytons Wine Merchants Limited
Laytons Wine Services Limited
Le Petit Wine Cellar Ltd
Legends of Drinks Ltd
Lemongrass and Cardamom Ltd
Leomar Limited
Leppelmann & Nie Limited
Les Caves de Camille Ltd
Les Vins de Latour Limited
Levin Trading Limited
Liberty Wines Limited
Life's A Bottle Limited
Lightbox Brands Limited
Limalimo UK Ltd
D.J. Limbrey Distilling Co. Ltd
Line Point Global UK Limited
Lion-Beer, Spirits & Wine (UK) Ltd
Lionel Export Agency Ltd
Lioness Paw UK Limited
Liquid Brand Marketing Limited
Liquid Projects International Ltd
Liquor Box Ltd
Liquor-Ish Ltd
Litchquor UK Ltd
Little Gems Wine Ltd
Little Grape Co Ltd
Little Vine Co Ltd
Littlemill Distillery Co Ltd
Liv-Ex Limited
Lizard Management Ltd

Loaded Spirits Ltd
Lobins Limited
Loch Lomond Distillers Limited
Loch Lomond Distillery Co Ltd
O.W.Loeb & Co Limited
Londinio Liqueurs Ltd.
London Ale UK Ltd
London Barrelhouse Limited
London Calling Sweden Ltd
London Drinks Limited
London Drinks Supplier Ltd
London Drinks and Beers Ltd
London Long Drink Limited
London Spiced Dry Limited
London Wholesale Ltd
London Wine Agencies Limited
London Wine Eis Limited
Loxwood Meadworks Ltd
Loyalty Wines Limited
Luxury Gourmet Ltd
Lyndon Drinks Limited
M Wines Limited
MB Whisky Limited
MCAL Merchant Limited
MCMCtrans Ltd
MDS International Ltd.
MJM Hospitality Ltd
MK Wine Art Ltd
MPS 64 Ltd
Simon Mace Wine Broking Ltd
Made in Little France Import Ltd
Madison Drinks Co Ltd
Maestral de Provence Ltd.
Maestrale Group Ltd
Magenta Wine Investors Limited
Magic Spells Brewery Limited
Magna Juice Ltd
Magnus Wines Ltd
Maha Cash & Carry Ltd
Maha Wholesale Ltd
Mahar Associates Ltd
Maiden Wines Limited
Mail-a-Wine Limited
Maison Sassy UK Limited
Maisons Marques et Domaines Ltd
Malts of Scotland Ltd
Mamada Ltd
Mamajuana UK Ltd
Manor Park Drinks Ltd.
Manteo Trading Co Ltd
Marc Fine Wines Limited
Markets It Ltd.
Marlonn Food & Wine Ltd
Marussia Beverages UK Limited
Mason & Mason Wines Limited
Master Spirits Limited
Master of Sake Ltd
Matteo Lupi Wines Ltd
Maxim & Co Limited
Maxwell's Trading Co Ltd
Mayfair Brands Limited
Mayfair Delivers Limited
Mead Ho! Limited
Meanwhile Drinks Ltd.
Medagio Limited
Mediterranean Farm Finest Ltd
Medoff UK Ltd
Melange Drinks Ltd
Melchior Limited
Melius Drinks Ltd.
Mellasat Wines Limited
Mentzendorff & Co Ltd

Mephisto Wine Merchants Ltd
Mercury Spirits Ltd
Metropolitan Spirits (U.K.) Ltd
Mezcal Reina Limited
Mezzaro Ltd
Mickey Finn's Liquor Co Ltd.
Milae Vodka Limited
Milk Vin Ltd
Mille Gusti Limited
Martin Miller's Gin Limited
Millesima Limited
Mina Collection Ltd
Minarda General Trade Ltd
Miracle Drinks Limited
Mo Madness Drinks Limited
Mode de Vie (Carbon) Limited
Modern Botanicals Limited
Modern Vintage Wines Ltd
Modest Merchant Limited
Moet Hennessy U.K. Limited
Mongoose Brewing Co Ltd
Monopole Wine Portfolio Management Ltd
Monteadria (UK) Limited
Montrachet Limited
Moore's Enterprises Limited
Duvel Moortgat UK Limited
More Wine Ltd
Murphy & Yeung Brewing Co Ltd
My Global Ventures Limited
Mymexico Global Ltd
Mzansi UK Ltd
N20winery Ltd
NCE Trading KFT Ltd
NJA Marketing Ltd
NTKS Ltd
NYSA International Ltd
Nat Trade SRL Ltd
Natural Bay Limited
Natural Marketing Ltd
Robin Navrozov Consulting Ltd
Near Beer Brewing Co. Ltd
Negociants Europe Limited
Negociants UK Limited
Neilward Ltd
Nekter Wines Ltd
Nephtis Limited
Neu Brandenburger Beer Co Ltd
New Claire Wine Ltd
New Fairdeal Drinks Limited
New Generation Wines Limited
New Muscovy Co Ltd
New World Trading Europe Ltd.
New Zealand Beer Collective Ltd
Newcomer Wines Limited
Nice Brewing Co Ltd
J & W Nicholson & Co Ltd
Nick Drinks Limited
Nifol Limited
Night Out Entertainments Ltd
Nightcap Global Limited
Nine Reigns Limited
Nino and Blue Spruce Ltd
Noble Green Wines Limited
Noble Wines (UK) Limited
Norfolk Rum Co Ltd
North West Industries Ltd
Novarto Drinks Ltd
Novel Spirits Collection Ltd
Novel Spirits Limited
Now This Is It Ltd
O & E Food Ltd
O & P Investments Limited

O'Donnell Moonshine Limited
OM Beers & Minerals Ltd
OX Bespoke Logistics Ltd
Oak Alliance Ltd.
Oak Group One P.L.C.
Obadec Enterprises Limited
Ocavia Wine & Spirits Ltd
Oeno Limited
Oenofuture Limited
Official Box Office UK Ltd
Ojo de Dios Ltd
Okowita Vodka Limited
Old Cellar Ltd
Old Red Lion Theatre Pub Ltd
Old Sport Limited
Old and Rare Whisky Limited
Oldschool Wines Limited
One Point Supplies Limited
One Stop East Limited
Ops Wines Ltd
Ora Brewing Co Ltd
Oracle Fine Wines Ltd.
Orale Ltd.
Organica Food & Wine Ltd
Oriental Drinks Limited
Original & Distinctive Limited
Oris Black Ltd
Ormos Trades Limited
Orsa Major Ltd
Oso Brew Co Ltd
Ossau Vins & Spiritueux Ltd
Otros Vinos Limited
Ourglass & Partners Ltd
Outlander Brands Limited
PMWine Trade Limited
PS Drinks Ltd
Padstow Brewing Company (2013) Ltd
Paisajes Trading Ltd
Pale Fox Wines Limited
Palinka UK Ltd
Palmer Traders Ltd
Panda Oriental Supermarket Ltd
Pandemonio Limited
Panemporium Ltd
Paramount Vintners Ltd
Parasol Wines Ltd
Parched Drinks Ltd
Park Royal Wholesale Limited
Passion Wine International Ltd
Peachy Glow Limited
Perfect Cellar Ltd
Pernod Ricard UK Limited
Personalised Care Solutions Ltd
Peruvian Enterprises Limited
Petrelli Ltd
PimentoDrinks UK Ltd
Pimlico Cellars (Agencies) Ltd
Pimlico Dozen Limited
Pinglestone Estate Limited
Pink City Cider Ltd
Pioneer Spirits Ltd
Pioneering Spirits Limited
Plant Relief Ltd
Plonq Wines Ltd
Plum Brandy Co Ltd
Polat International Ltd
Pollen Cider Ltd
Poltom Limited
Pongolo Ltd
Pop Cake Box Limited
Port City Brewing UK Limited
Portuguese Story Ltd

UK Wholesalers of Beers, Wines and Spirits

Poshmakers Ltd
Pot Still Drinks Ltd.
Potocki Spirits (Europe) Ltd
Mathieu Poulain Limited
Prasad Trading Co Ltd
Premier Beverages Limited
Premium Bottles Limited
Prime Cash & Carry Limited
Primos Group Ltd
Professional Wine Services Ltd
Project Urban Wines Ltd
Proof Drinks Limited
Prosit Wines Limited
Provenance Projects 2016 Ltd
Provence Impex Limited
Publik Wine Limited
Pull The Cork Limited
Punchline Ltd
Punchy Drinks Limited
Punjabi Ltd
Pure Techno Ltd
Python Controls Ltd
Qtranly Ltd
Quaich Whisky Investments Ltd
Quamina Quality Drinks Co Ltd
Quantum Vintners Limited
Quick Liquids Limited
R & B Wines Ltd
R Spirit Ltd
RCI Spirits Ltd
RJR Fort Ltd
RWM Holdings Limited
Ragtag Wines Ltd
Raisin Social Limited
Raks Suppliers Limited
Ramx Ltd
Rapid Fill Ltd
Rara Drinks Co Ltd
Rare Whisky Auctioneers Ltd
Rarewood (London) Limited
Ratherhavecava Ltd
Ravensbourne Wine Co Ltd
Readywine UK Ltd
Real Al Co Ltd
Real Grapes Ltd
Red Dragons Trading Limited
Red Fox Wines Limited
Red Squirrel Wine Ltd.
Redevined Wines Limited
Refined Wine Club Ltd.
Reformed Spirits Co Ltd
Refresh 24 Group Limited
Relais La Torre UK Ltd
Remfly Wines UK Limited
Retaliate Limited
Reva Drinks Ltd
Rexon Group Festivals Limited
Rich & Bad Ltd
Maurice Richard Ltd
Richmond Distillers (Zurich) Ltd
Richway Cash and Carry Ltd
Riding Wine Co Ltd
River Widow Brewery Ltd
Rivers Rum (UK) Limited
Robel Import Trading Ltd
Roberson Wine Merchant Limited
Rodica Wine and Spirits Ltd
Roland Wines Ltd
Robert Rolls & Co. Limited
Rome de Bellegarde Wines Ltd
Ross Earl Wine Co., Ltd.
Roust UK Ltd

Rovial Trans Ltd
Ruffnek Beer Limited
Rum Runna Ltd
Rum Shop Limited
Russian Doll Vodka Limited
Russian Investment II Limited
Rustic Tap Limited
Ryder Partners Limited
S & B Impex Ltd
SPP Wine Ltd
SW Group Spanish Wine Ltd
Sacred Spirits Holdings Ltd
Safeway Distribution Limited
Sageitude Ltd
Sagitha Ltd
Sagittarius Royaume-Uni Ltd
Sagittarius World Limited
Salto Cachaca Co Ltd
Sam-Gel Global Ventures Ltd
Sambath Trading Limited
Santa Code Limited
Sapling Spirits Ltd
Sardinia Wine Ltd
Sarpanch Food & Wine Distributors Ltd
Saucy Drinks Co Ltd
Schoenlaub Limited
Schuler Wine St. Jakob's Cellars Ltd
Seawoods Wine Ltd
See Squared Ltd
Select Whisky Limited
Sell My Wine Ltd
Senor Agave Limited
Separateflow Limited
Seth Ventures Limited
Sfuso Wine Limited
Shake's Ink Limited
Shamboozle Limited
Shocabo Ltd
Shonty Group Ltd
Shop Wine Limited
Shy Simba Ltd
Sibell Trading Limited
Signature Brew Ltd
Silly Point Wines Limited
Simply Drinks Distribution Ltd
Sin Shots (U.K.) Ltd.
Sip Sip Wine Limited
Sipping Liquor Ltd
Sixpenny Wines Limited
Skyden Spirits Ltd
Smiley Rhyme Limited
Snow Leopard Vodka Limited
Soho Wine Supply Limited
Solow Ltd
Soltano Wines Ltd
Somm in the Must Ltd
Sonvino Ltd.
Southwell Trading Ltd
Southwick Court Fine Wines (2012) Ltd
Special Cases Limited
Specialist Cellars Ltd
Speciality Brands Ltd
Speciality Drinks Limited
Spirit Cartel Limited
Spirit Generation Limited
Spirit Traders Ltd
Spirit of Bermondsey Ltd
Spirits International Management Ltd
Spirits Logistics Ltd
Spirits of Borough Ltd
Square Wholesale Ltd
Square Wine Ltd

St James's Fine Wine Limited
St. Max Wine Limited
Staid London Limited
Stallion Spirits Limited
Stay Gold Beer Co Ltd
Stewart Hill Walker UK Limited
J & G Stewart Scotch Whisky Ltd
Stida Beverages Ltd
Stockholm Distillers and Vintners
Stockwell Beverages Ltd
Stockwell Wholesalers Limited
Stoney Hospitality Limited
Street Food & Beverages Co Ltd
Sun Exports Limited
Sundown Vino & Liquor Ltd
Sunny Group Limited
Suntrack Ltd
Super Brit Bery Ltd
Supermalt UK Limited
Supermarket Solutions Limited
Surprising Wines Ltd
Swanbridge Fine Wines Ltd
Swara Trading International Ltd
Swig Wines Limited
Swimming Pigs Ltd.
Swipe (Wine) Limited
Swissgrapes Limited
Sybarite Cellars Limited
Sylvestre Limited
Symposia Wine Limited
T.M.B Wine Trading Ltd
T.W.S Wines Ltd
TBrands Distributor Ltd
TCG Winchester Limited
TL Step By Step Limited
TPSC Ltd
TVB Retail Limited
Bertrand Tailor Limited
Talbot & Barr Limited
Tall Blond UK Ltd
Tapp'd Cocktails Ltd
Tapp'd Ltd
Tasty Kameleon Ltd
Tata Trading Limited
Edward Tatham Champagne Ltd
Taunton Cider Co Ltd
Charles Taylor Wines Limited
Te Kano Estate Wines (UK) Ltd
Team Yebo Ltd
Teca Wines Limited
Tech-Beach UK Limited
Temple Wines (Cash & Carry) Ltd
Tender Vine Limited
Tequilas of Mexico Limited
Tewaina Ltd
Thagam UK Limited
Thames Distillers Limited
Thames Wholesale Ltd
Theatre of Wine Limited
Thomson & Scott Limited
Thrace Premium Drinks Ltd
Tiger Vines Ltd
Tikves London Ltd
Grace Tilly Limited
Tims Tuga Ltd
Tinnies Ltd
Tipple Brands Ltd
Toast Ale Ltd
Toff Wine Ltd
Topmost Foods Distribution Ltd.
Totally Awesome Wine Co Ltd
Tour de Force Wines Limited

Traderhorn Limited
Trading Import and Export Co Ltd
Trading Irmis Ltd
Trang Mai Exports Limited
Trebbiano Wines Ltd
Triage Wines Limited
Triangle Wines Limited
Tribeology Limited
Trinewine Ltd
Trusty Services Ltd
Ttow Ltd
Tudor Drinks Ltd
Turkish Kitchinn Wholesale Ltd
Glen Turner Co Ltd
Tutto Wines Limited
Two Heads Beer Co Limited
UK Blue Ribbon Group Beer Co., Ltd
UK McCullenvis Wine Group Ltd
UK McLouis Liquor Co Ltd
Ubicumque International Ltd
Ultimate Drinks Limited
Ultra Premium Drinks Limited
Uncharted Wine Co Ltd.
Uncle Nearest Ltd.
Under The Bonnet Wines Limited
United Spirit Brands Limited
United Wine Estates Limited
United Wines Ltd
Urbeer Ltd
Usedsoft Ltd
Uva Wines Ltd
V Beverages Limited
Valenta Wine Limited
Valentino & Finch Ltd
Valinch & Mallet Limited
Value Focused Solutions Ltd
Van Pur UK Ltd
Vegan Wine Company London Ltd
Vento Marino Ltd
Venus 14 Limited
Venus Wine & Spirit Merchants PLC
Veravinea Ltd
Verre Anglais Limited
Vertigo Beers Limited
Vickbar Limited
Victoria Island Beverage Co Ltd
Viktor and Walker Ltd
Vinafrica Limited
Vinals Wine & Food Limited
Vine & Cork Limited
Vinemporium Limited
Vineus Limited
Vinnaturo Ltd
Vinny Labs Ltd
Vino & Spirits Limited
Vino Unico Limited
Vinolex Ltd
Vinos Latinos Ltd
Vinovitaj Ltd
Vintage 1947 Limited
Vintner London Ltd
Vinum Limited
Vinvm Ltd
Viserra Limited
Vitesse Vintners Limited
Vitis-Terra Limited
Vranken Pommery UK Ltd.
WSB Investment and Consultancy Ltd
Walking Back The Cat Limited
Warwick Banks and Jenkins Ltd
Waterland Trading Limited
Wein Forum - Fine Wines Ltd

Weiser Taverns Beers & Minerals Ltd
Wenlen UK. Ltd
Werfa Holdings Ltd
West Coast Wines & Spirits Ltd.
West End Brands Ltd
West End Drinks Limited
Westbourne Drinks Co Ltd
Whisky Palate Limited
Whisky Work Play Ltd
Wild Life Botanicals Ltd
Wilkies International Ltd
Wilkinson Vintners Limited
William of Orange Brands Ltd
Wine & People Limited
Wine & Spirit International Ltd
Wine & Spirits Club SA Ltd
Wine Art Co Ltd
Wine Bliss Ltd
Wine Cru Limited
Wine Enterprise Investment Scheme
Wine Group Ltd
Wine IT Limited
Wine Online Ltd
Wine Outlet Ltd.
Wine People Europe Ltd
Wine Prophets Limited
Wine Treasury Limited
Wine UK Direct Limited
Wine for Drinking Limited
Wine-Invest Ltd
Wineaux Ltd
Winecraft Ltd
Wined Ltd
Winehood Ltd
Winelistphobia Ltd
Winemakers Club 2000 Limited
Wineologia Ltd
Wines Around Mediterranean Ltd
Wineservice Limited
Winesider UK Ltd
Wineworld Exchange UK Limited
Winning Invest & Trade Ltd
Winz International UK Ltd
Wisca Beverages Limited
Wisdom Whisky & Wine Limited
Witney Wine Limited
Wokka Spirits Limited
Wolf Leisure Limited
Workshy Brewing Ltd
World Brands Duty Free Limited
World Cider Box Limited
World Wine Imports Limited
Xeco Wines Limited
Xpress Bootleg Limited
Xpress Resolution Ltd
Yaad Rum Ltd
Young in Spirit Ltd
Zachicado Ltd
Zetas Ventures Ltd
Ziv & Zivka Ltd
Zonin UK Limited

Lothian [15]
Dramfool Ltd
Faking Bad Brewery Limited
Fidra Fine Spirits Limited
Gleninver Limited
Hedges & Butler Limited
Lang Brothers Limited
Largesse Corporate Gifts (2007) Ltd
Ian MacLeod Distillers Ltd
Ian MacLeod and Co Ltd

Wm Maxwell (Scotch Whisky) Ltd
PJ's Virtual Brewing Co Ltd
Peter J Russell & Co Ltd.
Spalathos Ltd.
Wildflower Wines Limited
Wincarnis Limited

Merseyside [65]
3 Lids Rum Ltd
Ali Booze Co Ltd
Altar Wines Limited
Alternative Rum Co Ltd
Amy's Wine House Limited
Art of Wine Ltd
Associated Church Clubs Ltd
BLSN Limited
Bajan Trading Co Ltd
Barwell & Jones Limited
Bearded Lion Drinks Co Ltd
Beerscellars (UK) Limited
Beverages Distribution Limited
Boar Wine Ltd
Boondales Limited
Booze Village Limited
Chalgrove Wines Limited
Clos Vintners Limited
Cornish Rum Co Ltd
Cosmopolitan Drinks Limited
Drinks R Us Limited
Drinkslynx Limited
FD Gin Co Ltd
Fabulous Gin Ltd
Fizz Guru Limited
Global Drinks (UK) Limited
W. Hall & Son (Holywell) Ltd
Hops and Barley (Group) Ltd
Hops and Barley (UK) Limited
Hops and Barley Limited
Hyde & Sons Limited
Incapico Inc Limited
Innovative Cocktails Ltd
Jackson & Seddon Ltd
Jimmy's Beer & Gas (Wirral) Ltd
Lpower Ltd
Lust Promotions Ltd
M & M Romanian Imports Ltd
Magic F & F Ltd
Main Rum Co Ltd
Adrian Mecklenburgh Limited
Middle Kingdom Ltd
Molvino Fine Wine & Spirits Co Ltd
Mywinelabel Limited
Nitrogenics Ltd
Nottage Bar Supplier Limited
O'Neill Fine Wines Limited
PPbeer Ltd.
Pemberton Central Limited
Pruno Wines Ltd
Quintrox Limited
Chalie Richards & Co Ltd
Sefton Beer Co Ltd
Ship & Mitre Brewing Co Ltd
Simply Spirits Limited
T & S Sales Limited
TP Retail Ltd
Think Wine Group Ltd
Three Graces Liverpool Ltd
Three Swallows Ltd
Tilted Penguin Gin Ltd
Victoria Garry Group Ltd
West Lancs Drinks Ltd
Wholesale Beer Supplies Ltd

Wine Agency Ltd

Middlesex [153]
A A Suppliers Ltd
Adonko Bitters (UK) Ltd
All Drinks Cash & Carry Ltd
Ambal Fuel Ltd
Anglo-African Trade Limited
Apical Breweries UK Ltd
Aquitania Ltd
Asante Distributors Limited
Bacchus Merchantry Limited
Bak Family Wines Limited
Bargain Food and Booze Limited
Barrys Discount Ltd.
Belabon Drinks Ltd
Best Bordeaux Wines Ltd
Beverage Boys Ltd
Brompton Wine Co Ltd
Brooks & Whitaker Limited
Bucks Spirits Ltd
Burgundy Tuscany Piedmont Ltd
Buzz Drinks Limited
CPT Trading Ltd
Champers (Wholesale) Limited
Cheng International Co Limited
Claret-E Limited
Co Stars London Ltd
Colchester Mann Limited
Comercio Ltd
Compasse Limited
Continental Cash & Carry Ltd
Coral MGT Limited
Coral Management Limited
Costadoria Ltd
F & M Cressi Limited
Cubed A Ltd
DNG Group Ltd
DNG Trading Ltd
DT Wine Importers Ltd
DW Brands Ltd
De Paolis Limited
Delbroo Ltd
Delecta Limited
Dhamecha Foods Limited
Diamond Aces Limited
Donaldson Reeves Limited
Doran Family Vintners Limited
Drinks 4 Less (UK) Limited
Eda Quality Foods North UK Ltd
Eight Brothers Corporation Ltd
Ellis of Richmond (Holdings) Ltd
Ellis of Richmond Limited
Epiphany Bars Limited
Euro Link Beverages Ltd
Eurochoice Limited
Europebro Wholesalers Ltd
Eurorock Trading Limited
Explore British Drinks Limited
Family of Hounds Limited
Fourteen Twelve Trading Ltd
Freerun Consulting Limited
GS Wholesalers Ltd
Gang of Five Ltd
Georges de la Chapelle Limited
German Beer Co Limited
Global Brands Trading Ltd
Global D & F Ltd
Golden Harvest Wholesale Ltd
HKK and Sons Ltd
HP Enterprises Limited
Hayk Corporation Ltd

Healthier Products Limited
Hungarian Wine Ltd
IBL Wines Ltd
Iceaction Limited
Indian Ice Gola Co Ltd
Tristan James Ltd
Kanlaon Limited
Karma Beverages Ltd
Khosla Wines Ltd
Kingdom Distillers Limited
Knights Catering Impex Ltd
Kuchh Hai Limited
LM Spirits Ltd
La Vigneronne Fine Wines Ltd
Lamjen Limited
Lebanese Fine Wines Limited
Levin Wines Limited
Liquor World Venture Ltd
London Creek Limited
Lordsworth Limited
Thomas Lowndes & Co. Limited
Lunzer Wine Group Limited
M & B Distributions (UK) Ltd
M M General Merchandise Ltd
Maximus Wholesale Limited
Meless Consortium Ltd
Meless Group Limited
Middlesex Wines Limited
Mysomm.Com Ltd
Noble Merchants Limited
North South Wines Limited
Northpole Crush Ltd
Norvic Ltd
Novus Drinks Ltd
Noy Brothers Enterprises Ltd
OM Wines Ltd
Offie Limited
Palms & Liquor Enterprises Ltd
Pan Euro Foods Limited
Panton Ventures Limited
Parmar Drinks & Wines Ltd
Premier UK Trading Limited
Premier Wines & Spirits Ltd
Premium Brands Distribution Ltd
Premium Bulgarian Wine Ltd
Prestige Vintners Limited
Prima Import & Export Ltd
Pristine Trades Ltd
Quintessential Decadence Ltd
RC Brands Ltd
RS Wholesale Limited
Ralph's Wines Ltd
Ray Jules Limited
Real Ale (Export) Limited
Real Ale (Retail) Limited
Real Ale (Wholesale) Limited
Real Ale Limited
Redvulette Ltd
Richmond Wine Agencies Limited
Rico Rico Ltd
Rondel Trading Ltd
Rosemille Ltd
Sarpe L & C Ltd
Savafrei Ltd
Savile Row Gin Limited
Sheila's Rum Punch Ltd
Signature Wines Ltd
Spar (UK) Limited
Star Direct Hospitality Ltd
Strategos Limited
Tasmanian Liquor Distributors Ltd
Terra Toda Ltd.

Tikka Beer Limited
Tioluxe Europe Limited
Tops Food and Wine Limited
Triple AAA Limited
Up Drinks Ltd
Urban Wholesalers Limited
Vintage Wine Investments Ltd
Wimbledon Wine Cellar Limited
Wine Raiders Limited
Wise Trading Limited
Xenon Wines & Spirits Limited
Yeast To West Ltd

Midlothian [75]
A Taste of The Caribbean Ltd
ANM Trading Limited
Alpha Whisky Ltd
Anderson Beverages Ltd
Applecart Drinks Limited
Atom Scotland Limited
Auld Acquaintance Whisky Co Ltd
Beer52 Limited
Bellissimo Vino Edinburgh Ltd
Bier UK Limited
Black Tartan Limited
Bottlers Limited
Brewgooder Foundation
Calduero Wine Importers Ltd
Cask Whisky Ltd
Chardon Wines Limited
Corkers Wine Limited
Crafty Connoisseur Limited
Cross Brew Ltd
De Burgh Fine Wine Limited
Deutsches Beer Limited
Deutsches Bier Limited
Dionysus Premium Drinks Ltd
Direct Wine Factory Ltd
Eastlin Alba Limited
Fine Products Exporters Ltd
Fine Wine Co Ltd
Finest Wine & Delicatessen Brokers Ltd.
French Sommelier with a Wee Dog Ltd
Frequency Enterprises Limited
From Cask To Bottle Limited
Gain Brands International (UK) Ltd
Gleann Mor Spirits Co Ltd
Glenalan Limited
Hannah Whisky Merchant's Ltd
J & M Whisky Limited
KLR & RCR Distribution Ltd
Kindman Brewing Ltd
Kingsbury Wine & Spirits Co Ltd
Leith Distillery Limited
MCAL Sweet Retail Limited
Milk Money Limited
Native Wines Ltd
New Wave (Scotland) Limited
Old Town Blending Co Ltd
Original Beer Co Ltd
Original Bier Co Ltd
Palmerston Fine Wines Ltd.
Peatreekers Limited
Prestige Whisky Worldwide Ltd
Pug Vodka Ltd
Quintessential Brands UK Ltd
RSD Whisky International Ltd
Raeburn Fine Wines Ltd.
Reality Bio Wine Ltd
Rebel Wine Club Ltd
T.M. Robertson & Son Limited
Rutherford, Shirlaw and Denholm Ltd

SOS Whisky Limited
Sco & Whisky Limited
Scotch Whisky International Ltd
Simpsons Wine Imports Limited
Slainte Mhath Ltd
Laurence Smith & Son (Edinburgh)
Snickering Pig Drinks Co Ltd
Spirits Development & Management Company (SDMC)
Spirits for Good CIC
Summerhall Distillery Asia Ltd
Village Selections Limited
Wemyss Vintage Malts Limited
Wemyss Wines and Spirits Ltd
Whigham Fergusson Limited
Whisky Merchants Trading Ltd
Wine Importers (Edinburgh) Ltd
Young Malt Co Ltd

Monmouthshire [11]
Azurapada Worldwide Ltd
Chesters Wine Merchants Ltd
Fines Master Spirit Co Ltd
Glacon Limited
Grwp Silwriad Cyf
Liquid Measure Limited
Morgan Jupe Limited
SJZP Limited
Stedman Bros. (Events) Limited
Valley Vineyards Limited
Wine Shop Limited

Norfolk [39]
Albert Altima Trade House Ltd
Barry Drinks Ltd
Bespoke London Wine Co Ltd
Beyond The Ale (GB) Limited
Bijou Bottles Limited
Bullards Spirits Limited
C C & C Limited
Campania Cucina Ltd
Carpe Vinum Ltd
Chateau Musar (U.K.) Limited
Chateau Musar International Ltd
Copper and Rye Limited
DC Imports UK Ltd
Diss Honest Brewing Co Ltd
Drink Kind Ltd
Drunk Maitre D Limited
Ephemeris Solutions Ltd
G.W. Fields & Sons (Great Yarmouth)
Ghost Drinks Ltd
Peter Graham Wines Limited
Home Farm Gin Limited
Lord Nelson Burnham Ltd
Made To Measure Ltd
Meadrising Limited
Norfolk Vineyard Ltd
Norwich Dry Gin Co Ltd
Number One Drinks Co Ltd
Rimpex-UK Limited
Rum Matters Limited
Sisserou Marketing Limited
TBD Tipples Ltd
TBpub Ltd
TFWF Ltd
Tamarind Drinks Limited
Tanner Brodin Limited
Taste Buds Wines Limited
V.C. Vintners Limited
Walnut Tree Distillery Ltd
Wanderlust Wine Limited

Northamptonshire [38]
8 Barrels Club Ltd
8 Drinks Ltd
AGS Vintners Limited
Alcohollect Ltd
Bar Joker Ltd
Batarak Limited
Benchmark Drinks Ltd
Bordeaux and Beyond Ltd
Buffet Restaurant Northampton Ltd
Cassels and Sons Brewing Europe Ltd
City Beer Limited
Cobblers Gin Limited
Compasses Gomshall Ltd
Dragonwood Limited
Drinks Club Ltd
Fieldscot Ltd
Gunners Cocktails Limited
Jerome Harlington Limited
Harlington Wine Limited
Independent Drinks Supplies Ltd
KB Suppliers Ltd
Kermis Bier Ltd
Kristal Spirits UK Limited
Libertine Spirits Ltd
Local Beer Delivered Ltd
Lounge Spirits Ltd
Magma Liquid Ltd
New Fine Wines Ltd
One Love Rum Co Ltd
Organic French Wines Limited
Original Herbale Brewing Co Ltd
RK Vodka Limited
Ruby & Claret Limited
S & N Products Ltd
Charles Samuel Imports & Exports Ltd
Thirstee Business Limited
Trailblazing Wine Ltd
Winery Jakubik UK Ltd

Northumberland [11]
Bath Sixteen Limited
Bigg Market Beer Co Ltd
Bigg Market Brewery Co Ltd
Brewis Beer Co Ltd
Dennhofer Wines Limited
Elliston Fine Wines Limited
Evil Spirits Ltd
First & Last Brewery Ltd
Half Cut Wines Limited
Lindisfarne Limited
North East Drinks Supplies Ltd

Nottinghamshire [35]
A. S. D. Wholesale Limited
Amayan Terroir Selections Ltd
Ann et Vin Limited
Antique Wine Co (Holdings) Ltd
Atlas Fine Wines Limited
Balkan Wines Ltd
Bang The Elephant Brewing Co Ltd
Bottle Drinks Co Ltd
Brand Central (UK) Limited
Cocktail Pickers Club Ltd
Corkhaus Ltd
Crafty Warehouse Ltd
Devine Distillates Group Ltd
Europemarca Limited
Green Cash & Carry Ltd
H & F Export Limited
K & A Eagle Limited
Konigsberg Seven Bridges Breweries Ltd
Left Coast Distribution Ltd
Les Vignerons de Saint Georges Ltd
M D (Cash & Carry) Limited
Mahal Enterprises Limited
Marta Vine Limited
More or Less Drinks Co Ltd
Myella Brands Ltd
Outstanding People Limited
P & P Distribution Limited
San Martino Limited
Scrumpy Wasp Limited
T & M Food Products Ltd
Tesh Beverages Limited
Vintage Wines Limited
WLL Wholesale Ltd
Weavers (Nottingham) Limited
Philip von Nell Wines Limited

Oxfordshire [51]
Absolutely Organic Limited
Adam & Herv Limited
Afco Traders Ltd
Amwell Springs Brewery Co Ltd
Artizen Raw Ltd
Bahamian Enterprise UK Limited
Bankside Brewing Limited
Bassen Ltd
Big Red D Ltd
Bobby Beer Co Ltd
W.H. Brakspear & Sons Limited
Coles Trading Limited
Colton Fox Trading Limited
Concha y Toro UK Limited
Coombe Castle Fine Wines Ltd
DGB Europe Limited
Dacastello Limited
Dedicated Wine Importers Ltd
Dedicated Wines Ltd
Different Wines Limited
Domaine Watson Ltd
Fine Wine Trading Limited
Finebatch Limited
Focus Beverages Ltd
Glug Limited
Heronsgate 7 Limited
Intertrade Wholesale Limited
S H Jones Wines Ltd
L'Altre VI Limited
Victor Lanson Brands Limited
Layered Cakes Ltd
Layered Ltd
Le Soula Limited
Liberty Liquors Ltd
Lock & Barrel Limited
MJLM Limited
Mastiha World Ltd
Noah Brothers Ltd
Noetic Wine Limited
Oxford Beer House Limited
Phone A Fix Ltd
Red Bottle Co Ltd
Slurp Wine Co Ltd
Smouse & Marchand Limited
Sourceror Ltd
Spokesuk Ltd
Tasteturkey Limited
Vieuxvino Investment Ltd
Vincisive Wines Limited
Winetraders (UK) Limited
Wyfold Vineyard Limited

UK Wholesalers of Beers, Wines and Spirits

Pembrokeshire [9]
Ascona Retail (Leases) Limited
Celtic Wines Limited
Chosen Wine Limited
Espana Imports Ltd
Lush Wines Ltd
Pembrokeshire Drinks Limited
Rhymney Brewery Western Ltd.
St Davids Gin Limited
Templeton Beer Wine & Spirit Co Ltd

Powys
Best of Hungary Ltd
L H Cellar Supplies Limited
Taste Merchants Ltd
Tirion Trading Co Ltd

Rhondda Cynon Taf
Celtavini.Com Limited
Truman's Drink Solutions Ltd

Rutland
H2vin Limited
Knight Trade (Oakham) Limited

Shropshire [28]
Wm.Addison (Newport) Limited
Apley Hall Wines Limited
Battlefield Beers Limited
Battlefield Brewery Limited
Bridgnorth Brewing Co Ltd
Buchanan Wines Ltd.
Giesen Wines UK Limited
Greek Wineshop Ltd
Hard To Find Wines Limited
Iron & Rose Ltd
Ironbridge Gorge Gin Co Ltd
Stanley Marlow & Son Limited
Momentum Wines Limited
Neil Morrissey Real Ale Co Ltd
Paso-Primero UK Ltd.
Terry Platt Wine Merchants Ltd
Pulling & Co.Limited
RD Wines Limited
Real Ale Direct Limited
Shropshire Beers Limited
Spain Link Ltd
Special Cider Co Ltd
TW Wine Solutions Ltd
Tanners (Shrewsbury) Limited
Tanners Cymru Limited
Tanners Wines Limited
Traditional Beer Co Ltd
Wine World Producers Limited

Somerset [86]
49 Wines Limited
7 Day Cellar Limited
A.I.M.S. (Refreshments) Ltd
Avalon Wholesale and Brewing Ltd
Azzurri Kitchen Ltd
B.D. (S/W) Ltd
Babicka Vodka (International) Ltd
Richard Banks & Co Ltd
Bath Gin Co Ltd
Bedminster Beer Co Ltd
Bibendum PLB Group Limited
Bibendum Wine Limited
Billings & Briggs Ltd

Bond Bar Ltd
Bristol Cider Co Ltd
Bristol Fine Wine Limited
Bristol Records Limited
Broadoak Cider Co Ltd
Casa Cocktails Limited
Chalk Farm Wines Ltd
Chandos Wines Ltd
Matthew Clark Bibendum Ltd
Matthew Clark Limited
Matthew Clark Wholesale Bond Ltd
Matthew Clark and Sons Ltd
Codorniu UK Limited
Corfu SW Limited
Crafty Wolf (Drinks) Limited
Crafty Wolf Limited
Creative Juices Bar Limited
Crest Cyder Co Ltd
D'Urberville Vineyard Limited
DBM Wines Limited
De-Laceys Tipples Limited
Enmore Wine Limited
Epic Beers Limited
Experience Wine Limited
J.T.Flanagan Trading Co Ltd
Gordano Wines Limited
Grape Opportunities Ltd
Himalaya Wines Limited
Imprint Wine Limited
Inro Drinks (Abtec) Limited
Intriguing Brands Limited
JJBrands Limited
C. & T. Licata & Son Limited
Lilley's Cider Limited
Little White Dog Limited
MGW World Ltd
Maison Shane et Filles Ltd
Mercanti Imports Limited
Mexican Spirits Carmen Del Rio Ltd
MyNaturalCo Ltd
D & M Nicholls Limited
Psychopomp Ltd
Quantock Abbey Wine Cellars Ltd
R S Wines Limited
Red & White Wines Limited
Regency Event Solutions Ltd
Reid Wines (1992) Limited
Responsible Trading Co Ltd
Sandhu Wholesale & Events Ltd
Scrawny Al Ltd
Snobby's Ltd
Somerset Craft Distillery Ltd
Spot Wines Limited
Steel Coulson Ltd
Stewart Wines Limited
Stokes Fine Wines Limited
Sunnyside Incorporated Limited
Temperley Wines Limited
Thorn-Clarke Wines (UK) Ltd
Thru The Glass Limited
Trade Wines Ltd
Two Pal's Co Ltd
Two Toes Ltd
Vine Trail Limited
Vine Wine Limited
Vineco Inco Ltd
Walker & Wodehouse Wines Ltd
West Country Wines Limited
White's Cellar Supplies (UK) Ltd
Wine Merchant Ltd
Wineclub Online Limited
Wolf Wine Limited

Xisto Wines Limited

Staffordshire [39]
3Squires Ltd
3Squires Wines Ltd
Ales. R. Russ Limited
Aspall Cyder Limited
Ballance Group Limited
Barkin Bars Ltd
Bogart Spirits Limited
Bourne & Co Solutions Ltd
Burton Drinks Limited
C G Supplies Limited
Cobra Beer Partnership Limited
Digby Fine English Ltd
Eden Garden Trading Limited
Euroofar Trading Limited
Fast Moving Goods Ltd
Halton Turner Brewing Co Ltd
In Vino Veritas Ltd
Innspired Taverns Limited
Ishke Brands Ltd
Ital Sardo Limited
Just Perfect Wines Ltd
Lucky Strike Pub Co Ltd
Maw Berwick Ltd
Midlands Drinks Limited
Mieland Limited
Molson Coors Brewing Co (UK) Ltd
Molson Coors Brewing International
Olive Wines Limited
Premier Pubco Limited
Presidente Wines Limited
Queen of The Moorlands Whisky Co Ltd
Ran Ales Ltd
Real Irish Whiskey Limited
Rock and Roll Spirit Co Ltd
Rok Drinks Limited
Simply Cask Ltd
Vino Italiano Ltd
Whitebridge Wines Limited
Wine Freedom Limited

Suffolk [30]
Adnams PLC
Beautiful Beers East Anglia (UK) Ltd
Beer & Co Distribution and Sales Ltd
Boxford Wine Co Ltd
Cameron Cavendish Fine Wines Ltd
Dragon Drinks Limited
Edmunds Cocktails Ltd
Fishers Gin Ltd
Go Brazil Wines & Spirits (UK) Ltd
Trevor Hughes Wines Limited
Imperial Wine Co Ltd
Ionica Wine Cellars Ltd
JD Group Enterprises Ltd
Lacons Brewery Limited
Lexington Trading Limited
Nowselect Limited
Old Empire Events Ltd
Orchard-Lisle Wines Ltd
Phil Cellars Ltd
Pioneer Gin Limited
Rest Wine Ltd
Thomas Ridley and Son,Limited
Say It With Champers Ltd
Seckford Wines Limited
Smashing Wines Limited
Top Deal Services Ltd
Vintage Capital II PLC

Waveney Ales and Ciders Ltd
Witek Spirits Ltd
World Sake Imports UK Ltd

Surrey [218]
10 International Limited
8000 Vintages Limited
97 Catering Ltd
A-Holding Ltd
Above Brand Limited
Added Pressure Ltd
Aizia Ltd
Ambassador Commodities Ltd
Andreev Services Ltd
Angola Beverages Holding Co Ltd
Anna Wine & Food Ltd
Appellations Limited
Asahi Premium Brands Ltd
Asahi UK Ltd
Ascott Invest Limited
Ashanti Drinks Limited
Asiana Mart Limited
Astrum Wine Cellars Limited
Athila Roos Ltd
Australian Vintage (Europe) Ltd
BCM Brewing Co Ltd
BFV International Limited
Bacchus Wine Auctions Limited
Bayede Wines UK Ltd
Beaumont Beverages Ltd.
Billecart - Salmon (UK) Ltd
Birdcage Gin Ltd.
Black Kola UK Limited
Blackadder International Ltd
Bondi Brands Limited
Bondi Brewery Limited
Bosman Wines UK Ltd
G. Bravo & Son Limited
Burgundys Collection Limited
CPC Business Limited
Carmelita Limited
Cellar Select Ltd
Chacalli-De Decker Ltd.
Checkmate Premium Brands Ltd
Church Road Mini Market Ltd
Henry C. Collison and Sons Ltd
D & K Capital Ltd
DH Global Wine Ltd
Dankan Ltd
De Wetshof International Ltd
Decanter Wines Limited
Deer & Badger Ltd
Dirty Drinks Ltd
Distell Europe Ltd.
Distell International Holdings Ltd
Drinks 2 You Limited
Drinks Network Ltd
Du Terroir A La Table Limited
Dumenil Champagne Limited
Eclipse Drinks Limited
Emporia Brands Limited
Evernex Ltd
Evocative Wines Limited
Exul Limited
Fabijhon Wine Ltd
Famille Clarke Limited
Fightback Brewing Co Ltd
Firkin Whisky Co Ltd
Four Corners Wine Co Ltd
G Life Limited
General Wine and Liquor Co Ltd
Glo-Rum Enterprise Limited

Global Ethics Liquor Co Ltd
Global Village Wines Limited
Global Wine & Spirits Ltd
Global24-7 (UK) Ltd
Good Life Gin Co Ltd
Good Living Brew Co Limited
Gourvid Limited
William Grant & Sons Brands Ltd
Grape Variety Ltd
Hannibal Brown Wine Services Ltd
Hapusa Spirits UK Ltd
Heath Trading Limited
Hi - Line Wines Limited
Hi-Spirits Ltd
Hic-Cup Wines Limited
Hidden Caveau Limited
Hop Drop Limited
Hoppl Wines Limited
House of Sparkling Ltd
Iberian Wine Shippers Limited
Impala Transportation Ltd
Independent Vintner Ltd
Inside Trax Limited
Interactive Stage Ltd
Island Drinks Limited
Italian Wine Buyers Club Ltd
Jabru Bevco Ltd
Kapaka Limited
Kato Enterprises Limited
Keg Delivery Service Ltd
Kingfisher Beer Ltd
L'Atelier Terroir Limited
La Guilde du Cognac Limited
Last Drop Distillers Limited
Laurence Leisure Limited
Les Caves de Pyrene Limited
Liquid Assets Group Ltd.
Liquid Ninja Limited
Litmus Wine Agencies Limited
Little Horse Wines Limited
London & Scottish International Ltd
London & Scottish Spirits Ltd
London Wine Shippers Limited
M & P Diffusion Limited
Manley Wines UK Limited
Manoj Navaladi Ltd
Sarah Marsh Ltd
Mast-Jaegermeister UK Holding Ltd
Mast-Jaegermeister UK Limited
Mayfly Wine Co Ltd.
McKenzie Fine Wines Limited
Meadow Trading Co Ltd
Medoc Wines Limited
Miraj Beers & Wines Limited
Mobay Drinks Ltd
Mondial Wine Limited
Montymac Vintners Ltd
More Sake Limited
My Nan's Favourite Ltd
Navaladi Ltd
Nordic Imports Ltd
Novus BH Magister Ltd
Oxford Brewery Limited
Oxford Brewing Co Ltd
Oyster Import Export Limited
Panache du Sud Ltd
Panda Trading International Ltd
Paradigm Red Limited
Pingu & Co Ltd
Portugal Winelist Ltd
Poulter Group UK Limited
Premier Distillers Ltd

Prime Drinks Ltd
Prime Wines Limited
Project Wines UK Limited
Quality Spirits International Ltd
Quicksip Ltd
RBW Fine Wines Limited
Rackham Investments Limited
A.H.Rackham Limited
Ragul Ltd
Realsa Wines Import & Export Ltd
Rhuby Limited
Rippingale Promotions Limited
River Drinks Ltd
Russbrit Ltd
S.A.R.D.V.M Ltd
SASC Enterprise Limited
Santat Wines Limited
Sauvignon Wines UK Ltd
Savage Wines UK Limited
Sazerac UK Limited
Vernon Scott Limited
Second Eger Ltd
Sharing The Best Limited
Single Cask Ltd
Six Rivers Limited
Smith & Humpston Ltd
Sober Limited
St Pierre Partners Limited
Stack United Limited
Starstock Ltd
Sterling Wine Agencies Limited
Superba London Wines Ltd
Swinging Vine Ltd
Szicsek Palinka Ltd
T Warriors Brewery UK Limited
T.C.T.C. Services Ltd
Teqcoola Limited
That Wineshop Limited
Thirsty Brands Ltd
Thiyagu Ltd
Tiny Vessel Brewing Co Ltd
Tokaj Merchants Ltd
Toro Industries Ltd
Trade Network Supplies Limited
Tump By Aj & Sonz Ltd
UK Beer & Soft Drinks Ltd
UK Vintners (of London) PLC
Unicodrinks ESP Ltd
Unique Wine Safaris Limited
Urban Beers and Wines Ltd
V & A Jobs UK Ltd
V I Wholsale Limited
VDK Import Export Limited
Valvai Cash & Carry Ltd
Valvai Ltd
Vektor Vodka UK Ltd
Vice Enterprises Limited
Vigneti Tardis UK Ltd
Vinimpo (U.K.) Limited
Vinissimo Limited
Vins Ltd
Vintage & Fine Wine International
Viscount Agencies Limited
Vitkovitch Brothers Limited
Warner Family Wines Limited
Whisky Baron Ltd.
Whisky Point Limited
Wine Pantry (Wholesale) Ltd
Wine Pantry Limited
Wine Place Limited
Winecall Limited
Winelink Limited

UK Wholesalers of Beers, Wines and Spirits — dellam

Woori Trade Ltd
World Wide Wines Limited
World of Drinks Limited
Worldewide Limited
Worthington Wine and Spirits UK Ltd
Wrights Lion Brewery Limited
Yoka Family Limited

Sussex [146]
A & S Drinks Ltd
ACK Trading Ltd
Abyss Brewing Ltd
Afterthought Spirits Co Ltd
Agrosale UK Limited
Airways Bonded Warehouse Ltd
All English Distribution Ltd.
Allied Wholesale Ltd
Amirante Empire Limited
W.J.Armstrong Limited
Atlasaim International Limited
Babco UK Ltd.
Bach & Co Solution Limited
Barton, Brownsdon & Sadler Ltd
Beer and Spirit Agencies International
Black Cat Brewery Limited
Blue Thorn Gin Limited
Bouquet Limited
Brazen Beer Limited
Brighton Brew Co Ltd
Brighton Soft Drinks Limited
Brighton and Hove Wine Co Ltd
Brix & Porter Ltd.
Brunswick Fine Wines and Spirits Ltd
Buckingtons Ltd
Bump Events U.K Limited
Burgundy Wines Limited
Bwinfusions Ltd
C & E Transport Ltd
C.O.D. Beers Limited
CBD Drinks Co Ltd
CSS On-Trade Limited
Cabezac Collections Limited
Cape Wines Limited
Carousel Wines Limited
Colemans ABC Ltd
Compass Supply Solutions Ltd
Copricom Ltd
Crackerjack Wines Limited
Cuestion Tequila EMEA Ltd
Cuestion Tequila Limited
D.C Enterprises (Import/Export) Ltd
DTB Distribution Ltd
Davenport Vineyards Limited
Delage & Haughton Limited
Deniz & Ada Limited
Drinksbot Limited
Elixir Wine Ltd
Fairview Wines Limited
Falcon Vintners Limited
Fifty One Forty Limited
Four Seasons Hastings Ltd
Foxhole Spirits Limited
Franc Wine Ltd
Freshfield Fine Wines Limited
Functional Drinks Co Limited
Garmence Limited
Giovanni Food & Wine Limited
Good Wine Limited
Guilty Libations Limited
Gunson Fine Wines Limited
Gusto Wines Ltd
Harp Wines & Spirits Ltd

Helver Wines Ltd
Hennings Wine Merchants Ltd
Highly Spirited Ltd
Hydraun Limited
International Diplomatic Supplies
Itedomum (UK) Ltd
Jam Consultants Global Limited
Kerry Wines Limited
Las Bodegas Limited
Latin Spirits & Beers (UK) Ltd
Lazy Lizard Beer Co Ltd
Le Venue Wine Warehouse Ltd
Les Producteurs et Vignerons de France
Les Vins de Sylvain Ltd
Lewes Gin Limited
Liquid Market Limited
Lord Krishna Trade Ltd
Lorelei Fine Wines Limited
Lost and Found Taprooms Ltd
Mayfield Distilling Co Ltd
Medusa Wines Ltd
MegaTradingLtd Limited
Melen London Ltd.
Message in a Bottle Ltd.
Midhurst Wine Shippers Limited
Morgan Classic Wines Limited
Amlot Morgan Fine Wines Ltd
Mothership Beer Ltd
Neon Brew Co Limited
Octagon Industries Ltd
Oliver's Beer and Wine Limited
Olivers Wine Agency Limited
Orbit Wines Limited
Pacta Connect UK Limited
Pigs Ears Beers Limited
Popjax Limited
Premia Brands Trading Limited
Present Tense Limited
Preston Wines Ltd
Provenance Fine Wines Ltd
Ratcliffe & Brown Wines and Spirits
Real Ales AT Limited
Revilo Group Limited
Richdells Wine Merchants Holdings
Route des Vins Limited
Rum Fellows Limited
SDC Wine Importers Ltd
SP (DPH) Exports Limited
Scarlettes Ltd
Seven Cellars Ltd.
Sheridan Cooper's Limited
Sheridan Wines Limited
Silver Rocket Brewing Ltd
Slightly Squiffy Limited
Smith & Harris Enterprises Ltd.
Society of Vintners Limited
South Downs Real Estate Ltd
Southbrew Co Ltd
Southern England Wines (UK) Ltd
Summerforever Ltd
Ultravino Limited
Vats Wine Co. Limited
Verrillo Partnership Limited
Villa Sofia Limited
Vin-X Enterprise Investment Scheme Ltd
Vinfinity Limited
Viniexport Limited
Viniguide Limited
Vintage Roots Limited
Wallis Ventures Ltd
Waverley Drinks Limited
Wine Divine Ltd

Wine Keg Co Ltd
Wineguise Limited
Winery Classic Limited
Wines of The Americas Limited
Withers Agencies Limited
Woodland Wine Store Limited
Michael Woolley Limited
World of Patria International Ltd
Xardins Wines and Cava Ltd
Xorta Global Management Ltd
Zing Vodk Limited

Tyne & Wear [40]
3F Leisure Limited
A Little Bit of French Ltd
CKW (Europe) Limited
CKW Trading Limited
Canny Class Ltd
Churnet Valley Drinks Limited
Clarence Spirits Limited
H.B.Clark & Co.(Successors) Ltd
Cullercoats Gin Co Ltd
Express Drinks Ltd
Gin Corporation Limited
Guest Wines & Co. Ltd
Head Thirst Ltd
House of Roo Ltd
Jetchill Ltd
Kaur's Convenience Store Ltd
Kitwave Limited
La Vigna Vini Ltd
Laneberg Wine Ltd
Lesont Ltd
Lucky Drinks 4 U Ltd
M.& M.Value Limited
NM Lesuire Ltd
North East Hold Limited
Northern Supplies (NE) Ltd
Oakmount Group Limited
Old Man Rum Co Ltd
Orion Cash & Carry Limited
Our Tino Ltd
Popaball Limited
QNGC Limited
George Sinclair & Sons Ltd
Smartprice (NE) Ltd
Sunderland Gin Limited
TFC Wholesale Ltd
Thorne Licence Wholesale Ltd
Tipple Transport Limited
Urban Wine Co. Ltd
Uropa Group Ltd
Wise Imports Limited

Warwickshire [58]
A Di Maria & Sons Ltd
Amore G.N.A. Limited
Appleton Estate Wines Ltd
BJ Drinks Ltd
Baby Bottles (Wholesale) Ltd
Beer Gonzo Ltd
Beer and Gas Man Limited
Bevimangia Limited
Brewbarge Limited
Brewed 4 U Ltd
Bull Trading Worldwide Ltd
Cana Import Limited
Caribbean Trade Ltd
Cider Centrum Ltd
Crazy Gin Ltd
Daysh Beers Wines & Spirits Ltd

Divergent Drinks Ltd
Double Measure Club Ltd
Dowbridge Distributors Ltd
Drinks2u Ltd
Dunarea Albastra Ltd
ERE Igga Ltd
Empress Ale Ltd
Fine Wine World Ltd
G B Consortium Wholesale Ltd
Gallachers Fine Wines Limited
Gelston Castle Fine Wines Ltd
Ghost Laboratories Limited
Goldbeach Trading Limited
Hunny Pot Pub Co. Limited
Imported Brands International Ltd
Invest Inns Limited
Law and Disorder Brew Co Ltd
Leamington Wine Co Ltd
Little Big Wine Co Ltd
Love and Labour Ltd.
M & T Wholesale Ltd
Malvern Ltd
Murray Brother's Whisky Ltd
ONCC Import Limited
Purity Brewing Co Ltd
Railway Bar & Grill Ltd
Sandhar & Kang (Birmingham) Ltd
Satellite Brands Limited
Smart Save Distribution Ltd
Srihari Haran Ltd
Stargold Wholesale Ltd
Tap HQ Ltd
Vin Neuf Limited
Vinitaly Limited
Volfram Ltd
Warwickshire Cash & Carry Ltd
Warwickshire Drinks Plus Ltd
Waters (1802) Limited
David J. Watt (Fine Wines) Ltd
Wine Cellar Midlands Limited
Wine House Warwick Limited
Wine Poole Limited

West Midlands [132]
101 Reykjavik UK Ltd
3 Tigers Limited
AB & R Import and Export Ltd
Ababio Express Limited
Approved Products Ltd
Articulate Drinks Co Ltd
Atanas Distributors Ltd
Bassrap Ltd
Beer Belly's Ltd
Beerco Limited
Beverage Boutique Ltd
Big D'Z Convenience and Winery Ltd
Bitter Lemons Gin Ltd
Blind Monkey Limited
Bordeaux Undiscovered Limited
Bosworthcruises Ltd
Bottle Butler Limited
Bottles on Demand Limited
Brewers Wholesale Limited
Budge Brands Ltd
C C and C London Ltd
Cador Limited
Capper & Co Ltd
Cask and Craft Direct Ltd
Central Pubs (UK) Limited
Champagne Charlie (Midlands) Ltd
Champagne Company (UK) Limited
Clarkes Drinks Direct Limited

Condor Wines Ltd
Connolly's (Wine Merchants) Ltd
County Catering (Midlands) Ltd
Cresco Import Exports Ltd
Cyprian Services Limited
D K Beers Ltd.
DC Cash and Carry Ltd
DT1 Ltd
Darlaston Drink Shop Limited
Desirable Drinks Ltd
Diabolus Limited
Drink Driver Ltd
Drinkintime Ltd.
Drinks Emporium Limited
Drinks To Go Plus Ltd
Earny Limited
East and West Foods Cash and Carry
Empire Star Limited
Euro Asia Distriubtion Limited
Euro Beer Distribution Ltd
Euro Speed Intl Ltd
Exivi Limited
Finedon Convenience Store Ltd
Franco Hetty Limited
Frazier's Wine Merchants Ltd.
Frontier Trading International Ltd
Frontier Trading Limited
Ftspot Limited
Fyre Festival UK Ltd
GBW Subscriptions Ltd
Gain & Coombs Ltd
Greenlink Enterprises Limited
Hardywood Park Craft Brewery Ltd.
Harris Filters Limited
R & J Harris Ltd
Heavenly Grapes Limited
Hollandwest Limited
Horizon Soft Drinks Limited
I I Wine Limited
JR First Choice Cash & Carry Ltd
Jascera UK Ltd
Jiggers Whistle Limited
Jupiter Wholesale Limited
KD Wholesale Ltd
Kan Trading Limited
Kay Distributions Ltd
Libra Drinks Wholesale Limited
Lonerider UK Ltd
MDF Wholesale Ltd
MSB Wholesale Services Limited
Magazin Romanesc Ltd
Magnate Drinks Ltd
Majlen Ltd
Marston's Acquisitions Limited
Mega Kegs Limited
Meridale Store Ltd
Mr Kegz Ltd
Murcotts Ltd.
Naked Spirit Co Ltd
Newhampton Wines Ltd
Nickolls & Perks Limited
Orso Wine Agencies Limited
Paloma & Pablo Import & Export Ltd
Pearl Leisure Limited
Point Beer UK Limited
Premier Inc. Ltd
Prostimo Ltd
Pulse Products Limited
Quest Leisure Limited
Quint-Essential JQ Ltd
R B M Leisure Limited
Paul Roberts Wines Limited

SJO Supplies Limited
Selectia Wine Ltd
Simply 1st Wine Co Ltd
Simply Beers Limited
Sips 'n' Nibbles Ltd
Spainorama Ltd
Spencers (Bromsgrove) Limited
Splendid Corks Limited
St.James Winery Ltd
Stour Valley Events Limited
Swallow (Soft Drinks, Beer and Cider Wholesalers)
Swallow Dispensed Drinks Solutions
TH Nightlife Ltd
Tenby Drinks (UK) Limited
Tequila Shop Ltd
Test Tube Products Limited
Thorne Wines Limited
Tipton Wines Limited
Transylvania's Finest Ltd
Truekeg UK Ltd
Trust in Global Food Ltd
V B Cash & Carry Ltd
Vine and Malt Ltd
Vitam Dare Limited
W S B C Limited
Wave Wine Ltd
Wedgbury Connections Ltd
White Pearl Ltd
Whittalls Wines Limited
Wine Carafe Limited
World Traveller Wines Limited
Yaved Ltd

Wiltshire [37]
Arkell's Brewery Limited
Balcony Wines Ltd
Beeble Liquor Limited
Beef and Burgundy Limited
Berkeley Cellars Limited
Bumble Mead Ltd
Cascade Drinks Limited
Cognac Growers' Collective Ltd
Crush Wines Ltd
Dark Revolution Ltd
Drink Artisan Ltd
Event Wine Solutions Limited
Freixenet Copestick Limited
Grainger Fine Wines Ltd
Hayloft Ventures Ltd
Imperial Capital D & G Ltd
Intercontinental Trade Solutions Ltd
Lisbon Wines Limited
Lombard Scotch Whisky Limited
Low-Key Essentials Ltd
Marlborough International (UK) Ltd
Museum Wines Limited
Nectar Imports Limited
Nexus Wine Trading Ltd
Peculiar Gin Co Ltd
Private Wine Shippers Ltd
Seb and Emma Ltd
Spiritory Ltd
Vin D'Oc Limited
Vino Italiano Importers Ltd
Vinterest Limited
Wadworth & Company (Burford) Ltd
Wadworth and Co Ltd
Whisky 78 Ltd
Wiltshire Liqueur Co Ltd
Wyld Rose Ltd
Yapp Brothers Limited

UK Wholesalers of Beers, Wines and Spirits

Worcestershire [18]
Alcohol By Volume Limited
Central Drinks Pub Co Ltd
Champagne Collection Limited
Fairytale Gin Limited
Hop Shed Limited
Investmentwine Ltd
JBD Booze Ltd
JSF Services Limited
Malpas Stallard Limited
Monkey Shed Estate Brewing Co Ltd
Pinckneys Gin Limited
Pryzm Cocktails Limited
Raer Scotch Whisky Ltd
Schnapp Lab Ltd
Shelsley Brewing Co Ltd
Twaites and Jones Limited
Vicar's Gin Ltd
Winehunters Ltd

Yorkshire [206]
3 Big Dogs Limited
ANA Distribution Limited
Adventure Brands Ltd
Afrogrocers Ltd
Ale Trader Ltd
Atlas Food Wholesale Ltd
Atom Brewing Co Limited
Avant Garde Drinks Ltd
Baijiu Beer Co Ltd
Baijiu Evolution Ltd
Barge & Barrell Inns Ltd
Barmaster (Independant Wholesalers)
Barn Direct Limited
Bazaar Store Ltd
Be Rude Not To Ltd
Beer Company (Exports) Ltd
Beer Company Consolidations Ltd
Beer Co Ltd
Beer Paradise (York) Limited
Beer People Limited
Beer Supply Limited
Bespoke Fine Wines Limited
Better Buy Ltd
Blue Island Limited
Blue Star Inns Limited
Bon Coeur Fine Wines Limited
Bone Machine Brewing Co Ltd
Booze Crew Leeds Ltd
Bosun's Brewery Tap Ltd
Brew Boxes Ltd
Broom House Investments Ltd
Bubbles for Friends Ltd.
Buon Vino Ltd
Can Man Ltd
Carpet Bagger Limited
Cellar 28 Ltd
Champagne One Ltd
Champagne Warehouse Ltd
Champions Cider Ltd
Chequers Distribution Ltd
Cider of Sweden Ltd
A.P. Claxton Ltd
Clique Wine Limited
Clubinn Together Limited
Conscious Collaborative Ltd
Cooper Hill Brewery Ltd
Corelli Wine Co Ltd
Cow West Yorkshire Limited
Creation Wines UK Limited
Crescent Fine Foods Ltd

Creswick Inns & Leisure Ltd
D & F Wines Ltd
Darley Abbey Wines Limited
Delta Western Distributions Ltd
Denby Dale Wines Limited
Nick Dobson Ltd
Domal Trading Limited
Drink Store Wholesale Limited
Drinkrite Limited
Drinks Depot Ltd
Drinks Direct Limited
Dutch Courage Drinks Consultants Ltd
Earle Wines Ltd.
Epicurean Food and Drink Corporation
Evokesomm Limited
Expressmode Limited
Extravision Security Systems Ltd
Field and Fawcett Wine Merchants and Delicatessen
Fiji Store Ltd
Fine Drinks Cooperative Ltd
Fine Food & Wine Limited
Fine Wine Works Limited
First Crew Ltd
Firth and Co Wine Merchants Ltd
Florin Wholesaler Ltd
G Point 7 Ltd
Grassington Spirit Co Ltd
Great Newsome Brewery Limited
Great Spirit Co Ltd
Great Whisky Co Ltd
Green Leaf Liquids Limited
Greenfield Bacon Limited
Halifax Wine Co Ltd
Hallamshire Wine Shipping Co. Ltd
Hanwood Limited
Harmonicande Vintners Ltd
Harp & Crown Cider Co Ltd
Hazewater Food Services Ltd
Hips Drinks Ltd
Hooton Management Limited
Hop Hideout Limited
Horsetown Beers Limited
Hotham's Spirits Ltd
House of Townend Limited
House of Wine Limited
Huddersfield Cash and Carry Ltd
Hutton & Mitchell Licensed Traders
I Caesar Limited
IKP Trading Limited
International Procurement and Logistics
International Wine Emporium Ltd.
Italy Abroad Network Limited
J W Wines Ltd
Jordan Sky Ltd
Just Incase Wines Ltd
Klostergut Limited
La Pata Negra Ltd
Label Bouchon Limited
Lamba Trading Co. Limited
Lamson Wine Co Ltd
Lancashire Beer Co Ltd
Landmark Wholesale Limited
Latitude Wine Limited
Laughing Ass Brewery Ltd
Le Bon Vin Limited
Lilo Beverages Ltd
Liquid Indulgence Ltd
Lupe's Imports Limited
MSM Foods Limited
Maharaja & Sons Ltd
Maison du Vin Ltd

Malton Brewery Limited
Medicare Health & Energy Drinks Ltd
Merchant Vintners Co Ltd
Meridian Centre Hospitality Ltd
Mirfield Brewery Limited
Henry Mitchell & Sons Limited
Mitchell's Vintners Limited
Molotov Brand Limited
Momento Vivere Holdings Ltd
Morosini Mills Limited
Mother of Wine Ltd
Najpol Ltd
Nandha Murgesan Ltd
Narang Wholesalers Limited
National Drink Distributors Ltd
Natural Wine Co Ltd
Nightingale Drinks Co Ltd
Noahs Estate Ltd
Perfect Pair Wines Ltd
Pivo Beverages Ltd
Pivovar Ltd
Play Limited
Pomona Island Brew Co Ltd
Pradeeprjm Limited
Premier Cru Fine Wine Ltd.
Premium Beverage Refreshments Ltd
Prestige Wine & Food (UK) Ltd
Prosecco 1754 Limited
Pulp Craft Cider Limited
Pyvo UK Ltd
Quarter Cafe Bar Limited
Quiqui Mezcal Ltd
Raven Hill Brewery Limited
Rawson Trading (Doncaster) Ltd
Rip Mountain Brewery Ltd.
Russells and Wrangham Limited
Russetglow Limited
S & T Wines Limited
Saravanan Traders (UK) Ltd
Sativatech Ltd
Sheffield Brewers Collective
Sherwood Outlaws Brewing Co Ltd
Shorty's Gins Ltd
Sinners Gin Ltd
Solitude Wines Limited
Spirit Beer Co Ltd
Steel City Exports Ltd
Sunset Wines Limited
Superyacht Supplies Limited
Tate-Smith Limited
Tattoo Limited
Tayler Beers Limited
This Is Not A Party Limited
Tirg Limited
Today's Wholesale Services Ltd
John Toma TDE Ltd
Transylvania Wine Ltd
Trinity Drinks Limited
Triple Point Brewing Ltd
Truly Spirited Ltd
Twilight Drinks Ltd
UK Lesiure Ltd
Union International Drinks Corporation
Veini Wine Co Ltd
Vett Limited
Vinceremos Wines & Spirits Ltd
Vines Wines Limited
Vino Pronto UK Ltd
A J Walsh Consultant Limited
Watermark Fine Wine Limited
Wetherby Brew Co Limited
White Willows Beers, Wines and Spirits

Whiteleys of Halifax Limited
Wickersley Fine Wines Ltd
Wine Library Limited
Wine Rascals Yorkshire Limited
Wine Tasting Angels Ltd

WinesOnline Ltd
Wineways (Harrogate) Limited
Wold Toppers Limited
Wright Wine Co Ltd
Yorkshire Beers Limited

Yorkshire Vino Ltd
Yorkshire Vintners Limited
Zinstream Wine Limited

Company Profiles

10 International Limited
Incorporated: 4 May 2006 *Employees:* 8
Net Worth: £372,658 *Total Assets:* £1,233,272
Registered Office: The Lodge, Guildford Road, Effingham, Leatherhead, Surrey, KT24 5PE
Shareholders: Toby Charles Petre Hancock; William Gerald Rolfe
Officers: Laurence Herbert, Secretary; Toby Charles Petre Hancock [1974] Director/Wine Merchant; Simon William Rolfe [1977] Director; William Generald Rolfe [1950] Director/Wine Merchant

100 Pipers (Whisky) Limited
Incorporated: 17 August 2001
Previous: Glenallachie Distillery Limited
Registered Office: 111-113 Renfrew Road, Paisley, Renfrewshire, PA3 4DY
Parent: Chivas Holdings (IP) Limited
Officers: Stuart MacNab [1964] Director/Accountant; Vincent Turpin [1978] Director/Chief Financial Officer [French]

100cl Limited
Incorporated: 10 November 2014
Net Worth Deficit: £61,878 *Total Assets:* £46,156
Registered Office: 299 Haggerston Road, London, E8 4EN
Major Shareholder: Roberta Sergio
Officers: Roberta Sergio [1975] Director/Scientist [Italian]

101 Reykjavik UK Ltd
Incorporated: 20 June 2016
Net Worth: £4,398 *Total Assets:* £11,618
Registered Office: 870 Tyburn Road, Birmingham, B24 9NT
Officers: Krzysztof Robert Szelbracikowski [1988] Director/Broker [Polish]

106 Business Solutions Limited
Incorporated: 8 August 2017
Registered Office: 3rd Floor, 86-90 Paul Street, London, EC2A 4NE
Officers: Peter Kehinde Egbo [1977] Director/Importer and Exporter

11:11 Gin Ltd
Incorporated: 2 November 2018
Registered Office: 150 Armistice Avenue, Springfield, Chelmsford, Essex, CM1 6AR
Major Shareholder: Luke von Schonenberger
Officers: Luke Von Schonenberger [1987] Director

180 East Limited
Incorporated: 10 December 2013
Net Worth: £298,180 *Total Assets:* £422,677
Registered Office: 85 Great Portland Street, London, W1W 7LT
Major Shareholder: William Jeremy Turnage
Officers: Nicholas James Whishaw Masters [1978] Director; James Geoffrey Bethune Taylor [1979] Director; William Turnage [1978] Director

1879 Brand Ventures Ltd.
Incorporated: 11 June 2018
Registered Office: 4th Floor, 150 West George Street, Glasgow, G2 2HG
Parent: Peter Holmes Group Ltd.
Officers: Fiona Alison Holmes [1980] Director/HR Consultant; Peter Andrew Holmes [1971] Managing Director

The 19th Beer Company Ltd
Incorporated: 6 August 2018
Registered Office: 53 Milburn Road, Bedford, MK41 0PD
Shareholders: Marc John Anderson; David Peter Welch
Officers: Marc John Anderson [1988] Director/Project Manager; David Peter Welch [1989] Director/Salesman

23 High Path Ltd
Incorporated: 8 May 2014
Net Worth: £9,767 *Total Assets:* £19,039
Registered Office: 23 High Path, London, SW19 2JY
Major Shareholder: Rodger Molyneux-Roberts
Officers: Rodger Molyneux-Roberts [1951] Director

23-7 Brewing Ltd
Incorporated: 25 October 2017
Registered Office: 5 Marsett Close, Norden, Rochdale, Lancs, OL12 7QT
Major Shareholder: Alexander David O'Mahony
Officers: Alexander David O'Mahony [1975] Director/Teacher

247 Enterprises UK Ltd
Incorporated: 15 June 2006
Net Worth: £1,031,953 *Total Assets:* £2,266,958
Registered Office: Unit 1 Astley Park, Chaddock Lane, Tyldesley, Manchester, M29 7JY
Shareholders: David Fashhou; Hani Fashhou
Officers: Hani Fashhou, Secretary; David Fashhou [1979] Director/Wholesaler; Hani Fashhou [1981] Director/Wholesaler

2I Whiskies Limited
Incorporated: 1 July 2014
Net Worth: £3,125,928 *Total Assets:* £3,571,489
Registered Office: 10 Ayr Road, Giffnock, Glasgow, G46 6RX
Officers: Iain Lindsay Hamilton, Secretary; Iain Lindsay Hamilton [1955] Director/Whisky Broker; Irene McKay Hamilton [1961] Director/Whisky Broker; Nichola Irene Hamilton [1988] Director/Whisky Broker

3 Barrel Company Limited
Incorporated: 5 April 2011
Registered Office: St Michaelsgate House, High Street, Waddington, Lincoln, LN5 9RF
Major Shareholder: James Tob-Ogu
Officers: James Tob-Ogu [1963] Director/Beverage Sales

3 Big Dogs Limited
Incorporated: 25 January 2017
Net Worth Deficit: £71,884 *Total Assets:* £126,482
Registered Office: 13 Yorkersgate, Malton, N Yorks, YO17 7AA
Officers: James Ian Parker [1990] Managing Director

3 Cities Brewing Company Ltd
Incorporated: 15 November 2017
Registered Office: 42 Hogarth Road, Whitwick, Coalville, Leics, LE67 5GF
Major Shareholder: Marcus Garry Edward Goddard
Officers: Marcus Garry Edward Goddard [1980] Director

3 Lids Rum Ltd
Incorporated: 29 September 2017
Net Worth: £900 *Total Assets:* £10,296
Registered Office: 1 Beechurst Road, Liverpool, L25 3PX
Shareholders: Andrew Robert John Laird; Andrew Robert John Laird
Officers: Andrew Robert John Laird [1985] Director

3 Tigers Limited
Incorporated: 10 December 2012 *Employees:* 3
Net Worth: £13,908 *Total Assets:* £128,341
Registered Office: 119c Baltimore Road, Great Barr, Birmingham, B42 1DD
Major Shareholder: Jaspal Liam Singh Purewal
Officers: Jaspal Liam Singh Purewal [1994] Director/Sales Assistant

3ABC Ltd
Incorporated: 14 February 2017
Net Worth: £5,617 *Total Assets:* £23,568
Registered Office: Flat 1, 180 St Pauls Road, London, N1 2LL
Shareholders: Akshit Raj Gupta; Ashwin Balivada; Aditya Nigudkar
Officers: Ashwin Balivada [1988] Director [Indian]; Akshit Raj Gupta [1988] Director/Operations [Indian]; Aditya Nigudkar [1983] Director/Cofounder [Indian]

3F Leisure Limited
Incorporated: 3 March 2006
Net Worth Deficit: £17,188 *Total Assets:* £59,771
Registered Office: 2 The Green, Southwick, Sunderland, Tyne & Wear, SR5 2JE
Shareholder: Ashish Vedhara
Officers: Ashish Vedhara [1973] Director

3R'SB Limited
Incorporated: 5 June 2017
Registered Office: 2 Prospect Street, Reading, Berks, RG1 7YG
Major Shareholder: Deepraj Bholah
Officers: Deepraj Bholah [1967] Director/Manager [Italian]

3Squires Ltd
Incorporated: 1 August 2018
Registered Office: 98 Lancaster Road, Newcastle-under-Lyme, Staffs, ST5 1DS
Shareholders: Kenton Hackney; Thomas Guy Scarlett
Officers: Kenton Hackney [1962] Director; Thomas Guy Scarlett [1980] Director

3Squires Wines Ltd
Incorporated: 15 May 2018
Registered Office: 98 Lancaster Road, Newcastle-under-Lyme, Staffs, ST5 1DS
Officers: Kenton Hackney [1962] Managing Director; Thomas Guy Scarlett [1980] Director/Chief Executive

4 Acre Brewing Co. Ltd
Incorporated: 31 December 2018
Registered Office: 198 Berechurch Hall Road, Colchester, Essex, CO2 9PN
Shareholders: Spencer Aaron Gilbert; Amir William Anbouche; Jack William James Snell
Officers: Amir William Anbouche [1992] Director

4 Rabbits Ltd
Incorporated: 11 February 2019
Registered Office: 72 Higher Blandford Road, Broadstone, Dorset, BH18 9AH
Officers: Andrew Richard Hill [1967] Director

4 Star (Leicester) Limited
Incorporated: 4 September 2006
Net Worth: £3,682 *Total Assets:* £23,855
Registered Office: 67 Uppingham Road, Leicester, LE5 3TB
Major Shareholder: Massimiliano Torre
Officers: Massimiliano Torre [1971] Director/Salesman [Italian]

414 Alcohols Limited
Incorporated: 16 August 2016
Net Worth Deficit: £7,802 *Total Assets:* £32,698
Registered Office: 51a High Street, Kirkcaldy, Fife, KY1 1LJ
Shareholders: John Alexander Thomson; Craig Edward Fell
Officers: James Thomson, Secretary; Craig Edward Fell [1983] Director; John Alexander Thomson [1979] Director

49 Wines Limited
Incorporated: 9 February 2015
Registered Office: Woodlands Grange, Woodlands Lane, Bradley Stoke, Bristol, BS32 4JY
Shareholders: Rajan Soni; Susan Carol Soni
Officers: Paul William Lawrence Redfern [1953] Director/Solicitor; Rajan Soni [1962] Director/Wine Merchant

55 Above Ltd
Incorporated: 25 April 2014
Net Worth Deficit: £90,586 *Total Assets:* £46,887
Registered Office: 4 Langford Court, Ongar Road, Kelvedon Hatch, Brentwood, Essex, CM15 0LB
Major Shareholder: Alan Colin Gilchrist
Officers: Alan Colin Gilchrist [1971] Director/IT Consultant

7 Day Cellar Limited
Incorporated: 31 October 2017
Registered Office: 1 New Street, Wells, Somerset, BA5 2LA
Major Shareholder: Timothy Edward Cullum
Officers: Timothy Edward Cullum [1969] Director; Mark Robert Harding [1963] Operations Director

79North Limited
Incorporated: 10 March 2016
Net Worth Deficit: £558 *Total Assets:* £1,389
Registered Office: Back Stable, Unit 2 Ash Park Business Centre, Ash Lane, Little London, Tadley, Hants, RG26 5FL
Major Shareholder: Rui Manuel Alves Ramos
Officers: Rui Manuel Alves Ramos [1979] Director/Sales [Portuguese]

8 Barrels Club Ltd
Incorporated: 19 October 2018
Registered Office: 2 Lings Local Centre, Lumbertubs, Northampton, NN3 8NQ
Major Shareholder: Nikesh Sushil Patel
Officers: Nikesh Sushil Patel [1989] Director

8 Drinks Ltd
Incorporated: 17 July 2017
Registered Office: 9 Debdale Road, Wellingborough, Northants, NN8 5AA
Major Shareholder: Rikul Patel
Officers: Rikul Patel [1992] Director

8000 Vintages Limited
Incorporated: 25 May 2018
Registered Office: 23 Consfield Avenue, New Malden, Surrey, KT3 6HB
Major Shareholder: Ioseb Natenadze
Officers: Ioseb Natenadze [1983] Director [Georgian]

88 Connect Ltd
Incorporated: 27 July 2011 *Employees:* 2
Net Worth Deficit: £15,387 *Total Assets:* £6,053
Registered Office: 33 Byron Avenue, Kingsbury, London, NW9 0ER
Shareholders: Jean Christophe Rousseau; Jalpesh Dinsukhrai Thakrar
Officers: Dinsukhrai Jagjavian Thakrar, Secretary; Jalpesh Dinsukhrai Thakrar [1973] Director/Self Employed

888 Global Trade Ltd
Incorporated: 21 April 2017
Net Worth Deficit: £3,152 *Total Assets:* £18,591
Registered Office: 10 Main Street, Doune, Perthshire, FK16 6BJ
Officers: LEA Cunningham [1977] Director/Property Manager; Stephen Cunningham [1976] Director/Cost Engineer

97 Catering Ltd
Incorporated: 15 January 2019
Registered Office: 2 Vulcan Way, Wallington, Surrey, SM6 9RY
Officers: Liam Wells [1997] Director

A & B Vintners Limited
Incorporated: 27 May 1998 *Employees:* 9
Net Worth: £717,551 *Total Assets:* £2,836,696
Registered Office: 43-45 Dorset Street, London, W1U 7NA
Major Shareholder: John Charles Arnold
Officers: Sally Ann Arnold, Secretary; John Charles Arnold [1964] Director/Wine Merchant; Simon Christopher Davies [1978] Director/Wine Merchant; Alexander Nicholas Kidney [1965] Director/Chartered Accountant

A & G Management Consultancy Ltd
Incorporated: 2 February 2018
Registered Office: 27 Old Gloucester Street, London, WC1N 3AX
Shareholders: Antonio Fernandes; Gabriel Antonio Fernandes
Officers: Gabriel Fernandes, Secretary; Antonio Fernandes [1953] Director/Operations Manager; Gabriel Antonio Fernandes [1957] Director/Finance Manager [Portuguese]

A & S Drinks Ltd
Incorporated: 20 September 2018
Registered Office: Flat 1, 11 Boundary Road, Hove, E Sussex, BN3 4EH
Major Shareholder: Umair Ahmed
Officers: Umair Ahmed [1991] Director

A A Suppliers Ltd
Incorporated: 16 November 2018
Registered Office: 83 Hayes End Drive, Hayes, Middlesex, UB4 8HE
Major Shareholder: Azrar Ahmed Ghuman Begum
Officers: Azrar Ahmed Ghuman Begum [1981] Director [Spanish]

A and R Fine Wines Limited
Incorporated: 23 November 2012
Net Worth Deficit: £38 *Total Assets:* £446
Registered Office: 7 Dodgewell Close, Blackwell, Alfreton, Derbys, DE55 5BH
Major Shareholder: Catherine Suzanne Genevieve Quinlan
Officers: Roger Alan Poulter [1971] Finance Director; Catherine Suzanne Genevieve Quinlan [1977] Director/Strategic Manager [French]

A Di Maria & Sons Ltd
Incorporated: 22 February 2019
Registered Office: Colinton House, Leicester Road, Bedworth, Warwicks, CV12 8AB
Officers: Adriano di Maria [1992] Director; Antonio di Maria [1960] Director

A Little Bit of French Ltd
Incorporated: 13 November 2018
Registered Office: Hel Reed, Floor C, Milburn House, Dean Street, Newcastle upon Tyne, NE1 1LE
Major Shareholder: Carl Edward James McDonald
Officers: Carl Edward James McDonald [1971] Director/Seller of Wine

A Little Luxury Distillery Ltd
Incorporated: 23 January 2019
Registered Office: 20-22 Wenlock Road, London, N1 7GU
Shareholders: Barbara Ann Daughtrey; Laura Elizabeth Daughtrey
Officers: Barbara Ann Daughtrey, Secretary; Barbara Ann Daughtrey [1953] Director; Laura Elizabeth Daughtrey [1981] Director

A Taste of The Caribbean Ltd
Incorporated: 30 October 2015
Registered Office: 29 York Place, Edinburgh, EH1 3HP
Shareholders: Ian Hallam Gittens; Bryan John Rankin
Officers: Ian Hallam Gittens [1946] Director [Barbadian]; Bryan John Rankin [1945] Director/Chartered Accountant

A-Holding Ltd
Incorporated: 30 October 2017 *Employees:* 1
Net Worth Deficit: £3,714 *Total Assets:* £1,530
Registered Office: Ashcombe Court, Woolsack Way, Godalming, Surrey, GU7 1LQ
Major Shareholder: Anna Maria Biernikowicz
Officers: Anna Maria Biernikowicz [1988] Director [Polish]

A-Z Spirits Ltd
Incorporated: 10 February 2017
Registered Office: 78 Glenshamrock Drive, Auchinleck, Cumnock, E Ayrshire, KA18 2EF
Major Shareholder: Marcin Zajaczkowski
Officers: Neil Edward Medine [1970] Director/Trader; Tomasz Sitarek [1979] Director/Trader [Polish]; Marcin Zajaczkowski [1984] Director/Trader [Polish]

A. S. D. Wholesale Limited
Incorporated: 1 November 1995 *Employees:* 27
Net Worth: £1,670,371 *Total Assets:* £3,350,733
Registered Office: Brookside Way, Huthwaite, Sutton in Ashfield, Notts, NG17 2NL
Parent: A.S.D. WH Holdings Limited
Officers: Christopher Allan Eaton, Secretary; Steven Seaman [1965] Director/Wholesaler

A.F.T. (Liquor Stores) Limited
Incorporated: 19 January 1972 *Employees:* 34
Net Worth: £2,265,545 *Total Assets:* £4,953,725
Registered Office: 1st Floor, 34 B-D Main Street, Moira, Co Down, BT67 0LE
Shareholder: Milltate LLP
Officers: Michael Moynagh, Secretary; Floyd Damien Maguire [1962] Director [Irish]; Andrew Terence John Montague [1953] Director/Solicitor [Irish]; Michael Moynagh [1948] Managing Director [Irish]; Jane Maria Reihill [1959] Director [Irish]

A.I.M.S. (Refreshments) Limited
Incorporated: 17 October 1994
Net Worth: £584,223 *Total Assets:* £719,223
Registered Office: 11 Selden Road, Stockwood, Bristol, BS14 8PS
Shareholders: Andrew Philip Warren; Susan Warren
Officers: Susan Warren, Secretary; Andrew Philip Warren [1947] Managing Director

A1 Resources Limited
Incorporated: 11 April 2013
Net Worth Deficit: £729 *Total Assets:* £27,120
Registered Office: 2 Oak Lodge, 6 Oak Lodge Drive, West Wickham, Kent, BR4 0RQ
Major Shareholder: Stephen John Rose
Officers: Stephen John Rose, Secretary; Stephen John Rose [1958] Director/Chartered Accountant

A2Z Drinks Limited
Incorporated: 7 February 2018
Registered Office: 1 Chestnut Avenue, Buckhurst Hill, Essex, IG9 6EN
Officers: Catalin Ifrim [1978] Director [Romanian]

A2Z Wines & Groceries Ltd
Incorporated: 27 December 2017
Registered Office: 15 Back Queen Street, Leigh, Lancs, WN7 1BN
Shareholders: Michaela Ladicova; Michaela Ladicova; Michaela Ladicova; Michaela Ladicova
Officers: Michaela Ladicova [1993] Director [Slovak]

AB & R Import and Export Limited
Incorporated: 13 June 2017
Registered Office: Flat 28, 235 Hamstead Road, Great Barr, Birmingham, B43 5EL
Major Shareholder: Clifford Alphanso Robinson
Officers: Clifford Robinson [1965] Director/Night Patrol Officer [Jamaican]

AB Care Connect Limited
Incorporated: 18 November 2011
Previous: Quality Art Project Limited
Net Worth Deficit: £23,900 Total Assets: £18,865
Registered Office: 10 Hazeleigh Gardens, Woodford Green, Essex, IG8 8DX
Major Shareholder: Amir Mahmood
Officers: Amir Mahmood [1973] Director/Business Analyst [Australian]

ABA Eaglesham Ltd
Incorporated: 24 January 1958 Employees: 3
Net Worth Deficit: £75,165 Total Assets: £1,821,470
Registered Office: 168 Bath Street, Glasgow, G2 4TP
Officers: Alexander Bulloch [1927] Director; Carol Anne Jagielko [1956] Director; Henry John Jagielko [1952] Director; Audrey Jane Scott-Larsen [1959] Director/Secretary; Gail Irene Allan Smith [1957] Director/Wine Merchant

Ababio Express Limited
Incorporated: 14 May 2018
Registered Office: 75 Yale Road, Willenhall, W Midlands, WV13 2JR
Major Shareholder: Biggy Ababio
Officers: Biggy Ababio [1980] Director/Chief Executive

Abbey Brands Limited
Incorporated: 6 May 2014
Registered Office: 51 Welbeck Street, London, W1G 9HL
Major Shareholder: Michael Joseph Francis Claessens
Officers: Michael Joseph Francis Claessens [1993] Director [Dutch]

Aben Wines Limited
Incorporated: 6 October 1992
Net Worth: £8,321 Total Assets: £71,250
Registered Office: Dolphin House, 12 Beaumont Gate, Shenley Hill, Radlett, Herts, WD7 7AR
Officers: Denise Natalie Aben, Secretary; Denise Natalie Aben [1958] Director/Agent; Maurice Joseph Aben [1949] Director/Wine Merchant [French]

Abercrombie Fine Wines Limited
Incorporated: 27 June 2013 Employees: 4
Net Worth: £22,004 Total Assets: £31,898
Registered Office: 3rd Floor, Paternoster House, 65 St Paul's Churchyard, London, EC4M 8AB
Major Shareholder: Thomas Edward Bradshaw
Officers: Thomas Edward Bradshaw [1978] Director; James Hamilton Low [1976] Director; Duncan William Harold Thomson [1983] Director

Aberdrinks Scotland Limited
Incorporated: 23 April 2013
Net Worth Deficit: £3,916 Total Assets: £14,162
Registered Office: 21 Fairfield Street, Dundee, DD3 8HX
Shareholders: Paul Michael Stewart; Philip McCardel
Officers: Philip McCardel, Secretary; Philip Andrew McCardel [1954] Director; Keith Alexander Mudie [1974] Director; Paul Michael Stewart [1977] Director

Abloc UK Ltd
Incorporated: 8 June 2017
Net Worth Deficit: £2,810 Total Assets: £1,338
Registered Office: 3 The Studios, 320 Chorley Old Road, Bolton, Lancs, BL1 4JU
Officers: Alistair Frederick Stirling [1969] Director

Above Brand Limited
Incorporated: 17 February 2017
Net Worth Deficit: £3,962 Total Assets: £12,966
Registered Office: Davis Burton Williams and Co, Unit B11, Sutton Business Centre, Restmor Way, Wallington, Surrey, SM6 7AH
Major Shareholder: Francesca Martorelli
Officers: John Kirk Saunderson Elsden [1952] Director/Company Chairman; Francesca Martorelli [1985] Director/Creative Entrepreneur [Italian]

ABR Restaurant Group Ltd
Incorporated: 23 June 2017
Registered Office: Abra Wholesales Ltd, 5 Picketts Lock Lane, London, N9 0AS
Officers: Bhavani Thayananthan [1972] Director/Entrepreneur; Thuraichamy Thayananthan [1972] Director/Entrepreneur

Abra Export UK Limited
Incorporated: 22 June 2017
Registered Office: Abra Wholesales Ltd, 5 Picketts Lock Lane, London, N9 0AS
Officers: Bhavani Thayananthan [1972] Director/Entrepreneur; Thuraichamy Thayananthan [1972] Director/Entrepreneur

AbruzzoWines Ltd
Incorporated: 12 October 2018
Registered Office: 16 Eagle Heights, 6 Bramlands Close, London, SW11 2LJ
Major Shareholder: Daniel Di Pompo
Officers: Daniel di Pompo [1989] Director [Italian]

Absolute Wholesale Limited
Incorporated: 21 March 2017
Registered Office: Rowlands House, Portobello Road, Birtley, Chester-le-Street, Co Durham, DH3 2RY
Major Shareholder: Imran Hussain
Officers: Imran Hussain [1971] Director/Landlord/Property Manager

Absolutely Organic Limited
Incorporated: 7 September 2000
Registered Office: Bourton House, Lonsdale Court, Great Rollright, Chipping Norton, Oxon, OX7 5RB
Shareholder: Colin David Townsend Green
Officers: Rachel Ellen Townsend Green, Secretary/Clerical Assistant; Colin David Townsend Green [1961] Director/Chartered Building Surveyor; Rachel Ellen Townsend Green [1960] Director/Housewife

Abyss Brewing Ltd
Incorporated: 6 October 2016
Net Worth Deficit: £18,155 *Total Assets:* £53,799
Registered Office: Pelham Arms, High Street, Lewes, E Sussex, BN7 1XL
Officers: Andrew Daniel Bridge [1975] Director/Marketing; Andrew Peter Mellor [1971] Director/Publican & Brewing

Acacia Drinks Ltd
Incorporated: 27 May 2005
Registered Office: 32 Ashurst Drive, Ilford, Essex, IG2 6SB
Major Shareholder: Jagjit Singh Singh
Officers: Jagjit Singh Singh [1973] Director

Ace Incorporation Ltd
Incorporated: 15 February 2017
Registered Office: Tree Tops, Burtons Lane, Chalfont St Giles, Bucks, HP8 4BD
Officers: Seema Ganatra, Secretary; Mahek Ganatra [1996] Director/Economist

Aceo Limited
Incorporated: 6 September 1999 *Employees:* 22
Net Worth: £7,297,945 *Total Assets:* £7,907,415
Registered Office: Hillside Farm, Rodley, Westbury on Severn, Glos, GL14 1QZ
Major Shareholder: Edward Odim
Officers: Edward Odim [1958] Director/Whisky Broker

ACK Trading Ltd
Incorporated: 15 August 2017
Net Worth Deficit: £11,038 *Total Assets:* £1,966
Registered Office: 66 Norman Road, St Leonards on Sea, E Sussex, TN38 0EJ
Shareholders: Casaba Balogh; Katalin Foldesi
Officers: Csaba Balogh [1971] Director

Acod S & C Ltd
Incorporated: 16 May 2016
Net Worth Deficit: £4,718 *Total Assets:* £567
Registered Office: 37 Rosemary Road, Poole, Dorset, BH12 3HA
Shareholders: Silviu Sorin Acodrinesei; Constantim Catalim Acodrinesei
Officers: Silviu Sorin Acodrinesei [1976] Director [Romanian]

Adaka Group Ltd
Incorporated: 3 April 2017
Net Worth Deficit: £12,154 *Total Assets:* £10,525
Registered Office: 71-75 Shelton Street, London, WC2H 9JQ
Major Shareholder: Christopher Sosomadina Adaka
Officers: Christopher Sosomadina Adaka [1995] Director

Adam & Herv Limited
Incorporated: 26 April 2016
Net Worth Deficit: £8,376 *Total Assets:* £8,480
Registered Office: Greenway House, Sugarswell Business Park, Shenington, Banbury, Oxon, OX15 6HW
Shareholders: Adam Saletti; Herve Landry
Officers: Herve Landry [1952] Director/Merchant [French]; Adam Saletti [1981] Director/Merchant [Swedish]

Added Pressure Ltd
Incorporated: 16 March 2016
Registered Office: 107 Friars Wood, Croydon, Surrey, CR0 9JL
Shareholders: Shaun Gordon; Ashley Scott
Officers: Shaun Gordon [1971] Director/Sales; Ashley Scott [1987] Director/Operations

Wm.Addison (Newport) Limited
Incorporated: 21 June 1961 *Employees:* 11
Net Worth: £150,237 *Total Assets:* £811,503
Registered Office: 19-20 Cedar Court, Halesfield 17, Telford, Salop, TF7 4PF
Shareholders: David Howard Horton; Jonathan William Addison Horton
Officers: David Howard Horton, Secretary/Joint Managing Director; David Howard Horton [1969] Joint Managing Director; Jonathan William Addison Horton [1971] Joint Managing Director; Lesley Anne Horton [1944] Director

Adnams PLC
Incorporated: 24 March 1890 *Employees:* 203
Net Worth: £28,642,000 *Total Assets:* £64,708,000
Registered Office: East Green, Southwold, Suffolk, IP18 6JW
Officers: Elizabeth Sarah Cantwell, Secretary; Jonathan Adnams [1956] Director; Nicola Joy Dulieu [1963] Director; Michael Guy Hilliard Heald [1950] Director; Karen Hester [1962] Director; Bridget Fiona McIntyre [1961] Director; Stephen Crommelin Pugh [1958] Director; Dr Steven Michael Sharp [1950] Marketing Director; Andrew Charles Wood [1960] Director

Adonko Bitters (UK) Ltd
Incorporated: 2 January 2019
Registered Office: 2nd Floor, College House, 17 King Edwards Road, Ruislip, Middlesex, HA4 7AE
Shareholders: Eric Antwi Nuamah; Felix Kelvin Bryant; Kofi Samuels
Officers: Felix Kelvin Bryant, Secretary; Felix Kelvin Bryant [1970] Director/Financial Broker; Eric Antwi Nuamah [1977] Operational Director

ADP Wines Ltd
Incorporated: 25 January 2007
Net Worth: £73,651 *Total Assets:* £161,030
Registered Office: Foxhole Farm, Little Horwood Road, Winslow, Buckingham, MK18 3JW
Major Shareholder: Patrick Nicolas Rosin
Officers: Patrick Nicolas Rosin [1964] Director/Wine Merchant

Adventure Brands Ltd
Incorporated: 27 July 2018
Registered Office: Corner House, Luton Street, Keighley, W Yorks, BD21 2LE
Shareholders: Jayne Margaret Watmough; George Watmough
Officers: George Watmough [1948] Director; Jayne Margaret Watmough [1958] Director/Company Secretary

AFC Direct Ltd
Incorporated: 25 May 2016
Net Worth: £32,556 *Total Assets:* £83,765
Registered Office: 2 Devonia Cottages, St Marks Road, Binfield, Bracknell, Berks, RG42 4AT
Major Shareholder: Francesco Cinque
Officers: Francesco Cinque [1988] Director

Afco Traders Ltd
Incorporated: 28 December 2016
Net Worth Deficit: £1,482 *Total Assets:* £812
Registered Office: 13 Catherine Street, Oxford, OX4 3AQ
Shareholders: Arturo Felipe Albacete; David Albacete
Officers: Hipolito Albacete, Secretary; Arturo Felipe Albacete [1992] Director/Web Developer [Spanish]; Hipolito Felipe Albacete [1962] Director/Salesman [Spanish]; David Nicolas Albacete Fernandez [1995] Director [Spanish]

Afrogrocers Ltd
Incorporated: 3 March 2014
Net Worth: £16,772 *Total Assets:* £39,652
Registered Office: 38 Warren House Road, Allerton Bywater, W Yorks, WF10 2FB
Major Shareholder: Adeoluwa Joel Akande
Officers: Adeoluwa Joel Akande [1974] Director; Hannah Adejumoke Akande [1983] Director

After Eight Alcohol Concierge Ltd
Incorporated: 31 August 2018
Registered Office: 20-22 Wenlock Road, London, N1 7GU
Major Shareholder: Zavon Miller
Officers: Zavon Miller [1990] Director/Self Employed [Zimbabwean]

Aftersunset Ltd
Incorporated: 4 May 2017
Net Worth: £8,409 *Total Assets:* £9,659
Registered Office: 25 Sirius Building, 3 Jardine Road, London, E1W 3WE
Shareholders: Jose Antonio Moreno Costa; Yoze Torres Martin
Officers: Jose Antonio Moreno Costa [1984] Director/Hospitality [Spanish]

Afterthought Spirits Company Ltd
Incorporated: 30 January 2018
Registered Office: Unit 43 Henfield Business Park, Henfield, W Sussex, BN5 9SL
Parent: Afterthought Group Ltd
Officers: Douglas Walford [1977] Director/Engineer

Agave Partners Limited
Incorporated: 28 February 2018
Registered Office: The White House, Clifton Marine Parade, Gravesend, Kent, DA11 0DY
Shareholder: Indie Spirits Limited
Officers: Douglas Brougham Cunningham [1968] Director

Agave Thieves Ltd
Incorporated: 17 May 2016
Registered Office: Greenlooms House, Martins Lane, Hargrave, Chester, CH3 7RX
Shareholders: Andrew Charles Lowe-Smith; Benjamin Richard Iles
Officers: Benjamin Richard Iles [1982] Director; Andrew Charles Lowe-Smith [1986] Director

Agave Union Limited
Incorporated: 8 March 2017
Net Worth: £100 *Total Assets:* £100
Registered Office: 163 Bath Street, Glasgow, G2 4SQ
Parent: Brougham Investments Limited
Officers: Andrew Douglas Bratten [1963] Director

Agencia Ltd
Incorporated: 11 February 2019
Registered Office: 20-22 Wenlock Road, London, N1 7GU
Major Shareholder: Shamsher Singh
Officers: Shamsher Singh [1964] Director

Agro Investment Ltd
Incorporated: 29 April 2015
Net Worth: £220,946 *Total Assets:* £943,864
Registered Office: 89 Worship Street, London, EC2A 2BF
Major Shareholder: Guido Andretta
Officers: Guido Andretta [1960] Director [Italian]

Agrosale UK Limited
Incorporated: 19 September 2016
Net Worth Deficit: £13,487
Registered Office: 2 Cricket Court, Hackenden Lane, East Grinstead, W Sussex, RH19 3DN
Major Shareholder: Alikhan Ali-Zade
Officers: Alikhan Ali-Zade [1964] Managing Director

AGS Vintners Limited
Incorporated: 12 January 2015
Net Worth: £6,274 *Total Assets:* £145,297
Registered Office: The Mill, Pury Hill Business Park, Alderton Road, Towcester, Northants, NN12 7LS
Shareholders: Saimir Haxhijani; Gentian Haxhijani
Officers: Saimir Haxhijani [1985] Director [Italian]

AGT Professional Services Limited
Incorporated: 24 October 2016
Registered Office: 52 Hoylake Drive, Farcet, Peterborough, PE7 3BE
Major Shareholder: Alain Gourou
Officers: Alain Gourou [1962] Director/Wine Trader [Ivorian]

Agua Piedra Mezcal & Co Ltd
Incorporated: 23 August 2016
Registered Office: 60 Tottenham Court Road, London, W1T 2EW
Major Shareholder: David Celso Eduardo Santillan Giles
Officers: David Celso Eduardo Santillan Giles [1988] Director/Business Management [Mexican]

Aims & Co Ltd
Incorporated: 15 April 2013
Net Worth Deficit: £18,033 *Total Assets:* £594
Registered Office: 84 Katherine Road, London, E6 1EN
Major Shareholder: Iftikhar Ahmed
Officers: Iftikhar Ahmed [1975] Director/Self Employed [Pakistani]

Airways Bonded Warehouse Limited
Incorporated: 24 January 1994
Registered Office: MacDonald House, 1 Lowfield Way, Lowfield Heath, Crawley, W Sussex, RH11 0PW
Shareholders: Gordon Ian Sankey; Barry Howard Smart
Officers: Deborah Gould, Secretary; Gordon Ian Sankey [1959] Director; Stephen Robert Wescott [1959] Director

Aizia Ltd
Incorporated: 20 March 2014
Net Worth: £26,054 *Total Assets:* £57,159
Registered Office: 3 Summerlay Close, Kingswood, Tadworth, Surrey, KT20 6HE
Officers: Mirjana Berecic-Hall [1968] Marketing Director

AK Cash & Carry Ltd
Incorporated: 21 January 2013
Net Worth Deficit: £6,877 *Total Assets:* £61,778
Registered Office: Unit 12 Merthyr Tydfil Industrial Park, Pentrebach, Merthyr Tydfil, CF48 4DR
Major Shareholder: Daljit Singh
Officers: Daljit Singh [1964] Director

AKM Trading Services Ltd
Incorporated: 17 September 2009 *Employees:* 2
Net Worth Deficit: £25,623 *Total Assets:* £109,015
Registered Office: Churchill House, 120 Bunns Lane, London, NW7 2AS
Shareholders: Costas Symeou; Andrew Anastasi Symeou
Officers: Constantine Symeou, Secretary; Andrew Symeou [1981] Director/Logistics Manager; Constantine Symeou [1984] Director/Buyer

AKS Brands Limited
Incorporated: 27 September 2017
Net Worth Deficit: £6,222 *Total Assets:* £2,860
Registered Office: 81 Bellegrove Road, Welling, Kent, DA16 3PG
Major Shareholder: Alison Alison Sawyer
Officers: Alison Sawyer [1976] Director

Al & Lu (UK) Ltd
Incorporated: 6 September 2018
Registered Office: 10 Coptic Street, London, WC1A 1NH
Major Shareholder: Mingxiang Chang
Officers: Mingxiang Chang [1983] Director [Chinese]

Al Liver Management Limited
Incorporated: 14 May 2018
Registered Office: 272 Bath Street, Glasgow, G2 4JR
Major Shareholder: Malkit Singh Bharj
Officers: Malkit Singh Bharj [1964] Director/Actor

Albert Altima Trade House Limited
Incorporated: 6 March 2017
Registered Office: 21 Pinder Road, Norwich, NR3 2EG
Major Shareholder: Vladislav Cudalb
Officers: Vladislav Cudalb [1986] Director/General Manager [Romanian]

Albion Distillery Ltd
Incorporated: 28 June 2018
Registered Office: 6-8 Bonhill Street, London, EC2A 4BX
Officers: Richard Mahoney [1986] Director/Accountant

Albion Fine Wines Ltd
Incorporated: 16 February 1998
Net Worth: £29,151 *Total Assets:* £52,583
Registered Office: 9 Mansfield Street, London, W1G 9NY
Shareholder: Susan Fiona Fotheringham
Officers: Laurentius Johannes Roosloot, Secretary; Phillip Amery [1956] Director; Susan Fiona Fotheringham [1956] Director/Education Consultant

Albion Gin Ltd
Incorporated: 28 June 2018
Registered Office: 51 The Maples, Harlow, Essex, CM19 4QZ
Major Shareholder: Harrison Aldrich Green
Officers: Harrison Aldrich Green [1997] Director/Chief Executive

Albion Wine Shippers Limited
Incorporated: 3 July 1986 *Employees:* 6
Net Worth: £274,697 *Total Assets:* £1,101,207
Registered Office: 9 Mansfield Street, London, W1G 9NY
Major Shareholder: Phillip Amery
Officers: Phillip Amery, Secretary; Phillip Amery [1956] Director/Retail Manager

Alchemist Brewery Limited
Incorporated: 11 March 2013
Registered Office: Beech House, 4A Newmarket Road, Cambridge, CB5 8DT
Major Shareholder: Alan Paul Chorlton
Officers: Dr Alan Paul Chorlton [1956] Director

Alchemy Drinks Ltd.
Incorporated: 26 February 2014 *Employees:* 29
Net Worth: £235,013 *Total Assets:* £2,202,683
Registered Office: Alchemy House, 28 Abbotsinch Road, Grangemouth, Stirlingshire, FK3 9UX
Major Shareholder: Thomas McMillan
Officers: Michael Joseph McShane, Secretary; Thomas McMillan [1972] Director/Business Executive; Michael Joseph McShane [1982] Director

Alchemy Inns Limited
Incorporated: 6 August 2001 *Employees:* 2
Net Worth: £2,194,748 *Total Assets:* £4,784,856
Registered Office: Alchemy House, 28 Abbotsinch Road, Grangemouth, Stirlingshire, FK3 9UX
Major Shareholder: Thomas McMillan
Officers: Michael Joseph McShane, Secretary; Thomas McMillan [1972] Director; Michael Joseph McShane [1982] Operations Director

Alcofrolics Ltd
Incorporated: 11 December 2018
Registered Office: 25 Cornwall Road, London, N4 4PH
Major Shareholder: Deborah Henry
Officers: Deborah Henry [1978] Director/Entrepreneur

Alcohol By Volume Limited
Incorporated: 20 January 2003
Net Worth: £159,086 *Total Assets:* £205,551
Registered Office: Springfields, 25 Three Springs Road, Pershore, Worcs, WR10 1HR
Major Shareholder: Ronald John Mackie
Officers: Jennifer Trethewey, Secretary; Ronald John Mackie [1947] Director/Sales Consultant

Alcohollect Ltd
Incorporated: 23 May 2018
Registered Office: 35 High Street, Wollaston, Wellingborough, Northants, NN29 7QE
Officers: Jason Paul Jordan [1980] Director/Project Manager

Alcohology Ltd
Incorporated: 10 September 2014
Net Worth Deficit: £1,166 *Total Assets:* £32,597
Registered Office: 3 The Old Brewery Yard, High Street, Falmouth, Cornwall, TR11 2BY
Major Shareholder: Peter Walker
Officers: Peter Walker [1972] Managing Director

Alcos Trade Limited
Incorporated: 29 November 2018
Registered Office: 30 Berkeley Street, Scunthorpe, N Lincs, DN15 6BJ
Major Shareholder: Lukasz Piorecki
Officers: Lukasz Piorecki [1977] Director [Polish]

The Ale Trader Ltd
Incorporated: 16 June 2017
Registered Office: 29 Marshall Drive, Pickering, N Yorks, YO18 7JT
Major Shareholder: Paul Littlewood
Officers: Paul Littlewood [1968] Managing Director

Alegri Trade Ltd.
Incorporated: 4 December 2017
Registered Office: 33 Springfield Road, Welling, Kent, DA16 1QN
Officers: Alexandru Aftinescu [1989] Director/Employee [Romanian]; Grigore Spac [1987] Director/Self Employed [Romanian]

Aleksic & Mortimer Ltd
Incorporated: 30 May 2008 Employees: 1
Net Worth Deficit: £28,218 Total Assets: £34,415
Registered Office: 109 Petherton Road, London, N5 2RS
Major Shareholder: Dragan Aleksic
Officers: Jocelyn Frances Pook, Secretary; Dragan Aleksic [1963] Director/Sculptor [Dutch]

Ales. R. Russ Limited
Incorporated: 11 October 2010
Net Worth: £25,065 Total Assets: £149,730
Registered Office: Unit 19 Longford Road Industrial Estate, Longford Road, Cannock, Staffs, WS11 0DG
Shareholder: Stephen John Russell
Officers: Sandra Glenys Russell [1950] Director; Stephen John Russell [1954] Director; Stuart Stephen Russell [1990] Director

David Alexander Wine Merchants Maidenhead Limited
Incorporated: 27 August 1987
Net Worth: £384 Total Assets: £3,422
Registered Office: Wedgewood, Cricket Green Lane, Hartley Wintney, Hook, Hants, RG27 8PH
Major Shareholder: David Franklin Thomas Wright
Officers: David Franklin Thomas Wright, Secretary; Martin Alexander Sloots [1957] Director; David Franklin Thomas Wright [1958] Director

Alexander Wines Ltd.
Incorporated: 7 March 2012 Employees: 14
Net Worth: £56,108 Total Assets: £582,193
Registered Office: Abercorn House, 79 Renfrew Road, Paisley, Renfrewshire, PA3 4DA
Parent: Dunns Food & Drinks Limited
Officers: Fraser Douglas Alexander [1956] Director/Wholesale Wine Merchant; Victoria Ruth Beckett [1978] Director; Julie Frances Dunn [1967] Director; Paul Alexander Graham [1980] Director; James Columba Rowan [1959] Director

Alexandria Partners Limited
Incorporated: 11 May 2012
Net Worth: £1,665 Total Assets: £2,074
Registered Office: 26 Inverness Mews, Fishguard Way, London, E16 2SP
Major Shareholder: Sebahattin Yildirim
Officers: Regimantas Mauragas [1986] Director [Lithuanian]; Sebahattin Yildirim [1967] Director [Turkish]

Alf Vini Limited
Incorporated: 7 September 2010
Net Worth Deficit: £4,650 Total Assets: £3,632
Registered Office: 33 Dukes Drive, Chesterfield, Derbys, S41 8QB
Major Shareholder: Alfonso Santoro
Officers: Alfonso Santoro [1951] Director [Italian]

Alfa Drinks Limited
Incorporated: 20 July 2017
Registered Office: 70 Seabourne Road, Bournemouth, BH5 2HT
Shareholders: Simon Preston; Wiebke Hertzenberg
Officers: Wiebke Hertzenberg [1977] Director [German]; Simon Preston [1975] Director

Algebra Drinks Ltd
Incorporated: 12 September 2014
Net Worth Deficit: £37,678 Total Assets: £7,979
Registered Office: Algebra Drinks Ltd, 20-22 Wenlock Road, London, N1 7GU
Shareholders: Yves Cosentino; Amarilla Ltd
Officers: Yves Cosentino [1974] Director [French]

Algodon Europe Limited
Incorporated: 23 September 2009
Net Worth Deficit: £355,475 Total Assets: £74,517
Registered Office: Market House, 10 Market Walk, Saffron Walden, Essex, CB10 1JZ
Parent: Algodon Wines & Luxury Development Group Inc
Officers: Anthony Charles Foster, Secretary; Anthony Charles Foster [1943] Director/Master of Wines; Peter Jessel Levay Lawrence [1933] Director

Ali Booze Company Limited
Incorporated: 7 March 2017 Employees: 4
Net Worth Deficit: £26,487 Total Assets: £9,169
Registered Office: 317 East Prescott Road, Knotty Ash, Liverpool, L14 2DD
Major Shareholder: Ali Safavand
Officers: Ali Safavand [1972] Director/Manager [Iranian]

Alice Wholesale Trading Limited
Incorporated: 13 October 2009
Net Worth: £298,573 Total Assets: £461,258
Registered Office: Tariff Works, Tariff Road, London, N17 0DY
Shareholder: Huseyin Dogan
Officers: Huseyin Dogan [1964] Director/Manager

Alinari Ltd
Incorporated: 11 January 2019
Registered Office: Kemp House, 160 City Road, London, EC1V 2NX
Shareholders: Riccardo Scaramelli; David Marcus
Officers: David Marcus [1986] Director; Riccardo Scaramelli [1975] Director [Italian]

Alivini (North) Limited
Incorporated: 14 December 1993 Employees: 13
Net Worth: £303,136 Total Assets: £1,077,817
Registered Office: Units 2 and 3, 199 Eade Road, London, N4 1DN
Parent: Franciacorta Limited
Officers: Stephen Dennis Bridgeman, Secretary; Stephen Dennis Bridgeman [1942] Director; Custudio Jose Dos Santos [1957] Director/Wine & Food Importer [Portuguese]; Jose de Nobrega Pires [1956] Director/Wine & Food Importer [Portuguese]; Antonio Pirozzi [1943] Director; Maria Vitoria Santos-Pires [1960] Director/Financier [Portuguese]; Gianni Segatta [1945] Director

Alivini Company Limited
Incorporated: 12 February 1985 Employees: 84
Net Worth: £4,616,283 Total Assets: £6,575,749
Registered Office: Units 2 and 3, 199 Eade Road, London, N4 1DN
Parent: Franciacorta Limited
Officers: Stephen Dennis Bridgeman, Secretary; Stephen Dennis Bridgeman [1942] Director; Custudio Jose Dos Santos [1957] Director/Wine & Food Importer [Portuguese]; Jose de Nobrega Pires [1956] Director/Wine & Food Importer [Portuguese]; Antonio Pirozzi [1943] Director; Maria Vitoria Santos-Pires [1960] Director/Financier [Portuguese]; Gianni Segatta [1945] Director/Wine & Food Importer

Alko Vintages UK Ltd
Incorporated: 19 April 2018
Registered Office: 71-75 Shelton Street, Covent Garden, London, WC2H 9JQ
Shareholders: Archard Lwihula Kati; Elkanah Ondieki Oenga
Officers: Archard Lwihula Kato [1960] Director [New Zealander]; Elkanah Ondieki Oenga [1984] Director [Kenyan]

Alky Limited
Incorporated: 2 May 2017
Registered Office: Tankard Wealth, Regus Office, 2 Tallis Street, London, EC4Y 0AB
Major Shareholder: Nicolai Hald
Officers: Nicolai Hald [1992] Director/Self Employed [Danish]; Jack David Smith [1997] Director/Student

All Drinks Cash & Carry Limited
Incorporated: 7 July 2016
Net Worth Deficit: £170,340 *Total Assets:* £416,958
Registered Office: c/o JSP Accountants Limited, First Floor, 10 College Road, Harrow, Middlesex, HA1 1BE
Shareholders: Kulwant Singh Gulati; Ajit Singh Chawla
Officers: Ajit Singh Chawla [1975] Director; Kulwant Singh Gulati [1966] Director

All English Distribution Ltd.
Incorporated: 25 September 2017
Registered Office: Flat 3, 31 The Avenue, Eastbourne, E Sussex, BN21 3YD
Officers: Patrick Guy Armstrong Carey [1972] Director/Entrepreneur

All Food Supplies Ltd
Incorporated: 19 February 2010 *Employees:* 3
Net Worth: £9,803 *Total Assets:* £21,710
Registered Office: 28 Marlyon Road, Ilford, Essex, IG6 3XN
Major Shareholder: Dhusyanthan Kanapathipillai
Officers: Dhusyanthan Kanapathipillai [1970] Director/Manager

All Market Europe Limited
Incorporated: 26 November 2009 *Employees:* 81
Net Worth: £2,711,573 *Total Assets:* £19,229,848
Registered Office: 2nd Floor, 55 Charterhouse Street, London, EC1M 6HA
Officers: Giles Thomas Turner Brook [1974] Director/CEO All Market Europe Ltd; Michael Kirban [1975] Director [American]

Alliance Foods Limited
Incorporated: 20 December 2011
Previous: First International Trading Limited
Net Worth: £4,185,969 *Total Assets:* £5,176,621
Registered Office: 86-90 Paul Street, London, EC2A 4NE
Officers: Dr Bilal Rana [1976] Director/Certified Chartered Accountant

Alliance Wine Company Limited
Incorporated: 29 October 1984 *Employees:* 69
Net Worth: £2,101,824 *Total Assets:* £12,006,068
Registered Office: 7 Beechfield Road, Willowyard Estate, Beith, N Ayrshire, KA15 1LN
Officers: Christian Bouteiller, Secretary; Christian Bouteiller [1958] Managing Director; Giles Cooke [1971] Sales Director; Karen Cunningham [1966] Administration Director; Charles Jonathan Kennett [1947] Director/Engineer; Miriam Spiers [1966] Director; Fergal Tynan [1972] Director [Irish]

Allied Ship Supplies (Ireland) Limited
Incorporated: 10 August 1998 *Employees:* 4
Net Worth: £850,928 *Total Assets:* £1,248,146
Registered Office: Unit 6 MacLean Road, Campsie, Co Derry, BT47 3XX
Major Shareholder: Owen Deehan
Officers: Lisa Brennan, Secretary; Owen Deehan [1965] Director

Allied Wholesale Ltd
Incorporated: 17 March 2017
Net Worth Deficit: £13,697 *Total Assets:* £29,398
Registered Office: Unit 25 Winterpick Business Park, Hurstpierpoint Road, Wineham, Henfield, W Sussex, BN5 9BJ
Major Shareholder: Jacob Sunny Abraham
Officers: Jacob Sunny Abraham [1986] Director [Indian]

Allson Sparkle Limited
Incorporated: 19 September 1984 *Employees:* 54
Net Worth: £5,053,407 *Total Assets:* £7,289,341
Registered Office: Unit S and Warehouse 5, Telford Road, Eastfield Industrial Estate, Glenrothes, Fife, KY7 4NX
Shareholders: Nicola Drysdale; Colin Jonathon Drysdale
Officers: Colin Jonathon Drysdale [1966] Executive Director; Nicola Drysdale [1969] Director

Allt A' Bhainne Distillery Limited
Incorporated: 17 August 2001
Previous: Chivas Brothers (Americas) Limited
Registered Office: 111-113 Renfrew Road, Paisley, Renfrewshire, PA3 4DY
Parent: Chivas Holdings (IP) Limited
Officers: Stuart MacNab [1964] Director/Accountant; Vincent Turpin [1978] Director/Chief Financial Officer [French]

Allum Limited
Incorporated: 6 June 1991
Net Worth Deficit: £30,458 *Total Assets:* £47,452
Registered Office: Bassetts, 107 Power Road, London, W4 5PY
Shareholder: Paul Justus Higgins
Officers: Paul Justus Higgins, Secretary; Paul Justus Higgins [1971] Director/Company Secretary; Hershey Tiffin [1978] Director/Sales

Almaster Limited
Incorporated: 23 May 2018
Registered Office: 24 Marlborough Crescent, Sevenoaks, Kent, TN13 2HP
Shareholder: Maciej Wodke
Officers: Maciej Wodke [1973] Director; Monika Wodke [1974] Director

Alpha Whisky Ltd
Incorporated: 26 September 2018
Registered Office: 14 South Trinity Road, Edinburgh, EH5 3NR
Major Shareholder: Alan MacDonald Watt
Officers: Alan MacDonald Watt [1966] Director/Chartered Accountant

Altamira Management Services Limited
Incorporated: 31 March 2016 *Employees:* 2
Net Worth: £143 *Total Assets:* £2,769
Registered Office: Pound House, 62A Highgate High Street, London, N6 5HX
Shareholders: Karen Ann Macadam; Richard Desmond Macadam
Officers: Karen Ann Macadam [1955] Director/Personal Assistant; Richard Desmond Macadam [1957] Director

Altar Wines Limited
Incorporated: 17 February 2017
Net Worth: £169 Total Assets: £5,131
Registered Office: 128 Leyfield Road, Liverpool, L12 9HB
Major Shareholder: Brendan Michael Gallagher
Officers: Helen Gallagher, Secretary; Brendan Michael Gallagher [1966] Director/Teacher

The Alternative Rum Company Limited
Incorporated: 15 December 2004 Employees: 2
Net Worth: £602 Total Assets: £3,512
Registered Office: 46 Hamilton Square, Birkenhead, Merseyside, CH41 5AR
Shareholder: Benjamine John Cross de Chevannes
Officers: Benjamine John Cross de Chavannes [1938] Director; Pauline Strahan [1950] Director

Always 20 Limited
Incorporated: 20 April 2018
Registered Office: 71-75 Shelton Street, London, WC2H 9JQ
Major Shareholder: Cheung Sai Mui
Officers: Cheung Sai Mui, Secretary; Cheung Sai Mui [1955] Director [Chinese]

Always Available Ltd
Incorporated: 26 October 2016
Registered Office: 26 Thorney Lane South, Iver, Bucks, SL0 9AE
Shareholders: Rajesh Batavia; Rajesh Batavia
Officers: Rajesh Batavia [1959] Director

Amarri Prosecco Limited
Incorporated: 20 July 2016
Registered Office: Unit 5 Parkburn Court, Parkburn Industrial Estate, Hamilton, S Lanarks, ML3 0QQ
Major Shareholder: Angela Maria Lynas
Officers: Angela Maria Lynas [1966] Director/Wholesaler

Amathus Drinks PLC
Incorporated: 30 December 1982 Employees: 233
Net Worth: £14,834,015 Total Assets: £30,882,864
Registered Office: 309 Elveden Road, Ealing, London, NW10 7ST
Shareholder: Chariton Platon Georgiou
Officers: Loucia Machlouzarides, Secretary; Chariton Platon Georgiou [1960] Director; Isabella Ava Georgiou [1987] Director; Loucia Machlouzarides [1974] Director

Amayan Terroir Selections Ltd
Incorporated: 29 December 2015
Net Worth: £1 Total Assets: £1
Registered Office: Stuart Norton, 17 Coningsby Road, Nottingham, NG5 4LG
Major Shareholder: Stephen Huse
Officers: Stephen Huse [1985] Director/Entrepreneur [French]

Ambal Fuel Ltd
Incorporated: 13 June 2017
Registered Office: 180 Lyon Park Avenue, Wembley, Middlesex, HA0 4HG
Major Shareholder: Pragash Loganathan
Officers: Pragash Loganathan [1981] Director

Ambassador Commodities Ltd
Incorporated: 5 October 2018
Registered Office: 46 Nova Road, Croydon, Surrey, CR0 2TL
Major Shareholder: Vito Marino
Officers: Ciro Gallo [1969] Director/Consultant [Italian]; Vito Marino [1978] Director/Consultant [Italian]

Ambessa Goods Ltd
Incorporated: 19 February 2018
Registered Office: 50 Novello Street, London, SW6 4JB
Shareholders: Maria Eugenia Planella Ferrer; Tudor David Rees-Williams
Officers: Maria Eugenia Planella Ferrer [1993] Director [Spanish]; Tudor David Rees-Williams [1991] Director/Importation and Distribution of Wine

AMC Trading Co Ltd
Incorporated: 15 March 2018
Registered Office: 272 Bath Street, Glasgow, G2 4JR
Major Shareholder: Alan McNaughton
Officers: Alan McNaughton, Secretary; Alan McNaughton [1984] Director

American Fizz (UK) Limited
Incorporated: 28 July 2011 Employees: 35
Net Worth: £1,090,945 Total Assets: £1,947,009
Registered Office: The Saxon Centre, 11 Bargates, Christchurch, Dorset, BH23 1PZ
Major Shareholder: Gholam Reza Aghajanzadeh-Langaroody
Officers: Gholam Reza Aghajanzadeh-Langaroody [1958] Director [Iranian]

Amirante Empire Limited
Incorporated: 23 June 2014
Net Worth Deficit: £5,485 Total Assets: £31,022
Registered Office: 11 Pine Walk, Uckfield, E Sussex, TN22 1TU
Shareholders: Esteban Amirante; Maria Lorena Zarate Avila
Officers: Esteban Amirante [1970] Director [Italian]; Maria Lorena Zarate Avila [1973] Director [Spanish]

Amis Trading Limited
Incorporated: 8 September 2010 Employees: 2
Net Worth: £468,371 Total Assets: £531,106
Registered Office: 36 Wattleton Road, Beaconsfield, Bucks, HP9 1SE
Shareholders: Imane Soussi; Abid Mahmood
Officers: Abid Mahmood [1979] Director; Imane Soussi [1986] Director

Amish Wholesalers Limited
Incorporated: 12 March 2008
Net Worth: £1,876,742 Total Assets: £3,572,830
Registered Office: Charter House, 8-10 Station Road, London, E12 5BT
Major Shareholder: Amish Thakkar
Officers: Amish Thakkar [1986] Director

AMK Distribution Ltd
Incorporated: 29 February 2016 Employees: 9
Net Worth Deficit: £22,557 Total Assets: £126,099
Registered Office: 13 Hailey Road, Erith, Kent, DA18 4AA
Shareholders: Dil Bahadur Thapa; Ishor Jung Gurung
Officers: Ishor Jung Gurung [1978] Director [Nepalese]

AMK Wholesale Ltd
Incorporated: 27 March 2002
Net Worth: £13,921 Total Assets: £193,212
Registered Office: Cambridge House, 27 Cambridge Park, Wanstead, London, E11 2PU
Officers: Dennis Saunders, Secretary; Angela Marie King [1954] Director

Amore G.N.A. Limited
Incorporated: 13 September 2016
Net Worth Deficit: £9,647 *Total Assets:* £9,171
Registered Office: 15 Niton Road, Nuneaton, Warwicks, CV10 0BX
Shareholders: Nicola Albanese; Giovanni Albanese
Officers: Giovanni Albanese [1977] Director/Engineer; Nicola Albanese [1980] Director/Hairdresser [Italian]; Vaughan Williams [1976] Director

Amphora Portfolio Management Limited
Incorporated: 12 February 2009 *Employees:* 4
Net Worth Deficit: £390,944 *Total Assets:* £1,204,884
Registered Office: 5 Fitzroy Square, London, W1T 5HH
Shareholder: David Jackson
Officers: James Grey Oliver Fletcher [1979] Director/Wine Merchant; David Jackson [1970] Director/Wine Merchant; Mike Steuart [1958] Director/Chartered Accountant

Amwell Springs Brewery Company Limited
Incorporated: 19 July 2017
Net Worth Deficit: £6,347 *Total Assets:* £33,156
Registered Office: Westfield Farm House, Westfield Road, Cholsey, Wallingford, Oxon, OX10 9LS
Officers: Andrew William Gibbons [1982] Director; David Ernest Gibbons [1951] Director; Michael David Gibbons [1979] Director; Thomas James Hammond [1982] Director; Darren Rudkin Pavitt [1967] Director

Amy's Wine House Limited
Incorporated: 15 March 2016 *Employees:* 3
Net Worth: £7,119 *Total Assets:* £25,570
Registered Office: 31 Coronation Drive, Crosby, Liverpool, L23 3BN
Major Shareholder: Elizabeth Mary Jones
Officers: Elizabeth Mary Jones [1983] Director

ANA Distribution Limited
Incorporated: 20 April 2012 *Employees:* 3
Net Worth: £12,735 *Total Assets:* £20,204
Registered Office: 46 Houghton Place, Bradford, W Yorks, BD1 3RG
Major Shareholder: Muhammed Akeel Parvez
Officers: Mohammed Akeel Parvez [1973] Director/Manager

Ana Express Ltd
Incorporated: 25 August 2018
Registered Office: 89 Tooting High Street, London, SW17 0SP
Major Shareholder: Elena Crecan
Officers: Elena Crecan [1968] Director [Romanian]

Anderson Beverages Ltd
Incorporated: 17 October 2017
Registered Office: 38 Sloan Street, Edinburgh, EH6 8PH
Shareholders: Caitlin Sian Anderson; Chloe Dawn Anderson
Officers: Caitlin Sian Anderson [1990] Director/Sales; Chloe Dawn Anderson [1998] Director/Administration

Andes Trading Limited
Incorporated: 9 March 2007
Net Worth Deficit: £36,359 *Total Assets:* £47,639
Registered Office: Exchange Building, 66 Church Street, Hartlepool, Cleveland, TS24 7DN
Shareholders: Robert Smedley; Robert Bryan Smedley
Officers: Robert Bryan Smedley [1986] Director; Robert Smedley [1951] Director

Andina Trade Ltd
Incorporated: 4 April 2016
Net Worth Deficit: £9,500 *Total Assets:* £20,277
Registered Office: 10 Field Street, Shepshed, Loughborough, Leics, LE12 9AL
Shareholders: Joaquin Meier; Monica Violeta Carreras Oliva
Officers: Monica Violeta Carreras Oliva [1970] Director [Spanish]; Joaquin Meier [1971] Director [German]

Andreev Services Ltd
Incorporated: 10 May 2007 *Employees:* 1
Net Worth Deficit: £21,681 *Total Assets:* £2,623
Registered Office: Flat 21, Glenrose House, 2 Benhill Wood Road, Sutton, Surrey, SM1 4HT
Major Shareholder: Andrey Andreev
Officers: Andrey Ivanov Andreev [1972] Director/Businessman [Bulgarian]

Andrews Beer & Mineral Company Limited
Incorporated: 14 June 2006 *Employees:* 13
Net Worth: £1,587,583 *Total Assets:* £1,780,222
Registered Office: 46 Northdown Road, Cliftonville, Margate, Kent, CT9 2RW
Shareholders: Jonathan Charles Ellis; Julian Ellis; Anthony Ellis; Denise Ellis
Officers: Anthony Ellis [1950] Director/Wholesaler; Denise Ellis [1956] Director/Wholesaler; Jonathan Charles Ellis [1983] Director/Wholesale Buyer & Representative; Julian Ellis [1980] Director/Transport and Office Manager

Andris Holdings Limited
Incorporated: 30 July 2018
Registered Office: 80 Long Acre, London, WC2E 9NG
Major Shareholder: Andris Praulitis
Officers: Andris Praulitis [1985] Director [Latvian]

Angel Feathers Limited
Incorporated: 5 July 2018
Registered Office: Oldfield, Forestry Road, Llanferres, Mold, Flintshire, CH7 5SH
Shareholders: Katharine Wilding; Mark Steven Wilding
Officers: Katharine Wilding [1968] Director; Mark Steven Wilding [1969] Director

Angel Wine & Spirit Group Co., Ltd.
Incorporated: 15 November 2017
Registered Office: Chase Business Centre, 39-41 Chase Side, London, N14 5BP
Major Shareholder: Chun-Kuang Tu
Officers: Chun-Kuang TU [1976] Director [Taiwanese]

Angeli Del Vino Limited
Incorporated: 25 August 2016
Net Worth Deficit: £3,691 *Total Assets:* £5,022
Registered Office: 22 Trentlea Way, Sandbach, Cheshire, CW11 3AZ
Shareholders: Johanna Gunn; Katie Elizabeth Webb
Officers: Johanna Gunn [1972] Director/Self Employed; Katie Elizabeth Webb [1980] Director/Assessor

Anglium Ltd
Incorporated: 24 March 2006 *Employees:* 1
Net Worth Deficit: £115,796 *Total Assets:* £30,590
Registered Office: Westwood House, Annie Med Lane, South Cave, Brough, N Humbers, HU15 2HG
Shareholders: Lodewijk Jozef Vleugels; Katrien Vleugels
Officers: Lodewijk Vleugels [1950] Director/Teacher [Belgian]

Anglo Drinks Limited
Incorporated: 3 September 1999 Employees: 3
Net Worth Deficit: £682,621 Total Assets: £40,098
Registered Office: Unit 6a Wakes Hall Business Centre, Colchester Road, Wakes Colne, Colchester, Essex, CO6 2DY
Parent: Standy Holdings Limited
Officers: Andrew Neil Howe, Secretary; Stuart Charles Davis [1970] Director/Sales Manager; Andrew Neil Howe [1966] Accounts Director

Anglo-African Trade Limited
Incorporated: 15 March 1995
Net Worth Deficit: £4,741 Total Assets: £323
Registered Office: 17 Neal Corner, 2 Bath Road, Hounslow, Middlesex, TW3 3HJ
Officers: Diana Rani Sirichand Jethwani [1982] Director/Finance Senior Manager; Meera Sirichand Jethwani [1945] Director/Housewife; Rajendra Sirichand Jethwani [1977] Director/Businessman; Sirichand Narumal Jethwani [1940] Director/Businessman; Kuravakalyil Thomas Thomas [1939] Director/Company Executive

Anglocolombian Ltd
Incorporated: 26 May 2015
Registered Office: 20 South Road, Weymouth, Dorset, DT4 9NR
Officers: Monica Avellaneda [1981] Director/Export/Distribution [Colombian]; Thomas Edward Ballard [1983] Director/Export/Distribution; Timothy Edward Ballard [1958] Director/Bricklayer

Angola Beverages Holding Company Limited
Incorporated: 12 April 2017
Registered Office: Avalon House, 72 Lower Mortlake Road, Richmond, Surrey, TW9 2JY
Parent: Distell International Holdings Limited
Officers: Karen Spy, Secretary; Werner Nolte [1976] Director/Head of Finance [South African]

Angove's (Europe) Limited
Incorporated: 28 June 2001
Registered Office: Thames Distillers, Timbermill Way, London, SW4 6LY
Parent: Angove's Pty Ltd
Officers: Andrew John Coombe, Secretary; John Carlyon Angove [1947] Director/Vigneron [Australian]

Angus Dundee Distillers PLC
Incorporated: 14 October 1950 Employees: 134
Net Worth: £141,472,272 Total Assets: £164,446,112
Registered Office: 20-21 Cato Street, London, W1H 5JQ
Shareholders: Tania Hillman; Aaron Nicholas Hillman
Officers: Jean Elizabeth Hillman, Secretary; Robert Fleming [1955] Distillery Director; Aaron Nicholas Hillman [1964] Director; Jean Elizabeth Hillman [1932] Director; Tania Hillman [1962] Director; Terence Michael Hillman [1933] Director; Michael Hubert Humphreys [1932] Director; Steven McNeil [1968] Director; Brian John Megson [1955] Director/Executive

Angus Wines Limited
Incorporated: 1 October 2012
Net Worth Deficit: £14,327 Total Assets: £159
Registered Office: 46 Gladstone Place, Aberdeen, AB10 6XA
Major Shareholder: Graeme Hetherington
Officers: Graeme Hetherington, Secretary; Graeme Hetherington [1972] Director/CA

Anjo Wines Limited
Incorporated: 18 August 1983
Net Worth: £713,765 Total Assets: £1,864,565
Registered Office: Guardian Chartered Accountants, 2 William Street, Newtownards, Co Down, BT23 4AH
Shareholder: Garrett Peter O'Reilly
Officers: Garrett Peter O'Reilly [1972] Director [Irish]; Kevin Michael O'Reilly [1976] Director [Irish]

ANM Trading Limited
Incorporated: 1 July 2014 Employees: 4
Net Worth Deficit: £12,298 Total Assets: £7,142
Registered Office: 6 Redheughs Rigg, Edinburgh, EH12 9DQ
Shareholders: Aimee Morris; Naomi Morris
Officers: Aimee Morris [1995] Director/Business Executive; Janet Morris [1964] Director/Business Executive; Naomi Morris [1998] Director/Business Executive; Scott John Morris [1967] Director/Business Executive

ANM Wholesale Limited
Incorporated: 15 May 2017
Registered Office: 6 Highwood Lane, Loughton, Essex, IG10 3LS
Major Shareholder: Deborah Iris Mechell
Officers: Deborah Iris Mechell [1960] Director/Wholesale

Ann et Vin Limited
Incorporated: 9 September 2003 Employees: 3
Net Worth Deficit: £21,356 Total Assets: £140,925
Registered Office: 23 Castle Gate, Newark on Trent, Notts, NG24 1AZ
Major Shareholder: Ann Margaret Hayes
Officers: Peter Courtney Duncan, Secretary/Director; Ann Margaret Hayes [1957] Director/Wine Shop Manageress

Anna Wine & Food Ltd
Incorporated: 7 November 2018
Registered Office: 52 Canterbury Road, Croydon, Surrey, CR0 3PW
Major Shareholder: Yemlihan Aydin
Officers: Yemilhan Aydin [1964] Director

Annessa Imports Limited
Incorporated: 15 September 1992 Employees: 63
Net Worth: £1,649,483 Total Assets: £3,934,850
Registered Office: Wellington House, 273-275 High Street, London Colney, Herts, AL2 1HA
Officers: Maria Giovanna Annessa, Secretary [Italian]; Gaetano Alfano [1964] Director; Domenico Annessa [1957] Director/Importer; Gianni Enrico Annessa [1958] Director/Importer; Maria Giovanna Annessa [1965] Director/Importer [Italian]

The Antipodean Sommelier Limited
Incorporated: 12 May 2011 Employees: 2
Net Worth: £37,584 Total Assets: £290,927
Registered Office: Barn End, 76 Cherry Orton Road, Orton Waterville, Peterborough, Cambs, PE2 5EH
Shareholder: Antony David Wellings
Officers: James Edward Leary [1980] Director/Trader [New Zealander]; Antony David Wellings [1968] Sales Director

The Antique Wine Co (Holdings) Limited
Incorporated: 27 March 1996
Net Worth: £4,731 Total Assets: £20,707
Registered Office: 86 Clifton Road, Ruddington, Nottingham, NG11 6DE
Major Shareholder: Stephen Williams
Officers: Leonard Heath, Secretary; Stephen Williams [1957] Director/Wine Merchant

Antrobus Brothers Limited
Incorporated: 10 January 2019
Registered Office: 24 Doric Avenue, Frodsham, Cheshire, WA6 6QG
Shareholders: Neil Antrobus; Ian Antrobus
Officers: Ian Antrobus [1959] Company Secretary/Director; Neil Antrobus [1960] Director

Anya Global Limited
Incorporated: 15 November 2016
Registered Office: 3rd Floor, 207 Regent Street, London, W1B 3HH
Major Shareholder: Yashpal Singh Yadav
Officers: Dr Arun Kumar Chauhan [1971] Director/Doctor; Yashpal Singh Yadav [1984] Director [Indian]

AOC Distribution Ltd
Incorporated: 31 July 2007
Net Worth Deficit: £39
Registered Office: 20 Lansdown, Stroud, Glos, GL5 1BG
Shareholders: Gerald Xavier Jose Gerald Beaumont; Sarah-Jane Beaumont
Officers: Sarah-Jane Beaumont, Secretary; Generald Xavier Jose Generald Beaumont [1970] Director/Sales/Marketing Manager [French]; Sarah-Jane Beaumont [1970] Director/Office Manager

Aotearoa Distribution Ltd
Incorporated: 21 October 2011
Net Worth: £184,538 *Total Assets:* £194,538
Registered Office: Unit 3, 62 Garman Road, London, N17 0UT
Parent: Venus Wine & Spirit Merchants PLC
Officers: Pantelis Christoforou [1970] Director; Kerry Michael [1959] Director

Apex Dispense Limited
Incorporated: 13 June 2017
Registered Office: The Admiral Drake, Kingston Crescent, North End, Portsmouth, PO2 8DH
Major Shareholder: Alexander David Leonard
Officers: Alexander David Leonard [1988] Director

Apical Breweries UK Ltd
Incorporated: 22 January 2018
Registered Office: 62 Long Drive, Greenford, Middlesex, UB6 8LZ
Major Shareholder: Robert Owen Subanney
Officers: Stephen Francis Howden [1993] Director; Brandon Robert Subanney [1994] Director; Robert Owen Subanney [1963] Director

Apley Hall Wines Limited
Incorporated: 29 March 2016 *Employees:* 4
Net Worth Deficit: £893 *Total Assets:* £4,096
Registered Office: 1 Brassey Road, Old Potts Way, Shrewsbury, Salop, SY3 7FA
Shareholders: Paul Simon Stroud; Anthony Lingard-Lane
Officers: John Howard Dove [1943] Director/Tribunal Judge (Retired); Anthony Lingard-Lane [1951] Director; Jane Margaret Lingard-Lane [1966] Director

Apna Distribution Ltd
Incorporated: 13 September 2017
Registered Office: Kemp House, 160 City Road, London, EC1V 2NX
Major Shareholder: Mohammed Nabil Nazir

Appellations Limited
Incorporated: 11 May 2010 *Employees:* 3
Net Worth: £1,233,400 *Total Assets:* £1,751,699
Registered Office: Aissela, 46 High Street, Esher, Surrey, KT10 9QY
Major Shareholder: Nicolas Hallet
Officers: Alan John Delamain [1968] Director/Financial Controller; Nicolas Hallet [1979] Director [French]; Jessica Clair Harris [1972] Director/Fund Raiser; Thomas James Mann [1978] Director

Applecart Drinks Limited
Incorporated: 19 February 2019
Registered Office: 101 Rose Street, South Lane, Edinburgh, EH2 3JG
Major Shareholder: Joseph Scott Ray
Officers: Joseph Scott Ray [1980] Director/Social Investment and Innovation Advisor

Applethwaite Wines Ltd
Incorporated: 2 February 2015 *Employees:* 1
Net Worth Deficit: £10,156 *Total Assets:* £19,208
Registered Office: 10 High Street, Windermere, Cumbria, LA23 1AF
Major Shareholder: Thomas Nicholas Hadfield
Officers: Thomas Nicholas Hadfield [1952] Director

Appleton Estate Wines Ltd
Incorporated: 5 February 2018
Registered Office: 63 Heath Road, Bedworth, Warwicks, CV12 0AW
Major Shareholder: Ranjeet Bains
Officers: Ranjeet Bains [1975] Director

Appletree Cider Limited
Incorporated: 9 May 2017
Registered Office: 71-75 Shelton Street, Covent Garden, London, WC2H 9JQ
Major Shareholder: Sam Tam
Officers: Sam Tam, Secretary; Sam Tam [1983] Director

Approved Products Ltd
Incorporated: 12 April 2007 *Employees:* 3
Net Worth: £302,356 *Total Assets:* £2,664,400
Registered Office: 121 Livery Street, Birmingham, B3 1RS
Shareholder: Budge Dhariwal
Officers: Budge Dhariwal [1961] Director

Aqua Vitae Vodka Limited
Incorporated: 5 December 2018
Registered Office: 5 Spenser Court, Spenser Road, Bedford, MK40 2BA
Shareholders: Maqhawe Mcabango Nkumane; Issac George Raymond
Officers: Maqhawe Mcabango Nkumane [1990] Director/Salesman; Issac George Raymond [1989] Director/Salesman

Aquitania Ltd
Incorporated: 8 October 2013
Net Worth: £28,764 *Total Assets:* £35,178
Registered Office: 11-12 Hallmark Trading Estate, Fourth Way, Wembley, Middlesex, HA9 0LB
Officers: Darren Mark Johnson [1989] Director/Sales

Aran Beers Limited
Incorporated: 9 September 2014
Registered Office: 171-173 Gray's Inn Road, London, WC1X 8UE
Major Shareholder: Frank Ganley
Officers: Frank Ganley [1943] Director [Irish]

Arcari & Sons Ltd.
Incorporated: 18 August 2016
Registered Office: 210 Huntingfield Road, Putney, London, SW15 5ES
Major Shareholder: Fabio Vittorio Arcari
Officers: Fabio Vittorio Arcari [1985] Managing Director

Archangel Wines Limited
Incorporated: 31 August 2000
Net Worth: £13,340 *Total Assets:* £101,992
Registered Office: 137 Croydon Road, Anerley, London, SE20 7TT
Major Shareholder: Enrico Roberto Martinez
Officers: Carla Victoria Martinez, Secretary; Enrico Roberto Martinez [1961] Managing Director

Arda Rohat Limited
Incorporated: 8 August 2016 *Employees:* 4
Net Worth: £6,199 *Total Assets:* £20,632
Registered Office: 31 Canonbury Road, London, N1 2DG
Shareholder: Fatma Tonbul
Officers: Fatma Tonbul [1978] Director/Businesswoman

Ariki Limited
Incorporated: 2 November 2018
Registered Office: Oliver Court, Spring Garden Lane, Gosport, Hants, PO12 1FW
Major Shareholder: Juraj Komara
Officers: Juraj Komara [1971] Director [Slovak]

Arisaig Distillers Ltd
Incorporated: 20 December 2016
Registered Office: Arisaig Gartocharn, Alexandria, W Dunbartonshire, G83 8ND
Major Shareholder: Sharon Newall
Officers: Sharon Newall, Secretary; Sharon Newall [1961] Director

Ark Inta Ltd
Incorporated: 26 November 2018
Registered Office: 6 North House, Monks Orchard Road, Beckenham, Kent, BR3 3BW
Major Shareholder: Jonathan Ashvin Unimke
Officers: Vincentia Ifeanyi Opara, Secretary; Jonathan Ashvin Unimke [1983] Director/Salesman [Belgian]

Arkell's Brewery Limited
Incorporated: 28 December 1927 *Employees:* 251
Net Worth: £44,568,540 *Total Assets:* £70,877,672
Registered Office: Kingsdown, Upper Stratton, Swindon, Wilts, SN2 7RU
Officers: Emma Louise Defty, Secretary; Alexander Thomas Arkell [1985] Director/Head Brewer; George James Arkell [1978] Brewery Director; James Rixon Arkell [1951] Director/Chairman; Nicholas Henry Arkell [1955] Director of Brewery Co; Barry John Russell [1961] Director/Chartered Accountant

Armit Holding Limited
Incorporated: 15 July 2008
Net Worth: £11,575,020 *Total Assets:* £13,029,346
Registered Office: 5 Royalty Studios, 105 Lancaster Road, London, W11 1QF
Parent: Baarsma Wine Group Holding BV
Officers: Karen Lesley Ellis [1973] Finance Director; Susan Harper [1971] Sales and Marketing Director; Kirsten Emma Kilby [1977] Managing Director

Armit Wines Limited
Incorporated: 27 January 1982 *Employees:* 50
Net Worth: £1,103,538 *Total Assets:* £11,612,215
Registered Office: 5 Royalty Studios, 105 Lancaster Road, London, W11 1QF
Officers: Karen Lesley Ellis [1973] Finance Director; Kirsten Emma Kilby [1977] Managing Director

W.J.Armstrong Limited
Incorporated: 25 April 1936 *Employees:* 13
Net Worth: £248,761 *Total Assets:* £798,807
Registered Office: 12 London Road, East Grinstead, W Sussex, RH19 1AG
Shareholders: Michael Armstrong; Mary Hunt
Officers: Alison Ruth Armstrong, Secretary; Michael Armstrong [1939] Director/Wine Spirit Merchant; Nigel Anthony Armstrong [1964] Director/Wine Spirit Merchant; Philip Michael Armstrong [1962] Director/Wine Spirit Merchant

Art Beer Company Ltd
Incorporated: 3 December 2018
Registered Office: Ailsa Craig, Newnham Road, Hook, Hants, RG27 9LX
Major Shareholder: Simon Brockwell
Officers: Simon Brockwell [1985] Commercial Director

Art Entertainment Ltd
Incorporated: 14 June 2018
Registered Office: Kemp House, 160 City Road, London, EC1V 2NX
Major Shareholder: Neil Gallery
Officers: Neil Gallery [1963] Director/Publican

The Art of Wine Ltd
Incorporated: 20 May 2015
Net Worth: £4,946 *Total Assets:* £11,505
Registered Office: Seymour Chambers, 92 London Road, Liverpool, L3 5NW
Major Shareholder: William Paul Askew
Officers: William Paul Askew [1966] Director

Artful Dodger Whisky Ltd
Incorporated: 1 August 2017
Registered Office: 37 Warren Street, London, W1T 6AD
Parent: Woolf Sung Limited
Officers: Sebastian Joseph Woolf [1980] Director

The Articulate Drinks Company Limited
Incorporated: 11 January 2018
Registered Office: Brook House, Moss Grove, Kingswinford, W Midlands, DY6 9HS
Shareholders: Sarah Priestly-Bingham; Georgina Priestly-Bingham
Officers: Georgina Priestly-Bingham [1978] Managing Director; Sarah Priestly-Bingham [1972] Director

Artisan Beer Import Co Ltd
Incorporated: 5 December 2011
Registered Office: 113 Holloway Road, London, N7 8LT
Major Shareholder: Martin Patrick Hayes
Officers: Martin Patrick Hayes [1980] Director/Publican

Artisan Lounge and Cellar Limited
Incorporated: 15 March 2016
Registered Office: 7 Church Road, Fleet, Hants, GU51 3RT
Major Shareholder: Nicola Anne Hutchens
Officers: Nicky Anne Hutchens [1984] Director/Hospitality

Artisan Wine Storage Ltd
Incorporated: 19 March 2014 *Employees:* 1
Net Worth Deficit: £31,170 *Total Assets:* £237,330
Registered Office: 8th Floor, South Reading Bridge House, George Street, Reading, Berks, RG1 8LS
Major Shareholder: Eamonn Peter Egan
Officers: Eamonn Peter Egan [1970] Director [Irish]

Artizen Raw Ltd
Incorporated: 28 March 2018
Registered Office: 76 Tony Humphries Road, Banbury, Oxon, OX16 0FF
Shareholders: Florent Remi Arcin; Sofia Taraf Kojok
Officers: Florent Remi Arcin [1980] Managing Director [French]; Sofia Taraf Kojok [1983] Director [French/Lebanese]

Arundo Limited
Incorporated: 24 April 2018
Registered Office: 70 Castellain Mansions, Castellain Road, London, W9 1HA
Major Shareholder: Archie Patrick Finton Reed
Officers: Archie Patrick Finton Reed [1994] Director

ASA Ventures Limited
Incorporated: 17 August 2009
Net Worth Deficit: £5,997 *Total Assets:* £15,484
Registered Office: Third Floor, 207 Regent Street, London, W1B 3HH
Shareholders: Axel Stahmer; Andreas Stahmer
Officers: Andreas Benno Frederik Stahmer [1984] Director/Manager [German]; Axel Frederik Stephan Stahmer [1980] Director/Manager [German]

Asahi Premium Brands Ltd
Incorporated: 9 February 2017 *Employees:* 12
Net Worth Deficit: £953,021 *Total Assets:* £7,887,753
Registered Office: One Forge End, Woking, Surrey, GU21 6DB
Parent: Asahi Europe Ltd
Officers: Edward Perks, Secretary; Rohan Cummings [1975] Director; Hector Gorosabel [1960] Director [Canadian]; Yusuke Naritsuka [1972] Director [Japanese]; Filippo Scandellari [1961] Managing Director [Italian]

Asahi UK Ltd
Incorporated: 23 December 2004 *Employees:* 188
Previous: Miller Brands (UK) Limited
Net Worth: £28,456,000 *Total Assets:* £109,625,000
Registered Office: One Forge End, Woking, Surrey, GU21 6DB
Parent: Asahi Europe Limited
Officers: Edward William Perks, Secretary; Timothy James Clay [1966] Managing Director; Rohan Cummings [1975] Director/Chief Financial Officer; Hector Gorosabel [1960] Managing Director Western Europe [Canadian]; Yusuke Naritsuka [1972] Director [Japanese]; Michael Richard Randles [1975] Director/Chartered Accountant

Asante Distributors Limited
Incorporated: 2 February 2018
Net Worth: £100 *Total Assets:* £100
Registered Office: 21 Jesmond Way, Stanmore, Harrow, Middlesex, HA7 4QR
Shareholders: Mahmoud Jiva Rayani; Ashwin Karsandas Padia; Kim Patrick Rawson
Officers: Ashwin Karsandas Padia [1958] Director [Kenyan]; Kim Patrick Rawson [1955] Director; Mahmoud Jiva Rayani [1952] Director/Wine Merchant

ASCO Foods Limited
Incorporated: 24 October 2000
Net Worth: £1,407,356 *Total Assets:* £5,103,317
Registered Office: Units 7 & 8 Amersham Commercial Park, Raans Road, Amersham, Bucks, HP6 6JY
Officers: Sundeep Singh Chadha, Secretary; Arshdeep Singh Chadha [1980] Director; Ravneet Singh Chadha [1970] Director; Sundeep Singh Chadha [1974] Director

Ascona Retail (Leases) Limited
Incorporated: 15 August 2015
Previous: Local Value Stores Limited
Registered Office: Unit 12 Bridge Innovation Centre, Pembrokeshire Science and Technology Park, Pembroke Dock, Pembrokeshire, SA72 6UN
Major Shareholder: Darren Charles Briggs
Officers: Darren Charles Briggs [1970] Director; Shane David Higgon [1969] Director; Duncan Eric Morris [1962] Director

Ascott Invest Limited
Incorporated: 24 August 2009
Net Worth Deficit: £77,455 *Total Assets:* £28,256
Registered Office: The Old Wheel House, 31-37 Church Street, Reigate, Surrey, RH2 0AD
Major Shareholder: Olivier Dubuisson
Officers: Craig Lambert, Secretary; Keri Nichole Griffith [1970] Director [American]

ASG Wines Limited
Incorporated: 27 January 2017
Net Worth Deficit: £9,632 *Total Assets:* £26,078
Registered Office: 18 Chelsea Manor Street, London, SW3 3UH
Major Shareholder: Gonzalo Aldaco
Officers: Gonzalo Aldaco [1983] Director/Architect [Hungarian]

Ashanti Drinks Limited
Incorporated: 29 August 2009
Net Worth: £84,727 *Total Assets:* £174,576
Registered Office: 204 Brigstock Road, Thornton Heath, Surrey, CR7 7JD
Officers: Noel Dempster [1958] Director/Food Trader

Asia-Pacific 11230699 Vitamin Beverage Co., Ltd
Incorporated: 28 February 2018
Registered Office: Unit G25, Waterfront Studios, 1 Dock Road, London, E16 1AH
Shareholders: Lili Song; Haibao Bu
Officers: Haibao BU [1977] Director [Chinese]

Asiana Mart Limited
Incorporated: 28 July 2016
Registered Office: 14 Bankside Close, Carshalton, Surrey, SM5 3SB
Officers: Gapjoong Kwon [1962] Director [South Korean]

Ask Drinks Ltd
Incorporated: 14 October 2014 *Employees:* 7
Net Worth: £151,158 *Total Assets:* £549,691
Registered Office: 54 Queen Street, Farnworth, Bolton, Lancs, BL7 4AH
Shareholder: Adam Christian Kirkpatrick
Officers: Adam Christian Kirkpatrick [1973] Director/Drinks Retail; Simon Kirkpatrick [1971] Director/Drinks Retail

Aspall Cyder Limited
Incorporated: 30 June 1986 Employees: 131
Net Worth: £950,877 Total Assets: £25,999,500
Registered Office: 137 High Street, Burton on Trent, Staffs, DE14 1JZ
Parent: Aspall Holdings Limited
Officers: Gemma Wisniewski, Secretary; Simon Kerry [1970] Director/Chief Finance Officer; James Christian Shearer [1980] Marketing Director; Philip Mark Whitehead [1977] Managing Director

Associated Church Clubs Limited
Incorporated: 18 June 1992 Employees: 1
Net Worth: £236,739 Total Assets: £262,038
Registered Office: Archdiocese of Liverpool, The Centre for Evangelisation, Croxteth Drive, Sefton Park, Liverpool, L17 1AA
Parent: Liverpool Roman Catholic Archdiocesan Trust
Officers: John Cowdall, Secretary; Reverend Edward Richard Cain [1955] Director/Roman Catholic Priest; Rev Sean Kirwin [1968] Director/Roman Catholic Priest; Carol Lawrence [1967] Director; Reverend Michael Anthony Thompson [1960] Director/Roman Catholic Priest

Asta Barista Baby Ltd
Incorporated: 14 June 2018
Registered Office: Green Hay, The Green, Churchdown, Glos, GL3 2LF
Officers: Daphne Brett [1971] Director/Change Manager; Jason Mortimer [1970] Director/Security Consultant

Astir Cigars & Wine Ltd
Incorporated: 14 January 2016
Previous: Astir Food & Wine Limited
Net Worth: £29,934 Total Assets: £97,036
Registered Office: 17 Hobart Place, London, SW1W 0HH
Major Shareholder: Michael Hani Bou Antoun
Officers: Michael Hani Bou Antoun [1983] Director/Food & Wine Supplier; Nauf Bou Antoun [1986] Director

Astonburgh Limited
Incorporated: 12 October 2005
Net Worth: £98,190 Total Assets: £109,433
Registered Office: 4th Floor, Clerks Well House, 20 Britton Street, London, EC1M 5UA
Major Shareholder: Laurent Vialette
Officers: Frances Ann Gordon [1954] Director

Astrum Wine Cellars Limited
Incorporated: 20 February 1997 Employees: 15
Net Worth: £110,385 Total Assets: £1,610,967
Registered Office: Unit 7 Falcon Business Centre, 14 Wandle Way, Mitcham, Surrey, CR4 4FG
Major Shareholder: Bruno Besa
Officers: Stefano Benato, Secretary [Italian]; Stefano Benato [1969] Operations Director [Italian]; Bruno Besa [1966] Managing Director [Italian]; Massimiliano Folli [1968] Sales Director [Italian]; Mark Perna [1965] Marketing Director [Italian]

At The Group Ltd
Incorporated: 2 February 2018
Registered Office: 4b Worsley Road, Worsley, Manchester, M28 2NL
Officers: Matthew William James Baker [1989] Director/Self Employed

Atanas Distributors Ltd
Incorporated: 31 December 2018
Registered Office: 720a Alum Rock Road, Birmingham, B8 3PP
Officers: Atanas Rashkov [1995] Director [Bulgarian]

Athila Roos Ltd
Incorporated: 14 December 2018
Registered Office: 5 Hexham Road, Morden, Surrey, SM4 6NH
Major Shareholder: Athila Roos
Officers: Athila Roos [1981] Director

Atkinson's Gin Ltd
Incorporated: 11 September 2018
Registered Office: Flat 5, Bridge House, Dover Road East, Gravesend, Kent, DA11 0RD
Major Shareholder: Leon Atkinson
Officers: Leon Atkinson [1993] Director

The Atlantic Craft Soda Company Ltd
Incorporated: 15 March 2016
Net Worth Deficit: £11,670 Total Assets: £2,472
Registered Office: 38 Middlehill Road, Colehill, Wimborne, Dorset, BH21 2SE
Major Shareholder: Gerard Brendan Gaughan
Officers: Felicity Jane Gaughan [1965] Finance Director; Gerard Brendan Gaughan [1966] Director/Management Consultant

Atlantis Iberica Ltd
Incorporated: 1 May 2014
Net Worth Deficit: £8,221 Total Assets: £10,966
Registered Office: 20-22 Wenlock Road, London, N1 7GU
Officers: Antonio Hernandez Hernandez [1957] Director [Spanish]

Atlas Fine Wines Limited
Incorporated: 7 September 2010 Employees: 13
Net Worth: £1,191,012 Total Assets: £2,950,437
Registered Office: Park View House, 58 The Ropewalk, Nottingham, NG1 5DW
Major Shareholder: Simon Larkin
Officers: Mark John Edwards [1954] Director; Simon Larkin [1973] Director/Master of Wine; Aidan Denis Treacy [1961] Director [Irish]

Atlas Food Wholesale Ltd
Incorporated: 8 October 2018
Registered Office: 231 East Bawtry Road, Rotherham, S Yorks, S60 4LH
Major Shareholder: Cihan Cocelli
Officers: Cihan Cocelli [1982] Director

Atlasaim International Limited
Incorporated: 28 October 1994 Employees: 3
Net Worth: £1,111,863 Total Assets: £1,288,761
Registered Office: 7 East Drive, Ham Manor, Angmering, Littlehampton, W Sussex, BN16 4JH
Major Shareholder: Miguel Velasco-Carrillo
Officers: Miguel Velasco-Carrillo, Secretary/Sales Manager [Spanish]; Miguel Velasco-Carrillo [1949] Director [Spanish]

Atom Brands Limited
Incorporated: 13 March 2018
Registered Office: Unit 1 Ton Business Park, 2-8 Morley Road, Tonbridge, Kent, TN9 1RA
Parent: Atom Supplies Limited
Officers: Joel John Kelly [1980] Director/Solicitor

Atom Brewing Co Limited
Incorporated: 25 June 2012
Net Worth: £25,019 Total Assets: £190,136
Registered Office: Unit 4 Food & Drink Park, Malmo Road, Sutton Fields Industrial Estate West, Hull, HU7 0YF
Shareholders: Allan Edward Rice; Sarah Jill Thackray
Officers: Allan Edward Rice [1980] Director; Dr Sarah Thackray [1982] Director

Atom Cask Holdings Limited
Incorporated: 13 March 2018
Registered Office: Unit 1 Ton Business Park, 2-8 Morley Road, Tonbridge, Kent, TN9 1RA
Parent: Atom Supplies Limited
Officers: Joel John Kelly [1980] Director/Solicitor

Atom Drinks Limited
Incorporated: 13 March 2018
Registered Office: Unit 1 Ton Business Park, 2-8 Morley Road, Tonbridge, Kent, TN9 1RA
Parent: Atom Supplies Limited
Officers: Joel John Kelly [1980] Director/Solicitor

Atom Group Limited
Incorporated: 13 March 2018
Registered Office: Unit 1 Ton Business Park, 2-8 Morley Road, Tonbridge, Kent, TN9 1RA
Parent: Atom Supplies Limited
Officers: Joel John Kelly [1980] Director/Solicitor

Atom Scotland Limited
Incorporated: 14 March 2018
Registered Office: Unit 9 A1 Industrial Estate, Sir Harry Lauder Road, Edinburgh, EH15 2QA
Parent: Atom Supplies Limited
Officers: Joel John Kelly [1980] Director/Solicitor

Atom Supplies Limited
Incorporated: 1 May 1996 *Employees:* 221
Net Worth: £4,185,871 *Total Assets:* £18,093,900
Registered Office: Unit 1 Ton Business Park, 2-8 Morley Road, Tonbridge, Kent, TN9 1RA
Parent: Pioneer Brewing Company Limited
Officers: Terri Francis, Secretary; Benedict James Olaf Ellefsen [1981] Director; Terri Nicole Francis [1986] Director/Lawyer [Australian]; Joel John Kelly [1980] Director/Solicitor; Andrew Kenneith Logan [1985] Ecommerce Director; Thomas Stanley McGuinness [1980] Director; Justin Toby Petszaft [1981] Managing Director

Attitude Spirits Ltd
Incorporated: 6 November 2017
Net Worth: £100 *Total Assets:* £100
Registered Office: 18 Wimpole Street, London, W1G 8GD
Shareholders: Teodor Goroszeniuk; Andrew Timothy Lawson; Christopher Lian Hock Chan
Officers: Teodor Goroszeniuk, Secretary; Christopher Lian Hock Chan [1967] Director/Consultant Surgeon; Teodor Goroszeniuk [1943] Director/Consultant in Pain Medicine and Anaesthesia; Andrew Timothy Lawson [1956] Director/Business and Brand Consultant

Au Vodka Ltd
Incorporated: 4 March 2015 *Employees:* 2
Net Worth Deficit: £3,866 *Total Assets:* £112,136
Registered Office: The Post House, Adelaide Street, Swansea, SA1 1SB
Shareholders: Charles Elliot Morgan; Jackson Aaron Quinn
Officers: Charles Elliot Morgan [1995] Director; Jackson Aaron Quinn [1993] Director

Auld Acquaintance Whisky Company Limited
Incorporated: 24 October 2018
Registered Office: 28 Jane Street, Edinburgh, EH6 5HD
Major Shareholder: Derek Joseph Mair
Officers: Derek Joseph Mair [1961] Director/Businessman

Aurora Ales Limited
Incorporated: 11 August 2016
Net Worth: £24,409 *Total Assets:* £25,500
Registered Office: 98 Church Street, Ilkeston, Derbys, DE7 8QG
Officers: Gillian Derbyshire, Secretary; Trevor James Bishop [1952] Director/Brewing; Mark Wayne Derbyshire [1963] Director/Brewing

Ausavenues Limited
Incorporated: 7 October 2014
Net Worth: £140 *Total Assets:* £108,156
Registered Office: 29 Rathnew Court, 5 Meath Crescent, London, E2 0QG
Major Shareholder: Jason Andrew Cameron
Officers: Jason Cameron, Secretary; Jason Cameron [1981] Director/Trade Manager [Australian]

Aussie Rules Ltd
Incorporated: 4 October 2013
Net Worth: £15,293 *Total Assets:* £120,974
Registered Office: 272 Bath Street, Glasgow, G2 4JR
Major Shareholder: Lee Barrie
Officers: Lee Barrie [1974] Director; Michelle Lisa Barrie [1977] Director

The Australian Cellar Ltd
Incorporated: 3 September 2018
Registered Office: Grand Union House, 20 Kentish Town Road, London, NW1 9NX
Major Shareholder: Melanie Brown
Officers: Melanie Brown [1983] Director [New Zealander]

Australian Vintage (Europe) Limited
Incorporated: 26 September 1994
Net Worth: £22,510 *Total Assets:* £39,710
Registered Office: Stephenson House, 2 Cherry Orchard Road, Croydon, Surrey, CR0 6BA
Officers: Michael Heinz Noack, Secretary; Jason Kaz Scott Kociolek [1972] Director [Australian]; Michael Heinz Noack [1958] Director/Chief Finance Officer [Australian]

Australian Wine Services Limited
Incorporated: 22 July 2002
Net Worth Deficit: £34,509 *Total Assets:* £1,232
Registered Office: 71 Peak Hill, Sydenham, London, SE26 4NS
Major Shareholder: David John Baldwin
Officers: David John Baldwin, Secretary/Wine Management; David John Baldwin [1971] Director/Wine Management

Authentic French Wines (Importers) Limited
Incorporated: 19 November 2015
Net Worth: £7,930 *Total Assets:* £9,890
Registered Office: 55 Western Avenue, Brentwood, Essex, CM14 4XR
Shareholders: Mark Edwards; Erwan Le Bohec; Olivier Porte
Officers: Mark Edwards [1965] Director/Telecommunications Technician; Erwan Le Bohec [1974] Director/Delicatessen Owner [French]; Olivier Porte [1967] Director/IT Manager [French]

Avalon Wholesale and Brewing Limited
Incorporated: 6 November 2015 *Employees:* 2
Net Worth: £6,484 *Total Assets:* £29,296
Registered Office: Four Fifty Partnership, Bath Street, Cheddar, Somerset, BS27 3AA
Shareholders: Arthur Josiah Frampton; Sandra Jane Frampton
Officers: Arthur Josiah Frampton [1956] Director; Sandra Jane Frampton [1962] Director

Avant Garde Drinks Ltd
Incorporated: 20 July 2011
Net Worth Deficit: £123,143 *Total Assets:* £111,273
Registered Office: Hardcores House, Rawson Spring Road, Sheffield, S6 1PD
Shareholders: David James Pickard; Andrew Peter Trudgill
Officers: David James Pickard [1983] Director; Robert Pickard [1954] Director; Andrew Peter Trudgill [1981] Director/Sales Manager

Avazak Ltd
Incorporated: 25 February 2019
Registered Office: 34 Piedmont Road, London, SE18 1TA
Shareholder: Vahe Karapetyan
Officers: Vahe Karapetyan [1987] Director/Trader [Armenian]

Axiom Brands Limited
Incorporated: 20 March 2013 *Employees:* 6
Net Worth: £101,123 *Total Assets:* £384,760
Registered Office: c/o Resolve Bulldog House, London Road, Twyford, Reading, Berks, RG10 9EU
Shareholders: Ian Mark Bayliss; Elizabeth Anne Cannon
Officers: Elizabeth Anne Canon [1957] Director

Ayr Brewing Company Limited
Incorporated: 28 May 2009
Net Worth: £32,922 *Total Assets:* £105,871
Registered Office: 17 Scaur O'Doon Road, Ayr, KA7 4EP
Shareholders: Paul Rossi; Anthony Valenti
Officers: Anthony Valenti, Secretary; Paul Rossi [1954] Director/Hotelier; Anthony Valenti [1961] Director/Restaurateur

Azienda Vitivinicola Stassi Ltd
Incorporated: 30 January 2018
Registered Office: Flat 5, 8-12 Hessel Street, London, E1 2LP
Major Shareholder: Luca Stassi
Officers: Luca Stassi [1992] Director/Bartender [Italian]

Aziken Ventures Limited
Incorporated: 22 September 2014
Registered Office: 35 Carolina Close, London, E15 1JR
Major Shareholder: Taiwo Odion Okun
Officers: Dr. Taiwo Odion Okun [1951] Director/Medical Practitioner

Azizi Drinks Ltd
Incorporated: 28 May 2014
Net Worth Deficit: £135,212 *Total Assets:* £873
Registered Office: Global House, 303 Ballards Lane, London, N12 8NP
Major Shareholder: Kaushik Amritlal Mody
Officers: Richard Geoffrey Martin [1954] Director/Consultant; Kaushik Amritlal Mody [1957] Director

Aztec Spirits Ltd
Incorporated: 23 July 2018
Registered Office: 17 Glyndwr Street, Port Talbot, SA13 1YH
Shareholders: Ritchie Lee Care; Owen Jones
Officers: Ritchie Lee Care [1983] Director/Laboratory Technician; Owen Jones [1991] Director/Analyst

Azurapada Worldwide Ltd
Incorporated: 30 January 2018
Registered Office: 2 Police Houses, Rassau, Blaenau Gwent, NP23 5TE
Major Shareholder: Jozsef Szasz
Officers: Jozsef Szasz [1983] Director/Aeronautical Engineer [Hungarian]

The Azzurri Kitchen Ltd
Incorporated: 15 April 2015
Registered Office: Unit 1 Smiths Forge Industrial Estate, North End Road, Yatton, Somerset, BS49 4AU
Parent: Price Technical Limited
Officers: Stephen Kenneth Price [1961] Director

B & B Drinks Ltd
Incorporated: 29 April 2013 *Employees:* 2
Net Worth Deficit: £4,785 *Total Assets:* £1
Registered Office: Moorside Road Farm, Moorside Road, Bolton, Lancs, BL7 0JZ
Major Shareholder: Jean Wood
Officers: Jean Wood [1952] Director/Tutor

B & D Clarke Limited
Incorporated: 16 March 2005
Net Worth: £685 *Total Assets:* £90,316
Registered Office: 5 John Fryer Avenue, Wincham, Northwich, Cheshire, CW9 6EG
Shareholders: Brian Peter Clarke; Dawn Mary Clarke
Officers: Brian Peter Clarke, Secretary; Brian Peter Clarke [1959] Director; Dawn Mary Clarke [1960] Director

B & F Enterprise UK Ltd
Incorporated: 14 May 2018
Registered Office: Kemp House, 160 City Road, London, EC1V 2NX
Officers: Dr Olufolake Akinduro-Aje, Secretary; Benson Aje [1972] Director/Criminologist

B & M Produce Limited
Incorporated: 4 July 2017
Registered Office: Ground Floor, 2 Woodberry Grove, London, N12 0DR
Major Shareholder: Maureen Fagon-Francis
Officers: Maureen Fagon-Francis, Secretary; Maureen Fagon-Francis [1965] Director

B & P Beverages Ltd
Incorporated: 31 October 2017
Registered Office: 58 Durham Road, Birtley, Chester-le-Street, Co Durham, DH3 2QJ
Officers: Lee Brown [1983] Director; Paul Peterson [1990] Director

B & W Distributors Limited
Incorporated: 8 December 2017
Registered Office: Unit 20 Grove Park Industrial Estate, Waltham Road, White Waltham, Maidenhead, Berks, SL6 3LW
Major Shareholder: Amrik Singh Aidan
Officers: Amrik Singh Aidan [1972] Director/Self Employed

B Wines Limited
Incorporated: 2 November 2018
Registered Office: 72 Old Brompton Road, London, SW7 3LQ
Major Shareholder: Bruno Cernecca
Officers: Bruno Cernecca [1971] Director [Italian]

B.D. (S/W) Ltd
Incorporated: 15 May 2003 *Employees:* 9
Net Worth: £42,145 *Total Assets:* £174,659
Registered Office: Mary Street House, Mary Street, Taunton, Somerset, TA1 3NW
Shareholders: Julian Alexander Murray; Lindsey Dawn Murray
Officers: Lindsey Dawn Murray, Secretary/Financial Controller; Alexander Julian Murray [1964] Director/Wholesaler; Lindsey Dawn Murray [1971] Director/Financial Controller

Babco UK Ltd.
Incorporated: 12 September 2000 Employees: 4
Net Worth: £22,732 Total Assets: £111,163
Registered Office: Suite 2a, 1st Floor, Warren Court, Park Road, Crowborough, E Sussex, TN6 2QX
Shareholders: World of Patria International Holdings Ltd; Christopher Peter Bowen
Officers: Christopher Peter Bowen [1960] Director/Marketing and Distribution; Andrew Michael Kerr [1969] Managing Director; Robert Ian Nichols [1968] Director; Steve William Smith [1961] Director

Babicka Vodka (International) Limited
Incorporated: 23 August 2013 Employees: 2
Net Worth Deficit: £117,672 Total Assets: £44,092
Registered Office: Redford House, Friggle Street, Frome, Somerset, BA11 5LP
Shareholder: Alex David Victor Clarke
Officers: Susan Jane Clarke, Secretary; Alex David Victor Clarke [1972] Director

Bablake Wines Limited
Incorporated: 3 February 1950 Employees: 89
Net Worth: £12,000 Total Assets: £12,000
Registered Office: 309 Elveden Road, Park Royal, London, NW10 7ST
Parent: Amathus Drinks PLC
Officers: Warren Charles Adams, Secretary; Warren Charles Adams [1965] Director/Accountant; Chariton Platon Georgiou [1960] Director; Isabella Ava Georgiou [1987] Director; Loucia Machlouzarides [1974] Director; Dale Wharton [1960] Operations Director

Babuji Ltd
Incorporated: 10 November 2011
Registered Office: 36 St Johns Road, Slough, Berks, SL2 5EZ
Major Shareholder: Muhammad Abbas
Officers: Muhammad Abbas [1981] Director/Sales [Pakistani]

Baby Bottles (Wholesale) Limited
Incorporated: 22 October 1986 Employees: 46
Net Worth: £669,334 Total Assets: £3,392,245
Registered Office: Crondal Road, Bayton Road Industrial Estate, Exhall, Coventry, Warwicks, CV7 9NH
Shareholders: Andrew Glyn Wright; Michael John Garnett; Keith James Harding
Officers: Andrew Glyn Wright, Secretary; Michael John Garnett [1960] Director; Keith James Harding [1965] Director; Andrew Glyn Wright [1967] Director

Babyboyempire. Ltd
Incorporated: 8 August 2018
Registered Office: 285 Fleetwood Road North, Thornton-Cleveleys, Lancs, FY5 4LE
Major Shareholder: Lauren Chadwick-Greer
Officers: Scott Clewlow [1985] Director

Bacana Sangria UK Limited
Incorporated: 14 March 2018
Registered Office: Brightwell Grange, Britwell Road, Slough, SL1 8DF
Shareholders: Rachael Robertson; Artur Claudino
Officers: James Robertson [1975] Director; Rachael Robertson [1970] Director

Bacardi-Martini Limited
Incorporated: 12 October 1935 Employees: 232
Net Worth: £48,721,000 Total Assets: £114,699,000
Registered Office: Bacardi Brown-Forman House, Kings Worthy, Winchester, Hants, SO23 7TW
Parent: Bacardi U.K. Limited
Officers: Amanda Claire Almond [1972] Managing Director; Ross Tomas Bilsland [1980] Finance Director

Bacchus Fine Wine & Food Limited
Incorporated: 18 October 2018
Registered Office: 70 Carmen Street, London, E14 6NW
Major Shareholder: Domenico de Ruosi
Officers: Domenico de Ruosi [1988] Director/Entrepreneur [Italian]

Bacchus London Limited
Incorporated: 24 September 2018
Registered Office: 15 Charter Court, Stroud Green Road, London, N4 3SG
Major Shareholder: Tolga Koymen
Officers: Tolga Koymen [1976] Director

Bacchus Merchantry Limited
Incorporated: 8 October 2018
Registered Office: 1052 Uxbridge Road, Hayes, Middlesex, UB4 0RJ
Major Shareholder: Nirmal Singh Sachdeva
Officers: Nirmal Singh Sachdeva, Secretary; Nirmal Singh Sachdeva [1983] Director [Indian]

Bacchus Vin Ltd
Incorporated: 26 April 2018
Registered Office: 14 Quill Lane, Putney, London, SW15 1NL
Major Shareholder: Stephane Gallice
Officers: Stephane Gallice [1973] Director [French]

Bacchus Wine Auctions Limited
Incorporated: 8 August 2016
Net Worth: £22,919 Total Assets: £43,459
Registered Office: 10 Courtlands Avenue, Esher, Surrey, KT10 9HZ
Shareholders: Christopher Hambleton; Helen Hambleton
Officers: Christopher Andrew Hambleton [1978] Director/Owner; Helen Louise Hambleton [1978] Director/Owner

Bacchus-Les-Vignobles de France Limited
Incorporated: 21 February 1975 Employees: 3
Net Worth: £333,868 Total Assets: £634,694
Registered Office: Bacchus House, 4 Grange Mills, Weir Road, London, SW12 0NE
Major Shareholder: Patrick Burckhard
Officers: Dr Patrick Burckhard [1944] Director [French]

Bach & Co Solution Limited
Incorporated: 19 December 2018
Registered Office: c/o Partners in Enterprise Ltd, First Floor Office, 5 Bartholomews, Brighton, BN1 1HG
Major Shareholder: Bachana Khachidze
Officers: Bachana Khachidze [1982] Director/Wine Merchant [Georgian]

Bad Girls Brew Limited
Incorporated: 7 November 2017
Registered Office: 22a Thorney Crescent, London, SW11 3TT
Major Shareholder: Barbara Elizabeth Gorna
Officers: Barbara Elizabeth Gorna, Secretary; Barbara Elizabeth Gorna [1955] Director

UK Wholesalers of Beers, Wines and Spirits   dellam

Bad Joke Brew Co. Ltd.
Incorporated: 13 April 2017
Net Worth: £3,462 *Total Assets:* £3,462
Registered Office: Unit 2C(A) Penn Street Works, Penn Street, Amersham, Bucks, HP7 0PX
Shareholders: Jessica Lucy Bailey; James Phillip Cross
Officers: Jessica Lucy Bailey [1992] Director/Brewer; James Phillip Cross [1993] Director/Brewer

Bahamian Enterprise UK Limited
Incorporated: 26 February 2018
Registered Office: 29 Ablett Close, Oxford, OX4 1XH
Shareholder: Oliver Keell
Officers: Isabella Keell [1993] Director; Oliver Keell [1993] Director

The Baijiu Beer Company Limited
Incorporated: 17 October 2016 *Employees:* 3
Net Worth: £100 *Total Assets:* £4,468
Registered Office: 8 Holyrood View, Sheffield, S10 4NG
Shareholders: Christopher James Spencer; Philip Craig Lee; Craig Butler
Officers: Craig Butler [1969] Director; Philip Craig Lee [1970] Director; Christopher James Spencer [1974] Director

Baijiu Evolution Ltd
Incorporated: 16 October 2018
Registered Office: 8 Holyrood View, Sheffield, S10 4NG
Shareholders: Christopher James Spencer; Philip Craig Lee; Craig Butler
Officers: Craig Butler [1969] Director; Christopher James Spencer [1974] Director

The Bajan Trading Company Limited
Incorporated: 20 September 2007
Net Worth: £222,996 *Total Assets:* £344,674
Registered Office: The Sovereign Distillery, Wilson Road, Huyton, Knowsley, Merseyside, L36 6AD
Parent: Halewood International Limited
Officers: Stewart Andrew Hainsworth [1969] Director/Chief Executive Officer; Alan William Robinson [1965] Finance Director; James Stocker [1967] Marketing Director; Stephen Keith Wallace [1966] Director/Marketing Consultant

Bak Family Wines Limited
Incorporated: 19 July 2018
Registered Office: Maple House, 11 Briar Road, Twickenham, Middlesex, TW2 6RB
Major Shareholder: Mickel Johan Frederik Bak
Officers: Mickel Johan Frederik Bak [1959] Director [Dutch]

Bakewell Road Brewery Ltd
Incorporated: 24 August 2018
Registered Office: The Woodlands, Bakewell Road, Matlock, Derbys, DE4 3AU
Shareholders: David Stuart Walsh; Cathy Walsh
Officers: Cathy Walsh [1978] Director; David Stuart Walsh [1978] Director

Balcony Wines Ltd
Incorporated: 7 June 2018
Registered Office: 2 West Dunley Farm Cottage, Grittleton, Chippenham, Wilts, SN14 6PY
Major Shareholder: Neil Adrian Perry
Officers: Neil Adrian Perry [1959] Director/Chartered Accountant

Balkan Wines Ltd
Incorporated: 10 October 2018
Registered Office: 3 Westerlands, Stapleford, Nottingham, NG9 7JE
Major Shareholder: Daniel James Amin
Officers: Daniel James Amin [1980] Managing Director

The Ballance Group Limited
Incorporated: 13 July 2005
Net Worth Deficit: £22,379 *Total Assets:* £2,431
Registered Office: Office Afloat, Barton Marina, Barton under Needwood, Burton on Trent, Staffs, DE13 8DZ
Officers: Peter Frederick Ballance, Secretary; Michael Peter Ballance [1961] Director

Ballers Brands Ltd
Incorporated: 28 January 2019
Registered Office: 71-75 Shelton Street, London, WC2H 9JQ
Major Shareholder: Alan Colton
Officers: Alan Colton, Secretary; Alan Colton [1981] Director

Balman Import & Export Limited
Incorporated: 4 May 2006
Net Worth: £68,802 *Total Assets:* £413,936
Registered Office: c/o Pitts & Seeus, Omnibus Business Centre, 39-41 North Road, London, N7 9DP
Major Shareholder: Balvinder Singh Bahra
Officers: Mandeep Kaur, Secretary [Indian]; Balvinder Singh Bahra [1982] Director

Balthazar Limited
Incorporated: 5 January 2001
Net Worth: £119,701 *Total Assets:* £303,821
Registered Office: Lynton House, 7-12 Tavistock Square, London, WC1H 9BQ
Shareholders: Charles Valentine Llewellyn Tapps Gervis Meyrick; Alexandra Dulcie Mary Meyrick
Officers: Alexandra Dulcie Mary Meyrick, Secretary; Charles Valentine Llewellyn Tapps Gervis Meyrick [1971] Director/Wine Spirit Wholesaler

Bancroft Wines Limited
Incorporated: 20 August 1999 *Employees:* 23
Net Worth: £108,544 *Total Assets:* £3,688,703
Registered Office: Woolyard, 54 Bermondsey Street, London, SE1 3UD
Major Shareholder: Peter Charles de Haan
Officers: Samantha Jayne Ghysen, Secretary; Barnaby Simon Davis [1972] Director; Peter Charles de Haan [1952] Director; Simon Christopher Johnson [1965] Director; Jonathan David Worsley [1976] Director

Bang The Elephant Brewing Co Ltd
Incorporated: 1 September 2017
Registered Office: 17 Craig Street, Long Eaton, Nottingham, NG10 1ET
Shareholders: Nigel Patton; Michael Shipman
Officers: Nigel Patton, Secretary; Michael Shipman, Secretary; Nigel Patton [1978] Director/Master Brewer; Michael Shipman [1982] Director/Master Brewer

Banini UK Ltd
Incorporated: 6 October 2014 *Employees:* 5
Net Worth Deficit: £216,312 *Total Assets:* £52,101
Registered Office: Summerfield Bungalow, Summerfield Drive, Prestwich, Manchester, M25 9XS
Major Shareholder: Lukasz Hall
Officers: Lukasz Hall [1979] Director [Polish]

Richard Banks & Co Ltd
Incorporated: 6 September 2010
Net Worth Deficit: £9,745 *Total Assets:* £84,610
Registered Office: c/o Business Control Ltd, Red Lion Yard, Odd Down, Bath, BA2 2PP
Shareholders: Richard John Banks; Alison Claire Banks
Officers: Alison Claire Banks, Secretary; Richard John Banks [1957] Director

Banks & Company (Vintners) Ltd.
Incorporated: 15 July 2011
Net Worth Deficit: £2,200 *Total Assets:* £3,432
Registered Office: 10 St Peter's Hill, Stamford, Lincs, PE9 2PE
Major Shareholder: Andrew William Banks
Officers: Andrew William Banks [1979] Director

Bankside Brewing Limited
Incorporated: 29 September 2017
Registered Office: Atrebates, Middle Road, Stanton St John, Oxford, OX33 1EX
Officers: Charles Jack Jeffrey Burt [1965] Director

Bar Joker Ltd
Incorporated: 5 December 2018
Registered Office: 52 Montague Street, Kettering, Northants, NN16 8RU
Officers: Marek Dluzak [1975] Director/Business Owner [Polish]

Georges Barbier of London Limited
Incorporated: 24 September 1984 *Employees:* 7
Net Worth: £2,019,451 *Total Assets:* £2,239,135
Registered Office: 267 Lee High Road, London, SE12 8RU
Shareholders: Georges Fernand Barbier; Mary Lynn Barbier
Officers: Mary Lynn Barbier, Secretary; Georges Fernand Barbier [1949] Director/Wine Merchant [French]; Mary Lynn Barbier [1951] Director/Wine Merchant

Barcalima Wines Limited
Incorporated: 5 April 2011
Net Worth Deficit: £3,498 *Total Assets:* £34
Registered Office: Unit 102 Bowen Court, St Asaph Business Park, St Asaph, Denbighshire, LL17 0JE
Major Shareholder: Philip Brooks
Officers: Philip James Brookes [1953] Director

J. & G. Barclay and Company Limited
Incorporated: 13 September 1993
Net Worth: £351,143 *Total Assets:* £370,663
Registered Office: 4 Eaglesham Road, Clarkston, Glasgow, G76 7BT
Officers: David Ellis Barclay, Secretary; Colin Shields Barclay [1958] Director [Canadian]; David Ellis Barclay [1991] Director/Lawyer; Fiona Adair Barclay [1961] Director/Consultant [Canadian]; Michael Shields Barclay [1989] Director/Electrician; Catharina Margaretha Zonneveld [1971] Director/Banker [Dutch]

Barcode Traders Limited
Incorporated: 30 July 2008 *Employees:* 2
Net Worth Deficit: £22,714 *Total Assets:* £993,804
Registered Office: 5th Floor, Ashford Commercial Quarter, 1 Dover Place, Ashford, Kent, TN23 1FB
Shareholders: Miron Fein; Uri Benenson
Officers: Uri Benenson [1954] Director [Israeli]; Miron Fein [1956] Director [Israeli]

Bargain Food and Booze Limited
Incorporated: 2 May 2018
Registered Office: 8 Gostling Road, Twickenham, Middlesex, TW2 6ER
Officers: Ivneet Singh [1993] Director/Shop Assistant

Bargate Drinks Limited
Incorporated: 11 October 2012
Registered Office: 82 Blind Lane, Bourne End, Bucks, SL8 5LD
Major Shareholder: Michael Agate
Officers: Michael Agate [1948] Director/Accountant

Barge & Barrell Inns Ltd
Incorporated: 23 April 2018
Registered Office: 2 South Lane, Elland, Halifax, W Yorks, HX5 0HG
Shareholder: Dylan Wheater
Officers: Dylan Wheater, Secretary; Dylan Wheater [1999] Director

Barkin Bars Ltd
Incorporated: 15 October 2015
Net Worth Deficit: £65,090 *Total Assets:* £27,581
Registered Office: 2 Main Street, Whittington, Lichfield, Staffs, WS14 9JU
Major Shareholder: Jamie Marie Lowe
Officers: Jamie Marie Lowe [1982] Director/Bar Manager

Barmaster (Independant Wholesalers) Limited
Incorporated: 15 September 1999
Net Worth: £423,402 *Total Assets:* £1,698,951
Registered Office: Unit 2 Highcliffe Mills, Bruntcliffe Lane, Morley, Leeds, LS27 9LR
Shareholders: Andrew Cooper; David Hill
Officers: Nicholas James Cooper, Secretary; Andrew Cooper [1956] Director; David Hill [1958] Director/Sales Manager

Barn Direct Limited
Incorporated: 7 July 1999 *Employees:* 18
Previous: Booze Barn Limited
Net Worth: £199,023 *Total Assets:* £797,389
Registered Office: Old Linen Court, 83-85 Shambles Street, Barnsley, S Yorks, S70 2SB
Shareholders: Narendra Chhotubhai Patel; Ushaben Narendra Patel
Officers: Narendra Chhotubhai Patel, Secretary/Director [Indian]; Narendra Chhotubhai Patel [1960] Director [Indian]; Ushaben Narendra Patel [1962] Director [Indian]

Barndiva Wine Company Limited
Incorporated: 7 August 2018
Registered Office: 305 Regents Park Road, Finchley, London, N3 1DP
Major Shareholder: Lukka Abramsky Feldman
Officers: Lukka Abramsky Feldman [1978] Director

Barokes Limited
Incorporated: 13 January 2006
Registered Office: 5 Fleet Place, London, EC4M 7RD
Officers: Steven John Anthony Barics, Secretary; Steven John Anthony Barics [1953] Director [Australian]; Alan Charles Rutland [1957] Director

Barrel Booze Limited
Incorporated: 22 June 1999 *Employees:* 14
Net Worth: £606,128 *Total Assets:* £4,874,818
Registered Office: 25 Park Street West, Luton, Beds, LU1 3BE
Major Shareholder: Amrik Singh Binning
Officers: Amarjit Singh Aujla, Secretary; Amrik Singh Binning [1958] Director

UK Wholesalers of Beers, Wines and Spirits   dellam

Barrique Vintners Limited
Incorporated: 7 November 2016 *Employees:* 1
Net Worth: £4,926,919 *Total Assets:* £5,804,571
Registered Office: Hyde Park House, 5 Manfred Road, London, SW15 2RS
Officers: Gary James Boom [1958] Director [Dutch]; Peter Anthony Lunzer [1959] Director

Barry Drinks Ltd
Incorporated: 18 October 2013
Net Worth: £27,400 *Total Assets:* £188,645
Registered Office: Unit 6 Lansdowne Road, Union Park, Norwich, NR6 6NF
Major Shareholder: Tamor Kaur
Officers: Ravinder Dahliwal [1982] Director; Dalil Singh [1979] Director

Barrys Discount Ltd.
Incorporated: 27 October 2010
Net Worth: £49,492 *Total Assets:* £1,025,938
Registered Office: 384-386 Staines Road, Feltham, Middlesex, TW14 8BT
Shareholder: Preet Singh Suri
Officers: Preet Singh Suri [1970] Director/Marketing Manager

E J Bartholomew Limited
Incorporated: 8 October 2014
Net Worth Deficit: £58,699 *Total Assets:* £295
Registered Office: 108 High Street, Stevenage, Herts, SG1 3DW
Shareholders: Sandy Angus; Virginia Clarke
Officers: Edward Bartholomew [1987] Director; Jack Bartholomew [1989] Director

T. & J.T. Barton (Bottlers) Limited
Incorporated: 19 January 1978 *Employees:* 42
Net Worth: £6,063,621 *Total Assets:* £8,811,326
Registered Office: 410 Bolton Road, Ashton in Makerfield, Wigan, Lancs, WN4 8UN
Parent: T. & J.T Barton (Holdings) Limited
Officers: John Thomas Barton, Secretary; John Thomas Barton [1947] Director; Margaret Gallagher [1943] Director

Barton, Brownsdon & Sadler Limited
Incorporated: 7 November 1985 *Employees:* 4
Net Worth: £138,178 *Total Assets:* £1,073,883
Registered Office: Unit 16 Star Road, Partridge Green, Horsham, W Sussex, RH13 8RA
Shareholders: Nicholas John Budibent; Giles Willson Budibent
Officers: Giles Willson Budibent [1973] Director; John Barry Budibent [1945] Director; Nicholas John Budibent [1975] Director

Barwell & Jones Limited
Incorporated: 30 December 2008 *Employees:* 7
Net Worth: £209,488 *Total Assets:* £299,874
Registered Office: The Sovereign Distillery, Wilson Road, Huyton, Knowsley, Merseyside, L36 6AD
Parent: Chalie Richards & Company Limited
Officers: Stewart Andrew Hainsworth [1969] Director/Chief Executive; Alan William Robinson [1965] Finance Director

Base Cachaca Import (UK) Ltd
Incorporated: 16 August 2011
Registered Office: 59 Windsor Road, London, N7 6JL
Major Shareholder: Sebastian Thomas Keuchel
Officers: Sebastian Thomas Keuchel [1970] Director

Basket Press Wines Ltd
Incorporated: 27 October 2016
Net Worth Deficit: £6,950 *Total Assets:* £5,909
Registered Office: 14 Alfred Road, London, W3 6LH
Officers: Zainab Juzer Barodawalla [1984] Director/Wine Sales Person [Indian]; Jiri Majerik [1975] Director/Hospitality Manager [Czech]

Bassen Ltd
Incorporated: 25 July 2018
Registered Office: 75 Gainsborough Green, Abingdon, Oxon, OX14 5JL
Shareholders: Gkor Tovmasian; Hayk Tovmasyan
Officers: Gkor Tovmasian [1991] Director/Self Employed [Greek]

Bassrap Ltd
Incorporated: 19 September 2017
Registered Office: 6 Turtons Croft, Bilston, W Midlands, WV14 9YA
Officers: Paramdeep Singh Bassra [1989] Managing Director/CEO

Batarak Limited
Incorporated: 20 March 2017
Registered Office: 3 Butlin Close, Rothwell, Kettering, Northants, NN14 6YA
Major Shareholder: Paul Lawrence Gamage
Officers: Paul Lawrence Gamage [1954] Director

Batch Cider Ltd
Incorporated: 30 January 2019
Registered Office: 12 Greenway, London, N14 6NN
Major Shareholder: Carl Reid
Officers: Carl Reid [1993] Director/Architect

The Bath Gin Company Limited
Incorporated: 4 June 2013 *Employees:* 5
Net Worth Deficit: £14,769 *Total Assets:* £101,798
Registered Office: 2-3 Queen Street, Bath, BA1 1HE
Shareholders: Peter Meacock; Harald Eric Bret
Officers: Harald Eric Bret [1979] Director [French]; Peter Meacock [1958] Director; Thomas Edward Hugh Pople [1987] Director/General Manager

Bath Sixteen Limited
Incorporated: 15 January 2016
Net Worth Deficit: £13,769 *Total Assets:* £41,083
Registered Office: 8 Linnet Court, Cawledge Business Park, Alnwick, Northumberland, NE66 2GD
Officers: Andrew George Deans, Secretary; Andrew George Deans [1991] Director; George Deans [1967] Director

Baton Rouge Limited
Incorporated: 20 April 1994
Net Worth Deficit: £155,720
Registered Office: 17 Cononbury Lane, London, N1 2AS
Major Shareholder: Ross Douglas Bull
Officers: Mary Christine Bull, Secretary; Mary Christine Bull [1947] Director; Ross Douglas Bull [1947] Director/Economist

Battlefield Beers Limited
Incorporated: 9 May 2006 *Employees:* 8
Net Worth: £85,851 *Total Assets:* £220,294
Registered Office: 6 Claremont Building, Claremont Bank, Shrewsbury, Salop, SY1 1RJ
Major Shareholder: John Pitcher
Officers: Gillian Pitcher, Secretary; John Pitcher [1961] Managing Director

Battlefield Brewery Limited
Incorporated: 12 February 2013 *Employees:* 6
Net Worth Deficit: £326,088 *Total Assets:* £162,528
Registered Office: Battlefield Brewery, Harlescott Lane, Shrewsbury, Salop, SY1 3AH
Shareholders: Graham David Boulger; Shane Brian Craig
Officers: Graham David Boulger [1958] Director; Susan Sharon Boulger [1962] Director

Battys Discount Drinks Store Limited
Incorporated: 8 August 2002 *Employees:* 12
Net Worth: £116,257 *Total Assets:* £201,729
Registered Office: 41 Brighton Street, Barrow in Furness, Cumbria, LA14 5HG
Shareholders: David Batty; Michelle Batty
Officers: Michelle Batty, Secretary; David William Batty [1969] Director/Manager; Michelle Batty [1972] Director/Manager

The Bavarian Beer Company Ltd
Incorporated: 7 February 2018
Registered Office: Lakeview House, 4 Woodbrook Crescent, Billericay, Essex, CM12 0EQ
Major Shareholder: Richard John Lewsey
Officers: Richard John Lewsey [1959] Director

Bayede Wines UK Ltd
Incorporated: 30 January 2019
Registered Office: 999 London Road, Thornton Heath, Surrey, CR7 6JE
Major Shareholder: Subhash Chander Sood
Officers: Subhash Chander Sood [1948] Director

Bazaar Store Ltd
Incorporated: 28 August 2018
Registered Office: Unit 7A-7B, Parkway Drive, Sheffield, S9 4WN
Major Shareholder: Gunel Zaidova
Officers: Cihan Cocelli, Secretary; Gunel Zaidova [1986] Managing Director

BB & R Limited
Incorporated: 28 June 2005 *Employees:* 270
Net Worth: £51,975,000 *Total Assets:* £254,874,000
Registered Office: 3 St James's Street, London, SW1A 1EG
Parent: Berry Bros. & Rudd Limited
Officers: Janet Ann Impey, Secretary; Christopher John Robinson [1969] Director; Elizabeth Margaret Rudd [1966] Director

BB & R Spirits Limited
Incorporated: 25 March 1943
Registered Office: One Fleet Place, London, EC4M 7WS
Parent: Highland Distillers Limited
Officers: Gemma May Robson, Secretary; Martin Alexander Cooke [1961] Director/Solicitor; Alan William Frizzell [1964] Director/Chartered Accountant

BCM Brewing Company Ltd
Incorporated: 15 February 2019
Registered Office: Hayles Bridge Offices, 228 Mulgrave Road, Cheam, Surrey, SM2 6JT
Officers: David Richard Johnson [1972] Director; Lesley Edna Meeson [1977] Director; Rosalyn Porter [1957] Director; Stephen John Porter [1955] Director

BD Wines Limited
Incorporated: 1 December 2016 *Employees:* 1
Net Worth: £2,807 *Total Assets:* £33,407
Registered Office: Dane John Works, Gordon Road, Canterbury, Kent, CT1 3PP
Major Shareholder: Benoit Dezecot
Officers: Benoit Dezecot [1985] Director [French]

BDDR Enterprises Limited
Incorporated: 16 December 2013
Registered Office: 26 Sudbrooke Road, London, SW12 8TG
Officers: Derek Shannon Moore, Secretary; Brandy Moore [1971] Director/IT Sales [American]; Derek Moore [1968] Director/IT Sales [American]

Bdellium Trading Company Limited
Incorporated: 9 May 2015
Registered Office: 51 Deer Park Way, Waltham Abbey, Essex, EN9 3YN
Major Shareholder: Kayode Adeniyi Oyetunde
Officers: Kayode Adeniyi Oyetunde [1972] Director/Trading

Be Hop Ltd
Incorporated: 30 November 2017
Registered Office: Flat 6, 23 Maud Street, London, E16 1YU
Major Shareholder: Lysander Demaiter
Officers: Lysander Demaiter [1992] Director [Belgian]

Be My Wine Ltd.
Incorporated: 14 March 2013 *Employees:* 10
Net Worth Deficit: £34,379 *Total Assets:* £235,710
Registered Office: 100 Nottingham Terrace, London, NW1 4QE
Shareholders: Geoffray Benat; Dan Cohen
Officers: Geoffray Benat [1985] Director [French]; Dan Cohen [1987] Director [French]

Be Organiq Limited
Incorporated: 5 May 2015
Previous: U.D.K.N. Limited
Net Worth: £13,583 *Total Assets:* £19,275
Registered Office: 1st Floor, Office 160, Block D, New Covent Garden, London, SW8 5LL
Officers: Nicolae Chitoraga [1993] Director/Wine Connoisseur [Moldovan]

Be Rude Not To Ltd
Incorporated: 11 June 2018
Registered Office: 4 Downe Close, East Cowick, Goole, E Yorks, DN14 9EY
Major Shareholder: David McIvor
Officers: David McIvor [1962] Director/Entrepreneur

Beacon Wines Limited
Incorporated: 25 January 2016
Net Worth: £4,819 *Total Assets:* £13,865
Registered Office: 3 Warwick Road, Beaconsfield, Bucks, HP9 2PE
Officers: Alison Jane Cadwell, Secretary; Alison Jane Cadwell [1965] Director/Wholesale and Retail of Wine and Other Alcohol; Simon Bryan Shaw Ronaldson [1966] Director/Wholesale and Retail of Wine and Other Alcohol

UK Wholesalers of Beers, Wines and Spirits   dellam

Bear Smyth Limited
Incorporated: 18 November 2013
Net Worth Deficit: £45,365 *Total Assets:* £373,714
Registered Office: 4th Floor, Allan House, 10 John Princes Street, London, W1G 0AH
Shareholders: Bjorn Filip Botvid Johansson; Gerard Anthony Smyth
Officers: Bjorn Filip Botvid Johansson [1978] Director/Management Consultant [Swedish]; Gerard Anthony Smyth [1966] Director/Consultant

Bearded Lion Drinks Company Ltd
Incorporated: 23 March 2018
Registered Office: 170 Hereford Drive, Bootle, Merseyside, L30 1QZ
Major Shareholder: Johnathan Charles Stewart
Officers: Johnathan Charles Stewart [1987] Director/Manager

Beattie & Roberts Imports Ltd
Incorporated: 1 November 2018
Registered Office: 14a Mountgrove Road, London, N5 2LS
Shareholders: Francis Alexander Roberts; Thomas Ian James Beattie
Officers: Thomas Ian James Beattie [1988] Director [Australian]; Francis Alexander Roberts [1987] Director

Beatville Limited
Incorporated: 2 January 1990 *Employees:* 4
Net Worth: £1,240,292 *Total Assets:* £1,337,569
Registered Office: 8B Laynes House, 526-528 Watford Way, Mill Hill, London, NW7 4RS
Officers: Urvashi Shah, Secretary; Dipak Lalji Shah [1963] Director; Javed Farhat Ullah [1941] Director

Beaumont Beverages Ltd.
Incorporated: 13 March 2017
Net Worth Deficit: £2,817 *Total Assets:* £3,615
Registered Office: 98 Stafford Road, Wallington, Surrey, SM6 9AY
Shareholder: Sophie Beaumont
Officers: Sophie Beaumont [1991] Director

Beautiful Beers East Anglia (UK) Limited
Incorporated: 11 January 2019
Registered Office: 1b St Johns Street, Bury St Edmunds, Suffolk, IP33 1SQ
Major Shareholder: Cornelis Fredericus Matheus Van Den Oort
Officers: Cornelis Fredericus Matheus Van Den Oort [1962] Director/Proprietor [Dutch]

Bedford Continental Wholesale Limited
Incorporated: 17 May 1979
Registered Office: Total Produce, Enterprise Way, Pinchbeck, Spalding, Lincs, PE11 3YR
Parent: Skoulikas Bedford Limited
Officers: Brendan Dermot Coakley [1953] Director/Chairman [Irish]

Bedminster Beer Company Limited
Incorporated: 18 June 2013
Net Worth: £58 *Total Assets:* £29,970
Registered Office: Suite 1, Liberty House, South Liberty Lane, Bristol, BS3 2ST
Shareholders: Paul Wratten; Danette Wratten
Officers: Danette Wratten [1977] Director; Paul Wratten [1985] Director/Pub Manager

Beeble Liquor Limited
Incorporated: 23 October 2018
Registered Office: Eastcourt House, Eastcourt, Malmesbury, Wilts, SN16 9HP
Shareholders: Matthew Campbell Brauer; Nicola Jane Reed
Officers: Matthew Campbell Brauer [1991] Director/Accountant; Nicola Jane Reed [1965] Director/Artist

Beef and Burgundy Limited
Incorporated: 21 July 2009
Net Worth: £22,824 *Total Assets:* £276,964
Registered Office: 4 Cleaves Avenue, Colerne, Chippenham, Wilts, SN14 8BX
Major Shareholder: Mark Haisma
Officers: Mark John Haisma [1972] Director [Australian]

Beefeater Distillery Limited
Incorporated: 31 March 1954
Previous: European Cellars (Germany) Limited
Registered Office: Chivas House, 72 Chancellors Road, London, W6 9RS
Parent: Allied Domecq Spirits & Wine Limited
Officers: Stuart MacNab [1964] Director/Accountant; Vincent Turpin [1978] Director/Chief Financial Officer [French]

Beer & Co Distribution and Sales Limited
Incorporated: 31 March 2017
Net Worth Deficit: £1,079 *Total Assets:* £1,205
Registered Office: 18 Bonny Crescent, Ipswich, Suffolk, IP3 9UN
Shareholders: Gregory Gary Cooper; Rachel Marie Jane Cooper
Officers: Gregory Gary Cooper [1973] Director; Rachel Marie Jane Cooper [1972] Director

Beer & Wine (Northern) Limited
Incorporated: 23 May 2018
Registered Office: 148 Jethro Street, Bolton, Lancs, BL2 2PL
Major Shareholder: Dax Owen
Officers: Dax Owen [1972] Director

The Beer and Gas Man Limited
Incorporated: 26 November 2009
Net Worth: £24,104 *Total Assets:* £150,710
Registered Office: The Barn, Wood Farm, Coal Pit Lane, Willey, Warwicks, CV23 0SL
Major Shareholder: Mark Joseph O'Neill
Officers: Mark Joseph O'Neill [1980] Director/Driver

Beer and Spirit Agencies International Limited
Incorporated: 21 January 1992 *Employees:* 2
Net Worth: £3,745 *Total Assets:* £15,528
Registered Office: 168 Church Road, Hove, E Sussex, BN3 2DL
Major Shareholder: Michael Cook
Officers: Michael Cook [1937] Director/Salesman; Karl Patrick Weddell [1972] Director

Beer Barrels & Minerals (Wales) Limited
Incorporated: 30 June 1995
Net Worth: £19,736 *Total Assets:* £319,029
Registered Office: Guardian House, 5a Squire Drive, Brynmenyn Industrial Estate, Bridgend, Mid Glamorgan, CF32 9TX
Shareholders: Gurmit Singh Bedesha; Rachel Bedesha
Officers: Gurmit Singh Bedesha [1962] Director/General Manager

The Beer Belly Company Incorporated Limited
Incorporated: 17 January 2014 *Employees:* 3
Net Worth: £96,532 *Total Assets:* £1,775,833
Registered Office: Onega House, 112 Main Road, Sidcup, Kent, DA14 6NE
Major Shareholder: Craig Johnathan Richards
Officers: Craig Johnathan Richards [1976] Director

Beer Belly's Ltd
Incorporated: 21 July 2014
Net Worth: £16,971 *Total Assets:* £50,515
Registered Office: Grosvenor House, 11 St Pauls Square, Birmingham, B3 1RB
Major Shareholder: Ravi Inder Singh Kaypee
Officers: Ravi Inder Singh Kaypee [1984] Director/Wholesale

The Beer Bottle Company Ltd
Incorporated: 20 February 2015
Registered Office: 7 Church Avenue, Newry, Co Armagh, BT34 1DY
Officers: Enda Julia McElherron [1969] Director

The Beer Boutique Ltd
Incorporated: 19 April 2011 *Employees:* 9
Net Worth: £38,033 *Total Assets:* £148,845
Registered Office: 78 St John's Hill, London, SW11 1SF
Parent: Two Heads Beer Co Limited
Officers: James Charles Hickson [1983] Director; Jonathan Russell Kaye [1973] Director/Investor; Marc Verlet [1975] Director/Banker [Belgian]

The Beer Company (Exports) Ltd
Incorporated: 10 July 2014
Net Worth: £100 *Total Assets:* £100
Registered Office: WH Prior, Railway Court, Doncaster, S Yorks, DN4 5FB
Parent: The Beer Company Limited
Officers: Philip Craig Lee [1970] Director; Joanne Taylor [1979] Director

The Beer Company Consolidations Limited
Incorporated: 30 May 2014
Net Worth: £162,664 *Total Assets:* £1,022,201
Registered Office: W H Prior, Railway Court, Doncaster, S Yorks, DN4 5FB
Parent: The Beer Company Limited
Officers: Joanne Taylor [1979] Director

The Beer Company Limited
Incorporated: 7 October 2008 *Employees:* 2
Net Worth: £263,980 *Total Assets:* £1,662,319
Registered Office: W H Prior, Railway Court, Doncaster, S Yorks, DN4 5FB
Major Shareholder: Joanne Taylor
Officers: Joanne Taylor, Secretary; Joanne Taylor [1979] Director

Beer Express Limited
Incorporated: 18 June 1998 *Employees:* 40
Net Worth: £550,822 *Total Assets:* £1,937,517
Registered Office: Unit 15 Derwent Mills Commercial Park, Cockermouth, Cumbria, CA13 0HT
Major Shareholder: Jasbir Singh
Officers: Michelle McAvoy, Secretary; Maureen McDonald [1966] Director/Sales; Michelle McAvoy [1972] Director

Beer Gonzo Ltd
Incorporated: 15 March 2010
Net Worth: £214 *Total Assets:* £117,416
Registered Office: 3a Earlsdon Street, Coventry, Warwicks, CV5 6EP
Shareholders: Anthony Charles Akers; Martin Stephen Paul Leape; Michael Christopher Leape
Officers: Anthony Charles Akers [1977] Director/Manager; Martin Stephen Paul Leape [1980] Director/Manager; Micheal Christopher Leape [1969] Director/Publican

Beer Journey Ltd
Incorporated: 31 January 2017
Registered Office: 5 Clos Tyniad Glo, Barry, Vale of Glamorgan, CF63 4QQ
Shareholders: Alex Martindale-Dopson; Joseph Thomas Williams
Officers: Alex Martindale-Dopson [1991] Director; Joseph Thomas Williams [1991] Director

Beer Land Ltd
Incorporated: 15 August 2017
Net Worth: £10 *Total Assets:* £10
Registered Office: 3 Chestnut Drive, London, E11 2TA
Major Shareholder: Andrius Talat-Kelpsa
Officers: Andrius Talat-Kelpsa [1975] Managing Director [Lithuanian]

Beer Me Now Ltd
Incorporated: 4 July 2018
Registered Office: 23 St Cyrus Road, Colchester, Essex, CO4 0NG
Major Shareholder: Evan Herbert
Officers: Evan Herbert [1991] Director

Beer Paradise (York) Limited
Incorporated: 14 October 2009 *Employees:* 9
Net Worth: £206,111 *Total Assets:* £307,477
Registered Office: Unit 20 Centre Park, Marston Moor Business Park, Tockwith, York, YO26 7QF
Officers: Karen Elizabeth Annely [1958] Director; Zak Avery [1970] Director

The Beer People Limited
Incorporated: 1 September 2014
Net Worth: £12,622 *Total Assets:* £29,801
Registered Office: 7 Manor Park Road, Cleckheaton, W Yorks, BD19 5BL
Shareholders: Pat Schoffield; Haseeb Qureshi
Officers: Haseeb Qureshi [1985] Director/Manager; Patricia Ann Schofield [1953] Director/Manager

Beer Rocks Brewery Ltd
Incorporated: 8 October 2012 *Employees:* 21
Net Worth Deficit: £1,384 *Total Assets:* £11,064
Registered Office: 34 Main Street, Cherry Burton, Beverley, N Humbers, HU17 7RF
Major Shareholder: Mark Antony Dallison
Officers: Mark Antony Dallison [1972] Director/Sales Marketing

Beer Seller Ltd
Incorporated: 14 November 2017
Registered Office: Halfway House, Horsmonden Road, Brenchley, Tonbridge, Kent, TN12 7AX
Major Shareholder: Samuel Louis Allen
Officers: Samuel Louis Allen [1990] Managing Director

Beer Supply Limited
Incorporated: 13 October 2009
Net Worth Deficit: £1,320 *Total Assets:* £1,001
Registered Office: Unit 2 Highcliffe Mill, Bruntcliffe Lane, Morley, Leeds, LS27 9LR
Major Shareholder: David Hill
Officers: David Hill [1958] Director; Nicky Lee Hill [1981] Director

Beer Traders UK Limited
Incorporated: 14 February 2018
Registered Office: 15 Charlton Lane, Leckhampton, Cheltenham, Glos, GL53 9DT
Major Shareholder: Grant MacDonald Cook
Officers: Grant MacDonald Cook [1959] Director

The Beer Warehouse (Maidenhead) Limited
Incorporated: 20 July 2001 *Employees:* 17
Net Worth: £452,984 *Total Assets:* £1,236,490
Registered Office: Suite 1, Unit A1 Tectonic Place, Holyport Road, Maidenhead, Berks, SL6 2YE
Shareholders: Michelle Rita McNulty; Ciaran McNulty
Officers: Ciaran McNulty [1969] Director

Beer52 Limited
Incorporated: 14 May 2013 *Employees:* 11
Net Worth: £433,395 *Total Assets:* £865,624
Registered Office: 26 Howe Street, Edinburgh, EH3 6TG
Shareholders: James Brown; Fraser Doherty
Officers: James Ronald Brown [1989] Director/Entrepreneur; Fraser Doherty [1988] Director

Beercall Ltd
Incorporated: 2 September 2015
Net Worth: £1,000 *Total Assets:* £1,000
Registered Office: 71-75 Shelton Street, Covent Garden, London, WC2H 9JQ
Officers: Arthur Saly [1968] Director

Beerco Limited
Incorporated: 18 January 2019
Registered Office: Kingsnorth House, Blenheim Way, Birmingham, B44 8LS
Major Shareholder: Joseph Alan Povey
Officers: Joseph Alan Povey [1989] Director

Beerfantastic Ltd
Incorporated: 4 February 2010
Registered Office: Warrens Farm, Brook Road, Great Tey, Colchester, Essex, CO6 1JG
Parent: Winefantastic Ltd
Officers: Katharine Esther Prestwich, Secretary; John Roland Greenwold [1967] Director; John Peter Williams [1964] Director; Andrew John Wolton [1966] Director

Beermaster Derby Ltd
Incorporated: 25 October 2010
Net Worth: £18,559 *Total Assets:* £294,002
Registered Office: 22 Melton Avenue, Littleover, Derby, DE23 1FY
Major Shareholder: Satnam Singh Dhamrait
Officers: Satnam Singh Dhamrait [1965] Director/Self Employed

Beerpol Ltd
Incorporated: 7 February 2018
Registered Office: Flat 3, 33 Westbere Road, London, NW2 3SP
Shareholders: Slawomir Lisek; Bogdan Piotr Niedbalec
Officers: Bogdan Piotr Niedbalec [1971] Director [Polish]

Beerscellars (UK) Limited
Incorporated: 7 February 2014
Previous: Hops and Barley Limited
Registered Office: Castor Street, Liverpool, L6 5AT
Parent: Hops and Barley (Group) Limited
Officers: John Kenneth Ravenscroft [1955] Director/Licencee

Beerspotters Ltd
Incorporated: 18 January 2012
Net Worth Deficit: £28,032 *Total Assets:* £2,037
Registered Office: 10 Bolton Street, Ramsbottom, Bury, Lancs, BL0 9HX
Major Shareholder: Leon John O'Callaghan
Officers: Leon John O'Callaghan [1967] Director

Beets Incorporated Ltd
Incorporated: 4 October 2017
Registered Office: 22 St Nicholas Street, Bodmin, Cornwall, PL31 1AD
Major Shareholder: Jolyon Alexander Donald Ferrier
Officers: Jolyon Alexander Donald Ferrier [1988] Director

Bekel Limited
Incorporated: 13 June 1989 *Employees:* 1
Net Worth Deficit: £51,945 *Total Assets:* £63,427
Registered Office: c/o Oran Mor, 731 Great Western Road, Glasgow, G12 8QX
Major Shareholder: Colin MacLean Beattie
Officers: Colin MacLean Beattie [1953] Director/Publican

Belabon Drinks Ltd
Incorporated: 16 May 2018
Registered Office: 18 Arnside Gardens, Wembley, Middlesex, HA9 8TJ
Major Shareholder: Nicholas Jaksic
Officers: Nicholas Jaksic [1984] Director/Entrepreneur

Belfast Distillery Company Limited
Incorporated: 18 October 2010
Previous: Belfast Distillery Limited
Net Worth Deficit: £1,912,616 *Total Assets:* £2,192,911
Registered Office: c/o Elliott Duffy Garrett, 40 Linenhall Street, Belfast, BT2 8BA
Major Shareholder: Mark Fuller
Officers: Joseph Raymond Babiec [1968] Managing Director [American]; Mark Benton Fuller [1953] Director/Management Consultant [American]

The Belgian Life Limited
Incorporated: 6 December 2016
Net Worth Deficit: £7,416 *Total Assets:* £5,696
Registered Office: Jubilee House, East Beach, Lytham St Annes, Lancs, FY8 5FT
Shareholders: Alexandra Theresa Cosgrave; Mark Duncan
Officers: Alexandra Theresa Cosgrave, Secretary; Alexandra Theresa Cosgrave [1965] Director/Estate Agent; Mark Duncan [1962] Director/Aircraft Sprayer

Belgrave Distribution Ltd
Incorporated: 5 December 2011
Registered Office: First Floor, 34-36 High Street, Barkingside, Essex, IG6 2DQ
Major Shareholder: Thirunavukarasu Prabaharan
Officers: Thirunavukarasu Prabaharan [1962] Director

Belizaire Drinks Ltd
Incorporated: 16 January 2019
Registered Office: Apartment 1708, City Heights, Victoria Bridge Street, Salford, M3 5AS
Major Shareholder: Aidan Ross Belizaire
Officers: Aidan Ross Belizaire [1986] Marketing Director

Bellissimo Vino Edinburgh Ltd
Incorporated: 16 May 2018
Registered Office: 20 Baberton Mains Loan, Edinburgh, EH14 3EP
Major Shareholder: Gary Cennerazzo
Officers: Gary Cennerazzo [1989] Managing Director [Scottish/Italian]

Belloni Limited
Incorporated: 22 February 2000
Net Worth: £33,291 *Total Assets:* £33,291
Registered Office: 9 Tileyard Road, London, N7 9AH
Shareholder: Ratilal Vadher
Officers: Ratilal Vadher, Secretary/Director; Carmine Carnevale [1941] Director [Italian]; Antonia Maroso [1954] Director [Italian]; Ratilal Vadher [1949] Director; Anna Vainella [1954] Director [Italian]

Bellwether Impex (UK) Limited
Incorporated: 19 July 2016
Registered Office: 21 Goldcraft Close, Heywood, Lancs, OL10 2QW
Major Shareholder: Moses Adedoyin Adegbite
Officers: Moses Adedoyin Adegbite [1975] Director/Business Person [Ghanaian]

Bellwether Wines Ltd
Incorporated: 21 July 2009
Registered Office: Rutland House, Minerva Business Park, Lynch Wood, Peterborough, Cambs, PE2 6PZ
Shareholders: Paul Robert Hook; John Bryan
Officers: John Bryan [1972] Director; Paul Robert Hook [1955] Director; Maurice Adrian Posnett [1963] Director

Belvoir Brewery Limited
Incorporated: 23 March 1995
Net Worth: £195,942 *Total Assets:* £238,945
Registered Office: Crown Park, Station Road, Old Dalby, Melton Mowbray, Leics, LE14 3NQ
Major Shareholder: Colin William Brown
Officers: Margaret Ruth Griffiths, Secretary; Colin William Brown [1959] Director/Businessman

Bemco International (UK) Limited
Incorporated: 2 December 2002 *Employees:* 1
Net Worth Deficit: £7,379 *Total Assets:* £9,473
Registered Office: 14 Bull Road, Stratford, London, E15 3HQ
Shareholder: Edward Osei-Tutu Bonsu
Officers: Anne Osei-Tutu Bonsu, Secretary; Edward Osei-Tutu Bonsu [1961] Director

Benchmark Drinks Ltd
Incorporated: 23 January 2018
Registered Office: Timsons Business Centre, Bath Road, Kettering, Northants, NN16 8NQ
Major Shareholder: Paul Michael Schaafsma
Officers: Paul Michael Schaafsma [1973] Managing Director; Oliver Sebastian Wessely [1972] Director

Bengal Foods Limited
Incorporated: 15 March 1996
Net Worth: £202,364 *Total Assets:* £338,487
Registered Office: Clarence House, 35 Clarence Street, Market Harborough, Leics, LE16 7NE
Officers: Abdul Majid [1959] Managing Director; Usman Goni Majid [1982] Director

Benjamin & Blum Limited
Incorporated: 27 February 2012
Net Worth: £34,701 *Total Assets:* £51,247
Registered Office: 17 Hanover Square, London, W1S 1BN
Shareholders: Paul Andrew Benjamin; Marta Magdalena Lejkowski
Officers: Paul Andrew Benjamin [1974] Director; Marta Magdalena Lejkowski [1975] Director [Polish]

Bent Distribution Ltd
Incorporated: 31 July 2015
Net Worth: £250 *Total Assets:* £104,484
Registered Office: 295A Heathway, Dagenham, Essex, RM9 5AQ
Major Shareholder: Robertas Uzukauskas
Officers: Robertas Uzukauskas [1972] Director [Lithuanian]

Berkeley Cellars Limited
Incorporated: 3 August 2018
Registered Office: 16a Vicarage Street, Warminster, Wilts, BA12 8JE
Major Shareholder: Andrew Grant Gulliver
Officers: Andrew Grant Gulliver [1961] Director

Berkmann Family Holdings Limited
Incorporated: 30 January 1964 *Employees:* 205
Net Worth: £10,311,973 *Total Assets:* £28,857,532
Registered Office: No 10-12 Brewery Road, London, N7 9NH
Major Shareholder: Joseph Berkmann
Officers: Nitkuna Raj Vimala Raj, Secretary; Ewa Smolinska Berkmann [1949] Director; Joseph Berkmann [1931] Director/Wine Merchant [Austrian]; Rupert Anthony Berkmann [1979] Director; Peter Haidacher [1943] Director [Austrian]

Berkmann Wine Cellars Limited
Incorporated: 10 November 1987 *Employees:* 205
Net Worth: £12,119,620 *Total Assets:* £30,443,210
Registered Office: 10-12 Brewery Road, London, N7 9NH
Parent: Berkmann Family Holdings Ltd
Officers: Sarah Jane Clark, Secretary; Joseph Berkmann [1931] Director/Wine Merchant [Austrian]; Rupert Anthony Berkmann [1979] Director; Michel Canard [1956] Director/Salesman [French]; Dinesh Changela [1956] Commercial Director; Alexander Julian Hunt [1979] Purchasing Director; William Peter Lowe [1961] Director/Wine Merchant; Charles Edward Marshall [1969] Director/Importation, Marketing, Sale of Alcoholic Beverage; Edward William Joseph Martin [1979] Director/Businessman; Bruno Richard [1958] Director/Salesman [French]; Nitkuna Raj Vimala-Raj [1966] Finance Director [Malaysian]

Bermondsey Gin Limited
Incorporated: 15 June 2004 *Employees:* 3
Net Worth: £7,595 *Total Assets:* £225,051
Registered Office: 75 Mutley Plain, Plymouth, PL4 6JJ
Major Shareholder: Christian Errboe Jensen
Officers: Alan Forrester, Secretary; Christian Errboe Jensen [1964] Director [Danish]

David Berryman Holdings Limited
Incorporated: 23 September 2016
Net Worth: £1,133,224 Total Assets: £1,133,224
Registered Office: New Orchard Estate, Unit B Airport Executive Park, President Way, Luton, Beds, LU2 9NY
Shareholders: Marianne Florence Pyrke; David Alec Berryman
Officers: David Alec Berryman, Secretary; Clare Miquette Bartholdi [1979] Director; David Alec Berryman [1942] Director; Tom David Berryman [1982] Director/Civil Servant [British/Swiss]; Rachel Joy Collins [1975] Managing Director; Robert Alan Shotton [1949] Director

David Berryman Limited
Incorporated: 29 October 1987 Employees: 37
Net Worth: £1,463,015 Total Assets: £5,656,133
Registered Office: New Orchard Estate, Unit B Airport Executive Park, President Way, Luton, Beds, LU2 9NY
Parent: David Berryman Holdings Limited
Officers: David Alec Berryman, Secretary; David Alec Berryman [1942] Director; Rachel Joy Collins [1975] Managing Director; Robert Alan Shotton [1949] Director

Bespoke Fine Wines Limited
Incorporated: 8 November 2018
Registered Office: 28 Bagdale, Whitby, N Yorks, YO21 1QL
Shareholders: Christopher Arthur Jones; Joshua James Richard Mullock
Officers: Christopher Arthur Jones [1961] Director; Joshua James Richard Mullock [1996] Director

The Bespoke London Wine Company Limited
Incorporated: 10 December 2010
Registered Office: Ivy Cottage, The Common, Barton Turf, Norwich, NR12 8BA
Major Shareholder: Gavin Robert Morgan Smith
Officers: Alan Warwick Morgan Smith, Secretary; Gavin Robert Morgan Smith [1979] Director/Wine Merchant; Shelagh Lesley Smith [1949] Director

Bespoke Wines Ltd
Incorporated: 24 October 2008
Net Worth: £63,916 Total Assets: £132,264
Registered Office: The Bottle Shop, 4 Pen-Y-Lan Road, Roath, Cardiff, CF24 3PF
Officers: Daniel Williams [1982] Director/Self Employed

Best Bordeaux Wines Ltd
Incorporated: 22 February 2019
Registered Office: 26 Holmwood Road, Enfield, Middlesex, EN3 6QJ
Major Shareholder: Gnaly Kore
Officers: Gnaly Kore [1973] Director [French]

Best Cask Ltd
Incorporated: 23 April 2018
Registered Office: 71-75 Shelton Street, London, WC2H 9JQ
Shareholders: Huibin Feng; Douglas George William Scott
Officers: Dr Huibin Feng [1973] Director [Chinese]; Douglas George William Scott [1963] Director

The Best of America Limited
Incorporated: 23 September 1997
Registered Office: 60 Pitshanger Lane, London, W5 1QY
Officers: Douglas Michael Harrison, Secretary/Director; Douglas Michael Harrison [1942] Director

The Best of Beaujolais Limited
Incorporated: 14 October 2005
Registered Office: 60 Pitshanger Lane, London, W5 1QY
Major Shareholder: Douglas Michael Harrison
Officers: Belinda Harrison, Secretary; Douglas Michael Harrison [1945] Director

The Best of Bordeaux Limited
Incorporated: 21 June 2005
Registered Office: The Studio, 60 Pitshanger Lane, London, W5 1QY
Officers: Belinda Harrison, Secretary; Douglas Michael Harrison [1945] Director

The Best of Burgundy Limited
Incorporated: 21 June 2005
Registered Office: The Studio, 60 Pitshanger Lane, London, W5 1QY
Officers: Belinda Harrison, Secretary; Douglas Michael Harrison [1945] Director

The Best of California Limited
Incorporated: 23 September 1997
Registered Office: 60 Pitshanger Lane, London, W5 1QY
Officers: Douglas Michael Harrison, Secretary/Director; Douglas Michael Harrison [1942] Director

Best of Champagne Limited
Incorporated: 7 February 2011
Registered Office: The Studio, 60 Pitshanger Lane, London, W5 1QY
Officers: Lydia Harrison [1983] Director

Best of France Limited
Incorporated: 7 February 2011
Registered Office: The Studio, 60 Pitshanger Lane, London, W5 1QY
Officers: Lydia Harrison [1983] Director

Best of Hungary Ltd
Incorporated: 10 November 2016
Net Worth: £1,491 Total Assets: £22,887
Registered Office: Brynhyfryd, Taliesin, Machynlleth, Powys, SY20 8JG
Shareholders: Monika Konstantina Gyenes; Zoltan Laszlo Kopacsi
Officers: Monika Konstantina Gyenes [1962] Director [Hungarian]; Zoltan Laszlo Kopacsi [1993] Director [Hungarian]

Best of Italy Limited
Incorporated: 7 February 2011
Registered Office: The Studio, 60 Pitshanger Lane, London, W5 1QY
Officers: Lydia Harrison [1983] Director

The Best of Loire Limited
Incorporated: 14 October 2005
Registered Office: 60 Pitshanger Lane, London, W5 1QY
Major Shareholder: Douglas Michael Harrison
Officers: Belinda Harrison, Secretary; Douglas Michael Harrison [1945] Director

Best of New World Limited
Incorporated: 7 February 2011
Registered Office: The Studio, 60 Pitshanger Lane, London, W5 1QY
Officers: Lydia Harrsion [1983] Director

Best of Portugal Limited
Incorporated: 7 February 2011
Registered Office: The Studio, 60 Pitshanger Lane, London, W5 1QY
Officers: Lydia Harrison [1983] Director

Best of Spain Limited
Incorporated: 7 February 2011
Registered Office: The Studio, 60 Pitshanger Lane, London, W5 1QY
Officers: Lydia Harrison [1983] Director

Best Price Retail and Wholesale Limited
Incorporated: 12 October 2009 *Employees:* 18
Net Worth: £73,096 *Total Assets:* £648,228
Registered Office: Unit 9 Lyndean Industrial Estate, Felixstowe Road, Abbeywood, London, SE2 9SG
Shareholders: Deepak Kumar Shrestha; Om Thapa
Officers: Deepak Kumar Shrestha [1971] Director [Nepalese]; Om Thapa [1973] Director [Nepalese]

Best-One Local Ltd
Incorporated: 6 February 2019
Registered Office: 123 Mawney Road, Romford, Essex, RM7 7BH
Major Shareholder: Pamela Marongui
Officers: Pamela Marongui [1993] Director [Italian]

Bestline Wholesale Ltd
Incorporated: 28 November 2011
Registered Office: 28 Marlyon Road, Ilford, Essex, IG6 3XN
Major Shareholder: Dhusyanthan Kanapathipillai
Officers: Dhusyanthan Kanapathipillai [1970] Director/Manager

Better Buy Ltd
Incorporated: 27 May 2015
Net Worth Deficit: £52,717 *Total Assets:* £32,979
Registered Office: 8 Turton Road, Ravenfield, Rotherham, S Yorks, S65 4GZ
Major Shareholder: Phillip Naughton
Officers: John Higgins [1964] Sales Director; Philip Naughton [1963] Director

Bevco Limited
Incorporated: 1 September 2015
Registered Office: c/o Ashcroft Cameron, The Mead Business Centre, Mead Lane, Hertford, SG13 7BJ
Major Shareholder: Brian McManus
Officers: Brian McManus [1965] Director [Irish]

The Beverage Boutique Ltd
Incorporated: 15 October 2018
Registered Office: 108 Ashdale Drive, Birmingham, B14 4TU
Shareholders: Sara Jean Bird; Ryan James Bird
Officers: Ryan James Bird [1987] Director/Retail Manager; Sara Jean Bird [1989] Director/Lunchtime Supervisor

Beverage Boys Ltd
Incorporated: 27 February 2018
Registered Office: 162 Ferrymead Avenue, Middlesex, Greenford, Middlesex, UB6 9TW
Major Shareholder: Jateen Kumar Chauhan
Officers: Jateen Kumar Chauhan [1988] Director

Beverage Brothers Limited
Incorporated: 6 December 2016
Registered Office: 4 Kingswood Court, Long Meadow, South Brent, Devon, TQ10 9YS
Major Shareholder: Philip Clark
Officers: Philip Clark [1959] Director

The Beverage Provider Limited
Incorporated: 30 May 2018
Registered Office: 6 Aldwych Buildings, Parker Mews, London, WC2B 5NT
Major Shareholder: Larry Dinell Patterson
Officers: Larry Dinell Patterson [1962] Director [American]

Beverages Distribution Limited
Incorporated: 30 March 2017
Registered Office: 3a Maple Close, Seaforth, Liverpool, L21 4PD
Major Shareholder: Swapnil Niranjan Shah
Officers: Swapnil Niranjan Shah [1981] Director [Indian]

Beveridge Wines Ltd
Incorporated: 13 December 2012
Net Worth: £33 *Total Assets:* £44,033
Registered Office: Rathmoyle, 7 Cable Road, Whitehead, Co Antrim, BT38 9PX
Major Shareholder: Andrew Fullerton
Officers: Andrew Fullerton [1974] Director

Bevimangia Limited
Incorporated: 3 October 2016
Registered Office: The Apex, 2 Sheriffs Orchard, Coventry, Warwicks, CV1 3PP
Major Shareholder: Chukwuemeka Victor Onyekwere
Officers: Chukwuemeka Victor Onyekwere [1976] Director/Engineer

Beviqua Ltd
Incorporated: 27 February 2009
Previous: Centra Trading Ltd
Net Worth: £860 *Total Assets:* £29,773
Registered Office: Crossways Cargo Centre, Galleon Boulevard, Crossways Business Park, Dartford, Kent, DA2 6QE
Major Shareholder: Ranjit Singh Chahal
Officers: Ranjit Singh Chahal [1971] Director/Engineer

Beylerbeyi UK Ltd
Incorporated: 7 December 2018
Registered Office: 32 Willoughby Road, London, N8 0JG
Shareholder: Cuneyt Ozgumus
Officers: Cuneyt Ozgumus [1981] Director [Turkish]

Beyond The Ale (GB) Limited
Incorporated: 15 May 1995
Net Worth: £2 *Total Assets:* £2
Registered Office: 3 East Barn, Market Weston Road, Thelnetham, Diss, Norfolk, IP22 1JJ
Shareholders: Margaret Mary Bernadette Churchouse; Stephen Ronald Churchouse
Officers: Margaret Mary Bernadette Churchouse, Secretary; Margaret Mary Bernadette Churchouse [1956] Director/Event Organisers; Stephen Ronald Churchouse [1956] Director

BF Wines UK Ltd
Incorporated: 17 May 2018
Registered Office: Kemp House, 160 City Road, London, EC1V 2NX
Officers: Dr Olufolake Akinduro-Aje, Secretary; Benson Aje [1972] Director/Criminologist

BFA Holdings Limited
Incorporated: 4 April 2006
Net Worth Deficit: £122,026 Total Assets: £35,361
Registered Office: Market House, 10 Market Walk, Saffron Walden, Essex, CB10 1JZ
Major Shareholder: Diana Jillian Foster
Officers: Diana Jillian Foster, Secretary; Anthony Charles Foster [1943] Director/Wine Shipper; Diana Jillian Foster [1945] Company Secretary/Director

BFV International Limited
Incorporated: 2 June 2016
Registered Office: Ashcombe Court, Woolsack Way, Godalming, Surrey, GU7 1LQ
Officers: Philip Andries Smith, Secretary; Jan Christoffel Bosman [1955] Director [South African]; Petrus Wilhelmus Jacobus Bosman [1981] Director [South African]

Bhanbore Trading Company PVT Ltd
Incorporated: 3 October 2014
Net Worth: £35,950 Total Assets: £550,337
Registered Office: T/A Ukrani Cash & Carry, Unit 8 Rippleside Commercial Estate, Renwick Road, Barking, Essex, IG11 0SB
Shareholder: Mohan Mal
Officers: Nisha Devi [1994] Director [Pakistani]; Mohan Mal [1962] Director [Pakistani]; Pesu Mal [1972] Director [Pakistani]

BI Wines and Spirits Limited
Incorporated: 26 November 1996 Employees: 41
Previous: Bordeaux Index Limited
Net Worth: £14,887,323 Total Assets: £48,678,520
Registered Office: 10 Hatton Garden, London, EC1N 8AH
Shareholder: Gary James Boom
Officers: Generald Robert Dreyer, Secretary; Gary James Boom [1958] Director [Dutch]; Andrew Robert Joel Brudenell-Bruce [1951] Director/Wine Merchant; Matthew Sam Gleave [1970] Director/Wine Merchant; Natasha Ann Lucas [1975] Director/Chartered Tax Advisor; Sebastian Elliot Rowe [1969] Director/Wine Merchant; Michael Alan Spencer [1955] Director/Businessman; David Michael Thomas [1970] Director/Wine Merchant; Colin Thomas West [1958] Director/Wine Merchant

Bianca Trading Wine Ltd
Incorporated: 13 February 2019
Registered Office: Marcher House, Marcher Court, Sealand Road, Chester, CH1 6BS
Major Shareholder: Bianca Lisowski
Officers: Juliusz Lisowski, Secretary; Bianca Lisowski [1956] Director

Bibendum PLB Group Limited
Incorporated: 13 March 2007
Net Worth: £19,997,000 Total Assets: £27,291,000
Registered Office: Whitchurch Lane, Whitchurch, Bristol, BS14 0JZ
Parent: Bibendum PLB (Topco) Limited
Officers: Andrea Pozzi [1971] Director/Group Chief Operating Officer; Ewan James Robertson [1982] Finance Director; Jonathan Solesbury [1965] Director/Group Chief Financial Officer

Bibendum Wine Limited
Incorporated: 9 February 1988 Employees: 261
Net Worth Deficit: £2,171,000 Total Assets: £2,109,000
Registered Office: Whitchurch Lane, Whitchurch, Bristol, BS14 0JZ
Parent: Bibendum PLB Group Limited
Officers: Andrea Pozzi [1971] Director/Group Chief Operating Officer; Ewan James Robertson [1982] Finance Director; Jonathan Solesbury [1965] Director/Group Chief Financial Officer

Bibere Ltd.
Incorporated: 20 December 2012
Net Worth Deficit: £57,922 Total Assets: £24,552
Registered Office: First Floor, Universal House, Unit 10, 88-94 Wentworth Street, London, E1 7SA
Major Shareholder: Andrea Amici
Officers: Andrea Amici [1968] Director

Bielo Limited
Incorporated: 22 February 2017 Employees: 3
Net Worth Deficit: £1,852 Total Assets: £328
Registered Office: 1st Floor, Commerce House, 1 Raven Road, South Woodford, London, E18 1HB
Shareholder: Jonathan William Glenny
Officers: Jonathan William Glenny [1965] Director; Damian Patrick Morgan [1961] Director [Irish]; John Francis O'Loughlin [1960] Director [Irish]

Bier UK Limited
Incorporated: 1 September 2014
Registered Office: 29 York Place, Edinburgh, EH1 3HP
Major Shareholder: Colin Makin
Officers: Colin Makin [1962] Director

Biercraft Ltd
Incorporated: 9 October 2012 Employees: 2
Net Worth: £125,716 Total Assets: £431,032
Registered Office: 53 Coopersale Road, Hackney, London, E9 6AU
Officers: Mary Fiona McLeod, Secretary; Ben Jon Michael Henshaw [1971] Director Wine Importer; Nicholas James Trower [1978] Director

Big D'Z Convenience and Winery Limited
Incorporated: 11 May 2015
Net Worth Deficit: £66,026 Total Assets: £1,486
Registered Office: Trilogy Suite, 9 Church Street, Wednesfield, Wolverhampton, W Midlands, WV11 1SR
Major Shareholder: Gursharn Singh Sandhu
Officers: Gursharn Singh Sandhu [1978] Director

Big Fish Brewing Company Limited
Incorporated: 15 June 2016
Net Worth Deficit: £10,771 Total Assets: £4,197
Registered Office: 45 Glenury Crescent, Stonehaven, Aberdeenshire, AB39 3LF
Major Shareholder: Alexander Frederick William Stockton
Officers: Alexander Frederick William Stockton [1972] Director

Big Mouth Wine Limited
Incorporated: 4 March 2017
Net Worth Deficit: £3,173 Total Assets: £41,827
Registered Office: 15 Bateman Street, London, W1D 3AQ
Major Shareholder: Victoria Helena Hart-Dale
Officers: Simon George Anderson [1968] Director; Thomas Northway [1976] Director

Big Red D Ltd
Incorporated: 19 August 2016
Net Worth Deficit: £8,590
Registered Office: 154 Ravencroft, Bicester, Oxon, OX26 6YF
Shareholder: Peter Dickens
Officers: Karen Dickens [1968] Director; Peter Dickens [1967] Director

Bigg Market Beer Company Ltd
Incorporated: 3 July 2017
Net Worth: £3 *Total Assets:* £3
Registered Office: 87 Station Road, Ashington, Northumberland, NE63 8RS
Shareholders: Raymond Black; James Bradford; Thomas Owen Jones
Officers: Raymond Black [1953] Director; James Bradford [1953] Director; Thomas Owen Jones [1985] Director

Bigg Market Brewery Company Ltd
Incorporated: 3 July 2017
Net Worth: £3 *Total Assets:* £3
Registered Office: 87 Station Road, Ashington, Northumberland, NE63 8RS
Shareholders: Raymond Black; Thomas Owen Jones; James Bradford
Officers: Raymond Black [1953] Director; James Bradford [1953] Director; Thomas Owen Jones [1985] Director

Bihl Ltd
Incorporated: 31 July 2017
Registered Office: 4 Stoney Bank, Gillingham, Kent, ME7 3AG
Shareholders: Radu Gheorghe Miclaus; Magnus Sean Clarke
Officers: Magnus Sean Clarke [1979] Director; Bojan Kambic [1981] Finance Director [Croatian]; Radu Gheorghe Miclaus [1963] Director

Bijou Bottles Limited
Incorporated: 27 August 2008 *Employees:* 15
Net Worth: £52,742 *Total Assets:* £514,690
Registered Office: Trafalgar House, Wellesley Road, Tharston, Norwich, NR15 2PD
Major Shareholder: Gordon Philip Hall
Officers: Gordon Philip Hall, Secretary/Wine Merchant; Gordon Philip Hall [1958] Director/Wine Merchant; Jerome Thomas Lambert [1977] Director/Wine Merchant [French]

Billecart - Salmon (UK) Limited
Incorporated: 10 March 1995 *Employees:* 6
Net Worth Deficit: £333,562 *Total Assets:* £1,071,725
Registered Office: Sudial House, 98 High Street, Horsell, Woking, Surrey, GU21 4SU
Officers: Colin John Palmer, Secretary/Director; Colin John Palmer [1961] Director; Mathieu Roland-Billcart [1981] Director [French]

Billings & Briggs Ltd
Incorporated: 7 September 2015
Net Worth Deficit: £24,353 *Total Assets:* £54,567
Registered Office: Unit 3, 2 Upper York Street, Bristol, BS2 8QN
Shareholders: Louise Markes; Daniel Patrick Briggs
Officers: Daniel Patrick Briggs [1980] Director/Wine Buyer AIWS; Louise Markes [1981] Director/Project Manager

Binning Trading Company Limited
Incorporated: 28 February 2017 *Employees:* 1
Net Worth Deficit: £23,836 *Total Assets:* £71,794
Registered Office: 87 Drewstead Road, London, SW16 1AX
Major Shareholder: Nirmal Jeet Singh Binning
Officers: Nirmal Jeet Singh Binning [1975] Director

Biotanica Ltd
Incorporated: 25 May 2018
Registered Office: Kemp House, 160 City Road, London, EC1V 2NX
Major Shareholder: Sally Wynter
Officers: Sally Wynter, Secretary; Sally Wynter [1994] Director/Producer

Birdcage Gin Ltd.
Incorporated: 26 November 2015
Registered Office: 20 Parvis Road, West Byfleet, Surrey, KT14 6HA
Shareholders: Christian Dominic Howard Emmans; Paloma Paradis Shakouri; James William Willetts
Officers: Christian Dominic Howard Emmans [1995] Director/Student; Paloma Paradis Shakouri [1995] Director/Student; James William Willetts [1993] Director/Student

Birds of Arcadia Ltd
Incorporated: 14 August 2017
Registered Office: Caer Dathyl, Rhosmeirch, Llangefni, Anglesey, LL77 7SJ
Major Shareholder: Thomas David Milburn
Officers: Thomas David Milburn [1989] Director

Birrificio Del Ducato London Limited
Incorporated: 6 June 2014
Net Worth Deficit: £57,094 *Total Assets:* £581,836
Registered Office: 15 Northfields Prospect, Northfields, London, SW18 1PE
Officers: Marco Acquistapace [1958] Director/Manager; Giovanni Campari [1977] Director [Italian]; Manuel Piccoli [1973] Director/Entrepreneur [Italian]

The Bitter End Limited
Incorporated: 18 July 2018
Registered Office: Downs & Co, 1-2 The Grange, High Street, Westerham, Kent, TN16 1AH
Shareholders: John Rothwell; Paul Swinney
Officers: John Rothwell [1954] Director; Paul Swinney [1961] Director

Bitter Lemons Gin Ltd
Incorporated: 14 June 2018
Registered Office: BSEEN, Aston University Innovation, Birmingham Campus, Faraday Wharf, Holt Street, Birmingham, B7 4BB
Major Shareholder: Luke Anthony Warren
Officers: Luke Anthony Warren [1996] Director/Student

Bittles Irish Whiskey Co Ltd
Incorporated: 18 September 2018
Registered Office: 4 Comber Street, Saintfield, Ballynahinch, Co Down, BT24 7AZ
Shareholders: John Bittles; Fergal Bittles; Ciaran Bittles
Officers: Ciaran Bittles [1994] Director/Bar Manager; Fergal Bittles [1996] Director/Bar Manager; John Bittles [1960] Director/Publican

BJ Drinks Ltd
Incorporated: 17 July 2017
Registered Office: 9 Torcross Avenue, Coventry, Warwicks, CV2 3NE
Major Shareholder: Jeyalakshmi Rathnavelu
Officers: Jeyalakshmi Rathnavelu [1983] Director [Sri Lankan]

BL Drinks Ltd
Incorporated: 22 March 2018
Registered Office: 16a The Parade, Yately, Hants, GU46 7UN
Shareholders: Paul Robert Lockhart; Darren Welch
Officers: Paul Robert Lockhart [1967] Director/Business Development; Darren Welch [1975] Director/Sales Manager

BL011 Limited
Incorporated: 5 April 2012
Net Worth Deficit: £227,332 *Total Assets:* £266,790
Registered Office: New Kings Court, Tollgate, Chandler's Ford, Eastleigh, Hants, SO53 3LG
Shareholders: Emma Alken; Stephanie Alken
Officers: Anthony Alken, Secretary; Anthony Alken [1955] Director [Irish]; Gregory Alken [1957] Director [Irish]

Black & Yellow Developments Limited
Incorporated: 14 August 2014
Previous: Premium Liquids Limited
Registered Office: 23 South Acre, Oakenshaw, Crook, Co Durham, DL15 0SZ
Major Shareholder: John Robert Foster
Officers: John Robert Foster [1980] Director

Black Cat Brewery Limited
Incorporated: 11 July 2012
Net Worth Deficit: £55,830 *Total Assets:* £23,795
Registered Office: Twitten Cottage, Southview Road, Crowborough, E Sussex, TN6 1HF
Shareholders: Kathryn Margaret Mary Wratten; Paul Wratten
Officers: Kathryn Margaret Mary Wratten [1962] Director/Brewery Owner; Paul Wratten [1964] Director/Brewery Owner

Black Dog Gin Company Limited
Incorporated: 16 November 2018
Registered Office: 243 Mill Road, Cambridge, CB1 3BE
Shareholders: David Elsom; Gary Hayes; Simon Durance
Officers: Simon Durance [1974] Director; David Elsom [1970] Director; Gary Hayes [1966] Director

Black Dog Wine Agency Limited
Incorporated: 14 April 2011
Net Worth Deficit: £148,916 *Total Assets:* £29,918
Registered Office: 31 Woodlands Park, Wash Lane, Allostock, Knutsford, Cheshire, WA16 9LG
Shareholders: David Paddle; Katie Butler
Officers: Katie Butler [1978] Director/Wine Trade; David Paddle [1969] Director/Wine Sales

Black Forest Beers Limited
Incorporated: 18 August 2006
Net Worth: £16,829 *Total Assets:* £288,751
Registered Office: 2 Cholseley Drive, Fleet, Hants, GU51 1HG
Major Shareholder: Sandip Praful Chandra Patidar
Officers: Ira Marika Patidar, Secretary; Sandip Praful Chandra Patidar [1966] Director/Importer and Retailer

Black Kola UK Limited
Incorporated: 18 July 2018
Registered Office: 3 Fullers Wood, Croydon, Surrey, CR0 8HZ
Officers: Anthony Olukayode Ogunfeibo [1960] Director/Lawyer

Black Tartan Limited
Incorporated: 20 January 2017
Registered Office: 157a Broughton Road, Edinburgh, EH7 4JJ
Shareholder: Tom Douglas Melville
Officers: Tom Douglas Melville [1974] Creative Director; Andrew George Campbell Skene [1967] Director

Blackadder International Limited
Incorporated: 7 March 1995 *Employees:* 3
Net Worth: £570,782 *Total Assets:* £1,280,294
Registered Office: c/o Lloyd & Co, 103-105 Brighton Road, Coulsdon, Surrey, CR5 2NG
Major Shareholder: Robin Michael Tucek
Officers: Robin Michael Tucek, Secretary; Hannah Eveline Tucek [1982] Director/Musician; Robin Michael Tucek [1948] Director

Blackcattaverns Ltd
Incorporated: 13 September 2018
Registered Office: 23 High Path, Merton, London, SW19 2JY
Shareholders: Rodger Molyneux-Roberts; Rowan Elizabeth Molyneux-Roberts
Officers: Rodger Molyneux-Roberts [1951] Director; Rowan Elizabeth Molyneux-Roberts [1990] Director

Blackedge Brewing Company Ltd
Incorporated: 30 November 2009 *Employees:* 5
Net Worth: £4 *Total Assets:* £87,173
Registered Office: Moreton Mill, Hampson Street, Horwich, Bolton, Lancs, BL6 7JH
Shareholder: Wayne Roper
Officers: Shaun Reynolds [1974] Director/Civil Servant; Rowena Rose Roper [1980] Director/Brewery Administrator; Wayne Roper [1975] Brewery Director

Blackstorm Rum Ltd
Incorporated: 19 January 2018
Registered Office: 174a Coningham Road, London, W12 8BY
Officers: Jeffrey Pope [1969] Director/Businessman

Sir Richard Blake & Associates Limited
Incorporated: 8 November 1976
Net Worth Deficit: £35,470 *Total Assets:* £30
Registered Office: Flat 1/01, 130 Chamberlain Road, Jordanhill, Glasgow, G13 1RT
Shareholders: Querida Alvis of Lee; Shireen Alvis of Lee
Officers: Querida Alvis of Lee, Secretary; Querida Alvis of Lee [1970] Director

Blakes Fine Wine Ltd
Incorporated: 21 June 2007
Net Worth Deficit: £71,219 *Total Assets:* £34,904
Registered Office: 5-6 Market Place, Derrylin, Enniskillen, Co Fermanagh, BT92 9LA
Shareholders: Patrick Declan Blake; Bernadette Ann Blake
Officers: Patrick Declan Blake, Secretary; Patrick Declan Blake [1955] Director/Wine Importer [Irish]

Blast Vintners Ltd
Incorporated: 31 January 2014 *Employees:* 1
Net Worth: £68,160 *Total Assets:* £162,028
Registered Office: 86-89 Paul Street, London, EC2A 4NE
Major Shareholder: Joseph Michael Gilmour
Officers: Joseph Michael Gilmour [1980] Director/Wine Merchant

Blends Wine Estates UK Ltd
Incorporated: 2 November 2004 *Employees:* 6
Net Worth: £9,504,345 *Total Assets:* £11,817,875
Registered Office: The Busworks, 39-41 North Road, London, N7 9DP
Parent: World Wine Investors UK Ltd
Officers: Simon Charles Farr [1953] Director; Erique Almagro Germa [1944] Director [Spanish]

Blind Monkey Limited
Incorporated: 3 August 2017
Net Worth Deficit: £7,138 *Total Assets:* £3,477
Registered Office: Trigate Business Centre, Hagley Road West, Oldbury, W Midlands, B68 0NP
Major Shareholder: William Richard Stephenson
Officers: William Richard Stephenson [1973] Director

Bloody Drinks Limited
Incorporated: 5 December 2017
Registered Office: 13A Chadwick Road, London, E11 1NE
Shareholders: Henry Robert Spencer Farnham; William Trevorian Stuart Best
Officers: William Trevorian Stuart Best [1985] Director/Entrepreneur; Henry Robert Spencer Farnham [1985] Director/Entrepreneur

The Bloomsbury Distillery Ltd
Incorporated: 11 September 2015
Net Worth: £71,826 *Total Assets:* £123,031
Registered Office: 44 Emerald Street, London, WC1N 3QH
Major Shareholder: Alan McQuillan
Officers: Benjamin Peter Harriman [1986] Commercial Director; Alan McQuillan [1982] Director [Irish]; Paul Nigel Wickman [1955] Director

Bloomsbury Drinks Ltd
Incorporated: 26 March 2013
Net Worth: £171,569 *Total Assets:* £391,988
Registered Office: Basement of Tavistock Hotel, Bedford Way, London, WC1H 9EU
Officers: Jonathan Charles Dalton [1973] Director [Australian]; Mark Corin Walton [1973] Director

BLSN Limited
Incorporated: 7 March 2018
Registered Office: Suite 9, Imperial Court, Exchange Street East, Liverpool, L2 3AB
Major Shareholder: Sinikweyinkosi Tshuma
Officers: Sinikweyinkosi Tshuma, Secretary; Lovemore Bhebhe [1976] Director [Zimbabwean]

Blu-Dot Commodities Limited
Incorporated: 13 February 2019
Registered Office: C A Pitts & Co, 114 Omnibus Business Centre, 39-41 North Road, London, N7 9DP
Parent: Blu-Dot Telecoms Ltd
Officers: Azhar Mohamed [1983] Director [South African]

Blue Diamond (UK) Ltd
Incorporated: 7 February 2013
Net Worth: £4,990 *Total Assets:* £175,951
Registered Office: 295A Heathway, Dagenham, Essex, RM9 5AQ
Major Shareholder: Arvydas Misiunas
Officers: Arvydas Misiunas [1962] Director [Lithuanian]

Blue Island Limited
Incorporated: 11 December 2003
Net Worth: £2,379 *Total Assets:* £20,134
Registered Office: 110 Causeway Head Road, Dore, Sheffield, S17 3DW
Major Shareholder: Susannah George Fullerton Sheppard
Officers: Susannah George Fullerton Sheppard, Secretary; Susannah George Fullerton Sheppard [1967] Director/Solicitor

Blue Magic Limited
Incorporated: 22 September 2016
Net Worth Deficit: £418 *Total Assets:* £153
Registered Office: Fairhavens, Mussenden Lane, Longfield, Dartford, Kent, DA3 8NX
Shareholders: Michael Lee; Vanzelo Lee
Officers: Michael Lee [1994] Director; Vanzelo Lee [1992] Director

Blue Marble Consultants Limited
Incorporated: 17 October 2014 *Employees:* 1
Net Worth: £61,686 *Total Assets:* £76,202
Registered Office: 1 Pengover Heights, Liskeard, Cornwall, PL14 3UA
Shareholder: Nicholas Ian Rogers
Officers: Nicholas Rogers, Secretary; Nicholas Ian Rogers [1965] Director/Accountant; Helen Frances Taylor [1963] Director

Blue Momentum Limited
Incorporated: 17 January 2017
Net Worth Deficit: £305 *Total Assets:* £100
Registered Office: Part of Unit 10 Tower Industrial Estate, Tower Lane, Eastleigh, Hants, SO50 6NZ
Major Shareholder: Amardip Singh Bhatti
Officers: Amardip Singh Bhatti [1980] Director

Blue Star Inns Limited
Incorporated: 14 December 2005 *Employees:* 12
Net Worth: £139,948 *Total Assets:* £163,039
Registered Office: Unit 3 Highcliffe Mill, Bruntcliffe Lane, Morley, Leeds, LS27 9LR
Shareholders: Andrew Cooper; David Hill
Officers: Nicky Lee Hill, Secretary; Andrew Cooper [1956] Director; David Hill [1958] Director/Sales Manager; Nicky Lee Hill [1981] Director/Warehouse Manager

Blue Thorn Gin Limited
Incorporated: 7 August 2018
Registered Office: 137 Gratton Field, Bishopstone, Seaford, E Sussex, BN25 2UF
Shareholders: Calum Jonathan Martin Waters; Richard Henry Cheeseman
Officers: Richard Henry Cheeseman [1995] Director; Richard Antony Cheeseman [1958] Director; Calum Jonathan Martin Waters [1996] Director; David Waters [1958] Director

Blue Tree Limited
Incorporated: 19 July 2001 *Employees:* 10
Net Worth: £2,627,925 *Total Assets:* £19,974,350
Registered Office: Beech House, Melbourn Science Park, Melbourn, Herts, SG8 6HB
Shareholders: Victoria Katharine Fowkes Bolt; Benjamin James Bolt
Officers: Nigel Anthony Watson, Secretary; Benjamin James Bolt [1971] Director/Commercial Manager; Victoria Katharine Fowkes Bolt [1970] Director/Marketing

Blue Wine Ltd
Incorporated: 9 January 2018
Registered Office: 181 Water Street, Cambridge, CB4 1PB
Major Shareholder: Maria de Los Angeles Oyono Tompson
Officers: Maria de Los Angeles Oyono Tompson [1980] Director [Spanish]

Bluetec Trading Services Ltd
Incorporated: 20 June 2018
Registered Office: 34 Clare Road, Maidenhead, Berks, SL6 4DG
Major Shareholder: Tariq Rashid
Officers: Tariq Rashid [1965] Director [Pakistani]

Blush Gin Distrubutors UK Ltd
Incorporated: 4 December 2018
Registered Office: 40 Childs Crescent, Swanscombe, Kent, DA10 0EA
Shareholders: John Justin Trotter; Tina Delivett
Officers: Tina Delivett [1958] Sales Director; John Justin Trotter [1961] Sales Director

Blux UK Import Ltd
Incorporated: 15 June 2015
Net Worth Deficit: £318,884 Total Assets: £95,611
Registered Office: First Floor, Rainham House, Manor Way, Rainham, Essex, RM13 8RH
Parent: Capital UK Partners Ltd
Officers: Kevin John Butcher, Secretary; Francis Ronald Mark Harding [1966] Director; Kevin Ivan Webb [1956] Director; Lee Trevor Webb [1993] Director

BM Wines Limited
Incorporated: 12 January 1996 Employees: 3
Net Worth: £635,486 Total Assets: £733,929
Registered Office: Suite 1, 2nd Floor, Henwood Pavilion, Henwood Industrial Estate, Ashford, Kent, TN24 8DH
Major Shareholder: Bernard Emile Mounier
Officers: Takashi Sasaki, Secretary; Bernard Emile Marie Mounier [1952] Director/Wine Agent/Broker [French]

Boar Wine Ltd
Incorporated: 10 November 2017
Registered Office: 40 Croft Avenue, Wirral, Merseyside, CH62 2BR
Major Shareholder: Matthew Sweeney
Officers: Matthew Sweeney [1990] Director/Consultant

Bobby Beer Company Limited
Incorporated: 5 August 2013
Net Worth Deficit: £113,287 Total Assets: £18,354
Registered Office: c/o Bronsens, Albion Street, Chipping Norton, Oxon, OX7 5BH
Shareholders: Georgina Elizabeth Pearman; Sam Murray Pearman
Officers: Georgina Elizabeth Pearman [1973] Director; Pearman Sam [1978] Director

Bodega Raffy UK Ltd
Incorporated: 12 August 2011
Net Worth Deficit: £122,131 Total Assets: £2,038
Registered Office: 1st Floor, 2 Woodberry Grove, North Finchley, London, N12 0DR
Officers: Guillaume Raffy [1981] Director/Entrepreneur [French]

Bodega Uncielo (UK) Limited
Incorporated: 9 March 2017 Employees: 1
Net Worth Deficit: £10,030 Total Assets: £14,883
Registered Office: Flat 5, 43 St Stephen's Terrace, London, SW8 1DL
Major Shareholder: Benjamin Daniel Hillman
Officers: Benjamin Daniel Hillman [1979] Director/Solicitor

Bogart Spirits Limited
Incorporated: 20 May 2014
Registered Office: Rok House, Kingswood Business Park, Holyhead Road, Albrighton, Staffs, WV7 3AU
Parent: Rok Stars PLC
Officers: Robbert Jan Franciscus de Klerk [1973] Director [American]; Jonathan Mark Kendrick [1957] Director; Bruce William Renny [1965] Director

Bohemia Beer House Limited
Incorporated: 12 June 1996 Employees: 4
Net Worth Deficit: £62,481 Total Assets: £491,943
Registered Office: Bayford Hall Coachhouse, Bayford, Hertford, SG13 8BR
Major Shareholder: George William Rowley
Officers: Bridget Jane Rowley, Secretary; George William Rowley [1964] Director/Broker

Bohemian Brands Limited
Incorporated: 15 December 2016 Employees: 1
Net Worth: £8,214 Total Assets: £208,123
Registered Office: 4 Prince Albert Road, London, NW1 7SN
Shareholders: Initial Rewards Limited; Julian David Piler
Officers: Julian David Piler [1967] Director; Jonathan Reuben [1981] Director; Martin Jack Reuben [1943] Director/Corporate Promotions Executive

PNJ Bolton International Ltd
Incorporated: 5 December 2018
Registered Office: 16 Tiller Road, London, E14 8PX
Major Shareholder: Philip Bolton
Officers: Philip Bolton [1951] Director

The Bombay Spirits Company Limited
Incorporated: 8 June 1998 Employees: 15
Net Worth: £1,699,000 Total Assets: £1,699,000
Registered Office: Laverstoke Mill, London Road, Laverstoke, Whitchurch, Hants, RG28 7NR
Parent: Bacardi U.K. Limited
Officers: John Michael Burke [1965] Marketing Director; Iain MacGregor Lochhead [1962] Director; Matthew James Phillips [1983] Finance Director

Bon Coeur Fine Wines Limited
Incorporated: 24 May 2005 Employees: 18
Net Worth: £690,964 Total Assets: £4,226,339
Registered Office: Moor Park, Moor Road, Melsonby, Richmond, N Yorks, DL10 5PR
Shareholders: James Henry Goodhart; Samantha Jane Goodhart
Officers: Jonathon Timothy Mann, Secretary; James Henry Goodhart [1970] Director/Wine Merchant; Samantha Jane Goodhart [1967] Director; Jonathon Timothy Mann [1976] Finance Director

Bon Vin Inc. Limited
Incorporated: 13 March 2001 Employees: 1
Net Worth Deficit: £44,351 Total Assets: £86,813
Registered Office: 27 New Dover Road, Canterbury, Kent, CT1 3DN
Officers: Sophie Marie Martine Holzberg [1958] Director/Independent Commercial Agent [French]

Bond Bar Ltd
Incorporated: 22 October 2018
Registered Office: 22 Wallace Scott Road, Weston Super Mare, Somerset, BS23 1UG
Major Shareholder: Siobhan Thomas
Officers: Siobhan Thomas, Secretary; Siobhan Thomas [1990] Director/Care Assistant

Bondi Brands Limited
Incorporated: 7 May 2015 Employees: 5
Net Worth Deficit: £17,397 Total Assets: £163,006
Registered Office: Ibex House, Baker Street, Weybridge, Surrey, KT13 8AH
Officers: Martin Hugo Hess [1959] Director; Sean Hughes [1953] Director; Alistair MacLeod [1955] CEO/Executive Director; Andrew John Pepper [1968] Director; Carl Rigby [1962] Director

Bondi Brewery Limited
Incorporated: 7 May 2015 *Employees:* 4
Net Worth Deficit: £229,625 *Total Assets:* £5,216
Registered Office: Ibex House, Baker Street, Weybridge, Surrey, KT13 8AH
Officers: Martin Hugo Hess [1959] Director; Alistair MacLeod [1955] CEO/Executive Director; Andrew John Pepper [1968] Director; Carl Rigby [1962] Director

Bone Machine Brewing Company Limited
Incorporated: 24 January 2017
Net Worth Deficit: £9,189 *Total Assets:* £29,508
Registered Office: Unit 1e Hampden Road, Pocklington Industrial Estate, York, YO42 1NR
Shareholders: Marko Antero Karjalainen; Kimmo Eerik Karjalainen
Officers: Kimmo Eerik Karjalainen [1984] Sales Director [Finnish]; Marko Antero Karjalainen [1987] Director/Brewer and Brewing Consultant [Finnish]

Bonfire Hill Limited
Incorporated: 21 December 2006
Net Worth: £54,457 *Total Assets:* £123,254
Registered Office: Blatchford Farm, Bridestowe, Okehampton, Devon, EX20 4HZ
Officers: John Walter Raymond Passmore, Secretary [Irish]; Edward Charles William Adams [1960] Director/Wine Merchant; Bruce Stanley Jack [1968] Director/Wine Merchant [South African]; John Walter Raymond Passmore [1976] Director/Consultant [Irish]

Bonny Gin Ltd
Incorporated: 6 November 2018
Registered Office: 22 Moorhouse Avenue, Glasgow, G13 4RB
Major Shareholder: Patrick Gahagan
Officers: Patrick Gahagan [1994] Director/Supply Chain Manager

Bonvoy Limited
Incorporated: 8 November 2018
Registered Office: 10 Tournament House, Bowling Green Lane, Penrith New Squares, Penrith, Cumbria, CA11 7GP
Major Shareholder: Chris Bonnie
Officers: Chris Bonnie [1979] Director

Boondales Limited
Incorporated: 28 February 1996 *Employees:* 10
Net Worth: £202,260 *Total Assets:* £243,804
Registered Office: Hanover Buildings, 11-13 Hanover Street, Liverpool, L1 3DN
Shareholder: David Francis Riley
Officers: David Francis Riley Riley, Secretary; David Francis Riley Riley [1957] Director/Licensee; Francis Joseph Riley [1953] Director; William Riley [1950] Director/Licensee

Boot Liquor Wholesale Limited
Incorporated: 28 May 2013
Net Worth: £28,682 *Total Assets:* £60,040
Registered Office: 20-22 Wenlock Road, London, N1 7GU
Major Shareholder: Michael Leslie Scott
Officers: Michael Leslie Scott [1990] Director

Booze 2 U Ltd
Incorporated: 9 July 2018
Registered Office: 71-75 Shelton Street, London, WC2H 9JQ
Shareholders: Christopher Cannon; Alan Thomas; Roy McGaw
Officers: Alan Thomas, Secretary; Christopher Canon [1985] Director; Roy McGaw [1980] Director; Alan Thomas [1962] Director

The Booze Bolton Limited
Incorporated: 14 November 2017
Registered Office: 333b Derby Street, Bolton, Lancs, BL3 6LR
Officers: Rashid Minhas [1978] Director [Pakistani]; Syed Javed Zaidi Kahtoon [1952] Director [Spanish]

Booze Crew Leeds Ltd
Incorporated: 6 April 2016
Net Worth Deficit: £5,084 *Total Assets:* £5,496
Registered Office: 208a Roundhay Road, Leeds, LS8 5AA
Major Shareholder: Mohammad Iltaf
Officers: Mohammad Iltaf [1983] Director

Booze Cruz Ltd
Incorporated: 20 June 2018
Registered Office: 429a Crownhill Road, Plymouth, PL5 2LJ
Major Shareholder: Chad James Franklin
Officers: Chad James Franklin [1987] Director/Manager

Booze Village Limited
Incorporated: 7 November 2018
Registered Office: 304 Green Hill Road, Liverpool, L18 9SZ
Officers: Swapnil Niranjan Shah [1981] Director [Indian]

Bopfags Services Ltd
Incorporated: 14 February 2019
Registered Office: Flat 6, Windspoint Drive, London, SE15 1SD
Major Shareholder: Babatunde Opeyemi Fagunwa
Officers: Babatunde Opeyemi Fagunwa [1979] Director/Warehouseman [Nigerian]

Bordeaux and Beyond Ltd
Incorporated: 2 April 2007
Net Worth Deficit: £7,126 *Total Assets:* £12,058
Registered Office: Thistle Down Barn, Holcot Lane, Sywell, Northampton, NN6 0BG
Shareholders: John Ramon Green; Anthony William Hill
Officers: John Ramon Green, Secretary/Director; John Ramon Green [1951] Director/Public Servant; Anthony William Hill [1951] Director/Consultant

Bordeaux Index Limited
Incorporated: 30 July 2012
Previous: BI Wines and Spirits Limited
Registered Office: 10 Hatton Garden, London, EC1N 8AH
Parent: BI Wines and Spirits Limited
Officers: Colin Thomas West [1958] Director/Wine Merchant

Bordeaux Undiscovered Limited
Incorporated: 9 November 2004 *Employees:* 2
Net Worth Deficit: £531,156 *Total Assets:* £50,305
Registered Office: 3rd Floor, Regent House, Bath Avenue, Wolverhampton, W Midlands, WV1 4EG
Major Shareholder: Nicholas Paul Stephens
Officers: Nicholas Stephens [1956] Director

Bordeaux Wine Investments Limited
Incorporated: 7 August 1998 *Employees:* 8
Net Worth Deficit: £35,606 *Total Assets:* £4,766,934
Registered Office: 2 The Mews, 16 Holly Bush Lane, Sevenoaks, Kent, TN13 3TH
Officers: Andrew Douglas Lench [1954] Director

UK Wholesalers of Beers, Wines and Spirits   dellam

Borders Distillers Limited
Incorporated: 23 April 2015
Registered Office: The Borders Distillery, Commercial Road, Hawick, Roxburghshire, TD9 7AQ
Parent: The Three Stills Company Limited
Officers: Timothy Ado Carton [1959] Director [Irish]; Laurence John Fordyce [1962] Director; Anthony Brian Roberts [1965] Director

Borders Distilling Limited
Incorporated: 20 December 2017
Registered Office: The Borders Distillery, Commercial Road, Hawick, Roxburghshire, TD9 7AQ
Parent: The Three Stills Company Limited
Officers: Timothy Ado Carton [1959] Director [Irish]; Laurence John Fordyce [1962] Director; Anthony Brian Roberts [1965] Director

Bosco-UK Limited
Incorporated: 22 January 2018
Registered Office: London 1st, 70 North End Road, London, W14 9EP
Officers: Zoe Elizabeth Andrews [1983] Director; Julia Gobert [1961] Director; Nelson Rawlins [1960] Director

Bosman Wines UK Ltd
Incorporated: 14 June 2016
Net Worth Deficit: £7,191 Total Assets: £10,850
Registered Office: Ashcombe Court, Woolsack Way, Godalming, Surrey, GU7 1LQ
Shareholder: BFV International Limited
Officers: Petrus Wilhelmus Jacobus Bosman [1981] Director [South African]; Pieter Gerhardus Du Toit [1981] Director [South African]; Lucy Margaret Faraday Warner [1966] Director/Sales & Marketing

The Bosun's Brewery Tap Ltd
Incorporated: 27 October 2015
Previous: Bosun's Market Place Ltd
Net Worth Deficit: £2,858 Total Assets: £2
Registered Office: c/o D & A Hill Chartered Accountants, No 18 T8/9, Brooke's Mill, Armitage Bridge, Huddersfield, W Yorks, HD4 7NR
Major Shareholder: Grahame Francis Andrews
Officers: Grahame Francis Andrews [1954] Director; Gordon Michael Hartley [1954] Director

Bosworthcruises Ltd
Incorporated: 12 September 2017
Registered Office: The Boat Journeyman, Gas Street Basin, Gas Street, Birmingham, B1 2JT
Major Shareholder: Michal Zdrojek
Officers: Catherine Elizabeth Hytner [1950] Director; Michal Zdrojek [1994] Director [Polish]

Botan Grey Ltd
Incorporated: 4 July 2018
Registered Office: 110 Wigmore Lane, Luton, Beds, LU2 8AD
Major Shareholder: Princess Serwah Adu-Gyamfi
Officers: Princess Serwah Adu-Gyamfi [1991] Director/Businesswoman

Botanicals and Hops Limited
Incorporated: 25 June 2018
Registered Office: The Manor House, West End, Sedgefield, Stockton on Tees, Cleveland, TS21 2BW
Major Shareholder: Matthew Philip Wilson
Officers: Matthew Philip Wilson [1986] Director/Chemical Engineer

Botella Imports Ltd
Incorporated: 22 March 2016
Net Worth: £2,337 Total Assets: £18,403
Registered Office: The Hermitage, 15a Shenfield Road, Brentwood, Essex, CM15 8AG
Major Shareholder: Eduardo Flores Flores
Officers: Eduardo Flores Flores [1976] Director/Wine Importer [Mexican]

The Bottle Bank Limited
Incorporated: 9 May 2016 Employees: 4
Net Worth Deficit: £5,197 Total Assets: £122,445
Registered Office: Maritime House, Discovery Quay, Falmouth, Cornwall, TR11 3XA
Shareholders: Nicholas David Hodginson; Lewis Elliot Matthews
Officers: Nicholas David Hodgkinson [1981] Director; Lewis Elliot Matthews [1981] Director

Bottle Butler Limited
Incorporated: 6 September 2012 Employees: 2
Net Worth: £6,199 Total Assets: £19,495
Registered Office: 18-22 Stoney Lane, Yardley, Birmingham, B25 8YP
Shareholders: Charnpaul Singh Kooner; Kiran Kaur Kooner
Officers: Kiran Kaur Kooner [1987] Director

The Bottle Drinks Company Ltd
Incorporated: 1 May 2013 Employees: 2
Net Worth Deficit: £51,804 Total Assets: £68,468
Registered Office: Ossington Chambers, 6-8 Castle Gate, Newark, Notts, NG24 1AX
Major Shareholder: Robert John Ratcliffe
Officers: Robert John Ratcliffe [1962] Director/Wine & Spirits Merchant

Bottle Green Limited
Incorporated: 1 March 1990
Net Worth: £3,926,000 Total Assets: £5,610,000
Registered Office: The Winery, Fairhills Road, Irlam, Manchester, M44 6BD
Parent: Kingsland Drinks Group Limited
Officers: Edmund Anthony Baker, Secretary; Edmund Anthony Baker [1973] Finance Director; Jonathan Ernest Eagle [1960] Commercial Director; Andrew Jonathan Sagar [1959] Managing Director

The Bottle Shop (Penarth) Limited
Incorporated: 4 November 2013
Net Worth: £20,775 Total Assets: £55,377
Registered Office: The Bottle Shop, Old Masonic Building, Station Approach, Penarth, S Glamorgan, CF64 3EE
Officers: Daniel Williams [1982] Director/Wine Merchant

The Bottlers Limited
Incorporated: 12 March 2002
Net Worth Deficit: £5,681 Total Assets: £50,982
Registered Office: 21-23 Comely Bank Road, Edinburgh, EH4 1DS
Shareholders: Zubair Mohamed; Roy Matthew Richards
Officers: Simon Vincent Le Druillenec, Secretary; Zubair Mohamed [1962] Director/Wine Merchant

Bottles on Demand Limited
Incorporated: 9 October 2017
Registered Office: 126 Claypit Lane, West Bromwich, W Midlands, B70 9UH
Major Shareholder: Rodane Anthony Bennett
Officers: Rodane Anthony Bennett [1994] Director

Bouquet Limited
Incorporated: 29 July 2016
Net Worth Deficit: £5,983 *Total Assets:* £4,816
Registered Office: 29 Gildredge Road, Eastbourne, E Sussex, BN21 4RU
Major Shareholder: Peter Ronald Castle
Officers: Erica Jane Castle, Secretary; Peter Ronald Castle, Secretary; Erica Jane Castle [1967] Director; Peter Ronald Castle [1961] Director/Wholesale

Bourgognes Only Limited
Incorporated: 4 July 2013
Net Worth Deficit: £6,817 *Total Assets:* £48,394
Registered Office: Third Floor, 20 Old Bailey, London, EC4M 7AN
Shareholders: Nathalie Anne Alberte Teilhard de Chardin; Philippe Henri Urbain Teilhard de Chardin
Officers: Nathalie Anne Alberte Teilhard de Chardin [1963] Director [French]; Philippe Henri Urbain Teilhard de Chardin [1963] Director [French]

Bourne & Co Solutions Ltd
Incorporated: 29 August 2017
Registered Office: 38 Gayle, Wilnecote, Tamworth, Staffs, B77 4DJ
Officers: Michael Kocon [1984] Director

Bournemouth Food Ltd
Incorporated: 16 March 2018
Registered Office: 151 West Green Road, London, N15 5EA
Shareholders: Deniz Metehan Baykara; Umit Ozcali
Officers: Deniz Metehan Baykara, Secretary; Umit Ozcali, Secretary; Deniz Metehan Baykara [1976] Director/Engineer; Umit Ozcali [1978] Director/Manager

Boutinot Canada Limited
Incorporated: 12 October 2018
Registered Office: Boundary House, Cheadle Point, Cheadle, Cheshire, SK8 2GG
Parent: Wine Vantage Limited
Officers: Michael Joseph Moriarty [1965] Director; Dennis Whiteley [1961] Director

Boutinot Limited
Incorporated: 25 November 1980 *Employees:* 140
Net Worth: £25,912,476 *Total Assets:* £82,608,976
Registered Office: Boundary House, Cheadle Point, Cheadle, Cheshire, SK8 2GG
Shareholders: Dennis Whiteley; Donna Whiteley; Araldica Castelvero SCA
Officers: Michael Joseph Moriarty, Secretary/Accountant; Antony Malcolm Brown [1957] Director; Iain Robert Davies [1970] Director; Claudio Manera [1963] Director [Italian]; Michael Joseph Moriarty [1965] Director/Accountant; Dennis Whiteley [1961] Deputy Managing Director

Boutinot USA Limited
Incorporated: 6 August 2018
Registered Office: Boundary House, Cheadle Point, Cheadle, Cheshire, SK8 2GG
Parent: Wine Vantage Limited
Officers: Michael Joseph Moriarty [1965] Director; Dennis Whiteley [1961] Director

Boutinot Wines Limited
Incorporated: 11 March 2011
Registered Office: Boundary House, Cheadle Point, Cheadle, Cheshire, SK8 2GG
Parent: Boutinot Limited
Officers: Michael Joseph Moriarty, Secretary; Nicola Jayne Lowe [1971] Director; Michael Joseph Moriarty [1965] Director/Accountant; Dennis Whiteley [1961] Director

Boutique Brands Limited
Incorporated: 29 July 2005 *Employees:* 4
Net Worth Deficit: £138,601 *Total Assets:* £413,115
Registered Office: c/o Hillier Hopkins LLP, First Floor, Radius House, 51 Clarendon Road, Watford, Herts, WD17 1HP
Major Shareholder: Olivier Scaramucci
Officers: Olivier Scaramucci [1963] Director/Executive

The Boutique Spirit Company Limited
Incorporated: 13 September 2012 *Employees:* 4
Net Worth Deficit: £59,985 *Total Assets:* £61,111
Registered Office: 34a Watling Street, Radlett, Herts, WD7 7NN
Shareholders: Roberto Fiorillo; Jassel Jagdish Patel
Officers: Shane Cody [1981] Director; Jass Patel [1974] Director

Bowsaw Bourbon Limited
Incorporated: 17 May 2018
Registered Office: 155-157 Donegall Pass, Belfast, BT7 1DT
Parent: Kirker Greer (Holdings) Limited
Officers: Steven Clark Pattison [1979] Director; Richard Ryan [1977] Director

Boxford Wine Company Limited (The)
Incorporated: 30 July 1982
Net Worth: £277,422 *Total Assets:* £302,021
Registered Office: Spring Cottage, Butchers Lane, Boxford, Sudbury, Suffolk, CO10 5EA
Major Shareholder: Hugh Nigel Phillips
Officers: Fiona Ann Phillips, Secretary; Fiona Ann Phillips [1946] Director; Hugh Nigel Phillips [1944] Director

J.Braham Everett Imports Ltd
Incorporated: 10 June 2013 *Employees:* 2
Net Worth: £23,425 *Total Assets:* £80,083
Registered Office: Office 4 Sudbury Stables, Sudbury Road, Downham, Billericay, Essex, CM11 1LB
Shareholders: Lorraine Mandy Braham-Everett; Jonathan Joseph Braham-Everett
Officers: Jonathan Joseph Braham-Everett [1982] Director/Shipping; Lorraine Mandy Braham-Everett [1982] Director

S.A.Brain & Company,Limited
Incorporated: 12 April 1897 *Employees:* 2,520
Net Worth: £74,859,000 *Total Assets:* £192,684,992
Registered Office: Dragon Brewery, Pacific Road, Cardiff, CF24 5HJ
Officers: Charles Nicholas Brain, Company Secretary; Alistair Grant Arkley [1947] Director; Charles Nicholas Brain [1971] Director/Company Secretary; Jonathan Bridge [1978] Operations Director; Alistair William Darby [1966] Director/Chief Executive; Martin Stuart Reed [1960] Director/Accountant; John Frederick William Rhys [1958] Director/Marketing Consultant; Peter John Wilson [1958] Director

W.H. Brakspear & Sons Limited
Incorporated: 28 January 1896 *Employees:* 25
Net Worth: £59,174,000 *Total Assets:* £106,872,000
Registered Office: Bull Courtyard, Bell Street, Henley on Thames, Oxon, RG9 2BA
Parent: J.T.D. Investments Limited
Officers: David Generald Nathan, Secretary; Michael Anthony Trehearne Davies [1953] Director; Thomas Anthony Trehearne Davies [1980] Director; David Generald Nathan [1970] Director

Brand Central (UK) Limited
Incorporated: 7 June 2010
Net Worth: £509 *Total Assets:* £47,541
Registered Office: Imogen House, 37 Moorbridge Road, Bingham, Nottingham, NG13 8GG
Major Shareholder: Paul Hinks
Officers: Paul Hinks [1968] Managing Director

Branda Ltd
Incorporated: 16 August 2013 *Employees:* 5
Net Worth: £195,567 *Total Assets:* £2,653,156
Registered Office: 10 Skylines Village, Limeharbour, London, E14 9TS
Shareholder: Julius Ledas
Officers: Julius Ledas [1979] Director [Lithuanian]

Branded Drinks Ltd
Incorporated: 16 September 1999 *Employees:* 24
Net Worth: £1,041,037 *Total Assets:* £3,886,575
Registered Office: The Bottling Works, Unit 1 The Business Park, Tufthorn Avenue, Coleford, Glos, GL16 8PN
Major Shareholder: Jonathan Charles Calver
Officers: Gray Bensted Olliver, Secretary; Jonathan Charles Calver [1970] Managing Director; Gray Bensted Olliver [1949] Sales & Marketing Director

G. Bravo & Son Limited
Incorporated: 15 October 1959 *Employees:* 3
Net Worth: £89,402 *Total Assets:* £380,978
Registered Office: Turnbull House, 226 Mulgrave Road, Cheam, Surrey, SM2 6JT
Major Shareholder: Giuseppe Franco Bravo
Officers: Giuseppe Franco Bravo, Secretary; Giuseppe Franco Bravo [1955] Director

Brayston Leisure Ltd.
Incorporated: 4 September 2015 *Employees:* 2
Net Worth: £21,542 *Total Assets:* £186,552
Registered Office: 123 Wellington Road South, Stockport, Cheshire, SK1 3TH
Major Shareholder: Michael Shepherd
Officers: Michael Shepherd [1971] Director/Beer Wholesaler

Brazen Beer Limited
Incorporated: 16 January 2019
Registered Office: 15-17 Middle Street, Brighton, BN1 1AL
Shareholders: Joseph Henry Herbie Ringwood; Aleksander Martin Levente
Officers: Aleksander Martin Levente [1987] Sales Director; Joseph Henry Herbie Ringwood [1987] Sales Director

Brazen Rum Ltd
Incorporated: 26 June 2018
Registered Office: Flat 1-2, 1167 Pollokshaws Road, Glasgow, G41 3NG
Shareholders: Frederick Drucquer; Douglas Alan Jeffries
Officers: Frederick Drucquer [1990] Director/Analyst; Douglas Alan Jeffries [1963] Sales Director

Brew Boxes Ltd
Incorporated: 15 August 2018
Registered Office: Permanent House, 1 Dundas Street, Huddersfield, W Yorks, HD1 2EX
Shareholders: Daniel Bromley; Steven Thomas Trow
Officers: Steven Thomas Trow, Secretary; Daniel Bromley [1977] Director; Steven Thomas Trow [1978] Director

Brewbarge Limited
Incorporated: 3 April 2018
Registered Office: 16 Glendower Approach, Heathcote, Warwick, CV34 6ET
Officers: Mark John Downey [1981] Director; Michael Christopher Healy [1983] Director

Brewed 4 U Ltd
Incorporated: 7 May 2008
Net Worth Deficit: £85,624 *Total Assets:* £86,478
Registered Office: The Railway Hotel, Boston Place, Coventry, Warwicks, CV6 5NN
Officers: Ana Magdalena Sumra [1976] Director [Romanian]

The Brewers Wholesale Limited
Incorporated: 14 January 2010 *Employees:* 8
Net Worth: £176,754 *Total Assets:* £952,342
Registered Office: Unit 2B Gainsborough Trading Estate, Rufford Road, Stourbridge, W Midlands, DY9 7ND
Parent: Avancez Holdings Limited
Officers: Mark Adrian Bryan Hill [1968] Director

The Brewgooder Foundation
Incorporated: 2 February 2016 *Employees:* 3
Net Worth: £28,422 *Total Assets:* £318,083
Registered Office: 1 St Colme Street, Edinburgh, EH3 6AA
Officers: Martin Dickie [1982] Director; Joshua Howard Littlejohn [1986] Director; Alan Mahon [1990] Managing Director [Irish]; James Bruce Watt [1982] Director

Brewgooder Limited
Incorporated: 9 December 2015 *Employees:* 3
Net Worth: £7,506 *Total Assets:* £316,047
Registered Office: Room 203, 54 Washington Street, Glasgow, G3 8AZ
Parent: Brewgooder Foundation
Officers: Shane Alexander Corstorphine [1979] Director; Simon John Hannah [1977] Managing Director; Joshua Howard Littlejohn [1986] Director; Scott MacDonald [1977] Commercial Director; Alan Mahon [1990] Managing Director [Irish]; Stephen McCranor [1978] Director; Christopher Stuart Miller [1971] Director

Brewis Beer Co Ltd
Incorporated: 11 December 2018
Registered Office: 3 West Close, Warkworth, Morpeth, Northumberland, NE65 0JZ
Shareholders: Christopher Brewis; Maxine Brewis
Officers: Christopher Brewis [1967] Director; Maxine Brewis [1964] Director

Brewland Ltd
Incorporated: 22 June 2017
Registered Office: 31 Brook Lodge, North Circular Road, London, NW11 9LG
Officers: Jakub Szymanowski [1991] Director

Brexit Import and Export Company Limited
Incorporated: 28 April 2018
Registered Office: 55 York Road, North Weald, Epping, Essex, CM16 6HT
Major Shareholder: Mary Ellen Jolley
Officers: Mary Ellen Jolley [1963] Director/Teacher

Brian Traders Ltd
Incorporated: 20 July 2016
Net Worth: £24,748 *Total Assets:* £31,519
Registered Office: 116a Barking Road, London, E6 3BD
Major Shareholder: Muhammad Irshad
Officers: Muhammad Irshad [1966] Director/Businessman [Portuguese]

Bric Commerce Ltd
Incorporated: 25 September 2013
Net Worth Deficit: £269
Registered Office: 5 Blakesley Court, 26 Blakesley Avenue, London, W5 2DU
Major Shareholder: Haralambos Michael Pastides
Officers: Haralambos Michael Pastides [1977] Director

Bridge Vintners Limited
Incorporated: 11 January 1983 *Employees:* 2
Net Worth: £34,609 *Total Assets:* £439,692
Registered Office: Navigation Warehouse, Riverhead Road, Louth, Lincs, LN11 0DA
Major Shareholder: Michael Howard Sowter
Officers: Michael Howard Sowter [1958] Director/Broker Consultant

Bridge Wine Limited
Incorporated: 26 February 2018
Registered Office: 1 Kings Road, London, SW19 8PL
Officers: Victoria Power [1977] Director

Bridgnorth Brewing Co. Ltd.
Incorporated: 5 January 2006
Net Worth: £19,172 *Total Assets:* £32,938
Registered Office: 46 High Street, Bridgnorth, Salop, WV16 4DX
Major Shareholder: Annabelle Beaman
Officers: Richard Edward Beaman, Secretary; Annabelle Beaman [1996] Director

The Brighton and Hove Wine Company Limited
Incorporated: 8 January 2018
Registered Office: 11 Colbourne Road, Hove, E Sussex, BN3 1TA
Major Shareholder: Brad Dyson
Officers: Brad Dyson [1976] Digital Director

Brighton Brew Co Ltd
Incorporated: 7 October 2015
Net Worth Deficit: £19,149 *Total Assets:* £1,025
Registered Office: 70 New Church Road, Hove, E Sussex, BN3 4FL
Major Shareholder: Max Danin
Officers: Max Danin [1991] Director

Brighton Soft Drinks Limited
Incorporated: 20 November 2005 *Employees:* 7
Previous: Ben Shaws Brighton Limited
Net Worth: £81,056 *Total Assets:* £413,205
Registered Office: 30-34 North Street, Hailsham, E Sussex, BN27 1DW
Parent: Southern Taxis (Brighton) Limited
Officers: Helen Burdett, Secretary; Andrew John Cheesman [1966] Director

Brindle Distillery Limited
Incorporated: 25 October 2017
Registered Office: Ollerton Fold Farm, Ollerton Lane, Withnell, Chorley, Lancs, PR6 8BW
Parent: Brindle Holdings Limited
Officers: Mark William Long [1987] Director/Manager; Catherine Singleton [1965] Director; Gerard Edmund John Singleton [1962] Director

Bringmevino (UK) Limited
Incorporated: 10 March 2016
Net Worth: £11,503 *Total Assets:* £218,885
Registered Office: PMB Taxation Services, 6b Hunter Street, Glasgow, G74 4LZ
Major Shareholder: Thomas Smith
Officers: Thomas Smith [1949] Director

Bristol Cider Company Ltd
Incorporated: 6 January 2015
Previous: Gas Lane Cider Company Ltd
Registered Office: 339 Two Mile Hill Road, Kingswood, Bristol, BS15 1AN
Shareholders: Jonathan Paul Kemp; Marcus Simon George Chappell
Officers: Marcus Simon George Chappell [1970] Director; Jonathan Paul Kemp [1972] Director

Bristol Fine Wine Limited
Incorporated: 6 April 2010
Net Worth Deficit: £51,442 *Total Assets:* £56,074
Registered Office: 91 Princess Victoria Street, Bristol, BS8 4DD
Major Shareholder: Charles James Hastings Lucas
Officers: Charles James Hastings Lucas [1969] Director

Bristol Records Limited
Incorporated: 29 August 2018
Registered Office: 4 Amberwood Mews, Hamp Green Rise, Bridgwater, Somerset, TA6 6AY
Shareholders: Paul Crossan; Morgan Jan Alial Erkhagen
Officers: Paul Crossan [1972] Director; Morgan Jan Alial Erkhagen [1972] Director [Swedish]

Briton Ferry Brewing Company Limited
Incorporated: 21 July 2016
Net Worth: £100 *Total Assets:* £100
Registered Office: 20 Ena Avenue, Neath, W Glamorgan, SA11 3AD
Major Shareholder: Rhys Phillip Davies
Officers: Rhys Phillip Davies [1973] Director

Brix & Porter Ltd.
Incorporated: 10 October 2017
Registered Office: Flat 9, Westgarth, 145 Marina, St Leonards on Sea, E Sussex, TN38 0BT
Shareholders: Jessica Louise Scarratt; Matthew James Wilson
Officers: Jessica Louise Scarratt [1980] Managing Director; Matthew James Wilson [1980] Director

Broad Street Brands Limited
Incorporated: 13 December 2011 *Employees:* 4
Previous: Broad Street Brands Public Limited Company
Net Worth: £32,220 *Total Assets:* £62,949
Registered Office: Level 17, Dashwood House, 69 Old Broad Street, London, EC2M 1QS
Officers: David Keith Papworth, Secretary; Richard Charles Quintin Ambler [1955] Director; Andrew William Burrows [1945] Director; Timothy Harold Garnett Lyle [1951] Director/Chartered Accountant; David Keith Papworth [1963] Director/Corporate Financier

Broadoak Cider Company Limited
Incorporated: 24 April 2007
Net Worth Deficit: £53,458 *Total Assets:* £457,775
Registered Office: Scott Cottage, Pagans Hill, Chew Stoke, Bristol, BS40 8UQ
Major Shareholder: Nina Maria Emily Brunt
Officers: Nina Maria Emily Brunt, Secretary; Nina Maria Emily Brunt [1950] Director; Steven Lee Brunt [1979] Director

The Broadway Drinks Company Ltd
Incorporated: 27 July 2017 *Employees:* 3
Net Worth Deficit: £33,742 *Total Assets:* £62,438
Registered Office: 2 Catford Broadway, London, SE6 4SP
Shareholder: Xhulio Sina
Officers: Natalie Caroline John [1979] Director; Xhulio Sina [1980] Director/Manager

Brockmans Gin Limited
Incorporated: 3 November 2006 *Employees:* 10
Net Worth Deficit: £2,866,239 *Total Assets:* £4,508,086
Registered Office: 40 Queen Anne Street, London, W1G 9EL
Shareholders: Kevin George Taylor; Lauren Cherie Willis; Graeme Walter Briggs
Officers: Marc Brownstein [1960] Director/President & Chief Executive Officer [American]; Anastasios Economou [1977] Director [Greek]; Neil John Everitt [1961] Director; Robert Andrew Fowkes [1957] Director; Alexandra Lesley Hincks [1967] Director/Consultant

Brocour Ltd.
Incorporated: 1 July 2015
Registered Office: 23 Sulina Road, London, SW2 4EJ
Major Shareholder: James Oliver Swann
Officers: James Oliver Swann [1976] Director/Wine Merchant

The Brompton Wine Company Limited
Incorporated: 5 March 2007
Net Worth: £5,851 *Total Assets:* £56,432
Registered Office: Kajaine House, 57-67 High Street, Edgware, Middlesex, HA8 7DD
Major Shareholder: Richard Edward Household
Officers: Richard Edward Household [1969] Director/Wine Merchant

Brookfield Beverages Limited
Incorporated: 14 August 2012 *Employees:* 9
Net Worth: £715,699 *Total Assets:* £4,741,928
Registered Office: Brookfield, 105 High Street, Sharnbrook, Bedford, MK44 1PE
Major Shareholder: Nigel Duncan McNally
Officers: Nigel Duncan McNally [1960] Director

Brookfield Drinks Limited
Incorporated: 21 August 2012 *Employees:* 9
Net Worth: £2,670,799 *Total Assets:* £4,574,059
Registered Office: Brookfield, 105 High Street, Sharnbrook, Bedford, MK44 1PE
Parent: Kestrel Brewing Company Limited
Officers: Nigel Duncan McNally [1960] Director

Brooks & Whitaker Limited
Incorporated: 5 September 2011
Net Worth: £4,096 *Total Assets:* £54,297
Registered Office: 11-12 Hallmark Trading Centre, Fourth Way, Wembley, Middlesex, HA9 0LB
Major Shareholder: Sam Brooks
Officers: Sam Brooks [1979] Managing Director

Jack Brooksbank Limited
Incorporated: 2 August 2016 *Employees:* 1
Net Worth: £14,390 *Total Assets:* £28,276
Registered Office: 5 Stirling Court Yard, Stirling Way, Borehamwood, Herts, WD6 2FX
Officers: Jack Brooksbank [1986] Director/Consultant

Broom House Investments Limited
Incorporated: 10 January 1974 *Employees:* 40
Net Worth: £6,716,149 *Total Assets:* £9,620,780
Registered Office: Unit 1 River Street, Brighouse, W Yorks, HD6 1LU
Major Shareholder: Ian James Clay
Officers: Ruth Ann Clay, Secretary; Ian James Clay [1953] Director; James Anthony Clay [1984] Director

Broughton Ales Limited
Incorporated: 14 August 1995 *Employees:* 9
Net Worth: £269,366 *Total Assets:* £502,688
Registered Office: Main Street, Broughton Village, Biggar, S Lanarks, ML12 6HQ
Shareholders: Stephen Lawrence McCarney; David Andrew McGowan; John Simon Hunt
Officers: John Simon Hunt [1963] Director; Stephen Lawrence McCarney [1961] Director; David Andrew McGowan [1963] Director

Browett & Fair Ltd
Incorporated: 7 November 2018
Registered Office: 2 Pickle Mews, London, SW9 0FJ
Shareholders: Nicholas William Fair; Ben David Hulton Browett
Officers: Ben David Hulton Browett [1992] Director/Wine Merchant; Nicholas William Fair [1993] Director/Accounts Manager

Brown Bear Tales Ltd
Incorporated: 27 February 2017
Registered Office: 4 Lambrigg Terrace, Kendal, Cumbria, LA9 4BB
Officers: Laura Horney [1989] Director; Mircea Ion Putanu [1989] Director [Romanian]

Andrew Bruce Fine Wines Limited
Incorporated: 4 June 2007
Registered Office: 10 Hatton Garden, London, EC1N 8AH
Parent: BI Wines and Spirits Limited
Officers: Generald Robert Dreyer, Secretary; Gary James Boom [1958] Director [Dutch]

Bruce Jack Wines Limited
Incorporated: 14 December 2017
Registered Office: 299 Cannon Hill Lane, London, SW20 9HQ
Major Shareholder: John Walter Raymond Passmore
Officers: John Walter Raymond Passmore [1976] Managing Director [Irish]

Bruist Trading Ltd
Incorporated: 12 January 2018
Registered Office: Unit 11-13 Cadzow Gait, 222 Low Waters Road, Hamilton, S Lanarks, ML3 7QR
Major Shareholder: Mahim Munir
Officers: Anum Nadia Iqbal [1989] Director; Mahim Munir [1995] Director

Brummells Gin Limited
Incorporated: 22 June 2006
Registered Office: 10a St Ann's Road, London, SW13 9LJ
Major Shareholder: Gary Elias Jamali Hazell
Officers: Gary Elias Jamali Hazell [1959] Director/Sales and Marketing

Brunswick Fine Wines and Spirits Limited
Incorporated: 21 March 2016 *Employees:* 4
Net Worth: £641,131 *Total Assets:* £1,443,417
Registered Office: Flat 1, 6 Vernon Terrace, Brighton, BN1 3JG
Shareholders: Carlos de Haan; Jamie Ambrose Kirke Graham
Officers: Carlos de Haan [1975] Director; Jamie Ambrose Kirke Graham [1967] Director/Wine Merchant; Kenneth Stewart [1965] Director/Wine Merchant

Bubbles & Wines Limited
Incorporated: 25 May 2010
Net Worth Deficit: £71,115 *Total Assets:* £251,393
Registered Office: 20 Moxon Street, London, W1U 4EU
Major Shareholder: Laurent Faure
Officers: Laurent Faure [1966] Director/Businessman [French]

Bubbles for Friends Ltd.
Incorporated: 17 October 2014
Registered Office: 43 Owston Road, Carcroft, Doncaster, S Yorks, DN6 8DA
Shareholders: Jaap Christiaan Veenstra; Jasper Rogier Groen
Officers: Jasper Rogier Groen [1974] Director/Entrepreneur [Dutch]; Jaap Christiaan Veenstra [1972] Director/Entrepreneur [Dutch]

Bubra Drinks Ltd
Incorporated: 21 January 2019
Registered Office: 86 Clarson House, 3 Midnight Avenue, London, SE5 0AF
Major Shareholder: Dennis Paul Tuffour-Kensah
Officers: Dennis Paul Tuffour-Kensah [1976] Director/Operational Manager

Buchanan Wines Ltd.
Incorporated: 24 November 2016 *Employees:* 1
Net Worth: £1,274 *Total Assets:* £11,553
Registered Office: 10 Rowton Close, Wellington, Telford, Salop, TF1 3PW
Major Shareholder: Peter Henry McKinnon Buchanan
Officers: Martin Thomas Buchanan [1982] Director/Wine Merchant; Peter Henry McKinnon Buchanan [1947] Director/Consultant

Buckingham Fine Wine Ltd
Incorporated: 13 January 2015
Registered Office: 19 Charles Street, London, W1J 5DT
Parent: Buckingham Securities and Investments PLC
Officers: Matthew Jason Bees [1972] Director/Project Manager

Buckingtons Ltd
Incorporated: 20 July 2017
Registered Office: 2 Halfway Cottages, East Dean Road, East Dean, Eastbourne, E Sussex, BN20 0BB
Major Shareholder: Jennifer Lisa Healey
Officers: Jennifer Lisa Healey [1971] Director

Bucklebury Brewers Ltd
Incorporated: 18 February 2019
Registered Office: Highgates, Broad Lane, Upper Bucklebury, Reading, Berks, RG7 6QJ
Officers: Stephen Harris [1966] Director; Raymond Peter Herbert [1956] Director/Engineer

Bucks Spirits Ltd
Incorporated: 18 January 2018
Registered Office: 209 The Heights, Northolt, Middlesex, UB5 4BX
Major Shareholder: Linda Heather Collis
Officers: Linda Heather Collis [1984] Director/Manager [Indian]

Budge Brands Ltd
Incorporated: 29 March 2005 *Employees:* 4
Net Worth: £319,397 *Total Assets:* £994,208
Registered Office: 78 Wharfdale Road, Birmingham, B11 2DE
Shareholder: Budge Dhariwal
Officers: Budge Dhariwal [1961] Director

Buffet Restaurant Northampton Ltd
Incorporated: 27 December 2018
Registered Office: 2 Northampton Road, Brixworth, Northampton, NN6 9DY
Major Shareholder: Razvan Tiberiu Vasile
Officers: Razvan Tiberiu Vasile [1979] Director/General Manager [Romanian]

Bugle and Co Ltd
Incorporated: 23 July 2009
Registered Office: The Yews, Cootes Lane, Fen Drayton, Cambs, CB24 4SL
Shareholders: Charles Dominic Owen Prymaka; Alexandra Mary Dain Prymaka
Officers: Alexandra Mary Dain Prymaka [1984] Director; Charles Dominic Owen Prymaka [1987] Director

Buke Limited
Incorporated: 11 January 2018
Net Worth: £458 *Total Assets:* £6,386
Registered Office: Unit 18 Ashley House, Ashley Road, Tottenham Hale, London, N17 9LZ
Major Shareholder: Ersin Coskun
Officers: Ersin Coskun [1976] Director [Turkish]

Bulgarsko Pivo Limited
Incorporated: 7 January 2019
Registered Office: 214 Seven Sisters Road, London, N4 3NX
Major Shareholder: Simeon Dimitrov Dimitrov
Officers: Simeon Dimitrov Dimitrov [1989] Director [Bulgarian]

Bull Trading Worldwide Ltd
Incorporated: 18 January 2018
Registered Office: 1110 Elliot Court Business Park, Herald Avenue, Coventry, Warwicks, CV5 6UB
Major Shareholder: Harvinder Singh Sunner
Officers: Harvinder Singh Sunner, Secretary; Harvinder Singh Sunner [1978] Director/Shopkeeper

Bullards Spirits Limited
Incorporated: 30 October 2017
Registered Office: 2 Chestnut Cottage, Bunwell Road, Spooner Row, Wymondham, Norfolk, NR18 9LH
Major Shareholder: Clare Joanne Evans
Officers: Craig Allison [1988] Director; Clare Joanne Evans [1969] Director

Bumble Mead Ltd
Incorporated: 1 February 2019
Registered Office: 18 The Causeway, Chippenham, Wilts, SN15 3DB
Major Shareholder: Thomas Edward Jenner
Officers: Thomas Edward Jenner [1985] Director/Dreyman

Bump Events U.K Limited
Incorporated: 3 April 2017
Registered Office: 25 Bidwell Avenue, Bexhill on Sea, E Sussex, TN39 4DB
Major Shareholder: Matthew Leslie Dawes
Officers: Matthew Leslie Dawes [1984] Director

The Bunnahabhain Distillery Company Limited
Incorporated: 7 January 2003
Registered Office: 8 Milton Road, College Milton North, East Kilbride, S Lanarks, G74 5BU
Parent: Distell International Limited
Officers: Karen Spy, Secretary; Fraser John Thornton [1969] Director

Buon Vino Ltd
Incorporated: 28 January 2008 *Employees:* 3
Net Worth: £51,261 *Total Assets:* £148,789
Registered Office: The Courtyard, Settle, Skipton, N Yorks, BD24 9JY
Major Shareholder: Robert William Bagot
Officers: Robert William Bagot, Secretary; Robert William Bagot [1976] Director/Wine Merchant

Burbage Wines Limited
Incorporated: 28 March 2006 *Employees:* 1
Net Worth: £114 *Total Assets:* £27,605
Registered Office: 1 Betony Close, Lutterworth, Leics, LE17 4UY
Major Shareholder: Richard Mark Pearson
Officers: Valerie Pearson, Secretary; Richard Mark Pearson [1963] Director/Wine Trader

Burble Foods and Beverages Limited
Incorporated: 8 February 2018
Registered Office: 71-75 Shelton Street, Covent Garden, London, WC2H 9JQ
Major Shareholder: Tolulope Ayomide Agbeyo
Officers: Tolulope Ayomide Agbeyo [1994] Director [Nigerian]

Burdett Wines Ltd
Incorporated: 22 March 2012
Net Worth: £8,550 *Total Assets:* £24,946
Registered Office: Tre-Ru House, The Leats, Truro, Cornwall, TR1 3AG
Shareholders: Carl Stuart Burdett; Lorraine Claire Burdett
Officers: Peter Stephen May, Secretary; Carl Stuart Burdett [1968] Director; Lorraine Burdett [1974] Director

Burgeon Allied Limited
Incorporated: 5 June 2017
Registered Office: 34 Francis Court, MacArthur Close, Erith, Kent, DA8 1DQ
Officers: Olalekan Lawal [1988] Director/Trader [Nigerian]

Burgundy Tuscany Piedmont Ltd
Incorporated: 26 March 2015
Registered Office: 3rd Floor, Vyman House, 104 College Road, Harrow, Middlesex, HA1 1BQ
Major Shareholder: Andrew Nicholas Pavli
Officers: Andrew Nicholas Pavli [1964] Director

Burgundy Wines Limited
Incorporated: 25 April 2000
Net Worth Deficit: £56,135 *Total Assets:* £12,531
Registered Office: 124 Brighton Road, Shoreham-by-Sea, W Sussex, BN43 6RH
Major Shareholder: Derek John Fowlie
Officers: Derek John Fowlie, Secretary; Derek John Fowlie [1948] Director/Wine Merchant

Burgundys Collection Limited
Incorporated: 19 February 2019
Registered Office: Laurel Bank Cottage, Bagshot Road, Chobham, Surrey, GU24 8BU
Shareholders: Olivier Bernstein; Hob
Officers: Olivier Bernstein [1966] Director [French]; Laura Jane Godwin [1988] Managing Director

Bruce Burlington and Company Limited
Incorporated: 25 May 1946
Registered Office: 146 New London Road, Chelmsford, Essex, CM2 0AW
Parent: G. A. Smith & Sons Limited
Officers: George Robert Peter Smith, Secretary; George Robert Peter Smith [1965] Director; Nicholas Roy Smith [1956] Director/Wine Merchant; Peter Overett Smith [1930] Director

Burn Stewart (U.S. Holdings) Limited
Incorporated: 12 July 2000
Registered Office: 8 Milton Road, College Milton North, East Kilbride, S Lanarks, G74 5BU
Shareholders: Distell International Limited; Distell Internatiional Limited
Officers: Karen Spy, Secretary; Nardus Oosthuizen [1968] Director/Accountant [South African]; Fraser John Thornton [1969] UK Sales Director

The Burnfield Trading Company Limited
Incorporated: 21 January 2002
Registered Office: Hamilton House, 70 Hamilton Drive, Glasgow, G12 8DR
Parent: G101 Off Sales Limited
Officers: Cynthia King [1942] Director; Stefan Paul King [1962] Director

Burnobennie Distillery Limited
Incorporated: 21 December 2018
Registered Office: 3 West Craibstone Street, Aberdeen, AB11 6YW
Major Shareholder: Michael Bain
Officers: Michael Bain [1973] Director; Liam John Pennycook [1993] Director

Oliver Burridge & Company Limited
Incorporated: 12 March 1937
Net Worth: £534,386 *Total Assets:* £565,828
Registered Office: 1 Vincent Square, London, SW1P 2PN
Parent: Fetchgold Limited
Officers: Teresa Maria Burridge, Secretary/Sales Manager; Edward Nicholas Burridge [1960] Director; Teresa Maria Burridge [1964] Sales Director

Burridges of Arlington St Ltd
Incorporated: 27 August 2016 *Employees:* 5
Net Worth: £20,756 *Total Assets:* £329,074
Registered Office: 1 Vincent Square, Westminster, London, SW1P 2PN
Shareholders: Edward Nicholas Burridge; Teresa Maria Burridge
Officers: Edward Nicholas Burridge [1960] Director; Teresa Maria Burridge [1964] Director

Burton Drinks Limited
Incorporated: 20 September 2018
Registered Office: 108 Broadway Street, Burton on Trent, Staffs, DE14 3ND
Major Shareholder: Imran Razak
Officers: Imran Razak [1982] Director/Self Employed

Burton Rd Brewing Co Limited
Incorporated: 17 November 2015
Net Worth: £9,156 *Total Assets:* £16,576
Registered Office: 65 Kingsfield Drive, Manchester, M20 6HX
Shareholders: James Philip Roberts; Tom Willliam Westcott; Richard Berry
Officers: Richard Berry [1981] Director; Tom Willliam Westcott [1976] Director

The Busted Cow Ltd
Incorporated: 10 September 2018
Registered Office: 20-22 Wenlock Road, London, N1 7GU
Major Shareholder: Thomas Ward
Officers: Thomas Ward [1996] Director

Buveur Ltd
Incorporated: 20 August 2018
Registered Office: Wisteria, Grange Barn, Pikes End, Pinner, London, HA5 2EX
Shareholders: Nicholas Patrick Andrew Wallis; Samuel Hunt
Officers: Samuel Hunt [1994] Director/Creative; Robert Wallis [1994] Director/Manager

Buzwine Limited
Incorporated: 14 June 2017
Net Worth: £17,671 *Total Assets:* £30,778
Registered Office: Kemp House, 160 City Road, London, EC1V 2NX
Officers: Joel Palous [1969] Director/Consultant [French]

Buzz Booze Ltd
Incorporated: 10 March 2018
Registered Office: Unit 1228, 356 Newport Road, Cardiff, CF23 9AE
Major Shareholder: Ferass Nadde
Officers: Ferass Nadde [1966] Director

Buzz Drinks Limited
Incorporated: 15 October 2018
Registered Office: 6a Hillside Road, Southall, Middlesex, UB1 2PD
Major Shareholder: Ravneet Singh Lalia
Officers: Ravneet Singh Lalia [1995] Director/Barman

The BV Group UK Limited
Incorporated: 12 October 2018
Registered Office: 1 Berkeley Street, London, W1J 8DJ
Major Shareholder: Harshit Mishra
Officers: Harshit Mishra [1995] Director/Distributor [Indian]

Bwinfusions Ltd
Incorporated: 5 January 2018
Registered Office: 3 Oxford Road, Worthing, W Sussex, BN11 1XG
Major Shareholder: Jack Luis Pablo Baeza-Wigzell
Officers: Jack Luis Pablo Baeza-Wigzell [1996] Director/Student

By His Grace Food Ltd
Incorporated: 26 February 2018
Registered Office: The Bull, Rainham Road South, Dagenham, Essex, RM10 8AQ
Major Shareholder: Stella Osunbor
Officers: Stella Osunbor [1960] Director

Anthony Byrne Fine Wines Limited
Incorporated: 11 April 1983 *Employees:* 12
Net Worth: £5,371,270 *Total Assets:* £6,094,454
Registered Office: Ramsey Business Park, Stocking Fen Road, Ramsey, Cambs, PE26 2UR
Shareholder: Anthony Edward Byrne
Officers: Rae Byrne, Secretary; Anthony Edward Byrne [1949] Director/Wine Consultant; Rae Byrne [1951] Director

C & C 2011 (NI) Limited
Incorporated: 22 June 1964
Registered Office: 15 Dargan Road, Belfast, BT3 9LS
Parent: C & C Holdings (NI) Limited
Officers: Stephen Glancey [1960] Director; Riona Heffernan [1980] Director/Chartered Accountant [Irish]; Patrick McMahon [1980] Director/Accountant [Irish]

C & D Exports Ltd
Incorporated: 22 November 2016
Registered Office: E K Business Centre, 14 Stroud Road, East Kilbride, G75 0YA
Shareholders: Colin Grant; David Murdoch
Officers: Colin Grant [1983] Director/Oil Engineer; David Murdoch [1972] Director/Firefighter

C & D Wines Limited
Incorporated: 15 January 1985 *Employees:* 22
Net Worth: £3,957,017 *Total Assets:* £5,799,325
Registered Office: 25 Metro Business Centre, Kangley Bridge Road, London, SE26 5BW
Shareholders: Felix Benito; Jennifer Christine Benito
Officers: David Charles Benito-Barnett, Secretary; Felix Benito [1948] Managing Director [Spanish]; Jennifer Christine Benito [1948] Director; David Charles Benito-Barnett [1980] Director/Businessman; Vicente Herrando [1950] Sales Director [Spanish]; Jose Velo-Rego [1950] Director/Wine Importer [Spanish]

C & E Transport Ltd
Incorporated: 5 April 2017
Net Worth: £1 *Total Assets:* £1
Registered Office: 10 Rylstone Road, Eastbourne, E Sussex, BN22 7HN
Major Shareholder: Max Samuel Morgan
Officers: Max Samuel Morgan [1990] Director

C & R Wines Limited
Incorporated: 4 September 2012 *Employees:* 2
Net Worth: £180,737 *Total Assets:* £270,373
Registered Office: 23-25 Queen Street, Coleraine, Co Londonderry, BT52 1BG
Shareholders: Richard Henderson; Crawford Henderson; Richard Henderson; Crawford Henderson
Officers: Crawford Henderson [1958] Director; Richard Henderson [1971] Director

C C & C Limited
Incorporated: 2 December 2003
Net Worth Deficit: £80,438 *Total Assets:* £948,594
Registered Office: Units 3 and 4, 49 Hurricane Way, Norwich, NR6 6JB
Shareholders: Mark Julian Feneron; Jeanette Anne Feneron
Officers: Patricia Ann Fox, Secretary; Mark Julian Feneron [1964] Director

C C and C London Ltd
Incorporated: 4 September 2018
Registered Office: 10 Southdown Avenue, Birmingham, B18 5LG
Major Shareholder: Danielle Young
Officers: Danielle Young [1985] Director

C G Supplies Limited
Incorporated: 12 July 2011
Net Worth: £52,115 *Total Assets:* £96,415
Registered Office: 29-31 Moorland Road, Stoke on Trent, Staffs, ST6 1DS
Shareholders: David Andrew Massey; Robert John Stamp
Officers: David Andrew Massey [1982] Director; Robert John Stamp [1978] Director

C N Drinks Limited
Incorporated: 4 January 2012 *Employees:* 2
Net Worth: £34,337 *Total Assets:* £122,059
Registered Office: 165 High Street, Honiton, Devon, EX14 1LQ
Shareholders: William Hiley; Christopher Norcott; Nicola Norcott
Officers: William John Haviland Hiley [1960] Director; Christopher John Norcott [1974] Director; Nicola May Norcott [1976] Director

C'est Nous UK Ltd
Incorporated: 8 May 2017
Net Worth: £1,472 *Total Assets:* £3,967
Registered Office: 3 Meadow Park, Stoke Mandeville, Aylesbury, Bucks, HP22 5XH
Shareholders: Angela Mary Granville; Michael Granville
Officers: Angela Mary Granville [1963] Director/Teacher; Michael Granville [1959] Director/Business Manager

C. & O. Wines Limited
Incorporated: 8 July 1992 *Employees:* 18
Net Worth: £438,760 *Total Assets:* £1,480,254
Registered Office: 14 Park Road Estate, Park Road, Timperley, Cheshire, WA14 5QH
Parent: Squarewalk Limited
Officers: May Haussels, Secretary; May Haussels [1949] Director/CS

C.O.D. Beers Limited
Incorporated: 26 October 1999 *Employees:* 4
Net Worth: £895 *Total Assets:* £83,906
Registered Office: 44-46 Old Steine, Brighton, BN1 1NH
Shareholders: Peter Bell; Lynn Margaret Brannigan-Bell
Officers: Lynn Margaret Brannigan-Bell, Secretary; Peter Bell [1963] Managing Director

C.P.A.'s Wine Limited
Incorporated: 30 May 1991
Net Worth: £23,799 *Total Assets:* £102,799
Registered Office: 15 Grange Crescent, West Cross, Swansea, SA3 5ET
Shareholder: Andrew John Hetherington
Officers: Andrew John Hetherington, Secretary; Paul Glyn Davies [1957] Director/Hotel Proprietor; Andrew John Hetherington [1959] Director/Hotel Proprietor

Cabal Estates Limited
Incorporated: 28 January 2019
Registered Office: 31a Appach Road, London, SW2 2LD
Major Shareholder: Edward George Clifford
Officers: Edward George Clifford [1988] Sales Director

Cabezac Collections Limited
Incorporated: 8 April 2010
Net Worth Deficit: £140,094 *Total Assets:* £10,096
Registered Office: 85 Church Road, Hove, E Sussex, BN3 2BB
Major Shareholder: Gontran Dondain
Officers: Stephanie Dondain, Secretary; Stephanie Dondain [1966] Director [French]; Sebastien Longerinas [1969] Director [French]

Cacheflow Ltd
Incorporated: 10 January 2019
Registered Office: 20-22 Wenlock Road, London, N1 7GU
Major Shareholder: Nana Natalie Dokua Anderson
Officers: Nana Natalie Dokua Anderson [1992] Director/Supervisor

William Cadenhead Limited
Incorporated: 22 December 1972 *Employees:* 16
Net Worth: £4,453,290 *Total Assets:* £4,739,575
Registered Office: 9 Bolgam Street, Campbeltown, Argyll, PA28 6HZ
Parent: J & A Mitchell and Co Ltd
Officers: Stuart Alexander Campbell, Secretary; Lilian Cunningham Campbell [1931] Director; Neil Clapperton [1958] Director; Alan Campbell Murray [1962] Director/Shopkeeper; Mr George Christopher Redpath [1936] Director/Design Consultant

Cadestin International Wines Limited
Incorporated: 13 February 2015 *Employees:* 1
Net Worth Deficit: £7,893 *Total Assets:* £20,644
Registered Office: 182 Ashmore Road, London, W9 3DE
Major Shareholder: Etienne Jose Cadestin
Officers: Etienne Jose Cadestin [1985] Director/Consultant [French]

Cadogan Wines Limited
Incorporated: 29 September 2011 *Employees:* 1
Net Worth Deficit: £18,670 *Total Assets:* £1,352
Registered Office: 14 Downlands, Walmer, Deal, Kent, CT14 7XA
Shareholders: Steven Russell Pettifer; Liia Pettifer
Officers: Steven Russell Pettifer [1964] Director

Cador Limited
Incorporated: 22 May 2014
Net Worth: £2 *Total Assets:* £2
Registered Office: Unit 3 Aston Expressway Industrial Estate, 64 Pritchett Street, Birmingham, B6 4EX
Shareholder: Natalie Anne Duff-Tytler
Officers: Natalie Anne Duff-Tytler [1970] Director; Simon Ransom Tester [1975] Financial Director

CADV Limited
Incorporated: 22 August 1929 *Employees:* 2
Previous: Chivas Allied Domecq Ventures Limited
Net Worth: £68,784,000 *Total Assets:* £73,567,000
Registered Office: 111-113 Renfrew Road, Paisley, Renfrewshire, PA3 4DY
Parent: ADIUK
Officers: Ailsa Mary Robertson Mapplebeck, Secretary; Stuart MacNab [1964] Director/Accountant; Vincent Turpin [1978] Director/Chief Financial Officer [French]

Calabria Family Wines (Europe) Limited
Incorporated: 29 January 2018
Registered Office: Kemp House, 160 City Road, London, EC1V 2NX
Officers: William Calabria [1948] Winemaker/Managing Director [Australian]

Calduero Wine Importers Limited
Incorporated: 1 November 2013 *Employees:* 4
Net Worth Deficit: £57,431 *Total Assets:* £2,365
Registered Office: 61 Dublin Street, Edinburgh, EH3 6NL
Major Shareholder: Peter Richard Brown
Officers: Elizabeth Jane Brown [1986] Director/Film Producer; Matthew Alexander Richard Brown [1982] Director/Freelance Television and Film Coordinator; Peter Richard Brown [1951] Director; Susan Brown [1954] Director

Calibre Brands Limited
Incorporated: 5 February 2001
Net Worth Deficit: £1,626,691 *Total Assets:* £699,253
Registered Office: Ground Floor, 5-6 Underhill Street, London, NW1 7HS
Major Shareholder: Gulnida Toichieva
Officers: Gulnida Toichieva [1970] Director [Kazakh]

Call-a-Keg (Scotland) Limited
Incorporated: 3 October 2011 *Employees:* 1
Previous: JF Kegs (Aberdeen) Limited
Net Worth: £100 *Total Assets:* £14,358
Registered Office: 4 Valentine Court, Dundee Business Park, Dundee, DD2 3QB
Major Shareholder: James Fyffe
Officers: James Fyffe [1969] Director

Call-a-Keg Beverages Ltd
Incorporated: 6 March 2009 *Employees:* 2
Net Worth Deficit: £35,899 *Total Assets:* £19,169
Registered Office: 31 Hawkhill, Dundee, DD1 5DH
Major Shareholder: Peter Kenneth Marr
Officers: James Michael Marr [1960] Director; Peter Kenneth Marr [1984] Director

Call-a-Keg Limited
Incorporated: 15 June 2016
Registered Office: 31 Hawkhill, Dundee, DD1 5DH
Major Shareholder: James Michael Marr
Officers: James Michael Marr [1960] Director

Cambridge Champagne Company Limited
Incorporated: 6 December 2017
Registered Office: Unit 3 The Enterprise Centre, Ditton Walk, Cambridge, CB5 8QD
Major Shareholder: Dennis Geoffrey Caswell
Officers: Dennis Geoffrey Caswell [1976] Director

Cambridge Wine Merchants Ltd
Incorporated: 25 February 1993
Net Worth: £522,521 *Total Assets:* £2,004,327
Registered Office: 46 Harvey Goodwin Avenue, Cambridge, CB4 3EU
Shareholders: Brett Alexander Charles Turner; Timothy Hal Quentin Wilson
Officers: Timothy Hal Quentin Wilson, Secretary; Brett Alexander Charles Turner [1965] Director/Wine Merchant; Timothy Hal Quentin Wilson [1967] Director

Camden Drinks Company Limited
Incorporated: 2 October 2018
Registered Office: 41 Great Portland Street, London, W1W 7LA
Shareholders: Brand Nation Limited; Marc Joseph Laventure
Officers: Justin Dennis James [1976] Director; Marc Joseph Laventure [1984] Director

Camii Punch Ltd
Incorporated: 16 November 2017
Registered Office: 20-22 Wenlock Road, London, N1 7GU
Major Shareholder: Janine Camille
Officers: Janine Camille [1991] Director

Camino Real Limited
Incorporated: 19 September 2016
Net Worth: £12,841 *Total Assets:* £12,841
Registered Office: c/o Premala Matthen, 25c Whiteheads Grove, London, SW3 3HB
Major Shareholder: Zachary Scott Elfman
Officers: Holly Zagor Elfman [1953] Director/Principal [American]; Zachary Scott Elfman [1984] Director/Winemaker [American]

Camis International Trading Co., Ltd.
Incorporated: 9 January 2019
Registered Office: 27 Old Gloucester Street, London, WC1N 3AX
Major Shareholder: Fuqing Yuan
Officers: Fuqing Yuan, Secretary; Fuqing Yuan [1992] Director [Chinese]

Campania Cucina Ltd
Incorporated: 8 February 2017
Registered Office: Gables Lodge, Whinburgh Road, Westfield, Dereham, Norfolk, NR19 1QJ
Shareholder: Simon William Henry Whiteley
Officers: Simon William Henry Whiteley, Secretary; Peter James Clark [1965] Director; Simon William Henry Whiteley [1953] Director

Campbell Inns Limited
Incorporated: 3 March 2005 *Employees:* 37
Net Worth: £747,799 *Total Assets:* £2,353,097
Registered Office: 11 Portland Road, Kilmarnock, E Ayrshire, KA1 2BT
Shareholders: John Leitch Campbell; Senga Campbell
Officers: Senga Campbell, Secretary; John Leitch Campbell [1961] Director

The Can Man Ltd
Incorporated: 21 February 2018
Registered Office: 3 Grasscroft, Almondbury, Huddersfield, W Yorks, HD5 8XG
Major Shareholder: Philip John Raworth
Officers: Philip John Raworth [1962] Director; Steven Walsh [1950] Director

Cana Import Limited
Incorporated: 4 October 2004 *Employees:* 2
Net Worth Deficit: £114,529 *Total Assets:* £65,756
Registered Office: 9 Margaret Close, Harbury, Leamington Spa, Warwicks, CV33 9JB
Shareholder: Robert Kenneth Darlison
Officers: Robert Kenneth Darlison, Secretary; Elizabeth Amanda Darlison [1959] Director; Robert Kenneth Darlison [1969] Director and Secretary

Canal Cellars Ltd
Incorporated: 22 January 2007 *Employees:* 9
Net Worth: £29,567 *Total Assets:* £461,177
Registered Office: Canal House, 100 Lissadel Street, Salford, M6 6BP
Shareholder: James Edward Prady
Officers: Dhiren Lalit Kotecha, Secretary; Dhiren Lalit Kotecha [1979] Director; James Edward Prady [1978] Director

Canapacampana Limited
Incorporated: 27 October 2017
Registered Office: 100 Elmington Road, London, SE5 7RB
Major Shareholder: Antonio Manzo
Officers: Antonio Manzo [1979] Director [Italian]

Candy Cotton Ltd
Incorporated: 23 August 2018
Registered Office: 19 Rogers House, Page Street, London, SW1P 4EX
Shareholders: Hanna Tegest Merzouk; Fadhilat Sope Fabiola Umar
Officers: Hanna Tegest Merzouk [1994] Director; Fadhilat Sope Fabiola Umar [1994] Director

Cangiani UK Ltd
Incorporated: 30 July 2015
Net Worth Deficit: £2,752 Total Assets: £69,637
Registered Office: c/o G Teoli & Co, Balfour House, 741 High Road, North Finchley, London, N12 0BP
Major Shareholder: Vincenzo Matrone
Officers: Vincenzo Matrone [1969] Director/Entrepreneur [Italian]

Canny Class Ltd
Incorporated: 15 November 2018
Registered Office: 30 Simpson Street, Crookhill, Ryton, Tyne & Wear, NE40 3EP
Shareholders: Lisa Ovenden Ferry; Leanne Ovenden
Officers: Leanne Ovenden [1984] Director/Learning Mentor; Lisa Ovenden Ferry [1987] Director/Bar Manager

Canopy Beer Company Ltd
Incorporated: 28 July 2014 Employees: 7
Net Worth: £24,013 Total Assets: £159,858
Registered Office: Arch 1127, 41 Norwood Road, London, SE24 9AJ
Shareholders: Matthew James Theobalds; Estelle Theobalds
Officers: Estelle Theobalds [1982] Director; Matthew James Theobalds [1984] Director/Head Brewer

Cantina Caputo Limited
Incorporated: 1 May 2008
Net Worth Deficit: £44,530 Total Assets: £2
Registered Office: 2 Hilliards Court, Chester Business Park, Chester, CH4 9PX
Major Shareholder: Paul Michael Caputo
Officers: Michael William Caputo [1951] Director/Chartered Accountant; Paul Michael Caputo [1984] Director/Wine Merchant

Cantium Spirit Ltd
Incorporated: 6 February 2019
Registered Office: 129 Maidstone Road, Borough Green, Sevenoaks, Kent, TN15 8HE
Major Shareholder: Kevin Lewis Andrews
Officers: Kevin Lewis Andrews [1973] Director/Producer

Capacha Limited
Incorporated: 9 April 2014 Employees: 1
Net Worth: £253,010 Total Assets: £851,588
Registered Office: 5th Floor, 89 New Bond Street, London, W1S 1DA
Major Shareholder: Sophie Anne Celine Decobecq
Officers: Sophie Anne Celine Decobecq [1977] Director [French]

Cape Secrets Limited
Incorporated: 5 July 2017
Registered Office: 21 Highnam Business Centre, Highnam, Gloucester, GL2 8DN
Shareholder: Paul Myatt
Officers: William Grant Humphreys [1960] Director/Administrator; Paul Anthony Myatt [1978] Director

Cape Wine Exporters (UK) Ltd
Incorporated: 5 September 2017
Registered Office: 84 Faroe Road, London, W14 0EP
Major Shareholder: Harry Rollo Gabb
Officers: Harry Rollo Gabb [1972] Director

Cape Wine Merchants Ltd
Incorporated: 6 August 2018
Registered Office: c/o Because, Suite 201 Berkshire House, 39 Ascot High Street, Ascot, Berks, SL5 7HY
Major Shareholder: Anthony Jon Papalia
Officers: Anthony Jon Papalia [1982] Director [Australian/Italian]

Cape Wines Limited
Incorporated: 23 August 2017
Registered Office: 1 Edenthorpe Lodge, 7 St Johns Road, Eastbourne, E Sussex, BN20 7JA
Shareholders: Michael Anthony Harrison; Cornelius Francois Meyer
Officers: Michael Anthony Harrison [1979] Managing Director; Cornelius Francois Meyer [1976] Managing Director [South African]

Capion Trading Limited
Incorporated: 25 August 2017
Net Worth Deficit: £11,934 Total Assets: £3,217
Registered Office: 6 St David's Square, Westferry Road, London, E14 3WA
Parent: Manuel Investments S.A.
Officers: Howard Seymour Laughton [1967] Director

Capital Languages Ltd
Incorporated: 7 July 2015
Registered Office: 10 Glandore Parade, Belfast, BT15 3FX
Officers: Miguel Escano [1978] Director/Food and Drink Importer [Spanish]

Capper & Co. Ltd.
Incorporated: 12 May 1925
Registered Office: Block F, Longacre Industrial Estate, Rosehill, Willenhall, W Midlands, WV13 2JP
Officers: Charles Peter Blakemore, Secretary; Peter Francis Blakemore [1943] Director; Scott Munro-Morris [1973] Finance Director; Simon Joseph Wiltshire [1964] Director

Caps Off Ltd.
Incorporated: 16 January 2017
Registered Office: 12 Liddell Way, Bishop Auckland, Co Durham, DL14 8EX
Shareholders: Alastair Wild; Chloe Danielle Suddes
Officers: Chloe Danielle Suddes [1994] Director; Alastair Wild [1990] Director

Capsule Wine Ltd
Incorporated: 17 September 2018
Registered Office: Flat 2, 29 Thornton Hill, London, SW19 4HU
Shareholders: Christopher Jeremy Leopold Anandan; Simon Peter Roger Jones
Officers: Christopher Jeremy Leopold Anandan [1983] Director/Advertising Consultant; Simon Peter Roger Jones [1974] Director/Advertising Consultant

Caribbean Collective Group Ltd
Incorporated: 29 September 2018
Registered Office: 71-75 Shelton Street, London, WC2H 9JQ
Major Shareholder: Alvin Delemico
Officers: Alvin Delemico [1976] Director/Media Sales Executive

Caribbean Trade Ltd
Incorporated: 13 June 2002
Net Worth Deficit: £31,705   Total Assets: £14,560
Registered Office: 171 Bell Green Road, Bell Green, Coventry, Warwicks, CV6 7GW
Officers: Fiona Quaynor, Secretary; Osbourne Victor Frank [1951] Director/Proprietor

Caribswede Ltd
Incorporated: 29 June 2011
Net Worth: £2   Total Assets: £2
Registered Office: 17 Cwm Cottage Road, Abertillery, Gwent, NP13 1AT
Shareholders: Anna Nina Jessica Coipell; Oliver Patrick Coipell
Officers: Anna Nina Jessica Coipell [1969] Director/Self Employed [Swedish]; Oliver Patrick Coipell [1970] Director/Engineer

Cariel Spirits International Limited
Incorporated: 17 May 2016
Net Worth: £100   Total Assets: £100
Registered Office: The White House, Clifton Marine Parade, Gravesend, Kent, DA11 0DY
Parent: Cariel Spirits AB
Officers: Douglas Brougham Cunningham [1968] Director

Carmelita Limited
Incorporated: 6 December 2010
Net Worth Deficit: £53,804   Total Assets: £56,972
Registered Office: Thorncroft, Old Reigate Road, Betchworth, Surrey, RH3 7DQ
Shareholders: Nicola Katherine Codling; James Robert Codling
Officers: James Robert Codling [1977] Director; Nicola Katherine Codling [1977] Director/Marketing Manager [Irish]

C Carnevale Limited
Incorporated: 27 March 2008   Employees: 162
Net Worth: £2,581,884   Total Assets: £11,901,745
Registered Office: 107 Blundell Street, London, N7 9BN
Major Shareholder: Carmine Carnevale
Officers: Lucia Gandolfi, Secretary; Carmine Carnevale [1941] Director/Cheesemaker [Italian]

Daniel Carnio Ltd
Incorporated: 5 July 2018
Registered Office: 71-75 Shelton Street, London, WC2H 9JQ
Shareholder: Daniel Carnio
Officers: Daniel Carnio [1987] Director [Italian]

The Carob Tree Limited
Incorporated: 27 May 2004
Net Worth: £227,044   Total Assets: £263,642
Registered Office: c/o GBP Associates LLP, 6th Floor, Aviation House, 125 Kingsway, London, WC2B 6NH
Major Shareholder: Trevor George Robinson
Officers: Lorna McKay [1955] Director; Nicholas McKay [1956] Director

Carousel Wines Limited
Incorporated: 16 April 2018
Registered Office: 20 Downlands Avenue, Bexhill on Sea, E Sussex, TN39 3PL
Officers: John Alexander McKinney [1981] Director

Carpe Vinum Ltd
Incorporated: 6 August 2018
Registered Office: Pastons Piece, Brundall Road, Blofield, Norwich, NR13 4LB
Officers: Ana Maria Toth [1968] Director [Hungarian]; Sandor Toth [1968] Director [Hungarian]; Andrew Christopher Verney [1960] Finance Director; Katharine Mary Verney [1963] Director

Carpet Bagger Limited
Incorporated: 3 July 2017
Registered Office: 67 Westgate End, Wakefield, W Yorks, WF2 9RL
Major Shareholder: Stephen Anderson
Officers: Stephen Anderson, Secretary; Billy Anderson [1998] Director; Stephen Anderson [1968] Director

Carson & Carnevale Limited
Incorporated: 2 September 2016   Employees: 4
Net Worth Deficit: £110,746   Total Assets: £539,350
Registered Office: Camburgh House, 27 New Dover Road, Canterbury, Kent, CT1 3DN
Shareholders: Via Monte Campo Ltd; Carson Wines Ltd
Officers: Luigi Carnevale [1981] Director/General Manager; Christopher Carson [1947] Director; Jonathan Carson [1984] Director; Antonia Maroso [1954] Commercial Director [Italian]

Carson Wines Ltd
Incorporated: 24 January 2014   Employees: 2
Net Worth Deficit: £197,956   Total Assets: £207,734
Registered Office: Camburgh House, 27 New Dover Road, Canterbury, Kent, CT1 3DN
Shareholders: Mark Charles Buffery; Christopher Carson
Officers: Christopher Carson, Secretary; Christopher Carson [1947] Director/Wine Merchant; Jonathan Carson [1984] Director/Wine Merchant

Carte Blanche Wines Limited
Incorporated: 5 October 2009   Employees: 5
Net Worth Deficit: £124,186   Total Assets: £230,725
Registered Office: Bridges Centre, Drybridge Park, Monmouth, Gwent, NP25 5AS
Shareholders: Benjamin William Thomas Llewelyn; Benjamin William Thomas Llewelyn
Officers: Tania Jeannette Amanda Bridge, Secretary; Benjamin William Thomas Llewelyn [1974] Director

Carter Importing Ltd
Incorporated: 21 February 2014
Net Worth Deficit: £44,489   Total Assets: £15,033
Registered Office: 56 Carbery Avenue, Bournemouth, BH6 3LG
Officers: Allan Carter [1948] Director/Retired; Phillip Carter [1980] Director/Senior Architectural Technologist MCIAT/Associate; Teresa Carter [1951] Director/Retired; Anna Monika Symonowicz [1984] Director/Customer Assistant [Polish]

The Cartmel Spirit Company Limited
Incorporated: 6 November 2017
Registered Office: 136 Highgate, Kendal, Cumbria, LA9 4HW
Major Shareholder: Edmund Wood
Officers: Edmund Wood [1989] Director

Cartwright Brothers Vintners Limited
Incorporated: 13 December 1999   Employees: 9
Net Worth Deficit: £76,007   Total Assets: £38,256
Registered Office: 30 City Road, London, EC1Y 2AB
Shareholders: Martin Cartwright; David Cartwright
Officers: Martin Cartwright, Secretary; David Cartwright [1949] Director/Fire Consultant; Martin Cartwright [1946] Director; Richard Charles Cartwright [1973] Director/Wine Merchant

Casa Ambar Limited
Incorporated: 3 March 2009
Net Worth Deficit: £40,552 *Total Assets:* £44,837
Registered Office: 85-87 Bayham Street, London, NW1 0AG
Major Shareholder: Isis Ramirez Gaytan
Officers: Isis Elizabeth Ramirez Gaytan [1982] Director [Mexican]

Casa Cocktails Limited
Incorporated: 3 August 2015
Net Worth Deficit: £268 *Total Assets:* £372
Registered Office: 22 Northumberland Road, Redland, Bristol, BS6 7BB
Shareholders: Christopher Harrington; Borja Banus
Officers: Borja Banus [1993] Director [Spanish]; Christopher Harrington [1992] Director

Casa Julia Limited
Incorporated: 28 April 1975 *Employees:* 64
Previous: Casa Julia PLC
Net Worth: £9,941,501 *Total Assets:* £13,883,850
Registered Office: 11 Springwood Drive, Springwood Industrial Estate, Braintree, Essex, CM7 2YR
Shareholder: Vinzenzo Santomauro
Officers: Gillian Christine Santomauro, Secretary; Carol Susan Evans [1960] Director/Accounts Manager; Lorna Clare Felton [1969] Director/Purchasing Manager; Julia Adelaide Santomauro [1974] Director/Research Psychologist; Nicola Elizabeth Santomauro [1971] Managing Director; Paula Ann Santomauro [1968] Director/Facilities Manager

Casa Leal Ltd
Incorporated: 23 March 2005
Net Worth Deficit: £8,721 *Total Assets:* £42,408
Registered Office: 499D Hackney Road, London, E2 9ED
Major Shareholder: Domingos Miguel Leal Da Silva
Officers: Jose Barrientos Cordova, Secretary; Domingos Miguel Leal Da Silva [1971] Director [Portuguese]

Cascade Drinks Limited
Incorporated: 9 November 1978 *Employees:* 21
Net Worth: £140,735 *Total Assets:* £924,119
Registered Office: 5 Merlin Way, Bowerhill Trading Estate, Melksham, Wilts, SN12 6TJ
Shareholders: JCM Investments Ltd; James Charles Mardell
Officers: James Charles Mardell [1958] Director; Sean Charles Mardell [1987] Director

Cascade Trade Services Ltd
Incorporated: 22 October 2018
Registered Office: Kemp House, 160 City Road, London, EC1V 2NX
Major Shareholder: Ajay Krishan Puri
Officers: Ajay Krishan Puri [1956] Director/Businessman [Indian]

Cascriva Ltd
Incorporated: 3 February 2014 *Employees:* 5
Net Worth: £221,665 *Total Assets:* £744,811
Registered Office: Office B, First Floor, 3 Sherrin Road, New Spitalfields Market, London, E10 5SG
Parent: Cascriva Holdings Ltd
Officers: Jose Javier Castello Escriva [1987] Director/Import/Export [Spanish]

Casella Family Brands (Europe) Limited
Incorporated: 29 April 1992 *Employees:* 16
Previous: Peter Lehmann Wines (UK) Limited
Net Worth: £2,036,380 *Total Assets:* £11,399,190
Registered Office: The Stores, Officers' Mess, Royston Road, Duxford, Cambridge, CB22 4QH
Major Shareholder: Giovanni Marcello Casella
Officers: Giovanni Marcello Casella [1959] Director [Australian]

The Cashew Apple Company Limited
Incorporated: 21 January 2019
Registered Office: Flat 16, Block F, Wild Street, London, WC2B 4BD
Shareholders: Artur Sebastiao Fernandes Da Costa; Anushka Leticia Gomes Da Costa
Officers: Artur Sebastiao Fernandes Da Costa [1981] Director/Depot Train Driver [Portuguese]

Cask and Craft Direct Ltd
Incorporated: 2 August 2018
Registered Office: 11 Welford Road, Sutton Coldfield, W Midlands, B73 5DP
Major Shareholder: Christopher David Morris
Officers: Helen Jarvis [1984] Sales Director; Christopher David Morris [1974] Director

Cask Hub Limited
Incorporated: 18 February 2019
Registered Office: 38 Craven Street, London, WC2N 5NG
Shareholders: Gio Parla; Thanh Tuan Mai
Officers: Gio Parla [1967] Director [Italian]

Cask Industries Ltd
Incorporated: 30 January 2018
Registered Office: 12 New Fetter Lane, London, EC4A 1JP
Parent: Barrel Industries Limited
Officers: Walid Fakhry [1968] Director/Investment Manager; Martyn Simpson [1986] Director/Self Employed

Cask Trade Ltd
Incorporated: 5 November 2018
Registered Office: 203 Linen Hall, 162-168 Regent Street, London, W1B 5TG
Major Shareholder: Simon Michael Aron
Officers: Simon Michael Aron [1967] Director; Dr Theodoros Empeslidis [1974] Director/Consultant Opthalmologist; Sir Colin George Hampden-White [1971] Director/TV Presenter/Producer; Lee John Tomlinson [1988] Director

Cask Whisky Ltd
Incorporated: 26 June 2015
Registered Office: 12 Brougham Street, Edinburgh, EH3 9JH
Major Shareholder: Callison Eaton
Officers: Callison Eaton [1961] Director

Caspian Black Limited
Incorporated: 8 February 2019
Registered Office: 76 Barry Road, London, SE22 0HP
Shareholders: Nicholas Charles Vedat Hitchins; Alasdair Hitchins
Officers: Nicholas Charles Vedat Hitchins [1988] Director/Chartered Engineer

Cassago Imports Limited
Incorporated: 28 April 2017
Net Worth Deficit: £1,006 *Total Assets:* £1,889
Registered Office: 16 Churchill Road, Stamford, Lincs, PE9 1JA
Shareholders: James Edward Baker; Peter Gaskell
Officers: Peter Gaskell [1987] Director

Cassels and Sons Brewing Europe Ltd
Incorporated: 19 October 2017
Registered Office: 1 Rushmills, Northampton, NN4 7YB
Parent: Cassels and Sons (2012) Ltd
Officers: Alasdair Lorne Cassels [1950] Director/Property Landlord [New Zealander]; Alex John Warren [1975] Director/Export Sales Manager [British/New Zealander]

Castillon International Limited
Incorporated: 15 December 2009
Registered Office: 17 Hampton Grove, Bury, Lancs, BL9 6PT
Major Shareholder: Brian Andrew Powell
Officers: Brian Andrew Powell [1957] Director

Castle Eden Beer Company Limited
Incorporated: 15 February 2011
Net Worth: £9,846 *Total Assets:* £63,656
Registered Office: c/o Milner Smeaton, Redcar Leisure & Community Heart, Ridley Street, Redcar, Cleveland, TS10 1TD
Shareholders: Limelight Brands Limited; Paul Baldwin
Officers: Paul Baldwin [1967] Director

Castle Eden Brewery Ltd
Incorporated: 22 March 2012
Net Worth: £118,530 *Total Assets:* £922,028
Registered Office: 8 East Cliff Road, Spectrum Business Park, Seaham, Co Durham, SR7 7PS
Shareholder: Cliff Walker
Officers: David Travers [1952] Director; Cliff Walker [1962] Director

Cathay Importers (London) Limited
Incorporated: 5 October 1973
Net Worth: £569,743 *Total Assets:* £827,408
Registered Office: No 188 High Road, Willesden, London, NW10 2PB
Major Shareholder: Ming Wah Wu
Officers: Ji Peng Wu, Secretary; Ming Wah Wu [1958] Director

Cathedral Wholesale and Events Limited
Incorporated: 25 July 2018
Registered Office: Unit 11b Beechburn Industrial Estate, Prospect Road, Crook, Co Durham, DL15 8RA
Major Shareholder: Julie Hinch
Officers: Julie Hinch [1966] Director

Cattier UK Limited
Incorporated: 8 October 1992 *Employees:* 2
Net Worth: £32,534 *Total Assets:* £109,070
Registered Office: c/o Browne Jacobson LLP, 6 Bevis Marks, London, EC3A 7BA
Officers: Philippe Eric Jean Claude Bienvenu [1963] Director/Wine Wholesaler [French]; Jean-Jacques Daniel Cattier [1944] Director/Wine Wholesaler [French]

Cava Spiliadis UK Limited
Incorporated: 20 January 2015 *Employees:* 2
Net Worth: £94,761 *Total Assets:* £153,038
Registered Office: 5 Elstree Gate, Elstree Way, Borehamwood, Herts, WD6 1JD
Major Shareholder: Elisa Cuccioletta
Officers: George Spiliadis [1980] Director/President of Cava Spiliadis [Canadian]

Cameron Cavendish Fine Wines Limited
Incorporated: 29 May 2001
Net Worth Deficit: £74,735 *Total Assets:* £102,784
Registered Office: Pearls Barn, Pearls Farmhouse, Ipswich Road, Helmingham, Stowmarket, Suffolk, IP14 6EN
Major Shareholder: Julian Cameron Bowden
Officers: Julian Cameron Bowden, Secretary/Wine Merchant; Julia Priscilla Bowden [1967] Travel Director; Julian Cameron Bowden [1969] Director/Wine Merchant

Caves de Pierre Limited
Incorporated: 29 December 2000
Net Worth: £395,866 *Total Assets:* £722,790
Registered Office: 14 Southgate Road, London, N1 3LY
Shareholder: Francois Domange
Officers: Mary Domange, Secretary/Journalist [French]; Francois Domange [1951] Director/Wine Dealer [French]

Cavoda Limited
Incorporated: 4 November 2013
Net Worth: £103,734 *Total Assets:* £192,998
Registered Office: 71 New Dover Road, Canterbury, Kent, CT1 3DZ
Officers: Peter Lampe [1951] Director

Cayenes Ltd
Incorporated: 22 August 2007
Net Worth Deficit: £14,582 *Total Assets:* £24,172
Registered Office: Southgate Office Village, 286b Chase Road, Southgate, London, N14 6HF
Major Shareholder: Sukhdeep Singh Dhillon
Officers: Sukhdeep Singh Dhillon [1976] Director

Cazcabel Drinks Limited
Incorporated: 11 March 2013 *Employees:* 3
Previous: Agave Tequila Limited
Net Worth Deficit: £179,009 *Total Assets:* £102,478
Registered Office: 41 Great Portland Street, London, W1W 7LA
Parent: Proof Drinks Limited
Officers: Paul Ferguson [1981] Director; James McDermott [1977] Director; James Vincent Neville- O'Brien [1942] Director [Irish]

Cazcabel Tequila Limited
Incorporated: 27 February 2019
Registered Office: 41 Great Portland Street, London, W1W 7LA
Shareholders: Paul Ferguson; James McDermott; James Vincent Neville-O'Brien
Officers: Paul Ferguson [1981] Director; James McDermott [1977] Director; James Vincent Neville- O'Brien [1942] Director [Irish]

CBD Drinks Company Limited
Incorporated: 18 June 2018
Registered Office: 98 Oving Road, Chichester, W Sussex, PO19 7EW
Major Shareholder: Robert John Wattie
Officers: Robert John Wattie [1976] Managing Director

CDGH Pub Co Ltd
Incorporated: 21 June 2018
Registered Office: Kemp House, 160 City Road, London, EC1V 2NX
Officers: Steven Dobby, Secretary; David Hart [1960] Director/Sales

Celebration Drinks Limited
Incorporated: 9 July 2010 *Employees:* 4
Net Worth Deficit: £52,141 *Total Assets:* £451,798
Registered Office: Trafalgar House, 712 London Road, West Thurrock, Essex, RM20 3JT
Shareholders: David George Heley; Michael Thomas Heley
Officers: David George Heley [1978] Director/General Manager; Michael Thomas Heley [1982] Director/Warehouse Manager

Celex Foods Limited
Incorporated: 20 January 2011 *Employees:* 5
Net Worth: £47,067 *Total Assets:* £250,615
Registered Office: 1 Beauchamp Court, 10 Victors Way, Barnet, Herts, EN5 5TZ
Major Shareholder: Ganeshamoorthy Kabilan
Officers: Ganeshamoorthy Kabilan [1978] Director

Cellar & Co Limited
Incorporated: 14 January 2016 *Employees:* 2
Net Worth: £4,301,320 *Total Assets:* £4,420,926
Registered Office: 4 & 5 The Cedars, Apex 12, Old Ipswich Road, Colchester, Essex, CO7 7QR
Officers: James Kelland [1966] Director; Hamid Nawaz-Khan [1952] Director/Chief Executive; Hugo David Rose [1953] Director/Consultant; Christopher Chris Villiers [1976] Director/Finance Advisor

Cellar 28 Ltd
Incorporated: 15 October 2002 *Employees:* 5
Net Worth: £46,980 *Total Assets:* £205,571
Registered Office: William Street, Rastrick, Brighouse, W Yorks, HD6 1HR
Major Shareholder: Anthony Vincent Mitchell
Officers: Anthony Mitchell, Secretary; Anthony Vincent Mitchell [1961] Director

Cellar Capital Limited
Incorporated: 18 December 2018
Registered Office: Flat 4, 43 Cornwall Gardens, London, SW7 4AA
Major Shareholder: Andrew Robertson Wylie
Officers: Andrew Robertson Wylie [1971] Director

Cellar Link Limited
Incorporated: 2 June 2008 *Employees:* 1
Net Worth: £124,534 *Total Assets:* £319,776
Registered Office: 8th Floor, South Reading Bridge House, George Street, Reading, Berks, RG1 8LS
Major Shareholder: Eamonn Peter Egan
Officers: Eamonn Peter Egan [1970] Director/General Manager [Irish]

Cellar Select Ltd
Incorporated: 16 January 2018
Registered Office: 1 Vineyard Mews, Preston Place, Richmond, Surrey, TW10 6DD
Major Shareholder: Olivia Lefort
Officers: Olivia Lefort [1985] Director/Executive Assistant [French]

Cellar Supplies Cheltenham Limited
Incorporated: 6 March 2003 *Employees:* 13
Net Worth: £130,112 *Total Assets:* £587,819
Registered Office: Midway House, Herrick Way, Staverton Technology Park, Staverton, Cheltenham, Glos, GL51 6TQ
Shareholders: Shaun Dandy; Peter George Cassidy; Jacqueline Lee Cassidy
Officers: Shaun Dandy, Secretary; Peter George Cassidy [1958] Director; Shaun Dandy [1962] Director

Cellar Supplies Limited
Incorporated: 14 March 2016
Registered Office: Midway House, Staverton Technology Park, Herrick Way, Staverton, Glos, GL51 6TQ
Major Shareholder: Peter George Cassidy
Officers: Peter George Cassidy [1958] Director

Cellar Trends Limited
Incorporated: 29 January 1999 *Employees:* 79
Net Worth: £7,201,901 *Total Assets:* £17,051,138
Registered Office: Rawdon House, Rawdon Terrace, Station Road, Ashby De La Zouch, Leics, LE65 2GN
Parent: Cellar Trends Holdings Limited
Officers: David Geoffrey Marriott, Secretary/Commission Agent; Seymour Paul Ferreira [1962] Director/Entrepreneur; David Geoffrey Marriott [1949] Director/Commission Agent; John Charles Marriott [1978] Director/National Accounts Manager; Hugues Michel Pietrini [1969] Director [French]; Geoffrey Fraser Watts [1977] Director/Manager; Martin Fraser Watts [1944] Director

Cellar Twelve Limited
Incorporated: 26 March 2004
Net Worth: £10,515 *Total Assets:* £516,459
Registered Office: Unit 6 Reeds Farm Estate, Cow Watering Lane, Writtle, Chelmsford, Essex, CM1 3SB
Shareholders: Damian Paul Barrett; David Graeme MacDonald
Officers: Damian Paul Barrett, Secretary/Wine Merchant; Damian Paul Barrett [1971] Director/Wine Merchant; David Graeme MacDonald [1970] Director/Wine Merchant

Cellarers (Wines) Limited
Incorporated: 22 November 1972
Net Worth: £2 *Total Assets:* £2
Registered Office: Lakeside Drive, Park Royal, London, NW10 7HQ
Parent: Diageo Great Britain Limited
Officers: James Matthew Crayden Edmunds [1974] Director/Solicitor; Gabor Kovacs [1980] Director [Hungarian]; Kara Elizabeth Major [1977] Director [American]

Cellartrade Ltd
Incorporated: 24 April 2017
Net Worth Deficit: £4,894 *Total Assets:* £1,449
Registered Office: Kintail Moor Road, Langham, Colchester, Essex, CO4 5NR
Shareholders: Paul Jeremy Armstrong; Susan Anne Armstrong
Officers: Paul Jeremy Armstrong [1961] Director

Cellarvino Limited
Incorporated: 20 November 2013
Registered Office: 25 Park Street West, Luton, Beds, LU1 3BE
Major Shareholder: Amrik Singh Binning
Officers: Amrinder Binning, Secretary; Amrik Singh Binning [1958] Director

Celtavini.Com Limited
Incorporated: 26 July 2017
Registered Office: 51 High Street, Ferndale, Rhondda Cynon Taf, CF43 4RH
Major Shareholder: Anthony Graham Watkins
Officers: Anthony Graham Watkins [1957] Director

Celtic Spirits Limited
Incorporated: 5 March 2012
Registered Office: Linnmhor House, Strathpeffer, Ross-shire, IV14 9BP
Major Shareholder: Michael MacKenzie
Officers: Michael MacKenzie [1964] Director/Wines and Spirits Merchant

Celtic Wines Limited
Incorporated: 8 October 2003 *Employees:* 16
Net Worth: £70,033 *Total Assets:* £1,001,423
Registered Office: Unit 1a Warrior Way, Pembroke Dock, Pembrokeshire, SA72 6UB
Parent: Celtic Vintners Ltd
Officers: Reginald Roy Roberts, Secretary; Peter Edward Caine [1949] Director; Reginald Roy Roberts [1949] Director

Cenimex Ltd
Incorporated: 9 November 2015
Net Worth Deficit: £6,349 *Total Assets:* £5,481
Registered Office: 20-22 Wenlock Road, London, N1 7GU
Shareholder: Berdia Qamarauli
Officers: Dennis Muriu [1973] Finance Director [Kenyan]; Berdia Qamarauli [1975] Managing Director

Central Drinks Pub Company Ltd
Incorporated: 4 April 2014
Registered Office: 14 The Square, Alvechurch, Worcs, B48 7LA
Shareholders: Khera Holdings Ltd; Stone Cross Hotel Ltd
Officers: Kuldip Singh Johal [1962] Director; Sukhjit Khera [1971] Director

Central Pubs (UK) Limited
Incorporated: 13 February 2004
Net Worth: £117,415 *Total Assets:* £416,704
Registered Office: 84-96 Lombard Street, Digbeth, Birmingham, B12 0QR
Shareholders: Darpun Kumar; Naresh Kumar
Officers: Darpun Kumar, Secretary; Darpun Kumar [1975] Director; Naresh Kumar [1977] Director; Surinder Singh [1952] Director

CGAVL Imports Limited
Incorporated: 11 May 2017
Net Worth Deficit: £2,781 *Total Assets:* £3,515
Registered Office: 20a Cyprus Avenue, London, N3 1ST
Major Shareholder: Alexander Vladimirovich Lushnikov
Officers: Aleksei Vladimirovich Lushnikov [1994] Director/Sparkling Wine Importer; Alexander Vladimirovich Lushnikov [1987] Director/Sparkling Wine Importer

Chacalli-De Decker Ltd.
Incorporated: 13 February 1996 *Employees:* 5
Net Worth Deficit: £406,239 *Total Assets:* £13,085
Registered Office: 81-82 High Street, Egham, Surrey, TW20 9HE
Parent: Flemingo International (BVI) Limited
Officers: Carlo Bernasconi [1960] Director [Swiss]

Chalgrove Wines Limited
Incorporated: 18 March 2010 *Employees:* 4
Net Worth: £65,616 *Total Assets:* £472,357
Registered Office: 5 Temple Square, Temple Street, Liverpool, L2 5RH
Major Shareholder: Timothy John Adam Scriven
Officers: Timothy John Adam Scriven [1965] Director

Chalk & Charcoal Limited
Incorporated: 17 March 2015
Net Worth: £306 *Total Assets:* £101,676
Registered Office: Audley House, Northbridge Road, Berkhamsted, Herts, HP4 1EH
Shareholders: Kate Marston; Benedict John Marston
Officers: Benedict John Marston [1972] Director/Marketing/Production; Kate Marston [1975] Director/Marketing/Production

Chalk Farm Wines Ltd
Incorporated: 27 October 2014
Registered Office: Whitchurch Lane, Whitchurch, Bristol, BS14 0JZ
Parent: Bibendum Wine Limited
Officers: Andrea Pozzi [1971] Director/Group Chief Operating Officer; Ewan James Robertson [1982] Finance Director; Jonathan Solesbury [1965] Director/Group Chief Financial Officer

Champagne Cellar Limited
Incorporated: 18 May 2018
Registered Office: 40a Chaucer Road, London, SE24 0NU
Shareholders: Alexandra Katherine Addison-Scott; James William Lance Ford
Officers: Alexandra Katherine Addison-Scott [1991] Director; James William Lance Ford [1989] Director

Champagne Charlie (Midlands) Limited
Incorporated: 12 May 2000
Registered Office: Grange Lane, Lye, Stourbridge, W Midlands, DY9 7HH
Major Shareholder: Desmond Barry Wilson
Officers: Jean Margaret Feher, Secretary; Desmond Barry Wilson [1946] Director [Irish]

The Champagne Collection Limited
Incorporated: 14 August 2012 *Employees:* 1
Net Worth Deficit: £50,361 *Total Assets:* £15,266
Registered Office: 3 Upton Road, Callow End, Worcester, WR2 4TG
Major Shareholder: Peter William Pedrick
Officers: Peter William Pedrick [1962] Director

The Champagne Company (UK) Limited
Incorporated: 10 October 2008
Net Worth: £125,674 *Total Assets:* £1,223,505
Registered Office: Aston Expressway Industrial Estate, Pritchett Street, Birmingham, B6 4EX
Shareholder: Natalie Anne Duff-Tytler
Officers: Natalie Anne Duff-Tytler [1970] Marketing Director; Simon Ransom Tester [1975] Director/Operations Manager

Champagne Duval-Leroy (UK) Limited
Incorporated: 11 August 1998 *Employees:* 2
Net Worth Deficit: £567,785 *Total Assets:* £52,913
Registered Office: 4th Floor, Lincoln House, 300 High Holborn, London, WC1V 7JH
Major Shareholder: Caroline Irma Elisabeth Duval
Officers: Carol Duval [1955] Director [Belgian]

Champagne G.H. Martel & Co. (U.K.) Ltd
Incorporated: 4 March 1998
Net Worth: £17,453 *Total Assets:* £19,671
Registered Office: 145 Dovehouse Street, Chelsea Square, London, SW3 6LB
Shareholder: Vincent Rapeneau
Officers: Jean Francois Rapeneau, Secretary [French]; Vincent Rapeneau [1978] Director [French]

Champagne House Ltd
Incorporated: 28 December 2016
Registered Office: 1 Seagrave Road, London, SW6 1RP
Officers: Jekaterina Barbulata [1986] Director [Latvian]

Champagne Imports Limited
Incorporated: 3 April 2003
Previous: Cognac Inc. Limited
Net Worth Deficit: £53,370
Registered Office: 41 Greek Street, Stockport, Cheshire, SK3 8AX
Shareholder: Elizabeth Anne Cross
Officers: Geoffrey Littman, Secretary; Elizabeth Anne Cross [1964] Executive Director [Canadian]; Geoffrey Littman [1942] Director/Solicitor

Champagne One Ltd
Incorporated: 10 December 2015
Net Worth Deficit: £24,858 *Total Assets:* £23,108
Registered Office: 830a Harrogate Road, Greengates Lodge, Bradford, W Yorks, BD10 0RA
Officers: Rajan Singh Johal [1994] Director/Retailer

Champagne Route Limited
Incorporated: 19 January 2018
Registered Office: 11 Waverley Gardens, London, E6 5TQ
Major Shareholder: Vida Keturakiene
Officers: Vida Keturakiene [1980] Finance Director [Lithuanian]

Champagne Warehouse Ltd
Incorporated: 25 October 2000 *Employees:* 9
Net Worth: £3,468,115 *Total Assets:* £4,992,298
Registered Office: Parkhill Business Centre, Walton Road, Wetherby, W Yorks, LS22 5DZ
Major Shareholder: Antony Stones
Officers: Helen Louise Stones, Secretary/Manager; Teresa Barnard [1969] Marketing Director; Antony Stones [1965] Managing Director; Helen Louise Stones [1967] Director

Champagnehub Limited
Incorporated: 27 October 2016
Registered Office: 2 Sheraton Street, London, W1F 8BH
Officers: Peter Kristoffer Cummings Nielsen [1976] Director [Danish]; Pia Helena Cummings Nielsen [1981] Director [Swedish]

Champagnes and Chateaux Ltd.
Incorporated: 24 May 1989 *Employees:* 10
Net Worth: £1,537,061 *Total Assets:* £2,560,485
Registered Office: Aston House, Cornwall Avenue, London, N3 1LF
Major Shareholder: Alain Thienot
Officers: Christophe Galez, Secretary; Christophe Galez [1964] Managing Director [French]; Thierry Jacques Morigeon [1972] Director [French]; Stanislas Thienot [1976] Director [French]

Champers (Wholesale) Limited
Incorporated: 1 October 2013 *Employees:* 57
Net Worth: £296,209 *Total Assets:* £7,854,751
Registered Office: 263 Water Road, Abbeydale Industrial Estate, Wembley, Middlesex, HA0 1HX
Parent: HT Drinks Holdings Ltd
Officers: Kilesh Patel [1972] Director; Sagar Thakrar [1985] Director; Sanjay Thakrar [1979] Director

Champers Wines Limited
Incorporated: 16 October 2002
Net Worth Deficit: £170,607 *Total Assets:* £213,525
Registered Office: 3 Montpelier Avenue, Bexley, Kent, DA5 3AP
Officers: Pareshkumar Vinubhai Patel [1968] Director/Retailer

Champions Cider Ltd
Incorporated: 7 February 2018
Registered Office: Champions Cider, Unit 2a Harwood Road, Northminster Business Park, Upper Poppleton, York, YO26 6QU
Major Shareholder: Charlie Simpson-Daniel
Officers: Charlie Simpson-Daniel [1989] Director/Consultant

Champsonthego.co.uk Ltd
Incorporated: 15 January 2016
Registered Office: Suite 5, 167 Holland Park Avenue, London, W11 4UR
Major Shareholder: Mike Babajide Adenuga
Officers: Mike Babajide Adenuga [1982] Director/Entrepreneur

J. Chandler & Company, Limited
Incorporated: 18 July 1925 *Employees:* 6
Net Worth: £1,373,515 *Total Assets:* £1,580,660
Registered Office: New Abbey House, Fyfield Road, Weyhill, Andover, Hants, SP11 8DN
Officers: Jonathan William Sharp, Secretary; Frances Marie Austin [1931] Director/Married/Housewife; George Evans [1929] Director; Gary Richard Joyce [1961] Production Director; Jane Carol Joyce [1967] Sales Director; Denis Morgan Moylan [1956] Director; Jonathan William Sharp [1966] Director; Peter Frederick Winckley [1960] Director

Chandos Wines Ltd
Incorporated: 23 October 2018
Registered Office: Flat 5, 41 Upper Belgrave Road, Clifton, Bristol, BS8 2XW
Major Shareholder: Andrew Dennis
Officers: Andrew Dennis [1961] Director

Chaps Group Limited
Incorporated: 15 June 2015
Net Worth Deficit: £1,076 *Total Assets:* £22,742
Registered Office: Construction House, Dumballs Road, Cardiff, CF10 5FE
Major Shareholder: Jamie Paul Stacey
Officers: Jamie Stacey [1979] Managing Director

GDD Chapuy Limited
Incorporated: 16 December 2015 *Employees:* 2
Net Worth Deficit: £107,120 *Total Assets:* £134,966
Registered Office: 43 Berkeley Square, Mayfair, London, W1J 5AP
Shareholders: Olutimilehin Adedeji; Momodou Adama Samba
Officers: Olutimilehin Adedeji, Secretary; Olutimilehin Adedayo Adedeji [1984] Director; Momodou Adama Samba [1981] Director

Chardon Wines Limited
Incorporated: 29 November 2006
Net Worth Deficit: £94,340 *Total Assets:* £921,578
Registered Office: 26 Charlotte Square, Edinburgh, EH2 4ET
Parent: Murray Capital Limited
Officers: Sir David Edward Murray [1951] Director; David Douglas Murray [1973] Director; Keith Andrew Murray [1975] Director

Charente Enterprises Limited
Incorporated: 2 May 1995
Net Worth Deficit: £189,081 *Total Assets:* £117,661
Registered Office: 55 Crown Street, Brentwood, Essex, CM14 4BD
Officers: Sheila Ann Mary Hornsby, Secretary; Neil Alistair Hornsby [1945] Director/Wine Importer; Sheila Ann Mary Hornsby [1947] Director/Secretary

Charter Brands Limited
Incorporated: 13 September 2011 *Employees:* 4
Net Worth Deficit: £311,900 *Total Assets:* £370,131
Registered Office: Testwood House, Testwood Park, Salisbury Road, Totton, Hants, SO40 2RW
Shareholders: Mark Robert Dawkins; Mark Andrew Crump
Officers: Mark Andrew Crump [1970] Director; Mark Robert Dawkins [1970] Director

Chateau de la Combe Ltd
Incorporated: 1 July 2014
Net Worth Deficit: £41,669 *Total Assets:* £25,322
Registered Office: 1 Kings Avenue, London, N21 3NA
Major Shareholder: Yuriy Lopatynskyy
Officers: Matvey Lopatinsky [1994] Director; Yuriy Lopatynskyy [1971] Director

Chateau de Sours Estates Limited
Incorporated: 13 March 1997
Net Worth: £5,992,532 *Total Assets:* £6,012,162
Registered Office: 18 Fitzhardinge Street, London, W1H 6EQ
Shareholders: Charlotte Krajewski; Martin Krajewski Esq
Officers: Martin John Krajewski, Secretary; Anil Dave [1955] Director/Chartered Accountant; Martin John Krajewski [1955] Director/Executive Search

Chateau Khornabuji Limited
Incorporated: 8 March 2018
Registered Office: 71-75 Shelton Street, London, WC2H 9JQ
Major Shareholder: Klaudiusz Kaiser-Helman
Officers: Klaudiusz Kaiser-Helman [1962] Director [Polish]

Chateau Miao Ltd
Incorporated: 12 May 2017
Registered Office: 110 Cromwell Road, Cambridge, CB1 3EG
Major Shareholder: Michael Christopher Brown
Officers: Michael Christopher Brown [1978] Managing Director

Chateau Musar (U.K.) Limited
Incorporated: 23 January 1980 *Employees:* 7
Net Worth: £309,461 *Total Assets:* £3,310,544
Registered Office: Faiers House, Gilray Road, Diss, Norfolk, IP22 4WR
Shareholders: Ronald Hochar; Gaston Hochar
Officers: Richard Hunt, Secretary; Gaston Hochar [1966] Director/Engineer [Lebanese]; Ronald Hochar [1944] Director/Wine Producer [Lebanese]

Chateau Musar International Limited
Incorporated: 16 February 1987
Registered Office: Faiers House, Gilray Road, Diss, Norfolk, IP22 4WR
Shareholders: Ronald Hochar; Gaston Hochar
Officers: Richard Hunt, Secretary; Ronald Hochar [1944] Director/Wine Producer [Lebanese]

Chateau Wines Ltd.
Incorporated: 18 April 2003
Net Worth: £38,670 *Total Assets:* £174,314
Registered Office: Windsor House, 103 Whitehall Road, Colchester, Essex, CO2 8HA
Major Shareholder: Richard James Hipkin
Officers: Richard James Hipkin [1966] Director

Checkmate Premium Brands Ltd
Incorporated: 6 August 2013
Net Worth Deficit: £221,049 *Total Assets:* £100
Registered Office: Ashcombe Court, Woolsack Way, Godalming, Surrey, GU7 1LQ
Shareholders: Stephen Charles Bishop; Patricia Lynn Dayton; Troy Dayton
Officers: Troy Dayton [1972] Director [American]

Chelsea Vintners London Limited
Incorporated: 31 July 2012 *Employees:* 6
Net Worth: £959,816 *Total Assets:* £1,614,420
Registered Office: 495 Green Lanes, Palmers Green, London, N13 4BS
Shareholders: Raymond Jonathon Eyles; Richard John Leighton; John Frederick Anderson
Officers: John Frederick Anderson [1965] Director [American]; Trevor de Yong [1978] Director [Australian]; Raymond Jonathon Eyles [1970] Director [Australian]; Richard John Leighton [1964] Director; Christopher James Dinsdale Wood [1984] Director

Cheng International Co Limited
Incorporated: 9 May 2018
Registered Office: 1st Floor, Healthaid House, Marlborough Hill, Harrow, Middlesex, HA1 1UD
Major Shareholder: Zhuqing Guan
Officers: Lue Dong [1983] Director [Chinese]; Zhuqing Guan [1988] Director/Wine Expert [Chinese]

Chequers Distribution Ltd
Incorporated: 22 June 2018
Registered Office: 15 Swabys Yard, Beverley, E Yorks, HU17 9BZ
Officers: Ian David Allott [1959] Director

Cheshire Gin Company Limited
Incorporated: 30 August 2018
Registered Office: Amtri House, Hulley Road, Macclesfield, Cheshire, SK10 2NE
Shareholders: Richard Buxton; Simon John Spurrell
Officers: Richard Buxton [1966] Director; Simon John Spurrell [1967] Director

Chesters Wine Merchants Ltd
Incorporated: 3 August 2017
Registered Office: 2 Stable Mews, Lewis Lane, Abergavenny, Monmouthshire, NP7 5BA
Shareholders: Lloyd Beedell; Ben Southon
Officers: Lloyd Beedell [1986] Director; Ben Southon [1989] Director

Chetan Wholesalers Limited
Incorporated: 16 July 1986
Net Worth: £762,075 *Total Assets:* £4,643,368
Registered Office: 47-49 River Road, Barking, Essex, IG11 0DA
Officers: Kishore Mandalia, Secretary; Dipin Mandalia [1956] Director; Kishore Mandalia [1954] Director; Nitin Mandalia [1960] Director

Cheti & Co Holdings Limited
Incorporated: 27 April 2018
Registered Office: 153-155 Hoxton Street, London, N1 6PJ
Shareholders: Ryan Chetiyawardana; Jonathan Charles Jackson; Grow Partners Limited
Officers: Ryan Chetiyawardana [1984] Director/Mixologist; Jonathan Charles Jackson [1982] Director/Consultant

Cheti & Co Limited
Incorporated: 12 November 2018
Registered Office: 153-155 Hoxton Street, London, N1 6PJ
Parent: Cheti & Co Holdings Limited
Officers: Ryan Chetiyawardana [1984] Director/Mixologist; Jonathan Charles Jackson [1982] Director/Consultant

Chevalier de Mentaubert Limited
Incorporated: 16 June 2015
Net Worth Deficit: £18,179 Total Assets: £60,107
Registered Office: 39 Park Cliff Road, Greenhithe, Kent, DA9 9FY
Shareholders: Kim Fung Yip; Alex Tran
Officers: Alex Tran [1985] Director/Manager; Kim Fung Yip [1980] Director

Chez Antoine Ltd
Incorporated: 20 September 2012
Net Worth Deficit: £792 Total Assets: £43,041
Registered Office: First Floor Flat, 206 Mare Street, London, E8 3RD
Major Shareholder: Antoine Herve Marie Riviere
Officers: Antoine Herve Marie Riviere [1960] Director [French]

Chic Fruit Ltd
Incorporated: 19 November 2018
Registered Office: Flat 2, 70a Charlton Church Lane, London, SE7 7AB
Major Shareholder: Juan Camilo Quiceno Cardona
Officers: Juan Camilo Quiceno Cardona [1980] Director [Colombian]

Childale Limited
Incorporated: 19 February 2002
Previous: Beer Direct Limited
Registered Office: Chilworth House, Little Chart, Ashford, Kent, TN27 0QB
Shareholders: Brian Robert Pettit; Martin David Johnson
Officers: Martin David Johnson, Secretary; Martin David Johnson [1952] Director/Importer and Wholesaler; Dr Brian Robert Pettit [1953] Director/Business Consultant

Chilli Brands (New Zealand) Limited
Incorporated: 18 May 2015
Registered Office: 4 Market Square Building, 85 High Street, Manchester, M4 1BD
Shareholders: Gareth Andrew Whittle; Christian Peter Barton; Kieron Mark Barton
Officers: Christian Peter Barton [1979] Director; Kieron Barton [1975] Director; Gareth Andrew Whittle [1976] Director

Chilli Brands Limited
Incorporated: 29 April 2015 Employees: 23
Net Worth Deficit: £4,613,409 Total Assets: £2,554,847
Registered Office: 4 Market Square Building, 85 High Street, Manchester, M4 1BD
Shareholders: Christian Peter Barton; Kieron Barton; Gareth Andrew Whittle
Officers: Christian Peter Barton [1979] Director; Kieron Mark Barton [1975] Director; Gareth Andrew Whittle [1976] Director

Chilli Marketing Brand Management Ltd
Incorporated: 19 May 2008 Employees: 3
Net Worth: £134,226 Total Assets: £5,563,390
Registered Office: 4 Market Square, 85 High Street, Manchester, M4 1BD
Parent: Chilli Brands Limited
Officers: Christian Peter Barton [1979] Director; Kieron Mark Barton [1975] Director; Gareth Andrew Whittle [1976] Director

Chilli Marketing Promotions Limited
Incorporated: 24 July 2003
Net Worth Deficit: £3,967 Total Assets: £8,500
Registered Office: 4 Market Square Building, 85 High Street, Manchester, M4 1BD
Shareholders: Gareth Andrew Whittle; Kieron Barton
Officers: Gareth Andrew Whittle, Secretary/Marketing & Promotion; Kieron Mark Barton [1975] Director; Gareth Andrew Whittle [1976] Director/Marketing & Promotion

Chillwines Limited
Incorporated: 5 August 2015
Net Worth Deficit: £15,582 Total Assets: £20,955
Registered Office: 56 Holland Road, Little Clacton, Clacton on Sea, Essex, CO16 9RS
Shareholders: Mark Sands; John Scully
Officers: John Scully, Secretary; Mark Sands [1966] Director

Chiltern Trading Ltd
Incorporated: 2 March 2016 Employees: 1
Net Worth: £5,839 Total Assets: £251,926
Registered Office: 5 Chiltern Avenue, Macclesfield, Cheshire, SK11 8LP
Major Shareholder: Paul Atherton
Officers: Paul Atherton [1957] Director

Chivalry Trading International Co. Ltd
Incorporated: 21 July 2017
Registered Office: 66 Canberra Road, London, SE7 8PE
Officers: Wei Li [1970] Director [Chinese]; Thomas Yucheng Xu [1965] Director [French]; Hongchun Zhang [1972] Director [Chinese]

Choice Drinks Limited
Incorporated: 1 June 2016
Registered Office: Units 1 & 2 Manchester Industrial Park, Holt Street, Manchester, M40 5AX
Shareholders: John Francis Risby; Christine Risby
Officers: Christine Risby, Secretary; Christine Risby [1961] Director; John Francis Risby [1971] Director

Choise Group Ltd
Incorporated: 28 August 2018
Registered Office: 71-75 Shelton Street, London, WC2H 9JQ
Major Shareholder: Serkan Aksakal
Officers: Serkan Aksakal, Secretary; Serkan Aksakal [1981] Director/Self Employed

Chosen Wine Limited
Incorporated: 8 November 2018
Registered Office: 74 High Street, Fishguard, Pembrokeshire, SA65 9AU
Shareholders: Alastair Huw Davies; Martin Robert Alan Kiss
Officers: Alastair Huw Davies [1975] Director; Martin Robert Alan Kiss [1961] Director

Church Road Mini Market Ltd
Incorporated: 20 December 2018
Registered Office: 172b Church Road, Mitcham, Surrey, CR4 3BW
Major Shareholder: Karthigesu Selvarasa
Officers: Karthigesu Selvarasa [1969] Director/Salesman [Norwegian]

Churchill Graham Limited
Incorporated: 9 August 1982
Net Worth Deficit: £378,459 *Total Assets:* £458,734
Registered Office: 8 Wigmore Street, London, W1V 2RD
Officers: Geoffrey Stephen Daw, Secretary; Anthony Maxwell Graham [1945] Director/Stockbroker; John Lochiel Graham [1952] Director/Wine Merchant

Churchill Vintners Limited
Incorporated: 17 January 1989
Registered Office: 10-12 Brewery Road, London, N7 9NH
Parent: Berkmann Wine Cellars Ltd
Officers: Rupert Anthony Berkmann [1979] Director

Churnet Valley Drinks Limited
Incorporated: 12 March 2015
Registered Office: Unit S3, Narvik Way, Tyne Tunnel Trading Estate, North Shields, Tyne & Wear, NE29 7XJ
Officers: Particia Ada Rice, Secretary; David Leonard Brind [1972] Director; John Frederick Hope [1969] Group Operations Director; Particia Ada Rice [1957] Director; Paul Victor Young [1957] Director

CHX Distillers Ltd
Incorporated: 18 April 2018
Registered Office: 90 Laitwood Road, London, SW12 9QJ
Shareholders: Timothy Emerson Welch; Kirstine Newton; Barnaby James Wharton
Officers: Kirstine Newton [1974] Media Director; Timothy Emerson Welch [1973] Director; Barnaby James Wharton [1976] Director/Tour Operator

Cibus Vitae Ltd.
Incorporated: 8 September 2016
Registered Office: 71-75 Shelton Street, Covent Garden, London, WC2H 9JQ
Shareholder: Luigi Lagonigro
Officers: Luigi Lagonigro [1975] Director [Italian]; Felice Russo [1979] Director [Italian]

Cibusrex Ltd
Incorporated: 21 July 2017
Registered Office: Flat 271, Shakespeare Tower, Barbican, London, EC2Y 8DR
Shareholder: Fabrizio Santarelli
Officers: Carlo Resta [1959] Director [Italian]

Cider Centrum Ltd
Incorporated: 26 October 2016
Registered Office: 24 Kingfisher Way, Alcester, Warwicks, B49 6RW
Major Shareholder: Jan Sostok
Officers: Jan Sostok [1975] Director [Czech]

Cider Is Wine Ltd
Incorporated: 8 June 2018
Registered Office: 23 Brill Close, Maidenhead, Berks, SL6 3EJ
Major Shareholder: Alistair John Morrell
Officers: Alistair John Morrell [1967] Director

Cider of Sweden Ltd
Incorporated: 26 June 2006 *Employees:* 39
Net Worth: £12,852,489 *Total Assets:* £48,552,928
Registered Office: Albion Court, 5 Albion Place, Leeds, LS1 6JL
Shareholder: Barry Thomas Connolly
Officers: Ciaran Michael Cleland, Secretary; Carl Eric Berg [1946] Director/Consultant [Swedish]; Peter Bronsman [1963] Director [Swedish]; Barry Thomas Connolly [1961] Director [Irish]

Ciderfex Limited
Incorporated: 3 April 2018
Registered Office: Middle Flat, 85 Tilehouse Street, Hitchin, Herts, SG5 2DY
Major Shareholder: Richard Clive Wilson
Officers: Richard Clive Wilson [1966] Director

Cincin Wines Ltd
Incorporated: 27 December 2017
Registered Office: 137 High Street, Lee on the Solent, Hants, PO13 9BU
Officers: Deborah Irene Watts [1960] Director; Michael John Watts [1960] Director

Circle View Business Consultancy Ltd
Incorporated: 16 December 2010
Net Worth: £3,863 *Total Assets:* £5,045
Registered Office: 49 St Albans Road, Seven Kings, Ilford, Essex, IG3 8NN
Major Shareholder: Jaspal Dosanjh
Officers: Jaspal Dosanjh [1972] Director

The Circle Wine Company Limited
Incorporated: 8 June 2005 *Employees:* 1
Net Worth Deficit: £2,796 *Total Assets:* £167,198
Registered Office: 47 Chesilton Road, London, SW6 5AA
Shareholder: Sara Penelope Ritchie Harrison
Officers: Sara Penelope Ritchie Harrison, Secretary; Sara Penelope Ritchie Harrison [1965] Director/Wine Trader

Circus Enjoy with Us Ltd
Incorporated: 8 February 2018
Registered Office: 33 Purser House, Tulse Hill, Brixton, London, SW2 2JA
Major Shareholder: Fausto Gottardo
Officers: Fausto Gottardo [1965] Director [Italian]

Citrone Limited
Incorporated: 21 June 2017
Registered Office: 80 West Central, Stoke Road, Slough, Berks, SL2 5PF
Officers: Frank Ikenye [1983] Director

Citrosoft Drinks Limited
Incorporated: 30 November 1987 *Employees:* 9
Net Worth: £500,184 *Total Assets:* £622,717
Registered Office: 11 Nicholas Street, Burnley, Lancs, BB11 2AL
Shareholders: Michelle Jayne Spence; Patricia Abraham
Officers: Lesley May Keegan, Secretary; Malcolm Joseph Abraham [1942] Director; Patricia Anne Abraham [1943] Director; Michelle Jayne Spence [1965] Director

City Beer Limited
Incorporated: 25 July 2003
Net Worth: £319,107 *Total Assets:* £566,142
Registered Office: 2 Everitt Close, Denington Industrial Estate, Wellingborough, Northants, NN8 2QE
Shareholders: Ketan Shah; Binny Shah
Officers: Binny Shah, Secretary/Director; Binny Shah [1963] Director; Kavit Shah [1988] Director; Ketan Shah [1959] Director

UK Wholesalers of Beers, Wines and Spirits dellam

City Wine Collection Limited
Incorporated: 18 July 2007 *Employees:* 3
Net Worth: £3,456 *Total Assets:* £741,908
Registered Office: 133 Chase Side, London, N14 5HD
Major Shareholder: Zoran Ristanovic
Officers: Zoran Ristanovic, Secretary; Norman Peter Gardner [1945] Director/Wine Merchant; Lukasz Gramza [1979] Director/Financial Controller [Polish]; Zoran Ristanovic [1963] Director/Wine Merchant

CKW (Europe) Limited
Incorporated: 27 July 2018
Registered Office: 6 Queens Court, Third Avenue, Gateshead, Tyne & Wear, NE11 0BU
Shareholders: Peter James Schroeder; Christina Kelway Wotherspoon
Officers: Peter James Schroeder [1962] Director [Canadian]

CKW Trading Limited
Incorporated: 20 May 2010 *Employees:* 3
Net Worth: £11,456 *Total Assets:* £1,373,444
Registered Office: Grainger Suite, Dobson House, Regent Centre, Gosforth, Newcastle upon Tyne, NE3 3PF
Shareholders: Peter James Schroeder; Christina Kelway Wotherspoon
Officers: Christina Wotherspoon, Secretary; Peter James Schroeder [1962] Director [Canadian]

Clapham Wine Company Limited
Incorporated: 18 May 2012 *Employees:* 1
Net Worth Deficit: £322,543 *Total Assets:* £233,097
Registered Office: 33 Queens Road, Tunbridge Wells, Kent, TN4 9LZ
Major Shareholder: Christopher Edward Bailey
Officers: Laura Jane Bailey, Secretary; Christopher Edward Bailey [1975] Director/Management Consultant

Clara Wines Limited
Incorporated: 3 April 2017
Net Worth: £11,780 *Total Assets:* £11,780
Registered Office: 68 Muncaster Road, London, SW11 6NU
Major Shareholder: Sarah Stimpson
Officers: Sarah Stimpson [1983] Director

Clarence Spirits Limited
Incorporated: 7 January 2019
Registered Office: 17 The Crescent, Whitley Bay, Tyne & Wear, NE26 2JG
Major Shareholder: Martin Nicholas Summers
Officers: Martin Nicholas Summers [1975] Director

Claret-E Limited
Incorporated: 19 May 2000 *Employees:* 1
Net Worth: £144,154 *Total Assets:* £1,494,315
Registered Office: 20 Sunningdale Close, Stanmore, Middlesex, HA7 3QL
Officers: Antony Guy Butterwick, Secretary; Antony Guy Butterwick [1966] Director/Fine Wine Trader

Claribes Limited
Incorporated: 2 February 1993
Net Worth Deficit: £16,823 *Total Assets:* £1,229
Registered Office: Postern Piece Farm, Bedford Street, Ampthill, Beds, MK45 2EX
Officers: Nicholas John Kinder, Secretary; Helen Janet Kelly [1956] Director/Consultant; Nicholas John Kinder [1956] Director/Sales and Marketing Consultant

H.B.Clark & Co.(Successors) Limited
Incorporated: 31 July 1913 *Employees:* 281
Net Worth: £6,754,456 *Total Assets:* £24,827,042
Registered Office: Unit S3, Narvik Way, Tyne Tunnel Trading Estate, North Shields, Tyne & Wear, NE29 7XJ
Officers: Patricia Ada Rice, Secretary; David Leonard Brind [1972] Director; John Frederick Hope [1969] Group Operations Director; Jay MacKay [1966] Managing Director; Patricia Ada Rice [1957] Director; Paul Victor Young [1957] Director

Matthew Clark (Scotland) Limited
Incorporated: 1 October 1963
Registered Office: Wellpark Brewery, 161 Duke Street, Glasgow, G4 0UL
Parent: Matthew Clark Bibendum (Holdings) Limited
Officers: Andrea Pozzi [1971] Director/Group Chief Operating Officer; Ewan James Robertson [1982] Finance Director; Jonathan Solesbury [1965] Director/Group Chief Financial Officer

Matthew Clark and Sons Limited
Incorporated: 11 April 2011
Registered Office: Whitchurch Lane, Whitchurch, Bristol, BS14 0JZ
Parent: Matthew Clark Bibendum Limited
Officers: Andrea Pozzi [1971] Director/Group Chief Operating Officer; Ewan James Robertson [1982] Finance Director; Jonathan Solesbury [1965] Director/Group Chief Financial Officer

Matthew Clark Bibendum Limited
Incorporated: 23 October 1990 *Employees:* 1,793
Previous: Conviviality Group Limited
Net Worth Deficit: £48,134,000 *Total Assets:* £302,287,008
Registered Office: Whitchurch Lane, Bristol, BS14 0JZ
Parent: Matthew Clark Bibendum (Holdings) Limited
Officers: Andrea Pozzi [1971] Director/Group Chief Operating Officer; Ewan James Robertson [1982] Finance Director; Jonathan Solesbury [1965] Director/Group Chief Financial Officer

Matthew Clark Limited
Incorporated: 12 April 2011
Registered Office: Whitchurch Lane, Whitchurch, Bristol, BS14 0JZ
Parent: Matthew Clark Bibendum Limited
Officers: Andrea Pozzi [1971] Director/Group Chief Operating Officer; Ewan James Robertson [1982] Finance Director; Jonathan Solesbury [1965] Director/Group Chief Financial Officer

Matthew Clark Wholesale Bond Limited
Incorporated: 12 April 2011
Registered Office: Whitchurch Lane, Whitchurch, Bristol, BS14 0JZ
Parent: Matthew Clark Bibendum Limited
Officers: Andrea Pozzi [1971] Director/Group Chief Operating Officer; Ewan James Robertson [1982] Finance Director; Jonathan Solesbury [1965] Director/Group Chief Financial Officer

Clarke Wholesale Limited
Incorporated: 8 March 2004 *Employees:* 5
Net Worth: £1,868,266 *Total Assets:* £3,840,743
Registered Office: 16 Cottage Road, Newry, Co Down, BT35 8RS
Shareholders: Declan Gerard Clarke; Sinead Eileen Clarke
Officers: Sinead Eileen Clarke, Secretary; Declan Gerard Clarke [1966] Director [Irish]; Sinead Eileen Clarke [1970] Director [Irish]

Clarkes Drinks Direct Limited
Incorporated: 15 June 2011
Net Worth: £1,030 *Total Assets:* £36,086
Registered Office: 53 All Saints Road, Wolverhampton, W Midlands, WV2 1EG
Major Shareholder: Manjinder Singh
Officers: Manjinder Singh [1978] Director/Sales Person

Classic Cask Limited
Incorporated: 14 February 2019
Registered Office: The Smithfield, Meadow Road, Derby, DE1 2BH
Major Shareholder: Emily Louise Bowler
Officers: Emily Louise Bowler [1984] Director/Publican

Classic Malts Limited
Incorporated: 26 May 2011
Net Worth: £40,935 *Total Assets:* £835,537
Registered Office: 93 Dromore Road, Banbridge, Co Down, BT32 4EF
Shareholders: Raymond Armstrong; Florence Elizabeth Armstrong
Officers: Jennifer Eadie, Secretary; Florence Elizabeth Armstrong [1950] Director; Raymond Armstrong [1948] Director

A.P. Claxton Ltd
Incorporated: 4 January 2011 *Employees:* 2
Net Worth Deficit: £10,922 *Total Assets:* £120,753
Registered Office: Administration Office, The Racecourse, Boroughbridge Road, Ripon, N Yorks, HG4 1UG
Shareholders: Adrian Hadley Leighton Hoose; Jack Edward Hoose
Officers: Adrian Hoose [1983] Development Director; Jack Edward Hoose [1953] Business Director

Clements Harrison Limited
Incorporated: 23 August 2017
Registered Office: 39 Thurloe Place, London, SW7 2HP
Shareholders: George Frederick Tearlach Clements; Edward Peter Douglas Harrison
Officers: George Frederick Tearlach Clements [1986] Director; Edward Peter Douglas Harrison [1981] Director

Cleveland Bar Supplies Limited
Incorporated: 18 March 2013
Net Worth: £13,055 *Total Assets:* £49,839
Registered Office: 22 Nursery Gardens, Yarm, Cleveland, TS15 9UY
Major Shareholder: John Thomas Lancaster
Officers: John Thomas Lancaster [1959] Director

Clique Wine Limited
Incorporated: 15 May 2018
Registered Office: 4 Brewery Place, Leeds, LS10 1NE
Major Shareholder: Nicholas Robert King
Officers: Nicholas Robert King [1973] Director

Clock Tower Distilleries Limited
Incorporated: 7 August 2017
Registered Office: Arquen House, 4-6 Spicer Street, St Albans, Herts, AL3 4PQ
Shareholders: Paul Anthony Marsh; Charlotte Trudy Carroll
Officers: Charlotte Trudy Carroll [1978] Director/Business Professional; Paul Anthony Marsh [1968] Business Consultant & Director

Clos Vintners Limited
Incorporated: 14 November 2014
Net Worth Deficit: £29,314 *Total Assets:* £1,047
Registered Office: 64 Derby Lane, Liverpool, L13 3DN
Major Shareholder: Jamie Blennerhassett
Officers: Jamie Blennerhassett [1995] Director

Cloud Wine Ltd
Incorporated: 25 October 2016
Registered Office: Flat 7, Oliver Court, 1 Cromwell Gardens, Bournemouth, BH5 2DG
Officers: Dalila Cordoni [1986] Director [Italian]; Salvatore Salpietro [1971] Director [Italian]

Club Belmont Ltd
Incorporated: 16 July 2018
Registered Office: 34a Western Avenue, London, W3 7TZ
Major Shareholder: Samuel Livingstone Aird
Officers: Samuel Livingstone Aird, Secretary; Samuel Livingstone Aird [1985] Director

Clubinn Together Limited
Incorporated: 20 November 2017
Registered Office: 187 The Wheel, Ecclesfield, Sheffield, S35 9ZA
Major Shareholder: Neil Thomas Travis
Officers: Neil Thomas Travis [1962] Director

The Clutha Distillery Company Limited
Incorporated: 13 February 2018
Registered Office: Radleigh House, 1 Golf Road, Clarkston, E Renfrewshire, G76 7HU
Major Shareholder: Ashley Cochrane
Officers: Ashley Cochrane [1993] Director

CMJ Pub Trade Ltd
Incorporated: 21 March 2018
Registered Office: 71-75 Shelton Street, London, WC2H 9JQ
Major Shareholder: Cavell Jarrett
Officers: Cavell Jarrett, Secretary; Cavell Jarrett [1987] Director/Publican

CMT (Wines) Limited
Incorporated: 4 September 1998 *Employees:* 3
Net Worth: £53,033 *Total Assets:* £131,511
Registered Office: 1 West Hill, Pathfields Business Park, South Molton, Devon, EX36 3BS
Major Shareholder: Charles Edward Hugh Cotton
Officers: Georgina Anne Gartside Cotton, Secretary; Charles Edward Hugh Cotton [1958] Managing Director

Co Stars London Ltd
Incorporated: 31 January 2014 *Employees:* 1
Net Worth Deficit: £20,495 *Total Assets:* £66,075
Registered Office: Unit 104 Qwest, Great West Road, Brentford, Middlesex, TW8 0GP
Major Shareholder: Bo Wei
Officers: Bo Wei [1985] Director/Manager

Co.Bru Limited
Incorporated: 9 April 2018
Registered Office: 11a Gwendwr Road, West Kensington, London, W14 9BQ
Major Shareholder: Michael Cockburn
Officers: Michael Cockburn [1988] Director/Entrepreneur

Cobblers Gin Limited
Incorporated: 25 May 2018
Registered Office: 3 Butlin Close, Rothwell, Kettering, Northants, NN14 6YA
Shareholders: Steven Paul Gamage; Paul Lawrence Gamage
Officers: Paul Lawrence Gamage [1954] Director; Steven Paul Gamage [1990] Managing Director

Cobev Limited
Incorporated: 9 May 2018
Registered Office: Charter House, 8-10 Station Road, Manor Park, London, E12 5BT
Major Shareholder: Amish Thakkar
Officers: Amish Thakkar [1986] Director

Cobra Beer Partnership Limited
Incorporated: 28 January 2009 Employees: 5
Net Worth: £12,104,656 Total Assets: £14,096,065
Registered Office: 137 High Street, Burton on Trent, Staffs, DE14 1JZ
Shareholders: Karan Faridoon Bilimoria; Molson Coors Brewing Company (UK) Limited
Officers: Gemma Louise Wisniewski, Secretary; Lord Karan Faridoon Bilimoria [1961] Director; Simon John Cox [1967] Director; Dynshaw Fareed Italia [1970] Director; James Christian Shearer [1980] Marketing Director; Philip Mark Whitehead [1977] Director

Coca-Cola Amatil (UK) Limited
Incorporated: 18 May 2015
Previous: Chilli Brands (Australia) Limited
Registered Office: c/o Intertrust, 35 Great St Helen's, London, EC3A 6AP
Officers: Michelle O'Flaherty [1973] Director

Cochin Heritage Ltd
Incorporated: 26 September 2014
Net Worth Deficit: £24,906 Total Assets: £122,397
Registered Office: 54 Ballards Lane, Finchley, London, N3 2BU
Major Shareholder: Pillai Vivekanand Raman
Officers: Vivekanand Raman Pillai [1976] Director/IT Consultant

Cocksure Brewing Company Limited
Incorporated: 27 April 2015 Employees: 2
Net Worth: £40,152 Total Assets: £51,883
Registered Office: c/o Cox Costello & Horne, 4th & 5th Floor, 14-15 Lower Grosvenor Place, London, W1W 0EX
Shareholders: Calum Doutch; Daniel Edward Snow
Officers: Calum Doutch [1985] Director/National Account Manager; Daniel Edward Snow [1986] Director/National Account Manager

Cocktail Express Ltd
Incorporated: 12 February 2013 Employees: 1
Net Worth: £258,192 Total Assets: £306,012
Registered Office: 52 Chandos Avenue, London, W5 4ER
Major Shareholder: Ahmed Helimi
Officers: Said Zamani [1975] Director/Business Consultancy [French]

The Cocktail Pickers Club Ltd
Incorporated: 24 May 2016
Net Worth Deficit: £36,219 Total Assets: £72,814
Registered Office: 19 The Square, Retford, Notts, DN22 6DQ
Major Shareholder: Jennifer Mary Hall
Officers: Jennifer Mary Hall [1986] Director

Coddington Hepburn Limited
Incorporated: 2 March 2000
Registered Office: 14 Berkley Court, Mill Street, Berkhamsted, Herts, HP4 2DT
Major Shareholder: Kenneth Andrew Hepburn
Officers: Kenneth Andrew Hepburn [1956] Director/Consultant

Codorniu UK Limited
Incorporated: 11 February 1999 Employees: 5
Net Worth: £1,570,449 Total Assets: £1,621,925
Registered Office: One Redcliff Street, Bristol, BS1 6TP
Officers: Ramon Raventos [1975] Director [Spanish]

Coe of Ilford Limited
Incorporated: 13 April 1960
Net Worth: £12,036,925 Total Assets: £12,040,525
Registered Office: 23 Cumberland Avenue, London, NW10 7RX
Parent: Enotria Winecellars Limited
Officers: Mark Huszczo, Secretary; Troy Christensen [1966] Director [American]

The Cognac Growers' Collective Limited
Incorporated: 3 August 2012
Registered Office: The Barn, Lotmead Business Village, Wanborough, Swindon, Wilts, SN4 0UY
Shareholder: Penelope Margaret Jackson
Officers: Peter Bowyer [1954] Director; Penelope Margaret Jackson [1963] Director

Colchester Mann Limited
Incorporated: 14 March 2006
Net Worth Deficit: £9,617 Total Assets: £6,091
Registered Office: Odeon House, 146 College Road, Harrow, Middlesex, HA1 1BH
Shareholders: Henry Robert Mann; Josephine Rachelle Mann
Officers: Josephine Rachelle Mann, Secretary/Company Executive; Henry Robert Mann [1947] Director/Company Executive; Josephine Rachelle Mann [1948] Director/Company Executive

Cold Black Label Limited
Incorporated: 5 November 2010
Net Worth Deficit: £184,688 Total Assets: £26,164
Registered Office: 5 Squire Drive, Brynmenyn Industrial Estate, Bridgend, Mid Glamorgan, CF32 9TX
Officers: Gurmit Singh Bedesha [1962] Director; Rachel Bedesha [1969] Director/Manager; Gurmeet Kaur Gill [1962] Director/Manager

Cold Formd Ltd
Incorporated: 19 July 2016
Net Worth Deficit: £1,509 Total Assets: £31,230
Registered Office: 52 Berkeley Square, London, W1J 5BT
Shareholder: Andrew George Michael
Officers: Andrew George Michael [1983] Director

Coleburn Distillery Limited
Incorporated: 20 March 2014
Registered Office: Coleburn Distillery, Rothes, Elgin, Moray, IV30 8SN
Major Shareholder: Edward Odim
Officers: Edward Odim [1958] Director/Whisky Distilling & Warehousing

Colemans ABC Ltd
Incorporated: 17 November 1993 Employees: 15
Net Worth: £24,137 Total Assets: £590,202
Registered Office: The Old Tram Depot, Bexhill Road, St Leonards on Sea, E Sussex, TN38 8BG
Officers: Teresa Ann Coleman, Secretary; David John Coleman [1956] Director/Soft Drinks Distributor; Teresa Ann Coleman [1956] Director/Company Secretary

Coles Trading Limited
Incorporated: 11 January 2005 Employees: 1
Net Worth Deficit: £5,235 Total Assets: £56,485
Registered Office: 89 High Street, Thame, Oxon, OX9 3EH
Major Shareholder: Timothy Richard Coles
Officers: Timothy Richard Coles [1958] Director

Collective Trading Limited
Incorporated: 17 August 2006 Employees: 1
Net Worth: £31,840 Total Assets: £46,063
Registered Office: 364-368 Cranbrook Road, Gants Hill, Ilford, Essex, IG2 6HY
Major Shareholder: Vasant Lakhani
Officers: Vasantkumar Dahyalal Lakhani [1948] Director/Businessman

Spencer Collings & Co Limited
Incorporated: 15 December 2005
Registered Office: 1 Lumley Street, Mayfair, London, W1K 6TT
Major Shareholder: Michael George Spencer Collings
Officers: Michael George Spencer Collings [1949] Director

Collins Wines Limited
Incorporated: 31 March 1977
Net Worth: £182,443 Total Assets: £186,637
Registered Office: Hawthorn Farm, Great Missenden, Bucks, HP16 0RL
Major Shareholder: Christopher Douglas Collins
Officers: Christopher Douglas Collins, Secretary; Christopher Douglas Collins [1940] Director; Susanne Collins [1948] Director

Henry C. Collison and Sons Limited
Incorporated: 21 March 1969 Employees: 2
Net Worth: £424,172 Total Assets: £518,826
Registered Office: Avalon House, 72 Lower Mortlake Road, Richmond, Surrey, TW9 2JY
Parent: Vins et Spiritueux Richelieu S.A.
Officers: Karen Spy, Secretary; Werner Nolte [1976] Finance Director [South African]; Fraser John Thornton [1969] Managing Director

Colne Confectionery Ltd
Incorporated: 22 December 2017
Registered Office: Blakewood Court, Anerley Park, Anerley, London, SE20 8NS
Officers: Diane Woolwich [1964] Director/Landlord

K. Colombier Limited
Incorporated: 16 August 1973 Employees: 3
Net Worth: £5,309 Total Assets: £366,959
Registered Office: 7 Torriano Mews, London, NW5 2RZ
Shareholders: Frank Kratky; Jaroslava Kratky
Officers: Jaroslava Kratky, Secretary; Frank Kratky [1945] Director; Jaroslava Kratky [1947] Director

Colombier Vins Fins Limited
Incorporated: 21 June 1974 Employees: 10
Net Worth: £2,665,104 Total Assets: £2,993,441
Registered Office: Colombier House, Cadley Hill Industrial Estate, Ryder Close, Swadlincote, Derbys, DE11 9EU
Major Shareholder: Jehu Attias
Officers: Lesley Anne Good, Secretary; Jehu Attias [1941] Director/Wine Merchant; Micheline Attias [1953] Director/Wine Importer

Colorado Craft Spirits Ltd
Incorporated: 28 February 2017
Net Worth Deficit: £7,480 Total Assets: £5,470
Registered Office: Marlbridge House, The Industrial Estate, Enterprise Way, Edenbridge, Kent, TN8 6HF
Shareholders: David Brogan; Alastair Brogan
Officers: David Andrew Brogan [1969] Director

Colosseum Wines Limited
Incorporated: 4 May 2007
Net Worth: £6,668 Total Assets: £88,487
Registered Office: c/o Goumal & Co, 3 Wedmore Street, London, N19 4RU
Shareholders: Massimiliano Scacchi; Glenna Scacchi
Officers: Glenna Scacchi, Secretary; Glenna Scacchi [1971] Director/Actress; Massimiliano Scacchi [1969] Director/Import Manager [Italian]

Colton Fox Trading Limited
Incorporated: 5 September 2017
Registered Office: 6 Newbury Street, Wantage, Oxon, OX12 8BS
Shareholder: Edward Penny
Officers: Edward Penny [1970] Director

Comercio Ltd
Incorporated: 22 May 2018
Registered Office: 9 Osterley Court, Great West Road, Isleworth, Middlesex, TW7 4PX
Officers: Raman Kappor [1974] Director/Management Consultant [Indian]

Compass Supply Solutions Limited
Incorporated: 21 March 1996 Employees: 34
Net Worth: £1,900,934 Total Assets: £7,536,151
Registered Office: Units 6-8 Birdham Business Park, Birdham Road, Chichester, W Sussex, PO20 7BT
Shareholders: Sharville Investments Ltd.; CSS Group Ltd
Officers: Paul William Hilder, Secretary; Paul William Hilder [1974] Finance Director; David Jonathan Wood [1971] Director

Compasse Limited
Incorporated: 16 July 2014
Net Worth Deficit: £17,396 Total Assets: £157
Registered Office: Insito Finance Ltd, Ashley House, 86-94 High Street, Hounslow, Middlesex, TW3 1NH
Shareholders: Karen Elizabeth Whelan; Susan Patricia Liburd
Officers: Susan Patricia Liburd [1962] Director/Business Development Manager; Karen Elizabeth Whelan [1948] Director/Business Consultant

The Compasses Gomshall Ltd
Incorporated: 14 June 2017
Registered Office: 165a Mill Road, Wellingborough, Northants, NN8 1PR
Officers: Omprakash Damodaran Arethedathu [1978] Director/Manager; Manisha Reddy Kondapalli [1991] Director/Manager; Kevin James Warder [1981] Director/Manager; Pavan Kumar Yenugula [1988] Director/Manager [Indian]

Con Gusto Wines Limited
Incorporated: 26 July 2016
Net Worth Deficit: £7,345 Total Assets: £17,763
Registered Office: 139-143 Union Street, Oldham, Lancs, OL1 1TE
Major Shareholder: Peter Dushko
Officers: Peter Dushko [1954] Director

Concha y Toro UK Limited
Incorporated: 20 December 2000 Employees: 61
Net Worth: £9,835,044 Total Assets: £45,458,360
Registered Office: 9 Ashurst Court, London Road, Wheatley, Oxon, OX33 1ER
Officers: Enrique Ortuzar, Secretary; Thomas Domeyko [1967] Corporate Director Foreign Subsidiaries [Chilean]; Osvaldo Solar [1961] Director/Corporate C.F.O [Chilean]

UK Wholesalers of Beers, Wines and Spirits   dellam

Concordia Wines Ltd
Incorporated: 16 July 2018
Registered Office: 30 Bolingbroke Road, London, W14 0AL
Major Shareholder: Deborah Louise Newberry
Officers: Deborah Louise Newberry [1975] Director/Lawyer

Condor Wines Ltd
Incorporated: 15 June 2011 *Employees:* 2
Net Worth: £29,667 *Total Assets:* £704,088
Registered Office: 19 Bourton Road, Solihull, W Midlands, B92 8AY
Officers: Lee Evans [1974] Director; Maria Evans [1972] Director [Argentinian]

Conic Brewing Limited
Incorporated: 12 June 2017
Net Worth: £100 *Total Assets:* £100
Registered Office: 5 Douglas Park Crescent, Glasgow, G61 3DS

Connecting Italian Food UK Ltd
Incorporated: 18 July 2018
Registered Office: 62 Church Square, Brandon, Co Durham, DH7 8EE
Major Shareholder: Jean Baptiste Podda
Officers: Jean Baptiste Podda [1973] Director/Salesman [Italian]

Connoisseur Estates Limited
Incorporated: 1 March 2002 *Employees:* 6
Net Worth Deficit: £185,059 *Total Assets:* £2,071,432
Registered Office: Binfield Vineyard, Forest Road, Wokingham, Berks, RG40 5SE
Shareholders: Norlin Events Ltd; Andrew George Steel
Officers: Richard Stephen Irwin [1973] Director; Andrew Steel [1959] Director/Salesman; Stephen Brian Symington [1980] Director

Connolly Wines Ltd
Incorporated: 28 March 2007 *Employees:* 4
Net Worth: £38,505 *Total Assets:* £118,584
Registered Office: 81 Leyland Road, Ballycastle, Co Antrim, BT52 6EZ
Shareholders: Garry Connolly; Noleen Connolly
Officers: Gary Anthony Connolly, Secretary; Gary Anthony Connolly [1972] Secretary & Director [Irish]; Noleen Connolly [1976] Director [Irish]

Connolly's (Wine Merchants) Limited
Incorporated: 25 November 1976
Net Worth: £590,421 *Total Assets:* £944,898
Registered Office: Arch 13, 220 Livery Street, Snow Hill, Birmingham, B3 1EU
Major Shareholder: Christopher Michael Connolly
Officers: Tania Elizabeth Connolly, Secretary; Christopher Michael Connolly [1959] Director/Wine Merchant; Tania Elizabeth Connolly [1963] Director

Connollys' Liquor Wholesale Limited
Incorporated: 15 October 2009 *Employees:* 42
Net Worth: £287,652 *Total Assets:* £2,890,990
Registered Office: 54 Glenshesk Road, Ballycastle, Co Antrim, BT54 6PY
Shareholders: Gerard Anthony Connolly; Mairead Connolly
Officers: Gary Anthony Connolly [1972] Director [Irish]; Mairead Connolly [1951] Director [Irish]

Conroy-Hood Limited
Incorporated: 31 October 2008
Net Worth Deficit: £89,038 *Total Assets:* £37,325
Registered Office: Rothsay House, 14 Rothsay Place, Bedford, MK40 3PX
Major Shareholder: Geraldine Conroy
Officers: Generaldine Conroy [1978] Director; Dr Sarah Louise Hood [1976] Director/Doctor

Conscious Collaborative Ltd
Incorporated: 13 February 2019
Registered Office: Balne Hall, Balne Hall Road, Goole, E Yorks, DN14 0EA
Shareholders: Phillip David White; Matthew Wood; Sam Weller
Officers: Sam Weller [1985] Director/Operations Manager; Phillip David White [1984] Managing Director; Matthew Wood [1990] Director/Chairman

Consolidated Wines Limited
Incorporated: 12 May 2018
Registered Office: 2 Old Rectory Close, Mersham, Ashford, Kent, TN25 6LZ
Major Shareholder: Andrew Gavin Murphy
Officers: Andrew Gavin Murphy [1964] Director

Consulting & Food Ltd
Incorporated: 5 January 2018
Registered Office: Flat 24, Ireton House, 3 Stamford Square, London, SW15 2BG
Major Shareholder: Franco Sabatini
Officers: Franco Sabatini [1961] Director [Italian]

Conti Coronini Ltd
Incorporated: 14 January 2019
Registered Office: 6 Coppice Drive, London, SW15 5BW
Major Shareholder: Alexia Coronini Cronberg
Officers: Alexia Coronini Cronberg [1979] Sales Director

Continental Beer Services Ltd
Incorporated: 15 June 2015
Net Worth: £3,480 *Total Assets:* £4,934
Registered Office: 18 Craven Road, Newbold, Chesterfield, Derbys, S41 7HJ
Shareholders: Steven Andrew Jackson; Michael Eugene Dooher
Officers: Michael Eugene Dooher, Secretary; Michael Eugene Dooher [1939] Director; Steven Jackson [1967] Director/Publican

Continental Cash & Carry Limited
Incorporated: 24 June 2014
Net Worth: £141,545 *Total Assets:* £1,015,835
Registered Office: 9A Long Drive, Kelvin Industrial Estate, Greenford, Middlesex, UB6 8GB
Major Shareholder: Dinesh Kumar Dhingra
Officers: Dinesh Kumar Dhingra [1969] Director/Trader [Indian]

Continental Wines Limited
Incorporated: 5 April 1982 *Employees:* 3
Net Worth: £33,637 *Total Assets:* £282,974
Registered Office: Cheribourne House, 45a Station Road, Willington, Bedford, MK44 3QL
Major Shareholder: Geoffrey Downing
Officers: Geoffrey Downing [1954] Director

Cool Apple Limited
Incorporated: 6 March 2009
Net Worth: £33,492 *Total Assets:* £73,556
Registered Office: Unit 4 Manor Farm Buildings, Churchend Lane, Charfield, Wotton under Edge, Glos, GL12 8LJ
Major Shareholder: Lisa Natalie Friel
Officers: Lisa Natalie Friel [1971] Director

Coombe Castle Fine Wines Limited
Incorporated: 23 May 1985
Net Worth: £843,658 *Total Assets:* £1,929,379
Registered Office: 41 Cornmarket Street, Oxford, OX1 3HA
Parent: Wardsend Ltd
Officers: Hamish Alexander Laing [1978] Director/Accountant; Ian Michael Laing [1946] Director; Benjamin Leroux [1975] Director/Winemaker [French]

Coombe Farm Wines Limited
Incorporated: 12 March 2010
Net Worth Deficit: £21,666 *Total Assets:* £19,306
Registered Office: Stowell Park Estate Ltd, The Estate Office, Yanworth, Cheltenham, Glos, GL54 3LQ
Major Shareholder: Samuel George Armstrong Vestey
Officers: Lord Samuel George Armstrong Vestey [1941] Director

Cooper Hill Brewery Ltd
Incorporated: 2 April 2004
Previous: Morley Brewery Ltd
Net Worth: £45,266 *Total Assets:* £47,760
Registered Office: Unit 4 Highcliffe Mills, Bruntcliffe Lane, Morley, Leeds, LS27 9LR
Shareholders: Andrew Cooper; David Hill
Officers: Andrew Cooper [1956] Director; David Hill [1958] Director/Sales Manager

Copper and Rye Leisure Ltd
Incorporated: 10 January 2019
Registered Office: 14 De Walden Drive, Kilmarnock, E Ayrshire, KA3 6AA
Shareholders: Ross Pollock; Christopher Storey
Officers: Ross Pollock [1988] Director; Christopher Storey [1988] Director

Copper and Rye Limited
Incorporated: 20 February 2015
Previous: Toro Bodega Limited
Registered Office: Barn 8, Manor Farm Barns, Back Lane, Martham, Norfolk, NR29 4PE
Shareholder: Annette Clark
Officers: Daniel Clark, Secretary; Annette Emily Clark [1990] Director/Purchasing Manager

Copper Still Company Limited
Incorporated: 28 March 2014
Net Worth Deficit: £42,910 *Total Assets:* £70,700
Registered Office: 52 Tottenham Court Road, London, W1T 2EH
Shareholders: Sophie Iris Hudson; Simon McDearmid Parkin
Officers: Simon McDearmid Parkin [1977] Director

Copricom Ltd
Incorporated: 12 April 2017
Net Worth: £100 *Total Assets:* £100
Registered Office: Unit 22 Bulrushes Business Park, Coombe Hill Road, East Grinstead, W Sussex, RH19 4LZ
Major Shareholder: Laszlo Adam
Officers: Laszlo Adam [1981] Director [Hungarian]

Coral Management Limited
Incorporated: 6 July 2005
Net Worth: £33,115 *Total Assets:* £1,038,267
Registered Office: Innovation House, Unit B, 292 Worton Road, Isleworth, Middlesex, TW7 6EL
Major Shareholder: Balvinder Singh Kaeda
Officers: Balvinder Singh Kaeda [1969] Director

Coral MGT Limited
Incorporated: 26 January 2007
Net Worth Deficit: £59,751 *Total Assets:* £754,854
Registered Office: 14 Adelaide Road, Heston, Middlesex, TW5 9AG
Major Shareholder: Hiren Kumar Patel
Officers: Hiren Kumar Patel [1969] Director

Corelli Wine Company Ltd
Incorporated: 21 August 2018
Registered Office: Low Springs, 16 Moorfield Road, Ilkley, W Yorks, LS29 8BL
Major Shareholder: Alexander George Lithgow
Officers: Alexander George Lithgow [1991] Director/Electrical Engineer

Corfu SW Limited
Incorporated: 26 March 2018
Registered Office: 128 Stoke Lane, Westbury on Trym, Bristol, BS9 3RJ
Officers: Sofoklis Kypriotis, Secretary; Demetrakis Andrew Demetriou [1959] Director; Sofoklis Kypriotis [1967] Director [Greek]

Corkers Wine Limited
Incorporated: 28 March 2007 *Employees:* 2
Net Worth: £219,959 *Total Assets:* £233,225
Registered Office: 49 Caroline Terrace, Edinburgh, EH12 8QX
Major Shareholder: Graeme Breslin
Officers: Susan Breslin, Secretary; Graeme Breslin [1964] Director

Corkhaus Ltd
Incorporated: 18 August 2016 *Employees:* 2
Net Worth Deficit: £8,807 *Total Assets:* £4,068
Registered Office: 4 Cross Street, Beeston, Nottingham, NG9 2NX
Major Shareholder: Steven Burnett
Officers: Steven Burnett [1994] Director

Corktalk Limited
Incorporated: 13 November 2013 *Employees:* 1
Net Worth Deficit: £17,460 *Total Assets:* £193
Registered Office: 26 Hopeman Close, College Town, Sandhurst, Berks, GU47 0XH
Major Shareholder: Rachel Jane Barnett
Officers: Rachel Jane Barnett [1982] Managing Director

Corney and Barrow Group Limited
Incorporated: 28 January 1969 *Employees:* 153
Net Worth: £22,555,000 *Total Assets:* £40,117,000
Registered Office: 1 Thomas More Street, London, E1W 1YZ
Shareholders: Nicholas Theobald Sibley; Percy Weatherall
Officers: Paul Stanton Masters, Secretary; Adam de La Falaise Brett Brett-Smith [1956] Director/Wine Merchant; Timothy George Freshwater [1944] Director; Bernard Candler Grigsby [1949] Director [American]; Paul Stanton Masters [1951] Director; Damian Theobald Oliver Sibley [1969] Managing Director; Edward Percy Keswick Weatherall [1957] Director/Merchant

Corney and Barrow Limited
Incorporated: 14 September 1988 *Employees:* 153
Net Worth: £14,712,000 *Total Assets:* £39,744,000
Registered Office: 1 Thomas More Street, London, E1W 1YZ
Parent: Corney & Barrow Merchanting Holdings Limited
Officers: Winston Spencer Brian Sanderson, Secretary; Adam de La Falaise Brett Brett-Smith [1956] Director/Wine Merchant; Simon Joseph Duffy [1976] Director; Timothy George Freshwater [1944] Director/Advisor; Bernard Candler Grigsby [1949] Director [American]; Oliver Hartley [1967] Export Director; Paul Stanton Masters [1951] Director; Damian Theobald Oliver Sibley [1969] Director/Company Owner; Edward Percy Keswick Weatherall [1957] Director/Chairman

Cornfield Foods and Beverages Limited
Incorporated: 8 February 2018
Registered Office: 71-75 Shelton Street, Covent Garden, London, WC2H 9JQ
Major Shareholder: Tolulope Ayomide Agbeyo
Officers: Tolulope Ayomide Agbeyo [1994] Director [Nigerian]

The Cornish Moonshine Company Limited
Incorporated: 3 December 2018
Registered Office: Goose Barn, Tubbs Mill, Caerhays, St Austell, Cornwall, PL26 6NB
Major Shareholder: Simon Duggan
Officers: Simon Duggan [1970] Director/Restaurateur

Cornish Point Wines UK Ltd
Incorporated: 5 May 1999 *Employees:* 2
Net Worth: £37,175 *Total Assets:* £91,864
Registered Office: 2 Station Road, Radlett, Herts, WD7 8JX
Officers: Nigel Greening, Secretary; Nicola Megan Jane Greening [1970] Director/Executive; Nigel Greening [1950] Director

The Cornish Rum Company Ltd
Incorporated: 3 July 2017
Registered Office: The Sovereign Distillery, Wilson Road, Huyton, Knowsley, Merseyside, L36 6AD
Parent: Halewood International Limited
Officers: John Andrew Bradbury [1971] Director; Stewart Andrew Hainsworth [1969] Director/Chief Executive Officer; Alan William Robinson [1965] Finance Director

Cornucopia Wines Limited
Incorporated: 29 May 2015
Registered Office: 3rd Floor, 114a Cromwell Road, London, SW7 4AG
Shareholders: Richard Alexander Bates; Mark Anthony Jackson
Officers: Richard Alexander Bates [1958] Director/Publishing [Irish]; Mark Anthony Jackson [1967] Director/Facilities Manager

Corvin Import Export Ltd
Incorporated: 4 June 2018
Registered Office: 41 Runbury Circle, London, NW9 8RX
Major Shareholder: Cristian Gabriel Dragomir
Officers: Cristian Gabriel Dragomir [1982] Director [Romanian]

Corvinus Beverages International Ltd
Incorporated: 10 July 2018
Registered Office: Apartment 2303, 26 Hertsmere Road, London, E14 4EF
Shareholder: Szabolcs Balasko
Officers: Szabolcs Balasko [1989] Director/Investment Professional [Hungarian]

Cosmic Services Limited
Incorporated: 27 May 2016 *Employees:* 1
Net Worth Deficit: £1,250 *Total Assets:* £4,994
Registered Office: Third Floor, 20 Old Bailey, London, EC4M 7AN
Major Shareholder: Nikolaos Mytilineos
Officers: Nikolaos Mytilineos [1977] Director [Greek]

Cosmopolitan Drinks Limited
Incorporated: 1 October 2010
Net Worth: £1 *Total Assets:* £1
Registered Office: Castor Street, Liverpool, L6 5AT
Major Shareholder: John Kenneth Ravenscroft
Officers: John Kenneth Ravenscroft [1955] Director/Licencee

Coss Wines Ltd.
Incorporated: 7 February 2012
Net Worth: £18 *Total Assets:* £18
Registered Office: 26 Fowlmere Road, Thriplow, Royston, Herts, SG8 7QU
Shareholders: Dale Michael Coss; Dale Michael Coss; Clare Marie Ansell
Officers: Clare Marie Ansell [1973] Director/General Manager; Dale Michael Coss [1971] Director/Business Owner

Cossart,Gordon and Co.Limited
Incorporated: 26 October 1907
Registered Office: Fells House, Station Road, Kings Langley, Herts, WD4 8LH
Parent: John E Fells & Sons Ltd
Officers: Louise Catherine Rimes, Secretary; David Cossart [1942] Director; Stephen Antony Moody [1960] Managing Director

Costadoria Ltd
Incorporated: 24 August 2017
Registered Office: Stanmore Business & Innovation Centre, Stanmore Place, Howard Road, Stanmore, Middlesex, HA7 1GB
Major Shareholder: Masadiq Mohamed Jaffer
Officers: Masadiq Mohamed Jaffer [1961] Director/Accountant

Cotrade Ltd
Incorporated: 9 June 2017
Net Worth: £424 *Total Assets:* £898
Registered Office: 71-75 Shelton Street, Covent Garden, London, WC2H 9JQ
Major Shareholder: Catalin Ionut Stan
Officers: Catalin Ionut Stan [1983] Director [Romanian]

The Cotswold Port Co. Ltd
Incorporated: 20 January 2016 *Employees:* 1
Net Worth Deficit: £4,052 *Total Assets:* £8,985
Registered Office: 3 Sussex Mews, Cheltenham, Glos, GL52 5FU
Major Shareholder: Emma Sally Phillips
Officers: Emma Sally Phillips [1978] Director

Cotswold Wines Ltd
Incorporated: 31 January 2019
Registered Office: 10 College Fields, Longlevens, Gloucester, GL2 0AG
Major Shareholder: Simon John Griffiths
Officers: Dean John Griffiths [1952] Director; Simon John Griffiths [1987] Director

Cotswolds Wine Company Limited
Incorporated: 2 July 2018
Registered Office: 7 Bakehouse Court, Long Hill Road, Ascot, Berks, SL5 8RZ
Major Shareholder: Anthony Charles Cowling
Officers: Anthony Charles Cowling [1964] Managing Director

Country Life Brewery Ltd
Incorporated: 22 November 2010 *Employees:* 3
Net Worth Deficit: £1,653 *Total Assets:* £42,879
Registered Office: 8 Greenfield Close, Bideford, Devon, EX39 3RY
Shareholder: Anna Clare Lacey
Officers: Anna Clare Lacey [1973] Director; Simon Roy Lacey [1968] Director

County Catering (Midlands) Limited
Incorporated: 27 February 1980 *Employees:* 2
Net Worth: £4,232 *Total Assets:* £416,102
Registered Office: Drayton Court, Drayton Road, Solihull, W Midlands, B90 4NG
Shareholders: Nicholas John Cockburn Underwood; Timothy Morris Underwood
Officers: Timothy Morris Underwood, Secretary; Philip Anthony Chamberlain [1952] Director/Wine Merchant; Nicholas John Cockburn Underwood [1953] Director/Wine Merchant; Timothy Morris Underwood [1958] Director/Wine Merchant

Michel Couvreur (Scotch Whiskies) Limited
Incorporated: 22 April 1988 *Employees:* 6
Net Worth: £1,514,178 *Total Assets:* £2,077,092
Registered Office: Meldrum House, Old Meldrum, Aberdeenshire, AB5 0AE
Parent: AI Spirit
Officers: Marthe Georgette Andree Couvreur [1932] Director [French]; Alexandra Marie Elisabeth Deschamps [1972] Director/Housewife [French]; Cyril Deschamps [1973] Director [French]; Jean Arnaud Frantzen [1973] Director [French]

Cow West Yorkshire Limited
Incorporated: 15 February 2019
Registered Office: Brown Cow, Pontefract Road, Ackworth, Pontefract, W Yorks, WF7 7EL
Major Shareholder: Tracy Chambers
Officers: Tracy Chambers, Secretary; Tracy Chambers [1971] Director/Publican; Christine McGuire [1958] Director/Carer

CPC Business Limited
Incorporated: 7 May 2008
Net Worth: £56,437 *Total Assets:* £61,297
Registered Office: 1 Station Approach, Hampton, Surrey, TW12 2HZ
Officers: Xu Dong Xu [1967] Director/General Manager

CPT Trading Ltd
Incorporated: 14 November 2018
Registered Office: 18 Blackmores Grove, Teddington, Middlesex, TW11 9AF
Major Shareholder: Marc Ralph Fourie
Officers: Marc Ralph Fourie [1977] Director/Entrepreneur

CRA Ltd
Incorporated: 23 June 2016
Net Worth: £90,532 *Total Assets:* £128,309
Registered Office: Hollinwood Business Centre, Albert Street, Oldham, Lancs, OL8 3QL
Major Shareholder: Anastasios Savvopoulos
Officers: Anastasios Savvopoulos [1977] Director [Greek]

Crabtrees Craft Pubs and Bottle Merchants Limited
Incorporated: 7 November 2018
Registered Office: 67 Chorley Old Road, Bolton, Lancs, BL1 3AJ
Major Shareholder: Margaret Ruth Crabtree
Officers: Margaret Ruth Crabtree [1976] Creative Director

Crackerjack Wines Limited
Incorporated: 3 October 2013
Registered Office: Tanners, River, Petworth, W Sussex, GU28 9AY
Shareholders: Rupert John Clevely; David James Hohnen
Officers: Rupert John Clevely [1957] Director; David James Hohnen [1949] Director/Winemaker [Australian]

The Cracking Little Wine Company Limited
Incorporated: 3 July 2017
Net Worth: £1 *Total Assets:* £1
Registered Office: Willow House, Orbital 24, Oldham Street, Denton, Manchester, M34 3SU
Parent: EF Limited
Officers: Paul Mizen [1959] Managing Director

Craddock Cocktails Ltd
Incorporated: 25 October 2018
Registered Office: 2 Englewood Road, London, SW12 9NZ
Major Shareholder: Richard Martin Evans
Officers: Richard Martin Evans [1989] Director/Consultant

The Craft Beer Collaborative Ltd
Incorporated: 21 November 2018
Registered Office: 25 Cedar Park Drive, Bolsover, Chesterfield, Derbys, S44 6XP
Major Shareholder: Darren John Filsell
Officers: Denise Jessica Louise Trueman, Secretary; Darren John Filsell [1972] Director

Craft Distillers Scotland Limited
Incorporated: 21 January 2014
Registered Office: 46 New Road, Milnathort, Kinross, KY13 9XT
Major Shareholder: George Preston Thomson
Officers: George Preston Thomson [1954] Director

The Craft Drink Co Ltd
Incorporated: 10 March 2009 *Employees:* 7
Previous: Cotswold Fine Food Limited
Net Worth Deficit: £78,051 *Total Assets:* £276,837
Registered Office: Unit 6 Draycott Business Ceentre, Draycott, Moreton in Marsh, Glos, GL56 9JY
Major Shareholder: Richard William David Chamberlain
Officers: Soraya Chamberlain, Secretary; Richard William David Chamberlain [1968] Director/Wholesaler

Craft Locals Limited
Incorporated: 23 January 2017
Net Worth Deficit: £84,783 *Total Assets:* £334,021
Registered Office: Arnos Arms, Bowes Road, London, N11 1AN
Major Shareholder: Daniel Peter Fox
Officers: Daniel Peter Fox [1979] Director

Craft Wines Ltd
Incorporated: 7 February 2019
Registered Office: 63 Turners Hill, Adeyfield, Hemel Hempstead, Herts, HP2 4LH
Shareholders: Paul Rance; Diane Rance
Officers: Diane Rance, Secretary; Paul Rance [1959] Director/Transport Manager

Crafted Beverages Limited
Incorporated: 8 July 2016
Net Worth Deficit: £10,700 *Total Assets:* £10,332
Registered Office: 27 Old Gloucester Street, London, WC1N 3AX
Shareholders: Emma Whiting; Andrew Whiting
Officers: Andrew George Whiting [1982] Director; Emma Whiting [1983] Director

Craftibeer Limited
Incorporated: 10 August 2016 Employees: 1
Net Worth Deficit: £5,374 Total Assets: £1,142
Registered Office: Office 4, 219 Kensington High Street, Kensington, London, W8 6BD
Major Shareholder: Corin Simon Hughes
Officers: Corin Simon Hughes [1975] Director

Craftmaster Social Ltd
Incorporated: 16 February 2018
Registered Office: Bewell House, Bewell Street, Hereford, HR4 0BA
Major Shareholder: Richard Butterworth
Officers: Richard Butterworth [1984] Director

Craftwater Brewing Company Limited
Incorporated: 23 July 2018
Registered Office: 11 Moorsend, Kingsteignton, Newton Abbot, Devon, TQ12 3JY
Shareholders: Russell Stanley Nixon; Christopher James Thackray; Christopher Andrew Ward
Officers: Christopher James Thackray [1983] Managing Director

Crafty Cask Wholesale Ltd
Incorporated: 11 January 2017
Registered Office: 21 Brockholes Crescent, Poulton-le-Fylde, Lancs, FY6 8HX
Officers: John Kieran Murphy [1982] Director/Salesperson

Crafty Connoisseur Limited
Incorporated: 12 November 2018
Registered Office: 148 Gilmerton Dykes Road, Edinburgh, EH17 8PE
Shareholders: Brenda McKenzie; Stephen Alexander McKenzie
Officers: Brenda McKenzie, Secretary; Stephen McKenzie, Secretary; Brenda McKenzie [1973] Marketing Director; Stephen Alexander McKenzie [1968] Import Export Director

Crafty Devil Brewing Ltd
Incorporated: 29 September 2014 Employees: 9
Net Worth: £31,533 Total Assets: £149,411
Registered Office: Unit 3 The Stone Yard, Ninian Park Road, Cardiff, CF11 6HE
Shareholders: Adam Michael Edinborough; Rhys David Watkins
Officers: Adam Michael Edinborough [1982] Director; Rhys David Watkins [1981] Director

Crafty Pint Limited
Incorporated: 18 August 2016
Registered Office: Low Bield, Knipe Fold, Outgate, Ambleside, Cumbria, LA22 0PU
Major Shareholder: Alastair Francis Kirk
Officers: Alastair Francis Kirk [1965] Director

Crafty Warehouse Ltd
Incorporated: 6 February 2018
Registered Office: Unit 4 Ashling Court, Iremonger Road, Nottingham, NG2 3JA
Major Shareholder: Gavin Kenneth Morrison
Officers: Gavin Kenneth Morrison [1980] Director

Crafty Wolf (Drinks) Limited
Incorporated: 12 September 2017
Registered Office: 4 Beaufort West, Bath, BA1 6QB
Major Shareholder: Glyn David Gronow
Officers: Glyn David Gronow [1959] Director

Crafty Wolf Limited
Incorporated: 12 September 2017
Registered Office: 4 Beaufort West, Bath, BA1 6QB
Major Shareholder: Glyn David Gronow
Officers: Glyn David Gronow [1959] Director

Craftyard Events Limited
Incorporated: 20 September 2017
Registered Office: Craftyard, 23a Walton Street, Aylesbury, Bucks, HP20 1TZ
Shareholder: Sarah-Jayne Cook
Officers: Sarah-Jayne Cook [1971] Director/Police Officer

Dudley Craig Wines Limited
Incorporated: 2 September 2014
Net Worth: £13,014 Total Assets: £176,539
Registered Office: Studio 1, 305a Goldhawk Road, London, W12 8EU
Major Shareholder: Richard Dudley Craig
Officers: Richard Dudley Craig [1964] Director/Wine Merchant

Crazy Brew UK Limited
Incorporated: 16 October 2018
Registered Office: 21-27 Summerstown, London, SW17 0BQ
Major Shareholder: Guilherme Campos Lopes
Officers: Guilherme Campos Lopes [1983] Director [Brazilian]

Crazy Gin Ltd
Incorporated: 27 January 2016 Employees: 1
Net Worth Deficit: £69,157 Total Assets: £22,638
Registered Office: Ground Floor, Warwick House Industrial Estate, Banbury Road, Southam, Warwicks, CV47 2PT
Major Shareholder: Sukhjinder Singh Nagra
Officers: Sukhjinder Nagra, Secretary; Sukhjinder Singh Nagra [1978] Director

CRC Delta Ltd
Incorporated: 3 May 2013
Net Worth: £43,830 Total Assets: £74,535
Registered Office: 157 Bellville House, 4 John Donne Way, London, SE10 9FW
Major Shareholder: Christopher Rodgerson
Officers: Christopher Rodgerson [1982] Director/IT Consultant

Creation Wines UK Limited
Incorporated: 21 November 2017
Registered Office: c/o Brosnans Birkby House, Bailiff Bridge, Brighouse, W Yorks, HD6 4JJ
Major Shareholder: Jean Claude Martin
Officers: Jonalthan Patrick Drake [1961] Director

Creative Juices Bar Limited
Incorporated: 16 May 2018
Registered Office: 11 Lynmouth Road, Bristol, BS2 9YH
Major Shareholder: Lisa Paige Calder
Officers: Lisa Paige Calder [1968] Director

Creative Juices Brewing Company Ltd
Incorporated: 19 March 2018
Registered Office: 72 Parkside Drive, Watford, Herts, WD17 3AZ
Shareholders: Ben Janaway; Sarah Jane Chiappi; Stuart Wallace
Officers: Sarah Jane Chiappi [1973] Director; Ben Janaway [1975] Director; Stuart Wallace [1978] Director

The Creative Whisky Company Limited
Incorporated: 12 November 2004 *Employees:* 5
Net Worth: £1,111,742 *Total Assets:* £2,279,288
Registered Office: Steading, New Cample Farm, Thornhill, Dumfries & Galloway, DG3 5EY
Shareholder: David James Millard Stirk
Officers: David Michael Stirk, Secretary; David James Millard Stirk [1976] Managing Director; Dawn Stirk [1981] Finance Director

Cremant Inc Ltd
Incorporated: 21 December 2018
Registered Office: 71-75 Shelton Street, London, WC2H 9JQ
Major Shareholder: Leigh Austin
Officers: Leigh Austin [1974] Director

Crescent Fine Foods Ltd
Incorporated: 21 January 2016
Net Worth: £90,937 *Total Assets:* £157,052
Registered Office: Suite 54, The Enterprise Hub, 62 Tong Street, Bradford, W Yorks, BD4 9LX
Major Shareholder: Mohammed Saber Ismael Hassan
Officers: Mohammed Saber Hassan, Secretary; Mohammed Saber Hassan [1958] Director/Food and Beverage Trader

Cresco Import Exports Ltd
Incorporated: 4 April 2014
Registered Office: 28 Ryecroft Avenue, Wolverhampton, W Midlands, WV4 5UQ
Major Shareholder: Gurmit Dheensa
Officers: Gurmit Dheensa [1974] Director/Self Employed

F & M Cressi Limited
Incorporated: 22 June 1995
Net Worth: £12,792 *Total Assets:* £15,802
Registered Office: 21 Albert Road, Hounslow, Middlesex, TW3 3RW
Shareholders: Felix-Johannes Peter Otto Kress von Wendland; Marcelle Michelle Georgina Maria von Wendland
Officers: Marcelle Michelle Georgina Maria Von Wendland, Secretary/Marketing Director [German]; Felix-Johannes Peter Otto Kress Von Wendland [1974] Managing Director [German]; Marcelle Michelle Georgina Maria Von Wendland [1970] Director/Marketing Manager [German]

The Crest Cyder Company Ltd
Incorporated: 6 March 2018
Registered Office: 176 Eaton Crescent, Taunton, Somerset, TA2 7UG
Major Shareholder: Alice Louise Fitzsimons
Officers: Alice Louise Fitzsimons [1988] Director

Creswick Inns & Leisure Ltd
Incorporated: 28 March 2008
Net Worth: £304,494 *Total Assets:* £354,225
Registered Office: 29 Creswick Lane, Grenoside, Sheffield, S35 8NL
Shareholders: Neil Thomas Travis; Beverley Travis
Officers: Beverley Jayne Travis, Secretary; Neil Thomas Travis [1962] Director

Cribbar Limited
Incorporated: 6 March 2003
Net Worth: £24,330 *Total Assets:* £145,647
Registered Office: Regent House, 29 Bank Street, Newquay, Cornwall, TR7 1DH
Officers: Christine Pearce, Secretary; Christine Pearce [1944] Director/Wholesaler; Michael Pearce [1946] Director/Wholesaler

Croatian Fine Wines Limited
Incorporated: 19 January 2011 *Employees:* 1
Net Worth Deficit: £215,232 *Total Assets:* £77,018
Registered Office: Winnington Hall, Winnington Lane, Winnington, Northwich, Cheshire, CW8 4DU
Parent: Anderson Bevan Limited
Officers: Mark Roberts, Secretary; Mark Roberts [1970] Director/Accountant

Cromfine Limited
Incorporated: 15 March 2013
Registered Office: 9 Cumberland Road, Birkdale, Southport, Lancaster, PR8 6NY
Shareholders: Jose Mendoza; Jose Mendoza
Officers: Jose Mendoza, Secretary; Jose Mendoza [1957] Director/Property Developer [Spanish]

Cropol Luxury Products Ltd
Incorporated: 10 September 2013
Registered Office: 20a Rossetti Gardens Mansions, Flood Street, London, SW3 5QY
Major Shareholder: David Michael Faktor
Officers: David Michael Faktor [1960] Director

Cross Brew Ltd
Incorporated: 20 August 2015
Registered Office: 16a Queen Street, Edinburgh, EH2 1JE
Shareholder: Michael Aikman
Officers: Michael Aikman [1978] Director; Daniel Bartley [1983] Director/Graphic Designer [Irish]; Ericka Duffy [1979] Director/Barista [Canadian]; Jason Scott [1974] Director

Crouch Vale Brewery Limited
Incorporated: 27 October 1980 *Employees:* 18
Net Worth: £2,504,246 *Total Assets:* £2,822,445
Registered Office: 23 Haltwhistle Road, South Woodham Ferrers, Chelmsford, Essex, CM3 5ZA
Shareholder: Colin John Bocking
Officers: Fiona Michelle Bocking, Secretary; Colin John Bocking [1954] Director; Fiona Michelle Bocking [1959] Director

Crown Cash & Carry Ltd
Incorporated: 16 October 2012
Net Worth: £88,267 *Total Assets:* £278,015
Registered Office: Unit 3 Kingsbridge Road, Barking, Essex, IG11 0BP
Major Shareholder: Syed Faisal Saddat Naqvi
Officers: Sayed Anis Nakvi [1971] Director [Polish]

Cru Classe Limited
Incorporated: 5 June 2018
Registered Office: Flat 4, 52 Queens Gardens, London, W2 3AA
Shareholders: Andrew James Scopes; Joshua Richard Sarais
Officers: Joshua Richard Sarais [1990] Director/Consultant; Andrew James Scopes [1993] Director/Student

Cru Prive Ltd
Incorporated: 6 October 2015
Net Worth Deficit: £489 *Total Assets:* £3,328
Registered Office: c/o Watson Syers Accountants Ltd, Evolve Business Centre, Cygnet Way, Rainton Bridge South Business Park, Houghton-le-Spring, Co Durham, DH4 5QY
Major Shareholder: Elena Gargani
Officers: Elena Gargani, Secretary; Elena Gargani [1974] Director [Italian]

Crucial Brands Holdings Limited
Incorporated: 16 July 2014
Net Worth Deficit: £399,986 *Total Assets:* £14
Registered Office: 29 Portland Street, Kilmarnock, E Ayrshire, KA1 2BY
Shareholders: Scott McMurray Watson; Brian David Woods
Officers: Norbert Muller [1965] Director [Belgian]; Scott McMurray Watson [1972] Director; Brian David Woods [1974] Director

Crucial Drinks US Holdings Ltd
Incorporated: 13 April 2017
Registered Office: 29 Portland Road, Kilmarnock, E Ayrshire, KA1 2BY
Officers: Scott McMurray Watson [1972] Director; Brian David Woods [1974] Director

Crudo Limited
Incorporated: 17 February 2014
Net Worth Deficit: £29,065 *Total Assets:* £295,469
Registered Office: 16 West Smithfield, London, EC1A 9HY
Major Shareholder: Andrea Mello Grosso
Officers: Giovanni Perri, Secretary; Andrea Mello Grosso [1965] Director [Italian]

W.& J.Cruickshank and Company Limited
Incorporated: 5 May 1978 *Employees:* 4
Net Worth: £1,178,406 *Total Assets:* £1,214,700
Registered Office: Cunningholes Industrial Estate, March Road, Buckie, Banffshire, AB56 4DA
Major Shareholder: William Cruickshank
Officers: William Cruickshank [1942] Director

Crundale Wines Limited
Incorporated: 10 July 2017
Net Worth: £100 *Total Assets:* £100
Registered Office: 8 Godwin Road, London, E7 0LE
Major Shareholder: Thomas David Hewson
Officers: Thomas David Hewson, Secretary; Thomas David Hewson [1985] Director/Musician

Crush Wines Ltd
Incorporated: 6 September 2005 *Employees:* 4
Net Worth: £95,645 *Total Assets:* £446,438
Registered Office: Bremhill Court, Bremhill, Calne, Wilts, SN11 9LA
Shareholders: Christopher Simon Ellis; Linda Christine Ellis
Officers: Christopher Simon Ellis [1958] Director

CRVC UK Limited
Incorporated: 26 January 1981 *Employees:* 10
Net Worth: £1,830,328 *Total Assets:* £4,620,381
Registered Office: Third Floor, The Broadgate Tower, 20 Primrose Street, London, EC2A 2RS
Officers: Pascal Lucien Emile Prudhomme [1962] Director [French]

Crystle Limited
Incorporated: 15 September 1999 *Employees:* 1
Net Worth: £349,169 *Total Assets:* £484,463
Registered Office: 60 Broad Road, Sale, Cheshire, M33 2BE
Shareholders: Peter Alan Gray; Pavlina Gray
Officers: Peter Alan Gray, Secretary; Pavlina Gray [1976] Director [Czech]; Peter Alan Gray [1955] Director

CS Wines Limited
Incorporated: 8 March 2013
Net Worth Deficit: £21,865 *Total Assets:* £235,567
Registered Office: 8 Royal Opera Arcade, London, SW1Y 4UY
Major Shareholder: Gilles Pierre Yves Corre
Officers: Gilles Pierre Yves Corre [1971] Director [French]

Csburrwine Ltd
Incorporated: 20 February 2019
Registered Office: Greenacres, 54 Cleat Hill, Ravensden, Bedford, MK41 8AN
Major Shareholder: Christopher Burr
Officers: Christopher Burr, Secretary; Christopher Burr [1951] Director/Master of Wine

CSS On-Trade Limited
Incorporated: 1 March 2008 *Employees:* 8
Previous: Chivertons of Sussex Limited
Net Worth Deficit: £231,359 *Total Assets:* £335,220
Registered Office: Units 6-8 Birdham Business Park, Birdham Road, Chichester, W Sussex, PO20 7BT
Shareholders: Sharville Investments Ltd.; Compass Supply Solutions Ltd
Officers: Paul William Hilder [1974] Finance Director; David Jonathan Wood [1971] Director

The Cuba Trading Company Ltd
Incorporated: 10 September 2018
Registered Office: Haydens Farm, High Easter, Chelmsford, Essex, CM1 4QU
Shareholders: William Richard Knight; Mark Ubsdell
Officers: William Richard Knight [1961] Film Director/Producer; Mark Ubsdell [1960] Film Director/Producer

Cubed A Ltd
Incorporated: 20 June 2017
Registered Office: 132 Clarence Street, Southall, Middlesex, UB2 5BW
Officers: Avtar Chand [1965] Director; Lekhika Chaudhary [1995] Director; Jaswinder Kaur [1965] Director

Cubic Brands Limited
Incorporated: 29 August 2002 *Employees:* 1
Net Worth: £212,428 *Total Assets:* £320,257
Registered Office: 15 Saxholm Way, Southampton, SO16 7HB
Major Shareholder: Robert Lee Preston
Officers: Elizabeth Louise Preston, Secretary; Elizabeth Louise Preston [1978] Director; Robert Lee Preston [1975] Director

Cuestion Tequila EMEA Ltd
Incorporated: 26 November 2018
Registered Office: Pear Tree Farm, West Chiltington Lane, Billingshurst, W Sussex, RH14 9DP
Major Shareholder: Jason Matthew Fandrich
Officers: Thomas Anthony Poulton [1990] Digital Director; Tracey Ruth Poulton [1969] Marketing Director

Cuestion Tequila Limited
Incorporated: 16 November 2018
Registered Office: Pear Tree Farm, West Chiltington Lane, Billingshurst, W Sussex, RH14 9DP
Shareholders: Tracey Ruth Poulton; Thomas Anthony Poulton
Officers: Thomas Anthony Poulton [1990] Digital Director; Tracey Ruth Poulton [1969] Marketing Director

Cullercoats Gin Company Ltd
Incorporated: 10 July 2017
Registered Office: 1 Two Ball Lonnen, Fenham, Newcastle upon Tyne, NE4 9RN
Major Shareholder: Daniel Humphreys
Officers: Daniel Humphreys [1958] Director/MD

Cumberland Bargin Booze Limited
Incorporated: 16 September 2016
Net Worth Deficit: £3,392 *Total Assets:* £207,133
Registered Office: Suite 21, 10 Churchill Square, Kings Hill, West Malling, Kent, ME19 4YU
Officers: Tracey Town [1962] Director

Cumbrae Supply Company Limited
Incorporated: 7 March 2006 *Employees:* 4
Net Worth: £34,336 *Total Assets:* £445,215
Registered Office: Houston House, 95 Wright Street, Renfrew, PA4 8AN
Major Shareholder: Jane Victoria MacDuff
Officers: Jane Victoria MacDuff, Secretary/Wholesaler; Jane Victoria MacDuff [1952] Director/Wholesaler

The Curious Wine Cellar Limited
Incorporated: 14 March 2013
Net Worth Deficit: £22,655 *Total Assets:* £3,542
Registered Office: Summer House, Meadow Court, Northleach, Cheltenham, Glos, GL54 3EP
Officers: Alan Charles Richell [1959] Director; Andrea Jane Richell [1968] Director; Annabel Mary Savage [1951] Director; Mark Savage [1949] Director

Cut Rum Limited
Incorporated: 12 January 2016 *Employees:* 2
Net Worth Deficit: £107,047 *Total Assets:* £20,211
Registered Office: 41 Great Portland Street, London, W1W 7LA
Parent: Proof Drinks Limited
Officers: Paul Ferguson [1981] Director; James McDermott [1977] Director

Cuvee Cavalier Limited
Incorporated: 22 November 2016
Net Worth Deficit: £684
Registered Office: 1st Floor, Chilworth Point, 1 Chilworth Road, Southampton, SO16 7JQ
Parent: The BCIP Group Limited
Officers: Betty Tanner, Secretary; Ioana Journoux [1978] Director; Betty Tanner [1957] Director

Cyprian Services Limited
Incorporated: 25 January 2018
Registered Office: 52 Ridgeway Road, Tipton, W Midlands, DY4 0TU
Officers: Cyprian Henryk Kazimierski [1984] Director [Polish]

Czech Beer Alliance Limited
Incorporated: 11 October 2018
Registered Office: Lower Ground Floor, 40 Bloomsbury Way, London, WC1A 2SE
Parent: CMP Venture Limited
Officers: Dr Filip Celadnik [1984] Director [Czech]

D & F Inns Ltd
Incorporated: 16 August 2018
Registered Office: 194 London Road, Hazel Grove, Stockport, Cheshire, SK7 4DQ
Shareholders: Danielle Lisa Tuite; Finbarr Andrew Tuite
Officers: Danielle Lisa Tuite [1988] Director; Finbarr Andrew Tuite [1973] Director [Irish]

D & F Wines Ltd
Incorporated: 31 January 2018
Registered Office: 4 Belle Vue Road, Kelso Heights, Leeds, LS3 1HN
Shareholder: Diego Izquierdo Cervantes
Officers: Diego Izquierdo Cervantes [1989] Director [Spanish]

D & K Capital Ltd
Incorporated: 15 March 2016
Net Worth Deficit: £8,086 *Total Assets:* £9,591
Registered Office: 46 Nova Road, Croydon, Surrey, CR0 2TL
Shareholder: Pallone Umberto
Officers: Umberto Pallone [1972] Director/Consultant [Italian]; Antonio Saracino [1981] Director/Consultant [Italian]

D & N Supplies Limited
Incorporated: 1 October 2018
Registered Office: 10 Craigton Road, London, SE9 1QF
Shareholders: Dipakkumar Babubhai Patel; Nalinaben Dipakkumar Patel
Officers: Dipakkumar Babubhai Patel [1957] Director; Nalinaben Dipakkumar Patel [1958] Director

D & V Wines Ltd
Incorporated: 23 May 2016
Net Worth: £29,608 *Total Assets:* £80,048
Registered Office: Warehouse K, Western Gateway, London, E16 1DR
Major Shareholder: John D'Ell Ross
Officers: John D'Ell Ross [1970] Director

D D S Food Imports Ltd
Incorporated: 7 June 1999
Net Worth Deficit: £35,443 *Total Assets:* £44,892
Registered Office: Raydean House, Western Parade, Great North Road, New Barnet, Barnet, Herts, EN5 1AH
Shareholders: Michele Brazza; Eleonora Brazza
Officers: Michele Brazza [1960] Director [Italian]

D K Beers Ltd.
Incorporated: 23 March 2016
Net Worth: £7,749 *Total Assets:* £28,132
Registered Office: 72 Overdale Road, Birmingham, B32 2QR
Major Shareholder: Dharnpal Khosla
Officers: Dharnpal Khosla [1965] Director

D K International (UK) Limited
Incorporated: 11 October 2013 *Employees:* 2
Net Worth: £1,979 *Total Assets:* £428,507
Registered Office: Colombo House, Colombo Street, Derby, DE23 8LW
Shareholders: Arjan Maldev Kana; Jake Kotecha
Officers: Arjan Maldev Kana [1977] Director/Salesman

D'Arcy Wine Merchants Limited
Incorporated: 8 November 2006 *Employees:* 2
Net Worth Deficit: £65,475 *Total Assets:* £464,565
Registered Office: 2 Lypiatt Terrace, Cheltenham, Glos, GL50 2SX
Shareholders: Ranulf Peter Middleton; Sanc Enterprises Ltd
Officers: Nigel David Cowan, Secretary; Ranulf Peter Middleton [1959] Director/Art Publisher

D'Urberville Vineyard Limited
Incorporated: 23 November 2016 *Employees:* 1
Net Worth: £1 *Total Assets:* £42,492
Registered Office: Mary Street House, Mary Street, Taunton, Somerset, TA1 3NW
Major Shareholder: Colin Charles Hawkins
Officers: Colin Charles Hawkins [1950] Director/Agriculture

D.C Enterprises (Import/Export) Limited
Incorporated: 3 July 1997
Net Worth Deficit: £44,136 *Total Assets:* £1
Registered Office: The Mews, St Nicholas Lane, Lewes, E Sussex, BN7 2JZ
Major Shareholder: Damon Deans Cane
Officers: Damon Deans Cane, Secretary; Damon Deans Cane [1972] Director; Yazmin Deans-Cane [1972] Director/Jeweller [Mexican]

D.Rock Champagne Ltd
Incorporated: 26 November 2018
Registered Office: Unit 2a The Connaught Business Centre, 22 Willow Lane, London, CR4 4NA
Major Shareholder: Mariyan Stoykov Stoykov
Officers: Mariyan Stoykov Stoykov [1981] Director [Bulgarian]

Da Vinci Finest Italian Products Limited
Incorporated: 12 April 2017
Net Worth: £100 *Total Assets:* £100
Registered Office: The Stable Yard, Vicarage Road, Stony Stratford, Milton Keynes, Bucks, MK11 1BN
Major Shareholder: Antonino Impera
Officers: Antonino Impera [1991] Director [Italian]; Mark Rhsk Lloyd [1988] Director

Da Vinci Traders Ltd
Incorporated: 11 September 2015
Net Worth Deficit: £43,237 *Total Assets:* £8,398
Registered Office: The Cabin, Leafy Lane, Gravesend, Kent, DA13 0DR
Major Shareholder: James Bolton
Officers: James Stacey Bolton [1981] Director/Business Owner

Da'mos Food & Beverages Limited
Incorporated: 23 September 2016
Net Worth Deficit: £633 *Total Assets:* £6,230
Registered Office: 61a Grays Place, Slough, Berks, SL2 5AF
Shareholders: Joanne Nicola Moseley; Da'mos Management Ltd
Officers: Joanne Nicola Moseley [1985] Director/Technical Coordinator

Dacastello Limited
Incorporated: 25 June 2013
Registered Office: 124 Churchill Road, Bicester, Oxon, OX26 4XD
Major Shareholder: Julian Paul Gardner
Officers: Julian Paul Gardner [1967] Director/Electronics Engineer

Dago Wines Ltd
Incorporated: 4 May 2012
Net Worth: £29,456 *Total Assets:* £140,752
Registered Office: 355a Barking Road, London, E6 1LA
Major Shareholder: Lucia Bonadies
Officers: Lucia Bonadies [1968] Director/Businesswoman [Italian]; Eugenio Ciccarelli [1971] Director/Wine Specialist [Italian]; Philippe Sylvian Christian Polleux [1981] Director/Restaurant Manager [French]; Jonathan Stevens [1970] Wine Regional Director Europe Vina Errazuriz

Dallyla Ltd
Incorporated: 9 October 2017
Registered Office: 357 Green Lane, Ilford, Essex, IG3 9TQ
Major Shareholder: Elena Glavana
Officers: Elena Glavana [1978] Director [Romanian]

Dalmunach Distillery Limited
Incorporated: 17 August 2001
Previous: Chivas Brothers (Europe) Limited
Registered Office: 111-113 Renfrew Road, Paisley, Renfrewshire, PA3 4DY
Parent: Chivas Holdings (IP) Limited
Officers: Stuart MacNab [1964] Director/Accountant; Vincent Turpin [1978] Director/Chief Financial Officer [French]

The Danish Snaps Company Ltd
Incorporated: 3 January 2018
Registered Office: 93 Golborne Road, London, W10 5NL
Shareholders: Jacqueline Skott; Kell Skott
Officers: Jacqueline Skott [1968] Director; Kell Skott [1965] Director [Danish]

Dankan Ltd
Incorporated: 11 May 2015
Net Worth: £2 *Total Assets:* £2
Registered Office: 35 St Clairs Road, Croydon, Surrey, CR0 5NE
Shareholders: Elisa Massaiu; Daniele Massaiu
Officers: Daniele Massaiu [1983] Director [Italian]

Danyal Ltd
Incorporated: 17 November 2009
Net Worth: £517 *Total Assets:* £2,811
Registered Office: 17 Green Lanes, London, N16 9BS
Major Shareholder: Tolga Serkan Danyal
Officers: Tolga Serkan Danyal [1979] Director/Tourism [Turkish]

Dark Revolution Ltd
Incorporated: 22 January 2015 *Employees:* 1
Net Worth: £11,331 *Total Assets:* £60,015
Registered Office: Unit 9 Lancaster Road, Sarum Business Park, Salisbury, Wilts, SP4 6FB
Shareholders: Gregory Hughes; Tanya Hughes
Officers: Gregory Hughes [1973] Director; Tanya Hughes [1974] Director

Darlaston Drink Shop Limited
Incorporated: 6 February 2019
Registered Office: Trilogy Suite, 9 Church Street, Wednesfield, Wolverhampton, W Midlands, WV11 1SR
Major Shareholder: Alap Madhusudan Bhausar
Officers: Alap Madhusudan Alap Madhusudan Bhausar [1981] Director [Indian]

Darley Abbey Wines Limited
Incorporated: 27 March 2017
Registered Office: c/o UHY Hacker Young, 6 Broadfield Court, Broadfield Way, Sheffield, S8 0XF
Major Shareholder: Andrew Malia Barlow
Officers: Andrew Malia Barlow [1977] Director; Nichol Malia Barlow [1982] Director

Dave and Dani Ltd
Incorporated: 15 March 2018
Registered Office: 57 Stroud Green Road, Finsbury Park, London, N4 3EG
Major Shareholder: Daniel Emanuel
Officers: Daniel Emanuel [1977] Director

Davenport Vineyards Limited
Incorporated: 27 June 2017
Registered Office: Limney Farm, Castle Hill, Rotherfield, E Sussex, TN6 3RR
Shareholders: Louisa Kate Arabella Belli; William Talbot John Davenport
Officers: Louisa Kate Arabella Belli [1969] Sales Director; William Talbot John Davenport [1964] Director/Winemaker; Philip Lewis Harris [1982] Director/Vineyard Manager

Daves Drinks Ltd
Incorporated: 7 June 2018
Registered Office: 81 Valiant House, Charlton, London, SE7 8BE
Major Shareholder: David Blackwood
Officers: David Blackwood, Secretary; David Blackwood [1983] Director

Davy & Company Limited
Incorporated: 13 June 1913 *Employees:* 47
Net Worth: £17,061,768 *Total Assets:* £19,024,476
Registered Office: 161-165 Greenwich High Road, London, SE10 8JA
Parent: Davy & Company (1997) Ltd
Officers: Noel Ramsden, Secretary; Nigel James Bunting [1967] Director; Andrew Chudley [1977] Director; James Richard John Davy [1967] Director; John Sydney Victor Davy [1930] Director/Free Vintner; Noel Ramsden [1955] Director

Dayboat Limited
Incorporated: 10 February 2017
Net Worth: £11,798 *Total Assets:* £12,689
Registered Office: 10 Hyde Place, Canterbury, Kent, CT3 3AL
Officers: Oliver Nicholas Leon [1988] Director

Daysh Beers Wines & Spirits Ltd
Incorporated: 16 July 2018
Registered Office: 231-233 Lower Hillmorton Road, Rugby, Warwicks, CV21 4AA
Major Shareholder: Simon Richard Daysh
Officers: Simon Richard Daysh [1985] Director/Shop Assistant

DBM Wines Limited
Incorporated: 15 February 2018
Registered Office: Spencer House, 6 Morston Court, Aisecombe Way, Weston-Super-Mare, Somerset, BS22 8NA
Major Shareholder: Richard Alan Davis
Officers: Richard Alan Davis [1965] Director/Wine Merchant

DC Cash and Carry Ltd
Incorporated: 8 September 2017
Registered Office: 61 Oakfield Road, Balsall Heath, Birmingham, B12 9PX
Major Shareholder: Narinder Singh Dosanjh
Officers: Narinder Singh Dosanjh [1989] Marketing Director

DC Imports UK Ltd
Incorporated: 9 January 2017
Net Worth Deficit: £5,359 *Total Assets:* £2,937
Registered Office: Abbeyfields, Back Lane, Castle Acre, Norfolk, PE32 2AR
Shareholders: Catherine Jill Frost; David Lawrence Nicholson
Officers: David Lawrence Nicholson, Secretary; Catherine Jill Frost [1961] Director; David Lawrence Nicholson [1957] Director

DC Wine Merchant Ltd
Incorporated: 21 August 2017
Registered Office: Flat 3, 98 Rope Street, London, SE16 7TQ
Officers: Dipansh Chopra [1986] Director [Indian]

DCFT Investments Ltd.
Incorporated: 11 June 2010
Previous: Modern Vintage Wines Ltd
Registered Office: 6 Malvern House, 1a Liverpool Grove, London, SE17 2JJ
Major Shareholder: Donald Wayne Howes
Officers: Donald Howes, Secretary; Donald Wayne Howes [1952] Director

De Burgh Fine Wine Limited
Incorporated: 22 October 2012 *Employees:* 6
Net Worth: £205,442 *Total Assets:* £697,403
Registered Office: Fordel Mains Steading, Dalkeith, Midlothian, EH22 2PQ
Major Shareholder: Tarquin de Burgh
Officers: Tarquin Rohan de Burgh [1970] Director; William Alexander Nicolson [1978] Director

De Christ Wines Ltd
Incorporated: 11 June 2014
Net Worth Deficit: £40,652 *Total Assets:* £2,040
Registered Office: 32 Layard Square, London, SE16 2JE
Major Shareholder: Franck Elvis N'Dolykhan Thierry Assemian
Officers: N'dolykhan Franck Elvis Thierry Assemian [1972] Director/Chief Executive Officer

De Facto Spirits Limited
Incorporated: 24 July 2018
Registered Office: Anderson House, 24 Rose Street, Aberdeen, AB10 1UA
Major Shareholder: Stuart Beange Duncan
Officers: Stuart Beange Duncan [1949] Director/Property Developer

De Paolis Limited
Incorporated: 30 September 2016 *Employees:* 1
Net Worth: £29,503 *Total Assets:* £266,613
Registered Office: Ryefield Court, 81 Joel Street, Northwood Hills, Northwood, Middlesex, HA6 1LL
Shareholders: Francesca Amanda de Paolis; Susie de Paolis
Officers: Lady Susan Blanche Louise Anglesey [1950] Director; Francesca Amanda de Paolis [1982] Director

De Wetshof International Limited
Incorporated: 20 February 2002
Registered Office: Munro House, Portsmouth Road, Cobham, Surrey, KT11 1PP
Shareholders: Danie de Wet; Daniel Jacobus Johannes de Wet; Lesca de Wet; Pieter Janz Dekema de Wet
Officers: Danie de Wet [1949] Director/Farmer [South African]; Lesca de Wet [1950] Director/Marketing [South African]; Kevin Patrick Gallagher [1944] Director/Accountant [Irish]

De-Laceys Tipples Limited
Incorporated: 7 November 2018
Registered Office: First Floor Office, 28 High Street, Shepton Mallet, Somerset, BA4 5AN
Major Shareholder: Helen Naomi Lacey
Officers: Helen Naomi Lacey [1975] Director

Decanter Trading Company Limited
Incorporated: 21 January 2000
Net Worth Deficit: £24,409 *Total Assets:* £15,115
Registered Office: 2b Maryport Street, Usk, Gwent, NP15 1AB
Major Shareholder: Mario Giolino
Officers: Mario Giolino [1958] Director/Wine Trader [Italian]

Decanter Wines Limited
Incorporated: 3 February 2003
Net Worth Deficit: £30,206 *Total Assets:* £53,185
Registered Office: Little Porch, Yarm Way, Leatherhead, Surrey, KT22 8RQ
Shareholders: James Peter Monks; Krystyna Bernadette Monks
Officers: Krystyna Bernadette Monks, Secretary; James Peter Monks [1956] Director; Krystyna Bernadette Monks [1956] Director

Deceptive Wines Limited
Incorporated: 20 February 2016
Registered Office: Chilcomb Manor, Chilcomb, Winchester, Hants, SO21 1HR
Shareholders: Alan John Morgan; Lorraine Claire Morgan
Officers: Lorraine Claire Morgan, Secretary; Alan John Morgan [1958] Director/Chartered Accountant; Lorraine Claire Morgan [1960] Director/Housewife

Deckers Restaurants Limited
Incorporated: 3 November 1987 *Employees:* 32
Net Worth: £2,648,640 *Total Assets:* £9,034,201
Registered Office: Unit F, Royle Pennine Trading Estate, Lynroyle Way, Rochdale, Lancs, OL11 3EX
Parent: Deckers Hospitality Group Ltd
Officers: Victoria Cosgrove, Secretary; Clifford Brierley [1950] Director/Restaurateur; Maxwell James Brierly [1974] Director/Hotelier; Andrew Waller [1960] Managing Director

Deco Spirits Limited
Incorporated: 26 July 2017
Registered Office: 55-57 High Street, Metheringham, Lincoln, LN4 3DZ
Shareholders: Samantha Ann Jones; Amy Jayne Havenhand
Officers: Amy Jayne Havenhand [1982] Director; Samantha Ann Jones [1985] Director

Decorum Vintners Limited
Incorporated: 29 July 1999 *Employees:* 5
Net Worth: £748,220 *Total Assets:* £1,132,594
Registered Office: Unit 1 Shaftesbury Centre, 85 Barlby Road, London, W10 6BN
Shareholders: Rupert Henry Monier-Williams; Mark James Lloyd Roberts
Officers: Rupert Henry Monier Williams, Secretary; Rupert Henry Monier Williams [1965] Director/Wine Merchant; Mark James Lloyd Roberts [1964] Director/Wine Merchant

Dedicated Wine Importers Limited
Incorporated: 13 January 1992
Net Worth: £763 *Total Assets:* £3,177
Registered Office: The Dairy, Manor Farm, Toot Baldon, Oxford, OX44 9NG
Shareholders: Christopher John Neville Lake; Jacqueline Maria Lake
Officers: Jacqueline Maria Lake, Secretary/Wine Importer; Christopher John Neville Lake [1954] Director

Dedicated Wines Ltd
Incorporated: 11 June 2005 *Employees:* 3
Net Worth: £684,523 *Total Assets:* £1,180,842
Registered Office: Unit 7 Hall Farm, High Street, South Moreton, Didcot, Oxon, OX11 9AG
Shareholders: Richard Neville Lewis Evans; Edward John Heskett Squires
Officers: Richard Neville Lewis Evans [1951] Director; Edward John Heskett Squires [1960] Director

Deer & Badger Ltd
Incorporated: 1 March 2018
Registered Office: 105 Church Road, Richmond, Surrey, TW10 6LS
Major Shareholder: Mario Tomekovic
Officers: Andrej Kustro [1993] Director/Chef [Croatian]; Mario Tomekovic [1984] Director/Sommelier [Croatian]

Deeti Wholesale Limited
Incorporated: 4 March 2015
Net Worth: £1,422 *Total Assets:* £16,136
Registered Office: Area A23, 7-11 Minerva Road, Park Royal, London, NW10 6HJ
Major Shareholder: Maulikkumar Ashokbhai Patel
Officers: Maulikkumar Ashokbhai Patel [1980] Director

DEF Investments Limited
Incorporated: 12 March 1892
Net Worth: £882,522 *Total Assets:* £885,686
Registered Office: Lakeside Drive, Park Royal, London, NW10 7HQ
Parent: Diageo Overseas Holdings Limited
Officers: James Matthew Crayden Edmunds [1974] Director/Solicitor; Kara Elizabeth Major [1977] Director [American]; Vinod Rao [1962] Director [Indian]; Prabhaharan Viswanathan [1972] Director [Australian]

Dega Trading Ltd
Incorporated: 5 October 2018
Registered Office: 783 Tottenham High Road, London, N17 8AH
Major Shareholder: Mert Can
Officers: Mert Can [1985] Director [Portuguese]

Deholjob Limited
Incorporated: 18 November 2003 *Employees:* 2
Net Worth: £8,538 *Total Assets:* £28,020
Registered Office: 19 Woodside Lane, Bexley, Kent, DA5 1JL
Major Shareholder: Folarin Olaopa
Officers: Olubunmi Olaopa, Secretary; Folarin Olaopa [1979] Director

Del Professore Limited
Incorporated: 23 March 2015 *Employees:* 1
Net Worth: £472,632 *Total Assets:* £764,753
Registered Office: 17 Grosvenor Street, Mayfair, London, W1K 4QG
Parent: Diageo DV Limited
Officers: Leonardo Leuci [1976] Director/Entrepreneur [Italian]; Dhruv Luthra [1977] Director; Carlo Quaglia [1971] Director [Italian]

Delage & Haughton Limited
Incorporated: 8 May 2018
Registered Office: 2 St Andrews Place, Lewes, E Sussex, BN7 1UP
Officers: Jaime Delage [1986] Director/Importer [Spanish]; Georgina Ruth Haughton [1986] Director; Thomas Patrick Haughton [1986] Director

Delbrew Ltd
Incorporated: 6 November 2018
Registered Office: Companies House, Default Address, Cardiff, CF14 8LH
Major Shareholder: Khorshed Mohamad
Officers: Khorshed Mohamad [1984] Director/General Manager [Syrian]

Delbroo Ltd
Incorporated: 20 November 2018
Registered Office: 2nd Floor, College House, 17 King Edwards Road, Ruislip, Middlesex, HA4 7AE
Major Shareholder: Khorshed Mohamad
Officers: Khorshed Mohamad [1984] Director [Syrian]

Delecta Limited
Incorporated: 1 March 2010
Net Worth Deficit: £3,327 *Total Assets:* £4,122
Registered Office: 180 Addison Road, Enfield, Middlesex, EN3 5LE
Major Shareholder: Aristides Kaizer
Officers: Aristides Kaizer [1952] Director

Delegat Europe Limited
Incorporated: 11 March 1998 *Employees:* 12
Net Worth: £2,203,058 *Total Assets:* £6,925,916
Registered Office: 4th Floor, 27-29 Cursitor Street, London, EC4A 1LT
Officers: Robert Lawrence Wilton, Secretary; Jakov Nikola Delegat [1949] Managing Director [New Zealander]; John Anthony Freeman [1974] Managing Director [Canadian]; Robert Lawrence Wilton [1943] Director/University Lecturer [Australian]

Delicatezze Siciliane Limited
Incorporated: 25 October 2017
Registered Office: 102 London Road, High Wycombe, Bucks, HP11 1DB
Major Shareholder: Harpreet Saini
Officers: Harpreet Saini [1993] Director [Italian]

Delicious Drinks Limited
Incorporated: 16 May 2018
Registered Office: 18 Lynedoch Crescent, Glasgow, G3 6EQ
Shareholders: Christopher George Leggat; Caraline Sara Leggat
Officers: Caraline Sara Leggat [1982] Director; Christopher George Leggat [1981] Director

Deliverance Dot Com Limited
Incorporated: 16 November 2009
Net Worth: £371 *Total Assets:* £36,864
Registered Office: 1 Glenburn Road, East Kilbride, S Lanarks, G74 5BA
Major Shareholder: Henry Allan Cunningham
Officers: Henry Allan Cunningham, Secretary; Henry Allan Cunningham [1955] Director/Consultant; Graeme Nigel Harrowell [1957] Director

Delivered Drinks Limited
Incorporated: 18 October 2010
Registered Office: 2 Redwood Avenue, Peel Park, East Kilbride, S Lanarks, G74 5PE
Major Shareholder: Henry Allan Cunningham
Officers: Henry Allan Cunningham [1955] Director

Delivering Happiness Limited
Incorporated: 21 November 2016 *Employees:* 2
Net Worth: £335 *Total Assets:* £17,188
Registered Office: Kemp House, 160 City Road, London, EC1V 2NX
Shareholders: Joe Revell; Olivier Santiago Navarro
Officers: Olivier Santiago Navarro [1977] Director/Entrepreneur [Irish]; Joe Revell [1987] Director/Entrepreneur

Delivery Offlicence Ltd
Incorporated: 23 May 2018
Registered Office: 55 Brooms Road, Luton, Beds, LU2 0JR
Major Shareholder: Shan Ali
Officers: Shan Ali [1984] Director

Delta Western Distributions Ltd
Incorporated: 22 December 2016
Registered Office: 75a Odsal Road, Bradford, BD6 1PN
Shareholders: Ogheneochuko Odudu; Delta Western Ltd
Officers: Ogheneochuko Odudu [1980] Director

Delta World Trading Limited
Incorporated: 20 June 2017
Registered Office: Suite 5, 39-41 Chase Side, Southgate, London, N14 5BP
Major Shareholder: Myat Min San
Officers: Myat Min San [1991] Director/Civil Engineer

Deluxe Wines Limited
Incorporated: 2 February 2016
Registered Office: 3 Lloyd Road, Station Gates, Broadstairs, Kent, CT10 1HY
Major Shareholder: Michael James Curtis
Officers: Michael James Curtis [1981] Director

Demball Limited
Incorporated: 6 October 1988 *Employees:* 2
Net Worth: £2,078,421 *Total Assets:* £2,080,221
Registered Office: c/o Finance Associates, 65 London Wall, London, EC2M 5TU
Parent: The Nikka Whisky Distilling Co., Ltd.
Officers: Taketoshi Kishimoto [1959] Managing Director [Japanese]; Yoshisuke Motojima [1964] Director/Office Worker [Japanese]

Demon Vodka Limited
Incorporated: 28 November 2017
Registered Office: 16 Radford Crescent, Billericay, Essex, CM12 0DG
Major Shareholder: Philip Andrew Notley
Officers: Philip Andrew Notley [1967] Managing Director

Denby Dale Wines Limited
Incorporated: 19 April 2006 *Employees:* 1
Net Worth: £9,819 *Total Assets:* £60,626
Registered Office: 41 Darton Road, Cawthorne, Barnsley, S Yorks, S75 4HY
Major Shareholder: Denise Mary Padgett
Officers: Phillip Padgett, Secretary; Denise Mary Padgett [1956] Director; Phillip Padgett [1956] Director

Deniz & Ada Limited
Incorporated: 7 June 2016 *Employees:* 1
Net Worth Deficit: £1,682 *Total Assets:* £18,984
Registered Office: 25 Copse Hill, Brighton, BN1 5GA
Major Shareholder: Agata Yolay
Officers: Ismail Yolay [1977] Director/Wine Merchant [Turkish]

Dennhofer Wines Limited
Incorporated: 18 October 1976 *Employees:* 10
Net Worth: £82,163 *Total Assets:* £335,021
Registered Office: The Rookery, Newton, Stocksfield, Northumberland, NE43 7UN
Major Shareholder: Heinz Dennhofer
Officers: Heinz Dennhofer, Secretary [German]; Heinz Dennhofer [1946] Director [German]; Maire Caithlin Dennhofer [1948] Director [Irish]

Rodney Densem Wines Limited
Incorporated: 14 July 2017
Registered Office: 7-9 Macon Court, Crewe, Cheshire, CW1 6EA
Major Shareholder: Simon Densem
Officers: Simon Densem [1972] Director; Steven Edmund Leonard [1968] Director

Deshi Bazar Ltd
Incorporated: 5 March 2018
Registered Office: 12 Meldon Road, Manchester, M13 0TZ
Major Shareholder: A T M Humaun Kabir
Officers: Mamun Ahmed [1973] Director/Manager; A T M Humaun Kabir [1978] Director

Desi Wines Ltd
Incorporated: 23 April 2018
Registered Office: 20-22 Wenlock Road, London, N1 7GU
Major Shareholder: Sunny Jassal
Officers: Sunny Jassal [1975] Director

Desideria Ltd
Incorporated: 18 October 2017
Registered Office: 9 Seagrave Road, London, SW6 1RP
Officers: Cristiano Ariu [1980] Director/Building Contractor [Italian]; Riccardo Steri [1973] Director/Entrepreneur [Italian]

Desirable Drinks Ltd
Incorporated: 11 February 2019
Registered Office: 151 Priory Road, Hall Green, Birmingham, B28 0SX
Major Shareholder: Iindeya Shabay Campbell
Officers: Iindeya Shabay Campbell [1989] Director; Abdon Laing [1982] Director

Deskbeers Limited
Incorporated: 14 October 2014 *Employees:* 2
Net Worth: £12,364 *Total Assets:* £38,619
Registered Office: 20 Allens Road, Southsea, Hants, PO4 0QB
Officers: Timothy James Morgan [1976] Director; Adam Rogers [1983] Director/Developer

Destilado London Limited
Incorporated: 14 May 2018
Registered Office: Unit P18, Bow Wharf, 221 Grove Road, London, E3 5SN
Shareholders: Alexander Michael Wolpert; Michael Sager
Officers: Marcis Alfred Dzelzainis [1982] Director; Trowbridge George McKay [1983] Director; Michael Sager [1983] Director [Swiss]; Alexander Michael Wolpert [1982] Director

Deutsches Beer Limited
Incorporated: 4 September 2014
Registered Office: 29 York Place, Edinburgh, EH1 3HP
Major Shareholder: Colin Makin
Officers: Colin Makin [1962] Director

Deutsches Bier Limited
Incorporated: 1 September 2014
Registered Office: 29 York Place, Edinburgh, EH1 3HP
Major Shareholder: Colin Makin
Officers: Colin Makin [1962] Director

Deutschlond Brewery Limited
Incorporated: 14 February 2018
Registered Office: 71-75 Shelton Street, Covent Garden, London, WC2H 9JQ
Major Shareholder: Marc-Oliver Lesch
Officers: Marc-Oliver Lesch [1984] Director [German]

Devine Distillates Group Limited
Incorporated: 5 June 2015 *Employees:* 1
Net Worth: £10,259 *Total Assets:* £294,420
Registered Office: Mercury House, Shipstones Business Centre, North Gate, Nottingham, NG7 7FN
Shareholder: Peter Joseph Robson
Officers: Peter Robson [1959] Director

Dew Hill Blending Company (Glasgow) Limited
Incorporated: 21 August 1958
Net Worth: £14,625 *Total Assets:* £14,662
Registered Office: Allan House, 25 Bothwell Street, Glasgow, G2 6NL
Parent: Herman Jansen Beverages International B.V.
Officers: Herman Diederik Jansen, Secretary; Henricus Theodorus Franciscus Jansen [1953] Director [Dutch]; Herman Diederik Jansen [1986] Export Director [Dutch]

John Dewar and Sons Limited
Incorporated: 24 October 1958 *Employees:* 356
Net Worth: £188,070,000 *Total Assets:* £537,265,024
Registered Office: c/o Bacardi-Martini Limited, Bacardi Brown-Forman House, Kings Worthy, Winchester, Hants, SO23 7TW
Parent: Bacardi U.K. Limited
Officers: Jean Marc Lambert [1965] Director, Supply Chain and Manufacturing [French]; Iain MacGregor Lochhead [1962] Director/Executive; Ian Stuart Lowthian [1959] Chairman/Global Technical Director; Matthew James Phillips [1983] Finance Director; Paolo Camillo Tucci [1963] Finance Director

A. Dewar Rattray Limited
Incorporated: 23 May 1939 *Employees:* 8
Net Worth: £615,532 *Total Assets:* £1,241,716
Registered Office: 32 Main Road, Kirkoswald, Maybole, S Ayrshire, KA19 8HY
Shareholders: Stanley Walker Morrison; Stanley Andrew Morrison
Officers: Nicholas John White, Secretary; Frances Dupuy [1957] Commercial Operations Director; Margaret Edith Morrison [1939] Director; Stanley Andrew Morrison [1977] Director of International Marketing and Sales; Stanley Walker Morrison [1941] Director/Whisky Broker; Nicholas John White [1966] Managing Director

DFG Distribution Ltd
Incorporated: 11 May 2016
Net Worth: £14,007 *Total Assets:* £37,614
Registered Office: 483 Green Lanes, London, N13 4BS
Major Shareholder: Xingrong Li
Officers: Xingrong Li [1984] Director [Chinese]

DGB Europe Limited
Incorporated: 21 October 2005 *Employees:* 7
Net Worth: £2,298,659 *Total Assets:* £4,039,832
Registered Office: Suite 216, 99 Park Drive, Milton Park, Milton, Abingdon, Oxon, OX14 4RY
Parent: DGB Pty Ltd
Officers: Henk Van Der Westhuyzen, Secretary; Garreth William Anderson [1964] Managing Director; Timothy Randolph Hutchinson [1951] Managing Director [South African]

DH Global Wine Ltd
Incorporated: 10 September 2007
Net Worth: £13,334 *Total Assets:* £283,207
Registered Office: 266-268 Wickham Road, Shirley, Croydon, Surrey, CR0 8BJ
Shareholders: Fuji Deng; Ruifen Huo
Officers: Ruifen Huo, Secretary/Wine Trade; Fuji Deng [1973] Director/Wine Trade

Dhamecha Foods Limited
Incorporated: 20 March 1974 *Employees:* 628
Net Worth: £76,463,000 *Total Assets:* £188,968,992
Registered Office: 2 Hathaway Close, Stanmore, Middlesex, HA7 3NR
Parent: Dhamecha Group Limited
Officers: Mukesh Manilal Vithlani, Secretary; Khodidas Ratanshi Dhamecha [1930] Director; Shantilal Ratanshi Dhamecha [1931] Director; Jitendra Patel [1959] Director

Dhesis Wholesale Ltd
Incorporated: 5 May 2005 *Employees:* 6
Net Worth: £20,475 *Total Assets:* £249,404
Registered Office: 164 Bedford Road, Kempston, Bedford, MK42 8BH
Shareholder: Gurdawar Singh Dhesi
Officers: Gurbinder Singh Dhesi, Secretary; Gurdawar Singh Dhesi [1958] Director/Wholesaler

Di Vine Importers Limited
Incorporated: 13 August 1999 *Employees:* 25
Net Worth: £1,590,664 *Total Assets:* £2,828,842
Registered Office: Unit A4, Springhead Enterprise Park, Northfleet, Gravesend, Kent, DA11 8HB
Major Shareholder: Felice Evola
Officers: Felice Evola [1956] Director [Italian]; Michael Francesco Evola [1988] Director/Food & Wine Importer

Di.Wine Limited
Incorporated: 14 November 2014
Net Worth Deficit: £6,867 *Total Assets:* £846
Registered Office: 147a Barking Road, East Ham, London, E6 1LD
Shareholders: Diletta Paoletti; Flavia Paoletti
Officers: Diletta Paoletti [1989] Director [Italian]; Flavia Paoletti [1987] Director [Italian]

Diabolus Limited
Incorporated: 20 June 2014 *Employees:* 2
Net Worth Deficit: £142,102 *Total Assets:* £65,385
Registered Office: 1623 Warwick Road, Knowle, Solihull, W Midlands, B93 9LF
Major Shareholder: James John Taylor
Officers: James John Taylor [1977] Director

Diageo Global Supply IBC Limited
Incorporated: 3 December 1951 *Employees:* 145
Net Worth: £19,762,000 *Total Assets:* £35,549,000
Registered Office: Third Floor, Capital House, 3 Upper Queen Street, Belfast, BT1 6QD
Officers: Aedin Kenealy, Secretary; Alyson Donaldson [1983] Finance Director; David Varian [1961] Director [Irish]

Diageo Great Britain Limited
Incorporated: 5 May 1952 *Employees:* 1,238
Net Worth: £2,988,000,000 *Total Assets:* £3,436,999,936
Registered Office: Lakeside Drive, Park Royal, London, NW10 7HQ
Parent: Grand Metropolitan Limited
Officers: Gavin Paul Crickmore [1958] Director/Chartered Accountant; James Matthew Crayden Edmunds [1974] Director/Solicitor; Sharon Lynnette Fennessy [1967] Director/Group Treasurer [Irish]; Kerryn Louise Haynes [1970] Director/Accountant; David Heginbottom [1970] Director/Group Treasurer; Hina Patel [1979] Director/Company Secretary Senior Assistant; Gabor Zeisler [1973] Director/General Manager [Hungarian]

Diageo Northern Ireland Limited
Incorporated: 24 September 1956 *Employees:* 136
Net Worth: £14,018,000 *Total Assets:* £38,528,000
Registered Office: Third Floor, Capital House, 3 Upper Queen Street, Belfast, BT1 6QD
Officers: Aedin Kenealy, Secretary; Rory Cowan [1979] Director/Accountant [Irish]; Kieran Gowing [1965] Director/Accountant [Irish]

Diageo United Kingdom Limited
Incorporated: 28 January 1956
Registered Office: Lakeside Drive, Park Royal, London, NW10 7HQ
Parent: Diageo Great Britain Limited
Officers: James Matthew Crayden Edmunds [1974] Director/Solicitor; Gabor Kovacs [1980] Director [Hungarian]; Kara Elizabeth Major [1977] Director [American]

Diamond Aces Limited
Incorporated: 9 February 2018
Registered Office: 211 Station Road, Harrow, Middlesex, HA1 2TP
Officers: Sunil Singh [1993] Director/Manager

Diamond Stag Importers Ltd.
Incorporated: 10 July 2014
Net Worth Deficit: £2,419
Registered Office: 16 Pocklington Close, Colindale, London, NW9 5WS
Major Shareholder: Richard Sanat Shah
Officers: Richard Sanat Shah [1995] Director/Chief Operating Officer

Diamonds & Pearl Trading Limited
Incorporated: 21 October 2014
Net Worth: £53,330 *Total Assets:* £82,428
Registered Office: 9 West Lodge Road, Colchester, Essex, CO3 3NL
Major Shareholder: Marcin Rafal Kotomski
Officers: Marcin Rafal Kotomski [1979] Director/Interior Designer [Polish]; Radoslaw Kotomski [1974] Managing Director [Polish]

F.L. Dickins Limited
Incorporated: 7 October 1949 *Employees:* 3
Net Worth: £53,169 *Total Assets:* £89,707
Registered Office: 89-91 High Street, Rickmansworth, Herts, WD3 1EF
Shareholders: Alison Jane Love; Karen Elizabeth Holloway
Officers: Betty Alma Dickins, Secretary; Betty Alma Dickins [1935] Director/Company Secretary; Karen Elizabeth Holloway [1961] Director; Alison Jane Love [1965] Director

Different Wines Limited
Incorporated: 22 January 2015
Net Worth Deficit: £22,547 *Total Assets:* £41,045
Registered Office: Meadowgrove, Letcombe Road, Wantage, Oxon, OX12 9NA
Shareholders: Andrew John McLeod; Alison Meriel McLeod
Officers: Alison McLeod, Secretary; Alison Meriel McLeod [1957] Director; Andrew John McLeod [1959] Director

Diffusion Food By Pina Company Ltd
Incorporated: 6 June 2018
Registered Office: 71-75 Shelton Street, London, WC2H 9JQ
Shareholders: Antonia Vitellino; Mirco Pizzoli
Officers: Antonia Vitellino [1982] Director [Italian]

Digby Fine English Ltd
Incorporated: 5 April 2012
Net Worth: £1,218,131 *Total Assets:* £1,218,131
Registered Office: c/o DPC, Vernon Road, Stoke on Trent, Staffs, ST4 2QY
Shareholders: Trevor Todd Clough; Jason John Humphries
Officers: Ewen Irving Cameron [1956] Director; Trevor Todd Clough [1975] Director; Dr Jason John Humphries [1971] Director; Weicheng Zhang [1989] Director [Chinese]

Digby Wine Ltd
Incorporated: 5 April 2012 *Employees:* 4
Net Worth Deficit: £431,322 *Total Assets:* £1,219,494
Registered Office: 1 Berkeley Street, Mayfair, London, W1J 8DJ
Parent: Digby Fine English Ltd
Officers: Ewen Irving Cameron [1956] Director; Trevor Todd Clough [1975] Director; Dr Jason John Humphries [1971] Director; Weicheng Zhang [1989] Director [Chinese]

Dillon Bass Limited
Incorporated: 11 September 1978 *Employees:* 26
Net Worth: £74,497 *Total Assets:* £9,290,578
Registered Office: 41A Stockmans Way, Belfast, BT9 7ET
Shareholders: Coleraine Distillery Limited; Jas. Hennessy & Co. Limited
Officers: Aishling Hourican, Secretary; Enrique Abad Acosta [1966] Finance & Operations Director [Spanish]; Jean-Baptiste Briot [1970] Director [French]; Brian Michael Brown [1971] Business Unit Director [Irish]; Conor McQuaid [1969] Director/CEO & Chairman [Irish]; Bertrand Steip [1965] Managing Director [French]; Claire Tolan [1976] Managing Director [Irish]

Dima's Vodka UK Ltd
Incorporated: 12 October 2016
Net Worth Deficit: £442 *Total Assets:* £45,001
Registered Office: First Floor, 15 Young Street, London, W8 5EH
Major Shareholder: Dmitry Deinega
Officers: Dmitry Deinega [1988] Director

Dion Wines & Food Limited
Incorporated: 8 November 2013
Net Worth Deficit: £40,334 *Total Assets:* £41,908
Registered Office: 26 Bon Accord Terrace, Aberdeen, AB11 6DU
Shareholders: Rodrigo Rendon; Gerardo Garcia
Officers: Rodrigo Rendon [1973] Director/Engineer [Irish]

Dionysius Importers Ltd
Incorporated: 17 May 2012
Net Worth Deficit: £44,346 *Total Assets:* £105,835
Registered Office: Third Floor, 207 Regent Street, London, W1B 3HH
Major Shareholder: Claudio Marangoni
Officers: Claudio Marangoni [1975] Director [Italian]

Dionysus Boutique Wine Merchants Ltd
Incorporated: 8 May 2018
Registered Office: 20-22 Wenlock Road, London, N1 7GU
Major Shareholder: Krzysztof Janusz Karecki
Officers: Krzysztof Karecki [1978] Director/Trader [Polish]

Dionysus Premium Drinks Ltd
Incorporated: 13 November 2017
Registered Office: 5-6 Loaning Crescent, Edinburgh, EH7 6JU
Major Shareholder: Serkan Tarakci
Officers: Serkan Tarakci [1993] Director [Turkish]

Direct Beers Limited
Incorporated: 28 July 2005 *Employees:* 1
Net Worth Deficit: £20,442 *Total Assets:* £19,715
Registered Office: Unit 6 Heritage Business Centre, Belper, Derbys, DE56 1SW
Major Shareholder: Stephen Trevor Gee
Officers: Stephen Trevor Gee [1966] Director

Direct Booze Limited
Incorporated: 7 May 2002 *Employees:* 4
Net Worth: £2,485,945 *Total Assets:* £2,924,597
Registered Office: 364-368 Cranbrook Road, Gants Hill, Ilford, Essex, IG2 6HY
Shareholders: Vasant Lakhani; Rishi Lakhani
Officers: Rishi Lakhani [1982] Director

Direct Wine Factory Ltd
Incorporated: 12 June 2013
Previous: Wine Factory Direct Ltd
Net Worth: £2,174,676 *Total Assets:* £2,174,676
Registered Office: Mitchell House, Mitchell Street, Edinburgh, EH6 7BD

Direct Wine Importers Limited
Incorporated: 30 March 2015
Registered Office: 9 Kendal Close, Chester, CH2 2PR
Shareholder: John George Hill
Officers: James Crossen [1954] Director/Engineer; John George Hill [1951] Sales Director; Tony Luongo [1957] Director/Hairdresser

Direct2door Food & Beverage Ltd.
Incorporated: 11 August 2014
Net Worth: £16,053 *Total Assets:* £54,610
Registered Office: 72 Atkinson Road, London, E16 3LS
Major Shareholder: Silmara Piagno
Officers: Silmara Piagno [1977] Director [Italian]

Dirt. Ltd
Incorporated: 9 July 2018
Registered Office: 40c Ockendon Road, London, N1 3NP
Major Shareholder: Mattia Bianchi
Officers: Mattia Bianchi [1981] Director/Restaurateur [Italian]

The Dirty Drinks Collective Limited
Incorporated: 12 April 2017
Registered Office: Unit 3, 33 North Cross Road, London, SE22 9ET
Shareholders: Magnum Brands Limited; Thirteen Innovation Holdings Ltd
Officers: Katherine Victoria Mafi [1977] Director

Dirty Drinks Ltd
Incorporated: 22 October 2018
Registered Office: Craven Lodge, Grosvenor Road, Godalming, Surrey, GU7 1PA
Shareholders: Matija Davor Keyworth Pisk; Oliver Murray Clements
Officers: Oliver Murray Clements [1992] Director/Business Executive; Matija Davor Keyworth Pisk [1993] Director/Business Executive

Discover Wine (UK) Ltd
Incorporated: 5 May 2009
Net Worth Deficit: £31,047 *Total Assets:* £28,119
Registered Office: Peridot, Anmore Road, Denmead, Waterlooville, Hants, PO7 6NW
Major Shareholder: Janine Mary Pert
Officers: Janine Pert, Secretary; Janine Mary Pert [1956] Director/Wine Merchant

Discover Wine Limited
Incorporated: 15 March 2002 *Employees:* 2
Net Worth: £2,276 *Total Assets:* £72,441
Registered Office: Burwash Manor Barns, New Road Barton, Cambridge, CB3 7AY
Shareholders: Deborah Patricia Cozzi; Jason Francis Cozzi
Officers: Jason Francis Cozzi, Secretary/Director; Deborah Patricia Cozzi [1969] Director; Jason Francis Cozzi [1968] Director

Disley Gin Ltd
Incorporated: 7 January 2019
Registered Office: 7 Daisy Way, High Lane, Stockport, Cheshire, SK6 8EF
Shareholders: Josef Ben Singleton; Marybeth Grace Singleton
Officers: Josef Ben Singleton [1983] Director/Joiner

The Diss Honest Brewing Company Limited
Incorporated: 24 October 2014
Registered Office: 11 King Street, King's Lynn, Norfolk, PE30 1ET
Parent: Poppi (Holdings) Ltd
Officers: Thomas Hector Atkins [1945] Director

Distant Lands Ltd
Incorporated: 9 August 2018
Registered Office: 31 Butt Lane, Milton, Cambridge, CB24 6DG
Shareholders: Samuel James Adamson; Edward Anthony Read
Officers: Samuel James Adamson [1992] Director; Edward Anthony Read [1974] Director

Distell Europe Ltd.
Incorporated: 26 May 1998
Net Worth: £1,743,509 *Total Assets:* £1,746,009
Registered Office: Avalon House, 72 Lower Mortlake Road, Richmond, Surrey, TW9 2JY
Parent: Distell International Holdings Limited
Officers: Karen Spy, Secretary; Werner Nolte [1976] Finance Director [South African]; Fraser John Thornton [1969] Managing Director

Distell International Holdings Limited
Incorporated: 8 April 2016
Net Worth: £16,970,308 *Total Assets:* £18,152,844
Registered Office: Avalon House, 72 Lower Mortlake Road, Richmond, Surrey, TW9 2JY
Parent: Distell Group Limited
Officers: Nwavudu Constance Ekebuisi, Secretary; Christopher John Blandford-Newson [1964] Director/Asset Management [British/South African]; Steven Jeffrey Nathan [1962] Director [South African]; Werner Nolte [1976] Finance Director [South African]; Fraser John Thornton [1969] Managing Director; Leonard Jacobus Volschenk [1971] Managing Director [South African]

Distell International Limited
Incorporated: 16 March 1988 *Employees:* 291
Previous: Burn Stewart Distillers Limited
Net Worth: £87,354,000 *Total Assets:* £171,064,992
Registered Office: 8 Milton Road, College Milton North, East Kilbride, S Lanarks, G74 5BU
Parent: Distell Group Limited
Officers: Nwavudu Constance Ekebuisi, Secretary; Werner Nolte [1976] Finance Director [South African]; Fraser John Thornton [1969] Director; Johan Van Zyl [1971] Supply Chain Director [South African]

Distilled Brands Limited
Incorporated: 1 October 2012
Net Worth: £9,626 *Total Assets:* £21,402
Registered Office: 1 Glenburn Road, East Kilbride, S Lanarks, G74 5BA
Major Shareholder: Henry Allan Cunningham
Officers: Henry Allan Cunningham [1955] Director

Distilled Liquor Company Limited
Incorporated: 2 November 2012
Registered Office: 18 Lynedoch Crescent, Glasgow, G3 6EQ
Officers: Frederick Hamilton Laing [1950] Managing Director

Distillers Direct Ltd
Incorporated: 27 May 2015
Net Worth Deficit: £2,670 *Total Assets:* £16,862
Registered Office: 16 Kernan Drive, Loughborough, Leics, LE11 5JF
Major Shareholder: Craig Allan Harris
Officers: Craig Allan Harris [1974] Sales Director; Anna Mikalina Werstyn [1962] Sales Director

Distillery 96 Limited
Incorporated: 28 September 2018
Registered Office: Heather Lea, Tockholes Road, Tockholes, Darwen, Lancs, BB3 0NR
Major Shareholder: Regan Toner
Officers: Regan Toner [1996] Director

Distinction Armagnac Limited
Incorporated: 21 November 2012
Registered Office: 6 Moss Street, Paisley, Renfrewshire, PA1 1BL
Major Shareholder: Kenneth John McLachlan
Officers: Kenneth John McLachlan [1947] Director

Distribev Ltd.
Incorporated: 23 April 2015
Registered Office: 50 The Meadway, Hoddesdon, Herts, EN11 8AS
Major Shareholder: Karol Kulis
Officers: Karol Kulis [1980] Managing Director [Polish]

Dita Grappolo Ltd
Incorporated: 1 June 2017 *Employees:* 2
Net Worth Deficit: £6,577 *Total Assets:* £1,004
Registered Office: 95 King Street, Lancaster, LA1 1RH
Shareholders: Marco Fanton; Grzegorz Jerzy Tomaszewicz
Officers: Grzegorz Jerzy Tomaszewicz [1988] Director [Norwegian]

Ditton Wine Traders Ltd
Incorporated: 17 February 2004 *Employees:* 3
Net Worth: £505,937 *Total Assets:* £2,137,418
Registered Office: Unit 4a, 3 Eastfields Avenue, Riverside Quarter, Wandsworth, London, SW18 1GN
Major Shareholder: Mark Andries Schuringa
Officers: Mark Andries Schuringa [1967] Director/Wine Trader [Dutch]; Bart Laurens Van Der Vliet [1967] Director [Dutch]

Divergent Drinks Ltd
Incorporated: 21 March 2017 *Employees:* 2
Net Worth Deficit: £145,052 *Total Assets:* £138,772
Registered Office: Fulford House, Newbold Terrace, Leamington Spa, Warwicks, CV32 4EA
Shareholders: Daniel James Cahill; David Molla-Diez
Officers: Daniel James Cahill [1974] Director; Stephen Edward Manning [1961] Director; David Molla-Diez [1980] Director [Spanish]

UK Wholesalers of Beers, Wines and Spirits dellam

Diverse Beers Limited
Incorporated: 12 February 2019
Registered Office: 1a Sandringham Drive, Spondon, Derby, DE21 7QL
Major Shareholder: Andrew Mark Kenworthy
Officers: Andrew Mark Kenworthy [1987] Director/Beer Wholesaler

Divine Associates Ltd
Incorporated: 17 April 2018
Registered Office: 801 Old Kent Road, London, SE15 1NX
Major Shareholder: Ihiukwu Obiora
Officers: Ihiukwu Obiora [1964] Director/Businessman [Nigerian]

Diwine London Ltd
Incorporated: 9 July 2015
Registered Office: 60 Windsor Avenue, Wimbledon, London, SW19 2RR
Major Shareholder: Borbala Szekely
Officers: Borbala Szekely [1981] Director [Hungarian]

Diwine Piemonte Limited
Incorporated: 2 September 2016
Net Worth Deficit: £309 *Total Assets:* £6,391
Registered Office: Flat 307, 1 Cording Street, Banbury Point, London, E14 6NR
Officers: Michele Bussi [1989] Director [Italian]

DLG Wholesale Ltd
Incorporated: 21 April 2017
Registered Office: 20 Westerham Avenue, London, N9 9BU
Major Shareholder: Dogan Ucar
Officers: Dogan Ucar [1974] Director

DLRF Limited
Incorporated: 20 June 2012
Net Worth: £10,428 *Total Assets:* £302,231
Registered Office: Malvern View, Kews Lane, Kilcot, Newent, Glos, GL18 1GH
Shareholders: David John Price; Elizabeth Anne Price
Officers: Elizabeth Anne Davis [1959] Director; David John Price [1959] Director

Dmomentum Ltd
Incorporated: 26 August 2016
Registered Office: 22 Artisan Mews, London, NW10 5GL
Shareholders: Lorenzo Sergi; Noemi Ribaric
Officers: Noemi Ribaric [1989] Director [Slovenian]; Lorenzo Sergi [1990] Director [Italian]

DN Pacifica Ltd
Incorporated: 13 June 2017
Net Worth Deficit: £114,812 *Total Assets:* £46,124
Registered Office: 9 Stratfield Park, Elettra Avenue, Waterlooville, Hants, PO7 7XN
Shareholders: Margaryta Denton; Anthony Denton
Officers: Anthony Denton [1976] Director; Margaryta Denton [1974] Director

DNG Group Ltd
Incorporated: 30 July 2018
Registered Office: 509 Kenton Road, Harrow, Middlesex, HA3 0UL
Major Shareholder: Dev Dhingra
Officers: Dev Dhingra [2000] Director [Indian]

DNG Trading Ltd
Incorporated: 2 July 2018
Registered Office: 509 Kenton Road, Harrow, Middlesex, HA3 0UL
Major Shareholder: Priya Dhingra
Officers: Priya Dhingra [1994] Director [Indian]

Do Trading Limited
Incorporated: 26 September 2018
Registered Office: 85 Brook Court, Watling Street, Radlett, Herts, WD7 7JA
Officers: Thi MY Hanh Nguyen [1986] Director/Beautician [Vietnamese]

Nick Dobson Ltd
Incorporated: 13 November 2002
Net Worth Deficit: £125,173 *Total Assets:* £151,484
Registered Office: 3 The Grove, Idle, W Yorks, BD10 9JS
Major Shareholder: Joelle Nebbe-Mornod
Officers: Joelle Nebbe-Mornod [1971] Director [Swiss]

Docklands Trading Company Limited
Incorporated: 22 October 1998
Net Worth: £198,834 *Total Assets:* £241,090
Registered Office: Units 22-23 The IO Centre, 59-71 River Road, Barking, Essex, IG11 0DR
Shareholders: Kaushik Amritlal Mody; Peter Millington
Officers: Peter Millington, Secretary; Peter Millington [1960] Director/Accountant; Kaushik Amritlal Mody [1957] Director

Doctor Bird Rum Ltd
Incorporated: 29 September 2017
Registered Office: 31b Grove Hill Road, London, SE5 8DF
Major Shareholder: Archibald Robert Burden
Officers: Archibald Robert Burden [1990] Director

Dodotraders UK Limited
Incorporated: 9 May 2012
Net Worth: £58,953 *Total Assets:* £155,933
Registered Office: 4 Hanover Walk, Hatfield, Herts, AL10 9EL
Major Shareholder: Baboo Taukoor
Officers: Baboo Oomeshwarsingh Taukoor [1973] Director

Domaine des Jeanne Limited
Incorporated: 29 April 2013 *Employees:* 2
Net Worth Deficit: £183,855 *Total Assets:* £56,445
Registered Office: Brockbourne House, 77 Mount Ephraim, Tunbridge Wells, Kent, TN4 8BS
Major Shareholder: Lady Jeanne Marie Davies
Officers: Lady Jeanne Marie Davies [1955] Director/Housewife

Domaine Direct Limited
Incorporated: 16 July 2002
Registered Office: 29 Wilmington Square, London, WC1X 0EG
Major Shareholder: Hilary Gibbs
Officers: Peter Derry, Secretary; Hilary Gibbs [1952] Director

Domaine Watson Ltd
Incorporated: 3 December 2014
Net Worth: £572 *Total Assets:* £6,096
Registered Office: Willowfield House, Fir Lane, Steeple Aston, Oxon, OX25 4SF
Major Shareholder: Elizabeth Watson
Officers: Elizabeth Watson, Secretary; Elizabeth Watson [1973] Director

Domal Trading Limited
Incorporated: 6 September 2017
Registered Office: Unit 1 Enfield Avenue, Leeds, LS7 1QN
Major Shareholder: Sajid Khan
Officers: Sajid Khan [1972] Director

Donaldson Reeves Limited
Incorporated: 20 January 2003
Net Worth Deficit: £10,331 *Total Assets:* £68,005
Registered Office: 86 Wigley Road, Feltham, Middlesex, TW13 5HF
Officers: Susan Jane Donaldson, Secretary/Director; Keith William Donaldson [1962] Director

Donatel Freres Limited
Incorporated: 4 December 1945 *Employees:* 16
Net Worth: £1,543,641 *Total Assets:* £1,851,869
Registered Office: 42 Old Compton Street, London, W1V 6LR
Major Shareholder: Malcolm George Mullin
Officers: Gillian Mullin [1952] Director; Malcolm George Mullin [1953] Managing Director

Donnelly Wholesale Limited
Incorporated: 14 February 2011
Net Worth: £2 *Total Assets:* £2
Registered Office: 2 Legmoylin Road, Silverbridge, Newry, Co Down, BT35 9LL
Major Shareholder: Rory Donnelly
Officers: Rory Donnelly [1969] Director

Donnington Brewery Limited
Incorporated: 20 January 2017
Registered Office: Donnington Brewery, Upper Swell, Stow on-the-Wold, Cheltenham, Glos, GL54 1EP
Major Shareholder: James Rixon Arkell
Officers: John Peter Arkell, Secretary; James Rixon Arkell [1951] Director/Brewer

Doran Family Vintners Limited
Incorporated: 14 December 2011
Net Worth Deficit: £16,755 *Total Assets:* £99,787
Registered Office: 104 Teddington Park Road, Teddington, Middlesex, TW11 8NE
Shareholders: Georgia Maeve Doran; Thomas Kavanagh Doran
Officers: Georgia Maeve Doran [1981] Director; Thomas Kavanagh Doran [1984] Director/Teacher

The Dorset Wine Company Limited
Incorporated: 15 February 2006 *Employees:* 3
Net Worth: £47,635 *Total Assets:* £141,997
Registered Office: Strathmore House, 11 Queen Mother Square, Poundbury, Dorchester, DT1 3DX
Shareholders: Jonathan Charles; Melanie Jane Lister Charles
Officers: Melanie Jane Lister Charles, Secretary; Jonathan David Gwyther Charles [1972] Director/Wine Merchant; Melanie Jane Lister Charles [1971] Director/Retail Merchandiser

Dorys Shop Ltd
Incorporated: 8 May 2017
Registered Office: 26 Charlton Road, London, N9 8EJ
Officers: Dorina Loizidis [1968] Director/Banksman [Romanian]

Dos Santos Bev Co UK Limited
Incorporated: 6 February 2019
Registered Office: Anumerate Limited, Office 1, 3rd Floor, W.M Promus, 132-144 High Street, Bromley, Kent, BR1 1EZ
Shareholders: Julian Paulo Dos Santos; Eugene Paulo Dos Santos
Officers: Eugene Paulo Dos Santos [1962] Director [Portuguese]; Julian Paulo Dos Santos [1969] Director [Portuguese]

The Double Hard Whiskey Company Ltd
Incorporated: 5 November 2018
Registered Office: 37 Pearson Close, Aylesbury, Bucks, HP19 7TH
Shareholders: Jake Corteen; Ashley Roche
Officers: Jake Corteen [1992] Director; Ashley Roche [1976] Director

Double Measure Club Ltd
Incorporated: 15 October 2018
Registered Office: 24 Elmsdale Avenue, Coventry, Warwicks, CV6 6ES
Major Shareholder: Jagdeep Gill
Officers: Jagdeep Gill [1990] Director

Douglas Export Agency Limited
Incorporated: 9 June 1953
Registered Office: 16 Park Circus, Glasgow, G3 6AX
Parent: Hunter Laing & Company Limited
Officers: Stewart Hunter Laing, Secretary; Stewart Hunter Laing [1946] Director

Dourthe UK Limited
Incorporated: 29 August 2000 *Employees:* 1
Net Worth: £1,161,738 *Total Assets:* £1,196,609
Registered Office: c/o Browne Jacobson LLP, 6 Bevis Marks, London, EC3A 7BA
Major Shareholder: Alain Thienot
Officers: Patrick Jean Marie Gilbert Jestin [1959] Director [French]

Dowbridge Distributors Ltd
Incorporated: 25 June 2010 *Employees:* 2
Net Worth: £10,467 *Total Assets:* £80,814
Registered Office: Unit 2 Grendon House Farm, Warton Lane, Atherstone, Warwicks, CV9 3DT
Shareholders: Alan Wood; Anita Pauline Wood; Elizabeth McCoubrey; David Andrew McCoubrey
Officers: David Andrew McCoubrey [1963] Director/Management Consultant; Elizabeth McCoubrey [1966] Director/Hairstylist; Alan Wood [1965] Director/Brewer; Anita Pauline Wood [1969] Director/Office Manager

Dr Dougan (Enterprises) Limited
Incorporated: 2 November 2016
Net Worth: £461 *Total Assets:* £26,569
Registered Office: Unit 4 Brent Road, Green Lane Trading Estate, Stockport, Cheshire, SK4 2JR
Major Shareholder: David Robert Dougan
Officers: David Robert Dougan [1987] Director/Warehousing

Dracula Wine House Ltd
Incorporated: 19 October 2018
Registered Office: 224 High Road Leytonstone, London, E11 3HU
Major Shareholder: Ruxanda Rodica Purcaru
Officers: Ruxanda Rodica Purcaru [1962] Director [Romanian]

Draft Link Limited
Incorporated: 23 July 2014
Net Worth: £1,117 *Total Assets:* £47,244
Registered Office: 6 Tadworth Parade, Hornchurch, Essex, RM12 5AS
Major Shareholder: Adam Tott
Officers: Dr Chloe Tott, Secretary; Adam Tott [1987] Director

Dragon Drinks Limited
Incorporated: 14 February 2012
Net Worth Deficit: £109,693 *Total Assets:* £15,016
Registered Office: The Spirit Lodge, Buntings Farm, Pentlow, Sudbury, Suffolk, CO10 7JL
Shareholders: Stephen David Harlow; Mark Blewitt
Officers: Mark Blewitt, Secretary; Mark Blewitt [1960] Director; John Harlow [1951] Director/Retired; Stephen David Harlow [1960] Director

Dragon Wines Limited
Incorporated: 13 February 2019
Registered Office: Suite 17, Apex House, Thomas Street, Caerphilly, Gwent, CF83 8DP
Shareholder: Gabriel Jacobus Beeslaar
Officers: Gabriel Jacobus Beeslaar [1974] Director/Winemaker [South African]; Joel Anthony Southby Bramwell [1975] Sales Director; Daniel Marcus Tracey [1979] Director/Chartered Quantity Surveyor

Dragonwood Limited
Incorporated: 11 January 2017
Net Worth: £5,624 *Total Assets:* £102,485
Registered Office: 9 Scirocco Close, Northampton, NN3 6AP
Major Shareholder: Sukhbir Singh Somel
Officers: Sukhbir Singh Somel [1979] Director

Dram-a-Drinks Ltd.
Incorporated: 28 October 1998
Registered Office: Suite 8, 2 Nevern Place, London, SW5 9PR
Major Shareholder: Harry Munro Singer
Officers: Harry Munro Singer [1953] Director/Consultant

Dramfool Ltd
Incorporated: 22 May 2015 *Employees:* 1
Net Worth: £8,476 *Total Assets:* £90,729
Registered Office: 4 Champany Holdings, Linlithgow, W Lothian, EH49 7NR
Major Shareholder: Bruce Farquhar
Officers: Bruce Farquhar [1972] Director/Commissioning Operator

Draught Services Ltd
Incorporated: 29 November 2016 *Employees:* 2
Net Worth: £260 *Total Assets:* £8,417
Registered Office: 25 Endsleigh Court, Colchester, Essex, CO3 3QT
Officers: Jason Allan Danes [1980] Director/Draught Beer Services and Cellar Technician

Drayman Drinks Ltd
Incorporated: 28 January 2013
Net Worth Deficit: £397 *Total Assets:* £292,009
Registered Office: 57 Windmill Street, Gravesend, Kent, DA12 1BB
Officers: Ranjit Singh Chahal [1971] Director

Drill Wholesale Limited
Incorporated: 17 April 2018
Registered Office: 8 Mill Road, Stock, Ingatestone, Essex, CM4 9BH
Major Shareholder: Raees Khan
Officers: Raees Khan [1980] Director

Drink Artisan Ltd
Incorporated: 21 June 2018
Registered Office: 2 West Dunley Farm Cottage, Grittleton, Chippenham, Wilts, SN14 6PY
Shareholders: Neil Adrian Perry; Richard Julian Perry
Officers: Neil Adrian Perry [1959] Director/Chartered Accountant; Richard Julian Perry [1966] Director

The Drink Connect Ltd
Incorporated: 27 March 2018
Registered Office: Kemp House, 160 City Road, London, EC1V 2NX
Major Shareholder: William Leach
Officers: William Leach, Secretary; William Leach [1991] Director/Founder

The Drink Driver Ltd
Incorporated: 9 March 2018
Registered Office: 7 Swanley Close, Halesowen, W Midlands, B62 0HQ
Major Shareholder: Ash Taleghani
Officers: Ash Taleghani [1994] Director/Student

Drink Free Ltd
Incorporated: 20 July 2018
Registered Office: Unit 1 High House Lane, Kenardington, Ashford, Kent, TN26 2LF
Major Shareholder: Andrew Iain Stewart Laughland
Officers: Andrew Iain Stewart Laughland [1965] Director

Drink Kind Ltd
Incorporated: 22 May 2018
Registered Office: 70 Silver Street, Norwich, NR3 4TU
Major Shareholder: Samantha Jayne Wilkinson
Officers: Samantha Jayne Wilkinson [1989] Director/Manager

Drink Link Grimsby Limited
Incorporated: 23 October 2017
Registered Office: 23 Chantry Lane, Grimsby, N E Lincs, DN31 2LP
Major Shareholder: Derrick Howard
Officers: Derrick Howard [1964] Director/Publican

Drink Store Limited
Incorporated: 25 January 2019
Registered Office: 41 Great Portland Street, London, W1W 7LA
Shareholders: Justin James; Gerard Kavanagh
Officers: Justin Dennis James [1976] Director; Gerard Kavanagh [1970] Director [Irish]

The Drink Store Wholesale Limited
Incorporated: 19 March 2015
Net Worth: £100 *Total Assets:* £100
Registered Office: Hussains Hall, 38 Devonshire Street, Keighley, W Yorks, BD21 2AU
Major Shareholder: Sukhraj Singh Chouhan
Officers: Sukhraj Singh Chouhan [1982] Director

Drink Warehouse Events Limited
Incorporated: 27 November 2015
Registered Office: 3 Lloyd Road, Station Gates, Broadstairs, Kent, CT10 1HY
Major Shareholder: Michael James Curtis
Officers: Michael James Curtis [1981] Director

Drink247 Ltd
Incorporated: 22 June 2018
Registered Office: 20-22 Wenlock Road, London, N1 7GU
Major Shareholder: Zoltan Sergiu-Vladut
Officers: Zoltan Sergiu-Vladut [1990] Director

Drinkable Ltd
Incorporated: 20 November 2017
Registered Office: 53a Selborne Road, London, N14 7DD
Officers: Sokol Veselaj [1971] Director

Drinkintime Ltd.
Incorporated: 15 April 2003
Net Worth: £12,192 *Total Assets:* £13,651
Registered Office: The Barn Pastoral Centre, 173 Church Road, Northfield, Birmingham, B31 2LX
Shareholders: Nicholas Robert Gay; Patricia Margaret Gay
Officers: Patricia Margaret Gay, Secretary; Nicholas Robert Gay [1947] Director/Drinks Wholesaler

Drinklink Limited
Incorporated: 26 April 1993
Registered Office: 63 Trevarthian Road, St Austell, Cornwall, PL25 4BY
Parent: St. Austell Brewery Company Limited
Officers: Colin John Stratton, Secretary/Accountant; Simon James Staughton [1959] Director

Drinkologie Limited
Incorporated: 22 January 2018
Registered Office: 9 Walsingham Place, Truro, Cornwall, TR1 2RP
Shareholders: Anne-Marie Hurst; Eleanor Annette Bradshaw
Officers: Eleanor Annette Bradshaw [1971] Director; Anne-Marie Hurst [1965] Director

Drinkrite Limited
Incorporated: 9 January 2009 *Employees:* 1
Net Worth: £240,667 *Total Assets:* £595,304
Registered Office: Stuart House, 15-17 North Park Road, Harrogate, N Yorks, HG1 5PD
Major Shareholder: Michael Joseph Slattery
Officers: Michael Joseph Slattery [1956] Director

Drinks 2 You Limited
Incorporated: 6 September 2017
Registered Office: PS7 Services Ltd, c/o Drinks 2 You, Unit D Block 2-3, Redhouse Road, Croydon, Surrey, CR0 3AQ
Officers: Selvin Engutsamy, Secretary; Selvin Engutsamy [1989] Director

Drinks 4 Less (UK) Limited
Incorporated: 5 September 2011
Net Worth: £9,711 *Total Assets:* £27,446
Registered Office: 115 Greenford Business Centre, Station Approach, Oldfield Lane North, Greenford, Middlesex, UB6 0AL
Major Shareholder: Anandpreet Singh Powar
Officers: Anandpreet Singh Powar [1986] Director [Indian]

The Drinks Agency Ltd
Incorporated: 14 June 2017
Net Worth: £550 *Total Assets:* £18,975
Registered Office: 13 Montpellier Arcade, Cheltenham, Glos, GL50 1SU
Major Shareholder: Michele Bodart
Officers: Michele Bodart, Secretary; Michele Bodart [1960] Director/Business Owner

The Drinks Bay Limited
Incorporated: 5 June 2018
Registered Office: Unit A3, Connaught Business Centre, Hyde Estate Road, London, NW9 6JL
Major Shareholder: Victoria Ibidun Ogunniyi
Officers: Victoria Ibidun Ogunniyi [1970] Director/Businesswoman

The Drinks Club Ltd
Incorporated: 30 August 2013
Net Worth: £508,205 *Total Assets:* £1,908,987
Registered Office: Biddlesden Abbey, Biddlesden, Brackley, Northants, NN13 5TR
Shareholders: Stuart Graham Randall; Randall Parker Food Group Limited
Officers: David Richard Brady, Secretary; Louis Jules Hydleman [1956] Director; Stuart Graham Randall [1987] Director/Entrepreneur

Drinks Depot Ltd
Incorporated: 18 May 2004
Net Worth: £6,640 *Total Assets:* £13,756
Registered Office: Unit 4 Rowan Trade Park, Neville Road, Bradford, W Yorks, BD4 8TQ
Major Shareholder: Jatinder Singh
Officers: Himat Singh, Secretary; Jatinder Singh [1978] Director

Drinks Direct Limited
Incorporated: 18 May 2004 *Employees:* 8
Previous: Drinksdirect.co.uk Ltd
Net Worth: £494,277 *Total Assets:* £787,686
Registered Office: Unit 6 Rowan Trade Park, Neville Road, Bradford, W Yorks, BD4 8TQ
Major Shareholder: Jatinder Singh
Officers: Himat Singh, Secretary; Himat Singh [1955] Director; Jatinder Singh [1978] Director

The Drinks Emporium Limited
Incorporated: 9 May 2014
Net Worth: £2 *Total Assets:* £2
Registered Office: 217 Aston Road, Birmingham, B6 4LH
Parent: Cador Limited
Officers: Natalie Anne Duff-Tytler [1970] Director; Simon Ransom Tester [1975] Financial Director

Drinks Factory Limited
Incorporated: 14 February 2012
Registered Office: 635 Bath Road, Slough, Berks, SL1 6AE
Major Shareholder: Rajinder Singh Birk
Officers: Rajinder Singh Birk [1980] Director/Entrepreneur

Drinks Global Ltd
Incorporated: 22 April 2008
Net Worth: £188,763 *Total Assets:* £286,091
Registered Office: c/o Pitts & Seeus, Omnibus Business Centre, 39-41 North Road, London, N7 9DP
Major Shareholder: Mandeep Kaur
Officers: Mandeep Kaur [1985] Director

The Drinks Guild Ltd
Incorporated: 28 April 1998
Net Worth Deficit: £51,338 *Total Assets:* £13,683
Registered Office: Barton Cottage, Basingstoke Road, Old Alresford, Alresford, Hants, SO24 9DS
Shareholders: Anthony Charles Gard; Ian Victor Lockwood
Officers: Martyn Victor Browne [1959] Director/Whisky Merchant; Anthony Charles Gard [1949] Marketing Director; Ian Victor Lockwood [1942] Director

Drinks Inc. Ltd
Incorporated: 19 January 2001 *Employees:* 119
Net Worth: £12,466,514 *Total Assets:* £28,128,664
Registered Office: 4 Falcon Road, Belfast, BT12 6SJ
Shareholder: Paul Martin Camplisson
Officers: Paul Martin Camplisson, Secretary; Stephen Joseph Brown [1958] Director/Warehouse Manager [Irish]; Catherine Camplisson [1969] Director [Irish]; Paul Martin Camplisson [1965] Director/Sales Marketing & Distribution [Irish]; Gareth Rory Nethercott [1969] Finance Director [Irish]

The Drinks Link International Limited
Incorporated: 22 July 2005
Net Worth Deficit: £36,000 *Total Assets:* £1,365
Registered Office: 187 Belswains Lane, Hemel Hempstead, Herts, HP3 9XA
Shareholders: Clive Thomas; Susan Thomas
Officers: Susan Thomas, Secretary; Clive Thomas [1952] Director

The Drinks Lover Ltd
Incorporated: 21 September 2010
Net Worth Deficit: £58,615
Registered Office: 18 Roneo Corner, Hornchurch, Essex, RM12 4TN
Major Shareholder: Roriki Dwayne Earl Hutchinson
Officers: Roriki Dwayne Earl Hutchinson [1972] Director

The Drinks Network Ltd
Incorporated: 7 January 2019
Registered Office: 53 Woodthorpe Road, Ashford, Surrey, TW15 2RP
Major Shareholder: Victoria Elizabeth Wilson
Officers: Victoria Elizabeth Wilson [1974] Director and Company Secretary

The Drinks Orchard Ltd
Incorporated: 19 February 2016
Net Worth: £929 *Total Assets:* £1,262
Registered Office: 109 Coleman Road, Leicester, LE5 4LE
Shareholders: Anna Iwona Pawelek; Tomasz Pawelek
Officers: Tomasz Pawelek [1976] Director [Polish]

Drinks R Us Limited
Incorporated: 8 March 2011
Registered Office: 48-52 Penny Lane, Mossley Hill, Liverpool, L18 1DG
Major Shareholder: Rakesh Ishwar Daryanani
Officers: Rakesh Ishwar Daryanani [1982] Director

Drinks To Go Plus Ltd
Incorporated: 17 November 2017
Registered Office: 146 Harvington Road, Birmingham, B29 5ER
Major Shareholder: Maryam Hatami
Officers: Maryam Hatami [1978] Director/Shopkeeper

Drinks21 Ltd
Incorporated: 23 November 2010
Net Worth: £103,155 *Total Assets:* £434,875
Registered Office: 9 Queen's Square, Ascot Business Park, Ascot, Berks, SL5 9FE
Parent: Drinks21 Group Ltd
Officers: Nigel Kevin Morton, Secretary; Stephen Michael Brogan [1969] Director

Drinks2u Ltd
Incorporated: 5 September 2018
Registered Office: 113 Maidavale Crescent, Coventry, Warwicks, CV3 6GE
Major Shareholder: Gurdip Singh Manak
Officers: Gurdip Singh Manak [1983] Director/Salesman

Drinksbot Limited
Incorporated: 8 March 2018
Registered Office: Telecom House, 125-135 Preston Road, Brighton, BN1 6AF
Shareholders: Andrew John Cant; Ekua Cant
Officers: Andrew John Cant [1989] Director; Ekua Cant [1984] Director

Drinkscraft Limited
Incorporated: 5 February 2016
Net Worth Deficit: £8,087 *Total Assets:* £34,295
Registered Office: Flat 1, 15 Woodfield Avenue, London, SW16 1LL
Major Shareholder: David John Bridge-Collyns
Officers: David John Bridge-Collyns [1978] Director/Alcoholic Drinks Wholesaler/Importer

Drinkslynx Limited
Incorporated: 22 July 2011
Registered Office: 48-52 Penny Lane, Mossley Hill, Liverpool, L18 1DG
Major Shareholder: Rakesh Ishwar Daryanani
Officers: Rakesh Ishwar Daryanani [1982] Director

Drinksman Limited
Incorporated: 29 July 2015 *Employees:* 1
Net Worth Deficit: £24,272 *Total Assets:* £9,282
Registered Office: White Owl, Conford, Liphook, Hants, GU30 7QN
Major Shareholder: James William Connolly
Officers: James William Connolly [1971] Director/Wine and Spirits Merchant

Drinksology Limited
Incorporated: 6 October 2017
Registered Office: 155-157 Donegall Pass, Belfast, BT7 1DT
Parent: Kirker Greer (Holdings) Limited
Officers: Steven Clark Pattison [1979] Director; Richard Ryan [1977] Director

Drinkss Cash and Carry Limited
Incorporated: 27 February 2018
Registered Office: 20-22 Wenlock Road, London, N1 7GU
Major Shareholder: Athaf Ratasaf
Officers: Athaf Ratasaf [1982] Director Manager

Drinktonics Limited
Incorporated: 18 December 2018
Registered Office: Trevella Manor, Trispen, Truro, Cornwall, TR4 9BD
Major Shareholder: Anne-Marie Hurst
Officers: Anne-Marie Hurst [1965] Director

Drinkz Ltd
Incorporated: 18 October 2018
Registered Office: 59 The Avenue, Leighton Bromswold, Huntingdon, Cambs, PE28 5AW
Shareholders: Joshua William Wills; Matheus de Almeida
Officers: Matheus de Almeida [1997] Director/Interior Designer [Italian]; Joshua William Wills [1994] Director/Financial Adviser

Dromedary Trading & Resources Limited
Incorporated: 13 February 2018
Registered Office: 18a/20 King Street, Maidenhead, Berks, SL6 1EF
Major Shareholder: Elizabeth Stefka Perry
Officers: Elizabeth Stefka Perry [1959] Director

Drop The Anchor Brewery Ltd
Incorporated: 9 November 2016
Net Worth: £216 *Total Assets:* £37,729
Registered Office: Avon Works, Bridge Street, Christchurch, Dorset, BH23 1DY
Major Shareholder: Neil Hodgkinson
Officers: Neil Hodgkinson [1976] Director

Droylsden Craft Limited
Incorporated: 3 September 2018
Registered Office: 50 Clough Road, Droylsden, Manchester, M43 7NG
Major Shareholder: Anthony Thomas Conway
Officers: Anthony Thomas Conway [1990] Director/Manager

Drum and Black Rum Company Limited
Incorporated: 3 October 2016
Net Worth Deficit: £1,175
Registered Office: 78 York Street, London, W1H 1DP
Shareholders: Daniel Buckland; Graham Cotton
Officers: Daniel Buckland [1985] Director; Graham Cotton [1978] Director

Drumgaw Holdings Ltd
Incorporated: 26 February 2019
Registered Office: 27 Drumgaw Road, Armagh, BT60 2AD
Major Shareholder: Gareth William John Megaw
Officers: Gareth William John Megaw [1988] Director/Engineer

Drumstick Products Company Limited
Incorporated: 26 June 2014
Net Worth: £1,171,504 *Total Assets:* £5,636,975
Registered Office: 5 North End Road, London, NW11 7RJ
Officers: Abraham Spitzer [1974] Director/Food Wholesaler; Esther Spitzer [1947] Director/Food Wholesaler; Neil Spitzer [1972] Director/Food Wholesaler; Richard Spitzer [1944] Director; Samuel Spitzer [1980] Director/Food Wholesaler

The Drunk Maitre D Limited
Incorporated: 4 April 2017
Net Worth Deficit: £3,376 *Total Assets:* £6,135
Registered Office: 190 Jex Road, Norwich, NR5 8XH
Shareholders: Laszlo Zupan; Laszlo Zupan
Officers: Laszlo Zupan [1982] Director/Wine Merchant [Hungarian]

DSC Imports Limited
Incorporated: 25 November 2015
Net Worth Deficit: £2,823 *Total Assets:* £16,349
Registered Office: No 1 Approach Road, London, SW20 8BA
Shareholder: Paul Belcher
Officers: Paul Belcher [1976] Director/Chef; Adrian James Copplestone [1977] Director/Chef

DT Wine Importers Ltd
Incorporated: 8 January 2019
Registered Office: 6 Walpole Road, Twickenham, Middlesex, TW2 5SN
Major Shareholder: Dominic Thranum
Officers: Dominic Thranum [1967] Director

DT1 Ltd
Incorporated: 30 October 2015 *Employees:* 2
Net Worth Deficit: £20,680 *Total Assets:* £19,723
Registered Office: 1623 Warwick Road, Knowle, Solihull, W Midlands, B93 9LF
Major Shareholder: James John Taylor
Officers: James John Taylor [1977] Director

DTA Drinks Ltd
Incorporated: 26 February 2019
Registered Office: 8 East Cliff Road, Dawdon, Seaham, Co Durham, SR7 7PS
Shareholders: David Travers; Stuart Travers
Officers: David Travers [1952] Director; Stuart Travers [1979] Director

DTB Distribution Ltd
Incorporated: 29 January 2019
Registered Office: 11 Theobalds Green, Heathfield, E Sussex, TN21 8BT
Shareholders: Libertad Luque Garcia; Ney Pacheco
Officers: Libertad Luque Garcia [1984] Director [Spanish]; Ney Pacheco [1962] Director [Brazilian]

DTdist Ltd
Incorporated: 27 September 2017
Registered Office: 494 Muswell Hill Broadway, London, N10 1BT
Major Shareholder: Bujar Leka
Officers: Bujar Leka [1969] Director

Du Terroir A La Table Limited
Incorporated: 18 November 2005
Net Worth: £3,518 *Total Assets:* £16,101
Registered Office: Pennyweights, 163 Welcomes Road, Kenley, Surrey, CR8 5HB
Officers: Christel Mireille Jeanne Lombard, Secretary; Christel Mireille Jeanne Lombard [1970] Director/Administrator [French]

Duchy Beverages Ltd
Incorporated: 11 June 2018
Registered Office: 1 Elm Cottages, Park Bottom, Redruth, Cornwall, TR15 3XJ
Major Shareholder: Dean Apollo Bungay
Officers: Dean Apollo Bungay [1988] Director

The Dulwich Spirits Company Limited
Incorporated: 10 January 2017
Net Worth Deficit: £3,402 *Total Assets:* £7,012
Registered Office: 6 Tell Grove, East Dulwich, London, SE22 8RH
Major Shareholder: Philippa Gee
Officers: Thomas Gee, Secretary; Philippa Gee [1988] Director

Dumenil Champagne Limited
Incorporated: 3 November 2016
Net Worth: £218 *Total Assets:* £12,977
Registered Office: Moorgate House, 7 Station Road West, Oxted, Surrey, RH8 9EE
Shareholders: Michael Peter Dumenil; Nicholas George Dumenil; Katharyn Laura Rose
Officers: Nicholas George Dumenil [1988] Director; Timothy Peter Dumenil [1953] Director

Dunarea Albastra Ltd
Incorporated: 27 September 2018
Registered Office: 83 Freeman Street, Coventry, Warwicks, CV6 5FF
Major Shareholder: Constantin Parvulescu
Officers: Constantin Parvulescu [1955] Director [Romanian]

Duncairn Wines Limited
Incorporated: 6 April 1965 *Employees:* 16
Net Worth: £441,437 *Total Assets:* £1,188,302
Registered Office: 5-7 Corporation Square, Belfast, BT1 3AJ
Shareholders: Peter McAlindon; Neal Edward McAlindon
Officers: Maureen Sarah McAlindon, Secretary; Kevin Peter McAlindon [1965] Director/Wine Merchant; Neal Edward McAlindon [1969] Director/Wine Buyer

Duple Social Club Sth Shore BPL . Ltd
Incorporated: 20 November 2018
Registered Office: 96a Bond Street, Blackpool, Lancs, FY4 1EX
Major Shareholder: Stephen Higham
Officers: Stephen Higham [1960] Club Director

Durrants Fine Wines Limited
Incorporated: 23 November 2005 *Employees:* 5
Net Worth: £2,359 *Total Assets:* £303,396
Registered Office: Unit 22 Maple Leaf Business Park, Manston, Ramsgate, Kent, CT12 5GD
Shareholders: Timothy Birch; Matthew St John Birch
Officers: Barry Desmond Birch, Secretary/Director; Barry Desmond Birch [1943] Director; Matthew St John Birch [1972] Sales Director; Timothy James Birch [1969] Director/Co-ordinator

Dutch Courage Drinks Consultants Ltd
Incorporated: 25 January 2019
Registered Office: Beck Farm, Crambe, York, YO60 7JR
Major Shareholder: George Ian MacNicol
Officers: George Ian MacNicol [1983] Director

DW Brands Ltd
Incorporated: 29 January 2019
Registered Office: 66 Rendlesham Road, Enfield, Middlesex, EN2 0TZ
Major Shareholder: Daniel Andrew Wing
Officers: Daniel Andrew Wing [1991] Director/Administrator

DWS Wholesale Limited
Incorporated: 3 May 2013
Net Worth: £15,135 *Total Assets:* £390,246
Registered Office: Unit 4 Acorn Court, Clarion Close, Swansea Enterprise Park, Swansea, SA6 8QU
Major Shareholder: Daryl William Stephens
Officers: Daryl William Stephens [1965] Director

E I Wines Limited
Incorporated: 29 April 2009 *Employees:* 21
Net Worth: £1,115,335 *Total Assets:* £7,530,545
Registered Office: Unit 23 The Ivories, 6-18 Northampton Street, London, N1 2HY
Officers: Paul Dominic Dauthieu, Secretary; Hugo Argyll Campbell [1961] Director; Mark Jonathan Chapman [1966] Director; Paul Dominic Dauthieu [1975] Director; Peter Joseph Paul Dauthieu [1971] Director; Peter Dominic Dauthieu [1944] Director

E.W.G.A. Limited
Incorporated: 19 March 2003 *Employees:* 58
Net Worth: £360,194 *Total Assets:* £4,036,547
Registered Office: EWGA, Hyning Home Farm, Dock Acres, Warton, Lancs, LA6 1HP
Major Shareholder: Adrian Christopher Moeckell
Officers: Janette Alison McLaughlin [1969] Sales Director; Adrian Christopher Moeckell [1960] Director/Wine Importer

Earle Wines Ltd.
Incorporated: 29 September 1998
Net Worth: £96,858 *Total Assets:* £353,346
Registered Office: Gardener's Cottage, Rudding Park, Follifoot, Harrogate, N Yorks, HG3 1JH
Shareholders: John Earle Jacobs; Patricia Rosemary Jacobs
Officers: Patricia Rosemary Jacobs, Secretary; John Earle Jacobs [1952] Director/Wine Importer; Patricia Rosemary Jacobs [1947] Director/Wine Importer

Earny Limited
Incorporated: 27 October 2011
Net Worth Deficit: £47,199 *Total Assets:* £236,197
Registered Office: Unit 3, 1161 Chester Road, Erdington, Birmingham, B24 0QY
Major Shareholder: Aaron Rico Singh Dhami
Officers: Aaron Rico Singh Dhami [1991] Director

Earth Elements Ltd
Incorporated: 20 September 2018
Registered Office: 20 Broughinge Road, Borehamwood, Herts, WD6 5AL
Shareholders: Dionigi Rassu; Elpidio Battistini
Officers: Dionigi Rassu [1963] Director [Italian]

Easier Sales Limited
Incorporated: 12 January 2016 *Employees:* 1
Net Worth: £21,346 *Total Assets:* £131,128
Registered Office: Unit 7 Clifton Bury Farm, Church Street, Clifton, Beds, SG17 5EX
Major Shareholder: Graham Abbott
Officers: Jon Royal, Secretary; Graham David Abbott [1964] Director

East and West Foods Cash and Carry Limited
Incorporated: 6 February 2019
Registered Office: 61b Caroline Street, Birmingham, B3 1UF
Officers: Surinder Singh [1974] Director/Wholesaler

East London Brewing Company Limited
Incorporated: 9 May 2011 *Employees:* 9
Net Worth: £12,081 *Total Assets:* £284,896
Registered Office: Units 44-45 Fairways Business Park, Lammas Road, London, E10 7QB
Shareholders: Claire Ashbridge-Thomlinson; Stuart Francis Lascelles
Officers: Claire Ashbridge-Thomlinson [1970] Director; Stuart Francis Lascelles [1969] Director

East Street Wine Company Limited
Incorporated: 22 June 2016 *Employees:* 2
Net Worth: £119,185 *Total Assets:* £263,444
Registered Office: 2nd Floor, Regis House, 45 King William Street, London, EC4R 9AN
Shareholders: Peter Andrew Smith; Daniel Spencer
Officers: Peter Andrew Smith [1964] Director; Daniel Spencer [1967] Director

East West Ales Limited
Incorporated: 28 May 1991 *Employees:* 7
Net Worth: £233,152 *Total Assets:* £3,091,366
Registered Office: Shadwell House, 65 Lower Green Road, Rusthall, Tunbridge Wells, Kent, TN4 8TW
Shareholders: Janet Cheeseman; David Aucutt
Officers: Janet Cheesman, Secretary; David Aucutt [1968] Director/Wholesalers & Distribution; Janet Cheesman [1947] Director/Wholesalers & Distribution

Eastcoast Supplies Ltd.
Incorporated: 10 March 2014
Previous: MRK Food Supplies Ltd
Net Worth: £3,025,891 Total Assets: £3,441,785
Registered Office: 45-47 Bond Street, South Shore, Blackpool, Lancs, FY4 1BW
Shareholder: Muhammad Rafiq Kahn
Officers: Roy Nigel Kearsley [1967] Director/Accountant; Muhammad Rafq Khan [1979] Director/Venture Capitalist

The Eastern Pantry Ltd
Incorporated: 21 June 2018
Registered Office: 70 Edinburgh Place, Coronation Square, Cheltenham, Glos, GL51 7SE
Shareholders: Leszek Ciesiolka; Rita Anna Krawczyk-Ciesiolka
Officers: Leszek Ciesiolka [1984] Director/Security Guard [Polish]; Rita Anna Krawczyk-Ciesiolka [1984] Director/Editor [Polish]

Eastlin Alba Limited
Incorporated: 8 August 2016
Net Worth Deficit: £12,412 Total Assets: £107,874
Registered Office: 42 Charlotte Square, Edinburgh, EH2 4HQ
Major Shareholder: Megan Elizebeth Brown
Officers: Megan Elizebeth Brown [1994] Director; Chinghung Tan [1991] Managing Director

Easy9 Limited
Incorporated: 30 December 2008
Registered Office: 5 Jupiter House, Calleva Park, Aldermaston, Reading, Berks, RG7 8NN
Major Shareholder: Founder Director Milan Papic
Officers: Milan Papic [1977] Director/Healer [Serbian]

Eataly Food Distributors Ltd
Incorporated: 5 September 2018
Registered Office: 2 London Mews, London, W2 1HY
Major Shareholder: Bruno Fracassi
Officers: Raimondo Demontis [1979] Director/Entrepreneur [Italian]

Ebenezer Leisure Limited
Incorporated: 22 March 2004 Employees: 1
Net Worth: £67,731 Total Assets: £133,766
Registered Office: 46 Union Street, Wick, Caithness, Sutherland, KW1 5ED
Major Shareholder: Donald Murray Lamont
Officers: Donald Murray Lamont [1957] Director/Business Proprietor

Ebony Drinks Limited
Incorporated: 27 June 2018
Registered Office: 38 Stangate Drive, Iwade, Sittingbourne, Kent, ME9 8UH
Major Shareholder: Doris Idowu Amodu
Officers: Doris Idowu Amodu [1965] Director/Management

Eclipse Drinks Limited
Incorporated: 19 March 2018
Registered Office: 54A Church Road, Ashford, Surrey, TW15 2TS
Major Shareholder: Amit Kochhar
Officers: Amit Kochhar [1976] Director

Eda Quality Foods North UK Limited
Incorporated: 23 March 2018
Registered Office: Unit 1-8 Centenary Estate, Centenary Road, Enfield, Middlesex, EN3 7UD
Shareholders: Eda Quality Foods North UK Ltd; Victoria Dincer
Officers: Victoria Dincer [1970] Director; Ercan Ucur [1970] Director

Eden Fine Wines Limited
Incorporated: 4 July 2006 Employees: 12
Net Worth: £351,665 Total Assets: £640,298
Registered Office: 6 School Court, Broompark, Co Durham, DH7 7RY
Major Shareholder: Gary Takhar
Officers: Gary Gurjinder Singh Takhar [1975] Director

Eden Garden Trading Limited
Incorporated: 29 August 2006
Registered Office: 256 Uxbridge Street, Burton on Trent, Staffs, DE14 3JX
Officers: Conceicao Pereira, Secretary/Director [Portuguese]; Conceicao Pereira [1957] Director [Portuguese]

Edgerton Holdings Limited
Incorporated: 21 May 2018
Registered Office: Flat 2, Studley Court, 166 Woodside Green, London, SE25 5EW
Major Shareholder: Martin James Edgerton Gill
Officers: Jacqueline Ann Webber, Secretary; Martin James Edgerton Gill [1939] Director

Edinburgh Cocktail Week Ltd
Incorporated: 16 February 2018
Registered Office: 40a Speirs Wharf, Glasgow, G4 9TH
Major Shareholder: Gary Anderson
Officers: Gary Anderson [1985] Director/Public Relations

Edition Spirits Ltd.
Incorporated: 15 April 2010
Registered Office: 16 Park Circus, Glasgow, G3 6AX
Parent: Hunter Laing & Company Limited
Officers: Scott Hepburn Laing, Secretary; Andrew William Douglas Laing [1982] Director

Edmunds Cocktails Ltd
Incorporated: 26 November 2018
Registered Office: 92 Barons Road, Bury St Edmunds, Suffolk, IP33 2LY
Major Shareholder: Tom Mayes
Officers: Tom Mayes [1988] Director/Salesman

Edrington European Travel Retail Limited
Incorporated: 14 February 2000
Previous: Maxxium Travel Retail Limited
Net Worth: £480,221 Total Assets: £6,514,611
Registered Office: 100 Queen Street, Glasgow, G1 3DN
Parent: Highland Distribution Company Limited
Officers: Gemma May Robson, Secretary; Kasper Moos Andersen [1977] Commercial Director [Danish]; Aristotelis Baroutsis [1973] Regional Managing Director [Swedish]; Jeremy McDowell Chaplin [1971] Director/Accountant; Scott John McCroskie [1967] Finance Director

Edrington International Brands Limited
Incorporated: 3 June 2005
Net Worth: £1,005,644 Total Assets: £1,871,262
Registered Office: 100 Queen Street, Glasgow, G1 3DN
Parent: Edrington Brands Limited
Officers: Martin Alexander Cooke, Secretary/Solicitor; Martin Alexander Cooke [1961] Director/Solicitor; Ian Barrett Curle [1961] Director; Paul Andrew Hyde [1972] Director; Scott John McCroskie [1967] Director

Edrington-Beam Suntory UK Distribution Limited
Incorporated: 4 February 2000 *Employees:* 195
Previous: Maxxium UK Limited
Net Worth: £36,735,000 *Total Assets:* £134,907,008
Registered Office: 191 West George Street, Glasgow, G2 2LD
Shareholders: Beam Suntory UK Limited; Highland Distribution Ventures Limited
Officers: Neville Douglas Ross, Secretary; Catarina Maria Alves Da Silva Toscano [1981] Director/Legal Counsel [Portuguese/British]; Aristotelis Baroutsis [1973] Managing Director [Swedish]; Jeremy McDowell Chaplin [1971] Director/Chartered Accountant; Iurii Grebenkin [1972] Managing Director [Russian]; Roman Jakob Bruno Kohler [1977] Finance Director [German]; Huw Charlton Pennell [1961] Director; Mark Riley [1972] Managing Director; Neville Douglas Ross [1971] Finance Director

Edwards Beers and Minerals Limited
Incorporated: 15 January 1986 *Employees:* 6
Net Worth: £655,829 *Total Assets:* £1,541,994
Registered Office: Unit 5 Grovebury Place Estate, Grovebury Road, Leighton Buzzard, Beds, LU7 4SH
Shareholders: Terrence Roy Edwards; Edwards Beers & Wines (Holdings) Ltd
Officers: Suzanne Edwards, Secretary; Suzanne Edwards [1953] Director; Terence Roy Edwards [1952] Managing Director

Edwards Beers and Wine Supplies Ltd
Incorporated: 28 November 2009 *Employees:* 46
Net Worth: £1,181,693 *Total Assets:* £3,517,661
Registered Office: Unit 5 Grovebury Place, Grovebury Road, Leighton Buzzard, Beds, LU7 4SH
Parent: Edwards Beers & Wines (Holdings) Ltd
Officers: Suzanne Edwards, Secretary; Graham Terrence Edwards [1980] Director/General Manager; Suzanne Edwards [1953] Director; Terence Roy Edwards [1952] Managing Director

Edwards Beers and Wines (Holdings) Ltd
Incorporated: 18 November 2010
Net Worth: £924,393 *Total Assets:* £968,966
Registered Office: Unit 5 Grovebury Place, Grovebury Road, Leighton Buzzard, Beds, LU7 4SH
Major Shareholder: Terence Roy Edwards
Officers: Suzanne Edwards [1953] Director; Terence Roy Edwards [1952] Managing Director

Morgan Edwards Limited
Incorporated: 23 January 2018
Registered Office: Knutsford Market Hall, Silk Mill Street, Knutsford, Cheshire, WA16 6DF
Officers: Edward Joseph Speakman [1991] Director; Morgan Ward [1991] Director

Edwards Wine Agencies Limited
Incorporated: 28 November 2009
Previous: Edwards Beers and Wine Merchants Ltd
Registered Office: Unit 5 Grovebury Place, Grovebury Road, Leighton Buzzard, Beds, LU7 4SH
Major Shareholder: Suzanne Edwards
Officers: Suzanne Edwards, Secretary; Suzanne Edwards [1953] Director; Terence Roy Edwards [1952] Managing Director

Eebria Limited
Incorporated: 21 January 2013
Net Worth: £525,694 *Total Assets:* £722,881
Registered Office: 15 Almond Road, London, SE16 3LR
Officers: David William Jackson [1986] Director; Rachael Sarah Jackson [1985] Director/Accountant

EFE Store Limited
Incorporated: 19 January 2016
Registered Office: 75 Hampton Road, London, E4 8NP
Major Shareholder: Haydar Gultekin
Officers: Haydar Gultekin [1980] Managing Director

Eight Brothers Corporation Limited
Incorporated: 22 February 2019
Registered Office: Flat 26, 88-98 College Road, Harrow on the Hill, Middlesex, HA1 1EQ
Major Shareholder: Carlos Emilio Raninqueo
Officers: Carlos Emilio Raninqueo [1983] Director [Spanish]

Eight Vodka Limited
Incorporated: 8 November 2018
Registered Office: 12th Floor, 6 New Street Square, London, EC4A 3BF
Shareholders: Juan David Vintimilla Palacios; Jason Kingsley Drummond
Officers: Jason Kingsley Drummond [1969] Director

EJ Orendale Ltd
Incorporated: 4 October 2018
Registered Office: 15 Mallow Street, Manchester, M15 5GE
Major Shareholder: Eunji Noh
Officers: Eunji Noh [1986] Director [South Korean]

El Brewery Limited
Incorporated: 18 April 2018
Registered Office: 36 Pasture Field Road, Manchester, M22 5JU
Major Shareholder: Eric John Hymas
Officers: Eric John Hymas [1982] Director/Wholesale Beer

EL IP Rights Limited
Incorporated: 16 August 2017
Registered Office: Belle House, Platform 1 Victoria Station, London, SW1V 1JT
Major Shareholder: Roman Park
Officers: Roman Park [1993] Director

El Toro Wines Limited
Incorporated: 6 April 2017
Net Worth: £21,809 *Total Assets:* £33,917
Registered Office: 3 West Hartlepool Road, Wolviston, Stockton on Tees, Cleveland, TS22 5JZ
Major Shareholder: Ana Maria Garcia Fernandez
Officers: Thomas John Hart, Secretary; Adrian Cortes Garcia [1992] Director/Business Manager [Spanish]; Ana Maria Garcia Fernandez [1971] Director/Retail Manager [Spanish]; Carlos Rodriguez Alonso [1976] Director/Retail Manager [Spanish]

Elements Eight Rum Company Limited
Incorporated: 31 August 2005
Net Worth: £3,055 *Total Assets:* £37,581
Registered Office: c/o Gallaghers, Titchfield House, 69-85 Tabernacle Street, London, EC2A 4BD
Shareholders: Carl Louis Stephenson; Andreas Redlefsen
Officers: Carl Louis Stephenson [1970] Director

Elicite Ltd
Incorporated: 22 September 2016 *Employees:* 9
Net Worth Deficit: £64,708 *Total Assets:* £508,250
Registered Office: The Biscuit Factory, Unit A302a, 100 Drummond Road, London, SE16 4DG
Parent: April Group SA
Officers: Jonathan Colin Fleetwood [1968] Managing Director

Elixir Wine Ltd
Incorporated: 6 February 2019
Registered Office: Methlyk, Beaconsfield Road, Chelwood Gate, Haywards Heath, W Sussex, RH17 7LE
Shareholders: Bryn Beach; Danielle Beach; Gary Beach
Officers: Bryn Beach [1972] Director; Danielle Beach [1972] Director; Gary Beach [1974] Director

Ellis of Richmond (Holdings) Limited
Incorporated: 21 July 1994 *Employees:* 75
Net Worth: £6,249,680 *Total Assets:* £9,633,510
Registered Office: Richmond House, Unit 1 The Links, Popham Close, Hanworth, Middlesex, TW13 6JE
Shareholder: Guy Maxwell Cunningham
Officers: William Derek Ellis, Secretary; Guy Maxwell Cunningham [1969] Director/Wine Merchant; Henry James Ellis [1960] Director/Wine Merchant; John Robert Henry Ellis [1963] Director/Wine Merchant; William Derek Ellis [1965] Director/Chartered Accountant; Graham Peter Triefus [1952] Director/Chartered Accountant

Ellis of Richmond Limited
Incorporated: 8 January 1944 *Employees:* 69
Net Worth: £3,879,142 *Total Assets:* £8,047,245
Registered Office: Richmond House, Unit 1 The Links, Popham Close, Hanworth, Middlesex, TW13 6JE
Parent: Ellis of Richmond (Holdings) Ltd
Officers: Henry James Ellis, Secretary; Guy Maxwell Cunningham [1969] Director/Wine Merchant; Henry James Ellis [1960] Director/Wine Merchant; John Robert Henry Ellis [1963] Director/Wine Merchant; William Derek Ellis [1965] Director/Chartered Accountant; Peter John Harwood [1953] Director/Wine Merchant; Martin Paul Longley [1947] Director/Wine Merchant; Graham Peter Triefus [1952] Director/Chartered Accountant

Ellis Wharton Wines Ltd
Incorporated: 13 June 2006 *Employees:* 4
Net Worth: £269,796 *Total Assets:* £391,998
Registered Office: The Old Carriage Works, Moresk Road, Truro, Cornwall, TR1 1DG
Shareholder: Charles Edward Clegg Wharton
Officers: David Michael Ellis, Secretary/Director; David Michael Ellis [1950] Director; Charles Edward Clegg Wharton [1971] Director

Ellismuir Limited
Incorporated: 6 February 2017
Net Worth Deficit: £12,782 *Total Assets:* £2,938
Registered Office: 9 Royal Crescent, Glasgow, G3 7SP
Major Shareholder: Sebajeevan Sebaratnam
Officers: John David Atkings [1948] Director; Robert Donald [1950] Director; Sebajeevan Sebaratnam [1976] Director [German]

Elliston Fine Wines Limited
Incorporated: 22 September 2003 *Employees:* 3
Net Worth: £31,262 *Total Assets:* £3,315,766
Registered Office: 19 Fenkle Street, Alnwick, Northumberland, NE66 1HW
Shareholders: Piers Harry North Dalrymple Methuen; Rebecca Methuen
Officers: Rebecca Methuen, Secretary; Piers Harry North Dalrymple Methuen [1966] Director/Business Executive; Rebecca Methuen [1969] Director/Secretary

Ellustria Limited
Incorporated: 9 June 2016
Net Worth Deficit: £9,367 *Total Assets:* £455,710
Registered Office: c/o Clintons, 55 Drury Lane, London, WC2B 5RZ
Officers: Roman Park [1993] Director

Ely & Sidney Limited
Incorporated: 30 June 1981 *Employees:* 3
Net Worth: £811,735 *Total Assets:* £6,741,256
Registered Office: 91 Brick Lane, London, E1 6QL
Shareholder: Ely & Sidney Holdings Limited
Officers: Jason Zeloof, Secretary; Jason Zeloof [1974] Director

Ely's Cocktails Ltd
Incorporated: 14 May 2018
Registered Office: Sagittarius, 4th Floor, Golderbrook House, 15-19 Great Titchfield Street, London, W1W 8AZ
Parent: Ely's Cocktails SAS
Officers: Ely Niang-Fall [1987] Director/Officer [French]; Guillaume Sudre [1985] Director/Chief Executive Officer (CEO) [French]

Eminent Life Limited
Incorporated: 27 April 2015
Net Worth Deficit: £47,411 *Total Assets:* £74,392
Registered Office: 1 Berkeley Street, London, W1J 8DJ
Major Shareholder: Jerome Jean Jacober
Officers: Jerome Jean Jacober [1981] Director [Swiss]

Eminent Wines Limited
Incorporated: 15 November 2006
Net Worth Deficit: £55,409 *Total Assets:* £2,892
Registered Office: 1 Berkeley Street, Mayfair, London, W1J 8DJ
Major Shareholder: Jerome Jean Jacober
Officers: Jerome Jean Jacober [1981] Director [Swiss]

Empire Drinks Ltd
Incorporated: 20 July 2018
Registered Office: 616D Green Lane, Ilford, Essex, IG3 9SE
Major Shareholder: Priya Bihal
Officers: Priya Bihal [1991] Director/Psychologist

Empire Star Limited
Incorporated: 26 June 1997 *Employees:* 35
Net Worth: £1,999,666 *Total Assets:* £7,355,451
Registered Office: c/o Patara Chartered Accountants, 352 Bearwood Road, Bearwood, Smethwick, W Midlands, B66 4ET
Shareholders: Baron Wayne Robert Davenport; Kulvinder Singh Uppal; Harbinder Singh Uppal
Officers: Rajinder Singh, Secretary; Baron Wayne Robert Davenport [1967] Director; Ian Edward Robinson [1974] Director; Harbinder Singh Uppal [1967] Director

Emporia Brands Limited
Incorporated: 6 July 1959 *Employees:* 14
Net Worth: £749,306 *Total Assets:* £2,805,689
Registered Office: The Church, 172 London Road, Guildford, Surrey, GU1 1XR
Major Shareholder: James Arthur Rackham
Officers: William Peter Duff, Secretary; William Peter Duff [1983] Finance Director; Jack Arthur Rackham [1987] Director/Bar Manager; James Arthur Rackham [1953] Director; Atherton John West [1954] Marketing Director

Emporium Import Ltd
Incorporated: 24 July 2013 *Employees:* 2
Net Worth Deficit: £224,057 *Total Assets:* £19,208
Registered Office: 5 Yeomans Court, Ware Road, Hertford, SG13 7HJ
Major Shareholder: Gary Frank Ronald Squibb
Officers: Gary Squibb [1956] Director; John Gary Squibb [1986] Director

Empress Ale Ltd
Incorporated: 14 May 2015
Net Worth: £110,746 *Total Assets:* £127,073
Registered Office: 18 Willes Road, Leamington Spa, Warwicks, CV32 4PY
Shareholders: Grenville Turner; Surjeeven Virk
Officers: Grenville Turner [1957] Director; Surjeeven Virk [1979] Managing Director

Emthea Ltd
Incorporated: 16 May 2018
Registered Office: Kemp House, 160 City Road, London, EC1V 2NX
Shareholder: Anthea Okolie
Officers: Chukwuemeka Okolie [1983] Director/Account Manager [Nigerian]

Englishman Supplies Limited
Incorporated: 19 November 2004 *Employees:* 4
Net Worth Deficit: £79,720 *Total Assets:* £47,859
Registered Office: 3 Clanricarde Gardens, Tunbridge Wells, Kent, TN1 1HQ
Shareholders: James Bruce MacNay; Cinzia Long
Officers: Bruce William MacNay, Secretary; John Vernon Carter [1950] Director; Cinzia Long [1974] Director/Tourism Consultant [Italian]; James Bruce MacNay [1977] Director

Enjoydrinks Limited
Incorporated: 18 November 2009
Net Worth: £14,957 *Total Assets:* £182,900
Registered Office: Windfall House, D1, The Courtyard, Alban Park, St Albans, Herts, AL4 0LA
Major Shareholder: Stephen Frederick Doggett
Officers: Stephen Frederick Doggett [1975] Managing Director

Enmore Wine Limited
Incorporated: 16 November 2010
Net Worth: £2,312 *Total Assets:* £3,225
Registered Office: Enmore Castle (West), Church Lane, Enmore, Bridgwater, Somerset, TA5 2DU
Major Shareholder: Anne Christine Stoye
Officers: Anne Christine Stoye [1953] Director/Administrator

Enny Wines Ltd
Incorporated: 10 July 2015
Net Worth Deficit: £4,199 *Total Assets:* £8,339
Registered Office: 1 Tower Road, Little Downham, Ely, Cambs, CB6 2TD
Shareholders: Julia Davis; John Hill
Officers: Julia Davis [1956] Director/Local Authority Officer; John Hill [1963] Director/Local Authority Officer

Enopoli Limited
Incorporated: 7 December 2004
Net Worth: £38,101 *Total Assets:* £45,150
Registered Office: Millennium Business Centre, Humber Trading Estate, Humber Road, Staples Corner, London, NW2 6DW
Major Shareholder: Gaetano Sallesio
Officers: Carla Grandoni, Secretary/Administrator [Italian]; Gaetano Sallesio [1971] Director [Italian]

Enotria Winecellars Limited
Incorporated: 14 September 1972 *Employees:* 280
Net Worth: £8,810,092 *Total Assets:* £91,997,264
Registered Office: 23 Cumberland Avenue, London, NW10 7RX
Parent: Enotria Holdings Limited
Officers: Mark Huszczo, Secretary; Troy Christensen [1966] Director [American]; Jon Pepper [1977] Director

Enovino Organic Ltd
Incorporated: 16 March 2012
Net Worth Deficit: £58,256 *Total Assets:* £15,801
Registered Office: 15H Dalgarno Gardens, London, W10 5JN
Major Shareholder: Adjet Jean Claude Kouame
Officers: Adjet Jean Claude Kouame [1963] Director

Enzo's Food and Wine Ltd
Incorporated: 7 February 2019
Registered Office: 20-22 Wenlock Road, London, N1 7GU
Major Shareholder: Vincenzo Maida
Officers: Vincenzo Maida [1958] Director [Italian]

Ephemeris Solutions Ltd
Incorporated: 4 April 2018
Registered Office: 56 Denbigh Road, Norwich, NR2 3HH
Major Shareholder: Katherine Hannah Evans
Officers: Katherine Hannah Evans [1988] Director/Consultant

Epic Beers Limited
Incorporated: 13 April 2017
Net Worth: £17,452 *Total Assets:* £82,604
Registered Office: The Brewery, West Hewish, Weston-Super-Mare, Somerset, BS24 6RR
Shareholders: Graham Dunbavan; Mark Charles Davey
Officers: Mark Charles Davey [1966] Director/Manager; Graham Dunbavan [1959] Director/Brewer; David Allen Turner [1974] Director

Epicure Wines Ltd
Incorporated: 21 June 2004 *Employees:* 1
Net Worth Deficit: £2,307 *Total Assets:* £75,355
Registered Office: 50 Weston Road, Rochester, Kent, ME2 3HA
Major Shareholder: Hughes Brisset
Officers: Hugues Brisset, Secretary/Director [French]; Hugues Brisset [1971] Director [French]

Epicurean Food and Drink Corporation Limited
Incorporated: 23 January 1978
Net Worth Deficit: £13,306 *Total Assets:* £46,041
Registered Office: Blemann House, Unit 3 Clayton Wood Industrial Estate, Clayton Wood Close, Leeds, LS16 6QE
Officers: Hilton Anthony Lorie, Secretary; Harris Mark Lorie [1986] Director; Hilton Anthony Lorie [1954] Director

Epiphany Bars Limited
Incorporated: 22 October 2018
Registered Office: 6a Hillside Road, Southall, Middlesex, UB1 2PD
Major Shareholder: Ravneet Singh Lalia
Officers: Ravneet Singh Lalia [1995] Director/Barman

ERE Igga Ltd
Incorporated: 8 January 2019
Registered Office: 139 Avon Street, Coventry, Warwicks, CV2 3GQ
Major Shareholder: Hawa Bari
Officers: Koko Tanoh, Secretary; Hawa Bari [1983] Director/Sales Professional

Erin Vintners Ltd
Incorporated: 5 February 2014
Net Worth: £135,050 *Total Assets:* £359,890
Registered Office: 27 Main Street, Rathmore, Belleek, Enniskillen, Co Fermanagh, BT93 3FY
Major Shareholder: Michael Gramsch
Officers: Catherine Gramsch, Secretary; Michael Gramsch [1959] Director/Businessman [German]

Espana Imports Ltd
Incorporated: 28 June 2016
Net Worth Deficit: £350 *Total Assets:* £100
Registered Office: Castle Chambers, 6 Westgate Hill, Pembroke, SA71 4LB
Shareholders: Tarulata Vinod Pitamber; Vinodlal Samji Pitamber
Officers: Vinodlal Samji Pitamber [1949] Director

Espir Baron & Solomon Limited
Incorporated: 17 September 2018
Registered Office: 2nd Floor, Gadd House, Arcadia Avenue, London, N3 2JU
Major Shareholder: Robert Aaron Espir
Officers: Daniel Baron Argeband [1985] Director; Robert Aaron Espir [1985] Director

Essenza Di Romagna Limited
Incorporated: 11 July 2016
Net Worth: £2 *Total Assets:* £6,002
Registered Office: 2 Stephyns Drive, Fleet, Hants, GU51 1GN
Shareholders: Robert Oates; Roderick Springett
Officers: Robert John Oades [1955] Director; Roderick Francis Springett [1953] Director

Essex Catering Supplies Limited
Incorporated: 14 October 2002 *Employees:* 1
Net Worth Deficit: £22,492 *Total Assets:* £87,387
Registered Office: Unit F, Wrexham Road, Basildon, Essex, SS15 6PX
Major Shareholder: Mohammad Mir-Tahmasebi
Officers: Mohammad Mirtahmasebi [1960] Director/Manager

Estelon Holdings Limited
Incorporated: 5 January 2018
Registered Office: Broad Water Lodge, Higham Road, London, N17 6NN
Officers: Uzaifa Katende [1989] Director

Ester Wines Limited
Incorporated: 21 May 2014 *Employees:* 1
Net Worth Deficit: £66,645 *Total Assets:* £127,600
Registered Office: 5 Jupiter House, Calleva Park, Aldermaston, Reading, Berks, RG7 8NN
Major Shareholder: Adam Louis Dugmore
Officers: Adam Louis Dugmore [1979] Director/Wine Importer

Estini Ltd
Incorporated: 3 August 2018
Registered Office: 1 Wellington House, 160 Upper Richmond Road, London, SW15 2SW
Shareholders: David Strang; Simon Edwin Peter Hardcastle
Officers: Simon Edwin Peter Hardcastle [1984] Director/Project Manager; David Strang [1972] Managing Director

Etna Food & Wine Ltd
Incorporated: 20 February 2016
Net Worth: £1,091 *Total Assets:* £35,758
Registered Office: Unit C, 111 Watery Lane, Darwen, Blackburn, BB3 2EB
Shareholders: Franco Lorusso; Antonino Turano
Officers: Antonino Turano, Secretary; Franco Lorusso [1970] Director [Italian]; Antonio Turano [1976] Director [Italian]

Euro Asia Distriubtion Limited
Incorporated: 8 December 2017
Registered Office: 11 Graham Road, West Bromwich, W Midlands, B71 4ED
Officers: Som Nath Sapkota [1974] Director [Portuguese]

Euro Beer Distribution Ltd
Incorporated: 1 June 2004 *Employees:* 2
Net Worth: £116 *Total Assets:* £998,000
Registered Office: 6 Short Street, Willenhall, W Midlands, WV12 4JS
Shareholder: Mandip Singh
Officers: Mandip Singh, Secretary; Rajinder Singh Sanghera [1973] Director; Mandip Singh [1977] Director

Euro Link Beverages Ltd
Incorporated: 17 August 2012 *Employees:* 2
Net Worth Deficit: £22,191 *Total Assets:* £1,401
Registered Office: 1 Old Park Road, 5 High Acres, Enfield, Middlesex, EN2 7DT
Major Shareholder: Tahir Isaac
Officers: Tahir Isaac [1954] Director

Euro Speed Intl Ltd
Incorporated: 13 January 2014
Net Worth Deficit: £16,822
Registered Office: Office 4, Brook House Business Centre, Brook Street, Tipton, W Midlands, DY4 9DD
Major Shareholder: Avtar Kular
Officers: Avtar Kular [1974] Director/Imports

Euro Wines (C & C) Limited
Incorporated: 9 March 2007
Net Worth: £661,224 *Total Assets:* £2,556,135
Registered Office: 5-9 Creekside, Deptford, London, SE8 4SA
Major Shareholder: Balbir Singh Ghuman
Officers: John Andrew Donald [1958] Director/Employee; Balbir Singh Ghuman [1967] Director

Euro-Trade and Finance Limited
Incorporated: 24 April 1991
Net Worth: £71,730 *Total Assets:* £165,092
Registered Office: 1 The Paddocks, Wood Street, Swanley, Kent, BR8 7PA
Officers: Ian Joseph Hercules [1978] Director/Accountant

Euroboozer Limited
Incorporated: 18 May 2001 *Employees:* 10
Net Worth Deficit: £55,575 *Total Assets:* £1,213,187
Registered Office: Notley Farm, Bedmond Road, Abbots Langley, Herts, WD5 0GX
Major Shareholder: Martyn Adam Railton
Officers: Jason Smith, Secretary; Martyn Adam Railton [1981] Director/Importer

Eurochoice Limited
Incorporated: 1 December 2008
Net Worth: £41,271 *Total Assets:* £5,293,382
Registered Office: Continental House, 497 Sunleigh Road, Wembley, Middlesex, HA0 4LY
Officers: Salmon Ahmed [1970] Director

Euroofar Trading Limited
Incorporated: 25 May 2016
Registered Office: 221 Horninglow Road, Burton on Trent, Staffs, DE14 2PY
Major Shareholder: Feilun Zheng
Officers: Fei Lun Zheng [1979] Director

Europa Drinks Limited
Incorporated: 22 March 2010 *Employees:* 1
Net Worth: £340,977 *Total Assets:* £404,998
Registered Office: 18 St Christophers Way, Pride Park, Derby, DE24 8JY
Officers: Devshi Kana [1974] Director

European Beer Exports Limited
Incorporated: 6 June 2018
Registered Office: 5 The Lodge, Rectory Farm, East Farndon Road, Marston Trussell, Market Harborough, Leics, LE16 9TU
Shareholders: Andrew Michael Caswell; Nicholas John Shuttleworth
Officers: Andrew Michael Caswell [1961] Director; Nicholas John Shuttleworth [1967] Director

European Beverages Ltd
Incorporated: 25 October 1999
Net Worth: £14,861 Total Assets: £125,805
Registered Office: 416 Green Lane, Ilford, Essex, IG3 9JX
Officers: Hassan Yildiz [1976] Director

European Brand Trading Limited
Incorporated: 26 August 2004
Net Worth Deficit: £698,953 Total Assets: £906,357
Registered Office: Cedarlea, 16 Barracks Lane, Ravensmoor, Nantwich, Cheshire, CW5 8PR
Parent: Gresty Holdings Limited
Officers: Mark Andrew Hassall, Secretary/Accountant; Catherine Ann Hassall [1945] Director; Norman Hassall [1943] Director

European Wine Brokers Limited
Incorporated: 22 April 2014
Registered Office: Carrayol Arch, 8 Church Crescent, London, N10 3ND
Major Shareholder: Demetri Demetriou
Officers: Demetri Demetriou [1952] Director/Wine Broker

Europebro Wholesalers Ltd
Incorporated: 17 November 2014
Net Worth: £5,006 Total Assets: £20,414
Registered Office: 41 Gainsborough Tower, Academy Gardens, Northolt, Middlesex, UB5 5PF
Major Shareholder: Daniel Coumarakichenane
Officers: Daniel Coumarakichenane [1971] Director [French]

Europemarca Limited
Incorporated: 29 March 2000 Employees: 2
Net Worth: £581,046 Total Assets: £938,276
Registered Office: 229 Greenwood Road, Bakersfield, Nottingham, NG3 7FU
Shareholders: Pierluigi Turatti; Jowita Sowinska-Turatti
Officers: Jowita Sowinska-Turatti [1975] Director/Manager [Polish]; Pierluigi Turatti [1949] Director/Importer [Italian]

Europlus Trading Limited
Incorporated: 21 January 2000 Employees: 1
Net Worth: £182,195 Total Assets: £626,419
Registered Office: Old Station Road, Loughton, Essex, IG10 4PL
Shareholders: Mary Catherine Green; Jonathan Paul Porter
Officers: Jonathan Paul Porter [1964] Director/General Trader

Europvin UK Limited
Incorporated: 29 September 1999
Net Worth Deficit: £2,121 Total Assets: £3,196
Registered Office: 5a Station Terrace, East Boldon, Co Durham, NE36 0LJ
Parent: Europvin SA
Officers: Pierre Codaccioni, Secretary; Beatriz Pilar [1974] Director/Manager [Spanish]; Julia Wilkinson [1961] Director/Wine Consultant

Eurorock Trading Limited
Incorporated: 15 March 2004 Employees: 1
Net Worth: £19,397 Total Assets: £38,860
Registered Office: 110 Carlton Avenue East, Wembley, Middlesex, HA9 8LY
Major Shareholder: Pravin Kara
Officers: Pravin Ratna Kara [1965] Director

Eurotrade Supply Limited
Incorporated: 20 September 2018
Registered Office: Kemp House, City Road, London, EC1V 2NX
Major Shareholder: Dennis Michael Dennis Michael Obrien
Officers: Dennis Michael Obrien [1964] Director

Eurovenus Limited
Incorporated: 7 February 1989
Net Worth Deficit: £682,173 Total Assets: £4,372,716
Registered Office: 56a Haverstock Hill, London, NW3 2BH
Officers: Pantelis Chrysostomou, Secretary; Pantelis Chrysostomou [1977] Director; Lucy Katsantonis [1970] Director

Eurovines Limited
Incorporated: 29 March 1994 Employees: 12
Net Worth: £1,012 Total Assets: £516,898
Registered Office: The Forge, Nettlestone Hill, Seaview, Isle of Wight, PO34 5DU
Shareholders: Timothy Martin Flint; Evelyn Flint
Officers: Evelyn Flint, Secretary; Evelyn Flint [1968] Director/Wholesale Wine Merchant; Timothy Martin Flint [1964] Director/Wine Merchant

Eurowines Limited
Incorporated: 13 July 1966 Employees: 15
Net Worth: £1,885,396 Total Assets: £4,884,157
Registered Office: Vintage House, 6 Heathmans Road, London, SW6 4TJ
Shareholders: Leonardo Addis; Nello Battistel
Officers: Nello Battistel, Secretary; Leonardo Addis [1967] Director [Italian]; Nello Battistel [1969] Sales Director

Euroworld Foods Limited
Incorporated: 14 May 2008
Registered Office: Berkeley Suite, 35 Berkeley Square, London, W1J 5BF
Officers: Abdul Shakoor [1967] Director

H.B. Evelyo Ltd.
Incorporated: 28 November 2017
Registered Office: 2nd Floor, Stratus House, Emperor Way, Exeter Business Park, Exeter, Devon, EX1 3QS
Major Shareholder: Philip Everett-Lyons
Officers: Philip Everett-Lyons [1983] Director

Event Wine Solutions Limited
Incorporated: 28 March 2013
Net Worth: £39,999 Total Assets: £135,693
Registered Office: Daisy Cottage, The Fields, Mere, Warminster, Wilts, BA12 6EA
Major Shareholder: Antony Paul Scaife
Officers: Antony Paul Scaife [1963] Director; Debra Jane Scaife [1962] Director

Eventus Global Ltd
Incorporated: 12 November 2014
Net Worth Deficit: £91,910 Total Assets: £107,092
Registered Office: The Tall House, 29a West Street, Marlow, Bucks, SL7 2LS
Shareholder: Mark Griffith
Officers: Mark Griffith [1971] Director

Ever-Tree Wholesale & Retail Limited
Incorporated: 4 July 2018
Registered Office: Unit 7-10 Station Approach, Hitchin, Herts, SG4 9UW
Major Shareholder: Sercihan Yusuf Ucur
Officers: Sercihan Yusuf Ucur [1995] Director

Everards Brewery Limited
Incorporated: 7 October 1936 *Employees:* 75
Net Worth: £81,160,000 *Total Assets:* £111,340,000
Registered Office: Devana Avenue, Optimus Point, Glenfield, Leicester, LE3 8JS
Major Shareholder: Richard Anthony Spencer Everard
Officers: Nigel Geoffrey Allen, Secretary; Nigel Geoffrey Allen [1975] Finance Director; Julian William Spencer Everard [1988] Director; Richard Anthony Spencer Everard [1954] Director; Stephen Gould [1968] Director; John Nicholas Lloyd [1948] Director; Serena Anne Richards [1952] Director; Charlotte Ione Vowles [1985] Director; Adrian Robert Weston [1935] Director

Evergreen Foods Limited
Incorporated: 12 February 2018
Registered Office: 71-75 Shelton Street, Covent Garden, London, WC2H 9JQ
Major Shareholder: Kalin Bambani
Officers: Kalin Bambani, Secretary; Kalin Bambani [1997] Director [Bulgarian]

Evernex Ltd
Incorporated: 30 September 2009
Net Worth Deficit: £22,598 *Total Assets:* £80,324
Registered Office: Unit 101 Kingspark Business Centre, Kingston Road, New Malden, Surrey, KT3 3ST
Major Shareholder: Dohyung Kim
Officers: Dohyung Kim, Secretary; Dohyung Kim [1969] Director

Everyday Wholesale Ltd
Incorporated: 27 January 2011
Net Worth Deficit: £363,870 *Total Assets:* £153,484
Registered Office: 67A Waterside Trading Centre, Trumpers Way, London, W7 2QD
Major Shareholder: Jatinder Singh Johal
Officers: Jatinder Singh Johal [1969] Director

Evil Spirits Ltd
Incorporated: 23 February 2017 *Employees:* 2
Net Worth: £1,809 *Total Assets:* £11,979
Registered Office: Tower Buildings, 9 Oldgate, Morpeth, Northumberland, NE61 1PY
Parent: Harper & Willow Ltd
Officers: Paul Andrew Brown, Secretary; Francis John Major [1978] Director; Helen Major [1981] Director

Evocative Wines Limited
Incorporated: 22 March 2017
Registered Office: Elm Farm, Woodstock Lane South, Claygate, Esher, Surrey, KT10 0TB
Major Shareholder: Michael Letellier
Officers: Michael Letellier [1948] Director/Wine Importer

Evok3 Ltd
Incorporated: 23 August 2018
Registered Office: Apartment 11, 70 Renforth Street, London, SE16 7JZ
Officers: Carlos Nelson Arano Nacif [1990] Director [Italian]; Jon Bazan Martinez [1991] Director [Spanish]

Evokesomm Limited
Incorporated: 18 November 2016
Net Worth Deficit: £19,416 *Total Assets:* £35,821
Registered Office: 97 Tewit Lane, Halifax, W Yorks, HX2 9SD
Major Shareholder: Jacqueline Sharp
Officers: Maxine Helliwell [1974] Director; Jacqueline Sharp [1967] Director

Evolution Drinks Ltd
Incorporated: 4 July 2018
Registered Office: John A Walker, 1a Davyhulme Circle, Urmston, Manchester, M41 0ST
Major Shareholder: John Frederick Terry
Officers: John Frederick Terry [1967] Managing Director

EW Bars Limited
Incorporated: 5 October 2018
Registered Office: 69 Unitt Road, Loughborough, Leics, LE12 8BX
Major Shareholder: Eleanar Wilson
Officers: Eleanar Wilson [1988] Director/Wholesaler

Ewer Limited
Incorporated: 4 March 1992
Net Worth Deficit: £301,127 *Total Assets:* £48,092
Registered Office: 21 Wavendon Avenue, Chiswick, London, W4 4NP
Officers: Elizabeth Eleanor Radaelli, Secretary; Patricia Etiennette Yveline Annick Coates [1939] Director/Retired; Elizabeth Eleanor Radaelli [1937] Director/Company Secretary; Ernesto Remo Radaelli [1943] Director/Wine Merchant [Italian]

Excess UK Limited
Incorporated: 5 April 2004 *Employees:* 3
Net Worth Deficit: £38,838 *Total Assets:* £222,559
Registered Office: Unit 5 Nimrod Industrial Estate, Nimrod Way, Reading, Berks, RG2 0EB
Major Shareholder: Imran Khan
Officers: Imran Khan [1969] Sales Director

Exeter Drinks Ltd
Incorporated: 6 August 2015
Net Worth Deficit: £21,128 *Total Assets:* £124,821
Registered Office: Unit 2 Aylesbeare Business Common Park, Aylesbeare, Exeter, EX5 2DG
Major Shareholder: Julian Simon Packer
Officers: Julian Packer, Secretary; Julian Simon Packer [1965] Director/Wine Merchant

Exigo (UK) Limited
Incorporated: 29 May 2007 *Employees:* 1
Net Worth: £23,263 *Total Assets:* £330,617
Registered Office: Barnside, 3-5 Church Street, Ampthill, Bedford, MK45 2PJ
Major Shareholder: Steven Adam Lamont
Officers: Steven Adam Lamont, Secretary; Steven Adam Lamont [1987] Director

Exivi Limited
Incorporated: 14 August 2018
Registered Office: 238 Birmingham Road, Great Barr, Birmingham, B43 7AH
Major Shareholder: Amarjeet Singh Kudhail
Officers: Amarjeet Singh Kudhail [1975] Director/Consultant

Exmoor Wines Limited
Incorporated: 29 July 2003
Net Worth Deficit: £14,423 Total Assets: £7,809
Registered Office: Lime Court, Pathfields Business Park, South Molton, Devon, EX36 3LH
Major Shareholder: James Edward Macmillan
Officers: Sophia Elizabeth Pares Macmillan, Secretary; James Edward Macmillan [1967] Director

Experience Wine Limited
Incorporated: 10 August 2007 Employees: 2
Net Worth Deficit: £322,953 Total Assets: £184,729
Registered Office: Winchester House, Deane Gate Avenue, Taunton, Somerset, TA1 2UH
Shareholder: Mark St John Graham Forbes
Officers: Chris Witherden, Secretary; Nigel James Ede [1972] Commercial Director; Kathryn Alexandra Forbes [1961] Director/Hotelier; Mark St John Graham Forbes [1956] Director/Hotelier

Expert Euro Exports Ltd
Incorporated: 11 September 2017
Registered Office: 61d Ashvale Place, Aberdeen, AB10 6QJ
Shareholders: Craig Davies; Andy Jastrzebski
Officers: Craig Davies [1989] Director; Andy Jastrzebski [1951] Director [Polish]

Explore British Drinks Limited
Incorporated: 21 December 2017
Registered Office: F27 Sabichi House, 5 Wadsworth Road, Perivale, Middlesex, UB6 7JD
Major Shareholder: Robert Neil Stanley
Officers: Robert Neil Stanley [1982] Director

Export and Import Trading Ltd
Incorporated: 15 February 2019
Registered Office: 1 Bowden Terminal, Luckyn Lane, Basildon, Essex, SS14 3AX
Major Shareholder: Richard John Hull
Officers: Richard John Hull [1959] Director

Express Drinks Ltd
Incorporated: 23 November 2012
Net Worth: £269,061 Total Assets: £514,914
Registered Office: Unit 3 Naylor Court, Patterson Street, Blaydon on Tyne, Tyne & Wear, NE21 5SD
Major Shareholder: Edwin Rayne
Officers: Edwin Rayne [1958] Director

Expression du Terroir Limited
Incorporated: 22 October 2014
Net Worth Deficit: £192,925 Total Assets: £1,391,073
Registered Office: Suite A, 4-6 Canfield Place, London, NW6 3BT
Officers: Muriel Hughette Chatel [1967] Director [French]

Expressmode Limited
Incorporated: 29 July 1998 Employees: 14
Net Worth: £419,870 Total Assets: £1,009,969
Registered Office: Suite 1, Aireside House, Royd Ings Avenue, Keighley, W Yorks, BD21 4BZ
Shareholders: David Paul Ambler; Stephen David Buckley
Officers: Stephen David Buckley, Secretary/Director; David Paul Ambler [1963] Director; Stephen David Buckley [1973] Director/Secretary

Extravision Security Systems Limited
Incorporated: 5 May 2005 Employees: 1
Net Worth Deficit: £17,048 Total Assets: £131,680
Registered Office: Roxy Venue, Wharf Street, Sowerby Bridge, W Yorks, HX6 2AE
Major Shareholder: Lee Nuttall
Officers: Lee Stuart Nuttall, Secretary; Lee Stuart Nuttall [1981] Director/Company Secretary

Exul Limited
Incorporated: 3 December 2018
Registered Office: 15 Hamilton Court, 66 Ashburton Road, Croydon, Surrey, CR0 6AN
Major Shareholder: Henrietta Sampene
Officers: Henrietta Sampene [1985] Director

Eythrope Wine Limited
Incorporated: 3 February 2016 Employees: 3
Net Worth: £1,128,654 Total Assets: £1,167,722
Registered Office: Windmill Hill, Silk Street, Waddesdon, Aylesbury, Bucks, HP18 0JZ
Major Shareholder: Nathaniel Charles Jacob Rothschild
Officers: Craig Christian Armstrong [1971] Director; Magnus James Goodlad [1972] Director; Ben Walter Howkins [1942] Director/Consultant

F & B Premium Brands Limited
Incorporated: 24 September 2010
Net Worth: £45,358 Total Assets: £156,788
Registered Office: Pantiles Chambers, 85 High Street, Tunbridge Wells, Kent, TN1 1XP
Major Shareholder: Denis Renty
Officers: Denis Jean Renty [1970] Director [Belgian]

F8t B8dgers Ltd
Incorporated: 5 October 2018
Registered Office: 9-11 Market Street, Stalybridge, Cheshire, SK15 2AL
Major Shareholder: Philip Waite
Officers: Philip Waite [1969] Director/Publican

Fabijhon Wine Ltd
Incorporated: 18 December 2017
Registered Office: 2 Lauriston Close, Knaphill, Woking, Surrey, GU21 2AU
Major Shareholder: Ion Panait
Officers: Ion Panait [1962] Director/Sale of Wine Products [Romanian]

Fabre Brothers Ltd
Incorporated: 27 February 2019
Registered Office: Flat 22, Courier Court, 2 Guardian Avenue, London, NW9 4AZ
Major Shareholder: Jean-Philippe Fabre
Officers: Jean-Philippe Fabre [1990] Director/Entrepreneur [French]

Fabulous Gin Ltd
Incorporated: 19 December 2018
Registered Office: 166 Linacre Road, Liverpool, L21 8JU
Shareholders: Gaynor Purcell; Susan Metcalf; Lisa Maria Copp
Officers: Lisa Maria Copp [1973] Director; Susan Metcalf [1966] Director; Gaynor Purcell [1977] Director

Fah Mai Holdings Limited
Incorporated: 14 June 2017
Registered Office: Unit 3 Merchant, Station Road, Smeeth, Ashford, Kent, TN25 6SX
Officers: Louis Haseman [1984] Director

Fair City Spirits Limited
Incorporated: 11 September 2017
Registered Office: Ruthven Villa, Montrose Road, Auchterarder, Perth & Kinross, PH3 1BZ
Major Shareholder: Robert Daniel Fergus Hartley
Officers: Robert Daniel Fergus Hartley [1965] Director

Fair Fayre Food & Wines Limited
Incorporated: 20 December 2013 *Employees:* 2
Net Worth: £34,443 *Total Assets:* £34,443
Registered Office: 16 Churchill Way, Cardiff, CF10 2DX
Officers: Anne Bowe, Secretary; Anne Bowe [1957] Director [Irish]; Paul Bowe [1953] Director [Irish]

Fairview Vineyard Ltd
Incorporated: 7 August 2017
Registered Office: Fairview, Goldford Lane, Bickerton, Malpas, Cheshire, SY14 8LL
Shareholders: William Smith; Robert Smith
Officers: Dr Liane Margaret Smith [1960] Director/Head of Estates; Robert Smith [1989] Assistant Director; William Smith [1987] Director

Fairview Wines Limited
Incorporated: 20 July 2015 *Employees:* 1
Net Worth Deficit: £28,911 *Total Assets:* £50,506
Registered Office: 98 Oving Road, Chichester, W Sussex, PO19 7EW
Shareholders: Robert John Wattie; Robert John Wattie
Officers: Robert John Wattie [1976] Director/Wine Merchant

Fairway Foods Limited
Incorporated: 30 May 2002
Net Worth: £58,799 *Total Assets:* £65,878
Registered Office: 20 Shepherds Bush Road, Hammersmith, London, W6 7PJ
Major Shareholder: Sajid Ishaq
Officers: Sajid Ishaq [1965] Director/Businessman

Fairytale Gin Limited
Incorporated: 31 December 2018
Registered Office: Old Manor Farm, Bockleton, Tenbury Wells, Worcs, WR15 8PP
Shareholders: Charlotte Elizabeth Pile; Mark Pile
Officers: Charlotte Elizabeth Pile [1976] Creative Director; Mark Pile [1975] Director/Head of Manufacturing

Faking Bad Brewery Limited
Incorporated: 30 November 2018
Registered Office: 32 Woodhall Road, Pencaitland, Tranent, E Lothian, EH34 5AR
Shareholders: Gareth Alun Evans; Gordon George Kidd
Officers: Gareth Alun Evans [1973] Director; Gordon George Kidd [1974] Director

Falcon Vintners Limited
Incorporated: 21 February 1995 *Employees:* 5
Net Worth: £508,739 *Total Assets:* £3,764,429
Registered Office: 93 Bohemia Road, St Leonards on Sea, E Sussex, TN37 6RJ
Shareholders: Eric Sabourin; Claire Elizabeth Sabourin; Falcon Vintners Holdings Ltd; Claire Elizabeth Sabourin; Falcon Vintners Holdings Limited
Officers: Claire Sabourin, Secretary; Jonathan Arcaini [1980] Director/Wine Merchant; Eric Sabourin [1968] Director/Wine Trade [Canadian]

Falcon Wholesaler Limited
Incorporated: 14 August 2017
Registered Office: 32 Landstead Road, London, SE18 2LH
Officers: Thomas Peter James Welch [1982] Director/Self Employed

Falugamaro International Ltd
Incorporated: 18 October 2018
Registered Office: 20-22 Wenlock Road, London, N1 7GU
Shareholders: Gabriele Rosella; Matteo Monti; Luciano Garau
Officers: Dr Luciano Garau [1995] Director [Italian]; Dr Matteo Monti [1995] Director [Italian]

Fameface Import Limited
Incorporated: 2 February 2017
Net Worth Deficit: £11,480 *Total Assets:* £46,000
Registered Office: Kemp House, 160 City Road, London, EC1V 2NX
Major Shareholder: Chukwuebuka Ukachukwu
Officers: Chukwuebuka Ukachukwu, Secretary; Chukwuebuka Ukachukwu [1987] Director/Energy Trader [Nigerian]

Famille Clarke Limited
Incorporated: 15 August 2016
Net Worth Deficit: £5,703 *Total Assets:* £7,571
Registered Office: 1 Broome Hall, Coldharbour, Dorking, Surrey, RH5 6HJ
Shareholders: Andrew Terence Clarke; Clare Alev Clarke
Officers: Andrew Terence Clarke [1958] Director/Lawyer; Clare Alev Clarke [1995] Director

Family Choice Wholesale Limited
Incorporated: 31 May 2017
Registered Office: 93 Heol Muston, Cardiff, CF5 4BD
Major Shareholder: Jeyaratnam Pathmasri
Officers: Jeyaratnam Pathmasri, Secretary; Jeyaratnam Pathmasri [1978] Director/Businessman

Family of Hounds Limited
Incorporated: 18 November 2016 *Employees:* 1
Net Worth Deficit: £60,267 *Total Assets:* £41,226
Registered Office: c/o Anthony Cowen, 1st Floor, Stanmore House, 15-19 Church Road, Stanmore, Middlesex, HA7 4AR
Shareholders: Andrea Frigerio; Lina Adeeb
Officers: Andrea Frigerio [1977] Director [Italian]

Far Out Wines Limited
Incorporated: 9 December 1998
Net Worth Deficit: £166,237 *Total Assets:* £135,806
Registered Office: Fifth Floor, 11 Leadenhall Street, London, EC3V 1LP
Major Shareholder: Gavin Charles Chavasse Quinney
Officers: Angela Claire Quinney, Secretary; Gavin Charles Chavasse Quinney [1960] Managing Director

Faridoon Wines Ltd
Incorporated: 5 March 2015
Registered Office: 1 Doughty Street, London, WC1N 2PH
Officers: Lady Lynne Heather Bilimoria [1965] Director; Lord Karan Bilimoria [1961] Director

Farr Vintners Limited
Incorporated: 10 October 1978 Employees: 23
Net Worth: £14,905,674 Total Assets: £40,755,556
Registered Office: Commodore House, Battersea Reach, Juniper Drive, London, SW18 1TW
Officers: Rajesh Arvind Patel, Secretary; Stephen John Browett [1959] Buying Director; Timothy Doe [1958] Director; Oliver Neil East [1978] Sales Director; Thomas Edward Hudson [1970] Sales Director; Rajesh Arvind Patel [1969] Finance Director; Joanne Michelle Purcell [1971] Director/Vintner; Mark Richard Ross [1979] Sales Director

Fast Moving Goods Ltd
Incorporated: 11 October 2016
Net Worth: £100 Total Assets: £100
Registered Office: 17 MacDonald Crescent, Stoke on Trent, Staffs, ST3 6JH
Officers: Arkadiusz Stencel [1979] Director [Polish]

Favela Cerveja Ltd
Incorporated: 2 November 2016
Registered Office: 10 The Crescent, Loughton, Essex, IG10 4PY
Officers: Charles Edward Gay [1986] Director; Frederick John Gay [1953] Director; Daniel James Osben [1985] Director/Business Development Manager

Favourite Beers Limited
Incorporated: 27 May 2010
Net Worth Deficit: £18,488 Total Assets: £32,448
Registered Office: 15 Stanbridge Way, Quedgeley, Gloucester, GL2 4RE
Shareholder: Leigh Richard Norwood
Officers: Roseanna Emily Ferner [1990] Director/Store Manager; Leigh Richard Norwood [1959] Director; Nicola Carole Norwood [1959] Director

Fcuk Ltd
Incorporated: 16 November 2018
Registered Office: 71-75 Shelton Street, London, WC2H 9JQ
Major Shareholder: Dene Bentley
Officers: Dene Bentley, Secretary; Dene Bentley [1965] Director

FD Gin Company Ltd
Incorporated: 5 March 2018
Registered Office: 12 Tramway Road, Liverpool, L17 7AY
Officers: James Michael Woods [1995] Director/Bar Supervisor

Feewcha Services Ltd
Incorporated: 15 January 2019
Registered Office: 5 Nash House, Prospect Hill, London, E17 3EW
Major Shareholder: Eldrun Charles
Officers: Eldrun Charles [1979] Director/Businessman

Fegan Wholesale Ltd
Incorporated: 28 September 2007 Employees: 2
Net Worth Deficit: £38,253 Total Assets: £41,827
Registered Office: 20 Carrive Road, Silverbridge, Newry, Co Armagh, BT35 9LJ
Major Shareholder: Gerard Fegan
Officers: Gerard Fegan, Secretary; Gerard Fegan [1965] Secretary and Director [Irish]; Jacqueline Fegan [1965] Director [Irish]

Felix Solis Avantis UK Ltd
Incorporated: 21 May 2013 Employees: 6
Net Worth: £451,682 Total Assets: £556,349
Registered Office: 3rd Floor, 24 Burgate, Canterbury, Kent, CT1 2HA
Officers: Richard Cochrane [1972] Managing Director; Alberto Jose Munoz Rubio [1973] Director [Spanish]; Felix Jose Solis Ramos [1973] Export and Marketing Director [Spanish]; Felix Solis Yanez [1945] Director/Chief Executive Manager [Spanish]

John E.Fells & Sons Limited
Incorporated: 1 May 1920 Employees: 50
Net Worth: £10,591,224 Total Assets: £27,073,200
Registered Office: Fells House, Station Road, Kings Langley, Herts, WD4 8LH
Parent: Atlantis Wine Holdings Ltd
Officers: Louise Catherine Rimes, Secretary; Alan Robert Campbell [1962] Sales Director; Nicholas John Gurney [1970] Director/Certified Chartered Accountant; Robert Wyndham Hill-Smith [1951] Managing Director [Australian]; Stephen Antony Moody [1960] Managing Director; John Andrew Douglas Symington [1960] Director/Port Producer; Paul Douglas Symington [1953] Director/Port Producer; Edward Jared MacLeod Thornton [1965] Development Director; Simon William Michael Thorpe [1966] Commercial Director; Miguel Torres Maczassek [1974] Director [Spanish]

Feni Global Limited
Incorporated: 9 April 2018
Registered Office: 38 Lower Belgrave Street, London, SW1W 0LN
Shareholder: Carl Vincent Le Blond
Officers: Dr. Timothy Alexander David Hyde [1967] Director; Carl Vincent Le Blond [1963] Director/Chairman; James Robinson [1978] Director; Anna Timblo [1976] Director

Ferintosh Distillery Limited
Incorporated: 28 June 2017
Registered Office: 28 Stark Avenue, Clydebank, W Dunbartonshire, G81 6EF
Major Shareholder: Kevin MacKinnon
Officers: Kevin MacKinnon [1979] Director/Wholesale Alcohol

Ferovinum Ltd
Incorporated: 26 March 2018
Registered Office: 71-75 Shelton Street, Covent Garden, London, WC2H 9JQ
Shareholders: Mitchel Fowler; Daniel James Gibney
Officers: Mitchel Fowler [1985] Director/Investment Banking; Daniel James Gibney [1979] Director/Finance Professional

Festina Drinks Ltd
Incorporated: 3 December 2014 Employees: 5
Net Worth: £177,648 Total Assets: £510,538
Registered Office: 44 Mortimers Lane, Fair Oak, Eastleigh, Hants, SO50 7BD
Shareholders: Robert Eric Gorst; Gina Blythe Gorst
Officers: Robert Eric Gorst, Secretary; Gina Blythe Gorst [1969] Director/Housewife; Robert Eric Gorst [1966] Director

Ffarm Vintners Limited
Incorporated: 1 February 2011 Employees: 6
Net Worth: £225,397 Total Assets: £326,870
Registered Office: Unit 1 Council Street West, Llandudno, Conwy, LL30 1ED
Shareholders: Jeremy Platt; Sean Connoly Appleton-Davies
Officers: Sean Appleton-Davies [1966] Director; Jeremy Platt [1961] Director

FFM Pasta Co Ltd
Incorporated: 6 November 2017
Registered Office: Flat 23, 6 Cranley Place, London, SW7 3AB
Shareholders: Filippo Giulio Gallenzi; Ivo Stjepan Jere Poklepovic
Officers: Filippo Giulio Gallenzi [1994] Director [Italian]

Alfie Fiandaca Limited
Incorporated: 10 December 1975 *Employees:* 12
Net Worth: £180,531 *Total Assets:* £705,667
Registered Office: Wellington House, 273-275 High Street, London Colney, Herts, AL2 1HA
Parent: Annessa Imports Limited
Officers: Gaetano Alfano [1964] Director; Domenico Annessa [1957] Director

Fidra Fine Spirits Limited
Incorporated: 22 September 2017
Registered Office: Ballencrieff Garden Cottage, Longniddry, E Lothian, EH32 0PJ
Shareholders: Alison Joanne Brydie; Emma Louise Bouglet
Officers: Emma Louise Bouglet [1975] Director; Alison Joanne Brydie [1974] Director

Field and Fawcett Wine Merchants and Delicatessen Limited
Incorporated: 10 November 2005 *Employees:* 12
Net Worth: £171,582 *Total Assets:* £735,254
Registered Office: Bingley House Farm, Grimston Bar, York, YO19 5LA
Shareholders: Peter Edward Fawcett; Cathryn Mary Fawcett
Officers: Peter Edward Fawcett, Secretary/Director; Cathryn Mary Fawcett [1967] Director; Peter Edward Fawcett [1963] Director

Field Bar Gin Limited
Incorporated: 12 October 2017
Net Worth Deficit: £1,162
Registered Office: 8 Turner Road, Cardiff, CF5 1HS
Shareholders: Matthew Robert Eaton; Alice Clare Eaton
Officers: Alice Clare Eaton, Secretary; Matthew Robert Eaton [1975] Director/Salesman

G.W. Fields & Sons (Great Yarmouth) Limited
Incorporated: 8 May 1975 *Employees:* 18
Net Worth: £2,690,843 *Total Assets:* £3,016,408
Registered Office: Yare Shipping Stores, Hewett Road, Great Yarmouth, Norfolk, NR31 0NN
Shareholders: Christopher George Fields; Jill Elizabeth Fields
Officers: Christopher George Fields, Secretary; Rejane Elizabeth Hammond, Secretary/Buyer; Christopher George Fields [1946] Director/Accountant; Rejane Elizabeth Hammond [1978] Director/Buyer

Fieldscot Ltd
Incorporated: 17 June 2004
Net Worth Deficit: £5,802
Registered Office: 191 Rowlett Road, Corby, Northants, NN17 2BY
Major Shareholder: Daniel Martin Woods
Officers: Daniel Martin Woods, Secretary; Daniel Martin Woods [1955] Director

Fifty One Forty Limited
Incorporated: 20 August 2015
Net Worth: £3,866 *Total Assets:* £14,092
Registered Office: Anova House, Wickhurst Lane, Broadbridge Heath, Horsham, W Sussex, RH12 3LZ
Officers: Gavin Klocek [1980] Director; Gary Mills [1981] Director; Alexander Joseph William Ruston [1974] Director; Nicholas David Thomas [1979] Director

The Fightback Brewing Company Limited
Incorporated: 30 November 2018
Registered Office: Milton House, 33a Milton Road, Hampton, Surrey, TW12 2LL
Shareholders: Richard James Murray Smith; Denzil Philip Thomas; Gary Prosser
Officers: Gary Prosser [1974] Director; Richard James Murray Smith [1972] Director; Denzil Philip Thomas [1965] Director/Advertising Consultant

Fiji Store Ltd
Incorporated: 19 January 2017
Registered Office: Kaiviti, Church Lane, Carlton, Goole, E Yorks, DN14 9PB
Major Shareholder: Jone Antonio Rabici Kama
Officers: Jone Antonio Rabici Kama [1974] Managing Director

Fill Macan Limited
Incorporated: 16 August 2018
Registered Office: Pavilion 1, Finnieston Business Park, Minerva Way, Glasgow, G3 8AU
Major Shareholder: Douglas Gordon Wheatley

J.W. Filshill International Limited
Incorporated: 2 April 2014
Net Worth Deficit: £148,490 *Total Assets:* £113,066
Registered Office: c/o J W Filshill Limited, Ainslie Avenue, off Hillington Road, Hillington, Glasgow, G52 4HE
Parent: J.W. Filshill Limited
Officers: Simon John Hannah [1977] Director; Christopher Stuart Miller [1971] Commercial Director; David Neill Moore [1970] Director

Fine & Rare Wines Limited
Incorporated: 8 September 1994 *Employees:* 78
Net Worth: £2,398,084 *Total Assets:* £29,503,260
Registered Office: Centennium House, 100 Lower Thames Street, London, EC3R 6DL
Shareholder: Mark Carlo Bedini
Officers: Andrew Peter Bottomley, Secretary; Marco Carlo Bedini [1957] Director; Andrew Peter Bottomley [1965] Director; William Twyman III Comfort [1966] Director [American]; Patrick O'Connor [1977] Director [Irish]; Andrew Daniel Wolfson [1969] Managing Director Financial Services

Fine Cider Limited
Incorporated: 10 April 2014
Net Worth Deficit: £69,093 *Total Assets:* £41,422
Registered Office: Third Floor, 22-27 The Oval, London, E2 9DT
Major Shareholder: Felix Matthew Nash
Officers: Edward Charles John Nash [1952] Director/Architect; Felix Nash [1989] Director/The Sale of Ciders and Perries

Fine Drinks Cooperative Limited
Incorporated: 15 July 2013
Net Worth Deficit: £32,570 *Total Assets:* £212,994
Registered Office: Parkhill Business Centre, Walton Road, Wetherby, W Yorks, LS22 5DZ
Shareholders: Barry Nigel Groves; Antony Stones
Officers: Barry Nigel Groves, Secretary; Barry Nigel Groves [1956] Director; Antony Stones [1965] Director

Fine Food & Wine Limited
Incorporated: 9 March 2018
Registered Office: 760 Ecclesall Road, Sheffield, S11 8TB
Officers: Mark Sutton [1966] Director

Fine Products Exporters Limited
Incorporated: 11 June 2014 *Employees:* 2
Net Worth: £169,397 *Total Assets:* £508,415
Registered Office: Admiral House, 29-30 Maritime Street, Edinburgh, EH6 6SE
Officers: David Kennedy Taylor [1945] Director/Architect; Philip Francis Taylor [1972] Director/Marketing

The Fine Wine (Old World) Trading Company Limited
Incorporated: 21 March 2017 *Employees:* 2
Net Worth: £396,096 *Total Assets:* £508,827
Registered Office: Aston House, Cornwall Avenue, London, N3 1LF
Shareholders: Russell Jonathan Gould; Yechuan Zhang
Officers: Russell Jonathan Gould [1974] Director; Yechuan Zhang [1985] Director [Chinese]

Fine Wine Company Limited
Incorporated: 5 November 2002 *Employees:* 5
Net Worth: £19,310 *Total Assets:* £264,603
Registered Office: 119 Portobello High Street, Edinburgh, EH15 1AR
Officers: Adam Rankine [1971] Director/Wine Merchant

Fine Wine Direct Limited
Incorporated: 18 September 2018
Registered Office: Kemp House, 160 City Road, London, EC1V 2NX
Major Shareholder: Sam Robin Earl
Officers: Sam Earl, Secretary; Andrew Earl [1955] Director Canary Wharf Group PLC; Sam Robin Earl [1980] Director/Entrepreneur

Fine Wine House Ltd
Incorporated: 1 February 2011
Registered Office: T1 Hurlingham Studios, Ranelagh Gardens, Fulham, London, SW6 3PA
Major Shareholder: Philip Anthony Slocombe
Officers: Philip Anthony Slocombe [1954] Director/Wine Merchant

The Fine Wine Trading Company (UK) Limited
Incorporated: 29 September 2015
Registered Office: 84 Gowan Avenue, London, SW6 6RG
Major Shareholder: Dominic Edwin Collier
Officers: Dominic Edwin Collier [1955] Director/Consultant

Fine Wine Trading Limited
Incorporated: 21 October 1999
Registered Office: 41 Cornmarket Street, Oxford, OX1 3HA
Major Shareholder: George Mark Somerset Clowes
Officers: Lady Rose Clowes, Secretary; George Mark Somerset Clowes [1954] Director

Fine Wine Works Limited
Incorporated: 17 July 2012
Net Worth: £45,582 *Total Assets:* £115,922
Registered Office: Triune Court, Monks Cross Drive, Huntington, York, YO32 9GZ
Shareholders: Nigel Howard Brotherton; Helen Christine Brotherton
Officers: Helen Christine Brotherton [1963] Director; Paul Stuart Lancaster [1958] Director/Chartered Accountant

Fine Wine World Ltd
Incorporated: 12 July 2017
Registered Office: Chestnut Field House, Chestnut Field, Rugby, Warwicks, CV21 2PD
Major Shareholder: Michael Robert Lindley
Officers: Michael Robert Lindley [1968] Director/Notary

Fine Wines Direct UK Limited
Incorporated: 22 May 2009
Registered Office: 242 Penarth Road, Cardiff, CF11 8TU
Officers: Nigel O'Sullivan [1957] Director; Gregory Thomas Williams [1970] Sales Director

Finebatch Limited
Incorporated: 8 August 1991
Net Worth: £8,090 *Total Assets:* £76,777
Registered Office: Gosford House, Kidlington, Oxon, OX5 2PX
Parent: Gusford Trust
Officers: James Leslie Sargent, Secretary; Michael Wilmer Watson [1962] Director/Self Employed; Peter Wilmer Watson [1933] Director Consultant

Finedon Convenience Store Limited
Incorporated: 7 May 2004
Previous: Costcutter Express Limited
Net Worth: £34,506 *Total Assets:* £90,579
Registered Office: Trilogy Suite, 9 Church Street, Wednesfield, Wolverhampton, W Midlands, WV11 1SR
Major Shareholder: Sukjinder Singh Bassi
Officers: Sukhjinder Singh Bassi [1983] Director

Fines Master Spirit Company Ltd
Incorporated: 28 February 2017
Registered Office: c/o UHY Hacker Young, Lanyon House, Mission Court, Newport, NP20 2DW
Shareholders: Patric Michael Cilliers; Michael Kenworthy Rhodes
Officers: Patric Michael Cilliers [1987] Director [South African]; Michael Kenworthy Rhodes [1987] Director/Professional Sportsman [South African]

Finest Wine & Delicatessen Brokers Ltd.
Incorporated: 7 September 1999
Registered Office: 52 Leith Walk, Edinburgh, EH6 5HW
Shareholder: Michael Laux
Officers: George Alexander Way, Secretary; Michael Laux [1962] Director/Lawyer [German]; Joachim Ries [1965] Director/Business Consultant [German]

Firewater Merchants Ltd
Incorporated: 25 February 2019
Registered Office: 23 Craddock Road, Canterbury, Kent, CT1 1YP
Shareholders: Kofo Olaniyan; Laurenzay Beckford-Miller
Officers: Laurenzay Beckford-Miller [1997] Director/Self Employed; Kofo Olaniyan [1997] Director/Self Employed

The Firkin Whisky Co Ltd
Incorporated: 20 April 2017
Registered Office: 103-105 Brighton Road, Coulsdon, Surrey, CR5 2NG
Major Shareholder: Michael George Spencer Collings
Officers: Deborah Leanne Collings [1961] Director; Michael George Spencer Collings [1949] Director; Nicholas Jonathan Lloyd Tilt [1961] Director/Production

The First & Last Brewery Ltd
Incorporated: 6 July 2016 *Employees:* 2
Net Worth Deficit: £20,186 *Total Assets:* £51,729
Registered Office: Caistron, Throughton, Morpeth, Northumberland, NE65 7LG
Shareholders: Emma Kellie; Sam Kellie
Officers: Emma Kellie [1979] Director/Brewer; Sam Kellie [1976] Director/Charity Worker

First Bar Supplies Limited
Incorporated: 17 December 2013 *Employees:* 2
Net Worth: £49,339 *Total Assets:* £568,781
Registered Office: C7-C8 Spectrum Business Centre, Anthony's Way, Rochester, Kent, ME2 4NP
Major Shareholder: Vondeira Thornton
Officers: Howard Thornton [1950] Director; Vondeira Thornton [1960] Administrative Director

First Cape Vineyards Ltd
Incorporated: 14 March 2017
Registered Office: Shakespeare House, 168 Lavender Hill, London, SW11 5TG
Parent: First Cape Vineyards (Pty) Ltd
Officers: Thomas Reuben Bosch, Secretary; Hendrik Jacobus Griessel [1968] Director [South African]; Willem Jacobus Van Der Vyver [1966] Managing Director [South African]

First Class Beverages Ltd
Incorporated: 13 September 2011
Net Worth: £135,362 *Total Assets:* £135,722
Registered Office: 52 Bury Old Road, Whitefield, Manchester, M45 6TL
Major Shareholder: Michael Delaney
Officers: Michael Delaney [1961] Director

First Crew Ltd
Incorporated: 8 February 2007
Net Worth Deficit: £1,234 *Total Assets:* £61,575
Registered Office: 43 Owston Road, Carcroft, Doncaster, S Yorks, DN6 8DA
Major Shareholder: Kevin Andrew McNamee
Officers: Kevin Andrew McNamee [1962] Director

First Whisky Limited
Incorporated: 19 September 2001
Net Worth: £1,695,090 *Total Assets:* £1,696,990
Registered Office: First Integrated House, Broadfold Road, Bridge of Don, Aberdeen, AB23 8EE
Major Shareholder: Ian Suttie
Officers: Ian Alexander Suttie [1947] Director

Firth and Co Wine Merchants Limited
Incorporated: 6 June 2009 *Employees:* 7
Net Worth Deficit: £6,909 *Total Assets:* £238,065
Registered Office: Newton Bank, Newton-le-Willows, Bedale, N Yorks, DL8 1TE
Shareholders: Andrew John Firth; Amanda Jane Firth
Officers: Amanda Jane Firth, Secretary; Andrew John Firth [1961] Managing Director; William James Charles Tilling [1986] Director/Wine Merchant

Fishers Gin Ltd
Incorporated: 4 December 2015
Net Worth Deficit: £98,802 *Total Assets:* £92,035
Registered Office: Beach Lodge, Brudenell Street, Aldeburgh, Suffolk, IP15 5DD
Major Shareholder: Andrew Michael Hilliard Heald
Officers: Joanna Marie Dennis [1962] Director; Andrew Michael Hilliard Heald [1987] Director/Businessman; Michael Guy Hilliard Heald [1950] Director; Antonia Alexandra Jamison [1972] Director; Timothy Alexander Veale [1989] Director/Senior National Account Manager

Fitlikey Brewery Ltd
Incorporated: 4 February 2019
Registered Office: 6a York Street, Aberdeen, AB11 5DD
Officers: Dr James Philip Olley [1988] Director and Company Secretary

Five Star Cash & Carry Ltd
Incorporated: 16 March 2018
Registered Office: 27a Beehive Lane, Ilford, Essex, IG1 3RG
Major Shareholder: Salman Javed
Officers: Salman Javed [1956] Director

Fizz Guru Limited
Incorporated: 11 April 2014
Net Worth Deficit: £2,099 *Total Assets:* £33,093
Registered Office: 131 High Street, Newton-le-Willows, St Helens, Merseyside, WA12 9SL
Shareholders: Alison Wilson; Alexandra Myhill
Officers: Alexandra Myhill [1981] Director/Marketing Manager; Alison Wilson [1975] Director

Flagship Brands Ltd
Incorporated: 30 March 2005 *Employees:* 1
Net Worth: £135,866 *Total Assets:* £264,669
Registered Office: Suite 203, 275 Deansgate, Manchester, M3 4EL
Major Shareholder: Paul Baxendale
Officers: Paul Baxendale [1962] Director

J.T.Flanagan Trading Company Ltd
Incorporated: 25 August 2017
Registered Office: The Old Shed, Highercombe Farm, Dulverton, Somerset, TA22 9PT
Major Shareholder: James Anthony Flanagan
Officers: James Anthony Flanagan [1981] Director

Flava Foods Ltd
Incorporated: 13 December 2018
Registered Office: 40 Brookfield House, Selden Hill, Hemel Hempstead, Herts, HP2 4FA
Major Shareholder: Adenrele Bankole
Officers: Adenrele Bankole [1992] Director

Flavour Foods & Drinks Ltd
Incorporated: 10 August 2016
Registered Office: 28 Bonsall Avenue, Derby, DE23 6JW
Officers: Sandeep Shinde [1974] Director

Flawless Spirits Ltd
Incorporated: 13 August 2018
Registered Office: Library Chambers, 48 Union Street, Hyde, Cheshire, SK14 1ND
Shareholders: Jessica Elizabeth Mortimer; Samuel John Mortimer; Christopher Daniel Neville
Officers: Jessica Elizabeth Mortimer [1989] Director; Samuel John Mortimer [1992] Director

Rodney Fletcher Vintners Ltd
Incorporated: 20 April 2010 *Employees:* 1
Net Worth: £32,324 *Total Assets:* £357,884
Registered Office: c/o Premier UK Business, Lyndum House, 12-14 High Street, Petersfield, Hants, GU32 3JG
Officers: Timothy Wyndham Fletcher [1968] Director/Vintner

Flint Wines Limited
Incorporated: 8 March 2006 *Employees:* 14
Net Worth: £979,109 *Total Assets:* £4,387,308
Registered Office: 16 Stannary Street, London, SE11 4AA
Shareholders: Samuel Balfour Clarke; Jason Clive Patrick Haynes
Officers: Samuel Balfour Clarke [1973] Director; Gearoid Edmund Devaney [1975] Director/Wine Dealer; Jason Clive Patrick Haynes [1968] Director/Wine Buyer

Flobegill Wines UK Ltd
Incorporated: 8 November 2010
Registered Office: 12 Kempsford Gardens, London, SW5 9LH
Officers: Nanaweikule Steve Dorgu [1964] Director

Flora Fine Wines Ltd
Incorporated: 6 December 2018
Registered Office: 58 Ellesmere Road, Dollis Hill, London, NW10 1JR
Major Shareholder: Abbi Nicol Moreno
Officers: Abbi Nicol Moreno [1971] Managing Director

Florin Wholesaler Ltd
Incorporated: 14 December 2018
Registered Office: 33 Fife Street, Sheffield, S9 1NN
Major Shareholder: Florin Badea
Officers: Florin Badea [1989] Director [Romanian]

The Flower Miners Limited
Incorporated: 8 January 2019
Registered Office: Trevella, Trispen, Truro, Cornwall, TR4 9BD
Major Shareholder: Anne-Marie Hurst
Officers: Anne-Marie Hurst [1965] Director

Flying Firkin Distribution Limited
Incorporated: 9 January 1995 *Employees:* 8
Net Worth: £46,302 *Total Assets:* £426,482
Registered Office: Unit 3 Holker Mill, Burnley Road, Colne, Lancs, BB8 8EG
Shareholders: Siba Commercial Services Ltd; Nina Diane Bates
Officers: Sara Knox, Secretary; Nina Diane Bates [1972] Director/Beer Wholesaler; Michael Peter Benner [1966] Director; John Blair Hart [1956] Director; Nicholas Rowland Stafford [1958] Director

Focus Beverages Ltd
Incorporated: 14 April 2015
Registered Office: The Dairy, Manor Farm, Toot Baldon, Oxford, OX44 9NG
Officers: Frank Van Horne [1974] Director [Dutch]; Pascal Weijers [1969] Director [Dutch]

Foodiebusters Epic Food Authority Ltd
Incorporated: 26 November 2018
Registered Office: 27 Old Gloucester Street, London, WC1N 3AX
Shareholders: Iago Vazquez; Josep Guirao
Officers: Josep Guirao, Secretary; Iago Vazquez, Secretary; Josep Guirao [1968] Director/Entrepreneur [Andorran]; Iago Vazquez [1986] Director/Entrepreneur [Spanish]

For Goodness Sake Ltd
Incorporated: 31 January 2018
Registered Office: 29 Twickenham Road, Leyton, London, E11 4BN
Major Shareholder: Matthew James Dominic Kennedy
Officers: Matthew James Dominic Kennedy [1986] Director/Chief Executive

For The Love of Wine Limited
Incorporated: 19 February 2013 *Employees:* 4
Net Worth Deficit: £27,523 *Total Assets:* £367,028
Registered Office: 42 Corvette Avenue, Warsash, Southampton, SO31 9AP
Shareholders: Nicola Elizabeth Bradbeer; Robert James Douglas Steel
Officers: Nicola Elizabeth Bradbeer, Secretary; Nicola Elizabeth Bradbeer [1969] Financial Director; Robert James Douglas Steel [1966] Wine Sales Director

Force Brewery Limited
Incorporated: 20 February 2012
Net Worth: £29,262 *Total Assets:* £29,262
Registered Office: Unit 2 Bulley Poultry Farm, Bulley, Gloucester, GL2 8BJ
Major Shareholder: Charles Neville Wyndham Malet
Officers: Charles Neville Wyndham Malet [1976] Director

Forest Hill Brewing Company Limited
Incorporated: 12 February 2018
Registered Office: 14b Ryecroft Road, Lewisham, London, SE13 6EZ
Major Shareholder: Thomas Dennis
Officers: Thomas Dennis [1991] Director/Self Employed Musician

Forest Road Brewing Co Ltd
Incorporated: 15 July 2014 *Employees:* 6
Previous: Ferment London Ltd
Net Worth Deficit: £27,602 *Total Assets:* £76,406
Registered Office: 355 Westgate Street, London, E8 3RL
Officers: Ian McRae, Secretary; Peter Maclin Brown [1985] Director/Brewer [American]; Ian McRae [1989] Director/Brewer [Irish]

Forth Wines Limited
Incorporated: 28 January 2010
Registered Office: 7 Evanton Drive, Thornliebank Industrial Estate, Thornliebank, Glasgow, G46 8HL
Parent: William Morton Ltd
Officers: Brian Douglas Robertson, Secretary; Ewen Irving Cameron [1956] Director; Ian Cumming [1962] Commercial Director; Brian Douglas Robertson [1962] Director/Financial Controller; Stephen Gerard Russell [1953] Director

Fortmount Trading Limited
Incorporated: 13 May 1999 *Employees:* 6
Net Worth: £2,176,438 *Total Assets:* £4,307,544
Registered Office: 8B Laynes House, 526-528 Watford Way, Mill Hill, London, NW7 4RS
Officers: Urvashi Shah, Secretary; Dipak Lalji Shah [1963] Director/Businessman; Javed Farhat Ullah [1941] Director/Salesman

Fortunae Limited
Incorporated: 27 April 2016 *Employees:* 1
Net Worth Deficit: £84,860 *Total Assets:* £21,730
Registered Office: Fortunae Ltd, P O Box 74349, London, EC1P 1ZL
Major Shareholder: Tugba Erem
Officers: Tugba Erem [1981] Director [Turkish]

Fortunella Spirits Ltd
Incorporated: 28 January 2019
Registered Office: 20-22 Wenlock Road, London, N1 7GU
Shareholders: Lukasz Stafin; Dariusz Plazewski
Officers: Dariusz Plazewski [1977] Director [Polish]; Lukasz Stafin [1984] Director [Polish]

Forty Acres Ltd
Incorporated: 3 April 2014 *Employees:* 2
Net Worth Deficit: £7,968 *Total Assets:* £118,114
Registered Office: 21 Barnards Hill, Marlow, Bucks, SL7 2NX
Major Shareholder: David Joel Peek
Officers: David Joel Peek [1980] Director

Forward Moving Limited
Incorporated: 5 November 2018
Registered Office: Flat 2, 7 Rayners Road, London, SW15 2AY
Major Shareholder: Gianfranco Cianti
Officers: Gianfranco Cianti [1987] Director [Italian]

Four Corners Wine Company Limited
Incorporated: 16 December 2015 *Employees:* 3
Net Worth: £126,390 *Total Assets:* £188,168
Registered Office: Albury Mill, Mill Lane, Chilworth, Guildford, Surrey, GU4 8RU
Major Shareholder: Stuart Young
Officers: Stuart Young [1977] Managing Director

Four Seasons Hastings Ltd
Incorporated: 3 December 2015
Net Worth: £14,352 *Total Assets:* £55,947
Registered Office: 68-70 Bohemia Road, St Leonards on Sea, E Sussex, TN37 6RQ
Major Shareholder: Thushya Inthirakumar
Officers: Thushya Inthirakumar [1986] Director

Fourteen Drops Ltd
Incorporated: 24 April 2017 *Employees:* 4
Net Worth Deficit: £1,827 *Total Assets:* £91,269
Registered Office: 3 Innovation Court, Yarm Road, Stockton on Tees, Cleveland, TS18 3DA
Shareholders: Fiona Eleanor McLain; Andrea Bruno Asciamprener
Officers: Andrea Bruno Asciamprener [1985] Director/Sales Manager [Italian]; Dr Bruce Irving McLain [1959] Director/Doctor; Fiona Eleanor McLain [1987] Director/Wine Buyer; Sarah McLain [1959] Director Sally and Sarah Care

Fourteen Twelve Trading Limited
Incorporated: 22 June 2017
Registered Office: 7 Trevor Gardens, Edgware, Middlesex, HA8 0EY
Major Shareholder: Jafar Shareef
Officers: Jafar Shareef [1990] Director

Fox Fitzgerald Whisky Trading Company Limited
Incorporated: 16 October 2013 *Employees:* 4
Net Worth: £703,811 *Total Assets:* £983,193
Registered Office: 3 Clive Street, Hereford, HR1 2SB
Shareholders: Bocarisa Enterprises Limited; Fox Fitzgerald Limited
Officers: Eamonn FitzGenerald Jones [1963] Director/Sales Executive; Aidan Stuart Smith [1956] Director/Sales Executive

Foxbusiness Tobacco Ltd
Incorporated: 5 July 2018
Registered Office: 352 Fulham Road, London, SW10 9UH
Major Shareholder: Kristijan Savic
Officers: Kristijan Savic [1985] Director [Croatian]

Foxhole Spirits Limited
Incorporated: 10 February 2016 *Employees:* 3
Net Worth Deficit: £87,925 *Total Assets:* £20,333
Registered Office: Bolney Wine Estate, Foxhole Lane, Bolney, Haywards Heath, W Sussex, RH17 5NB
Major Shareholder: James Philip Marsden-Smedley
Officers: Graham John Linter, Secretary; Graham John Linter [1964] Director; Samantha Martha Linter [1968] Director; James Philip Marsden-Smedley [1989] Director

Foxstead Limited
Incorporated: 1 November 2005 *Employees:* 6
Net Worth: £140,992 *Total Assets:* £410,626
Registered Office: Pillar House, 113-115 Bath Road, Cheltenham, Glos, GL53 7LS
Major Shareholder: Iain James Crockett
Officers: Iain James Crockett [1965] Managing Director

Clark Foyster Wines Limited
Incorporated: 25 May 1994 *Employees:* 4
Net Worth: £550,114 *Total Assets:* £1,061,456
Registered Office: 15 South Ealing Road, London, W5 4QT
Shareholders: Isabelle Anne Clark; Lance Edmund Foyster
Officers: Isabelle Anne Clark [1963] Director/Accountant; Lance Edmund Foyster [1961] Director/Wine Merchant

Franc Wine Ltd
Incorporated: 3 August 2018
Registered Office: The English Wine Centre, Berwick, Polegate, E Sussex, BN26 5QS
Shareholders: Franck Sottou; Robert James Blackman
Officers: Robert James Blackman [1963] Director; Franck Sottou [1970] Director [French]

France Domaines Limited
Incorporated: 2 March 1987 *Employees:* 2
Net Worth: £113,760 *Total Assets:* £134,795
Registered Office: First Floor, Thavies Inn House, 3-4 Holborn Circus, London, EC1N 2HA
Major Shareholder: Eric Gerard Deren
Officers: Eric Gerard Deren, Secretary/Director [French]; Eric Gerard Deren [1958] Director [French]; Agathe Metayer [1983] Director [French]

Franchiserv Limited
Incorporated: 16 September 1994
Net Worth: £437,354 *Total Assets:* £439,040
Registered Office: Lowin House, Tregolls Road, Truro, Cornwall, TR1 2NA
Shareholders: Brenda Rose Sellers; Paul Thomas Garfield Sellers
Officers: Brenda Rose Sellers, Secretary; Brenda Rose Sellers [1949] Director/Management Consultant; Paul Thomas Garfield Sellers [1947] Director/Management Consultant

Franciacorta Limited
Incorporated: 9 March 1993 *Employees:* 104
Net Worth: £4,044,907 *Total Assets:* £6,786,359
Registered Office: Units 2 and 3, 199 Eade Road, London, N4 1DN
Shareholder: Antonio Pirozzi
Officers: Stephen Dennis Bridgeman, Company Secretary; Stephen Dennis Bridgeman [1942] Director; Custudio Jose Dos Santos [1957] Director/Wine & Food Importer [Portuguese]; Jose de Nobrega Pires [1956] Director/Wine & Food Importer [Portuguese]; Antonio Pirozzi [1943] Director; Maria Vitoria Santos-Pires [1960] Director/Financier [Portuguese]; Gianni Segatta [1945] Director/Wine & Food Importer

Francis Fine Wines Ltd
Incorporated: 29 August 2002 *Employees:* 3
Net Worth: £3,347 *Total Assets:* £214,774
Registered Office: 6 Charter Point Way, Ashby Park, Ashby-De-La-Zouch, Leics, LE65 1NF
Shareholders: Matthew Charles Francis; Melanie Francis
Officers: Melanie Francis, Secretary; Matthew Charles Francis [1967] Director

Franco Hetty Limited
Incorporated: 31 March 2016
Net Worth Deficit: £320 *Total Assets:* £523
Registered Office: 121 Livery Street, Birmingham, B3 1RS
Major Shareholder: Raji Kaur Dhariwal
Officers: Budge Dhariwal [1961] Director; Raji Kaur Dhariwal [1989] Managing Director

Franklyn Road Brewing Ltd
Incorporated: 29 January 2019
Registered Office: 20-22 Wenlock Road, London, N1 7GU
Major Shareholder: Shem Wallis-Jones
Officers: Shem Wallis-Jones [1976] Director/Brewer

Franko's Food Ltd
Incorporated: 27 February 2018
Registered Office: 113 Bradenham Road, West Wycombe, High Wycombe, Bucks, HP14 4EZ
Major Shareholder: Franko Cetinich
Officers: Franko Cetinich [1952] Director

Frazier's Wine Merchants Ltd.
Incorporated: 20 October 1972 *Employees:* 11
Net Worth: £831,382 *Total Assets:* £1,851,550
Registered Office: 2 Stirling Road, Shirley, Solihull, W Midlands, B90 4NE
Shareholders: William Jerome Frazier; John Lewis Reginald Frazier
Officers: Georgina Frazier, Secretary; Georgina Frazier [1947] Director/Company Secretary; John Lewis Reginald Frazier [1941] Director/Wine Merchant; William Jerome Frazier [1972] Director/Manager

Frederick's Wine Company Limited
Incorporated: 10 December 2018
Registered Office: Willow Cottage, Reading Road, Mattingley, Hants, RG27 8JU
Officers: Lisa June Bowman-Hood [1968] Director; Stuart Gregory Bowman-Hood [1965] Director; Laura Anne Evans [1962] Director; Guy Christopher Smith [1964] Director

The Free from Beer Co Ltd
Incorporated: 27 April 2018
Registered Office: Towngate House, 2-8 Parkstone Road, Poole, Dorset, BH15 2PW
Shareholders: Michael Sears; Thomas Paul Sears
Officers: Michael Sears [1956] Director; Thomas Paul Sears [1982] Director

Free Spirits Group Ltd
Incorporated: 2 October 2018
Registered Office: 20-22 Wenlock Road, London, N1 7GU
Shareholders: Tristan Ramsay; Claire Ramsay
Officers: Claire Ramsay [1980] Director; Tristan Ramsay [1979] Director

Free Trade Beers and Minerals Limited
Incorporated: 8 April 1991 *Employees:* 16
Net Worth: £138,509 *Total Assets:* £832,558
Registered Office: 227-247 Gascoigne Road, Barking, Essex, IG11 7LN
Shareholders: Satwant Singh; Ranveer Singh Mohal; Baljit Kaur Mohal
Officers: Ranveer Singh Mohal [1986] Director; Satwant Singh [1952] Director

Freerun Consulting Limited
Incorporated: 17 October 2006 *Employees:* 2
Net Worth: £11,715 *Total Assets:* £64,555
Registered Office: 31-33 College Road, Harrow, Middlesex, HA1 1EJ
Shareholders: Diana Iaghanashvili; Giorgi Sulkhanishvili
Officers: Diana Iaghanashvili, Secretary/Consultant; Diana Iaghanashvili [1983] Director/Accountant; Giorgi Sulkhanishvili [1964] Director/Wine Consultant [Georgian]

Freight Brewing Co. Ltd
Incorporated: 9 January 2017
Net Worth Deficit: £10,164 *Total Assets:* £130
Registered Office: 119 Cranbrook Road, Poole, Dorset, BH12 3BR
Shareholders: Anthony Grigori Tonu Probert; Remy Chaloner
Officers: Remy Chaloner [1993] Director/Brewer; Anthony Grigori Tonu Probert [1993] Director/Arborist

Freixenet Copestick Limited
Incorporated: 27 May 2005 *Employees:* 29
Previous: Copestick Murray Limited
Net Worth: £2,351,225 *Total Assets:* £22,577,178
Registered Office: 8 Woodstock Court, Blenheim Road, Marlborough, Wilts, SN8 4AN
Parent: Henkell International GmbH
Officers: Nicholas George Bryan, Secretary; Dr Andreas Brokemper [1969] Director [German]; Damian Michael Clarke [1970] Director; Robin Peto Copestick [1963] Director; Pedro Ferrer [1958] Director [Spanish]

Freixenet UK Ltd
Incorporated: 13 January 1964 *Employees:* 22
Net Worth: £3,055,006 *Total Assets:* £8,232,514
Registered Office: Freixenet House, Wellington Business Park, Dukes Ride, Crowthorne, Berks, RG45 6LS
Officers: Michael Derek Goddard, Secretary; Damian Michael Clarke [1970] Managing Director; Pedro Ferrer [1958] Director/Chairman [Spanish]; Michael Derek Goddard [1963] Finance Director; Bernd Friedrich Kurt Halbach [1953] Director [German]

The French Sommelier with a Wee Dog Ltd
Incorporated: 15 February 2018
Registered Office: 7 Dene Guest House, Eyre Place, Edinburgh, EH3 5ES
Major Shareholder: Jean-Pierre Chauvin
Officers: Jean-Pierre Chauvin [1986] Director/Consultant [French]

The French Wine Project Limited
Incorporated: 10 June 2015
Net Worth Deficit: £39,830 *Total Assets:* £52,851
Registered Office: 9 Devonshire Mews, London, W4 2HA
Major Shareholder: Jean-Charles Adam
Officers: Jean-Charles Adam [1965] Director/Manager [French]

Frenchbubbles Limited
Incorporated: 24 June 2008 *Employees:* 2
Net Worth: £46,211 *Total Assets:* £133,556
Registered Office: South View, Lower Wall Road, West Hythe, Hythe, Kent, CT21 4NW
Shareholders: Stefano Frigerio; Maud Fierobe
Officers: Stefano Frigerio, Secretary; Maud Fierobe [1974] Director [French]; Stefano Frigerio [1970] Director [Italian]

Frenchvines Limited
Incorporated: 7 February 2005 *Employees:* 1
Net Worth: £29,764 *Total Assets:* £57,333
Registered Office: 7 Josselin Court, Wollaston Industrial Estate, Basildon, Essex, SS13 1QE
Major Shareholder: Ulaganathan Suppiah
Officers: Suppiah Celia Joyce, Secretary; Ulaganathan Suppiah [1952] Director/Engineer

Frequency Enterprises Limited
Incorporated: 9 November 2017
Registered Office: 93 George Street, Edinburgh, EH2 3ES
Officers: Daryl Demarco [1982] Creative Director

Freshfield Fine Wines Limited
Incorporated: 15 January 2009 *Employees:* 1
Net Worth: £27,577 *Total Assets:* £72,730
Registered Office: Myosotis, Isle of Thorns Lane, Chelwood Gate, E Sussex, RH17 7LA
Major Shareholder: Marcus Thorold
Officers: Marcus Thorold, Secretary; Marcus Guy Francis Thorold [1955] Director/Wine Merchant

Friarwood Fine Wines Limited
Incorporated: 9 December 2014 *Employees:* 10
Net Worth: £171,043 *Total Assets:* £1,355,171
Registered Office: Ground Floor, 26 New Kings Road, London, SW6 4ST
Shareholders: Benjamin Robert Carfagnini; Jay Anthony Carfagnini
Officers: Benjamin Robert Carfagnini [1988] Director/Fine Wine Salesman [Canadian]; Jay Anthony Carfagnini [1956] Director/Lawyer [Canadian]

Friends of Wine Ltd
Incorporated: 4 August 2006 *Employees:* 3
Net Worth: £455 *Total Assets:* £19,533
Registered Office: Bushbury House, 435 Wilmslow Road, Withington, Manchester, M20 4AF
Officers: James Hovington, Secretary; Catherine Maria Hovington [1952] Director; James Hovington [1980] Director; Peter Anthony Hovington [1952] Director

Friendship Adventure Ltd.
Incorporated: 5 May 2017 *Employees:* 3
Net Worth Deficit: £4,434 *Total Assets:* £3,911
Registered Office: 6 George Mews, London, SW9 7AB
Shareholders: Toby Julian Ejsmond-Frey; Neil Edward Wates; Jeremy Adam Caspar Scharf
Officers: Toby Julian Ejsmond-Frey [1988] Director/Marketing Manager; Neil Edward Wates [1986] Director/Project Manager

Frizzenti Limited
Incorporated: 18 February 2013 *Employees:* 5
Net Worth: £49,232 *Total Assets:* £337,435
Registered Office: Pennant House, 1-2 Napier Court, Napier Road, Reading, Berks, RG1 8BW
Shareholders: Daniel Spinath; George Edward Workman
Officers: Daniel Spinath [1964] Director [German]; George Edward Workman [1980] Director

From Cask To Bottle Limited
Incorporated: 6 December 2018
Registered Office: 196/17 Lindsay Road, Edinburgh, EH6 6ND
Major Shareholder: Ross Sivills
Officers: Ross Sivills [1980] Managing Director

Fronsacdirect Limited
Incorporated: 30 July 1998
Registered Office: 6 Parc Y Fro, Creigiau, Cardiff, CF15 9SA
Officers: Frances Ann Willmott, Secretary; Kevin Nash Knight Willmott [1951] Director/Wine Merchant

Fronsacwines Limited
Incorporated: 30 July 1998
Registered Office: 6 Parc Y Fro, Creigiau, Cardiff, CF15 9SA
Officers: Frances Ann Willmott, Secretary; Kevin Nash Knight Willmott [1951] Director/Wine Merchant

Frontier Trading International Limited
Incorporated: 23 July 2008 *Employees:* 2
Net Worth: £65,135 *Total Assets:* £739,750
Registered Office: Finch House, 28-30 Wolverhampton Street, Dudley, W Midlands, DY1 1DB
Shareholders: Richard James Price; Caroline Jane Price
Officers: Caroline Jane Price, Secretary; Caroline Jane Price [1966] Director/Business Executive; Richard James Price [1966] Director

Frontier Trading Limited
Incorporated: 29 July 1997
Net Worth Deficit: £478,129 *Total Assets:* £70,635
Registered Office: Finch House, 28-30 Wolverhampton Street, Dudley, W Midlands, DY1 1DB
Shareholders: Caroline Jane Price; Richard James Price
Officers: Caroline Jane Price, Secretary/Business Executive; Caroline Jane Price [1966] Director/Business Executive; Richard James Price [1966] Director

Ftspot Limited
Incorporated: 9 September 2015
Net Worth Deficit: £8,348 *Total Assets:* £30,029
Registered Office: 87 Oldacre Road, Oldbury, W Midlands, B68 0RL
Major Shareholder: Lukasz Marcin Rys
Officers: Paulina Pelczar, Secretary; Lukasz Marcin Rys [1977] Managing Director [Polish]

Full Logistic Ltd
Incorporated: 15 November 2016 *Employees:* 2
Net Worth: £311 *Total Assets:* £17,848
Registered Office: 18 Horsley Road, London, E4 7HX
Major Shareholder: Florentin Alexandru Achim
Officers: Ionela Girea, Secretary; Florentin Alexandru Achim [1984] Director/Driver [Romanian]

Functional Drinks Co Limited
Incorporated: 28 February 2019
Registered Office: 29 Lutener Road, Easebourne, Midhurst, W Sussex, GU29 9AT
Major Shareholder: Robert John Wattie
Officers: Robert John Wattie [1976] Director/Drinks Distributor

The Funemployed Agency Ltd
Incorporated: 20 April 2018
Registered Office: The White House, Clifton Marine Parade, Gravesend, Kent, DA11 0DY
Parent: The Funemployed Ltd
Officers: Douglas Brougham Cunningham [1968] Director; Sean Cunningham [1963] Director; Christina Gallon [1984] Director

The Funemployed Ltd
Incorporated: 20 April 2018
Registered Office: The White House, Clifton Marine Parade, Gravesend, Kent, DA11 0DY
Major Shareholder: Douglas Brougham Cunningham
Officers: Douglas Brougham Cunningham [1968] Director; Sean Cunningham [1963] Director; Christina Gallon [1984] Director

The Funky Beer Company Limited
Incorporated: 7 August 2013
Registered Office: 20 Mannin Way, Lancaster Business Park, Lancaster, LA1 3SW
Major Shareholder: Loic Jordan Cross
Officers: Loic Jordan Cross [1983] Director

FV Craft Beers Ltd
Incorporated: 10 May 2018
Registered Office: 19 Cotswold Close, Cirencester, Glos, GL7 1XP
Major Shareholder: Richard Francis Dodd
Officers: Melanie Jane Dodd, Secretary; Richard Francis Dodd [1971] Director/Ecologist

FV Trading Europe Ltd
Incorporated: 27 February 2014
Registered Office: Dalton House, 60 Windsor Avenue, London, SW19 2RR
Shareholders: Daniel Ferdinand; Jaromir Vonka
Officers: Daniel Ferdinand [1988] Director/Trader [Slovak]; Jaromir Vonka [1982] Director/Trader [Czech]

FVFC Limited
Incorporated: 21 April 2017
Net Worth Deficit: £8,409 *Total Assets:* £12,808
Registered Office: 33 Inner Loop Road, Beachley, Chepstow, Glos, NP16 7HF
Shareholders: Christine Eve Voisin; Fabien Voisin
Officers: Christine Eve Voisin [1972] Director [French]; Fabien Voisin [1973] Director [French]

Fyre Festival UK Ltd
Incorporated: 23 January 2019
Registered Office: 3 Archer Drive, Cheswick Green, Solihull, W Midlands, B90 4LG
Major Shareholder: Ryan James Snook
Officers: Ryan James Snook [1982] Director/General Manager

G & G International BCN Ltd
Incorporated: 27 December 2018
Registered Office: 302 Riemann Court, 44 Bow Common Lane, London, E3 4FU
Shareholders: Ignasi Guzman; Xavier Grau
Officers: Ignasi Guzman [1989] Director [Spanish]

G B Consortium Wholesale Limited
Incorporated: 9 September 2015
Registered Office: 5 Albany Road, Earlsdon, Coventry, Warwicks, CV5 6JQ
Major Shareholder: Sukhwinder Singh
Officers: Sukhwinder Singh [1971] Director [Indian]

G Life Limited
Incorporated: 7 February 2007
Net Worth Deficit: £118,689 *Total Assets:* £18,764
Registered Office: The Church, 172 London Road, Guildford, Surrey, GU1 1XR
Officers: Lyubov Rackham, Secretary; James Arthur Rackham [1953] Director

G M Drinks Limited
Incorporated: 3 December 2012 *Employees:* 1
Net Worth: £693 *Total Assets:* £600,103
Registered Office: The Old School House, West Street, Southwick, Fareham, Hants, PO17 6EA
Major Shareholder: Marc Patch
Officers: Gemma Nicole Patch [1979] Director; Marc Patch [1979] Director/Sales Manager

G M Drinks of Hampshire Limited
Incorporated: 16 October 2015
Registered Office: The Old School House, West Street, Southwick, Fareham, Hants, PO17 6EA
Shareholders: Marc Patch; Gemma Nicole Patch
Officers: Gemma Nicole Patch [1979] Director; Marc Patch [1979] Director/Sales Manager

G Point 7 Ltd
Incorporated: 4 May 2011
Net Worth: £61,456 *Total Assets:* £664,538
Registered Office: Unit 8 & 9, Shaw Lane Industrial Estate, Ogden Road, Doncaster, S Yorks, DN2 4SQ
Officers: Lev Muradov, Secretary; Andrejs Jefimovs [1976] Director [Latvian]; Dimitry Muradov [1980] Director [Israeli]; Danis Parum [1966] Director [Israeli]; Vladimer Sanadze [1958] Director/Operations Manager

G Sake Company Limited
Incorporated: 25 October 1993 *Employees:* 23
Net Worth: £4,109 *Total Assets:* £189,907
Registered Office: Three Counties House, 18a Victoria Street, Dunstable, Beds, LU6 3BA
Major Shareholder: Chee Leong Lau
Officers: Maki Yanagida, Secretary/Sake Trader [Japanese]; Chee Leong Lau [1965] Director/Food & Drink Retailer/Wholesaler; Maki Yanagida [1967] Director/Secretary [Japanese]

Gabby & Bello Enterprises Ltd
Incorporated: 14 July 2009
Net Worth Deficit: £20,350 *Total Assets:* £37,436
Registered Office: 10 Fourth Avenue, Clayton, Manchester, M11 4LZ
Major Shareholder: Gbola Daud Bello
Officers: Gbola Daud Bello [1961] Director [Nigerian]

Gain & Coombs Ltd
Incorporated: 14 December 2018
Registered Office: Unit B11, Park Lane, Birmingham, B35 6AN
Major Shareholder: Simon Gain
Officers: Simon Gain [1970] Director

Gain Brands International (UK) Ltd
Incorporated: 20 May 2015 *Employees:* 1
Net Worth Deficit: £19,345 *Total Assets:* £37,933
Registered Office: 148 Gilmerton Dykes Road, Edinburgh, EH17 8PE
Shareholders: Stephen Alexander McKenzie; Brenda Jane McKenzie; Gain Brands International PTE Ltd
Officers: Stephen Alexander McKenzie, Secretary; Brenda Jane McKenzie [1973] Marketing Director; Stephen Alexander McKenzie [1968] Director/Accountant

The Gala Drinks Company Limited
Incorporated: 19 May 2004 *Employees:* 10
Net Worth: £64,965 *Total Assets:* £2,048,900
Registered Office: 57 New Walk, Leicester, LE1 7EA
Shareholders: Kirtan Shah; Nirav Shah
Officers: Kirtan Shah, Secretary/Distributor; Kirtan Shah [1973] Director/Distributor; Nirav Shah [1971] Director/Distributor

Galette Wines Limited
Incorporated: 26 January 2012 *Employees:* 2
Net Worth: £638 *Total Assets:* £37,937
Registered Office: Silwood Villa, Netley Road, Southsea, Hants, PO5 3NB
Major Shareholder: Russell Mark Payne
Officers: Russell Mark Paine [1960] Director

Gallachers Fine Wines Limited
Incorporated: 1 December 2017
Registered Office: Fulford House, Newbold Terrace, Leamington Spa, Warwicks, CV32 4EA
Major Shareholder: Deborah Elizabeth Gallacher
Officers: Deborah Elizabeth Gallacher [1970] Director

Galldachd Na H-Alba Brewing Ltd
Incorporated: 22 September 2017
Registered Office: Sunnybrae, Old Well Road, Moffat, Dumfries & Galloway, DG10 9AP
Major Shareholder: Michael Stuart Tough
Officers: Thomas Joseph Barr, Secretary; Michael Stuart Tough [1965] Managing Director

G & G Gallo Enterprises Limited
Incorporated: 29 March 1995 *Employees:* 39
Net Worth: £3,299,715 *Total Assets:* £4,811,061
Registered Office: 430-450 Avenue West, Skyline 120, Great Notley, Braintree, Essex, CM77 7AA
Major Shareholder: Gerardo Santomauro
Officers: Giuseppina Santomauro, Secretary [Italian]; Gerardo Santomauro [1955] Managing Director [Italian]; Giuseppina Santomauro [1956] Director/Teacher [Italian]; Pasquale Luca Santomauro [1988] Director [Italian]

The Galloping Wine Nose Limited
Incorporated: 21 November 2017
Registered Office: Sean Rowe, Office K Dutch Barn, Ford End, Chelmsford, Essex, CM3 1LN
Major Shareholder: Benjamin Lewis
Officers: Benjamin Lewis [1977] Director

Gandhi Wine Suppliers Limited
Incorporated: 25 September 1984 *Employees:* 27
Net Worth: £870,662 *Total Assets:* £3,017,932
Registered Office: Units 22-23 The IO Centre, 59-71 River Road, Barking, Essex, IG11 0DR
Major Shareholder: Kaushik Amritlal Mody
Officers: Kaushik Amritlal Mody, Secretary; Kaushik Amritlal Mody [1957] Director

Gang of Five Ltd
Incorporated: 21 September 2017
Registered Office: 39 Hill Road, Pinner, Middlesex, HA5 1LB
Major Shareholder: Leslie Paul Jarvis
Officers: Leslie Paul Jarvis [1957] Director/Administrator

Pascal Garcia Consulting Limited
Incorporated: 25 April 2006
Registered Office: Tricor Suite, 4th Floor, 50 Mark Lane, London, EC3R 7QR
Major Shareholder: Pascal Claude Jacques Garcia
Officers: Pascal Claude Jacques Garcia [1968] Director/Chairman [French]

Gargara Limited
Incorporated: 13 June 2017
Net Worth Deficit: £2,616
Registered Office: 5 Ramsey Road, Whittlesey, Peterborough, PE7 1DR
Major Shareholder: Tomasz Jan Zagorowski
Officers: Tomasz Jan Zagorowski [1974] Managing Director [Polish]

Garmence Limited
Incorporated: 5 August 2015
Net Worth Deficit: £51,261 *Total Assets:* £8,174
Registered Office: Martlet House, E1 Yeoman Gate, Yeoman Way, Worthing, W Sussex, BN13 3QZ
Shareholders: Charlotte Catherine Marie Calvet; Benoit Patrice Marie Alain Calvet; Valerie Sophie Marie Calvet
Officers: Benoit Patrice Marie Alain Calvet [1956] Director/Wine Merchant [French]; Charlotte Catherine Marie Calvet [1985] Sales Director [French]; Valerie Sophie Marie Calvet [1960] Director [French]

Garumbas Ltd
Incorporated: 15 January 2018
Registered Office: 1b Annes Terrace, Milford, Co Armagh, BT60 3NU
Shareholders: Santiago Casas Rodriguez; Alberto Viva Rol
Officers: Santiago Casas Rodriguez [1985] Director/Software Engineer [Spanish]; Alberto Viva Rol [1985] Director/Trade Agent [Spanish]

Martinez Gassiot & Company Limited
Incorporated: 16 June 1903
Registered Office: Chivas House, 72 Chancellors Road, London, W6 9RS
Parent: Allied Domecq (Holdings) Limited
Officers: Stuart MacNab [1964] Director/Accountant; Vincent Turpin [1978] Director/Chief Financial Officer [French]

Gather 77 Limited
Incorporated: 7 September 2018
Registered Office: Unit C1, Mulleys Farm, Little Bromley, Essex, CO11 2PL
Officers: Adam Catchpole [1977] Director; Matthew George Keeling [1976] Director

GBW Subscriptions Ltd
Incorporated: 6 September 2018
Registered Office: Halfpenny Green Vineyards, Upper Whittimere, Bobbington, Stourbridge, W Midlands, DY7 5EP
Officers: Jodi Hugget [1974] Director; Andrew John Kewin [1965] Director; Clive Martin Charles Vickers [1967] Director; Lisa Christine Vickers [1970] Director

GCBW Catrine Ltd
Incorporated: 18 May 1943 *Employees:* 3
Net Worth: £25,823 *Total Assets:* £1,375,964
Registered Office: 1 Anthony Road, Largs, N Ayrshire, KA30 8EQ
Parent: ABA Eaglesham Ltd
Officers: Henry John Jagielko, Secretary/Accountant; Carol Anne Bulloch [1956] Director/Clerkess; Henry John Jagielko [1952] Director/Accountant; Alexander Reynolds [1955] Director/Manager

GDK Drinks Ltd
Incorporated: 26 January 2009 *Employees:* 2
Net Worth Deficit: £46,631 *Total Assets:* £232,870
Registered Office: PKF-FPM Accountants Limited, Dromalane Mill, The Quays, Newry, Co Down, BT35 8QS
Major Shareholder: Philip Russell
Officers: David Michael Russell [1984] Director/Sales & Brand Manager; Patricia Russell [1952] Director/Bank Official [Irish]; Philip Russell [1954] Director [Irish]

Gelston Castle Fine Wines Limited
Incorporated: 9 February 1989
Net Worth Deficit: £46,050 *Total Assets:* £502,935
Registered Office: The Apex, 2 Sheriffs Orchard, Coventry, Warwicks, CV1 3PP
Major Shareholder: Alexander Douglas Scott
Officers: Lucinda Jane Scott, Secretary; Alexander Douglas Scott [1959] Director/Wine Merchant

Gem Wines Ltd
Incorporated: 14 October 2016
Net Worth Deficit: £17,920 *Total Assets:* £11,195
Registered Office: 71-75 Shelton Street, Covent Garden, London, WC2H 9JQ
Shareholder: Elena Selezneva
Officers: Dr Elena Selezneva, Secretary; Dr Elena Selezneva [1976] Director/Entrepreneur

Gemeaux Limited
Incorporated: 29 October 2012
Net Worth Deficit: £33,122 *Total Assets:* £15,516
Registered Office: Suite A, 10th Floor, Maple House, High Street, Potters Bar, Herts, EN6 5BS
Shareholders: Ian Dibbs; Karen Dibbs
Officers: Ian Dibbs [1958] Director; Karen Dibbs [1958] Director

General Bilimoria Wines Limited
Incorporated: 28 January 2009
Net Worth: £5,295 *Total Assets:* £152,257
Registered Office: 1 Doughty Street, London, WC1N 2PH
Shareholders: Karan Faridoon Bilimoria; Lady Lynne Heather Bilimoria
Officers: Lord Karan Faridoon Bilimoria [1961] Director

General Wine and Liquor Company Limited
Incorporated: 14 August 1986 *Employees:* 25
Net Worth: £732,210 *Total Assets:* £1,885,791
Registered Office: The Old Steppe House, Brighton Road, Godalming, Surrey, GU7 1NS
Shareholders: Alan David Snudden; Alan David Snudden
Officers: Nichola Jane Snudden, Secretary; Sara Elizabeth Bangert [1967] Director; Angus John Snell McDonald [1972] Director/Wine Merchant; Alan David Snudden [1958] Director/Vintner

Genesis Wines Limited
Incorporated: 2 December 2003 *Employees:* 7
Net Worth Deficit: £1,437,951 *Total Assets:* £326,713
Registered Office: 68 South Lambeth Road, Vauxhall, London, SW8 1RL
Major Shareholder: Tom Heywood-Lonsdale
Officers: Tom Norman Heywood Lonsdale, Secretary; Tom Norman Heywood Lonsdale [1953] Director/Wine Merchant

Gente Di Mare Ltd
Incorporated: 20 September 2017
Registered Office: 9 Woburn Close, London, SW19 1DS
Officers: Andrea Boriassi, Secretary; Alexandro Caracoi [1990] Director [Italian]

Georges de la Chapelle Limited
Incorporated: 29 September 2003 *Employees:* 1
Net Worth: £26,823 *Total Assets:* £33,475
Registered Office: 10 Bideford Road, Ruislip, Middlesex, HA4 0UB
Major Shareholder: Aurelia Yveline Prat
Officers: Franck Zaire, Secretary; Aurelia Yveline Prat [1977] Director [French]

Georgian British Company Ltd
Incorporated: 21 May 2014
Registered Office: Unit 2 Invicta Park, Sandpit Road, Dartford, Kent, DA1 5BU
Major Shareholder: Henry Mchedlishvili
Officers: Henry Mchedlishvili [1976] Director

Georgian Wine Company Ltd
Incorporated: 10 October 2018
Registered Office: 122 Boundary Road, London, NW8 0RH
Major Shareholder: Zura Kokorashvili
Officers: Zura Kokorashvili [1983] Director/Businessman

Gergovie Wines Limited
Incorporated: 13 April 2011 *Employees:* 10
Net Worth: £213,397 *Total Assets:* £362,686
Registered Office: 70 Druid Street, London, SE1 2HQ
Shareholders: Stephen Williams; Henry Charles Lester; Raef Thomas Le Roy Hodgson
Officers: Raef Thomas Le Roy Hodgson [1983] Director; Henry Charles Lester [1976] Director; Stephen Williams [1982] Director/Head Chef

The German Beer Co Limited
Incorporated: 1 May 2013
Registered Office: 30 Greenford Gardens, Greenford, Middlesex, UB6 9LY
Officers: Timo Alexander Breunig [1981] Director [German]; Kshtiz Jude Gaur [1981] Director [Australian]

Ghost Drinks Ltd
Incorporated: 9 April 2015 *Employees:* 1
Net Worth Deficit: £55,450 *Total Assets:* £249,428
Registered Office: 1st Floor, Woburn House, 84 St Benedicts Street, Norwich, NR2 4AB
Shareholders: Hugh Francis Bower; Anthony Kenneth Brett
Officers: Hugh Francis Bower [1988] Director

Ghost Laboratories Limited
Incorporated: 16 August 2017
Registered Office: Highdown House, 11 Highdown Road, Leamington Spa, Warwicks, CV31 1XT
Major Shareholder: Steven Alexander Smith
Officers: Steven Alexander Smith [1970] Director

Gianni. B. Limited
Incorporated: 20 March 2009
Net Worth: £48,675 *Total Assets:* £63,070
Registered Office: Unit 003 Parma House, Clarendon Road, London, N22 6UL
Shareholders: Mark Gurrieri; Jonathan Gurrieri
Officers: Giovanni Gian Battista Gurrieri [1945] Director; Jonathan Gurrieri [1981] Director

The Gibraltar Gin Company Limited
Incorporated: 21 September 2018
Registered Office: Morants Hall, Colchester Road, Great Bromley, Colchester, Essex, CO7 7TN
Major Shareholder: Michael Joseph Volf
Officers: Michael Joseph Volf [1959] Director/Owner Care Group

Giesen Wines UK Limited
Incorporated: 27 May 2010 *Employees:* 1
Net Worth: £24,970 *Total Assets:* £36,219
Registered Office: c/o Dyke Yaxley, 1 Brassey Road, Old Potts Way, Shrewsbury, Salop, SY3 7FA
Shareholders: Alexander Giesen; Marcel Giesen; Theodor Giesen
Officers: Alexander Giesen [1959] Director [New Zealander]; Marcel Giesen [1965] Director [New Zealander]; Theodor Giesen [1958] Director [New Zealander]

Gift Creation and Design Limited
Incorporated: 28 November 2009 *Employees:* 9
Net Worth Deficit: £394,047 *Total Assets:* £1,221,853
Registered Office: Unit 12 Westby Close, Whitehills Drive, Whitehills Business Park, Blackpool, Lancs, FY4 5LW
Parent: Gift Creation and Design (Holdings) Ltd
Officers: Shohil Thakrar [1991] Director

Gigglewater Productions Ltd
Incorporated: 6 October 2017
Registered Office: 44 Honeyman Close, London, NW6 7AZ
Major Shareholder: Catherine Monahan
Officers: Catherine Monahan, Secretary; Catherine Monahan [1975] Director/CEO/Founder [Irish]

Gill Cash & Carry Limited
Incorporated: 30 October 2013
Net Worth: £48,946 *Total Assets:* £122,982
Registered Office: 9-11 Sunbeam Road, London, NW10 6JP
Major Shareholder: Daljit Singh Gill
Officers: Daljit Singh Gill [1961] Director/Businessman

Gill's Drams Ltd.
Incorporated: 15 June 2018
Registered Office: 8 Luggieburn Walk, Coatbridge, N Lanarks, ML5 1EE
Major Shareholder: Gillian Kirkland
Officers: Gillian Kirkland [1980] Director

The Gin Cooperative Ltd
Incorporated: 9 January 2018
Registered Office: Mayfield, Oyne, Insch, Garioch, Aberdeenshire, AB52 6QT
Major Shareholder: Natalie Anne Reid
Officers: Natalie Anne Reid [1983] Director/Owner

Gin Corporation Limited
Incorporated: 25 May 2017
Net Worth Deficit: £1,429 *Total Assets:* £13,109
Registered Office: 224 Park View, Whitley Bay, Tyne & Wear, NE26 3QR
Shareholder: Mark Ions
Officers: Mark Ions [1976] Director/Co Founder

The Gin Dobry Gin Company Ltd
Incorporated: 9 February 2018
Registered Office: 1 Harmer Court, Park Road, Southborough, Tunbridge Wells, Kent, TN4 0NZ
Major Shareholder: Daniel Robert Dudgeon
Officers: Daniel Robert Dudgeon [1980] Director

Gin Fizz Ltd
Incorporated: 2 October 2014
Net Worth: £839,142 *Total Assets:* £869,640
Registered Office: 182 Hamilton Road, Manchester, M13 0PX
Officers: Haroon Hussain [1988] Director; Ryan Jack Taylor [1996] Director

The Gin Room Scotland Ltd
Incorporated: 30 August 2016
Net Worth: £1 *Total Assets:* £1
Registered Office: 7 Wood Street, Aberdeen, AB11 9QD
Major Shareholder: Jayne Carmichael Norrie
Officers: Jayne Carmichael Norrie [1981] Director

Ginkhana Limited
Incorporated: 7 February 2018
Registered Office: Sunnyside Croft, Blairs, Aberdeen, AB12 5YT
Shareholders: David Lawson; Leeanne Lawson
Officers: Jill Bedawi, Secretary; Jill Bedawi [1969] Director; David Lawson [1973] Director; Leeanne Lawson [1976] Director/Housewife

Ginvino Ltd
Incorporated: 8 July 2016
Net Worth Deficit: £8,414 *Total Assets:* £77,222
Registered Office: 19 Langford Court, 22 Abbey Road, London, NW8 9DN
Parent: Tsovan Holdings Ltd
Officers: Zaruhi Serobyan [1980] Director/Accountant

Giovanni Food & Wine Limited
Incorporated: 21 June 2007 *Employees:* 14
Net Worth: £50,704 *Total Assets:* £177,652
Registered Office: Premier House, 36-48 Queen Street, Horsham, W Sussex, RH13 5AD
Shareholders: Franco James Barozzi; Maurizia Ascani
Officers: Maurizia Ascani [1975] Director/Manager of Cafe [Italian]; Franco James Barozzi [1986] Director

Giuseppe's Wines Limited
Incorporated: 15 December 2015 *Employees:* 2
Net Worth Deficit: £16,740 *Total Assets:* £13,808
Registered Office: 131 Old Manse Road, Wishaw, N Lanarks, ML2 0EW
Officers: Giuseppe Chierchia [1959] Director [Italian]; Maria Anne Chierchia [1991] Director

Glacon Limited
Incorporated: 7 April 2016
Net Worth Deficit: £42,910 *Total Assets:* £57,519
Registered Office: Merlin House, Langstone Business Village, Priory Drive, Langstone, Newport, NP18 2HJ
Major Shareholder: Matthew John Southall
Officers: Joseph Matthew Southall [1991] Director

Glam Drinks Ltd
Incorporated: 13 June 2018
Registered Office: 68 Mainsacre Drive, Stonehouse, S Lanarks, ML9 3QH
Major Shareholder: Margaret Carboni
Officers: Dr Margaret Carboni, Secretary; Dr Margaret Carboni [1990] Director/Research Scientist

Glamorgan Brewing Company Limited
Incorporated: 7 November 1994
Previous: The Glamorgan Beer Company Limited
Net Worth: £275,883 *Total Assets:* £2,357,248
Registered Office: Unit B, Llantrisant Business Park, Llantrisant, Pontyclun, Mid Glamorgan, CF72 8LF
Parent: G B C (Holdings) Limited
Officers: Richard Morgan Anstee, Secretary; John Anstee [1947] Director; Rhys Thomas Anstee [1980] Director; Richard Morgan Anstee [1974] Director/Manager; David John Atkins [1977] Financial Director

UK Wholesalers of Beers, Wines and Spirits

Glasgow Distillers Limited
Incorporated: 31 December 2003
Net Worth: £1,160,262 *Total Assets:* £1,160,452
Registered Office: 5th Floor, 45 Hope Street, Glasgow, G2 6AE
Major Shareholder: Elspeth Revie
Officers: Susanne Le May, Secretary; Kenneth George Le May [1951] Director/Chartered Accountant

Gleann Mor Spirits Company Limited
Incorporated: 19 March 2015
Net Worth: £23,059 *Total Assets:* £163,812
Registered Office: 28 Jane Street, Edinburgh, EH6 5HD
Major Shareholder: Derek Joseph Mair
Officers: Karin Mair, Secretary; Derek Joseph Mair [1961] Director/Businessman

Gleeson N.I. Limited
Incorporated: 27 May 2004
Net Worth Deficit: £343,957 *Total Assets:* £8,152,965
Registered Office: 15 Dargan Road, Belfast, BT3 9LS
Parent: C & C Group PLC
Officers: Ryan Knox [1976] Director/Commercial Manager; Thomas Michael McCusker [1957] Managing Director; Patrick McMahon [1980] Finance Director [Irish]

Glen Monarch Distillery Limited
Incorporated: 9 June 2017
Registered Office: Flat 1, 180 St Pauls Road, London, N1 2LL
Shareholder: Ashwin Balivada
Officers: Ashwin Balivada [1988] Director [Indian]; Dr Mohan Krishna Balivada [1959] Director/Businessman [Indian]

Glen Scotia Distillery Company Limited
Incorporated: 19 July 2013 *Employees:* 3
Net Worth: £73,773,000 *Total Assets:* £154,226,000
Registered Office: 30 Broadwick Street, London, W1F 8JB
Parent: Loch Lomond Distillery Company Limited
Officers: Colin Matthews [1965] Director; Richard Miles [1966] Director; Nicholas Rose [1957] Director

Glenalan Limited
Incorporated: 11 January 1993
Net Worth: £1,940 *Total Assets:* £8,850
Registered Office: Laverockdale Lodge, Dreghorn Loan, Edinburgh, EH13 0DB
Major Shareholder: Alan Gordon Henry Macpherson
Officers: Dr Alan Gordon Henry Macpherson [1952] Director/Medical Practitioner

The Glenallachie Distillers Co Limited
Incorporated: 1 March 2017 *Employees:* 1
Net Worth Deficit: £93,774 *Total Assets:* £476,095
Registered Office: Glenallachie Distillery, Glenallachie, Aberlour, Banffshire, AB38 9LR
Shareholders: William James Walker; Alistair James Graham Stevenson
Officers: Patricia Bridget Savage, Secretary; Patricia Bridget Savage [1959] Commercial Director; Alistair James Graham Stevenson [1958] Director; William James Walker [1945] Managing Director

Glenbrynth Limited
Incorporated: 10 July 2018
Registered Office: c/o Brodies LLP, 110 Queen Street, Glasgow, G1 3BX
Officers: Brenda Venestia Nathan [1959] Director/Businesswoman [South African]; Brian Nathan [1941] Director/Businessman [South African]; Michael Darren Nathan [1988] Director/Businessman [South African]

Gleneagles Distillery Limited
Incorporated: 20 December 2018
Registered Office: Briven House, Main Road, Aberuthven, Auchterarder, Perthshire, PH3 1HB
Major Shareholder: Graham Charles Bennett
Officers: Graham Charles Bennett [1958] Director

Glenforest Limited
Incorporated: 22 July 2010 *Employees:* 2
Net Worth: £186,361 *Total Assets:* £9,290,394
Registered Office: 16 Muir Street, Hamilton, S Lanarks, ML3 6EP
Parent: Malasi S.A.
Officers: Simone Polini [1970] Director [Italian]

Gleninver Limited
Incorporated: 14 June 2000
Registered Office: c/o Marchwood Accountancy Services Ltd, The Old Bakehouse, 77a High Street, Linlithgow, W Lothian, EH49 7ED
Major Shareholder: Ian David MacDonald
Officers: Richard Ian Jasper [1965] Director; Ian David MacDonald [1947] Director

The Glenlatterach Whisky Co Ltd
Incorporated: 12 May 2017
Net Worth: £1,360 *Total Assets:* £1,360
Registered Office: Brokentore, Kellas, Elgin, Moray, IV30 8TS
Major Shareholder: Alexander Tomas Christie
Officers: Alexander Tomas Christie [1980] Director/Exporter

Glennlay & Co Ltd
Incorporated: 11 November 2016
Registered Office: 67 Bathurst Walk, Iver, Bucks, SL0 9EF
Major Shareholder: Vijay Selvaraj
Officers: Vijay Selvaraj [1975] Director

Glenreidh Liquor Company Ltd
Incorporated: 6 April 2018
Registered Office: 272 Bath Street, Glasgow, G2 4JR
Major Shareholder: Abhishek Bagchi
Officers: Abhishek Bagchi [1978] Director [American]

Glenroy Spirits Limited
Incorporated: 21 August 2014
Net Worth Deficit: £133,073 *Total Assets:* £35
Registered Office: Durat House, Finch Way, Strathclyde Business Park, Bellshill, N Lanarks, ML4 3PR
Major Shareholder: Amir Eisa Bawi
Officers: Amir Eisa Bawi [1957] Director

Glenturret Limited
Incorporated: 17 December 2018
Registered Office: 100 Queen Street, Glasgow, G1 3DN
Parent: Highland Distillers Limited
Officers: Martin Alexander Cooke [1961] Director/Company Secretary

Glo-Rum Enterprise Limited
Incorporated: 11 September 2017
Registered Office: 1 Hanbury Mews, Croydon, Surrey, CR0 7DW
Shareholders: Aston Wilson; Bianca Bailey Wilson
Officers: Rosanna Bailey, Secretary; Aston Wilson [1979] Director/Senior Account Executive; Dr Bianca Bailey Wilson [1985] Director/Higher Education Researcher

Matthew Gloag & Son Limited
Incorporated: 14 April 1939
Registered Office: 100 Queen Street, Glasgow, G1 3DN
Parent: Highland Distillers Group Limited
Officers: Martin Alexander Cooke, Secretary; Martin Alexander Cooke [1961] Company Secretary/Director; Suzy Smith [1972] Director

Global Beer Company Ltd
Incorporated: 10 February 2015
Net Worth: £12,110 Total Assets: £199,145
Registered Office: 71-75 Shelton Street, London, WC2H 9JQ
Officers: David Stewart Brown [1957] Director

Global Brands Trading Ltd
Incorporated: 26 January 2018
Registered Office: 215b Kenton Lane, Harrow, Middlesex, HA3 8RP
Major Shareholder: Veneshen Govender
Officers: Veneshen Govender [1978] Director

Global D & F Ltd
Incorporated: 31 May 2018
Registered Office: 13 The Broadway, Southall, Middlesex, UB1 1JR
Major Shareholder: Ramona Schmidt
Officers: Ramona Schmidt [1960] Director [German]

Global Drinks (UK) Limited
Incorporated: 1 October 2010
Net Worth: £6,050 Total Assets: £7,358
Registered Office: Castor Street, Liverpool, L6 5AT
Major Shareholder: John Kenneth Ravenscroft
Officers: John Kenneth Ravenscroft [1955] Director/Licencee

Global Ethics Liquor Co Limited
Incorporated: 4 July 2014
Previous: Global Ethics Financial Services Limited
Net Worth Deficit: £166,366 Total Assets: £125,804
Registered Office: Steel House, 13-17 Princes Road, Richmond, Surrey, TW10 6QD
Major Shareholder: Duncan Hugh Goose
Officers: Duncan Hugh Goose [1968] Managing Director; Ian John Spooner [1971] Director/Head of Brand

Global Foods Limited
Incorporated: 18 August 1981 Employees: 117
Net Worth: £11,201,317 Total Assets: £19,162,588
Registered Office: 1-3 Stadium Close, off Penarth Road, Cardiff, CF11 8TS
Major Shareholder: Mohammed Yaqub
Officers: Nina Ahmad-Vellani [1965] Director/HR Manager; Mubarik Ali [1939] Director/Wholesaler; Qaiser Aziz [1975] Director/Sales Manager [Pakistani]; David Owen Davies [1958] Director/General Manager; Shahid Iqbal [1966] Director/Accountant; Sophie Gamela Kriss [1978] Director/Business Executive; Abdul Wahid [1957] Director/Businessman [Pakistani]; Mohammed Yaqub [1934] Director

Global Trade & Consulting Ltd
Incorporated: 1 November 2018
Registered Office: 20-22 Wenlock Road, London, N1 7GU
Major Shareholder: Sergio Pancolini
Officers: Sergio Pancolini [1967] Director/Manager [Italian]

Global Village Wines Limited
Incorporated: 7 May 2009
Registered Office: Ibex House, Baker Street, Weybridge, Surrey, KT13 8AH
Major Shareholder: Joseph Richard Minerva
Officers: Tommaso Minerva, Secretary; Joseph Richard Minerva [1960] Director/Wine Importer

Global Wine & Spirits Ltd
Incorporated: 27 November 2018
Registered Office: 6 Westville Road, Thames Ditton, Surrey, KT7 0UJ
Major Shareholder: Maxwell John Maxey
Officers: Maxwell John Maxey [1956] Marketing Director

Global Wine Distributors Limited
Incorporated: 20 November 2013
Net Worth: £82,100 Total Assets: £325,144
Registered Office: 8 College Green, Bangor, Co Down, BT20 5FA
Parent: Thisway Scot Ltd
Officers: John Michael Botros [1948] Director/Barrister; Graeme David Paton [1965] Director

The Global Wine Trading Company Limited
Incorporated: 4 May 2017
Net Worth: £149 Total Assets: £2,848
Registered Office: 49 Berkeley Square, London, W1J 5AZ
Officers: Richard Maria [1969] Director/General Manager [French]; Timothy John McCandless [1971] Director/Personal Assistant

Global World Wide Beer Limited
Incorporated: 13 April 2015
Registered Office: Office 4, 219 Kensington High Street, Kensington, London, W8 6BD
Major Shareholder: Hratschja Sargsjan
Officers: Hratschja Sargsjan, Secretary; Hratschja Sargsjan [1978] Director [German]

Global24-7 (UK) Ltd
Incorporated: 10 March 2010
Net Worth Deficit: £25,384 Total Assets: £96,864
Registered Office: The Courtyard, Pennyfarthing House, Brighton Road, South Croydon, Surrey, CR2 6AW
Major Shareholder: Keith Stock
Officers: Keith Stock [1957] Director/Sales

Globe Logistics Limited
Incorporated: 22 September 2015
Registered Office: 230 Narborough Road, Leicester, LE3 2AN
Major Shareholder: Igors Kormilcevs
Officers: Igors Kormilcevs [1986] Managing Director [Latvian]

Globus Wines (UK) Ltd
Incorporated: 7 August 2009
Net Worth: £36,697 Total Assets: £191,132
Registered Office: 9 Parkfield, Chorleywood, Rickmansworth, Herts, WD3 5AY
Major Shareholder: Aashima Hariyani
Officers: Aashima Hariyani [1978] Director

Glow Glow Ltd.
Incorporated: 9 August 2012
Registered Office: Suite 3, 95 Wilton Road, London, SW1V 1BZ
Major Shareholder: Isaac Chriqui
Officers: Isaac Chriqui [1958] Director/Chairman & CEO [French]

Glug Limited
Incorporated: 2 September 2004
Net Worth: £51,988 *Total Assets:* £383,225
Registered Office: 5 Minton Place, Victoria Road, Bicester, Oxon, OX26 6QB
Major Shareholder: David Walkden
Officers: Kevin Stirrat, Secretary; David Walkden [1961] Director

Glugged! Ltd
Incorporated: 18 May 2018
Registered Office: 93 Thornton Road, Manchester, M14 7NT
Officers: Callum Alexander Ferguson [1988] Director/Wine Merchant; Robert Andrew Johnson [1973] Director/Wine Merchant

Glugit Limited
Incorporated: 16 May 2017
Registered Office: Kemp House, 160 City Road, London, EC1V 2NX
Major Shareholder: Jason Rivolta
Officers: Jason Rivolta [1967] Director/Sales & Marketing

GM Catering Supplies Ltd
Incorporated: 2 February 2016
Net Worth: £51,329 *Total Assets:* £93,753
Registered Office: The Gate Business Centre, Keppoch Street, Cardiff, CF24 3JW
Shareholder: Mian Gul
Officers: Mian Gul [1987] Director

GNR Distillery Limited
Incorporated: 21 June 2018
Registered Office: Manwood Barn, Mersea Road, Abberton, Colchester, Essex, CO5 7NS
Shareholder: Gavin Miklaucich
Officers: Susan Miklaucich, Secretary; Richard Fletcher Frost [1972] Director; Gavin Miklaucich [1966] Director

Go Brazil Wines & Spirits (UK) Ltd
Incorporated: 24 May 2010
Net Worth Deficit: £92,051 *Total Assets:* £21,895
Registered Office: Basepoint Business Centre, 70-72 The Havens, Ipswich, Suffolk, IP3 9BF
Major Shareholder: Nicholas Charles Roderick Corfe
Officers: Nicholas Charles Roderick Corfe [1962] Director/Export Consultant

Godin Tepe Limited
Incorporated: 4 April 2018
Registered Office: 67 Lower Road, Chalfont St Peter, Gerrards Cross, Bucks, SL9 9AS
Shareholder: Dariush Dezfulli
Officers: Dariush Dezfulli [1959] Director

Goedhuis & Company Limited
Incorporated: 23 June 1981 *Employees:* 24
Net Worth: £1,801,735 *Total Assets:* £17,668,416
Registered Office: 3rd Floor, 12 Gough Square, London, EC4A 3DW
Officers: Justin Randall, Secretary; Oliver Robert Morgan Bolitho [1967] Director/Investor; Georgina Lucy Crawley [1977] Director/Wine Merchant; Jonathan Daniel Goedhuis [1949] Director/Wine Shipper [Dutch]; James Hamilton Low [1976] Director/Wine Merchant; Gareth David Pearce [1953] Director/Chartered Accountant; Justin Randall [1966] Director/Accountant; David William Roberts [1962] Director; Thomas Nigel Stopford Sackville [1968] Director/Wine Merchant; James Edward Strutt [1969] Director/Wine Merchant; Philippa Jane Graeme Wright [1969] Director/PR and Marketing

Gold Max Distribution Limited
Incorporated: 12 October 2009
Net Worth Deficit: £102,884 *Total Assets:* £82,512
Registered Office: The White House, Clifton Marine Parade, Gravesend, Kent, DA11 0DY
Major Shareholder: Amrik Singh Channa
Officers: Amrik Singh Channa [1977] Director

Gold Tooth Limited
Incorporated: 13 June 2018
Registered Office: 93 Great Eastern Street, London, EC2A 3HZ
Shareholders: Sam James Orrock; Matthew Jefrey Allen Whiley
Officers: Sam James Orrock [1984] Director; Matthew Jefrey Allen Whiley [1980] Director

Goldbeach Trading Limited
Incorporated: 12 August 2008 *Employees:* 7
Net Worth: £70,565 *Total Assets:* £431,136
Registered Office: 5 Albany Road, Earlsdon, Coventry, Warwicks, CV5 6JQ
Major Shareholder: Makhan Singh
Officers: Makhan Singh [1963] Director

Goldcrest Drinks Limited
Incorporated: 20 May 2011
Previous: Falcon International Beverages Ltd
Net Worth: £157,830 *Total Assets:* £222,213
Registered Office: 53 Leamington Road, Hockley, Essex, SS5 5HH
Officers: Gary Alan Biddiss [1961] Director

Golden Coin Trading Limited
Incorporated: 17 July 2018
Registered Office: Flat 22, 7 Yeoman Street, London, SE8 5DT
Major Shareholder: Nghia Thanh Duong
Officers: Nghia Thanh Duong [1987] Director/Accountant

Golden Crust & Co Limited
Incorporated: 27 May 2011
Net Worth Deficit: £755 *Total Assets:* £1,144
Registered Office: 1386 London Road, Leigh on Sea, Essex, SS9 2UJ
Parent: Regional GD Limited
Officers: Gary Edward Downham [1965] Director

Golden Decanters Limited
Incorporated: 11 March 2015 *Employees:* 2
Net Worth: £1,332 *Total Assets:* £32,534
Registered Office: Ferniehill House, Stanley, Perth, PH1 4QD
Shareholders: Ann Kirsty Medlock; Julia MacKenzie-Gillanders
Officers: Julia MacKenzie-Gillanders [1981] Director; Ann Kirsty Medlock [1965] Director

Golden Everest Limited
Incorporated: 24 July 2014
Net Worth Deficit: £21,392 *Total Assets:* £105,799
Registered Office: Unit 19 Autumn Park Industrial Estate, Dysart Road, Grantham, Lincs, NG31 7EU
Major Shareholder: Kalpit Bhandari
Officers: Kalpit Bhandari [1991] Director

Golden Harvest Wholesale Limited
Incorporated: 12 September 2008
Net Worth Deficit: £73,712 *Total Assets:* £4,719,372
Registered Office: 170 Draycott Avenue, Harrow, Middlesex, HA3 0BZ
Major Shareholder: Divyesh Kurji Karsan
Officers: Divyesh Kurji Karsan [1969] Director

Golden Whisky Limited
Incorporated: 23 October 2018
Registered Office: 11 Stoneywood Brae, Aberdeen, AB21 9DW
Major Shareholder: Zhenzhen Zhang
Officers: Zhenzhen Zhang [1989] Director/Manager [Chinese]

Goldex International Ltd
Incorporated: 16 August 2017
Registered Office: 57 Moresby Road, London, E5 9LE
Major Shareholder: Jehuda Goldenberg
Officers: Jehuda Goldenberg [1949] Director

Goldfinch Whisky Merchants Ltd
Incorporated: 28 November 2018
Registered Office: Langcroft, Buchanan Castle Estate, Drymen, Glasgow, G63 0HX
Major Shareholder: Andrew John MacDonald-Bennett
Officers: Andrew John MacDonald-Bennett [1974] Director

Goldy Gin Limited
Incorporated: 23 December 2016
Registered Office: Flat 2, 23 Mount Street, London, W1K 2RP
Major Shareholder: Justin Daniel O'Shea
Officers: Antonio Michele Conigliaro [1971] Director/Bar Owner; Ramon Mac-Crohon Ron [1975] Director/Entrepreneur [Spanish]; Justin Daniel O'Shea [1979] Director/Entrepreneur [Australian]

Goldy Limited
Incorporated: 3 April 2017
Registered Office: Flat 2, 23 Mount Street, London, W1K 2RP
Major Shareholder: Justin Daniel O'Shea
Officers: Justin Daniel O'Shea [1979] Director [Australian]

Goldy's Corner Shop Ltd
Incorporated: 18 May 2018
Registered Office: 5 Mount Stuart Square, Cardiff, CF10 5LR
Officers: Annabelle Singh [1984] Director/Collections Advisor; Satnam Singh [1988] Director/HGV Driver [Indian]

Gonzalez Byass UK Limited
Incorporated: 6 February 2004 *Employees:* 29
Net Worth: £3,965,572 *Total Assets:* £8,145,926
Registered Office: c/o Rayner Essex LLP, Tavistock House South, Tavistock Square, London, WC1H 9LG
Officers: Maria Romero Garcia-Delgado, Secretary; Manuel Jimenez Aguilar [1974] Director [Spanish]; Mauricio Gonzalez-Gordon Lopez de Carrizosa [1960] Director [Spanish]; Jorge Alberto Grosse Mac Dougall [1953] Director/General Manager [Spanish/Argentinian]; Pedro Andres Rebuelta Del Pedredo Gonzalez [1960] Executive Director [Spanish]

Good Food Wines Limited
Incorporated: 8 February 1984 *Employees:* 27
Net Worth: £9,018,130 *Total Assets:* £10,668,573
Registered Office: 3 Manor Road, Chatham, Kent, ME4 6AE
Officers: Kathleen Alice Haselden [1943] Director; Kevin William Geoffrey Haselden [1950] Director

The Good Life Gin Company Ltd
Incorporated: 7 December 2017
Registered Office: Anchor House, Burgoine Quay, 8 Lower Teddington Road, Kingston upon Thames, Surrey, KT1 4EU
Major Shareholder: Samuel Rupert Berry
Officers: Samuel Rupert Berry [1989] Director

Good Living Brew Co Limited
Incorporated: 16 March 2018
Registered Office: Sundial House, High Street, Horsell, Woking, Surrey, GU21 4SU
Major Shareholder: Brett Jason Venter
Officers: Danielle Bekker [1976] Director/Engineer [South African]; Brett Jason Venter [1976] Director [South African]

Good Spirits Ltd
Incorporated: 29 May 2018
Registered Office: 28 Crieff Road, London, SW18 2EA
Shareholders: James Henry Newton Kaye; James Edward Prowse
Officers: James Henry Newton Kaye [1996] Director; James Edward Prowse [1996] Director

Good Wine Limited
Incorporated: 1 August 2018
Registered Office: Tree Tops, Beacon Hill, Ovingdean, Brighton, BN2 7BN
Major Shareholder: Matthew Mundroina
Officers: Matthew Mundroina [1994] Director

Goodeataly Ltd
Incorporated: 27 September 2018
Registered Office: 1st Floor, 26 Fouberts Place, London, W1F 7PP
Officers: Fabrizio Bertoni [1966] Director [Italian]; Cristian Salamini [1976] Director [Italian]

Gordano Wines Limited
Incorporated: 11 April 2001 *Employees:* 11
Net Worth: £98,908 *Total Assets:* £825,243
Registered Office: 2 Chesterfield Buildings, Westbourne Place, Clifton, Bristol, BS8 1RU
Major Shareholder: Roland Henry Bagnall
Officers: Roland Henry Bagnall [1959] Director/Wines & Spirits Wholesaler

Gordon & MacPhail Limited
Incorporated: 16 February 2017
Registered Office: George House, Boroughbriggs Road, Elgin, Moray, IV30 1JY
Parent: Speymalt Whisky Distributors Limited
Officers: Norman Ross, Secretary; Ewen Cameron Mackintosh [1968] Director

Gordons (Bolton) Limited
Incorporated: 7 October 1933 *Employees:* 7
Net Worth: £1,988,249 *Total Assets:* £2,927,824
Registered Office: Carlyle House, 78 Chorley New Road, Bolton, Lancs, BL1 4BY
Shareholder: Gordon Richard Seymour
Officers: Gordon Richard Seymour [1968] Director/Motor Dealer; Gordon Lewis Seymour [1949] Director/Motor Engineer; Marjorie Seymour [1945] Director/Secretary; Natalie Victoria Seymour [1975] Director; Nicola Rachel Seymour [1972] Director

The Gort Inn Ltd
Incorporated: 5 February 2018
Registered Office: 57 Main Street, Gortin, Omagh, Co Tyrone, BT79 8NH
Major Shareholder: Michael McGuigan
Officers: Michael McGuigan, Secretary; Michael McGuigan [1982] Director/Publican [Irish]

UK Wholesalers of Beers, Wines and Spirits   dellam

Gourvid Limited
Incorporated: 6 June 2016
Net Worth: £3,171   Total Assets: £92,098
Registered Office: 28 Church Grove, Kingston upon Thames, Surrey, KT1 4AL
Shareholders: Juan Manuel Matas Carnero; Maria Celina Giroldi
Officers: Juan Manuel Matas Carnero [1981] Director/Entrepreneur [Argentinian]

The Gower Gin Company Limited
Incorporated: 17 October 2017
Registered Office: 44 St Helen's Road, Swansea, SA1 4BB
Shareholders: Sian Margaret Brooks; Andrew Crawford Brooks
Officers: Andrew Crawford Brooks [1964] Director; Sian Margaret Brooks [1966] Director

Grace Wines (UK) Limited
Incorporated: 5 January 2017   Employees: 2
Net Worth Deficit: £11,544   Total Assets: £32,641
Registered Office: 15 Towcester Road, Old Stratford, Milton Keynes, Bucks, MK19 6AN
Shareholders: John Paul Crook; Sheena Salah
Officers: John Paul Crook [1965] Director; Sheena Salah [1961] Director

Grafham Brewing Company Ltd
Incorporated: 29 November 2017
Registered Office: 30 Breach Road, Grafham, Cambs, PE28 0BA
Major Shareholder: Paul Robinson
Officers: Paul Robinson [1974] Director/Designer

Graftyset Limited
Incorporated: 4 November 2003
Net Worth Deficit: £271,651   Total Assets: £661,876
Registered Office: Victoria House, 12 Hatherley Road, Sidcup, Kent, DA14 4DT
Major Shareholder: Bertrand Velge
Officers: Bertrand Roger Velge [1959] Director

Gordon Graham & Company Limited
Incorporated: 7 January 2003
Registered Office: 8 Milton Road, College Milton North, East Kilbride, S Lanarks, G74 5BU
Parent: Distell International Limited
Officers: Karen Spy, Secretary; Fraser John Thornton [1969] Director

Peter Graham Wines Limited
Incorporated: 2 March 2000   Employees: 13
Net Worth: £43,783   Total Assets: £1,114,312
Registered Office: Unit 2 Gales Business Park, Ayton Road, Wymondham, Norfolk, NR18 0QQ
Major Shareholder: Louisa Caroline Bacos
Officers: Louisa Caroline Turner, Secretary; Louisa Caroline Turner [1970] Director

Grainger Fine Wines Ltd
Incorporated: 18 October 2010
Net Worth Deficit: £59,497   Total Assets: £6,652
Registered Office: The Stone Barn, Noble Street, Sherston, Malmesbury, Wilts, SN16 0NA
Officers: Simon Grainger [1951] Director

Grand Vin Wine Merchants Ltd
Incorporated: 2 October 2014
Registered Office: 2 The Mews, 16 Holly Bush Lane, Sevenoaks, Kent, TN13 3TH
Major Shareholder: Andrew Douglas Lench
Officers: Andew Lench [1954] Director/Wine Trade

Grande Marque Food & Beverage Limited
Incorporated: 3 May 2017
Registered Office: 6 Edge View Crescent, Merrymans Lane, Alderley Edge, Cheshire, SK9 7TB
Major Shareholder: Antony Brian Kensington
Officers: Ian David Jenner [1969] Director

Grandi Vini Limited
Incorporated: 4 March 2014
Net Worth: £3,179   Total Assets: £34,528
Registered Office: Experience House, 5 Port Hill, Hertford, SG14 1PJ
Major Shareholder: Roberto Dimostrato
Officers: Roberto Dimostrato [1977] Director [Italian]

Grandor Limited
Incorporated: 24 May 2018
Registered Office: 49 Greek Street, London, W1D 4EG
Shareholders: Andrew Grant Rennie; Danielle Rose Rennie
Officers: Paul David Beare, Secretary; Andrew Grant Rennie [1966] Director [Canadian]; Danielle Rose Rennie [1965] Director [Canadian]

Grands Vins de France Limited
Incorporated: 18 January 2008   Employees: 1
Net Worth: £17,277   Total Assets: £305,139
Registered Office: Milton House, Gatehouse Road, Aylesbury, Bucks, HP19 8EA
Major Shareholder: Demetri Demetriou
Officers: Karina Kiersztan, Secretary; Demetri Demetriou [1952] Director/Wine Broker

William Grant & Sons Brands Limited
Incorporated: 31 January 2014   Employees: 115
Net Worth: £100,693,000   Total Assets: £251,652,000
Registered Office: Independence House, 84 Lower Mortlake Road, Richmond, Surrey, TW9 2HS
Parent: William Grant & Sons Limited
Officers: Gregory Justin Bargeton, Secretary; Douglas John Bagley [1967] Director [Australian]; Gregory Justin Bargeton [1973] Director/Global Head of Legal; Gary William Brewer [1961] Director; Philip Andrew Gladman [1970] Marketing Director; Rita Marie Greenwood [1968] Director; Ewan John Henderson [1968] Director; Simon John Hunt [1971] Director [Australian/British]; Michael Lamont [1960] Director/Accountant; Christopher Wesley Mason [1953] Director; Paul Henry Rochford [1963] Director/Accountant; Jonathan Mark Yusen [1970] Director [American]

William Grant & Sons UK Limited
Incorporated: 19 August 1988   Employees: 143
Net Worth: £821,000   Total Assets: £146,531,008
Registered Office: Form 1 Bartley Wood Business Park, Bartley Way, Hook, Hants, RG27 9XA
Parent: William Grant & Sons Investments Limited
Officers: Karen Louise Forbes, Secretary; Neil Peter Barker [1963] Managing Director [British/Australian]; Rita Marie Greenwood [1968] Director; Ewan John Henderson [1968] Director/Group Tax and Company Secretary; Christopher Wesley Mason [1953] Managing Director; Paul Henry Rochford [1963] Director; Iain David Short [1981] Director/Chartered Accountant

Grants-EU Limited
Incorporated: 21 January 2002
Net Worth: £4,054,572   Total Assets: £4,054,572
Registered Office: Suite 1, Bowden Terminal, Luckyn Lane, Basildon, Essex, SS14 3AX
Major Shareholder: William Francis de Fries
Officers: William Francis de Fries [1953] Director

Grape and Grain Management Limited
Incorporated: 15 October 2012
Net Worth: £10,283 Total Assets: £91,690
Registered Office: 31 St Johns Crescent, Whitchurch, Cardiff, CF14 7AF
Shareholders: Clare Lynne Hardwicke-Wall; Graham Meredith Wall
Officers: Clare Lynne Hardwicke-Wall [1967] Director; Graham Meredith Wall [1961] Director

Grape and Nectar Ltd
Incorporated: 19 November 2018
Registered Office: 4 Linden Avenue, Maidenhead, Berks, SL6 6HB
Shareholders: Katherine Emma Dart; Fiona Ann Hayes
Officers: Katherine Emma Dart [1975] Director; Fiona Ann Hayes [1984] Director

Grape Drinks (UK) Limited
Incorporated: 25 January 2013
Net Worth: £2,675 Total Assets: £52,651
Registered Office: 18-20 Parliament Square, Hertford, SG14 1EZ
Major Shareholder: Ali Canbolat
Officers: Ali Canbolat [1967] Director

The Grape Escape Limited
Incorporated: 11 March 2004
Registered Office: c/o Hughes & Co, Unit 1 Vantage Court, Riverside Business Park, Barrowford, Lancs, BB9 6BP
Shareholders: Stuart Lester Walton; Carole Shutt
Officers: Carole Shutt, Secretary; Stuart Lester Walton [1947] Director/Manager

Grape Merchants Ltd
Incorporated: 5 December 2018
Registered Office: 29 Wexham Road, Slough, Berks, SL2 5HF
Officers: Amit Singh Bassi [1982] Director/Recruitment Consultant; Sergio Rojas Buitrago [1982] Director/IT Consultant [Spanish]; Taranjeet Singh Sandhu [1984] Director/Banker

Grape Opportunities Ltd
Incorporated: 16 September 2013
Registered Office: 22 Yeo Way, Clevedon, Somerset, BS21 7UP
Officers: David Christopher John Nicholls [1950] Director/Retired

Grape Passions Limited
Incorporated: 3 April 2001 Employees: 8
Net Worth: £1,099,266 Total Assets: £1,381,747
Registered Office: Unit 7 Rosewood Business Park, Eastways, Witham, Essex, CM8 3AA
Major Shareholder: Mark Nicholas Soudah
Officers: Kay Madeline Soudah, Secretary/Sales Manager; Kay Madeline Soudah [1965] Director/Company Secretary; Mark Nicholas Soudah [1965] Director

The Grape Variety Ltd
Incorporated: 5 January 2018
Registered Office: 21-23 Croydon Road, Caterham, Surrey, CR3 6PA
Shareholders: Thomas Alexander Johnson; Steven Garry Bishop
Officers: Steven Garry Bishop [1980] Director; Thomas Alexander Johnson [1987] Director

Grape Wines Services Ltd
Incorporated: 25 August 2017
Registered Office: 10 Elm Park Road, London, SE25 6UA
Major Shareholder: Stuart Anthony Williams
Officers: Natalia Fudali Lara, Secretary; Natalia Fudali Lara [1987] Director/Manager [Brazilian]; Stuart Anthony Williams [1967] Managing Director

Grapebee Ltd
Incorporated: 8 November 2016
Net Worth Deficit: £6,352 Total Assets: £17,958
Registered Office: 79 Essex Road, Islington, London, N1 2SF
Major Shareholder: Valerio Rosellini
Officers: Valerio Rosellini [1985] Director/Wine Merchant [Italian]

Grapes of Hungary Ltd
Incorporated: 3 June 2014 Employees: 1
Net Worth Deficit: £22,088 Total Assets: £8,355
Registered Office: 4 Albert Place, Perth, PH2 8JE
Major Shareholder: Csilla Sebestyen
Officers: Csilla Sebestyen [1980] Director/Sommelier [Hungarian]

Grassington Spirit Company Limited
Incorporated: 25 September 2018
Registered Office: 13 Main Street, Grassington, Skipton, N Yorks, BD23 5AD
Officers: Angela Mary Beetham [1966] Director/Legal Secretary; Andrew Michael Booth [1961] Director; Karen Linda Darwin [1963] Director/Jeweller; Philip Andrew Johnson [1950] Director/Retired; Jacqueline Carol Sugden [1957] Director

Gravity Drinks Ltd
Incorporated: 31 August 2016
Net Worth Deficit: £8,269 Total Assets: £192,069
Registered Office: G01 Charrington Tower, 11 Biscayne Avenue, London, E14 9AY
Major Shareholder: Matthew Joseph Maslin
Officers: Matthew Joseph Maslin [1974] Director

Graysons Freight Services Limited
Incorporated: 23 April 1980 Employees: 10
Net Worth: £125,087 Total Assets: £459,955
Registered Office: 124-126 Church Hill, Loughton, Essex, IG10 1LH
Major Shareholder: Stuart Paul Jackson
Officers: Stuart Jackson, Secretary; Stuart Paul Jackson [1970] Managing Director; Joanne May [1983] Director

The Great Newsome Brewery Limited
Incorporated: 7 September 2006 Employees: 9
Net Worth: £109,907 Total Assets: £279,828
Registered Office: Great Newsome Farm, South Frodingham, Hull, HU12 0NR
Parent: I M Hodgson & Son Limited
Officers: Matthew Hodgson, Secretary; Jonathan Hodgson [1976] Director/Farmer; Laurence Hodgson [1950] Director/Farmer; Matthew Hodson [1973] Director/Farmer

Great Orme Drinks Co. Ltd
Incorporated: 1 September 2018
Registered Office: Avalon, Tan Y Fron Road, Abergele, Clwyd, LL22 9BA
Officers: Jeremy Platt [1961] Director; Carolyn Sylvia Plattt [1959] Director/Teacher

The Great Smattsby Limited
Incorporated: 9 March 2017
Registered Office: 16 Wetherby Gardens, London, SW5 0JP
Parent: Coldharbour Holdings Limited
Officers: Ashley John Smatt [1980] Director

The Great Spirit Company Ltd
Incorporated: 7 December 2015
Registered Office: Unit 3, 61a Osbaldwick Lane, York, YO10 3AY
Major Shareholder: Edward Ludlow
Officers: Edward Ludlow [1972] Director

Great Western Wine Company Limited (The)
Incorporated: 2 September 1983
Net Worth: £395,250 Total Assets: £395,251
Registered Office: 23 Cumberland Avenue, London, NW10 7RX
Parent: Enotria Group Limited
Officers: Mark Huszczo, Secretary; Troy Christensen [1966] Director [American]

The Great Whisky Company Ltd
Incorporated: 30 March 2012
Net Worth Deficit: £1,393 Total Assets: £53,229
Registered Office: Unit 3, 61a Osbaldwick Lane, York, YO10 3AY
Major Shareholder: Amanda Lynn Ludlow
Officers: Amanda Lynn Ludlow [1967] Director

The Great Wine Group Limited
Incorporated: 28 July 2016
Registered Office: 11 Red Lion Way, Wooburn Green, High Wycombe, Bucks, HP10 0HT
Officers: Ewen Irving Cameron [1956] Director; Penelope Ann Heyes [1960] Director; John Donald Philips [1957] Director [Irish]; Graham Paul Sumeray [1963] Director

Greatdrams Ventures Limited
Incorporated: 24 October 2017
Registered Office: Brook House, Park Lane, Poynton, Stockport, Cheshire, SK12 1RG
Major Shareholder: Gregory Dillon
Officers: Gregory Dillon [1985] Director/Marketing Consultant; Kirsty Dillon [1984] Marketing Director

Greater London Beer Exports Ltd
Incorporated: 24 October 2017
Registered Office: Marlborough Arms, 36 Torrington Place, London, WC1E 7LY
Major Shareholder: Alan Blues
Officers: Alan Blues [1980] Director/Manager

Greatvine Ltd
Incorporated: 11 May 2016
Net Worth: £21,537 Total Assets: £49,807
Registered Office: Titanic Suites, 55-59 Adelaide Street, Carryduff, Belfast, BT2 8FE
Shareholder: Sherril Soliman
Officers: Mohamed Soliman [1945] Director/Wine Seller [Egyptian]; Sherril Soliman [1965] Director/Wine Seller

GreatWineDirect Limited
Incorporated: 19 May 2015
Net Worth Deficit: £54,019 Total Assets: £18,165
Registered Office: Flexi Spaces, 40 Ashton Old Road, Manchester, M12 6LP
Major Shareholder: Heath Donnelly
Officers: Heath Donnelly [1971] Director

The Greek Wineshop Ltd
Incorporated: 9 November 2016 Employees: 2
Net Worth Deficit: £572
Registered Office: 1 Brassey Road, Old Potts Way, Shrewsbury, Salop, SY3 7FA
Shareholders: Georgios Papanikolaou; Eirini Lagoumidi
Officers: Eirini Lagoumidi [1977] Director/Vice President of Greek Commercial Company [Greek]; Georgios Papanikolaou [1978] Director/Merchant [Greek]

Green Cash & Carry Ltd
Incorporated: 8 February 2019
Registered Office: 15 Herbert Road, Kirkby in Ashfield, Nottingham, NG17 9DD
Major Shareholder: Octavian Rusu
Officers: Octavian Rusu [1988] Director [Romanian]

Green Heart Wines Ltd
Incorporated: 10 August 2018
Registered Office: 2 Stadium Street, London, SW10 0PS
Major Shareholder: Richard Patrick Jacques
Officers: Richard Patrick Jacques [1968] Director

Green Island (UK) Limited
Incorporated: 17 January 2005
Net Worth Deficit: £123,962 Total Assets: £169,539
Registered Office: Stirling House, 107 Stirling Road, London, N22 5BN
Major Shareholder: Yogendranath Bacha
Officers: Yogendranath Bacha [1976] Director/Chartered Accountant; Hishan Jackaria [1977] Director/Accountant

Green Leaf Liquids Limited
Incorporated: 25 February 2019
Registered Office: 45a Balby Road, Doncaster, S Yorks, DN4 0RD
Shareholders: Kuldip Chopra; Ravinder Paul Pabial
Officers: Kuldip Chopra [1977] Director/Civil Servant; Ravinder Paul Pabial [1978] Director/Accounts Manager

Rachael Green Limited
Incorporated: 28 June 2017
Registered Office: 107 Castle Street, Stockport, Cheshire, SK3 9AR
Major Shareholder: Rachael Green
Officers: Mark Green [1966] Director/Bar Manager; Rachael Green [1972] Director/Manager

Green Room Ales Limited
Incorporated: 16 March 2009
Net Worth Deficit: £14,892
Registered Office: Levalsa House, St Stephens Road, Sticker, St Austell, Cornwall, PL26 7HA
Major Shareholder: Stephen Charles Burton
Officers: Stephen Charles Burton [1983] Director

John Greenacre Limited
Incorporated: 22 October 2010 Employees: 2
Net Worth Deficit: £9,029 Total Assets: £296
Registered Office: Greenacres, Halstead Road, Tilton on the Hill, Leicester, LE7 9LB
Shareholders: Henry Bruce Deane; Joy Gwyneth Deane
Officers: Henry Bruce Deane [1967] Director/IT Consultant; Joy Gwyneth Deane [1966] Director

Greencroft Bottling Company Limited
Incorporated: 18 May 2003 Employees: 230
Net Worth: £12,070,858 Total Assets: £29,484,372
Registered Office: Unit 1 Greencroft Estate, Tower Road, Annfield Plain, Stanley, Co Durham, DH9 7XP
Shareholders: Anthony Austin Cleary; Veronica Anne Cleary
Officers: Alexandra Louise Cleary [1986] Director; Anthony Austin Cleary [1952] Director; Benjamin William Andrew Cleary [1988] Director; Caroline Robyn Cleary [1990] Director; Veronica Anne Cleary [1954] Director; Mark Anthony Satchwell [1964] Managing Director

Greenfield Bacon Limited
Incorporated: 6 April 1976 Employees: 8
Net Worth: £239,738 Total Assets: £565,797
Registered Office: 55a Wakefield Road, Gildersome, Leeds, LS27 7HH
Officers: Joan Brooke, Secretary; Joan Brooke [1942] Director/Housewife

Greenlink Enterprises Limited
Incorporated: 14 May 2012
Net Worth Deficit: £9,925 Total Assets: £1,344
Registered Office: 4a Beacon Road, Great Barr, Birmingham, B43 7BP
Shareholders: Jason Mark Anthony Jones; Sampath Sudesh Sundar
Officers: Jason Mark Anthony Jones, Secretary; Jason Mark Anthony Jones [1975] Director; Sampath Sudesh Sundar [1968] Director/Importer

Greenmount Holdings Limited
Incorporated: 5 May 2015
Net Worth Deficit: £7,728 Total Assets: £3,577
Registered Office: Safestore Ltd, Unit 125, 2 Colville Court, Winwick Quay, Warrington, Cheshire, WA2 8QT
Major Shareholder: Dariusz Trela
Officers: Dariusz Krzysztof Trela [1978] Director [Polish]

Greens Beers Limited
Incorporated: 12 October 2011
Net Worth: £75,753 Total Assets: £240,948
Registered Office: Kenann House, Unit 32 Newby Road Industrial Estate, Newby Road, Hazel Grove, Stockport, Cheshire, SK7 5DA
Major Shareholder: David John Ware
Officers: Adele Anne Ware, Secretary; David John Ware [1957] Director

Greens Wholesale Ltd
Incorporated: 4 October 2017
Registered Office: 7 Glass Street, Markinch, Fife, KY7 6DP
Shareholders: Harris Shahzad Aslam; Raza Rehman
Officers: Harris Shahzad Aslam [1996] Director; Raza Rehman [1990] Director

Greenwood Distillers Limited
Incorporated: 9 March 2018
Registered Office: 49 St James's Street, London, SW1A 1JT
Officers: Barthelemy Timothee Lawrence Edvard Brosseau [1989] Director [French]; Andrew William Rankin [1957] Director; Dan Lawrence Zaum [1965] Director

Greenwood Spirits Limited
Incorporated: 30 September 2015 Employees: 1
Net Worth Deficit: £1,411,896 Total Assets: £7,645,300
Registered Office: 49 St James's Street, London, SW1A 1JT
Officers: Barthelemy Timothee Lawrence Edvard Brosseau [1989] Director [French]; Andrew William Rankin [1957] Director; Dan Lawrence Zaum [1965] Director

Gremi Wine Trading (UK) Limited
Incorporated: 1 February 2018
Registered Office: Office 8, 176 Finchley Road, London, NW3 6BT
Major Shareholder: Iurii Melnychenko
Officers: Iurii Melnychenko [1985] Director [Ukrainian]

Grey Cardinal Limited
Incorporated: 9 July 2012
Previous: 08134813 Limited
Net Worth Deficit: £25,020 Total Assets: £664
Registered Office: Mint Accounting c/o Tax by Design, Park Terrace, Worcester Park, London, KT4 7JZ
Major Shareholder: Latif Mammadaliyev
Officers: Latif Mammadaliyev [1994] Director [Azerbaijani]

Grizzly Endeavours Ltd
Incorporated: 19 July 2018
Registered Office: 135 Norse Road, Glasgow, G14 9EH
Major Shareholder: Ryan Grant
Officers: Ryan Grant [1985] Director/Self Employed

Group93 Ltd
Incorporated: 17 January 2019
Registered Office: 71-75 Shelton Street, London, WC2H 9JQ
Shareholder: Lopa Sudhir Vibhakar
Officers: Lopa Sudhir Vibhakar, Secretary; Dipesh Vibhakar [1991] Director; Sudhir Vibhakar [1959] Director

Groupe Prestige Ltd
Incorporated: 15 August 2011
Net Worth Deficit: £5,000 Total Assets: £30,000
Registered Office: 104 Sternhold Avenue, London, SW2 4PP
Major Shareholder: Aymeric Bruneau
Officers: Aymeric Valere Raymond Bruneau, Secretary; Aymeric Valere Raymond Bruneau [1979] Director/Entrepreneur [French]; Alexandre Claude Lucien Caillol [1978] Sales Director [French]

Grwp Silwriad Cyf
Incorporated: 20 September 2018
Registered Office: 16 East Roedin, Coed Eva, Cwmbran, NP44 7DX
Shareholders: Trefor Puw; Steffan Ap Breian; David Jeffrey Rees
Officers: Steffan Ap Breian [1959] Director/Bee Keeper

GS Wholesalers Ltd
Incorporated: 15 May 2014
Net Worth Deficit: £60,534 Total Assets: £327,235
Registered Office: Unit B, Belvue House, Belvue Road, Northolt, Middlesex, UB5 5QJ
Shareholder: Gulzar Stanickzi
Officers: Gulzar Stanickzi, Secretary; Gulzar Stanickzi [1979] Managing Director

GS Wines Ltd
Incorporated: 8 November 2017
Registered Office: Kemp House, 160 City Road, London, EC1V 2NX

GSWD Catrine Ltd
Incorporated: 4 August 1994
Registered Office: 1 Anthony Road, Largs, N Ayrshire, KA30 8EQ
Parent: LLDY Alexandria Ltd
Officers: Henry John Jagielko, Secretary/Accountant; Alexander Bulloch [1927] Director; Henry John Jagielko [1952] Director/Accountant

GSYB Ltd
Incorporated: 14 January 2019
Registered Office: Unit 1 Roding House, 2 Cambridge Road, Barking, Essex, IG11 8NL
Shareholders: Alicia Prats Perez; Estrella Gabriela Padilla Docampo
Officers: Estrella Gabriela Padilla Docampo [1983] Director [Spanish]; Alicia Prats Perez [1988] Director [Spanish]

Gudfish Limited
Incorporated: 6 June 2015
Net Worth Deficit: £12,373 *Total Assets:* £32,143
Registered Office: 111-115 Hammersmith Grove, London, W6 0NQ
Shareholders: Robert Joseph Fishel; Thor Hallgrimur Ragnarsson Gudmundsson
Officers: Robert Joseph Fishel [1992] Director; Thor Hallgrimur Gudmundsson [1963] Director

Guest Wines & Co. Ltd
Incorporated: 11 January 2019
Registered Office: 1 Windermere Terrace, North Shields, Tyne & Wear, NE29 0PG
Shareholders: Kelvyn Guest; Lian Zang
Officers: Kelvyn Guest [1975] Director; Ruth Guest [1975] Director; Lian Zhang [1988] Director

Guilty Libations Limited
Incorporated: 9 August 2016
Net Worth: £5,944 *Total Assets:* £49,384
Registered Office: 39 Portsmouth Wood Close, Lindfield, Haywards Heath, W Sussex, RH16 2DQ
Major Shareholder: Paul Stanley
Officers: Paul Stanley [1975] Director

Guinexport Trade and Services Limited
Incorporated: 3 November 2014
Net Worth Deficit: £13,789 *Total Assets:* £1,872
Registered Office: 7 Venus Way, Peterborough, Cambs, PE2 8GF
Major Shareholder: Dionisio Bisan-Etame Mayer
Officers: Dionisio Bisan-Etame Mayer [1969] Director/Trader [Spanish]

Samuel Gulliver & Co. Limited
Incorporated: 7 December 2018
Registered Office: 21 Bedford Square, London, WC1B 3HH
Shareholders: Stuart Thomas Gulliver; Justin Paul Horsman
Officers: Stuart Thomas Gulliver [1963] Director; Justin Paul Horsman [1977] Director

Gunners Cocktails Limited
Incorporated: 6 July 2016
Net Worth Deficit: £24,384 *Total Assets:* £31,414
Registered Office: 10 Canberra House, Corbygate Business Park, Corby, Northants, NN17 5JG
Major Shareholder: Giles Michael Gummer Fuchs
Officers: David Charles John Bedford [1964] Director/Chartered Surveyor; Giles Michael Gummer Fuchs [1964] Director

Gunson Fine Wines Limited
Incorporated: 13 December 2000
Net Worth: £15,544 *Total Assets:* £152,238
Registered Office: 66 Milward Crescent, Hastings, E Sussex, TN34 3RU
Shareholder: Dion John Gunson
Officers: Lisa Gunson, Secretary; Dion John Gunson [1966] Director

Gurkha Beer Ltd
Incorporated: 13 January 2015
Previous: Gurkha Beer (UK) Limited
Net Worth Deficit: £27,555 *Total Assets:* £327,881
Registered Office: Room 3, 1st Floor, Conduit Business Centre, 2 The Mews, London, SE18 7AP
Officers: Lov Bikram Gautam [1977] Director; Sachin Shrestha [1980] Director

Gusto Wines Ltd
Incorporated: 20 August 2012 *Employees:* 6
Net Worth: £90,013 *Total Assets:* £239,936
Registered Office: 20 Elbridge Avenue, Bognor Regis, W Sussex, PO21 5AD
Shareholders: Simon Peter Wallace; Clare Emma Wallace
Officers: Clare Emma Wallace [1972] Finance Director; Simon Peter Wallace [1972] Managing Director

Gvino Limited
Incorporated: 21 November 2016
Net Worth: £1,105 *Total Assets:* £7,089
Registered Office: Unit 4 Vista Place, Coy Pond Business Park, Ingworth Road, Poole, Dorset, BH12 1JY
Shareholders: Diana Mercedes Fernandez Tello; Danilo Tysoe Di Salvo
Officers: Danilo Tysoe di Salvo [1986] Director

GW Wines Limited
Incorporated: 13 March 1991 *Employees:* 2
Net Worth: £112,909 *Total Assets:* £287,195
Registered Office: Denzell House, Denzell Gardens, Dunham Road, Altrincham, Cheshire, WA14 4QF
Major Shareholder: Timothy Arthur Littler
Officers: Timothy Arthur Littler, Secretary; Lynne Georgina Littler [1948] Director; Timothy Arthur Littler [1950] Managing Director

GWB Associates Limited
Incorporated: 12 August 1999
Net Worth Deficit: £21,873 *Total Assets:* £10,817
Registered Office: 8 Luffman Road, London, SE12 9SX
Major Shareholder: Graham William Beever
Officers: Patricia Beever, Secretary; Graham William Beever [1952] Director

H & F Export Limited
Incorporated: 8 January 2019
Registered Office: 35 Sherwood Street, Warsop, Mansfield, Notts, NG20 0JR
Officers: Francis Austin O'Neill [1983] Director/Consultant; Xiangyu Wei [1990] Director [Chinese]

H & G Corporation Ltd
Incorporated: 30 August 2011
Net Worth Deficit: £6,660 *Total Assets:* £21,437
Registered Office: 7 St Peters Avenue, Aylesbury, Bucks, HP19 9LY
Major Shareholder: Armando Rodriguez Herrero
Officers: Armando Herrero Rodriguez [1975] Director/Self Employed [Spanish]

H & W Cash & Carry Ltd
Incorporated: 6 April 2018
Registered Office: 178 Richmond Road, Ilford, Essex, IG1 2XL
Officers: Shah Nawaz Khan [1980] Director/Self Employed [Pakistani]

H & W Wines Limited
Incorporated: 4 July 2002
Net Worth Deficit: £3,393 *Total Assets:* £31,998
Registered Office: Manor Farm House, 18 Main Street, Burrough on the Hill, Leics, LE14 2JQ
Major Shareholder: Peter James Howkins
Officers: Peter James Howkins, Secretary; Peter James Howkins [1950] Director

H R Drinks (Wholesale) Ltd
Incorporated: 24 August 2017
Registered Office: Suite 302 EW, Sterling House, Langston Road, Loughton, Essex, IG10 3TS
Officers: Devinder Kaur Dhillon [1981] Director

H2vin Limited
Incorporated: 30 July 2009 *Employees:* 6
Net Worth: £94,786 *Total Assets:* £913,483
Registered Office: 22 Melton Road, Whissendine, Oakham, Rutland, LE15 7EU
Shareholder: Christian Pierre Honorez
Officers: Christian Pierre Honorez [1954] Director/Wine Merchant [French]; Matthew Robert Wilkin [1971] Director/Wine Merchant

Half Cut Wines Limited
Incorporated: 21 December 2015
Net Worth Deficit: £1,347 *Total Assets:* £11,539
Registered Office: Victoria House, Bondgate Within, Alnwick, Northumberland, NE66 1TA
Major Shareholder: Ronald George Watson
Officers: Ronald George Watson [1954] Director

Halifax Wine Company Ltd
Incorporated: 24 April 2015 *Employees:* 2
Net Worth: £12,440 *Total Assets:* £47,194
Registered Office: Equitable House, 55 Pellon Lane, Halifax, W Yorks, HX1 5SP
Shareholders: Andrew Paterson; Karen Paterson
Officers: Andrew Paterson [1959] Director/Wine Merchant; Karen Paterson [1969] Director/Wine Merchant

W. Hall & Son (Holywell) Limited
Incorporated: 27 June 2008
Net Worth: £1,012,630 *Total Assets:* £1,642,509
Registered Office: Castor Street, Liverpool, L6 5AT
Parent: Beerscellars (UK) Limited
Officers: Caroline Doran [1979] Director; John Kenneth Ravenscroft [1955] Director

Hall & Woodhouse Limited
Incorporated: 8 June 1898 *Employees:* 1,419
Net Worth: £118,890,000 *Total Assets:* £206,032,992
Registered Office: The Brewery, Blandford St Mary, Dorset, DT11 9LS
Officers: Marianne Susie Jarvis, Secretary; Timothy Clarke [1957] Director; Lucinda Rachel Gray [1979] Director; David Harry Christopher Hoare [1964] Director; Mark James [1972] Director/Solicitor; Matthew Richard Kearsey [1972] Director; Dean James Livesey [1977] Director; Michael James Owen [1970] Finance Director; James Martin Scott [1959] Director; Michael Anthony Street [1947] Director; Anthony William Woodhouse [1965] Director; Mark John Michael Woodhouse [1955] Director

Hallamshire Wine Shipping Co. Limited
Incorporated: 1 June 1994 *Employees:* 2
Net Worth Deficit: £102,402 *Total Assets:* £59,319
Registered Office: 52 School Green Lane, Sheffield, S10 4GR
Shareholders: Richard Walter Ibbotson; Julie Ibbotson
Officers: Richard Walter Ibbotson, Secretary; Richard Walter Ibbotson [1955] Director/Solicitor; Robert Charles Rusby [1955] Director/Restaurateur/CD

Hallgarten Wines, Limited
Incorporated: 2 April 1947 *Employees:* 102
Net Worth: £7,799,690 *Total Assets:* £17,434,252
Registered Office: Dallow Road, Luton, Beds, LU1 1UR
Officers: Jayne Elizabeth Foster, Secretary; Andrew Nicholas Bewes [1964] Sales Director; Howard Warren Falk [1963] Finance Director

Halton Turner Brewing Company Ltd
Incorporated: 26 March 2018
Registered Office: 11 Whitley Avenue, Amington, Tamworth, Staffs, B77 3QU
Shareholders: Christopher Paul Turner; Giles Halton
Officers: Christopher Paul Turner [1983] Director

Hameed Investments Limited
Incorporated: 24 May 2002
Net Worth: £1,200,993 *Total Assets:* £1,781,003
Registered Office: Exchange Building, 66 Church Street, Hartlepool, Cleveland, TS24 7DN
Major Shareholder: Riaz Mohammad Hameed
Officers: Riaz Mohammad Hameed, Secretary; Riaz Mohammad Hameed [1973] Director [Turkish]

Hamer & Perks Limited
Incorporated: 8 April 1999 *Employees:* 2
Net Worth Deficit: £20,731 *Total Assets:* £57,598
Registered Office: Unit D, Constellation Mill, Higher Ainsworth Road, Radcliffe, Bury, Lancs, M26 4AD
Major Shareholder: Frederick John Thomas Rushton
Officers: Frederick Johnthomas Rushton [1966] Director/Salesman

Hammonds of Knutsford PLC
Incorporated: 28 May 1999 *Employees:* 27
Net Worth: £12,739,735 *Total Assets:* £22,859,692
Registered Office: Warford Grange Farm, Pedley House Lane, Great Warford, Knutsford, Cheshire, WA16 7SP
Major Shareholder: Jonathan Hammond
Officers: Jonathan Hammond, Secretary; Jonathan Hammond [1970] Director/Wholesaler; Sarah Lucy Hancock Hammond [1971] Director

Hamptons Wine Ltd
Incorporated: 10 April 2013 *Employees:* 4
Previous: Wine Mill (Orpington) Ltd
Net Worth: £311,299 *Total Assets:* £454,477
Registered Office: Suite 302 EW, Sterling House, Langston Road, Loughton, Essex, IG10 3TS
Major Shareholder: Devinder Kaur Dhillon
Officers: Devinder Kaur Dhillon [1981] Director

Hanging Ditch Wine Merchants Ltd
Incorporated: 26 October 2007 *Employees:* 5
Net Worth Deficit: £54,412 *Total Assets:* £58,811
Registered Office: Britannic Buildings, 42-44 Victoria Street, Manchester, M3 1ST
Shareholders: Benjamin Edward Francis Stephenson; Jeffrey Ian Bell; Roger Francis Stephenson
Officers: Benjamin Edward Francis Stephenson [1975] Director/Wine Merchant; Roger Stephenson [1946] Director

Hannah Whisky Merchant's Ltd
Incorporated: 3 May 2012
Net Worth: £9,693 *Total Assets:* £200,839
Registered Office: Suite 4, 81-85 Portland Street, Edinburgh, EH6 4AY
Major Shareholder: Gregor Hannah
Officers: Gregor Hannah [1987] Director

Hannibal Brown Wine Services Limited
Incorporated: 7 May 2010
Net Worth Deficit: £70,363 Total Assets: £9,299
Registered Office: Regency House, 61a Walton Street, Walton on the Hill, Tadworth, Surrey, KT20 7RZ
Major Shareholder: Pamela Gregory
Officers: Pamela Gregory [1966] Director; Judith King [1981] Director

Hanwood Limited
Incorporated: 6 February 1986
Registered Office: Trafalgar Mills, Leeds Road, Huddersfield, W Yorks, HD2 1YY
Officers: Peter John Taylor, Secretary; Peter John Taylor [1957] Director/Accountant

Happy Girl Beverage Company Limited
Incorporated: 24 October 2018
Registered Office: 6 Forrest Gardens, London, SW16 4LP
Major Shareholder: Keleigh Ann-Marie Johnson
Officers: Keleigh Ann-Marie Johnson [1983] Director

Hapusa Spirits UK Ltd
Incorporated: 24 July 2018
Registered Office: c/o PBSL, The Courtyard, 14a Sydenham Road, Croydon, Surrey, CR0 2EE
Officers: Hoshang Rohinton Noria [1978] Director/Consultant

Harama Trading Ltd
Incorporated: 26 July 2018
Registered Office: 20-22 Wenlock Road, London, N1 7GU
Major Shareholder: Antonio Jorge Gomes Inacio Pinto
Officers: Antonio Jorge Gomes Inacio Pinto [1960] Director/Salesman [Portuguese]

Hard Back Rum Limited
Incorporated: 7 November 2018
Registered Office: 26 Brimston Close, Hartlepool, Cleveland, TS26 0QA
Major Shareholder: Charlie James Clark
Officers: Charlie James Clark [1990] Director/Construction Estimator

Hard To Find Wines Limited
Incorporated: 28 November 2006
Net Worth Deficit: £575,169 Total Assets: £718,629
Registered Office: The Tasting Room, Unit 7 High Grosvenor, Bridgnorth, Salop, WV15 5PN
Parent: ICC Five Limited
Officers: Emma Thomas, Secretary; Christopher Joseph Davies [1946] Director; Mark Robert Davies [1979] Director

HardyDistillery Ltd
Incorporated: 3 September 2018
Registered Office: 51-53 Church Street, Little Lever, Bolton, Lancs, BL3 1BL
Shareholders: Linda Elizabeth Walker; Danielle Louise Cunniff
Officers: Danielle Louise Cunniff [1995] Director/Bar Staff; Linda Elizabeth Walker [1967] Director/Licensee

Hardywood Park Craft Brewery Ltd.
Incorporated: 4 January 2017 Employees: 2
Net Worth Deficit: £7,982 Total Assets: £63,024
Registered Office: 1st Floor, Copthall House, New Road, Stourbridge, W Midlands, DY8 1PH
Shareholders: Edward Firth; Mark Edward Charles Smith
Officers: Edward Firth [1967] Director; Eric Scott McKay [1980] Director/President [American]; Ricahrd John Miller [1962] Director/Vice President; James Patrick Murtaugh [1979] Director/Co-Founder [American]; Mark Edward Charles Smith [1974] Director

Harlequin (Stockport) Limited
Incorporated: 29 January 1997 Employees: 22
Net Worth: £262,033 Total Assets: £721,713
Registered Office: Units 3-4 Tilson Road, Roundthorn Industrial Estate, Manchester, M23 9GF
Shareholders: Lucy Mansour Dehghan; Abdol Reza Mansour Dehghan
Officers: Hamid Reza Davarbakhsh, Secretary; Abdol Reza Mansour Dehghan [1961] Director

Jerome Harlington Limited
Incorporated: 14 July 2014
Registered Office: The Mill, Pury Hill Business Park, Alderton Road, Paulerspury, Towcester, Northants, NN12 7LS
Major Shareholder: Jerome Alexander Harlington
Officers: Jerome Alexander Harlington [1972] Director

Harlington Wine Limited
Incorporated: 24 August 2005
Net Worth Deficit: £445,080 Total Assets: £50,938
Registered Office: The Mill, Pury Hill Business Park, Alderton Road, Towcester, Northants, NN12 7LS
Shareholders: Beaufort Nominees Ltd; Jerome Alexander Harlington
Officers: Irene Alexander Harlington, Secretary; Jerome Alexander Harlington [1972] Director/Wine Retailer

Harmonicande Vintners Ltd
Incorporated: 25 March 2010
Net Worth Deficit: £23,125 Total Assets: £16,475
Registered Office: 32 Mulberry Way, Armthorpe, Doncaster, S Yorks, DN3 3UE
Major Shareholder: Paola de Martin
Officers: Paola de Martin, Secretary; Paola de Martin [1976] Director [Italian]

Harmony Wines Limited
Incorporated: 20 April 2018
Registered Office: 12 Northfields Prospect, Putney Bridge Road, London, SW18 1PE
Major Shareholder: Lois Dufouleur
Officers: Lois Dufouleur [1988] Director/Wine Producer/Importer [French]

Harp & Crown Cider Company Limited
Incorporated: 5 March 2018
Registered Office: Bridge House, 64-72 Mabgate, Leeds, LS9 7DZ
Major Shareholder: Robert (Elias) Wilson
Officers: Robert Wilson [1941] Director (CEO)

Harp Wines & Spirits Ltd
Incorporated: 2 January 2014 Employees: 2
Net Worth: £5,416 Total Assets: £973,779
Registered Office: 30-34 North Street, Hailsham, E Sussex, BN27 1DW
Major Shareholder: Praful Patel
Officers: Praful Patel [1959] Director

Harris Filters Limited
Incorporated: 17 February 2014
Previous: R & J Harris Ltd
Registered Office: 42 and 43 Zoar Street, Lower Gornal, Dudley, W Midlands, DY3 2PA
Officers: Julie Ann Harris [1968] Director; Robert John Harris [1961] Director

R & J Harris Ltd
Incorporated: 8 March 2018
Registered Office: 42 & 43 Zoar Street, Lower Gornal, Dudley, W Midlands, DY3 2PA
Parent: R & J Harris Ltd
Officers: Julie Ann Harris [1968] Director; Robert John Harris [1961] Director

Harrisons Fine Wines Limited
Incorporated: 2 May 2017 *Employees:* 4
Net Worth Deficit: £1,642 *Total Assets:* £153,451
Registered Office: Harrisons Fine Wines, 1a Galvelmore Street, Crieff, Perthshire, PH7 4DN
Shareholders: Simon Nicholas Harrison; Susan Rose Harrison
Officers: Simon Nicholas Harrison [1962] Director/Wine Merchant; Susan Rose Harrison [1959] Director/Wine Merchant

Harrow & Hope Limited
Incorporated: 1 April 2003 *Employees:* 2
Previous: H. J. H Barrel Wines Limited
Net Worth Deficit: £308,681 *Total Assets:* £1,254,141
Registered Office: Marlow Winery, Pump Lane North, Marlow, Bucks, SL7 3RD
Major Shareholder: Henry John Hugh Laithwaite
Officers: Kaye Louise Laithwaite, Secretary; Henry John Hugh Laithwaite [1980] Director/Wine Merchant; Kaye Louise Laithwaite [1980] Director/General Manager

Harry Bromptons Ltd
Incorporated: 1 August 2013
Registered Office: c/o Tudor Drinks Ltd, Office 5, Wingate Business Exchange, Wingate Square, London, SW4 0AF
Officers: Ian Martin O'Donohue [1980] Director; Martin Odonohue [1946] Director

Harry's Road Fine Wine Limited
Incorporated: 18 January 2006
Net Worth Deficit: £138,247
Registered Office: Pearl Assurance House, 2 Donegall Square East, Belfast, BT1 5HB
Shareholders: Brian Hubert Hamilton Nelson; Julia Maxine Nelson
Officers: Julia Maxine Nelson, Secretary; Grace Emma Mary Morrow [1986] Director; Brian Hubert Hamilton Nelson [1937] Director

Harrydev Limited
Incorporated: 17 January 2006
Net Worth: £35,689 *Total Assets:* £80,523
Registered Office: 83 Colchester Road, London, E10 6HB
Major Shareholder: Shivcharan Singh Sanghera
Officers: Sukhwinder Sanghera, Secretary; Shivcharan Singh Sanghera [1969] Director

Ian Hart Distilling Limited
Incorporated: 4 December 2017
Registered Office: 5 Talbot Road, London, N6 4QS
Parent: Sacred Spirits Holdings Ltd
Officers: Ian Nicholas Hart, Secretary; Ian Nicholas Hart [1965] Director; Hilary Susan Jones [1962] Director

Richard Harvey Wines Limited
Incorporated: 11 March 1997
Net Worth: £8,457 *Total Assets:* £173,369
Registered Office: Bucknowle House, Bucknowle, Wareham, Dorset, BH20 5PQ
Shareholders: Richard Neville Harvey; Sara Lorelei Harvey
Officers: Richard Neville Harvey, Secretary/Wine Merchant; Richard Neville Harvey [1951] Director/Wine Merchant; Sara Lorelei Harvey [1952] Director

Harvey's Wholesale Limited
Incorporated: 14 January 2009 *Employees:* 7
Net Worth Deficit: £102,701 *Total Assets:* £178,200
Registered Office: Unit 4 Ponthir Road, Caerleon, Gwent, NP18 3NY
Major Shareholder: David Reginald Barton
Officers: David Reginald Barton [1963] Director

Harvies of Edinburgh Limited
Incorporated: 23 May 2002
Net Worth Deficit: £32,682 *Total Assets:* £11
Registered Office: Westwaters, Belmont Business Park, Durham, DH1 1TW
Parent: Speyside Distillers Company Limited
Officers: Yu Hung Ho [1964] Director [Taiwanese]; John McDonough [1956] Director/Manager

H Harwood Ltd
Incorporated: 11 July 2018
Registered Office: Kernow, Ventonraze, Illogan, Redruth, Cornwall, TR16 4RY
Major Shareholder: Holly Harwood
Officers: Holly Harwood [1989] Director

Haslemere Wine Merchants Limited
Incorporated: 29 April 2014
Net Worth Deficit: £12,484 *Total Assets:* £65,470
Registered Office: 20 Bradmore Way, Brookmans Park, Hatfield, Herts, AL9 7QX
Shareholders: Avgerinos Yiangou; Deborah Michelle Yiangou
Officers: Avgerinos Yiangou [1960] Director; Deborah Michelle Yiangou [1965] Director

Hatch Mansfield Cellars Limited
Incorporated: 18 February 2010
Registered Office: New Bank House, Brockenhurst Road, Ascot, Berks, SL5 9DJ
Parent: Hatch Mansfield Agencies Ltd
Officers: Paul Andrew Hughes-D'aeth, Secretary; Paul Andrew Hughes-D'aeth [1962] Director; Patrick William McGrath [1960] Director

Hatton & Edwards Fine Wine Merchants Limited
Incorporated: 20 September 2013 *Employees:* 3
Net Worth: £581,475 *Total Assets:* £656,041
Registered Office: 39a Welbeck Street, London, W1G 8DH
Shareholders: Timothy Block; Edward Kennedy
Officers: Timothy Michael Block [1989] Director

Hatton Wholesale Ltd
Incorporated: 9 October 2018
Registered Office: 24 Crossland, Milton Keynes, Bucks, MK14 6AX
Officers: Antony Suthagaran Jeyaseelan [1981] Director

James Hawker and Company Limited
Incorporated: 26 March 1927
Registered Office: Chivas House, 72 Chancellors Road, London, W6 9RS
Parent: Allied Domecq Spirits & Wine Limited
Officers: Stuart MacNab [1964] Director/Accountant; Vincent Turpin [1978] Director/Chief Financial Officer [French]

Hay Hampers Limited
Incorporated: 8 October 1991 Employees: 13
Net Worth: £747,592 Total Assets: £1,104,457
Registered Office: The Taste House, Roman Bank, Bourne, Lincs, PE10 9LQ
Shareholders: Gabriele Da Re; Elisabeth Och
Officers: Gabriele Da Re, Secretary; Gabriele Da Re [1972] Director/Food & Wine Merchant [Italian]; Elisabeth Och [1973] Director/Food & Wine Merchant [Italian]

The Haycock's Drinks Company Ltd
Incorporated: 15 August 2014
Net Worth Deficit: £32,093 Total Assets: £38,660
Registered Office: 1 Kings Avenue, London, N21 3NA
Major Shareholder: Andrew Campana
Officers: Andrew Campana [1976] Director

Haycock's No.9 UK Ltd
Incorporated: 15 August 2014
Net Worth Deficit: £73,489 Total Assets: £44,096
Registered Office: 1 Kings Avenue, London, N21 3NA
Major Shareholder: James Joseph Campana
Officers: James Joseph Campana [1972] Director

Hayk Corporation Ltd
Incorporated: 31 August 2018
Registered Office: 627 Field End Road, Ruislip, Middlesex, HA4 0RF
Major Shareholder: Hiren Vinodchandra Trivedi
Officers: Hiren Vinodchandra Trivedi [1973] Director [Indian]

Hayloft Ventures Ltd
Incorporated: 10 July 2018
Registered Office: The Hayloft, Poughcombe Farmhouse, Ogbourne St Andrew, Marlborough, Wilts, SN8 1SE
Shareholders: David Joel Peek; Paul David Alan Murray
Officers: Paul David Alan Murray [1963] Director; David Joel Peek [1980] Director

Hayward Bros (Wines) Limited
Incorporated: 13 January 1951 Employees: 10
Net Worth: £1,830,345 Total Assets: £2,846,043
Registered Office: Suite 5, Jamaica Wharf, 2 Shad Thames, London, SE1 2YU
Shareholders: Robert Brandon Hayward; Joanna Elizabeth Beeston
Officers: Sarah Jayne Hayward, Secretary; Joanna Elizabeth Beeston [1974] Director/Wine Shipper; Brandon Hayward [1944] Director/Wine Shipper; James Brandon Hayward [1969] Director/Banker; Robert Brandon Hayward [1971] Director/Wine Shipper; Sarah Jayne Hayward [1972] Director/Wine Shipper; Susan Margaret Knight [1948] Non-Executive Director; Anthony Schendel [1964] Director

Hazelbank Limited
Incorporated: 21 September 2016
Net Worth Deficit: £62,884 Total Assets: £12,116
Registered Office: 9 Upper Strand Street, Sandwich, Kent, CT13 9EE
Major Shareholder: Amanda Clare Felton
Officers: Amanda Clare Felton [1967] Director

Hazewater Food Services Ltd
Incorporated: 29 June 2010 Employees: 21
Previous: Hazewater Services Ltd
Net Worth: £909,477 Total Assets: £1,075,189
Registered Office: East Suite, 1st Floor, Waterfront, Salts Mill Road, Shipley, Bradford, BD17 7TD
Officers: Michael Sidney Kwashie [1970] Director

HBN Ltd
Incorporated: 3 April 2018
Registered Office: 33 Moorgate Road, Carrbrook, Stalybridge, Cheshire, SK15 3NF
Officers: Steven Harrison [1965] Director/Wholesale

HD Wine & Spirit Ltd
Incorporated: 13 October 2017
Registered Office: 141C High Road, Loughton, Essex, IG10 4LT
Major Shareholder: Huseyin Demir
Officers: Huseyin Demir [1982] Director [Turkish]; Hasret Ergin [1985] Director [French]

Head Thirst Ltd
Incorporated: 13 April 2018
Registered Office: 19 George Street East, Sunderland, Tyne & Wear, SR3 1HG
Shareholders: Neil Anthony; Aaron Bate
Officers: Neil Anthony [1988] Director/Brewer

Headline Wines Ltd
Incorporated: 16 March 2018
Registered Office: 36 Water Road, Reading, Berks, RG30 2NN
Shareholders: Leslie Owensby; William Beeson
Officers: William Beeson [1985] Director [American]; Leslie Owensby [1977] Director

Healthier Products Limited
Incorporated: 15 August 2017
Registered Office: Holm Oak, Mount Park Avenue, Harrow, Middlesex, HA1 3JN
Major Shareholder: Paul Gareth Catherall
Officers: Paul Gareth Catherall [1962] Director

Healthy Wines Ltd
Incorporated: 29 February 2016
Net Worth Deficit: £8,155 Total Assets: £12,365
Registered Office: 71-75 Shelton Street, Covent Garden, London, WC2H 9JQ
Major Shareholder: Christopher Celegrat
Officers: Christopher Celegrat [1979] Director [Polish]

Heath London Limited
Incorporated: 6 June 2018
Registered Office: Kemp House, 160 City Road, London, EC1V 2NX
Major Shareholder: Richard Heath
Officers: Richard Heath [1988] Director/Owner

Heath Trading Limited
Incorporated: 10 July 2017
Net Worth: £9,775 Total Assets: £960,763
Registered Office: Global House, 1 Ashley Avenue, Epsom, Surrey, KT18 5FL
Major Shareholder: Nicholas Henry Wilson
Officers: Nicholas Henry Wilson [1988] Director/Export Manager

Heavenly Grapes Limited
Incorporated: 11 July 2017
Registered Office: 15 Bluebell Croft, Northfield, Birmingham, B31 1FF
Shareholders: Saravanan Velliangattur Senniappan; Thirunavukkarasu Kulandaisamy
Officers: Thirunavukkarasu Kulandaisamy [1964] Director; Saravanan Velliangattur Senniappan [1971] Director

Hedges & Butler Limited
Incorporated: 9 September 1998
Registered Office: Russell House, Dunnet Way, Broxburn, W Lothian, EH52 5BU
Parent: Ian MacLeod Distillers Ltd
Officers: Michael James Younger, Secretary; Leonard Stuart Russell [1961] Director

Heidi Beers Limited
Incorporated: 6 April 2009 *Employees:* 17
Net Worth: £60,090 *Total Assets:* £4,032,332
Registered Office: Suite 204, Templeton Business Centre, Binnie Place, Glasgow, G40 1AW
Parent: Heidi Beers Holdings Limited
Officers: Petra Margareta Wetzel [1974] Director [German]

Hellenic Agora Limited
Incorporated: 27 June 2018
Registered Office: 178 Seven Sisters Road, London, N7 7PX
Major Shareholder: Panagiotis Soiledis
Officers: Panagiotis Soiledis [1963] Director [Greek]

Helluva... Limited
Incorporated: 4 May 2012
Net Worth: £6,564 *Total Assets:* £9,246
Registered Office: 48 Granville Avenue, Hartlepool, Cleveland, TS26 8NB
Officers: Pamela Connolly, Secretary; Jamie Francis Connolly [1973] Director [New Zealander]

Helver Wines Ltd
Incorporated: 24 December 2018
Registered Office: c/o Richard Matthew Accountancy, The Courtyard, 30 Worthing Road, Horsham, W Sussex, RH12 1SL
Major Shareholder: Oliver Douglas Farquharson
Officers: Helen Sheila Farquharson [1973] Director; Oliver Douglas Farquharson [1973] Director

Henderik & Co Limited
Incorporated: 4 August 2016
Net Worth Deficit: £380 *Total Assets:* £100
Registered Office: 39a Welbeck Street, London, W1G 8DH
Major Shareholder: Brian Bickley
Officers: Brian Bickley [1964] Director

Hennings Wine Merchants Limited
Incorporated: 2 August 1960 *Employees:* 32
Net Worth: £1,310,051 *Total Assets:* £2,359,742
Registered Office: The Wine Cellars, Station Approach, Pulborough, W Sussex, RH20 1AQ
Parent: Hennings Investment Holdings Limited
Officers: Alison Victoria Howard, Secretary; Edward Charles Hennings [1944] Director/Victualler; Matthew Edward Hennings [1970] Sales Director

Heritiers Domec Ltd
Incorporated: 30 October 2017
Net Worth: £100 *Total Assets:* £100
Registered Office: Walkhurst Lodge, Walkhurst Road, Benenden, Cranbrook, Kent, TN17 4DR
Major Shareholder: Baudouin Roger Marie Cuchet
Officers: Baudouin Roger Marie Cuchet [1969] Director

Heroes Drinks Company C.I.C.
Incorporated: 20 August 2012 *Employees:* 6
Previous: Heroes Drinks Company Ltd
Net Worth Deficit: £64,586 *Total Assets:* £160,603
Registered Office: 20-22 Wenlock Road, London, N1 7GU
Major Shareholder: Christopher Thomas Gillan
Officers: Brian Townsend Davidson [1965] Director; Dr Anthony John Douglas [1957] Director/Associate Professor; Christopher Thomas Gillan [1979] Managing Director; Brendan Walsh [1955] Director

Heronsgate 7 Limited
Incorporated: 22 August 2016
Registered Office: 49B Market Square, Witney, Oxon, OX28 6AG
Shareholders: Marco Alessandro Bosisio; Marco Alessandro Bosisio
Officers: Marco Alessandro Bosisio [1975] Director/Export Manager

HG & S Ltd
Incorporated: 3 January 2017
Net Worth Deficit: £9,253 *Total Assets:* £14,161
Registered Office: 86-90 Paul Street, London, EC2A 4NE
Shareholders: David William Fortune; David Smith
Officers: David William Fortune [1962] Director; David Smith [1967] Director

HG Wine Limited
Incorporated: 14 March 2008 *Employees:* 2
Net Worth Deficit: £46,819 *Total Assets:* £639,970
Registered Office: 26 St John Street, London, EC1M 4AY
Shareholders: Trevor Gulliver; Alexander Giles Fergus Henderson
Officers: Christopher James Gosling [1984] Director/Accountant; Trevor Gulliver [1953] Director/Restaurateur; Alexander Giles Fergus Henderson [1963] Director/Restaurateur

Hi - Line Wines Limited
Incorporated: 6 November 2003 *Employees:* 50
Net Worth: £528,808 *Total Assets:* £5,220,125
Registered Office: Unit 2, 40 Purley Way, Croydon, Surrey, CR0 3JP
Major Shareholder: Sharmmila Jeganmogan
Officers: Sharmmila Jeganmogan [1979] Director

Hi-Spirits Ltd
Incorporated: 13 August 2002 *Employees:* 25
Net Worth: £4,355,371 *Total Assets:* £9,584,388
Registered Office: 60 Marina Place, Hampton Wick, Kingston upon Thames, Surrey, KT1 4BH
Major Shareholder: William Alan Goldring
Officers: Christopher Douglas Ritchie [1972] Director [Canadian]; Christopher Robin Skinger [1974] Director [American]; Magdalena Ewa Tadych [1978] Director [Polish]

Hic-Cup Wines Limited
Incorporated: 15 February 2001
Registered Office: Albury Mill, Mill Lane, Chilworth, Guildford, Surrey, GU4 8RU
Major Shareholder: Phillip Dougherty
Officers: Sarah Dougherty, Secretary; Nicholas Allen [1986] Director; Phillip Martin Dougherty [1962] Director/Contract Caterer; Gordon Roy Wigginton [1951] Director

Walter Hicks Limited
Incorporated: 26 November 1993
Registered Office: 63 Trevarthian Road, St Austell, Cornwall, PL25 4BY
Parent: St. Austell Brewery Company Limited
Officers: Colin John Stratton, Secretary/Chartered Accountant; Simon James Staughton [1959] Director

Hidden Caveau Limited
Incorporated: 17 April 2018
Registered Office: 3 Church Path, Woking, Surrey, GU21 6EJ
Shareholder: Joanne de Magneval
Officers: Joanne de Magneval [1981] Director; Thierry de Magneval [1981] Director [French]

Hidden Gem - Urban Artisan Spirit Ltd
Incorporated: 14 March 2017
Registered Office: 103 Chorley Road, Swinton, Manchester, M27 4AA
Major Shareholder: Carmel Heeran
Officers: Carmel Heeran [1972] Director/Alcohol Production and Sales

The Hidgate Ltd
Incorporated: 10 July 2017
Registered Office: Unit 203 Canalot Studios, 222 Kensal Road, London, W10 5BN
Major Shareholder: Andrey Kugaevskikh
Officers: Andrey Kugaevskikh, Secretary; Andrey Kugaevskikh [1976] Director [Russian]

Hierarchy Brewing Company Limited
Incorporated: 25 June 2018
Registered Office: The Manor House, West End, Sedgefield, Stockton on Tees, Cleveland, TS21 2BW
Major Shareholder: Matthew Philip Wilson
Officers: Matthew Philip Wilson [1986] Director/Chemical Engineer

High Jinks Limited
Incorporated: 21 May 2018
Registered Office: The Old Vicarage, Boughton Hill, Dunkirk, Faversham, Kent, ME13 9LE
Officers: Vicky Louise Roberts [1980] Director/General Manager

Highball Brands Limited
Incorporated: 11 February 2016 *Employees:* 2
Net Worth Deficit: £58,067 *Total Assets:* £79,685
Registered Office: First Floor, 60 Tottenham Court Road, London, W1T 2EW
Officers: Fabrice Pierre Michel Limon [1976] Managing Director

Highfern Limited
Incorporated: 20 August 2013 *Employees:* 1
Net Worth Deficit: £53,364 *Total Assets:* £169,909
Registered Office: 109 Douglas Street, Glasgow, G2 4HB
Shareholders: William Robert Ransom; Jean Frances Walker
Officers: William Robert Ransom [1975] Director; James Walker [1946] Director; Jean Frances Walker [1976] Director

Highland Distillers Limited
Incorporated: 19 June 1995 *Employees:* 202
Net Worth: £96,600,000 *Total Assets:* £374,300,000
Registered Office: 100 Queen Street, Glasgow, G1 3DN
Parent: 1887 Company Limited
Officers: Gemma May Robson, Secretary; Aristotelis Baroutsis [1973] Director [Swedish]; Jeremy McDowell Chaplin [1971] Director; Graham Robert Hutcheon [1963] Director; Scott John McCroskie [1967] Director/Chartered Accountant

Highland Drinks Ltd
Incorporated: 1 November 2017
Net Worth: £10 *Total Assets:* £10
Registered Office: The Tower, 103 High Street, Elgin, Moray, IV30 1EB
Major Shareholder: Craig Douglas
Officers: Craig Douglas [1971] Director

Highland Liquor Company Ltd
Incorporated: 19 February 2018
Registered Office: 23 Market Street, Ullapool, Ross-shire, IV26 2XE
Shareholders: Robert James Hicks; Helen Chalmers
Officers: Helen Chalmers [1981] Director; Robert James Hicks [1971] Director

The Highland Malt Whisky Company Limited
Incorporated: 28 May 1998
Registered Office: 308 Albert Drive, Glasgow, G41 5RS
Shareholders: Alfred Lockhart Bryden; Nuala Naughton
Officers: Nuala Naughton, Secretary; Alfred Lockhart Bryden [1925] Director/Commodity Merchant; Nuala Naughton [1960] Director

The Highland Scotch Whisky Company Limited
Incorporated: 30 January 1997
Registered Office: 45 Coylton Crescent, Hamilton, S Lanarks, ML3 9NL
Shareholder: David John Atkings
Officers: John David Atkings, Secretary; John David Atkings [1948] Director; George Todorov Minev [1955] Director/Businessman [Bulgarian]

Highland Vintners Ltd
Incorporated: 17 August 2016
Net Worth Deficit: £779 *Total Assets:* £200
Registered Office: 272 Bath Street, Glasgow, G2 4JR
Officers: Sebastian Robertson [1966] Director

Highlands & Islands Scotch Whisky Company Limited
Incorporated: 30 April 1997
Net Worth Deficit: £217 *Total Assets:* £2,014
Registered Office: 2 Stewart Street, Milngavie, Glasgow, G62 6BW
Shareholders: Harry Brian Crook; Caroline Crawford Crook
Officers: Caroline Crawford Crook, Secretary; Harry Brian Crook [1942] Director

Highlands Whisky Company Ltd
Incorporated: 22 June 2007
Net Worth: £871 *Total Assets:* £15,763
Registered Office: 30 Bonnethill Road, Pitlochry, Perthshire, PH16 5BS
Major Shareholder: Christophe Maurice Gauthier
Officers: Ruth Taggart Gauthier, Secretary; Christophe Maurice Eric Gabriel Gauthier [1967] Director/Business Executive [French]

Highly Spirited Ltd
Incorporated: 24 June 2013
Net Worth Deficit: £27,726 *Total Assets:* £15,682
Registered Office: 2-4 Ash Lane, Rustington, Littlehampton, W Sussex, BN16 3BZ
Shareholders: Mark Avellano; Christopher Edgcumbe Rendle; Alan Michael Shapiro
Officers: Mark Avellano, Secretary; Mark Avellano [1970] Director/Brand Developer; Christopher Edgcumbe Rendle [1958] Director/Brand Developer; Alan Michael Shapiro [1962] Director/Company President [American]

Hiline Wines Peterborough Ltd
Incorporated: 13 February 2018
Registered Office: 20 Royce Road, Peterborough, Cambs, PE1 5YB
Officers: Sharmmila Jeganmogan [1979] Director

Geo Hill (Grocers) Limited
Incorporated: 6 October 1931 *Employees:* 6
Net Worth: £97,331 *Total Assets:* £281,414
Registered Office: The Gables, Bishop Meadow Road, Loughborough, Leics, LE11 5RE
Major Shareholder: Andrew Steven Hill
Officers: Gillian Mary Leeson, Secretary; Andrew Steven Hill [1946] Director/Wine Merchant

Hillbridge Estates Limited
Incorporated: 4 November 1997
Net Worth Deficit: £4,034,896 *Total Assets:* £32,039
Registered Office: First Floor, Roxburghe House, 273-287 Regent Street, London, W1B 2HA
Parent: Quistec Limited
Officers: Serge Despont [1964] Director/Accountant [Swiss]

Hillcrest Wines Limited
Incorporated: 18 September 2015
Net Worth Deficit: £8,002 *Total Assets:* £84,398
Registered Office: 1 Freemans Yard Lane, Cheriton, Alresford, Hants, SO24 0AY
Shareholder: Andrew William Seden
Officers: Jacob Leadley [1980] Director; Rebecca Anne Leadley [1979] Director; Andrew William Seden [1982] Director; Marilyn Elizabeth Seden [1950] Director; William Edward Seden [1950] Director

Hills Prospect Holdings Ltd
Incorporated: 9 November 2015 *Employees:* 144
Net Worth: £3,147,887 *Total Assets:* £9,307,573
Registered Office: Hills Prospect PLC, Consolidated House, Faringdon Avenue, Romford, Essex, RM3 8SP
Shareholders: Trevor Bowers; Nicholas Callaghan
Officers: Trevor Bowers [1958] Director; Nicholas Callaghan [1970] Director

Hills Prospect PLC
Incorporated: 23 July 2001 *Employees:* 144
Net Worth: £3,471,074 *Total Assets:* £9,251,692
Registered Office: Hills Prospect PLC, Consolidated House, Faringdon Avenue, Romford, Essex, RM3 8SP
Officers: Michael Lomotey, Secretary; Trevor Bowers [1958] Director; Nicholas Callaghan [1970] Director; Lisa Richards [1966] Director; Darren Smart [1969] Director; Collette Whittington-Bowers [1967] Director

Hilton & Rowley Ltd
Incorporated: 20 October 2017 *Employees:* 2
Net Worth: £2 *Total Assets:* £2
Registered Office: 5 Clarence Crescent, London, SW4 8LH
Shareholders: Adam James Hilton; Mark Christopher Rowley
Officers: Adam James Hilton [1991] Director/Real Estate; Mark Christopher Rowley [1991] Director/Charity Work

Himalaya Wines Limited
Incorporated: 4 February 2015
Net Worth Deficit: £6,499 *Total Assets:* £12,546
Registered Office: 16 Canterbury Street, Barton Hill, Bristol, BS5 9BF
Officers: Gurnam Singh [1971] Director/Ground Worker/Property Manager

Hindsight Collective Ltd
Incorporated: 20 January 2017
Net Worth Deficit: £788 *Total Assets:* £1,711
Registered Office: 37 Chelsfield Grove, Chorlton, Manchester, M21 7SU
Shareholders: Marcus James Baxendale; Jess James Hutchinson
Officers: Marcus James Baxendale [1990] Director; Jess James Hutchinson [1991] Director

Hingston & Co. Ltd
Incorporated: 11 January 2017
Net Worth Deficit: £16,616 *Total Assets:* £23,046
Registered Office: Unit 106, 15 Pundersons Gardens, London, E2 9QG
Shareholders: Kuleen Piyush Khimasia; Casey Sorenson
Officers: Kuleen Piyush Khimasia [1993] Director; Casey Sorenson [1991] Director/Founder

Hips Drinks Ltd
Incorporated: 3 September 2018
Registered Office: 10 Swarcliffe Road, Leeds, LS14 5LE
Major Shareholder: Martin Thornton
Officers: Kieren Lee Riley-Hicken [1992] Director

Hitchin Brewery Ltd
Incorporated: 6 October 2017
Registered Office: 16 Thatchers End, Hitchin, Herts, SG4 0PD
Shareholder: Carl Robert Paddison
Officers: Carl Robert Paddison [1977] Director/Paramedic

Hitchin Distillery Limited
Incorporated: 14 November 2018
Registered Office: 18 Victoria Road, Hitchin, Herts, SG5 2LS
Major Shareholder: Kerry James Burrows
Officers: Kerry James Burrows [1977] Director/Distiller

The Hitchin Wine Company Limited
Incorporated: 10 February 2012 *Employees:* 3
Net Worth: £27,708 *Total Assets:* £163,327
Registered Office: The Wyevale Centre, Cambridge Road, Hitchin, Herts, SG4 0JT
Major Shareholder: Paul O' Connor
Officers: Paul Oconnor [1953] Director/Wine Merchant

Hix & Buck Ltd
Incorporated: 15 May 2009
Net Worth Deficit: £195,845 *Total Assets:* £113,007
Registered Office: 50 Mount Nod Road, London, SW16 2LL
Major Shareholder: Jaysri Chix Chandaria
Officers: Jaysri Chix Chandaria [1968] Director/Importer

HKK and Sons Ltd
Incorporated: 29 January 2018
Registered Office: 38 Dudley Road, South Harrow, Middlesex, HA2 0PR
Major Shareholder: Hina Kirit Kumar
Officers: Hina Kirit Kumar [1961] Director [Portuguese]

HM47 Investment Projects Ltd
Incorporated: 16 August 2002
Previous: HM47 Investment Ltd
Registered Office: 67 Kings Grove, London, SE15 2NA
Major Shareholder: Robert Campbell Hall
Officers: Robert Campbell Hall, Secretary; Robert Campbell Hall [1952] Director

HNB Trade Ltd
Incorporated: 15 November 2011 Employees: 1
Net Worth: £8,350 Total Assets: £273,735
Registered Office: 5 North End Road, London, NW11 7RJ
Major Shareholder: Virutthasalam Prabhakaran
Officers: Virutthasalam Prabhakaran [1976] Director

Hobnobber Ltd
Incorporated: 22 February 2018
Registered Office: Appledore, 95 Fairview Road, Headley Down, Hants, GU35 8JB
Major Shareholder: Michael Sharp
Officers: Michael Sharp, Secretary; Michael Sharp [1964] Director

Hobo Beer & Co. Ltd.
Incorporated: 10 February 2012
Net Worth: £83,284 Total Assets: £133,004
Registered Office: 1st Floor, 50-51 Berwick Street, London, W1F 8SJ
Officers: Scott Collins [1971] Director; Stuart William Ekins [1968] Director; Richard Stanley Herbert [1973] Director; Ben Aneurin McFarland [1976] Director/Journalist; Thomas Edward Horan Sandham [1977] Director/Journalist; Sharon Denise Young [1966] Director/Accountant

Hobros Limited
Incorporated: 21 September 2018
Registered Office: Level 3, 207 Regent Street, London, W1B 3HH
Shareholders: Timothy Tinloch Ho; Anthony Tinchon Ho
Officers: Anthony Tinchon Ho [1978] Director/Manager; Timothy Tinloch Ho [1969] Director

Hochfeld International Ltd
Incorporated: 19 January 2017 Employees: 1
Net Worth: £671,671 Total Assets: £2,844,874
Registered Office: Orchard Place, Comp Road, Borough Green, Sevenoaks, Kent, TN15 8LW
Parent: Richard Hochfeld Management Ltd
Officers: Edward Charles Hickford, Secretary; Alan Claude Guindi [1961] Director; Martin Patrick O'Sullivan [1980] Director

James Hocking Wine Limited
Incorporated: 5 February 2019
Registered Office: Stag Gates House, 63-64 The Avenue, Southampton, SO17 1XS
Major Shareholder: James Rylett Hocking
Officers: James Rylett Hocking [1971] Director/Wine Merchant; Joscelyn Frances Hocking [1979] Director/Financial Controller

Hofmeister Enterprises Ltd
Incorporated: 22 April 2016 Employees: 6
Net Worth Deficit: £1,024,535 Total Assets: £132,914
Registered Office: Nexus House, 2 Cray Road, Sidcup, Kent, DA14 5DA
Parent: The Hofmeister Brewing Company Limited
Officers: John Byrne [1973] Director; Spencer Chambers [1974] Director; Richard Nicholas Longhurst [1971] Director

Hoghton Brewery Limited
Incorporated: 25 April 2013
Net Worth Deficit: £1,159 Total Assets: £4,000
Registered Office: 39 Long Acre, Covent Garden, London, WC2E 9LG
Shareholders: Duccio Matteo Faraoni; Elena Susanna Isabella Faraoni
Officers: Duccio Matteo Faraoni [1970] Director [Italian]; Elena Susanna Isabella Faraoni [1976] Director/Management Consultant

Holborn Gin Company Limited
Incorporated: 16 August 2018
Registered Office: 46 Kiln Garth, Rothley, Leicester, LE7 7LZ
Major Shareholder: Ross Evans
Officers: Ross Evans [1976] Director

Holcombe Gin Ltd
Incorporated: 26 October 2018
Registered Office: 73 Harwood Road, Tottington, Bury, Lancs, BL8 4AF
Major Shareholder: Paul Andrew Coupe
Officers: Paul Andrew Coupe [1961] Director

Holdsworth Spirits & Company Limited
Incorporated: 20 March 2014 Employees: 3
Net Worth: £299,092 Total Assets: £430,575
Registered Office: Waterworks House, Pluckley Road, Charing, Kent, TN27 0AH
Shareholders: Mark Philip Holdsworth; Claire Denise Holdsworth
Officers: Claire Denise Holdsworth [1973] Director/Consultant; Mark Philip Holdsworth [1973] Director/Consultant

Hollandwest Limited
Incorporated: 31 March 2003 Employees: 6
Net Worth: £1,056,022 Total Assets: £2,453,779
Registered Office: 78 Wharfdale Road, Tyseley, Birmingham, B11 2DE
Shareholder: Budge Dhariwal
Officers: Budge Dhariwal [1961] Director

Holy Grape Ltd
Incorporated: 10 September 2018
Registered Office: 56 Sherfield Gardens, London, SW15 4PP
Major Shareholder: Eleftherios Spiliopoulos
Officers: Eleftherios Spiliopoulos [1990] Director [Greek]

Home Farm Gin Limited
Incorporated: 21 December 2018
Registered Office: Home Farm, Ketteringham Lane, Hethersett, Norwich, NR9 3DF
Shareholders: Paul William Dunnett; Neville Leverett
Officers: Paul William Dunnett [1971] Director; Neville Leverett [1993] Director

Home2.0beer UK Ltd
Incorporated: 29 June 2018
Registered Office: The Sphere, 110-112 Silvertown Way, London, E16 1EA
Major Shareholder: Tomas Lebedevas
Officers: Tomas Lebedevas [1978] Managing Director [Lithuanian]

Honeybee Farm Ltd
Incorporated: 16 August 2018
Registered Office: 97 Chelsfield Grove, Chorlton, Manchester, M21 7BD
Major Shareholder: Tunde Finni
Officers: Tunde Finni [1971] Director; Rachel Naylor [1974] Director

Honkytonk Wine Library Limited
Incorporated: 7 June 2018
Registered Office: 2 North East Quay, Plymouth, PL4 0BN
Shareholders: Fitzroy Joseph Spencer; Zoe Brodie
Officers: Zoe Brodie [1973] Director; Fitzroy Joseph Spencer [1965] Director

Hoops and Champagne Ltd
Incorporated: 15 July 2015
Net Worth Deficit: £1,340 *Total Assets:* £1,094
Registered Office: 19 Woolstaplers Way, London, SE16 3UT
Officers: Andrea Barsottini [1988] Director [Italian]; Abel Sinkovicz [1984] Director [Hungarian]; Ben Frieda Emiel Van de Meutter [1971] Director/Sommelier [Belgian]

Hooton Management Limited
Incorporated: 17 January 2014
Net Worth Deficit: £1,998 *Total Assets:* £20,709
Registered Office: 39 Moorland View, Aston, Sheffield, S26 2FR
Major Shareholder: Daniel Hooton
Officers: Karen Hooton [1976] Director

Hop Drop Limited
Incorporated: 4 July 2018
Registered Office: The Gallery, Outwood Common, Outwood, Redhill, Surrey, RH1 5PW
Major Shareholder: James Joseph Rushforth
Officers: James Joseph Rushforth [1985] Director

Hop Hideout Limited
Incorporated: 17 January 2019
Registered Office: 19 Kirkstone Road, Sheffield, S6 2PN
Major Shareholder: Julia Rosemary Wingate Gray
Officers: Julia Rosemary Wingate Gray [1979] Director/Businesswoman

The Hop Shed Limited
Incorporated: 8 October 2015 *Employees:* 3
Previous: The Unity Brew House Limited
Net Worth Deficit: £81,083 *Total Assets:* £131,130
Registered Office: Elmhurst, Alfrick, Worcs, WR6 5EY
Shareholders: Hani Omar Saleh; Sarah Louise Saleh
Officers: Hani Omar Saleh [1974] Director; Sarah Louise Saleh [1974] Director

Hop To The Vine Limited
Incorporated: 15 January 2019
Registered Office: 52 Western Way, Letchworth Garden City, Herts, SG6 4SJ
Major Shareholder: Jason Newton Garwood Cole
Officers: Jason Newton Garwood Cole [1987] Director/Musician

Hope Sisters Limited
Incorporated: 24 January 2019
Registered Office: Room 203, 54 Washington Street, Glasgow, G3 8AZ
Major Shareholder: Alan Mahon
Officers: Alan Mahon [1990] Director [Irish]

Hopper House Brew Farm Ltd
Incorporated: 7 January 2019
Registered Office: Hopper House, Brew Farm, Racecourse Road, Sedgefield, Co Durham, TS21 2HL
Shareholders: Stephen Brown; Ian Grieve
Officers: Stephen Brown [1969] Director/Farmer; Ian Grieve [1962] Director/Retired

Hoppl Wines Limited
Incorporated: 2 September 2002
Registered Office: 71 Rosebery Road, Langley Vale, Epsom Downs, Surrey, KT18 6AB
Major Shareholder: Alastair Neil Kerr
Officers: Alastair Neil Kerr, Chartered Secretary; Alastair Neil Kerr [1949] Director/Chartered Secretary; Jacqueline Carol Kerr [1958] Director/Solicitor

Hoppy Days Inn Ltd
Incorporated: 24 August 2017
Registered Office: Whiteleys, Sovereign House, 155-157 High Street, Aldershot, Hants, GU11 1TT
Shareholders: Martin Stacey; Tracy Clarke
Officers: Martin Stacey, Secretary; Tracy Clarke [1964] Director/Landlady; Martin Stacey [1957] Director/Landlord

Hops and Barley (Group) Limited
Incorporated: 7 February 2014
Registered Office: Castor Street, Liverpool, L6 5AT
Major Shareholder: John Kenneth Ravenscroft
Officers: John Kenneth Ravenscroft [1955] Director/Licencee

Hops and Barley (UK) Limited
Incorporated: 7 February 2014
Registered Office: Castor Street, Liverpool, L6 5AT
Parent: Hops and Barley (Group) Limited
Officers: John Kenneth Ravenscroft [1955] Director/Licencee

Hops and Barley Limited
Incorporated: 31 July 1991 *Employees:* 83
Previous: Beerscellars (UK) Limited
Net Worth: £1,547,394 *Total Assets:* £3,913,148
Registered Office: Castor Street, Liverpool, L6 5AT
Major Shareholder: John Kenneth Ravenscroft
Officers: Caroline Doran, Secretary/Director; Caroline Doran [1979] Director; John Kenneth Ravenscroft [1955] Director/Licencee

Hops and Dots Brewing Company Ltd
Incorporated: 28 June 2018
Registered Office: 8 Orchard Road, Middlesbrough, Cleveland, TS5 5PW
Shareholders: John Chester; Hugh Grime
Officers: John Chester [1982] Director/Teacher; Hugh Grime [1981] Director/Lawyer

Hoptimism Limited
Incorporated: 19 February 2014 *Employees:* 1
Net Worth: £140 *Total Assets:* £10,915
Registered Office: Albion House, 32 Pinchbeck Road, Spalding, Lincs, PE11 1QD
Major Shareholder: Robert James Stanley Doyle
Officers: Robert James Stanley Doyle [1982] Director

Horizon Soft Drinks Limited
Incorporated: 30 March 1983 *Employees:* 36
Net Worth: £1,293,420 *Total Assets:* £2,201,561
Registered Office: Anchor Brook Business Park, Wharf Approach, Aldridge, W Midlands, WS9 8BX
Major Shareholder: Barry John Stevens
Officers: Andrew Cooper [1979] Finance Director; Barry John Stevens [1946] Director/Soft Drinks Wholesaler; David Barry Stevens [1979] Director/Drinks Wholesaler and Installation of Water Cooler

Horizons Enterprise Ltd
Incorporated: 23 November 2017
Registered Office: Soane Point, 6-8 Market Place, Reading, Berks, RG1 2EG
Major Shareholder: Joanne Bharwani
Officers: Joanne Bharwani [1972] Director

Horsetown Beers Limited
Incorporated: 7 July 2016
Net Worth: £15,022 *Total Assets:* £15,022
Registered Office: 30 Yorkersgate, Malton, N Yorks, YO17 7AW
Major Shareholder: Howard Kinder
Officers: Howard Kinder [1961] Director/Racing Groom

K & S Hosking Ltd
Incorporated: 21 February 2007
Net Worth: £265,123 *Total Assets:* £356,598
Registered Office: The Park House, 75 Parkstone Road, Poole, Dorset, BH15 2NZ
Shareholders: Keith Hosking; Shaughan Hosking
Officers: Keith Hosking, Secretary/Drinks Wholesaler; Keith Hosking [1965] Director/Drinks Wholesaler; Shaughan Hosking [1962] Director/Drinks Wholesaler

Hot Corks Limited
Incorporated: 22 September 2003
Net Worth Deficit: £11,848 *Total Assets:* £23,548
Registered Office: 3 Draysfield, Wormshill, Sittingbourne, Kent, ME9 0TY
Officers: Nicholas Malcolm Gee, Secretary; Denise Pauline Gee [1952] Director/Accounts Manager; Michael Noble Gee [1953] Director; Nicholas Malcolm Gee [1961] Director

Hotham's Spirits Ltd
Incorporated: 28 January 2019
Registered Office: 20-22 Hepworth's Arcade, Kingston upon Hull, HU1 1UJ
Officers: Simon Pownall, Secretary; Emma Kinton [1975] Director; Simon Pownall [1971] Director

Mike Hothersall Wines Limited
Incorporated: 7 September 2016
Net Worth: £21,897 *Total Assets:* £40,068
Registered Office: Quayside House, Highland Terrace, Barrington Street, Tiverton, Devon, EX16 6PT
Major Shareholder: Michael Henry Hothersall
Officers: Michael Henry Hothersall [1956] Director; Valerie Hothersall [1956] Director

House of Hops Limited
Incorporated: 3 April 2018
Registered Office: 16 St Lukes Road, Salford, M6 5DH
Shareholder: Claire Fisher
Officers: Scott Daniels [1985] Director; Claire Fisher [1985] Director

The House of Roo Ltd
Incorporated: 10 October 2017
Registered Office: 15 Bancroft Terrace, Sunderland, Tyne & Wear, SR4 7SS
Shareholders: Bryn Jones; Richard Nelson
Officers: Bryn Jones [1963] Director; Richard Nelson [1987] Director

House of Sparkling Ltd
Incorporated: 2 November 2011
Registered Office: 3 Rosebriars, Esher, Surrey, KT10 9NN
Officers: Preben Jensen Saxlund [1946] Director/Retired [Danish]

House of Townend Limited
Incorporated: 3 May 1962 *Employees:* 76
Net Worth: £1,280,018 *Total Assets:* £6,687,892
Registered Office: House of Townend, Wyke Way, Melton, North Ferriby, E Yorks, HU14 3BQ
Parent: J Townend & Sons (Hull) Ltd
Officers: Angus Joseph Whitehead, Secretary; David George Archibald [1972] Director; Neil Robert Goldie [1963] Director; Derek Hill [1945] Director; Alexandra Louise Townend [1967] Director/Hotel General Manager; Jennifer Ann Townend [1940] Director; John Charles Townend [1965] Director; Alan John Whitehead [1951] Director; Angus Joseph Whitehead [1965] Director/Chartered Accountant

House of Wine Limited
Incorporated: 4 April 2018
Registered Office: 5 Walker Road, Horsforth, Leeds, LS18 4AJ
Shareholder: Michael Charles Hoult
Officers: Stephen Paul Gilroy [1982] Director; Michael Charles Hoult [1981] Director

Hoversy Technologies Ltd
Incorporated: 23 October 2018
Registered Office: 70 Carmen Street, London, E14 6NW
Major Shareholder: Domenico de Ruosi
Officers: Domenico de Ruosi [1988] Director/Entrepreneur [Italian]

HP Enterprises Limited
Incorporated: 19 May 2015 *Employees:* 19
Net Worth Deficit: £187,921 *Total Assets:* £191,095
Registered Office: First Floor, 100 College Road, Harrow, Middlesex, HA1 1BQ
Shareholders: Hanish Kumar Patel; Kunal Kumar Patel
Officers: Hanish Patel [1980] Director/Wholesale of Alcoholic Beverages; Kunal Kumar Patel [1982] Director

HS13 Trading Ltd
Incorporated: 14 December 2018
Registered Office: 9 Brewers Court, Willeys Avenue, Exeter, EX2 8EZ
Major Shareholder: Harry Strong
Officers: Harry Strong [1997] Director

The HSE of Drinks Ltd
Incorporated: 7 August 2018
Registered Office: Unit 212, 26 Cheering Lane, East Village, Stratford, London, E20 1BD
Major Shareholder: Cerise Alexander-Johnson
Officers: Cerise Alexander-Johnson [1982] Director

HT Drinks Ltd
Incorporated: 15 May 1985 *Employees:* 112
Previous: HT & Co (Drinks) Limited
Net Worth: £18,111,000 *Total Assets:* £37,335,000
Registered Office: 31-37 Park Royal Road, Park Royal, London, NW10 7LQ
Parent: HT Drinks Holdings Ltd
Officers: Prakash Thakrar, Secretary; Prakash Thakrar [1949] Director; Sagar Thakrar [1985] Director/Business Executive; Sanjay Thakrar [1979] Director

Huddersfield Cash and Carry Ltd
Incorporated: 20 July 2018
Registered Office: 314 Bradford Road, Huddersfield, W Yorks, HD1 6LQ
Officers: Safdar Ali Choudhry [1977] Director/Manager

Trevor Hughes Wines Limited
Incorporated: 26 June 2013 *Employees:* 2
Net Worth Deficit: £78,439 *Total Assets:* £73,967
Registered Office: 5 Station Way, Brandon, Suffolk, IP27 0BH
Major Shareholder: Trevor Keith Hughes
Officers: Trevor Hughes [1950] Director

Human Brands PLC
Incorporated: 23 November 2017
Registered Office: Hill Dickinson LLP, The Broadgate Tower, 20 Primrose Street, London, EC2A 2EW
Major Shareholder: Ryan Dolder
Officers: Ryan Dolder, Secretary; Janon Ajene Costley [1973] Director [American]; Ryan Dolder [1977] Director [American]

Humble Group Ltd
Incorporated: 17 June 2009 *Employees:* 20
Net Worth: £1,514,562 *Total Assets:* £2,103,920
Registered Office: 2 Battersea Rise, London, SW11 1ED
Major Shareholder: James Fyfe Dawson
Officers: James Fyfe Dawson [1972] Director/Business Manager

Humo International Limited
Incorporated: 12 August 2014
Previous: Expomedconsulting Limited
Net Worth Deficit: £7,159 *Total Assets:* £51,332
Registered Office: The Old Studio, High Street, West Wycombe, Bucks, HP14 3AB
Shareholders: Pavel Nesterenko; Aleksandra Oserzska
Officers: Pavel Nesterenko [1985] Director/Legal Consultant [Russian]; Aleksandra Ozerska [1990] Director [Latvian]

Hungarian Wine Ltd
Incorporated: 16 May 2014
Net Worth Deficit: £26,554 *Total Assets:* £2,044
Registered Office: 50 Salisbury Road, Hounslow, Middlesex, TW4 6JQ
Major Shareholder: Zsigmond Zsebok
Officers: Zsigmond Zsebok [1977] Director [Hungarian]

Hunny Pot Pub Co. Limited
Incorporated: 6 October 1999
Net Worth: £48,807 *Total Assets:* £420,770
Registered Office: 87 De Montfort Way, Cannon Park, Coventry, Warwicks, CV4 7DU
Shareholder: Charanjit Singh Sohal
Officers: Baljit Kaur, Company Secretary; Charanjit Singh Sohal [1958] Director; Jagdeep Singh Sohal [1987] Director

Thorman Hunt & Co Limited
Incorporated: 3 August 1978 *Employees:* 14
Net Worth: £1,565,268 *Total Assets:* £3,703,488
Registered Office: 4 Pratt Walk, Lambeth, London, SE11 6AR
Major Shareholder: Jeremy Hunt
Officers: John Anthony Willan, Secretary; Nigel Wooldridge Brown [1945] Director/Insurance Broker; Timothy Charles French [1974] Director; Charles Hunt [1984] Director/Salesman; Jeremy John Thorman Hunt [1944] Director/Wine Shipper; Richard Edward Lashbrook [1960] Director/Wine Shipper; John Anthony Willan [1943] Director/Chartered Accountant

Hunter Douglas Scotch Whisky Limited
Incorporated: 11 March 2015
Net Worth: £100 *Total Assets:* £100
Registered Office: c/o Cloch Solicitors, 94 Hope Street, Glasgow, G2 6PH
Parent: The Shieling Scotch Whisky Co Ltd
Officers: Andrew Ross Crombie [1964] Director/Stonemason

J. & J. Hunter Limited
Incorporated: 4 September 1924 *Employees:* 4
Net Worth: £72,704 *Total Assets:* £88,109
Registered Office: Whitecliff Inn, 2 Chester Avenue, Whitehead, Co Antrim, BT38 9QQ
Shareholders: John Nugent Donnelly; Whitecliff Holdings Limited
Officers: Christopher Donnelly, Secretary; Eileen Donnelly [1938] Director [Irish]; James Ivan Donnelly [1976] Director [Irish]; James T Donnelly [1931] Director; John Nugent Donnelly [1934] Director [Irish]; Richard Donnelly [1973] Director/Investment Consultant [Irish]

Hurlingham Wine Merchants Limited
Incorporated: 15 September 1998 *Employees:* 2
Net Worth Deficit: £15,883 *Total Assets:* £2,255
Registered Office: Abacus House, 70-72 High Street, Bexley, Kent, DA5 1AJ
Officers: Nicholas Leonard Philip Darton-Bigg [1949] Director/Accountant; Victoria Joan Darton-Bigg [1951] Director/Market Researcher

Hurmiz UK Ltd
Incorporated: 15 July 2016
Net Worth: £305 *Total Assets:* £1,561
Registered Office: Basement, 312 Wilmslow Road, Manchester, M14 6XQ
Major Shareholder: Miran Hurmiz
Officers: Miran Hurmiz [1986] Director

The Hurns Beer Co. Limited
Incorporated: 18 March 1994 *Employees:* 27
Net Worth: £571,806 *Total Assets:* £4,630,683
Registered Office: Hurns House, Kingsway Business Centre, Fforestfach, Swansea, SA5 4DL
Shareholders: Claire Frances Parry; Constance Patricia Parry
Officers: Constance Patricia Parry, Secretary; Claire Frances Parry [1967] Director; Constance Patricia Parry [1957] Director; William Thomas Parry [1959] Director/Solicitor

Hurns Mineral Water Co. Limited
Incorporated: 21 April 1966 *Employees:* 3
Net Worth: £509,028 *Total Assets:* £3,167,253
Registered Office: The Kingsway, Fforestfach Industrial Estate, Fforestfach, Swansea, SA5 4DL
Officers: Claire Frances Parry [1967] Director; Constance Patricia Parry [1957] Director; William Thomas Parry [1959] Director/Solicitor

Hurricane Rum Company Limited
Incorporated: 29 January 2018
Registered Office: 1 Stephen Street, London, W1T 1AL
Major Shareholder: Arlo Brady
Officers: Arlo Brady [1977] Director

Hutton & Mitchell Licensed Traders Limited
Incorporated: 3 April 2007 *Employees:* 14
Net Worth: £1,440,583 *Total Assets:* £1,931,190
Registered Office: 13-17 Paradise Square, Sheffield, S1 2DE
Shareholders: Claire Ann Hutton; Robert Hutton
Officers: Robert Hutton, Secretary; Robert Hutton [1968] Director

Hyde & Sons Limited
Incorporated: 14 December 1955
Net Worth: £43,742 *Total Assets:* £47,157
Registered Office: 40 Dunbar Crescent, Southport, Merseyside, PR8 3AB
Shareholder: Patricia Mary Hyde
Officers: Patricia Mary Hyde, Secretary; Matthew John Hyde [1968] Director/Wine & Book Salesman; Patricia Mary Hyde [1935] Director/Wine Merchant

UK Wholesalers of Beers, Wines and Spirits   dellam

Hydes' Brewery Limited
Incorporated: 27 December 1912 *Employees:* 623
Net Worth: £19,511,056 *Total Assets:* £38,585,184
Registered Office: The Beer Studio, 30 Kansas Avenue, Salford, M50 2GL
Officers: Charles Adam Hyde, Secretary; Brian Bagnall [1961] Director; Christopher Thomas Howard Hopkins [1961] Director/Chief Executive; Charles Adam Hyde [1954] Director/Chartered Accountant; Paul David Jefferies [1965] Director/Brewer; Peter Johnson [1942] Director/Chartered Accountant; Richard Mainon [1973] Director/Financial Adviser; Adam James Mayers [1975] Finance Director

Hydraun Limited
Incorporated: 16 September 2015
Net Worth Deficit: £8,575 *Total Assets:* £14,851
Registered Office: Unit 1a, Little Meadow Bilsham Road, Yapton, Arundel, W Sussex, BN18 0JY
Major Shareholder: Robert Artur Skorupa
Officers: Robert Artur Skorupa [1993] Director [Polish]

I Caesar Limited
Incorporated: 6 March 2018
Registered Office: Union International Drinks Corporation, Bridge House, 64-72 Mabgate, Leeds, LS9 7DZ
Major Shareholder: Robert (Elias) Wilson
Officers: Robert Wilson [1941] Director (CEO)

I I Wine Limited
Incorporated: 9 November 2001
Net Worth Deficit: £2,100,352 *Total Assets:* £452,415
Registered Office: 3rd Floor, Regent House, Bath Avenue, Wolverhampton, W Midlands, WV1 4EG
Major Shareholder: Nicholas Paul Stephens
Officers: Nicholas Stephens [1956] Director; Robert Peter Turton [1952] Director/Chartered Accountant

Tom l'Anson Wines Ltd
Incorporated: 5 April 2012 *Employees:* 1
Net Worth: £16 *Total Assets:* £44,388
Registered Office: McGills, Oakley House, Tetbury Road, Cirencester, Glos, GL7 1US
Major Shareholder: Thomas Peter l'Anson
Officers: Thomas Peter l'anson [1977] Director

I'll Ask The Boys Ltd
Incorporated: 14 November 2018
Registered Office: 20-22 Wenlock Road, London, N1 7GU
Shareholders: Neil Grayshon; Giulio Bernardello; Jacob Hamilton Rosen
Officers: Giulio Bernardello [1992] Director [Italian]; Neil Grayshon [1982] Director/Wine Merchant; Jacob Hamilton Rosen [1987] Director/Chef

I.G.T. Management Ltd
Incorporated: 24 May 2013
Net Worth: £11,447 *Total Assets:* £15,368
Registered Office: 163 Gordon Road, London, EN2 0QA
Shareholder: Dario Langella
Officers: Dario Langella [1976] Director/Operation Manager [Italian]

I8 MGT Limited
Incorporated: 27 February 2017
Registered Office: 32b Gordon Road, London, W5 2AH
Major Shareholder: David de la Torre Canaveras
Officers: David de La Torre Canaveras [1984] Director [Spanish]

Ian MacBarrel & Spirits Ltd
Incorporated: 5 December 2018
Registered Office: 2 Albert Place, Dufftown, Keith, Moray, AB55 4AY
Shareholders: Radoslaw Jarecki; Krzysztof Maruszewski
Officers: Radoslaw Jarecki [1977] Director [Polish]; Krzysztof Maruszewski [1979] Director [Polish]

Iberian Wine Shippers Limited
Incorporated: 20 December 2011
Net Worth Deficit: £649 *Total Assets:* £5,056
Registered Office: Doshi Accountants Ltd, 6th Floor, Amp House, Dingwall Road, Croydon, Surrey, CR0 2LX
Major Shareholder: Suneet Chirag Patel
Officers: Suneet Chirag Patel [1988] Director

Iberiandrinks UK Ltd
Incorporated: 7 November 2012
Net Worth: £10,583 *Total Assets:* £120,745
Registered Office: 188 Mitcham Road, London, SW17 9NJ
Major Shareholder: Diego Munoz Somoza
Officers: Diego Munoz Somoza, Secretary; Diego Munoz Somoza [1975] Director/Sales & Marketing [Spanish]

IBL Wines Ltd
Incorporated: 26 October 2017
Registered Office: 215 Kenton Lane, Harrow, Middlesex, HA3 8RP
Major Shareholder: Sudesh Singh
Officers: Sudesh Singh [1963] Director

Iceaction Limited
Incorporated: 23 March 1995
Net Worth Deficit: £3,648,977 *Total Assets:* £86,496
Registered Office: 215b Kenton Lane, Harrow, Middlesex, HA3 8RP
Officers: Sudesh Singh [1963] Director

Icknield Stores Ltd
Incorporated: 22 November 2012 *Employees:* 5
Net Worth: £4,466 *Total Assets:* £48,967
Registered Office: 164 Bedford Road, Kempston, Bedford, MK42 8BH
Shareholders: Gurmej Singh Dhesi; Gurmukh Singh
Officers: Gurmej Singh Dhesi [1973] Director; Gurmukh Singh [1952] Director

Icomex London Limited
Incorporated: 30 November 2018
Registered Office: 71-75 Shelton Street, London, WC2H 9JQ
Major Shareholder: Pablo Antar
Officers: Pablo Antar, Secretary; Pablo Antar [1979] Director [Argentinian]

Identity Drinks Brands Limited
Incorporated: 12 February 2015 *Employees:* 6
Net Worth: £51,088 *Total Assets:* £720,984
Registered Office: Waterworks House, Pluckley Road, Charing, Kent, TN27 0AH
Parent: Cognac Ferrand
Officers: Alexander Gabriel [1966] Director [French]; Jaye Iwanowski [1978] Director/Marketing Consultant [Australian]; Nicholas Rodgers [1971] Director/Consultant

The Idle Hour Spirit Company Ltd
Incorporated: 8 March 2016
Net Worth Deficit: £5,007 Total Assets: £19,462
Registered Office: Unit 2 Sheen Stables, rear of 119 Sheen Lane, London, SW14 8AE
Shareholders: Peter Gutierrez; Stephen Thorp
Officers: Peter Gutierrez [1962] Director; Stephen Thorp [1965] Director/Drinks Creator

If Eaglesham Ltd
Incorporated: 5 February 1962
Registered Office: 1 Anthony Road, Largs, N Ayrshire, KA30 8EQ
Parent: LLDY Alexandria Limited
Officers: Henry John Jagielko, Secretary/Accountant; Carol Anne Bulloch [1956] Director

IGW Brokers Limited
Incorporated: 13 July 2011
Net Worth Deficit: £7,425 Total Assets: £113,619
Registered Office: 24 Bedford Row, London, WC1R 4TQ
Major Shareholder: Vimal Jawahar Chatwani
Officers: Vimal Chatwani [1981] Director

IKP Trading Limited
Incorporated: 24 September 2013
Net Worth: £71,450 Total Assets: £1,784,731
Registered Office: Bradavon, 45 The Dales, Cottingham, E Yorks, HU16 5JS
Major Shareholder: Ian Kinloch Paver
Officers: Deborah Jane Paver, Secretary; Ian Kinloch Paver [1963] Director

Il Palagio Ltd
Incorporated: 4 February 2014
Net Worth: £27,425 Total Assets: £371,554
Registered Office: Tower Bridge House, St Katherine's Way, London, E1W 1DD
Parent: Steerpike Limited
Officers: Fiona Claire Fowler [1967] Director; Veronica Pradines [1974] Finance Director [Irish]; Anita Marie Sumner [1963] Director

Il Tastevin Ltd
Incorporated: 4 January 2017
Net Worth Deficit: £749 Total Assets: £15,621
Registered Office: 396 Fulham Palace Road, London, SW6 6HU
Major Shareholder: Marcello Muiesan
Officers: Marcello Muiesan [1971] Director/Sommelier [Italian]

Il Tipico Italiano Ltd
Incorporated: 9 February 2018
Registered Office: Kemp House, 160 City Road, London, EC1V 2NX
Officers: George Richard Smith [1990] Director

The Illicit Spirit Co. Limited
Incorporated: 20 April 2017
Registered Office: Titanium 1, King's Inch Road, Glasgow, G51 4BP
Shareholders: Tania Hillman; Aaron Nicholas Hillman
Officers: Aaron Nicholas Hillman [1964] Director; Tania Hillman [1962] Director

Imbibe Ltd
Incorporated: 21 February 2019
Registered Office: 6 Avon Street, Tunbridge Wells, Kent, TN1 2JG
Major Shareholder: Emma Melville
Officers: Emma Melville [1975] Director

Imbibros Ltd
Incorporated: 22 October 2004 Employees: 1
Net Worth Deficit: £33,518 Total Assets: £94,171
Registered Office: 73b Pelham Road, London, SW19 1NX
Major Shareholder: Paul Sinclair Young
Officers: Paul Sinclair Young, Secretary; Paul Sinclair Young [1967] Director/Chartered Accountant

IMC Business Group Limited
Incorporated: 2 April 2015
Net Worth Deficit: £2,393 Total Assets: £432
Registered Office: 199 Kemp House, 152-160 City Road, London, EC1V 2NX
Major Shareholder: Hugo Tolomei
Officers: Hugo Tolomei [1982] Director [Italian]

Impala Transportation Ltd
Incorporated: 22 November 2010 Employees: 1
Net Worth Deficit: £1,391 Total Assets: £25
Registered Office: 48 Nutfield Road, Merstham, Redhill, Surrey, RH1 3EP
Major Shareholder: Nabil Joseph
Officers: Nabil Joseph [1962] Director

Imperial 21 Joya Ltd
Incorporated: 23 May 2018
Registered Office: 67 Ayres Road, Old Trafford, Manchester, M16 9NH
Major Shareholder: Yanzhong Xu
Officers: Dr Yanzhong Xu [1959] Director

Imperial Capital D & G Ltd
Incorporated: 18 June 2018
Registered Office: 18a High Street, Devizes, Wilts, SN10 1AT
Major Shareholder: Dimitar Dimitrov
Officers: Dimitar Dimitrov [1974] Director/Lawyer [American]

Imperial Cash & Carry Limited
Incorporated: 5 June 1987 Employees: 26
Net Worth: £17,360,170 Total Assets: £27,892,548
Registered Office: Imperial House, 18 Eley Road, Eley Industrial Estate, Edmonton, London, N18 3BB
Shareholders: Phatachand Ghanshamdas Mulchandani; Manoher Ghanshamdas Mulchandani
Officers: Manoher Ghanshamdas Mulchandani, Secretary; Manoher Ghanshamdas Mulchandani [1959] Director/Wine Merchant; Phatachand Ghanshamdas Mulchandani [1956] Director (Wine Merchant)

Imperial Distillers Co. Limited
Incorporated: 28 January 1987
Registered Office: 8 Milton Road, East Kilbride, S Lanarks, G74 5BU
Shareholders: Henry C Collison & Sons Limited; Henry C. Collison and Sons Limited
Officers: Karen Spy, Secretary; Werner Nolte [1976] Finance Director [South African]; Fraser John Thornton [1969] Managing Director

The Imperial Wine Company Limited
Incorporated: 30 January 1989
Registered Office: 7 Trinity Street, Bungay, Suffolk, NR35 1EH
Officers: Sandra Jane Flatt, Secretary; Sandra Jane Flatt [1956] Director

Impexpo Ltd
Incorporated: 12 March 2018
Registered Office: 71-75 Shelton Street, London, WC2H 9JQ
Officers: Konstantinos Souliotis [1956] Director/Broker [Greek]

Import Brothers Limited
Incorporated: 29 January 2013
Registered Office: 9 Parkwood Road, London, SW19 7AQ
Shareholders: Daniel Robert Harrison; Robert Andrew Simpson
Officers: Daniel Robert Harrison [1980] Director/Consultant; Robert Andrew Simpson [1979] Director/Consultant

Imported Brands International Limited
Incorporated: 9 March 1992 *Employees:* 1
Net Worth: £128,787 *Total Assets:* £244,730
Registered Office: The Robbins Building, Albert Street, Rugby, Warwicks, CV21 2SD
Major Shareholder: John David Vaughan Seth-Smith
Officers: John David Vaughan Seth Smith [1946] Director/Wine Merchant; William Jonathan Cory Seth-Smith [1985] Director

Impression Beverages Ltd
Incorporated: 8 May 2017
Registered Office: 71-75 Shelton Street, Covent Garden, London, WC2H 9JQ
Major Shareholder: Tamoy Carter
Officers: Tamoy Carter [1982] Director

Imprint Wine Limited
Incorporated: 15 February 2019
Registered Office: The Lodge, Park Road, Shepton Mallet, Somerset, BA4 5BS
Shareholders: Martin John Salter; Camilla Jane Wood
Officers: Nicola Claydon, Secretary; Martin John Salter [1961] Director; Camilla Jane Wood [1972] Director

Impulse Global Ltd
Incorporated: 16 August 2010
Net Worth Deficit: £61,333 *Total Assets:* £47,254
Registered Office: 17 Pickford Close, Bexleyheath, Kent, DA7 4RB
Major Shareholder: Saravpreet Sahni
Officers: Saravpreet Sahni [1977] Director

In Vino Bidco Limited
Incorporated: 7 February 2013
Net Worth: £6,392,794 *Total Assets:* £27,959,740
Registered Office: Boundary House, Cheadle Point, Cheadle, Cheshire, SK8 2GG
Parent: In Vino Limited
Officers: Michael Joseph Moriarty, Secretary; Claudio Manera [1963] Director [Italian]; Michael Joseph Moriarty [1965] Director; Dennis Whiteley [1961] Director

In Vino Limited
Incorporated: 7 February 2013 *Employees:* 147
Net Worth: £14,220,430 *Total Assets:* £74,332,672
Registered Office: Boundary House, Cheadle Point, Cheadle, Cheshire, SK8 2GG
Shareholders: Dennis Whiteley; Donna Whiteley; Araldica Castelvero S.C.A.
Officers: Michael Joseph Moriarty, Secretary; Claudio Manera [1963] Director [Italian]; Michael Joseph Moriarty [1965] Director; Dennis Whiteley [1961] Director

In Vino Veritas Ltd
Incorporated: 16 April 2002
Net Worth: £377,186 *Total Assets:* £1,305,784
Registered Office: The Stables, 27 Main Road, Shuttington Village, Tamworth, Staffs, B79 0DP
Major Shareholder: Nigel Francis O'Mara
Officers: Ian William Sawyer, Secretary/Business Consultant; Nigel Francis O'Mara [1968] Director/Wine Dealer

In Wine & Spirit Solutions, Ltd
Incorporated: 27 November 2018
Registered Office: 71-75 Shelton Street, London, WC2H 9JQ
Major Shareholder: Manuel Ribeiro
Officers: Manuel Ribeiro, Secretary; Manuel Ribeiro [1979] Director/Wine & Spirits Expert [Portuguese]

Incapico Inc Limited
Incorporated: 12 November 2018
Registered Office: 11 Penrhyd Road, Wirral, Merseyside, CH61 2XJ
Major Shareholder: Max Leon Furlong
Officers: Max Leon Furlong [1996] Managing Director

Inception Drinks Limited
Incorporated: 6 February 2019
Registered Office: 1a Rook Hill Road, Christchurch, Dorset, BH23 4DZ
Major Shareholder: Kristian Michael Thomas Gaffney-Dodds
Officers: Kristian Michael Thomas Gaffney-Dodds [1989] Sales Director

Inconcept Ltd
Incorporated: 15 March 2016
Net Worth: £100 *Total Assets:* £221
Registered Office: 22 Fisher Street, London, E16 4DH
Major Shareholder: Aleksandr Anikejenko
Officers: Aleksandr Anikejenko [1970] Director [Lithuanian]

Independent Drinks Supplies Limited
Incorporated: 16 December 2005 *Employees:* 2
Net Worth: £17,874 *Total Assets:* £154,958
Registered Office: Rylands, Church Road, Hargrave, Wellingborough, Northants, NN9 6BQ
Shareholders: David Tayler; Shelley Tayler
Officers: Shelley Elizabeth Taylor, Secretary; David Edward Taylor [1974] Director/Drinks Wholesaler

The Independent Vintner Ltd
Incorporated: 13 September 2012 *Employees:* 1
Net Worth: £35,876 *Total Assets:* £45,635
Registered Office: Suite 7, Claremont House, 22-24 Claremont Road, Surbiton, Surrey, KT6 4QU
Major Shareholder: Giles Iain Smith Walker
Officers: Giles Iain Smith Walker [1975] Director/Wine Consultant

India Gold Limited
Incorporated: 22 May 2013
Registered Office: 60 Beckett Street, Lees, Oldham, Lancs, OL4 3JY
Shareholders: Christopher Paul Callaghan; Naunit Mistry; Daniel John Hutchings
Officers: Christopher Paul Callaghan [1964] Director/Retailer; Daniel John Hutchings [1977] Director/Accountant; Naunit Mistry [1962] Director

The Indian Ice Gola Co Ltd
Incorporated: 9 February 2017
Registered Office: 22 Pettsgrove Avenue, Wembley, Middlesex, HA0 3AF
Shareholders: Mitesh Sevani; Chetan Shivji Varsani
Officers: Mitesh Sevani, Secretary; Chetan Varsani, Secretary; Mitesh Sevani [1981] Director/Project Manager; Chetan Shivji Varsani [1981] Director/Electrician

The Indian Runner Drinks Company Limited
Incorporated: 15 April 2013
Net Worth Deficit: £124,174 *Total Assets:* £45,524
Registered Office: 3 Rotherbrook Court, Bedford Road, Petersfield, Hants, GU32 3QG
Shareholder: William Huw Harris
Officers: Andrew Burdon [1967] Director

Indie Brands Ltd.
Incorporated: 24 August 2011 *Employees:* 7
Net Worth: £328,960 *Total Assets:* £3,829,331
Registered Office: The White House, Clifton Marine Parade, Gravesend, Kent, DA11 0DY
Major Shareholder: Douglas Brougham Cunningham
Officers: Andrew Douglas Bratten [1963] Director; Douglas Brougham Cunningham [1968] Director; Grant Cunningham [1972] Director/Consultant

Indie Spirits Limited
Incorporated: 29 November 2016
Net Worth: £1 *Total Assets:* £1
Registered Office: The White House, Clifton Marine Parade, Gravesend, Kent, DA11 0DY
Parent: Tribe of Indie (Holdings) Limited
Officers: Andrew Douglas Bratten [1963] Director; Douglas Brougham Cunningham [1968] Director; Grant Cunningham [1972] Director

Indie Wines Limited
Incorporated: 20 December 2016
Net Worth: £1 *Total Assets:* £1
Registered Office: The White House, Clifton Marine Parade, Gravesend, Kent, DA11 0DY
Parent: Tribe of Indie (Holdings) Limited
Officers: Douglas Brougham Cunningham [1968] Director

Indigo Drinks Limited
Incorporated: 20 March 2003 *Employees:* 4
Net Worth: £129,198 *Total Assets:* £288,428
Registered Office: Charnwood House, Harcourt Way, Meridian Business Park, Leicester, LE19 1WP
Shareholders: Victoria Cox; Jason Dobbs
Officers: Victoria Cox, Secretary/Director; Victoria Cox [1975] Director; Jason Dobbs [1967] Director

Indigo Wine Limited
Incorporated: 10 April 2003 *Employees:* 7
Net Worth: £265,361 *Total Assets:* £1,118,623
Registered Office: Bon Marche Centre, 241 Ferndale Road, London, SW9 8BJ
Major Shareholder: Ben Jon Michael Henshaw
Officers: Ben Jon Michael Henshaw, Secretary/Director Wine Importer; Ben Jon Michael Henshaw [1971] Director Wine Importer; Stacey Caroline Henshaw [1970] Director/Interior Design

Indra Beverages Limited
Incorporated: 18 April 2018
Registered Office: 249 Cranbrook Road, Ilford, Essex, IG1 4TG
Major Shareholder: Hardeep Singh Bhandal
Officers: Hardeep Singh Bhandal [1984] Director

Ineffable LDN Limited
Incorporated: 23 July 2018
Registered Office: 32 Missenden, Roland Way, London, SE17 2HS
Shareholders: Paul Kevin Yiminyi; Daniel Royes
Officers: Daniel Royes [1988] Director; Paul Kevin Yiminyi [1991] Director

Infinite Session Ltd
Incorporated: 1 November 2017
Registered Office: 32 Chroma Mansions, 14 Penny Brookes Street, London, E20 1BP
Shareholders: Christopher John Hannaway; Thomas Eamon Hannaway
Officers: Christopher John Hannaway [1989] Director; Thomas Eamon Hannaway [1987] Director

Infinity Wines Limited
Incorporated: 23 May 2015 *Employees:* 1
Net Worth: £2,467 *Total Assets:* £26,993
Registered Office: Suite A, 10th Floor, Maple House, High Street, Potters Bar, Herts, EN6 5BS
Major Shareholder: Sarah Pollock
Officers: Sarah Pollock [1964] Director

Infinitygroup1 Limited
Incorporated: 28 February 2019
Registered Office: 35 Stanley Street, Derby, DE22 3GU
Major Shareholder: Adedolapo Adepoju
Officers: Adedolapo Adepoju [1991] Director/Musician [Nigerian]

Infotonomy Ltd
Incorporated: 6 June 2016
Net Worth Deficit: £3,323 *Total Assets:* £7,675
Registered Office: Hollinwood Business Centre, Albert Street, Oldham, Lancs, OL8 3QL
Shareholder: Evridiki Batistatou
Officers: Evridiki Batistatou [1977] Director; Anastasios Savvopoulos [1977] Director

Inkd Limited
Incorporated: 14 August 2018
Registered Office: 7 Durweston Street, London, W1H 1EN
Major Shareholder: Hooman Jamshidi
Officers: Hooman Jamshidi [1980] Director

Inn Control Management Services Ltd
Incorporated: 24 July 2003
Net Worth: £29,442 *Total Assets:* £72,990
Registered Office: Head Office, The Bakewell Bakery, Unit 14 Riverside Business Park, Bakewell, Derbys, DE45 1GS
Major Shareholder: Nicholas James Beagrie
Officers: Jemma Lynne Beagrie, Secretary; Nicholas James Beagrie [1966] Director

Innovative Cocktails Ltd
Incorporated: 27 March 2018
Registered Office: Royal Institution, 24 Colquitt Street, Liverpool, L1 4DE
Shareholders: Ryan Francis McMahon; Daniel Murphy; Thomas Hardwick
Officers: Thomas Hardwick [1987] Director/Solicitor; Ryan Francis McMahon [1982] Director; Daniel Murphy [1983] Director

Innspired Taverns Limited
Incorporated: 25 May 1999
Registered Office: Jubilee House, Second Avenue, Burton on Trent, Staffs, DE14 2WF
Parent: Innspired Group Limited
Officers: Francesca Appleby, Secretary; Edward Michael Bashforth [1973] Director; Stephen Peter Dando [1972] Director/Chartered Accountant

Innvino Ltd
Incorporated: 17 April 2014 Employees: 2
Previous: Wine and Tradition Ltd
Net Worth: £37,022 Total Assets: £126,454
Registered Office: 376 Chiswick High Road, Chiswick, London, W4 5TF
Shareholders: Sebastien Faelens; David Mrjias
Officers: Sebastien Faelens [1983] Director [French]

Inro Drinks (Abtec) Limited
Incorporated: 3 July 2003 Employees: 10
Net Worth: £68,005 Total Assets: £157,215
Registered Office: Thomas Westcott, 7 Castle Street, Bridgwater, Somerset, TA6 3DT
Shareholders: Trevor Paul Odierno; Susan Mary Odierno
Officers: Susan Mary Odierno, Secretary/Drinks Wholesaler; Susan Mary Odierno [1949] Director/Drinks Wholesaler; Trevor Paul Odierno [1946] Director/Drinks Wholesaler

Inside Trax Limited
Incorporated: 18 May 2012
Net Worth: £6,008 Total Assets: £60,072
Registered Office: Moorgate House, 7b Station Road West, Oxted, Surrey, RH8 9EE
Shareholders: Christine Ann Wilson; David John Wilson
Officers: Christine Ann Wilson [1956] Director; David John Wilson [1955] Director

Insignia Spirits Limited
Incorporated: 20 February 2018
Registered Office: 71-75 Shelton Street, Covent Garden, London, WC2H 9JQ
Major Shareholder: John O'Donovan
Officers: Robert O'Donovan, Secretary; John O'Donovan [1983] Director [Irish]; Robert O'Donovan [1987] Director [Irish]

Instabooze Limited
Incorporated: 26 February 2018
Registered Office: 6 Westfield, Sherborne, Dorset, DT9 6AY
Officers: Nathan James Park [1982] Director

Intelligent Trade Limited
Incorporated: 21 December 2012
Registered Office: Kemp House, 152 City Road, London, EC1V 2NX
Major Shareholder: Amardeep Singh
Officers: Amardeep Singh [1990] Director/Buying and Selling

Inter Trading Leicester Limited
Incorporated: 16 January 1996 Employees: 9
Net Worth: £3,134,287 Total Assets: £4,810,791
Registered Office: 44 Cobden Street, Leicester, LE1 2LB
Shareholder: Dilip Bharania
Officers: Bharat Mohanlal Bharania, Secretary; Bharat Mohanlal Bharania [1960] Director/Manager; Dilip Bharania [1951] Director/Manager

Interactive Stage Ltd
Incorporated: 7 November 2018
Registered Office: 3A Dee Road, Vision House, Richmond, Surrey, TW9 2JN
Major Shareholder: Monika Kray
Officers: Monika Kray [1976] Director [Polish]

Intercellar Distribution Limited
Incorporated: 11 December 2012
Net Worth: £122,395 Total Assets: £239,592
Registered Office: Bezant House, Bradgate Park View, Chellaston, Derby, DE73 5UH
Major Shareholder: Leigh Simon Wilkinson
Officers: Leigh Simon Wilkinson [1974] Director

Intercontinental Trade Solutions Limited
Incorporated: 18 December 2018
Registered Office: 76 Padstow Road, Churchward, Swindon, Wilts, SN2 2EG
Officers: Samwel Maina [1989] Director

Interlink UK Exports Limited
Incorporated: 25 April 1997
Registered Office: 72 Cedar Lawn Avenue, Barnet, Herts, EN5 2LN
Shareholder: Aleksandra Stanley
Officers: Mark Stanley, Secretary; Aleksandra Stanley [1967] Director

International Business Solutions Ltd
Incorporated: 28 September 2016
Net Worth: £6,664 Total Assets: £102,784
Registered Office: 85 Great Portland Street, London, W1W 7LT
Officers: Barbara Greco [1983] Director [Italian]

International Diplomatic Supplies Limited
Incorporated: 14 April 2005 Employees: 12
Net Worth: £210,325 Total Assets: £2,040,367
Registered Office: Ground Floor, 1-7 Station Road, Crawley, W Sussex, RH10 1HT
Shareholders: John Maitland Coe; Patrick Henry Doyle
Officers: Noeleen Patricia Alexopoulou, Secretary; John Maitland Coe [1955] Director; Patrick Henry Doyle [1964] Director [Irish]

International Procurement and Logistics Limited
Incorporated: 16 April 2004 Employees: 2,137
Net Worth: £105,085,000 Total Assets: £260,690,000
Registered Office: Asda House, South Bank, Great Wilson Street, Leeds, LS11 5AD
Parent: Asda Stores Limited
Officers: Varinder Rehal, Secretary; John Fallon [1970] Director; James Edward Fasey [1973] Finance Director; Varinder Rehal [1975] Director and Company Secretary; Max Sandiford Smith Hilliard [1958] Director; Michael John Bland Snell [1964] Director

The International Spirit Vault Ltd
Incorporated: 8 September 2018
Registered Office: 20-22 Wenlock Road, London, N1 7GU
Shareholders: Leslie Brian McCall; Julie McCall; Zoe Graham; Richard McCall
Officers: Zoe Graham [1985] Director; Julie McCall [1962] Director; Leslie Brian McCall [1959] Director; Richard McCall [1988] Director

International Wine Emporium Ltd.
Incorporated: 20 February 2017
Registered Office: Lodge Farm Office, Chantry Lane, Hazlewood, Tadcaster, N Yorks, LS24 9NH
Officers: Henry Oliver Smith [1991] Director/Sales

International Wine Forwarding Limited
Incorporated: 4 October 1983
Registered Office: The International Wine Centre, Dallow Road, Luton, Beds, LU1 1UR
Officers: Jayne Elizabeth Foster, Secretary; Howard Warren Falk [1963] Finance Director

Interseel Ltd
Incorporated: 26 September 2017
Registered Office: 20-22 Wenlock Road, London, N1 7GU
Major Shareholder: Laszlo Szilagyi
Officers: Laszlo Szilagyi [1974] Director [Hungarian]

Intertrade Wholesale Limited
Incorporated: 3 October 2002 *Employees:* 4
Net Worth: £1,621,036 *Total Assets:* £1,972,373
Registered Office: 1 Spinners Court, 55 West End, Witney, Oxon, OX25 1NH
Major Shareholder: Vasant Lakhani
Officers: John Radley [1955] Sales Director

Intriguing Brands Limited
Incorporated: 28 May 2012
Net Worth Deficit: £132,790 *Total Assets:* £8,820
Registered Office: 26 St Marys Road, Burnham on Sea, Somerset, TA8 2AZ
Major Shareholder: Paul Francis Mills
Officers: Paul Francis Mills, Secretary; Paul Francis Mills [1960] Sales and Operations Director

Inverarity Vaults Limited
Incorporated: 22 February 1991
Net Worth: £53,660 *Total Assets:* £53,660
Registered Office: 7 Evanton Drive, Thornliebank Industrial Estate, Thornliebank, Glasgow, G46 8HL
Parent: William Morton Ltd
Officers: Brian Douglas Robertson, Secretary; Brian Douglas Robertson [1962] Director/Financial Controller; Stephen Gerard Russell [1953] Director; Gail Irene Allan Smith [1957] Director

Inverglen Scotch Whisky Co. Limited
Incorporated: 21 May 1970
Net Worth: £100 *Total Assets:* £100
Registered Office: 25 Northfield Park, Largs, N Ayrshire, KA30 8NZ
Officers: Anthony Miles Clarkson, Secretary; Anthony Miles Clarkson [1954] Director/Accountant; Kenneth John McLachlan [1947] Director/Chartered Accountant

Inverheath Limited
Incorporated: 12 February 1997
Registered Office: Edradour Distillery, Pitlochry, Perthshire, PH16 5JP
Major Shareholder: Andrew William Symington
Officers: Graham Keith Cox, Secretary; Andrew William Symington [1963] Director

Inverroche Ireland Ltd
Incorporated: 29 July 2016 *Employees:* 2
Net Worth Deficit: £8,441 *Total Assets:* £16,761
Registered Office: 15 Church Street, Belfast, BT1 1PG
Parent: Oberon Estates Limited
Officers: Jonathan Millar [1963] Director/Business Consultancy

Invest Inns Limited
Incorporated: 2 April 2013
Registered Office: 52 Queen Street, Cubbington, Leamington Spa, Warwicks, CV32 7NA
Shareholders: Jeremy William Lewitt; Graham Barry Soden
Officers: Jeremy William Lewitt [1949] Director; Graham Barry Soden [1943] Director

Investmentwine Ltd
Incorporated: 27 April 2011 *Employees:* 1
Net Worth: £183 *Total Assets:* £5,811
Registered Office: 7 Fivewood Barns, Yew Tree Farm, Money Lane, Bromsgrove, Worcs, B61 0QY
Officers: Peter James Higgins [1949] Director/Wine Merchant

Invino Vitalis Ltd
Incorporated: 12 January 2017
Net Worth Deficit: £2,943 *Total Assets:* £17,424
Registered Office: 39 Highcombe Close, London, SE9 4QH
Officers: Petko Yordanov Petkov [1963] Director

Ionica Wine Cellars Ltd
Incorporated: 3 June 2014
Net Worth: £12,423 *Total Assets:* £75,942
Registered Office: 53 High Street, Cheveley, Newmarket, Suffolk, CB8 9DQ
Shareholder: Dritan Doda
Officers: Dritan Doda [1979] Director/Sales

Ireland Craft Beers Ltd
Incorporated: 30 December 2014
Net Worth: £84,030 *Total Assets:* £207,406
Registered Office: Suite 125, 21 Botanic Avenue, Belfast, BT7 1JJ
Officers: Liam Brogan [1985] Director [Irish]; Shane McCarthy [1986] Director [Irish]

Iridium Supplies Limited
Incorporated: 10 July 2018
Registered Office: 48 Warwick Road, Carlisle, Cumbria, CA1 1DN
Major Shareholder: Benjamin Howard Turnbull
Officers: Benjamin Howard Turnbull [1984] Director

The Irish Gin Company Ltd
Incorporated: 19 April 2018
Registered Office: 35 Legilly Road, Dungannon, Co Tyrone, BT70 1QG
Major Shareholder: Cathal Peter McVeigh
Officers: Cathal Peter McVeigh [1989] Director

Iron & Rose Ltd
Incorporated: 8 February 2016 *Employees:* 1
Net Worth: £764 *Total Assets:* £22,893
Registered Office: 10 Cavell Drive, Shrewsbury, Salop, SY3 8GD
Shareholders: Robin Owen Nugent; Marguerite Katherine Nugent
Officers: Marguerite Katherine Nugent [1971] Director/Curator; Robin Owen Nugent [1969] Director/Wine Merchant

Iron Pier Brewery Limited
Incorporated: 17 March 2017
Net Worth Deficit: £67,347 *Total Assets:* £60,568
Registered Office: Units 6 & 7 May Avenue Industrial Estate, Northfleet, Gravesend, Kent, DA11 8RU
Shareholders: James Hayward; Charles Malcolm Venner
Officers: James Hayward [1982] Director; Caroline Jane Stroud [1973] Director; Charles Malcolm Venner [1976] Director; John Anthony Leslie Warden [1969] Director

The Ironbridge Gorge Gin Company Ltd
Incorporated: 17 January 2019
Registered Office: 25 Croppings Park, Lightmoor, Telford, Salop, TF4 3GB
Major Shareholder: Derek Clive Bowen
Officers: Derek Clive Bowen [1963] Director/Salesman

Isake International Limited
Incorporated: 29 October 2001
Net Worth: £44,610 *Total Assets:* £102,146
Registered Office: Flat 54, Newlands Terrace, 157 Queenstown Road, London, SW8 3RN
Major Shareholder: Xavier Chapelou
Officers: Xavier Rene Chapelou, Secretary [French]; Xavier Rene Chapelou [1965] Director/Sommelier [French]; Kumiko Ohta [1967] Director [Japanese]

DBS Isherwood Limited
Incorporated: 13 November 1997 *Employees:* 4
Net Worth: £1,965,292 *Total Assets:* £2,116,006
Registered Office: 133b High Street, Holywood, Co Down, BT18 9LG
Major Shareholder: Derek Barney Sealy Isherwood
Officers: Fiona Catherine Isherwood, Secretary; Derek Barney Sealy Isherwood [1944] Director/Merchant; Fiona Catherine Isherwood [1958] Director/Administrator; Allen Charles Michael Kearney [1985] Director

Ishka Wines and Spirits UK Limited
Incorporated: 14 December 2016
Net Worth: £28,722 *Total Assets:* £28,722
Registered Office: Flat 10, 17-19 Shacklewell Lane, London, E8 2BY
Major Shareholder: Patrick Ryan
Officers: Dr Eugene Ryan [1959] Director/Doctor [Irish]; Patrick Ryan [1988] Director/Entrepreneur [Irish]

Ishke Brands Ltd
Incorporated: 1 February 2019
Registered Office: Stafford Business Village, Dyson Way, Stafford, ST18 0TW
Shareholders: Patrick Gerald McGuckian; Stephen Anthony O'Neill
Officers: Patrick Generald McGuckian [1965] Director; Stephen Anthony O'Neill [1965] Director

Island Ales Limited
Incorporated: 24 March 1993 *Employees:* 20
Net Worth: £212,077 *Total Assets:* £546,994
Registered Office: 9 St Johns Place, Newport, Isle of Wight, PO30 1LH
Shareholders: Stephen Thomas Minshull; Thomas Minshull
Officers: Stephen Thomas Minshull [1958] Director; Thomas Minshull [1937] Director; Christopher Barnet Mousley [1956] Sales Director

Island Drinks Limited
Incorporated: 28 March 2018
Registered Office: 32 Gemini Court, 852 Brighton Road, Purley, Surrey, CR8 2FD
Shareholders: Jeremy John Martyn May; Lucy Katherine Wright
Officers: Jeremy John Martyn May [1985] Director; Lucy Katherine Wright [1989] Director

Isle of Bute Gin Company Limited
Incorporated: 26 January 2018
Registered Office: Pavilion 1, Finnieston Business Park, Minerva Way, Glasgow, G3 8AU
Shareholders: Simon Tardivel; Merchant City Brewing Company Limited
Officers: Allan Douglas Rimmer [1982] Director; Simon Tardivel [1986] Director/Distiller; Douglas Gordon George Wheatley [1959] Director

Isle of Wight Brewery Limited
Incorporated: 24 September 2009 *Employees:* 4
Net Worth: £80,222 *Total Assets:* £139,346
Registered Office: 9 St Johns Place, Newport, Isle of Wight, PO30 1LH
Shareholders: Stephen Thomas Minshull; Thomas Minshull
Officers: Stephen Thomas Minshull [1958] Director; Thomas Minshull [1937] Director; Christopher Mousley [1956] Sales Director

It's A Gin Thing Ltd
Incorporated: 6 December 2018
Registered Office: 32 Mount Pleasant Walk, Radcliffe, Manchester, M26 4FJ
Major Shareholder: Ryan Lee Walters
Officers: Ryan Lee Walters [1980] Director

Ital Sardo Limited
Incorporated: 19 October 2015
Registered Office: Office Afloat, Barton Marina, Burton on Trent, Staffs, DE13 8DZ
Shareholder: Michael Peter Ballance
Officers: Michael Peter Ballance [1961] Director; Guy Laurant Conzinu [1985] Director [Dutch]; Jill Hartley [1961] Director

Italia Wine and Food Ltd
Incorporated: 6 June 2018
Registered Office: 19 Park Road, Lytham St Annes, Lancs, FY8 1PW
Major Shareholder: Noemio Bruno Carpenito
Officers: Noemio Bruno Carpenito [1970] Director

Italian Appellations Limited
Incorporated: 19 January 2010 *Employees:* 1
Net Worth Deficit: £39,685 *Total Assets:* £67,433
Registered Office: 16 Comely Park, Dunfermline, Fife, KY12 7HU
Shareholders: Steven Francis Turbull; John Malcolm Flinn
Officers: John Malcolm Flinn [1952] Director; Steven Francis Turnbull [1972] Director

Italian Importers Ltd
Incorporated: 2 February 2016 *Employees:* 2
Net Worth Deficit: £5,654 *Total Assets:* £551
Registered Office: Glyncoed, Penrhyncoch, Aberystwyth, Ceredigion, SY23 3EE
Shareholder: Susan Jones
Officers: David Clive Jenkins [1968] Director; Susan Jones [1961] Director

Italian Wine Buyers Club Limited
Incorporated: 21 April 2016
Net Worth Deficit: £11,093 *Total Assets:* £5,357
Registered Office: Allen House, 1 Westmead Road, Sutton, Surrey, SM1 4LA
Major Shareholder: Nichola Patchett
Officers: Nichola Patchett [1963] Director/Retail Manager

The Italian Wine Club Ltd
Incorporated: 28 November 2003
Net Worth: £3,459 *Total Assets:* £6,763
Registered Office: 28 Milton Park, Highgate, London, N6 5QA
Shareholder: Andrew Geoffry Scoones
Officers: Andrew Geoffry Scoones, Secretary; Alison Jane Fry [1959] Director/Nurse; Dr Richard Paul William Fry [1957] Director/Doctor of Medicine

Italicus Ltd
Incorporated: 21 May 2016
Net Worth: £594,403 *Total Assets:* £924,740
Registered Office: Studio 34, 65 Alfred Road, London, W2 5EU
Major Shareholder: Giuseppe Gallo
Officers: Ron Anderson [1956] Director; Giuseppe Gallo [1980] Director/Consultant; Valeria Piovesana [1972] Director [Italian]

Italimport (Wessex) Limited
Incorporated: 27 August 2009
Net Worth Deficit: £2,525 *Total Assets:* £61,609
Registered Office: 58 Kinson Road, Bournemouth, BH10 4AN
Shareholders: Paola Macarena Tondreaus Acevedo; Carlos Luis Chacin Lorenzo
Officers: Carlos Luis Chacin-Lorenzo [1965] Director

Italy Abroad Network Limited
Incorporated: 13 November 2003
Net Worth Deficit: £65,581 *Total Assets:* £121,498
Registered Office: Oak Mill, Topcliffe Lane, Morley, Leeds, LS27 0HL
Major Shareholder: Andrea D'Ercole
Officers: Dercole Andrea [1975] Director [Italian]

Italy on Tap Ltd
Incorporated: 31 October 2006
Previous: Costello Bookkeeping Services Limited
Net Worth Deficit: £44,982 *Total Assets:* £26,298
Registered Office: 29a High Street, West Wickham, Kent, BR4 0LP
Major Shareholder: Paul Louis Jemetta
Officers: Paul Louis Jemetta [1965] Director/Accountant

Italy Service UK Ltd
Incorporated: 9 January 2018
Net Worth Deficit: £488
Registered Office: 44 Maiden Lane, London, WC2E 7LN
Shareholder: Giuliano Manoli
Officers: Giuliano Manoli, Secretary; Nicola Laurino [1965] Director/Commerce [Italian]; Giuliano Manoli [1959] Commercial Director [Italian]

Itasca Wines Limited
Incorporated: 22 January 2018
Registered Office: Studio 5, The Old Kiln, Penncroft Farm, Itchel Lane, Crondall, Hants, GU10 5PX
Shareholders: Simon Porter; Malcolm Thomas Walker
Officers: Simon Porter [1959] Director/Farmer; Malcolm Thomas Walker [1958] Director/Film Producer

Itedomum (UK) Ltd
Incorporated: 22 April 2015
Net Worth: £1,702 *Total Assets:* £104,497
Registered Office: c/o Evla, 30 Worthing Road, Horsham, W Sussex, RH12 1SL
Major Shareholder: Veronika Bagoly
Officers: Attila Marton [1967] Director [Hungarian]

Iturn Global Ltd
Incorporated: 5 September 2017
Registered Office: Kemp House, 160 City Road, London, EC1V 2NX
Officers: Sankalp Rajen Sikka [1997] Director/Self Employed [Indian]

J & A Drinks Limited
Incorporated: 8 December 2011 *Employees:* 7
Net Worth: £1,145,679 *Total Assets:* £1,686,432
Registered Office: c/o Bulpitt Crocker Taxation Limited, Burlington House, Old Christchurch Road, Bournemouth, BH1 2HZ
Shareholders: Anthony Ernest Horton; Jonathan Michael Horton
Officers: Anthony Ernest Horton [1988] Director; Jonathan Michael Horton [1988] Director

J & D Wholesalers Ltd
Incorporated: 30 May 2018
Registered Office: Kemp House, 160 City Road, London, EC1V 2NX
Officers: Luxan Sriskantharajah [1994] Director [Sri Lankan]

J & De Limited
Incorporated: 3 April 2017
Registered Office: Ash House, School Lane, Chittering, Cambs, CB25 9PW
Shareholders: Damien Egan; Jenny Willatt
Officers: Damien Egan [1978] Director/Sales Manager; Jenny Willatt [1984] Director/Experience Designer

J & M Whisky Limited
Incorporated: 5 April 2017
Registered Office: Cowan & Partners Limited, 60 Constitution Street, Leith, Edinburgh, EH6 6RR
Shareholders: James Andrew; Somax Vertriebs & Vermittlungs GmbH
Officers: James Andrew [1961] Director; Mario Gorlach [1964] Director [German]

J A Glass Limited
Incorporated: 15 September 2011
Registered Office: 7 Evanton Drive, Thornliebank Industrial Estate, Glasgow, G46 8HL
Parent: William Morton Ltd
Officers: Brian Douglas Robertson [1962] Director/Financial Controller; Stephen Gerard Russell [1953] Director

J K Wholesales Ltd
Incorporated: 1 September 2018
Registered Office: 33 Cowley Road, Ilford, Essex, IG1 3JL
Major Shareholder: Theerththiga Sathiyaseelan
Officers: Theerththiga Sathiyaseelan [1991] Director/Administration [Sri Lankan]

J M & D Limited
Incorporated: 20 February 2009 *Employees:* 8
Net Worth: £81,929 *Total Assets:* £1,122,880
Registered Office: The Chancery, 58 Spring Gardens, Manchester, M2 1EW
Major Shareholder: Daniel Michael Hassall
Officers: Daniel Michael Hassall [1984] Director/FMCS Sales

J W Wines Ltd
Incorporated: 13 November 2003 *Employees:* 3
Net Worth: £1,164,323 *Total Assets:* £1,475,867
Registered Office: The Quadrant, 99 Parkway Avenue, Sheffield, S9 4WG
Major Shareholder: Wajid Mahmood
Officers: Wajid Mahmood [1982] Director

J.G. Distillers Limited
Incorporated: 9 May 1991 Employees: 36
Net Worth: £3,512,240 Total Assets: £14,977,495
Registered Office: 3 Peel Park Place, East Kilbride, S Lanarks, G74 5LW
Officers: Caroline Purdie, Secretary; Colin Shields Barclay [1958] Director/Merchant [Canadian]; Gerrard McSherry [1956] Director/Accountant; Caroline Amy Purdie [1983] Director

J.R.G. Investments Limited
Incorporated: 11 January 1965
Net Worth Deficit: £3,561 Total Assets: £43,823
Registered Office: 92 Dover Crescent, Bedford, MK41 8QH
Shareholder: Adrian Peter Stephan Luto
Officers: Ronald Basil Winslow, Secretary; Adrian Peter Stephen Luto [1956] Director/Solicitor; Ronald Basil Winslow [1943] Director/Accountant

J.W.G. PLC
Incorporated: 11 July 1984 Employees: 118
Net Worth: £3,580,942 Total Assets: £7,685,623
Registered Office: Gremista Industrial Estate, Lerwick, Isle of Shetland, ZE1 0PX
Shareholders: George Hepburn; Anna Hepburn
Officers: Anna Mary Hepburn [1946] Director/Housewife; George Garland Hepburn [1948] Director/Publican; Iain Robert Johnston [1971] Director/General Operations Manager

J.W.L Wholesale Drinks Ltd
Incorporated: 5 February 2010
Net Worth Deficit: £3,427 Total Assets: £30,992
Registered Office: 8 Station Road, Llanelli, Carmarthenshire, SA15 1AL
Major Shareholder: Elvet Wynne Lewis
Officers: Elvet Wynne Lewis [1957] Director

Jabru Bevco Ltd
Incorporated: 10 November 2016
Net Worth Deficit: £17,846 Total Assets: £17,036
Registered Office: 4 Waterside Mews, Stoughton Road, Guildford, Surrey, GU1 1LA
Officers: James Andrew Thomas Van Der Watt [1977] Director/Founder [Irish]

Jackrabbit Brewing Co. Ltd
Incorporated: 29 January 2019
Registered Office: 198 Berechurch Hall Road, Colchester, Essex, CO2 9PN
Shareholders: Amir William Anbouche; Spencer Aaron Gilbert
Officers: Amir William Anbouche [1992] Director

Jackson & Seddon Ltd
Incorporated: 19 July 2017
Net Worth: £643 Total Assets: £13,338
Registered Office: c/o Stuart McBain Ltd (Accountants), Unit 18 Tower Street, Brunswick Business Park, Liverpool, L3 4BJ
Major Shareholder: Robert James Seddon
Officers: Robert James Seddon [1978] Director/Owner

Jackson Nugent Vintners Limited
Incorporated: 23 May 1979 Employees: 14
Net Worth: £2,434,102 Total Assets: £2,999,574
Registered Office: 30 Homefield Road, Wimbledon, London, SW19 4QF
Shareholders: Caroline O'Shaughnessy; Caroline O' Shaughnessy; Julie Frances Jackson
Officers: Margaret Jackson, Secretary; Alan Alfred Webster Jackson [1935] Director/Chairman; Julie Frances Jackson [1960] Managing Director; Caroline O' Shaughnessy [1962] Director; Caroline O'Shaughnessy [1962] Director

Jade General Merchants Ltd
Incorporated: 26 April 2018
Registered Office: 238 Bexley Road, Erith, Kent, DA8 3HB
Major Shareholder: Ade Williams
Officers: Ade Williams [1965] Director/IT Consultant

The Jaded Group Limited
Incorporated: 20 February 2017
Net Worth: £927 Total Assets: £1,607
Registered Office: 42 The Square, Chagford, Newton Abbot, Devon, TQ13 8AH
Shareholders: Gillian Michelle Mann; Brian Hamilton Renwick
Officers: Gillian Michelle Mann [1962] Director/Wine Retail; Brian Hamilton Renwick [1939] Director/Consultant

Jaguar Beverage Ltd
Incorporated: 5 October 2018
Registered Office: Kemp House, 160 City Road, London, EC1V 2NX
Officers: Saeed Mohammadi [1971] Director [Canadian]

Jaitly Trading Co Ltd
Incorporated: 6 August 2008
Net Worth: £120,488 Total Assets: £651,497
Registered Office: Unit 67 Crayford Industrial Estate, Swaisland Drive, Crayford, Dartford, Kent, DA1 4HS
Major Shareholder: Ajay Sharma
Officers: Ajay Sharma [1968] Director/Wholesaler [Indian]

Jam Consultants Global Limited
Incorporated: 20 June 2012 Employees: 2
Net Worth: £669 Total Assets: £30,507
Registered Office: 2-4 Ash Lane, Rustington, Littlehampton, W Sussex, BN16 3BZ
Major Shareholder: Mark Avellano
Officers: Mark Avellano, Secretary; Mark Avellano [1970] Director/Brand Developer & Consultant; Jane Storey [1970] Director/Brand Developer & Consultant

William James & Sons Ltd
Incorporated: 15 August 2018
Registered Office: 453 Cranbrook Road, Ilford, Essex, IG2 6EW
Major Shareholder: Bhimji Nanji Patel
Officers: Bhimji Nanji Patel [1969] Director/Chief Executive [Indian]; Dhara Bhimji Patel [1993] Director [Indian]; Kunal Bhimji Patel [1991] Managing Director [Indian]; Kunver Bhimji Patel [1974] Director [Indian]

Anthony James Beverages Limited
Incorporated: 19 February 2019
Registered Office: 12 The Turnstones, Gravesend, Kent, DA12 5QD
Major Shareholder: Anthony James Foord
Officers: Alexander Buller [1986] Director/Designer; Anthony James Foord [1986] Director

James Fine Wines Limited
Incorporated: 26 May 2016 *Employees:* 1
Net Worth: £61,662 *Total Assets:* £373,611
Registered Office: c/o Tayabali Tomlin & White, 5 High Green, Great Shelford, Cambridge, CB22 5EG
Major Shareholder: James Graham Read
Officers: James Graham Read [1976] Director

Nicholas James Gin Ltd
Incorporated: 30 May 2018
Registered Office: 1 Walkden Road, Worsley, Manchester, M28 3DA
Major Shareholder: Nicholas James McCance
Officers: Nicholas James McCance [1992] Managing Director

Edward James Limited
Incorporated: 16 November 2006
Net Worth Deficit: £68,134 *Total Assets:* £65,238
Registered Office: 91 Cobham Road, Ilford, Essex, IG3 9JL
Major Shareholder: Jagmohan Singh
Officers: Jagmohan Singh [1985] Director/Self Employed

Tristan James Ltd
Incorporated: 1 August 2011
Net Worth: £3,998 *Total Assets:* £29,204
Registered Office: 11a Uxbridge Road, Hillingdon, Middlesex, UB10 0LR
Shareholder: Wesley Wesley James Daly
Officers: Wesley Daly [1984] Director

Janemac Ltd
Incorporated: 12 February 2018
Registered Office: 71-75 Shelton Street, Covent Garden, London, WC2H 9JQ
Major Shareholder: Jane Dunham
Officers: Jane Dunham [1966] Director

Japan Gourmet (UK) Limited
Incorporated: 16 January 2014
Net Worth Deficit: £125,226 *Total Assets:* £17,928
Registered Office: Suite E, 1-3 Canfield Place, London, NW6 3BT
Major Shareholder: Jorg Muller
Officers: Xiaye Li, Secretary; Xiaye Li [1989] Director [Chinese]; Jorg Muller [1963] Director [German]

Jascera UK Ltd
Incorporated: 16 January 2018
Registered Office: 39 Richards House, Burrowes Street, Walsall, W Midlands, WS2 8NN
Major Shareholder: Ogonna Solomon Anolue
Officers: Ogonna Solomon Anolue [1975] Director/Entrepreneur [Nigerian]

Jascots Wine Merchants Limited
Incorporated: 12 February 2014 *Employees:* 41
Net Worth: £303,490 *Total Assets:* £3,023,350
Registered Office: The Observatory, Pinnacle House, 260 Old Oak Common Lane, London, NW10 6DX
Shareholders: John Simon Charnock; Miles Thomas MacInnes
Officers: Ian James Carter [1964] Director/Wine Merchant; John Simon Charnock [1965] Director; Miles Thomas MacInnes [1982] Director; Adam James Porter [1982] Director/Wine Merchant; Jonathan James Scott [1962] Director

Jassim Limited
Incorporated: 11 August 2008
Net Worth: £424,367 *Total Assets:* £2,438,942
Registered Office: Unit A3, Oyo Business Units, Crabtree Manorway North, Belvedere, Kent, DA17 6AX
Major Shareholder: Jaspreet Anand
Officers: Jaspreet Anand, Secretary; Jaspreet Anand [1974] Director and Secretary

Jays Beverages Limited
Incorporated: 8 April 2010
Net Worth: £7,780 *Total Assets:* £43,562
Registered Office: Uglow Farm, Broadhead Road, Turton, Bolton, Lancs, BL7 0JN
Major Shareholder: Jagdish Parbat Savani
Officers: Jagdish Parbat Savani [1981] Director

Jays Trading Ltd
Incorporated: 16 June 2010
Net Worth: £10,945 *Total Assets:* £20,685
Registered Office: 299 Littleton Road, Salford, M7 3TA
Officers: Kevin Green [1955] Director/Self Employed

JB Champagne & Co Ltd
Incorporated: 21 February 2018
Registered Office: Wilberforce House, Station Road, London, NW4 4QE
Major Shareholder: Jean-Baptiste Sory
Officers: Jean-Baptiste Sory [1993] Director [French]

JBD Booze Ltd
Incorporated: 15 January 2019
Registered Office: 1 Leigh Sinton Road, Malvern, Worcs, WR14 1JL
Major Shareholder: Shamsher Singh
Officers: Shamsher Singh [1964] Director

JC Wholsale and Distribution Ltd
Incorporated: 28 June 2017
Registered Office: Unit 30 Paisley Self Storage, 115 Abercrombie Street, Paisley, Renfrewshire, PA3 4AT
Officers: Craig Gibson [1983] Director/Aircraft Engineer; Jonathan McCall [1982] Director/Aircraft Engineer

JC Wine Events Ltd
Incorporated: 18 October 2010
Net Worth Deficit: £16,426 *Total Assets:* £7,199
Registered Office: Forge House, Lower Oddington, Moreton in Marsh, Glos, GL56 0XD
Shareholders: Julian Seymour Chamberlen; Caroline Chamberlen
Officers: Caroline Chamberlen [1966] Director/School Tour Guide; Julian Seymour Chamberlen [1964] Director/Wine Merchant

JD Group Enterprises Ltd
Incorporated: 7 December 2017
Registered Office: 15 Ellenbrook Green, Ipswich, Suffolk, IP2 9RR
Major Shareholder: Johny Habib Karromi Shaia
Officers: Johny Habib Karromi Shaia [1989] Director [Iraqi]

JD's Sports Bar Ltd
Incorporated: 20 June 2014
Net Worth: £39,854 *Total Assets:* £82,774
Registered Office: JD's Sports Bar, 1 Glencairn Street, Motherwell, N Lanarks, ML1 1TT
Major Shareholder: Karen Cullen
Officers: Karen Cullen [1967] Director/Manager

JDS Trading Limited
Incorporated: 7 January 2014
Net Worth Deficit: £111,080 *Total Assets:* £70,771
Registered Office: 266-268 High Street, Waltham Cross, Herts, EN8 7EA
Major Shareholder: Julian David Piler
Officers: Julian David Piler [1967] Director/Futures Trader

JDT Drinks Company Ltd
Incorporated: 12 April 2018
Registered Office: Unit 12A, Ash Park Business Centre, Tadley, Hants, RG26 5EL
Major Shareholder: John Parker
Officers: John Parker [1983] Director

Mark Jefferson Wines Limited
Incorporated: 20 May 2004 *Employees:* 2
Net Worth Deficit: £59,397 *Total Assets:* £72,451
Registered Office: 177 Sandown Road, Belfast, BT5 6GX
Major Shareholder: Mark Harold Jefferson
Officers: Dr Victoria Louise Kett, Secretary; Mark Harold Jefferson [1970] Director/Wine Merchant

Jeffries Vintage Drinks Ltd
Incorporated: 31 October 2017
Registered Office: Park House, 37 Clarence Street, Leicester, LE1 3RW
Shareholders: Leon Williamson; Lee Thomas John Jeffries
Officers: Lee Thomas Jeffries [1981] Director; Leon Williamson [1980] Director

Jelly Bowl Ltd
Incorporated: 17 February 2004
Net Worth Deficit: £84,052 *Total Assets:* £33,447
Registered Office: 1st Floor, 36 Albemarle Street, Mayfair, London, W1S 4JE
Major Shareholder: Biren Gala
Officers: Biren Gala [1979] Director/Consultant

Jenkins and Beckers Fine Wine Limited
Incorporated: 27 May 2015 *Employees:* 5
Net Worth: £827,721 *Total Assets:* £1,241,363
Registered Office: 1a Mill Yard, Childerley, Dry Drayton, Cambridge, CB23 8BA
Officers: Alison Carolyn Cumming [1949] Director; Hester Chloe Mary Cumming [1983] Director; Phoebe Alice Elizabeth Cumming [1988] Director; Robert Alexander Cumming [1945] Director; Chloe Jenkins [1929] Director

Jenuine Jamaican Products Limited
Incorporated: 1 February 2013
Net Worth: £3,142 *Total Assets:* £3,858
Registered Office: Flat 8, Saint Augustines Court, Lynton Road, Bermondsey, London, SE1 5DP
Shareholder: Douglas Cowan
Officers: Douglas Cowan [1958] Director/Import/Export [Jamaican]; Arlene Patricia Ellis [1973] Director/Import/Export [Jamaican/British]

Jervis Trading Limited
Incorporated: 12 July 2017
Registered Office: 6 Station View, Chester, CH2 3DT
Shareholders: Peter Jervis; Laura Jervis
Officers: Laura Jervis [1987] Director; Peter Jervis [1986] Director

Jetchill Ltd
Incorporated: 14 May 2009 *Employees:* 2
Net Worth Deficit: £14,675 *Total Assets:* £69,547
Registered Office: Hadrian House, Beaminster Way East, Unit 9 Kingston Park, Newcastle upon Tyne, NE3 2ER
Officers: Robert David Flunder [1982] Director; Colin Myers [1972] Managing Director

Jezba Ltd
Incorporated: 26 April 2017
Registered Office: 33 Corvette Court, Cardiff, CF10 4NL
Officers: Mohammed Hikki [1987] Director

JF Kegs (Scotland) Limited
Incorporated: 14 August 2007 *Employees:* 17
Net Worth: £750,567 *Total Assets:* £1,852,500
Registered Office: Block 24 Kilspindie Road, Dunsinane Industrial Estate, Dundee, DD2 3QH
Major Shareholder: James Fyffe
Officers: James Fyffe [1969] Director

JF Tobias Limited
Incorporated: 22 November 2013
Net Worth Deficit: £22,068 *Total Assets:* £334,456
Registered Office: The Stables, 23B Lenten Street, Alton, Hants, GU34 1HG
Major Shareholder: George Frederick Augustus Rodgers
Officers: Gus Frederick Augustus Rodgers [1983] Director

JH Wine Agencies Ltd
Incorporated: 6 January 2012
Net Worth Deficit: £1,433 *Total Assets:* £19,490
Registered Office: 210 Spalding Road, Pinchbeck, Spalding, Lincs, PE11 3PB
Shareholders: John Robert William Walker; Howard Jonathan Frish
Officers: Howard Jonathan Frish [1964] Director; John Robert William Walker [1951] Director

Jia Bo Rui International Trade Limited
Incorporated: 30 April 2018
Registered Office: 28 Cottall Avenue, Chatham, Kent, ME4 6HG
Major Shareholder: Ruizi Jiang
Officers: Ruizi Jiang [1985] Director/Self Employed [Chinese]

Jiangsu Wine Trading Company Ltd
Incorporated: 2 October 2018
Registered Office: Apartment 4, Fusion 5, 10 Middlewood Street, Salford, M5 4LN
Shareholders: Peter-Francis Crameri; Haiping Gu
Officers: Peter-Francis Crameri, Secretary; Peter-Francis Crameri [1967] Director; Haiping Gu [1975] Director [Chinese]

The Jiggers Whistle Limited
Incorporated: 14 September 2017
Registered Office: 5-7 High Street, Brownhills, Walsall, W Midlands, WS8 6ED
Shareholder: Teresa Cragg
Officers: Colin Cragg [1972] Director/Publican

Jimmy's Beer & Gas (Wirral) Limited
Incorporated: 17 January 2017 *Employees:* 4
Net Worth Deficit: £13,075 *Total Assets:* £29,446
Registered Office: 210-218 New Chester Road, Rock Ferry, Birkenhead, Merseyside, CH41 9BG
Major Shareholder: James Hunstone
Officers: James Hunstone [1963] Director

The Jin Bar Ltd
Incorporated: 3 January 2017
Registered Office: 4 Pathfinder Way, Warboys, Cambs, PE28 2RD
Shareholders: James Leivers; Hayley Leivers
Officers: Hayley Leivers [1987] Director/Designer; James Leivers [1983] Director/Network Engineer

Jivana Spirits Ltd.
Incorporated: 13 November 2017
Registered Office: Flat 1, Philips House, 8 Ravenswood Road, London, SW12 9PL
Shareholders: Rachitha Seneviratne; Caishenkama Ltd
Officers: Vikram Pathak [1992] Director/Investments; Rachitha Seneviratne [1991] Director/Marketing [Australian]

JJ Wholesalers Ltd
Incorporated: 6 August 2009
Net Worth: £25,003 *Total Assets:* £58,138
Registered Office: Sellars View, Sellars Road, Hardwicke, Gloucester, GL2 4QD
Major Shareholder: Jaswinder Mann
Officers: Jennifer Mann, Secretary; Jaswinder Mann [1975] Director/Wholesaler

JJBrands Limited
Incorporated: 5 December 2011 *Employees:* 1
Net Worth Deficit: £33,086 *Total Assets:* £2,658
Registered Office: 26 St Marys Road, Burnham on Sea, Somerset, TA8 2AZ
Major Shareholder: Paul Francis Mills
Officers: Xiuyue Mills, Secretary; Paul Francis Mills [1960] Director/Sales Agency & Distributor

JKVK International Import and Export Ltd
Incorporated: 25 February 2019
Registered Office: 9 Nelson Road, London, E4 9AP
Shareholders: Keith Gill; Kenneth Cupid
Officers: Kenneth Cupid, Secretary; Keith Gill [1957] Sales Director

JN Trading Limited
Incorporated: 5 April 2018
Registered Office: 7-9 Killyleagh Street, Crossgar, Co Down, BT30 9DQ
Parent: James Nicholson Wine Limited
Officers: Nicola Davies, Secretary; Nicola Davies [1972] Director/Accountant; James Nicholson [1953] Director/Wine Merchant

Michael Jobling Wines Ltd
Incorporated: 28 June 1988
Net Worth Deficit: £34,237 *Total Assets:* £45,757
Registered Office: Collingwood House, Church Square, Hartlepool, Cleveland, TS24 7EN
Major Shareholder: Michael Jobling
Officers: Geoffrey Michael Jobling [1948] Director/Vintner

Jocks and Peers Brewing Company Limited
Incorporated: 24 July 2018
Registered Office: 180 St Pauls Road, London, N1 2LL
Shareholders: Akshit Raj Gupta; Ashwin Balivada; Aditya Nigudkar
Officers: Ashwin Balivada [1988] Sales Director [Indian]; Akshit Raj Gupta [1988] Director/Operations Manager [Indian]; Aditya Nigudkar [1983] Marketing Director [Indian]

ND John Wine Limited
Incorporated: 5 July 2011
Net Worth: £1 *Total Assets:* £1
Registered Office: 90 Walter Road, Swansea, SA1 4QF
Major Shareholder: Nick John
Officers: Nicholas David John [1963] Director

N D John Wine Merchants Limited
Incorporated: 25 September 2000 *Employees:* 13
Net Worth: £287,821 *Total Assets:* £1,178,240
Registered Office: Unit 2 Millbrook Trading Estate, Siloh Road, Landore, Swansea, SA1 2NT
Major Shareholder: Nicholas David John
Officers: Peter Garfield John, Secretary; Nicholas David John [1963] Director/Wine Merchant

Jolly Good Beer Ltd
Incorporated: 9 March 2017
Registered Office: 7 Church Street, Willingham, Cambridge, CB24 5HS
Major Shareholder: Yvan Jack Seth
Officers: Yvan Jack Seth [1980] Director [Australian]

Aston Jones Limited
Incorporated: 17 June 2003 *Employees:* 2
Net Worth Deficit: £72,919 *Total Assets:* £48,514
Registered Office: 10 Miners Park Road, Llay Industrial Estate, Llay, Wrexham, Clwyd, LL12 0PQ
Major Shareholder: Angus Gordon Smellie
Officers: Jane Marie Smellie, Secretary

S H Jones Wines Ltd
Incorporated: 29 August 1978 *Employees:* 30
Net Worth: £50,424 *Total Assets:* £898,359
Registered Office: 2 Riverside Tramway Road, Banbury, Oxon, OX16 5TU
Major Shareholder: Richard Nicholas Jones
Officers: Gregory Norman Shaw, Secretary; Harry Alexander Sircom Jones [1989] Director/Chartered Accountant; Richard Nicholas Jones [1957] Director/Wine Merchant; Gregory Norman Shaw [1966] Director/General Manager

Jonesborough Wholesale Ltd
Incorporated: 11 August 2011
Net Worth: £110,396 *Total Assets:* £271,009
Registered Office: 67 The Village, Jonesborough, Newry, Co Down, BT35 8HR
Major Shareholder: Seamus Philip McNamee
Officers: Seamus Philip McNamee [1959] Director/Shop Owner [Irish]; Seamus McNamee [1991] Director/Student [Irish]; Siofra McNamee [1987] Director [Irish]

Jordan Sky Ltd
Incorporated: 3 April 2018
Registered Office: 514 Hall Road, Hull, HU6 9BS
Officers: Jordan Sky, Secretary; Jordan Sky [1984] Director/Manager

JPHA Ltd
Incorporated: 25 January 2019
Registered Office: 29 The Glade, Woodford Green, Essex, IG8 0QA
Major Shareholder: James Pham
Officers: James Pham [1995] Director

UK Wholesalers of Beers, Wines and Spirits

JR First Choice Cash & Carry Ltd
Incorporated: 16 January 2015
Net Worth Deficit: £63,416 Total Assets: £62,142
Registered Office: 34 Great Western Industrial Estate, Great Western Close, Birmingham, B18 4QF
Shareholders: Jaroslaw Marek Zawodny; Rafal Kowzan
Officers: Rafal Kowzan [1983] Director [Polish]; Jaroslaw Marek Zawodny [1987] Director [Polish]

JSF Services Limited
Incorporated: 25 February 2009 Employees: 2
Net Worth: £367 Total Assets: £38,522
Registered Office: 5 Woodedge Drive, Droitwich, Worcs, WR9 7GB
Shareholders: Justin Stephen Farr; Deborah Ann Farr
Officers: Deborah Ann Farr, Secretary; Deborah Ann Farr [1980] Director; Justin Stephen Farr [1975] Director/IT Consultant

Jub Club Top Bar Ltd
Incorporated: 30 October 2018
Registered Office: 20-22 Wenlock Road, London, N1 7GU
Major Shareholder: Walter Geoge Balloch
Officers: Walter Geoge Balloch [1963] Director

Junga Ltd
Incorporated: 22 February 2019
Registered Office: 71-75 Shelton Street, Covent Garden, London, WC2H 9JQ
Major Shareholder: Sinnathurai Rajenthiram
Officers: Sinnathurai Rajenthiram [1963] Director [Sri Lankan]

Jupiter Wholesale Limited
Incorporated: 10 January 2017 Employees: 1
Net Worth Deficit: £12,195 Total Assets: £408
Registered Office: 16 Warwick Gardens, Tividale, Oldbury, W Midlands, B69 3JB
Officers: Pardeep Singh Rai [1980] Director/Manager

Just A Splash Limited
Incorporated: 15 February 2016 Employees: 1
Net Worth Deficit: £75,632 Total Assets: £102,767
Registered Office: Brent House, 382 Gloucester Road, Cheltenham, Glos, GL51 7AY
Shareholders: Anil Varma; Pia Varma
Officers: Anil Varma [1954] Director/Sales; Pia Varma [1982] Director/Sales

Just Incase Wines Ltd
Incorporated: 17 September 2018
Registered Office: 16 Hunter Hill Road, Sheffield, S11 8UE
Officers: Thomas Dunning-Lewis [1994] Director; Gary Maudsley [1993] Director; Cole Peter Procter [1994] Marketing Director; Marco Thompson [1992] Director

Just Miniatures Limited
Incorporated: 9 January 2003
Net Worth: £76,004 Total Assets: £336,914
Registered Office: Alexander House, 3 Clifford Finch Way, Crockatt Road, Hadleigh, Essex, IP7 6RD
Major Shareholder: Amareet Mattu
Officers: Gavin John Alexander [1976] Director; Amareet Mattu [1994] Director

Just Perfect Wines Ltd
Incorporated: 15 November 2013
Registered Office: 31 Chervil Close, Stoke on Trent, Staffs, ST3 7YD
Major Shareholder: Julia Elizabeth Phillips
Officers: Julia Elizabeth Phillips [1971] Director

Justerini & Brooks, Limited
Incorporated: 22 December 1900 Employees: 51
Net Worth: £1,399,778,048 Total Assets: £1,432,017,024
Registered Office: 61 St James's Street, London, SW1A 1LZ
Parent: Diageo Great Britain Limited
Officers: Gavin Paul Crickmore [1958] Director/Chartered Accountant; James Matthew Crayden Edmunds [1974] Director/Solicitor; Sharon Lynnette Fennessy [1967] Director/Group Treasurer [Irish]; David Heginbottom [1970] Director/Group Treasurer; Aniko Mahler [1976] Director/Head of Statutory Compliance [Hungarian]; Kara Elizabeth Major [1977] Director [American]; Edward Martin Peachey [1973] Commercial Financial Director

Jean Juviniere Limited
Incorporated: 10 October 1989 Employees: 7
Net Worth: £565,140 Total Assets: £724,432
Registered Office: Unit 26 Graphite Way, Hadfield, Glossop, Derbys, SK13 1QH
Major Shareholder: Ronald Scorer
Officers: Julia Scorer, Secretary; Steven Murtagh [1980] Director; Claire Scorer [1982] Director; Julia Scorer [1949] Director/Secretary; Ronald Scorer [1953] Director/Wine Wholesaler

JW Corporation Ltd
Incorporated: 5 September 2018
Registered Office: 3rd Floor, 86-90 Paul Street, London, EC2A 4NE
Major Shareholder: Ming-Chi Chin
Officers: Ming-Chi Chin [1991] Director [Taiwanese]

JWM Vintners Limited
Incorporated: 29 October 2001
Net Worth Deficit: £8,005 Total Assets: £12,441
Registered Office: 9 Great Chesterford Court, London Road, Great Chesterford, Saffron Walden, Essex, CB10 1PF
Shareholders: Jonathan William May; Neil Vasey
Officers: Stuart May, Secretary; Jonathan William May [1969] Director/Wine Merchant

K & A Eagle Limited
Incorporated: 29 December 2017
Registered Office: 243 Radford Road, Nottingham, NG7 5GU
Major Shareholder: Sebastian Slusarczyk
Officers: Sebastian Slusarczyk [1997] Managing Director [Polish]

K & G Spirits Ltd
Incorporated: 3 January 2019
Registered Office: 29 Hilders Road, Leicester, LE3 6HE
Shareholders: Krzysztof Ozarowski; Gurjinder Singh Surana
Officers: Krzysztof Ozarowski [1980] Director [Polish]; Gurjinder Singh Surana [1981] Director

K R Wines & Beers Ltd
Incorporated: 13 April 2015
Net Worth: £37,622 Total Assets: £128,289
Registered Office: Unit 12 Lower Wharf Street, Ashton under Lyne, Lancs, OL6 7PE
Shareholders: Ritesh Jethwa; Mukesh Jethwa
Officers: Mukesh Jethwa, Secretary; Mukesh Jethwa [1958] Director/Sales; Ritesh Jethwa [1984] Director/Sales

Kairos Solutions Ltd
Incorporated: 23 March 2017 Employees: 1
Net Worth: £2,289 Total Assets: £17,630
Registered Office: St Madoc Christian Youth Camp, Llanmadoc, Swansea, SA3 1DE
Shareholders: Alison Holland; Martin Holland
Officers: Alison Holland [1961] Director/Centre Manager; Martin Holland [1960] Sales Director

Kal Wine Source UK Ltd
Incorporated: 2 December 2010
Net Worth Deficit: £1,104,329 *Total Assets:* £3,302,196
Registered Office: 76 New Cavendish Street, London, W1G 9TB
Officers: Celine Bannino [1972] Director [French]

Kaleboard Limited
Incorporated: 17 June 2013
Net Worth: £728,284 *Total Assets:* £811,531
Registered Office: 124-126 Littleton Road, Salford, M7 3TW
Major Shareholder: Ranjeev Singh
Officers: Ranjeev Singh [1972] Director

Kallwin Limited
Incorporated: 14 January 1992 *Employees:* 2
Net Worth: £1,364,846 *Total Assets:* £2,264,425
Registered Office: 3-37 Autumn Street, Bow, London, E3 2TT
Shareholders: Retnakumar Govindaraju; Manjit Singh Sambhi
Officers: Manjit Singh Sambhi, Secretary; Retnakumar Govindaraju [1964] Director/Shopkeeper; Manjit Singh Sambhi [1962] Director/Electrician

Kamros Cash and Carry Limited
Incorporated: 25 May 2010 *Employees:* 24
Net Worth: £668,353 *Total Assets:* £4,624,249
Registered Office: Unit 1 Firtree House, Creek Road, Barking, Essex, IG11 0JH
Major Shareholder: Idris Abdullah
Officers: Idris Abdullah [1977] Director/Chief Executive Officer

Kan Trading Limited
Incorporated: 8 July 2009
Net Worth Deficit: £5,645 *Total Assets:* £37,008
Registered Office: Unit 6, 17 Thorp Street, Birmingham, B5 4AT
Major Shareholder: Chi Chiu Kan
Officers: Jen Yeh Goh [1982] Commercial Director [Malaysian]; Chi Chiu Kan [1977] Director

Kane Republik Ltd
Incorporated: 2 October 2013
Previous: Cape To Rio Ltd
Net Worth: £100 *Total Assets:* £100
Registered Office: 30a Earl's Court Square, London, SW5 9DQ
Parent: RCI Spirits Ltd
Officers: Rafik Ishani [1980] Director/Chartered Accountant; Tim Reuter [1982] Director/Company Secretary

Kanj Wholesale Ltd
Incorporated: 12 December 2018
Registered Office: 5 Chamber House Farm, Rochdale Road East, Heywood, Lancs, OL10 1SD
Major Shareholder: Antonio Lloyd Rizzelli
Officers: Antonio Lloyd Rizzelli [1993] Director/Sales Person [Italian]

Kanlaon Limited
Incorporated: 7 June 2011 *Employees:* 1
Net Worth: £2,457,348 *Total Assets:* £4,288,873
Registered Office: 2 Jardine House, The Harrovian Business Village, Bessborough Road, Harrow, Middlesex, HA1 3EX
Major Shareholder: Stephen James Carroll
Officers: Stephen James Carroll [1966] Director

Kanpai (London) Food and Beverage Management Co., Ltd.
Incorporated: 27 October 2017
Registered Office: c/o TFC Legal, 80 Coleman Street, London, EC2R 5BJ
Officers: Soji Hiraide [1974] Director [Taiwanese]; Richy Low [1980] Director [Malaysian]; Megumu Mekata [1980] Director [Japanese]

Kapaka Limited
Incorporated: 13 March 2018
Registered Office: Hope House, Barton Road, Bramley, Guildford, Surrey, GU5 0EA
Major Shareholder: Aaron Marcus Hibbert
Officers: Aaron Marcus Hibbert [1981] Director/Businessman

Karla & Co. Spirits Limited
Incorporated: 29 July 2015
Net Worth Deficit: £8,059 *Total Assets:* £12,166
Registered Office: 71-75 Shelton Street, Covent Garden, London, WC2H 9JQ
Shareholder: Veronika Karlova
Officers: Veronika Karlova [1986] Director [Slovak]

Karma Beverages Ltd
Incorporated: 15 December 2014
Net Worth: £25,321 *Total Assets:* £31,807
Registered Office: 54 Mildred Avenue, Hayes, Middlesex, UB3 1TP
Major Shareholder: Nirmal Panesar
Officers: Nirmal Panesar [1974] Director

Kasgo Limited
Incorporated: 15 November 2018
Registered Office: 15 Butterwick, Watford, Herts, WD25 9SD
Shareholders: Malgorzata Malinowska; Kasun Tharindu Madushanka Karunakara Arachchige
Officers: Kasun Tharindu Madushanka Karunakara Arachchige, Secretary; Malgorzata Malinowska, Secretary; Kasun Tharindu Madushanka Karunakara Arachchige [1987] Director/Postman [Sri Lankan]; Malgorzata Malinowska [1985] Director/Assistant Manager [Polish]

Kash & Karry Supplies Ltd
Incorporated: 5 November 2012
Net Worth Deficit: £20,911 *Total Assets:* £106,382
Registered Office: Unit 7 Aqueduct Street, Preston, Lancs, PR1 7JN
Officers: Krushnakumar Nandwana [1985] Director [Indian]

Kater Four (Cash & Carry) Limited
Incorporated: 31 July 1973 *Employees:* 12
Net Worth: £324,157 *Total Assets:* £984,235
Registered Office: Unit 16 Kernan Drive, Bishop Meadow Industrial Estate, Loughborough, Leics, LE11 5JF
Shareholders: Craig Allan Harris; Anna Mikalina Werstyn
Officers: Anna Mikalina Werstyn, Secretary; Craig Allan Harris [1974] Director/Manager; Anna Mikalina Werstyn [1962] Director/Company Secretary

Kato Enterprises Limited
Incorporated: 1 October 1996 *Employees:* 13
Net Worth: £745,099 *Total Assets:* £1,954,357
Registered Office: Endurance House, 71 Sumner Road, Croydon, Surrey, CR0 3LN
Shareholder: Kayode Sunday Toyinbo
Officers: Kayode Sunday Toyinbo, Secretary; Lynn Mann [1959] Director/Marketing; Kayode Sunday Toyinbo [1958] Director/Banking

Kaur's Convenience Store Limited
Incorporated: 14 May 2018
Registered Office: 135-137 Boldon Lane, South Shields, Tyne & Wear, NE34 0NE
Officers: Esha Kaur [1981] Director/Businesswoman

Kay Distributions Ltd
Incorporated: 22 October 2015
Net Worth Deficit: £8,571
Registered Office: Unit 95 and 96 One Stop Storage, Aston Lane, Birmingham, B20 3BT
Major Shareholder: Kayode Ajibola Ogunbola
Officers: Kayode Ajibola Ogunbola [1979] Director/Businessman [Nigerian]

Kayzar Ltd
Incorporated: 14 March 2018
Registered Office: 20-22 Wenlock Road, London, N1 7GU
Major Shareholder: Donus Tiskaya
Officers: Donus Tiskaya [1983] Director [Turkish]

KB Agencies Ltd
Incorporated: 11 August 2014
Net Worth: £62,794 Total Assets: £117,488
Registered Office: 12 Strathkelvin Lane, East Kilbride, G75 8GD
Officers: Jacqui Brown [1962] Director; Kenneth Brown [1953] Director

KB Suppliers Ltd
Incorporated: 22 March 2018
Registered Office: 26 Parkfield Road, Park Field, Longbuckby, Northants, NN6 7QJ
Major Shareholder: Bikram Singh
Officers: Bikram Singh [1979] Director

KBB Components Ltd
Incorporated: 5 November 2018
Registered Office: 20-22 Wenlock Road, London, N1 7GU
Major Shareholder: Maurizio Grigiante
Officers: Alessandra Susana [1963] Director/Teacher [Italian]

KBE Drinks Enterprises Limited
Incorporated: 30 January 2019
Registered Office: Springfield House, Sandling Road, Maidstone, Kent, ME14 2LP
Parent: Kingfisher Beer Europe Ltd
Officers: Mark Edward Davis, Secretary; Damon William Thornton Swarbrick [1974] Director

KC Brothers Ltd
Incorporated: 1 August 2018
Registered Office: 132 Tulketh Brow, Ashton on Ribble, Preston, Lancs, PR2 2SJ
Shareholders: Niraj Kc; Suraj Kc
Officers: Niraj Kc [1983] Director/Student

KD Wholesale Ltd
Incorporated: 5 July 2012 Employees: 1
Net Worth: £49,727 Total Assets: £149,391
Registered Office: 29 Waterloo Road, Wolverhampton, W Midlands, WV1 4DJ
Major Shareholder: Karamjit Singh Saini
Officers: Karamjit Singh Saini [1941] Director

Kedem Europe Limited
Incorporated: 25 March 1993 Employees: 13
Net Worth: £2,039,415 Total Assets: £3,672,280
Registered Office: Block B, OCC Estate, 105 Eade Road, London, N4 1TJ
Shareholder: Morris Herzog
Officers: Morris Herzog, Secretary; Benjamin Stern, Secretary; Mordecai Halpern [1946] Director; Morris Herzog [1978] Director/Salesman; Benjamin Stern [1970] Director/Food Distributor

Joseph Keegan & Sons Limited
Incorporated: 25 March 1949 Employees: 21
Net Worth: £520,411 Total Assets: £868,490
Registered Office: Centenary Buildings, Cleveland Avenue, Holyhead, Anglesey, LL65 2LB
Shareholders: Peter Francis Campbell; Jonathan Nathaniel Campbell
Officers: Jonathan Nathaniel Campbell, Secretary/Director; Jonathan Nathaniel Campbell [1971] Director; Peter Francis Campbell [1959] Director

Keeling Andrew & Co Limited
Incorporated: 15 September 2016 Employees: 2
Net Worth: £50,163 Total Assets: £129,934
Registered Office: 51 Lambs Conduit Street, London, WC1N 3NB
Shareholders: Mark Peter Andrew; Daniel Benjamin Keeling
Officers: Mark Peter Andrew [1980] Director; Daniel Benjamin Keeling [1975] Director

Keep Control Ltd
Incorporated: 27 October 2015 Employees: 1
Net Worth: £799 Total Assets: £1,882
Registered Office: Unit 5 Hale House, 296a Green Lanes, Palmers Green, London, N13 5TP
Major Shareholder: Alessandro Ciccariello
Officers: Alessandro Ciccariello [1979] Director [Italian]

Keepr's Ltd
Incorporated: 15 August 2018
Registered Office: Unit 3 Vista Place, Ingworth Road, Poole, Dorset, BH12 1JY
Parent: The British Honey Company Ltd
Officers: Alistair Luke Wallace [1974] Director; Michael Williams [1943] Director

Keeps Lager Co Ltd
Incorporated: 5 June 2018
Registered Office: 20-22 Wenlock Road, London, N1 7GU
Major Shareholder: David Joseph Cornell
Officers: David Joseph Cornell, Secretary; David Joseph Cornell [1991] Director/Professional Sportsman

The Keg & Bottle Ltd
Incorporated: 1 August 2007 Employees: 2
Net Worth: £742 Total Assets: £23,097
Registered Office: 17 Catshole Lane, Bideford, Devon, EX39 3DQ
Officers: Linda Margaret Scoynes, Secretary; Arthur William John Scoynes [1951] Director/Retail Manager; Linda Margaret Scoynes [1952] Director/Administrator

The Keg Company (N.I.) Ltd
Incorporated: 18 January 2011
Net Worth: £32,637 Total Assets: £106,340
Registered Office: 108 Glen Road, Andersonstown, Belfast, BT11 8BH
Shareholders: Anne Quinn; Seamus McGlone
Officers: James Joseph McGlone [1973] Director [Irish]; Anne Quinn [1969] Director [Irish]

Keg Delivery Service Ltd
Incorporated: 14 April 2012 Employees: 3
Net Worth: £48,133 Total Assets: £129,647
Registered Office: 2 Castle Business Village, Station Road, Hampton, Surrey, TW12 2BX
Shareholder: Rajiv Vedi
Officers: Rahul Vedi [1957] Director/Wholesale Beer & Wine Supplier; Rajiv Vedi [1958] Director/Wholesale Beer & Wine Supplier

Kegs of Camberley Limited
Incorporated: 11 July 2011
Net Worth: £20,841 Total Assets: £43,688
Registered Office: Martket House, 19-21 Market Place, Wokingham, Berks, RG40 1AP
Shareholders: Steve Skinner; Michelle Skinner
Officers: Michelle Skinner [1969] Director; Steve Skinner [1966] Director/Fireman

Kegs R Us (Leicester) Ltd
Incorporated: 15 February 2019
Registered Office: Unit 4 Iliffe House, Iliffe Avenue, Oadby, Leicester, LE2 5JB
Officers: Paresh Govindji Bathia [1959] Director

Kegs R Us Ltd
Incorporated: 10 June 2011 Employees: 2
Net Worth: £264 Total Assets: £246,361
Registered Office: Unit 4 Iliffe House, Iliffe Avenue, Oadby, Leicester, LE2 5LS
Major Shareholder: Paresh Govindji Bathia
Officers: Amal Bathia [1994] Director/Consultant; Paresh Govindji Bathia [1959] Director/Wholesaler

Kegspertise Ltd
Incorporated: 28 March 2017
Registered Office: 70a Ardarroch Road, Aberdeen, AB24 5QS
Major Shareholder: John Wemyss
Officers: John Wemyss [1979] Director/Manager

Keltek Cornish Brewery Limited
Incorporated: 27 March 1997 Employees: 12
Net Worth Deficit: £70,024 Total Assets: £550,492
Registered Office: 3 Chapel Street, Redruth, Cornwall, TR15 2BY
Parent: The Optoelectronic Manufacturing Corporation (UK) Ltd
Officers: Richard Stuart Heath [1986] Director/Business Development; Stuart Heath [1953] Director; William Generald Charles Heath [1983] Director/Business Development

Kentish Pip Ltd
Incorporated: 1 June 2016
Net Worth Deficit: £91,970 Total Assets: £139,648
Registered Office: Woolton Farm, Bekesbourne, Canterbury, Kent, CT4 5EA
Officers: David Walton, Secretary; Sam Alexander Mount [1985] Director

Kermis Bier Ltd
Incorporated: 5 June 2018
Registered Office: The Mill, Pury Hill Business Park, Alderton Road, Towcester, Northants, NN12 7LS
Major Shareholder: Paul Watson
Officers: Paul Watson [1962] Director

Kernow Rum Company Limited
Incorporated: 22 December 2017
Registered Office: Queens Hotel, High Street, St Ives, Cornwall, TR26 1RR
Parent: The Cornwall Pub Company Ltd
Officers: Neythan Edward Hayes [1971] Director

Kerry Wines Limited
Incorporated: 25 July 2001
Net Worth: £32 Total Assets: £32
Registered Office: 3 Queens Drive, Maresfield, E Sussex, TN22 2HX
Major Shareholder: John Anthony Wilkinson
Officers: Paulene Wilkinson, Secretary; John Anthony Wilkinson [1939] Director/Sales Executive

Kese International Ltd
Incorporated: 15 December 2014
Previous: Kese International Beverage Ltd
Net Worth: £60,000 Total Assets: £60,000
Registered Office: Ground Floor, 2 Woodberry Grove, London, N12 0DR
Officers: Bob Kese Kawi [1978] Director/International Alcohol Broker

Kestrel Brewing Company Limited
Incorporated: 14 August 2012
Net Worth: £2,030,652 Total Assets: £4,419,432
Registered Office: Brookfield, 105 High Street, Sharnbrook, Bedford, MK44 1PE
Parent: Brookfield Beverages Limited
Officers: Nigel Duncan McNally [1960] Director

Key Brands International Ltd
Incorporated: 3 December 2008 Employees: 3
Net Worth: £845,911 Total Assets: £1,898,084
Registered Office: 28 Landport Terrace, Portsmouth, PO1 2RG
Shareholders: Zoe Rachel Shore; Michael John Shore
Officers: Michael John Shore [1970] Director; Zoe Rachel Shore [1975] Director/Administrator

Khosla Wines Ltd
Incorporated: 9 February 2010 Employees: 26
Net Worth: £438,658 Total Assets: £1,750,464
Registered Office: 1 Warner House, Harrovian Business Village, Bessborough Road, Harrow, Middlesex, HA1 3EX
Major Shareholder: Ram Kumar Khosla
Officers: Atul Khosla [1990] Director/Manager [Indian]; Ram Kumar Khosla [1980] Director [Indian]

Kibo Wines Ltd
Incorporated: 18 June 2018
Registered Office: 26 Newbiggen Street, Thaxted, Dunmow, Essex, CM6 2QR
Major Shareholder: Martyn Pollock
Officers: Martyn Pollock [1985] Managing Director

KIC Inventories Limited
Incorporated: 8 January 2014
Previous: KIC Bottlers Limited
Net Worth: £105,320 Total Assets: £5,077,631
Registered Office: Kincardine House, Abergargie, Perth, PH2 9LX
Parent: KIC (Holdings) Limited
Officers: Jamie Walker Stanley Pringle Morrison, Secretary; Jamie Walker Stanley Pringle Morrison [1973] Director

Kicking Horse Ltd.
Incorporated: 20 September 2013 Employees: 9
Net Worth Deficit: £235,460 Total Assets: £449,312
Registered Office: Littlewood, Wood End, Marlow, Bucks, SL7 2HW
Shareholders: Thomas William Farnorth Higginson; William Bucknall
Officers: William Bucknall [1984] Director; Thomas William Farnorth Higginson [1985] Director

Kikijee Global Services Limited
Incorporated: 7 November 2018
Registered Office: Kemp House, 160 City Road, London, EC1V 2NX
Officers: Azeez Fatoye, Secretary; Kikelomo Fatoye [1974] Director/Support Worker

Kilo Wines Ltd
Incorporated: 6 July 2016
Net Worth Deficit: £628 *Total Assets:* £16,032
Registered Office: 102 Barrow Road, Quorn, Loughborough, Leics, LE12 8DL
Major Shareholder: Nicholas Kent Robinson
Officers: Nicholas Kent Robinson [1980] Director

Kilted Drinks Limited
Incorporated: 26 July 2017
Registered Office: 1 West Regent Street, Glasgow, G2 1RW

Kimbland Distillery Ltd
Incorporated: 16 August 2017
Registered Office: 53a Hertford Road, Stevenage, Herts, SG2 8SA
Shareholder: Sebastian James Anthony Aiden Hadfield-Hyde
Officers: Sebastian James Anthony Aiden Hadfield-Hyde [1985] Overseas Director

Kindman Brewing Ltd
Incorporated: 12 February 2018
Registered Office: Flat 5, 47 South Gyle Broadway, Edinburgh, EH12 9LR
Shareholders: Kyle James Naples; Lindsey Elizabeth Ross Hunter
Officers: Lindsey Elizabeth Ross Hunter [1989] Director/Computer Programmer; Kyle James Naples [1990] Director/Analyst

Kindred Spirit Partnership Limited
Incorporated: 25 May 2017
Registered Office: The Cabin, Paradise Lane, Kincardine, Alloa, Clackmannanshire, FK10 4LR
Shareholder: Murdina Anne MacLeod
Officers: Su Jung Lee [1972] Director [Taiwanese]; Murdina Anne MacLeod [1967] Director; Leigh Helen McGrotty [1973] Director

Kingdom Distillers Limited
Incorporated: 5 April 2018
Registered Office: 47 Clitheroe Avenue, Harrow, Middlesex, HA2 9UU
Major Shareholder: Jaskaran Singh Dhaliwal
Officers: Jaskaran Singh Dhaliwal [1975] Director/Entrepreneur [Canadian]

Kingdom Foods & Drinks Limited
Incorporated: 10 April 2014
Net Worth Deficit: £3,435 *Total Assets:* £240,439
Registered Office: Brulimar House, Jubilee Road, Middleton, Manchester, M24 2LX
Major Shareholder: Mousin Ali
Officers: Mousin Ali [1982] Director

Kingfisher Beer Europe Limited
Incorporated: 31 March 1989
Net Worth: £619,282 *Total Assets:* £3,646,017
Registered Office: Springfield House, Sandling Road, Maidstone, Kent, ME14 2LP
Officers: Mark Edward Davis, Secretary; Doctor Vijay Mallya [1955] Director [Indian]; Shekar Ramamurthy [1961] Director/Deputy President [Indian]; Damon William Thornton Swarbrick [1974] Director

Kingfisher Beer Ltd
Incorporated: 10 September 2018
Registered Office: Flat 3, 508 London Road, Ashford, Surrey, TW15 3AE
Officers: Ravinder Randhawa [1990] Director

Kingsbury Wine & Spirits Co. Ltd.
Incorporated: 26 November 1993 *Employees:* 1
Net Worth: £338,341 *Total Assets:* £711,068
Registered Office: Princes Exchange, 1 Earl Grey Street, Edinburgh, EH3 9AQ
Major Shareholder: Katsuhiko Tanaka
Officers: Masako Tanaka, Secretary; Katsuhiko Tanaka [1959] Director [Japanese]; Gordon Henry Wright [1963] Director/Whisky Broker

Kingsland Drinks Group Limited
Incorporated: 24 August 2004 *Employees:* 369
Previous: Marplace (Number 638) Limited
Net Worth: £10,493,000 *Total Assets:* £68,237,000
Registered Office: The Winery, Fairhills Road, Irlam, Manchester, M44 6BD
Officers: Edmund Anthony Baker, Secretary; Mark Dixon [1968] Director; Michael Forde [1964] Director; Andrew Jonathan Sagar [1959] Director; Karen Wilson [1967] Director

Kingsland Drinks Limited
Incorporated: 4 March 1994 *Employees:* 369
Net Worth: £15,792,000 *Total Assets:* £79,140,000
Registered Office: The Winery, Fairhills Road, Irlam, Manchester, M44 6BD
Parent: Kingsland Drinks Group Limited
Officers: Edmund Anthony Baker, Secretary; Mark Dixon [1968] Director; Michael Forde [1964] Director; Andrew Jonathan Sagar [1959] Director; Karen Wilson [1967] Director

Kinkell Brewery Ltd
Incorporated: 9 November 2016
Net Worth Deficit: £2,814 *Total Assets:* £10,684
Registered Office: Kinkell House, St Andrews, Fife, KY16 8PN
Shareholders: Camilla Fyfe; Rory Fyfe
Officers: Camilla Fyfe [1977] Director/Teacher; Rory John Fyfe [1976] Director/Entrepreneur

Kinkladze Limited
Incorporated: 14 September 2018
Registered Office: 349 Bury Old Road, Prestwich, Manchester, M25 1PY
Major Shareholder: William Thomas Croston
Officers: Giorgi Kinkladze [1974] Director [Georgian]

Kirker & Greer Whiskey Limited
Incorporated: 23 April 2018
Registered Office: 155-157 Donegall Pass, Belfast, BT7 1DT
Parent: Kirker Greer (Holdings) Limited
Officers: Richard Ryan [1977] Director; Pattison Steven [1979] Director

Kirklee Scotch Whisky Limited
Incorporated: 20 February 2004 *Employees:* 2
Net Worth: £1,494,371 *Total Assets:* £1,580,819
Registered Office: 14 Mirrlees Drive, Glasgow, G12 0SH
Officers: Alan William Lundie, Secretary/Scotch Whisky Blender & Broker; Alan William Lundie [1951] Director/Scotch Whisky Blender & Broker; Anne Marion Young Lundie [1949] Director/Teacher

The Kitchen Table Wine Co. Ltd
Incorporated: 5 August 2005
Net Worth: £85,697 *Total Assets:* £208,129
Registered Office: 16 Holford Way, London, SW15 5FB
Shareholder: Polychronis Pateras
Officers: Mary Elizabeth Pateras, Secretary; Mary Elizabeth Pateras [1953] Director/Wine Buyer; Polychronis Pateras [1950] Director/Shipping Agent [Greek]

Kitwave Limited
Incorporated: 24 March 1987
Net Worth: £14,011 *Total Assets:* £63,259,264
Registered Office: Unit S3, Narvik Way, Tyne Tunnel Trading Estate, North Shields, Tyne & Wear, NE29 7XJ
Officers: Patrica Ada Rice, Secretary; David Leonard Brind [1972] Director; John Frederick Hope [1969] Group Operations Director; Jay MacKay [1966] Director/Retail Manager; Ben Maxted [1983] Frozen Divison Director; Alan McCartney [1980] IT Director; David Terrence Yolland [1965] Director; Michael Young [1988] Commercial Director; Paul Victor Young [1957] Director/Accountant

Klostergut Limited
Incorporated: 22 June 1977 *Employees:* 3
Net Worth: £653,455 *Total Assets:* £732,496
Registered Office: Church Fold, Leathley Lane, Leathley, Otley, W Yorks, LS21 2JX
Major Shareholder: Jurgen Kaiser
Officers: Jurgen Kaiser, Secretary; Christian James Kaiser [1979] Director/Account Manager; Jurgen Kaiser [1939] Director/Wine Merchant [German]; Marcus Jurgen Kaiser [1975] Director/Surveyor

KLR & RCR Distribution Ltd
Incorporated: 9 March 2016
Net Worth: £12,000 *Total Assets:* £16,892
Registered Office: 120 Dundas Street, Edinburgh, EH3 5DQ
Major Shareholder: Kyle Lewis Reid
Officers: Kyle Lewis Reid [1989] Director; Ronald Chisholm Reid [1958] Director

Knight Trade (Oakham) Limited
Incorporated: 22 September 2011 *Employees:* 2
Net Worth: £309,508 *Total Assets:* £310,833
Registered Office: 2 Cold Overton Road, Cold Overton, Oakham, Rutland, LE15 7QD
Shareholders: Jane Elizabeth Knight; Stephen Knight
Officers: Jane Elizabeth Knight [1960] Director; Stephen Knight [1957] Director

Knightrate Wines Ltd
Incorporated: 4 January 2018
Registered Office: 12 Nicholas Hawksmoor Drive, Borehamwood, Herts, WD6 1AZ
Major Shareholder: Amritraj Singh
Officers: Amritraj Singh [1987] Director/Business Person

Knights Catering Impex Ltd
Incorporated: 6 October 2017
Registered Office: 41 Stoneleigh Avenue, Enfield, Middlesex, EN1 4HJ
Major Shareholder: Mesut Bayram
Officers: Mesut Bayram [1988] Director/Manager

The Knotted Vine Limited
Incorporated: 19 June 2012 *Employees:* 3
Net Worth: £6,403 *Total Assets:* £324,852
Registered Office: c/o Chaddesley Sanford, 3rd Floor, 3 Fitzhardinge Street, London, W1H 6EF
Major Shareholder: David Frederick William Knott
Officers: David Frederick William Knott [1982] Director

Koa Brewing Limited
Incorporated: 14 May 2018
Registered Office: Koa Brewing, P O Box 73694, London, W12 2GJ
Officers: Steven James Human [1988] Director/Marketing Consultant

Koha Distribution Limited
Incorporated: 12 January 2012
Net Worth Deficit: £197 *Total Assets:* £9,421
Registered Office: 5 Irving Street, London, WC2H 7AT
Major Shareholder: Fadil Maqedonci
Officers: Fadil Maqedonci [1974] Director/Restaurant Owner

Kohisar Limited
Incorporated: 27 December 2018
Registered Office: 1a Hurstbourne Gardens, Barking, Essex, IG11 9UY
Shareholders: Mohan Mal; Pesu Mal
Officers: Mohan Mal [1962] Director [Pakistani]; Pesu Mal [1972] Director [Pakistani]

Kol App Ltd
Incorporated: 22 December 2016 *Employees:* 3
Net Worth: £89,770 *Total Assets:* £93,020
Registered Office: 593 Wandsworth Road, London, SW8 3JD
Officers: Martin Louis Leon Gunther [1990] Director/Consultant [French]; Pierre Andre Lucien Nicolet [1990] Director/Consultant [French]

Kold Group Limited
Incorporated: 8 February 2013 *Employees:* 3
Previous: Kold Ltd
Net Worth Deficit: £498,631 *Total Assets:* £61,807
Registered Office: Studio 6, Fairbank Studios 2, 65-69 Lots Road, London, SW10 0RN
Shareholders: Demetre Sotiropoulos; Nicholas Sotiropoulos
Officers: Victoria Carlaw [1985] Director; Nick Sotiropoulos [1985] Director

Kolden Ltd
Incorporated: 7 January 2019
Registered Office: Brenton Court, 2 Mabley Street, London, E9 5RX
Major Shareholder: Elody Kodelne Tchuente
Officers: Elody Kodelne Tchuente [1994] Director/Restaurateur [French]

Kolson Energy Limited
Incorporated: 16 December 2014
Previous: Kolson 1896 Limited
Net Worth Deficit: £158,759 *Total Assets:* £25,939
Registered Office: Livermore House, High Street, Dunmow, Essex, CM6 1AW
Officers: Stewart Rowley [1981] Director

Konigsberg Seven Bridges Breweries Ltd
Incorporated: 12 August 2014 *Employees:* 4
Net Worth Deficit: £342,854 *Total Assets:* £342,764
Registered Office: Konigsberg Seven Bridges Breweries Ltd, Meden Road, Boughton, Newark, Notts, NG22 9ZD
Shareholders: Richard Andrew Smyth; Graham Roy Lawrence
Officers: Graham Lawrence, Secretary; Robert Mark Handy [1988] Director/Brewer; Graham Roy Lawrence [1946] Director; Richard Andrew Smyth [1962] Director

Konik's Tail Limited
Incorporated: 30 July 2009
Net Worth: £45,207 *Total Assets:* £73,119
Registered Office: 33 Cavendish Square, London, W1G 0PW
Major Shareholder: Pleurat Shabani
Officers: Pleuat Shabani [1971] Director

Koomor Brewing Company Ltd
Incorporated: 21 November 2017
Registered Office: 8 Awliscombe Road, Welling, Kent, DA16 3JT
Shareholders: Joshua Michael Morrin; Kevin Koo
Officers: Kevin Koo, Secretary; Kevin Koo [1989] Director; Joshua Michael Morrin [1989] Director/IT Administrator

Korzinka Taste of Europe Limited
Incorporated: 5 April 2012 *Employees:* 12
Previous: Global Import Limited
Net Worth: £84,898 *Total Assets:* £221,870
Registered Office: 69 Argyle Street, Boston, Lincs, PE21 8PJ
Major Shareholder: Suayp Dogan
Officers: Suayp Dogan [1983] Director [Turkish]

Kosher Wines Limited
Incorporated: 21 March 2018
Registered Office: 124 Thanet Street, London, WC1H 9QE
Major Shareholder: Sacha Anoufa
Officers: Sacha Anoufa [1997] Director [French]

Kozuba & Sons Limited
Incorporated: 25 June 2015
Registered Office: Highlands House, Basingstoke Road, Spencers Wood, Reading, Berks, RG7 1NT
Major Shareholder: Zbigniew Kozuba
Officers: Maciej Kozuba, Secretary; Jakub Kozuba [1982] Director/Manager [Polish]; Maciej Kozuba [1976] Director/Manager [Polish]

Kraft Beer UK Ltd
Incorporated: 18 March 2014 *Employees:* 4
Previous: Roku Trade Ltd
Net Worth Deficit: £204,542 *Total Assets:* £51,731
Registered Office: The Sphere, 110-112 Silvertown Way, London, E16 1EA
Major Shareholder: Tomas Lebedevas
Officers: Tomas Lebedevas [1978] Managing Director [Lithuanian]

Kramjar Limited
Incorporated: 8 March 2012
Net Worth Deficit: £2,518 *Total Assets:* £14,264
Registered Office: Sigma House, Oak View Close, Edginswell Park, Torquay, Devon, TQ2 7FF
Shareholders: The Offie Limited; Lovegate Marketing Limited
Officers: Mark Andrew Crump [1970] Director; Rajesh Hargovind Jasraj [1964] Director

KRD Distribution Company Ltd
Incorporated: 18 August 2017
Registered Office: 22 Woodgarston Drive, Basingstoke, Hants, RG22 4YJ
Major Shareholder: Kassandra Russell-Davis
Officers: Generald Russell-Davis [1957] Director; Kassandra Russell-Davis [1970] Managing Director; Nicola Walwyn [1968] Director

Kristal Spirits UK Limited
Incorporated: 23 November 2017
Registered Office: 6 Aster Close, Northampton, NN3 3XG
Shareholder: Rikul Patel
Officers: Rikul Patel [1992] Managing Director; Arun Aditya Singla [1970] Financial Director [Indian]

KRW Leisure Limited
Incorporated: 11 May 2018
Registered Office: 20-22 Wenlock Road, London, N1 7GU
Officers: Kieran Richard Walton [1994] Director/Landlord

KSS Drinks Limited
Incorporated: 11 November 1999
Net Worth: £100 *Total Assets:* £100
Registered Office: 3 Montpelier Avenue, Bexley, Kent, DA5 3AP
Officers: Pareshkumar Vinubhai Patel [1968] Director/Retailer

KT Global Ltd
Incorporated: 6 April 2017
Registered Office: 71-75 Shelton Street, Covent Garden, London, WC2H 9JQ
Major Shareholder: Kishore Shendgay
Officers: Kishore Shendgay [1973] Director

Kuchh Hai Limited
Incorporated: 25 June 2018
Registered Office: First Floor, 10 College Road, Harrow, Middlesex, HA1 1BE
Major Shareholder: Jaideep Singh
Officers: Jaideep Singh [1981] Director

Kudos Drinks Ltd
Incorporated: 25 April 2013
Net Worth: £38,964 *Total Assets:* £328,645
Registered Office: 2B Etherow Industrial Estate, Woolley Bridge Road, Hadfield, Glossop, Derbys, SK13 2NS
Shareholder: Mark Richard Littlewood
Officers: Mark Richard Littlewood [1979] Director

Kudu Food and Wine Ltd
Incorporated: 16 December 2016
Registered Office: 20-22 Wenlock Road, London, N1 7GU
Major Shareholder: Peter Brian Kettle
Officers: Amanda Dorothy Kettle, Secretary; Peter Brian Kettle [1971] Director

Kukuruz Limited
Incorporated: 10 August 2017
Registered Office: 21 Arlington Street, London, SW1A 1RN
Major Shareholder: Rashid Mohamad Ibrahim
Officers: Rashid Mohamad Ibrahim, Secretary; Rashid Mohamad Ibrahim [1953] Director

Kwik-Keg Limited
Incorporated: 21 November 2002 *Employees:* 16
Net Worth: £3,690,033 *Total Assets:* £6,776,864
Registered Office: Lynnet Leisure Group, 23 Royal Exchange Square, Glasgow, G1 3AJ
Officers: Lynn Mortimer, Secretary; Annette Hunter [1966] Director/Manager

KWM Supplies Ltd
Incorporated: 3 August 2018
Registered Office: 38 Greencastle Street, Kilkeel, Co Down, BT34 4BH
Officers: Andrew Imrie, Secretary; Andrew Imrie [1979] Director/Victualler

Kylemore Trading Ltd
Incorporated: 4 September 2018
Registered Office: 5 Eastbourne Road, London, E15 3LH
Major Shareholder: Tyrone Velinor
Officers: Tyrone Velinor [1985] Director

L H Cellar Supplies Limited
Incorporated: 17 October 1994 *Employees:* 4
Net Worth: £115,441 *Total Assets:* £347,843
Registered Office: Bishop House, 10 Wheat Street, Brecon, Powys, LD3 7DG
Shareholders: Judith Ann Jones; Derrick Jones
Officers: Derrick Jones, Secretary; Derrick Jones [1945] Director; Judith Ann Jones [1939] Director

L'Altre VI Limited
Incorporated: 29 December 2015
Net Worth: £8,437 *Total Assets:* £8,676
Registered Office: 190 Upper Road, Kennington, Oxford, OX1 5LR
Shareholders: Rachel Nuria Everett; Ruben Felix Loayza Everett
Officers: Rachel Nuria Everett [1964] Director/Self Employed; Ruben Felix Loayza Everett [1989] Director/Student

L'Atelier Terroir Limited
Incorporated: 2 October 2017
Registered Office: 31 Chertsey Street, Guildford, Surrey, GU1 4HD
Shareholders: Victoria Vladimirovna Greenhalgh; Paul Robert Greenhalgh; Mauro Azoia Sardinheiro
Officers: Paul Robert Greenhalgh [1963] Director; Victoria Vladimirovna Greenhalgh [1963] Director; Mauro Azoia Sardinheiro [1985] Director/Wine Maker [Portuguese]

L'Atypique Ltd
Incorporated: 12 September 2017
Registered Office: 11 Rosebery Court, London, EC1R 5HP
Major Shareholder: James Joseph Galbraith
Officers: James Joseph Galbraith [1980] Managing Director

L.A. Drinks Company Limited
Incorporated: 11 July 1995 *Employees:* 29
Net Worth: £1,837,901 *Total Assets:* £4,665,195
Registered Office: 3 Silverwood Industrial Estate, Silverwood Road, Lurgan, Co Armagh, BT66 6LN
Shareholders: Laurence Creaney; Ann Creaney
Officers: Laurence Creaney, Secretary; Ann Creaney [1944] Director; Laurence Creaney [1944] Director; Barry Martin McCaughley [1967] Director/Sales Manager [Irish]; Elaine Mary McCaughley [1968] Director/Manager [Irish]

La Aurora Ltd
Incorporated: 24 January 2019
Registered Office: 20-22 Wenlock Road, London, N1 7GU
Major Shareholder: Bernabe Augusto Gramajo Caballero
Officers: Bernabe Augusto Gramajo Caballero [1987] Director/Freelance Journalist [Argentinian]

La Cerveceria Limited
Incorporated: 9 January 2018
Registered Office: Kemp House, 160 City Road, London, EC1V 2NX
Major Shareholder: Manuel Padilla
Officers: Manuel Padilla [1984] Director [Mexican]

La Collina Biologica Ltd
Incorporated: 3 May 2016
Net Worth: £2 *Total Assets:* £2
Registered Office: Sterling House, Fulbourne Road, Walthamstow, London, E17 4EE
Shareholder: Francesco Cirelli
Officers: Francesco Cirelli [1980] Director [Italian]

La Delizia UK Limited
Incorporated: 26 July 2017
Registered Office: London 1st Accounting Services, 70 North End Road, London, W14 9EP
Officers: Zoe Elizabeth Andrews [1983] Director; Julia Gobert [1961] Director/Sales; Nelson Rawlins [1960] Director/Sales

La Diva Drinks & Food Ltd
Incorporated: 6 November 2008 *Employees:* 12
Net Worth: £74,692 *Total Assets:* £690,577
Registered Office: Unit 5 Catford Hill, Catford, London, SE6 4NU
Shareholders: Hasan Mustafa Ozkoc; Erol Mustafa Ozkoc
Officers: Hasan Ozkoc, Secretary; Erol Mustafa Ozkoc [1989] Director; Hasan Ozkoc [1987] Director/Marketing Consultant

La Guilde du Cognac Limited
Incorporated: 10 May 2018
Registered Office: Independence House, 84 Lower Mortlake Road, Richmond, Surrey, TW9 2HS
Parent: William Grant & Sons Investments Limited
Officers: Philip Andrew Gladman [1970] Marketing Director; Paul Geoffrey Hancock [1969] Director/Accountant; Jean-Sebastien Robicquet [1966] Director [French]; Didier Rolland [1967] Director [French]

LA International Trading Ltd
Incorporated: 20 March 2014
Previous: Rocket Chips Limited
Net Worth Deficit: £45,467 *Total Assets:* £157,658
Registered Office: 31 Abbey Parade, London, SW19 1DG
Major Shareholder: Daniel Roger La
Officers: Daniel Roger La [1984] Director

La Madeleine Wines Limited
Incorporated: 11 June 2018
Registered Office: Studio 1, 305a Goldhawk Road, London, W12 8EU
Officers: Roberto Freddi [1981] Director/Chef [Italian]; Allegra Sarah McEvedy [1970] Director/Chef; Paul Colin Warren Smith [1965] Director/Accountant

La Pata Negra Ltd
Incorporated: 26 May 2015
Registered Office: 160 Leeds Road, Lofthouse, Wakefield, W Yorks, WF3 3LR
Major Shareholder: Joseph Goiti
Officers: Joseph Goiti [1987] Director; Thomas Goiti [1985] Director

La Peira Limited
Incorporated: 1 July 2014
Net Worth: £13,345 *Total Assets:* £118,372
Registered Office: Kemp House, 160 City Road, London, EC1V 2NX
Major Shareholder: Robert Dougan
Officers: Karine Ah-Ton [1974] Director [French]; Robert Don Hunter Dougan [1969] Director [Australian]

La Vigna Vini Ltd
Incorporated: 9 November 2016
Net Worth Deficit: £14,207 *Total Assets:* £12,000
Registered Office: 13 Mary Street, Sunderland, Tyne & Wear, SR1 3NH
Major Shareholder: Fabio Rinaldi
Officers: Fabio Rinaldi [1992] Director [Italian]

La Vigneronne Fine Wines Limited
Incorporated: 15 May 1981
Net Worth: £5,658 Total Assets: £31,218
Registered Office: 2 Parkfield Gardens, Harrow, Middlesex, HA2 6JR
Shareholders: Michael William Berry; Elizabeth Jane Rosemary Berry
Officers: Michael William Berry, Secretary; Elizabeth Jane Rosemary Berry [1949] Director/Wine Merchant; Michael William Berry [1952] Director/Wine Merchant

Label Bouchon Limited
Incorporated: 8 July 2016
Net Worth Deficit: £2,789 Total Assets: £46,150
Registered Office: 51 Clarkegrove Road, Sheffield, S10 2NH
Major Shareholder: Simeon James Goodman
Officers: Simeon James Goodman [1974] Director/Self Employed Food and Beverage Consultant

Labrat Brewing Limited
Incorporated: 19 November 2018
Registered Office: 33 Bernham Avenue, Stonehaven, Aberdeenshire, AB39 2WD
Major Shareholder: Peter Douglas Erland MacKenzie
Officers: Peter Douglas Erland MacKenzie [1979] Director/Doctor

Lacons Brewery Limited
Incorporated: 27 September 1993 Employees: 62
Previous: J.V. Trading Ltd.
Net Worth: £1,250,906 Total Assets: £5,394,371
Registered Office: 3 Cooke Road, South Lowestoft Industrial Estate, Lowestoft, Suffolk, NR33 7NA
Major Shareholder: Michael Joseph Carver
Officers: Michael Joseph Carver [1968] Director; Sean Michael Gregory [1978] Finance & Operations Director

Lafferty & Sons Ltd
Incorporated: 2 October 2018
Registered Office: Alloa Business Centre, The Whins, Alloa, Clackmannanshire, FK10 3SA
Major Shareholder: Alberto Borin
Officers: Alberto Borin [1981] Director [Italian]; Claudia G Ina Gamberucci [1979] Director [Italian]

Andrew Laing & Company Limited
Incorporated: 11 March 2015
Net Worth: £100 Total Assets: £100
Registered Office: c/o Cloch Solicitors, 94 Hope Street, Glasgow, G2 6PH
Parent: The Shieling Scotch Whisky Co Ltd
Officers: Andrew Ross Crombie [1964] Director/Stonemason

Douglas Laing & Company Limited.
Incorporated: 31 March 1950 Employees: 23
Net Worth: £7,048,651 Total Assets: £11,683,044
Registered Office: Douglas House, 18 Lynedoch Crescent, Glasgow, G3 6EQ
Major Shareholder: Frederick Hamilton Laing
Officers: Alexander Melville Bisset [1961] Director/Chartered Accountant; Frederick Hamilton Laing [1950] Director; Caraline Sara Leggat [1982] Director of Whisky; Christopher George Leggat [1981] Commercial Director; Danny MacLennan [1975] Financial Director

Laing Shipping & Export Agency Ltd. (The)
Incorporated: 10 October 1950
Registered Office: Douglas House, 18 Lynedoch Crescent, Glasgow, G3 6EQ
Officers: Frederick Hamilton Laing [1950] Director

The Laing Whisky Co Ltd
Incorporated: 29 January 2013
Registered Office: 18 Lynedoch Crescent, Glasgow, G3 6EQ
Officers: Caraline Sara Laing [1982] Director/Manager

Laki & G Ltd
Incorporated: 14 December 2018
Registered Office: Kemp House, 160 City Road, London, EC1V 2NX
Officers: Gurmail Singh [1986] Director/Auditor

Lamba Trading Co. Limited
Incorporated: 1 November 1967 Employees: 10
Net Worth: £11,490,549 Total Assets: £14,359,649
Registered Office: 3 Park Square, Leeds, LS1 2NE
Shareholder: Michael Lamba
Officers: Michael Lamba, Secretary; Aaron Ishan Lamba [1988] Director; Bimla Lamba [1933] Director; Kabir Raj Lamba [1982] Director; Kamal Lamba [1957] Director [Malaysian]; Michael Lamba [1956] Director/Wholesale Grocer

Daniel Lambert Wines Limited
Incorporated: 1 April 2003
Net Worth: £28,520 Total Assets: £320,114
Registered Office: 5 Clos Iechyd, Cavendish Green, Penyfai, Bridgend, Mid Glamorgan, CF31 4BF
Major Shareholder: Daniel Sebastian Jeremy Lambert
Officers: Helen Elizabeth Lambert, Secretary; Daniel Sebastian Jeremy Lambert [1971] Director; Helen Elizabeth Lambert [1970] Director

Lamberton Whisky & Spirits Limited
Incorporated: 20 February 2012
Net Worth: £175,154 Total Assets: £191,576
Registered Office: 47-49 The Square, Kelso, Roxburghshire, TD5 7HW
Shareholders: John Charles Alexander McDougall; Patricia McDougall
Officers: John Charles Alexander McDougall [1941] Director/Manager

Lamjen Limited
Incorporated: 21 November 1980
Net Worth: £57,162 Total Assets: £101,757
Registered Office: 131 Broomgrove Gardens, Edgware, Middlesex, HA8 5RJ
Officers: Chih Pin Yoong, Secretary; Ann Yoong [1955] Director; Chih Pin Yoong [1951] Director

Lamson Wine Company Limited
Incorporated: 6 March 2018
Registered Office: Health & Energy Drinks, Bridge House, 64-72 Mabgate, Leeds, LS9 7DZ
Major Shareholder: Robert (Elias) Wilson
Officers: Robert Wilson [1941] Director (CEO)

Lanark House Investments Limited
Incorporated: 19 January 2017
Net Worth: £728,700 Total Assets: £746,812
Registered Office: 19 New Street, Ledbury, Herefords, HR8 2DX
Major Shareholder: David Michael Elliston
Officers: Mary Frances Diggins [1947] Director; David Michael Elliston [1945] Director; Margaret Ruth Elliston [1952] Director

Lancashire Beer Company Limited
Incorporated: 15 January 2014 *Employees:* 5
Net Worth: £23,071 *Total Assets:* £397,390
Registered Office: High Grain Farm, Wigglesworth, Skipton, N Yorks, BD23 4SN
Shareholder: Glen Wildman
Officers: Glen Wildman [1960] Director

Lancaster Wines Limited
Incorporated: 12 April 2013 *Employees:* 3
Net Worth: £6,229 *Total Assets:* £58,043
Registered Office: 26 St Georges Quay, Lancaster, LA1 1RD
Shareholders: Barry Peter Howarth; Fiona Mary Howarth
Officers: Barry Peter Howarth [1956] Director; Fiona Mary Howarth [1957] Director

Lanchester Wine Cellars Limited
Incorporated: 12 September 1980 *Employees:* 214
Net Worth: £5,172,519 *Total Assets:* £34,806,348
Registered Office: Unit 2 Greencroft Estates, Tower Road, Annfield Plain, Stanley, Co Durham, DH9 7XP
Shareholders: Anothony Austin Cleary; Veronica Anne Cleary
Officers: Adam Richard Black [1968] Director; Anthony Austin Cleary [1952] Director/Wine Importer; Veronica Anne Cleary [1954] Director/Human Resources Manager; Mark Anthony Satchwell [1964] Director

Lanchester Wine Sales Limited
Incorporated: 25 April 2012
Net Worth Deficit: £371,619
Registered Office: Unit 2 Greencroft Estates, Tower Road, Annfield Plain, Stanley, Co Durham, DH9 7XP
Parent: Lanchester Wine Cellars Limited
Officers: Anthony Austin Cleary [1952] Director/Wine Importer; Veronica Anne Cleary [1954] Director; Mark Anthony Satchwell [1964] Director

Land'oc Wines Ltd
Incorporated: 1 May 2018
Registered Office: 28 Main Street, Kelty, Fife, KY4 0AA
Shareholders: Jean-Michel Hubert Gauffre; Karen Gauffre
Officers: Jean-Michel Hubert Gauffre [1954] Director [French]; Karen Gauffre [1963] Director

Land's End Gin Limited
Incorporated: 15 January 2019
Registered Office: 10 Tremayne Close, Devoran, Truro, Cornwall, TR3 6QE
Shareholders: Roger Wolens; Michael Bearcroft
Officers: Michael Bearcroft [1945] Director; Roger Wolens [1940] Director

Landmark Wholesale Limited
Incorporated: 17 May 1960 *Employees:* 39
Net Worth: £2,834,511 *Total Assets:* £13,090,641
Registered Office: 3 Carolina Court, Wisconsin Drive, Doncaster, S Yorks, DN4 5RA
Officers: Andrew Mark Thewlis, Secretary/Director; Shamir Bihal [1974] Director; David Grimes [1965] Director; George Garland Hepburn [1948] Director; Sharmmila Jeganmogan [1979] Director; Manmohan Khurana [1957] Director; Geoffrey Norman John Mills [1958] Managing Director; Amaan Ramzan [1987] Director; James William Oxley Russell [1977] Director; Marcus Singh [1979] Director; Jehangir Suterwalla [1970] Director; Andrew Mark Thewlis [1964] Director; William Christopher Wilcox [1955] Director; Gurdashan Singh Wouhra [1960] Managing Director

Laneberg Wine Ltd
Incorporated: 4 September 2017
Registered Office: 20 Kingsway Interchange, Eleventh Avenue, Team Valley Trading Estate, Gateshead, Tyne & Wear, NE11 0JY
Shareholders: Marie Elise Lane; Nicholas Anthony Lawrie Lane
Officers: Marie Elise Lane [1980] Managing Director

Lang Brothers Limited
Incorporated: 25 April 2003
Registered Office: Russell House, Dunnet Way, Broxburn, W Lothian, EH52 5BU
Parent: Ian MacLeod Distillers Ltd
Officers: Michael James Younger, Secretary; Leonard Stuart Russell [1961] Director

Langstone Beer Exports Ltd
Incorporated: 26 October 2017
Registered Office: 42 Langcliffe Park, Mumbles, Swansea, SA3 4JF
Major Shareholder: Myles Anthony Langstone
Officers: Myles Anthony Langstone [1993] Director

Languedoc Imports Ltd
Incorporated: 8 March 2016 *Employees:* 1
Net Worth: £186,977 *Total Assets:* £189,497
Registered Office: Enterprise House, Beesons Yard, Bury Lane, Rickmansworth, Herts, WD3 1DS
Major Shareholder: Nicholas Robin Kent
Officers: Nicholas Robin Kent [1962] Director/Consultant

The Langwith Brewing Company Limited
Incorporated: 17 July 2015 *Employees:* 3
Net Worth Deficit: £72,226 *Total Assets:* £81,617
Registered Office: 207 Knutsford Road, Grappenhall, Warrington, Cheshire, WA4 2QL
Shareholders: David Wilson; Cathryn Mary Wilson
Officers: Stephen Michael Pownall [1983] Director; Cathryn Mary Wilson [1957] Director; David Wilson [1977] Director

Victor Lanson Brands Limited
Incorporated: 13 February 2017
Registered Office: Graffix House, Newtown Road, Henley on Thames, Oxon, RG9 1HG
Major Shareholder: Victor Barbara Lanson
Officers: Roderick Neal McLoughlin [1959] Commercial Director

Lanson International UK Limited
Incorporated: 2 February 1996 *Employees:* 22
Net Worth: £4,592,000 *Total Assets:* £18,322,000
Registered Office: 18 Bolton Street, London, W1J 8BJ
Parent: SNC Lanson International Diffusion
Officers: Nicolas Roulleaux Dugage, Secretary; Philippe Baijot [1949] Director/Chairman [French]; Paul Edward Beavis [1970] Managing Director

Lant Street Wine Company Limited
Incorporated: 4 April 2014 *Employees:* 3
Net Worth Deficit: £75,979 *Total Assets:* £301,842
Registered Office: 171-173 Gray's Inn Road, London, WC1X 8UE
Shareholders: Kate Abigail Nelson; David Roy Wilcock
Officers: Ben Mark Wilcock [1980] Director; David Roy Wilcock [1953] Director/Accountant

Lanty Slee Liquor Co Ltd
Incorporated: 26 November 2018
Registered Office: Kemp House, 160 City Road, London, EC1V 2NX
Shareholders: Joe Nichols; John Walmsley
Officers: Joe Nichols [1984] Director/Manager; John Walmsley [1979] Director/Manager

Laravita Ltd
Incorporated: 21 September 2018
Registered Office: Branksome Lodge, 4 Loudwater Lane, Rickmansworth, Herts, WD3 4AP
Major Shareholder: Irina Laravita
Officers: Irina Laravita [1970] Director/Company Manager

Largesse Corporate Gifts (2007) Limited
Incorporated: 23 January 2007
Net Worth Deficit: £77,757 *Total Assets:* £21,274
Registered Office: Unit 3 Whin Park Industrial Estate, Cockenzie, E Lothian, EH32 9SF
Major Shareholder: Donald Stuart Brown
Officers: Donald Stuart Brown, Secretary; Donald Stuart Brown [1961] Director/Self Employed

Las Bodegas Limited
Incorporated: 7 July 2004
Net Worth: £802,251 *Total Assets:* £1,302,005
Registered Office: Unit 2 Wellbrook Farm, Berkeley Road, Mayfield, E Sussex, TN20 6EH
Shareholder: Carlos Maria Criado Perez Trefault
Officers: Laurence William Webster, Secretary; Carlos Maria Criado Perez Trefault [1952] Director; Jose Luis Criado-Perez [1953] Director/Engineer; Laurence William Webster [1968] CEO/Director

The Last Drop Distillers Limited
Incorporated: 2 April 2007 *Employees:* 10
Net Worth: £280,368 *Total Assets:* £2,955,156
Registered Office: 60 Marina Place, Hampton Wick, Kingston upon Thames, Surrey, KT1 4BH
Parent: Sazerac UK Limited
Officers: Kent Broussard [1959] Director [American]; Caroline May Geraedts-Espey [1982] Director; Rebecca Lucy Martin [1958] Managing Director; Christopher Douglas Ritchie [1972] Director [Canadian]; Christopher Robin Skinger [1974] Director [American]

The Last Word Drinks Company Ltd
Incorporated: 7 August 2018
Registered Office: 27 Old Gloucester Street, London, WC1N 3AX
Major Shareholder: Prodromos Pavli
Officers: Prodromos Pavli, Secretary; Prodromos Pavli [1961] Director

Late Night Liquor Ltd
Incorporated: 29 August 2018
Registered Office: 20-22 Wenlock Road, London, N1 7GU
Major Shareholder: Sophie Savage
Officers: Sophie Savage [1992] Managing Director; Natasha Chantel Walfall [1979] Director

Late Shop Ltd
Incorporated: 5 July 2017
Registered Office: 31 Astley, Dukinfield, Cheshire, SK16 4JU
Officers: Adil Kurshid [1980] Director [Pakistani]

Latin Spirits & Beers (UK) Ltd
Incorporated: 17 March 2008 *Employees:* 4
Net Worth: £5,290 *Total Assets:* £387,787
Registered Office: Third Floor, Montpelier House, 99 Montpelier Road, Brighton, BN1 3BE
Major Shareholder: David de Souza
Officers: David de Souza [1977] Director

Latitude Wine Limited
Incorporated: 24 February 2010 *Employees:* 5
Net Worth: £69,865 *Total Assets:* £253,070
Registered Office: 5 Cherry Tree Walk, Leeds, LS2 7EB
Major Shareholder: Christopher Charles Hill
Officers: Anthony Charles Hill, Secretary; Christopher Charles Hill [1974] Director

Louis Latour Limited
Incorporated: 16 March 1990
Net Worth: £1,389,682 *Total Assets:* £5,521,704
Registered Office: 12-14 Denman Street, London, W1D 7HJ
Officers: Louis Fabrice Latour, Secretary; John Davis Clevely [1927] Director/Chairman; Eric Andre Armand Fougere [1967] Director/CFO Maison Louis Latour [French]; Louis Fabrice Latour [1964] Managing Director [French]; Richard Anthony Nunn [1963] Director Marketing; Charles William Oatley [1971] Managing Director; Bruno Nicolas Pepin [1964] Sales Director [French]; Michael Veniat [1942] Sales Director [French]

Laughing Ass Brewery Ltd
Incorporated: 20 February 2018
Registered Office: 49 Thorn Road, Hedon, E Yorks, HU12 8HN
Shareholders: Simon Paul North; Kelvin Hurd
Officers: Kelvin Hurd [1971] Director; Simon Paul North [1970] Director

The Laughing Pug Ltd
Incorporated: 10 October 2018
Registered Office: 7 King Edward Close, Shanklin, Isle of Wight, PO37 7DW
Major Shareholder: Barrie Wade
Officers: Barrie Wade [1967] Director

Laurence Leisure Limited
Incorporated: 3 May 2017
Net Worth: £186 *Total Assets:* £12,809
Registered Office: 6th Floor, Amp House, Dingwall Road, Croydon, Surrey, CR0 2LX
Shareholders: Debora Casaca; Ashley Charles Letchford
Officers: Ashley Letchford [1980] Director

Laurent-Perrier (UK) Limited
Incorporated: 10 August 1978 *Employees:* 22
Net Worth: £3,004,214 *Total Assets:* £8,502,846
Registered Office: 66-68 Chapel Street, Marlow, Bucks, SL7 1DE
Shareholders: Laurent-Perrier, S.A.; Alexandra Pereyre; Stephanie Meneux
Officers: Stephane Branislav Demetre Dalyac [1962] Director [French]; Maurice Jouan de Kervenoael [1936] Director [French]; Bernard de La Giraudiere [1931] Director [French]; Adam John Guy [1976] Finance and Operations Director; Michael David Hesketh [1958] Managing Director; Malcolm Brian Johnston Kimmins [1937] Director; Stephanie Meneux [1963] Director [French]; Alexandra Pereyre [1959] Director [French]

Laurito Ltd
Incorporated: 9 April 2018
Registered Office: 86a Elgin Avenue, London, W9 2HD
Shareholders: The Hon Damian Vesey; Jack 86a Foreman; Marco Bella
Officers: Marco Bella [1991] Director/Barista/Consultant [Italian]; Jack Foreman [1986] Director/Graphic Designer/Creative Digital; The Hon Damian Vesey [1985] Director/Auctioneer

Laurus Brands Limited
Incorporated: 7 July 2008 Employees: 1
Net Worth: £55,631 Total Assets: £114,203
Registered Office: Testwood House, Testwood Park, Salisbury Road, Totton, Hants, SO40 2RW
Major Shareholder: Mark Robert Dawkins
Officers: Mark Robert Dawkins [1970] Managing Director; Jeremy Rockett [1966] Director

Lavinia UK Limited
Incorporated: 1 November 2004
Net Worth: £1 Total Assets: £1
Registered Office: 71 Queen Victoria Street, London, EC4V 4BE
Shareholders: Charlotte Laurence Marie Servant; Pauline Claude Marine Servant; Thomas Jacques Jean Servant
Officers: Charlotte Laurence Marie Servant [1986] Director [French]

Law and Disorder Brew Co Ltd
Incorporated: 20 February 2019
Registered Office: Kitchens Bridge Cottage, Polesworth Road, Grendon, Atherstone, Warwicks, CV9 3DW
Shareholders: Simon David Watson-Burge; Alison Jayne Watson-Burge
Officers: Alison Jayne Watson-Burge [1977] Director/Publican; Simon David Watson-Burge [1983] Director/Project Manager

Lay & Wheeler Limited
Incorporated: 6 March 2006 Employees: 24
Net Worth: £3,603,000 Total Assets: £16,707,000
Registered Office: Majestic House, The Belfry, Colonial Way, Watford, Herts, WD24 4WH
Parent: Majestic Wine Warehouses Limited
Officers: Alex Iapichino, Secretary; James Crawford [1977] Finance Director; Rowan Gormley [1962] Director [Irish]; Kathryn Dibble Andersen Keating [1986] Director/Businesswoman [American]

Layered Cakes Ltd
Incorporated: 18 February 2019
Registered Office: 79 Walker Drive, Faringdon, Oxon, SN7 7FY
Shareholders: Scott Thomas Holden; Amelia Grace Holden
Officers: Scott Thomas Holden [1973] Director/Artist

Layered Ltd
Incorporated: 18 February 2019
Registered Office: 79 Walker Drive, Faringdon, Oxon, SN7 7FY
Shareholders: Scott Thomas Holden; Amelia Grace Holden
Officers: Amelia Grace Holden [1984] Director/Designer; Scott Thomas Holden [1973] Director/Artist

Laytons Wine Merchants Limited
Incorporated: 10 February 1997 Employees: 8
Net Worth Deficit: £1,971,841 Total Assets: £1,424,482
Registered Office: 43 Portland Road, London, W11 4LJ
Parent: Jeroboams Limited
Officers: Caroline Ann Hall, Secretary; Peter John Birney Mitchell [1972] Director/Sales Manager and Wine Buyer; Peter Charles Rich [1954] Director; Michael Victor Andrew Robins [1973] Director; Hugh Francis Dering Sturges [1957] Director/Chief Executive Officer

Laytons Wine Services Limited
Incorporated: 18 February 2002 Employees: 15
Net Worth: £1,570,114 Total Assets: £7,711,524
Registered Office: 43 Portland Road, London, W11 4LJ
Parent: Jeroboams Limited
Officers: Caroline Ann Hall, Secretary; Peter John Birney Mitchell [1972] Director/Sales Manager and Wine Buyer; Peter Charles Rich [1954] Director; Hugh Francis Dering Sturges [1957] Director/Chief Executive Officer

Lazy Drinks Ltd.
Incorporated: 24 July 2017
Registered Office: 6 Station View, Chester, CH2 3DT
Shareholders: Peter Jervis; Laura Jervis
Officers: Laura Jervis [1987] Director

The Lazy Hare Limited
Incorporated: 26 November 2018
Registered Office: 1 Cwrt Henri Cottages, Dryslwyn, Carmarthen, SA32 8RU
Major Shareholder: Miriam Roseanna Holmes
Officers: Miriam Roseanna Holmes [1996] Director/Equestrian Groom

Lazy Lizard Beer Company Ltd
Incorporated: 27 November 2015 Employees: 2
Net Worth Deficit: £53,768 Total Assets: £7,700
Registered Office: Ground Floor, 19 New Road, Brighton, BN1 1UF
Shareholders: Lynn Flower; David James Flower
Officers: David James Flower [1970] Director; Lynn Flower [1969] Director

LC Wine Brokers Limited
Incorporated: 13 November 2007 Employees: 3
Net Worth: £157,096 Total Assets: £219,712
Registered Office: c/o Redford & Co Limited, 1st Floor, 64 Baker Street, London, W1U 7GB
Shareholders: Camille Jaques Benoist; Leopold Ernst-Gunther Cordier
Officers: Camille Benoist, Secretary; Leopold Ernst-Gunther Cordier [1978] Director [French]

LCW (Glasgow) Ltd
Incorporated: 25 August 2015
Net Worth Deficit: £187 Total Assets: £4,762
Registered Office: 115 Rimsdale Street, Glasgow, G40 3DP
Officers: Sunil Kumar Marwaha [1976] Director

LDC Scotland Limited
Incorporated: 26 April 2012 Employees: 8
Net Worth: £270,007 Total Assets: £1,550,313
Registered Office: 29 Portland Road, Kilmarnock, E Ayrshire, KA1 2BY
Officers: Kenneth James Rose [1973] Director [Australian]; Scott McMurray Watson [1972] Director; Brian David Woods [1974] Director

LDW Wines Limited
Incorporated: 26 January 2016 Employees: 2
Net Worth Deficit: £62,616 Total Assets: £40,750
Registered Office: 1st Floor, Audit House, 151 High Street, Billericay, Essex, CM12 9AB
Shareholders: Lucy Elizabeth Whittaker; David Whittaker
Officers: David Whittaker [1970] Director/Wine Sales; Lucy Elizabeth Whittaker [1976] Director/Student

Le Bon Vin Limited
Incorporated: 11 December 2000 Employees: 27
Net Worth: £599,499 Total Assets: £1,284,345
Registered Office: 340 Brightside Lane, Sheffield, S9 2SP
Shareholders: Dianne Marie Jouan; Patrick Yves Victor Jouan
Officers: Andrew King, Secretary; Noel Hirst [1974] Director/IT Manager; Dianne Marie Jouan [1967] Director; Patrick Yves Victor Jouan [1958] Director [French]

Le Petit Wine Cellar Ltd
Incorporated: 2 October 2018
Registered Office: Kemp House, 152-160 City Road, London, EC1V 2NX
Officers: Joanna Mary Brunt [1973] Director; Peter William Brunt [1942] Director; Michael Patrick Dougan [1968] Director

Le Soula Limited
Incorporated: 22 December 2010 Employees: 1
Net Worth Deficit: £14,770 Total Assets: £1,472,643
Registered Office: Units 4 & 5 Swinford Farm, Eynsham, Oxford, OX29 4BL
Major Shareholder: Mark George Hedley Walford
Officers: Mark George Hedley Walford [1952] Director

Le Venue Wine Warehouse Limited
Incorporated: 24 October 2017
Registered Office: Unit 1B, The Iron Works, Rye, E Sussex, TN31 7HW
Major Shareholder: Louis Swann
Officers: Louis Swann [1958] Director

Le Vignoble Ltd
Incorporated: 16 February 2012 Employees: 5
Net Worth: £40,865 Total Assets: £182,526
Registered Office: New Cooperage, Royal William Yard, Plymouth, PL1 3RP
Major Shareholder: Yannick Loue
Officers: Yannick Loue [1982] Director [French]

Lea & Sandeman Group of Companies Limited
Incorporated: 17 December 2009 Employees: 35
Net Worth: £1,655,663 Total Assets: £6,227,559
Registered Office: Brooks House, 1 Albion Place, Maidstone, Kent, ME14 5DY
Major Shareholder: Charles Algernon Lea
Officers: Charles Algernon LEA [1957] Director/Wine Merchant

The Leamington Wine Company Limited
Incorporated: 1 December 2015 Employees: 5
Net Worth: £50,182 Total Assets: £147,415
Registered Office: Fulford House, Newbold Terrace, Leamington Spa, Warwicks, CV32 4EA
Major Shareholder: Anita Elizabeth Mannion
Officers: Anita Elizabeth Mannion [1963] Director

Lebanese Fine Wines Limited
Incorporated: 21 May 2010 Employees: 3
Net Worth: £32,464 Total Assets: £401,347
Registered Office: 74 Bengarth Road, Northolt, Middlesex, UB5 5LJ
Major Shareholder: Pierre Chidiac
Officers: Pierre Chidiac [1970] Director/Trade/Retail

Ledbury Wine Limited
Incorporated: 29 July 2010
Net Worth Deficit: £18,027 Total Assets: £15,976
Registered Office: Walton Cardiff Manor, Walton Cardiff, Tewkesbury, Glos, GL20 7BL
Officers: Henry Alistair Samuel Sandbach [1944] Director

Left Coast Distribution Limited
Incorporated: 2 September 2013 Employees: 1
Net Worth: £6,114 Total Assets: £7,873
Registered Office: 12 Ashling Court, Nottingham, NG2 3JA
Parent: Junkbars Nottingham Ltd
Officers: Nigel Malcolm Garlick [1968] Director

Legacy Wines & Beverages UK Ltd
Incorporated: 13 February 2017
Registered Office: 8 Bay Horse Drive, Hala Hill, Lancaster, LA1 4LA
Shareholder: Miles Andrew Corish
Officers: Samir Chaturvedi [1980] Director [Indian]; Miles Corish [1970] Director/Wine Merchant [Australian]; Kaushik Rony Ghosh [1964] Director; Sujith Sudevan Thannikkatt [1983] Director [Indian]

Legends of Drinks Ltd
Incorporated: 26 October 2017
Registered Office: 9 Margaret McMillian House, Hazellville Road, Islington, London, N19 3BW
Officers: Frank Samuel [1983] Director/Driver

Leinburn Limited
Incorporated: 7 September 2006
Net Worth Deficit: £1,400 Total Assets: £10,509
Registered Office: Alkowna, Burnside Road, Garmouth, Fochabers, Moray, IV32 7NY
Major Shareholder: David John Bremner
Officers: David John Bremner, Secretary; David John Bremner [1966] Director

Leith Distillery Limited
Incorporated: 2 December 2015
Net Worth: £1 Total Assets: £1
Registered Office: 28 Jane Street, Edinburgh, EH6 5HD
Major Shareholder: Derek Joseph Mair
Officers: Derek Joseph Mair [1961] Director/Businessman

Lemongrass and Cardamom Ltd
Incorporated: 3 September 2018
Registered Office: 49 Maskelyne Close, London, SW11 4AE
Major Shareholder: Jasper Edwards
Officers: Jasper Edwards [1971] Director/Consultant

Leo Global Limited
Incorporated: 5 September 2012 Employees: 1
Previous: Leo Wholesale Limited
Net Worth: £23,630 Total Assets: £45,485
Registered Office: Hamilton Office Park, 31 High View Close, Leicester, LE4 9LJ
Major Shareholder: Jothappar Singh Randhawa
Officers: Jothappar Singh Randhawa [1960] Director

Leo's Cash & Carry Ltd
Incorporated: 31 March 2017
Registered Office: Office 18, 4th Floor, Centenary House, 1 Centenary Way, Salford, M50 1RF
Major Shareholder: Khuram Ali
Officers: Shahid Amber [1989] Director [Pakistani]

Leomar Limited
Incorporated: 7 May 2014 Employees: 2
Net Worth: £90,165 Total Assets: £365,410
Registered Office: New Bridge Street House, 30-34 New Bridge Street, London, EC4V 6BJ
Major Shareholder: Christos Argyrou
Officers: Christos Argyrou [1952] Director/Businessman [Greek]; Leonidas Argyrou [1986] Director [Greek]; Jeremy Winslow Parsons [1962] Director

Leppelmann & Nie Limited
Incorporated: 19 July 2018
Registered Office: 209C Gloucester Terrace, London, W2 6HX
Shareholders: Zhonglun Nie; Flora Maria Leppelmann
Officers: Flora Maria Leppelmann [1992] Director [German]; Zhonglun NIE [1991] Director [Chinese]

Les Caves de Camille Ltd
Incorporated: 5 February 2007
Net Worth: £3,445 *Total Assets:* £9,568
Registered Office: 35 Magdalen Road, London, SW18 3ND
Shareholder: Olivier Michel Marty
Officers: Isabelle Branson, Secretary; Olivier Michel Marty [1964] Director [French]

Les Caves de Pyrene Limited
Incorporated: 5 May 1995 *Employees:* 46
Net Worth: £2,910,006 *Total Assets:* £12,672,123
Registered Office: Pew Corner, Old Portsmouth Road, Artington, Guildford, Surrey, GU3 1LP
Parent: Quarrymoor Limited
Officers: Amy Victoria Morgan, Secretary; Eric Serge Narioo [1963] Director [French]

Les Producteurs et Vignerons de France Limited
Incorporated: 25 September 1984 *Employees:* 5
Net Worth: £545,944 *Total Assets:* £1,083,751
Registered Office: Pavilion View, 19 New Road, Brighton, BN1 1EY
Shareholders: Denise Lavaud; Cecile Marie Lavaud-White
Officers: Madame Denise Lavaud, Secretary [French]; Denise Lavaud [1946] Director/Wine Importer [French]; Monsieur Francois Paul Andre Lavaud [1942] Director/Wine Importer [French]; Cecile Marie Lavaud White [1971] Director/Wine Importer [French]

Les Vignerons de Saint Georges Limited
Incorporated: 6 November 1974
Net Worth: £24,740 *Total Assets:* £56,136
Registered Office: Mill Cottage, Main Street, Granby, Nottingham, NG13 9PQ
Shareholders: Gerrard Vincent Price; Ann Elizabeth Price
Officers: Gerard Vincent Price, Secretary; Ann Elizabeth Price [1953] Director/Restaurateur; Gerard Vincent Price [1955] Director/Restaurateur; Barrington Philip Zarach [1943] Director/Accountant

Les Vins de Latour Limited
Incorporated: 27 December 2018
Registered Office: Kemp House, 160 City Road, London, EC1V 2NX
Major Shareholder: Emmanuel Antoine Xuereb
Officers: Maria Christoforou, Secretary; Emmanuel Antoine Xuereb [1949] Sales Director

Les Vins de Sylvain Ltd
Incorporated: 3 August 2017
Registered Office: 4 Boltro Road, Haywards Heath, W Sussex, RH16 1BL
Officers: Sylvain Roger Bertheleme [1983] Director [French]

Lesont Ltd
Incorporated: 23 August 2012
Net Worth Deficit: £18,526 *Total Assets:* £1,022
Registered Office: 3 Gowan Terrace, Newcastle upon Tyne, NE2 2PS
Major Shareholder: Tommy Liao Wenkai
Officers: Gobi Krishnan Sivagnanam [1985] Managing Director [Singaporean]

Let There Be Beer Ltd
Incorporated: 24 April 2015 *Employees:* 4
Net Worth: £4,439 *Total Assets:* £65,080
Registered Office: 39-41 The Pantiles, Tunbridge Wells, Kent, TN2 5TE
Shareholders: Geoffrey Wentworth; Josephine Downing
Officers: Josephine Downing [1971] Director; Geoffrey Wentworth [1957] Director

Levenridge Limited
Incorporated: 1 October 2003 *Employees:* 2
Net Worth: £112,246 *Total Assets:* £3,135,767
Registered Office: Lynnet Leisure Group, 23 Royal Exchange Square, Glasgow, G1 3AJ
Officers: Lynn Mortimer, Secretary; Annette Hunter [1966] Director/Manager; Lynn Mortimer [1967] Director

Leverre Ltd
Incorporated: 25 July 2018
Registered Office: Stirling House, Denny End Road, Waterbeach, Cambridge, CB25 9PB
Major Shareholder: Nathanail Kechagias
Officers: Nathanail Kechagias [1969] Director [Greek]

Levin Trading Limited
Incorporated: 23 January 2019
Registered Office: 2nd Floor, 100 Cannon Street, London, EC4N 6EU
Major Shareholder: Steve Hanlon
Officers: Daniel Hawkins [1979] Director

Levin Wines Limited
Incorporated: 12 November 1990 *Employees:* 1
Net Worth Deficit: £1,013,070 *Total Assets:* £3,382,464
Registered Office: 467 Rayners Lane, Pinner, Middlesex, HA5 5ET
Shareholders: Lynne Julie Levin; David Levin
Officers: David Levin [1935] Director/Hotelier; Lynne Julie Levin [1955] Export Director [Australian]

Lewes Gin Limited
Incorporated: 31 December 2018
Registered Office: 50 Middle Way, Lewes, E Sussex, BN7 1NL
Major Shareholder: Andrew Gary Kerr
Officers: Andrew Gary Kerr [1977] Director

Lexington Trading Limited
Incorporated: 13 November 2018
Registered Office: Lexington School Road, Earsham, Bungay, Suffolk, NR35 2TF
Major Shareholder: Jessica Lily Jackson
Officers: Jessica Lily Jackson [1990] Director/Businesswoman

Leyland Home Brew Limited
Incorporated: 3 September 2012 *Employees:* 1
Net Worth: £4,541 *Total Assets:* £41,205
Registered Office: 15 Chapel Brow, Leyland, Preston, Lancs, PR5 2NH
Shareholders: Joseph Fredrick Coulson; Joseph Fredrick Coulson; Teresa Leokadia Coulson
Officers: Joseph Fredrick Coulson [1953] Director; Teresa Leokadia Coulson [1955] Director

LGVA Solutions Limited
Incorporated: 28 July 2008
Net Worth: £16,670 *Total Assets:* £936,895
Registered Office: Unit 1 Chelsea Fields, Western Road, Merton, London, SW19 2QA
Major Shareholder: Harpreet Singh Kahlon
Officers: Harpreet Singh Kahlon [1982] Director

LHK Fine Wines Limited
Incorporated: 24 September 2009
Net Worth: £12,682 *Total Assets:* £638,997
Registered Office: 102 Fulham Palace Road, Hammersmith, London, W6 9PL
Shareholder: Thomas James Mann
Officers: Patrick Maurice Magill [1965] Director/Wine Merchant; Thomas James Mann [1978] Director

Libertine Spirits Ltd
Incorporated: 16 October 2009
Net Worth Deficit: £371,980 *Total Assets:* £45,629
Registered Office: Biddlesden Park, Biddlesden, Brackley, Northants, NN13 5TR
Shareholders: Stuart Graham Randall; Libertine Company Limited
Officers: Stuart Randall, Secretary; Stuart Graham Randall [1987] Director/Self Employed

Liberty Liquors Ltd
Incorporated: 10 May 1988
Net Worth Deficit: £2,655
Registered Office: 30 St Giles, Oxford, OX1 3LE
Major Shareholder: Patrick Julian Stephenson
Officers: Patrick Julian Stephenson, Secretary; Patrick Julian Stephenson [1955] Director/Liquor Retailer/Wholesaler [Australian]

Liberty Wines Limited
Incorporated: 17 December 1996 *Employees:* 143
Net Worth: £15,189,086 *Total Assets:* £31,104,502
Registered Office: 6 Timbermill Way, London, SW4 6LY
Officers: Luciann Flynn, Secretary; Neville Victor Abraham [1937] Director/Management Consultant; Luciann Siobhan Flynn [1965] Director/Wine Merchant; David Charles Gleave [1956] Director/Wine Merchant; Henri Louis Hess [1938] Director/Consultant [German]; Michael Sidney Hill Smith [1954] Director/Wine Producer [Australian]; Andrew Knott [1965] Finance Director; Goncalo Sousa Machado [1978] Export Director [Portuguese]; Victoria Jane Nobles [1958] Director/Consultant; Thomas Matthew Fairley Platt [1979] Sales Director; Robert John Ratcliffe [1957] Director/Management Consultant; Gary Paul Wyatt [1966] Director/Chief Operating Officer

Libra Drinks Wholesale Limited
Incorporated: 10 June 2005 *Employees:* 44
Net Worth: £905,243 *Total Assets:* £3,107,849
Registered Office: Lifford Hall, Lifford Lane, Kings Norton, Birmingham, B30 3JN
Parent: Symmons & Allen Limited
Officers: Gary Robert Beagley [1970] Director; James Hugh McMurtry [1965] Director

Library Design Studio Ltd.
Incorporated: 25 August 2017
Net Worth Deficit: £3,546 *Total Assets:* £10,388
Registered Office: 9A Five Mile Business Park, Washingborough, Lincoln, LN4 1BF
Shareholder: James Edward Cann
Officers: James Edward Cann [1991] Director/Designer; Elizabeth Mercer [1991] Director/Designer

C. & T. Licata & Son Limited
Incorporated: 6 January 2003
Net Worth: £1,186,351 *Total Assets:* £1,233,339
Registered Office: 36 Picton Street, Montpelier, Bristol, BS6 5QA
Shareholders: Stefano Licata; Carmelo Licata
Officers: Stefano Licata, Secretary/Wholesaler and Retailer; Josephine Lattuca [1957] Director/Wholesaler and Retailer; Carmelo Licata [1932] Director/Wholesaler and Retailer; Stefano Licata [1959] Director/Wholesaler and Retailer; Teresa Licata [1936] Director/Wholesaler and Retailer [Italian]

Life Science Limited
Incorporated: 30 December 1996
Registered Office: 10 Forest Vale Road, Forest Vale Industrial Estate, Cinderford, Glos, GL14 2PH
Major Shareholder: Executors of Mr Alvin Clive Matthews
Officers: David John Twiss [1975] Director

Life's A Bottle Limited
Incorporated: 9 March 2012
Net Worth Deficit: £21,752 *Total Assets:* £709
Registered Office: 9 Bonhill Street, London, EC2A 4DJ
Major Shareholder: Martin Andrew Tunnicliffe-Squirrell
Officers: Thomas Jones [1978] Director; Lucinda Jane Tunnicliffe-Squirrell [1982] Director; Martin Andrew Tunnicliffe-Squirrell [1964] Director

Lightbox Brands Limited
Incorporated: 17 December 2014 *Employees:* 2
Net Worth Deficit: £115,844 *Total Assets:* £126,227
Registered Office: Flat 1, 300 Seven Sisters Road, London, N4 2AG
Major Shareholder: Patrick O'Reilly
Officers: Patrick O'Reilly [1977] Director [Irish]

Lilley's Cider Limited
Incorporated: 12 May 2003 *Employees:* 35
Previous: Catering Leisure Services Ltd
Net Worth: £671,527 *Total Assets:* £2,567,968
Registered Office: Unit 7B, Handlemaker Road, Frome, Somerset, BA11 4RW
Shareholders: Christopher Stanley Alfred Lilley; Marc Lilley
Officers: Marc Lilley, Secretary; Christopher Stanley Alfred Lilley [1957] Director/Cater; Marc Lilley [1980] Director/Caterer

Lilo Beverages Ltd
Incorporated: 25 June 2018
Registered Office: Royd House Barn, Royd House, Almondbury, Huddersfield, W Yorks, HD4 6SX
Shareholders: Andrew Mark Schofield; Victoria Louise Marriott
Officers: Victoria Louise Marriott [1969] Director; Andrew Mark Schofield [1963] Director

Limalimo UK Ltd
Incorporated: 7 April 2018
Registered Office: Flat 15, 17-18 Meredith Street, London, EC1R 0AE
Officers: Wassihun Yimenu Tesfa [1960] Director/Business Owner

D.J. Limbrey Distilling Co. Limited
Incorporated: 10 January 2014
Net Worth: £100,976 *Total Assets:* £237,767
Registered Office: 34 South Molton Street, Mayfair, London, W1K 5RG
Shareholders: Dominic James Limbrey; Chai Lin Limbrey; 3O Limited
Officers: Chai Lin Limbrey, Secretary; Chai Lin Limbrey [1967] Director; Dominic James Limbrey [1968] Director

Limbrey's Wine and Spirits Limited
Incorporated: 2 December 2010 *Employees:* 1
Net Worth Deficit: £47,726 *Total Assets:* £63
Registered Office: 21 Bell College Court, South Road, Saffron Walden, Essex, CB11 3FA
Major Shareholder: Sean Limbrey
Officers: Sean Limbrey [1970] Director/Spirit Brand Owner

Lincoln West End Limited
Incorporated: 24 February 2010
Net Worth: £5,251 *Total Assets:* £222,606
Registered Office: The Old Reservoir, 51a Horncastle Road, Woodhall Spa, Lincs, LN10 6UY
Major Shareholder: John Charles Russel Watkin
Officers: John Watkin [1961] Director

Lincolnshire Gin Ltd
Incorporated: 15 August 2017
Registered Office: 15 Barnes Close, Sleaford, Lincs, NG34 8BF
Major Shareholder: Barbara Ann Daughtrey
Officers: Barbara Ann Daughtrey [1953] Director

Lindisfarne Limited
Incorporated: 3 June 1975 *Employees:* 18
Net Worth: £240,502 *Total Assets:* £811,398
Registered Office: St Aidan's Winery, Holy Island, Northumberland, TD15 2RX
Parent: Harry Hotspur Holdings Limited
Officers: Keith Caville Stephenson, Secretary; Ian Booth Robinson [1947] Director; Keith Caville Stephenson [1954] Director; Ronald Thomas Tait [1953] Director/Pottery Manager; Christopher Darryl Walwyn-James [1952] Director

Line Point Global UK Limited
Incorporated: 11 September 2013 *Employees:* 2
Net Worth Deficit: £47,788 *Total Assets:* £288,860
Registered Office: 16 Great Queen Street, Covent Garden, London, WC2B 5AH
Major Shareholder: Dan Shekel
Officers: Dan Shekel [1949] Director/Manager [Israeli]

Lion-Beer, Spirits & Wine (UK) Ltd
Incorporated: 15 November 2017
Registered Office: One Wood Street, London, EC2V 7WS
Parent: Kirin Holdings Co Ltd.
Officers: Elizabeth Mary Fay Davidson, Secretary; Stephanie Louise Nixon [1972] Director [Australian]; Matthew John Purcell Tapper [1969] Director [New Zealander]

Lionel Export Agency Ltd
Incorporated: 2 November 2016
Net Worth Deficit: £5,101 *Total Assets:* £15,718
Registered Office: 4th Floor, 18 St Cross Street, London, EC1N 8UN
Shareholders: Lionel Parent; Viviane Moreau
Officers: Viviane Moreau [1983] Managing Director [French]

Lioness Paw UK Limited
Incorporated: 26 September 2018
Registered Office: Kemp House, 160 City Road, London, EC1V 2NX
Major Shareholder: Serwan Tektas
Officers: Katarzyna Ropiak [1994] Director [Polish]; Serwan Tektas [1993] Director [Polish]

Liptons Food & Wine Limited
Incorporated: 20 April 1995 *Employees:* 2
Net Worth: £5,568 *Total Assets:* £45,434
Registered Office: 27 Latham Road, Bexleyheath, Kent, DA6 7NW
Shareholders: Edward John Stimpson; Kim Joanna Stimpson
Officers: Edward John Stimpson, Secretary/Director; Edward John Stimpson [1956] Director; Kim Joanna Stimpson [1958] Director

Liqueurs de France Limited
Incorporated: 27 March 2002 *Employees:* 1
Net Worth Deficit: £12,584 *Total Assets:* £15,358
Registered Office: Venture House, The Tanneries, East Street, Titchfield, Fareham, Hants, PO14 4AR
Major Shareholder: Ian George Hutton
Officers: Ian George Hutton [1955] Director/Consultant

Liquid Assets Group Ltd.
Incorporated: 2 January 2018
Registered Office: Unit 12 Trade City, Avro Way, Brooklands Business Park, Weybridge, Surrey, KT13 0YF
Major Shareholder: Jamie Moulding
Officers: Jamie Moulding [1974] Director

Liquid Brand Exports Limited
Incorporated: 9 May 2018
Registered Office: 14 Merton Drive, Derby, DE22 4JJ
Major Shareholder: Kathryn Walker
Officers: Kathryn Walker, Secretary; Kathryn Walker [1983] Director

Liquid Brand Marketing Limited
Incorporated: 17 June 2016 *Employees:* 3
Net Worth: £54 *Total Assets:* £8,177
Registered Office: 41 Great Portland Street, London, W1W 7LA
Shareholders: Marc Joseph Laventure; Brand Nation Limited; Anurag Vrat Chandan
Officers: Justin Dennis James [1976] Director; Marc Joseph Laventure [1984] Director

Liquid Indulgence Ltd
Incorporated: 8 December 2010 *Employees:* 1
Net Worth Deficit: £7,368 *Total Assets:* £85,762
Registered Office: 21 Back Lane South, Wheldrake, York, YO19 6DT
Major Shareholder: Alan Terry
Officers: Alan Terry [1949] Director

Liquid Lounge Drinks Co. Ltd
Incorporated: 6 November 2017
Registered Office: 5 Horsepool Road, Sheviock, Torpoint, Cornwall, PL11 3EP
Major Shareholder: Thomas B L Pennington
Officers: Thomas B L Pennington [1978] Director

The Liquid Market Limited
Incorporated: 15 November 2016
Registered Office: The Clock Tower, Chelwood Gate Road, Nutley, E Sussex, TN22 3HE
Major Shareholder: Brett Jamie Akker
Officers: Brett Jamie Akker [1975] Director

Liquid Measure Limited
Incorporated: 2 October 2003 *Employees:* 11
Net Worth: £437,883 *Total Assets:* £853,996
Registered Office: Cedar House, Hazell Drive, Newport, NP10 8FY
Shareholders: Jayne Williams; Michael Williams
Officers: Jayne Williams, Secretary; Michael Williams [1960] Director

Liquid Ninja Limited
Incorporated: 13 February 2017
Registered Office: Old Gunn Court, North Street, Dorking, Surrey, RH4 1DE
Major Shareholder: Christina Jocelyn Minter
Officers: Christina Jocelyn Minter [1970] Director/Consultancy

Liquid Projects International Limited
Incorporated: 9 September 2015
Net Worth Deficit: £9,578 *Total Assets:* £325,768
Registered Office: 21-22 Maiden Lane, London, WC2E 7NA
Officers: Elliot Hughes [1993] Director [Irish]; Liam Lahart [1959] Director [Irish]; Peter Mosley [1970] Director [Irish]

Liquid Solutions Distribution (N.I.) Limited
Incorporated: 20 August 2015
Net Worth Deficit: £3,384 *Total Assets:* £47,462
Registered Office: 138 University Street, Belfast, BT7 1HJ
Parent: Liquid Solutions Distribution Ltd
Officers: Alan Keane, Secretary; Killian McGrath [1975] Director [Irish]

Liquid Vision Enterprise Limited
Incorporated: 3 March 2011 *Employees:* 5
Net Worth: £333,571 *Total Assets:* £1,202,885
Registered Office: 116a High Street, Sevenoaks, Kent, TN13 1UZ
Shareholders: Monika Wodke; Maciej Wodke
Officers: Monika Wodke, Secretary; Maciej Wodke [1973] Director

The Liquor Box Ltd
Incorporated: 21 December 2018
Registered Office: 270-276 York Way, London, N7 9PQ
Shareholders: Cagdas Soguksu; Ali Sahin
Officers: Ali Sahin [1993] Director; Cagdas Soguksu [1995] Director

Liquor World Venture Ltd
Incorporated: 9 November 2017
Registered Office: 31 Yeading Gardens, Hayes, Middlesex, UB4 0DN
Officers: Kamaljit Singh Bajaj [1980] Director [Indian]

Liquor-Ish Ltd
Incorporated: 30 July 2018
Registered Office: Kemp House, 152-160 City Road, London, EC1V 2NX
Shareholders: Deepak Kumar Malhotra; Sachin Sabharwal
Officers: Deepak Kumar Malhotra [1969] Director; Sachin Sabharwal [1990] Director

Lisaavo Ltd
Incorporated: 7 March 2018
Registered Office: Unit 5 Trafalgar Court, Widnes, Cheshire, WA8 0SZ
Major Shareholder: Lisa Atherton
Officers: Lisa Atherton, Secretary; Lisa Atherton [1972] Director/Consultant

Lisbon Wines Limited
Incorporated: 25 March 2016
Net Worth Deficit: £10,158 *Total Assets:* £22,343
Registered Office: 7 St Paul Street, Chippenham, Wilts, SN15 1LJ
Major Shareholder: Victor Ribeiro
Officers: Victor Ribeiro [1975] Director [Portuguese]

Litchquor UK Ltd
Incorporated: 19 February 2015
Registered Office: c/o Gordon Dadds Corporate Services Limited, Aldgate Tower, 2 Leman Street, London, E1 8QN
Officers: Frederic Joseph Nicholas Bestel [1971] Managing Director [Mauritian]

Lithuanian Beer Limited
Incorporated: 27 March 2002 *Employees:* 7
Net Worth: £443,233 *Total Assets:* £1,208,640
Registered Office: 23a Thames Road, Barking, Essex, IG11 0HN
Shareholders: Aira Ruta Jakimaviciene; Egonas Jakimavicius
Officers: Aira Ruta Jakimaviciene, Secretary; Egonas Jakimavicius [1962] Director [Lithuanian]

Litmus Wine Agencies Limited
Incorporated: 25 July 2009 *Employees:* 1
Previous: Elevage Limited
Net Worth: £38,302 *Total Assets:* £99,063
Registered Office: c/o Witney and Co, 39 Guildford Road, Lightwater, Surrey, GU18 5SA
Parent: Litmus Wines Limited
Officers: John Robert Worontschak [1961] Director/Wine Consultant

The Little Big Wine Company Limited
Incorporated: 22 June 2011
Net Worth Deficit: £10,065 *Total Assets:* £3
Registered Office: 6 New Street, Shipston on Stour, Warwicks, CV36 4EN
Officers: Lawrence John Hall [1978] Director/Public Relations Manager; Peter Taylor [1946] Director

Little Gems Wine Ltd
Incorporated: 26 September 2013
Net Worth Deficit: £8,080 *Total Assets:* £2,720
Registered Office: 483 Green Lanes, London, N13 4BS
Officers: Robert Donald Kennedy [1938] Director

The Little Grape Company Limited
Incorporated: 13 April 2017
Net Worth Deficit: £609 *Total Assets:* £244
Registered Office: Lower Ground Floor, 40 Bloomsbury Way, London, WC1A 2SE
Shareholder: Soraya Sohal
Officers: Soraya Sohal [1982] Director/Legal Executive

Little Horse Wines Limited
Incorporated: 9 October 2017
Registered Office: 65 Woodbridge Road, Guildford, Surrey, GU1 4RD
Shareholders: Justin Bache; Tara Lawrence
Officers: Justin Bache [1969] Director; Tara Lawrence [1969] Director

Little Rock Wine Company Limited
Incorporated: 11 December 1995 *Employees:* 22
Net Worth Deficit: £154,919 *Total Assets:* £2,272,073
Registered Office: 3 Silverwood Industrial Area, Silverwood Road, Craigavon, Co Armagh, BT66 6LN
Shareholder: Laurence Creaney
Officers: Laurence Creaney, Secretary; Ann Creaney [1944] Director; Laurence Creaney [1944] Director; Barry Martin McCaughley [1967] Director [Irish]; Elaine Mary McCaughley [1968] Director [Irish]

The Little Vine Company Ltd
Incorporated: 23 June 2017
Registered Office: 267 Drake House, St George Wharf, London, SW8 2LS
Major Shareholder: Christina Dayman
Officers: Sally Anne Cook [1980] Director [South African]; Christina Dayman [1985] Director

Little White Dog Limited
Incorporated: 3 July 2018
Registered Office: Ashtree Lodge, Studley Lane, Wanstrow, Shepton Mallet, Somerset, BA4 4TG
Shareholders: Jake Michael Forth; Emily Sarah Stidwill
Officers: Jake Michael Forth [1987] Director/Project Manager [Australian]; Emily Sarah Stidwill [1988] Director/Project Manager

The Littlemill Distillery Company Limited
Incorporated: 19 July 2013 *Employees:* 3
Net Worth Deficit: £699,000 *Total Assets:* £110,479,000
Registered Office: 30 Broadwick Street, London, W1F 8JB
Parent: Loch Lomond Holdings 1 Limited
Officers: Colin Matthews [1965] Director; Richard Miles [1966] Director; Nicholas Rose [1957] Director

Liv-Ex Limited
Incorporated: 10 November 1999 *Employees:* 39
Net Worth: £4,222,000 *Total Assets:* £6,500,368
Registered Office: Studio 10, Battersea Studios 2, 82 Silverthorne Road, London, SW8 3HE
Shareholder: Henry James Pearson Miles
Officers: Simon Anthony Robert Cottee, Secretary; Simon Anthony Robert Cottee [1972] Director/Accountant; Toby Augustine Courtauld [1968] Director/Property Investor; Justin Geoffrey Gibbs [1969] Director/Sales [Australian]; Ashley Hopkins [1980] Director; Gregory Kilborn Lockwood [1962] Director/Investor [Canadian]; Anthony Terence Maxwell [1974] Director/Wine Trade; Henry James Pearson Miles [1969] Finance Director; Sir Robert Brian Williamson [1945] Director/Banker

Lizard Management Ltd
Incorporated: 19 June 2018
Registered Office: Kemp House, 160 City Road, London, EC1V 2NX
Major Shareholder: Churchill Ordor
Officers: Churchill Ordor, Secretary; Churchill Ordor [1974] Director

LJW Wholesale Limited
Incorporated: 26 April 2018
Registered Office: Unit 13 Waddington Street, Oldham, Lancs, OL9 6QH
Major Shareholder: Paul James Wakelin
Officers: Paul James Wakelin [1982] Director

Lloyds Wines Limited
Incorporated: 17 November 2015
Net Worth Deficit: £26,695 *Total Assets:* £110,176
Registered Office: Brandon House, 90 The Broadway, Chesham, Bucks, HP5 1EG
Shareholders: Simon Godfrey Lloyd; Sally Anne Lloyd
Officers: Sally Anne Lloyd, Secretary; Simon Godfrey Lloyd [1968] Director

LM Spirits Ltd
Incorporated: 3 July 2018
Registered Office: 2 High Road, Pinner, Middlesex, HA5 2EW
Major Shareholder: Gabriel Carstoiu
Officers: Gabriel Carstoiu [1985] Director [Romanian]

Loaded Spirits Ltd
Incorporated: 30 January 2018
Registered Office: 71-75 Shelton Street, Covent Garden, London, WC2H 9JQ
Officers: Sean Roche [1993] Director; Thomas Scott [1990] Director

Lobins Limited
Incorporated: 10 February 1994 *Employees:* 2
Net Worth: £2 *Total Assets:* £30,965
Registered Office: 28 College Crescent, London, NW3 5DR
Shareholders: Rinkal Shivam Ray; Shivam Champakbhai Ray
Officers: Shivam Champakbhai Ray, Secretary; Rinkal Shivam Ray [1991] Director/Teacher [Indian]

Local Beer Delivered Ltd
Incorporated: 23 October 2018
Registered Office: 609 Harlestone Road, Northampton, NN5 6NU
Shareholders: Jack Justin Whitby Hay; Harry Oliver Thornton
Officers: Jack Justin Whitby Hay [1995] Director

Loch Lomond Distillers Limited
Incorporated: 12 September 2013 *Employees:* 217
Net Worth: £30,660,000 *Total Assets:* £217,186,000
Registered Office: 30 Broadwick Street, London, W1F 8JB
Parent: Glen Scotia Distillery Company Limited
Officers: Colin Matthews [1965] Director; Richard Miles [1966] Director; Nicholas Rose [1957] Director

Loch Lomond Distillery Company Limited
Incorporated: 19 July 2013 *Employees:* 3
Net Worth Deficit: £35,812,000 *Total Assets:* £154,226,000
Registered Office: 30 Broadwick Street, London, W1F 8JB
Parent: The Littlemill Distillery Company Limited
Officers: Colin Matthews [1965] Director; Richard Miles [1966] Director; Nicholas Rose [1957] Director

Lock & Barrel Limited
Incorporated: 14 January 2015
Registered Office: Home Park, Grove Road, Bladon, Oxon, OX20 1FX
Parent: Premier Partners Ltd
Officers: Deane Michael Ingram [1970] Director

O.W.Loeb & Co Limited
Incorporated: 3 March 1938 *Employees:* 10
Net Worth: £2,442,968 *Total Assets:* £7,223,783
Registered Office: 107 Charterhouse Street, London, EC1M 6HW
Officers: Mohamad Khaled Oueida [1950] Director/Accountant

Logistic Park Ltd
Incorporated: 14 September 2011
Net Worth: £100 *Total Assets:* £100
Registered Office: 40c Princess Margaret Road, Tilbury, Essex, RM18 8RH
Officers: Arkadiusz Burkowski [1974] Director [Polish]; Dariusz Waldemar Burkowski [1975] Director [Polish]; Pawel Janelt [1976] Director [Polish]; Rafal Loba [1977] Director [Polish]

Lombard Scotch Whisky Limited
Incorporated: 19 November 1985
Registered Office: 7 Orchard Close, Calne, Wilts, SN11 8HA
Officers: Margaret Elizabeth Lombard-Chibnall [1937] Director/Retired; Richard Anthony Lombard-Chibnall [1964] Sales Director

Londinio Liqueurs Ltd.
Incorporated: 9 February 2018
Net Worth: £1,795 *Total Assets:* £1,795
Registered Office: Basement Flat, 198 Munster Road, London, SW6 6AU
Major Shareholder: Jake Coventry
Officers: Jake Coventry [1991] Director

London & Scottish International Limited
Incorporated: 18 January 1994 *Employees:* 5
Net Worth: £186,472 *Total Assets:* £836,843
Registered Office: The Old Stables, Wiggins Yard, Bridge Street, Godalming, Surrey, GU7 1HW
Officers: Stephen Andrew Bonney, Secretary; Alexander William Parker [1973] Director; Heather Patricia Parker [1941] Director

London & Scottish Spirits Limited
Incorporated: 28 July 1992
Net Worth Deficit: £256,709
Registered Office: The Old Stables, Wiggins Yard, Bridge Street, Godalming, Surrey, GU7 1HW
Major Shareholder: Christopher Ronald Parker
Officers: Christopher Ronald Parker [1941] Director; Heather Patricia Parker [1941] Director

London Ale UK Ltd
Incorporated: 27 October 2017
Registered Office: c/o Furuichoi & Co, Winchester House, 259-269 Old Marylebone Road, London, NW1 5RA
Parent: London Ale and Co.
Officers: Jee Young Ra [1987] Director [South Korean]

London and East India Drinks Company Limited
Incorporated: 28 January 2008
Registered Office: 5 St James' Road, Tunbridge Wells, Kent, TN1 2JY
Shareholders: Richard Alexander Bruce Woodhouse; Frazer Douglas Thompson; Guy Vincent Tresnan
Officers: Richard Alexander Bruce Woodhouse, Secretary; Frazer Douglas Thompson [1959] Managing Director; Guy Tresnan [1961] Director/Sales & Marketing; Richard Alexander Bruce Woodhouse [1973] Finance Director

London Barrelhouse Limited
Incorporated: 5 February 2019
Registered Office: c/o Chandler & Georges, 75 Westow Hill, Crystal Palace, London, SE19 1TX
Shareholders: Peter Charalambous; Antony Ring Davis Charalambous
Officers: Antony Ring Davis Charalambous [1976] Director; Peter Charalambous [1975] Director

London Calling Sweden Ltd
Incorporated: 5 July 2017
Net Worth Deficit: £60,341 Total Assets: £31,101
Registered Office: Railway Arch, 72 Enid Street, London, SE16 3RA
Major Shareholder: Alireza Gol Mohammad
Officers: Alireza Gol Mohammad [1979] Director/Business Consultant [Swedish]

London Cash & Carry Ltd
Incorporated: 28 August 2013
Net Worth Deficit: £178,318 Total Assets: £325,943
Registered Office: London House, 135a Hastings Road, Bromley, Kent, BR2 8NH
Major Shareholder: Intikab Idrees
Officers: Intikab Idrees [1973] Managing Director [Sri Lankan]

London Creek Limited
Incorporated: 25 July 2015
Net Worth Deficit: £2,448 Total Assets: £555
Registered Office: Unit 4 Trading Estate, Pasadena Close, Hayes, Middlesex, UB3 3NQ
Major Shareholder: Nazir Qaiser
Officers: Qaiser Nazir, Secretary; Qaiser Nazir [1972] Director/Manager

London Drinks and Beers Ltd
Incorporated: 8 August 2015
Net Worth: £67 Total Assets: £11,821
Registered Office: 10 Almond Avenue, London, W5 4AA
Major Shareholder: Marcin Kryzwda
Officers: Marcin Krzywda [1983] Director [Polish]

London Drinks Limited
Incorporated: 14 December 2011 Employees: 2
Net Worth: £31,559 Total Assets: £237,089
Registered Office: Unit 5 Bolina Road, Bermondsey, London, SE16 3LF
Major Shareholder: Folarin Olaopa
Officers: Folarin Olaopa [1979] Director/Business Manager

London Drinks Supplier Ltd
Incorporated: 29 December 2017
Registered Office: 20-22 Wenlock Road, London, N1 7GU
Major Shareholder: Ali Ulcay
Officers: Ali Ulcay [1992] Director/Mature Student

London Long Drink Limited
Incorporated: 22 February 2019
Registered Office: 208 The Chart House, Burrells Wharf Square, London, E14 3TN
Shareholders: Harri Huuskonen; Carl Strickland
Officers: Harri Huuskonen [1969] Director [Finnish]

London SCC Group Ltd
Incorporated: 6 December 2012
Previous: Unionway Investment (UK) Ltd.
Registered Office: 909 Oldham Road, Manchester, M40 2EE
Shareholder: Kwok Man Wan
Officers: Kwok Man Wan, Secretary; Kwok Man Wan [1959] Director/Building Contractor

London Spiced Dry Limited
Incorporated: 9 October 2017
Net Worth: £100 Total Assets: £100
Registered Office: 85 Eaststand Apartments, Highbury Stadium Square, London, N5 1FF
Shareholders: Steven Stellakis Kyprianou; Georgi Dinkov Radev
Officers: Steven Stellakis Kyprianou [1974] Director; Georgi Dinkov Radev [1981] Director; Samuel Benzie Robson [1986] Director [Australian]

London Wholesale Ltd
Incorporated: 11 August 2011
Net Worth Deficit: £34,585 Total Assets: £234,661
Registered Office: G5 Hastingwood Trading Estate, 35 Harbet Road, Edmonton, London, N18 3HT
Major Shareholder: Shahbaz Ali Amjad Sheikh
Officers: Shahbaz Ali Amjad Sheikh [1949] Director

London Wine Agencies Limited
Incorporated: 9 September 2009
Net Worth: £219,318 Total Assets: £276,242
Registered Office: 55 St John Street, London, EC1M 4AN
Officers: David Michael Berliand [1935] Director; Robert Jonathan Rolls [1952] Director/Wine Merchant

London Wine Eis Limited
Incorporated: 18 July 2013
Net Worth: £116,787 Total Assets: £147,513
Registered Office: International House, 24 Holborn Viaduct, London, EC1A 2BN
Officers: Andrew Gulliver, Secretary; Andrew Grant Gulliver [1961] Director/Fund Manager; Simon Antony Frederick Walker [1964] Director/Wine Merchant

London Wine Shippers Limited
Incorporated: 17 March 1995 *Employees:* 1
Previous: Christopher Wells & Co Limited
Net Worth: £24,500 *Total Assets:* £118,139
Registered Office: Bourne House, Queen Street, Gomshall, Guildford, Surrey, GU5 9LY
Officers: Stephen Michael Johnson, Secretary; Elliot James Michael Awin [1987] Director; Michael Hugh Awin [1958] Director/Wine Trader; Richard Alan Kenneth Bacon [1943] Director; Christopher Gerard Wells [1949] Director/Wine Merchant

Lonerider UK Ltd
Incorporated: 26 August 2016 *Employees:* 2
Net Worth Deficit: £82,709 *Total Assets:* £26,429
Registered Office: 1st Floor, Copthall House, 1 New Road, Stourbridge, W Midlands, DY8 1PH
Shareholders: Brand Positioning Limited; EF Enterprises; Mark Edward Charles Smith; Edward Firth
Officers: Edward Firth [1967] Director; Mark Edward Charles Smith [1974] Director

Longview Wines Ltd
Incorporated: 6 September 2006
Net Worth: £2 *Total Assets:* £2
Registered Office: Broyan House, Priory Street, Cardigan, Ceredigion, SA43 1BZ
Officers: Leon Erman Saturno, Secretary; Leon Erman Saturno [1949] Director [Australian]

Loopland Brewing Company Ltd
Incorporated: 9 February 2017
Registered Office: Flat 1, 120a Orby Drive, Castlereagh, Co Down, BT5 6BB
Shareholders: Martin Briggs; Robert Murphy
Officers: Martin Briggs [1976] Director; Robert Murphy [1968] Director

Lora Trading (Europe) Ltd
Incorporated: 13 October 2015
Net Worth: £10,726 *Total Assets:* £179,773
Registered Office: The Pinnacle, 170 Midsummer Boulevard, Milton Keynes, Bucks, MK9 1BP
Major Shareholder: Sonya Ramakrishnan
Officers: Sonya Ramakrishnan [1997] Director

Lord Krishna Trade Ltd
Incorporated: 21 October 2013
Previous: Lord Krishna Food & Wine Ltd
Net Worth Deficit: £12,584 *Total Assets:* £64
Registered Office: 3rd Floor, Pinnacle, Central Court, Station Way, Crawley, W Sussex, RH10 1JH
Major Shareholder: Shinoj Vasudevan
Officers: Shinoj Vasudevan, Secretary; Shinoj Vasudevan [1975] Director

Lord Nelson Burnham Ltd
Incorporated: 30 April 2018
Registered Office: 2 Chestnut Cottage, Bunwell Road, Spooner Row, Wymondham, Norfolk, NR18 9LH
Major Shareholder: Clare Joanne Evans
Officers: Clare Joanne Evans [1969] Director

Lordsworth Limited
Incorporated: 6 January 2017
Net Worth: £100 *Total Assets:* £100
Registered Office: Unit 17f Dominion Industrial Estate, Dominion Road, Southall, Middlesex, UB2 5DP
Major Shareholder: Priya Dhingra
Officers: Jeyalakshmi Rathmnavelu [1983] Director [Sri Lankan]; Rajvir Singh Sahota [1983] Director/Consultant

Lorelei Fine Wines Limited
Incorporated: 27 May 1983
Net Worth Deficit: £30,573 *Total Assets:* £4,032
Registered Office: Rookery Farm, Nyetimber, W Sussex, PO21 3PY
Major Shareholder: Joerg Gottlob Paul-Heinz Arnhold
Officers: Sally Arnhold, Secretary; Joerg Gottlob Paul-Heinz Arnhold [1947] Director/Salesman [German]

Los Perros Sueltos Brewing Co Ltd
Incorporated: 19 February 2019
Registered Office: 20 South Mill Court, Southmill Road, Bishop's Stortford, Herts, CM23 3DA
Shareholders: Dominick Chad Hollinshead; Marco Biga; Francesco Lo Bue
Officers: Dominick Chad Hollinshead [1979] Director; Francesco Lo Bue [1992] Director/Brewer [Italian]

Lost and Found Taprooms Ltd
Incorporated: 18 April 2017
Registered Office: 168 Church Road, Hove, E Sussex, BN3 2DL
Shareholders: Simon John Checkley; Christopher Anthony Angelkov; Jonathan David Rutter
Officers: Christopher Anthony Angelkov [1974] Director; Simon John Checkley [1973] Director

The Lost Distillery Company Limited
Incorporated: 27 August 2013
Registered Office: 29 Portland Street, Kilmarnock, E Ayrshire, KA1 2BY
Shareholders: Scott McMurray Watson; Crucial Brands Holdings Limited; Brian David Woods
Officers: Scott McMurray Watson [1972] Director; Brian David Woods [1974] Director

Lost Rivers Beer Company Limited
Incorporated: 22 May 2018
Registered Office: Top Floor, Claridon House, London Road, Stanford-le-Hope, Essex, SS17 0JU
Major Shareholder: Barry Cross
Officers: Barry Cross [1971] Director

Lothbury Wine Shippers Limited
Incorporated: 19 January 1984
Registered Office: 3 Canonium Mews, Kelvedon, Colchester, Essex, CO5 9EF
Officers: Anne Metzger, Secretary; Anne Metzger [1942] Director/Secretary; Geoffrey Hugh Metzger [1941] Director/Retired; Lynne Watts [1951] Director/Secretary; Peter Watts [1943] Director/Wine Importer

Lough Neagh Distillers - 1837 Ltd
Incorporated: 26 November 2018
Registered Office: Inverlodge, 51 Bannfoot Road, Derrytrasna, Co Armagh, BT66 6PH
Major Shareholder: Vernon Fox
Officers: Vernon Fox [1973] Director [Irish]

Loughborough Student Services Limited
Incorporated: 29 March 1985
Net Worth: £166,056 *Total Assets:* £414,904
Registered Office: Union Building, Ashby Road, Loughborough, Leics, LE11 3TT
Shareholder: Paul Jonathan Barlow
Officers: Gary Chamberlain, Secretary; Fraser Barclay [1996] Director/Student; Paul Jonathan Barlow [1964] Director/Deputy General Manager; Sam Hanys [1996] Director/Union Executive Officer; Rahul Mathasing [1994] Director/Student; Trevor Andrew Page [1965] Union Director; Rory Pears [1996] Director/Student Executive Officer

Lounge Spirits Ltd
Incorporated: 4 July 2018
Registered Office: Manor House, Rectory Lane, Holcot, Northampton, NN6 9SR
Shareholders: Jason Stanley King; Emma Jane King
Officers: Emma Jane King [1975] Director; Jason Stanley King [1974] Director

Love and Labour Ltd.
Incorporated: 3 February 2017
Net Worth: £1,845 *Total Assets:* £8,837
Registered Office: 14 West Street, Shipston on Stour, Warwicks, CV36 4HD
Shareholders: Katie Scott; James Jensen
Officers: James Jensen [1986] Director/Operations Manager; Katie Scott [1989] Director/Operations Manager

Low-Key Essentials Ltd
Incorporated: 13 August 2018
Registered Office: 55 Henley Drive, Swindon, Wilts, SN6 7JU
Major Shareholder: Siddanta Pun
Officers: Siddanta Pun [1990] Director/Chief Executive

Thomas Lowndes & Co. Limited
Incorporated: 11 January 1935
Registered Office: 2 Longwalk Road, Stockley Park, Uxbridge, Middlesex, UB11 1BA
Parent: Beam Suntory UK Holdings Limited
Officers: Nadim Assi [1967] Director/CFO International [Canadian]; Madame Del Pino Bermudez de La Puente Sanchez-Aguilera [1974] Director/Associate General Counsel [Spanish]

Loxwood Meadworks Ltd
Incorporated: 7 June 2018
Registered Office: The Shed, 54 Oakfield Road, London, N14 6LX
Major Shareholder: Daniel Joseph Bacon
Officers: Daniel Joseph Bacon [1985] Director

Loyalty Wines Limited
Incorporated: 1 June 2016
Registered Office: House of Initiatives, 19 Elers Road, London, W13 9QB
Major Shareholder: Rodger Shiak Burns Craig
Officers: Rodger Shiak Burns Craig [1954] Director

Lpower Ltd
Incorporated: 8 May 2018
Registered Office: 22 South Road, Liverpool, L22 5PQ
Officers: Lee Power [1977] Director/Manager

Luca Wine Limited
Incorporated: 18 July 2017
Registered Office: Cotton Court, Church Street, Preston, Lancs, PR1 3BY
Major Shareholder: Luca Miserere
Officers: Luca Miserere [1968] Director/Wine Importer [Italian]

Lucky Drinks 4 U Ltd
Incorporated: 2 October 2007 *Employees:* 1
Net Worth Deficit: £1,408 *Total Assets:* £39,644
Registered Office: Unit 1151 Business & Innovation Centre, Sunderland Enterprise Park, Sunderland, Tyne & Wear, SR5 2TA
Major Shareholder: Satnam Singh
Officers: Satnam Singh [1972] Director

Lucky Spirits Ltd
Incorporated: 13 March 2012
Net Worth Deficit: £140,859 *Total Assets:* £10,367
Registered Office: 114a Bellegrove Road, Welling, Kent, DA16 3QR
Major Shareholder: Vladimir Samokhvalov
Officers: Vladimir Samokhvalov [1981] Director [Russian]

The Lucky Strike Pub Company Ltd
Incorporated: 2 October 2018
Registered Office: Tam O'Shanter, Ceder Drive, Gillway, Tamworth, Staffs, B79 8QL
Officers: Natalie Price [1991] Director/Manager

Lunzer Wine Group Limited
Incorporated: 9 July 2015
Net Worth: £9,294 *Total Assets:* £49,915
Registered Office: 1 Morley Road, Twickenham, Middlesex, TW1 2HG
Shareholder: Peter Anthony Lunzer
Officers: Anna-Sofia Ulrika Lunzer [1972] Director/Marketing Consultant [Swedish]; Peter Anthony Lunzer [1959] Director/Wine Consultant

Lupe's Imports Limited
Incorporated: 19 April 2018
Registered Office: 204-206 Cardigan Road, Leeds, LS6 1LF
Shareholders: Tansy Louise Garcia; Leon Rodolfo Garcia
Officers: Leon Rodolfo Garcia [1968] Director/Chef; Tansy Louise Garcia [1969] Director/Waiter

Lupton Wine Limited
Incorporated: 29 August 2012
Net Worth: £12,622 *Total Assets:* £40,358
Registered Office: The Weirs, Chilton Foliat, Hungerford, Berks, RG17 0TG
Major Shareholder: Mark Robertson
Officers: Mark Robertson [1974] Director/Wine Merchant

Lush Wines Ltd
Incorporated: 23 October 2017
Registered Office: 21 Heol Caradog, Fishguard, Pembrokeshire, SA65 9AY
Shareholders: Martin Robert Alan Kiss; Alastair Huw Davies
Officers: Alastair Huw Davies [1975] Managing Director; Martin Robert Alan Kiss [1961] Director

Lust Promotions Ltd
Incorporated: 19 October 2009
Net Worth: £1,588 *Total Assets:* £3,062
Registered Office: Penny Lane Business Centre, 374 Smithdown Road, Liverpool, L15 5AN
Major Shareholder: Simon Neale Davies
Officers: Simon Neale Davies, Secretary; Simon Neale Davies [1972] Director/Sales Manager; Hayley Keogh [1984] Director/Florist

Lusus Wines Ltd
Incorporated: 14 December 2018
Registered Office: 7 Princes Court, Billericay, Essex, CM12 0FH
Shareholders: Alexis Ross Baker; Claire Louise Baker
Officers: Alexis Ross Baker [1981] Director; Claire Louise Baker [1982] Director

Lux Ex Dignitas Limited
Incorporated: 29 October 2018
Registered Office: 45 Cavendish Gardens, Barking, Essex, IG11 9DU
Major Shareholder: Igor Butucel
Officers: Igor Butucel [1995] Director/Crane Supervisor [Romanian]

Luxury Alcohols Limited
Incorporated: 14 December 2010
Net Worth: £10,180 *Total Assets:* £10,180
Registered Office: 14 Derncleugh Gardens, Dawlish, Devon, EX7 0JG
Shareholder: Solomon Ani
Officers: Joshua Solomon Ani [1984] Director; Solomon Ani [1954] Director

Luxury Gourmet Ltd
Incorporated: 14 May 2018
Registered Office: 20-22 Wenlock Road, London, N1 7GU
Major Shareholder: Andrea Melis
Officers: Andrea Melis [1976] Director/Chef [Italian]

LVB Limited
Incorporated: 31 January 2017
Net Worth: £173,610 *Total Assets:* £182,668
Registered Office: New Cooperage, Royal William Yard, Plymouth, PL1 3RP
Major Shareholder: Yannick Loue
Officers: Yannick Loue [1982] Director [French]

LWC Drinks Limited
Incorporated: 21 June 2011 *Employees:* 724
Net Worth: £31,397,912 *Total Assets:* £72,563,552
Registered Office: Unit 3 Stainburn Road, Openshaw, Manchester, M11 2DN
Parent: Licensed Wholesale Company Limited
Officers: Peter Douglas Sumner, Secretary; Robin MacEwan Gray [1951] Director; Ebrahim Kassam Mukadam [1957] Director

Lynch Associates Ltd
Incorporated: 21 May 2010
Net Worth: £46,897 *Total Assets:* £63,078
Registered Office: St George's House, 215-219 Chester Road, Manchester, M15 4JE
Officers: Fiona Lynch [1966] Director/Engineering Geologist; Jonathan Richard Lynch [1970] Director/Engineering Geologist

Lyndon Drinks Limited
Incorporated: 12 June 2014
Net Worth: £1,920,185 *Total Assets:* £2,080,058
Registered Office: Hudson Court, Stane Close, London, SW19 2XQ
Officers: Aidan Turner [1983] Director/Manager

Lytham Brewery Limited
Incorporated: 25 September 2007 *Employees:* 4
Net Worth Deficit: £61,361 *Total Assets:* £107,621
Registered Office: Unit 2 Olympic Court, Whitehills Business Park, Blackpool, Lancs, FY4 5GU
Major Shareholder: James Anthony Booker
Officers: James Anthony Booker, Secretary; Andrew Mark Booker [1964] Director/Manager; James Anthony Booker [1987] Director/Brewer; Julie Louise Booker [1965] Director/Manager

M & B Distributions (UK) Ltd
Incorporated: 29 May 2013
Net Worth: £10,753 *Total Assets:* £12,573
Registered Office: 5 Martinbridge Industrial Estate, Lincoln Road, Enfield, Middlesex, EN1 1SP
Major Shareholder: Zenel Bytyqi
Officers: Zenel Bytyqi [1964] Director/Businessman

M & M Community Development Initiatives Limited
Incorporated: 24 April 2015
Registered Office: Suite 2, Stewart House, 56 Longbridge Road, Barking, Essex, IG11 8RW
Shareholder: Prince Michael Waddy Adjei-Ampofo
Officers: Margaret Naa Ode Kwafo, Secretary; Prince Michael Waddy Adjei-Ampofo [1969] Director/Project Manager

M & M Romanian Imports Ltd
Incorporated: 6 February 2019
Registered Office: 48-52 Penny Lane, Mossley Hill, Liverpool, L18 1DG
Shareholders: Franco Andres Meza; Ionut Mitrache
Officers: Franco Andres Meza [1974] Director; Ionut Mitrache [1989] Director [Romanian]

M & P Diffusion Limited
Incorporated: 8 March 2004
Net Worth: £1,000 *Total Assets:* £1,000
Registered Office: 6 Clarewood House, Clarewood, Drive, Camberley, Surrey, GU15 3TE
Shareholders: Matthew David Bowden; Phillipe Naon
Officers: Matthew David Bowden, Secretary; Matthew David Bowden [1968] Director

M & T Wholesale Ltd
Incorporated: 17 February 2003
Net Worth: £35,974 *Total Assets:* £147,750
Registered Office: Bridge House, 9-13 Holbrook Lane, Coventry, Warwicks, CV6 4AD
Major Shareholder: Tejaswir Jagdishbhai Patel
Officers: Tejaswir Jagdishbhai Patel [1966] Director [British/Indian]

M D (Cash & Carry) Limited
Incorporated: 17 June 2014
Net Worth Deficit: £35,896 *Total Assets:* £44,579
Registered Office: Unit 3 Palm Court, Nottingham, NG7 7HU
Major Shareholder: Mahir Deniz
Officers: Mahir Deniz [1977] Director

M M General Merchandise Ltd
Incorporated: 7 February 2018
Registered Office: 144 Cranford High Street, Cranford, Hounslow, Middlesex, TW5 9WB
Officers: Van Der Klugt Hermanus Jacobus Maria [1957] Director [Dutch]

M Wines Limited
Incorporated: 16 August 2016
Registered Office: 71-75 Shelton Street, Covent Garden, London, WC2H 9JQ
Major Shareholder: Mark Parrett
Officers: Mark Parrett, Secretary; Mark Parrett [1963] Finance Director

M.& M.Value Limited
Incorporated: 17 March 1960 *Employees:* 44
Net Worth: £1,656,882 *Total Assets:* £16,719,293
Registered Office: Unit S3, Narvik Way, Tyne Tunnel Trading Estate, North Shields, Tyne & Wear, NE29 7XJ
Officers: Patricia Ada Rice, Secretary; David Leonard Brind [1972] Finance Director; John Frederick Hope [1969] Group Operations Director; Patricia Ada Rice [1951] Director/Accountant; Stephen Rycroft [1963] Director/Buyer; Linda Jayne Wilson [1963] Director; Paul Victor Young [1957] Director/Accountant

MA Wine and Spirit Imports Limited
Incorporated: 4 February 2016
Net Worth Deficit: £37,725 *Total Assets:* £10,055
Registered Office: Jubilee House, East Beach, Lytham St Annes, Lancs, FY8 5FT
Major Shareholder: Mel Abert
Officers: Mel Abert [1970] Director [American]

James MacArthur & Co Limited
Incorporated: 15 October 1982 *Employees:* 1
Net Worth: £34,340 *Total Assets:* £47,982
Registered Office: 343 Kelvindale Road, Glasgow, G12 0QU
Shareholder: Arthur Hamilton Brown Winning
Officers: Mary MacArthur Winning, Secretary; Arthur Hamilton Brown Winning [1941] Director

Simon Mace Wine Broking Limited
Incorporated: 31 January 1997 *Employees:* 1
Net Worth Deficit: £471,395 *Total Assets:* £3,594
Registered Office: 83 Cambridge Street, Pimlico, London, SW1V 4PS
Shareholder: Simon Paul Mace
Officers: Andrew Peter Charles Fox, Secretary; Simon Paul Mace [1970] Director/Wine Broker

Tom MacFarlane and Company Limited
Incorporated: 6 April 1983 *Employees:* 2
Net Worth: £7,741,087 *Total Assets:* £8,903,972
Registered Office: 2 Otterburn Drive, Giffnock, Glasgow, G46 6UJ
Major Shareholder: Scott Robertson MacFarlane
Officers: Leigh MacFarlane, Secretary; Scott Robertson MacFarlane [1971] Director; Leigh McFarlane [1971] Director

Ian MacLeod and Company Limited
Incorporated: 24 May 1966
Registered Office: Russell House, Dunnet Way, Broxburn, W Lothian, EH52 5BU
Parent: Ian MacLeod Distillers
Officers: Michael James Younger, Secretary; Angela Mary Russell [1965] P.R. Director; David William Hodder Russell [1940] Director/Whisky Broker; Edith Stuart Russell [1932] Director/Housewife; Leonard Stuart Russell [1961] Marketing Director; Peter James Sidney Russell [1927] Director/Whisky Broker

Ian MacLeod Distillers Limited
Incorporated: 26 November 1957 *Employees:* 153
Net Worth: £62,203,000 *Total Assets:* £145,944,992
Registered Office: Russell House, Dunnet Way, Broxburn, W Lothian, EH52 5BU
Shareholders: Leonard Stuart Russell; Leonard Stuart Russell and Others as Trustees of The Leonard Stuart Russell 2003 Family Trust
Officers: Michael James Younger, Secretary; Gordon John Doctor [1959] Director/Whisky Blender; Richard William Farrar [1958] Director; Laura Agnes Anne Rankine [1979] HR Director; Angela Mary Russell [1965] P.R. Director; David William Hodder Russell [1940] Director/Whisky Broker; Edith Stuart Russell [1932] Director/Housewife; Leonard Stuart Russell [1961] Managing Director; Peter James Sidney Russell [1927] Director/Whisky Broker; Ian Alexander Shackleton [1965] Sales Director; Michael James Younger [1960] Finance Director

The Mad Batchers Ltd
Incorporated: 15 October 2018
Registered Office: 2B North Avenue, Exeter, EX1 2DU
Shareholders: Christy Shane Ormandy; Sam Robert Mooney
Officers: Sam Robert Mooney [1994] Director/Financial Adviser; Christy Shane Ormandy [1993] Director/Chef

Made in Little France Import Limited
Incorporated: 27 October 2014 *Employees:* 2
Net Worth: £17,142 *Total Assets:* £118,612
Registered Office: 397 St John Street, London, EC1V 4LD
Major Shareholder: Maxence Masurier
Officers: Maxence Masurier [1980] Director [French]

Made To Measure Ltd
Incorporated: 12 February 2019
Registered Office: The Old Jolly Farmers, Wood Dalling, Norwich, NR11 6AQ
Shareholders: Jonathan Robert Boyd; Fergus Christopher Partridge; Sarah Penelope Briggs
Officers: Jonathan Robert Boyd [1961] Director [Irish]; Sarah Penelope Briggs [1963] Director; Fergus Christopher Partridge [1968] Director

The Madison Drinks Company Limited
Incorporated: 26 July 1996
Net Worth: £10,000 *Total Assets:* £10,000
Registered Office: Unit 3 Venus House, 62 Garman Road, London, N17 0UT
Parent: Aotearoa Distribution Ltd
Officers: Pantelis Christoforou [1970] Director; Kerry Michael [1959] Director

Maestral de Provence Ltd.
Incorporated: 13 June 2017
Registered Office: 12 Ryecroft Street, London, SW6 3TT
Major Shareholder: Stuart Hamilton
Officers: Stuart Hamilton [1993] Director/Entrepreneur [French]

Maestrale Group Ltd
Incorporated: 29 September 2017
Registered Office: 11 Wingford Road, London, SW2 4DR
Shareholders: Vincenzo Mugnano; Alessio de Laureto
Officers: Alessio de Laureto [1986] Director [Italian]; Maria Mugnano [1992] Director [Italian]; Vincenzo Mugnano [1984] Director [Italian]

Magazin Romanesc Ltd
Incorporated: 20 December 2018
Registered Office: 582 Green Lane, Birmingham, B9 5QG
Officers: Cezar Darius Gheorghe [2000] Director/Shopkeeper [Romanian]

Magenta Wine Investors Limited
Incorporated: 20 August 2009
Net Worth: £67,760 *Total Assets:* £618,649
Registered Office: 47 Marylebone Lane, London, W1U 2NT
Shareholders: Shahram David Elghanayan; Roger Metta; Jimmy Metta
Officers: Shahram David Elghanayan [1975] Director; Jimmy Metta [1980] Director; Roger Metta [1973] Director

Magic F & F Ltd
Incorporated: 16 August 2017
Registered Office: Brasserie Chalon, 12 Barrow Street, St Helens, Merseyside, WA10 1RX
Officers: Rob Freeman [1979] Director/Licensee

Magic Spells Brewery Limited
Incorporated: 10 October 2016
Net Worth Deficit: £32,764 *Total Assets:* £17,236
Registered Office: 24 Rigg Approach, Leyton, London, E10 7QN
Major Shareholder: Jasdip Hare
Officers: Jasdip Hare [1976] Director

Magik Drinks Limited
Incorporated: 30 July 2004
Net Worth: £67,065 *Total Assets:* £100,361
Registered Office: Polhill Business Centre, London Road, Polhill, Halstead, Kent, TN14 7AA
Major Shareholder: Daljit Kaur Dhanoa
Officers: Daljit Kaur Dhanoa, Secretary; Harinder Paul Singh Dhanoa [1966] Director/Businessman

Magma Liquid Ltd
Incorporated: 14 September 2018
Registered Office: Royal Hotel, Market Place, Kettering, Northants, NN16 0AJ
Major Shareholder: Balraj Puni
Officers: Balraj Puni [1968] Director/Owner

Magna Juice Ltd
Incorporated: 21 June 2018
Registered Office: 20-22 Wenlock Road, London, N1 7GU
Officers: Zavon Miller [1990] Director/Self Employed [Zimbabwean]; Tapiwa Tutisani [1992] Director/Marketing Executive

Magnate Drinks Ltd
Incorporated: 23 April 2014
Registered Office: 164 Albion Street, Wolverhampton, W Midlands, WV1 3EJ
Major Shareholder: Patryk Stanislaw Konaszczuk
Officers: Patryk Stanislaw Konaszczuk [1990] Director [Polish]

Magnetic Brands Limited
Incorporated: 12 December 2016
Net Worth Deficit: £25,531 *Total Assets:* £102,269
Registered Office: 36 London Road, Braintree, Essex, CM7 2LG
Shareholder: Matthew Charles William McKee
Officers: Matthew Charles William McKee [1972] Commercial Director

Magnus Wines Ltd
Incorporated: 4 May 2018
Registered Office: 45 Horsford Road, London, SW2 5BP
Officers: Duncan McCredie [1980] Director/Banker

Maha Cash & Carry Ltd
Incorporated: 9 February 2015
Net Worth Deficit: £178,623 *Total Assets:* £72,802
Registered Office: Unit 9P, Kynoch Road, Eley Estate, Edmonton, London, N18 3BD
Major Shareholder: Nagarajan Kandeepan
Officers: Nagarajan Kandeepan [1979] Director [Sri Lankan]

Maha Wholesale Ltd
Incorporated: 29 August 2018
Registered Office: 72 Christchurch Road, London, SW19 2PB
Major Shareholder: Vijayakumaran Mahalingam
Officers: Vijayakumaran Mahalingam [1969] Director/Manager [Swiss]

Mahal Enterprises Limited
Incorporated: 7 March 2013
Net Worth: £3,974 *Total Assets:* £46,032
Registered Office: 8 Humber Road, Beeston, Nottingham, NG9 2EF
Major Shareholder: Harjinder Singh Mahal
Officers: Harjinder Singh Mahal [1963] Director

Mahar Associates Ltd
Incorporated: 29 November 2018
Registered Office: Kemp House, 160 City Road, London, EC1V 2NX
Officers: Aijaz Ahmed Mahar [1987] Director/Retail

Maharaja & Sons Ltd
Incorporated: 27 February 2018
Registered Office: 36 Cemetery Road, Bradford, BD8 9RY
Major Shareholder: Jasvinder Pal Singh
Officers: Jasvinder Pal Singh [1964] Director

Maiden Wines Limited
Incorporated: 16 November 2018
Registered Office: Kemp House, 160 City Road, London, EC1V 2NX
Shareholders: Stanislav Ciobanu; James Legg
Officers: Stanislav Ciobanu [1985] Director [Romanian]; James Legg [1986] Director

Maidenhead Wine Company Limited
Incorporated: 17 July 2002 *Employees:* 15
Net Worth: £1,052,585 *Total Assets:* £2,823,087
Registered Office: The Vineyard, Cordwallis Street, Maidenhead, Berks, SL6 7BE
Officers: Susan Elizabeth Warner, Secretary; Roland Street [1957] Director/Wine Wholesaler

Mail-a-Wine Limited
Incorporated: 20 February 2019
Registered Office: 6 Lawrence Road, London, SE25 5AA
Major Shareholder: Afamdi Maduabuchi Unaka
Officers: Afamdi Maduabuchi Unaka [1976] Director

Main Rum Company Limited (The)
Incorporated: 13 September 1984 *Employees:* 4
Net Worth: £4,296,208 *Total Assets:* £5,558,230
Registered Office: 46 Hamilton Square, Birkenhead, Merseyside, CH41 5AR
Parent: E & A Scheer BV
Officers: Christine Margaret Southern, Secretary; Ian William Smith [1974] Managing Director; Eric Edward Strahan [1949] Director; Carsten Erik Vlierboom [1964] Director [Dutch]

Main Sail Trading Company Limited
Incorporated: 1 May 2002
Net Worth Deficit: £11,382 Total Assets: £39,151
Registered Office: The White House, Clifton Marine Parade, Gravesend, Kent, DA11 0DY
Shareholder: Ian Ledger
Officers: Antony John Ould, Secretary; Christopher Peter Bowen [1960] Director

Maison du Vin Ltd
Incorporated: 25 February 2015
Net Worth: £16,582 Total Assets: £35,822
Registered Office: 22 Market Place, Malton, N Yorks, YO17 7LX
Major Shareholder: Matthew Beevers
Officers: Matthew Beevers, Secretary; Matthew Beevers [1984] Director

Maison Liedberg Limited
Incorporated: 12 February 2001
Net Worth: £33,322 Total Assets: £41,001
Registered Office: Avaland House, 110 London Road, Hemel Hempstead, Herts, HP3 9SD
Shareholders: Harry Billy Winks; N & D Project Management Limited; Nicolas David Ryman
Officers: Nigel James Palmer [1967] Managing Director; Nicolas David Ryman [1976] Director

Maison Maurice Limited
Incorporated: 21 January 1977 Employees: 35
Net Worth: £5,183,348 Total Assets: £6,645,845
Registered Office: K1-K5 Northfleet Industrial Estate, Lower Road, Northfleet, Gravesend, Kent, DA11 9BL
Shareholders: Adrian John Sundin; Jonathan Mark Sundin
Officers: Jonathan Mark Sundin, Secretary; Adrian John Sundin [1955] Director/Executive; Jonathan Mark Sundin [1956] Director/Executive

Maison Sassy UK Limited
Incorporated: 19 March 2018
Registered Office: 15-19 Great Titchfield Street, London, W1W 8AZ
Shareholders: Pierre Jourdren; Xavier D'Audiffret-Pasquier
Officers: Xavier D'Audiffret-Pasquier [1988] Director [French]; Aymeric Perret [1989] Director [French]

Maison Shane et Filles Ltd
Incorporated: 22 August 2018
Registered Office: 8 Nelson Place West, Bath, BA1 2SP
Major Shareholder: Shane Egan
Officers: Shane Egan [1969] Director/Company Secretary [Irish]

Maisons Marques et Domaines Limited
Incorporated: 16 July 1985 Employees: 17
Net Worth: £1,424,872 Total Assets: £7,306,545
Registered Office: 9A Compass House, Smugglers Way, London, SW18 1DB
Officers: Stuart Cole, Secretary; Alain Beydon [1946] Director [French]; Richard Edward Billett [1968] Managing Director; Stuart Cole [1955] Director/Chartered Accountant; Erwan Faiveley [1979] Director/Wine Producer [French]; Frederic Heidsieck [1957] Export Director [French]; Frederick Rouzaud [1967] Director [French]

Majestic Wine PLC
Incorporated: 28 July 1988 Employees: 1,528
Net Worth: £121,761,000 Total Assets: £251,967,008
Registered Office: Majestic House, The Belfry, Colonial Way, Watford, Herts, WD24 4WH
Officers: Alex Iapichino, Secretary; Justin James Apthorp [1962] Director/Buyer; James Crawford [1977] Finance Director; Rowan Gormley [1962] Director/Chief Executive Officer [Irish]; Ian Andrew Harding [1964] Director/Company Executive; Brian Gregory Hodder [1952] Director; David Anthony Stead [1958] Director/Auditor

Majestic Wine Warehouses Limited
Incorporated: 30 October 1981 Employees: 1,168
Net Worth: £86,652,000 Total Assets: £138,679,008
Registered Office: Majestic House, The Belfry, Colonial Way, Watford, Herts, WD24 4WH
Parent: Majestic Wine PLC
Officers: Alex Iapichino, Secretary; Nicholas James Bell [1985] Director; James Crawford [1977] Director; Olivia FitzGenerald [1972] Director/Businesswoman; Rowan Gormley [1962] Director/Chief Executive [Irish]; Stuart Christopher Lane [1981] Finance Director; Joshua Benjamin Geoffrey Lincoln-Creese [1984] Managing Director; Suzanne Louise Roberts [1974] Supply Chain Director; Natalie Th'ng [1986] Customer Director

Majlen Ltd
Incorporated: 23 October 2018
Registered Office: 171 Kitts Green, Birmingham, B33 9QN
Shareholders: Jakub Kozlowski; Milan Olichwier
Officers: Jakub Kozlowski [1985] Director [Polish]; Milan Olichwier [1989] Director [Polish]

Malpas Stallard Limited
Incorporated: 30 July 1956 Employees: 2
Net Worth: £168,651 Total Assets: £316,801
Registered Office: The Cellars, Fish Street, Worcester, WR1 2HN
Major Shareholder: Nigel Gerald Lind Smith
Officers: Rosalind Jean Carlyon Smith, Secretary; Nigel Generald Lind Smith [1944] Director/Wine Merchant; Rosalind Jean Carlyon Smith [1949] Director/Wine Trade

Malt Whisky Agency Ltd
Incorporated: 24 August 2015 Employees: 3
Net Worth Deficit: £14,183 Total Assets: £29,602
Registered Office: 25 Manor Street, Falkirk, Stirlingshire, FK1 1NH
Shareholders: Alexander Graham; Helen Graham; Alasdair Innes Henderson Graham
Officers: Alasdair Innes Henderson Graham [1990] Director/Building Services Engineer; Alexander Graham [1955] Director/Builder; Helen Graham [1949] Director/Housewife

The Malt Whisky Company Limited
Incorporated: 2 July 2004 Employees: 1
Net Worth: £451,743 Total Assets: £635,943
Registered Office: 56 Druids Park, Murthly, Perth, PH1 4EJ
Shareholders: Stuart Nickerson; Wilma Nickerson
Officers: Stuart Nickerson [1956] Director/General Manager; Wilma Nickerson [1959] Director

Malthouse Inns PLC
Incorporated: 16 November 1998 Employees: 1
Net Worth: £42,645 Total Assets: £178,213
Registered Office: Park House, 200 Drake Street, Rochdale, Lancs, OL16 1PJ
Major Shareholder: Bohdan Matwijczuk
Officers: Bohdan Matwijczuk, Secretary/Director; Anna Matwijczuk [1953] Director/Local Government Officer; Bohdan Matwijczuk [1951] Director/Accounts Manager

Malthub Ltd
Incorporated: 12 December 2018
Registered Office: The Old Post Office, Holt Lane, Lea, Matlock, Derbys, DE4 5GQ
Major Shareholder: Craig Lonie
Officers: Craig Lonie [1968] Managing Director

Malton Brewery Limited
Incorporated: 9 March 2018
Registered Office: 20 Westfield Avenue, Norton, Malton, N Yorks, YO17 8DN
Major Shareholder: Howard Kinder
Officers: Howard Kinder [1961] Director/Racing Groom

Malts of Scotland Ltd
Incorporated: 8 January 2008 *Employees:* 1
Net Worth Deficit: £5,367 *Total Assets:* £16,373
Registered Office: Amadeus House, 27b Floral Street, London, WC2E 9DP
Major Shareholder: Thomas Ewers
Officers: Thomas Ewers [1970] Managing Director [German]

Malvern Ltd
Incorporated: 8 May 2012
Net Worth Deficit: £20,052 *Total Assets:* £41,527
Registered Office: Suite 9, Lake View House, Wilton Drive, Warwick, CV34 6RG
Major Shareholder: Harvinder Singh Deo
Officers: Harvinder Singh Deo [1983] Director/Self Employed

Mamada Ltd
Incorporated: 4 February 2019
Registered Office: 1a Boundary Road, London, E13 9PS
Shareholders: Gergana Georgieva Dragneva; Cesar Alberto Santos Pimentel Dragneva
Officers: Gergana Georgieva Dragneva [1994] Director/General Manager [Bulgarian]

Mamajuana UK Ltd
Incorporated: 14 June 2018
Registered Office: 61 Forge Building, Wharf Road, London, N1 7GP
Officers: Tolga Tezgor [1984] Director

Manchester Drinks Company Ltd
Incorporated: 8 June 2005 *Employees:* 4
Net Worth: £3,931,489 *Total Assets:* £6,903,282
Registered Office: Suite 412, Warth Road, Bury, Lancs, BL9 9TB
Shareholders: Brian Colin Levine; Ricard Benjamin
Officers: Brian Colin Levine, Secretary/Director; Richard Marc Benjamin [1970] Director; Brian Colin Levine [1968] Director

Manchester Merchant Wines Ltd
Incorporated: 30 October 2003
Net Worth Deficit: £8,625 *Total Assets:* £7,341
Registered Office: 123 Wellington Road South, Stockport, Cheshire, SK1 3TH
Officers: David John Croft, Secretary; Anna Patricia Carden [1953] Director/Dentist; Simon Dennis Carden [1955] Director/Architect; David John Croft [1949] Director/Architectural Technician; Elaine Croft [1950] Director/Dance Teacher; Jon Croft [1969] Director/Wine Merchant

Manchester Trading Limited
Incorporated: 25 September 2015 *Employees:* 1
Net Worth Deficit: £71,182 *Total Assets:* £1,764,238
Registered Office: The Robert Street Hub, 12-14 Robert Street, Manchester, M3 1EY
Shareholders: Suleman Nurez Kamani; Nurez Abdullah Kamani
Officers: Suleman Nurez Kamani [1989] Director

Mangrove Global Limited
Incorporated: 3 September 2013 *Employees:* 22
Net Worth: £1,132,809 *Total Assets:* £7,298,294
Registered Office: 53 Redbridge Lane East, Ilford, Essex, IG4 5EY
Shareholders: John Maitland Coe; Nicholas James Gillett
Officers: John Maitland Coe [1955] Director/Wine and Spirit Merchant; Nicholas James Gillett [1972] Managing Director

Manley Wines UK Limited
Incorporated: 8 August 2018
Registered Office: 5 Broomfield Road, Kew, Richmond, Surrey, TW9 3HR
Major Shareholder: David Ovenden
Officers: David Ovenden [1958] Director

Manoj Navaladi Ltd
Incorporated: 6 June 2018
Registered Office: 199A Lower Addiscombe Road, Croydon, Surrey, CR0 6RA
Officers: Manoj Navaladi [1995] Director/Businessman [Indian]

Manor Park Drinks Ltd.
Incorporated: 17 July 2014 *Employees:* 2
Net Worth: £15,368 *Total Assets:* £30,102
Registered Office: Manor Park Drinks Ltd, 50 Purland Road, London, SE28 0AT
Shareholders: Richard John Hone; George Richard Hone
Officers: George Richard Hone [1992] Director/Drinks Supplier; Richard John Hone [1960] Director/Drinks Supplier

Manor Wholesale Ltd
Incorporated: 5 November 2018
Registered Office: 24 Woolston Manor, Abridge Road, Chigwell, Essex, IG7 6BX
Officers: Mohammed Khan [1985] Director

Manteo Trading Company Limited
Incorporated: 25 May 2018
Registered Office: 71-75 Shelton Street, London, WC2H 9JQ
Major Shareholder: Paul Woolnough
Officers: Paul Woolnough, Secretary; Paul Woolnough [1967] Director

Mantra Trading Limited
Incorporated: 21 February 2018
Registered Office: 42 Royle Close, Chalfont St Peter, Gerrards Cross, Bucks, SL9 0BB
Officers: Sachin Kanaiyalal Chokshi [1980] Director

Manzi Developments Limited
Incorporated: 13 July 2011
Net Worth: £1,527,710 *Total Assets:* £2,085,243
Registered Office: 42 Springfield Drive, Westcliff on Sea, Essex, SS0 0RA
Major Shareholder: Luigi Francesco Manzi
Officers: Carol Ann Reeve, Secretary; Luigi Francesco Manzi [1945] Director; Carol Ann Reeve [1950] Director

Marani Wines Limited
Incorporated: 26 July 2016
Net Worth: £1,449 *Total Assets:* £42,603
Registered Office: Unit 2 Invicta Park, Sandpit Road, Dartford, Kent, DA1 5BU
Officers: Tamta Giguashvili [1990] Director [Georgian]

Marathon Beverages Ltd
Incorporated: 12 October 2017
Registered Office: Rutland House, 90-92 Baxter Avenue, Southend on Sea, Essex, SS2 6HZ
Shareholders: Barbara Arlene Goldberg; Sheldon Francis Goldberg
Officers: Jacqueline Margaret O'Donoghue [1963] Director/Sales Manager

Marathon Food Limited
Incorporated: 18 July 1986
Net Worth: £1,246,250 *Total Assets:* £1,501,561
Registered Office: Francis House, 2 Park Road, Barnet, Herts, EN5 5RN
Major Shareholder: Sotera Papanicolaou
Officers: Sotera Shimitra, Secretary; Sotera Shimitra [1959] Managing Director

Marc Fine Wines Limited
Incorporated: 10 October 2001
Net Worth Deficit: £9,731,479 *Total Assets:* £9,258,172
Registered Office: 107 Charterhouse Street, London, EC1M 6HW
Officers: Mohamad Khaled Oueida, Secretary; Marlon Ralph Pietro Abela [1975] Director [Lebanese]; Mohamad Khaled Oueida [1950] Director/Accountant

Marcin & Son Ltd
Incorporated: 4 December 2018
Registered Office: 21 Travers Street, Salford, M7 3DN
Major Shareholder: Marcin Tadeusz Siudaj
Officers: Marcin Tadeusz Siudaj [1984] Sales Director [Polish]

Markets It Ltd.
Incorporated: 7 April 2017
Net Worth: £330 *Total Assets:* £37,442
Registered Office: Kemp House, 152 City Road, London, EC1V 2NX
Officers: Simone Stronati [1992] Director [Italian]

Marlborough International (UK) Limited
Incorporated: 15 March 2002
Net Worth Deficit: £31,250 *Total Assets:* £111,398
Registered Office: Amber Cottage, Burbage, Marlborough, Wilts, SN8 3BU
Shareholder: Peter Bowyer
Officers: Peter Bowyer, Secretary; Nigel George Ashley [1954] Director; Peter Bowyer [1954] Director

Marlico Limited
Incorporated: 11 April 2003
Net Worth: £606,698 *Total Assets:* £2,078,893
Registered Office: Sigma House, Oak View Close, Edginswell Park, Torquay, Devon, TQ2 7FF
Shareholders: Lisa Louise Crump; Mark Andrew Crump
Officers: Lisa Louise Crump, Secretary; Mark Andrew Crump [1970] Director

Marlonn Food & Wine Ltd
Incorporated: 17 July 2015
Net Worth: £1 *Total Assets:* £1
Registered Office: Charan House, 18 Union Road, London, SW4 6JP
Major Shareholder: Herman Stallone Gomes de Barros
Officers: Herman Stallone Gomes de Barros [1986] Director [Portuguese]

Stanley Marlow & Son Limited
Incorporated: 10 April 2014
Registered Office: 4 Woundale, Bridgnorth, Salop, WV15 5PR
Shareholder: David Hollyhead
Officers: David Hollyhead [1948] Director/Property Consultant; Mark William Luckman [1958] Director

The Marlow Wine Company Limited
Incorporated: 1 July 2016
Registered Office: Suite 1, Unit A1 Tectonic Place, Holyport Road, Maidenhead, Berks, SL6 2YE
Major Shareholder: Ciaran McNulty
Officers: Ciaran McNulty [1969] Director

Sarah Marsh Ltd
Incorporated: 16 February 2005
Net Worth Deficit: £11,197 *Total Assets:* £167,614
Registered Office: 20 Westlands Way, Oxted, Surrey, RH8 0ND
Major Shareholder: Sarah Anne Marsh
Officers: Pamela Kathleen Manster, Secretary; Sarah Anne Marsh [1967] Director/Wine Writer and Consultant

Marston's Acquisitions Limited
Incorporated: 20 July 1887
Net Worth: £32,300,000 *Total Assets:* £44,600,000
Registered Office: Marston's House, Brewery Road, Wolverhampton, W Midlands, WV1 4JT
Parent: Marston's Corporate Holdings Limited
Officers: Anne Marie Brennan, Secretary; Andrew Andonis Andrea [1969] Director; Ralph Graham Findlay [1961] Director/Chief Executive; Edward Hancock [1975] Director; Iain Kenneth Jackson [1969] Director/Chartered Surveyor; William Whittaker [1958] Director

Marta Vine Limited
Incorporated: 11 April 2010 *Employees:* 2
Net Worth Deficit: £23,463 *Total Assets:* £64,946
Registered Office: 7 Vicarage Road, Southwell, Notts, NG25 0NN
Major Shareholder: Kevin James Bowers
Officers: Marta Santos Branco de Aires Mateus, Secretary; Kevin James Bowers [1975] Director

Marta's Vinyard Limited
Incorporated: 8 February 2000
Net Worth Deficit: £233,941 *Total Assets:* £49,260
Registered Office: Heritage House, 34b North Cray Road, Bexley, Kent, DA5 3LZ
Major Shareholder: Malcolm McLeod Falconer
Officers: Marta Lunardi, Secretary; Malcolm McLeod Falconer [1956] Cabin Service Director; Marta Lunardi [1968] Commercial Director

Martin Enterprises Limited
Incorporated: 2 January 1981
Net Worth: £224,646 *Total Assets:* £227,679
Registered Office: 2 Highfield Park, Marlow, Bucks, SL7 2DE
Major Shareholder: Martin Alexander Sloots
Officers: Rita Kathleen Sloots, Secretary; Martin Alexander Sloots [1957] Director

Marussia Beverages UK Limited
Incorporated: 21 January 1988 *Employees:* 24
Net Worth: £1,207,309 *Total Assets:* £6,667,441
Registered Office: Palladium House, 1-4 Argyll Street, London, W1F 7LD
Officers: John Neil MacLeod Mathieson, Secretary; Etienne de Salins [1966] Managing Director [French]; John Neil MacLeod Mathieson [1961] Managing Director; Bruce Perry [1966] Managing Director; Eric Charles Turner [1959] Director

Mason & Mason Wines Limited
Incorporated: 8 November 2002
Net Worth Deficit: £139,896
Registered Office: Woolyard, 54 Bermondsey Street, London, SE1 3UD
Parent: Bancroft Wines Limited
Officers: Samantha Ghysen, Secretary; Barnaby Simon Davis [1972] Director; Peter Charles de Haan [1952] Director; Simon Christopher Johnson [1965] Director; Nicholas Adam Mason [1966] Director/Wine Buyer; Jonathan David Worsley [1976] Director

Jake Mason Ltd
Incorporated: 11 February 2008
Net Worth: £6,741 *Total Assets:* £540,582
Registered Office: 27 St Cuthberts Street, Bedford, MK40 3JG
Shareholder: Jayesh Kotecha
Officers: Jayesh Kotecha [1967] Director/Salesman

Mast-Jaegermeister UK Holding Limited
Incorporated: 12 August 2013
Net Worth: £6,805,000 *Total Assets:* £6,805,000
Registered Office: 1st Floor, Building 11, Riverside Way, Watchmoor Park, Camberley, Surrey, GU15 3YL
Shareholders: Florian Rehm; Christina Fluegel
Officers: Brett Hugh Keartland [1975] Finance Director; Guy Edward Lawrence [1965] Director/Chief Executive Officer

Mast-Jaegermeister UK Limited
Incorporated: 12 August 2013 *Employees:* 72
Net Worth: £11,296,000 *Total Assets:* £28,586,000
Registered Office: 1st Floor, Building 11, Riverside Way, Watchmoor Park, Camberley, Surrey, GU15 3YL
Parent: Mast-Jaegermeister UK Holding Limited
Officers: Brett Hugh Keartland [1975] Finance Director; Guy Edward Lawrence [1965] Director/Chief Executive Officer

Master of Malt Limited
Incorporated: 12 March 2018
Registered Office: Unit 1 Ton Business Park, 2-8 Morley Road, Tunbridge Wells, Kent, TN9 1RA
Parent: Atom Supplies Limited
Officers: Joel John Kelly [1980] Director/Solicitor

Master of Sake Ltd
Incorporated: 25 September 2018
Registered Office: 44 Shrewsbury Lane, London, SE18 3JF
Shareholders: Chun Yip Andy Chan; Global Wisdom Ltd
Officers: Chun Yip Andy Chan [1978] Director

Master Spirits Limited
Incorporated: 26 September 2015 *Employees:* 2
Net Worth: £150,403 *Total Assets:* £151,069
Registered Office: Office 7, 35-37 Ludgate Hill, London, EC4M 7JN
Shareholders: Michael Stefan Alwin Sauerbrey; Steven Joseph Haag
Officers: Steven Joseph Haag [1984] Director/Business Consultant [American]; Michael Stefan Alwin Sauerbrey [1977] Director/Consultant [German]

Masters of Malt Limited
Incorporated: 12 March 2018
Registered Office: Unit 1 Ton Business Park, 2-8 Morley Road, Tunbridge Wells, Kent, TN2 3EF
Parent: Atom Supplies Limited
Officers: Joel John Kelly [1980] Director/Solicitor

Mastiha World Ltd
Incorporated: 12 August 2014
Net Worth Deficit: £34,711 *Total Assets:* £18,440
Registered Office: Flat C, 206 Iffley Road, Oxford, OX4 1SD
Major Shareholder: George Economides
Officers: George Economides [1985] Director [Greek]

Matheson Brewers Ltd
Incorporated: 27 November 2018
Registered Office: Burns Cottage, Cornhill, Banff, Aberdeenshire, AB45 2DL
Shareholders: Angus Iain Matheson; Meg Walker Matheson
Officers: Angus Iain Matheson [1988] Director/Master Brewer

Matteo Lupi Wines Ltd
Incorporated: 16 January 2017 *Employees:* 1
Net Worth: £26,992 *Total Assets:* £185,815
Registered Office: 12 Brightling Road, London, SE4 1SQ
Major Shareholder: Matteo Lupi
Officers: Matteo Lupi [1971] Director [Italian]

Maverick Brands Limited
Incorporated: 13 March 2018
Registered Office: Unit 1 Ton Business Park, 2-8 Morley Road, Tonbridge, Kent, TN9 1RA
Parent: Atom Supplies Limited
Officers: Joel John Kelly [1980] Director/Solicitor

Maverick Drinks Limited
Incorporated: 12 March 2018
Registered Office: Unit 1 Ton Business Park, 2-8 Morley Road, Tonbridge, Kent, TN9 1RA
Parent: Atom Supplies Limited
Officers: Joel John Kelly [1980] Director/Solicitor

Maverick Spirits Limited
Incorporated: 13 March 2018
Registered Office: Unit 1 Ton Business Park, 2-8 Morley Road, Tonbridge, Kent, TN9 1RA
Parent: Atom Supplies Limited
Officers: Joel John Kelly [1980] Director/Solicitor

Maverick Ventures UK Ltd
Incorporated: 10 November 2006
Net Worth: £4,076 *Total Assets:* £17,328
Registered Office: 8 School Lane, St Erth, Hayle, Cornwall, TR27 6HN
Shareholders: Angelo Michael Spencer-Smith; Phoebe Elizabeth Sampson
Officers: Angelo Michael Spencer-Smith, Secretary; Phoebe Elizabeth Sampson [1977] Director/Regional Co-ordinator; Angelo Michael Spencer-Smith [1974] Director/Freelance Marketing, Management Consultant

Maw Berwick Ltd
Incorporated: 16 August 2018
Registered Office: 42 Bagot Grove, Sneyd Green, Stoke on Trent, Staffs, ST1 6JF
Major Shareholder: Michael Anthony Wilton
Officers: Michael Anthony Wilton [1967] Director/Bar Management

Maxim & Co Limited
Incorporated: 19 July 2017
Registered Office: 409 Charrington Tower, 11 Biscayne Avenue, London, E14 9AY
Officers: Maxim Puiu [1993] Director/Owner [Romanian]

Maximus Wholesale Limited
Incorporated: 7 August 2017
Registered Office: 224 Ash Grove, Hounslow, Middlesex, TW5 9DT
Major Shareholder: Francis Uraon
Officers: Francis Uraon [1967] Director

Wm Maxwell (Scotch Whisky) Limited
Incorporated: 27 July 1990
Registered Office: Russell House, Dunnett Way, Broxburn, W Lothian, EH52 5BU
Parent: Ian MacLeod Distillers
Officers: Michael James Younger, Secretary; David William Hodder Russell [1940] Director/Whisky Broker; Leonard Stuart Russell [1961] Managing Director; Peter James Sidney Russell [1927] Director/Whisky Broker

Maxwell's Trading Company Limited
Incorporated: 28 February 2019
Registered Office: Business Solutions, 67 Fernhead Road, London, W9 3EY
Officers: Bogdan-Costin Firuleasa [1975] Director [Romanian]

Mayday Island Limited
Incorporated: 17 May 2018
Registered Office: 155-157 Donegall Pass, Belfast, BT7 1DT
Parent: Kirker Greer (Holdings) Limited
Officers: Steven Clark Pattison [1979] Director; Richard Ryan [1977] Director

Mayfair Brands Limited
Incorporated: 27 August 2010
Net Worth Deficit: £206,198 *Total Assets:* £297,724
Registered Office: Hyde Park House, 5 Manfred Road, London, SW15 2RS
Officers: Stephen Joseph Duffy [1960] Director [Irish]; Roger Hatfield [1946] Director/Accountant; Michael Alexander Peirce [1942] Director [Irish]

Mayfair Delivers Limited
Incorporated: 18 August 2008 *Employees:* 1
Net Worth Deficit: £16,445 *Total Assets:* £236,199
Registered Office: Suite 589, Kemp House, 152-160 City Road, London, EC1V 2NX
Shareholder: Rui Amorim
Officers: Rui Amorim [1981] Director [Portuguese]

Mayfield Distilling Company Ltd
Incorporated: 6 February 2017
Registered Office: Woodlands, Mayfield Grange, Little Trodgers Lane, Mayfield, E Sussex, TN20 6BF
Parent: A.H. Rackham Ltd
Officers: James Arthur Rackham [1953] Director/Chairman

Mayfly Wine Company Ltd.
Incorporated: 19 August 2016
Net Worth: £375 *Total Assets:* £61,160
Registered Office: 1 The Paddock, Guildford, Surrey, GU1 2RQ
Officers: Mark Shilton Barlow, Secretary; Peter Edward Goss [1980] Director/Wine Merchant [Norwegian]

MB Whisky Limited
Incorporated: 2 August 2018
Registered Office: 20-22 Wenlock Road, London, N1 7GU
Major Shareholder: Matthew Gerald Rhoades-Brown
Officers: Matthew Genergal Rhoades-Brown [1987] Director

MBM Resource Trading International Limited
Incorporated: 25 February 1999 *Employees:* 3
Net Worth: £592,766 *Total Assets:* £833,833
Registered Office: Tennyson House, Cambridge Business Park, Cambridge, CB4 0WZ
Shareholders: Roland Alexander Jones; Private Cellar Limited
Officers: Angela Patricia Wilding, Secretary; Andrew Charles Ramsay Gordon [1964] Director/Wine Merchant; Daniel Patrick Maley [1944] Director/Petroleum Consultant [American]

MBW Traders Ltd
Incorporated: 5 February 2018
Registered Office: Flat 4, Door 44, Telegraph Mews, Goodmayes, Essex, IG3 8TF
Major Shareholder: Roy Clement
Officers: Roy Clement [1985] Director/Engineer

MC Drinks Limited
Incorporated: 20 April 2010 *Employees:* 3
Net Worth: £139,772 *Total Assets:* £206,340
Registered Office: 3 Harpenden Road, St Albans, Herts, AL3 5LW
Shareholders: Michael Andrew Morris; Susan Coralie Morris
Officers: Michael Andrew Morris [1959] Director; Susan Coralie Morris [1955] Director

MCAL Merchant Limited
Incorporated: 16 October 2003 *Employees:* 61
Net Worth: £32,093 *Total Assets:* £566,623
Registered Office: 81 Oxford Street, London, W1D 2EU
Shareholder: Mike Olov Christopherson
Officers: Anna Elisabeth Lagervist Christopherson, Secretary; Anna Elisabeth Lagervist Christopherson [1975] Director/Advisor [Swedish]; Mike Olov Christopherson [1968] Director/Advisor [Swedish]

MCAL Sweet Retail Limited
Incorporated: 8 December 1999 *Employees:* 3
Net Worth: £3,365 *Total Assets:* £80,722
Registered Office: 14 Summerside Place, Edinburgh, EH6 4NZ
Shareholder: Mike Olov Christopherson
Officers: Mike Christopherson, Secretary; Mike Olov Christopherson [1968] Director [Swedish]; Anna Elisabeth Lagerqvist Christopherson [1975] Director [Swedish]

James E. McCabe Limited
Incorporated: 4 February 1975 *Employees:* 572
Net Worth: £48,506,976 *Total Assets:* £65,369,696
Registered Office: 4 Annagh Drive, Portadown, Craigavon, Co Armagh, BT63 5WF
Parent: Golf Holdings Limited
Officers: William Stewart Wilson, Secretary; Robert James Davis [1952] Director/Certified Accountant; James Patrick Hunt [1976] Director [Irish]; James Oliver Hunt [1946] Director; Patrick Michael Paul Hunt [1973] Director; Patrick Mark Paul Hunt [1948] Director

Alistair McCoist & Jeff East (Vintners) Ltd
Incorporated: 28 March 2018
Registered Office: 12 Royal Crescent, Glasgow, G3 7SL
Shareholders: Alistair Murdoch McCoist; Jeffrey P M East
Officers: Jeffrey PM East [1968] Director; Alistair Murdoch McCoist [1962] Director

Douglas McGibbon & Co. Limited
Incorporated: 26 December 1947
Registered Office: Douglas House, 18 Lynedoch Crescent, Glasgow, G3 6EQ
Officers: Frederick Hamilton Laing [1950] Director

McGin - The Glasgow Gin Ltd
Incorporated: 8 August 2017
Registered Office: 17 Hope Street, Glasgow, G2 6AB
Major Shareholder: Celeste Sara McGinn
Officers: Celeste Sara McGinn [1966] Director

McGrath's Brewing Limited
Incorporated: 5 January 2018
Registered Office: 155-157 Donegall Pass, Belfast, BT7 1DT
Parent: Kirker Greer (Holdings) Limited
Officers: Steven Clark Pattison [1979] Director; Richard Ryan [1977] Director

Marshall McGregor Limited
Incorporated: 14 December 1992
Net Worth: £1,758,805 Total Assets: £1,762,976
Registered Office: 100 Queen Street, Glasgow, G1 3DN
Shareholders: Edrington Distillers Limited; Highland Distillers Group Limited
Officers: Martin Alexander Cooke, Secretary; Martin Alexander Cooke [1961] Director/Company Secretary; Ian Barrett Curle [1961] Director/Chief Executive; Paul Andrew Hyde [1972] Director; Scott John McCroskie [1967] Director

McKenzie Fine Wines Limited
Incorporated: 6 November 2007
Net Worth: £33,550 Total Assets: £42,176
Registered Office: Brook House, Mint Street, Godalming, Surrey, GU7 1HE
Major Shareholder: James McKenzie
Officers: James McKenzie [1967] Director [South African]

McLean's Gin Ltd
Incorporated: 11 January 2018
Registered Office: Burnbank Farm, Strathaven, S Lanarks, ML10 6QF
Major Shareholder: Colin McLean
Officers: Colin McLean [1989] Director/Head Ginologist

N. McLoone & Co. Ltd
Incorporated: 6 April 1993
Net Worth: £1,698,042 Total Assets: £2,466,941
Registered Office: Heathersage, 77 Glen Road, Derry, BT48 0BZ
Shareholder: Patrick Duffy
Officers: Caroline Duffy, Secretary; Caroline Duffy [1963] Director [Irish]; Patrick Duffy [1963] Director [Irish]

MCMCtrans Ltd
Incorporated: 27 February 2018
Registered Office: 71-75 Shelton Street, Covent Garden, London, WC2H 9JQ
Major Shareholder: Milan Michalisko
Officers: Milan Michalisko [1994] Director [Czech]

McNicoll and Cairnie Limited
Incorporated: 19 April 2017 Employees: 3
Net Worth Deficit: £27,463 Total Assets: £31,848
Registered Office: 100 Gray Street, Broughty Ferry, Dundee, DD5 2DN
Shareholders: Euan McNicoll; Alexander Small Cairnie
Officers: Alexander Small Cairnie [1961] Director; Euan McNicoll [1963] Director/Wine Merchant

MDF Wholesale Ltd
Incorporated: 15 October 2013 Employees: 2
Net Worth Deficit: £6,181 Total Assets: £86,037
Registered Office: 13 Wolverhampton Road, Codsall, Wolverhampton, W Midlands, WV8 1PT
Major Shareholder: Giovanna Emmanuela Denaro
Officers: Giovanna Emmanuela Denaro [1976] Director [Italian]

MDS International Ltd.
Incorporated: 12 August 2016
Net Worth: £100 Total Assets: £100
Registered Office: 45 Cascade Court, 1 Sopwith Way, London, SW11 8NS
Major Shareholder: Cuneyt Ozgumus
Officers: Cuneyt Ozgumus [1981] Director/Manager [Turkish]

Mead Ho! Limited
Incorporated: 22 June 2015
Net Worth Deficit: £3,384 Total Assets: £1,233
Registered Office: 9c Rumsey Road, London, SW9 0TR
Shareholders: Matthew Joseph Shapiro; Emily Sanne; Alexander Leadill
Officers: Emily Sanne [1991] Director/Insight Executive; Joseph Shapiro [1988] Director/Civil Servant

Meadow Trading Company Limited
Incorporated: 26 June 2002
Net Worth: £24,664 Total Assets: £71,010
Registered Office: 11 Longdown Road, Epsom, Surrey, KT17 3PT
Major Shareholder: Susan Margaret Minihan
Officers: Susan Margaret Minhan [1969] Director

Meadrising Limited
Incorporated: 30 September 2013
Net Worth Deficit: £64,625 Total Assets: £120,316
Registered Office: 21 Tombland, Norwich, NR3 1RF
Shareholders: Jane Deborah Seymour; Gordon Philip Hall
Officers: Jane Deborah Seymour [1957] Director/Event Manager

Meanwhile Drinks Ltd.
Incorporated: 20 June 2016
Net Worth Deficit: £24,019 Total Assets: £51,920
Registered Office: 32 Steeles Road, London, NW3 4RE
Major Shareholder: Benjamin Schroder
Officers: William Nott [1991] Director; Benjamin Schroder [1992] Director

Adrian Mecklenburgh Limited
Incorporated: 25 February 1980 Employees: 27
Net Worth: £1,339,643 Total Assets: £2,129,189
Registered Office: Laurel House, Woodlands Park, Ashton Road, Newton-le-Willows, St Helens, Merseyside, WA12 0HH
Parent: Vimto (Out of Home) Limited
Officers: Timothy Croston, Secretary; Timothy John Croston [1963] Director; Nicholas Yates [1974] Sales & Operations Director

Medagio Limited
Incorporated: 2 June 2016
Net Worth Deficit: £8,700 Total Assets: £1,521
Registered Office: Level 3, 207 Regent Street, London, W1B 3HH
Major Shareholder: Georgios Iordanidis
Officers: Georgios Iordanidis [1983] Director [Greek]

Medicare Health & Energy Drinks Limited
Incorporated: 26 February 2018
Registered Office: Bridge House, 64-72 Mabgate, Leeds, LS9 7DZ
Major Shareholder: Diane Wilson
Officers: Diane Wilson [1944] Director/Company Formation Agent Semi-Retired

Mediterranean Farm Finest Limited
Incorporated: 25 May 2016
Registered Office: Unit 5 Hale House, 296a Green Lanes, Palmers Green, London, N13 5TP
Shareholders: Georgios Kastoris; Evangelos Arkalakis
Officers: Georgios Kastoris [1974] Director [Greek]

Medoc Wines Limited
Incorporated: 10 April 2006 *Employees:* 1
Net Worth: £334,345 *Total Assets:* £714,367
Registered Office: Ashcombe House, 5 The Crescent, Leatherhead, Surrey, KT22 8DY
Major Shareholder: Dominic John Earle Welby
Officers: Dominic John Earle Welby [1960] Director/Wine Investor

Medoff UK Ltd
Incorporated: 11 July 2018
Registered Office: 62 Frith Street, Soho, London, W1D 3JN
Major Shareholder: Percy Parker
Officers: Percy Parker [1967] Director/Manager

Medusa Wines Ltd
Incorporated: 28 September 2018
Registered Office: Flat 19, Dulcima House, 16 Carfax, Horsham, W Sussex, RH12 1EZ
Major Shareholder: Meriem Benlamkadem
Officers: Meriem Benlamkadem [1988] Director [Moroccan]

Mega Kegs Limited
Incorporated: 27 May 2011
Net Worth: £19,914 *Total Assets:* £144,328
Registered Office: Quadrant Court, 44-45 Calthorpe Road, Edgbaston, Birmingham, B15 1TH
Major Shareholder: Bimla Kumari Tank
Officers: Anil Tank [1996] Director; Bimla Kumari Tank [1964] Director and Company Secretary

MegaTradingLtd Limited
Incorporated: 30 January 2018
Registered Office: 2 St Matthews Road, Worthing, W Sussex, BN11 4AU
Officers: Scott Michael Allison, Secretary; Scott Michael Allison [1981] Director/Tiler

Melange Drinks Ltd
Incorporated: 6 February 2019
Registered Office: 32 Hofland Road, London, W14 0LN
Shareholders: Alec John Price; Harry Benjamin Sain
Officers: Alec John Price [1993] Director/Consultant; Harry Benjamin Sain [1994] Director/Teacher

Melchior Limited
Incorporated: 25 January 2019
Registered Office: Flat 45, Beaufort Mansions, Beaufort Street, London, SW3 5AG
Officers: Jamie Marchant [1991] Director

Melen London Ltd.
Incorporated: 6 March 2012 *Employees:* 1
Net Worth Deficit: £14,354 *Total Assets:* £227
Registered Office: 48 Preston Road, Brighton, BN1 4QF
Major Shareholder: Osman Senkul
Officers: Osman Senkul [1959] Director [Turkish]; Barbaros Tanc [1959] Director/Contractor

Meless Consortium Ltd
Incorporated: 10 January 2018
Registered Office: 8 Eastmead Avenue, Greenford, Middlesex, UB6 9RA
Officers: Jean-Jacques Dally Koudou, Secretary; Nathanael Lasme [1959] Director [Ivorian]

Meless Group Limited
Incorporated: 21 August 2002
Net Worth Deficit: £10,658 *Total Assets:* £780
Registered Office: 8 Eastmead Avenue, Greenford, Middlesex, UB6 9RA
Shareholders: Nathanael Lasme; Srikanthan Shanmugalingam

Melius Drinks Ltd.
Incorporated: 25 February 2014 *Employees:* 3
Net Worth Deficit: £119,416 *Total Assets:* £174,948
Registered Office: 64 New Cavendish Street, London, W1G 8TB
Shareholders: Joseph Knopfler; Samuel Francis Showering
Officers: Hamish de Run [1976] Director; Adam John Fairbrother [1968] Director; Thomas Elliot Hockedy [1987] Director; Joseph Knopfler [1987] Director; Samuel Francis Showering [1987] Director/Sales

Mellasat Wines Limited
Incorporated: 11 January 1999 *Employees:* 1
Net Worth Deficit: £512,447
Registered Office: 3rd Floor, 12 Gough Square, London, EC4A 3DW
Major Shareholder: Stephen Michael Richardson
Officers: Sharon Jayne Monsey, Secretary; Stephen Michael Richardson [1958] Director/Farmer

Russell Mellor and Company Limited
Incorporated: 19 January 1944
Net Worth: £22,068 *Total Assets:* £63,183
Registered Office: 16 Cheriton Avenue, Bromley, Kent, BR2 9DD
Major Shareholder: Russell Lawrence Mellor
Officers: Generaldine Mellor, Secretary; Russell Lawrence Mellor [1937] Director

Mentzendorff & Company Limited
Incorporated: 24 July 1968 *Employees:* 41
Net Worth: £5,436,152 *Total Assets:* £23,962,904
Registered Office: The Woolyard, 52 Bermondsey Street, London, SE1 3UD
Parent: Societe Jacques Bollinger
Officers: Andrew John Smith, Secretary/Chartered Accountant; Etienne Bizot [1962] Managing Director [French]; Adrian William Michael Bridge [1963] Director; James Elliot Dodsworth [1975] Director of National Accounts; Andrew James Hawes [1964] Director/Wine Shipper; Jerome Henri Philipon [1962] Director/PDG - Champagne Bollinger [French]; Andrew John Smith [1965] Director/Chartered Accountant

Mephisto Wine Merchants Limited
Incorporated: 23 October 2007
Net Worth Deficit: £29,337 *Total Assets:* £58,404
Registered Office: 84 Warwick Avenue, London, W9 2PU
Major Shareholder: Laszlo Hesley
Officers: Janos Orgyan, Secretary; Laszlo Hesley [1981] Director; Janos Orgyan [1970] Director/Wine Merchant [Hungarian]

Mercanti Imports Limited
Incorporated: 21 December 2016
Net Worth: £10,273 *Total Assets:* £646,703
Registered Office: 1 Premier Estate, William Street, Bristol, BS2 0RG
Shareholders: Jean-Claude Gulotta; Lucia Rosina Gulotta; Luca David Gulotta
Officers: Lucia Rosina Gulotta, Secretary; Jean-Claude Gulotta [1984] Director

Merchant Vintners Company Limited (The)
Incorporated: 20 July 1967 *Employees:* 3
Net Worth: £695,270 *Total Assets:* £2,298,168
Registered Office: House of Townend, Wyke Way, Melton West Industrial Estate, Melton, E Yorks, HU14 3BQ
Officers: James Peter Robson, Secretary; Anthony Austin Cleary [1952] Director; James John Eustace [1969] Director/Wine Merchant; Nicholas Hillman [1956] Director/Wine Merchant; James Jonathan Tanner [1968] Director/Wine Merchant; John Charles Townend [1965] Director/Wine Merchant; Mary Elizabeth Trease [1969] Director

Mercurial Brewing Limited
Incorporated: 4 August 2017
Registered Office: Barngates House, Church Lane, Binfield, Bracknell, Berks, RG42 5NS
Officers: Christopher Fisher [1988] Director

Mercurion Ltd
Incorporated: 23 July 2018
Registered Office: Flat 6, 48 Ilford Hill, Ilford, Essex, IG1 2AT
Major Shareholder: Ionel Ciobanu
Officers: Ionel Ciobanu [1995] Director

Mercury Spirits Ltd
Incorporated: 26 July 2017 *Employees:* 2
Net Worth: £36,143 *Total Assets:* £45,984
Registered Office: Suite 213, Portland House, Bressenden Place, London, SW1E 5RS
Shareholders: Rebecca Elizabeth Kwee; Danilo Tersigni; Filippo Previero
Officers: Filippo Previero [1990] Director [Italian]; Danilo Tersigni [1988] Director [Italian]

Meridale Store Ltd
Incorporated: 20 June 2018
Registered Office: 78 Merridale Road, Wolverhampton, W Midlands, WV3 9RH
Major Shareholder: Muhammad Tahir Altaf Bibi
Officers: Muhammad Tahir Altaf Bibi [1967] Director [Spanish]

Meridian Centre Hospitality Ltd
Incorporated: 28 May 2014
Net Worth: £2,316 *Total Assets:* £3,191
Registered Office: 201 Queen Street, Withernsea, E Yorks, HU19 2HH
Parent: The Meridian Centre Withernsea CIO
Officers: Terry Dagnall [1957] Director; Keith Hardcastle [1942] Director/Retired

Message in a Bottle Ltd.
Incorporated: 25 April 2018
Registered Office: 18 Sissinghurst Close, Crawley, W Sussex, RH10 7FX
Officers: Mr Stephen Dunn [1964] Director

Metropolitan Spirits (U.K.) Limited
Incorporated: 2 December 2010 *Employees:* 2
Net Worth Deficit: £174,327 *Total Assets:* £51,907
Registered Office: 3rd Floor, Paternoster House, 65 St Paul's Churchyard, London, EC4M 8AB
Major Shareholder: Sven Ladefoged Olsen
Officers: Sven Ladefoged Olsen [1965] Director/Businessman [Danish]; Mark David Stringer [1970] Director/Businessman

Mexcal Ltd
Incorporated: 8 January 2018
Registered Office: 264 High Street, Beckenham, Kent, BR3 1DZ
Major Shareholder: Keiron Jermaine Wright
Officers: Kieron Wright [1984] Director

Mexican Spirits Carmen Del Rio Limited
Incorporated: 25 January 2019
Registered Office: 31 Warden Road, Bristol, BS3 1BU
Shareholders: Enrique Coss Adame; Erika Fernanda Cortes Resendiz
Officers: Marco Antonio Marco Antonio Vazquez [1967] Director/Accountant [Spanish]

Mezcal Reina Limited
Incorporated: 7 November 2016
Registered Office: 65 Oakwood Court, London, W14 8JF
Shareholder: Monica Torroella
Officers: Susana Franyutti [1977] Director/PR and Marketing; Monica Torroella [1978] Director/Designer [British/Mexican]

Mezzaro Ltd
Incorporated: 10 December 2018
Registered Office: Flat 5, 128 Belgrave Road, London, SW1V 2BL
Shareholders: Igor Mijavec; Sharan Shashikant Shah
Officers: Igor Mijavec [1991] Director/Consultant [Canadian]; Sharan Shashikant Shah [1991] Director/Banking [Kenyan]

MGW World Ltd
Incorporated: 18 August 2016
Net Worth Deficit: £11,762 *Total Assets:* £8,764
Registered Office: 63 Turtlegate Avenue, Bristol, BS13 8NN
Major Shareholder: Marek Widlarz
Officers: Marek Widlarz [1974] Director/Driver [Polish]

Mickey Finn's Liquor Company Ltd.
Incorporated: 25 September 2000
Registered Office: 10 Orange Street, Haymarket, London, WC2H 7DQ
Major Shareholder: Mark Anthony Wilson
Officers: Ken Doyle, Secretary; Mark Anthony Wilson [1961] Director/General Manager [Irish]

Middle Kingdom Ltd
Incorporated: 21 June 2018
Registered Office: 8 The Village, Bebington, Wirral, Merseyside, CH63 7PW
Major Shareholder: Colin Austin Ling
Officers: Colin Austin Ling [1954] Director

Middlesex Wines Limited
Incorporated: 1 February 2012
Net Worth: £206,911 *Total Assets:* £702,272
Registered Office: Unit 2 Waterway Business Park, Rigby Lane, Hayes, Middlesex, UB3 1EY
Shareholders: Dalil Singh; Tarmon Kaur
Officers: Dalil Singh [1979] Director

Middleton Associates Limited
Incorporated: 18 July 1995 *Employees:* 10
Net Worth: £678,093 *Total Assets:* £3,593,650
Registered Office: Mentor House, Ainsworth Street, Blackburn, BB1 6AY
Parent: Middleton Associates Holdings Ltd
Officers: Sandra Ashton, Secretary; Stephen Robert Ashton [1969] Director

Midhurst Wine Shippers Limited
Incorporated: 11 April 1997
Net Worth: £28,709 *Total Assets:* £52,436
Registered Office: Airworthy House, Zok Building, Elsted Marsh, Midhurst, W Sussex, GU29 0JT
Shareholder: Linda Mary Cartwright
Officers: Linda Mary Cartwright, Secretary; Paul Beck [1952] Director; Linda Mary Cartwright [1949] Director/Marketing Manager

Midlands Drinks Limited
Incorporated: 17 April 2013
Net Worth: £349 *Total Assets:* £49,265
Registered Office: 108 Broadway Street, Burton on Trent, Staffs, DE14 3ND
Major Shareholder: Imran Razak
Officers: Imran Razak [1982] Director/Self Employed

Mieland Limited
Incorporated: 3 March 1981
Net Worth: £73,500 *Total Assets:* £75,448
Registered Office: Chantry Stables, Thorney Lanes, Hoar Cross, Burton on Trent, Staffs, DE13 8QT
Shareholders: John Garstone; Dorothy Anne Garstone
Officers: Dorothy Anne Garstone, Secretary; Dorothy Anne Garstone [1931] Director/Teacher; Dr John Garstone [1931] Director/Metallurgist

Milae Vodka Limited
Incorporated: 6 August 2018
Registered Office: First Floor, Thavies Inn House, 3-4 Holborn Circus, London, EC1N 2HA
Shareholders: Justin Grant; Evan Singh Luthra; Nino Vang Vojvodic
Officers: Nino Vang Vojvodic [1983] Director [Swedish]

Milk Money Limited
Incorporated: 22 July 2015
Net Worth Deficit: £7,619 *Total Assets:* £5,528
Registered Office: 43 Rae's Gardens, Bonnyrigg, Midlothian, EH19 2DW
Shareholder: James Angus Stuart-Gammie
Officers: James Angus Stuart-Gammie [1974] Director

Milk Vin Ltd
Incorporated: 17 July 2018
Registered Office: 3a Vincent House, Vincent Square, London, SW1P 2NB
Major Shareholder: Thomas James Strickland
Officers: Thomas Strickland, Secretary; Thomas James Strickland [1988] Managing Director

Mill Distributors Limited
Incorporated: 23 January 2017 *Employees:* 1
Net Worth Deficit: £10,922 *Total Assets:* £13
Registered Office: 54 Sun Street, Waltham Abbey, Essex, EN9 1EJ
Major Shareholder: Leon William Miller
Officers: Leon William Miller [1976] Director

Mille Gusti Limited
Incorporated: 25 February 2005
Net Worth Deficit: £47,399 *Total Assets:* £152,171
Registered Office: 17 Rosebery Gardens, Ealing, London, W13 0HD
Officers: Barbara Singh, Secretary; Dalbir Singh [1941] Director/Wine Merchant

Millennium Cash & Carry Limited
Incorporated: 8 December 1999 *Employees:* 73
Net Worth: £20,582,116 *Total Assets:* £53,710,732
Registered Office: 364-368 Cranbrook Road, Gants Hill, Ilford, Essex, IG2 6HY
Major Shareholder: Panna Mashru
Officers: Rishi Lakhani [1982] Director

Martin Miller's Gin Limited
Incorporated: 21 October 1999 *Employees:* 14
Previous: Reformed Spirits Company Limited
Net Worth Deficit: £3,863,782 *Total Assets:* £3,377,683
Registered Office: 535 Kings Road, London, SW10 0SZ
Shareholders: Diego Zamora S.A; Living Capital Limited
Officers: Jacob Ehrenkrona, Secretary/Investment Manager [Swedish]; Thomas Daniel Michel Clamens [1965] Director [French]; Jacob Ehrenkrona [1975] Director [Swedish]; Lorenzo Guerra Fagalde [1968] Commercial Director [Spanish]; Emilio Restoy Cabrera [1969] Director/Chief Executive Officer [Spanish]; Andreas Mikael Versteegh [1969] Director [Swedish]

Millesima Limited
Incorporated: 26 May 1998
Net Worth: £431,903 *Total Assets:* £1,649,820
Registered Office: Wilberforce House, Station Road, London, NW4 4QE
Parent: Millesima SA
Officers: Fabrice Bernard [1973] Director [French]; Jean Bernard [1955] Director [French]

Mina Collection Ltd
Incorporated: 5 September 2017
Registered Office: 11 Bressenden Place, London, SW1E 5BY
Officers: Michael Adjovi [1997] Director [French]; Nadina Grigoras [1996] Director [Romanian]

Minarda General Trade Ltd
Incorporated: 4 October 2018
Registered Office: 27 Old Gloucester Street, London, WC1N 3AX
Parent: Minarda General Trade LLC
Officers: Antonio Cobino, Secretary; Antonio Cobino [1976] Director/Manager [Italian]

Miracle Drinks Limited
Incorporated: 25 June 2016
Registered Office: 30 Earhart House, Aerodrome Road, London, NW9 5ZQ
Shareholders: Harshad Kumar Raja; M Harshad Kumar Raja
Officers: Harshad Kumar Raja [1962] Director/Entrepreneur

Miraj Beers & Wines Limited
Incorporated: 25 October 2013 *Employees:* 4
Net Worth: £43,222 *Total Assets:* £178,217
Registered Office: 148 Chesterfield Road, Ashford, Surrey, TW15 3PD
Shareholder: Rahul Vedi
Officers: Rahul Vedi [1987] Director/Wholesale Beer and Wine Supplier; Rajiv Vedi [1958] Director/Beer Distributor

Mirfield Brewery Limited
Incorporated: 26 May 2018
Registered Office: 36 Holroyd Hill, Bradford, BD6 1PQ
Major Shareholder: Darren Ludbrook
Officers: Darren Ludbrook [1976] Director

Henry Mitchell & Sons Limited
Incorporated: 22 February 1936 *Employees:* 7
Net Worth: £224,524 *Total Assets:* £302,124
Registered Office: South Lane, Holmfirth, W Yorks, HD9 1HN
Shareholders: Stephen Crossland; David Crossland
Officers: Lorna Crossland, Secretary; David Crossland [1967] Director/Manager; Stephen Crossland [1942] Director/Grocer

Charles Mitchell Wines Limited
Incorporated: 30 September 1981 *Employees:* 6
Net Worth: £135,362 *Total Assets:* £255,540
Registered Office: Excalibur Way, Northbank Industrial Park, Irlam, Manchester, M44 5DL
Shareholders: Howard Charles Domney; Christopher Mitchell Pacey
Officers: Howard Charles Domney, Secretary; Helen Domney [1961] Director; Howard Charles Domney [1959] Director/Wine Importer and Distributor; Tracey Pacey [1964] Director

Mitchell's Vintners Limited
Incorporated: 25 March 1999 *Employees:* 10
Net Worth: £306,095 *Total Assets:* £518,717
Registered Office: 354 Meadowhead, Sheffield, S8 7UJ
Major Shareholder: John Dennis Mitchell
Officers: John Dennis Mitchell, Secretary; John Dennis Mitchell [1951] Director/Wines & Spirit Merchant

Mixed & Co By A Limited
Incorporated: 21 August 2018
Registered Office: 9/1, 503 Stobcross Street, Glasgow, G3 8GL
Major Shareholder: Ashley Jane MacLachlan
Officers: Ashley Jane MacLachlan [1997] Director/Student

The Mixed Case Limited
Incorporated: 28 July 2006
Net Worth Deficit: £75,717 *Total Assets:* £13,631
Registered Office: HSA & Co, Chartered Accountants, Lewis House, Great Chesterford Court, Great Chesterford, Essex, CB10 1PF
Shareholders: Stefanie Anna Maria Steil; Johanna Marie Ledwidge; Eamonn Patrick Ledwidge; Aoife Emily Ledwidge
Officers: Aoife Emily Ledwidge, Secretary; Aoife Emily Ledwidge [1985] Director [Irish]; Johanna Marie Ledwidge [1978] Director [Irish]

The Mixology Collection Ltd
Incorporated: 8 January 2019
Registered Office: Ash House, School Lane, Chittering, Cambs, CB25 9PW
Shareholders: Jenny Willatt; Damien Egan
Officers: Damien Egan, Secretary; Damien Egan [1978] Director/Sales Manager; Jenny Willatt [1984] Director/UX Researcher

MJLM Limited
Incorporated: 23 July 2002
Net Worth: £10,847 *Total Assets:* £85,050
Registered Office: Applejack Cottage, Taston, Oxon, OX7 3JL
Major Shareholder: Michael John Leonard Morgan
Officers: Didier Garnier, Secretary; Michael Morgan [1949] Director/Wine Merchant

MJM Hospitality Ltd
Incorporated: 21 September 2017
Registered Office: 25 Timbrell Place, London, SE16 5HU
Major Shareholder: Matthew John Mawtus
Officers: Matthew John Mawtus [1985] Director

MK Sales Training Limited
Incorporated: 22 January 2015 *Employees:* 1
Net Worth: £16,854 *Total Assets:* £31,896
Registered Office: 3 Crossways, Romford, Essex, RM2 6AA
Major Shareholder: Matthew John Knight
Officers: Matthew John Knight [1991] Director/Sales Trainer

MK Wine Art Ltd
Incorporated: 30 July 2014
Net Worth Deficit: £69,425 *Total Assets:* £1,248,979
Registered Office: 2nd Floor, 22 Eastcheap, London, EC3M 1EU
Major Shareholder: Mirko Kusturin
Officers: Mirko Kusturin [1971] Director [Italian]

MM Drinks Ltd
Incorporated: 27 March 2017
Net Worth: £207 *Total Assets:* £7,201
Registered Office: 110 Bitterne Road West, Southampton, SO18 1AQ
Shareholders: Marcin Miroslaw Rybak; Marta Katarzyna Rybarczyk
Officers: Marcin Miroslaw Rybak [1985] Director [Polish]; Marta Katarzyna Rybarczyk [1984] Director [Polish]

MMC Sales and Marketing Limited
Incorporated: 16 January 2017
Net Worth: £3,034 *Total Assets:* £9,366
Registered Office: 19 Willow Grove, Horden, Peterlee, Co Durham, SR8 4SA
Major Shareholder: Michelle McLean
Officers: Ian McLean [1966] Director; Michelle McLean [1972] Director/Sales and Marketing

MMGT Limited
Incorporated: 7 November 2018
Registered Office: 50 The Common, Parbold, Wigan, Lancs, WN8 7EA
Major Shareholder: Dave John Mountain
Officers: Dave John Mountain [1988] Finance Director

Mo Madness Drinks Limited
Incorporated: 10 November 2017
Registered Office: Mo'Madness Drinks, Suite 638, 26 Cheering Lane, East Village, Stratford, London, E20 1BD
Major Shareholder: Monique Senior
Officers: Monique Senior [1990] Director/Mixologist

Moa Group Ltd
Incorporated: 5 September 2018
Registered Office: 235a Harwoods Road, Watford, Herts, WD18 7RU
Major Shareholder: Octavian-Gabriel Chirila-Filip
Officers: Octavian-Gabriel Chirila-Filip [1986] Director [Romanian]; Vasilica-Andreea Chirila-Filip [1988] Director [Romanian]

Mobay Drinks Ltd
Incorporated: 2 October 2018
Registered Office: 57 Coldharbour Road, Croydon, Surrey, CR0 4DY
Major Shareholder: Joshua Ferguson
Officers: Joshua Ferguson [1999] Director/Entrepreneur

Mode de Vie (Carbon) Limited
Incorporated: 17 October 2017
Registered Office: 581-583 Battersea Park Road, London, SW11 3BH
Major Shareholder: Matthew John Valentine
Officers: Matthew John Valentine [1969] Director/Fund Manager

Modern Botanicals Limited
Incorporated: 7 February 2019
Registered Office: 71-75 Shelton Street, London, WC2H 9JQ
Major Shareholder: Nikita Stepanov
Officers: Nikita Stepanov, Secretary; Nikita Stepanov [1996] Director [Russian]

Modern Vintage Wines Ltd
Incorporated: 20 June 1995
Previous: Daft Investments Ltd.
Net Worth: £10,733 Total Assets: £153,820
Registered Office: 6 Malvern House, 1a Liverpool Grove, London, SE17 2JJ
Major Shareholder: Donald Wayne Howes
Officers: Donald Wayne Howes, Secretary; Catherine Margaret Howes [1951] Director; Donald Wayne Howes [1952] Director

The Modest Merchant Limited
Incorporated: 30 May 2018
Registered Office: Flat 605, Friesian House, 160 Buckhurst Street, London, E2 6FU
Major Shareholder: Alexander Percy
Officers: Alexander Percy [1985] Director/Wine Merchant [French]

Moet Hennessy U.K. Limited
Incorporated: 12 December 1941 Employees: 123
Net Worth: £24,912,524 Total Assets: £102,096,768
Registered Office: 18 Grosvenor Gardens, London, SW1W 0DH
Shareholders: Diageo PLC; LVMH Moet Hennessy Louis Vuitton
Officers: James Alexander Neil Cockeram [1955] Director; Gillian Irene Mackwood [1955] Director; Maryse Elisabeth Malicet [1966] Director [French]; Bertrand Steip [1965] Managing Director [French]; Jolyon Kenneth Thornton [1970] Director

Mojito Bar Ltd
Incorporated: 9 March 2018
Registered Office: 44 Hamlet Road, Southend on Sea, Essex, SS1 1HH
Major Shareholder: Clay Salter
Officers: Clay Salter [1993] Director/Salesman

Moke Fine Wines Limited
Incorporated: 22 January 2010
Net Worth: £970 Total Assets: £34,964
Registered Office: 302 Cirencester Business Park, Love Lane, Cirencester, Glos, GL7 1XD
Shareholder: Mark Willoughby John Norrie
Officers: Mark Willoughby John Norrie [1972] Director; Penelope Jane Norrie [1975] Director/Wine Merchant

Molendinar Spirits Limited
Incorporated: 6 February 2018
Registered Office: 272 Bath Street, Glasgow, G2 4JR
Major Shareholder: Judith Blaney
Officers: Judith Blaney [1973] Director/Qualified Management Accountant

Molotov Brand Limited
Incorporated: 5 February 2018
Registered Office: 43 Park Place, Leeds, LS1 2RY
Officers: Vanessa Heidi Javed [1972] Director; Dayle Ivan Roane [1970] Managing Director

Molson Coors Brewing Company (UK) Limited
Incorporated: 3 March 1888 Employees: 1,993
Net Worth: £332,433,984 Total Assets: £878,267,008
Registered Office: 137 High Street, Burton on Trent, Staffs, DE14 1JZ
Parent: Molson Coors Holdings Limited
Officers: Kristin Wolfe, Secretary; Simon Kerry [1970] Director; James Christian Shearer [1980] Marketing Director; Philip Mark Whitehead [1977] Director

Molson Coors Brewing International Limited
Incorporated: 21 November 1997
Registered Office: 137 High Street, Burton on Trent, Staffs, DE14 1JZ
Parent: Molson Coors Brewing Company
Officers: Simon Kerry [1970] Commercial Director; Philip Rutherford [1979] Tax Director; Philip Mark Whitehead [1977] Director

Molvino Fine Wine & Spirits Company Ltd
Incorporated: 22 May 2009 Employees: 4
Net Worth Deficit: £467,664 Total Assets: £259,011
Registered Office: c/o Langtons, 11th Floor, The Plaza, 100 Old Hall Street, Liverpool, L3 9QJ
Major Shareholder: Lawrence Jamieson Howie
Officers: Adriana Dinte [1974] Director [Moldovan]; Craig Howie [1955] Director; Lawrence Jamieson Howie [1958] Director; Mark Ingram [1968] Business Development Director

Momento Vivere Holdings Limited
Incorporated: 17 October 2018
Registered Office: 11 Springwood View, Penistone, Sheffield, S36 6SX
Officers: Thomas Bagley [1993] Director/Engineer; Thomas Richard Cadzow [1993] Director/Chartered Accountant; Michael Edward Dodds [1985] Director/Salesman; Bradley Alan Dean Gaunt [1993] Director/Salesman

Momentum Wines Limited
Incorporated: 17 May 2005 Employees: 8
Net Worth: £38,478 Total Assets: £387,972
Registered Office: 8 Mile End Business Park, Maes-Y-Clawdd, Oswestry, Salop, SY10 8NN
Major Shareholder: Howard Edward Jones
Officers: Howard Edward Jones, Company Secretary; Mark Braithwaite [1964] Director; Howard Edward Jones [1971] Director/Company Secretary; Joanne Elizabeth Jones [1966] Director

Monaghan Marketing Limited
Incorporated: 18 August 2004 Employees: 2
Net Worth Deficit: £48,613 Total Assets: £37,997
Registered Office: 7 Tummel Road, Wemyss Bay, Inverclyde, PA18 6BN
Officers: Angela Ruth Monaghan, Secretary; Paul Monaghan [1955] Director

Mondial Wine Limited
Incorporated: 10 April 1985 Employees: 18
Net Worth: £222,828 Total Assets: £3,054,799
Registered Office: 2nd Floor, 33 Brighton Road, South Croydon, Surrey, CR2 6EB
Major Shareholder: Matterino Dogliani
Officers: Gnaneswaran Kumaraswamy, Secretary; Stefano Bartholomeo Guisseppe Fiori [1952] Director/Sales Manager; Alessandro Riga [1970] Director [Italian]

Mongoose Brewing Company Limited
Incorporated: 15 December 2009 *Employees:* 3
Net Worth Deficit: £218,824 *Total Assets:* £184,260
Registered Office: Global House, 303 Ballards Lane, London, N12 8NP
Shareholders: Gandhi Oriental Foods Limited; Docklands Trading Company Limited
Officers: Jayantilal Chunilal Gandhi [1941] Director; Kaushik Amritlal Mody [1957] Director

Monkey Shed Estate Brewing Co Ltd
Incorporated: 9 June 2017
Registered Office: Beaumont, Woodbury Lane, Norton, Worcester, WR5 2PT
Major Shareholder: Richard Bakewell Phillips
Officers: Richard Bakewell Phillips [1966] Director/Farmer

Monolith (UK) Ltd
Incorporated: 18 June 2004 *Employees:* 135
Net Worth: £2,324,631 *Total Assets:* £4,647,557
Registered Office: Unit 3 Thames Gateway Park, Choats Road, Dagenham, Essex, RM9 6RH
Officers: Swetlana Kuhn, Secretary; Evaldas Bernotavicius [1980] Director [Lithuanian]

Monopole Wine Portfolio Management Ltd
Incorporated: 19 November 2012
Net Worth: £141,397 *Total Assets:* £213,753
Registered Office: 8 Porchester Place, London, W2 2BS
Shareholder: David Zwi William Farber
Officers: David John Chermont [1969] Director/Investment Banking [French]; David Zwi William Farber [1974] Director [French]; John Nielsen [1974] Director [Danish]; Nima Habibollah Sarikhani [1980] Director; Thierry Tomasin [1969] Director/Restaurant Owner [French]

Montann Limited
Incorporated: 31 August 2016
Net Worth Deficit: £2,099 *Total Assets:* £26,774
Registered Office: 132-134 Great Ancoats Street, Manchester, M4 6DE
Shareholders: Jasmine Elaine Coleman; Helen Jane Crompton
Officers: Jasmine Elaine Coleman [1982] Director; Helen Jane Crompton [1971] Director

Monteadria (UK) Limited
Incorporated: 26 September 1994
Net Worth Deficit: £9,178 *Total Assets:* £339
Registered Office: 1st Floor, Shropshire House, 179 Tottenham Court Road, London, W1T 7NZ
Parent: Agrokombinat 13 July DD
Officers: Brian Arthur Ractliffe, Secretary; Jovan Mihailovic [1942] Director

Montrachet Limited
Incorporated: 31 March 2004
Registered Office: 11 Catherine Place, London, SW1E 6DX
Shareholders: Charles Edward Taylor; Louisa Jane Defaye Perkins
Officers: Jenny Frances Blanks, Secretary; Louisa Jane de Faye Perkins [1968] Director/Wine Merchant; Charles Edward Taylor [1961] Director/Wine Merchant

Montymac Vintners Ltd
Incorporated: 25 May 2010
Registered Office: 34 Anyards Road, Cobham, Surrey, KT11 2LA
Major Shareholder: Neill Harrowell
Officers: Neill Anthony Harrowell [1964] Director

The Moody Spirit Company Ltd
Incorporated: 2 August 2018
Registered Office: 99 Westmorland Avenue, Blackpool, Lancs, FY1 5PF
Major Shareholder: Glen Michael Moody
Officers: Glen Michael Moody [1971] Director/Civil Servant

Moonberries Ltd
Incorporated: 21 January 2019
Registered Office: The Old Vicarage, High Street, Brenchley, Tonbridge, Kent, TN12 7NQ
Major Shareholder: Emily Jane Moon
Officers: Emily Jane Moon [1983] Marketing Director

Moonshine Traders Ltd
Incorporated: 2 April 2013 *Employees:* 2
Net Worth Deficit: £13,572 *Total Assets:* £33,603
Registered Office: Unit 1 Waverley Road, Mitchelston Industrial Estate, Kirkcaldy, Fife, KY1 3NH
Shareholders: Callum Donaldson Burt; Stephen McKerron Bremner
Officers: Stephen McKerron Bremner [1954] Director/Consultant; Callum Donaldson Burt [1988] Director/Financial Services

Moore's Enterprises Limited
Incorporated: 9 June 2000
Net Worth Deficit: £88,303 *Total Assets:* £64,977
Registered Office: 90a Walm Lane, London, NW2 4QY
Major Shareholder: Martin John Moore
Officers: Martin John Moore [1951] Director [Irish]

Duvel Moortgat UK Limited
Incorporated: 22 May 2006
Net Worth: £624,052 *Total Assets:* £1,777,542
Registered Office: 62 Wilson Street, London, EC2A 2BU
Parent: Duvel Moortgat N.V.
Officers: Herbert de Loose, Secretary; Anouk Sophie Lagae [1975] Finance Director [Belgian]; Michel Luc Marie Jozef Moortgat [1967] Director [Belgian]

More Beer Wholesale Limited
Incorporated: 16 May 2013 *Employees:* 7
Net Worth: £32,647 *Total Assets:* £938,416
Registered Office: Newgate, White Lund Industrial Estate, Morecambe, Lancs, LA3 3PT
Major Shareholder: Loic Jordan Cross
Officers: Loic Jordan Cross [1983] Director

More or Less Drinks Company Limited
Incorporated: 10 January 2013
Net Worth: £297,953 *Total Assets:* £595,876
Registered Office: 18 The Ropewalk, Nottingham, NG1 5DT
Major Shareholder: Stephen Hedley Norris
Officers: Christopher Arrigoni [1981] Director; Stephen Hedley Norris [1973] Director

More Sake Limited
Incorporated: 20 July 2012
Net Worth: £59,010 *Total Assets:* £68,957
Registered Office: 1 Parkshot, Richmond, Surrey, TW9 2RD
Shareholders: Rudolph Galand; Diana Aphrodite Salevourakis; Nicolas Gael Verhoye
Officers: Rudolph Galand [1984] Director/Sommelier [French]; Diana Aphrodite Salevourakis [1957] Director/Journalist; Nicolas Gael Verhoye [1981] Director/Sommelier [French]

More Wine Ltd
Incorporated: 17 April 2018
Registered Office: 71-75 Shelton Street, London, WC2H 9JQ
Major Shareholder: Richard Hamblin
Officers: Richard Hamblin [1972] Director/Wine Merchant

Morecambe Bay Wines Limited
Incorporated: 25 January 2013 *Employees:* 28
Net Worth: £521,594 *Total Assets:* £1,638,859
Registered Office: Morecambe Bay Wines, Newgate, White Lund Industrial Estate, Morecambe, Lancs, LA3 3PT
Major Shareholder: Peter Michael Cross
Officers: Qi [1986] Director [Chinese]; Peter Michael Cross [1958] Director; Malcolm John Savage [1955] Director

Moreno Wine Importers Company Limited
Incorporated: 11 August 1988 *Employees:* 7
Net Worth Deficit: £289,511 *Total Assets:* £916,970
Registered Office: c/o in Vino Limited, Boundary House, Cheadle Point, Cheadle, Cheshire, SK8 2GG
Parent: In Vino Limited
Officers: Iain Davies, Secretary; Iain Robert Davies [1970] Director/Accountant; Shaun Michael English [1974] Sales Director; Michael Joseph Moriarty [1965] Director; Dennis Whiteley [1961] Director

Morgan Classic Wines Limited
Incorporated: 16 June 1999 *Employees:* 3
Net Worth: £30,942 *Total Assets:* £914,429
Registered Office: 1 West Street, Lewes, E Sussex, BN7 2NZ
Shareholders: Carol Ann Morgan; John Peter Morgan
Officers: Carol Ann Morgan, Secretary; John Peter Morgan [1957] Director; Sophia Louise Morgan [1985] Director; Thomas Drummond Morgan [1988] Director

Amlot Morgan Fine Wines Ltd
Incorporated: 27 July 2010
Net Worth Deficit: £1,728 *Total Assets:* £3,100
Registered Office: 280 Cooden Drive, Bexhill on Sea, E Sussex, TN39 3AB
Shareholder: Dylan James Amlot
Officers: Vikash Tanna, Secretary; Dylan James Amlot [1971] Director of Events Company; Peter Lloyd Amlot [1944] Director/Retired; Ilse Amlot Hoffmann [1943] Director/Retired; Adam Geoffrey Morgan [1971] Director/Barrister; Gail Wilkinson [1973] Director

Morgan Jupe Limited
Incorporated: 1 June 2012
Net Worth: £1,730 *Total Assets:* £100,793
Registered Office: Lanyon House, Mission Court, Newport, NP20 2DW
Shareholders: Joshua Morgan; Jessica Anne Frances Hitchen
Officers: Jessica Anne Frances Hitchen [1991] Sales Director; Joshua William Ellis Morgan [1988] Managing Director

Morgenrot Group PLC
Incorporated: 18 August 1970 *Employees:* 23
Net Worth: £1,405,864 *Total Assets:* £4,192,147
Registered Office: Unit 2 Canary Way, Agecroft Commerce Park, Swinton, Manchester, M27 8AW
Officers: Andrew Ernest Southworth, Secretary; Carl Michael Plath [1979] Director/Accountant; Rudi Michael Plath [1942] Director/CEO Chairman [German]; Valerie Mary Plath [1944] Director

Morley Way Limited
Incorporated: 15 August 2018
Registered Office: 31 Westwood Park Road, Peterborough, PE3 6JL
Parent: Nene Charter Company Limited
Officers: Paul Robert Hook [1955] Director

Morosini Mills Limited
Incorporated: 13 May 1977 *Employees:* 4
Net Worth: £291,072 *Total Assets:* £523,037
Registered Office: 121 City Road, Bradford, W Yorks, BD8 8JR
Parent: Beer Express Limited
Officers: Alfie Fiandaca, Secretary/Director [Italian]; Alfie Fiandaca [1942] Director [Italian]; Jyotika Wahi [1984] Director/Business Manager [Indian]

Morrish & Banham Ltd
Incorporated: 27 May 2015 *Employees:* 2
Net Worth: £1,220 *Total Assets:* £75,699
Registered Office: 1 Pope Street, Brewery Square, Dorchester, DT1 1GW
Major Shareholder: Mark Stephen Banham
Officers: Mark Stephen Banham [1974] Director/Wine Merchant; Caroline Rachael Morrish-Banham [1972] Director/Local Government Officer

Neil Morrissey Real Ale Company Ltd
Incorporated: 19 June 2014
Net Worth: £6,417 *Total Assets:* £7,330
Registered Office: Nobold Farm, Nobold Lane, Nobold, Shrewsbury, Salop, SY5 8NW
Shareholder: Richard Slingsby
Officers: Christopher Edward Hamilton [1950] Director/Financial Adviser; Neil Anthony Morrissey [1962] Director/Actor; Richard Slingsby [1965] Director/Manager

William Morton Limited
Incorporated: 26 August 1974 *Employees:* 197
Net Worth: £3,454,011 *Total Assets:* £25,315,952
Registered Office: 7 Evanton Drive, Thornliebank Industrial Estate, Glasgow, G46 8HL
Shareholder: ABA Equity Limited
Officers: Brian Douglas Robertson, Secretary; Alexander Bulloch [1927] Director; Carol Anne Jagielko [1956] Director; Henry John Jagielko [1952] Director; Stephen Gerard Russell [1953] Director; Gail Irene Allan Smith [1957] Director; James Douglas Turnbull [1961] Director

Most Popular Limited
Incorporated: 30 October 2018
Registered Office: 7 School Green, Shinfield, Reading, Berks, RG2 9EE
Major Shareholder: Mayur Patel
Officers: Mayur Patel, Secretary; Mayur Patel [1965] Director/Self Employed

Mother Kelly's Distribution Limited
Incorporated: 18 November 2015
Net Worth Deficit: £56,526 *Total Assets:* £117,705
Registered Office: c/o Interax Accountancy Services Ltd, Basepoint, Oakfield Close, Tewkesbury, Glos, GL20 8SD
Shareholder: Nigel Henry Patrick Owen
Officers: Andrew Danahy [1981] Director; Nigel Henry Patrick Owen [1981] Director

Mother of Wine Ltd
Incorporated: 6 September 2018
Registered Office: Ground Floor, 30 Victoria Avenue, Harrogate, N Yorks, HG1 5PR
Major Shareholder: Ionut Matei
Officers: Ionut Matei [1983] Director [Romanian]

Mothership Beer Ltd
Incorporated: 8 December 2014
Previous: Jane Barnes Ltd
Net Worth: £1,917 *Total Assets:* £7,661
Registered Office: The Manse, Station Road, Plumpton Green, Lewes, E Sussex, BN7 3BX
Major Shareholder: Jane Barnes
Officers: Jane Barnes [1982] Director

Mount Fetti Ltd
Incorporated: 29 May 2018
Registered Office: Apartment 24, Fusion 6, 8 Middlewood Street, Salford, M5 4LN
Major Shareholder: Joshua Matthew Richards
Officers: Joshua Matthew Richards [1991] Director/Engineer

Mountcharge Limited
Incorporated: 23 September 2002
Net Worth Deficit: £213,196 *Total Assets:* £3,012
Registered Office: 14 Stulpfield Road, Grantchester, Cambridge, CB3 9NL
Shareholder: Graham Wilson
Officers: Joyce Elizabeth Wilson, Secretary; Graham Wilson [1947] Director; Joyce Elizabeth Wilson [1957] Director

MPS 64 Ltd
Incorporated: 18 October 2018
Registered Office: 35 Swete Street, London, E13 0BU
Major Shareholder: Ivan Stoyanov Stoyanov
Officers: Marina Pavlova Velinska, Secretary; Ivan Stoyanov Stoyanov [1972] Director/Manager [Bulgarian]

Mr Kegz Ltd
Incorporated: 5 September 2018
Registered Office: 22 Burgh Way, Walsall, W Midlands, WS2 7RG
Major Shareholder: Conor Aston Johns
Officers: Conor Aston Johns [1992] Director/Support Worker

Mr. Alba International Trading Company Limited
Incorporated: 10 August 2016 *Employees:* 1
Net Worth: £29,174 *Total Assets:* £42,888
Registered Office: 272 Bath Street, Glasgow, G2 4JR
Shareholders: Rougang Li; Wenqi Hou
Officers: Xiaobing, Secretary; Wenqi Hou, Secretary; Wenqi Hou [1968] Director/Manager [Chinese]; Rougang Li [1963] Director/Manager [Chinese]

MSB Wholesale Services Limited
Incorporated: 6 December 2016 *Employees:* 3
Net Worth Deficit: £61,305 *Total Assets:* £143,097
Registered Office: The Sahota Centre, Unit 3 & 4 Heath Street, Smethwick, W Midlands, B66 2QY
Shareholder: Jasmohinder Bihal
Officers: Jasmohinder Bihal [1994] Director

MSD Wholesale Limited
Incorporated: 19 January 2012 *Employees:* 8
Net Worth: £24,726 *Total Assets:* £2,604,655
Registered Office: MSD Warehouse, 31 Second Avenue, Chatham, Kent, ME4 5AU
Officers: Bakshish Kaur [1942] Director [Indian]

MSM Foods Limited
Incorporated: 7 March 2008
Net Worth: £4,407 *Total Assets:* £141,893
Registered Office: Unit 5, M62 Trading Estate, New Potter Grange Road, Goole, E Yorks, DN14 6BZ
Shareholder: Sebastian Remigiusz Szczesny
Officers: Sebastian Remigiusz Szczesny, Secretary/Director [Polish]; Marek Lozowski [1962] Director [Polish]; Sebastian Remigiusz Szczesny [1979] Director, Secretary [Polish]

MSSC (NW) Limited
Incorporated: 11 February 2019
Registered Office: 1 Westcroft Industrial Estate, Manchester Old Road, Middleton, Manchester, M24 4GJ
Officers: Joanne Lowrey [1973] Director; Norman Lee Lowrey [1970] Director

Alexander Muir & Son Limited
Incorporated: 18 February 1993
Net Worth Deficit: £188,992 *Total Assets:* £65,903
Registered Office: Regent Court, 70 West Regent Street, Glasgow, G2 2QZ
Major Shareholder: James Alexander Frederic Aykroyd
Officers: John Nicol, Secretary; Sir James Alexander Frederic Aykroyd [1943] Director

The Mullwood Wine Company Limited
Incorporated: 7 June 2001
Net Worth: £237,233 *Total Assets:* £1,190,697
Registered Office: Unit 4 Firefly Square, Plantation Road, Burscough, Ormskirk, Lancs, L40 8JT
Major Shareholder: David Spencer Fleetwood
Officers: Karen Elizabeth Fleetwood, Secretary; David Spencer Fleetwood [1964] Director; Karen Elizabeth Fleetwood [1962] Director/Secretary

Mumbles Brewery Ltd
Incorporated: 19 September 2011 *Employees:* 5
Net Worth: £17,097 *Total Assets:* £93,326
Registered Office: 23 Oakland Road, Mumbles, Swansea, SA3 4AQ
Shareholders: Robert Stephen Turner; Peter Graham Turner
Officers: Peter Graham Turner [1955] Director; Robert Stephen Turner [1956] Director

Mundus Wines Limited
Incorporated: 10 February 1999 *Employees:* 3
Net Worth: £153,319 *Total Assets:* £421,576
Registered Office: 3 Kensington Road, Belfast, BT5 6NG
Shareholders: Andrew Terence John Montague; James Eugene Bonner
Officers: James Eugene Bonner, Secretary; James Eugene Bonner [1961] Director [Irish]; Andrew Terence John Montague [1953] Director/Solicitor [Irish]

Muratina Limited
Incorporated: 21 March 2016
Net Worth Deficit: £419 *Total Assets:* £5
Registered Office: 25 Watercress Road, Cheshunt, Waltham Cross, Herts, EN7 6XJ
Major Shareholder: King'ori Wambaki
Officers: King'ori Wambaki, Secretary; King'ori Wambaki [1990] Director/Economist

Murcotts Ltd.
Incorporated: 3 February 2016
Net Worth: £977,615 *Total Assets:* £980,838
Registered Office: 11 St Margarets, Sutton Coldfield, W Midlands, B74 4HU
Major Shareholder: Robert Murcott
Officers: Robert Murcott [1964] Director

Murphy & Yeung Brewing Company Limited
Incorporated: 12 July 2018
Registered Office: 114 Colindale Avenue, Colindale, London, NW9 5GX
Shareholders: Tak Wai Yeung; Mark Edward Murphy
Officers: Mark Edward Murphy [1966] Director; Tak Wai Yeung [1964] Director

Murray Brother's Whisky Ltd
Incorporated: 4 March 2014
Registered Office: 7 Avonlea Rise, Leamington Spa, Warwicks, CV32 6HS
Shareholders: Christopher Cox; Thomas Edward Nicholls
Officers: Christopher Cox [1983] Director/Businessman [American]; Thomas Edward Nicholls [1984] Director/Businessman

Museum Wines Limited
Incorporated: 8 March 2006 *Employees:* 5
Net Worth Deficit: £10,777 *Total Assets:* £376,197
Registered Office: Chequers Court, 35 Brown Street, Salisbury, Wilts, SP1 2AS
Major Shareholder: Alex John Boon
Officers: Daniel Stephen Grigg [1986] Wine Director

MV Distribution Ltd
Incorporated: 3 July 2017
Registered Office: Roodscroft, Hatt, Saltash, Cornwall, PL12 6PJ
Major Shareholder: Max Venables
Officers: Max Venables [1989] Director/Transport Manager

MWH Wine Agencies Ltd
Incorporated: 3 October 2012
Registered Office: Meadow View, Tidmarsh, Reading, Berks, RG8 8ER
Officers: Michael Wellington Hall [1955] Director

MWH Wine Merchants Limited
Incorporated: 28 December 2006 *Employees:* 1
Net Worth Deficit: £24,726 *Total Assets:* £498,196
Registered Office: Meadow View, The Street, Tidmarsh, Reading, Berks, RG8 8ER
Major Shareholder: Michael Wellington Hall
Officers: Sarah Catherine Hall, Secretary; Michael Wellington Hall [1955] Director/Wine Merchant

My Cocktail Club Limited
Incorporated: 20 October 2017
Registered Office: 316 Blackpool Road, Fulwood, Preston, Lancs, PR2 3AE
Major Shareholder: Jake Arthur James Whittington
Officers: Jake Arthur James Whittington [1992] Director

My Gin My Way Ltd
Incorporated: 29 September 2018
Registered Office: 1st Floor, 44 Linthorpe Road, Middlesbrough, Cleveland, TS1 1RD
Officers: Laurence Stephen Brannigan [1985] Director; Adam Hillier [1981] Director; Jonathan Lee Neal [1983] Director; Stuart Ferguson Nicoll [1978] Director

My Global Ventures Limited
Incorporated: 6 July 2015
Previous: Irenin Limited
Net Worth: £10 *Total Assets:* £807
Registered Office: 25 Copenhagen Gardens, Chiswick, London, W4 5NN
Parent: Energian UK Limited
Officers: Ypatios Moysiadis [1979] Director [Greek]

My Nan's Favourite Ltd
Incorporated: 22 February 2019
Registered Office: Pitch Cottage, Pitch Place, Thursley, Godalming, Surrey, GU8 6QW
Major Shareholder: Christopher Jon Frederick
Officers: Christopher Jon Frederick [1982] Director

Myella Brands Ltd
Incorporated: 26 May 2016
Registered Office: Park House, 1 Piccadilly Close, Mansfield Woodhouse, Notts, NG19 8RX
Major Shareholder: Steve Charles Ward
Officers: Mark Kingerley [1978] Director/Area Manager; Steve Charles Ward [1982] Director/Senior National Account Manager

Myliko International (Wines) Ltd.
Incorporated: 13 September 1991 *Employees:* 13
Net Worth: £1,441,075 *Total Assets:* £4,399,963
Registered Office: Canal House, 100 Lissadel Street, Salford, M6 6BP
Major Shareholder: Hemant Dahyalal Kotecha
Officers: Nishit Dahyalal Kotecha, Secretary; Hemant Dahyalal Kotecha [1954] Director

Mymexico Global Ltd
Incorporated: 24 July 2018
Registered Office: 71-75 Shelton Street, Covent Garden, London, WC2H 9JQ
Major Shareholder: Amanda Regan
Officers: Amanda Regan, Secretary; Amanda Regan [1974] Director/Engineering Manager

MyNaturalCompany Limited
Incorporated: 19 July 2017
Net Worth: £15,099 *Total Assets:* £20,512
Registered Office: 1 Church Road, Frenchay, Bristol, BS16 1NB
Major Shareholder: Frederic Le Berre
Officers: Isabelle Stephanie Marie-Joseph Francoise Le Berre, Secretary; Frederic Le Berre [1971] Director [French]

Myrlex Southend Limited
Incorporated: 8 February 2016 *Employees:* 1
Net Worth: £57,645 *Total Assets:* £186,872
Registered Office: The Mechanics Workshop, New Lanark, Lanark, ML11 9DB
Major Shareholder: Alexander John Adamson Wilson
Officers: Alexander John Adamson Wilson, Secretary; Alexander John Adamson Wilson [1975] Director/Chartered Surveyor

Mysomm.Com Ltd
Incorporated: 11 September 2016
Net Worth: £7,528 *Total Assets:* £7,528
Registered Office: 33 Talbot Road, Twickenham, Middlesex, TW2 6SJ
Officers: Victoria Jane Stillwell [1984] Director

Mythop Gardens Limited
Incorporated: 20 July 2009
Net Worth Deficit: £70,266 *Total Assets:* £330,039
Registered Office: Old Bakery, Green Street, Lytham St Annes, Lancs, FY8 5LG
Parent: Windmill Holdings Limited
Officers: Peter John Whitehead, Secretary; Nicola Elizabeth Whitehead [1960] Director/Shop Manageress; Peter John Whitehead [1957] Director

Mywinelabel Limited
Incorporated: 25 November 2013
Net Worth: £7,758 *Total Assets:* £194,020
Registered Office: 71 Devonshire Road, Prenton, Wirral, Merseyside, CH43 1TN
Major Shareholder: Wahab Ziane
Officers: Wahab Ziane [1949] Director

Mzansi UK Ltd
Incorporated: 1 September 2018
Registered Office: 20-22 Wenlock Road, London, N1 7GU
Major Shareholder: Ngwako Ernest Mathole
Officers: Ngwako Ernest Mathole [1985] Director/Technician [South African]

N & M Wholesale Ltd
Incorporated: 30 August 2017
Net Worth Deficit: £9,192 *Total Assets:* £361,001
Registered Office: 77 Chapel Street, Billericay, Essex, CM12 9LR
Major Shareholder: Prashanth Nellutla
Officers: Nellutla Prashanth [1976] Director [Indian]

N G K Wholesale Limited
Incorporated: 25 June 2007
Net Worth Deficit: £3,096 *Total Assets:* £27,083
Registered Office: Suite D, Weller House, 58-60 Longbridge Road, Barking, Essex, IG11 8RT
Major Shareholder: Jasvinder Singh
Officers: Jasvinder Singh [1952] Director

N R Wines Limited
Incorporated: 23 January 2002
Net Worth: £4 *Total Assets:* £11,104
Registered Office: Dingle Brow, 10 Ravenscroft Close, Sandbach, Cheshire, CW11 1ZX
Major Shareholder: Nicholas Howard Reed
Officers: Jane Marie Reed, Secretary; Jane Marie Reed [1957] Director/Nurse; Nicholas Howard Reed [1957] Director/Wine Merchant

N.Double and Company Limited
Incorporated: 12 August 1948 *Employees:* 4
Net Worth: £217,341 *Total Assets:* £267,561
Registered Office: Arena, Holyrood Close, Poole, Dorset, BH17 7FJ
Shareholders: Stephen Kelly Ivan Double; Sophie Elizabeth Double
Officers: Stephen Kelly Ivan Double, Secretary; Sophie Elizabeth Double [1963] Director/Manager

N20winery Ltd
Incorporated: 24 January 2018
Registered Office: 16 Church Crescent, London, N20 0JP
Major Shareholder: Ian Nicholas Blackman
Officers: Ian Nicholas Blackman [1962] Director

Najpol Ltd
Incorporated: 14 September 2017
Registered Office: Unit 5, M62 Trading Estate, New Potter Grange Road, Goole, E Yorks, DN14 6BZ
Shareholders: Sebastian Remigiusz Szczesny; Marek Lozowski
Officers: Marek Lozowski [1962] Director [Polish]; Sebastian Remigiusz Szczesny [1979] Director [Polish]

Naked Fine Wine Bonds PLC
Incorporated: 18 July 2013 *Employees:* 2
Net Worth Deficit: £120,000 *Total Assets:* £6,093,000
Registered Office: Majestic House, The Belfry, Colonial Way, Watford, Herts, WD24 4WH
Parent: Naked Wines International Limited
Officers: Alex Iapichino, Secretary; James Crawford [1977] Finance Director; Rowan Gormley [1962] Director [Irish]

The Naked Spirit Company Ltd
Incorporated: 25 July 2018
Registered Office: The Office, 20 Sutton Oak Road, Sutton Coldfield, W Midlands, B73 6TL
Major Shareholder: Rajan Sudera
Officers: Rajan Sudera [1987] Director/Service Engineer

Naked Wines Prepayments Trustee Company Limited
Incorporated: 13 November 2008
Net Worth Deficit: £10,000 *Total Assets:* £13,361,000
Registered Office: Majestic House, The Belfry, Colonial Way, Watford, Herts, WD24 4WH
Parent: www.nakedwines.com Limited
Officers: Alex Iapichino, Secretary; James Crawford [1977] Director; Eamon William FitzGenerald [1984] Director/COO, Naked Wines [Irish]

Nandha Murgesan Ltd
Incorporated: 2 January 2019
Registered Office: 3 Popplewell Close, Belton, Doncaster, S Yorks, DN9 1TF
Major Shareholder: Nandhakumar Murugesan
Officers: Nandhakumar Murugesan, Secretary; Nandhakumar Murugesan [1997] Director/Businessman [Indian]

Narang Wholesalers Limited
Incorporated: 25 July 1995
Net Worth: £5,304,966 *Total Assets:* £10,358,287
Registered Office: Narang House, 121 City Road, Bradford, W Yorks, BD8 8JR
Parent: Narang Group Limited
Officers: Jagjeet Singh Kalsi, Secretary; Mohammed Younis Hussain [1971] Director/Wholesalers; Jagjeet Singh Kalsi [1951] Director/Wholesalers; Jasbir Singh Narang [1966] Director

Nat Trade SRL Ltd
Incorporated: 4 December 2018
Registered Office: Kemp House, 160 City Road, London, EC1V 2NX
Major Shareholder: Keith Stock
Officers: Keith Stock, Secretary; Keith Stock [1957] Director

National Drink Distributors Limited
Incorporated: 12 March 2014
Registered Office: 3 Carolina Court, Doncaster, S Yorks, DN4 5RA
Parent: Today's Wholesale Services Ltd
Officers: John Schofield [1954] Director

Native Oracle Limited
Incorporated: 11 February 2013
Net Worth Deficit: £5,537 *Total Assets:* £11,851
Registered Office: 111 Bell Street, Glasgow, G4 0TQ
Major Shareholder: Donald Anderson
Officers: Donald Andrew James Anderson [1971] Director; Navdeep Basi [1970] Director

Native Wines Ltd
Incorporated: 12 July 2017
Registered Office: 21/5 Stead's Place, Edinburgh, EH6 5DY
Shareholder: Valerio Lo Coco
Officers: Valerio Lo Coco [1980] Director/Wine Merchant [Italian]

Natural Bay Limited
Incorporated: 26 October 2016
Net Worth Deficit: £16,086 *Total Assets:* £20,990
Registered Office: Unit 8-10 Pembroke Buildings, Scrubs Lane, London, NW10 6RE
Shareholders: Pietro Genco; Alberto Antonini
Officers: Alberto Antonini [1972] Director [Italian]; Giulio Neri [1973] Director [Italian]

The Natural Beer Company Limited
Incorporated: 7 September 2018
Registered Office: 24 Reay Avenue, East Kilbride, S Lanarks, G74 1QT
Major Shareholder: Nicholas Young
Officers: Nicholas Young [1984] Director

Natural Marketing Ltd
Incorporated: 18 June 2003
Net Worth: £691 *Total Assets:* £828
Registered Office: 352 Fulham Road, London, SW10 9UH
Officers: Goran Tresic, Secretary; Miro Barac [1973] Director/Consulting Services [Croatian]; Henry Leonard Gewanter [1954] Director [American]; Saso Ilik [1968] Director/Economist

The Natural Wine Company Ltd
Incorporated: 3 August 2017
Registered Office: Scarfield, The Mains, Giggleswick, Settle, N Yorks, BD24 0AX
Major Shareholder: Robert William Bagot
Officers: Robert William Bagot [1976] Director Wine Business

Navaladi Ltd
Incorporated: 15 January 2018
Registered Office: 199A Lower Addiscombe Road, Croydon, Surrey, CR0 6RA
Officers: Manoj Navaladi [1995] Director/Businessman [Indian]

Robin Navrozov Consulting Limited
Incorporated: 1 June 2017
Registered Office: 5 Thistle Grove, London, SW10 9RR
Shareholders: The Ingenius Events Companyltd; Robin Lee Navrozov
Officers: William Twyman Comfort III [1966] Director [American]; Robin Lee Navrozov [1968] Director [American]

NCE Trading KFT Ltd
Incorporated: 21 December 2017
Registered Office: 6 Neville Road, London, E7 9QX
Major Shareholder: Sandip Navnitbhai Patel
Officers: Sandip Navnitbhai Patel [1967] Director

NDG (Hartlepool) Limited
Incorporated: 11 March 2016
Net Worth: £108 *Total Assets:* £1,343
Registered Office: Collingwood House, Church Square, Hartlepool, Cleveland, TS24 7EN
Officers: Natalie Gallagher [1982] Director

The Near Beer Brewing Co. Ltd
Incorporated: 30 August 2018
Registered Office: 91 Nunhead Lane, London, SE15 3QE
Officers: Thomas Joseph Blackwood [1986] Director; Berin Chesney Bowen-Thomas [1982] Director; Gregory Paul Farrington [1985] Director; Suneil Steven Paul Saraf [1980] Director

Neat Drinks Limited
Incorporated: 25 April 2017
Net Worth: £1 *Total Assets:* £1
Registered Office: 163 Bath Street, Glasgow, G2 4SQ
Parent: Brougham Investments Limited
Officers: Andrew Douglas Bratten [1963] Director

Neatly London Limited
Incorporated: 11 May 2018
Registered Office: 26-28 Southernhay East, Exeter, Devon, EX1 1NS
Shareholders: Gemma Heidi Blattler; Louis Blattler
Officers: Daniel Blattler [1968] Director/Consultant

Nectar Imports Limited
Incorporated: 14 June 1990 *Employees:* 103
Net Worth: £2,574,708 *Total Assets:* £7,579,812
Registered Office: Cold Berwick Hill, Berwick St Leonard, Salisbury, Wilts, SP3 5SN
Parent: Fuller, Smith & Turner P.L.C.
Officers: Severine Pascale Bequin, Secretary; Simon Ray Dodd [1974] Director; Simon Emeny [1965] Director; Richard Hamilton Fleetwood Fuller [1960] Director; Jonathon David Swaine [1971] Director

Needhams Wines Limited
Incorporated: 24 September 2014
Net Worth: £3,157 *Total Assets:* £13,073
Registered Office: Bank House, High Street, Chipstead, Sevenoaks, Kent, TN13 2RR
Major Shareholder: Kim Gordon Moss

Negociants Europe Limited
Incorporated: 8 November 2007
Registered Office: 6 St Andrew Street, London, EC4A 3AE
Major Shareholder: Robert Wyndham Hill-Smith
Officers: Karl Shane Martin, Secretary; Robert Wyndham Hill-Smith [1951] Managing Director [Australian]; Nicholas Burns Waterman [1962] Managing Director [Australian]

Negociants UK Limited
Incorporated: 30 July 1990 *Employees:* 17
Net Worth: £7,820,000 *Total Assets:* £12,991,000
Registered Office: 6 St Andrew Street, London, EC4A 3AE
Shareholders: Samuel Hill-Smith; Robert Wyndham Hill-Smith
Officers: Karl Shane Martin, Secretary; Robert Wyndham Hill-Smith [1951] Managing Director [Australian]; Nicholas Burns Waterman [1962] Director [Australian]

Neill & Company Wine Importers Ltd
Incorporated: 13 May 2008 *Employees:* 3
Net Worth: £17,958 *Total Assets:* £357,565
Registered Office: 6 Ballycrochan Drive, Bangor, Co Down, BT19 7LB
Major Shareholder: Robert Samuel Neill
Officers: Maureen Johnston, Secretary; Maureen Johnston [1969] Director/Accountant [Irish]; Robert Samuel Neill [1971] Director

Neilward Ltd
Incorporated: 29 June 2018
Registered Office: 20-22 Wenlock Road, London, N1 7GU
Major Shareholder: Neil Robert Ward
Officers: Neil Robert Ward [1971] Director/Landlord

Nekter Wines Ltd
Incorporated: 22 February 2016
Net Worth Deficit: £54,039 *Total Assets:* £7,619
Registered Office: 94 Cyprus Steet, London, E2 0NN
Major Shareholder: Jonothan Michael Davey
Officers: Jonothan Michael Davey [1978] Director/Management Consultant

Nele Drinks Limited
Incorporated: 14 August 2017
Registered Office: 21 Racavan Road, Broughshane, Ballymena, Co Antrim, BT42 4PH
Major Shareholder: Niall Edward Lloyd Esler
Officers: Niall Edward Lloyd Esler [1985] Director/Solicitor

Nene Charter Company Limited
Incorporated: 21 September 1994
Net Worth: £2,250,635 *Total Assets:* £3,063,589
Registered Office: 31 Westwood Park Road, Peterborough, PE3 6JL
Major Shareholder: Paul Robert Hook
Officers: Paul Robert Hook [1955] Director

Neon Brew Co Limited
Incorporated: 2 May 2017
Registered Office: Flat 1, 51 Clarendon Villas, Hove, E Sussex, BN3 3RE
Officers: Brett Preston, Secretary; David Richtor, Secretary; Brett Preston [1990] Director/Senior Venue Lead; David Richtor [1981] Director/Venue Lead

Nephtis Limited
Incorporated: 27 June 2018
Registered Office: Kemp House, 169 City Road, London, EC1V 2NX
Major Shareholder: Anthony Bulimwengu
Officers: Anthony Bulimwengu [1982] Director/Chairman [French]

Neptune Rum Ltd
Incorporated: 8 November 2016
Net Worth Deficit: £203,812 *Total Assets:* £9,292
Registered Office: 71 Rodney Road, Cheltenham, Glos, GL50 1HT
Major Shareholder: Richard Graham Davies
Officers: Richard Graham Davies [1971] Director; Barry Timothy Hyman [1968] Director; James Edward Molloy [1973] Director; Andrew Thomas Wall [1972] Director

Nestle James & Company Ltd
Incorporated: 14 September 2018
Registered Office: Commerce House, South Street, Elgin, Moray, IV30 1JE
Major Shareholder: Roderick Nestle James MacKenzie
Officers: Lucinda Jane MacKenzie [1965] Director; Roderick Nestle James MacKenzie [1963] Director

Neu Brandenburger Beer Company Limited
Incorporated: 7 October 1991
Net Worth: £2 *Total Assets:* £2
Registered Office: c/o George Hay & Co, 83 Cambridge Street, Pimlico, London, SW1V 4PS
Officers: Thomas Reitz, Secretary; Thomas Reitz [1956] Director/Wine Salesman [German]

New Age Wines Ltd
Incorporated: 20 August 2003 *Employees:* 2
Net Worth Deficit: £40,581 *Total Assets:* £6,366
Registered Office: 59 Feney Road, Craigavon, Co Armagh, BT67 0RF
Officers: Jayne Louise FitzGenerald, Secretary; Clement David Mark FitzGenerald [1954] Director; Jayne Louise FitzGenerald [1976] Director/International Aid Manager

New Claire Wine Ltd
Incorporated: 10 April 2012
Net Worth: £4,884 *Total Assets:* £86,090
Registered Office: 25 Balham High Road, London, SW12 9AL
Shareholders: Bhim Bhattachan; Kul Paudel
Officers: Bhim Bhattachan [1978] Director/Employment; Kul Bahadur Paudel [1975] Director/Employment [Nepalese]

New Fairdeal Drinks Limited
Incorporated: 24 July 2017
Registered Office: 152 Forest Road, London, E17 6JQ
Officers: Mohammad Hussain [1962] Director

New Fine Wines Ltd
Incorporated: 12 August 2002
Net Worth Deficit: £2,039 *Total Assets:* £91
Registered Office: 114 Birchfield Road, Northampton, NN1 4RH
Shareholder: Gregory Norman Shaw
Officers: Nicola Shaw, Secretary; Gregory Norman Shaw [1966] Director/Manager

New Generation Wines Limited
Incorporated: 17 July 2000 *Employees:* 17
Net Worth: £63,716 *Total Assets:* £1,894,149
Registered Office: 14 Kennington Road, London, SE1 7BL
Parent: F & B Holdings Limited
Officers: Kevin David Saunby, Secretary; Richard Edward Michael Boote [1969] Director/Wine Merchant; James Arthur Booth [1973] Director/Wine Consultant; James Robert Furze [1954] Director; Geoffrey Austin Harvey [1972] Marketing Export Director [South African]; Andrew Joseph Muscat [1969] Director/Wine Merchant; Gybertus Du Toit Naude [1966] Financial Director [South African]; Anthony Record [1939] Director; Hamish Gavin Young [1967] Commercial Director

The New Muscovy Company Limited
Incorporated: 29 September 1998 *Employees:* 2
Net Worth Deficit: £868,725 *Total Assets:* £6,072
Registered Office: 85 Great Portland Street, London, W1W 7LT
Shareholder: Lyndisfarne Partners Limited
Officers: Dmitry Yurievich Chalov [1976] Director; Dmitry Chebotarev [1965] Director; Anton Yurievich Zakharov [1970] Director

New School Wines Limited
Incorporated: 24 February 2010
Net Worth: £853 *Total Assets:* £23,599
Registered Office: 4 Barkers Field, Long Clawson, Melton Mowbray, Leics, LE14 4PL
Shareholders: Matthew John Gant; John Retsas
Officers: Matthew John Gant [1974] Director; John Retsas [1968] Director [Australian]

New Wave (Scotland) Limited
Incorporated: 18 November 2015
Net Worth Deficit: £34,496 Total Assets: £896,696
Registered Office: 4 Hope Street, Edinburgh, EH2 4DB
Shareholders: Christopher Alexander Mair; Caledonian Heritable Limited
Officers: Robert Graeme Arnott [1957] Director; Christopher Alexander Mair [1977] Director; Gordon Iain Russell [1971] Director/Accountant; Jamie Wightman [1987] Director

New World Trading Europe Ltd.
Incorporated: 18 July 2001
Net Worth Deficit: £3,108 Total Assets: £7,694
Registered Office: 29 Andrewes House, Barbican, London, EC2Y 8AX
Major Shareholder: Jonathan Paul Bear
Officers: Kurt Janson, Secretary/Tourism Policy Consultant [New Zealander]; Jonathan Bear [1970] Director/Consultant [New Zealander]; Patrick Anthony Gill [1971] Director/Accountant [New Zealander]

New Zealand Beer Collective Ltd
Incorporated: 26 January 2016 Employees: 3
Net Worth Deficit: £49,105 Total Assets: £150,630
Registered Office: 9d Lebanon Road, Wandsworth, London, SW18 1RE
Major Shareholder: Todd Brian Nicolson
Officers: Todd Brian Nicolson [1975] Director

Newchesters Ltd
Incorporated: 3 October 2018
Registered Office: 18 Seven Bar, 187 Front Street, Chester-le-Street, Co Durham, DH3 3AX
Major Shareholder: Mary Wright
Officers: Mark Walker [1970] Business Director; Mary Wright [1944] Director

Newcomer Wines Limited
Incorporated: 21 October 2013 Employees: 3
Net Worth Deficit: £6,212 Total Assets: £394,616
Registered Office: c/o Peter Honegger, Newcomer Wines Ltd, 5 Dalston Lane, London, E8 3DF
Shareholders: Daniela Pillhofer; Peter Honegger
Officers: Peter Honegger [1991] Director/CEO & Co-Founder [Austrian]; Daniela Pillhofer [1993] Director/CEO & Co-Founder [Austrian]

Newhampton Wines Ltd
Incorporated: 23 May 2018
Registered Office: 114-115 Newhampton Road West, Wolverhampton, W Midlands, WV6 0RR
Major Shareholder: Satwant Kaur
Officers: Satwant Kaur [1959] Director

Nexus Wine Trading Ltd
Incorporated: 2 February 2017
Net Worth: £22,546 Total Assets: £150,089
Registered Office: 1 The Green, Marlborough, Wilts, SN8 1AL
Major Shareholder: Georgie Bevan
Officers: Georgie Bevan [1977] Director

Nice Brewing Company Ltd
Incorporated: 23 April 2018
Registered Office: 20-22 Wenlock Road, London, N1 7GU
Shareholders: Roger Anthony John Savage; Lauren May Camacho
Officers: Lauren May Camacho [1989] Director/Charity Worker; Roger Anthony John Savage [1986] Director/Charity Worker

D & M Nicholls Limited
Incorporated: 4 March 2017
Net Worth Deficit: £2,707 Total Assets: £6,659
Registered Office: 22 Yeo Way, Clevedon, Somerset, BS21 7UP
Shareholder: David Christopher John Nicholls
Officers: David Christopher John Nicholls [1950] Director/Retired

J & W Nicholson & Co Ltd
Incorporated: 12 July 2016 Employees: 1
Previous: W Nicholson & Co Ltd
Net Worth: £168,055 Total Assets: £301,009
Registered Office: c/o PKF Littlejohn, 2nd Floor, 1 Westferry Circus, Canary Wharf, London, E14 4HD
Shareholders: Julia Suzanne Clifford Walker; Nicholas Ainger Browne
Officers: Nicholas Ainger Browne [1962] Director

James Nicholson Wine Limited
Incorporated: 26 July 2006 Employees: 21
Net Worth: £738,678 Total Assets: £3,623,122
Registered Office: 7-9 Killyleagh Street, Crossgar, Co Down, BT30 9DQ
Shareholders: James Nicholson; Elspeth Nicholson
Officers: Nicola Louise Davies, Secretary; Nicola Louise Davies [1972] Director/Accountant; James Nicholson [1953] Director/Wine Merchant

Nick Drinks Limited
Incorporated: 15 March 2018
Registered Office: 58 Grosvenor Road, London, N3 1EX
Officers: Lindorf Nicholas Amado [1973] Director/Programmer

Nickolls & Perks Limited
Incorporated: 30 October 1963 Employees: 19
Net Worth: £2,856,524 Total Assets: £5,081,055
Registered Office: 37 High Street, Stourbridge, W Midlands, DY8 1TA
Parent: Nickolls and Perks Holdings Limited
Officers: David Ernest Gardener, Secretary; David Squire Gardener [1935] Director/Wine Merchant; William John Gardener [1966] Director

Nielsen McKinsey Global Tourism & Hospitality Consulting Ltd
Incorporated: 31 May 2011
Registered Office: 6 Sussex Road, Weymouth, Dorset, DT4 0PL
Shareholders: Carlos Manuel Ferreira Duarte Almeida; Carlos Manuel Ferreira Duarte Almeida
Officers: Carlos Manuel Ferreira Duarte Almeida [1969] Director/Business Consulting [Portuguese]

Nifol Limited
Incorporated: 6 June 2018
Registered Office: Coker Isah & Co, 74 Church Road, London, SE19 2EZ
Major Shareholder: Folake Omoshalewa Oyebanji-Kofoworola
Officers: Folake Omoshalewa Oyebanji-Kofoworola [1976] Director/Trader

Night Out Entertainments Ltd
Incorporated: 9 October 2018
Registered Office: 71-75 Shelton Street, London, WC2H 9JQ
Major Shareholder: Beth Emma Freeman
Officers: Beth Emma Freeman [1974] Director

Nightcap Global Limited
Incorporated: 10 October 2016
Registered Office: 64c Shacklewell Lane, London, E8 2EY
Major Shareholder: Ciaran Thomas McNicholas
Officers: Ciaran Thomas McNicholas [1985] Director

The Nightingale Drinks Company Ltd
Incorporated: 30 October 2017
Registered Office: Unit 9 Darton Business Park, Barnsley Road, Darton, Barnsley, S Yorks, S75 5QX
Major Shareholder: David Owens
Officers: David Owens [1977] Director/F&B Development

Nightrep Limited
Incorporated: 8 December 2016
Net Worth Deficit: £2,715 *Total Assets:* £1,197
Registered Office: 28 Innerleithen Way, Perth, PH1 1RN
Major Shareholder: Iain James McDonald
Officers: Iain James McDonald [1966] Director/Consultant

Nine Reigns Limited
Incorporated: 6 June 2017
Registered Office: c/o Buzzacott LLP, 130 Wood Street, London, EC2V 6DL
Major Shareholder: Ranjeet Varma
Officers: Ranjeet Varma [1971] Director [Indian]

NineTailsDistillery Ltd
Incorporated: 28 August 2018
Registered Office: Iso:Fitness, Church Street, Pontardawe, Swansea, SA8 4JB
Major Shareholder: Cerith James Thomas
Officers: Cerith James Thomas [1991] Director/Businessman

Nino and Blue Spruce Ltd
Incorporated: 26 October 2018
Registered Office: 27 Old Gloucester Street, London, WC1N 3AX
Major Shareholder: Nino Mamukashvili
Officers: Nino Mamukashvili, Secretary; Nino Mamukashvili [1980] Director [Georgian]

Nisar Traders Ltd
Incorporated: 22 March 2018
Registered Office: 5 Ryeburne Street, Oldham, Lancs, OL4 2BP
Officers: Ammara Nisar [1980] Director/Manager

Nitrogenics Ltd
Incorporated: 10 January 2017
Registered Office: 2 Beech Avenue, Liverpool, L17 7EN
Officers: Paul Michael Coleman [1983] Events Director

NJA Marketing Ltd
Incorporated: 23 August 2012
Net Worth: £2,041 *Total Assets:* £10,759
Registered Office: Suite 29c, Imperial House, 64 Willoughby Lane, London, N17 0SP
Major Shareholder: Nicholas James Anderson
Officers: Nicholas James Anderson [1982] Director/Head of Sales

NM Lesuire Ltd
Incorporated: 20 December 2017
Registered Office: New Mill, Chesterton Road, South Shields, Tyne & Wear, NE34 9HG
Officers: Charlene Guthrie [1988] Director

NMWLeisure Ltd
Incorporated: 12 February 2018
Registered Office: 1 Manchester Road, Denton, Manchester, M34 3JU
Officers: Nicole Marie Webb [1996] Director/Licensee

No.9 Leisure Limited
Incorporated: 28 April 2004 *Employees:* 2
Net Worth Deficit: £934 *Total Assets:* £17,419
Registered Office: 9 Town Street, Duffield, Belper, Derbys, DE56 4EH
Shareholder: John Edward Morris
Officers: Sally Ann Morris, Secretary; John Edward Morris [1964] Director

Noah Brothers Ltd
Incorporated: 9 January 2019
Registered Office: 75 Gainsborough Green, Abingdon, Oxon, OX14 5JL
Major Shareholder: Gkor Tovmasian
Officers: Gkor Tovmasian [1991] Director [Greek]

Noahs Estate Ltd
Incorporated: 8 March 2018
Registered Office: 36 Park Lane, Wilberfoss, York, YO41 5PW
Major Shareholder: Jonathan Atkin
Officers: Jonathan Atkin [1984] Director/Businessman

Noble Green Wines Limited
Incorporated: 11 November 2005 *Employees:* 8
Net Worth Deficit: £1,974,777 *Total Assets:* £258,597
Registered Office: Lynton House, 7-12 Tavistock Square, London, WC1H 9LT
Shareholders: Jane Elizabeth Buckley; Peter Ralph Buckley
Officers: Jane Elizabeth Buckley, Secretary; Jane Elizabeth Buckley [1958] Director; Peter Ralph Buckley [1959] Director; Michael John Gould [1961] Director

Noble Merchants Limited
Incorporated: 1 July 2004 *Employees:* 3
Net Worth: £366 *Total Assets:* £369,660
Registered Office: Kings Suite, 4th Floor, Amba House, 15 College Road, Harrow, Middlesex, HA1 1BA
Shareholders: Jayesh Khamar; Samir Khamar
Officers: Jayesh Khamar, Secretary; Jayesh Khamar [1964] Director/Sales; Rajendra Khamar [1952] Director/Businessman; Samir Khamar [1959] Director/Sales

Noble Wines (UK) Limited
Incorporated: 3 July 2012
Net Worth Deficit: £69,904 *Total Assets:* £19,850
Registered Office: The Gatehouse, 2 Devonhurst Place, Heathfield Terrace, London, W4 4JD
Major Shareholder: Philippe Alexandre Mouche
Officers: Philippe Alexandre Mouche [1972] Director [French]

Noetic Wine Limited
Incorporated: 31 January 2019
Registered Office: 63 Churchward Close, Grove, Wantage, Oxon, OX12 0QZ
Major Shareholder: Timothy James Bayley
Officers: Timothy James Bayley [1976] Director

The Nolo Drinks Co. Ltd.
Incorporated: 18 October 2018
Registered Office: Central Chambers, 227 London Road, Hadleigh, Benfleet, Essex, SS7 2RF
Officers: Joanne Claire Birkitt [1976] Director

Nordic Imports Ltd
Incorporated: 31 October 2018
Registered Office: 84 Fleece Road, Long Ditton, Surbiton, Surrey, KT6 5JS
Shareholders: Markku St.John; Alex Morbin
Officers: Alex Morbin [1980] Director [British/Finnish]; Markku St.John [1980] Director [Finnish/American]

Noreast Beers (N.I.) Ltd
Incorporated: 17 February 1983 Employees: 12
Net Worth: £261,226 Total Assets: £407,015
Registered Office: 7 Church Avenue, Newry, Co Down, BT34 1DY
Shareholders: Enda Julia McElherron; David McElherron
Officers: Daisy McElherron [1998] Director; David McElherron [1969] Director [Irish]; Enda Julia McElherron [1969] Director

The Norfolk Rum Company Ltd
Incorporated: 7 January 2019
Registered Office: 20-22 Wenlock Road, London, N1 7GU
Major Shareholder: Susan Richman
Officers: Susan Richman [1972] Director

The Norfolk Vineyard Ltd
Incorporated: 5 March 2014
Net Worth Deficit: £12,941 Total Assets: £464
Registered Office: 2 Chestnut Cottage, Bunwell Road, Spooner Row, Wymondham, Norfolk, NR18 9LH
Shareholders: Clare Joanne Evans; Michael John McAully
Officers: Clare Joanne Evans [1969] Director; Michael John McAully [1951] Director/Designer

Norlin Distribution Limited
Incorporated: 21 June 2017
Registered Office: 14 Gresham Street, Belfast, BT1 1JN
Parent: Norlin Ventures Limited
Officers: Richard Stephen Irwin [1973] Director; Stephen Brian Symington [1980] Director

North East Drinks Supplies Ltd
Incorporated: 22 June 2010
Net Worth: £20,383 Total Assets: £119,429
Registered Office: DTS Business Park, Nelson Park West, Cramlington, Northumberland, NE23 1WG
Officers: Richard Farrell [1976] Director; Clifford James Waterston [1969] Director

North East Hold Limited
Incorporated: 5 August 2014
Net Worth: £2,854 Total Assets: £7,962
Registered Office: Unit 13 Coast Business Park, 1 Wesley Way, Benton Square Industrial Estate, Killingworth, Tyne & Wear, NE12 9TA
Major Shareholder: Terence Paul Borley
Officers: Christopher Borley [1988] Director

North of Scotland Distilling Company Limited
Incorporated: 16 February 1995 Employees: 2
Net Worth: £526,210 Total Assets: £1,481,745
Registered Office: 21 Forbes Place, Paisley, Renfrewshire, PA1 1UT
Shareholders: Roderick George Christie; Priscilla Joyce Craig
Officers: Priscilla Joyce Craig, Secretary/Interior Designer; Roderick George Christie [1952] Director; Priscilla Joyce Craig [1958] Director/Interior Designer

North South Wines Limited
Incorporated: 18 February 2014 Employees: 16
Net Worth: £530,677 Total Assets: £3,382,827
Registered Office: Unit 3 Britannia Court, The Green, West Drayton, Middlesex, UB7 7PN
Officers: Hamish Peregrine Curzon Gillespie, Secretary; Victor de Bortoli [1969] Director [Australian]; Joy Edmondson [1977] Brand Development Director; Hamish Peregrine Curzon Gillespie [1979] Finance Director; Stefano Girelli [1959] Director/Wine Producer [Italian]; Robert John Ratcliffe [1957] Director; Kim Jane Wilson [1981] Commercial Director

North Star Spirits Ltd.
Incorporated: 29 March 2016 Employees: 1
Net Worth: £118,212 Total Assets: £202,105
Registered Office: Ashfield House, Gartocharn, Alexandria, W Dunbartonshire, G83 8NB
Major Shareholder: Iain Andrew Croucher
Officers: Iain Andrew Croucher [1975] Director; Zoe Wight [1980] Director/Sales

North West Industries Ltd
Incorporated: 6 November 2018
Registered Office: 20-22 Wenlock Road, London, N1 7GU
Major Shareholder: Balazs Pillar
Officers: Balazs Pillar [1996] Director [Hungarian]

North West Spirits Limited
Incorporated: 24 August 2017
Net Worth Deficit: £19,713 Total Assets: £36,980
Registered Office: 18 Lawton Street, Congleton, Cheshire, CW12 1RP
Shareholders: Christopher Carsons; Martin David Holmes
Officers: Peter John Billingsley [1991] Director; Christopher Timothy Carsons [1982] Director; Oliver Dodwell [1988] Director; Martin David Holmes [1979] Director

Northern Hospitality (MCR) Limited
Incorporated: 6 November 2018
Registered Office: Egan Roberts, Unit 46 Manor Court, Salesbury Hall Road, Ribchester, Preston, Lancs, PR3 3XR
Shareholders: John Richard Brearley; Andrew Stewart Blackburn
Officers: Andrew Stewart Blackburn [1963] Director; John Richard Brearley [1961] Director

Northern Supplies (NE) Ltd
Incorporated: 29 January 2018
Registered Office: 3 Riverside Court, South Shields, Tyne & Wear, NE33 1EH
Major Shareholder: Santino Welsh
Officers: Santino Welsh [1996] Director; Shan Roheel Zaman [1991] Director

Northgate Wines Limited
Incorporated: 18 October 1996
Net Worth: £18,038 Total Assets: £28,121
Registered Office: Northgate, River Road, Caversham, Berks, RG4 7EH
Shareholders: Martin Game; Martin Game
Officers: Jonathan Game, Secretary; Martin Game [1968] Director

Northpole Crush Ltd
Incorporated: 29 August 2018
Registered Office: 89 Lansbury Road, Enfield, Middlesex, EN3 5NJ
Major Shareholder: Craig Donaldson
Officers: Craig Donaldson [1988] Director

Northwest Drinks Ltd
Incorporated: 6 March 2013 Employees: 8
Net Worth: £12,967 Total Assets: £142,050
Registered Office: Unit 5 Henrietta Trading Estate, Lennox Street, Ashton under Lyne, Lancs, OL6 6HW
Shareholder: Thomas Price
Officers: Thomas Price [1952] Director/Operations Manager; Gillian Shore [1977] Director/General Manager

Norvic Ltd
Incorporated: 11 December 2006 Employees: 1
Net Worth Deficit: £354,961 Total Assets: £1,039,063
Registered Office: 26 Garrick Road, Greenford, Middlesex, UB6 9HT
Major Shareholder: Alex Ghazarians
Officers: Alex Ghazarians [1978] Director

Norwich Dry Gin Company Ltd
Incorporated: 8 March 2016 Employees: 1
Net Worth Deficit: £54,263 Total Assets: £94,035
Registered Office: Evolution House, Iceni Court, Delft Way, Norwich, NR6 6BB
Shareholders: Simon Melton; Alison Rose Melton
Officers: Peter Richard Margree [1972] Director; Alison Rose Melton [1962] Director; Simon Melton [1961] Director

Nothing But The Grape Limited
Incorporated: 14 January 2011
Net Worth Deficit: £31,234 Total Assets: £193,132
Registered Office: Unit 1 Stoney Hill Industrial Estate, Whitchurch, Ross on Wye, Herefords, HR9 6BX
Shareholders: Karen Fiona Birch; Rupert Sylvester Birch
Officers: Rupert Sylvester Birch, Secretary; Karen Fiona Birch [1961] Director; Magnus Courtenay Birch [1987] Director; Rupert Sylvester Birch [1959] Director; Imogen Clare Birch Throckmorton [1991] Director

Nottage Bar Supplier Limited
Incorporated: 16 July 2012 Employees: 1
Net Worth Deficit: £6,508 Total Assets: £153,464
Registered Office: 28-30 Grange Road West, Birkenhead, Merseyside, CH41 4DA
Major Shareholder: Michael David Roberts
Officers: Michael David Roberts [1954] Director

Novarto Drinks Ltd
Incorporated: 2 July 2018
Registered Office: Flat 11, Middlesex Building, 4 Copt Place, London, NW7 1FT
Shareholders: Oleh Bashutskyy; Joao Paulo Marino de Oliveira
Officers: Oleh Bashutskyy [1979] Managing Director [Ukrainian]; Joao Paulo Marino de Oliveira [1987] Managing Director [Italian]

Novel Spirits Collection Limited
Incorporated: 5 February 2018
Registered Office: 12a Linden Grove, London, SE26 5PH
Officers: Mel Abert [1970] Director [American]

Novel Spirits Limited
Incorporated: 5 February 2018
Registered Office: 12a Linden Grove, London, SE26 5PH
Officers: Mel Abert [1970] Director [American]

Novus BH Magister Ltd
Incorporated: 21 November 2016 Employees: 3
Net Worth Deficit: £8,109 Total Assets: £11,474
Registered Office: 32 London Road, Guildford, Surrey, GU1 2AB
Shareholders: Aliona Braileanu; Sergiu Hriplivii; Irina Hriplivii
Officers: Aliona Braileanu [1980] Marketing and Sales Director [Romanian]; Irina Hriplivii [1984] Financial and Sales Director [Romanian]; Sergiu Hriplivii [1981] Logistics Director [Romanian]

Novus Drinks Ltd
Incorporated: 25 October 2018
Registered Office: Unit B, 292 Worton Road, Isleworth, Middlesex, TW7 6EL
Major Shareholder: Balvinder Singh Kaeda
Officers: Balvinder Singh Kaeda [1969] Director

Now This Is It Ltd
Incorporated: 25 May 2018
Registered Office: 71-75 Shelton Street, London, WC2H 9JQ
Shareholders: Graham Bellwood; Christopher Vipond
Officers: Graham Bellwood, Secretary; Graham Bellwood [1945] Director/Retired; Christopher Vipond [1956] Director/Financial Adviser

Nowselect Limited
Incorporated: 22 July 1987 Employees: 1
Net Worth Deficit: £285,115 Total Assets: £20,420
Registered Office: The Rookery, Eyke, Woodbridge, Suffolk, IP12 2RR
Major Shareholder: Andrew Charles Sheepshanks
Officers: Christopher James Sheepshanks, Secretary; Andrew Charles Sheepshanks [1960] Director

Noy Brothers Enterprises Ltd
Incorporated: 16 June 2017
Registered Office: 37 Greenhill Gardens, Northolt, Middlesex, UB5 6BU
Shareholders: Hayk Tovmasyan; Navasard Alexanian; Karine Alexanian; Navasard Alexanian
Officers: Karine Alexanian [1960] Director; Navasard Alexanian [1975] Director [Armenian]

NTKS Ltd
Incorporated: 7 September 2018
Registered Office: 54 Charles Grinling Walk, London, SE18 5BE
Major Shareholder: Kuberan Tharmaraja
Officers: Kuberan Tharmaraja [1983] Director/Accountant

Nue Innovations Limited
Incorporated: 14 March 2017
Net Worth Deficit: £1,187 Total Assets: £8,213
Registered Office: 27 Fleming Close, Cheshunt, Waltham Cross, Herts, EN7 6AY
Major Shareholder: Nnamdi Ekwem
Officers: Nnamdi Ekwem [1980] Director

Number One Drinks Company Limited
Incorporated: 24 July 2006 Employees: 1
Net Worth: £242,657 Total Assets: £450,252
Registered Office: St Johns House, 25 St John Maddermarket, Norwich, NR2 1DN
Major Shareholder: Marcin Adam Miller
Officers: Eleanor Joy Miller, Secretary; Marcin Adam Miller [1964] Director

Nutricont Ltd
Incorporated: 19 January 2018
Registered Office: 18 Old Forge, Armagh, BT60 4LP
Shareholders: Laszlo Zsolt Goldfinger; Csaba Domokos
Officers: Csaba Domokos [1976] Director [Hungarian]

NYSA International Ltd
Incorporated: 22 May 2017
Net Worth: £69,072 *Total Assets:* £70,000
Registered Office: First Floor, 15 Young Street, London, W8 5EH
Shareholder: Andrew Heald
Officers: Louis Bertrand Marie Henri Bizouard de Montille [1982] Director [French]; Ludovic Luc Marie Lazare Bizouard de Montille [1955] Managing Director [French]

O & E Food Ltd
Incorporated: 17 September 2018
Registered Office: 99 Grays Inn Road, London, WC1X 8TY
Shareholders: Ozan Yadirgi; Erdal Karadag
Officers: Erdal Karadag [1975] Director; Ozan Yadirgi [1980] Director

O & P Investments Limited
Incorporated: 21 October 2010
Net Worth Deficit: £23,375 *Total Assets:* £14,157
Registered Office: Suite 103, Davina House, 137-149 Goswell Road, London, EC1V 7ET
Shareholder: Raufu Adedamola Ojosipe
Officers: Raufu Adedamola Ojosipe, Secretary; Raufu Adedamola Ojosipe [1975] Director/Consultant

O'Donnell Moonshine Limited
Incorporated: 11 November 2016
Net Worth Deficit: £5,083 *Total Assets:* £101,787
Registered Office: Unit 9CI Queens Yard, White Post Lane, London, E9 5EN
Parent: O'Donnell Moonshine GmbH
Officers: George Oliver Mossman, Secretary; Hugo Cooke [1992] Director; Philip Morsink [1987] Director [German]; August Ullrich [1988] Director [German]

O'Neill Fine Wines Limited
Incorporated: 11 November 1985
Net Worth Deficit: £6,564 *Total Assets:* £56,376
Registered Office: c/o McKenzie Philips Accountants, 22 Coronation Road, Crosby, Merseyside, L23 5RQ
Shareholder: Malcolm Alexander O'Neill
Officers: Generaldine Veronica O'Neill, Secretary; Generaldine Veronica O'Neill [1953] Director/Teacher; Malcolm Alexander O'Neill [1937] Director/Wine Merchant

O'Vineyards Ltd
Incorporated: 1 June 2016
Registered Office: Brent House, 382 Gloucester Road, Cheltenham, Glos, GL51 7AY
Major Shareholder: Brigitte O'Connell
Officers: Brigitte O'Connell, Secretary; Brigitte O'Connell [1947] Director [French]

OAB Ventures Limited
Incorporated: 10 October 2017
Registered Office: Flat 8, 5 Cray View Close, Orpington, Kent, BR5 3FH
Major Shareholder: Benson Afasy-Brown
Officers: Abena Oduro, Secretary; Benson Afasy-Brown [1978] Director/Met CCTV

The Oak Alliance Ltd.
Incorporated: 9 November 2015
Net Worth: £2 *Total Assets:* £2
Registered Office: 118 Fairmont Avenue, London, E14 9PL
Major Shareholder: Alaa Merajuddin
Officers: Alaa Merajuddin [1986] Director/Finance [Bahraini]

Oak Cask Distribution Ltd
Incorporated: 21 February 2013
Net Worth Deficit: £31,066 *Total Assets:* £11,756
Registered Office: Marsh Cottage, Robertsend Lane, Long Green, Glos, GL19 4QH
Major Shareholder: Jonah David Costello
Officers: Jonah David Costello, Secretary; Jonah Costello [1988] Director/Builder

Oak Group One P.L.C.
Incorporated: 8 January 2019
Registered Office: 3 Gower Street, London, WC1E 6HA
Officers: Mike Peter Adams [1967] Director [Finnish]; Paavo Ollipekka Vahvaselkae [1971] Director [Finnish]

Oak Wines Limited
Incorporated: 21 November 2017
Registered Office: Stalk Farm, High Street, Mawdesley, Ormskirk, Lancs, L40 3TD
Officers: Michelle Knowles, Secretary; Michelle Knowles [1980] Director

Oakmount Group Limited
Incorporated: 30 January 2018
Registered Office: Flat 5C, 52 Grainger Park Road, Newcastle upon Tyne, NE4 8RQ
Officers: Fred Rene [1992] Director/Founder

Obadec Enterprises Limited
Incorporated: 26 September 2005
Registered Office: 16 Portmeadow Walk, Abbeywood, London, SE2 9UL
Officers: Titilope Gisanrin, Secretary; Babajide Adelekan Adeyemi [1960] Director/Chemical Engineering; Titilope Adeyemi [1966] Director/Health Professional

Ocavia Wine & Spirits Ltd
Incorporated: 11 October 2018
Registered Office: Suite 9, 4th Floor, 44 Broadway, London, E15 1XH
Major Shareholder: Iurie Bivol
Officers: Iurie Bivol [1972] Director

Occidental & Oriental Cellars Limited
Incorporated: 29 July 2009 *Employees:* 5
Net Worth: £81,211 *Total Assets:* £1,638,564
Registered Office: 146 High Street, Billericay, Essex, CM12 9DF
Major Shareholder: Yu Jin Desmond Lim
Officers: Oliver Christian Wynn Holtam, Secretary; Claire Rosalie Bailey [1969] Sales Director; Lee Raymond Crymble [1976] Managing Director; David Lindsay Emerson Hamilton [1957] Director; Oliver Christian Wynn Holtam [1976] Finance Director; Aby Juan Poo Tan [1974] Director/Wine Merchant [Singaporean]

Ocean Wines Limited
Incorporated: 22 January 2018
Registered Office: 18 Kettlewell Walk, Manchester, M18 8JW
Major Shareholder: Ishtiaq Ahmed
Officers: Ishtiaq Ahmed [1982] Director [Italian]

Octagon Industries Ltd
Incorporated: 19 February 2018
Registered Office: 23 Grafton Street, Brighton, BN2 1AQ
Shareholder: Daniel Marcos-Ashworth
Officers: Daniel Marcos-Ashworth [1998] Director/Businessman

Oeno Limited
Incorporated: 29 November 2000
Net Worth: £624,446 *Total Assets:* £1,925,795
Registered Office: 1 Lancaster Place, London, WC2E 7ED
Major Shareholder: Simon Charles Farr
Officers: Peri Batliwala, Secretary; Peri Batliwala [1959] Director/Consultant; Simon Charles Farr [1953] Director/Consultant

Oenofuture Limited
Incorporated: 15 June 2015 *Employees:* 1
Net Worth Deficit: £21,828 *Total Assets:* £7,651
Registered Office: Level 30, The Leadenhall Building, 122 Leadenhall Street, London, EC3V 4AB
Major Shareholder: Daniel Eros Carnio
Officers: Daniel Eros Carnio [1987] Director [Italian]

Official Box Office UK Ltd
Incorporated: 10 October 2018
Registered Office: Kemp House, 160 City Road, London, EC1V 2NX
Major Shareholder: Craig Williams
Officers: Craig Williams [1989] Director/Events & Marketing

The Offie Limited
Incorporated: 26 March 2003 *Employees:* 1
Net Worth: £2,011,597 *Total Assets:* £5,089,589
Registered Office: 34 Queensbury Station Parade, Edgware, Middlesex, HA8 5NN
Officers: Bhavna Jasraj, Secretary; Rajesh Hargovind Jasraj [1964] Director

Ohsake Ltd
Incorporated: 9 July 2018
Registered Office: 3 Lisle Close, Newbury, Berks, RG14 1PT
Major Shareholder: Alistair Neil McCallum
Officers: Alistair Neil McCallum [1990] Director/Entrepreneur

Ojo de Dios Ltd
Incorporated: 9 November 2018
Registered Office: 4 Ingestre Road, London, E7 0DY
Shareholders: Michael Neil John Cloke; Eduardo Gomez Resendiz; Barry Christopher Halstead
Officers: Michael Neil John Cloke [1984] Director/Marketing Consultant; Eduardo Gomez Resendiz [1981] Sales Director; Barry Christopher Halstead [1981] Director/Marketing Consultant

Okowita Vodka Limited
Incorporated: 15 September 2015 *Employees:* 1
Net Worth Deficit: £64,586 *Total Assets:* £26,480
Registered Office: 5th Floor, 89 New Bond Street, London, W1S 1DA
Major Shareholder: Jan Felix Michael Woroniecki
Officers: Jan Felix Michael Woroniecki [1959] Director

Old and Rare Whisky Limited
Incorporated: 31 December 2018
Registered Office: Kemp House, 160 City Road, London, EC1V 2NX
Major Shareholder: The Nguyen
Officers: The Nguyen [1984] Director

Old Brenin Distillery Ltd
Incorporated: 26 June 2018
Registered Office: Unit 30 Pontygwindy Industrial Estate, Caerphilly, Gwent, CF83 3HU
Major Shareholder: Carl Antony Simmonds
Officers: Carl Antony Simmonds [1968] Managing Director

Old Butcher's Wine Cellar Limited
Incorporated: 13 April 2012 *Employees:* 3
Net Worth: £24,715 *Total Assets:* £96,199
Registered Office: Old Butcher's Wine Cellar, High Street, Cookham, Berks, SL6 9SQ
Shareholders: Angela Louise Stratford; Paul Victor Stratford
Officers: Angela Louise Stratford [1974] Director; Paul Victor Stratford [1959] Director

The Old Cellar Ltd
Incorporated: 21 June 2011
Net Worth: £2,791 *Total Assets:* £7,075
Registered Office: 14 Parkfields Avenue, London, SW20 0QS
Officers: Stoyan Ivanov Stoyanov [1980] Director [Bulgarian]

Old Empire Events Ltd
Incorporated: 12 July 2018
Registered Office: 22 St Johns Place, Bury St Edmunds, Suffolk, IP33 1SW
Shareholders: Anthony Mark Woolnough; Darren Keath Mulvaney

The Old Man Rum Company Limited
Incorporated: 27 April 2015
Net Worth Deficit: £21,557 *Total Assets:* £8,568
Registered Office: 32 Portland Terrace, Newcastle upon Tyne, NE2 1QP
Shareholder: John Raymond Dickson
Officers: John Raymond Dickson [1962] Director

Old Red Lion Theatre Pub Limited
Incorporated: 11 January 2012 *Employees:* 15
Net Worth: £3,625 *Total Assets:* £89,025
Registered Office: 418 St John Street, London, EC1V 4NJ
Major Shareholder: Damien Devine
Officers: Damien Devine [1960] Managing Director; Helen Devine [1977] Managing Director

Old Sport Limited
Incorporated: 5 March 2015
Net Worth Deficit: £7,371 *Total Assets:* £26,371
Registered Office: First Floor, 15 Young Street, London, W8 5EH
Shareholder: Sagittarius 2 B
Officers: Guillaume Pierre Marie Eric Frerejean Taittinger [1978] Director [French]; Rodolphe Frerejean Taittinger [1986] Director [French]; Florestan Frederic Marie Loriot de Rouvray [1990] Director [French]

Old St.Andrews Limited
Incorporated: 9 July 2003 *Employees:* 2
Net Worth: £825,096 *Total Assets:* £1,968,533
Registered Office: Unit 7 Maidstone Road, Platt, Sevenoaks, Kent, TN15 8FD
Parent: Gorton Business Management Limited
Officers: Susan Elizabeth Gorton, Secretary; Robert David Gorton [1953] Director

UK Wholesalers of Beers, Wines and Spirits   dellam

Old Town Blending Company Ltd
Incorporated: 24 July 2014
Net Worth Deficit: £9,779 *Total Assets:* £52,228
Registered Office: 15 Atholl Crescent, Edinburgh, EH3 8HA
Shareholder: Gregor Alexander Jack Mathieson
Officers: Iain Lindsay Hamilton [1955] Director; Gregor Alexander Jack Mathieson [1967] Director; Gordon Robert Watt [1965] Director

Old Tullymet Whisky Company Ltd
Incorporated: 20 April 2017
Registered Office: 29 Portland Road, Kilmarnock, E Ayrshire, KA1 2BY
Officers: Scott McMurray Watson [1972] Director; Brian David Woods [1974] Director

Old Wine House Ltd
Incorporated: 28 December 2017
Registered Office: 58 New Bedford Road, Luton, Beds, LU1 1SH
Officers: Lilian Rotaru [1974] Director [Romanian]

Oldschool Wines Limited
Incorporated: 27 November 1963
Net Worth Deficit: £18,225 *Total Assets:* £69,835
Registered Office: 116-118 Islington High Street, Camden Passage, London, N1 8EG
Major Shareholder: Stephen Richard Oldschool
Officers: Stephen Richard Oldschool, Secretary; Dohne Arnold [1952] Director/Surveyor; Stephen Richard Oldschool [1947] Director/Solicitor

Olive Wines Limited
Incorporated: 30 April 2015
Net Worth: £90 *Total Assets:* £53,653
Registered Office: Electric House, Ninian Way, Wilnecote, Tamworth, Staffs, B77 5DE
Parent: Foster Healthcare Limited
Officers: Samuel Lister Olive [1981] Director

Oliver & Bird Limited
Incorporated: 22 January 2004
Net Worth: £1,024 *Total Assets:* £51,165
Registered Office: 5 Pellew Arcade, Teign Street, Teignmouth, Devon, TQ14 8EB
Major Shareholder: David Morley
Officers: David Morley [1954] Director

Oliver's Beer and Wine Limited
Incorporated: 24 November 2005 *Employees:* 29
Net Worth: £50,113 *Total Assets:* £1,730,247
Registered Office: Falcon Park, Hophurst Lane, Crawley Down, Crawley, W Sussex, RH10 4XF
Officers: Paul Andrew Oliver, Secretary; Paul Andrew Oliver [1971] Director; Yusuf Osman Tary [1970] Director; Allan Winton [1963] Sales Director

Olivers Wine Agency Limited
Incorporated: 8 March 2011
Net Worth Deficit: £63,602 *Total Assets:* £63,686
Registered Office: Unit 17-18 Borers Yard, Borers Arms Road, Copthorne, Crawley, W Sussex, RH10 3LH
Major Shareholder: Paul Andrew Oliver
Officers: Paul Andrew Oliver [1971] Director

Olley (NE) Limited
Incorporated: 9 August 2013
Net Worth: £6,885 *Total Assets:* £27,752
Registered Office: 27 Saddleston Close, Hillside Estate, Hartlepool, Cleveland, TS26 0EZ
Major Shareholder: Frank Olley
Officers: Frank Olley [1946] Director/Business Consultant

OM Beers & Minerals Ltd
Incorporated: 4 April 2003 *Employees:* 13
Net Worth: £17,454 *Total Assets:* £272,556
Registered Office: Cambridge House, 27 Cambridge, House, Wanstead, London, E11 2PU
Officers: Sabina Vedi, Secretary; Gaurav Vedi [1981] Director/Accountant

OM Wines Ltd
Incorporated: 4 June 2015
Net Worth: £1 *Total Assets:* £1
Registered Office: 3 Plumpton Close, Northolt, Middlesex, UB5 4EQ
Major Shareholder: Kumarathasan Kumarasamy
Officers: Kumarathasan Kumarasamy [1974] Director/Business Development Manager [Sri Lankan]

ONCC Import Limited
Incorporated: 5 February 2018
Registered Office: Flat 9, Hamilton Court, St Nicholas Street, Coventry, Warwicks, CV1 4BW
Officers: Constantin Oncica [1986] Director/Self Employed [Romanian]

One Love Rum Company Limited
Incorporated: 8 December 2016
Net Worth Deficit: £4,569 *Total Assets:* £10,218
Registered Office: 3 Butlin Close, Rothwell, Kettering, Northants, NN14 6YA
Major Shareholder: Steven Paul Gamage
Officers: Steven Paul Gamage [1990] Managing Director

One Point Supplies Limited
Incorporated: 22 June 2012 *Employees:* 2
Net Worth: £121,213 *Total Assets:* £349,919
Registered Office: Unit 1 Frontier Works, 33 Queen Street, London, N17 8JA
Major Shareholder: Dipum Patel
Officers: Dipum Patel [1979] Director

One Source Global Limited
Incorporated: 16 February 2018
Registered Office: 11 Kiloran Place, Newton Mearns, Glasgow, G77 6WT
Shareholder: Sandeep Singh
Officers: Sandeep Singh [1977] Director

One Stop East Limited
Incorporated: 27 November 2018
Registered Office: 29 Pangbourne Avenue, London, W10 6DJ
Major Shareholder: Aaisha Dadral
Officers: Aaisha Dadral [1986] Director

Ooberstock Limited
Incorporated: 2 July 2010
Net Worth: £113,427 *Total Assets:* £1,592,134
Registered Office: 9 Queens Square, Ascot Business Park, Ascot, Berks, SL5 9FE
Parent: Drinks21 Group Ltd
Officers: Nigel Kevin Morton, Secretary; Stephen Michael Brogan [1969] Director

The Opendoor Gin Company Ltd
Incorporated: 27 July 2016 *Employees:* 2
Net Worth Deficit: £13,908 *Total Assets:* £11,760
Registered Office: Beechey House, 87 Church Street, Crowthorne, Berks, RG45 7AW
Shareholders: Michael Ian Pollen; Suzanne Gail Pollen
Officers: Michael Ian Pollen [1957] Director; Suzanne Gail Pollen [1960] Director

Openwine Limited
Incorporated: 11 March 2008 *Employees:* 2
Net Worth: £39,554 *Total Assets:* £109,071
Registered Office: Willow Cottage, Reading Road, Mattingley, Hants, RG27 8JU
Shareholders: Stuart Gregory Bowman-Hood; Lisa June Bowman-Hood
Officers: Stuart Gregory Bowman-Hood, Secretary; Lisa June Bowman-Hood [1968] Director/Lecturer; Stuart Gregory Bowman-Hood [1965] Director/Sales Manager

Ops Wines Ltd
Incorporated: 4 October 2018
Registered Office: Flat 21, Centenary Heights, Larkwood Avenue, London, SE10 8GE
Major Shareholder: Pedro Miguel Queiros Mota
Officers: Pedro Miguel Queiros Mota [1986] Director [Portuguese]

Opus Cellars Limited
Incorporated: 28 July 2016
Net Worth: £291 *Total Assets:* £20,604
Registered Office: 3 Acorn Business Centre, Northarbour Road, Cosham, Portsmouth, PO6 3TH
Shareholders: Jean Victor Lanson; Roderick Neal McLoughlin
Officers: Roderick Neal McLoughlin [1959] Director

Opus Wines Limited
Incorporated: 6 August 1991
Registered Office: The Lodge, Odell, Bedford, MK43 7BB
Shareholders: Mark Glenn Bridgman Shaw; Lesley Shaw
Officers: Mark Glenn Bridgman Shaw, Secretary/Director; Mark Glenn Bridgman Shaw [1947] Director

Ora Brewing Company Ltd
Incorporated: 18 January 2016
Net Worth Deficit: £12,193 *Total Assets:* £10,286
Registered Office: 24 Eleanor Close, London, SE16 6PE
Shareholder: Daniele Zaccarelli
Officers: Daniele Costa Zaccarelli [1984] Director [Italian]; Emanuele Antonio Poletti [1984] Director [Italian]; Pietro Rubbianesi [1984] Director [Italian]

Oracle Fine Wines Ltd.
Incorporated: 28 March 2018
Registered Office: Office 32, 19-21 Crawford Street, London, W1H 1PJ
Major Shareholder: Gareth Howard Charlton
Officers: Gareth Charlton, Secretary; Gareth Howard Charlton [1966] Director

Orale Ltd.
Incorporated: 13 September 2016
Registered Office: 27 Old Gloucester Street, London, WC1N 3AX
Shareholders: Janusz Wojciech Sosnierz; Michael Ivonne Mendoza Tirado
Officers: Michael Ivonne Mendoza Tirado [1976] Trade and Investment Director [Mexican]; Janusz Wojciech Sosnierz [1977] Director/Operations Manager [Polish]

Orbit Wines Limited
Incorporated: 24 March 2017 *Employees:* 1
Net Worth: £2,387 *Total Assets:* £81,246
Registered Office: Flat 1, 6 Vernon Terrace, Brighton, BN1 3JG
Major Shareholder: Nebojsa Gusic
Officers: Nebojsa Gusic [1966] Director/Wine Merchant

Orchard Wine Co Ltd
Incorporated: 28 June 2016
Registered Office: Unit 7 Win Business Park, Newry, Co Down, BT35 6PH
Shareholders: Aoibheann Bellew; Bernard Murchan
Officers: Bernard Murchan [1979] Director/Manager [Irish]

Orchard-Lisle Wines Ltd
Incorporated: 16 July 2018
Registered Office: The Chimneys, 7 Church Road, Snape, Saxmundham, Suffolk, IP17 1SZ
Shareholders: James Comrie Orchard-Lisle; Eleanor Hepta Scarlett
Officers: James Comrie Orchard-Lisle [1977] Director/Sound Engineer; Eleanor Hepta Scarlett [1979] Director/Lawyer

Organic Country Drinks Ltd
Incorporated: 29 March 2005
Net Worth Deficit: £688 *Total Assets:* £1,449
Registered Office: Sportsman Farm, St Michaels, Tenterden, Kent, TN30 6SY
Shareholders: William Roy Cook; Irma Cook
Officers: Richard Michael Marney, Secretary; Irma Cook [1957] Director/Administrator; William Roy Cook [1946] Director/Wine Producer

Organic French Wines Limited
Incorporated: 13 December 2016
Registered Office: 3 Tunnel Hill Mews, Knock Lane, Blisworth, Northampton, NN7 3DA
Major Shareholder: John Eric Meadows
Officers: John Eric Meadows [1956] Director/Insurance Broker

Organic Wine Company Limited (The)
Incorporated: 20 December 1985
Net Worth: £37,700 *Total Assets:* £37,700
Registered Office: 1 Brands Hill Avenue, High Wycombe, Bucks, HP13 5PZ
Officers: Jonathan Lloyd Clifford-Smith, Secretary; Anthony Frank Mason [1944] Director/Marketing Consultant

Organica Food & Wine Ltd
Incorporated: 22 May 2015
Net Worth Deficit: £77,479 *Total Assets:* £107,758
Registered Office: Churchill House, 137-139 Brent Street, Hendon, London, NW4 4DJ
Major Shareholder: Onder Korkmaz
Officers: Onder Korkmaz [1979] Director [German]

Oriental Drinks Limited
Incorporated: 8 December 2016
Net Worth: £1 *Total Assets:* £1
Registered Office: 38 Portland Road, London, SE25 4PF
Officers: Tong Zhu [1980] Director [Chinese]

Origin Drinks Limited
Incorporated: 26 July 2011
Registered Office: 29 Montgomery Road, Newbury, Berks, RG14 6HT
Major Shareholder: Ben Tagoe
Officers: Ben Tagoe [1983] Director/HR Manager

Origin Wine Limited
Incorporated: 20 May 2004 Employees: 13
Net Worth: £2,665,196 Total Assets: £10,213,517
Registered Office: Rivermead House, 7 Lewis Court, Grove Park, Enderby, Leicester, LE19 1SD
Officers: Yves Bernard Adrien Fontannaz [1967] Director [Swiss]

Original & Distinctive Limited
Incorporated: 25 November 2013
Registered Office: 180 Piccadilly, London, W1J 9HF
Major Shareholder: Kenneth John Davey
Officers: Kenneth John Davey [1955] Director

The Original Beer Company Limited
Incorporated: 3 September 2014
Registered Office: 29 York Place, Edinburgh, EH1 3HP
Major Shareholder: Colin Makin
Officers: Colin Makin [1962] Director

The Original Bier Company Limited
Incorporated: 1 September 2014
Net Worth Deficit: £31,860 Total Assets: £24,702
Registered Office: 29 York Place, Edinburgh, EH1 3HP
Major Shareholder: Colin Makin
Officers: Colin Makin [1962] Director

The Original Herbale Brewing Company Ltd
Incorporated: 22 July 2015
Net Worth Deficit: £16,279 Total Assets: £15,302
Registered Office: 21 Barons Way, Kingsthorpe, Northampton, NN2 8HP
Major Shareholder: James David Tze-Ming Gouldsmith
Officers: James David Tze-Ming Gouldsmith [1967] Director/Manager

Original Liqueur Co Ltd
Incorporated: 25 July 2012
Net Worth Deficit: £738 Total Assets: £8,126
Registered Office: 4 Falcon Road, Belfast, BT12 6SJ
Shareholder: Paul Martin Camplisson
Officers: Paul Martin Camplisson [1965] Director [Irish]; Sarah-Jane Noelle McClure [1984] Director [Irish]; Gareth Rory Nethercott [1969] Director [Irish]; Eunan Joseph Ryan [1963] Director [Irish]

Original Wooden Case Limited
Incorporated: 22 January 2014
Net Worth: £49 Total Assets: £34,211
Registered Office: The Workshop, 3rd Floor, 32-40 Tontine Street, Folkestone, Kent, CT20 1JU
Shareholder: Simon Richard Trevor
Officers: Alexander Stephen James Pearce [1987] Director/Investment Analyst; Simon Richard Trevor [1958] Director/Wine Importer

Orion Cash & Carry Limited
Incorporated: 17 November 2006
Net Worth Deficit: £58,809 Total Assets: £72,900
Registered Office: 499a Stanhope Road, South Shields, Tyne & Wear, NE33 4QX
Shareholder: Liaqat Ali
Officers: Liaqat Ali, Secretary; Liaqat Ali [1954] Director/Businessman; Yasar Razwan Ali [1978] Director/Businessman; Talat Naheed [1958] Director/Businesswoman

Oris Black Ltd
Incorporated: 3 April 2017
Registered Office: 2 Waterside House, Theed Street, London, SE1 8ST
Major Shareholder: Oresiri Erhuero
Officers: Oresiri Erhuero [1968] Director/Designer

Ormos Trades Limited
Incorporated: 10 September 2012 Employees: 5
Net Worth: £6,451 Total Assets: £255,924
Registered Office: 35 Grafton Way, London, W1T 5DB
Major Shareholder: Konstantinos Grigoriou
Officers: Konstantinos Grigoriou [1988] Director [Greek]

Orsa Major Ltd
Incorporated: 8 October 2014 Employees: 4
Net Worth: £2,846,042 Total Assets: £2,895,828
Registered Office: 1 Kings Avenue, London, N21 3NA
Shareholders: Carlo Canavera; Severino Canavera; Renato Canavera
Officers: Giovanni Brumana [1958] Director [Italian]; Rasiklal Devshi Shah [1945] Director

Orso Wine Agencies Limited
Incorporated: 24 May 2005
Net Worth: £340,581 Total Assets: £379,709
Registered Office: Suite SBRO, Morgan Reach House, 136 Hagley Road, Birmingham, B16 9NX
Major Shareholder: Daniel Orsolini
Officers: Daniel Orsolini, Secretary; Daniel Orsolini [1965] Director/Wine Merchant [French]; Nicola Jane Orsolini [1968] Director/International Rights Manager

Peter Osborne Fine Wines Ltd
Incorporated: 29 July 2003 Employees: 2
Net Worth: £14,320 Total Assets: £63,725
Registered Office: 2 Lake End Court, Taplow Road, Taplow, Maidenhead, Berks, SL6 0JQ
Major Shareholder: Martin Robert Chapman
Officers: Thessa Lonica Chapman, Secretary; Martin Robert Chapman [1949] Director

Oso Brew Co Ltd
Incorporated: 27 February 2018
Registered Office: 19 Dolben Court, Montaigne Close, London, SW1P 4BB
Shareholders: Patrick Lloyd Tuck; David George Ross
Officers: Peter John Tuck, Secretary; David George Ross [1986] Director; Patrick Lloyd Tuck [1986] Director

Ossau Vins & Spiritueux Ltd
Incorporated: 15 May 2014 Employees: 3
Net Worth Deficit: £177,915 Total Assets: £245,778
Registered Office: 7 The Shrubberies, George Lane, London, E18 1BD
Shareholders: Olivier Carsoule; Antoine Gravouil; Eric Lafon
Officers: Antoine Gravouil [1979] Director [French]

Othello Food and Wine Limited
Incorporated: 31 January 2018
Registered Office: 70 Blakiston Street, Fleetwood, Lancs, FY7 6EW
Major Shareholder: Lee Dann
Officers: Lee Dann [1970] Director and Driver

Other World Wines Limited
Incorporated: 21 May 2018
Registered Office: 24 The Green, Edlesborough, Dunstable, Beds, LU6 2JF
Shareholders: Jack Alexander Blumsom; Gleb Petrenko
Officers: Jack Alexander Blumsom [1994] Director/Chief Executive; Gleb Petrenko [1994] Director/Chief Executive

Otros Vinos Limited
Incorporated: 21 January 2015
Net Worth Deficit: £10,179   *Total Assets:* £39,171
Registered Office: 1 Kings Avenue, London, N21 3NA
Major Shareholder: Fernando Berry
Officers: Fernando Berry [1984] Director [Australian]

Oui Vino Limited
Incorporated: 9 October 2018
Registered Office: 43 Polmor Road, Crowlas, Penzance, Cornwall, TR20 8DW
Shareholder: Hamish William Ludbrook
Officers: Hamish William Ludbrook [1983] Managing Director [New Zealander]

Our Tino Ltd
Incorporated: 10 April 2017   *Employees:* 1
Net Worth Deficit: £4,188   *Total Assets:* £6,190
Registered Office: Seven Mile House Farm, Old Great North Road, Seaton Burn, Newcastle upon Tyne, NE13 6BS
Major Shareholder: Brooke Davison
Officers: Brooke Davison [1990] Director of Our Tino

Ourglass & Partners Ltd
Incorporated: 3 May 2017
Net Worth Deficit: £9,990   *Total Assets:* £4
Registered Office: 3a Shaftesbury Road, London, N19 4QW
Officers: Martin Thomas Buchanan [1983] Director/Consultant; Benedict Edward Groves Johnson [1982] Director/Consultant

Ourlocal Limited
Incorporated: 18 April 2018
Registered Office: 21 Strickland Avenue, Dartford, Kent, DA1 5JR
Major Shareholder: Thamayanthy Janarthanan
Officers: Thamayanthy Janarthanan [1985] Director/Self Employed [Sri Lankan]

Outlander Brands Limited
Incorporated: 30 November 2017
Registered Office: 71-75 Shelton Street, Covent Garden, London, WC2H 9JQ
Major Shareholder: Carly Watson
Officers: Andrew Watson, Secretary; Andrew Watson [1980] Sales Director

Outstanding People Limited
Incorporated: 30 May 2017
Net Worth: £1,350   *Total Assets:* £1,350
Registered Office: H5 Ash Tree Court, Nottingham Business Park, Nottingham, NG8 6PY
Officers: Antonio Miguel Garcia Rodrigues Da Cruz [1974] Director [Portuguese]

OX Bespoke Logistics Ltd
Incorporated: 15 August 2017
Registered Office: 86 Lincoln Court, Bethune Road, London, N16 5EA
Officers: Mikolaj Jaworski [1983] Director [Polish]

OX Wines Ltd
Incorporated: 23 January 2019
Registered Office: 4 Amwell Place, Hertford Heath, Hertford, SG13 7SE
Major Shareholder: Xeniya Otkidych
Officers: John Richard Farquhar Parry, Secretary; Xeniya Otkidych [1991] Director [Kazakh]

Oxford Beer House Limited
Incorporated: 18 July 2018
Registered Office: 20 Foxwell Drive, Headington, Oxford, OX3 9QB
Major Shareholder: Ming Keong Choy
Officers: Ming Keong Choy [1986] Director/Operations Manager [British/Malaysian]

Oxford Brewery Limited
Incorporated: 20 December 2018
Registered Office: Mount Manor House, 16 The Mount, Guildford, Surrey, GU2 4HN
Major Shareholder: Moira Allan Ross
Officers: Moira Allan Ross [1953] Director

The Oxford Brewing Company Limited
Incorporated: 24 August 2017
Registered Office: Mount Manor House, 16 The Mount, Guildford, Surrey, GU2 4HN
Major Shareholder: Moira Allan Ross
Officers: Moira Allan Ross [1953] Director

Oxus Gin Ltd.
Incorporated: 2 June 2016
Net Worth Deficit: £7,936   *Total Assets:* £1,135
Registered Office: 4 Shaws Close, Prestwood, Great Missenden, Bucks, HP16 0SL
Officers: Elliot Mark Lacour [1992] Founder and Director; Samuel Mellett [1993] Director

Oyster Import Export Limited
Incorporated: 28 December 2016
Registered Office: 86 Homestead Way, New Addington, Croydon, Surrey, CR0 0AQ
Major Shareholder: Sami Safadi
Officers: Sami Safadi [1960] Director/Entrepreneur

Ozpax Limited
Incorporated: 31 July 2018
Registered Office: Durham House, 38 Street Lane, Ripley, Denby, Derbys, DE5 8NE
Major Shareholder: Andrew James Ogilvy
Officers: Stanley Yeomans [1944] Director

P & P Distribution Limited
Incorporated: 24 April 2018
Registered Office: 54 Dunvegan Drive, Rise Park, Nottingham, NG5 5DY
Shareholders: Pouya Mehran; Pouria Mehran
Officers: Pouria Mehran [1989] Director; Pouya Mehran [1989] Director

P & P Vino Limited
Incorporated: 8 August 2017
Registered Office: 30 Nelson Street, Leicester, LE1 7BA
Major Shareholder: Rajesh Pandya
Officers: Rajesh Pandya [1973] Director

Pacta Connect UK Limited
Incorporated: 8 December 2009
Net Worth: £23,554 *Total Assets:* £23,554
Registered Office: 36 Upper St James's Street, Brighton, BN2 1JN
Shareholder: Trevor Long
Officers: Judith Elaines Burns [1959] Director; Trevor Long [1953] Director

Padlock Brewery Ltd.
Incorporated: 4 January 2019
Registered Office: 247 Burton Road, Manchester, M20 2WA
Shareholders: Patrick Joseph Madigan; Nathan Boyes
Officers: Nathan Boyes [1993] Director; Patrick Joseph Madigan [1992] Director

Padstow Brewing Company (2013) Ltd
Incorporated: 4 October 1999 *Employees:* 2
Previous: Precise Consulting Limited
Net Worth: £24,371 *Total Assets:* £26,362
Registered Office: 62 Wilson Street, London, EC2A 2BU
Shareholders: Desmond John Archer; Caron Patricia Archer
Officers: Caron Patricia Archer [1960] Director/Customer Manager; Desmond John Archer [1958] Director

Pago Wines Limited
Incorporated: 24 September 2018
Registered Office: 49 Forth Park, Stirling, FK9 5NT
Major Shareholder: Samuel James Burns
Officers: Samuel James Burns [1984] Director/Shop Assistant

Paisajes Trading Ltd
Incorporated: 14 March 2018
Registered Office: The Old Truman Brewery c/o Yes Please, 91 Brick Lane, London, E1 6QL
Shareholders: Andrew James Law; Caroline Natasha Beashel
Officers: Caroline Natasha Beashel [1985] Director/Press Officer; Andrew James Law [1986] Director/Video Commissioner

Pale Fox Wines Limited
Incorporated: 5 April 2017 *Employees:* 1
Net Worth: £36,176 *Total Assets:* £39,639
Registered Office: Unit 1A Hazlewood Tower, Golborne Gardens, London, W10 5DT
Shareholders: Harry Cooke; Mark Douglas Hill
Officers: Harry Cooke [1992] Director/Entrepreneur; Mark Douglas Hill [1977] Director/Entrepreneur

Palinka UK Ltd
Incorporated: 27 July 2018
Registered Office: 20-22 Wenlock Road, London, N1 7GU
Shareholders: Robert James Lacey; Katalin Eva Vinter
Officers: Robert James Lacey [1973] Director; Katalin Eva Vintner [1978] Director

Pallet Price Wholesale Ltd
Incorporated: 31 October 2017
Registered Office: 203 Western Road, Mickleover, Derby, DE3 9GU
Major Shareholder: Bhupinder Singh Sohal
Officers: Bhupinder Singh Sohal [1982] Director/Entrepreneur

Palmer Traders Ltd
Incorporated: 9 May 2018
Registered Office: 20-22 Wenlock Road, London, N1 7GU
Major Shareholder: Lucca Fabbri
Officers: Lucca Fabbri [1984] Director/Sales Manager [Italian]

Palmerston Fine Wines Ltd.
Incorporated: 13 July 1993
Net Worth Deficit: £8,688
Registered Office: 48 Raeburn Place, Edinburgh, EH4 1HL
Shareholder: Simon John Lloyd
Officers: Simon John Lloyd, Secretary; Simon John Lloyd [1974] Director/Wine Merchant

Palms & Liquor Enterprises Limited
Incorporated: 4 December 2017
Registered Office: 75 Bradstowe House, Headstone Road, Harrow, Middlesex, HA1 1EH
Major Shareholder: Adetola Adebukunla James-Odukoya
Officers: Eniye Tawari, Secretary; Adetola Adebukunla James-Odukoya [1991] Managing Director; Eniye Blessing Tawari [1991] Director

Paloma & Pablo Import & Export Ltd
Incorporated: 8 February 2019
Registered Office: Vulcan Road, Bilston, Wolverhampton, W Midlands, WV14 7LF
Major Shareholder: Victor Nwamaziogbu Chukwudi
Officers: Victor Nwamaziogbu Chukwudi [1973] Director [Spanish]

Pan Euro Foods Limited
Incorporated: 2 March 2005 *Employees:* 1
Net Worth: £13,340 *Total Assets:* £18,448
Registered Office: 146 Berkeley Avenue, Hounslow, Middlesex, TW4 6LB
Officers: Jaswinder Kaur Rai, Secretary; Rajinder Singh Rai [1954] Director/Manager [Indian]

Panache du Sud Ltd
Incorporated: 24 January 2019
Registered Office: 49 Mount Ararat Road, Richmond, Surrey, TW10 6PL
Shareholders: Matthew Jeremy Newcomb; Alexander Slater
Officers: Matthew Jeremy Newcomb [1971] Director/Business Executive; Alexander Slater [1970] Director/Business Executive

Panache Natural Flavour Infusions Limited
Incorporated: 18 August 2017
Registered Office: Unit 6 Cockers Farm, Long Lane, Heath Charnock, Chorley, Lancs, PR6 9EE
Shareholders: Lee Paul Gaskell; Phillip John Booth
Officers: Phillip John Booth [1984] Director; Lee Paul Gaskell [1991] Director

Panda Oriental Supermarket Ltd
Incorporated: 8 June 2018
Registered Office: 27 Old Gloucester Street, London, WC1N 3AX
Officers: Simon Galway, Secretary; Linghua Li [1980] Director

Panda Trading International Limited
Incorporated: 16 October 2017
Registered Office: Springfield House, 23 Oatlands Drive, Weybridge, Surrey, KT13 9LZ
Shareholders: Jian Sun; Takahiro Matsui
Officers: Takahiro Matsui [1961] Director [Japanese]; Jian Sun [1980] Director

Pandemonio Limited
Incorporated: 18 November 2009 *Employees:* 7
Net Worth: £55,240 *Total Assets:* £524,620
Registered Office: 85 Leonard Street, London, EC2A 4QS
Shareholders: Luca Dusi; Federico Bruschetta
Officers: Federico Bruschetta [1969] Director [Italian]; Luca Dusi [1974] Director [Italian]

Pandemonium Wines Ltd
Incorporated: 14 September 2018
Registered Office: 82 High Street, Golborne, Warrington, Cheshire, WA3 3DA
Major Shareholder: Viliam Tomcanyi
Officers: Viliam Tomcanyi [1987] Director/Sales Manager [Slovak]

Panemporium Ltd
Incorporated: 17 January 2018
Registered Office: 27 Longshore, London, SE8 3DF
Major Shareholder: Panagiotis Dimaras
Officers: Panagiotis Dimaras [1971] Director/Trading Agent [Greek]

Pant y Foel Gin Ltd
Incorporated: 29 October 2018
Registered Office: Pant Y Foel, Saron, Denbigh, LL16 4TL
Major Shareholder: Lesley Karan Haythorne
Officers: Lesley Karan Haythorne [1965] Director/Dietitian

Panton Ventures Limited
Incorporated: 16 August 2011
Net Worth Deficit: £1,664 Total Assets: £24,604
Registered Office: 32 Totternhoe Close, Kenton, Harrow, Middlesex, HA3 0HS
Major Shareholder: Feisal Mehmood Khan
Officers: Feisal Mehmood Khan [1981] Director

Paradigm Red Limited
Incorporated: 23 April 2018
Registered Office: 66 Blagdon Road, New Malden, Surrey, KT3 4AE
Shareholders: Alexander James Wallbank; Xiangshou An
Officers: Guinan [1980] Director/Designer [Chinese]; Xiangshou [1983] Director/Senior IT Project Manager [Chinese]; Alexander James Wallbank [1984] Director/Head of Finance

Paragon Brands Limited
Incorporated: 19 May 2017 Employees: 4
Net Worth: £90 Total Assets: £2,190
Registered Office: Warford Grange Farm, Pedley House Lane, Great Warford, Knutsford, Cheshire, WA16 7SP
Shareholders: Christopher Jones; Jonathan Hammond
Officers: Jonathan Hammond [1970] Director; Christopher Jones [1970] Director

Paragon Wines Limited
Incorporated: 26 July 2006
Registered Office: 712 London Road, West Thurrock, Grays, Essex, RM20 3JT
Shareholders: Michael Schultz; Robert Miller
Officers: Adrian Philip Bird, Secretary; Luis Javier Tricio [1953] Director/Trading Manager

Paramount Vintners Ltd
Incorporated: 21 August 2012
Net Worth: £32,500 Total Assets: £32,500
Registered Office: Kemp House, 160 City Road, London, EC1V 2NX
Major Shareholder: Marvin Julian Calvin Roberts
Officers: Marvin Julian Calvin Roberts [1985] Director

Parasol Wines Ltd
Incorporated: 29 March 2018
Registered Office: 125 Purves Road, London, NW10 5TH
Major Shareholder: Michael Robert Blake Campbell
Officers: Michael Robert Blake Campbell [1972] Director

Parched Drinks Ltd
Incorporated: 23 October 2018
Registered Office: Kemp House, 160 City Road, London, EC1V 2NX
Officers: Simon Cormack, Secretary; Christopher White [1981] Sales Director

Park Place Drinks Limited
Incorporated: 4 November 2008 Employees: 1
Net Worth Deficit: £98,416 Total Assets: £26,259
Registered Office: 7 Park Place, Dollar, Clackmannanshire, FK14 7AA
Major Shareholder: Martin Traquair Price
Officers: Martin Traquair Price [1966] Director; Susan Jane Price [1966] Director

Park Royal Wholesale Limited
Incorporated: 8 February 2002 Employees: 2
Net Worth: £477,813 Total Assets: £519,414
Registered Office: Unit 18 The Metro Centre, Britannia Way, Park Royal, London, NW10 7PA
Major Shareholder: Parul Keshavlal Malde
Officers: Reshma Parul Malde, Secretary; Parul Keshavlal Malde [1971] Director

Parkers Newsagents Ltd
Incorporated: 16 August 2018
Registered Office: 3 Norfolk Place, Middlesbrough, Cleveland, TS3 7PB
Major Shareholder: Celia Parker
Officers: Celia Parker [1932] Director/Retired

Parmar Drinks & Wines Ltd
Incorporated: 10 November 2011
Net Worth Deficit: £6,190 Total Assets: £30,253
Registered Office: 2 Gemini Grove, Northolt, Middlesex, UB5 6ER
Officers: Kamaljit Singh [1976] Director

Parthenon Import Company Ltd
Incorporated: 5 February 2019
Registered Office: 1-2, 61 Orleans Avenue, Glasgow, G14 9NG
Major Shareholder: Christoforos Lomvardos
Officers: Christoforos Lomvardos [1964] Director/General Manager [Greek]

Party Drinks Company Limited
Incorporated: 2 April 2016 Employees: 2
Net Worth Deficit: £3,711 Total Assets: £585
Registered Office: c/o Francis Clark LLP, North Quay House, Sutton Harbour, Plymouth, PL4 0RA
Shareholders: David Laws; Marie Laws
Officers: David Laws [1960] Director/Sole Trader; Marie Laws [1959] Director/Housewife

Parverre Marketing Limited
Incorporated: 23 August 1996
Registered Office: Unit 2 Greencroft Estate, Tower Road, Annfield Plain, Stanley, Co Durham, DH9 7XP
Parent: Lanchester Wine Cellars Limited
Officers: Anthony Austin Cleary [1952] Director/Wine Importer

Paso-Primero UK Ltd.
Incorporated: 24 July 2015
Net Worth Deficit: £12,817 Total Assets: £35,507
Registered Office: 35 Moreton Crescent, Shrewsbury, Salop, SY3 7BY
Shareholder: Thomas William Holt
Officers: Thomas William Holt [1985] Director/Wine Trading; Emma Williams [1983] Director/Wine Trading

Passion Wine International Limited
Incorporated: 24 January 2012
Net Worth: £44,917 Total Assets: £79,227
Registered Office: 71 Peak Hill, London, SE26 4NS
Shareholders: David John Baldwin; Antonello Moresi
Officers: David John Baldwin [1971] Director; Antonello Moresi [1970] Director

Pastai di Serino Italian Food and Wine Excellence Ltd
Incorporated: 27 September 2018
Registered Office: 7 Swannington Road, Leicester, LE3 9AG
Major Shareholder: Danilo Ginolfi
Officers: Danilo Ginolfi [1987] Director/Manager [Italian]

PatelCashAndCarry Limited
Incorporated: 22 September 2017
Registered Office: Unit 15 Broadmead Center, Navestock Crescent, Liston Way, Woodford Green, Essex, IG8 7BN
Officers: Akash Sudhirkumar Patel [1991] Managing Director [Indian]

W.G. Paterson & Son Limited
Incorporated: 5 November 1981 Employees: 2
Net Worth: £22,844 Total Assets: £28,790
Registered Office: 16 Castle Street, Banff, Aberdeenshire, AB45 1DL
Shareholders: Isobel Paterson; Ian Paterson
Officers: Ian Paterson, Secretary; Isobel Paterson [1946] Director/Housewife

Pau Drinks Limited
Incorporated: 7 August 2018
Registered Office: 11 Forest Drive, Woodford Green, Essex, IG8 9NG
Shareholders: Kanta Kaur; Amit Jayantilal Pau
Officers: Kanta Kaur [1974] Director/Sales Person; Amit Jayantilal Pau [1976] Director/Sales Person

Peace Bond Ltd
Incorporated: 25 April 2018
Registered Office: East Burne Farm, Bickington, Newton Abbot, Devon, TQ12 6PA
Parent: Nash Inc Limited
Officers: Jacob Nash [1969] Director

Peachy Glow Limited
Incorporated: 8 August 2015
Net Worth Deficit: £2,236 Total Assets: £245
Registered Office: c/o Niren Blake LLP, 2nd Floor, Solar House, 915 High Road, London, N12 8QJ
Major Shareholder: Michael Oliver Baker
Officers: Michael Oliver Baker [1992] Director

Pearl Leisure Limited
Incorporated: 13 March 2014 Employees: 2
Net Worth: £10,801 Total Assets: £44,964
Registered Office: Lalita Buildings, 378 Walsall Road, Perry Barr, Birmingham, B42 2LX
Major Shareholder: Andrew Jones
Officers: Christopher O'Brien, Secretary; Andrew Jones [1964] Director; Christopher David O'Brien [1961] Director

Pearly Queen Beer Company Ltd
Incorporated: 20 July 2015
Net Worth Deficit: £15,015 Total Assets: £3,570
Registered Office: Unit 10, 80 Lytham Road, Fulwood, Preston, Lancs, PR2 3AQ
Shareholders: John Edward Leiper; Meetal Patel
Officers: John Edward Leiper [1983] Director/Founder; Meetal Patel [1983] Director/Co Founder

Peatreekers Limited
Incorporated: 31 January 2017
Net Worth: £29,110 Total Assets: £37,267
Registered Office: Top Floor, Admiral House, 29-30 Maritime Street, Edinburgh, EH6 6SE
Major Shareholder: Calum Liam Leslie
Officers: Calum Liam Leslie [1991] Director

The Peculiar Gin Company Ltd
Incorporated: 15 March 2018
Registered Office: 1 Market Hill, Calne, Wilts, SN11 0BT
Major Shareholder: Lisa Flack
Officers: Lisa Ann Flack [1970] Managing Director; Sara Witham [1980] Director

Pellegrino Wine and Food Distribution Ltd
Incorporated: 24 January 2017 Employees: 2
Net Worth Deficit: £4,248 Total Assets: £13,835
Registered Office: 45 Salisbury Road, Cardiff, CF24 4AB
Shareholder: Daniela Robustelli
Officers: Marco Pellegrino [1993] Director [Italian]; Leah Katherine Alice Thomas [1990] Director

Pemberton Central Limited
Incorporated: 9 June 2010
Net Worth Deficit: £58,554 Total Assets: £1
Registered Office: Castor Street, Liverpool, L6 5AT
Parent: Beerscellars (UK) Limited
Officers: Caroline Doran [1979] Director; John Kenneth Ravenscroft [1955] Director/Licencee

Pembrokeshire Drinks Limited
Incorporated: 9 February 2004 Employees: 21
Net Worth: £1,440 Total Assets: £35,575
Registered Office: Kidbraesons, Jameston, Tenby, Pembrokeshire, SA70 8QE
Shareholders: Marcia Kidney; Phillip John Kidney
Officers: Marcia Kidney, Secretary; Phillip John Kidney [1963] Director/Sales Representative

Penny Prize Limited
Incorporated: 6 October 2017
Registered Office: 147 Titwood Road, Glasgow, G41 4BN
Major Shareholder: Sajjad Soofi
Officers: Sajjad Soofi [1970] Director

Penryn Spirits Limited
Incorporated: 26 July 2018
Registered Office: Bickland House, Bickland Water Road, Falmouth, Cornwall, TR11 4SB
Shareholders: Willoughby Oliver Werner; Peter Edward Mack
Officers: Peter Edward Mack [1989] Director; Willoughby Oliver Werner [1986] Director

Penzance Gin Ltd
Incorporated: 17 December 2018
Registered Office: 27 Market Place, Penzance, Cornwall, TR18 2JD
Shareholders: Stephanie Vivian McCrindle; Sarah Elizabeth Shaw; Sarah Elizabeth Fowles-Laity
Officers: Sarah Elizabeth Shaw [1965] Director/Retailer

Peoplegood Limited
Incorporated: 1 September 2018
Registered Office: 3 Princes Avenue, Woodford Green, Essex, IG8 0LL
Shareholders: Stephen Andrew Johnson; Hisanori Shimoi
Officers: Stephen Andrew Johnson [1968] Director; Hisanori Shimoi [1968] Director/Real Estate Leasing [Japanese]

The Perfect Cellar Ltd
Incorporated: 19 November 2009
Net Worth: £90,451 *Total Assets:* £453,022
Registered Office: 3rd Floor North, 224-236 Walworth Road, London, SE17 1JE
Major Shareholder: Shamsia Nourmamod
Officers: Shamsia Nourmamod, Secretary; Moez Seraly [1973] Director/Chief Executive [French]

Perfect Pair Wines Ltd
Incorporated: 21 February 2018
Registered Office: 21 John Calvert Road, Woodhouse, Sheffield, S13 7PU
Shareholders: Daniel Hague; Staci Hague
Officers: Daniel Hague [1991] Director; Staci Hague [1991] Director

Perkins Independent Wine Traders Limited
Incorporated: 28 April 2009 *Employees:* 3
Net Worth: £27,258 *Total Assets:* £135,180
Registered Office: 34 Church Street, Appleby Magna, Swadlincote, Derbys, DE12 7BW
Shareholders: Matthew Perkins; Vanessa Estelle Perkins
Officers: Matthew Perkins [1972] Director/Wine Wholesaler; Vanessa Estelle Perkins [1973] Director/Consultant

Pernod Ricard UK Limited
Incorporated: 10 December 1984 *Employees:* 252
Net Worth: £490,279,008 *Total Assets:* £576,435,968
Registered Office: Building 12, Chiswick Park, 566 Chiswick High Road, London, W4 5AN
Parent: Chivas Investments Limited
Officers: Gilles Pierre Francis Bogaert [1969] Managing Director [French]; Thomas Yves Marie D'Aboville [1980] Finance Director [French]; David Anthony Haworth [1962] Managing Director; Stuart MacNab [1964] Director/Accountant; Anne-Louise Varroquier [1980] Director/General Counsel [French]

Perscot Ltd
Incorporated: 24 January 2018
Registered Office: 4 Albert Place, Perth, PH2 8JE
Shareholders: Lucy Burghard; Waldyr Wildo Aylas Aliaga
Officers: Waldyr Wildo Aylas Aliaga [1973] Director [Peruvian/British]; Lucy Burghard [1971] Director

Personalised Care Solutions Ltd
Incorporated: 3 December 2008
Net Worth: £34,641 *Total Assets:* £36,494
Registered Office: 9 Rees Street, Islington, London, N1 7AR
Shareholders: Kelly de Burgh Gaddes; Kathleen Julia Bondar
Officers: Kathleen Julia Bondar [1962] Director/Consultant; Kelly de Burgh Gaddes [1964] Director/Consultant [Australian]

The Perth Distillery Company Limited
Incorporated: 13 February 2018
Registered Office: 28 Innerleithen Way, Perth, PH1 1RN
Major Shareholder: Iain James McDonald
Officers: Elaine Brady [1967] Director; Iain James McDonald [1966] Director

Peruvian Enterprises Limited
Incorporated: 10 May 2004 *Employees:* 1
Net Worth Deficit: £115,914 *Total Assets:* £48,638
Registered Office: 37 Warren Street, London, W1T 6AD
Major Shareholder: Enrique Eduardo Aguilar-Cabrera
Officers: Menashy David Cohen, Secretary; Enrique Eduardo Aguilar Cabrera [1945] Director

Pesodeocho Wines Ltd
Incorporated: 31 October 2014
Net Worth Deficit: £1,765 *Total Assets:* £439
Registered Office: Honeybee Cottage, Folly Lane, Hough on the Hill, Grantham, Lincs, NG32 2BA
Major Shareholder: Stephen Martin Pickard
Officers: Stephen Martin Pickard [1957] Director

Petrelli Ltd
Incorporated: 28 August 2018
Registered Office: 20-22 Wenlock Road, London, N1 7GU
Shareholders: Barish Mata; Jean Mata
Officers: Jean Mata [1993] Director

PFG Marketing Ltd
Incorporated: 18 October 2011 *Employees:* 1
Net Worth: £11,790 *Total Assets:* £42,705
Registered Office: 252 Head Road, Annalong, Newry, Co Down, BT34 4RL
Shareholders: Paul Fredrick Gibson; Shirley Helen Gibson
Officers: Paul Fredrick Gibson [1960] Director/Marketing Consultant; Shirley Helen Gibson [1961] Director/Housewife

PFS Business Services Limited
Incorporated: 30 September 2016
Net Worth: £759 *Total Assets:* £1,546
Registered Office: 109 Down Hall Road, Rayleigh, Essex, SS6 9LN
Major Shareholder: Peter Frank Storey
Officers: Peter Frank Storey, Secretary; Peter Frank Storey [1968] Director/Accountant

Phil Cellars Ltd
Incorporated: 28 August 2014
Registered Office: 7 Warren Avenue, Saxmundham, Suffolk, IP17 1GF
Major Shareholder: Sam Merton Phillips
Officers: Sam Merton Phillips [1973] Director/Sales

Phil Macan Limited
Incorporated: 16 August 2018
Registered Office: Pavilion 1, Finnieston Business Park, Minerva Way, Glasgow, G3 8AU
Major Shareholder: Douglas Gordon Wheatley
Officers: Allan Douglas Rimmer [1982] Director; Lewis Scott Wheatley [1967] Director

Philipshill Retirement Village Ltd
Incorporated: 9 November 2016
Net Worth: £100 *Total Assets:* £100
Registered Office: 1 Cambuslang Court, Cambuslang, Glasgow, G32 8FH
Major Shareholder: Iain Gilchrist
Officers: Iain Gilchrist [1967] Director

UK Wholesalers of Beers, Wines and Spirits dellam

Philsner Ltd
Incorporated: 1 June 2018
Registered Office: 19 Gosforth Crescent, Dronfield, Derbys, S18 1PT
Officers: Debra Ann Hempshall [1960] Director/Personal Assistant; Emma Louise Hempshall [1989] Director/Commercial Manager; Kerry Alissia Hempshall [1992] Director/Buyer; Philip Charles Hempshall [1955] Director/Procurement

Phoenix Premium Drinks Limited
Incorporated: 1 September 2011 Employees: 5
Net Worth: £156,235 Total Assets: £371,713
Registered Office: 100 Shore Road, Greenisland, Carrickfergus, Co Antrim, BT38 8UE
Major Shareholder: Niall Martin McMullan
Officers: Niall Martin McMullan, Secretary; Jolene Doyle [1993] Director [Irish]; Niall Martin McMullan [1968] Director [Irish]

Phoenix Spirits Ltd
Incorporated: 1 May 2018
Registered Office: 36 The Headlands, Market Harborough, Leics, LE16 7DH
Major Shareholder: Liam Cockerill
Officers: Liam Cockerill [1989] Director

Phone A Fix Ltd
Incorporated: 3 January 2019
Registered Office: 17 Finsbury Place, Chipping Norton, Oxon, OX7 5LS
Major Shareholder: Wayne Adam Ryan
Officers: Wayne Adam Ryan [1993] Director

Piaff Trading UK Limited
Incorporated: 25 April 2017
Net Worth Deficit: £116,113 Total Assets: £30,503
Registered Office: 21 Sunnybank Avenue, Heaton Mersey, Stockport, Cheshire, SK4 3PR
Officers: Victoria Margaret Anne Bennett, Secretary; Victoria Margaret Anne Bennett [1971] Director/Marketer; Eileen Low [1954] Director/Administrator

Pick N Deliver Ltd
Incorporated: 29 June 2016
Registered Office: 5 The Lows, Oldham, Lancs, OL4 1AQ
Major Shareholder: Mohammed Junaid
Officers: Mohammed Junaid [1968] Director

Pierhead Drinks Limited
Incorporated: 18 April 2012 Employees: 7
Net Worth Deficit: £180,791 Total Assets: £261,856
Registered Office: 1 The Paddocks, Wood Street, Swanley, Kent, BR8 7PA
Officers: Amanda Nokes [1977] Director

Pieroth Limited
Incorporated: 18 July 1961 Employees: 312
Net Worth: £1,739,551 Total Assets: £5,232,441
Registered Office: The International Wine Centre, Dallow Road, Luton, Beds, LU1 1UR
Officers: Jayne Elizabeth Foster, Secretary; Howard Warren Falk [1963] Finance Director; David Huw Samuel [1961] Sales Director

Pigs Ears Beers Limited
Incorporated: 27 July 2011 Employees: 28
Net Worth Deficit: £147,848 Total Assets: £999,197
Registered Office: Unit 5 & 6 Ridge Farm, Horsham Road, Rowhook, Horsham, W Sussex, RH12 3QB
Major Shareholder: Andrew Noel Fisher
Officers: Andrew Noel Fisher, Secretary; David Melvyn Allen [1945] Director; Richard Mark Curtis [1963] Director; Stuart Roger Richard Curtis [1960] Director; Andrew Noel Fisher [1972] Director; Antonia Skinner [1985] Director

PimentoDrinks UK Ltd
Incorporated: 9 October 2018
Registered Office: Flat 38, Sovereign House, 19-23 Fitzroy Street, London, W1T 4BP
Officers: Oscar Panizzon [1971] Director/Consultant [Italian]

Pimlico Cellars (Agencies) Limited
Incorporated: 29 June 1998
Net Worth: £1 Total Assets: £1
Registered Office: 33 Churton Street, London, SW1V 2LT
Major Shareholder: John Morgan Trevena
Officers: Helen Joy Trevena, Secretary; John Morgan Trevena [1952] Director/Wine Merchant

Pimlico Dozen Limited
Incorporated: 25 November 1985 Employees: 2
Net Worth: £272,521 Total Assets: £421,306
Registered Office: 33 Churton Street, London, SW1V 2LT
Major Shareholder: John Morgan Trevena
Officers: John Morgan Trevena [1952] Director/Wine Merchant

Pinckneys Gin Limited
Incorporated: 21 September 2017
Registered Office: Wood Farm, Boraston, Tenbury Wells, Worcs, WR15 8NB
Major Shareholder: Charles Pinckney
Officers: Charles William Pinckney [1962] Director

Pinewood Vyntners Limited
Incorporated: 16 May 2016 Employees: 1
Net Worth Deficit: £6,487 Total Assets: £7,131
Registered Office: 414 West Wycombe Road, High Wycombe, Bucks, HP12 4AH
Shareholders: David Smyth; Valerie Smyth
Officers: Valerie Smyth, Secretary; David Smyth [1957] Director/Aeronautical Engineer

Pinglestone Estate Limited
Incorporated: 15 December 2016
Net Worth Deficit: £60,872 Total Assets: £2,147,771
Registered Office: 1st Floor, 128 Buckingham Palace Road, London, SW1W 9SA
Major Shareholder: Paul-Francois Edouard Joseph Vranken
Officers: Clement Albert Pierlot [1980] Director/General Manager [French]; Gaylord Carlos Aurelien Sequeira [1985] Operations Director [French]; Paul-Francois Edouard Joseph Vranken [1947] Director/Chairman [French]

Pingu & Co Ltd
Incorporated: 13 April 2017
Registered Office: 21 Albert Road, Richmond, Surrey, TW10 6DJ
Major Shareholder: Nathan Engelbrecht
Officers: Nathan Engelbrecht [1982] Director

Pink City Cider Ltd
Incorporated: 11 January 2019
Registered Office: 25 Ramsgate Street, London, E8 2NA
Major Shareholder: Talin Leask
Officers: Talin Leask [1983] Director/Operations Manager

The Pink Gin Company Ltd
Incorporated: 9 December 2016
Registered Office: Arisaig Gartocharn, Alexandria, W Dunbartonshire, G83 8ND
Major Shareholder: Sharon Newall
Officers: Sharon Newall [1961] Director

Pioneer Gin Limited
Incorporated: 22 October 2018
Registered Office: Highrow House, High Road East, Felixstowe, Suffolk, IP11 9PU
Shareholders: Sean Patrick Diarmaid Crean; Bruce Mervyn Beardwood
Officers: Sean Patrick Diarmaid Crean [1971] Director/Solicitor

Pioneer Spirits Ltd
Incorporated: 9 January 2018
Registered Office: 71-75 Shelton Street, Covent Garden, London, WC2H 9JQ
Officers: James Dimock [1981] Director/Chartered Accountant; Paul Karim [1977] Commercial Director; Daniel Parsons [1971] Director/Council Officer; Andrew Taylor [1978] Director/Banker

Pioneering Spirits Limited
Incorporated: 14 January 2019
Registered Office: Lower Ground Floor, 51 Welbeck Street, London, W1G 9HL
Major Shareholder: Michael Joseph Francis Claessens
Officers: Michael Joseph Francis Claessens [1993] Director [Dutch]

Pipehouse Gin Limited
Incorporated: 20 November 2017
Registered Office: 62 Juniper, Bracknell, Berks, RG12 7ZF
Officers: Ben Larcombe [1989] Director; Katherine Louise Larcombe [1991] Director; Emma Clare Priestley [1989] Director; Samuel Francis Priestley [1989] Director

Christopher Piper Wines Limited
Incorporated: 29 July 1980 Employees: 20
Net Worth: £1,012,509 Total Assets: £1,647,033
Registered Office: 1 Silver Street, Ottery St Mary, Devon, EX11 1DB
Shareholders: Christopher Charles Neville Piper; John Roderick Earle
Officers: John Roderick Earle, Secretary; John Roderick Earle [1956] Director/Wine Merchant; Christopher Charles Neville Piper [1957] Director/Wine Merchant

Pirate's Grog Rum Ltd
Incorporated: 23 May 2012 Employees: 3
Net Worth: £21,068 Total Assets: £195,202
Registered Office: 4 Capricorn Centre, Cranes Farm Road, Basildon, Essex, SS14 3JJ
Shareholders: Bethan Jones; Robert van der Weg; Gareth Noble
Officers: Bethan Jones [1986] Marketing Director; Gareth Noble [1987] Operations Director

Pivo Beverages Ltd
Incorporated: 12 June 2018
Registered Office: Suite 10, Sheepscar Court, Northside Business Park, Leeds, LS7 2BB
Major Shareholder: Mandeep Singh
Officers: Jasdeep Singh [1981] Director; Mandeep Singh [1978] Director

Pivovar Ltd
Incorporated: 12 December 2003 Employees: 16
Net Worth: £477,434 Total Assets: £1,074,325
Registered Office: Home Farm, Melbourne, York, YO42 4SX
Shareholders: James Andrew Hawksworth; Jonathan Brook Holdsworth
Officers: James Andrew Hawksworth, Secretary; James Andrew Hawksworth [1976] Director; Jonathan Holdsworth [1976] Director

PJ's Virtual Brewing Company Limited
Incorporated: 17 October 2017
Registered Office: 17a Bank Street, Mid Calder, Livingston, W Lothian, EH53 0AS
Major Shareholder: Peter James Smillie
Officers: Peter James Smillie [1971] Director

Places Trading (Suppliers) Limited
Incorporated: 1 November 1989
Net Worth: £100 Total Assets: £100
Registered Office: 28B Hempsted Lane, Gloucester, GL2 5JA
Officers: Patricia Hurley, Secretary; Barry Neil Hurley [1950] Director/Publican

Planet Wine Trading and Consulting Limited
Incorporated: 25 January 1999 Employees: 1
Net Worth Deficit: £300,788 Total Assets: £35,297
Registered Office: 31 Sackville Street, Manchester, M1 3LZ
Major Shareholder: Alexis Lichine
Officers: Charles Emanuel Prager, Secretary; Alexis Lichine [1960] Director/Wine Merchant [French]; Charles Emanuel Prager [1949] Director/Accountant

Plant Relief Ltd
Incorporated: 29 November 2018
Registered Office: Ground Floor, 2 Woodberry Grove, London, N12 0DR
Major Shareholder: Nicholas Regan
Officers: Kathryn Regan [1992] Director/Chief Marketing Officer (CMO); Nicholas Regan [1987] Director/Chief Executive Officer

Platinum Gin Ltd
Incorporated: 11 October 2018
Registered Office: 26 Walcot Close, Plymouth, PL6 8TG
Major Shareholder: James Congdon Alford
Officers: James Congdon Alford [1984] Director

Terry Platt Wine Merchants Limited
Incorporated: 8 April 1999
Registered Office: 26 Wyle Cop, Shrewsbury, Salop, SY1 1XD
Parent: Tanners (Shrewsbury) Limited
Officers: Robert John Morgan, Secretary; Robert John Morgan [1971] Director/Chartered Accountant; James Jonathan Tanner [1968] Director

Play Limited
Incorporated: 11 November 2016
Net Worth Deficit: £15,416 Total Assets: £13,843
Registered Office: 10 Mill Hill, Leeds, LS1 5DQ
Major Shareholder: Philip Layton
Officers: Philip Layton [1979] Director

Plonq Wines Ltd
Incorporated: 30 April 2018
Registered Office: Ground Floor Flat, 69 The Chase, London, SW4 0NP
Major Shareholder: Elizabeth Katherine Carter
Officers: Elizabeth Katherine Carter [1992] Director/Businesswoman

The Plum Brandy Company Limited
Incorporated: 13 September 2016
Net Worth Deficit: £5,623 *Total Assets:* £9,090
Registered Office: 352 Fulham Road, London, SW10 9UH
Shareholders: Mladen Jovasevic; Mladen Jovasevic
Officers: Mladen Jovasevic [1960] Director/Accountant

The Plymouth Rum Company Ltd
Incorporated: 6 June 2018
Registered Office: 99 Fore Street, Kingsbridge, Devon, TQ7 1AB
Shareholders: Dominic Graham Trounce; Alan Gibson Norchi
Officers: Alan Gibson Norchi [1966] Director; Dominic Graham Trounce [1966] Director

PMWine Trade Limited
Incorporated: 17 September 2010 *Employees:* 1
Net Worth: £55,421 *Total Assets:* £599,781
Registered Office: 67 Pall Mall, London, SW1Y 5ES
Officers: Miles Eric Ashton, Secretary; Grant William Sandiford Ashton [1967] Director/Businessman

Point Beer UK Limited
Incorporated: 18 July 2012
Net Worth Deficit: £39,431 *Total Assets:* £215,331
Registered Office: 1st Floor, Copthall House, New Road, Stourbridge, W Midlands, DY8 1PH
Major Shareholder: Jim Wiechmann
Officers: Edward Firth [1967] Company Secretary/Director; Mark Edward Charles Smith [1974] Director; Jim Wiechmann [1938] Director [American]

Polaris Wines Ltd
Incorporated: 24 November 2014 *Employees:* 1
Net Worth Deficit: £26,802 *Total Assets:* £6,309
Registered Office: 3 Farm Cottage, Higher Berrycourt, Donhead St Mary, Shaftesbury, Dorset, SP7 0ES
Major Shareholder: John Thorne
Officers: John William Thorne [1960] Director/Wine Merchant

Polat International Ltd
Incorporated: 21 October 2016
Previous: Safest D Limited
Net Worth: £12,222 *Total Assets:* £28,180
Registered Office: Broad Water Lodge, Higham Road, London, N17 6NN
Officers: Uzaifa Katende [1990] Director

Poleczka Limited
Incorporated: 3 August 2016
Registered Office: 10 Northdown Road, Hatfield, Herts, AL10 8JZ
Major Shareholder: Romuald Jan Hipner
Officers: Romuald Jan Hipner [1952] Director [Polish]

Pollen Cider Ltd
Incorporated: 6 October 2014
Net Worth Deficit: £16,747 *Total Assets:* £28,787
Registered Office: 1 Linnet Mews, London, SW12 8JE
Major Shareholder: Benjamin John Slater
Officers: Benjamin John Slater [1980] Director/Production and Sale of Cider

Polskie Wodki Ltd
Incorporated: 26 February 2014
Net Worth: £100 *Total Assets:* £25,658
Registered Office: 78 London Road, Slough, SL3 7HR
Major Shareholder: Lukasz Piotr Szmajdzinski
Officers: Lukasz Piotr Szmajdzinski [1980] Director/Manager [Polish]

Poltom Limited
Incorporated: 21 April 2004
Net Worth: £598,442 *Total Assets:* £835,534
Registered Office: 407 Britannia House, 11 Glenthorne Road, London, W6 0LH
Shareholders: Monika Anna Dalek; Tomasz Konstanty Dalek
Officers: Monika Anna Dalek, Secretary; Tomasz Konstanty Dalek [1973] Director [Polish]

Pomona Island Brew Co Ltd
Incorporated: 31 July 2017
Registered Office: 1 Shawcroft Hill, Hebden Bridge, W Yorks, HX7 8TD
Shareholders: Nicholas Anthony Greenhalgh; Ryan Thompson; Gareth Richard Bee
Officers: Gareth Richard Bee [1982] Director; Nicholas Anthony Greenhalgh [1981] Director; Ryan Thompson [1978] Director

Pongolo Ltd
Incorporated: 12 September 2018
Registered Office: Flat 2, 1-6 Rowhill Mansions, Rowhill Road, London, E5 8ED
Shareholders: Alexander Michael Woods; Henry John Magoveny Pescod
Officers: Henry John Magoveny Pescod [1983] Director/Chartered Surveyor; Alexander Michael Woods [1982] Director/Businessman

Pop Cake Box Limited
Incorporated: 28 December 2017
Registered Office: 5 Roseneath Place, London, SW16 2NA
Officers: Lina Kulthum Nayiga, Secretary; Lina Kulthum Nayiga [1997] Director/Baker

Popaball Limited
Incorporated: 11 August 2010 *Employees:* 42
Previous: The Tea Shed Limited
Net Worth: £1,076,566 *Total Assets:* £2,755,478
Registered Office: Benfield Business Park, Benfield Road, Newcastle upon Tyne, NE6 4NQ
Major Shareholder: Julia Fiona Quinn
Officers: Julia Fiona Quinn, Secretary; Julia Fiona Quinn [1988] Director

Popjax Limited
Incorporated: 8 November 2018
Registered Office: The Old Casino, 28 Fourth Avenue, Hove, E Sussex, BN3 2PJ
Major Shareholder: Stephen Robert Ford
Officers: Steven Robert Ford [1973] Director

Port City Brewing UK Limited
Incorporated: 24 April 2018
Registered Office: 55 Baker Street, London, W1U 7EU
Shareholders: Karen Assandri Butcher; George William Butcher III
Officers: George William Butcher III [1966] Director/Manager [American]; Edward Firth [1967] Director; Mark Edward Charles Smith [1974] Director

Port Ellen Distillery Company Limited
Incorporated: 3 December 2015
Net Worth: £90 Total Assets: £90
Registered Office: Ferniehill, Stanley, Perthshire, PH1 4QD
Shareholders: Hamish Curran; Kenneth Robert Robertson; Ann Kirsty Medlock
Officers: Hamish Curran [1962] Director; Ann Kirsty Medlock [1965] Director; Kenneth Robert Robertson [1950] Director

Port Ellen Distilling Limited
Incorporated: 3 December 2015
Net Worth: £90 Total Assets: £90
Registered Office: Ferniehill, Stanley, Perthshire, PH1 4QD
Shareholders: Hamish Curran; Kenneth Robert Robertson; Ann Kirsty Medlock
Officers: Hamish Curran [1962] Director; Ann Kirsty Medlock [1965] Director; Kenneth Robert Robertson [1950] Director

Portal Dingwall & Norris Limited
Incorporated: 19 March 2002
Net Worth: £193,889 Total Assets: £365,232
Registered Office: 48 Main Road, Emsworth, Hants, PO10 8AU
Shareholder: Philip Jeremy Portal
Officers: Anthony Portal, Secretary; Anthony Portal [1932] Director/Tax Consultant; Jane Marcella Portal [1963] Director/Wine Merchant; Philip Jeremy Portal [1963] Director/Wine Importer & Purveyor

Portavadie Distillery Limited
Incorporated: 25 July 2007 Employees: 1
Net Worth: £71,709 Total Assets: £1,110,483
Registered Office: Craig Lodge, Ostel Bay, Tighnabruaich, Argyll & Bute, PA21 2AH
Major Shareholder: Sarah Stow
Officers: George James Riddell, Secretary; Alexander Bulloch [1927] Director; Sarah Stow [1963] Director

The Porterage Co Ltd
Incorporated: 6 October 2010 Employees: 3
Net Worth Deficit: £16,703 Total Assets: £99,303
Registered Office: Unit 4B Crakeside Business Park, Greenodd, Ulverston, Cumbria, LA12 7RT
Shareholders: Judith Elaine Cropley; Colin Richard Cropley
Officers: Judith Elaine Cropley, Secretary; Colin Richard Cropley [1970] Director/Wine & Spirits Wholesaler

The Portsmouth Gin Company Limited
Incorporated: 11 April 2018
Registered Office: 77 North Wallington, Fareham, Hants, PO16 8TJ
Major Shareholder: Jake Jefferson Ryan Naylor
Officers: Jake Jefferson Ryan Naylor [1989] Director

Portugal Winelist Ltd
Incorporated: 3 September 2018
Registered Office: 21 Amis Avenue, New Haw, Addlestone, Surrey, KT15 3ET
Major Shareholder: Mark Richard Punter
Officers: Mark Richard Punter [1962] Director

The Portuguese Fine Wine Company Limited
Incorporated: 5 January 2016
Net Worth Deficit: £13,493 Total Assets: £13,280
Registered Office: Unit 7 The Forum, Icknield Way Industrial Estate, Icknield Way, Tring, Herts, HP23 4JY
Shareholder: Matthew William Bonner
Officers: Matthew William Bonner [1978] Director/Wine Merchant

Portuguese Story Ltd
Incorporated: 1 September 2011 Employees: 4
Net Worth Deficit: £27,273 Total Assets: £79,129
Registered Office: 3rd Floor, 28 Ely Place, London, EC1N 6TD
Shareholder: Roman Gonitel
Officers: Dr Roman Gonitel [1974] Director/Research Specialist

The Portuguese Winery Limited
Incorporated: 28 March 2017
Registered Office: 14 Wedderlea Drive, Glasgow, G52 2SS
Officers: Nikos James Thaniotis [1985] Director/IT Manager

The Poshmakers Ltd
Incorporated: 15 April 2010
Net Worth: £12,875 Total Assets: £22,287
Registered Office: William Sturges & Co, Burwood House, 14-16 Caxton Street, London, SW1H 0QY
Shareholders: Francisco Jose Ameijeiras; Ellenor Joy Baker
Officers: Ellenor Joy Baker [1981] Director; Jose Rodriguez-Ameijeiras Blanco [1976] Director

Pot Still Drinks Ltd.
Incorporated: 26 March 2018
Registered Office: 23 Brompton Square, London, SW3 2AD
Shareholders: Christopher Samuel Jackson; Matthew Nicholas Sonny Blain
Officers: Mathew Nicholas Sonny Blain [1993] Director; Christopher Samuel Jackson [1991] Director

Potocki Spirits (Europe) Limited
Incorporated: 12 November 2001
Net Worth Deficit: £77,330 Total Assets: £54,651
Registered Office: Penhurst House, 352-356 Battersea Park Road, London, SW11 3BY
Parent: Livadia Limited
Officers: Robin David Erskine [1948] Director/Accountant; Jan Roman Potocki [1971] Director/Vodka Supplier [French]

Mathieu Poulain Limited
Incorporated: 22 May 2013
Net Worth Deficit: £26,858 Total Assets: £8,047
Registered Office: 11 Scarborough Road, London, N4 4LX
Officers: Kevin Maxime Poulain, Secretary; Frederic Francois Poulain [1984] Director [French]; Mathieu Alex Poulain [1988] Director [French]

Poulter Group UK Limited
Incorporated: 12 January 2016
Net Worth: £566,248 Total Assets: £3,915,320
Registered Office: c/o Sable International, 13th Floor, One Croydon, 12-16 Addiscombe Road, Croydon, Surrey, CR0 0XT
Shareholder: Stephen John Poulter
Officers: Stephen John Poulter [1961] Director [New Zealander]

PPbeer Ltd.
Incorporated: 9 February 2016
Net Worth: £100 Total Assets: £100
Registered Office: 151 Picton Road, Wavertree, Liverpool, L15 4LG
Major Shareholder: Jerzy Jarzebowicz
Officers: Jerzy Jarzebowicz [1959] Director [Polish]; Oleh Senechko [1967] Director [Ukrainian]

Praban Na Linne Limited
Incorporated: 12 July 1976 Employees: 1
Net Worth: £391,542 Total Assets: £635,317
Registered Office: An Oifig, Eilean Iarmain, An T-Eilean, Sgitheanach, Isle of Skye, IV43 8QR
Parent: Praban Gu Leir Limited
Officers: Lady Lucilla Charlotte James Noble [1959] Director/Artist

Pradeeprjm Limited
Incorporated: 24 May 2018
Registered Office: 15 Rothay Road, Sheffield, S4 8BD
Officers: Pradeep Rajamanickam [1989] Director [Indian]

Prasad Trading Company Limited
Incorporated: 20 February 2019
Registered Office: 71-75 Shelton Street, London, WC2H 9JQ
Major Shareholder: Rahul Prasad
Officers: Rahul Prasad [1988] Director [Burmese]

Premia Brands Trading Limited
Incorporated: 16 April 2015 Employees: 1
Previous: BKT Consulting Limited
Net Worth Deficit: £4,903 Total Assets: £7,723
Registered Office: Springfield House, Springfield Road, Horsham, W Sussex, RH12 2RG
Major Shareholder: Matthew James Betts
Officers: Matthew James Betts [1984] Director

Premier Beverages Limited
Incorporated: 7 September 2017
Registered Office: 72 Meridian Place, London, E14 9FF
Shareholder: Paulo Nyambane Ratemo
Officers: Tetyana Kondratyuk [1981] Director/Fashion Designer; Paulo Nyambane Ratemo [1979] Director [American]

Premier Cru Fine Wine Ltd.
Incorporated: 20 March 2002 Employees: 4
Net Worth Deficit: £196,359 Total Assets: £168,238
Registered Office: 13a South Hawksworth Street, Ilkley, W Yorks, LS29 9DX
Shareholders: John Mathew Patrick Oddy; Richard John Carr
Officers: John Mathew Patrick Oddy, Secretary/Accountant; Richard John Carr [1968] Director/Self Employed; John Mathew Patrick Oddy [1969] Director/Accountant

Premier Distillers Ltd
Incorporated: 21 October 2015
Registered Office: 308 High Street, Croydon, Surrey, CR0 1NG
Officers: Miroslav Siba, Secretary; Reubin a Matticx [1934] Director [American]

Premier Inc. Ltd
Incorporated: 9 May 2012
Net Worth: £17,636 Total Assets: £193,238
Registered Office: Office 1, Izabella House, 24-26 Regent Place, Birmingham, B1 3NJ
Shareholders: Hardip Todd; Sukhwinder Todd
Officers: Hardip Todd [1976] Sales Director; Sukhwinder Todd [1977] Director

Premier Pubco Limited
Incorporated: 22 March 2001
Net Worth: £44,186 Total Assets: £209,606
Registered Office: 21 Navigation Way, Cannock, Staffs, WS11 7XU
Major Shareholder: James Barry Thomas
Officers: James Barry Thomas [1971] Operations Director; Susan Thomas [1960] Director

Premier UK Trading Limited
Incorporated: 2 June 2011 Employees: 2
Net Worth: £226,261 Total Assets: £1,353,211
Registered Office: Unit A4 & F1, 283 Water Road, Wembley, Middlesex, HA0 1HX
Major Shareholder: Himanshu Shah
Officers: Himanshu Shah [1977] Director

Premier Wines & Spirits Limited
Incorporated: 6 September 1991
Registered Office: York House, Empire Way, Wembley, Middlesex, HA9 0FQ
Parent: Ledrop Exports Limited
Officers: Hugh William Paul Clift [1948] Director/Chief Executive

Premium Beverage Refreshments Ltd
Incorporated: 20 December 2013 Employees: 3
Net Worth Deficit: £18,181 Total Assets: £824
Registered Office: 120 Mangham Road, Barbot Hall Industrial Estate, Rotherham, S Yorks, S62 6EF
Shareholders: Marvin James Henshaw; Daryl Moss
Officers: James Michael Barker [1980] Director; Marvin James Henshaw [1971] Director; Daryl Moss [1971] Director; Anthony Ashton Woodhouse [1968] Director

Premium Bottles Limited
Incorporated: 29 May 2018
Registered Office: 16 Andre Street, London, E8 2AA
Major Shareholder: Ferhat Yeter
Officers: Ferhat Yeter [1998] Director/Self Employed

Premium Brands Distribution Limited
Incorporated: 12 October 2012
Net Worth: £29,516 Total Assets: £184,462
Registered Office: Vista Centre, 50 Salisbury Road, Hounslow, Middlesex, TW4 6JQ
Major Shareholder: Harbeer Dhillon
Officers: Harbeer Dhillon [1972] Director

Premium Bulgarian Wine Ltd
Incorporated: 17 February 2016
Net Worth: £602 Total Assets: £17,109
Registered Office: Flat 8, Langdale Court, 308 West End Road, Ruislip, Middlesex, HA4 6QL
Major Shareholder: Petya Ivanova Mincheva
Officers: Petya Ivanova Mincheva [1979] Managing Director [Bulgarian]

Premium Vineyard Company UK Limited
Incorporated: 12 November 2014 Employees: 1
Net Worth: £480,116 Total Assets: £1,928,770
Registered Office: 19-20 Bourne Court, Southend Road, Woodford Green, Essex, IG8 8HD
Shareholders: Jean-Pierre Perrin; Francois Perrin
Officers: Marc-Olivier Pierre Jacques Francois Perrin [1970] Director [French]; Matthieu Pierre Marcel Joseph Perrin [1981] Director [French]

Present Tense Limited
Incorporated: 15 December 2016
Net Worth: £1,519 Total Assets: £6,049
Registered Office: 2-4 Ash Lane, Rustington, Littlehampton, W Sussex, BN16 3BZ
Major Shareholder: David Andrew Plant
Officers: David Andrew Plant [1974] Director

Presidente Wines Limited
Incorporated: 10 September 2018
Registered Office: 23 Lodge Hill, Tutbury, Burton on Trent, Staffs, DE13 9HF
Major Shareholder: Alan Platts
Officers: Alan Platts [1967] Director/Wine Agent; Hayley Fiona Platts [1968] Director/Administrator

Prestige Vintners Limited
Incorporated: 23 June 1983 *Employees:* 1
Net Worth: £9,162 *Total Assets:* £35,134
Registered Office: 194 Stanley Road, Teddington, Middlesex, TW11 8UE
Major Shareholder: Theres Smallridge
Officers: Theres Smallridge, Secretary; Theres Smallrdge [1949] Director [Swiss]

Prestige Whisky Worldwide Ltd
Incorporated: 4 September 2018
Registered Office: 81 Comiston Road, Morningside, Edinburgh, EH10 6AG
Major Shareholder: Tod Luke Bradbury
Officers: Tod Luke Bradbury [1982] Director

Prestige Wine & Food (UK) Ltd
Incorporated: 7 January 2016
Net Worth: £100 *Total Assets:* £100
Registered Office: Hussains Hall, 38 Devonshire Street, Keighley, W Yorks, BD21 2AU
Major Shareholder: Agostino Raia
Officers: Agostino Raia [1966] Director/Entrepreneur [Italian]

Preston Wines Ltd
Incorporated: 14 April 2014 *Employees:* 5
Net Worth Deficit: £25,332 *Total Assets:* £69,593
Registered Office: 62 Preston Street, Brighton, BN1 2HE
Shareholders: Alper Gonultas; Kamil Buer
Officers: Kamil Buer [1980] Director [Turkish]; Alper Gonultas [1994] Director [Turkish]

Prestonfield Whisky Company Limited
Incorporated: 4 April 1990
Registered Office: Edradour Distillery, Pitlochry, Perthshire, PH16 5JP
Major Shareholder: Andrew William Symington
Officers: Graham Keith Cox, Secretary; Andrew William Symington [1963] Director

Norman Price Wines Limited
Incorporated: 17 May 2006 *Employees:* 2
Net Worth: £335,073 *Total Assets:* £555,659
Registered Office: Heath Cottage, Tavistock Road, Yelverton, Devon, PL20 6EF
Major Shareholder: Charlotte Louise Price
Officers: Charlotte Louise Price, Secretary/Lecturer; Charlotte Louise Price [1954] Director/Lecturer; Timothy Charles Rose Price [1991] Director

Prima Import & Export Ltd
Incorporated: 23 September 2015
Registered Office: Flat 2, 25 Cedar Drive, Pinner, Middlesex, HA5 4BY
Major Shareholder: Mayank Kapadia
Officers: Mayank Kapadia [1977] Director [German]

Prime Cash & Carry Limited
Incorporated: 13 September 2012 *Employees:* 16
Net Worth Deficit: £104,496 *Total Assets:* £479,785
Registered Office: Unit 7c Angel Road Works, Advent Way, London, N18 3AH
Major Shareholder: Mohd Arsadul Quadri
Officers: Mohd Arsadul Quadri [1985] Director

Prime Drinks Ltd
Incorporated: 4 January 2019
Registered Office: 78 The Cravens, Smallfield, Horley, Surrey, RH6 9QT
Major Shareholder: Brian Haite
Officers: Brian Haite [1973] Director/Salesman

Prime Wines Limited
Incorporated: 12 April 2016
Net Worth: £3,156 *Total Assets:* £46,260
Registered Office: 4 Osier Way, Banstead, Surrey, SM7 1LL
Major Shareholder: George Alec John Toogood
Officers: George Toogood, Secretary; George Alec John Toogood [1941] Director/Wine Shipper

Primo Drinks (Lancashire) Ltd
Incorporated: 5 February 2007 *Employees:* 12
Previous: Same Day Beers (Fylde) Limited
Net Worth: £317,270 *Total Assets:* £859,005
Registered Office: Same Day Beers, Corrie Way, Bredbury Park Industrial Estate, Bredbury, Stockport, Cheshire, SK6 2ST
Shareholders: Gavin Michael Wright; Brian Michael Wright
Officers: Gavin Wright, Secretary; Brian Michael Wright [1958] Director; Gavin Wright [1982] Director

Primo Drinks (Merseyside) Ltd
Incorporated: 21 December 2005 *Employees:* 15
Previous: Same Day Beers (Wirral) Limited
Net Worth: £427,418 *Total Assets:* £986,116
Registered Office: Corrie Way, Bredbury Park Industrial Estate, Bredbury, Stockport, Cheshire, SK6 2ST
Shareholders: Gavin Michael Wright; Brian Michael Wright
Officers: Gavin Wright, Secretary; Brian Michael Wright [1958] Director; Gavin Michael Wright [1982] Director

Primo Drinks (North East) Ltd
Incorporated: 10 February 2012 *Employees:* 6
Previous: Same Day Beers Limited
Net Worth: £66,421 *Total Assets:* £860,570
Registered Office: Same Day Beers, Corrie Way, Bredbury Park Industrial Estate, Bredbury, Stockport, Cheshire, SK6 2ST
Shareholders: Gavin Michael Wright; Brian Michael Wright
Officers: Gavin Wright, Secretary; Brian Michael Wright [1958] Director; Gavin Michael Wright [1982] Director

Primo Drinks (Staffordshire) Ltd
Incorporated: 29 January 2008 *Employees:* 12
Previous: Same Day Beers (Stoke) Limited
Net Worth: £308,824 *Total Assets:* £487,937
Registered Office: Corrie Way, Bredbury, Stockport, Cheshire, SK6 2ST
Shareholders: Gavin Michael Wright; Brian Michael Wright
Officers: Gavin Wright, Secretary; Brian Michael Wright [1958] Director; Gavin Wright [1982] Director

Primo Drinks (Yorkshire) Ltd
Incorporated: 17 September 2009 *Employees:* 17
Previous: Same Day Beers (Yorkshire) Limited
Net Worth: £299,034 *Total Assets:* £787,971
Registered Office: Corrie Way, Bredbury Park Industrial Estate, Bredbury, Stockport, Cheshire, SK6 2ST
Shareholders: Brian Michael Wright; Gavin Michael Wright
Officers: Gavin Wright, Secretary; Brian Michael Wright [1958] Director; Gavin Wright [1982] Director

Primo Drinks Ltd
Incorporated: 7 July 2003 Employees: 50
Previous: Primo Drinks (Greater Manchester) Ltd
Net Worth: £377,454 Total Assets: £3,183,989
Registered Office: Same Day Beers, Corrie Way, Bredbury Industrial Estate, Bredbury, Stockport, Cheshire, SK6 2ST
Shareholders: Gavin Michael Wright; Brian Michael Wright
Officers: Gavin Wright, Secretary; Brian Michael Wright [1958] Director; Gavin Wright [1982] Director

The Primos Group Ltd
Incorporated: 26 February 2018
Registered Office: Flat 21, King's Quay, Chelsea Harbour, London, SW10 0UX
Shareholders: Renato de Paula Mezencio; Raquel Melo Milreu
Officers: Renato de Paula Mezencio [1987] Director/Entrepreneur [Italian]; Raquel Melo Milreu [1985] Director/Entrepreneur [Brazilian/Italian]

Pristine Trades Ltd
Incorporated: 5 June 2018
Registered Office: 7 Carisbrooke Close, Whitton, Hounslow, Middlesex, TW4 5PD
Major Shareholder: Ashmeet Singh
Officers: Ashmeet Singh [1998] Director

Private Wine Shippers Ltd
Incorporated: 4 October 2018
Registered Office: Grafton Jones, 2 New Road, Chippenham, Wilts, SN15 1EJ
Major Shareholder: Nigel Steven Savage
Officers: Nigel Steven Savage [1962] Director

Prodolce Ltd
Incorporated: 29 June 2018
Registered Office: 3 Park Place, Cheltenham, Glos, GL50 2QS
Major Shareholder: Jason Hamilton Whinfield Curl
Officers: Jason Hamilton Whinfield Curl [1966] Managing Director

Professional Wine Services Limited
Incorporated: 5 September 2012
Net Worth: £7,360 Total Assets: £78,263
Registered Office: 33 Swaffield Road, London, SW18 3AQ
Major Shareholder: James Brian Price
Officers: James Brian Price [1965] Director/Wine Merchant

Profile Wines Limited
Incorporated: 11 January 2017 Employees: 2
Net Worth: £801 Total Assets: £12,119
Registered Office: Barrington House, 41-45 Yarm Lane, Stockton on Tees, Cleveland, TS18 3EA
Shareholder: Jack Frederick Bowles
Officers: Jack Frederick Bowles [1981] Director/Business Owner; Eleanor Jane Richmond [1975] Director/Chef Proprietor

Prohibition Limited
Incorporated: 21 November 2013
Net Worth Deficit: £18,033 Total Assets: £128,808
Registered Office: 10 Castleglen Way, Dundrum, Co Down, BT33 0WN
Major Shareholder: Felicia Mary Matheson
Officers: Felicia Mary Matheson [1982] Director

Project Urban Wines Ltd
Incorporated: 22 January 2019
Registered Office: Flat 1, 2a Cambray Road, London, SW12 0DY
Major Shareholder: Freddie Cobb
Officers: Freddie Cobb [1984] Director

The Project Wines UK Limited
Incorporated: 27 August 2016
Registered Office: Ashcombe Court, Woolsack Way, Godalming, Surrey, GU7 1LQ
Shareholders: Thys Louw; Duncan Alexander Savage
Officers: Thys Louw [1982] Director/Winemaker [South African]; Duncan Alexander Savage [1978] Director/Winemaker [South African]; Lucy Margaret Faraday Warner [1966] Director/Sales & Marketing

Proof Drinks Limited
Incorporated: 8 April 2008 Employees: 19
Net Worth: £568,366 Total Assets: £1,817,175
Registered Office: 41 Great Portland Street, London, W1W 7LA
Parent: JPJ (UK) Limited
Officers: Paul Ferguson [1981] Director; James McDermott [1977] Director; James Vincent Neville-O'Brien [1942] Director [Irish]

The Proper Wine Company Limited
Incorporated: 27 February 2009
Registered Office: 13 Stockwell Street, Cambridge, CB1 3ND
Shareholder: Jonathan David Thomas
Officers: Jonathan David Thomas [1968] Director/Consultant; Stewart Travers [1975] Director/Wine Merchant

Prosecco 1754 Limited
Incorporated: 3 September 2013
Net Worth: £49,995 Total Assets: £181,161
Registered Office: 19 Appleton Court, Calder Park, Wakefield, W Yorks, WF2 7AR
Shareholders: Julian Robert Billington; Marcus James Hilton
Officers: Julien Robert Billington [1965] Director; Lindsey Anne Fellowes-Freeman [1982] Director; Marcus James Hilton [1977] Director; Gemma Lucy Rawson [1986] Director

Prosit Wines Limited
Incorporated: 30 June 2014
Net Worth Deficit: £8,142 Total Assets: £524
Registered Office: 570 Kingston Road, Raynes Park, London, SW20 8DR
Major Shareholder: Augusto Grotto
Officers: Augusto Grotto [1959] Director/IT Consultant [Italian]

Prostimo Ltd
Incorporated: 21 August 2002
Net Worth: £24,797 Total Assets: £46,733
Registered Office: Estate Office, Stag Industrial Estate, Oxford Street, Bilston, W Midlands, WV14 7HZ
Major Shareholder: Rajvinder Singh Sangha
Officers: Rajvinder Singh Sangha [1970] Director

Provenance Fine Wines Ltd
Incorporated: 12 December 1990 Employees: 1
Net Worth Deficit: £81,304 Total Assets: £437,805
Registered Office: Bailey House, 4-10 Barttelot Road, Horsham, W Sussex, RH12 1DQ
Parent: Vin-X Limited
Officers: Peter Robert Shakeshaft [1958] Director

Provenance Marketing Ltd
Incorporated: 13 April 2006 Employees: 2
Net Worth Deficit: £46,700 Total Assets: £285,688
Registered Office: 89 King Street, Maidstone, Kent, ME14 1BG
Officers: Richard Montgomerie Phillips, Secretary; Gruffald Benjamin Salter [1994] Director/Businessman

Provenance Projects 2016 Ltd
Incorporated: 16 June 2016 *Employees:* 2
Net Worth Deficit: £6,910 *Total Assets:* £5,421
Registered Office: 4th Floor, Tuition House, 27-37 St George's Road, Wimbledon, London, SW19 4EU
Shareholders: Louise Deegan-Riley; Benjamin Keene Leonard
Officers: Benjamin Keene Leonard [1975] Director/Banking

Provence Impex Limited
Incorporated: 6 February 2007 *Employees:* 1
Net Worth: £9,919 *Total Assets:* £52,141
Registered Office: 208 Jaquard Court, 32 Bishops Way, London, E2 9HB
Major Shareholder: Stephane Calme-Magnan
Officers: Jean Voisin, Secretary; Stephane Calme-Magnan [1965] Administrative/Legal Director [French]

Provino Limited
Incorporated: 22 August 2016
Net Worth: £4,573 *Total Assets:* £13,561
Registered Office: 19 Bridge Road, Lancaster, LA1 4UN
Shareholders: Alberto Zambianchi; Jared Matthew Williamson
Officers: Jared Matthew Williamson [1976] Director; Alberto Zambianchi [1970] Director [Italian]

Pruno Wines Ltd
Incorporated: 26 April 2018
Registered Office: 45 Lugard Road, Liverpool, L17 0BA
Major Shareholder: Sean Lionel Millar
Officers: Sean Lionel Millar [1967] Director

Pryzm Cocktails Limited
Incorporated: 23 April 2018
Registered Office: 10 Mynors Crescent, Wythall, Bromsgrove, Worcs, B47 5JG
Major Shareholder: Tye Smith
Officers: Tye Smith, Secretary; Tye Smith [1996] Director

PS Drinks Ltd
Incorporated: 13 May 2017
Net Worth Deficit: £37,029 *Total Assets:* £106,210
Registered Office: 43 Craven Park Road, Harlesden, London, NW10 8SE
Shareholder: Davinder Pal Singh Chawla
Officers: Davinder Pal Singh Chawla [1958] Director/Businessman; Poonam Chawla [1964] Director/Housewife; Ramneek Chawla [1992] Director/Businessman

PSB Trading Limited
Incorporated: 6 September 2011
Net Worth: £400 *Total Assets:* £7,994
Registered Office: 53 St Marys Road, Ilford, Essex, IG1 1QU
Major Shareholder: Parminder Singh Bassi
Officers: Parminder Singh Bassi [1988] Director

PSR Distribution Limited
Incorporated: 3 March 2017 *Employees:* 4
Net Worth: £49,589 *Total Assets:* £155,334
Registered Office: 54 Sun Street, Waltham Abbey, Essex, EN9 1EJ
Major Shareholder: Paul Burnham
Officers: Paul Simon Burnham [1974] Director

Psychopomp Ltd
Incorporated: 4 April 2014
Net Worth: £134,853 *Total Assets:* £187,351
Registered Office: 44 St Andrews Road, Montpelier, Bristol, BS6 5EH
Shareholders: Daniel Lee Walker; Liam Scott Hirt
Officers: Dr Liam Scott Hirt [1978] Director; Daniel Lee Walker [1982] Director

PT Drinks Ltd
Incorporated: 11 July 2018
Registered Office: 616D Green Lane, Ilford, Essex, IG3 9SE
Shareholders: Tia Bihal; Priya Bihal
Officers: Priya Bihal [1991] Director/Psychologist; Tia Bihal [1995] Director/Civil Servant

Pub Pool (711) Limited
Incorporated: 29 November 2006 *Employees:* 1
Net Worth: £65,361 *Total Assets:* £167,336
Registered Office: Fleece House, 213 Accrington Road, Burnley, Lancs, BB11 5ES
Officers: Amanda Grogan, Secretary; Amanda Grogan [1959] Director; Terry Grogan [1959] Director

Publik Wine Limited
Incorporated: 29 May 2018
Registered Office: Flat 3, 106 Priory Road, London, NW6 3NS
Major Shareholder: Jennifer Catherine Nel
Officers: Jennifer Catherine Nel [1979] Director/Accountant

Pug Vodka Ltd
Incorporated: 5 September 2016
Registered Office: 101 Rose Street, South Lane, Edinburgh, EH2 3JG
Shareholder: Lewis Geoff Green
Officers: Lee James Fascia [1980] Director; Lewis Geoff Green [1983] Director

Pull The Cork Limited
Incorporated: 18 January 2013
Previous: Savour The Investment Ltd
Net Worth: £2 *Total Assets:* £2
Registered Office: 74 Biscay Road, London, W6 8JN
Major Shareholder: James Douglas Nathan
Officers: Moritz Walter Bak [1989] Director [Dutch]; James Douglas Nathan [1989] Director

Pulling & Co. Limited
Incorporated: 30 September 1926
Registered Office: 26 Wyle Cop, Shrewsbury, Salop, SY1 1XD
Parent: Tanners (Shrewsbury) Limited
Officers: Robert John Morgan, Secretary; Robert John Morgan [1971] Director/Chartered Accountant; James Jonathan Tanner [1968] Director

Pulp Craft Cider Limited
Incorporated: 12 April 2017
Registered Office: Unit 10d Topland Country Business Park, Cragg Vale, Hebden Bridge, W Yorks, HX7 5RW
Officers: Jodie Jowett [1989] Director; Emma Sweaney [1975] Director

Pulse Products Limited
Incorporated: 6 May 1997 *Employees:* 2
Net Worth: £95,659 *Total Assets:* £317,469
Registered Office: 91 Soho Hill, Hockley, Birmingham, B19 1AY
Parent: NNA Properties Limited
Officers: Ajminder Singh [1974] Director

Punchline Ltd
Incorporated: 2 May 2018
Registered Office: 20a Southbrook Road, London, SE12 8LQ
Shareholders: Amari Boothe; Curtis Dixon; Ryan Banton
Officers: Ryan Banton [1987] Director; Amari Boothe [1989] Director; Curtis Dixon [1989] Director/Accounts Manager

Punchy Drinks Limited
Incorporated: 9 November 2017
Registered Office: 43 Adelaide Avenue, London, SE4 1LF
Major Shareholder: Paddy Charles Arthur Cavanagh-Butler
Officers: Daniel Bowers [1976] Director; Patrick Charles Arthur Cavanagh-Butler [1993] Director/Chief Executive; Charles Howard Hobhouse [1992] Director

Punjabi Ltd
Incorporated: 9 May 2018
Registered Office: 71-75 Shelton Street, London, WC2H 9JQ
Major Shareholder: Manjit Singh Hanjra
Officers: Manjit Singh Hanjra, Secretary; Manjit Singh Hanjra [1966] Director/Engineer

Pure Organic Drinks Limited
Incorporated: 26 April 2018
Registered Office: Hamilton Office Park, 31 High View Close, Leicester, LE4 9LJ
Major Shareholder: The Arl Corporation Limited
Officers: Carmel Charmain Arthur [1975] Director; Thomas William Charles Lamb [1947] Director; Christopher Edward Ryan [1970] Director

Pure Techno Ltd
Incorporated: 14 January 2019
Registered Office: First Floor, 112 Malden Crescent, London, NW1 8BL
Major Shareholder: Danial Aramesh
Officers: Danial Aramesh [1991] Director/Barman [Iranian]

Purity Brewing Company Limited
Incorporated: 27 August 2003 *Employees:* 40
Net Worth: £2,430,198 *Total Assets:* £5,428,463
Registered Office: The Brewery, Upper Spernall Farm, Spernall Lane, Great Alne, Alcester, Warwicks, B49 6JF
Parent: Purity Brewing Group Limited
Officers: James Philip Minkin, Secretary; Paul Halsey [1962] Director/Self Employed; James Philip Minkin [1966] Director/Accountant

Python Controls Ltd
Incorporated: 2 August 2018
Registered Office: 20-22 Wenlock Road, London, N1 7GU
Officers: Neil Humphrey [1969] Director/Software Engineer; Sandra Carol Humphrey [1961] Director

Pyvo UK Ltd
Incorporated: 5 January 2016
Net Worth: £483 *Total Assets:* £2,945
Registered Office: 105 Quaker Lane, Liversedge, W Yorks, WF15 8DF
Shareholders: Ewhen Chymera; Martyn Zenovij Chymera; Chrystyna Chymera-Holloway
Officers: Ewhen Chymera [1987] Director; Doctor Martyn Zenovij Chymera [1981] Director; Chrystyna Chymera-Holloway [1984] Director

QNGC Limited
Incorporated: 29 April 2014
Registered Office: 1a Dukesway Court, Team Valley Trading Estate, Gateshead, Tyne & Wear, NE11 0PJ
Parent: Falcombe Holdings Limited
Officers: Phillip Nigel Blain, Secretary; David James Horrocks [1959] Financial Director; William Edward Philip Noble [1988] Director

Qtranly Ltd
Incorporated: 23 July 2018
Registered Office: 198 St Anns Road, London, N15 5RP
Major Shareholder: Huy Quang Ly
Officers: Huy Quang Ly, Secretary; Huy Quang Ly [1995] Director [Vietnamese]

Quaich Whisky Investments Limited
Incorporated: 16 December 2016
Registered Office: Regina House, 124 Finchley Road, London, NW3 5JS
Major Shareholder: Piers Benedict Adam
Officers: Piers Benedict Adam [1964] Director

Quality Spirits International Limited
Incorporated: 3 March 1986 *Employees:* 12
Net Worth: £112,124,000 *Total Assets:* £116,992,000
Registered Office: Independence House, 84 Lower Mortlake Road, Richmond, Surrey, TW9 2HS
Parent: William Grant & Sons Enterprises Limited
Officers: Karen Louise Forbes, Secretary; Alexander John Davies [1982] Director/Head of Finance & Business Development; John Michael Harvey [1956] Managing Director; Ewan John Henderson [1968] Director; Michael Lamont [1960] Director

Quamina Quality Drinks Company Ltd
Incorporated: 24 January 2019
Registered Office: 257 Victoria Road, London, N22 7XH
Shareholders: Klinton Gilbert; Damilola Whitfield; Jamil Quamina
Officers: Klinton Gilbert [1981] Director/Teacher; Jamil Quamina [1985] Director/Manager; Damilola Whitfield [1991] Director/Self Employed

Quantock Abbey Wine Cellars Limited
Incorporated: 17 November 2011 *Employees:* 6
Net Worth: £63,906 *Total Assets:* £305,776
Registered Office: Mill Farm, Weston Bampfylde, Yeovil, Somerset, BA22 7HY
Shareholders: Christopher Staniland; Andrew Cecil Mangles
Officers: Andrew Mangles [1960] Director/Wine Supplier; Emma Ramage [1962] Director/Administrator; Christopher Staniland [1960] Director/Wine Supplier; Philippa Staniland [1962] Director/Administrator

Quantum Vintners Limited
Incorporated: 19 October 2012
Net Worth: £28,255 *Total Assets:* £72,940
Registered Office: c/o Arthur G Mead Ltd, Fitzrovia House, 153-157 Cleveland Street, London, W1T 6QW
Major Shareholder: Anthony James Russell
Officers: Anthony Russell [1967] Director

The Quarter Cafe Bar Limited
Incorporated: 6 June 2017
Net Worth Deficit: £11,144 *Total Assets:* £17,136
Registered Office: 4 Wood Street, Wakefield, W Yorks, WF1 2ED
Major Shareholder: Jake Winfield
Officers: Jake Winfield, Secretary; Timothy Winfield [1967] Director/Bar Staff

Quartz Group Scotland Ltd
Incorporated: 9 March 2000
Previous: Quartz Developments Limited
Net Worth: £582,754 *Total Assets:* £615,716
Registered Office: The Coutyard, 22 Hayburn Street, Glasgow, G11 6DG
Shareholders: Iain MacLean; William Knox
Officers: William Knox, Secretary; William Knox [1960] Director; Iain MacLean [1970] Director

The Queen of The Moorlands Whisky Company Ltd
Incorporated: 15 November 2005
Registered Office: 22 Russell Street, Leek, Staffs, ST13 5JF
Parent: Wine and Whisky Limited
Officers: Anne-Marie Marie Alexander [1969] Sales Director

Quercus Wines Ltd
Incorporated: 14 June 2018
Registered Office: 2 Pigdown Farm Cottages, Pigdown Lane, Hever, Edenbridge, Kent, TN8 7LX
Major Shareholder: Matthew John Iles
Officers: Matthew John Iles [1984] Director/Wine Merchant

Quero Enterprise Ltd
Incorporated: 27 April 2010
Net Worth: £223 *Total Assets:* £5,956
Registered Office: 41 High Street, Sandbach, Cheshire, CW11 1AL
Major Shareholder: Robert Keppel
Officers: Robert Keppel [1963] Director/Off Licence Manager

Quest Leisure Limited
Incorporated: 18 December 1992
Net Worth: £65,628 *Total Assets:* £70,494
Registered Office: Amar House, Broad Street, Wolverhampton, W Midlands, WV1 1HP
Officers: Sohan Singh Gill, Secretary; Sandeep Singh Gill [1978] Director; Sohan Singh Gill [1953] Managing Director

Quick Liquids Limited
Incorporated: 31 October 2016
Net Worth Deficit: £11,262 *Total Assets:* £13,443
Registered Office: 20-22 Wenlock Road, London, N1 7GU
Major Shareholder: George Edward Nightingale
Officers: George Edward Nightingale [1984] Director/Developer

Quick Whisky Limited
Incorporated: 1 September 2017
Registered Office: 20 Barnton Street, Stirling, FK8 1NA
Major Shareholder: Bartosz Czernia
Officers: Bartosz Czernia [1975] Director/Builder [Polish]

Quick-Keg Limited
Incorporated: 16 June 2006 *Employees:* 2
Net Worth: £42,952 *Total Assets:* £134,102
Registered Office: Windsor House, 26 Mostyn Avenue, Craig-Y-Don, Llandudno, Conwy, LL30 1YY
Shareholders: Craig Paul Davies; David Anthony Davies
Officers: Craig Paul Davies [1976] Director/Drinks Wholesaler; David Anthony Davies [1965] Director/Drinks Wholesaler

Quicksip Ltd
Incorporated: 8 May 2017
Registered Office: Pear Tree Cottage, Green Lane Farm, Shamley Green, Guildford, Surrey, GU5 0RD
Officers: Tom Marchant [1982] Director

Quint-Essential JQ Ltd
Incorporated: 24 August 2017
Registered Office: 61A St Pauls Square, Jewelley Quarter, Birmingham, B3 1QS
Major Shareholder: Harpinder Singh
Officers: Jaspreet Kaur Barns, Secretary; Harpinder Singh [1976] Director/Retailer

Quintessential Brands Premium Brands Limited
Incorporated: 27 March 2014 *Employees:* 16
Previous: Quintessential Brands Company Limited
Net Worth Deficit: £932,000 *Total Assets:* £5,544,000
Registered Office: Distribution Point, Melbury Park, Clayton Road, Birchwood, Warrington, Cheshire, WA3 6PH
Parent: Quintessential Brands UK Group Limited
Officers: Michael Clifford, Secretary; Warren Michael Scott [1963] Director/Businessman; Vincenzo Visone [1955] Director/Businessman [Italian]

Quintessential Brands Spirit Solutions Limited
Incorporated: 14 April 2011 *Employees:* 12
Previous: Essential Drinks Company Limited
Net Worth: £254,000 *Total Assets:* £9,515,000
Registered Office: Distribution Point, Melbury Park, Clayton Road, Birchwood, Warrington, Cheshire, WA3 6PH
Parent: Quintessential Brands UK Group Limited
Officers: Michael Clifford, Secretary; Warren Michael Scott [1963] Director/Businessman; Vincenzo Visone [1955] Director/Businessman [Italian]

Quintessential Brands UK Limited
Incorporated: 9 November 1973 *Employees:* 13
Previous: Marblehead Brand Development Limited
Net Worth: £8,277 *Total Assets:* £1,266,546
Registered Office: Quartermile One, 15 Lauriston Place, Edinburgh, EH3 9EP
Parent: Quintessential Spirits UK Limited
Officers: Michael Clifford, Secretary; Warren Michael Scott [1963] Director/Businessman; Vincenzo Visone [1955] Director [Italian]

Quintessential Decadence Ltd
Incorporated: 13 June 2017
Registered Office: 1 Alexandra Parade, Northolt Road, Harrow, Middlesex, HA2 8HE
Shareholders: Sheron de Sa Pinto; Francisco de Sa Pinto; Sandro Peres
Officers: Sheron de SA Pinto [1979] Director; Sandro Peres [1976] Director [Portuguese]

Quintessential Spirits Holdings Limited
Incorporated: 13 June 2012
Registered Office: Distribution Point, Melbury Park, Clayton Road, Birchwood, Warrington, Cheshire, WA3 6PH
Parent: Quintessential Spirits UK Limited
Officers: Michael Clifford, Secretary; Warren Michael Scott [1963] Director; Vincenzo Visone [1955] Director/Businessman [Italian]

Quintessential Spirits Limited
Incorporated: 13 June 2012
Registered Office: Distribution Point, Melbury Park, Clayton Road, Birchwood, Warrington, Cheshire, WA3 6PH
Parent: Quintessential Spirits Holdings Limited
Officers: Michael Clifford, Secretary; Warren Michael Scott [1963] Director; Vincenzo Visone [1955] Director/Businessman [Italian]

Quintessential Spirits UK Limited
Incorporated: 29 July 2011
Net Worth: £2 *Total Assets:* £176,535
Registered Office: Distribution Point, Melbury Park, Clayton Road, Birchwood, Warrington, Cheshire, WA3 6PH
Shareholders: Warren Michael Scott; Vincenzo Visone
Officers: Michael Clifford, Secretary; Warren Michael Scott [1963] Director/Businessman; Vincenzo Visone [1955] Director [Italian]

Quintessential Wines Holdings Limited
Incorporated: 13 June 2012
Registered Office: Distribution Point, Melbury Park, Clayton Road, Birchwood, Warrington, Cheshire, WA3 6PH
Parent: Quintessential Spirits UK Limited
Officers: Michael Clifford, Secretary; Warren Michael Scott [1963] Director; Vincenzo Visone [1955] Director/Businessman [Italian]

Quintessential Wines Limited
Incorporated: 13 June 2012
Registered Office: Distribution Point, Melbury Park, Clayton Road, Birchwood, Warrington, Cheshire, WA3 6PH
Parent: Quintessential Wines Holdings Limited
Officers: Michael Clifford, Secretary; Warren Michael Scott [1963] Director; Vincenzo Visone [1955] Director/Businessman [Italian]

Quintrox Limited
Incorporated: 18 May 2009 *Employees:* 1
Net Worth: £17,771 *Total Assets:* £37,629
Registered Office: 34 Manchester Road, Southport, Merseyside, PR9 9AZ
Major Shareholder: David Victor Porter
Officers: David Victor Porter, Secretary; David Victor Porter [1971] Director

Quiqui Mezcal Ltd
Incorporated: 6 August 2013 *Employees:* 1
Net Worth Deficit: £604 *Total Assets:* £78,069
Registered Office: BCL House, Royds Hall Road, Leeds, LS12 6AJ
Officers: Melanie Symonds [1977] Director

R & B Drinks Ltd
Incorporated: 17 February 2012 *Employees:* 8
Net Worth: £216,761 *Total Assets:* £539,978
Registered Office: Unit 7 Beaumont Business Centre, Boston Road, Gorse Hill, Beaumont Leys, Leicester, LE4 1AA
Major Shareholder: Harjinder Singh
Officers: Harjinder Singh [1973] Director

R & B Wines Ltd
Incorporated: 21 April 1999 *Employees:* 2
Net Worth: £103,390 *Total Assets:* £311,760
Registered Office: Suite 507, 28 Old Brompton Road, London, SW7 3SS
Major Shareholder: Henk Rudolf de Boer
Officers: Brigitte Katharina de Boer, Secretary [Swiss]; Brigitte Katharina de Boer [1947] Director [Swedish]; Henk Rudolf de Boer [1946] Director/Wine Consultant [Dutch]

R & M Chateau Wines Ltd
Incorporated: 10 July 2012 *Employees:* 3
Net Worth: £5,870 *Total Assets:* £101,445
Registered Office: Unit 10 Ministry Wharf, Wycombe Road, Saunderton, High Wycombe, Bucks, HP14 4HW
Major Shareholder: Michelle Goldsmith
Officers: Michelle Goldsmith [1978] Director; Richard Thomas Goldsmith [1966] Director/Wine Merchant

R B M Leisure Limited
Incorporated: 18 July 2001
Registered Office: 9 Church Street, Wednesfield, Wolverhampton, W Midlands, WV11 1SR
Major Shareholder: Harbans Lal
Officers: Harbans Lal [1969] Director

R S Wines Limited
Incorporated: 23 April 1999 *Employees:* 3
Net Worth: £12,478 *Total Assets:* £370,297
Registered Office: Woodlands Grange, Woodlands Lane, Bradley Stoke, Bristol, BS32 4JY
Shareholders: Rajan Soni; Susan Carol Soni
Officers: Susan Carol Soni, Secretary; Krishan Soni [1967] Director/Accountant; Rajan Soni [1962] Director/Wine Merchant

R Spirit Ltd
Incorporated: 18 January 2011
Net Worth: £115,674 *Total Assets:* £174,583
Registered Office: Suite 126, Higham Hill JSC, 313 Billet Road, London, E17 5PX
Officers: Dagmar Klongova, Secretary; Andrejs Jefimovs [1976] Director [Latvian]; Dimitry Muradov [1980] Director [Israeli]; Radoslav Semancik [1974] Director [Slovak]; Stanislav Trenciansky [1971] Director [Slovak]

R. St Barth Limited
Incorporated: 31 October 2016
Registered Office: 2 Hawsted, High Road, Buckhurst Hill, Essex, IG9 5SS
Shareholder: Mikael Sammy Silvestre
Officers: Carole Van T Hof, Secretary; Mikael Sammy Silvestre [1977] Director [French]; Severine Laetitia Silvestre [1975] Director [French]; Carole Anne Van T Hof [1946] Director

R.L.G. Trading Limited
Incorporated: 21 June 2007
Net Worth: £121,578 *Total Assets:* £313,696
Registered Office: 118 Cockmuir Street, Glasgow, G21 4XE
Officers: Stuart Alexander, Secretary; George Lynch [1959] Director

Rackham Investments Limited
Incorporated: 18 October 1960
Net Worth: £240,270 *Total Assets:* £417,811
Registered Office: The Church, 172 London Road, Guildford, Surrey, GU1 1XR
Major Shareholder: James Arthur Rackham
Officers: Willam Peter Duff, Secretary; Jack Arthur Rackham [1987] Director/Bar Manager; James Arthur Rackham [1953] Director

A.H.Rackham Limited
Incorporated: 8 July 1959 *Employees:* 1
Net Worth: £74,497 *Total Assets:* £437,254
Registered Office: The Church, 172 London Road, Guildford, Surrey, GU1 1XR
Major Shareholder: James Arthur Rackham
Officers: William Peter Duff, Secretary; James Arthur Rackham [1953] Director

Radleigh Wines Limited
Incorporated: 29 January 2010
Net Worth: £106,445 *Total Assets:* £117,643
Registered Office: Kincardine House, Aberargie, Perth, PH2 9LX
Major Shareholder: Jamie Walker Stanley Pringle Morrison
Officers: Jamie Walker Stanley Pringle Morrison [1973] Director

Raeburn Fine Wines Ltd.
Incorporated: 13 October 2014 Employees: 11
Net Worth: £980,296 Total Assets: £2,719,305
Registered Office: 23 Comely Bank Road, Edinburgh, EH4 1DS
Shareholders: Taher Mohamed; Zubair Mohamed
Officers: Taher Mahmud [1954] Director/Wine Merchant; Zubair Mohamed [1962] Director/Wine Merchant

Raer Scotch Whisky Ltd
Incorporated: 5 April 2012
Previous: Philipshill Retirement Village Ltd
Net Worth Deficit: £241,696 Total Assets: £1,141,138
Registered Office: Cognitor Accountancy Limited, Forbes House, Harris Business Park, Hanbury Road, Stoke Prior, Bromsgrove, Worcs, B60 4BD
Major Shareholder: James Kean
Officers: Jacob Kean [1996] Director; James Harkins Kean [1960] Director

Raer Whisky Company Limited
Incorporated: 9 November 2016
Net Worth: £100 Total Assets: £100
Registered Office: 1 Cambuslang Court, Cambuslang, Glasgow, G32 8FH
Major Shareholder: Iain Gilchrist
Officers: Iain Gilchrist [1967] Director

Raer Whisky Limited
Incorporated: 31 January 2017
Net Worth: £100 Total Assets: £100
Registered Office: 1 Cambuslang Court, Cambuslang, Glasgow, G32 8FH
Major Shareholder: Iain Gilchrist
Officers: Iain Gilchrist [1967] Director

Rafine Limited
Incorporated: 29 February 1984 Employees: 6
Net Worth: £1,406,972 Total Assets: £2,737,212
Registered Office: St John's Court, Easton Street, High Wycombe, Bucks, HP11 1JX
Shareholders: Michael Charles Raffety; Sarah Wendy Raffety
Officers: Michael Charles Raffety, Secretary; Adam Raffety [1982] Director; Michael Charles Raffety [1954] Director/Wine Broker; Sarah Wendy Raffety [1956] Director/Wine Broker

Rafti Ltd.
Incorporated: 18 May 2015 Employees: 2
Net Worth Deficit: £86,833 Total Assets: £13,608
Registered Office: 95 King Street, Lancaster, LA1 1RH
Major Shareholder: Tomasz Barczynski
Officers: Tomasz Barczynski [1975] Director [Polish]

Ragarfield International Limited
Incorporated: 10 September 2008
Net Worth Deficit: £43,429 Total Assets: £42,477
Registered Office: 31 Milton Road, Gravesend, Kent, DA12 2RF
Shareholders: Ashok Kumar Sharma; Neelu Sharma
Officers: Ashok Kumar Sharma [1947] Director; Neelu Sharma [1951] Director

Ragtag Wines Ltd
Incorporated: 30 May 2018
Registered Office: 71-75 Shelton Street, London, WC2H 9JQ
Major Shareholder: Richard Hamblin
Officers: Richard Hamblin, Secretary; Richard Hamblin [1972] Director/Wine Merchant

Ragul Ltd
Incorporated: 11 January 2018
Registered Office: 199A Lower Addiscombe Road, Croydon, Surrey, CR0 6RA
Officers: Ragul Periyasamy Manoharan [1994] Director/Businessman [Indian]

Railway Bar & Grill Ltd
Incorporated: 27 February 2014
Net Worth: £66,420 Total Assets: £183,724
Registered Office: 5 Albany Road, Earlsdon, Coventry, Warwicks, CV5 6JQ
Major Shareholder: Deepak Nagra
Officers: Deepak Nagra [1993] Director

Raisin Social Limited
Incorporated: 17 October 1986 Employees: 9
Net Worth: £1,547,805 Total Assets: £3,772,493
Registered Office: Savoy House, Savoy Circus, London, W3 7DA
Major Shareholder: Simon George Halliday
Officers: Martha Maria Halliday, Secretary; Patrick Lovell Halliday [1960] Director/Sales Manager; Simon George Halliday [1957] Managing Director; Alan John Watson [1941] Director

Rajpoot Traders Ltd
Incorporated: 25 July 2018
Registered Office: 35 Thornway Drive, Ashton under Lyne, Lancs, OL7 0AA
Major Shareholder: Waseem Sarwar
Officers: Waseem Sarwar [1984] Director/Businessman

Raks Suppliers Limited
Incorporated: 20 August 2014 Employees: 3
Net Worth Deficit: £11,349 Total Assets: £88,004
Registered Office: 81 Moordown, Woolwich, London, SE18 3NA
Shareholders: Rajan Somasutharam; Kaushikkumar Rambhai Patel
Officers: Kaushikkumar Rambhai Patel [1959] Director/Entrepreneur; Rajan Somasutharam [1979] Director/Entrepreneur

Raleigh (Glasgow) Limited
Incorporated: 10 March 1953
Registered Office: 16 Park Circus, Glasgow, G3 6AX
Parent: Hunter Laing & Company Limited
Officers: Stewart Hunter Laing, Secretary; Stewart Hunter Laing [1946] Director

Ralph's Wines Ltd
Incorporated: 11 April 2008 Employees: 1
Net Worth: £31,334 Total Assets: £96,170
Registered Office: 78 High Street, Whitton, Twickenham, Middlesex, TW2 7LS
Major Shareholder: Ralph Timothy Smith
Officers: Geoffrey Lilley Smith [1955] Director/University Professor; Ralph Timothy Smith [1980] Director

Ramstrad Trading Ltd
Incorporated: 9 February 2016
Registered Office: 3 Montpelier Avenue, Bexley, Kent, DA5 3AP
Major Shareholder: Ranjit Singh
Officers: Ranjit Singh [1971] Director

Ramx Ltd
Incorporated: 17 December 2018
Registered Office: Apartment 25.03, Twofiftyone Building, 251 Southwark Bridge Road, Elephant and Castle, London, SE1 6FN
Major Shareholder: Ross Andrew Murphy
Officers: Ross Andrew Murphy [1994] Director/Analyst [Irish]; Timothy Albert William Wheeler [1995] Director

Ran Ales Ltd
Incorporated: 23 July 2014 *Employees:* 2
Net Worth Deficit: £22,138 *Total Assets:* £38,453
Registered Office: Unit 8 Imex Business Park, Ormonde Street, Stoke on Trent, Staffs, ST4 3NP
Major Shareholder: Neville Mark Smith
Officers: Neville Mark Smith [1961] Director

Rando Global Alliance Limited
Incorporated: 18 May 2017
Registered Office: 566-568 Hyde Road, Manchester, M18 7EE
Major Shareholder: William Osuji Odefa
Officers: William Osuji Odefa [1986] Director

Rapid Fill Ltd
Incorporated: 25 February 2019
Registered Office: 5 Roxford Devas Street, London, E3 3LN
Major Shareholder: Tameil Ingram
Officers: Tameil Ingram [1989] Managing Director

Rara Drinks Company Ltd
Incorporated: 5 September 2017
Registered Office: Tulip House, 70 Borough High Street, London, SE1 1XF
Major Shareholder: Craig Chidgey
Officers: Craig Stewart Chidgey [1976] Director/Entrepreneur; Louise Robertson [1985] Director

Rare Whisky Auctioneers Ltd
Incorporated: 23 July 2018
Registered Office: 71-75 Shelton Street, Covent Garden, London, WC2H 9JQ
Officers: Geoffrey Philip Drage [1955] Director/Business Owner; Louis Haseman [1984] Director

Rarewood (London) Limited
Incorporated: 12 January 2018
Registered Office: Studio 1, 305a Goldhawk Road, London, W12 8EU
Officers: Tessa Elizabeth Jayne John [1972] Director

Rarus Ltd
Incorporated: 25 August 2011
Net Worth Deficit: £33,154 *Total Assets:* £1,815,626
Registered Office: 13 Hudson Street, Loughborough, Leics, LE11 1EJ
Shareholders: Maheshkumar Ramanlal Patel; Nainaben Maheshkumar Patel
Officers: Maheshkumar Ramanlal Patel, Secretary; Maheshkumar Ramanlal Patel [1966] Director; Nainaben Maheshkumar Patel [1969] Director

Rasputin Leisure Ltd
Incorporated: 22 May 2012 *Employees:* 10
Net Worth: £36,908 *Total Assets:* £319,093
Registered Office: c/o Henry Brown & Co, 26 Portland Road, Kilmarnock, E Ayrshire, KA1 2EB
Major Shareholder: John Doyle
Officers: Generald Francis Doyle [1981] Director; John Doyle [1960] Director

Ratcliffe & Brown Wines and Spirits Limited
Incorporated: 22 December 1999 *Employees:* 4
Net Worth: £397,155 *Total Assets:* £3,042,079
Registered Office: Office FF10, Brooklands House, 58 Marlborough Road, Lancing, W Sussex, BN15 8AF
Officers: Annalee Louise Morrow, Secretary; Andrew Percival Brown [1961] Director/General Manager; Annalee Louise Morrow [1974] Director/Accountant

Ratherhavecava Ltd
Incorporated: 26 July 2018
Registered Office: 3 Meadway, London, N14 6NY
Shareholders: Angela Finn; Breda Kelly
Officers: Angela Finn [1971] Director/Consultant

Raven Hill Brewery Limited
Incorporated: 28 March 2018
Registered Office: Raven Hill Farm, Kilham, Driffield, E Yorks, YO25 4EG
Major Shareholder: Mark William Savile
Officers: Mark William Savile [1985] Director

Raven Spirits Limited
Incorporated: 15 November 2017
Registered Office: 2 Old Skene Road, Kingswells, Aberdeen, AB15 8QA
Shareholders: Callum Downie Sim; Alison Jane Sim
Officers: Alison Jane Sim [1967] Director/Lawyer; Callum Downie Sim [1962] Director/Lawyer; Peter Robert Sim [1964] Director

Ravensbourne Wine Company Limited
Incorporated: 6 June 1986
Net Worth Deficit: £3,001 *Total Assets:* £94,410
Registered Office: 38 Penberth Road, London, SE6 1ES
Shareholder: Terence Reginald Short
Officers: Stephen John Williams, Secretary; Terence Reginald Short [1946] Director; Stephen John Williams [1949] Company Secretary and Director

Rawson Trading (Doncaster) Limited
Incorporated: 20 May 2014 *Employees:* 4
Net Worth: £69,463 *Total Assets:* £304,023
Registered Office: Lazarus Properties, 3 Lazarus Court, Doncaster, S Yorks, DN1 3NF
Major Shareholder: Benjamin Thomas Stephen Parr
Officers: Simon Campbell Barnett [1973] Director; Ben Robinson Muirhead [1983] Director/Delivery Driver; Benjamin Thomas Stephen Parr [1987] Director

Ray Jules Limited
Incorporated: 11 December 2015
Net Worth: £5,058 *Total Assets:* £66,035
Registered Office: 2 Candle Court, Heath Road, Hounslow, Middlesex, TW3 2NB
Major Shareholder: Babulal Shah
Officers: Babulal Shah [1941] Director/Carer

RBW Fine Wines Limited
Incorporated: 8 February 2019
Registered Office: Rosebank Cottage, Vann Lane, Chiddingfold, Surrey, GU8 4XU
Major Shareholder: Robin Frederick Baum
Officers: Robin Frederick Baum [1945] Director/Solicitor

RC Brands Ltd
Incorporated: 2 December 2015
Net Worth Deficit: £8,640 *Total Assets:* £9,164
Registered Office: 11-12 Hallmark Trading Centre, Fourth Way, Wembley, Middlesex, HA9 0LB
Major Shareholder: Babina Kaur Chawla
Officers: Babina Kaur Chawla [1974] Director

RCI Spirits Ltd
Incorporated: 6 March 2013
Previous: A Piece of Africa Ltd
Registered Office: 30a Earl's Court Square, London, SW5 9DQ
Shareholders: Tim David Reuter; Rafik Ishani
Officers: Rafik Ishani [1980] Director/Chartered Accountant; Tim David Reuter [1982] Director/Company Secretary

RD Wines Limited
Incorporated: 28 September 1998
Previous: Rodney Densem Wines Limited
Net Worth: £608,350 *Total Assets:* £3,260,000
Registered Office: Unit F, Halesfield 10, Telford, Salop, TF7 4QP
Shareholder: Margie Densem
Officers: Margaret Densem, Secretary/Retail Manager; Margaret Densem [1948] Director; Simon Densem [1972] Director; Nicholas James Gent [1976] Director; Keith Andrew Knight [1970] Director; Steven Edmund Leonard [1968] Managing Director

RDF Paper Ltd
Incorporated: 4 April 2014
Previous: Smartship Trading Ltd
Registered Office: Unit 3 Templewood Stock Road, West Hanningfield, Chelmsford, Essex, CM2 8LA
Shareholders: RDF Waste Ltd; PFL Investments Ltd; John Cashmore-Thorley
Officers: John James Cashmore Thorley [1968] Director

RDM Wines Limited
Incorporated: 4 July 2008 *Employees:* 28
Net Worth: £1,550,724 *Total Assets:* £3,350,739
Registered Office: 242 Penarth Road, Cardiff, CF11 8TU
Major Shareholder: Nigel O'Sullivan
Officers: Callum James O'Sullivan [1992] Director; Nigel O'Sullivan [1957] Managing Director; Renata Paula O'Sullivan [1964] Director; Gregory Thomas Williams [1970] Sales Director

RDV Spirits Ltd
Incorporated: 25 April 2013 *Employees:* 2
Net Worth: £122,323 *Total Assets:* £564,104
Registered Office: Soanepoint, 6-8 Market Place, Reading, Berks, RG1 2EG
Major Shareholder: Joanne Bharwani
Officers: Joanne Bharwani [1972] Director

Re:Stalk Ltd
Incorporated: 3 April 2018
Registered Office: 3/2 116 Dundrennan Road, Glasgow, G42 9SH
Major Shareholder: Grant David Hutchison
Officers: Grant David Hutchison [1984] Director/Musician

Readywine UK Ltd
Incorporated: 19 June 2017
Registered Office: Suite 35, Star Wharf, 40 St Pancras Way, London, NW1 0QX
Parent: Sixiang Holding Limited

The Real Al Company Limited
Incorporated: 29 March 2016
Net Worth: £45,402 *Total Assets:* £183,278
Registered Office: Unit 4 Ravenswood Industrial Estate, Shernhall Street, London, E17 9HQ
Officers: Alice Joy Churchward [1986] Director

Real Ale (Export) Limited
Incorporated: 21 December 2018
Registered Office: Flat 8, Old Lodge Place, Twickenham, Middlesex, TW1 1RQ
Parent: Real Ale Limited
Officers: Nicholas Joseph Dolan [1976] Director; Peter Dolan [1944] Director/Geologist; Zephaniah Oury King [1976] Managing Director

Real Ale (Retail) Limited
Incorporated: 21 December 2018
Registered Office: Flat 8, Old Lodge Place, Twickenham, Middlesex, TW1 1RQ
Parent: Real Ale Limited
Officers: Nicholas Joseph Dolan [1976] Director; Peter Dolan [1944] Director/Geologist; Zephaniah Oury King [1976] Managing Director

Real Ale (Wholesale) Limited
Incorporated: 21 December 2018
Registered Office: Flat 8, Old Lodge Place, Twickenham, Middlesex, TW1 1RQ
Parent: Real Ale Limited
Officers: Nicholas Joseph Dolan [1976] Director; Peter Dolan [1944] Director/Geologist; Zephaniah Oury King [1976] Managing Director

Real Ale Direct Limited
Incorporated: 26 February 2016
Net Worth: £46,607 *Total Assets:* £186,360
Registered Office: Unit 1 Station Yard, Station Road, Hadnall, Shrewsbury, Salop, SY4 3DD
Shareholders: Mathew Ian Davies; Julia Goodall
Officers: Mathew Ian Davies [1982] Director/Operations Manager; Julia Goodall [1980] Director/Administrative Manager

Real Ale Limited
Incorporated: 7 September 2004 *Employees:* 16
Net Worth: £561,035 *Total Assets:* £1,656,962
Registered Office: 8 Old Lodge Place, Twickenham, Middlesex, TW1 1RQ
Parent: Real Ale (Group) Limited
Officers: Zephaniah Oury King, Secretary; Nicholas Joseph Dolan [1976] Director/Retail Salesman; Peter Dolan [1944] Director/Geologist; Zephaniah Oury King [1976] Managing Director

Real Ales AT Limited
Incorporated: 13 October 2016
Net Worth Deficit: £29,001 *Total Assets:* £25,981
Registered Office: 63 High Street, Hurstpierpoint, W Sussex, BN6 9RE
Shareholder: Colin Ripley Bates
Officers: Colin Ripley Bates [1969] Director/Retail Sales

Real Grapes Ltd
Incorporated: 21 September 2015
Registered Office: 59-60 The Market Square, London, N9 0TZ
Major Shareholder: Simon Tskouaseli
Officers: Simon Tskouaseli [1984] Director [Greek]

Real Irish Whiskey Limited
Incorporated: 18 March 2013
Net Worth: £6 *Total Assets:* £6
Registered Office: Rok House, Kingswood Business Park, Holyhead Road, Albrighton, Staffs, WV7 3AU
Parent: Rok Stars PLC
Officers: Thomas Christopher FitzGenerald Doorley [1959] Director [Irish]

Real Wine Cellar Limited
Incorporated: 3 October 2013
Net Worth Deficit: £70,844
Registered Office: 85 London Road, Cheltenham, Glos, GL52 6HL
Major Shareholder: Filippo Migliuolo
Officers: Filippo Migliuolo [1992] Director [Italian]

Reality Bio Wine Ltd
Incorporated: 5 April 2018
Registered Office: 4-9 Hermitage Park Lea, Edinburgh, EH6 8DY
Major Shareholder: Gabriela Emilova Dimitrova
Officers: Gabriela Emilova Dimitrova [1992] Director/Manager [Bulgarian]

Realsa Wines Import & Export Ltd
Incorporated: 19 December 2014
Net Worth Deficit: £22,642 *Total Assets:* £58
Registered Office: No 1 Finns Farm, Smalls Hill Road, Norwood Hill, Horley, Surrey, RH6 0HR
Officers: Zack Kutty [1979] Director/Trading; Shinoj Vasudevan [1975] Director

Rebel Pi Limited
Incorporated: 21 August 2018
Registered Office: 1st Floor, 50 High Street, Cosham, Portsmouth, PO6 3AG
Major Shareholder: Jacquelyn Fast
Officers: Jacquelyn Fast [1983] Managing Director [Canadian]

The Rebel Wine Club Ltd
Incorporated: 27 July 2018
Registered Office: 24 Boswall Road, Edinburgh, EH5 3RN
Shareholders: Christine Jane Dobbin; William Jackson Todd
Officers: Christine Jane Dobbin [1983] Director; William Jackson Todd [1985] Director

Rebel Wine Ltd.
Incorporated: 25 July 2016
Net Worth Deficit: £19,848 *Total Assets:* £1,357
Registered Office: 71 Vernham Row, Vernham Dean, Andover, Hants, SP11 0LH
Major Shareholder: Rupert St Aubyn
Officers: Davina Katharine St Aubyn [1969] Director/Office Manager; Rupert St Aubyn [1963] Director

Recolte Wines Limited
Incorporated: 31 October 2013
Registered Office: 54 Hertford Street, Cambridge, CB4 3AQ
Major Shareholder: Jeremy John Thorman Hunt
Officers: John Willan, Secretary; Adrian John Lake [1954] Director

Red & White Wines Limited
Incorporated: 15 June 2005
Net Worth: £21,737 *Total Assets:* £66,854
Registered Office: Park House, 10 Park Street, Bristol, BS1 5HX
Officers: Liam James Steevenson [1975] Director/Wine Merchant

Red Bay Brewing Company Limited
Incorporated: 31 July 2018
Registered Office: 9 Bellisk Park, Cushendall, Ballymena, Co Antrim, BT44 0AF
Shareholders: Fergus Oliver Wheeler; Emmet Patrick Connon
Officers: Fergus Oliver Wheeler, Secretary; Emmet Patrick Connon [1982] Director/Electrical Engineer; Fergus Oliver Wheeler [1978] Director/Lawyer

Red Bonny Rum Limited
Incorporated: 9 October 2017
Registered Office: 155-157 Donegall Pass, Belfast, BT7 1DT
Parent: Kirker Greer (Holdings) Limited
Officers: Steven Clark Pattison [1979] Director; Richard Ryan [1977] Director

The Red Bottle Company Limited
Incorporated: 4 November 2013 *Employees:* 1
Net Worth: £7,806 *Total Assets:* £45,524
Registered Office: c/o F S Distribution Limited, Dormer Road, Thame, Oxon, OX9 3FS
Major Shareholder: David Alan Vernau
Officers: Tara Joanne Hollis, Secretary; David Alan Vernau [1963] Director

Red Door Gin Company Ltd
Incorporated: 6 April 2018
Registered Office: George House, Boroughbriggs Road, Elgin, Moray, IV30 1JY
Parent: Speymalt Whisky Distributors Limited
Officers: Norman Ross, Secretary; Ewen Cameron Mackintosh [1968] Director

Red Dragon Brewery Ltd.
Incorporated: 11 May 2017
Net Worth Deficit: £15,010 *Total Assets:* £52,740
Registered Office: Unit 24 Ard Business Park, New Inn, Pontypool, Gwent, NP4 0PN
Major Shareholder: Mark Hillman
Officers: Mark Hillman [1966] Director

Red Dragons Trading Limited
Incorporated: 16 July 2014
Registered Office: First Floor, 66 Shaftesbury Avenue, London, W1D 6LX
Major Shareholder: Kym Yune Lewis Ip
Officers: Kym Yune Lewis IP [1988] Director/Business Executive

Red Fox Wines Limited
Incorporated: 24 January 2007
Previous: Red Fox Landscapes Limited
Registered Office: 21 Bedford Square, London, WC1B 3HH
Shareholders: Julian Charles Elsden; Oliver Jack Elsden; Clive James Elsden
Officers: Clive James Elsden [1981] Managing Director; Julian Charles Elsden [1979] Director; Oliver Jack Elsden [1991] Director

Red Rose Drinks Limited
Incorporated: 4 April 2002 *Employees:* 6
Net Worth: £115 *Total Assets:* £107,830
Registered Office: Unit 18 Phoenix Close Industrial Estate, Green Lane, Heywood, Lancs, OL10 2JG
Major Shareholder: Derek Nuttall
Officers: Judith Nuttall, Secretary; Derek Nuttall [1952] Director/Manager

Red Squirrel Brewery Limited
Incorporated: 1 December 2010
Net Worth Deficit: £192,338 *Total Assets:* £574,906
Registered Office: Unit 18 Boxted Farm, Berkhamsted Road, Hemel Hempstead, Herts, HP1 2SG
Parent: Red Squirrel Group Limited
Officers: Gregory Francis Blesson [1966] Director; Jason Duncan Duncan-Anderson [1975] Director

Red Squirrel Wine Ltd.
Incorporated: 27 July 2012 *Employees:* 4
Net Worth: £117,984 *Total Assets:* £449,814
Registered Office: 3 Spice Court, Ivory Square, Plantation Wharf, London, SW11 3UE
Shareholder: Nicholas James Darlington
Officers: Gavin Leslie Brook Darlington [1949] Director/Retired; Nicholas James Darlington [1986] Director; Mark Douglas Holford [1950] Director; Charlotte Clementine Keenan [1981] Director/Businesswoman; George Alexander Bryson Kynoch [1946] Director/Chairman

Redevined Wines Limited
Incorporated: 16 November 2017
Registered Office: 176e Mitcham Lane, London, SW16 6NS
Shareholders: Patrick Bernard Bernie; Anthony John Cunliffe
Officers: Patrick Bernard Bernie [1984] Director/Accountant [Irish]; Dr Anthony John Cunliffe [1975] Director/Doctor

Redoor Limited
Incorporated: 21 January 2013
Net Worth: £1,000 *Total Assets:* £1,000
Registered Office: 26 Renwick Drive, Bromley, Kent, BR2 9GS
Major Shareholder: Xiaofei Qi
Officers: Wenbo Zhang, Secretary; Xiaofei Qi [1987] Director/Education Services [Chinese]; Jing Zhao [1981] Director/Education Services [Chinese]

Redvulette Ltd
Incorporated: 7 July 2017 *Employees:* 1
Net Worth Deficit: £7,642 *Total Assets:* £4,836
Registered Office: 4 Sten Close, Enfield, Middlesex, EN3 6UF
Major Shareholder: Beverley Arlene Dowridge
Officers: Beverley Arlene Dowridge [1961] Director

Refined Wine Club Ltd.
Incorporated: 29 September 2017
Registered Office: Block B, OCC Estate, 105 Eade Road, London, N4 1TJ
Officers: Morris Herzog [1978] Director

Reformed Spirits Company Limited
Incorporated: 19 October 2018
Registered Office: Unit 3.22, 535 Kings Road, London, SW10 0SZ
Major Shareholder: Carl Jakob Alistair Ehrenkrona
Officers: Carl Jakob Alistair Ehrenkrona [1975] Director [Swedish]

Refresh 24 Group Limited
Incorporated: 18 September 2018
Registered Office: 71-75 Shelton Street, London, WC2H 9JQ
Major Shareholder: Adam Gardner
Officers: Adam Gardner [1976] Managing Director

Regency Event Solutions Ltd
Incorporated: 14 February 2002
Net Worth: £50,984 *Total Assets:* £113,841
Registered Office: Grand Pier, Marine Parade, Weston Super Mare, Somerset, BS23 1AL
Shareholders: Axentis Panayiotou Demetriou; AGM Holdings Limited
Officers: Michelle Michael, Secretary; Axentis Panayiotou Demetriou [1979] Director; Kerry Michael [1959] Director

Regency Wines Limited
Incorporated: 22 April 2003 *Employees:* 13
Net Worth: £318,388 *Total Assets:* £619,567
Registered Office: 22 Apple Lane, Trade City, Sowton Industrial Estate, Exeter, Devon, EX2 5GL
Shareholder: Ian Marks
Officers: April Deliah Marks, Secretary/Wine Wholesale; April Deliah Marks [1967] Director/Wine Wholesale; Ian Marks [1970] Director/Wine Wholesale

Regent Wines Limited
Incorporated: 16 August 2006 *Employees:* 3
Net Worth: £14,072 *Total Assets:* £102,608
Registered Office: 157 Hope Street, Glasgow, G2 2UQ
Shareholders: Alastair Stewart Boogert; Jan Olof Johansson; Trimalgam Investments Limited
Officers: Alastair Stewart Boogert [1948] Director; Jan Olof Johansson [1953] Director/Restaurant Owner [Swedish]; James Anthony Walford [1946] Director

Reid Wines (1992) Limited
Incorporated: 10 February 1992 *Employees:* 4
Net Worth: £715,699 *Total Assets:* £1,177,055
Registered Office: Ground Floor, 11 Manvers Street, Bath, BA1 1JQ
Major Shareholder: David Martin Boobbyer
Officers: David Martin Boobbyer, Secretary; David Martin Boobbyer [1959] Director/Wine Merchant; William Howard Booty [1954] Director

Reids Gold Brewing Company Ltd
Incorporated: 31 January 2017 *Employees:* 1
Net Worth Deficit: £3,305 *Total Assets:* £5,305
Registered Office: 61 Provost Barclay Drive, Stonehaven, Aberdeenshire, AB39 2GE
Major Shareholder: Barry Reid
Officers: Barry Reid [1977] Director/Brewer

Rekhi Wholesale Ltd
Incorporated: 4 July 2017
Registered Office: 24 Barnehurst Avenue, Erith, Kent, DA8 3NF
Major Shareholder: Guneal Singh Rekhi
Officers: Guneal Singh Rekhi [1977] Director

Relais La Torre UK Ltd
Incorporated: 27 December 2018
Registered Office: 189 Applegarth House, Nelson Square, London, SE1 0PZ
Shareholders: Aisha Dad; Omar Mehmoud; Omar Ahmed Salah
Officers: Aisha Dad, Secretary; Omar Ahmed Salah [1995] Director [Italian]

Relaxandrinks Limited
Incorporated: 10 April 2017
Registered Office: P O Box 26965, Unit 12367 Baird Street, Glasgow, G1 9BW
Major Shareholder: Yiyang Tsai
Officers: Tsai Yiting, Secretary; Yiyang Tsai [1990] Director [Taiwanese]

Remfly Wines UK Limited
Incorporated: 5 December 2018
Registered Office: 133 Whitechapel High Street, London, E1 7QA
Major Shareholder: Ying Ming Lin
Officers: Yingming Lin [1969] Director

Remy Cointreau UK Distribution Limited
Incorporated: 4 July 2012 *Employees:* 57
Net Worth Deficit: £323,968 *Total Assets:* £15,852,757
Registered Office: Mazars LLP, The Pinnacle, 160 Midsummer Boulevard, Milton Keynes, Bucks, MK9 1FF
Parent: Remy Cointreau UK Limited
Officers: Madame Valerie Marie Anne Chapoulaud-Floquet [1962] Managing Director [French]; Spyridon Ghikas [1959] Director [Greek]; Peter John Sant [1960] Managing Director

Rendog Gin Ltd
Incorporated: 14 August 2018
Registered Office: 44 Meadow Walk, Tyldesley, Manchester, M29 7FA
Major Shareholder: Alison Reynolds
Officers: Alison Reynolds [1971] Director

Renwick MacDonald Bars Ltd
Incorporated: 26 September 2018
Registered Office: Holme Bank, Holme Road, Matlock Bath, Matlock, Derbys, DE4 3NU
Shareholders: Robbie MacDonald; Martin Renwick
Officers: Robbie MacDonald [1987] Director; Martin Renwick [1987] Director

Reservedwines Ltd
Incorporated: 19 December 2018
Registered Office: 9 Aylesbury Drive, Holland on Sea, Clacton on Sea, Essex, CO15 5QS
Shareholders: Kim Masters; Reese Barnard
Officers: Kim Masters [1966] Managing Director

The Responsible Trading Company Limited
Incorporated: 27 November 2007
Net Worth: £59,617 *Total Assets:* £115,867
Registered Office: Unit 5 Avon Gorge Industrial Estate, Portview Road, Avonmouth, Bristol, BS11 9LQ
Major Shareholder: William Henry Stockley
Officers: William Henry Stockley [1979] Director/Salesman

Rest Wine Ltd
Incorporated: 30 April 2018
Registered Office: Saxon House, Fornham All Saints, Bury St Edmunds, Suffolk, IP28 6JY
Shareholders: Stephen Lawrence Parker Lott; Rebecca Lott
Officers: Rebecca Lott, Secretary; Stephen Lawrence Parker Lott [1976] Director

Retaliate Limited
Incorporated: 13 October 2015 *Employees:* 1
Net Worth: £18,319 *Total Assets:* £35,207
Registered Office: 2nd Floor, 130 Shaftesbury Avenue, London, W1D 5EU
Major Shareholder: Georgios Chalaris
Officers: Georgios Chalaris [1987] Director [Greek]

Retro Shotz Limited
Incorporated: 29 June 2017
Registered Office: 28 Alexandra Terrace, Exmouth, Devon, EX8 1BD
Major Shareholder: Mark Edward Hewings
Officers: Mark Edward Hewings [1962] Director

Reva Drinks Ltd
Incorporated: 22 May 2018
Registered Office: Flat 18, Long Island House, Warple Way, London, W3 0RG
Shareholders: Jack Julius Williams; Andrew John Craig; Oliver Morley James Spencer
Officers: Andrew John Craig [1986] Director; Oliver Morley James Spencer [1986] Director; Jack Julius Williams [1987] Director

Revilo Group Limited
Incorporated: 5 October 2018
Registered Office: Unit 12 Borers Yard, Borers Arms Road, Copthorne, Crawley, W Sussex, RH10 3LH
Major Shareholder: Paul Andrew Oliver
Officers: Paul Andrew Oliver [1971] Managing Director

Rexon Group Festivals Limited
Incorporated: 9 March 2018
Registered Office: Kemp House, 160 City Road, London, EC1V 2NX
Major Shareholder: Alan Colton
Officers: Alan Colton, Secretary; Alan Colton [1945] Director

Raymond Reynolds Limited
Incorporated: 24 May 1990 *Employees:* 4
Net Worth: £61,944 *Total Assets:* £347,211
Registered Office: Unit 5 Furness Vale Industrial Estate, Station Road, Furness Vale, High Peak, Derbys, SK23 7SW
Officers: Raymond Martin Hunter Reynolds, Secretary; Martin John Hunter Reynolds [1929] Director/Solicitor (Retired); Raymond Martin Hunter Reynolds [1959] Director/Winemaker

RHM Retail Ltd
Incorporated: 30 January 2017
Net Worth Deficit: £20,430 *Total Assets:* £145,322
Registered Office: 10 Berwick View, Moira, Co Down, BT67 0SX
Shareholders: Lorna Maguire; Phillip Maguire
Officers: Lorna Maguire [1984] Director; Phillip Maguire [1980] Director/Account Manager

Rhuby Limited
Incorporated: 22 August 2011
Net Worth Deficit: £105,017
Registered Office: 30 Chertsey Road, Woking, Surrey, GU21 5AJ
Major Shareholder: Ylva Binder
Officers: Ylva Binder [1971] Director [Swedish]

Rhymney Brewery Western Ltd.
Incorporated: 16 January 2007 *Employees:* 1
Net Worth Deficit: £57,031 *Total Assets:* £5,216
Registered Office: Unit 3 Johnston Business Park, Johnston, Haverfordwest, Pembrokeshire, SA62 3PL
Shareholders: Stewart Longhurst; Janice Longhurst
Officers: Janice Longhurst, Secretary; Janice Longhurst [1958] Director/Local Government Officer; Stewart Longhurst [1953] Director

Ribox Quality Goods Ltd
Incorporated: 19 October 2017
Registered Office: 49 Winstanley Road, Saffron Walden, Essex, CB11 3EQ
Shareholder: Joan Marc Riera-Duocastella
Officers: Joan Marc Riera-Duocastella [1981] Director/Systems Administration [Spanish]

Rich & Bad Ltd
Incorporated: 26 April 2018
Registered Office: 136a Brooke Road, London, N16 7RS
Major Shareholder: Joshua Samuels
Officers: Joshua Samuels [1986] Director and Company Secretary

Maurice Richard Ltd
Incorporated: 5 November 2018
Registered Office: First Floor, 85 Great Portland Street, London, W1W 7LT
Shareholders: Alain Maurice Illi; Moreno Gasser; Sandro Richard Gianini
Officers: Moreno Gasser [1987] Director [Swiss]; Sandro Richard Gianini [1987] Director [Swiss]; Alain Maurice Illi [1986] Director [Swiss]

Chalie Richards & Company Limited
Incorporated: 1 May 1991 *Employees:* 2
Net Worth Deficit: £228,000 *Total Assets:* £1,051,000
Registered Office: The Sovereign Distillery, Huyton Business Park, Wilson Road, Huyton, Knowsley, Merseyside, L36 6AD
Parent: Halewood Wines and Spirits PLC
Officers: Stewart Andrew Hainsworth [1969] Director/Chief Executive; Alan William Robinson [1965] Director/Accountant

Richdells Wine Merchants Holdings Limited
Incorporated: 25 January 2018
Registered Office: 2 Warwick Place, Worthing, W Sussex, BN11 3EU
Shareholders: Keith Robert Richbell; David William Harold Swindells
Officers: Keith Robert Richbell [1957] Director; David William Harold Swindells [1968] Director; Harry Robert John Swindells [1992] Director; Jack David Swindells [1995] Director

Richmond Distillers (Zurich) Limited
Incorporated: 25 January 1949
Net Worth: £39,655 *Total Assets:* £45,195
Registered Office: 4th Floor, Imperial House, 8 Kean Street, London, WC2B 4AS
Officers: Nigel James Armstrong, Secretary; Nigel James Armstrong [1952] Director/Accountant; Berthold Pluznik [1945] Director/Merchant [Swiss]

Richmond Wine Agencies Limited
Incorporated: 8 February 2002
Registered Office: Richmond House, Unit 1 The Links, Popham Close, Hanworth, Middlesex, TW13 6JE
Parent: Ellis of Richmond Ltd
Officers: William Derek Ellis, Secretary; Henry James Ellis [1960] Director/Wine Merchant

Richway Cash and Carry Ltd
Incorporated: 21 December 2016
Net Worth Deficit: £23,082 *Total Assets:* £51,545
Registered Office: 265 Haydons Road, London, SW19 8TY
Shareholders: Mohanaraj Paramagurusamy; N Consulting Limited
Officers: Mohanaraj Paramagurusamy [1974] Director; Kirubanandam Swayamprakasam [1977] Director

Rico Rico Ltd
Incorporated: 1 December 2017
Registered Office: 80 Waverley Road, Enfield, Middlesex, EN2 7AQ
Shareholders: Mark Stuart Dobson; Sara Hoare Aranda
Officers: Mark Stuart Dobson [1983] Director/Manager; Sara Hoare Aranda [1984] Director/Tour Operator [Spanish]

Ricordo Ltd
Incorporated: 3 July 2017
Registered Office: Francis House, 2 Park Road, High Barnet, Barnet, Herts, EN5 5RN
Officers: Francesca Pilla [1951] Director; Giovanni Pilla [1948] Director [Italian]

William Riddell & Sons Limited
Incorporated: 16 January 2007
Net Worth Deficit: £292,991 *Total Assets:* £1,132,326
Registered Office: 10 Lynedoch Crescent, Glasgow, G3 6EQ
Major Shareholder: Guido Marini
Officers: Rudolf Jozef Koopmans [1956] Director [Belgian]

The Riding Wine Company Ltd
Incorporated: 15 March 2018
Registered Office: 16 Parklands, 22 Mount Park Road, London, W5 2RS
Shareholders: Vikram Singh Mertia; Jesal Thakker
Officers: Vikram Singh Mertia [1976] Managing Director; Jesal Thakker [1978] Managing Director

Thomas Ridley and Son, Limited
Incorporated: 17 October 1917 *Employees:* 210
Net Worth: £9,054,543 *Total Assets:* £19,910,284
Registered Office: Rougham Industrial Estate, Rougham, Bury St Edmunds, Suffolk, IP30 9ND
Parent: Ridley Godfrey (Holdings) Limited
Officers: Hugh Edward Godfrey, Secretary; Hugh Edward Godfrey [1944] Director/Chartered Accountant; Jennifer Patricia Godfrey [1946] Director; Justin Alexander Godfrey [1975] Director/Chartered Accountant

Riedango Limited
Incorporated: 9 June 2014
Net Worth Deficit: £1,293 *Total Assets:* £602
Registered Office: Flat 7, Grove Court, 36 Grove Road, Bournemouth, BH1 3DY
Parent: Bernd Riedemann
Officers: Bernd Riedemann [1943] Director/Consultant [German]

Rimpex-UK Limited
Incorporated: 29 January 2019
Registered Office: Rookery Nook, Church Street, Reepham, Norfolk, NR10 4JW
Shareholder: Alan Arthur Buckwell
Officers: Alan Arthur Buckwell [1950] Director/Proprietor

Rip Mountain Brewery Ltd.
Incorporated: 14 January 2014
Net Worth: £58,129 *Total Assets:* £58,528
Registered Office: 43 Owston Road, Carcroft, Doncaster, S Yorks, DN6 8DA
Shareholders: Black Brick BV; Voorhuis Beheer BV
Officers: Paul Christiaan Jozef Rijk [1965] Director/Entrepreneur [Dutch]

Ripped Earth Wines Limited
Incorporated: 13 October 2016
Registered Office: Sigma House, Oak View Close, Torquay, Devon, TQ2 7FF
Shareholders: Mark Andrew Crump; Mark Robert Dawkins
Officers: Mark Andrew Crump [1970] Director; Mark Robert Dawkins [1970] Director

UK Wholesalers of Beers, Wines and Spirits — dellam

Rippingale Promotions Limited
Incorporated: 18 December 2000 Employees: 7
Net Worth: £78,008 Total Assets: £694,587
Registered Office: Unit 6 Orchard Business Centre, Bonehurst Road, Redhill, Surrey, RH1 5EL
Shareholders: Lesley Ann Teasdale; Ian Kenneth Halliday
Officers: Ian Halliday, Secretary; Ian Kenneth Halliday [1960] Director; Lesley Ann Teasdale [1966] Director

Rive Gauche Wines (UK) Limited
Incorporated: 17 May 2011
Net Worth Deficit: £12,145 Total Assets: £2,810
Registered Office: 3 Montpelier Avenue, Bexley, Kent, DA5 3AP
Major Shareholder: Benedict Michael Kennedy
Officers: Benedict Michael Kennedy [1969] Director/Wine Merchant

River Drinks Ltd
Incorporated: 2 October 2018
Registered Office: 25 Bramble Rise, Cobham, Surrey, KT11 2HP
Shareholders: Max Christian Friedrich Gruenefeld; Fritz Gruenefeld
Officers: Fritz Gruenefeld [1959] Director [German]; Max Christian Friedrich Gruenefeld [1991] Director/Marketing Consultant [German]

River Widow Brewery Ltd
Incorporated: 25 January 2017
Registered Office: 15 Huxley Road, London, E10 5QT
Officers: Andrew Adwick [1984] Director/Accountant; Edmund Bussey [1983] Director/Professional Musician; Marcus Hibbert [1984] Director/Teacher

Rivers Rum (UK) Limited
Incorporated: 6 July 1992
Registered Office: 27 Mortimer Street, London, W1T 3BL
Major Shareholder: Raphael Nathaniel Edgar
Officers: Elizabeth Anne Edgar, Secretary; Raphael Nathaniel Edgar [1939] Director/Fire Prevention & Security Consultant [British/Grenadian]

RJR Fort Ltd
Incorporated: 18 April 2018
Registered Office: 8 Hilary Road, London, W12 0QB
Shareholders: Romana Vitas; Joze Anzic; Rajko Kumse
Officers: Joze Anzic, Secretary; Romana Vitas [1970] Director [Slovenian]

RK Vodka Limited
Incorporated: 31 July 2015 Employees: 1
Net Worth Deficit: £3,018 Total Assets: £7,895
Registered Office: Station House, Banbury Road, Charwelton, Daventry, Northants, NN11 3YY
Major Shareholder: Kiron Thomas Phillips
Officers: Kiron Thomas Phillips [1994] Director; Zanesh Joseph Phillips [1997] Director

Robb Brothers Wine Merchants Ltd
Incorporated: 2 April 2014
Net Worth: £855,021 Total Assets: £3,913,172
Registered Office: 20 + 20a Portadown Road, Lurgan, Craigavon, Co Armagh, BT66 8RE
Shareholder: Philip Norman James Robb
Officers: Norma Patricia Rompante, Secretary; Charles John Edward Robb [1960] Director/Sales Manager; Philip Norman James Robb [1958] Director/Clerical Manager; Norma Patricia Rompante [1961] Director/Accountants Manager

Robb Trading Ltd
Incorporated: 14 August 2015
Net Worth Deficit: £725 Total Assets: £3,309
Registered Office: 33b Church Street, Antrim, BT41 4BE
Major Shareholder: Denver Robb
Officers: Denver Robb [1977] Managing Director

Robel Import Trading Ltd
Incorporated: 12 May 2018
Registered Office: Unit 38 Eurolink Business Centre, 49 Effra Road, London, SW2 1BZ
Major Shareholder: Pawlos Habtezghi
Officers: Pawlos Habtezghi [1978] Director

Roberson Wine Merchant Limited
Incorporated: 17 October 1977
Registered Office: 21-27 Seagrave Road, London, SW6 1RP
Major Shareholder: Cliff John Roberson
Officers: Clifford John Roberson [1940] Managing Director

Quellyn Roberts (Wine Merchants) Limited
Incorporated: 26 March 1982
Registered Office: Watergate Chambers, 15a Watergate Row, Chester, CH1 2LE
Parent: Quellyn Roberts & Co Ltd
Officers: Paul Quellyn Roberts, Secretary; Jon Ashwoode Mathias [1945] Director/Chartered Accountant; Paul Quellyn Roberts [1945] Director/Wine Merchant

Paul Roberts Wines Limited
Incorporated: 6 December 2002 Employees: 4
Net Worth: £640,193 Total Assets: £877,245
Registered Office: 4 Grove Avenue, Moseley, Birmingham, B13 9RU
Major Shareholder: Paul Norman Roberts
Officers: Benita Helen Roberts, Secretary; Paul Norman Roberts [1961] Director/Wine Merchant

T.M. Robertson & Son Limited
Incorporated: 25 July 1947
Registered Office: Unit 12, 230-232 Sir Harry Lauder Road, Portobello, Edinburgh, EH15 2QA
Parent: Berkmann Wine Cellars Ltd
Officers: Rupert Anthony Berkmann [1979] Director

Roblex Ltd
Incorporated: 4 February 2009
Net Worth: £77,841 Total Assets: £137,954
Registered Office: 45 Main Street, Dunlop, Ayrshire, KA3 4AF
Shareholders: Craig Robertson; Fiona Robertson
Officers: Craig Robertson [1978] Managing Director; Fiona Robertson [1986] Director/Postmaster

The Rock and Roll Spirit Company Limited
Incorporated: 20 June 2018
Registered Office: Brook Farm, Chorley, Lichfield, Staffs, WS13 8DQ
Officers: Christopher Charles Abbot [1967] Director; Timothy Stuart Abbot [1958] Director

Rock Beverages Limited
Incorporated: 23 April 2018
Registered Office: 14 Argyle Street, Darwen, Lancs, BB3 1EX
Shareholders: John Martin Christopher; Jon-Michael Joseph Christopher
Officers: John Martin Christopher [1955] Director/Self Employed

Rockin Robin Brewery Ltd
Incorporated: 18 November 2013
Net Worth: £11,979 *Total Assets:* £83,159
Registered Office: 6 Pickering Street, Maidstone, Kent, ME15 9RS
Shareholders: Robin Christopher Smallbone; Stuart John Osgood
Officers: Robin Christopher Smallbone [1966] Director/Quality Engineer

Rockstar Spirits Limited
Incorporated: 8 June 2017
Registered Office: 53 Lumber Lane, Worsley, Salford, M28 2GJ
Officers: Thomas Hurst [1975] Director/Business Professional; Daren Paul Newman [1976] Director/Designer

Rodica Wine and Spirits Limited
Incorporated: 30 November 2017
Registered Office: 27 Old Gloucester Street, London, WC1N 3AX
Major Shareholder: Ales Rodica
Officers: Ales Rodica [1994] Director/Wine Trade [Slovenian]

Rok Drinks Limited
Incorporated: 5 January 2012
Net Worth: £118,278 *Total Assets:* £827,765
Registered Office: Rok House, Kingswood Business Park, Holyhead Road, Albrighton, Staffs, WV7 3AU
Parent: Rok Stars PLC
Officers: David Graham Higgins [1967] Director; Mark Graham Jones [1967] Director; Bruce William Renny [1965] Director

Roland Wines Ltd
Incorporated: 4 January 2017
Net Worth Deficit: £9,511 *Total Assets:* £60,574
Registered Office: 178 New Cross Road, London, SE14 5AA
Major Shareholder: Roland Szimeiszter
Officers: Roland Szimeiszter [1989] Director [Hungarian]

Robert Rolls & Co. Limited
Incorporated: 12 January 1982 *Employees:* 4
Net Worth: £241,570 *Total Assets:* £955,388
Registered Office: 55 St John Street, London, EC1M 4AN
Major Shareholder: Robert Jonathan Rolls
Officers: Robert Jonathan Rolls [1952] Director/Wine Merchant

Rome de Bellegarde Wines Ltd
Incorporated: 4 September 2018
Registered Office: 32 Woodstock Grove, Shepherds Bush, London, W12 8LE
Major Shareholder: David Smeralda
Officers: David Smeralda [1986] Director [French]

Rondel Trading Ltd
Incorporated: 10 June 2016 *Employees:* 2
Net Worth: £11,218 *Total Assets:* £111,415
Registered Office: c/o Kaman, 50 Salisbury Road, Hounslow, Middlesex, TW4 6JQ
Major Shareholder: Veronica Nastase
Officers: Veronica Nastase [1982] Director [Romanian]; Davinder Talwar [1967] Director

Roohop Ltd
Incorporated: 18 May 2015
Net Worth Deficit: £338,438 *Total Assets:* £31,416
Registered Office: Unit A3, Oyo Business Units, Crabtree Manorway North, Belvedere, Kent, DA17 6AX
Major Shareholder: Jaspreet Anand
Officers: Jaspreet Anand [1974] Director

Rosemille Ltd
Incorporated: 3 September 2018
Registered Office: Heaton Road, Lyncroft Gardens, Hounslow, Middlesex, TW3 2QT
Major Shareholder: Florin Cristian Nita
Officers: Florin Cristian Nita [1975] Director/Driver [Romanian]

Rosemount Pub Co. Limited
Incorporated: 22 September 1999 *Employees:* 6
Net Worth: £82,267 *Total Assets:* £453,595
Registered Office: 5 Fitzroy Place, Glasgow, G3 7RH
Officers: Harvey Samuel Fields, Secretary; Craig Bruce [1962] Director; Harvey Samuel Fields [1954] Director; Joshua Fields [1991] Director

Rosie & Gin Limited
Incorporated: 6 November 2018
Registered Office: 53 King Street, Manchester, M2 4LQ
Shareholders: Wayne Stephen Davies; Rosie Anna Williams
Officers: Wayne Stephen Davies [1987] Director; Rosie Anna Williams [1991] Director

Ross Earl Wine Co., Ltd.
Incorporated: 21 August 2018
Registered Office: Chase Business Centre, 39-41 Chase Side, London, N14 5BP
Shareholders: Hongxiao Wang; Xuefeng Wang; Dianbo Zhao
Officers: Hongxiao Wang [1973] Director [Chinese]

Rossendale Brew Co Ltd
Incorporated: 27 February 2019
Registered Office: Suite G1 (E), Adelphi Mill, Grimshaw Lane, Bollington, Cheshire, SK10 5JB
Major Shareholder: Luke John Williams
Officers: John Richard Williams [1947] Director/Bus Driver

Roust UK Ltd
Incorporated: 23 April 2013
Registered Office: Thomas House, 84 Eccleston Square, London, SW1V 1PX
Parent: Roust Trading Limited
Officers: Elina Fruin [1967] Director

Route des Vins Limited
Incorporated: 30 September 2004
Net Worth: £1,314 *Total Assets:* £1,314
Registered Office: 4th Floor, Park Gate, 161-163 Preston Road, Brighton, BN1 6AF
Major Shareholder: Andrew Reginald Wiseman
Officers: Andrew Reginald Wiseman, Secretary; Andrew Reginald Wiseman [1966] Director/Wine Merchant

Michel Roux Limited
Incorporated: 22 June 1984 *Employees:* 3
Net Worth: £474,315 *Total Assets:* £941,924
Registered Office: No 1 Bettoney Vere, Brayon Thames, Berks, SL6 2BA
Parent: Roux Waterside Inn Limited
Officers: Derek Charles Brown [1944] Director/Consultant; Claude Grant [1957] Director [French]; Alain Albert Roux [1968] Director/Chef

Rovial Trans Ltd
Incorporated: 2 July 2018
Registered Office: 40 Eton Grove, London, NW9 9LH
Major Shareholder: Dragos Vitega
Officers: Dragos Vitega [1974] Director/Van Driver [Romanian]

Row & Company Limited
Incorporated: 13 February 1934
Net Worth: £14,988,040 Total Assets: £16,136,183
Registered Office: 100 Queen Street, Glasgow, G1 3DN
Shareholder: Edrington Distillers Limited
Officers: Gemma May Robson, Secretary; Yves Audo [1962] Director [French]; Jeremy McDowell Chaplin [1971] Finance Director; Massimo Antonio Fabris [1970] Commercial Director [Italian]; Frederic Gourgeon [1970] Director [French]

Royal Tokaji Wines of Hungary Limited
Incorporated: 2 September 2009
Registered Office: Pelham Farm Office, Newton Valence, Alton, Hants, GU34 3NQ
Major Shareholder: Damon Patrick de Laszlo
Officers: Howard Stanley Mighell, Secretary; Damon Patrick de Laszlo [1942] Director

Roydon Flavours Ltd
Incorporated: 25 February 2019
Registered Office: 1 Roydon Mews, 17 High Street, Roydon, Essex, CM19 5EA
Major Shareholder: Laura Bridge
Officers: Laura Bridge [1964] Director

RR Whisky Ltd
Incorporated: 12 July 2018
Registered Office: Collessie Mill House, Collessie, Cupar, Fife, KY15 7RQ
Shareholders: Laura Kirstin Anderson; Richard William Farrar
Officers: Laura Kirstin Anderson [1972] Director

RRK Supplies Limited
Incorporated: 28 September 2017
Registered Office: 34 Hardy Avenue, Dartford, Kent, DA1 2FE
Major Shareholder: Syeda Monika Mustafa
Officers: Syeda Monika Mustafa [1991] Director [Bangladeshi]

RS Wholesale Limited
Incorporated: 27 July 2017
Registered Office: 1 Agincourt Villas, Uxbridge Road, Hillingdon, Middlesex, UB10 0NX
Major Shareholder: Ravneet Singh
Officers: Ravneet Singh [1984] Director

RSD Whisky International Ltd
Incorporated: 10 October 2017
Registered Office: 8 Bruntsfield Terrace, Edinburgh, EH10 4EX
Major Shareholder: Iain Clunes Shirlaw
Officers: Iain Clunes Shirlaw [1954] Director/Advisor

Ruby & Claret Limited
Incorporated: 4 September 2018
Registered Office: 11 High Street, Earls Barton, Northampton, NN6 0JG
Officers: Peter Karl Meister, Secretary; Clare Deer [1982] Director; Mark Deer [1980] Director

Rude Mechanicals Limited
Incorporated: 10 May 2018
Registered Office: Boundary House, Cheadle Point, Cheadle, Cheshire, SK8 2GG
Shareholders: Michael Joseph Moriarty; Dennis Whiteley
Officers: Michael Joseph Moriarty [1965] Director and Company Secretary; Dennis Whiteley [1961] Director; Matthew Whiteley [1989] Director; Thomas Whiteley [1987] Director

Ruffnek Beer Limited
Incorporated: 28 February 2019
Registered Office: 41 Great Portland Street, London, W1W 7LA
Shareholders: Paul Ferguson; James McDermott; James Vincent Neville-O'Brien
Officers: Paul Ferguson [1981] Director; James McDermott [1977] Director; James Vincent Neville- O'Brien [1942] Director [Irish]

The Rum Club Ltd
Incorporated: 1 September 2015
Net Worth Deficit: £17,948 Total Assets: £8,515
Registered Office: 25 Malvern Road, Southsea, Hants, PO5 2LZ
Shareholders: Giles Thomas Collighan; Vincent Robert Amos Noyce
Officers: Giles Thomas Collighan [1968] Director/Management Consultant; Vincent Robert Amos Noyce [1968] Director/Port Operations Manager; Richard Alexander Oatley [1974] Director/Sales and Marketing

Rum Fellows Limited
Incorporated: 31 January 2018
Registered Office: Cissbury, Nepcote Lane, Findon, Worthing, W Sussex, BN14 0SR
Shareholders: Jack William Spencer; Cissbury Enterprises Limited
Officers: Jack William Spencer [1988] Director; Hugh Geoffrey Robert Wyatt [1961] Director

Rum Matters Limited
Incorporated: 9 August 2016
Net Worth: £100 Total Assets: £100
Registered Office: Sackville Place, Magdalen Street, Norwich, NR3 1JU
Major Shareholder: Jeremy David Viner Element
Officers: Jeremy David Viner Element [1965] Director/Businessman

Rum Runna Ltd
Incorporated: 16 August 2017
Registered Office: 10 Court Farm Road, London, SE9 4JH
Officers: Olivia Ama Ansah [1995] Director; Yasmin Bluette Ansah [1995] Director; Kieron Andre-Evans Campbell [1995] Director

The Rum Shop Limited
Incorporated: 13 October 2005
Net Worth: £1,045 Total Assets: £3,255
Registered Office: Stirling House, 107 Stirling Road, London, N22 5BN
Major Shareholder: Yogendranath Bacha
Officers: Hishan Jackaria [1977] Director/Accountant

Rumbaclaat Ltd
Incorporated: 25 September 2018
Registered Office: Flat 4, 57 Star Lane, Orpington, Kent, BR5 3LJ
Major Shareholder: Lee Martell Smith
Officers: Lee Martell Smith, Secretary; Lee Martell Smith [1987] Director

Rurkee Trading Company Limited
Incorporated: 21 June 2005
Net Worth: £19,603 Total Assets: £44,236
Registered Office: 6 Roding Lane South, Ilford, Essex, IG4 5NX
Major Shareholder: Satwinder Singh
Officers: Satwinder Singh [1958] Director/Shop Assistant [Indian]

Russbrit Ltd
Incorporated: 11 January 2017
Registered Office: 28 Jubilee Road, Mytchett, Camberley, Surrey, GU16 6BE
Shareholders: David Bowcock; Egor Shestakov
Officers: David Bowcock [1986] Director; Egor Shestakov [1985] Director [Russian]

Peter J Russell & Company Ltd.
Incorporated: 16 July 2003
Registered Office: Russell House, Dunnet Way, Broxburn, W Lothian, EH52 5BU
Parent: Ian MacLeod Distillers Limited
Officers: Michael James Younger, Secretary; Leonard Stuart Russell [1961] Marketing Director; Lucinda Russell [1966] Director/Race Horse Trainer

Philip Russell Limited
Incorporated: 11 July 1968 *Employees:* 245
Net Worth: £17,039,422 *Total Assets:* £26,927,764
Registered Office: Alanbrooke Road, Castlereagh Industrial Estate, Belfast, BT6 9PR
Parent: Golf Holdings Limited
Officers: William Stewart Wilson, Secretary; Robert James Davis [1952] Director; James Patrick Hunt [1976] Director [Irish]; James Oliver Hunt [1946] Director; Patrick Michael Paul Hunt [1973] Director; Patrick Mark Paul Hunt [1948] Director

Russells and Wrangham Limited
Incorporated: 14 October 2018
Registered Office: 5 Navigation Wharf, off Yorkersgate, Malton, N Yorks, YO17 7AA
Major Shareholder: Howard Kinder
Officers: Howard Kinder [1961] Director/Racing Groom

Russetglow Limited
Incorporated: 8 April 1987 *Employees:* 1
Net Worth: £218,358 *Total Assets:* £301,001
Registered Office: William Street, Rastrick, Brighouse, W Yorks, HD6 1HR
Major Shareholder: Anthony Vincent Mitchell
Officers: Anthony Mitchell, Secretary; Anthony Vincent Mitchell [1961] Director

Russian Doll Vodka Limited
Incorporated: 12 November 2018
Registered Office: Flat 1, Carlow House, Miller Street, London, NW1 7DN
Major Shareholder: Jordan Ashley Bookman
Officers: Jordan Ashley Bookman [1979] Director

Russian Investment II Limited
Incorporated: 8 November 2018
Registered Office: 71-75 Shelton Street, Covent Garden, London, WC2H 9JQ
Shareholders: Jiri Pokorny; Kostadin Vasilev Bilev
Officers: Jiri Pokorny, Secretary; Kostadin Vasilev Bilev [1983] Director [Bulgarian]; Jiri Pokorny [1969] Director/Manager [Czech]

The Rustic Tap Limited
Incorporated: 5 April 2018
Registered Office: Kemp House, 160 City Road, London, EC1V 2NX
Officers: Lee Valentino, Secretary; Lee Valentino [1973] Director

Rutherford, Shirlaw and Denholm Limited
Incorporated: 12 January 2016
Previous: J & G Stuart Ltd
Net Worth: £39,962 *Total Assets:* £41,012
Registered Office: 8 Bruntsfield Terrace, Edinburgh, EH10 4EX
Major Shareholder: Robert Campbell Shirlaw
Officers: Olga Shirlaw, Secretary; Robert Campbell Shirlaw [1957] Director/Business Manager

Rutherglen Scotch Whisky Co. Ltd.
Incorporated: 26 August 1996
Net Worth: £21,889 *Total Assets:* £41,912
Registered Office: 7-11 Baronald Street, Rutherglen, Glasgow, G73 1AF
Major Shareholder: Eric Carlisle
Officers: Eric Carlisle, Secretary/Accountant; Eric Carlisle [1935] Director

RWM Holdings Limited
Incorporated: 25 March 2002 *Employees:* 29
Net Worth: £7,287,044 *Total Assets:* £8,782,118
Registered Office: 21-27 Seagrave Road, London, SW6 1RP
Major Shareholder: Clifford John Roberson
Officers: Clifford John Roberson [1940] Director/Chairman; Talya Roberson [1968] Managing Director

Ryder Partners Limited
Incorporated: 25 January 2019
Registered Office: 28 Pellipar Close, London, N13 4AG
Shareholders: Maksim Vassiljev; Kanwar Gurmohan Singh
Officers: Kanwar Gurmohan Singh [1978] Director/Operations Manager; Maksim Vassiljev [1983] Director [Estonian]

S & B Impex Ltd
Incorporated: 11 July 2018
Registered Office: 3 Station Place, Finsbury Park, London, N4 2DH
Major Shareholder: Tamar Otarashvili
Officers: Tamar Otarashvili [1985] Director [Georgian]

S & F Drinks Limited
Incorporated: 21 October 2003 *Employees:* 3
Net Worth: £16,333 *Total Assets:* £453,804
Registered Office: Kings Building, Hill Street, Lydney, Glos, GL15 5HE
Shareholders: Fay Alison Martin; Stewart Glanmore Martin
Officers: Fay Alison Martin, Secretary; Brad Stewart Martin [1988] Director/Drinks Wholesaler; Fay Alison Martin [1953] Director/Drinks Wholesaler; Stewart Glanmore Martin [1952] Director/Drinks Wholesaler

S & N Products Ltd
Incorporated: 12 June 2012 *Employees:* 4
Net Worth: £80,772 *Total Assets:* £232,587
Registered Office: 210 Rockingham Road, Kettering, Northants, NN16 9AH
Major Shareholder: Mukesh Joshi
Officers: Mukesh Joshi [1966] Director

S & T Wines Limited
Incorporated: 24 July 2018
Registered Office: 30 Westgate, Otley, W Yorks, LS21 3AS
Major Shareholder: Tony James Garwood
Officers: Kay Lorene Whiteley Jackson, Secretary; Tony James Garwood [1975] Director; Sharful Islam [1975] Director

S and S Wines Limited
Incorporated: 20 February 2004 Employees: 7
Net Worth: £332,097 Total Assets: £574,373
Registered Office: 50 Dysart Way, Leicester, LE1 2JY
Major Shareholder: Roger Paul Haddrell
Officers: Roger Paul Haddrell, Secretary; Roger Paul Haddrell [1973] Director

S.A.R.D.V.M Ltd
Incorporated: 3 September 2018
Registered Office: 11 Church Road, Great Bookham, Leatherhead, Surrey, KT23 3PB
Officers: Ansuya Devi Rathoar [1975] Director/Businesswoman [Mauritian]

S.X Prosecco Party Limited
Incorporated: 18 May 2018
Registered Office: 1 Ailward Road, Aylesbury, Bucks, HP19 9TX
Shareholders: Sadije Peposhi; Xhemile Peposhi
Officers: Sadije Peposhi [2000] Director/Student; Xhemile Peposhi [1975] Director/Housewife

Saam Wine Company Limited
Incorporated: 23 April 2007
Net Worth: £1,157 Total Assets: £2,340
Registered Office: 307 Perry Street, Billericay, Essex, CM12 0RB
Parent: Perdeberg Wines (Pty) Ltd
Officers: Christoffel Jacobus Briers Louw [1957] Director/Farmer [South African]; Dr Colin David Phillips Bryant [1958] Director/Consultant [South African]

Sacred Spirits Holdings Ltd
Incorporated: 14 September 2017
Registered Office: 5 Talbot Road, London, N6 4QS
Shareholders: Hilary Susan Jones; Ian Nicholas Hart
Officers: Ian Hart, Secretary; Ian Nicholas Hart [1965] Director; Hilary Susan Jones [1962] Director

Saddleworth Real Ale Ltd
Incorporated: 3 December 2013
Net Worth: £3 Total Assets: £2,825
Registered Office: 8 Sam Road, Diggle, Saddleworth, Oldham, Lancs, OL3 5PU
Major Shareholder: Catherine Elizabeth O'Neill
Officers: Catherine Elizabeth O'Neill [1974] Director

Safeway Distribution Limited
Incorporated: 4 August 2014
Net Worth: £40,240 Total Assets: £54,693
Registered Office: 74 Church Road, London, SE19 2EZ
Officers: Hotchand Sawlani [1953] Director/Self Employed; Hotchard Sawlani [1953] Director/Distributor [Indian]

Sageitude Ltd
Incorporated: 17 October 2018
Registered Office: Flat 12, Quayside Court, Abbotshade Road, London, SE16 5RG
Major Shareholder: Nnaemeka Francis Onwuka
Officers: Nnaemeka Francis Onwuka [1978] Director

Sagitha Ltd
Incorporated: 13 March 2017
Registered Office: 81 Wellington Road, London, E6 2RQ
Major Shareholder: Kayilapillai Elangcheliyan
Officers: Kayilapillai Elangcheliyan [1975] Director [Sri Lankan]

Sagittarius Royaume-Uni Limited
Incorporated: 21 January 2015
Net Worth Deficit: £214,004 Total Assets: £349,547
Registered Office: 15-19 Great Titchfield Street, London, W1W 8AZ
Major Shareholder: Michael Guy Hilliard Heald
Officers: Andrew Michael Hilliard Heald [1987] Managing Director; Michael Guy Hilliard Heald [1950] Director

Sagittarius World Limited
Incorporated: 10 June 2015
Net Worth Deficit: £6,567 Total Assets: £38,132
Registered Office: First Floor, 15 Young Street, London, W8 5EH
Officers: Rodolphe Frerejean Taittinger [1986] Director [French]; Andrew Michael Hilliard Heald [1987] Managing Director

Sai Soft Drinks Ltd
Incorporated: 11 March 2014
Net Worth Deficit: £47,879
Registered Office: 3 Beamway, Dagenham, Essex, RM10 8XR
Major Shareholder: Manish Pathak
Officers: Manish Pathak [1969] Director [Indian]

Sailortown Brewing Limited
Incorporated: 23 April 2018
Registered Office: 155-157 Donegall Pass, Belfast, BT7 1DT
Parent: Kirker Greer (Holdings) Limited
Officers: Steven Clark Pattison [1979] Director; Richard Ryan [1977] Director

Saints Row Brewing Co. Ltd.
Incorporated: 24 November 2016
Net Worth: £17,490 Total Assets: £17,490
Registered Office: 18 Maude Street, Darlington, Co Durham, DL3 7PW
Major Shareholder: Michal Czubak
Officers: Michal Czubak [1992] Brewer/Director [Polish]

Saj Holdings Ltd
Incorporated: 29 August 2018
Registered Office: 26 Kenilworth Close, Slough, SL1 2BA
Major Shareholder: Sajjad Ashraf
Officers: Sajjad Ashraf, Secretary; Sajjad Ashraf [1967] Director

The Salford Rum Company Limited
Incorporated: 20 February 2018
Registered Office: 51 Radcliffe Park Road, Salford, M6 7WP
Shareholders: James Harrison; Thomas Gaughan
Officers: Thomas Gaughan [1988] Director; James Harrison [1987] Director

The Salmon Lady Limited
Incorporated: 6 May 2016
Registered Office: 23 Chantry Lane, Grimsby, N E Lincs, DN31 2LP
Major Shareholder: David John Smith
Officers: David John Smith [1963] Sales Director

Salonica Limited
Incorporated: 1 February 2007
Net Worth Deficit: £26,570 Total Assets: £18,050
Registered Office: 120 Pyrles Lane, Loughton, Essex, IG10 2NW
Major Shareholder: Efthymios Tzechilidis
Officers: Efthymios Tzechilidis [1964] Director/Manager

The Salt Rock Liquor Company Limited
Incorporated: 13 September 2017
Registered Office: 47 Vernon Street, Saltcoats, N Ayrshire, KA21 5HE
Major Shareholder: Alexander Stewart Wilkie
Officers: Alexander Stewart Wilkie [1958] Director

The Salto Cachaca Company Limited
Incorporated: 2 April 2009
Net Worth Deficit: £40,622 Total Assets: £63,412
Registered Office: 31 Coniger Road, London, SW6 3TB
Major Shareholder: Stephen Matthew Wedgwood Drawbell
Officers: Annette Patricia Drawbell [1967] Director/Accounts Manager; Stephen Matthew Wedgwood Drawbell [1966] Director/Marketing

Saltrock Brewing Company Limited
Incorporated: 30 January 2019
Registered Office: 70 Porterfield, Comrie, Dunfermline, Fife, KY12 9XG
Major Shareholder: Peter Daniel Rossborough
Officers: Peter Daniel Rossborough [1979] Director/Businessman

Sam-Gel Global Ventures Limited
Incorporated: 9 June 2014
Net Worth: £15,386 Total Assets: £19,208
Registered Office: 56 Greenwood Road, London, E8 1AB
Major Shareholder: Samuel Omonforma
Officers: Samuel Pius Omonforma [1967] Director/General Business

Sambath Trading Limited
Incorporated: 11 June 2018
Registered Office: Kemp House, 160 City Road, London, EC1V 2NX
Officers: Sambathkumar Tamilazhagan, Secretary; Sambathkumar Tamilazhagan [1989] Director/Businessman [Indian]; Sambathkumar Tamilazhagan [1989] Director/Businessman [Indian]

Sambatha Ltd
Incorporated: 30 May 2018
Registered Office: 32 Melbourne Road, Leicester, LE2 0DR
Officers: Sambathkumar Tamilazhagan [1989] Director/Businessman [Indian]

Samco Global Foods Ltd
Incorporated: 17 May 2011
Net Worth: £1,181 Total Assets: £5,420
Registered Office: Unit 6 Tulketh Industrial Estate, Manchester, M40 9LY
Shareholder: Kenechukwu Chukwuemeka Orazu
Officers: Kenechukwu Chukwuemeka Orazu [1983] Director/Manager; Virginia Uju Orazu [1960] Director/Trading [Nigerian]

Same Day Beers Group Ltd
Incorporated: 20 May 2016
Registered Office: Bredbury Park Ind Est, Corrie Way, Bredbury, Stockport, Cheshire, SK6 2ST
Officers: Brian Michael Wright [1958] Director; Gavin Michael Wright [1982] Director

Sammartini Ltd
Incorporated: 24 June 2015
Net Worth Deficit: £4,195 Total Assets: £4,938
Registered Office: 2nd Floor, 1 City Road East, Manchester, M15 4PN
Major Shareholder: Anamaria Veglio
Officers: Annamaria Veglio [1971] Director [Italian]

Samphire Drinks Ltd
Incorporated: 18 February 2019
Registered Office: 1 Peterville, St Agnes, Cornwall, TR5 0QU
Shareholders: Peter Timothy Bawden; George Parry
Officers: Peter Timothy Bawden [1967] Director/Manager; George Parry [1998] Director/Sales Manager

Charles Samuel Imports & Exports Ltd
Incorporated: 6 October 2017
Registered Office: 9 Scirocco Close, Northampton, NN3 6AP
Officers: Charles Samuel Cornish [1989] Director; Daniel Joseph Lewell [1975] Director

Samuels Brewing Company Ltd
Incorporated: 14 June 2017 Employees: 2
Net Worth Deficit: £13,111 Total Assets: £12,933
Registered Office: Blick Studios, 46 Hill Street, Belfast, BT1 2LB
Major Shareholder: Gary Clarke
Officers: Gary Clarke [1974] Director [Irish]; Sean Clarke [1968] Director [Irish]

San Martino Limited
Incorporated: 17 September 2018
Registered Office: 48 Colliery Close, Nottingham, NG2 1PF
Shareholder: Gabriele Bolgeri
Officers: Dr Charles Edward Dall'omo [1983] Director; Stephanie Claire Dall'omo [1982] Director

Sandbar German Beer Ltd
Incorporated: 2 April 2002 Employees: 3
Net Worth: £115,448 Total Assets: £200,022
Registered Office: 48 Sutton Road, Stockport, Cheshire, SK4 2PW
Shareholder: Michael Andrew Flint
Officers: Michael Andrew Flint, Secretary; Joanne Ruth Flint [1974] Director/Marketing Manager; Michael Andrew Flint [1963] Director

Sandham Wine Merchants Ltd
Incorporated: 20 August 2003 Employees: 9
Net Worth: £433,437 Total Assets: £693,696
Registered Office: 3 South Street, Caistor, Lincoln, LN7 6UB
Shareholders: Jeremy John William Sandham; Helga Sandham
Officers: Jeremy John William Sandham, Secretary; Helga Sandham [1960] Director/Wine Merchant; Jeremy John William Sandham [1964] Director/Wine Merchant

Sandhar & Kang (Birmingham) Limited
Incorporated: 8 July 1994
Net Worth Deficit: £1,370,688 Total Assets: £548
Registered Office: 84 Albion Court, Attleborough Road, Nuneaton, Warwicks, CV11 4JJ
Parent: Sandhar & Kang Limited
Officers: Udham Singh Kang, Secretary/Director; Avtar Singh Kang [1943] Director; Swarn Singh Kang [1927] Director; Udham Singh Kang [1939] Director

Sandhu IT Services Ltd
Incorporated: 10 March 2016
Net Worth: £26,066 Total Assets: £51,440
Registered Office: 62 Mayfair Road, Dartford, Kent, DA1 5AQ
Shareholders: Parmjit Singh Sandhu; Rajpreet Sandhu
Officers: Parmjit Singh Sandhu [1974] Director/Consultant

Sandhu Wholesale & Events Limited
Incorporated: 24 April 2016
Net Worth Deficit: £18,377
Registered Office: 30-31 St James Place, Mangotsfield, Bristol, BS16 9JB
Major Shareholder: Arvinder Singh Sandhu
Officers: Arvinder Singh Sandhu [1989] Director

Sanghera Rum Company Limited
Incorporated: 23 March 2017
Registered Office: The Abbotts, Oak Hill Road, Stapleford Abbotts, Essex, RM4 1JL
Major Shareholder: Taj Sanghera
Officers: Tajinder Singh Sanghera [1983] Director/Self Employed

Sangiovesa Ltd
Incorporated: 2 March 2018
Registered Office: 43d Taylors Lane, Dundee, DD2 1AP
Major Shareholder: Oberdan Faini
Officers: Oberdan Faini [1955] Director/Wine Merchant [Italian]

Santa Code Limited
Incorporated: 28 August 2018
Registered Office: 2 Sutherland Court, Marylands Road, London, W9 2DT
Officers: Giorgio Codeghini [1982] Director/Businessman; Giselle Almeida Codeghini [1986] Director/Businesswoman

Santat Wines Limited
Incorporated: 30 June 1988
Net Worth: £275,006 Total Assets: £276,256
Registered Office: Pew Corner, Old Portsmouth Road, Artington, Guildford, Surrey, GU3 1LP
Parent: Les Caves de Pyrene Ltd
Officers: Amy Victoria Morgan, Secretary; Eric Serge Narioo [1963] Director [French]

Sanwin Ltd
Incorporated: 9 October 2017
Registered Office: 107 Saddlery Way, Chester, CH1 4LZ
Shareholders: Olivera Ristanovic-Santrac; Miroslav Santrac
Officers: Olivera Ristanovic-Santrac [1970] Director/Translator/Interpreter [Serbian]; Miroslav Santrac [1966] Director/Chemical Engineer [Slovenian]

Sapling Spirits Ltd
Incorporated: 21 March 2018
Registered Office: 19a Pavilion Terrace, London, W12 0HT
Shareholders: Ivo Edmund Devereux; Edward Theo Faulkner
Officers: Ivo Edmund Devereux [1995] Director; Edward Theo Faulkner [1995] Director

SAPM Commercial Ltd
Incorporated: 21 March 2016
Net Worth Deficit: £9,385 Total Assets: £74,254
Registered Office: 27 Elstow Road, Dagenham, Essex, RM9 6AX
Major Shareholder: Petar Dimitrov Dzhandarmov
Officers: Petar Dimitrov Dzhandarmov [1980] Director [Bulgarian]

Saravanan Traders (UK) Ltd
Incorporated: 7 January 2019
Registered Office: 3 Popplewell Close, Belton, Doncaster, S Yorks, DN9 1TF
Major Shareholder: Saravanan Elangovan
Officers: Saravanan Elangovan, Secretary; Saravanan Elangovan [1996] Director/Businessman [Indian]

Sardinia Wine Ltd
Incorporated: 11 November 2004
Net Worth: £28,025 Total Assets: £222,346
Registered Office: 36 Glebe Road, Finchley, London, N3 2AX
Shareholder: Roberto Zintu
Officers: Roberto Zintu, Secretary; Roberto Zintu [1960] Director [Italian]

Sarpanch Food & Wine Distributors Ltd
Incorporated: 13 June 2012
Net Worth Deficit: £22,515 Total Assets: £20,926
Registered Office: Unit 106, 6 The Broadway, Mill Hill, London, NW7 3LL
Major Shareholder: Sukhvir Singh Grewal
Officers: Solvita Zahare, Secretary; Sukhvir Singh Grewal [1987] Director [Indian]

Sarpe L & C Ltd
Incorporated: 30 August 2018
Registered Office: 25 Lyncroft Gardens, Hounslow, Middlesex, TW3 2QT
Major Shareholder: Anamaria Prioteasa
Officers: Anamaria Prioteasa [1983] Director/Salesman [Romanian]

SASC Enterprise Limited
Incorporated: 9 April 2018
Registered Office: 37 Banstead Road, Caterham, Surrey, CR3 5QG
Major Shareholder: Athavan Ramakrishnalal
Officers: Athavan Ramakrishnalal [1988] Director

Satellite Brands Limited
Incorporated: 28 September 2018
Registered Office: The Apex, 2 Sheriffs Orchard, Coventry, Warwicks, CV1 3PP
Major Shareholder: Wayne Alan Scrivener
Officers: Wayne Alan Scrivener [1980] Director/International Trade

Sativatech Ltd
Incorporated: 18 October 2018
Registered Office: Armadillo MUMB#81355, 8 Parkway Avenue, Sheffield, S9 4WA
Major Shareholder: Jordan Gors
Officers: Jordan Gors, Secretary; Jordan Gors [1994] Director [Australian]

The Saucy Drinks Company Limited
Incorporated: 26 August 2016
Registered Office: Kemp House, 160 City Road, London, EC1V 2NX
Major Shareholder: Colin George Berry
Officers: Colin George Berry [1949] Director

Sauvignon Wines UK Ltd
Incorporated: 19 May 2016
Registered Office: Ashcombe Court, Woolsack Way, Godalming, Surrey, GU7 1LQ
Shareholders: Matthys Michael Louw; Lucy Margaret Faraday Warner
Officers: Matthys Michael Louw [1982] Director/Winemaker [South African]; Lucy Margaret Faraday Warner [1966] Director/Sales & Marketing

Savafrei Ltd
Incorporated: 7 January 2019
Registered Office: 37 Eastcote Road, Pinner, Middlesex, HA5 1EL
Major Shareholder: Sava Ionut Onofrei
Officers: Sava Ionut Onofrei [1992] Director/Entrepreneur [Romanian]

Savage Selection Limited
Incorporated: 26 February 1988
Net Worth: £102,535 *Total Assets:* £651,355
Registered Office: The Ox House, Market Place, Northleach, Cheltenham, Glos, GL54 3EG
Major Shareholder: Mark Savage
Officers: Annabel Mary Savage, Secretary; Annabel Mary Savage [1951] Director; Mark Savage [1949] Director/Master of Wine; Michael Charles Storey [1947] Director/Chartered Accountant

Savage Wines UK Limited
Incorporated: 7 November 2016
Registered Office: Ashcombe Court, Woolsack Way, Godalming, Surrey, GU7 1LQ
Major Shareholder: Duncan Alexander Savage
Officers: Duncan Alexander Savage [1978] Director/Winemaker [South African]

Savile Row Gin Limited
Incorporated: 11 December 2017
Registered Office: 54-58 High Street, Edgware, Middlesex, HA8 7EJ
Major Shareholder: Stewart David Lee
Officers: Stewart David Lee [1972] Director

Say It With Champers Ltd
Incorporated: 4 June 2018
Registered Office: South Barn, Cross Green, Cockfield, Bury St Edmunds, Suffolk, IP30 0LG
Major Shareholder: Didier Penine
Officers: Didier Penine [1979] Director/Quantity Surveyor

Sazerac UK Limited
Incorporated: 28 February 2003 *Employees:* 25
Net Worth Deficit: £368,640 *Total Assets:* £33,908,028
Registered Office: 60 Marina Place, Hampton Wick, Kingston upon Thames, Surrey, KT1 4BH
Major Shareholder: William Alan Goldring
Officers: Rebecca Lucy Martin [1958] Managing Director; Christopher Douglas Ritchie [1972] Director [Canadian]; Christopher Robin Skinger [1974] Director [American]; Magdalena Ewa Tadych [1978] Finance Director [Polish]

Scarlettes Ltd
Incorporated: 1 November 2018
Registered Office: Oak Cottage, Hyde Street, Upper Beeding, Steyning, W Sussex, BN44 3TG
Major Shareholder: Debbie Fernanda Eaton
Officers: Debbie Fernanda Eaton [1969] Director/Recruitment Consultant

Scavelli's Limited
Incorporated: 16 June 2000
Net Worth: £15,348 *Total Assets:* £305,151
Registered Office: Paddock Farm, Sutton Lane, Sutton Scarsdale, Chesterfield, Derbys, S44 5UW
Major Shareholder: Vito Scavelli
Officers: Ausilia Scavelli, Secretary; Vito Scavelli [1965] Sales Director

Schnapp Lab Ltd
Incorporated: 8 October 2018
Registered Office: 12 Alexander Avenue, Droitwich, Worcs, WR9 8NH
Shareholders: David John Drury; Maxeen Ann Turton
Officers: David John Drury [1981] Director Development; Maxeen Ann Turton [1982] Director Marketing

Schoenlaub Limited
Incorporated: 20 November 2018
Registered Office: 7-9 Ferdinand Street, London, NW1 8ES
Major Shareholder: Thomas Schonlaub
Officers: Thomas Schonlaub [1974] Managing Director [German]

Schuler Wine St. Jakob's Cellars Limited
Incorporated: 30 January 1986
Net Worth Deficit: £30,817 *Total Assets:* £11,600
Registered Office: The St Botolph Building, 138 Houndsditch, London, EC3A 7AR
Shareholders: Jakob Schuler; Schuler & Cie A.G
Officers: Anton Real, Secretary; Andrew John Robertson [1950] Director/Part Time Lecturer; Jakob Schuler [1948] Director/Wine Importer [Swiss]

Scimedex Limited
Incorporated: 25 May 2016
Net Worth Deficit: £3,742 *Total Assets:* £6,002
Registered Office: 129a Sibson Road, Birstall, Leicester, LE4 4ND
Major Shareholder: William Paul Rushton
Officers: William Paul Rushton [1963] Director/Merchant

Sco & Whisky Limited
Incorporated: 13 March 2018
Registered Office: 3F1, 16 East Mayfield, Edinburgh, EH9 1SE
Major Shareholder: Mirko Grkajac
Officers: Alexandar Perisic, Secretary; Mirko Grkajac [1985] Director/Worker [Serbian]; Alexandar Perisic [1960] Director/Worker

Scot Bottle Limited
Incorporated: 5 July 2001
Net Worth: £12,429 *Total Assets:* £14,339
Registered Office: Carse of South Coldoch, Gargunnock, Stirling, FK8 3DF
Major Shareholder: Alan Ronald Graham
Officers: Peter Carnegie Gibson Graham, Secretary; Alan Ronald Graham [1969] Director/Business Development Manager; Janet Shirley Graham [1976] Director/Doctor

Scotch Whisky International Limited
Incorporated: 28 December 1995
Net Worth: £1,940 *Total Assets:* £8,850
Registered Office: Laverockdale Lodge, Dreghorn Loan, Edinburgh, EH13 0DB
Major Shareholder: Alan Gordon Henry Macpherson
Officers: Dr Alan Gordon Henry Macpherson [1952] Director/Medical Practitioner

Scotia Blending Company Limited
Incorporated: 10 May 2010
Net Worth: £4,283 *Total Assets:* £7,620
Registered Office: Chappell House, Chappell Street, Barrhead, E Renfrewshire, G78 1EL
Shareholder: John Neilson Turnbull
Officers: John Neilson Turnbull, Secretary; Alastair Robert Frazer Sinclair [1937] Director; John Neilson Turnbull [1952] Director

Scotland Grindlay Limited
Incorporated: 24 March 2015
Net Worth Deficit: £3,257 *Total Assets:* £27,009
Registered Office: c/o Callanders Limited, 53 High Street, Dumbarton, G82 1LS
Shareholder: George Scotland Gindlay
Officers: George Scotland Grindlay [1959] Director; Moira Elizabeth Grindlay [1960] Director

UK Wholesalers of Beers, Wines and Spirits   dellam

Vernon Scott Limited
Incorporated: 15 May 2013
Registered Office: Bank House, 81 St Judes Road, Englefield Green, Surrey, TW20 0DF
Shareholders: Matthew Vernon Hooper; Jody Scott Tucker
Officers: Matthew Vernon Hooper [1973] Director/General Manager - Wine Filtration [Australian]; Jody Scott Tucker [1968] Director/Designer [Australian]

Scott's of Quorn (Wine Bar & Vintners) Limited
Incorporated: 15 April 2014 Employees: 2
Net Worth Deficit: £8,459 Total Assets: £9,822
Registered Office: 78 Loughborough Road, Quorn, Leics, LE12 8DX
Shareholder: Stephen Robert Scott
Officers: Anne Scott, Secretary; Stephen Robert Scott [1967] Director/Surveyor

Scozia Grappa Ltd
Incorporated: 6 September 2018
Registered Office: 1 Beauchamp Court, 10 Victors Way, Barnet, Herts, EN5 5TZ
Major Shareholder: Amer Yousif Hanna Makenchi
Officers: Amer Yousif Hanna Makenchi [1962] Director [Iraqi]

Scrawny Al Ltd
Incorporated: 2 June 1995
Net Worth Deficit: £72,190 Total Assets: £28,432
Registered Office: 1 Elm Grove, Taunton, Somerset, TA1 1EG
Shareholders: Alasdair MacDonald; Anna Fay MacDonald
Officers: Alasdair MacDonald, Secretary; Alasdair MacDonald [1956] Director/Systems Analyst; Anna Fay MacDonald [1982] Director/Airline Crew

Scrumpy Wasp Limited
Incorporated: 16 September 2011
Net Worth Deficit: £194,289 Total Assets: £97,664
Registered Office: Rose Dean Farm, Mark Lane, East Markham, Newark, Notts, NG22 0QU
Shareholders: Timothy Paul Needham; Leanda Daphne Needham
Officers: Leanda Daphne Needham [1971] Director/P.A; Timothy Paul Needham [1960] Director/Brewer

SDC Wine Importers Ltd
Incorporated: 12 June 2017
Net Worth: £97 Total Assets: £233,822
Registered Office: Gloucester House, Church Walk, Burgess Hill, W Sussex, RH15 9AS
Major Shareholder: Lucy Ruth Minshaw Driver
Officers: Giles William John Cutlack [1975] Sales Director; Lucy Ruth Minshaw Driver [1970] Director/Independent Wine Merchant

Seabrook Wines Limited
Incorporated: 13 March 2012
Net Worth Deficit: £17,884 Total Assets: £6,873
Registered Office: Fairacre, Chiltern Road, Ballinger, Great Missenden, Bucks, HP16 9LJ
Shareholders: Julian Graham Seabrook; Samantha Rachel Seabrook
Officers: Samantha Seabrook, Secretary; Julian Graham Seabrook [1970] Director

Seafire Brewing Co. Ltd
Incorporated: 22 February 2019
Registered Office: 10 Seafire Place, Dalgety Bay, Dunfermline, Fife, KY11 9GY
Major Shareholder: Kiera Browne
Officers: Kiera Browne [1982] Director/Chief Executive

Seawoods Wine Ltd
Incorporated: 28 February 2017
Net Worth: £2,000 Total Assets: £2,000
Registered Office: Seawoods Wine Ltd, P O Box 73805, London, E11 9FU
Major Shareholder: Hua Zhong
Officers: Qiao Yu [1981] Director [Chinese]; Hua Zhong [1973] Director

Seb and Emma Ltd
Incorporated: 22 November 2011
Net Worth Deficit: £10,186 Total Assets: £118
Registered Office: 13 Sidmouth Street, Devizes, Wilts, SN10 1LD
Shareholders: Emma Barron; Sebastien Liegeard
Officers: Emma Barron [1973] Director; Sebastien Liegeard [1969] Director [French]

Seckford Agencies Limited
Incorporated: 21 May 1996 Employees: 12
Net Worth: £613,600 Total Assets: £2,404,807
Registered Office: Old Barn Farm, Harts Lane, Ardleigh, Colchester, Essex, CO7 7XQ
Major Shareholder: Philippa Jane Woods
Officers: David Antony Cartwright [1961] Sales Director; Richard William Harvey-Jones [1948] Director/Chairman; Philippa Jane Woods [1958] Director

Seckford Wines Limited
Incorporated: 21 June 1985 Employees: 26
Net Worth: £3,888,644 Total Assets: £6,382,622
Registered Office: Dock Lane, Melton, Woodbridge, Suffolk, IP12 1PE
Major Shareholder: Richard Harvey Jones
Officers: Richard William Harvey-Jones, Secretary/Wine Merchant; Julian Conway Downing [1964] Director/Wine Merchant; Charles Godwin [1973] Director/Wine Broker; Richard William Harvey-Jones [1948] Director/Wine Merchant; Marcus Millward Titley [1965] Director/Wine Broker

Second Eger Ltd
Incorporated: 19 October 2018
Registered Office: 23 Chiltern Drive, Surbiton, Surrey, KT5 8LP
Major Shareholder: Janos Peter Besenyi
Officers: Janos Peter Besenyi [1964] Director/Engineer [Argentinian]

Sedgemoor Drinks Limited
Incorporated: 7 January 2009 Employees: 2
Net Worth: £50,002 Total Assets: £50,002
Registered Office: Western House, Silverhills Road, Decoy Industrial Estate, Newton Abbot, Devon, TQ12 5ND
Officers: James Charles Mardell [1958] Managing Director; Steven Charles Mardell [1984] Director/Commercial Manager

See Squared Ltd
Incorporated: 30 May 2018
Registered Office: Ground Floor, 22 Steerforth Street, London, SW18 4HH
Major Shareholder: Christopher Cokayne
Officers: Christopher Cokayne [1974] Director

Sefton Beer Company Limited
Incorporated: 13 January 2016
Net Worth Deficit: £9,661 Total Assets: £234,681
Registered Office: Unit D5 Kingfisher Business Park, Hawthorne Road, Bootle, Merseyside, L20 6PF
Officers: Ian Robert Horrigan [1973] Director

Select Whisky Limited
Incorporated: 10 April 2016
Net Worth Deficit: £1,226 *Total Assets:* £282,970
Registered Office: New Burlington House, 1075 Finchley Road, London, NW11 0PU
Shareholders: Harry Zvi Ephraim Greenberg; Riki Greenberg
Officers: Riki Greenberg [1991] Director; Shelley Lucy Kelaty [1973] Director

The Select Wine Company Limited
Incorporated: 8 May 1998
Registered Office: 6 Benheim Terrace, Castle Street, Reading, Berks, RG1 7ST
Major Shareholder: Paul James Griffiths
Officers: Robert Vivian Grant, Secretary; Paul James Griffiths [1965] Director

Selectia Wine Ltd
Incorporated: 4 October 2018
Registered Office: 20 Campden Green, Solihull, W Midlands, B92 8HG
Major Shareholder: Jose Ignacio Clavijo Barrio
Officers: Jose Ignacio Clavijo Barrio [1968] Commercial Director [Spanish]; Francisca Isabel Marquez [1969] Director/Manager [Spanish]

Sell My Wine Ltd
Incorporated: 9 November 2016 *Employees:* 2
Net Worth: £36,644 *Total Assets:* £315,432
Registered Office: 1 Stockton Court, Greycoat Street, Westminster, London, SW1P 2QE
Shareholder: Paul Reece Clarke
Officers: Paul Reece Clarke [1971] Director; Daniel Joseph Haigh [1978] Director/Wine Trader

Senor Agave Limited
Incorporated: 11 August 2017
Registered Office: 38a Paddenswick Road, London, W6 0UB
Major Shareholder: Olivia Katie McSweeney
Officers: Olivia Katie McSweeney [1986] Director

Separateflow Limited
Incorporated: 1 November 2016
Net Worth: £15,477 *Total Assets:* £15,477
Registered Office: 2 Guy Street, London, SE1 3RF
Officers: Marco Floridia [1982] Director/Project, Account Manager [Italian]

Seriously Vodka Limited
Incorporated: 7 February 2017
Net Worth: £100 *Total Assets:* £100
Registered Office: 163 Bath Street, Glasgow, G2 4SQ
Parent: Indie Spirits Limited
Officers: Douglas Brougham Cunningham [1968] Director; Per Anders Jonsson [1960] Director [Swedish]

Seth Ventures Limited
Incorporated: 25 September 2012
Net Worth: £41,096 *Total Assets:* £44,480
Registered Office: Flat A, 1 Randolph Gardens, London, NW6 5EH
Major Shareholder: Arjun Seth
Officers: Arjun Seth [1973] Director

Seven Cellars Ltd.
Incorporated: 4 November 2015 *Employees:* 4
Net Worth Deficit: £26,659 *Total Assets:* £77,143
Registered Office: Station Studios, 96 Ethel Street, Hove, E Sussex, BN3 3LL
Shareholders: Anna Michelle Olivia Lowe; Louise Oliver
Officers: Anna Michelle Olivia Lowe [1971] Director; Louise Oliver [1974] Director

Sfuso Wine Limited
Incorporated: 1 June 2011
Net Worth Deficit: £7,073 *Total Assets:* £61,820
Registered Office: 1 Kings Avenue, London, N21 3NA
Major Shareholder: Marina Jankovic
Officers: Marina Jankovic [1977] Director

Shack Drinks Limited
Incorporated: 16 March 2017
Registered Office: Brickhouse Farm, Edwyn Ralph, Bromyard, Herefords, HR7 4LU
Shareholders: James David Manning; Richard Manning
Officers: James David Manning [1987] Director; Richard Manning [1990] Director

Shake's Ink Limited
Incorporated: 20 November 2018
Registered Office: Flat 101, Golden Lane Estate, London, EC1Y 0SJ
Major Shareholder: Oscar Lawrence Toma
Officers: Oscar Lawrence Toma [1974] Director

Shamboozle Limited
Incorporated: 28 August 2018
Registered Office: Flat 30, 2a Highshore Road, London, SE15 5AA
Major Shareholder: Sham Sundar Mahabir
Officers: Sham Sundar Mahabir [1976] Director; James Andrew Togut [1966] Director

Shandy Shack Ltd
Incorporated: 14 August 2018
Registered Office: 18 The Parkway, Southampton, SO16 3PQ
Shareholders: Frederick Joseph York Gleadowe; Edward Stapleton; Thomas Peter Stevens
Officers: Dr Frederick Joseph York Gleadowe [1991] Managing Director; Edward Stapleton [1992] Managing Director; Dr Thomas Peter Stevens [1991] Managing Director

Sharing The Best Limited
Incorporated: 7 April 2014
Net Worth Deficit: £39,970 *Total Assets:* £7,972
Registered Office: Cranfield, Southfields Road, Woldingham, Surrey, CR3 7BQ
Shareholders: Eny Cristina Millard; Andrew Christopher Glanvile Millard
Officers: Andrew Christopher Glanvile Millard [1963] Director; Eny Cristina Millard [1961] Director

Sharpham Wine Limited
Incorporated: 14 January 2019
Registered Office: Owl's Roost, Beenleigh, Harbertonford, Totnes, Devon, TQ9 7EF
Major Shareholder: Mark Richard William Sharman
Officers: Mark Richard William Sharman [1959] Director/Winemaker

Sheffield Brewers Collective
Incorporated: 13 March 2017
Registered Office: Office 209, J C Albyn Complex, Burton Road, Neepsend, Sheffield, S3 8BZ
Officers: Peter Andrew Rawlinson [1964] Director/Solicitor; Peter John Roberts [1969] Director; Andrew Neil Stephens [1978] Director/Publican

Sheikh Super Store Ltd
Incorporated: 21 September 2018
Registered Office: 94 Market Place, Romford, Essex, RM1 3ER
Major Shareholder: Muhammad Usman Nisar
Officers: Muhammad Usman Nisar [1983] Director/Entrepreneur [Pakistani]

Sheila's Rum Punch Ltd
Incorporated: 6 December 2018
Registered Office: 35 Bridge Close, Enfield, Middlesex, EN1 4LH
Major Shareholder: Sheila Bvuure-Gaynor
Officers: Caroline Nyasha Zata, Secretary; Sheila Bvuure-Gaynor [1983] Director/Manager [Zimbabwean]; Anthony Vivian Gaynor [1961] Director/Manager

Shellys Drinks Limited
Incorporated: 22 March 2017
Net Worth: £6,352 *Total Assets:* £52,397
Registered Office: Unit 17 Holme Mills Industrial Estate, Holme, Carnforth, Lancs, LA6 1RD
Major Shareholder: Michelle Partington
Officers: Michelle Partington [1973] Director

Shelsley Brewing Company Ltd
Incorporated: 31 January 2019
Registered Office: Lilac Cottage, Camp Lane, Shelsley Beauchamp, Worcester, WR6 6RL
Shareholders: James Allen; Ruth Elliker
Officers: James Allen [1966] Director; Ruth Elliker [1974] Director

Shepherd Neame Limited
Incorporated: 9 November 1914 *Employees:* 1,569
Net Worth: £201,052,000 *Total Assets:* £334,227,008
Registered Office: 17 Court Street, Faversham, Kent, ME13 7AX
Officers: Robin Neil Duncan, Secretary; George Harold Abbott Barnes [1954] Director; William John Brett [1965] Director; Nigel James Bunting [1967] Retail Director; Jonathan Beale Neame [1964] Director; Richard John Oldfield [1955] Director; Mark John Rider [1976] Finance Director; Hilary Susan Riva [1957] Director; Miles Howard Templeman [1947] Director/Consultant

Sheridan Cooper's Limited
Incorporated: 11 February 2003 *Employees:* 14
Net Worth: £28,056 *Total Assets:* £1,044,434
Registered Office: 4th Floor, Park Gate, 161-163 Preston Road, Brighton, BN1 6AF
Major Shareholder: Andrew Reginald Wiseman
Officers: Andrew Reginald Wiseman [1966] Director

Sheridan Wines Limited
Incorporated: 22 December 2009
Registered Office: 4th Floor, Park Gate, 161-163 Preston Road, Brighton, BN1 6AF
Major Shareholder: Sheridan Phyllis Wiseman
Officers: Sheridan Phyllis Wiseman [1966] Director/Finance Manager

Sherwood Outlaws Brewing Company Limited
Incorporated: 25 February 2017
Net Worth Deficit: £107 *Total Assets:* £2,949
Registered Office: W H Prior, Railway Court, Doncaster, S Yorks, DN4 5FB
Officers: Gareth Ball [1983] Director; Daniel Ironmonger Derry [1974] Director; Joanne Taylor [1979] Director

The Shieling Scotch Whisky Co Ltd
Incorporated: 11 March 2015
Net Worth: £100 *Total Assets:* £100
Registered Office: c/o Cloch Solicitors, Standard Buildings, 94 Hope Street, Glasgow, G2 6PH
Major Shareholder: Andrew Ross Crombie
Officers: Andrew Ross Crombie [1964] Director/Stonemason

Shindigger Craft Beer Ltd
Incorporated: 19 December 2012 *Employees:* 5
Net Worth: £171,547 *Total Assets:* £315,103
Registered Office: 6 Cross Keys Street, Manchester, M4 5ET
Major Shareholder: Paul Delamere
Officers: Paul Delamere [1989] Director; George Grant [1990] Director

The Ship & Mitre Brewing Company Limited
Incorporated: 17 May 2016
Net Worth Deficit: £22,341 *Total Assets:* £12,051
Registered Office: 133 Dale Street, Liverpool, L2 2JH
Shareholders: Steven Dobby; Benjamin Robert James Garner
Officers: Steven Richard Dobby [1974] Director; Benjamin Robert James Garner [1971] Director

Shires Wine Services Limited
Incorporated: 11 May 2012
Net Worth Deficit: £6,789 *Total Assets:* £405
Registered Office: 65 Rayneham Road, Ilkeston, Derbys, DE7 8RJ
Shareholders: Paul Anthony Waddingham; Tina Waddingham
Officers: Paul Anthony Waddingham [1955] Director; Tina Waddingham [1959] Director

Shocabo Ltd
Incorporated: 8 March 2018
Registered Office: 55 Chancellor House, Rotherhithe New Road, London, SE16 3FP
Shareholders: CDT Contracting Limited; Sholly It Limited; Darkshell Limited
Officers: Adegbenga Olusola Jibodu [1975] Director; Ombolaji Jibodu [1978] Director; Carl Tucker [1986] Director

Shonty Group Ltd
Incorporated: 15 June 2016
Net Worth: £8,416 *Total Assets:* £8,783
Registered Office: Kemp House, 152-160 City Road, London, EC1V 2NX
Officers: Shalinder Singh [1990] Director [Indian]

Shop Wine Limited
Incorporated: 22 January 2019
Registered Office: 83 Falmouth Road, London, SE1 4JN
Major Shareholder: Gian Philipp Schenkelberg
Officers: Gian Philipp Schenkelberg, Secretary; Gian Philipp Schenkelberg [1991] Director [German]

Shorty's Gins Ltd
Incorporated: 25 April 2018
Registered Office: Unit G5, St Hilda's Business Centre, The Ropery, Whitby, N Yorks, YO22 4ET
Major Shareholder: Rachael Conisbee
Officers: Rachael Conisbee [1970] Director

Shree Sai Trading Ltd
Incorporated: 16 February 2011
Net Worth: £621,444 Total Assets: £1,426,703
Registered Office: Unit 21 Clipper Park Industrial Estate, Thurrock Park Way, Tilbury, Essex, RM18 7HG
Major Shareholder: Surag Narpatsinh Sayania
Officers: Surag Narpatsinh Sayania [1984] Director

Shropshire Beers Limited
Incorporated: 12 May 2018
Registered Office: St Annes Chruch, Lea Cross, Shrewsbury, Salop, SY5 8JE
Major Shareholder: Christopher Julius Jones
Officers: Christopher Julius Jones [1963] Director/Entrepreneur

Shy Simba Ltd
Incorporated: 18 April 2018
Registered Office: International House, 12 Constance Street, London, E16 2DQ
Major Shareholder: Lauren Rebecca Elaine Dooley
Officers: Lauren Rebecca Elaine Dooley [1994] Director

Sibell Trading Limited
Incorporated: 10 May 2002
Net Worth Deficit: £61,271 Total Assets: £219,299
Registered Office: Hallswelle House, 1 Hallswelle Road, London, NW11 0DH
Officers: Esther Waldman, Secretary [Israeli]; Mordecai Leib Waldman [1969] Director

Siderea Consulting Limited
Incorporated: 17 January 2014 Employees: 1
Net Worth: £6,458 Total Assets: £35,173
Registered Office: 46 New Road, Milnathort, Kinross, KY13 9XT
Major Shareholder: George Preston Thomson
Officers: George Preston Thomson [1954] Director

Signatory Vintage Scotch Whisky Company Limited
Incorporated: 23 August 1988 Employees: 23
Net Worth: £37,594,184 Total Assets: £44,839,152
Registered Office: Edradour Distillery, Pitlochry, Perthshire, PH16 5JP
Major Shareholder: Andrew William Symington
Officers: Graham Keith Cox, Secretary; Graham Keith Cox [1947] Director/Solicitor; Andrew William Symington [1963] Managing Director

Signature Brew Ltd
Incorporated: 26 October 2011 Employees: 8
Net Worth: £135,947 Total Assets: £471,671
Registered Office: Unit 25 Leyton Business Centre, Etloe Road, London, E10 7BT
Shareholders: Thomas Bott; Sam Alistair McGregor
Officers: Tom Bott [1988] Director; Sam Alistair McGregor [1985] Director

Signature Wine Gifts Ltd
Incorporated: 15 February 2018
Registered Office: 80 Gresty Terrace, Crewe, Cheshire, CW1 5EW
Major Shareholder: Benjamin Robert Burrow
Officers: Benjamin Robert Burrow [1993] Director

Signature Wines Ltd
Incorporated: 9 August 2013
Net Worth Deficit: £122,051 Total Assets: £89,881
Registered Office: 20 Belvue Business Centre, Belvue Road, Northolt, Middlesex, UB5 5QQ
Major Shareholder: Deepak Bhatia
Officers: Deepak Bhatia [1975] Director/Businessman

Signorellis Deli Ltd
Incorporated: 4 May 2016 Employees: 10
Net Worth Deficit: £82,904 Total Assets: £214,119
Registered Office: 17 Burleigh Street, Cambridge, CB1 1DG
Major Shareholder: Alessandro Signorelli
Officers: Alessandro Signorelli [1982] Director [Italian]

Silence of The Drams Limited
Incorporated: 19 November 2018
Registered Office: 2 Ellis Lane, Frodsham, Cheshire, WA6 7HX
Major Shareholder: Christopher Mark Farrell
Officers: Christopher Mark Farrell [1974] Director; Sarah Jane Lewis [1980] Director

Silenus Limited
Incorporated: 22 March 2017
Registered Office: 47 Walkern Road, Stevenage, Herts, SG1 3RA
Shareholders: Derya Demirci de la Fuente; Loreto Capital Limited; Resultem
Officers: Derya Demirci de La Fuente [1986] Director/Sales Manager [Spanish]; Jean-Pierre Gintrac [1972] Director/Company Manager [French]; Jorge Gomez [1976] Business Director [Spanish]

Silly Point Wines Limited
Incorporated: 4 July 2012 Employees: 1
Net Worth Deficit: £36,126 Total Assets: £52,790
Registered Office: 21 Bedford Square, London, WC1B 3HH
Major Shareholder: Indira Thambiah
Officers: Indira Thambiah [1968] Director

Silver Fox Wines Ltd
Incorporated: 24 October 2017
Registered Office: 15 Keats Way, Cottam, Preston, Lancs, PR4 0NL
Officers: Kevin Thomas [1959] Director/Owner of Silver Fox Wines; Lesley Thomas [1959] Director/Owner of Silver Fox Wines

Silver Rocket Brewing Ltd
Incorporated: 17 January 2018
Registered Office: 6 Meadows, Hassocks, W Sussex, BN6 8EH
Shareholders: Matthew Christopher McGuire; Ben McCully
Officers: Ben McCully [1976] Director; Matthew Christopher McGuire [1974] Director and Company Secretary

Silverlite Cash & Carry Ltd
Incorporated: 27 October 2015 Employees: 1
Net Worth Deficit: £72,043 Total Assets: £99,471
Registered Office: 4 Sextant Park, Neptune Close, Medway City Estate, Rochester, Kent, ME2 4LU
Shareholders: Suganja Kartheepan; Kartheepan Parameswaran
Officers: Kartheepan Parameswaran [1985] Director/Businessman [Sri Lankan]

Silvertip Imports Limited
Incorporated: 1 November 2017
Registered Office: 17 The Drummonds, Epping, Essex, CM16 4PJ
Officers: Paul D Grundy, Secretary; Paul Donald Grundy [1983] Director

Simavin Limited
Incorporated: 22 May 2013 Employees: 1
Net Worth Deficit: £45,374 Total Assets: £31,816
Registered Office: 17 Burleigh Street, Cambridge, CB1 1DG
Major Shareholder: Alessandro Signorelli
Officers: Alessandro Signorelli [1982] Director/Sales and Marketing [Italian]

Simply 1st Wine Company Limited
Incorporated: 12 August 1998
Net Worth: £4,153 *Total Assets:* £137,412
Registered Office: Rutland House, 148 Edmund Street, Birmingham, B3 2FD
Shareholder: Alan Clift
Officers: Alan Clift, Secretary; John Henry Barnes [1939] Director/Importer; Alan Clift [1957] Director Secretary; Jeremy Frank Doyle [1965] Director/Computer Engineer

Simply Beers Limited
Incorporated: 8 July 2011
Net Worth Deficit: £5,845 *Total Assets:* £27,084
Registered Office: Harpal House, 14 Holyhead Road, Handsworth, Birmingham, B21 0LT
Shareholder: Kulwinder Singh
Officers: Krishna Kaur, Secretary; Kulwinder Singh [1963] Director

Simply Cask Ltd
Incorporated: 18 July 1996
Net Worth: £2,915 *Total Assets:* £108,975
Registered Office: 5 Peartree Road, Boon Hill, Bignall End, Stoke on Trent, Staffs, ST7 8NH
Major Shareholder: Phillip George Grocott
Officers: Generald Paul Snape, Secretary; Philip George Grocott [1953] Director

Simply Drinks Distribution Limited
Incorporated: 18 October 2018
Registered Office: 1st Floor, Global House, 303 Ballards Lane, London, N12 8NP
Shareholders: Andrew Bradley Seton Cotterill; Isabella Antollini
Officers: Isabella Antollini [1994] Director [Italian]; Andrew Bradley Seton Cotterill [1995] Director

Simply Spirits Limited
Incorporated: 3 February 2011
Registered Office: 48-52 Penny Lane, Liverpool, L18 1DG
Major Shareholder: Rakesh Ishwar Daryanani
Officers: Rakesh Ishwar Daryanani [1982] Director/Publican

Simpsons Wine Imports Limited
Incorporated: 12 February 2002 *Employees:* 2
Previous: Serenity Wines Limited
Net Worth Deficit: £65,211 *Total Assets:* £11,098
Registered Office: Princes Exchange, 1 Earl Grey Street, Edinburgh, EH3 9EE
Officers: Ruth Elizabeth Simpson, Secretary; Charles William Simpson [1969] Director; Ruth Elizabeth Simpson [1971] Director

Sin Shots (U.K.) Ltd.
Incorporated: 3 February 2006
Registered Office: 28 Rosslyn Hill, Hampstead, London, NW3 1NH
Major Shareholder: Surinderjit Sidhu
Officers: Surinderjit Sidhu [1971] Director/Business Owner

George Sinclair & Sons Limited
Incorporated: 31 December 1925 *Employees:* 2
Net Worth Deficit: £5,951 *Total Assets:* £28,960
Registered Office: The Old Post Office, 63 Saville Street, North Shields, Tyne & Wear, NE30 1AY
Officers: Alistair Robert Fraser Sinclair, Secretary; Alistair Robert Fraser Sinclair [1937] Director; Edith May Sinclair [1942] Director

Sindherfoods Limited
Incorporated: 5 December 2011
Net Worth: £19,255 *Total Assets:* £81,374
Registered Office: 46 High Street, Merthyr Tydfil, Mid Glamorgan, CF47 8DE
Major Shareholder: Daljit Singh
Officers: Daljit Singh [1964] Director/Self Employed

The Single Cask Ltd
Incorporated: 9 August 2016
Net Worth Deficit: £36,978 *Total Assets:* £238,030
Registered Office: 21 Verdant House, Levett Square, Richmond, Surrey, TW9 4FE
Shareholder: Benjamin Curtis
Officers: Benjamin Curtis [1974] Director

Single Malts Limited
Incorporated: 15 March 2005
Net Worth Deficit: £71,033 *Total Assets:* £49,701
Registered Office: 28 Albyn Place, Aberdeen, AB10 1YL
Major Shareholder: Euan Coutts Shand
Officers: Euan Coutts Shand [1956] Director

Singolo Vino Limited
Incorporated: 23 August 2018
Registered Office: 7a Station Parade, London Road, Sunningdale, Ascot, Berks, SL5 0EP
Officers: Kevin Brian Edward Dougall [1958] Director; William Lewis [1955] Director [Canadian]

Sinners Gin Ltd
Incorporated: 23 February 2018
Registered Office: Unit A, Thornes Lane, Wakefield, W Yorks, WF1 5RW
Shareholders: Alexander George Oates; Thomas Richard Marsden
Officers: Thomas Richard Marsden [1994] Director; Alexander George Oates [1993] Director

Sip Sip Wine Limited
Incorporated: 10 November 2017
Registered Office: 76 Florence Road, London, N4 4DP
Major Shareholder: Amanda Jane Sefton
Officers: Amanda Jane Sefton [1972] Director

Sipping Liquor Ltd
Incorporated: 24 April 2017 *Employees:* 1
Net Worth Deficit: £16,208 *Total Assets:* £167
Registered Office: 5 Luke Street, London, EC2A 4PX
Major Shareholder: Andrew John Rummer
Officers: Andrew John Rummer [1981] Director

Sips 'n' Nibbles Ltd
Incorporated: 14 January 2019
Registered Office: The Crown, 1 Wood Road, Codsall, Wolverhampton, W Midlands, WV8 1DB
Major Shareholder: Rachel Jane Mulkeen
Officers: Rachel Jane Mulkeen [1972] Director

Siris Trading Ltd
Incorporated: 12 October 2017
Registered Office: 616D Green Lane, Ilford, Essex, IG3 9SE
Major Shareholder: Retnakumar Govindaraju
Officers: Retnakumar Govindaraju [1964] Director/Businessman

Sisserou Marketing Limited
Incorporated: 17 December 2002
Net Worth Deficit: £93,581 *Total Assets:* £1,548
Registered Office: 120 College Road, Norwich, NR2 3JB
Major Shareholder: Julia Antonia La Ronde
Officers: Julia Antonia La Ronde [1967] Director

Six Rivers Limited
Incorporated: 9 June 2014
Net Worth Deficit: £44,739 *Total Assets:* £120,166
Registered Office: 6th Floor, Amp House, Dingwall Road, Croydon, Surrey, CR0 2LX
Major Shareholder: Kultar Singh Bhatoa
Officers: Kultar Singh Bhatoa [1963] Director

Sixpenny Wines Limited
Incorporated: 29 August 2013 *Employees:* 2
Net Worth: £152,977 *Total Assets:* £198,939
Registered Office: 13 Hurlingham Studios, Ranelagh Gardens, London, SW6 3PA
Officers: Caroline Cordelia Ridley Brocklehurst [1959] Director/Horse Breeder and Farmer

SJ Wines Ltd
Incorporated: 28 June 2016
Net Worth Deficit: £11,388 *Total Assets:* £12,349
Registered Office: 63 Bartholomew Street, Newbury, Berks, RG14 7BE
Major Shareholder: Stephen John Miles
Officers: Jacqueline May Miles, Secretary; Stephen John Miles [1982] Director

SJO Supplies Limited
Incorporated: 11 November 2011 *Employees:* 4
Net Worth Deficit: £22,232 *Total Assets:* £112,970
Registered Office: Lion House, 72 Chapel Street, Netherton, W Midlands, DY2 9PN
Major Shareholder: Stanley John Owen
Officers: Stanley John Owen [1944] Director

SJZP Limited
Incorporated: 16 April 2013
Net Worth Deficit: £19,243 *Total Assets:* £90,751
Registered Office: 10 Corporation Road, Newport, NP19 0AR
Shareholders: Anthony Charles Parsons; Lesley Ann Parsons
Officers: Anthony Charles Parsons [1972] Director/Business Innovation Manager; Lesley Ann Parsons [1969] Director/Business Manager

SK Trading (N.I.) Ltd
Incorporated: 3 March 2017
Net Worth: £162,159 *Total Assets:* £163,359
Registered Office: 62 Victoria Gate, Londonderry, BT47 2TP
Major Shareholder: James Deehan
Officers: James Deehan [1977] Director [Irish]

Skinny Booze Limited
Incorporated: 25 October 2012 *Employees:* 1
Net Worth Deficit: £45,698 *Total Assets:* £18,846
Registered Office: 102 Brookfield Road, Cheadle, Cheshire, SK8 1EX
Major Shareholder: Thomas Neale Bell
Officers: Stephen Malcolm Bell, Secretary; Thomas Neale Bell [1989] Managing Director

Skull X Ltd
Incorporated: 5 May 2017
Net Worth: £710 *Total Assets:* £35,710
Registered Office: 20 Vale Industrial Estate, Southern Road, Aylesbury, Bucks, HP19 9EW
Major Shareholder: Aman Chopra
Officers: Aman Chopra, Secretary; Aman Chopra [1973] Director

Sky Wines Limited
Incorporated: 9 May 2011
Registered Office: Ashby Lodge, Ashby Lane, Bitteswell, Lutterworth, Leics, LE17 4LW
Major Shareholder: Gary Michael Nimmo
Officers: Gary Michael Nimmo [1968] Director/Consultant; Lucinda Vivienne Nimmo [1970] Director/Manager; Duncan Piers Southwell-Sander [1968] Director/Consultant

Sky9 Ltd
Incorporated: 15 March 2018
Registered Office: 85a Farley Hill, Luton, Beds, LU1 5EG
Major Shareholder: Rimvydas Stankevicius
Officers: Rimvydas Stankevicius [1982] Director [Lithuanian]

Skyden Spirits Ltd
Incorporated: 21 June 2018
Registered Office: 8 Wadham Avenue, London, E17 4HT
Major Shareholder: Hung Duy Nguyen
Officers: Hung Duy Nguyen [1982] Director

Skyfall Distribution Limited
Incorporated: 10 April 2016
Net Worth Deficit: £17,643 *Total Assets:* £15,617
Registered Office: Ground Floor, Belmont Place, Belmont Road, Maidenhead, Berks, SL6 6TB
Shareholders: Christopher John Arbery; David Stephen Arbery
Officers: Christopher John Arbery [1976] Director; David Stephen Arbery [1980] Director/Consultant

Sladecs247 Ltd
Incorporated: 27 November 2018
Registered Office: 11 Hallam Close, Westminster House, Watford, Herts, WD24 4RJ
Major Shareholder: Rizwan Sheikh
Officers: Rizwan Sheikh, Secretary; Rizwan Sheikh [1983] Director [Kenyan]

Slainte Mhath Ltd
Incorporated: 9 November 2018
Registered Office: 2-20 Western Harbour Breakwater, Edinburgh, EH6 6PA
Major Shareholder: Josephine Elizabeth Kinsley
Officers: Josephine Elizabeth Kinsley [1971] Director/Manager

Slanj Whisky Ltd
Incorporated: 6 August 2018
Registered Office: Slanj, 82 St Vincent Street, Glasgow, G2 5UB
Shareholders: Brian Dundas Halley; Craig Halley
Officers: Brian Dundas Halley [1969] Director/Retailer; Craig Halley [1972] Director/Retailer

Slightly Squiffy Limited
Incorporated: 13 August 2018
Registered Office: 35 Waterside, East Grinstead, W Sussex, RH19 3XS
Officers: Ian Robert Goldie [1956] Director [Australian]; Caroline Elizabeth Taylor [1962] Director

UK Wholesalers of Beers, Wines and Spirits   dellam

Slim Gin Ltd
Incorporated: 15 January 2019
Registered Office: Beech House, The Meadows, Ingrave, Brentwood, Essex, CM13 3RL
Major Shareholder: Amanda Joy Ladlow
Officers: Amanda Joy Ladlow [1979] Director and Company Secretary

Sloane Home Ltd
Incorporated: 14 November 2013
Net Worth Deficit: £19,094 Total Assets: £31,948
Registered Office: The Rectory, Llandow, Cowbridge, Vale of Glamorgan, CF71 7NT
Major Shareholder: Leanne Peta Johns
Officers: Leanne Peta Johns [1971] Director

Slopemeister Brewing Company Limited
Incorporated: 24 August 2018
Registered Office: Oak House, Airth Castle Estate, Airth, Falkirk, FK2 8JF
Shareholders: Thomas Hendrie Sloper; Karen McLean
Officers: Karen McLean [1980] Marketing Director; Thomas Hendrie Sloper [1977] Managing Director

Sloshed Puppy Ltd
Incorporated: 19 September 2018
Registered Office: 36 The Normans, Slough, Berks, SL2 5TY
Major Shareholder: Marion Williams
Officers: Marion Williams [1944] Managing Director

Slurp Wine Company Limited
Incorporated: 13 April 2017 Employees: 16
Net Worth: £517,772 Total Assets: £935,089
Registered Office: 2 Riverside, Tramway Road, Banbury, Oxon, OX16 5TU
Shareholders: Copestick Murray Limited; Hugh Taylor; Richard Nicholas Jones
Officers: Stuart Andrew Bond [1977] Commercial Director; Robin Peto Copestick [1963] Managing Director; Richard Nicholas Jones [1957] Director/Wine Merchant; James Patrick Alexander Keef [1965] Director; Thilo Rieser [1972] Director [German]; Hugh Taylor [1965] Director

Small Batch Bottlers Scotland Limited
Incorporated: 17 January 2014
Registered Office: 46 New Road, Milnathort, Kinross, KY13 9XT
Major Shareholder: George Preston Thomson
Officers: George Preston Thomson [1954] Director

Small Beer Limited
Incorporated: 16 August 1990 Employees: 49
Net Worth: £1,041,051 Total Assets: £2,453,937
Registered Office: Unit 1 Churchill Business Park, Sleaford Road, Bracebridge Heath, Lincoln, LN4 2FF
Shareholders: Judith Anne Eastwood; Anthony William Eastwood
Officers: Anthony William Eastwood, Secretary; Anthony William Eastwood [1948] Director/Wholesaler; Judith Anne Eastwood [1949] Director/Wholesaler; Karen Louise Eastwood [1976] Director; Robert William Eastwood [1976] Commercial Director

Smart Save Distribution Limited
Incorporated: 21 October 2015
Net Worth Deficit: £8,742 Total Assets: £63,909
Registered Office: 1110 Elliott Court, Coventry Business Park, Herald Avenue, Coventry, Warwicks, CV5 6UB
Major Shareholder: Satvinder Singh
Officers: Satvinder Singh [1995] Director

Smartprice (NE) Ltd
Incorporated: 3 November 2010
Net Worth Deficit: £1,195,051 Total Assets: £286,070
Registered Office: 1 Willowdene, Washington, Tyne & Wear, NE37 1BF
Major Shareholder: Daljit Singh
Officers: Daljit Singh [1970] Director

Smashing Wines Limited
Incorporated: 18 January 2016 Employees: 3
Net Worth Deficit: £100,728 Total Assets: £52,454
Registered Office: 12 Quay Street, Woodbridge, Suffolk, IP12 1BX
Shareholders: Rebecca Luise Murland; Clement Florent Gerald Emmanuel Honore Sigaut
Officers: Rebecca Luise Murland [1983] Director; Clement Sigaut [1985] Director [French]

SMCA Enterprises Ltd.
Incorporated: 4 September 2015 Employees: 3
Net Worth: £4,538 Total Assets: £157,107
Registered Office: 123 Wellington Road South, Stockport, Cheshire, SK1 3TH
Officers: Sammy-Jo Ainsworth [1989] Director; Timothy Stewart Ainsworth [1981] Director

Smiley Rhyme Limited
Incorporated: 19 January 2012
Net Worth Deficit: £136,890 Total Assets: £65,126
Registered Office: 3rd Floor, 9 St Clare Street, London, EC3N 1LQ
Major Shareholder: Xiaoyun She
Officers: Beibei Tang [1961] Director [Chinese]

Smith & Harris Enterprises Ltd.
Incorporated: 28 September 2018
Registered Office: 11 Primrose Place, Worthing, W Sussex, BN13 3FQ
Shareholders: Mathew Smith; Josh Alan Micheal Paul Harris
Officers: Beth Kelly, Secretary; Josh Alan Micheal Paul Harris [1997] Director; Mathew David Stanley Smith [1991] Director

Smith & Humpston Ltd
Incorporated: 31 October 2018
Registered Office: 25 Melliss Avenue, Richmond, Surrey, TW9 4BQ
Major Shareholder: Benjamin Smith
Officers: Benjamin Smith [1994] Director/Marketing Consultant

Laurence Smith & Son (Edinburgh) Limited
Incorporated: 31 January 1956 Employees: 6
Net Worth: £758,241 Total Assets: £887,021
Registered Office: 60 Constitution Street, Leith, Edinburgh, EH6 6RR
Major Shareholder: Laurence Rognvald Smith
Officers: Colin Eric Christison, Secretary; Colin Eric Christison [1955] Director/Wine Merchant; Duncan Ross Smith [1961] Director; Laurence Rognvald Smith [1924] Director/Wine Merchant

Russell Smith F & B Limited
Incorporated: 15 November 2017
Registered Office: Lake House, Market Hill, Royston, Herts, SG8 9JN
Major Shareholder: Edward Nicholas Russell Smith
Officers: Robert Giles Russell Smith, Secretary; Edward Nicholas Russell Smith [1981] Director

Smouse & Marchand Limited
Incorporated: 8 May 2014 *Employees:* 3
Net Worth: £148,244 *Total Assets:* £646,991
Registered Office: 41 Cornmarket Street, Oxford, OX1 3HA
Shareholders: Rebecca Louise Kelley; Richard Paul Kelley
Officers: Rebecca Louise Kelley [1960] Director; Richard Paul Kelley [1961] Director

SmsZee Limited
Incorporated: 7 August 2018
Registered Office: 57 Cornwall Street, Grangetown, Cardiff, CF11 6PP
Officers: Waheeda Tasleem Sattar, Secretary; Abdul Sattar [1970] Director; Sahar Sattar [1988] Director; Sana Sattar [1996] Director; Waheeda Tasleem Sattar [1974] Director

The Snickering Pig Drinks Co Limited
Incorporated: 6 March 2018
Registered Office: Summerhall Distillery, 1 Summerhall, Edinburgh, EH9 1PL
Parent: Summerhall Distillery Limited
Officers: Matthew David Malcolm Gammell [1975] Director; Marcus George Pickering [1974] Director

Snobby's Ltd
Incorporated: 21 June 2018
Registered Office: 64 Sydenham Road, Cotham, Bristol, BS6 5SJ
Major Shareholder: Nicholas Alexander Bethell
Officers: Nicholas Alexander Bethell [1990] Director

Snow Beer UK Ltd
Incorporated: 9 April 2018
Registered Office: 10 Derbyshire Drive, Castle Donnington, Derbys, DE74 2EP
Major Shareholder: He Cui
Officers: HE Cui [1984] Director

Snow Leopard Vodka Limited
Incorporated: 31 October 2005
Net Worth Deficit: £1,375,791 *Total Assets:* £426,693
Registered Office: One Fleet Place, London, EC4M 7WS
Parent: The Edrington Group Limited
Officers: Gemma May Robson, Secretary; Paul Andrew Hyde [1972] Director/Accountant; Stephen Roger Sparrow [1970] Director/Businessman

Snowy Taverns Ltd
Incorporated: 16 May 2018
Registered Office: 27 North Gate Street, Chester, CH1 2HA
Major Shareholder: Paul Frost
Officers: Paul Frost [1985] New Director

SO & T Consulting Limited
Incorporated: 3 May 2017
Net Worth Deficit: £1,350 *Total Assets:* £8,099
Registered Office: 9 Aland Gardens, Broughton Astley, Leicester, LE9 6NE
Major Shareholder: Matthew James Swinfen
Officers: Matthew James Swinfen [1967] Director

Soar Valley Bar Supplies Ltd
Incorporated: 1 May 2007 *Employees:* 2
Net Worth: £32,761 *Total Assets:* £117,846
Registered Office: 78 Loughborough Road, Quorn, Loughborough, Leics, LE12 8DX
Major Shareholder: Michael Lemon
Officers: Jill Lemon, Secretary; Michael William Lemon [1956] Director

Sober Limited
Incorporated: 14 January 2019
Registered Office: 12 Medway Close, Croydon, Surrey, CR0 7YG
Major Shareholder: Moesha Mansa Boateng-Dampte
Officers: Moesha Mansa Boateng-Dampte [1998] Director/Student

The Society of Vintners Limited
Incorporated: 18 October 1974 *Employees:* 2
Net Worth: £869,609 *Total Assets:* £2,089,065
Registered Office: Cawley Place, 15 Cawley Road, Chichester, W Sussex, PO19 1UZ
Officers: John Lawrence St Pier Mansfield, Secretary; Martin John Barette [1961] Director/Wine Importer; Jessie Pearl Glover [1962] Director/Wine Merchant; April Deliah Marks [1967] Director/Wine Merchant; Lawrence Anthony Page [1936] Director/Wine Merchant; James Columba Rowan [1959] Director; Paul Thomas Tate-Smith [1962] Managing Director; Andrew Paul Wild [1962] Director/Wine Merchant

Sofibel Ltd
Incorporated: 11 December 2012
Net Worth Deficit: £1,620 *Total Assets:* £5,870
Registered Office: 65 Brookdene Avenue, Bushey, Herts, WD19 4LG
Major Shareholder: Chirag Jeetendra Patel
Officers: Chirag Jeetendra Patel [1978] Director

Soho Wine Supply Limited (The)
Incorporated: 24 January 1945 *Employees:* 9
Net Worth: £846,116 *Total Assets:* £1,119,884
Registered Office: 18 Percy Street, London, W1T 1DX
Shareholder: Klitos Sotiri
Officers: Panayiotis Sotiri, Secretary; Klitos Sotiri [1937] Director/Wine Merchant; Kyriacos Sotiri [1965] Director/Wine Merchant; Panayiotis Sotiri [1963] Director/Wine Merchant

Sol Regem Ltd.
Incorporated: 5 June 2017
Registered Office: Apollo Business Village, Heol Persondy, Pen-Y-Bond Ar Ogwr, Aberkenfig, Bridgend, Mid Glamorgan, CF32 9TF
Major Shareholder: Andrea Belsole
Officers: Andrea Belsole [1990] Director [Italian]

Solaris Wines Ltd
Incorporated: 1 December 2017
Registered Office: First Floor, CQL House, Alington Road, Little Barford, St Neots, Cambs, PE19 6YH
Major Shareholder: Andrew George Walker
Officers: Andrew George Walker [1963] Director

Solent Off-License Ltd
Incorporated: 23 April 2018
Registered Office: 43a Leigh Road, Unit 1 Withy Park, Withy Meadows, Dutton Lane, Eastleigh, Hants, SO50 6AB
Major Shareholder: Seref Tut
Officers: Seref Tut [1964] Director/Sales Manager

Solitude Wines Limited
Incorporated: 4 December 2015
Registered Office: BCL House, 2 Pavilion Business Park, Royds Hall Road, Leeds, LS12 6AJ
Major Shareholder: Phillip Ball
Officers: Phillip Ball [1958] Director

Solow Ltd
Incorporated: 31 May 2018
Registered Office: Flat 2, St James Court, Wricklemarsh Road, London, SE3 0NE
Shareholders: Simon James Liddle; Vanessa Lee
Officers: John Stewart Liddle, Secretary; Vanessa Lee [1981] Director; Simon James Liddle [1974] Managing Director

Soltano Wines Ltd
Incorporated: 17 August 2016
Registered Office: 5 Chigwell Road, London, E18 1LR
Officers: Daljit Singh [1982] Director

Solway Spirits Ltd
Incorporated: 4 May 2018
Registered Office: 1 Railway Cottage, Cummertrees, Annan, Dumfries & Galloway, DG12 5QG
Major Shareholder: Andrew Emmerson
Officers: Kathryn Edith Rimmer, Secretary; Andrew Emmerson [1968] Director/Brewer and Distiller

Somborne Valley Vineyard Limited
Incorporated: 23 March 2001
Net Worth Deficit: £106,161 *Total Assets:* £125,200
Registered Office: Hoplands Estate, Kings Somborne, Stockbridge, Hants, SO20 6QH
Shareholders: Nigel Wolsenholme; Jacqueline Wolsenholme
Officers: Kenneth John Stratton, Secretary/Accountant; Vicki Alison Cook [1964] Director/Personal Assistant; Jacqueline Wolstenholme [1960] Director/Administrator; Nigel Timothy Wolstenholme [1956] Director/Surveyor

Somerset Craft Distillery Ltd
Incorporated: 9 October 2018
Registered Office: Barton Lower Farm, Gosling Street, Barton St David, Somerset, TA11 6GS
Shareholders: Barry Davies; Mandy Davies
Officers: Barry Davies [1956] Director; Mandy Davies [1959] Director

Somm in the Must Ltd
Incorporated: 5 December 2017
Registered Office: Wework, 115 Mare Street, London, E8 4RU
Shareholders: Nicolas Pierron; Pierrick Gorrichon
Officers: Pierrick Gorrichon [1993] Director/Assistant Head Sommelier [French]; Nicolas Pierron [1982] Director/Head Sommelier [French]

Sommeliers Choice Limited
Incorporated: 12 October 1999
Net Worth: £506,683 *Total Assets:* £949,527
Registered Office: 79 Grange Road, Crofton, Kent, BR6 8EB
Shareholders: Timothy Richard McLaughlin-Green; Alison Mary McLaughlin-Green
Officers: Alison Mary McLaughlin-Green, Secretary; Alison Mary McLaughlin-Green [1963] Director/Communications Manager; Timothy Richard McLaughlin-Green [1965] Director

Sonvino Ltd.
Incorporated: 15 June 2015
Net Worth: £741 *Total Assets:* £741
Registered Office: B805, 60 Holland Street, London, SE1 9JF
Major Shareholder: Serhat Narsap
Officers: Serhat Narsap [1978] Director/Wholesaler

Sophie's Choice Limited
Incorporated: 27 June 2007
Registered Office: Camburgh House, 27 New Dover Road, Canterbury, Kent, CT1 3DN
Officers: Sophie Marie Martine Holzberg [1958] Director/Wine [French]

Sopwell Gin Company Limited
Incorporated: 25 September 2017
Registered Office: Flat 2, 14 Prospect Road, St Albans, Herts, AL1 2AX
Shareholders: Des Slatter; Abby Hughes
Officers: Abby Hughes [1977] Director; Des Slatter [1975] Director

SOS Whisky Limited
Incorporated: 4 December 2018
Registered Office: 6 Logie Mill, Edinburgh, EH4 4HG
Major Shareholder: Andrew George Campbell Skene
Officers: Rini Marayana, Secretary; Rini Marayana [1979] Director [Indonesian]

Sotus Limited
Incorporated: 16 April 2018
Registered Office: 61 Norton Road, Reading, Berks, RG1 3QH
Shareholders: Hanh Van Le; Thi Hong Duyen Nguyen
Officers: Hanh Van Le [1988] Director/RVQ/NVQ Assessor; Thi Hong Duyen Nguyen [1997] Director/Teacher & RVQ/NVQ Assessor [Vietnamese]

Soul Spirits Ltd
Incorporated: 26 March 2014 *Employees:* 2
Net Worth Deficit: £2,215 *Total Assets:* £38,601
Registered Office: The Old Carriage Works, Moresk Road, Truro, Cornwall, TR1 1DG
Shareholders: Rubina Tyler-Street; William Gannel Tyler-Street
Officers: Rubina Tyler-Street [1967] Director; William Gannel Tyler-Street [1965] Director/Entrepreneur

Source 360 Ltd
Incorporated: 16 May 2018
Registered Office: 55 Tring Road, Wilstone, Tring, Herts, HP23 4PE
Shareholders: James Francis McKenzie Brown; Nicholas John Benson
Officers: Nicholas John Benson [1965] Commercial Director; James Francis McKenzie Brown [1967] Managing Director

The Sourceror Ltd
Incorporated: 16 October 2018
Registered Office: Unit G187 Cherwell Business Village, Southam Road, Banbury, Oxon, OX16 2SP
Shareholders: Satnam Singh Darar; Benedick Fowler
Officers: Satnam Singh Darar [1977] Director; Benedick Fowler [1968] Director

JG Sousa Limited
Incorporated: 11 April 2018
Registered Office: Unit 3 Whitehills Drive, Whitehills Business Park, Blackpool, Lancs, FY4 5LW
Major Shareholder: Jacob Andrew Grimshaw
Officers: Jacob Andrew Grimshaw [1996] Director

South Downs Real Estate Limited
Incorporated: 10 February 2005
Net Worth: £12,089,356 *Total Assets:* £62,515,272
Registered Office: Nyetimber Vineyard, Gay Street, West Chiltington, W Sussex, RH20 2HH
Parent: Nyetimber Wines Limited
Officers: Robert Andrew MacDonald Watson, Secretary; Eric Niels Heerema [1960] Director [Dutch]

South Eastern Beers & Minerals Limited
Incorporated: 23 December 1994 *Employees:* 6
Net Worth: £454,616 *Total Assets:* £916,374
Registered Office: The Beech Depot, Sheephurst Lane, Marden, Tonbridge, Kent, TN12 9NU
Major Shareholder: Adrian Gerald Simmons
Officers: Edmund William John Simmons, Secretary; Trevor Royston Simmons, Secretary; Adrian Generald Simmons [1951] Director

South WLC Limited
Incorporated: 9 July 1993
Net Worth Deficit: £73,307
Registered Office: Wheat Glade House, Woods Lane, Cliddesden, Basingstoke, Hants, RG25 2JG
Major Shareholder: Christopher Henry Williams
Officers: Christopher Henry Williams [1972] Director

Southbourne Brewing Limited
Incorporated: 15 August 2013
Net Worth: £208,576 *Total Assets:* £219,633
Registered Office: 40 Clingan Road, Bournemouth, BH6 5PZ
Shareholders: Jennifer Alison Tingay; Sheldon Ashley Young
Officers: George William Arthur West, Secretary; Paul Richard Ryder [1962] New Business Director; Jennifer Alison Tingay [1976] Director/Brewer; George William Arthur West [1991] Director/Teacher; Sheldon Ashley Young [1969] Director/Architectural Technologist

Southbrew Company Ltd
Incorporated: 23 July 2018
Registered Office: 13 Penlands Way, Steyning, W Sussex, BN44 3PN
Shareholders: Paul Michael Robertson; Christopher Stephen Bowen
Officers: Christopher Stephen Bowen [1976] Director/Platform Product Manager; Paul Michael Robertson [1977] Director/Management Accountant

Southern England Wines (UK) Ltd
Incorporated: 22 March 2016 *Employees:* 3
Net Worth: £2,593,435 *Total Assets:* £2,754,968
Registered Office: Amelia House, Crescent Road, Worthing, W Sussex, BN11 1QR
Shareholder: John Richard Ball
Officers: John Richard Ball [1962] Director; Michael Norman Smith [1953] Director

Southern Wine Roads Limited
Incorporated: 28 July 2014
Net Worth Deficit: £70,138 *Total Assets:* £148,809
Registered Office: 23 Ruskin Drive, Orpington, Kent, BR6 9RP
Major Shareholder: Maria Moutsou
Officers: Dr. Maria Moutsou [1969] Director/Medical Doctor

Southern Wines Limited
Incorporated: 1 December 2009 *Employees:* 2
Previous: St. Aubyn Leschallas Wines Limited
Net Worth Deficit: £116,468 *Total Assets:* £328,975
Registered Office: Dane John Works, Gordon Road, Canterbury, Kent, CT1 3PP
Shareholders: Rupert St Aubyn; Armajaro Holdings Limited
Officers: Anthony Simon Leschallas [1955] Director; Rupert St. Aubyn [1963] Director; Anthony Richard Bangor Ward [1960] Director/Trader

Southover Drinks Limited
Incorporated: 10 February 2012 *Employees:* 1
Net Worth Deficit: £478,472 *Total Assets:* £17,807
Registered Office: Higher Herringston Farmhouse, Herringston, Dorchester, DT2 9PU
Shareholders: Joanna Elizabeth Wallington; Jonathan Christopher Gerrard Wallington
Officers: Joanna Wallington, Secretary; Jonathan Christopher Gerrard Wallington [1962] Director

The Southsea Gin Company Ltd
Incorporated: 25 February 2019
Registered Office: 13 Craneswater Park, Southsea, Hants, PO4 0NX
Shareholders: Jonathan Richard Rawlinson; Katharine Jane Rawlinson
Officers: Jonathan Richard Rawlinson [1980] Director; Katharine Jane Rawlinson [1981] Director/Housewife

Southwell Trading Ltd
Incorporated: 29 November 2018
Registered Office: 31 Perry Hill, Catford, London, SE6 4LF
Major Shareholder: David Neil French
Officers: David Neil French [1985] Director

Southwick Court Fine Wines (2012) Ltd
Incorporated: 28 September 2012 *Employees:* 3
Net Worth: £56,506 *Total Assets:* £1,350,018
Registered Office: Harben House, Harben Parade, Finchley Road, London, NW3 6LH
Shareholder: George Dafydd Rhys
Officers: George Dafydd Rhys [1965] Director/Wine Dealer

SP (DPH) Exports Limited
Incorporated: 9 December 2013
Net Worth Deficit: £75,522 *Total Assets:* £239,841
Registered Office: 1-2 The Cloisters, Laughton Road, Ringmer, E Sussex, BN8 5SD
Major Shareholder: Diego Palacio Hernandez
Officers: Diego Palacio Hernandez [1952] Director [Spanish]

Spain Link Ltd
Incorporated: 12 January 2010
Net Worth Deficit: £1,281 *Total Assets:* £1,184
Registered Office: Stone House Farm, Cleestanton Lane, Bitterley, Ludlow, Salop, SY8 3HQ
Major Shareholder: Philip Hipkiss
Officers: Fiona Louise Harrison [1976] Director; Natalie Jane Walker [1974] Director

Spainorama Ltd
Incorporated: 4 October 2018
Registered Office: 20 Campden Green, Solihull, W Midlands, B92 8HG
Major Shareholder: Jose Ignacio Clavijo Barrio
Officers: Jose Ignacio Clavijo Barrio [1968] Commercial Director [Spanish]; Jose Ignacio Clavijo Tejero [1997] Director/Project Manager [Spanish]

Spalathos Ltd.
Incorporated: 13 March 2017
Net Worth Deficit: £1,559 *Total Assets:* £876
Registered Office: 22 Vert Court, Haldane Avenue, Haddington, E Lothian, EH41 3PX
Major Shareholder: Neven Crljenak
Officers: Neven Crljenak [1975] Director/Whole Trader [Croatian]

Spalco Ltd
Incorporated: 12 March 2016
Net Worth: £12,255 *Total Assets:* £103,979
Registered Office: Unit 7 Agecroft Enterprise Park, Shearer Way, Swinton, Manchester, M27 8WA
Shareholders: Pawel Andrzej Stegierski; Karolina Gladysz
Officers: Karolina Gladysz [1988] Director [Polish]; Pawel Andrzej Stegierski [1974] Director/Sales Manager [Polish]

Spar (UK) Limited
Incorporated: 4 August 1959 *Employees:* 74
Net Worth: £13,187 *Total Assets:* £24,605,934
Registered Office: Hygeia Building, 66-68 College Road, Harrow, Middlesex, HA1 1BE
Officers: Mark Steven Keeley [1962] Director/Retail; Christopher William Lewis [1968] Trading Director; Jacqueline Elizabeth MacKenzie [1967] Director/Chief Information Officer; Deborah Mary Robinson [1965] Director; Ian David Taylor [1965] Retail Director

Special Cases Limited
Incorporated: 5 March 2013 *Employees:* 1
Net Worth: £141,966 *Total Assets:* £229,264
Registered Office: 53 Ashfield Road, London, W3 7JF
Shareholder: Elise Brugues
Officers: Elise Brugues [1977] Director [French]

The Special Cider Company Limited
Incorporated: 29 September 2016 *Employees:* 4
Net Worth Deficit: £3,072 *Total Assets:* £79,727
Registered Office: Building 15, Stanmore Industrial Estate, Bridgnorth, Salop, WV15 5HP
Shareholders: Mark Richard Jackson; Julia Sian Jackson
Officers: Julia Sian Jackson [1976] Director; Mark Richard Jackson [1964] Director

Specialist Cellars Ltd
Incorporated: 28 October 2013 *Employees:* 4
Previous: The New Zealand Cellar Ltd
Net Worth Deficit: £25,320 *Total Assets:* £49,004
Registered Office: Grand Union House, 20 Kentish Town Road, Camden, London, NW1 9NX
Major Shareholder: Melanie Paula Brown
Officers: Melanie Paula Brown [1983] Director [New Zealander]

Speciality Brands Ltd
Incorporated: 3 July 2007 *Employees:* 11
Net Worth: £1,545,625 *Total Assets:* £3,195,152
Registered Office: Elixir House, Whitby Avenue, Park Royal, London, NW10 7SF
Shareholders: Rajbir Singh Sawhney; Sukhinder Singh Sawhney; Christopher Charles Victor Seale
Officers: Sukhinder Singh Sawhney, Secretary; Rajbir Singh Sawhney [1971] Director/Wines & Spirits Specialist; Sukhinder Singh Sawhney [1968] Director/Wines & Spirits Specialist; Chris Seale [1967] Director

Speciality Drinks Limited
Incorporated: 28 May 2002 *Employees:* 148
Net Worth: £33,773,780 *Total Assets:* £49,235,136
Registered Office: Elixir House, Whitby Avenue, Park Royal, London, NW10 7SF
Officers: Sukhinder Singh Sawhney, Secretary/Wines Spirits Specialist; Rajbir Singh Sawhney [1971] Director/Wines Spirits Specialist; Sukhinder Singh Sawhney [1968] Director/Wine Spirit Specialist

Spencers (Bromsgrove) Limited
Incorporated: 17 September 1999
Net Worth: £212,281 *Total Assets:* £1,087,337
Registered Office: 102 Tettenhall Road, Wolverhampton, W Midlands, WV6 0BW
Shareholders: Kerry Verbeet; Mark Francis King
Officers: Mark Francis King, Secretary; Stephen Paul Thompson [1957] Director

Speymalt Whisky Distributors Limited
Incorporated: 11 April 1962 *Employees:* 154
Net Worth: £38,177,164 *Total Assets:* £43,225,660
Registered Office: George House, Boroughbriggs Road, Elgin, Moray, IV30 1JY
Officers: Norman Ross, Secretary; James Andrew Bishop [1959] Director; Ian Michael Chapman [1974] Marketing Director; David Thomas King [1964] Sales Director; Ewen Cameron Mackintosh [1968] Director; Stephen Alexander Masson Rankin [1971] Director; Norman Ross [1974] Director/Chartered Accountant; Neil Edward Urquhart [1975] Director; Stuart David Urquhart [1981] Operations Director; Gillian Anne McGregor Watson [1964] Director

Speyside Bonding Company Limited
Incorporated: 20 September 1967
Registered Office: 197 Bath Street, Glasgow, G2 4HU
Parent: Speyside Distillers Company Limited
Officers: Yung Sheng Chang [1953] Director [Taiwanese]; Yu Hung Ho [1964] Director [Taiwanese]; John McDonough [1956] Director

Speyside Distillers Company Limited
Incorporated: 2 September 1999 *Employees:* 14
Net Worth: £3,719,146 *Total Assets:* £12,144,597
Registered Office: 197 Bath Street, Glasgow, G2 4HU
Parent: Hoe International Ltd
Officers: Yung Sheng Chang [1953] Director [Taiwanese]; Yu Hung Ho [1964] Director [Taiwanese]; John McDonough [1956] Director

Speyside Trading Company Limited
Incorporated: 12 April 2016
Net Worth Deficit: £14,351 *Total Assets:* £248,919
Registered Office: Regent Court, 70 West Regent Street, Glasgow, G2 2QZ
Shareholders: John McDonough; Joanna McDonough
Officers: Joanna McDonough [1967] Director; John McDonough [1956] Director

Spiced Wine Company Limited
Incorporated: 18 August 2010
Net Worth: £312,328 *Total Assets:* £355,702
Registered Office: 80 Elms Avenue, Littleover, Derby, DE23 6FD
Shareholders: Paul Humphries; Carol Anne Humphries
Officers: Carol Anne Humphries, Secretary; Carol Anne Humphries [1953] Director; Paul Humphries [1953] Director

Spirimix Limited
Incorporated: 20 February 2015
Net Worth Deficit: £27,867 *Total Assets:* £34,937
Registered Office: Unit 9 Forest Industrial Park, Forest Road, Ilford, Essex, IG6 3HL
Major Shareholder: Charmaine Louisa Hayzelden
Officers: Charmaine Louisa Hayzelden [1977] Director

The Spirit Beer Company Limited
Incorporated: 17 October 2016 Employees: 4
Net Worth: £105 Total Assets: £105
Registered Office: 8 Holyrood View, Sheffield, S10 4NG
Shareholders: Philip Craig Lee; Craig Butler; Christopher James Spencer
Officers: Craig Butler [1969] Director; Nik Andrew Entwistle [1977] Director; Philip Craig Lee [1970] Director; Christopher James Spencer [1974] Director

Spirit Cartel Limited
Incorporated: 6 April 1973
Registered Office: 10-12 Brewery Road, London, N7 9NH
Parent: Berkmann Wine Cellars Ltd
Officers: Rupert Anthony Berkmann [1979] Director

Spirit Generation Limited
Incorporated: 2 February 2018
Registered Office: 10 Queen Street Place, London, EC4R 1AG
Shareholders: New Generation Wines Limited; Peter David Brian McKinley
Officers: James Arthur Booth [1973] Director; Peter David Brian McKinley [1946] Director/Consultant

Spirit O' Clyde Drinks Company Ltd
Incorporated: 19 February 2019
Registered Office: 76 Dumbarton Road, Clydebank, Glasgow, G81 1UG
Shareholders: Caroline Ross; Simon Ross
Officers: Caroline Ross [1966] Director; Simon Ross [1966] Director

Spirit of Bermondsey Ltd
Incorporated: 18 January 2019
Registered Office: 52 Chaucer Road, London, SE24 0NU
Major Shareholder: Nicholas Dominic Bernard Johnson
Officers: Nicholas Dominic Bernard Johnson [1969] Managing Director

Spirit of Glasgow Ltd
Incorporated: 3 May 2016 Employees: 1
Net Worth Deficit: £6,754 Total Assets: £1,036
Registered Office: 272 Bath Street, Glasgow, G2 4JR
Major Shareholder: Christopher Joseph Ross Bradley
Officers: Christopher Joseph Ross Bradley [1988] Director/Vehicle Technician

Spirit Still Ltd
Incorporated: 8 December 2015
Registered Office: Park House Business Centre, South Street, Elgin, Moray, IV30 1JB
Major Shareholder: Markus Hunger
Officers: Markus Hunger [1982] Director/Manager [German]

Spirit Traders Ltd
Incorporated: 27 October 2015
Previous: Uni Students Limited
Net Worth: £2,000,001 Total Assets: £2,000,001
Registered Office: 3rd Floor, 86-90 Paul Street, London, EC2A 4NE
Major Shareholder: Balwant Singh
Officers: Balwant Singh, Secretary; Balwant Singh [1971] Director/Broker

Spirit Valley France Limited
Incorporated: 4 September 2017
Registered Office: 2a Swordfish Business Park, Swordfish Close, Higgins Lane, Burscough, Lancs, L40 8JW
Major Shareholder: Patrick Lenehan
Officers: Patrick Lenehan [1959] Director/Self Employed

Spirito Limited
Incorporated: 3 July 2018
Registered Office: Cambridge House, 16 High Street, Saffron Walden, Essex, CB10 1AX
Major Shareholder: Peter Thomas Godden
Officers: Peter Thomas Godden [1946] Director

The Spiritory Ltd
Incorporated: 17 April 2018
Registered Office: Crewkerne Farmhouse, Pitton Road, West Winterslow, Wilts, SP5 1SA
Shareholder: Mark Westmacott
Officers: Mark Westmacott [1969] Director

Spirits Development & Management Company (SDMC) Limited
Incorporated: 16 December 2013
Net Worth: £631,395 Total Assets: £3,439,762
Registered Office: Citypoint, 65 Haymarket Terrace, Edinburgh, EH12 5HD
Major Shareholder: Michel Picard
Officers: Michel Bernard Picard [1942] Director [French]

Spirits for Good CIC
Incorporated: 11 October 2016 Employees: 5
Net Worth Deficit: £9,791 Total Assets: £21,646
Registered Office: Summerhall Distillery, 1 Summerhall, Edinburgh, EH9 1PL
Officers: Matthew David Malcolm Gammell [1975] Director and Engineer; David Neill Moore [1970] Director; David Owen Mullen [1968] Executive Creative Director; Marcus George Pickering [1974] Director/Co-Founder

Spirits International Management Limited
Incorporated: 21 November 2013
Net Worth: £21,354 Total Assets: £32,605
Registered Office: 2 Prince Edward Mansions, Hereford Road, London, W2 4WB
Major Shareholder: Roger Barnes
Officers: Roger Paul Barnes [1962] Director; Mischa Nara Manderson Mills [1966] Director/Strategic Consultant [British/Jamaican]

Spirits Logistics Ltd
Incorporated: 28 March 2018
Registered Office: Suite 6, 5 Percy Street, Fitzrovia, London, W1T 1DG
Major Shareholder: Solomon Gvajaia
Officers: Solomon Gvajaia [1960] Director [Georgian]

Spirits of Borough Ltd
Incorporated: 5 February 2019
Registered Office: 20-22 Wenlock Road, London, N1 7GU
Major Shareholder: Arthur Guillaume Marie de Chalus
Officers: Arthur Guillaume Marie de Chalus [1980] Director [French]

Spitfire Heritage Distillers Limited
Incorporated: 14 March 2016 Employees: 2
Net Worth Deficit: £28,369 Total Assets: £67,961
Registered Office: Meadow View, Meadow Lane, Mawdesley, Ormskirk, Lancs, L40 2QA
Shareholders: Ian Hewitt; Sarah Vanessa Jane Hewitt
Officers: Ian Hewitt [1965] Director; Sarah Vanessa Jane Hewitt [1965] Director/Teacher

Splendid Corks Limited
Incorporated: 11 January 2013
Net Worth Deficit: £22,264 *Total Assets:* £1,743
Registered Office: Virginia House, 56 Warwick Road, Solihull, W Midlands, B92 7HX
Major Shareholder: Alan Clift
Officers: Alan Clift [1957] Director; Jeremy Frank Doyle [1965] Director

Spokesuk Ltd
Incorporated: 5 November 2018
Registered Office: 1 Gordon Way, Witney, Oxon, OX28 4EH
Shareholders: Martin Peter Smith; Jacob David Walcott; John William Elliott
Officers: John William Elliott [1992] Director/Design Manager; Martin Peter Smith [1995] Director/I.T & Systems Operator; Jacob David Walcott [1992] Director/Head of Operations

Sporting Benefits Limited
Incorporated: 29 September 1997
Net Worth: £9,328 *Total Assets:* £46,461
Registered Office: 98 Acre Lane, Cheadle Hulme, Cheadle, Cheshire, SK8 7PA
Major Shareholder: David Alexander James Connor
Officers: Robert Edward Martin, Secretary; David Alexander James Connor [1944] Director/Insurance Broker; Linda Gertrude Connor [1947] Director/Marketing; Robert Edward Martin [1950] Director/Consultant; Howard Arthur Middleton [1944] Director/Lending Consultant

Spot Wines Limited
Incorporated: 3 April 2014
Net Worth: £7,512 *Total Assets:* £51,408
Registered Office: 37 Chamberlain Street, Wells, Somerset, BA5 2PQ
Major Shareholder: Andrew Kinnersley
Officers: Andrew Kinnersley [1979] Director/Wine Merchant

Spowart Wines Limited
Incorporated: 25 September 2013
Net Worth Deficit: £38,607 *Total Assets:* £8,557
Registered Office: 3 Garfield Road, Ryde, Isle of Wight, PO33 2PS
Major Shareholder: Kathleen Ross Spowart
Officers: Kathleen Ross Spowart [1967] Director

SPP Wine Ltd
Incorporated: 21 March 2018
Registered Office: 27 Broadway Market, London, E8 4PH
Shareholders: Iwo Jacimowicz; Liam Bede Kelleher
Officers: Iwo Jacimowicz [1979] Director/Wine Maker [Australian/Polish]; Liam Bede Kelleher [1984] Managing Director [New Zealander]; James Daniel Noble [1982] Director/Programmer

Springbank Distillers Limited
Incorporated: 22 October 1964 *Employees:* 13
Net Worth: £3,985,820 *Total Assets:* £4,160,030
Registered Office: 9 Bolgam Street, Campbeltown, Argyll, PA28 6HZ
Parent: J & A Mitchell and Co Ltd
Officers: Stuart Alexander Campbell, Secretary; Lilian Cunningham Campbell [1931] Director; Neil Clapperton [1958] Director; Alan Campbell Murray [1962] Director/Shopkeeper; Mr George Christopher Redpath [1936] Director/Design & Printing Consultant

Square Wholesale Ltd
Incorporated: 3 December 2018
Registered Office: 965 Romford Road, London, E12 5JR
Major Shareholder: Mahmud Ur Rasul
Officers: Mahmud Ur Rasul [1968] Director [Spanish]

Square Wine Ltd
Incorporated: 19 December 2018
Registered Office: 37a Dancer Road, London, SW6 4DU
Shareholders: Sandra Marie Falque; Sylvain Jehan Marie Arthur Philippon
Officers: Sandra Marie Falque [1988] Director/Management Consultant [French]; Sylvain Jehan Marie Arthur Philippon [1988] Director/Banker [French]

Squarewalk Limited
Incorporated: 12 March 1985
Net Worth: £570,243 *Total Assets:* £829,701
Registered Office: Unit 14 Park Road Estate, Park Road, Timperley, Cheshire, WA14 5QH
Major Shareholder: May Haussels
Officers: May Haussels, Secretary; May Haussels [1949] Director/Secretary

Srihari Haran Ltd
Incorporated: 22 January 2018
Registered Office: 227 Humber Avenue, Coventry, Warwicks, CV1 2AQ
Officers: Srihari Haran Esayanoor Sridharan [1993] Director/Businessman [Indian]

SSG Service Ltd
Incorporated: 10 July 2018
Registered Office: 272 Bath Street, Glasgow, G2 4JR
Major Shareholder: Gulzar Hussain
Officers: Gulzar Hussain, Secretary; Gulzar Hussain [1977] Director [Italian]

SSL Leisure Limited
Incorporated: 15 February 2012 *Employees:* 3
Net Worth Deficit: £8,623 *Total Assets:* £96,946
Registered Office: 32-36 Chorley New Road, Bolton, Lancs, BL1 4AP
Major Shareholder: James Greaves
Officers: James Greaves [1980] Director

St Davids Gin Limited
Incorporated: 15 January 2019
Registered Office: Flat 13-14, Cross Square, St Davids, Haverfordwest, Pembrokeshire, SA62 6SE
Major Shareholder: Neil Walsh
Officers: Neil Walsh [1975] Director; Ruth Louise Walsh [1982] Director and Company Secretary

St George's Beer Co. of St Austell Ltd
Incorporated: 15 February 2018
Registered Office: 34 Brook Place, Lea, Preston, Lancs, PR2 1TE
Major Shareholder: Victor Penrith
Officers: Victor Penrith [1946] Director

The St Ives Grog Company Limited
Incorporated: 27 February 2018
Registered Office: 16a Penwith Road, St Ives, Cornwall, TR26 2HX
Officers: Stuart Lawton [1978] Director/Manager

St James's Fine Wine Limited
Incorporated: 14 November 2014
Net Worth: £77,422 *Total Assets:* £94,743
Registered Office: 67 Pall Mall, London, SW1Y 5ES
Shareholders: Christopher Michael Tuffey; Claus Jorgensen
Officers: Grant William Sandiford Ashton [1967] Director/Entrepreneur

St Pierre Partners Limited
Incorporated: 4 November 2014
Registered Office: Woodlands Green Dene, East Horsley, Leatherhead, Surrey, KT24 5RG
Shareholders: Andrew George Steel; Janet Steel
Officers: Andrew Steel [1959] Director

St. Max Wine Limited
Incorporated: 25 April 2016
Registered Office: Kemp House, 169 City Road, London, EC1V 2NX
Major Shareholder: Tianle Ma
Officers: Ma Tianle [1981] Director/Manager [Chinese]

St.Austell Brewery Company Limited
Incorporated: 17 January 1910 Employees: 1,553
Net Worth: £100,660,000 Total Assets: £188,327,008
Registered Office: 63 Trevarthian Road, St Austell, Cornwall, PL25 4BY
Officers: Colin John Stratton, Secretary; Gerard Hugh Barnes [1968] Director; Gillian Caseberry [1965] Director; Kevin Roger Georgel [1970] Director/Chief Executive; Thomas Adam Luck [1956] Director; William Franck Michelmore [1959] Director; Simon James Staughton [1959] Director; Colin John Stratton [1965] Director/Chartered Accountant; Piers Michael Thompson [1971] Director/Regional National Sales Manager; Stephen John Worrall [1969] Director

St.James Winery Ltd
Incorporated: 4 April 2011
Net Worth: £2 Total Assets: £2
Registered Office: 44-45 Calthorpe Road, Edgbaston, Birmingham, B15 1TH
Major Shareholder: Bimla Kumari Tank
Officers: Bimla Kumari Tank [1964] Director

Stableyard Wines Limited
Incorporated: 23 July 2003 Employees: 1
Net Worth: £8,827 Total Assets: £36,671
Registered Office: Christopher House, 94b London Road, Leicester, LE2 0QS
Major Shareholder: Jon Burn
Officers: Rachel Elizabeth Francese Burn, Secretary/Wine Merchant; Jon Burn [1963] Director/Wine Merchant

Stack United Limited
Incorporated: 13 April 2017
Net Worth: £2 Total Assets: £2
Registered Office: 44 Queens Court Ride, Cobham, Surrey, KT11 1BB
Major Shareholder: Kemasiri Wickramage
Officers: Kemasiri Wickramage, Secretary; Kemasiri Wickramage [1975] Director [Sri Lankan]

Stag Ales Ltd
Incorporated: 15 August 2018
Registered Office: 2 Gibb Avenue, Darlington, Co Durham, DL1 1NQ
Major Shareholder: Andrew Trevor William Danby-Knight
Officers: Andrew Trevor William Danby-Knight [1992] Director/Entrepreneur

Stag Brewery Ltd
Incorporated: 6 January 2017
Net Worth: £9,000 Total Assets: £9,000
Registered Office: Little Engeham Farm, Woodchurch, Ashford, Kent, TN26 3QY
Officers: Jolian Robert McErlean [1971] Director/Brewer

Staibano Ltd
Incorporated: 30 April 2015 Employees: 1
Net Worth Deficit: £16,914 Total Assets: £41,001
Registered Office: Aldwych House, Winchester Street, Andover, Hants, SP10 2EA
Major Shareholder: Pier-Francesco Amodio
Officers: Catherine Susan Gilmour, Secretary; Pier-Francesco Amodio [1990] Director; Lawrence Stuart Mallinson [1957] Director; Thomas McGregor Shields [1950] Director/Author

Staid London Limited
Incorporated: 21 August 2012
Net Worth: £63,150 Total Assets: £126,278
Registered Office: 12 Mulberry Place, Pinnell Road, London, SE9 6AR
Officers: William Aspinall [1959] Director/Business Consultant

Frank Stainton Wines Limited
Incorporated: 19 February 1999 Employees: 8
Net Worth: £766,704 Total Assets: £1,475,790
Registered Office: 1 Station Yard, Station Road, Kendal, Cumbria, LA9 6BT
Shareholders: Frank Evan Stainton; Jennifer Stainton
Officers: Jennifer Stainton, Secretary/Director; Christopher Edward Leather [1965] Director/Wine Merchant; Frank Evan Stainton [1945] Director/Wine Merchant; Jennifer Stainton [1946] Director

Stallion Spirits Limited
Incorporated: 1 December 2017
Registered Office: 77 Avery Hill Road, London, SE9 2BJ
Shareholders: Vilmar Zampieron; Rui Cesar Teixeira
Officers: Rui Cesar Teixeira [1981] Director [Italian]; Vilmar Zampieron [1983] Director [Italian]

Star Beers Ltd
Incorporated: 13 November 1998 Employees: 6
Net Worth: £115,760 Total Assets: £182,742
Registered Office: Adams & Moore House, Instone Road, Dartford, Kent, DA1 2AG
Major Shareholder: Gurnam Singh
Officers: Gurnam Singh [1968] Director

Star Direct Hospitality Limited
Incorporated: 21 November 2017
Registered Office: 254 Staines Road, Twickenham, Middlesex, TW2 5AR
Major Shareholder: Kapil Mahendra Thakrar
Officers: Kapil Mahendra Thakrar [1967] Director

Star Value Limited
Incorporated: 13 February 1997
Net Worth Deficit: £464,677 Total Assets: £214,828
Registered Office: Heathersage, 77 Glen Road, Londonderry, BT48 0BZ
Shareholder: William Duffy
Officers: Siobhan Duffy, Secretary; Karen Duffy [1962] Director [Irish]; Siobhan Duffy [1959] Director [Irish]; William Duffy [1931] Director [Irish]

Stargold Wholesale Ltd
Incorporated: 27 February 2014
Net Worth: £79,641 Total Assets: £114,287
Registered Office: 5 Albany Road, Earlsdon, Coventry, Warwicks, CV5 6JQ
Major Shareholder: Poonam Nagra
Officers: Poonam Nagra [1993] Director

Starstock Ltd
Incorporated: 1 August 2012 *Employees:* 2
Net Worth: £587,278 *Total Assets:* £885,973
Registered Office: Mill House, 58 Guildford Street, Chertsey, Surrey, KT16 9BE
Shareholders: Samuel Maximillian Ulph; Tiffany Frances Ulph
Officers: Samuel Maximillan Ulph, Secretary; Neil Robert Ceidrych Griffiths [1961] Director; Samuel Maximillian Ulph [1982] Director

Stay Gold Beer Company Ltd
Incorporated: 28 September 2018
Registered Office: Flat 31, Drake Court, Tylney Avenue, London, SE19 1LW
Shareholders: Thomas Ewing; Harry Ewing
Officers: Harry Ewing [1994] Director; Thomas Ewing [1988] Director

Steamin' Billy (Property) Limited
Incorporated: 17 March 2004 *Employees:* 2
Previous: Steamin' Billy Brewing Co Limited
Net Worth: £1,929,572 *Total Assets:* £4,027,760
Registered Office: Granville Hall, Granville Road, Leicester, LE1 7RU
Parent: Steamin' Billy Brewing Co Limited
Officers: Barry Lount, Secretary/Director; William Charles Baden Allingham [1971] Director/Brewer; Barry Lount [1944] Director

Stedman Bros. (Events) Limited
Incorporated: 28 July 1939 *Employees:* 8
Net Worth: £468,756 *Total Assets:* £637,713
Registered Office: 25 Star Trading Estate, Ponthir, Newport, NP18 1PQ
Shareholder: Christopher Barry Stedman
Officers: Christopher Barry Stedman, Secretary/Director; Mark Hewitson [1978] Director/Operations Manager; Christopher Barry Stedman [1956] Director

Steel City Exports Ltd
Incorporated: 12 February 2019
Registered Office: 507 Herringthorpe Valley Road, Rotherham, S Yorks, S60 4LD
Major Shareholder: Liam Ryder Page
Officers: Liam Ryder Page [1988] Director

Steel Coulson Ltd
Incorporated: 10 October 2016
Net Worth: £9,333 *Total Assets:* £9,333
Registered Office: First Floor, 85 Kingsdown Parade, Bristol, BS6 5UJ
Shareholders: Jane Dutson; Glen Dawkins
Officers: Glen Dawkins [1971] Director

Steevenson Wines Limited
Incorporated: 5 June 2003 *Employees:* 12
Previous: Charles Steevenson Wines Limited
Net Worth: £87,345 *Total Assets:* £474,692
Registered Office: Unit 22-24 Plymouth Road Industrial Estate, Tavistock, Devon, PL19 9QN
Shareholders: Charles Patrick Carson Steevenson; Moira Ann Steevenson
Officers: Moira Ann Steevenson, Secretary/Wine Merchant; Charles Patrick Carson Steevenson [1956] Director/Wine Merchant; Moira Ann Steevenson [1952] Director/Wine Merchant

Sterling Wine Agencies Limited
Incorporated: 16 November 2006
Net Worth Deficit: £1,124,480 *Total Assets:* £175,008
Registered Office: Doshi Accountants Ltd, 6th Floor, Amp House, Dingwall Road, Croydon, Surrey, CR0 2LX
Shareholders: Jayanti Patel; Diptiben Chetankumar Sandesara
Officers: Diptiben Chetankumar Sandesara [1964] Director [Indian]

Stewart Hill Walker UK Limited
Incorporated: 29 September 2014
Previous: Stewart Lee Limited
Net Worth: £1 *Total Assets:* £1
Registered Office: 4314X, 9 Howick Place, London, SW1X 7ZJ
Major Shareholder: Lucilda Stewart
Officers: Lucilda Stewart [1962] Director/Lawyer

J & G Stewart Scotch Whisky Ltd
Incorporated: 17 January 2018
Registered Office: 71-75 Shelton Street, Covent Garden, London, WC2H 9JQ
Major Shareholder: Campbell Shirlaw
Officers: Campbell Shirlaw [1957] Managing Director

Stewart Wines Limited
Incorporated: 20 October 2005 *Employees:* 7
Net Worth: £218,046 *Total Assets:* £596,969
Registered Office: Springfield House, 45 Welsh Back, Bristol, BS1 4AG
Shareholders: Richard Andrew Stewart; Judith Helena Stewart
Officers: Judith Helena Stewart, Secretary; Richard Andrew Stewart [1955] Director

Stida Beverages Ltd
Incorporated: 27 November 2018
Registered Office: P O Box 6945, Office 20166, 207 Regent Street, London, W1A 6US
Shareholders: Stefan Courtney Green; Nida Shakoor
Officers: Stefan Courtney Green [1993] Director

The Stirling Whisky Company Ltd
Incorporated: 25 May 2018
Registered Office: 5 Rutherford Avenue, Bearsden, Glasgow, G61 4SE
Shareholders: John Clark Moore; George Michael Lunn; Jamie Lunn
Officers: George Michael Lunn [1942] Director; Jamie Lunn [1978] Director/Property Developer; John Clark Moore [1971] Director

STM Traders & Services Ltd
Incorporated: 16 May 2017
Registered Office: 19 Mafeking Avenue, Ilford, Essex, IG2 7AW
Shareholders: Thiruchittampalam Thirumaran; Lazarus Cruz Sujanthan
Officers: Lazarus Cruz Sujanthan [1981] Director [Sri Lankan]; Thiruchittampalam Thirumaran [1981] Director

Stockholm Distillers and Vintners Limited
Incorporated: 26 July 2016
Registered Office: 133a Kingston Road, London, SW19 1LT
Major Shareholder: Mukesh Jain
Officers: Mukesh Jain, Secretary; Mukesh Jain [1969] Director [Indian]

Stockport Gin Ltd
Incorporated: 5 November 2018
Registered Office: 17 Orchard Road, Compstall, Stockport, Cheshire, SK6 5JS
Shareholders: Cheryl Anne Sharrocks; Paul John Sharrocks
Officers: Cheryl Anne Sharrocks [1980] Director/Hairdresser; Paul John Sharrocks [1984] Director/Architect

Stockwell Beverages Ltd
Incorporated: 21 September 2017
Registered Office: 71-75 Shelton Street, London, WC2H 9JQ
Officers: Nicu Bogdan Bascau [1983] Director/Manager [Romanian]; Sonya Dholliwar [1978] Director

Stockwell Wholesalers Limited
Incorporated: 7 March 2018
Registered Office: 71-75 Shelton Street, London, WC2H 9JQ
Major Shareholder: Anuvinder Kaur
Officers: Anuvinder Kaur, Secretary; Anuvinder Kaur [1986] Director/Doctor

Stokes Fine Wines Limited
Incorporated: 8 July 1987
Net Worth: £34,197 Total Assets: £418,610
Registered Office: Pawlett House, West Street, Somerton, Somerset, TA11 7PS
Officers: Charles Farr [1961] Director/Businessman; Timothy James Parkins [1956] Director/Wine Merchant

Stoney Hospitality Limited
Incorporated: 8 May 2018
Registered Office: Flat 4, 41 Davies Street, London, W1K 4LT
Major Shareholder: Olukun Mukaila
Officers: Olukun Mukaila [1975] Director/Entrepreneur [French]

Storesrealm Limited
Incorporated: 6 October 1978 Employees: 10
Net Worth: £238,126 Total Assets: £404,033
Registered Office: 39 Deacons Hill Road, Elstree, Borehamwood, Herts, WD6 3HZ
Shareholder: John Daniel Donavan
Officers: John Daniel Donovan, Secretary; David Donovan [1961] Director/Warehouse Manager; John Daniel Donovan [1953] Director

Stour Valley Events Limited
Incorporated: 30 May 2017
Registered Office: 17 South Avenue, Stourbridge, W Midlands, DY8 3XY
Officers: James Bentley [1974] Director/Civil Servant

Stow Brewery Limited
Incorporated: 8 June 2015 Employees: 2
Net Worth: £6,762 Total Assets: £6,762
Registered Office: Plenploth House, Old Stage Road, Stow, Galashiels, Selkirkshire, TD1 2SU
Shareholders: Andrew Ronald Clark Hutchison; Jeremy William Fraser; Nigel Miller
Officers: Jeremy William Fraser, Secretary; Jeremy William Fraser [1962] Director; Nigel Alexander Miller [1954] Director/Farmer

Strategos Limited
Incorporated: 19 October 2009
Net Worth Deficit: £2,795 Total Assets: £1,265
Registered Office: Suite 1, 4th Floor, Office 5, Congress House, 14 Lyon Road, Harrow, Middlesex, HA1 2EN
Officers: Romina Andrea Curotto [1976] Director; Luis Emilio Vargas Hidalgo [1977] Director

Stratford's Wine Shippers and Merchants Limited
Incorporated: 7 September 2012
Registered Office: The Winery, Fairhills Road, Irlam, Manchester, M44 6BD
Parent: Kingsland Drinks Limited
Officers: Edmund Anthony Baker, Secretary; Andrew Jonathan Sagar [1959] Director

The Street Food & Beverages Company Ltd
Incorporated: 17 January 2017
Registered Office: 12 Cool Oak Lane, London, NW9 7BJ
Major Shareholder: Mitesh Sevani
Officers: Mitesh Sevani [1981] Director/Project Manager

Street Wines Limited
Incorporated: 25 July 2011
Net Worth Deficit: £5,940 Total Assets: £75,667
Registered Office: Unit 3 Uphall Farm, Salmons Lane, Coggeshall, Colchester, Essex, CO6 1RY
Major Shareholder: Neils Dubro
Officers: Neils Alex Dubro [1978] Director

Strongwells Limited
Incorporated: 13 November 2015 Employees: 1
Net Worth Deficit: £230 Total Assets: £18,994
Registered Office: 6 The Old Quarry, Nene Valley Business Park, Oundle, Peterborough, PE8 4HN
Major Shareholder: Antonio Beneforti
Officers: Antonio Beneforti [1969] Director/Entrepreneur [Italian]

Jack Sullivan (Properties) Limited
Incorporated: 10 September 1997
Net Worth: £5,121 Total Assets: £48,042
Registered Office: c/o Millbrook Trading Estate, Siloh Road, Landore, Swansea, SA1 2NU
Shareholders: John Sullivan; Michael Sullivan
Officers: Michael Sullivan, Secretary; John Sullivan [1944] Director; Michael Sullivan [1948] Director

Jack Sullivan Limited
Incorporated: 12 January 1973 Employees: 14
Net Worth: £737,054 Total Assets: £1,164,695
Registered Office: Bay E, Unit 3 Millbrook Trading Estate, Siloh Road, Landore, Swansea, SA1 2NU
Shareholder: Sonia Anne Wignall
Officers: Michael Sullivan, Secretary; John Sullivan [1944] Director; Michael Sullivan [1948] Director

Summerforever Ltd
Incorporated: 19 November 2018
Registered Office: Flat 2, 38 Brunswick Square, Brighton, BN3 1EE
Shareholders: Selina Lal; Yinyin Huang; Daomeng Wu
Officers: Yinyin Huang [1990] Director/Seller [Chinese]; Selina Lal [1983] Director/Buyer; Daomeng Wu [1990] Director/Seller [Chinese]

Summerhall Distillery Asia Limited
Incorporated: 6 March 2018
Registered Office: Summerhall Distillery, 1 Summerhall, Edinburgh, EH9 1PL
Shareholders: Matthew David Malcolm Gammell; Marcus George Pickering
Officers: Matthew David Malcolm Gammell [1975] Director; Marcus George Pickering [1974] Director

Sun Exports Limited
Incorporated: 10 August 2018
Registered Office: 3rd Floor, 207 Regent Street, London, W1B 3HH
Major Shareholder: Sunita Jogani
Officers: Sunita Jogani [1962] Director

Sunbird Wines UK Ltd
Incorporated: 1 August 2012
Registered Office: Old Barn Farm, Harts Lane, Ardleigh, Colchester, Essex, CO7 7QQ
Major Shareholder: Philippa Jane Woods
Officers: Philippa Jane Woods [1958] Director

Sunderland Gin Limited
Incorporated: 31 August 2017
Registered Office: 92 Greenbank Drive, Sunderland, Tyne & Wear, SR4 0JX
Major Shareholder: Stephen Anthony Brace
Officers: Stephen Anthony Brace [1991] Director/Business Development Executive

Sundown Vino & Liquor Ltd
Incorporated: 7 January 2019
Registered Office: 120 Panfield Road, London, SE2 9DE
Major Shareholder: Nana Ama Werehemaa Asare
Officers: Nana Ama Werehemaa Asare [1995] Director/Client/Project Coordinator [Ghanaian]

Sunny Group Limited
Incorporated: 3 August 2011 *Employees:* 1
Previous: Sunny Travel Ltd
Net Worth Deficit: £23,983 *Total Assets:* £10,312
Registered Office: Churchill House, 120 Bunns Lane, London, NW7 2AP
Major Shareholder: Yu Sun
Officers: Yu Sun [1976] Managing Director

Sunnyside Incorporated Limited
Incorporated: 21 August 1997
Net Worth: £307,072 *Total Assets:* £586,723
Registered Office: 2 Stafford Place, Weston-Super-Mare, Somerset, BS23 2QZ
Officers: Gregory James Dudd, Secretary; Gregory James Dudd [1970] Director/Hotelier; Jonathan Howell Dudd [1967] Director/Hotelier

Sunset Wines Limited
Incorporated: 14 June 2000 *Employees:* 14
Net Worth: £127,752 *Total Assets:* £492,294
Registered Office: Unit 3 Cleveland Road, Scarborough, N Yorks, YO12 7BG
Shareholder: Andrew Sample
Officers: Tracey Elizabeth Sample, Secretary; Andrew Sample [1963] Managing Director; Carl Sample [1983] Director/Manager; Matthew Paul Sample [1988] Director/Sales Executive

Suntrack Ltd
Incorporated: 23 January 2019
Registered Office: 6 Plaistow Park Road, London, E13 0SD
Major Shareholder: Moshiur Karim Mesu
Officers: Moshiur Karim Mesu [1990] Director/Manager [Bangladeshi]

Super Brit Bery Ltd
Incorporated: 25 October 2017
Registered Office: 81 Quinta Drive, London, EN5 3DA
Major Shareholder: Robert Kowal
Officers: Robert Kowal [1973] Managing Director [Polish]

Super Cooper Ltd
Incorporated: 3 October 2018
Registered Office: Monachyle Beag, Balquhidder, Lochearnhead, Stirling, FK19 8PQ
Shareholders: Tom Osbourne Lewis; Lisa May Lewis
Officers: Tom Osbourne Lewis, Secretary; Lisa May Lewis [1970] Director/Hotelier

Superba London Wines Ltd
Incorporated: 30 August 2017
Registered Office: 12 London Road, Morden, Surrey, SM4 5BQ
Officers: Gianluca Berardi [1990] Director/Manager [Italian]

Superior Import/Export Limited
Incorporated: 14 August 2001 *Employees:* 2
Net Worth: £548,321 *Total Assets:* £653,431
Registered Office: Crown House, Home Gardens, Dartford, Kent, DA1 1DZ
Major Shareholder: Harpreet Singh Johal
Officers: Harpreet Singh Johal [1979] Director/Sales & Marketing Import & Export

Supermalt UK Limited
Incorporated: 8 July 1991 *Employees:* 9
Net Worth: £1,465,655 *Total Assets:* £2,572,578
Registered Office: P1-004, Old Truman Brewery, 91 Brick Lane, London, E1 6QL
Parent: Royal Unibrew A/S
Officers: Patrick Topsoe-Jensen Plucnar, Secretary; Stephen David Gray [1972] Managing Director; Lars Jensen [1973] Director [Danish]; Johannes Fredericus Christiaan Maria Savonije [1956] Director [Dutch]

Supermarket Solutions Limited
Incorporated: 25 February 2009 *Employees:* 1
Net Worth: £100 *Total Assets:* £37,961
Registered Office: 2nd Floor, 1-5 Clerkenwell Road, London, EC1M 5PA
Major Shareholder: John Scanlon
Officers: John Scanlon [1958] Director

Superyacht Supplies Limited
Incorporated: 20 January 2003 *Employees:* 9
Net Worth: £236,849 *Total Assets:* £439,175
Registered Office: Parva Dene, Little Hatfield, E Yorks, HU11 4UZ
Shareholder: Ian Frank Jarvis
Officers: Carla Jarvis, Secretary; Carla Jarvis [1946] Director [Italian]; Ian Jarvis [1950] Director

Surprising Wines Ltd
Incorporated: 19 February 2018
Registered Office: 37 Clinton Road, London, E7 0HD
Major Shareholder: Frederic Tanoh-Koutoua
Officers: Frederic Tanoh-Koutoua [1973] Director [French]

Suwalki-UK Ltd
Incorporated: 30 June 2017
Registered Office: 120 Roding Road, Loughton, Essex, IG10 3EJ
Major Shareholder: Lubov Kravciv
Officers: Greta Luinyte [1988] Director

SW Group Spanish Wine Ltd
Incorporated: 12 September 2018
Registered Office: 119 Seagrave Road, London, SW6 1SS
Shareholders: Pedro de Los Bueis Andres; Maria Sonia Garcia Vicente
Officers: Pedro de Los Bueis Andres [1969] Managing Director [Spanish]

Swallow (Soft Drinks, Beer and Cider Wholesalers) Limited
Incorporated: 21 June 1995 *Employees:* 24
Net Worth: £1,487,882 *Total Assets:* £2,730,827
Registered Office: Stonehouse Lane, Bartley Green, Birmingham, B32 3AH
Major Shareholder: Stephen Thomas Land
Officers: Craig Stephen Land, Secretary; Stephen Thomas Land [1956] Director/Soft Drinks Wholesaler

Swallow Dispensed Drinks Solutions Limited
Incorporated: 2 October 2015 *Employees:* 2
Net Worth Deficit: £141,695 *Total Assets:* £453,365
Registered Office: Stonehouse Lane, Bartley Green, Birmingham, B32 3AH
Parent: Swallow Soft Drinks (Beer and Cider Wholesalers) Limited
Officers: Stephen Thomas Land [1956] Director

Swanbridge Fine Wines Ltd
Incorporated: 14 March 2017
Registered Office: The Pavilion, 96 Kensington High Street, London, W8 4SG
Shareholder: Xavier Jacques Jean-Paul de la Rochefoucauld
Officers: Amaury Christian Charles de La Rochefoucauld [1986] Director [French]; Stanislas Jean Baudouin de La Rochefoucauld [1987] Director [French]; Xavier Jacques Jean-Paul de La Rochefoucauld [1959] Director [French]

Swara Trading International Limited
Incorporated: 17 August 2007 *Employees:* 5
Net Worth: £1,179,483 *Total Assets:* £1,436,683
Registered Office: 132 Upper Richmond Road West, London, SW14 8DS
Shareholders: Anis Sobhag Shah; Minal Anis Shah
Officers: Anis Sobhag Shah, Secretary/Director; Anis Sobhag Shah [1970] Director; Minal Anis Shah [1969] Director

Swig Wines Limited
Incorporated: 30 October 2006 *Employees:* 8
Net Worth: £265,070 *Total Assets:* £744,403
Registered Office: 9 Bonhill Street, London, EC2A 4DJ
Major Shareholder: Robin Paul Francis Davis
Officers: Damon Thomas Quinlan, Secretary; Robin Paul Francis Davis [1968] Director/Wine Merchant

Swimming Pigs Ltd.
Incorporated: 21 February 2019
Registered Office: 71-75 Shelton Street, London, WC2H 9JQ
Major Shareholder: Anthony Christian M Reckley
Officers: Anthony Christian M Reckley [1986] Director [Bahamian]

Swinging Vine Ltd
Incorporated: 5 December 2018
Registered Office: 20 Linkfield Street, Redhill, Surrey, RH1 6BW
Shareholders: Tom Ellmann; Sazan Aljija
Officers: Sazan Aljija [1986] Director/Food and Beverage Manager [Italian]; Tom Ellmann [1997] Director/Student

Swinkels Snackery and Backery Limited
Incorporated: 6 March 2015
Registered Office: 23 Chantry Lane, Grimsby, N E Lincs, DN31 2LP
Major Shareholder: David John Smith
Officers: Michael David Elms [1953] Director; David John Smith [1963] Director

Swipe (Wine) Limited
Incorporated: 18 June 2018
Registered Office: Flat 2, 151 King Henrys Road, London, NW3 3RD
Major Shareholder: Frank Mannion
Officers: Frank Mannion [1972] Director/Producer & Distributor [Irish]

Swissgrapes Limited
Incorporated: 8 March 2017 *Employees:* 1
Net Worth: £100 *Total Assets:* £100
Registered Office: Kemp House, 160 City Road, London, EC1V 2NX
Major Shareholder: Yannick Mir
Officers: Yannick Mir, Secretary; Yannick Mir [1986] Director/Investment Banker [Swiss]

Sybarite Cellars Limited
Incorporated: 19 May 2016
Net Worth Deficit: £2,687 *Total Assets:* £3,766
Registered Office: 33 Keats House, Churchill Gardens, Pimlico, London, SW1V 3HY
Major Shareholder: Oliver Colin Robert Hill
Officers: Oliver Colin Robert Hill [1972] Director/Fine Wine Merchants

Sylvestre Limited
Incorporated: 31 March 2010
Net Worth Deficit: £4,124 *Total Assets:* £43,864
Registered Office: 140 Lansdowne Road, Tottenham, London, N17 9XX
Officers: Jean Sylvestre Akouete KOfficer [1976] Director [Ivorian]

Symposia Wine Limited
Incorporated: 16 May 2018
Registered Office: Flat 32, Groveside Court, 4 Lombard Road, London, SW11 3RQ
Major Shareholder: Patrick Andrew Rankine
Officers: Patrick Andrew Rankine [1980] Director [Australian]

Szicsek Palinka Ltd
Incorporated: 14 January 2016
Net Worth Deficit: £9,202 *Total Assets:* £5,262
Registered Office: 1 Rose Cottage, Guildford Road, Shamley Green, Guildford, Surrey, GU5 0RS
Major Shareholder: Aniko Szicsek
Officers: Aniko Szicsek [1970] Director/Wine and Spirits Retailer [Hungarian]

T & M Food Products Ltd
Incorporated: 15 December 2017
Registered Office: 8 Perivale Close, Nuthall, Nottingham, NG16 1QG
Shareholder: Fathali Moumchi
Officers: Fathali Moumchi [1957] Director [Iranian/British]

T & S Sales Limited
Incorporated: 3 June 2014 *Employees:* 2
Net Worth Deficit: £34,115 *Total Assets:* £920
Registered Office: Penny Lane Business Centre, 374 Smithdown Road, Liverpool, L15 5AN
Shareholder: Simon Neale Davies
Officers: Simon Davies, Secretary; Antonio Child [1963] Director; Simon Neale Davies [1972] Director

UK Wholesalers of Beers, Wines and Spirits

T J Wines Ltd
Incorporated: 8 March 2002 *Employees:* 3
Net Worth: £131,521 *Total Assets:* £310,170
Registered Office: Lakin Rose, Pioneer House, Vision Park, Histon, Cambridge, CB24 9NL
Shareholders: Tracey Jane Wadsworth; Steven Wadsworth
Officers: Steven Wadsworth, Secretary; Emily Louise Wadsworth [1992] Director; Oliver James Wadsworth [1996] Director; Steven Wadsworth [1963] Director; Tracey Jane Wadsworth [1966] Director/Wine Wholesaler

T Warriors Brewery UK Limited
Incorporated: 1 September 2017
Registered Office: 96 Thorkhill Road, Thames Ditton, Surrey, KT7 0UW
Parent: Ruyi Investment Limited
Officers: Feng Chen [1976] Director

T.C.T.C. Services Ltd
Incorporated: 15 August 2003
Net Worth: £1 *Total Assets:* £1
Registered Office: 163 Welcomes Road, Kenley, Surrey, CR8 5HB
Officers: Christel Mireille Jeanne Lombard [1970] Director/Housewife [French]

T.M.B Wine Trading Ltd
Incorporated: 24 March 2014
Net Worth: £22,220 *Total Assets:* £99,934
Registered Office: 320 Garratt Lane, London, SW18 4EJ
Shareholder: WCS Nominees Limited
Officers: Paul Nicholas Bedford [1957] Finance Director; William Thomas George Buckland [1982] Director

T.W.S Wines Ltd
Incorporated: 11 October 2018
Registered Office: 7 Dennington House, Dennington Park Road, London, NW6 1AU
Major Shareholder: Tal Isreael Groinen
Officers: Tal Isreael Groinen [1991] Director [Polish]

Taabs Investment UK Limited
Incorporated: 4 January 2019
Registered Office: 25 The Beeches, Tilbury, Essex, RM18 8ED
Officers: Babatunde Banjo [1964] Director

Bertrand Tailor Limited
Incorporated: 25 May 2017
Registered Office: 178 Seven Sisters Road, London, N7 7PX
Shareholders: Nikolaos Konstantinou; Georgios Drakakis-Kastrinakis
Officers: Nikolaos Konstantinou [1974] Director

Talbot & Barr Limited
Incorporated: 15 May 2015 *Employees:* 2
Net Worth Deficit: £34,045 *Total Assets:* £28,966
Registered Office: Suite 1, 3rd Floor, 11-12 St James's Square, London, SW1Y 4LB
Major Shareholder: Hugh Francis Froggatt
Officers: Hugh Francis Froggatt [1947] Director/Retired; Craig Martin William Van Der Venter [1963] Managing Director [South African]

Talking Wines Limited
Incorporated: 1 October 2003 *Employees:* 9
Net Worth: £18,349 *Total Assets:* £349,610
Registered Office: 3 Emmervale Court, Midland Road, Cirencester, Glos, GL7 1PZ
Shareholders: Simon David Thomson; Freya Elderkin Thomson
Officers: Freya Elderkin Thomson, Secretary; Simon David Thomson [1961] Managing Director

The Tall Blond UK Ltd
Incorporated: 24 December 2018
Registered Office: 71-75 Shelton Street, Covent Garden, London, WC2H 9JQ
Major Shareholder: Natalja Romanova
Officers: Aleksandre Grivach [1990] Director/The Head of Business Development Department [Georgian]

Tamarind Drinks Limited
Incorporated: 24 August 2017
Registered Office: 11 Prince Rupert Way, Norwich, NR7 0TS
Major Shareholder: David Stephen Newstead
Officers: Steven Matsell [1965] Director; David Stephen Newstead [1980] Director; Elliott James Norris [1979] Director

Tan Dowr Limited
Incorporated: 17 July 2017
Registered Office: Lowin House, Tregolls Road, Truro, Cornwall, TR1 2NA
Shareholders: Warwick James Royden; Charles Mitchell Gebhard
Officers: Warwick James Royden [1994] Director

Tanner Brodin Limited
Incorporated: 22 February 1985 *Employees:* 21
Net Worth: £891,469 *Total Assets:* £2,564,310
Registered Office: Nelson Yard, South Denes Road, Great Yarmouth, Norfolk, NR30 3PR
Shareholders: Lewis Loizos Ntjortjis; Kyriakos Kikis Ntjortjis
Officers: Kyriakos Kikis Ntjortjis, Secretary; Kyriakos Kikis Ntjortjis [1957] Director/Grocer and Food Wholesaler; Lewis Loizos Ntjortjis [1963] Director/Grocer and Food Wholesaler

Tanners (Shrewsbury) Limited
Incorporated: 9 August 1910 *Employees:* 109
Net Worth: £5,594,000 *Total Assets:* £10,743,567
Registered Office: 26 Wyle Cop, Shrewsbury, Salop, SY1 1XD
Major Shareholder: James Jonathan Tanner
Officers: Robert John Morgan, Secretary; Robert John Morgan [1971] Director/Chartered Accountant; James Jonathan Tanner [1968] Director/Wine Merchant; Katherine Elizabeth Anne Tanner [1969] Director

Tanners Cymru Limited
Incorporated: 24 July 1967
Registered Office: 26 Wyle Cop, Shrewsbury, Salop, SY1 1XD
Parent: Tanners (Shrewsbury) Limited
Officers: Robert John Morgan, Secretary; Stephen John Lloyd [1957] Sales Director; Robert John Morgan [1971] Director/Chartered Accountant; James Jonathan Tanner [1968] Director/Wine Merchant

Tanners Wines Limited
Incorporated: 18 September 1972 Employees: 109
Net Worth: £2,286,228 Total Assets: £7,556,743
Registered Office: 26 Wyle Cop, Shrewsbury, Salop, SY1 1XD
Parent: Tanners (Shrewsbury) Limited
Officers: Robert John Morgan, Secretary; Robert Charles Boutflower [1965] Sales Director; Stephen David Crosland [1959] Director; Stephen John Lloyd [1957] Sales Director; Robert John Morgan [1971] Director/Chartered Accountant; Adrian James Patterson [1955] Sales Director; James Jonathan Tanner [1968] Director/Wine Merchant

The Tap HQ Ltd
Incorporated: 5 September 2018
Registered Office: 20 Brierley Road, Coventry, Warwicks, CV2 1RS
Major Shareholder: Martin Luther Junior Maramba
Officers: Martin Luther Junior Maramba [1991] Director/Self Employed

Tapp'd Cocktails Ltd
Incorporated: 21 January 2019
Registered Office: 20-22 Wenlock Road, London, N1 7GU
Shareholders: James O'Hara; Luke Matthew Davis
Officers: Luke Matthew Davis [1989] Director/Landscaper; James O'Hara [1983] Director/IT Consultant

Tapp'd Ltd
Incorporated: 16 July 2018
Registered Office: 2 Englewood Road, London, SW12 9NZ
Shareholders: Richard Martin Evans; James O'Hara; Luke Matthew Davis
Officers: Richard Martin Evans [1989] Director/Consultant

Tasmanian Liquor Distributors Ltd
Incorporated: 14 June 2018
Registered Office: 89 Whitton Road, Twickenham, Middlesex, TW1 1BZ
Major Shareholder: Jefferson Luther King Campbell St John
Officers: Jefferson Luther King Campbell St John [1986] Director

Taste Buds Wines Limited
Incorporated: 31 August 2004 Employees: 1
Net Worth Deficit: £34,257 Total Assets: £23,384
Registered Office: 4b Church Street, Diss, Norfolk, IP22 4DD
Major Shareholder: Stephen Hearnden
Officers: Glen Justin Hearnden, Secretary; Stephen Hearnden [1945] Director/Wine Importer

Taste Italia Limited
Incorporated: 7 March 2017
Net Worth Deficit: £1,450 Total Assets: £27,923
Registered Office: 5 Ribblesdale Place, Preston, Lancs, PR1 8BZ
Shareholders: Samuel James William Ascroft; Alessandra Anita de Palma
Officers: Samuel James William Ascroft [1990] Director; Alessandra Anita de Palma [1993] Director

Taste Merchants Ltd
Incorporated: 16 February 2015 Employees: 10
Previous: Taste Traders Limited
Net Worth: £961,251 Total Assets: £1,234,247
Registered Office: 41 Mochdre Enterprise Park, Newtown, Powys, SY16 4LE
Officers: Craig Andrew Hawgood [1980] Director; Dale Peter Hawgood [1987] Director; Duncan James Hawgood [1973] Director; Geoffrey Frank Hawgood [1945] Director; Neville John Hawgood [1969] Director; Rosemary Ann Hawgood [1946] Director

Taste of Alcohol Ltd
Incorporated: 22 August 2017
Registered Office: 52 Muirend Road, Perth, PH1 1JU
Shareholders: Michal Adam Ciemniewicz; Rocio de la Purificacion Blazquez
Officers: Michal Adam Ciemniewicz [1973] Director/Manager [Polish]; Rocio de La Purificacion Blazquez [1978] Director/Bookkeeper [Spanish]

Taste of Georgia Limited
Incorporated: 30 May 2017
Net Worth Deficit: £3,646 Total Assets: £24,421
Registered Office: Northside House, 69 Tweedy Road, Bromley, Kent, BR1 3WA
Shareholders: Richard Cox; Ekaterine Cox
Officers: Ekaterine Cox [1976] Director; Richard Cox [1964] Director

Tasteturkey Limited
Incorporated: 26 March 2007
Previous: Tasteturkey.Com Limited
Net Worth: £11,926 Total Assets: £124,606
Registered Office: Sadler Talbot, 5 Minton Place, Victoria Road, Bicester, Oxon, OX26 6QB
Major Shareholder: Mark Hopkins
Officers: Mark Hopkins [1966] Director

The Tasting Barn Ltd
Incorporated: 4 November 2014
Previous: Binfield Fine Wine Agencies Limited
Registered Office: Binfield Vineyard, Forest Road, Wokingham, Berks, RG40 5SE
Shareholders: Helene Rose Haggitt; Andrew George Steel
Officers: Helene Rose Haggitt [1969] Director; Timothy Charles Parkinson [1962] Director; Andrew Steel [1959] Director

Tasty Kameleon Ltd
Incorporated: 19 September 2018
Registered Office: 20-22 Wenlock Road, London, N1 7GU
Shareholders: Felix-Johannes Peter Otto Kress von Wendland; Marcelle Michelle Georgina Maria von Wendland
Officers: Felix-Johannes Peter Otto Kress Von Wendland [1974] Director [German]; Marcelle Michelle Georgina Maria Von Wendland [1970] Director [German]

Tata Trading Limited
Incorporated: 26 July 2018
Registered Office: Kemp House, 160 City Road, London, EC1V 2NX
Shareholder: Nageshwar Rao Kuyya
Officers: Sateesh Rathna [1977] Director [Indian]

Tate-Smith Limited
Incorporated: 21 March 1960 Employees: 45
Net Worth: £2,500,703 Total Assets: £3,811,111
Registered Office: Sundella House, Castlegate, Malton, N Yorks, YO17 7EE
Officers: Catherine Louise Tate-Smith, Secretary/Company Accountant; Catherine Louise Tate-Smith [1963] Director/Company Secretary; Constance Maria Tate-Smith [1932] Director [Dutch]; Paul Thomas Tate-Smith [1962] Managing Director

Edward Tatham Champagne Limited
Incorporated: 13 April 2015
Net Worth Deficit: £292 Total Assets: £10,376
Registered Office: 6 Gilbert Street, London, W1K 5HH
Officers: Edward Jeremy Tatham [1963] Director/Champagne Broker

Tattoo Limited
Incorporated: 22 August 2017
Registered Office: 8 Holyrood View, Sheffield, S10 4NG
Shareholders: Philip Craig Lee; Nik Andrew Entwistle; Christopher James Spencer
Officers: Nik Andrew Entwistle [1977] Director; Philip Craig Lee [1970] Director; Christopher James Spencer [1974] Director

The Taunton Cider Company Limited
Incorporated: 15 April 2015 *Employees:* 10
Net Worth: £54,503 *Total Assets:* £303,318
Registered Office: 7 John Street, London, WC1N 2ES
Major Shareholder: Alison Louise Simpson
Officers: John Martin Brodie Clark [1946] Director; Alison Louise Simpson [1969] Director

Tayler Beers Limited
Incorporated: 19 November 2014
Net Worth: £148 *Total Assets:* £100,471
Registered Office: Unit C4, Wyther Lane Industrial Estate, Kirkstall, Leeds, LS5 3AP
Shareholders: Ian Elliott; David Andrew Stephenson
Officers: Ian Elliott [1972] Director; David Stephenson [1972] Director

Duncan Taylor Scotch Whisky Limited
Incorporated: 5 July 1961 *Employees:* 23
Net Worth: £5,810,554 *Total Assets:* £15,140,837
Registered Office: 28 Albyn Place, Aberdeen, AB10 1YL
Parent: Duncan Taylor & Company Holdings Limited
Officers: Kirsty Alison McLeod [1973] Director/Sales Manager; Euan Coutts Shand [1956] Director

Charles Taylor Wines Limited
Incorporated: 23 May 1986 *Employees:* 16
Net Worth: £1,043,899 *Total Assets:* £1,945,855
Registered Office: 11 Catherine Place, London, SW1E 6DX
Shareholders: Charles Edward Taylor; Louisa Jane Taylor
Officers: Louisa Jane Taylor, Secretary; Charles Edward Taylor [1961] Director/Wine Merchant; Louisa Jane Taylor [1968] Director/Wine Importer

Tayst Ltd
Incorporated: 30 July 2015 *Employees:* 4
Net Worth Deficit: £51,964 *Total Assets:* £43,253
Registered Office: Unit 5 Eastlake Close, Litchard Industrial Estate, Bridgend, CF31 2AL
Officers: Richard Morris [1983] Director/Food Wholesale

TBD Tipples Ltd
Incorporated: 28 December 2018
Registered Office: 34 Nelson Close, Harleston, Norfolk, IP20 9HL
Major Shareholder: Daniel William Curtis
Officers: Daniel William Curtis [1976] Director

TBpub Ltd
Incorporated: 30 April 2018
Registered Office: 2 Chestnut Cottage, Bunwell Road, Spooner Row, Wymondham, Norfolk, NR18 9LH
Officers: Russell Barrie Evans [1962] Director

TBrands Distributor Ltd
Incorporated: 21 February 2019
Registered Office: 20-22 Wenlock Road, London, N1 7GU
Major Shareholder: Tariq Rashid
Officers: Tariq Rashid [1965] Director/Business Executive [Pakistani]

TCG Winchester Limited
Incorporated: 25 January 2019
Registered Office: 3rd Floor, 207 Regent Street, London, W1B 3HH
Major Shareholder: David Fordham
Officers: David Fordham [1939] Director/Businessman

Te Kano Estate Wines (UK) Limited
Incorporated: 6 August 2018
Registered Office: 22 Chancery Lane, London, WC2A 1LS
Major Shareholder: Brian Lloyd
Officers: David Aldridge-Sutton, Secretary; Francisca May Han Lloyd [1987] Director/Accountant [New Zealander]

Team Spirit Beverage Ltd
Incorporated: 19 September 2017
Registered Office: c/o Pocket Rocket Creative Ltd, Unit 2 Touch Business Centre, Touch Road, Stirling, FK8 3AQ
Shareholders: Gary Doherty; Derek Downie Sneddon; Gary Dawson
Officers: Gary Dawson [1974] Director; Gary Doherty [1969] Director; Derek Downie Sneddon [1967] Director

Team Yebo Ltd
Incorporated: 29 November 2018
Registered Office: 133 Marsh Drive, London, NW9 7QG
Major Shareholder: Salomon Payne
Officers: Salomon Payne [1996] Director

Tec-Sol Limited
Incorporated: 25 August 2010
Net Worth: £64,105 *Total Assets:* £347,016
Registered Office: 8a Wingbury Courtyard Business Village, Leighton Road, Wingrave, Bucks, HP22 4LW
Major Shareholder: Ettore Brambilla
Officers: Ettore Brambilla [1975] Director/Manufacturing Consultant

Teca Wines Limited
Incorporated: 6 April 2017
Registered Office: 1 Maltings Place, 169 Tower Bridge Road, London, SE1 3JB
Major Shareholder: Sam Harris
Officers: Sam Harris [1975] Director/Wine Trader

Tech-Beach UK Limited
Incorporated: 13 February 2015
Registered Office: 27 Charlwood Road, Putney, London, SW15 1QA
Major Shareholder: John O'Connor
Officers: John O'Connor [1963] Managing Director [Australian]

Telser & Pauli Ltd
Incorporated: 28 March 2017
Registered Office: Carpenter Court, 1 Maple Road, Bramhall, Stockport, Cheshire, SK7 2DH
Shareholders: Marcel Telser; Arno Pauli
Officers: Marcel Telser [1971] Director [Liechtensteiner]

Temperley Wines Limited
Incorporated: 13 October 2009
Registered Office: Thorney House, Thorney, Langport, Somerset, TA10 0DR
Officers: Susan Elizabeth Temperley, Secretary; Humphrey Peter Neville Temperley [1948] Director/Farmer; Susan Elizabeth Temperley [1954] Director/Housewife

Templar Wines Ltd
Incorporated: 31 January 2008 *Employees:* 6
Net Worth: £115,380 *Total Assets:* £337,936
Registered Office: 2 Slader Business Park, Witney Road, Nuffield Industrial Estate, Poole, Dorset, BH17 0GP
Major Shareholder: Maxwell Charles Bracher
Officers: Maxwell Charles Bracher [1962] Director/Wine Merchant

Temple Wines (Cash & Carry) Limited
Incorporated: 27 September 1991 *Employees:* 19
Net Worth: £7,947,957 *Total Assets:* £9,808,691
Registered Office: 472 Church Lane, Kingsbury, London, NW9 8UA
Officers: Nalin Kataria, Secretary; Rajni Kataria [1947] Director/Manager

Templeton Beer Wine & Spirit Co Ltd
Incorporated: 21 September 2007 *Employees:* 21
Net Worth: £162,380 *Total Assets:* £657,601
Registered Office: Goose Green, Templeton, Narberth, Pembrokeshire, SA67 8SD
Major Shareholder: Lyndon Bernard Belt
Officers: Lyndon Belt, Secretary; Lyndon Bernard Belt [1971] Director/Haulage Contractor

Tenby Drinks (UK) Limited
Incorporated: 24 August 2015
Net Worth: £246,513 *Total Assets:* £344,409
Registered Office: 24 Finney Well Close, Bilston, W Midlands, WV14 9XN
Major Shareholder: Jaswinder Singh
Officers: Jaswinder Singh [1976] Director [Portuguese]

Tender Vine Limited
Incorporated: 24 October 2018
Registered Office: 22 Byards Croft, London, SW16 5EY
Major Shareholder: Amrita Ghosh
Officers: Amrita Ghosh [1983] Director

Tengu Sake Limited
Incorporated: 6 November 2012 *Employees:* 1
Net Worth: £125,092 *Total Assets:* £229,906
Registered Office: Old Mill, Mill Lane, Blockley, Moreton in Marsh, Glos, GL56 9HT
Major Shareholder: Oliver Rupert Hilton-Johnson
Officers: Oliver Rupert Hilton-Johnson [1981] Director

Tennent Caledonian Breweries UK Limited
Incorporated: 8 July 2009 *Employees:* 296
Net Worth: £60,250,000 *Total Assets:* £263,192,000
Registered Office: Wellpark Brewery, 161 Duke Street, Glasgow, G31 1JD
Parent: C & C Holdings (NI) Limited
Officers: Stephen Glancey [1960] Director; Andrea Pozzi [1971] Director - Manufacturing; Ewan James Robertson [1982] Finance Director; Richard Joseph Webster [1986] Finance Director

Tennent Caledonian Breweries Wholesale Limited
Incorporated: 26 January 1983 *Employees:* 145
Net Worth: £41,007,784 *Total Assets:* £62,979,348
Registered Office: Crompton Way, North Newmoor Industrial Estate, Irvine, N Ayrshire, KA11 4HU
Parent: Wallaces Express Limited
Officers: Stephen Glancey [1960] Director; Andrea Pozzi [1971] Director - Manufacturing; Ewan James Robertson [1982] Finance Director; Richard Joseph Webster [1986] Finance Director

Tenuta Tremollito Wines Ltd
Incorporated: 30 July 2015
Net Worth Deficit: £5,119 *Total Assets:* £11,230
Registered Office: 1st Floor, 87-89 High Street, Hoddesdon, Herts, EN11 8TL
Shareholders: Margherita Giordano; Vincenzo Giordano
Officers: Margherita Giordano [1960] Director; Vincenzo Giordano [1959] Director [Italian]

Teqbev Ltd
Incorporated: 6 April 2018
Registered Office: 28-30 North Street, Dalry, N Ayrshire, KA24 5DW
Officers: Jaspal Bassi [1980] Director/Retailer; Manpreet Bawa [1986] Director/Retailer [Indian]

Teqcoola Limited
Incorporated: 12 October 2016
Net Worth Deficit: £7,482 *Total Assets:* £10,690
Registered Office: Flat H, 82 Ewell Road, Surbiton, Surrey, KT6 6EX
Shareholders: Petra Jurciakova; Charlotte Felicity Hammond
Officers: Charlotte Felicity Hammond [1988] Director/Business Person; Petra Jurciakova [1984] Director/Business Person [Slovak]

The Tequila Shop Ltd
Incorporated: 5 November 2018
Registered Office: 56 Ivy Road, Stirchley, Birmingham, B30 2NU
Major Shareholder: Raj Dhokia
Officers: Raj Dhokia [1987] Director

Tequilas of Mexico Limited
Incorporated: 3 November 2009 *Employees:* 1
Net Worth Deficit: £3,570 *Total Assets:* £123,147
Registered Office: 10 Queen Street Place, London, EC4R 1AG
Major Shareholder: Cleo Rocos
Officers: Cleo Rocos [1962] Director

Terra Toda Ltd.
Incorporated: 30 March 2016
Net Worth: £1,838 *Total Assets:* £1,838
Registered Office: 6 Cloister Close, Teddington, Middlesex, TW11 9ND
Shareholders: Simon Andrew Broad; Fiona Marion McCready
Officers: Simon Andrew Broad [1978] Director/Wine Merchant; Fiona Marion McCready [1979] Advertising Accounts Director

Terra Wines Limited
Incorporated: 24 May 2012
Net Worth Deficit: £24,160 *Total Assets:* £15,215
Registered Office: The Magpies Eye, Kettleby Drive, The Driveway, Eye Kettleby, Melton Mowbray, Leics, LE14 2TD
Major Shareholder: Patrick Whenham-Bossy
Officers: Patrick Whenham-Bossy [1965] Director/Wine Retailer [Swiss]

Terrae Vinariae Limited
Incorporated: 8 September 2016
Net Worth: £9,783 *Total Assets:* £180,177
Registered Office: Suite 5, Olympic House, Bennett Street, Ardwick, Manchester, M12 5NL
Officers: Barry Burrows [1953] Director; Michael James Burrows [1970] Director; Francis Austin O'Neill [1983] Director; Antonio Giorgio Sanguineti [1965] Director [Italian]

Tesh Beverages Limited
Incorporated: 13 February 2017
Registered Office: 38 Slant Lane, Mansfield, Notts, NG20 8QW
Major Shareholder: Franz Kwame Fritz
Officers: Franz Kwame Fritz [1991] Director/Consultant

Test Tube Products Limited
Incorporated: 14 August 2003 *Employees:* 2
Net Worth: £772 *Total Assets:* £31,491
Registered Office: c/o Bissell & Brown Ltd, Charter House, 56 High Street, Sutton Coldfield, W Midlands, B72 1UJ
Shareholders: Ralph Edmund Coombs; Sasha Nekic
Officers: Sasha Nekic, Secretary/Accountant; Ralph Edmund Coombs [1956] Director/Sales; Sasha Nekic [1967] Director/Accountant

Tewaina Ltd
Incorporated: 24 September 2018
Registered Office: 71-75 Shelton Street, Covent Garden, London, WC2H 9JQ
Shareholders: Victoria Khan; Andrey Li
Officers: Victoria Khan [1977] Director/Lawyer [Russian]

TFC Wholesale Ltd
Incorporated: 7 December 2005
Net Worth: £401,775 *Total Assets:* £479,969
Registered Office: 108a Lobley Hill Road, Gateshead, Tyne & Wear, NE8 4YG
Shareholders: Trentino Carpinelli; Denise Carpinelli; Francesco Carpinelli
Officers: Denise Carpinelli, Secretary; Denise Carpinelli [1956] Director/Wholesaler; Francesco Carpinelli [1980] Director/Wholesaler; Trentino Carpinelli [1955] Director/Wholesaler

TFWF Ltd
Incorporated: 16 June 2015
Net Worth: £9,069 *Total Assets:* £94,309
Registered Office: Vale House, Ivy Todd, Necton, Swaffham, Norfolk, PE37 8JB
Major Shareholder: Edward Hartland Sharples
Officers: Edward Hartland Sharples [1967] Director/Wholesale and Retailing of Beers Wines and Spirits

TH Nightlife Ltd
Incorporated: 18 January 2019
Registered Office: 67 South Parade, Sutton Coldfield, W Midlands, B72 1QU
Major Shareholder: Anthony Hammond
Officers: Anthony Hammond, Secretary; Anthony Hammond [1970] Director

Thagam UK Limited
Incorporated: 3 January 2018
Registered Office: Second Floor, 1081 Garrat Lane, London, SW17 0LN
Officers: Senthuran Nithiyanandan [1984] Director

Thames Cash & Carry (Birmingham) Limited
Incorporated: 9 October 2018
Registered Office: Thames Cash & Carry Ltd, 1-3 Deacon Way, Tilehurst, Reading, Berks, RG30 6AZ
Officers: Nileshkumar Agrawal [1976] Director [Indian]

Thames Distillers Limited
Incorporated: 6 December 1996 *Employees:* 17
Net Worth Deficit: £896,208 *Total Assets:* £1,204,068
Registered Office: A E Chapman and Son Ltd, Timbermill Way, Gauden Road, London, SW4 6LY
Shareholder: A E Chapman & Son Ltd
Officers: Wellwood George Charles Maxwell, Secretary; Anthony Edward Chapman [1938] Director/Company Chairman; Christopher Frank Hayman [1947] Director; Ian Victor Lockwood [1942] Director; Wellwood George Charles Maxwell [1952] Director/Distiller

Thames Wholesale Ltd
Incorporated: 17 January 2019
Registered Office: Flat 77, Longland Court, Rolls Road, London, SE1 5HB
Major Shareholder: David Santos Jimenez
Officers: David Santos Jimenez [1958] Director [Spanish]

Thameside Rum Company Ltd
Incorporated: 28 August 2018
Registered Office: 2 Duke Street, Windsor, Berks, SL4 1SA
Major Shareholder: Matthew Rex Perkins
Officers: Matthew Rex Perkins [1986] Director/Management Accountant

Thameside Wines Limited
Incorporated: 1 March 2000 *Employees:* 1
Net Worth: £700,011 *Total Assets:* £875,597
Registered Office: 5th Floor, Ashford Commercial Quarter, 1 Dover Place, Ashford, Kent, TN23 1FB
Major Shareholder: Fiona Jane Cavanagh
Officers: Fiona Jane Cavanagh, Secretary/Managing Director; Fiona Jane Cavanagh [1957] Managing Director

That Wineshop Limited
Incorporated: 14 October 2009 *Employees:* 2
Previous: Tastespot Limited
Net Worth Deficit: £257,579 *Total Assets:* £3,174
Registered Office: 17 Manor Road, East Molesey, Surrey, KT8 9JU
Parent: T-International AS
Officers: Tore Hofstad [1963] Director [Norwegian]

Theatre of Wine Limited
Incorporated: 12 April 2002 *Employees:* 17
Net Worth: £149,880 *Total Assets:* £407,638
Registered Office: 75 Trafalgar Road, London, SE10 9TS
Shareholders: Daniel Illsley; Jonathan Christopher Jackson
Officers: Thomas Alexander Fedrick-Illsley [1985] Director/Wine Merchant; Daniel Illsley [1967] Director/Wine Merchant; Jonathan Christopher Jackson [1969] Director/Wine Merchant; Jason David Millar [1985] Director/Wine Merchant

Themirtis Limited
Incorporated: 9 March 2011
Net Worth Deficit: £6,602
Registered Office: 19 Durham Avenue, Woodford Green, Essex, IG8 7NH
Major Shareholder: Francesco Mirti
Officers: Carmeluccia di Grigoli [1978] Director [Italian]; Francesco Mirti [1974] Director [Italian]

TheTipsyTransit Ltd
Incorporated: 27 November 2017
Registered Office: Wheatsheaf Cottage, Free Street, Bishops Waltham, Southampton, SO32 1EE
Shareholder: Grace Elizabeth Georgia Tredre
Officers: Grace Elizabeth Georgia Tredre [1996] Director/Waiter

Think Wine Group Ltd
Incorporated: 23 October 2018
Registered Office: 9 Garston Old Road, Liverpool, L19 9AF
Shareholders: Katherine Maria Jones; Nana Anowa Hughes
Officers: Nana Anowa Hughes [1975] Director/Finance; Katherine Maria Jones [1989] Director/Sales

Thirstee Business Limited
Incorporated: 17 July 2000 *Employees:* 3
Net Worth: £50,866 *Total Assets:* £116,767
Registered Office: 15 High Street, Brackley, Northants, NN13 7DH
Major Shareholder: Anthony Timothy Wynter
Officers: Anthony Timothy Wynter, Secretary/Director; Anthony Timothy Wynter [1961] Director/Machine Dispenser

Thirsty Brands Ltd
Incorporated: 17 September 2015 *Employees:* 1
Net Worth: £10,322 *Total Assets:* £44,283
Registered Office: 105 Oyster Lane, West Byfleet, Surrey, KT14 7JF
Major Shareholder: David Evans McNabb
Officers: David Evans McNabb [1972] Director; Hannah Louise McNabb [1977] Director/Lawyer

This Is Not A Party Limited
Incorporated: 1 June 2017 *Employees:* 1
Net Worth Deficit: £7,719 *Total Assets:* £1,667
Registered Office: 51 Clarkegrove Road, Sheffield, S10 2NH
Major Shareholder: Sereen Ford
Officers: Sereen Ford [1976] Director

Thiyagu Ltd
Incorporated: 25 August 2018
Registered Office: 38c Canning Road, Croydon, Surrey, CR0 6QE
Officers: Karthikeyan Thiyagarajan [1994] Director [Indian]

Thomson & Scott Limited
Incorporated: 7 November 2013
Net Worth: £153,225 *Total Assets:* £448,107
Registered Office: 23 Exmouth Market, London, EC1R 4QL
Shareholders: Amanda Hussain Thomson; Ian Arthur McAinsh Thomson
Officers: Amanda Hussain Thomson [1971] Director/Champagne & Wine Sales; Ian Arthur McAinsh Thomson [1971] Director/PR Consultant

Thorn-Clarke Wines (UK) Limited
Incorporated: 19 February 2007
Registered Office: The Paragon, Counterslip, Bristol, BS1 6BX
Officers: Samuel David Clarke, Secretary; David Brian Clarke [1948] Director [Australian]; Samuel David Clarke [1970] Director/Business Manager [Australian]

Thorne Licence Wholesale Limited
Incorporated: 17 December 2015
Registered Office: Unit S3, Narvik Way, Tyne Tunnel Trading Estate, North Shields, Tyne & Wear, NE29 7XJ
Officers: Patricia Ada Rice, Secretary; David Leonard Brind [1972] Director; John Frederick Hope [1969] Group Operations Director; Patricia Ada Rice [1957] Director; Paul Victor Young [1957] Director

Thorne Wines Limited
Incorporated: 8 September 2017 *Employees:* 4
Net Worth: £27,078 *Total Assets:* £35,071
Registered Office: 19 Highfield Road, Edgbaston, Birmingham, B15 3BH
Shareholders: Malcolm Roger Thorne; Sarah Ann Thorne
Officers: Paula Marie Powell, Secretary; George Edward Thorne [1991] Director; James Harry Thorne [1988] Director; Malcolm Roger Thorne [1955] Director; Sarah Ann Thorne [1959] Director

Thrace Premium Drinks Ltd
Incorporated: 13 June 2018
Registered Office: 60 Millmead Business Centre, Mill Mead Road, London, N17 9QU
Officers: Leyla Turgut [1975] Director [Turkish]

The Three Graces Liverpool Ltd
Incorporated: 22 August 2017
Net Worth: £82 *Total Assets:* £13,454
Registered Office: 5 Church Road South, Liverpool, L25 7RJ
Officers: Alan Hutchinson [1946] Director [British/Canadian]; Drew Hutchinson [1980] Director [British/Canadian]; Samuel Raymond Mercer [1987] Director

Three Shires Distillery Ltd
Incorporated: 16 July 2018
Registered Office: Hawkshead Quarry, Leek Old Road, Sutton, Macclesfield, Cheshire, SK11 0JB
Shareholders: Richard Anthony Buxton; Shelly Frances Buxton
Officers: Joseph Buxton [2000] Director; Richard Anthony Buxton [1966] Director; Shelly Frances Buxton [1967] Director; Sophie Buxton [1999] Director

The Three Stills Company Limited
Incorporated: 13 March 2013 *Employees:* 6
Net Worth: £696,926 *Total Assets:* £9,540,301
Registered Office: The Borders Distillery, Commercial Road, Hawick, Roxburghshire, TD9 7AQ
Officers: Janine Watson, Secretary; Michael Frank Beamish [1957] Director; Timothy Ado Carton [1959] Director/International Drinks Industry Executive [Irish]; Pierre Dharcourt [1958] Director [French]; Laurence John Fordyce [1962] Director/Project Consultant; John Ronald Kerr Glen [1959] Director; Malcolm Ian Offord [1964] Director; Anthony Brian Roberts [1965] International Commercial Director

Three Swallows Ltd
Incorporated: 4 October 2010
Net Worth: £3,530 *Total Assets:* £15,916
Registered Office: Whitfield Buildings, Pensby Road, Heswall, Wirral, Merseyside, CH60 7RJ
Major Shareholder: Michael William Wynn
Officers: Michael William Wynn [1947] Director/Wine Merchant

Thru The Glass Limited
Incorporated: 23 March 2015 *Employees:* 1
Net Worth: £15,061 *Total Assets:* £22,297
Registered Office: 12 Avon Road, Keynsham, Bristol, BS31 1LJ
Major Shareholder: Nicola Jane Burston
Officers: James Burston, Secretary; Nicola Jane Burston [1971] Director

Tiger Vines Ltd
Incorporated: 4 July 2017
Registered Office: 47 Avondale Rise, London, SE15 4AJ
Major Shareholder: James Christopher Macpherson Thomas
Officers: Karan Anand Gokani [1984] Director [Indian]; Sunaina Gokani [1987] Director; Harash Pal Sethi [1950] Director; James Christopher Macpherson Thomas [1983] Director

Tikka Beer Limited
Incorporated: 19 April 2002
Net Worth Deficit: £163,704 *Total Assets:* £25,906
Registered Office: Devonshire House, 582 Honeypot Lane, Stanmore, Middlesex, HA7 1JS
Shareholders: Rohit Dhirajlal Amin; Sarvista Rohit Amin
Officers: Sarvista Rohit Amin, Secretary; Rohit Dhirajlal Amin [1953] Director/Trade Agent

Tikves London Ltd
Incorporated: 25 August 2010 *Employees:* 1
Previous: Hyde Park FM Ltd
Net Worth: £611 *Total Assets:* £12,193
Registered Office: 9c Sunderland Terrace, London, W2 5PA
Major Shareholder: Zak Pavlovski
Officers: Zak Pavlovski [1962] Director

Grace Tilly Limited
Incorporated: 29 March 2018
Registered Office: 71-75 Shelton Street, London, WC2H 9JQ
Major Shareholder: Clive Bay
Officers: Clive Bay [1961] Director

Tilted Penguin Gin Ltd
Incorporated: 31 May 2018
Registered Office: Landmark House, 43-45 Merton Road, Liverpool, L20 7AP
Shareholder: Frances Hudson
Officers: Tiffany Fleur Garstang [1968] Director/Consultant; Frances Hudson [1972] Director/Consultant

Time & Tide Brewing Limited
Incorporated: 29 August 2013 *Employees:* 3
Net Worth Deficit: £50,235 *Total Assets:* £178,562
Registered Office: Statenborough Farm, Felderland Lane, Worth, Deal, Kent, CT14 0BX
Shareholders: Samuel Robert Gordon Weller; Kerry Alicia Campling
Officers: Kerry Alicia Campling [1977] Director/HR Manager

Tims Tuga Ltd
Incorporated: 4 December 2018
Registered Office: Kemp House, 160 City Road, London, EC1V 2NX
Major Shareholder: Tim Armstrong
Officers: Tim Armstrong [1958] Director

Tinkture Ltd
Incorporated: 17 July 2017
Registered Office: Trelay, Penwartha Road, Bolingey, Perranporth, Cornwall, TR6 0DH
Shareholders: Hannah Rory Lamiroy; Sam Kwinten Lamiroy
Officers: Hannah Rory Lamiroy [1977] Director/Founder; Sam Kwinten Lamiroy [1976] Director; Mark Timothy Webster [1971] Director

Tinnies Ltd
Incorporated: 18 January 2018
Registered Office: 14a Wynell Road, London, SE23 2LN
Major Shareholder: Oliver Harkus
Officers: Oliver Harkus [1987] Director

Tiny Vessel Brewing Company Limited
Incorporated: 2 August 2006
Previous: Exquisite Essentials Ltd
Net Worth Deficit: £23,181 *Total Assets:* £3,599
Registered Office: Unit 505 Platts Eyot, Lower Sunbury Road, Hampton, Surrey, TW12 2HF
Major Shareholder: Ivailo Penchev Penev
Officers: Ivailo Penchev Penev [1979] Director [Bulgarian]

Tioluxe Europe Limited
Incorporated: 12 September 2017
Registered Office: Scottish Provident House, 76-80 College Road, Harrow, Middlesex, HA1 1BQ
Major Shareholder: Lilaram Bharvani Rajan
Officers: Kannuswamy Venguswamy [1967] Director/Sales Marketing [Singaporean]

Tipo Loco Drinks Co. Limited
Incorporated: 26 January 2018
Registered Office: Bishop's Court, 29 Albyn Place, Aberdeen, AB10 1YL
Major Shareholder: Michael Alexander Ballantyne
Officers: Karina Lianne Jayne Ballantyne [1985] Director; Michael Alexander Ballantyne [1983] Director

Tipple Brands Ltd
Incorporated: 30 July 2014
Net Worth: £204,666 *Total Assets:* £278,487
Registered Office: 86-90 Paul Street, Shoreditch, London, EC2A 4NE
Shareholders: Paritosh Bhandari; Vishal Sagar Mair
Officers: Paritosh Bhandari [1974] Director [Indian]; Vishal Sagar Mair [1978] Director

Tipple Spirits Company Limited
Incorporated: 24 January 2019
Registered Office: 81 Gairn Road, Aberdeen, AB10 6AP
Shareholders: Laura Bowman Punzano; Neil Michael Thomson
Officers: Laura Bowman Punzano [1980] Director/Accounts Manager [Scottish/Spanish]; Neil Michael Thomson [1987] Director/Mechanical Engineer

Tipple Transport Limited
Incorporated: 23 July 2018
Registered Office: Spaceworks, Benton Park Road, Newcastle upon Tyne, NE7 7LX
Officers: David Robinson-Young, Secretary; Brian Clifford Hunt [1946] Director

Tipsy Events Ltd
Incorporated: 5 March 2018
Registered Office: 12 Anmore Road, Denmead, Waterlooville, Hants, PO7 6NP
Major Shareholder: Janine Mary Pert
Officers: Janine Mary Pert [1956] Director [Australian]

Tipsy Tea Limited
Incorporated: 15 February 2019
Registered Office: 75 Winifred Road, Stockport, Cheshire, SK2 6HF
Shareholders: Thomas Matthew Bailey; James Bailey; Karnis Kate Bailey
Officers: James Bailey [1979] Director; Karnis Kate Bailey [1984] Director; Thomas Matthew Bailey [1982] Director

Tipton Wines Limited
Incorporated: 25 September 2018
Registered Office: Trilogy Suite, 9 Church Street, Wednesfield, Wolverhampton, W Midlands, WV11 1SR
Shareholders: Surinder Pal; Krishi Kiritkumar Soni
Officers: Krishi Kiritkumar Soni [1984] Director [Indian]

Tirg Limited
Incorporated: 20 November 2018
Registered Office: 7 Chapel Street, Leeds, LS15 7RN
Shareholders: Ryan Martin Greaves; Thomas David Idle
Officers: Ryan Martin Greaves [1996] Director/Plumber; Thomas David Idle [1986] Director/Tiler

The Tirion Trading Company Limited
Incorporated: 22 March 2006
Net Worth: £14,631 *Total Assets:* £207,062
Registered Office: 51 High Street, Brecon, Powys, LD3 7AP
Major Shareholder: Gareth Johns
Officers: Gareth Johns, Secretary; Margaret Johns, Secretary; Gareth Johns [1977] Director

Titanic Distillers Belfast Ltd
Incorporated: 15 August 2018
Registered Office: 8 Station Road, Holywood, Co Down, BT18 0BP
Shareholders: Richard Irwin; Peter Martin Lavery
Officers: Richard Irwin [1973] Director; Peter Martin Lavery [1961] Director [Irish]

Titanic Distillers Limited
Incorporated: 17 August 2018
Registered Office: 43 Waring Street, Belfast, BT1 2DY
Officers: Richard Stephen Irwin [1973] Director; Stephen Brian Symington [1980] Director

Titanic Holdings Japan Ltd
Incorporated: 6 June 2018
Registered Office: 22 Mount Charles, Belfast, BT7 1NZ
Parent: Titanic Holdings Co., Ltd.
Officers: Cartan McLaughlin [1971] Director

Titanic Wines Limited
Incorporated: 15 November 2017
Registered Office: 33 Croft Road, Holywood, Co Down, BT18 0PR
Major Shareholder: Elizabeth Mary Bottomley
Officers: Elizabeth Mary Bottomley [1974] Managing Director

TJC Corporate Events Limited
Incorporated: 9 January 2006 *Employees:* 3
Net Worth Deficit: £61,722 *Total Assets:* £89,197
Registered Office: Meadowlands, 55 Golden Ridge, Freshwater, Isle of Wight, PO40 9LF
Shareholders: Trevor John Coles; Sandra Coles
Officers: Sandra Coles, Secretary; Trevor John Coles [1954] Director

TL Step By Step Limited
Incorporated: 12 August 2013
Net Worth Deficit: £256 *Total Assets:* £23,096
Registered Office: 85 Condell Road, London, SW8 4HS
Major Shareholder: Ana Cristina Lozano-Quintana
Officers: Ana Cristina Lozano-Quintana [1970] Director/Chemical Engineer [Colombian]

Toast Ale Ltd
Incorporated: 22 December 2015
Net Worth Deficit: £102,550 *Total Assets:* £119,400
Registered Office: 105 Sustainable Bankside, Sumner Street, London, SE1 9HZ
Major Shareholder: Tristram James Avondale Stuart
Officers: Emma Carrasco [1960] Director/Chief Marketing and Engagement Officer [American]; Helen Victoria Jones [1958] Director; Serge Robert Guy Kremer [1966] Director [Luxembourger]; Paul John Lindley [1966] Director; Tristram James Avondale Stuart [1977] Director/Author & Campaigner; Robert John Niven Wilson [1983] Director/Chief Executive

Today's Wholesale Services Limited
Incorporated: 3 August 2011 *Employees:* 29
Net Worth: £3,118,000 *Total Assets:* £12,075,000
Registered Office: 3 Carolina Court, Wisconsin Drive, Doncaster, S Yorks, DN4 5RA
Officers: John Schofield, Secretary; John Charles Baines [1956] Trading Director; Darren Paul Goldney [1970] Managing Director; John FitzGenerald Kinney [1963] Retail Director; John Schofield [1954] Finance Director

Todd Vintners Limited
Incorporated: 29 October 1987
Registered Office: 17 Court Street, Faversham, Kent, ME13 7AX
Shareholder: Jonathan Beale Neame
Officers: Robin Neil Duncan, Secretary; Jonathan Beale Neame [1964] Director; Mark John Rider [1976] Director

Toff Wine Ltd
Incorporated: 3 April 2018
Registered Office: 2 Wimpole Mews, London, W1G 8PE
Major Shareholder: Rohan Tawadey
Officers: Rohan Tawadey [1985] Managing Director

Tokaj Merchants Ltd
Incorporated: 9 May 2012
Net Worth Deficit: £5,702 *Total Assets:* £9,575
Registered Office: 18 Ashburnham Road, Richmond, Surrey, TW10 7NF
Major Shareholder: Csaba Toth
Officers: Csaba Toth [1983] Managing Director [Hungarian]

Toke Commodity Electro Limited
Incorporated: 11 September 2018
Registered Office: Park House, 37 Clarence Street, Leicester, LE1 3RW
Major Shareholder: Tomas Morejon Hernandez
Officers: Tomas Morejon Hernandez [1975] Director [Spanish]

Tolchards Limited
Incorporated: 23 September 2009 *Employees:* 89
Net Worth: £2,033,008 *Total Assets:* £6,623,436
Registered Office: Tolchards House, Woodland Road, Torquay, Devon, TQ2 7AX
Major Shareholder: James Charles Mardell
Officers: Alan Stanley Jeavons [1943] Director; James Charles Mardell [1958] Director; Karen Michelle Mardell [1971] Director; Sean Charles Mardell [1988] Commercial Director; Steven Charles Mardell [1984] Operations Director; Robert Kenneth Lewis Phillips [1952] Director

Tolmid International Ltd
Incorporated: 5 March 2018
Registered Office: 5 Dent Close, South Ockendon, Essex, RM15 5DS
Shareholders: Olufemi Tolulope Elemide; Olaide Olubunmi Jinadu; Oluwaseyi Grace Elemide-Emis
Officers: Oluwaseyi Grace Elemide-Emis, Secretary; Olufemi Tolulope Elemide [1967] Director/Engineer [Nigerian]; Olaide Olubunmi Jinadu [1970] Director/Manager [Irish]

Tolsta Brands Limited
Incorporated: 20 September 2011
Net Worth: £100,001 *Total Assets:* £126,624
Registered Office: 17 Racecourse Business Park, 69 Bothwell Road, Hamilton, S Lanarks, ML3 0DW
Major Shareholder: John McAulay
Officers: John John McAulay [1951] Director/Consultant

Tom's Tap and Brewhouse Ltd
Incorporated: 15 March 2018
Registered Office: 4-5 Thomas Street, Crewe, Cheshire, CW1 2BD
Officers: Jacqui Ayling, Secretary; Jacqui Ayling [1962] Director/Bar Manager; Sean Edward Ayling [1967] Director/Brewer; Thomas Andrew Farmer [1985] Director/Insurance Professional

John Toma TDE Ltd
Incorporated: 28 December 2017
Registered Office: 44 Elmham Road, Sheffield, S9 4PR
Officers: Ioan Toma [1961] Director [Romanian]

Tomlinson Whisky Merchants Limited
Incorporated: 25 April 2018
Registered Office: 68 Charnwood Crescent, Newton, Alfreton, Derbys, DE55 5SH
Shareholders: Lee John Tomlinson; Rebecca Louise Papworth
Officers: Rebecca Louise Papworth [1988] Company Secretary/Director; Lee John Tomlinson [1988] Director

Rodney Tompkin Fine Wines Limited
Incorporated: 21 May 1999
Net Worth Deficit: £21,676 *Total Assets:* £4,795
Registered Office: 11 Marsh Road, Weymouth, Dorset, DT4 8JD
Shareholders: Rodney Arthur Tompkin; Paul Tompkin
Officers: Rodney Arthur Tompkin, Secretary; Rodney Arthur Tompkin [1950] Director/Wine Merchant

Toorank UK Limited
Incorporated: 16 February 1998
Net Worth Deficit: £209,691 *Total Assets:* £6,155,354
Registered Office: Silbury Court, 420 Silbury Boulevard, Central Milton Keynes, Bucks, MK9 2AF
Major Shareholder: Antoon Cornelis Jan Blij
Officers: Antoon Cornelis Jan Blij [1948] Director/Chairman [Dutch]

Top Alco Ltd
Incorporated: 17 February 2017
Net Worth Deficit: £2,075 *Total Assets:* £7,328
Registered Office: 80a Clarendon Road, Christchurch, Dorset, BH23 2AA
Shareholders: Daniel Maksymilian Sulimierski; Krzysztof Piotr Dziebowski; Sebastian Rafal Kubaczka
Officers: Krzysztof Piotr Dziebowski [1977] Managing Director [Polish]; Sebastian Rafal Kubaczka [1979] Managing Director [Polish]; Daniel Maksymilian Sulimierski [1977] Managing Director [Polish]

Top Deal Services Ltd
Incorporated: 20 November 1998 *Employees:* 3
Net Worth: £118,639 *Total Assets:* £120,857
Registered Office: John Phillips & Co Ltd, 81 Claydon Business Park, Great Blakenham, Ipswich, Suffolk, IP6 0NL
Major Shareholder: Lee Antony Robert Gifkins
Officers: Lee Antony Robert Gifkins [1964] Director/Commodity Dealer

Top Spirits Ltd
Incorporated: 1 February 2012 *Employees:* 4
Net Worth: £20,100 *Total Assets:* £206,821
Registered Office: 109 Coleman Road, Leicester, LE5 4LE
Shareholders: Tomasz Pawelek; Anna Iwona Pawelek
Officers: Anna Iwona Pawelek, Secretary; Tomasz Pawelek [1976] Director [Polish]

Topmost Foods Distribution Ltd.
Incorporated: 18 June 2018
Registered Office: 65 Samuel Street, London, SE18 5LF
Parent: Topmost Foods Limited
Officers: Adekunle Akanji Ademola [1955] Director

Tops Food and Wine Limited
Incorporated: 27 March 2018
Registered Office: 25 Shrewsbury Walk, Isleworth, Middlesex, TW7 7DE
Major Shareholder: Nabeela Baig
Officers: Nabeela Baig [1971] Director

Toro Industries Ltd
Incorporated: 5 June 2018
Registered Office: 82 Reigate Avenue, Sutton, Surrey, SM1 3JJ
Officers: Juan Diego Toro Figueroa [1991] Director/Recruitment Consultant [Colombian]

Tortuga Brands Limited
Incorporated: 4 September 2017 *Employees:* 2
Net Worth: £1,168 *Total Assets:* £147,489
Registered Office: 53 Redbridge Lane East, Ilford, Essex, IG4 5EY
Officers: Peter Alexander Denis Davie [1960] Director; Nicholas James Gillett [1972] Director; Jeremy Winslow Parsons [1962] Director

The Totally Awesome Wine Company Limited
Incorporated: 11 May 2017
Registered Office: 62 Wilson Street, London, EC2A 2BU
Major Shareholder: Thomas Byrne
Officers: Thomas Byrne [1956] Director

Tour de Force Wines Limited
Incorporated: 17 March 2015 *Employees:* 1
Net Worth Deficit: £9,760 *Total Assets:* £15,510
Registered Office: 26 Gordon Road, London, N11 2PB
Major Shareholder: Adam John Williams
Officers: Elizabeth Grace Williams [1981] Director

Tower International Limited
Incorporated: 19 March 2004
Net Worth: £140,075 *Total Assets:* £336,076
Registered Office: 416 Green Lane, Ilford, Essex, IG3 9JX
Shareholder: Salih Hassan
Officers: Belgin Hassan, Secretary; Salih Hassan [1950] Director; Alpay Hilmi [1968] Director

Town Centre Inns Limited
Incorporated: 7 May 2002 *Employees:* 8
Net Worth: £2,141,922 *Total Assets:* £2,899,131
Registered Office: Numeric House, 98 Station Road, Sidcup, Kent, DA15 7BY
Shareholders: Town Centre Holdings Limited; Kenneth Roy Ryan
Officers: Julia Annette Defries, Secretary; Kenneth Roy Ryan [1946] Director

TP Retail Ltd
Incorporated: 21 February 2019
Registered Office: 36 Ince Road, Thornton, Liverpool, L23 4UF
Officers: Tom Pritchard [1999] Director/Shopkeeper

TPA Trading Limited
Incorporated: 24 October 2016
Registered Office: Unit 1B Townfoot Industrial Estate, Brampton, Cumbria, CA8 1SW
Major Shareholder: James Kent
Officers: James Kent [1948] Director/Accountant

TPDirect Ltd
Incorporated: 20 September 2018
Registered Office: 13 Poplar Road, Ramsgate, Kent, CT11 9SL
Major Shareholder: Paul Adams
Officers: Paul Adams [1974] Director

TPSC Ltd
Incorporated: 1 June 2018
Registered Office: 3 Whatcotts Yard, Palatine Road, London, N16 8ST
Major Shareholder: Bortolo Garibaldo
Officers: Bortolo Garibaldo [1964] Director [Italian]

Tractor Shed Brewing Limited
Incorporated: 17 February 2009
Previous: Mitchell Krause Brewing Limited
Net Worth Deficit: £79,533 *Total Assets:* £134,127
Registered Office: The Tractor Shed, Calva Brow, Workington, Cumbria, CA14 1DB
Shareholder: Thomas Graeme Mitchell
Officers: Rachel Ann Mitchell [1969] Director; Thomas Graeme Mitchell [1967] Director

Trade Network Supplies Limited
Incorporated: 27 January 2015
Net Worth Deficit: £78,574 *Total Assets:* £22,934
Registered Office: Unit 2 Coomber Way, Croydon, Surrey, CR0 4TQ
Major Shareholder: Imran Patel
Officers: Imran Patel [1985] Director

Trade Wines Ltd
Incorporated: 31 March 2010
Registered Office: Burnt House Farm, Old Fosse Road, Bath, BA2 2SS
Officers: Roderick Humphris [1966] Director/Publican

Traderhorn Limited
Incorporated: 21 November 1967
Net Worth Deficit: £272,802 *Total Assets:* £99
Registered Office: 43-45 Dorset Street, London, W1U 7NA
Shareholder: Anker Horn
Officers: Sally Horn, Secretary; Anker Horn [1936] Director [Danish]; Sally Horn [1939] Director

Trading Import and Export Company Limited
Incorporated: 9 June 2010
Registered Office: Unit 349 Camberwell Business Centre, 99-103 Lomond Grove, London, SE5 7HN
Major Shareholder: Philippe Raymond Menguini
Officers: Philippe Raymond Menguini [1965] Director/Business Executive [Cameroonian]

Trading Irmis Ltd
Incorporated: 29 April 2014
Registered Office: 36 Lincoln Road, London, E7 8QW
Officers: Irmantas Petkus [1983] Director [Lithuanian]

Traditional Beer Company Ltd
Incorporated: 29 January 2013 *Employees:* 2
Net Worth Deficit: £32,919 *Total Assets:* £64,508
Registered Office: 32 Talbot Street, Whitchurch, Salop, SY13 1PS
Major Shareholder: Richard James Lever
Officers: Richard James Lever [1972] Director and Company Secretary

The Traditional Italian Wine Company Limited
Incorporated: 23 February 2017
Registered Office: 21 Navigation Business Village, Navigation Way, Ashton on Ribble, Preston, Lancs, PR2 2YP
Major Shareholder: Lee Aaron Brobson
Officers: Lee Aaron Brobson [1985] Director

Trailblazing Wine Ltd
Incorporated: 4 March 2015
Net Worth: £590 *Total Assets:* £8,255
Registered Office: The Mill, Pury Hill Business Park, Alderton Road, Towcester, Northants, NN12 7LS
Shareholders: Jerome Alexander Harlington; Beaufort Nominees Limited
Officers: Jerome Alexander Harlington [1972] Director

Trang Mai Exports Limited
Incorporated: 5 September 2018
Registered Office: 178 Seven Sisters Road, London, N7 7PX
Major Shareholder: Thi Doan Trang Le
Officers: Thi Doan Trang Le [1975] Director

Transylvania Wine Ltd
Incorporated: 16 February 2015
Net Worth: £30,456 *Total Assets:* £37,166
Registered Office: The Shacks House, Roils Head, Halifax, W Yorks, HX2 0SX
Major Shareholder: Ovidiu Emilian Draghici
Officers: Ovidiu Emilian Draghici [1975] Director/Manager; Dr. Teodora Mirela Draghici [1977] Director/Doctor

Transylvania's Finest Ltd
Incorporated: 2 August 2018
Registered Office: Kingsnorth House, Blenheim Way, Birmingham, B44 8LS
Shareholders: Trevor Gordon Dyer; Ioan Nemes; David Gordon Rawson

Trebbiano Wines Ltd
Incorporated: 20 September 2017
Registered Office: 22 Artisan Mews, Warfield Road, Brent, London, NW10 5GL
Shareholders: Matteo Cali; Riccardo Basile
Officers: Riccardo Basile, Secretary; Matteo Cali, Secretary; Matteo Cali [1994] Director [Italian]

Trendbev Ltd.
Incorporated: 10 May 2017
Net Worth: £120 *Total Assets:* £120
Registered Office: Unit 27 Harwood Court, Bowes Road, Middlesbrough, Cleveland, TS2 1PU
Shareholder: Robert William Tillston
Officers: Mark Alan Robinson [1963] Director; Robert William Tillston [1947] Director

Triage Wines Limited
Incorporated: 18 October 2013
Net Worth: £94,691 *Total Assets:* £97,523
Registered Office: 43-45 Dorset Street, London, W1U 7NA
Parent: A & B Vintners Limited
Officers: John Charles Arnold, Secretary; John Charles Arnold [1964] Director/Wine Merchant; Simon Christopher Davies [1978] Director/Wine Merchant; Alexander Nicholas Kidney [1965] Director/Chartered Accounts

Triangle Wines Limited
Incorporated: 19 October 2017
Registered Office: Bon Marche Centre, 241 Ferndale Road, London, SW9 8BJ
Shareholders: Benedict Jon Michael Henshaw; Alvaro Ribalta Millan
Officers: Benedict Jon Michael Henshaw [1971] Director; Alvaro Ribalta Millan [1982] Director/Sales Manager [Spanish]

Tribeology Limited
Incorporated: 11 October 2017
Registered Office: 235 Wandsworth Bridge Road, London, SW6 2TU
Officers: Charles Thomas Markland [1983] Director/Consultant

Triberg Limited
Incorporated: 5 October 1992
Net Worth: £436,585 *Total Assets:* £516,563
Registered Office: 133B High Street, Holywood, Co Down, BT18 9LG
Major Shareholder: Derek Barney Sealy Isherwood
Officers: Fiona Catherine Isherwood, Secretary; Derek Barney Sealy Isherwood [1944] Director/Wine Merchant; Fiona Catherine Isherwood [1958] Director/Administrator

Trilogy Beverage Brands Ltd
Incorporated: 25 April 2013
Net Worth: £341,947 *Total Assets:* £407,707
Registered Office: Laurel House, 173 Chorley New Road, Bolton, Lancs, BL1 4QZ
Major Shareholder: Darius Burrows
Officers: Darius Burrows [1980] Director; James Winstanley [1981] Director

Trinewine Ltd
Incorporated: 6 August 2018
Registered Office: 133 Barnet Road, Viewpoint House, London, EN5 3JX
Shareholder: Manisha Hooda
Officers: Manisha Hooda, Secretary; Manisha Hooda [1978] Director/Entrepreneur

Trinity Drinks Limited
Incorporated: 2 July 2018
Registered Office: 118 Silcoates Lane, Wrenthorpe, Wakefield, W Yorks, WF2 0PE
Shareholder: Liam Aaron Brennan
Officers: Liam Aaron Brennan [1994] Director

Triple AAA Limited
Incorporated: 20 January 2006 *Employees:* 1
Net Worth: £184,370 *Total Assets:* £1,055,789
Registered Office: Kajaine House, 57-67 High Street, Edgware, Middlesex, HA8 7DD
Shareholders: Phatachand Ghanshamdas Mulchandani; Manoher Ghanshamdas Mulchandani
Officers: Naseem Sultan Mohammed [1963] Director

Triple Point Brewing Ltd
Incorporated: 15 November 2018
Registered Office: 178 Shoreham Street, Sheffield, S1 4SQ
Major Shareholder: Michael Jonathan Brook
Officers: Michael Jonathan Brook [1961] Director

Triumph Foodservice Limited
Incorporated: 13 August 2014
Net Worth: £19,131 *Total Assets:* £76,650
Registered Office: 165b Ravensbourne Avenue, Shortlands, Bromley, Kent, BR2 0AY
Shareholder: Jijan Uddin
Officers: Sarah Chaudhry [1980] Director; Jijan Uddin [1980] Director/Owner

Tropical Ltd
Incorporated: 29 September 2015
Net Worth: £4,591 *Total Assets:* £7,788
Registered Office: 272 Bath Street, Glasgow, G2 4JR
Major Shareholder: Bejoy Pallithazhe
Officers: Bejoy Pallithazhe [1976] Director [Indian]

Truekeg UK Ltd
Incorporated: 24 August 2018
Registered Office: Flat 41, Little Sutton Lane, Sutton Coldfield, W Midlands, B75 6SE
Major Shareholder: Rajiv Khanna
Officers: Rajiv Khanna [1970] Director/Entrepreneur [Italian]

Truk Limited
Incorporated: 26 February 2019
Registered Office: 224 Fosse Road South, Leicester, LE3 0FU
Major Shareholder: Mahfuz Balkaya
Officers: Mahfuz Balkaya [1976] Director

Truly Spirited Ltd
Incorporated: 20 March 2018
Registered Office: 31 Olive Walk, Harrogate, N Yorks, HG1 4RL
Major Shareholder: Harvey Roe
Officers: Harvey Roe [1966] Managing Director

Truman's Drink Solutions Limited
Incorporated: 6 May 2015 *Employees:* 1
Net Worth Deficit: £5,188
Registered Office: O'Brien & Partners, Highdale House, 7 Centre Court, Main Avenue, Treforest Industrial Estate, Pontypridd, Rhondda Cynon Taf, CF37 5YR
Major Shareholder: Robert Paul Truman
Officers: Robert Paul Truman [1960] Director

Trust in Global Food Ltd
Incorporated: 24 September 2013
Net Worth Deficit: £13,049 *Total Assets:* £9,260
Registered Office: 116 Stechford Road, Birmingham, B34 6BJ
Major Shareholder: Vikram Verma
Officers: Vikram Verma [1976] Director [Indian]

Trusty Services Ltd
Incorporated: 14 August 2018
Registered Office: Kemp House, 160 City Road, London, EC1V 2NX
Major Shareholder: Michael Carr
Officers: Michael Carr [1982] Director

Trywines Expertise Limited
Incorporated: 31 July 2003 *Employees:* 1
Net Worth: £150,880 *Total Assets:* £279,181
Registered Office: Griffins Court, 24-32 London Road, Newbury, Berks, RG14 1JX
Shareholders: Helen Amadi; Edoardo Amadi
Officers: Edoardo Amadi [1961] Wine Director [Italian]; Helen Amadi [1967] Director/PA

TST Ventures Limited
Incorporated: 5 October 2018
Registered Office: Unit 5 Belvedere Business Park, Crabtree Manorway South, Belvedere, Kent, DA17 6AH
Major Shareholder: Thanh Tuan Mai
Officers: Thanh Tuan Mai [1986] Director

TTO Limited
Incorporated: 2 July 2009
Net Worth Deficit: £19,292 *Total Assets:* £7,320
Registered Office: 7 Cooks Lane, Southbourne, Emsworth, Hants, PO10 8LG
Major Shareholder: Thomas Francis Williams
Officers: Thomas Francis Williams [1977] Director/Sales

Ttow Ltd
Incorporated: 21 June 2018
Registered Office: 5 The Mall, London, W5 2PJ
Shareholders: Bartosz Wiktor Wozniak; Rafal Piotr Krukowski
Officers: Bartosz Wiktor Wozniak [1985] Director [Polish]

Tudor Drinks Ltd
Incorporated: 8 November 2012 Employees: 3
Net Worth Deficit: £31,203 Total Assets: £334,737
Registered Office: 3rd Floor, 207 Regent Street, London, W1B 3HH
Major Shareholder: Ian Martin O'Donohue
Officers: Simon Green [1973] Director; Ian Martin O'Donohue [1980] Director; Martin Odonohue [1946] Director/Retired

Tulaich Ltd
Incorporated: 27 April 2017
Registered Office: Inchbreck House, Kirkintilloch, Glasgow, G66 1RS
Officers: Diane Murray, Secretary; Steven Craig Murray [1971] Director; Hung Tran [1971] Director

Tump By Aj & Sonz Ltd
Incorporated: 7 February 2018
Registered Office: 62b Selsdon Road, South Croydon, Surrey, CR2 6PE
Major Shareholder: Anthony Joseph
Officers: Anthony Joseph [1983] Director

Turkish Kitchinn Wholesale Ltd
Incorporated: 7 June 2017
Registered Office: 449 West Green Road, London, N15 3PL
Major Shareholder: Emre Kars
Officers: Emre Kars [1983] Managing Director

Glen Turner Company Limited
Incorporated: 4 November 1981 Employees: 127
Net Worth: £250,004,000 Total Assets: £302,870,016
Registered Office: 2nd Floor, Regis House, 45 King William Street, London, EC4R 9AN
Officers: Jean Pierre Cayard [1942] Director [French]

Tutto Wines Limited
Incorporated: 7 March 2014
Net Worth: £44,285 Total Assets: £242,289
Registered Office: 303 Hoxton Street, London, N1 5JX
Shareholders: Damiano Fiamma; Alexander William Whyte
Officers: Damiano Fiamma [1987] Director [Italian]; Alexander William Whyte [1986] Director

TVB Retail Limited
Incorporated: 4 June 2018
Registered Office: 172 Cannon Workshops, Cannon Drive, London, E14 4AS
Major Shareholder: Robert John Edwards
Officers: Robert John Edwards [1984] Managing Director

TW Wine Solutions Ltd
Incorporated: 10 November 2015
Registered Office: Rectory Fields, Lowe Hill Road, Wem, Shrewsbury, Salop, SY4 5UA
Major Shareholder: Thomas Steven Walmsley
Officers: Thomas Walmsley [1991] Director of Consulting

Twaites and Jones Limited
Incorporated: 23 March 2010
Net Worth: £387,771 Total Assets: £523,910
Registered Office: Orchard House, Victoria Square, Droitwich, Worcs, WR9 8DS
Officers: Dany Louise Jones, Secretary; Hayley Marie Twaites, Secretary; Oliver John Jones [1979] Director; Christopher Matthew Twaites [1969] Director

Twilight Drinks Ltd
Incorporated: 17 December 2018
Registered Office: Flat 105, Bradfield Road, Sheffield, S6 2BP
Major Shareholder: Marcis Sarguns
Officers: Marcis Sarguns [1991] Director/Entrepreneur [Latvian]

The Two Essentials Ltd.
Incorporated: 29 September 2017
Registered Office: Kingsley House, Elm Road, Leigh on Sea, Essex, SS9 1SN
Shareholder: Charles Norman Ryland
Officers: Charles Norman Ryland [1984] Managing Director

Two Heads Beer Co Limited
Incorporated: 31 August 2017 Employees: 4
Net Worth: £80,584 Total Assets: £111,576
Registered Office: 78 St John's Hill, London, SW11 1SF
Major Shareholder: Jonathan Russell Kaye
Officers: James Charles Hickson [1983] Director/Retail Development Manager; Jonathan Russell Kaye [1973] Director; Marc Johan Robert Verlet [1975] Director/Banker [Belgian]

Two Pal's Company Limited
Incorporated: 13 September 2018
Registered Office: 47 Upper Perry Hill, Southville, Bristol, BS3 1NJ
Shareholders: Mark Richard James Furze; Benjamin James Coulson
Officers: Mark Richard James Furze, Secretary; Benjamin James Coulson [1988] Director/Front End Developer; Mark Richard James Furze [1987] Director/Product Manager

Two Toes Ltd
Incorporated: 15 October 2018
Registered Office: 21B Self Store, Norton Fitzwarren, Taunton, Somerset, TA2 6NS
Shareholders: Charlie Harris; Ozzy Flowers; Luke Harris
Officers: Charlie Harris [1994] Director

Ty Nant Spring Water Limited
Incorporated: 14 November 1988
Net Worth Deficit: £55,032 Total Assets: £3,366,041
Registered Office: Bethania, Llanon, Ceredigion, SY23 5LS
Officers: Hywel John Davies, Secretary; Pietro Biscaldi [1958] Managing Director [Italian]

UBI Drinks Enterprises Limited
Incorporated: 4 February 2019
Registered Office: Springfield House, Sandling Road, Maidstone, Kent, ME14 2LP
Parent: United Breweries International (U.K.) Limited
Officers: Mark Edward Davis, Secretary; Damon William Thornton Swarbrick [1974] Director

Ubicumque International Ltd
Incorporated: 18 July 2017
Net Worth: £1,000 Total Assets: £1,000
Registered Office: 27 Old Gloucester Street, London, WC1N 3AX
Major Shareholder: Sergio Rosciglione
Officers: Dr Sergio Rosciglione [1943] Director/Retired [Italian]

Ufton Travel Retail Limited
Incorporated: 7 October 2009 *Employees:* 2
Net Worth: £46,406 *Total Assets:* £64,648
Registered Office: Ufton Court, The Paddock, West Ridge, Sittingbourne, Kent, ME10 1UH
Officers: Alan John Snelling [1948] Director/Agent; Margaret Helena Anne Snelling [1949] Director/Agent; Mark Snelling [1987] Director

Uisce Ard Ltd
Incorporated: 6 October 2008
Net Worth: £172,118 *Total Assets:* £7,833,778
Registered Office: Unit 6 The Mead Business Centre, Mead Lane, Hertford, SG13 7BJ
Major Shareholder: Paul Martin Camplisson
Officers: Paul Martin Camplisson, Secretary; Paul Martin Camplisson [1965] Director [Irish]; Gareth Rory Nethercott [1969] Director [Irish]

Uist Distillery Ltd
Incorporated: 10 May 2018
Registered Office: 198, Stoneybridge, South Uist, HS8 5SD
Major Shareholder: Christopher Panaro
Officers: Christopher Panaro [1962] Director/Retired

UK Beer & Soft Drinks Ltd
Incorporated: 9 June 2015
Net Worth Deficit: £959 *Total Assets:* £1
Registered Office: 6th Floor, Amp House, Dingwall Road, Croydon, Surrey, CR0 2LX
Major Shareholder: Yostinappu Philip Thavarajah
Officers: Yostinappu Philip Thavarajah [1970] Director/Delivery Manager

UK Blue Ribbon Group Beer Co., Ltd
Incorporated: 2 November 2018
Registered Office: Unit G25, Waterfront Studios, 1 Dock Road, London, E16 1AH
Major Shareholder: Xiuyun Wang
Officers: Xiuyun Wang [1960] Director [Chinese]

UK Foods & Drinks Ltd
Incorporated: 6 October 2004
Net Worth Deficit: £46,483 *Total Assets:* £178
Registered Office: 4a Rufford Drive, Whitefield, Manchester, M45 8PL
Major Shareholder: Zahid Ali
Officers: Zahid Rana Ali [1973] Director

UK Lesiure Ltd
Incorporated: 11 May 2009
Net Worth: £149,036 *Total Assets:* £282,582
Registered Office: 15 High Street, Wombwell, Barnsley, S Yorks, S73 0DA
Major Shareholder: James Harper
Officers: James Harper [1970] Director/Manager; Demi Leigh Peters [1989] Director/Manager

UK McCullenvis Wine Group Ltd
Incorporated: 3 May 2018
Registered Office: Fifth Floor, 3 Gower Street, London, WC1E 6HA
Major Shareholder: Zhiliang Wang
Officers: Zhiliang Wang, Secretary; Zhiliang Wang [1968] Director [Chinese]

UK McLouis Liquor Company Limited
Incorporated: 5 February 2018
Registered Office: Kemp House, 152-160 City Road, London, EC1V 2NX
Major Shareholder: Clariephine Almoguerra Angeles
Officers: Clariephine Almoguerra Angeles [1981] Director [Filipino]

UK Vintners (of London) PLC
Incorporated: 25 March 2015 *Employees:* 3
Net Worth Deficit: £833,238 *Total Assets:* £479,256
Registered Office: Amp House, Dingwall Road, Croydon, Surrey, CR0 2LX
Officers: Robert John Edwards, Secretary; Charles Brodie Agutter [1982] Director/Manager; Peter Anthony Solle [1956] Director/Manager

UK Wine & Food Supplies Ltd
Incorporated: 23 April 2012
Net Worth: £154 *Total Assets:* £14,014
Registered Office: 58 Fisher Hill Way, Radyr, Cardiff, CF15 8DR
Major Shareholder: Simon Symeonides
Officers: Simon Symeonides [1959] Director [Greek]

UKAFDS Limited
Incorporated: 31 January 2019
Registered Office: 44 Bevill Square, Salford, M3 6BB
Shareholders: Andrew Robert Ferguson; Duran Selvi; Ugur Kayan
Officers: Andrew Robert Ferguson [1982] Director/Restaurateur; Ugur Kayan [1977] Director/Restaurateur; Duran Selvi [1972] Director/Restaurateur

Ultimate Drinks Limited
Incorporated: 15 March 2018
Registered Office: Kemp House, 152-160 City Road, London, EC1V 2NX
Major Shareholder: Neil Macwan
Officers: Neil Macwan [1985] Director

Ultra Premium Drinks Limited
Incorporated: 4 October 2018
Registered Office: 25 Balham High Road, London, SW12 9AL
Major Shareholder: Nick Giorgio
Officers: Nick Giorgio [1969] Director/Consultant

Ultracomida Trading Co. Limited
Incorporated: 29 April 2010 *Employees:* 3
Net Worth: £76,943 *Total Assets:* £483,179
Registered Office: Unit 10 Glan Yr Afon Industrial Estate, Llanbadarn Fawr, Aberystwyth, Ceredigion, SY23 3JQ
Parent: Ultracomida Limited
Officers: Paul William Grimwood [1970] Director/Restaurateur; Shumana Palit [1973] Director/Restaurateur

Ultravino Limited
Incorporated: 23 June 2017 *Employees:* 2
Net Worth: £85,823 *Total Assets:* £106,897
Registered Office: Appledram Barns, Birdham Road, Chichester, W Sussex, PO20 7EQ
Shareholders: Dylan Morgan; Gabriele Bertone; Angela Masella
Officers: Gabriele Bertone [1985] Director [Italian]; Angela Masella [1968] Director

Uncharted Wine Company Ltd.
Incorporated: 26 May 2017
Net Worth Deficit: £114,084 Total Assets: £386,290
Registered Office: Unit 16 Containerville, 35 Corbridge Crescent, London, E2 9EZ
Shareholder: Rupert James Taylor
Officers: Patrick John Headlam [1967] Director/Wine Merchant; Louise Holstein [1967] Director/Wine Merchant; Rupert James Taylor [1980] Director/Wine Merchant; Alexander James Thompson [1966] Director

Uncle Nearest Ltd.
Incorporated: 15 February 2018
Registered Office: Suite 106, 268 Belsize Road, London, NW6 4BT
Parent: Uncle Nearest, Inc.
Officers: Dominique Nichole Johnson [1984] Director/Business Executive [American]; Fawn Weaver [1976] Director/Owner/CEO [American]

Under The Bonnet Wines Limited
Incorporated: 27 February 2015
Net Worth: £19,889 Total Assets: £211,653
Registered Office: Flat 6, Woodfield House, Dacres Estate, Dacres Road, London, SE23 2BL
Shareholder: Basile Hubert Serge Gueret
Officers: Basile Hubert Serge Gueret [1988] Director/Restaurant Manager [French]

Underground Spirits Limited
Incorporated: 23 January 2017
Net Worth Deficit: £6,729 Total Assets: £57,393
Registered Office: 2 Green Acres, Welwyn Garden City, Herts, AL7 4LJ
Major Shareholder: Claudia Roughley
Officers: Claudia Roughley [1978] Director/Owner [Australian]

Unfiltered Wines Limited
Incorporated: 21 February 2018
Registered Office: Kirk Rice LLP, The Courtyard, High Street, Ascot, Berks, SL5 7HP
Officers: Margaux Aubry Sharratt [1987] Director [French]; Jade Anne-Marie Febvre [1987] Director [French]

Unicodrinks ESP Ltd
Incorporated: 12 March 2018
Registered Office: 5 Dawnay Road, Bookham, Leatherhead, Surrey, KT23 4PE
Shareholders: Viral Patel; Jaymish Patel
Officers: Jaymish Patel [1992] Director/Biofuel Evolution Ltd; Viral Patel [1988] Managing Director

Union Brands Ltd
Incorporated: 23 March 2011 Employees: 2
Net Worth: £2,550 Total Assets: £3,123
Registered Office: 701 Stonehouse Park, Sperry Way, Stonehouse, Glos, GL10 3UT
Shareholders: William Howard Austin; Philip John Warren
Officers: Philip Warren, Secretary; William Austin [1974] Director; Philip Warren [1975] Director

Union Drinks Ltd
Incorporated: 23 January 2019
Registered Office: The Old Rectory, Mill Lane, Smeeton Westerby, Leics, LE8 0QL
Major Shareholder: Jonathan Mark Chapman
Officers: Alison Clare Chapman [1968] Director; Jonathan Mark Chapman [1966] Director

Union International Drinks Corporation Limited
Incorporated: 6 March 2018
Registered Office: Bridge House, 64-72 Mabgate, Leeds, LS9 7DZ
Major Shareholder: Robert (Elias) Wilson
Officers: Robert Wilson [1941] Director (CEO)

Union XV Gin Co Ltd
Incorporated: 8 October 2018
Registered Office: Ogilvie Munro, 6 Woodside Place, Charing Cross, Glasgow, G3 7QF
Major Shareholder: John MacSporran
Officers: John MacSporran [1959] Director/Sales Manager

Unique Wine Safaris Limited
Incorporated: 5 July 2018
Registered Office: 1-7 Park Road, Caterham, Surrey, CR3 5TB
Major Shareholder: George Alec John Toogood
Officers: David Michael Kelly [1965] Director/Administrator; George Alec John Toogood [1941] Director/Administrator

United Breweries International (U.K.) Limited
Incorporated: 21 December 1982 Employees: 34
Net Worth: £580,891 Total Assets: £3,493,883
Registered Office: Springfield House, Sandling Road, Maidstone, Kent, ME14 2LP
Officers: Mark Edward Davis, Secretary; Dr Vijay Mallya [1955] Director/Industrialist and Business Executive [Indian]; Mahadevan Narayanan [1958] Director [Indian]

United Phoenix Limited
Incorporated: 12 May 2010 Employees: 1
Net Worth Deficit: £19,964 Total Assets: £47,097
Registered Office: 2nd Floor, Suite A, Kennedy House, 31 Stamford Street, Altrincham, Cheshire, WA14 1ES
Major Shareholder: Lihong Fan
Officers: Lihong Fan [1968] Director [Norwegian]

United Spirit Brands Limited
Incorporated: 6 May 2008
Net Worth Deficit: £39,060 Total Assets: £2
Registered Office: Suite 1, 3rd Floor, 11-12 St James's Square, London, SW1Y 4LB
Major Shareholder: Pleurat Shabani
Officers: Pleuat Shabani [1971] Director

United Supplies Limited
Incorporated: 20 October 1986
Net Worth: £761,238 Total Assets: £1,173,117
Registered Office: United House, 6 Regent Road, Aberdeen, AB11 5NS
Shareholders: Ian Watt Strachan; Douglas Martin Gallacher
Officers: Ian Watt Strachan, Secretary; Douglas Martin Gallacher [1947] Director; Ian Watt Strachan [1944] Director

United Wholesale Grocers Limited
Incorporated: 14 September 1982 Employees: 143
Net Worth: £9,422,780 Total Assets: £25,720,696
Registered Office: 246 Flemington Street, Springburn, Glasgow, G21 4BY
Parent: United Holdings UK Ltd
Officers: Kamran Javed, Secretary; Waqas Badar [1971] Director/Trading Controller; Amaan Ramzan [1987] Operations Director; Mohammad Ramzan [1957] Director; Nabeel Ramzan [1982] Director

UK Wholesalers of Beers, Wines and Spiritsdellam

United Wine Estates Limited
Incorporated: 17 October 1984
Net Worth Deficit: £45,342 *Total Assets:* £1,352
Registered Office: 83 Cambridge Street, Pimlico, London, SW1V 4PS
Major Shareholder: Thomas Reitz
Officers: Thomas Reitz [1956] Director/Wine Merchant [German]

United Wine Merchants Limited
Incorporated: 15 April 1985 *Employees:* 48
Net Worth: £8,011,573 *Total Assets:* £16,961,920
Registered Office: Unit 5 Silverwood Business Park, Lurgan, Craigavon, Co Armagh, BT66 6SY
Parent: Rossmoyle Trading Ltd
Officers: Siobhan McSorley, Secretary; Connor Hyland [1970] Finance Director [Irish]; Martin Francis McAuley [1959] Managing Director; Maarten Schuurman [1969] Managing Director [Dutch]

United Wines Ltd
Incorporated: 7 December 2011
Registered Office: 19 Wharfdale Road, London, N1 9SB
Shareholders: Angel Chorbov; Ivan Teodorov Ivanov
Officers: Angel Chorbov [1985] Director/Lawyer [Bulgarian]; Ivan Teodorov Ivanov [1986] Director/Manager [Bulgarian]

Universal Drinks Ltd
Incorporated: 11 March 2004
Net Worth Deficit: £23,772 *Total Assets:* £14,594
Registered Office: 57 Kings Avenue, Chadwell Heath, Romford, Essex, RM6 6BD
Major Shareholder: Salih Hakan
Officers: Hakan Salih [1964] Director

Universal Wines & Spirits Limited
Incorporated: 7 January 2005
Registered Office: Unit 2 Greencroft Estate, Tower Road, Annfield Plain, Stanley, Co Durham, DH9 7XP
Parent: Lanchester Wine Cellars Limited
Officers: Anthony Austin Cleary [1952] Director; Veronica Anne Cleary [1954] Director; Bee Sarah Eustace [1964] Director; Robert Andrew Eustace [1963] Director

Unwined Limited
Incorporated: 17 June 2003
Net Worth Deficit: £48,063
Registered Office: 40 Clarence Road, Chesterfield, Derbys, S40 1LQ
Major Shareholder: Thomas Edward White
Officers: Thomas Edward White [1972] Director

Uokka Limited
Incorporated: 22 September 2016
Net Worth Deficit: £3,951 *Total Assets:* £16,894
Registered Office: Duart House, Finch Way, Strathclyde Business Park, Bellshill, N Lanarks, ML4 3PR
Major Shareholder: Luke Anthony Kilcoyne
Officers: Generald Kilcoyne [1963] Director; Luke Anthony Kilcoyne [1995] Director

Up Drinks Ltd
Incorporated: 31 May 2018
Registered Office: 13 The Broadway, Southall, Middlesex, UB1 1JR
Major Shareholder: Zawar Hussain Shah
Officers: Zawar Hussain Shah [1959] Director

Up Front Brewing Limited
Incorporated: 25 March 2015
Net Worth: £2,059 *Total Assets:* £19,927
Registered Office: 1/1, 27 Skirving Street, Glasgow, G41 3AB
Major Shareholder: Jacob Griffin
Officers: Dr Jacob Griffin, Secretary; Dr Jacob Griffin [1984] Director

Urban Beers and Wines Ltd
Incorporated: 1 April 2016
Registered Office: Pennyfarthing House, Novitt Bamford, Brighton Road, South Croydon, Surrey, CR2 6AW
Major Shareholder: Keith Stock
Officers: Keith Stock, Secretary; Keith Stock [1957] Director

Urban Warehousing Limited
Incorporated: 9 March 2016
Net Worth Deficit: £11,837 *Total Assets:* £82,965
Registered Office: The Enterprise Centre, Cranborne Road, Potters Bar, Herts, EN6 3DQ
Major Shareholder: Rizwan Azmat Sandhu
Officers: Rizwan Azmat Sandhu [1979] Director/Consultant

Urban Wholesalers Limited
Incorporated: 20 June 2013 *Employees:* 2
Net Worth: £2,578 *Total Assets:* £12,582
Registered Office: 18 Brunel Close, Hounslow, Middlesex, TW5 9RP
Shareholder: Manpreet Singh
Officers: Sudesh Chauhan [1984] Director [Indian]; Manpreet Singh [1981] Director [Indian]

Urban Wine Co. Ltd
Incorporated: 21 August 2018
Registered Office: 5 Cradock Avenue, Hebburn, Tyne & Wear, NE31 2TJ
Major Shareholder: Susanne Patricia Winton
Officers: Susanne Patricia Winton [1982] Managing Director

Urbeer Ltd
Incorporated: 23 April 2018
Registered Office: Kemp House, 160 City Road, London, EC1V 2NX
Major Shareholder: Yen-Kai Lee
Officers: Yen-Kai Lee [1993] Director/Student [Taiwanese]

Uropa Group Ltd
Incorporated: 11 October 2018
Registered Office: Spaceworks, Benton Park Road, Newcastle upon Tyne, NE7 7LX
Officers: Natalia Ramade [1986] Director/General Manager [Uruguayan]; Rodrigo Ramade [1989] Director [Uruguayan]

Usedsoft Ltd
Incorporated: 30 October 2012
Registered Office: 3rd Floor, 207 Regent Street, London, W1B 3HH
Shareholders: Klaus-Peter Kraatz; Gerard Donat
Officers: Gerard Donat [1954] Director/Contractor [French]; Klaus-Peter Kraatz [1956] Director/Contractor [German]

USSR Limited
Incorporated: 7 April 2005 *Employees:* 5
Net Worth: £109,487 *Total Assets:* £450,417
Registered Office: Unit 8 Bankside Park Industrial Estate, 28 Thames Road, Barking, Essex, IG11 0HZ
Major Shareholder: Oleh Hodovanets
Officers: Oleh Hodovanets [1979] Director

Ustuner Ltd
Incorporated: 28 April 2017
Registered Office: 83 Park Lane, Peterborough, Cambs, PE1 5JJ
Officers: Ali Ustuner [1996] Managing Director

Utku Emre Ltd
Incorporated: 23 March 2015
Net Worth Deficit: £112,819 *Total Assets:* £34,798
Registered Office: 53-55 Lothair Road, Leicester, LE2 7QE
Major Shareholder: Hasan Karaoglan
Officers: Hasan Karaoglan [1972] Director

Uva Hitchin Ltd
Incorporated: 21 August 2018
Registered Office: 26 Bucklersbury, Hitchin, Herts, SG5 1BG
Shareholders: Duncan George Gammie; Antonio Miceli
Officers: Antonio Miceli [1965] Director/Businessman [Italian]

Uva Wines Ltd
Incorporated: 25 October 2018
Registered Office: 115a Albion Road, London, N16 9PL
Major Shareholder: Emilia Marinig
Officers: Emilia Marinig [1977] Managing Director [Italian]

UWD Limited
Incorporated: 12 January 2017
Registered Office: Glencairn Cottage, Percy Street, Plymouth, PL5 1QH
Officers: Richard John Ellery Butler [1990] Director/Catering; Claudia Rebelo de Oliveira [1990] Director [Portuguese]

V & A Jobs UK Ltd
Incorporated: 19 November 2013
Net Worth Deficit: £2,193 *Total Assets:* £1,230
Registered Office: 48 Nutfield Road, Merstham, Redhill, Surrey, RH1 3EP
Major Shareholder: Mircea-Calin Voinea
Officers: Matt John Austin [1974] Director; Stefan Mitica [1976] Director/IT Consultant [Romanian]

V B Cash & Carry Ltd
Incorporated: 18 January 2019
Registered Office: 21 Bowyer Road, Birmingham, B8 1EX
Officers: Beniamin Vaduva [1999] Director/Owner [Romanian]

V Beverages Limited
Incorporated: 19 April 2017
Registered Office: 32 Curzon Street, London, W1J 7WS
Major Shareholder: Andrew Eddy
Officers: Max Roberto Derek Chater [1987] Director; Andrew Eddy [1982] Director

V G International Trading Limited
Incorporated: 24 May 2010
Net Worth Deficit: £32,454 *Total Assets:* £26,710
Registered Office: Unit 10 Royal Shopping Centre, 299 High Street, Slough, SL1 1BD
Major Shareholder: Gurvade Soyan
Officers: Gurvade Soyan [1983] Director

V I Wholsale Limited
Incorporated: 6 December 2018
Registered Office: 1 Chance Mead, Mayfield Avenue, New Haw, Addlestone, Surrey, KT15 3AG
Major Shareholder: Veronica-Isabela Dragoi
Officers: Veronica-Isabela Dragoi [1985] Director/Businesswoman [Romanian]

V.C. Vintners Limited
Incorporated: 20 December 2000 *Employees:* 9
Net Worth: £554,982 *Total Assets:* £826,967
Registered Office: Unit One Marine Park, Gapton Hall Road, Gapton Industrial Estate, Great Yarmouth, Norfolk, NR31 0NL
Shareholders: Paul John Scott; Jessie Pearl Glover
Officers: Joseph Paul Scott, Secretary/Director; Jessie Pearl Glover [1962] Sales Director; Paul John Scott [1956] Director

Valenta Wine Limited
Incorporated: 13 March 2017
Net Worth Deficit: £3,387 *Total Assets:* £131
Registered Office: 112 Lanson Building, Chelsea Bridge Wharf, 348 Queenstown Road, London, SW11 8QQ
Major Shareholder: Christoffer Valenta
Officers: Christoffer Valenta [1989] Director/Office Worker [Danish]

Valentino & Finch Ltd
Incorporated: 29 September 2016
Registered Office: 71-75 Shelton Street, Covent Garden, London, WC2H 9JQ
Major Shareholder: Darren Jenkins
Officers: Eileen Jenkins, Secretary; Amanda James [1970] Director; Darren Jenkins [1969] Managing Director

Valentino Platinum Ltd
Incorporated: 1 March 2012
Net Worth: £65,264 *Total Assets:* £109,780
Registered Office: 121 Brooker Road, Waltham Abbey, Essex, EN9 1JH
Major Shareholder: Valentinas Januska
Officers: Valentinas Januska [1971] Director [Lithuanian]

Valerieblue Ltd
Incorporated: 24 January 2018
Registered Office: 79 Roodegate, Basildon, Essex, SS14 2AX
Major Shareholder: Taylor Hadley
Officers: Taylor Hadley [1967] Director

Valinch & Mallet Limited
Incorporated: 4 September 2015
Net Worth: £11,896 *Total Assets:* £55,616
Registered Office: Flat 6, 50 Pont Street, London, SW1X 0AE
Major Shareholder: Davide Romano
Officers: Davide Romano [1985] Director [Italian]

Valley Vineyards Limited
Incorporated: 26 February 2009 *Employees:* 2
Net Worth: £29,440 *Total Assets:* £274,558
Registered Office: 1 Llanwenarth Road, Govilon, Abergavenny, Monmouthshire, NP7 9PN
Shareholders: Richard James; Richard Addison
Officers: Richard Addison [1967] Marketing Director; Richard James [1965] Director/Marketing & Sales

Valley Wines, Beer & Spirits Limited
Incorporated: 16 October 2015
Net Worth Deficit: £1,194 *Total Assets:* £16,590
Registered Office: 487 Newchurch Road, Rawtenstall, Rossendale, Lancs, BB4 7TG
Shareholder: Andrew Nicholas Parker
Officers: Andrew Nicholas Parker [1973] Director

Value Focused Solutions Limited
Incorporated: 7 December 2016
Registered Office: Office 56, Mill Mead Business Centre, Mill Mead Road, South Tottenham, London, N17 9QU
Major Shareholder: Sebastian Czerniejewski
Officers: Pawel Kedziora, Secretary; Sebastian Czerniejewski [1978] Managing Director [Polish]

Valvai Cash & Carry Ltd
Incorporated: 4 October 2015
Registered Office: 149 Wingate Crescent, Croydon, Surrey, CR0 3AP
Major Shareholder: Komathi Varatharaj
Officers: Komathi Varatharaj [1976] Director; Kumareswararaja Varatharaj [1973] Director/Marketing

Valvai Ltd
Incorporated: 4 October 2015
Registered Office: 149 Wingate Crescent, Croydon, Surrey, CR0 3AP
Major Shareholder: Komathi Varatharaj
Officers: Komathi Varatharaj [1976] Director; Kumareswararaja Varatharaj [1973] Director/Marketing

Van Pur UK Ltd
Incorporated: 15 January 2018
Registered Office: 6th Floor, First Central 200, 2 Lakeside Drive, London, NW10 7FQ
Major Shareholder: Zbigniew Wantusiak
Officers: Nicholas Jaksic, Secretary; Ryszard Czopik [1967] Director/Vice-President [Polish]; Nicholas Jaksic [1984] Director/Entrepreneur

Vanilla Blue Limited
Incorporated: 1 March 2013
Net Worth Deficit: £52,312 Total Assets: £3,674
Registered Office: 32 Whitehill Road, Dartford, Kent, DA1 4AA
Officers: Janice Nicholls, Secretary; Janice Nicholls [1981] Director/Chief Operating Officer; Uchenna Donald Nwachukwu [1979] Director/Chief Executive

Varmont Ltd
Incorporated: 19 January 2012 Employees: 4
Net Worth Deficit: £4,317 Total Assets: £39,061
Registered Office: 13 Quay Street, Cardiff, CF10 1EA
Officers: Antonio Cersosimo [1976] Director [Italian]; Angelo Montuori [1974] Sales Director [Italian]; Luca Montuori [1977] Operational Director [Italian]; Enrico Varchetta [1974] Director [Italian]

Vats Wine Co. Limited
Incorporated: 11 July 1989 Employees: 1
Net Worth: £6,341 Total Assets: £17,070
Registered Office: Pump Cottage, Beddingham, Lewes, E Sussex, BN8 6JY
Major Shareholder: David John Allcorn
Officers: Caroline Jane Allcorn, Secretary; David John Allcorn [1956] Director/Wine Salesman

Henry de Vaugency Ltd
Incorporated: 19 February 2016
Net Worth Deficit: £6,498 Total Assets: £18,537
Registered Office: Brook Studios, Chipping, Buntingford, Herts, SG9 0PG
Shareholders: Pascal Elie Albert Henry; Delphine Huguette Marie Henry
Officers: Delphine Henry [1974] Director/Wine Grower [French]; Pascal Henry [1975] Director/Wine Grower [French]

VDK Import Export Limited
Incorporated: 8 March 2018
Registered Office: 6 Park Road, Godalming, Surrey, GU7 1SH
Shareholders: Dimitrios Kalfakis; Sofia Athanasiadou
Officers: Sofia Athanasiadou [1976] Director [Greek]; Dimitrios Kalfakis [1967] Director [Greek]

VDS UK Limited
Incorporated: 31 July 2000 Employees: 6
Net Worth: £223,405 Total Assets: £1,067,140
Registered Office: First Floor, 39 High Street, Billericay, Essex, CM12 9BA
Shareholders: Stephen Frederick Brown; Paul MacGregor
Officers: Stephen Frederick Brown [1953] Director; Paul MacGregor [1959] Director

Veda UK Limited
Incorporated: 21 May 2008
Net Worth: £23,661 Total Assets: £115,706
Registered Office: Onega House, 112 Main Road, Sidcup, Kent, DA14 6NE
Officers: Craig Johnathan Richards [1976] Director

Vegan Wine Company London Ltd
Incorporated: 21 June 2018
Registered Office: Flat 305, Southgate Road, London, N1 3JH
Shareholders: Declan Emmet Cotterill Gallivan; Gabriel Llandin Churchill
Officers: Gabriel Llandin Churchill [1991] Director/Entrepreneur; Declan Emmet Cotterill Gallivan [1992] Director/Solicitor

Veini Wine Company Limited
Incorporated: 10 May 2018
Registered Office: The Old Chapel, Park Lane, Baildon, Shipley, W Yorks, BD17 7QH
Major Shareholder: Philip Scott Wellings
Officers: Philip Scott Wellings [1969] Finance Director

Vektor Vodka UK Ltd
Incorporated: 26 January 2018
Registered Office: Little Orchard, Raleigh Drive, Claygate, Esher, Surrey, KT10 9DE
Officers: Mark Bloom [1967] Director; Lewis Paul Casserley [1994] Director; Jordan Fearnley Brown [1994] Director; Darius Kent [1973] Director [Canadian]

Vendange (European) Limited
Incorporated: 4 February 2003
Registered Office: P O Box 1074, TMAC House, Sandhurst, Berks, GU47 8YG
Officers: Philippa Lynn Perera, Secretary; Dillon Ladislaus Perera [1950] Director/Wine Exporter

Vento Marino Ltd
Incorporated: 28 February 2007
Previous: Bikinissimi Limited
Net Worth Deficit: £53,438 Total Assets: £1,223
Registered Office: 135 Notting Hill Gate, London, W11 3LB
Major Shareholder: Anna Veronica Moretti Degli Adimari
Officers: Anna Veronica Moretti, Secretary; Anna Veronica Moretti [1979] Director

Venus 14 Limited
Incorporated: 7 March 1997
Net Worth: £1,341,503 Total Assets: £1,873,599
Registered Office: 58 Lower Clapton Road, London, E5 0RN
Major Shareholder: Balvinder Singh Johal
Officers: Rajwant Kaur, Secretary; Balvinder Singh Johal [1951] Director/Store Manager

Venus Wine & Spirit Merchants PLC
Incorporated: 27 January 2006 Employees: 150
Net Worth: £9,195,024 Total Assets: £24,123,172
Registered Office: Unit 3 Venus House, 62 Garman Road, London, N17 0UT
Officers: Pantelis Christoforou [1970] Director; Kerry Michael [1959] Director; Lakis Michaelides [1964] Director; Christos Kyrillos Ioannou Papaloizou [1964] Director/Architect

Veravinea Ltd
Incorporated: 25 June 2013
Net Worth: £191,287 Total Assets: £211,170
Registered Office: Flat 11, Doddington Grove, London, SE17 3TG
Major Shareholder: Alain Riviere
Officers: Alain Riviere [1967] Director/Fine Wine Salesman [French]

Verre Anglais Limited
Incorporated: 4 August 2015
Net Worth Deficit: £6,422 Total Assets: £263,719
Registered Office: 3 London Wall Buildings, London, EC2M 5PD
Major Shareholder: Sarah Jane Goodwin
Officers: Sarah Jane Goodwin [1977] Director/Marketing Professional

The Verrillo Partnership Limited
Incorporated: 1 March 2017
Net Worth Deficit: £46,046 Total Assets: £117,415
Registered Office: 168 Church Road, Hove, E Sussex, BN3 2DL
Shareholders: Sergio Milan Verrillo; Lynsey Abernethy Verrillo
Officers: Lynsey Abernethy Verrillo [1981] Director/Senior Manager; Sergio Milan Verrillo [1981] Director/Winemaker [Hungarian]

Vertigo Beers Limited
Incorporated: 7 February 2017
Net Worth: £12,329 Total Assets: £17,056
Registered Office: 1 St Peters Mews, Warham Road, London, N4 1BT
Officers: Terence Corless, Secretary; Terence Corless [1989] Director/Craft Drinks Distributor

Vett Limited
Incorporated: 28 May 2002
Net Worth Deficit: £109,730 Total Assets: £3,006
Registered Office: 1 Top Farm Court, Top Street, Bawtry, Doncaster, S Yorks, DN10 6TF
Major Shareholder: William Francis Alan de Fries
Officers: William Francis Alan de Fries [1953] Director

Via Academia Vocatus Ltd
Incorporated: 10 August 2018
Registered Office: 272 Bath Street, Glasgow, G2 4JR
Major Shareholder: David Matthew Hughes
Officers: David Matthew Hughes [1978] Director/Entrepreneur

Viader Vintners Limited
Incorporated: 7 April 2006 Employees: 3
Net Worth: £8,692 Total Assets: £190,043
Registered Office: Unit 14 Waterside Business Park, Lamby Way, Cardiff, CF3 2ET
Major Shareholder: Gilbert Viader
Officers: Claire Viader, Secretary; Gilbert Viader [1957] Director/Vintner [French]

Vicar's Gin Ltd
Incorporated: 14 October 2018
Registered Office: 2 Francis Road, Stourport on Severn, Worcs, DY13 8PL
Major Shareholder: Naomi Joy Joy
Officers: Naomi Joy Joy [1976] Director

Vicarage Spirit Limited
Incorporated: 6 March 2018
Registered Office: The Old Vicarage, Main Road, Hursley, Winchester, Hants, SO21 2JW
Shareholder: David John Warwick
Officers: David John Warwick [1962] Director; Janet Anne Warwick [1960] Director

Vice Enterprises Limited
Incorporated: 15 February 2012
Registered Office: 102 Ruden Way, Epsom, Surrey, KT17 3LP
Major Shareholder: Richard Charles Yolland
Officers: Richard Charles Yolland [1972] Director/Investment Banker

Vickbar Limited
Incorporated: 10 August 1981
Net Worth Deficit: £567,269 Total Assets: £37,990
Registered Office: 4th Floor, 24-26 Baltic Street West, London, EC1Y 0RP
Major Shareholder: George James Demetrius Lemos
Officers: Anastasia Aglaia Lemos, Secretary; George James Demetrius Lemos [1955] Director/Merchant

Vickery Wines Limited
Incorporated: 3 February 1999 Employees: 1
Net Worth Deficit: £128,468 Total Assets: £5,029
Registered Office: 16 Lindler Court, Leighton Buzzard, Beds, LU7 1TS
Major Shareholder: Islay Joy Kennedy
Officers: Islay Joy Kennedy [1949] Director/Wine Importer

Vicomte Bernard de Romanet Limited
Incorporated: 16 February 1967
Net Worth Deficit: £300,000
Registered Office: International Wine Centre, Dallow Road, Luton, Beds, LU1 1UR
Officers: Jayne Elizabeth Foster, Secretary; Howard Warren Falk [1963] Finance Director; David Huw Samuel [1961] Director

Victoria Garry Group Ltd
Incorporated: 23 February 2015
Net Worth: £78,199 Total Assets: £88,430
Registered Office: The Sunbeam, 34 Old Wargrave Road, Newton-le-Willows, Merseyside, WA12 8LU
Major Shareholder: Steven William Hewitt
Officers: Stephen William Hewitt [1978] Director/Publican

The Victoria Island Beverage Company Ltd
Incorporated: 29 August 2018
Registered Office: 40 Bloomsbury Way, London, WC1A 2SE
Major Shareholder: Itua Jude Ehimuan
Officers: Emmanuel Omologbe Ehimuan [1992] Director [Nigerian]; Itua Jude Ehimuan [1988] Marketing Director [Nigerian]

Victory Global Ltd
Incorporated: 24 February 2012
Net Worth Deficit: £515 Total Assets: £4,485
Registered Office: 2116 Davenport House, 261 Bolton Road, Bury, Lancs, BL8 2NZ
Shareholders: Victor Yarbrough; Lydia Keys-Yarbrough
Officers: Victor Yarbrough [1979] Managing Director [American]

Vieuxvino Investment Ltd
Incorporated: 22 October 2018
Registered Office: 8 St Lawrence Road, South Hinksey, Oxford, OX1 5AZ
Major Shareholder: Qian Li
Officers: Dr Qian Li [1986] Director/Consultant

Vigneti Tardis UK Ltd
Incorporated: 1 August 2017
Registered Office: E-Accountants Limited, 36 Bardolph Road, Richmond, Surrey, TW9 2LH
Shareholders: Jack James Peter Lewens; Bruno de Conciliis
Officers: Bruno de Conciliis [1962] Director [Italian]; Jack James Peter Lewens [1977] Director

Viking Enterprises Limited
Incorporated: 4 July 2013
Net Worth: £10,425 *Total Assets:* £159,180
Registered Office: Unit 1 Kingsbridge Road, Barking, Essex, IG11 0BP
Major Shareholder: Latif Ahmed Qureshi
Officers: Latif Ahmed Qureshi [1959] Director/Businessman

Viktor and Walker Ltd
Incorporated: 3 July 2018
Registered Office: Kemp House, 160 City Road, London, EC1V 2NX
Major Shareholder: Adam Mitchell
Officers: Adam Mitchell, Secretary; Adam Mitchell [1986] Director/Nutritionist

Villa Sofia Limited
Incorporated: 3 January 2013
Net Worth Deficit: £50,194 *Total Assets:* £20,103
Registered Office: 20 Havelock Road, Hastings, E Sussex, TN34 1BP
Major Shareholder: Giuseppe Di Palma
Officers: Giuseppe di Palma [1971] Director [Italian]

Village Cottages (Cornwall) Limited
Incorporated: 15 January 1970 *Employees:* 3
Net Worth Deficit: £6,944 *Total Assets:* £23,370
Registered Office: 15 Alverton Street, Penzance, Cornwall, TR18 2QP
Shareholders: John Holden; Max Yashar Holden; Susie Umran Mehmet-Salih
Officers: John Holden, Secretary; John Holden [1955] Director/Wine Merchant; Max Yashar Holden [1987] Director/Wine Merchant; Susie Umran Mehmet-Salih [1954] Director/Retired

Village Selections Limited
Incorporated: 26 September 2013
Net Worth Deficit: £86,266 *Total Assets:* £2,212,201
Registered Office: 54 Bankhead Crossway South, Edinburgh, EH11 4EP
Major Shareholder: Daniel Arthur Fisher
Officers: Daniel Arthur Fisher [1982] Director/Executive [American]

John Villar Wines Limited
Incorporated: 16 October 2006 *Employees:* 1
Net Worth: £3,049 *Total Assets:* £133,468
Registered Office: 7 Phillips Acre, Yarpole, Leominster, Herefords, HR6 0DA
Major Shareholder: John Gaspard Villar
Officers: Clare Amelia Villar, Secretary; John Gaspard Villar [1966] Director/Wine Merchant

Vin D'Oc Limited
Incorporated: 14 November 2003
Net Worth: £10,861 *Total Assets:* £11,544
Registered Office: 10 St Ann Street, Salisbury, Wilts, SP1 2DN
Shareholders: Jennifer Mary Hibberd; Robin Victor Bruce Hibberd
Officers: Jennifer Mary Hibberd, Secretary; Jennifer Mary Hibberd [1950] Director/Secretary; Robin Victor Bruce Hibberd [1943] Director/Wine Maker

Vin Est... Ltd
Incorporated: 20 January 2010 *Employees:* 2
Net Worth: £95,060 *Total Assets:* £188,148
Registered Office: Walnut Tree, Fyfield, Lechlade, Glos, GL7 3NT
Shareholders: Rachel Anne Jenkins; Michael David Jenkins
Officers: Michael David Jenkins [1966] Director; Rachel Anne Jenkins [1968] Director/Finance

Vin Neuf Limited
Incorporated: 24 December 2001 *Employees:* 2
Net Worth: £53,578 *Total Assets:* £115,685
Registered Office: 6B Union Street, Stratford upon Avon, Warwicks, CV37 6QT
Major Shareholder: James Shirley Hart Richards
Officers: James Shirley Hart Richards, Secretary; James Shirley Hart Richards [1972] Director/Wine Trader

Vin-X Enterprise Investment Scheme Ltd
Incorporated: 4 July 2013
Net Worth: £189,728 *Total Assets:* £288,937
Registered Office: Bailey House, 4-10 Barttelot Road, Horsham, W Sussex, RH12 1DQ
Shareholder: Clive Richard Sharpe
Officers: Peter Robert Shakeshaft [1958] Director

Vinafrica Limited
Incorporated: 14 February 1991
Net Worth: £726 *Total Assets:* £726
Registered Office: Savoy House, Savoy Circus, London, W3 7DA
Shareholder: Simon George Halliday
Officers: Simon George Halliday, Secretary; Mario Forge Gomes Monteiro, Secretary; Simon George Halliday [1957] Director/Company Secretary

Vinals Wine & Food Limited
Incorporated: 15 July 2014
Net Worth: £12,429 *Total Assets:* £229,764
Registered Office: 10 Philpot Lane, London, EC3M 8AA
Major Shareholder: Rolando Vinals
Officers: Rolando Vinals [1972] Director [Italian]

Vinandar Wines Limited
Incorporated: 14 September 2018
Registered Office: Kirkrigg, Lake Road, Windermere, Cumbria, LA23 2DB
Parent: Wine Vantage Limited
Officers: Deborah Brooks [1962] Director; Michael Joseph Moriarty [1965] Director; Dennis Whiteley [1961] Director

Vinature Ltd
Incorporated: 7 October 2018
Registered Office: Highland Cottage, Bredwardine, Hereford, HR3 6BZ
Major Shareholder: James Wesley Robson
Officers: James Wesley Robson [1978] Director/Chef

Vinceremos Wines & Spirits Limited
Incorporated: 4 July 1991 *Employees:* 5
Net Worth: £216,155 *Total Assets:* £503,628
Registered Office: Royal House, Sovereign Street, Leeds, LS1 4BJ
Major Shareholder: Jeremy Christopher Gardener
Officers: Kellie Samantha Sykes, Secretary; Jeremy Christopher Gardener [1956] Director/Wine Merchant

Vincisive Wines Limited
Incorporated: 30 November 2011
Net Worth: £1,031 *Total Assets:* £54,045
Registered Office: 88 Sheep Street, Bicester, Oxon, OX26 6LP
Shareholders: Mark Chamberlain; John Edwards; Darren Joseph Brogden
Officers: Darren Joseph Brogden [1969] Director/Wine Merchant; Mark Chamberlain [1975] Director; John Edwards [1967] Director

Vine & Cork Limited
Incorporated: 30 August 2017
Registered Office: 71-75 Shelton Street, Covent Garden, London, WC2H 9JQ
Shareholders: Andrea Perticati; Tiziano Mario Caldera; Gianpiero Rocca
Officers: Andrea Perticati [1970] Director/Program Manager [Italian]; Dr Gianpiero Rocca [1981] Director/Manager [Italian]

The Vine and Malt Ltd
Incorporated: 15 June 2018
Registered Office: 143 Hamstead Road, Great Barr, Birmingham, B43 5BB
Major Shareholder: Rohan Chouhan
Officers: Rohan Chouhan [1999] Managing Director

Vine Street Wine Company Limited
Incorporated: 24 August 2017
Registered Office: 1st Floor, 5 Century Court, Tolpits Lane, Watford, Herts, WD18 9PX
Major Shareholder: Mark Cancea
Officers: Mark Cancea [1960] Director

Vine Trail Limited
Incorporated: 28 August 2002 *Employees:* 10
Net Worth: £1,428,068 *Total Assets:* £1,852,899
Registered Office: Boyces Building, Regent Street, Clifton, Bristol, BS8 4HU
Shareholders: Catherine Lucy Brookes; James Nicholas William Brookes
Officers: Catherine Lucy Brookes, Secretary; Catherine Lucy Brookes [1951] Director/Wine Merchant; James Nicholas William Brookes [1960] Director/Wine Merchant

Vine Wine Limited
Incorporated: 21 May 2015 *Employees:* 2
Net Worth: £3,891 *Total Assets:* £61,468
Registered Office: The Old Emporium, Bow Street, Langport, Somerset, TA10 9PQ
Major Shareholder: Patrick Maurice Magill
Officers: Patrick Maurice Magill [1965] Director; Sophie Emma Grace Magill [1963] Director

Vineco Inco Ltd
Incorporated: 18 May 2018
Registered Office: Unit D, 6 Clay Hill, Bristol, BS5 7EU
Shareholder: Dinish Kuriakose Kattakkayam
Officers: Dinish Kuriakose Kattakkayam [1988] Director/Management Accountant [Indian]

Vinemporium Limited
Incorporated: 24 October 2013
Registered Office: Sterling House, Fulbourne Road, Walthamstow, London, E17 4EE
Major Shareholder: Stavros Chambi
Officers: Stavros Chambi [1976] Director

Vines Wines Limited
Incorporated: 5 November 2012
Registered Office: Bennick House, Airedale View, Rawdon, Leeds, LS19 6QF
Officers: Ian Michael Vinall, Secretary; Ian Michael Vinall [1969] Director; Rachel Louisa Vinall [1982] Director

Vineus Limited
Incorporated: 14 September 2018
Registered Office: Suite 5, 2nd Floor, Innovation Centre, 225 Marsh Wall, London, E14 9FW
Officers: Marina Petrova [1982] Director

Vinexcel Limited
Incorporated: 17 July 1987
Net Worth Deficit: £11,311 *Total Assets:* £897
Registered Office: 106-108 Reddish Lane, Manchester, M18 7JL
Shareholders: John Spencer Comyn; Evelyn Belle Comyn
Officers: Evelyn Belle Comyn, Secretary; Evelyn Belle Comyn [1939] Director/Secretary; John Spencer Comyn [1939] Sales Director

Vineyard Belfast Limited-The
Incorporated: 27 September 2002 *Employees:* 11
Net Worth: £506,283 *Total Assets:* £761,643
Registered Office: Lindsay House, 10 Callender Street, Belfast, BT1 5BN
Shareholders: Geraldine McGurran; Anthony McGurran
Officers: Generaldine McGurran, Secretary; Anthony McGurran [1954] Director/Wine & Spirit Merchant

Vinfinity Limited
Incorporated: 3 August 2015
Net Worth: £37,044 *Total Assets:* £213,392
Registered Office: Falcon Park, Hophurst Lane, Crawley Down, Crawley, W Sussex, RH10 4XF
Shareholder: Martin Game
Officers: Martin Game [1968] Director/Salesman; Paul Andrew Oliver [1971] Director

Viniexport Limited
Incorporated: 30 March 2016
Registered Office: Martlet House, E1 Yeoman Gate, Yeoman Way, Worthing, W Sussex, BN13 3QZ
Major Shareholder: Eugenio Picca
Officers: Eugenio Picca [1984] Director [Italian]

Viniguide Limited
Incorporated: 15 December 2003 *Employees:* 1
Net Worth Deficit: £19,944 *Total Assets:* £13,700
Registered Office: 49 Station Road, Polegate, E Sussex, BN26 6EA
Shareholder: Paul Boyer
Officers: Paul Henri Boyer [1975] Director/Wine Consultant [French]

Vinimpo (U.K.) Limited
Incorporated: 5 March 1996 *Employees:* 1
Net Worth: £108,943 *Total Assets:* £1,834,266
Registered Office: Ibex House, Baker Street, Weybridge, Surrey, KT13 8AH
Major Shareholder: Joseph Richard Minerva
Officers: Tommaso Minerva, Secretary; Joseph Richard Minerva [1960] Director/Wine Importer

Vinissimo Limited
Incorporated: 23 January 1996   Employees: 12
Net Worth: £261,543   Total Assets: £1,031,826
Registered Office: DS House, 306 High Street, Croydon, Surrey, CR0 1NG
Officers: Chantal Santoro, Secretary; Paul John Evangelista Santoro [1967] Sales Director

Vinitaly Limited
Incorporated: 13 February 2007   Employees: 1
Net Worth: £10,382   Total Assets: £104,602
Registered Office: 52 Leicester Street, Bulkington, Bedworth, Warwicks, CV12 9NG
Shareholders: Giacomo Nucci; Giulia Nucci
Officers: Elio Nucci [1954] Director [Italian]; Giacomo Nucci [1990] Director; Giulia Nucci [1987] Director

Vinnaturo Ltd
Incorporated: 12 June 2013
Net Worth Deficit: £8,611   Total Assets: £66,409
Registered Office: Flat 4, 106 Oxford Gardens, London, W10 6NG
Major Shareholder: Tom Craven
Officers: Thomas Craven, Secretary; Thomas Craven [1984] Director/Wine Merchant

Vinny Labs Ltd
Incorporated: 1 November 2017
Registered Office: 18-20 Scrutton Street, London, EC2A 4RX
Major Shareholder: Sebastian Sheiky Lyall
Officers: Sebastian Sheiky Lyall [1982] Director

Vino & Spirits Limited
Incorporated: 3 November 2016
Registered Office: First Floor, 85 Great Portland Street, London, W1W 7LT
Major Shareholder: Alan Sasa Perisin
Officers: Alan Sasa Perisin [1969] Director/Programmer

Vino Italiano Importers Limited
Incorporated: 27 March 2015
Net Worth: £2,349   Total Assets: £36,123
Registered Office: Bank House, 2-4 Wood Street, Swindon, Wilts, SN1 4AB
Shareholders: Candido Nigris; Gianni Pau; Pier Luigi Turatti
Officers: Candido Nigris [1967] Director [Italian]

Vino Italiano Ltd
Incorporated: 4 May 2018
Registered Office: Suite 8, 146 High Street, Burton on Trent, Staffs, DE14 1JE
Major Shareholder: Guy Laurant Conzimu
Officers: Guy Laurant Conzimu [1985] Director [Dutch]

Vino Merchant Limited
Incorporated: 19 February 2018
Registered Office: Lower Brimscombe Mill, Brimscombe, Stroud, Glos, GL5 2SB
Shareholder: Martin Rudolf Lomberg
Officers: Ashley Lomberg [1987] Director; Martin Rudolf Lomberg [1962] Director

Vino Pronto UK Ltd
Incorporated: 11 September 2016
Net Worth Deficit: £240   Total Assets: £9,431
Registered Office: 7 Manor Croft, Bishop Wilton, York, YO42 1TG
Officers: Luke Hirst [1974] Director; Richard Kilian [1972] Director; Daniel Peel [1974] Director

Vino Unico Limited
Incorporated: 13 June 2018
Registered Office: Kemp House, 160 City Road, London, EC1V 2NX
Shareholders: Delia Babiciu; Scott Evans
Officers: Delia Babiciu [1978] Director/Lawyer; Scott Evans [1983] Director/Lawyer [Australian]

Vino Vero Ltd
Incorporated: 11 January 2013
Net Worth: £31,605   Total Assets: £71,077
Registered Office: 105 Leigh Road, Leigh on Sea, Essex, SS9 1JL
Shareholders: Charlotte Emma Brown; Sam Dixon Brown
Officers: Charlotte Emma Brown [1984] Director; Sam Dixon Brown [1982] Director

Vinolex Ltd
Incorporated: 19 September 2017
Registered Office: JSA Partners, 41 Skylines Business Village, Limeharbour, Canary Wharf, London, E14 9TS
Major Shareholder: Zsolt Szente
Officers: Zsolt Szente [1975] Director [Hungarian]

The Vinorium Limited
Incorporated: 23 June 2005   Employees: 15
Previous: Z & B Vintners Limited
Net Worth: £1,296,295   Total Assets: £3,392,663
Registered Office: Ashmill House, Ashford Road, Lenham, Maidstone, Kent, ME17 2GQ
Major Shareholder: Stuart William McCloskey
Officers: Stuart William McCloskey [1972] Director

Vinos Latinos Ltd
Incorporated: 16 December 2009
Previous: Winesofuruguay.co.uk. Ltd
Registered Office: 33 Felhampton Road, London, SE9 3NT
Major Shareholder: Carla Antonella Bertellotti
Officers: Carla Antonella Bertellotti, Secretary; Carla Antonella Bertellotti [1976] Director/Wine Importer [Italian]

Vinotrans Ltd
Incorporated: 26 October 2016
Net Worth Deficit: £3,993   Total Assets: £4,217
Registered Office: Unit 21 Dale House, Vickers Street, Manchester, M40 8EF
Major Shareholder: Dan Dimbu
Officers: Dan Dimbu [1990] Director [Romanian]

Vinova Export Limited
Incorporated: 12 January 2017
Registered Office: Fleming Court, Leigh Road, Eastleigh, Hants, SO50 9PD
Major Shareholder: Eusebio Novas Hay
Officers: Eusebio Novas Hay [1985] Director/Entrepreneur [Spanish]

Vinoveritas (Europe) Limited
Incorporated: 18 April 2016
Net Worth Deficit: £4,327   Total Assets: £423
Registered Office: Carrick House, Lypiatt Road, Cheltenham, Glos, GL50 2QJ
Shareholders: Samuel Archibald Hyman; Howard Jonathan Hyman
Officers: Howard Jonathan Hyman [1949] Director/Strategic Adviser; Samuel Archibald Hyman [1979] Director

Vinovest Limited
Incorporated: 15 May 2017
Net Worth: £95 *Total Assets:* £50,563
Registered Office: 43 Cornelius House, 5 Handley Page Road, Barking, Essex, IG11 0UY
Officers: Ethem Ozdemir [1974] Director/Sales Manager

Vinovitaj Ltd
Incorporated: 25 November 2011
Net Worth Deficit: £5,111 *Total Assets:* £159
Registered Office: Flat 3, 5 Milton Road, London, E17 4SP
Shareholder: Barbora Bartosova
Officers: Barbora Bartosova [1984] Managing Director [Czech]

Vins Ltd
Incorporated: 26 February 2018
Registered Office: Keelers, High Street, Limpsfield, Oxted, Surrey, RH8 0DT
Officers: Benjamin Paul Chatfield [1974] Director/Marketing Consultant; Peter Andrew Hames [1979] Director

Vintage & Fine Wine International Limited
Incorporated: 15 May 1985 *Employees:* 3
Net Worth: £4,106,649 *Total Assets:* £8,774,116
Registered Office: Church House, 10 Chesham Road, Guildford, Surrey, GU1 3LS
Officers: Paul Nunnerley Hall, Secretary; Tracey Anne Daniell [1961] Director/Office Administrator; Clare Juliet Jackson [1962] Director/Wine Broker

Vintage 1947 Limited
Incorporated: 5 August 2013
Net Worth: £591,141 *Total Assets:* £687,989
Registered Office: 63 Highgate High Street, Highgate, London, N6 5JX
Shareholders: Jordi Orriols-Gil; Benjamin Rick; Jason Francis Feasey
Officers: Deniz Akgul [1977] Director/Trader Hedge Fund; Patrick Robert Badenoch [1977] Director/Hedge Fund Manager; Jason Francis Feasey [1972] Director/Portfolio Manager Hedge Fund; Lydia Hollas [1983] Director/Solicitor; Jordi Orriols-Gil [1975] Director/Trader; Benjamin Rick [1972] Director/Fund Manager

Vintage Capital II PLC
Incorporated: 9 February 2016
Net Worth: £4,401,037 *Total Assets:* £5,029,026
Registered Office: Somerville Rooms, Queensberry Road, Newmarket, Suffolk, CB8 9AU
Officers: William Henry Sporborg, Secretary; Jonathan Daniel Goedhuis [1949] Director [Dutch]; Christopher Holdsworth Hunt [1942] Director; Simon David Marsh [1962] Director/Racing Manager; William Henry Sporborg [1965] Director

The Vintage Malt Whisky Company Limited
Incorporated: 13 March 1992 *Employees:* 7
Net Worth: £4,030,349 *Total Assets:* £5,031,725
Registered Office: 2 Stewart Street, Milngavie, Glasgow, G62 6BW
Shareholders: Harry Brian Crook; Andrew Brian Crook
Officers: Caroline Sanderson James, Secretary; Andrew Brian Crook [1976] Managing Director; Caroline Crawford Crook [1943] Director; Harry Brian Crook [1942] Director/Chairman; Caroline Sanderson James [1968] Director/Solicitor

Vintage Roots Limited
Incorporated: 14 October 1996 *Employees:* 17
Net Worth: £1,378,304 *Total Assets:* £2,340,761
Registered Office: Barttelot Court, Barttelot Road, Horsham, W Sussex, RH12 1DQ
Shareholders: Neil Palmer; Lance Pigott
Officers: Neil Palmer, Secretary/Director; Neil Palmer [1960] Director; Lance Pigott [1959] Director

Vintage Wine Investments Limited
Incorporated: 11 October 2017
Registered Office: 21 Culverlands Close, Stanmore, Middlesex, HA7 3AG
Officers: Denis Hartnett [1975] Director [Irish]

Vintage Wines Limited
Incorporated: 12 September 1953 *Employees:* 8
Net Worth: £220,224 *Total Assets:* £629,429
Registered Office: 116 Derby Road, Nottingham, NG1 5FB
Major Shareholder: Terry Albert Rockley
Officers: Katarzyna Magdalena Zawadzka, Secretary; Terry Albert Rockley [1964] Sales Director

Vinterest Limited
Incorporated: 13 June 2014 *Employees:* 2
Net Worth Deficit: £26,915 *Total Assets:* £11,351
Registered Office: Windover House, St Ann Street, Salisbury, Wilts, SP1 2DR
Shareholders: Angus James McKellen Fordyce; Nuno Dorring de Brito E Cunha
Officers: Nuno Brito E Cunha [1983] Director; Angus James McKellen Fordyce [1984] Director

The Vintner London Ltd
Incorporated: 17 March 2010 *Employees:* 19
Net Worth: £349,579 *Total Assets:* £2,076,235
Registered Office: Unit F, 19 Heathmans Road, London, SW6 4TJ
Shareholders: Martin's Family Holdings Limited; Thomas Edward Gilbey; Beth Christian Gilbey
Officers: Tony Harb, Secretary; Julia Helena Beran [1982] Director/Wine Merchant; Thomas Edward Gilbey [1972] Director/Wine Merchant

Vinum Fine Wines Limited
Incorporated: 11 September 2015 *Employees:* 12
Net Worth: £947,697 *Total Assets:* £7,417,750
Registered Office: 146 High Street, Billericay, Essex, CM12 9DF
Major Shareholder: Yu Jin Desmond Lim
Officers: Claire Rosalie Bailey [1969] Sales Director; Lee Raymond Crymble [1976] Managing Director; David Lindsay Emerson Hamilton [1957] Director/Vice Chairman; Oliver Christian Wynn Holtam [1976] Finance Director

Vinum Limited
Incorporated: 8 February 2008 *Employees:* 16
Net Worth Deficit: £441,955 *Total Assets:* £1,591,607
Registered Office: 7 Torriano Mews, London, NW5 2RZ
Shareholders: Valeria Nibbio; Angelo Cane
Officers: Angelo Cane, Secretary/Director [Italian]; Angelo Cane [1964] Director [Italian]; Valeria Nibbio [1964] Director [Italian]

Vinvm Ltd
Incorporated: 16 April 2018
Registered Office: 80 Long Acre, London, WC2E 9NG
Shareholders: Daniel Edward Elswood; Andris Praulitis; Igo Konrads
Officers: Daniel Edward Elswood [1988] Director; Igo Konrads [1985] Director [Latvian]; Andris Praulitis [1985] Director [Latvian]

VIP Bottles Ltd
Incorporated: 22 May 2014 Employees: 4
Net Worth: £64,940 Total Assets: £277,325
Registered Office: 42 Welford Road, Leicester, LE2 7AA
Shareholder: Bhupinder Singh Gill
Officers: Bhupinder Singh Gill [1989] Director/IT Technician; Avtar Singh Uppal [1948] Director/Taxi Driver

VIP Services Scotland Ltd
Incorporated: 20 November 2018
Registered Office: 14 Stormyhill Road, Portree, Isle of Skye, IV51 9DY
Major Shareholder: Vitalie Cacicovschi
Officers: Vitalie Cacicovschi [1972] Director [Romanian]

Viscount Agencies Limited
Incorporated: 21 January 1980 Employees: 4
Net Worth: £864,636 Total Assets: £1,067,907
Registered Office: Concept House, 3 Dene Street, Dorking, Surrey, RH4 2DR
Officers: Janette Lesley Rexha, Secretary; Julian Nicholas Candish Furnell [1961] Director

Viserra Limited
Incorporated: 9 March 2011 Employees: 14
Net Worth: £174,613 Total Assets: £594,758
Registered Office: Unit 1, 112A Warner Road, London, SE5 9HQ
Major Shareholder: Vera Isabel Ramos
Officers: Vera Isabel Rodrigues Ramos [1982] Director/Administrator [Portuguese]

Vitam Dare Limited
Incorporated: 20 May 2015
Net Worth: £1,486 Total Assets: £43,478
Registered Office: 472b Bearwood Road, Smethwick, W Midlands, B66 4HA
Major Shareholder: Houman Chitsaz Esfahani
Officers: Houman Chitsaz Esfahani [1973] Director [French]

Vitena Wines Ltd
Incorporated: 8 June 2017
Registered Office: Companies House, Default Address, Cardiff, CF14 8LH
Officers: Jessica Bella [1992] Director/Consultant [Italian]

Vitesse Vintners Limited
Incorporated: 23 August 2011
Net Worth Deficit: £860 Total Assets: £8,212
Registered Office: 70 Upper Richmond Road, London, SW15 2RP
Officers: Peter Henry Borer [1944] Director/Executive Chairman; Michael Haynes [1947] Director/Rail Transport Consultant; John William Sampson Hine [1951] Director/Management Consultant; Michael Robert Edwards Jones [1947] Director/Consultant

Vitis-Terra Limited
Incorporated: 6 September 2016
Net Worth Deficit: £2,131
Registered Office: 4 Stannary Street, London, SE11 4AA
Major Shareholder: Franck Cedric Tienta
Officers: Aboh Roger Albert Cairo [1980] Director [French]; Patrick Alexandre Fomethe Momo [1976] Director [French]; Franck Cedric Tienta [1981] Director [French]

Vitkovitch Brothers Limited
Incorporated: 25 January 2006
Net Worth: £1,903 Total Assets: £8,278
Registered Office: Greensleeves House, Highfield, Banstead, Surrey, SM7 3LJ
Shareholder: Angela Caroline Gray
Officers: Thomas Oliver Gray, Secretary; Angela Caroline Gray [1962] Director

Vito International Ltd
Incorporated: 6 November 2015 Employees: 2
Net Worth: £605,298 Total Assets: £2,628,447
Registered Office: Hill House, Farm Barbers Lane, Antrobus, Northwich, Cheshire, CW9 6JT
Major Shareholder: Barbara Powell
Officers: Babara Powell [1957] Director/Housewife; Brian Andrew Powell [1957] Director/Wine Merchant

Vitosha Wine Ltd
Incorporated: 10 January 2019
Registered Office: 7 Victoria Road, Alton, Hants, GU34 2DH
Shareholders: Umesh Prasad; Neelesh Prasad
Officers: Umesh Prasad [1965] Director

Vivir Drinks Ltd
Incorporated: 19 September 2018
Registered Office: 75 The Cottages, Beacon Hill, Penn, High Wycombe, Bucks, HP10 8NH
Officers: Navindh Grewal, Secretary; Navindh Grewal [1988] Director; Paul Hayes [1982] Director

Volfram Ltd
Incorporated: 31 October 2011
Net Worth: £4,063 Total Assets: £4,063
Registered Office: Apex, 2 Sheriffs Orchard, Coventry, Warwicks, CV1 3PP
Officers: Daniil Panpurin [1985] Director [Russian]

Philip von Nell Wines Limited
Incorporated: 4 February 2009 Employees: 1
Net Worth: £49,769 Total Assets: £91,378
Registered Office: Charnwood Cottage, 1a Charnwood Grove, West Bridgford, Nottingham, NG2 7NT
Major Shareholder: David Alexander Lazaro
Officers: David Alexander Lazaro [1986] Director/Salesman

Voubearst Limited
Incorporated: 9 January 2018
Registered Office: Companies House, Default Address, Cardiff, CF14 8LH
Major Shareholder: Yajun Tian
Officers: Yajun Tian [1975] Director [Chinese]

Vranac Stonecastle Limited
Incorporated: 11 March 2018
Registered Office: 6 Roding Lane South, Ilford, Essex, IG4 5NX
Major Shareholder: Qazim Sokoli
Officers: Qazim Sokoli [1969] Director

Vranken Pommery UK Ltd.
Incorporated: 31 December 1996 Employees: 11
Net Worth: £952,501 Total Assets: £4,929,697
Registered Office: Lincoln House, 300 High Holborn, London, WC1V 7JH
Parent: Vranken-Pommery Monopole SA
Officers: Sara Louise Hicks [1962] Director; Nicholas Andrew Travers Hyde [1947] Director; Cyrille Laupie [1972] Director [French]; Julien Lonneux [1989] Director [Belgian]; Nathalie Jeanne Marie Odile Vranken [1964] Director [French]; Paul Francois Edouard Joseph Vranken [1947] Chairman & Managing Director [French]

Vyce Ltd
Incorporated: 22 February 2019
Registered Office: 6 High Street, Wheathampstead, St Albans, Herts, AL4 8AA
Shareholders: John Edward Turner; Steve Fishhwick
Officers: John Edward Turner [1971] Director

W D L Wholesale Limited
Incorporated: 13 October 2017
Registered Office: WD Estates, Office 11, Green Industrial Estate, The Roe, St Asaph, Denbighshire, LL17 0LT
Officers: Joshua Lewis, Secretary; Gary Durkin [1954] Director; Ryan Lewis [1975] Director

W S B C Limited
Incorporated: 13 July 2007
Registered Office: 10 The Hogan, Selwyn Road, Edgbaston, Birmingham, B16 0SP
Major Shareholder: Sukvinder Singh
Officers: Sukvinder Singh [1967] Director

Wadworth & Company (Burford) Limited
Incorporated: 20 May 1930
Registered Office: Northgate Brewery, Devizes, Wilts, SN10 1JW
Parent: Wadworth and Company Limited
Officers: Alison Jane Skedd, Secretary; Charles John Eric Bartholomew [1951] Managing Director/Chairman; Anthony Frederick West [1951] Sales Director

Wadworth and Company Limited
Incorporated: 18 November 1889 Employees: 1,043
Net Worth: £83,381,000 Total Assets: £152,864,992
Registered Office: Northgate Brewery, Devizes, Wilts, SN10 1JW
Officers: Alison Jane Skedd, Secretary; Nigel John Bewley Atkinson [1953] Director; Rupert Bagnall [1970] Operations Director - Managed Houses; Charles John Eric Bartholomew [1951] Managing Director/Chairman; John Edward Beard [1962] Director; Edward Scandrett Harford [1948] Director/Computer Consultant; Alison Jane Skedd [1963] Director/Accountant; Nicola Claire Stenhouse [1979] Director; Lloyd John Stephens [1957] Tenanted Trade Director; Jonathan Thomas [1964] Sales Director; Christopher Welham [1970] Director/Chief Executive Officer

Wagner Spirits Ltd
Incorporated: 14 December 2016
Net Worth: £10 Total Assets: £10
Registered Office: 14 Carswell Gardens, Glasgow, G41 2DH
Major Shareholder: Donald Alasdair MacLellan
Officers: Donald Alasdair MacLellan [1981] Director/Export Sales Manager (Spirits)

Waistcoat Wines Ltd
Incorporated: 16 July 2015
Net Worth: £829 Total Assets: £46,445
Registered Office: Unit 17 Foxes Bridge Road, Forest Vale Industrial Estate, Cinderford, Glos, GL14 2PQ
Shareholder: Kelly Mortimer
Officers: Kelly Mortimer [1980] Director; James Wormleighton [1983] Director

Walker & Wodehouse Wines Limited
Incorporated: 17 June 2009
Net Worth Deficit: £130,459 Total Assets: £30,326
Registered Office: Whitchurch Lane, Whitchurch, Bristol, BS14 0JZ
Parent: Bibendum PLB Group Limited
Officers: Andrea Pozzi [1971] Director/Group Chief Operating Officer; Ewan James Robertson [1982] Finance Director; Jonathan Solesbury [1965] Director/Group Chief Financial Officer; Robin Nigel Wodehouse [1943] Director/Consultant

Alistair Walker Whisky Company Ltd
Incorporated: 13 March 2018
Registered Office: 1st Floor, Building 3, Earls Court, Earls Gate Business Park, Grangemouth, Stirlingshire, FK3 8ZE
Major Shareholder: Alistair Craig Walker
Officers: Alistair Craig Walker [1974] Managing Director

Walking Back The Cat Limited
Incorporated: 28 September 2018
Registered Office: 843 Finchley Road, London, NW11 8NA
Major Shareholder: Yosef Schwartz
Officers: Yosef Schwartz [1959] Director [Israeli]

Wall2wall Wines Limited
Incorporated: 28 February 2019
Registered Office: 2 Oldfield Road, Bocam Park, Bridgend, CF35 5LJ
Shareholders: Jonathan Hugh Wall; Benjamin Wall
Officers: Benjamin Wall [1995] Director; Jonathan Hugh Wall [1961] Director

Wallaces Express Limited
Incorporated: 2 April 2003
Net Worth: £26,346,260 Total Assets: £26,347,828
Registered Office: Crompton Way, North Newmoor Industrial Estate, Irvine, N Ayrshire, KA11 4HU
Parent: C & C Group PLC
Officers: Stephen Glancey [1960] Director; Andrea Pozzi [1971] Director - Manufacturing; Ewan James Robertson [1982] Finance Director

Wallis Ventures Ltd
Incorporated: 11 August 2017
Net Worth: £25 Total Assets: £25
Registered Office: 11 The Brambles, Cuckfield, Haywards Heath, W Sussex, RH17 5BF
Major Shareholder: Barnaby George Wallis
Officers: Barnaby George Wallis [1998] Director

Walnut Tree Distillery Ltd
Incorporated: 3 September 2018
Registered Office: Walnut Tree Farm, Easthaugh Road, Lyng Easthaugh, Norwich, NR9 5LN
Shareholders: Graham Paul Mills; Emma Louise Brigham
Officers: Emma Louise Brigham [1976] Director; Graham Paul Mills [1969] Director

A J Walsh Consultant Limited
Incorporated: 26 March 2018
Registered Office: The Office Suite, 2 Greno House, School Lane, Grenoside, Sheffield, S35 8QU
Major Shareholder: Adrian James Walsh
Officers: Adrian James Walsh [1964] Director

Wanderlust Wine Limited
Incorporated: 11 September 2015
Net Worth Deficit: £52,641 *Total Assets:* £52,198
Registered Office: Evolution House, Iceni Court, Delft Way, Norwich, NR6 6BB
Major Shareholder: Richard Ellison
Officers: Richard Peter Ellison, Secretary; Richard Peter Ellison [1982] Director

Warner Family Wines Limited
Incorporated: 12 November 2015
Registered Office: Ashcombe Court, Woolsack Way, Godalming, Surrey, GU7 1LQ
Major Shareholder: Lucy Margaret Faraday Warner
Officers: Lucy Margaret Faraday Warner [1966] Director/Sales & Marketing

Warwick Banks and Jenkins Limited
Incorporated: 10 July 2006 *Employees:* 1
Previous: Active Tourism Limited
Net Worth Deficit: £22,222 *Total Assets:* £152,641
Registered Office: 47 Marylebone Lane, London, W1U 2NT
Shareholders: Nigel John Jenkins; Oliver Graham Warwick Banks; Howard John Jenkins
Officers: Howard John Jenkins [1984] Director; Nigel John Jenkins [1952] Director; Oliver Graham Warwick Banks [1987] Director

Warwickshire Cash & Carry Limited
Incorporated: 29 December 2014
Net Worth: £12,305 *Total Assets:* £144,498
Registered Office: 151 Rugby Road, Cubbington, Leamington Spa, Warwicks, CV32 7JJ
Major Shareholder: Amarpal Singh Khera
Officers: Amarpal Singh Khera [1994] Director/Salesman; Dalbire Singh Khera [1977] Director/Manager

Warwickshire Drinks Plus Limited
Incorporated: 6 January 2005
Net Worth: £845,011 *Total Assets:* £1,211,173
Registered Office: 151 Rugby Road, Cubbington, Leamington Spa, Warwicks, CV32 7JJ
Major Shareholder: Dalbire Singh Khera
Officers: Dalbire Singh Khera [1977] Director/Manager

Waterland Trading Limited
Incorporated: 12 July 2018
Registered Office: 71-75 Shelton Street, Covent Garden, London, WC2H 9JQ
Parent: Lumbock Ventures Limited
Officers: Jan Honing, Secretary; Jan Honing [1974] Director/Consultant [Dutch]

Watermark Fine Wine Limited
Incorporated: 28 March 2014 *Employees:* 1
Net Worth: £1,648,196 *Total Assets:* £1,831,386
Registered Office: Headon Yard Cottage, Wydale, Brompton-by-Sawdon, Scarborough, N Yorks, YO13 9DG
Officers: Gary James Boom [1958] Director/Wine Merchant [Dutch]; Andrew Haughton Davison [1967] Director

Waters (1802) Limited
Incorporated: 29 January 1925
Net Worth: £665,527 *Total Assets:* £684,422
Registered Office: 27 High Street, Warwick, CV34 4AX
Major Shareholder: Robert Gordon Woodruff Caldicott
Officers: Dame Fiona Caldicott, Secretary; Dame Fiona Caldicott [1941] Director/NHS Trust Chairman; Robert Gordon Woodruff Caldicott [1941] Director

Watson Food & Beverages Ltd
Incorporated: 15 November 2011
Net Worth Deficit: £71,773 *Total Assets:* £54,532
Registered Office: Unit 31 Longsight Business Park, 69 Hamilton Road, Manchester, M13 0PD
Major Shareholder: Malik Aftab Hussain
Officers: Malik Aftab Hussain [1958] Director/Businessman [German]

David J. Watt (Fine Wines) Limited
Incorporated: 16 August 1983
Net Worth: £1,017,458 *Total Assets:* £1,222,138
Registered Office: South Hill Farm, Appleby Hill, Austrey, Atherstone, Warwicks, CV9 3ER
Shareholders: David James Sinclair Watt; Frances Elizabeth Mary Watt
Officers: Frances Elizabeth Mary Watt, Secretary; David James Sinclair Watt [1945] Director; Frances Elizabeth Mary Watt [1957] Director/Company Secretary

Waud Wines Limited
Incorporated: 28 April 2015
Net Worth: £38,922 *Total Assets:* £124,698
Registered Office: 4-6 Dudley Road, Tunbridge Wells, Kent, TN1 1LF
Officers: Martin Vivian Athey [1955] Director/Solicitor; Jeremy Charles Waud [1961] Director

Wave Wine Ltd
Incorporated: 18 January 2019
Registered Office: Unit 2 Mount Street Business Park, Nechells, Birmingham, B7 5QU
Shareholder: Yang Guo
Officers: Yang Guo [1980] Director

Waveney Ales and Ciders Limited
Incorporated: 14 June 2012 *Employees:* 3
Net Worth: £11,871 *Total Assets:* £64,827
Registered Office: Unit 4 Belvedere Road, Lowestoft, Suffolk, NR33 0PR
Shareholders: Steven Moore; Darren Moore
Officers: Steven Moore, Secretary; Angela Moore [1955] Director; Darren Moore [1978] Director; Michelle Moore [1985] Director; Steven Moore [1955] Director

Waverley Drinks Limited
Incorporated: 10 July 2013
Registered Office: Bishopstone, 36 Crescent Road, Worthing, W Sussex, BN11 1RL
Major Shareholder: Paul Barnes
Officers: Paul Barnes [1976] Director

The Way Outback Brewery Limited
Incorporated: 26 July 2018
Registered Office: 146 Seabourne Road, Bournemouth, BH5 2JA
Major Shareholder: Richard Brown
Officers: Richard Brown [1984] Director

Weavers (Nottingham) Limited
Incorporated: 7 June 1938 *Employees:* 17
Net Worth: £127,433 *Total Assets:* £743,664
Registered Office: 1 Castle Gate, Nottingham, NG1 7AQ
Shareholders: Alan William Trease; Mary Elizabeth Trease
Officers: Philip Geoffrey Trease, Secretary/Director; Alan William Trease [1937] Director/Wine Merchant; Diana Kay Trease [1944] Director/Wine Merchant; Mary Elizabeth Trease [1969] Director/Wine Merchant; Philip Geoffrey Trease [1973] Director

Webdrinks Ltd
Incorporated: 5 September 2014
Net Worth Deficit: £390 *Total Assets:* £56
Registered Office: X92 Cody Technology Park, Old Ively Road, Farnborough, Hants, GU14 0LX
Parent: Inchora Limited
Officers: Anthony Banham [1957] Director; Darren Stanley [1967] Director; Steve Dennis Whatley [1961] Director

The Wedding Wine Shop Ltd
Incorporated: 8 February 2019
Registered Office: 1a Spey Road, Tilehurst, Reading, Berks, RG30 4DJ
Major Shareholder: Toby James Underwood
Officers: Toby James Underwood [1990] Director/Operations Manager

Wedgbury Connections Ltd
Incorporated: 12 September 2017
Registered Office: 8 Conway Crescent, Willenhall, W Midlands, WV12 5TP
Major Shareholder: Sarah Louise Wedgbury
Officers: Sarah Louise Wedgbury [1971] Director

The Wee Vinoteca Ltd
Incorporated: 9 October 2018
Registered Office: 3 New Court, Woolmer Green, Knebworth, Herts, SG3 6LJ
Major Shareholder: Duncan George Gammie
Officers: Duncan George Gammie [1988] Director

Wein Forum - Fine Wines Limited
Incorporated: 18 June 2013
Net Worth: £2,514 *Total Assets:* £2,514
Registered Office: 27 Old Gloucester Street, London, WC1N 3AX
Major Shareholder: Christof Martin
Officers: Ludwig Martin Rohde [1970] Director/Entrepreneur [German]

Weiser Taverns Beers & Minerals Ltd
Incorporated: 4 July 2006 *Employees:* 3
Net Worth Deficit: £133,874 *Total Assets:* £123,459
Registered Office: 1st Floor, Commerce House, 1 Raven Road, South Woodford, London, E18 1HB
Major Shareholder: Joseph Grehan
Officers: Christopher Courtney, Secretary; Christopher Courtney [1982] Director

Welford Retail Limited
Incorporated: 4 June 2010
Net Worth: £35,611 *Total Assets:* £106,850
Registered Office: 66-64 Granby Street, Leicester, LE1 1DH
Major Shareholder: Nilesh Vadoliya
Officers: Nilesh Kanjibhai Vadoliya [1977] Director

Charles Wells Brewery Limited
Incorporated: 24 February 2006 *Employees:* 204
Previous: Wells & Young's Brewing Company Limited
Net Worth: £7,753,000 *Total Assets:* £65,067,000
Registered Office: The Brewery, Havelock Street, Bedford, MK40 4LU
Parent: Charles Wells Limited
Officers: Anthony Robert Fryer [1973] Finance Director; William Andrew Justin Phillimore [1962] Director; Paul Richard Wells [1958] Director

Charles Wells, Limited
Incorporated: 7 January 1910 *Employees:* 365
Net Worth: £75,246,000 *Total Assets:* £141,250,000
Registered Office: Eagle Brewery, Havelock Street, Bedford, MK40 4LU
Officers: Anthony Robert Fryer [1973] Finance Director; Robert Lewis Ivell [1952] Director; William Andrew Justin Phillimore [1962] Director/Chief Executive; Paul Stephen Rawlinson [1959] Director; Geoffrey Charles Vaughan Wells [1970] Director/Lawyer [Canadian]; Paul Richard Wells [1958] Director; Peter John Wells [1970] Director

Wellsh Brewers Cardiff Ltd
Incorporated: 22 August 2016
Registered Office: Guardian House, 5 Squire Drive, Bridgend, Mid Glamorgan, CF32 9TX
Officers: Gurmit Singh Bedesha [1962] Director

Wemyss Vintage Malts Limited
Incorporated: 6 January 2005 *Employees:* 8
Net Worth: £3,693,481 *Total Assets:* £15,660,336
Registered Office: 4 Melville Crescent, Edinburgh, EH3 7JA
Parent: The Wemyss Development Company Limted
Officers: Isabella Wemyss, Secretary; Karen Margaret Stewart [1968] Director of Marketing; Isabella Alethea Wemyss [1968] Director; William John Wemyss [1970] Director/Company Chairman

Wemyss Wines and Spirits Limited
Incorporated: 14 May 2007
Registered Office: 4 Melville Crescent, Edinburgh, EH3 7JA
Parent: Wemyss Vintage Malts Limited
Officers: Isabella Wemyss, Secretary; Isabella Alethea Wemyss [1968] Director; William John Wemyss [1970] Director

Wenlen UK. Ltd
Incorporated: 14 November 2016
Registered Office: 71-75 Shelton Street, Covent Garden, London, WC2H 9JQ
Major Shareholder: Lena Thomas
Officers: Lena Marshall, Secretary; Lena Marshall [1972] Director/Subject Specialist [Irish]

Werfa Holdings Ltd
Incorporated: 13 August 2018
Registered Office: 20-22 Wenlock Road, London, N1 7GU
Shareholders: Jonathan Alan Oliveira Moore; Shafiq Karim
Officers: Shafiq Karim [1984] Director/Marketing Consultant; Jonathan Alan Oliveira Moore [1984] Director/Financial Analyst

The Wessex Wine Company Ltd
Incorporated: 16 August 2018
Registered Office: The Wincombe Centre, Wincombe Business Park, Shaftesbury, Dorset, SP7 9QJ
Officers: Joseph Pestell, Secretary; Joseph Pestell [1957] Director/Vineyard Manager

West Coast Wines & Spirits Ltd.
Incorporated: 3 August 2015
Net Worth Deficit: £49,331 Total Assets: £67,600
Registered Office: 71-75 Shelton Street, Covent Garden, London, WC2H 9JQ
Major Shareholder: Paul Haley
Officers: Paul Haley, Secretary; Paul Haley [1958] Director [American]

West Country Wines Limited
Incorporated: 28 July 2016
Registered Office: 178-180 Lawrence Hill, Bristol, BS5 0DN
Major Shareholder: Hardev Singh
Officers: Hardev Singh [1961] Director

West End Brands Ltd
Incorporated: 30 March 2005
Net Worth Deficit: £455,309
Registered Office: 4th Floor, Cardinal House, 39-40 Albemarle Street, London, W1S 4TE
Major Shareholder: Howard Wyndham Raymond
Officers: Alexandra Georgina Robson, Secretary; Howard Wyndham Raymond [1959] Property Director; Alexandra Georgina Robson [1968] Director/Consultant

West End Drinks Limited
Incorporated: 31 May 2012 Employees: 5
Net Worth: £155,208 Total Assets: £451,839
Registered Office: 4th Floor, Cardinal House, 39-40 Albemarle Street, London, W1S 4TE
Shareholders: Howard Wyndham Raymond; Alexandra Georgina Robson
Officers: Alexandra Robson, Secretary; Howard Wyndham Raymond [1959] Director; Alexandra Georgina Robson [1968] Director

West Lancs Drinks Ltd
Incorporated: 15 February 2019
Registered Office: 7 West Dene, 34 Lulworth Road, Southport, Merseyside, PR8 2JW
Major Shareholder: Stephen Tipping
Officers: Stephen Tipping [1964] Director

West Spirits MCR Ltd
Incorporated: 18 October 2018
Registered Office: 4 The Birchin, Joiner Street, Manchester, M4 1PH
Officers: Samuel Paul Crick [1996] Director/Barman

The Westbourne Drinks Company Limited
Incorporated: 19 March 2013 Employees: 3
Net Worth: £133,847 Total Assets: £266,091
Registered Office: Duppy Share HQ, Great Western Studios, 65 Alfred Road, London, W2 5EU
Shareholder: George Paradine Frost
Officers: George Frost [1987] Director

Westend Cash and Carry Ltd
Incorporated: 21 August 2017
Registered Office: Regus Slough Town Centre, 18 Stoke Road, Slough, Berks, SL2 5AG
Officers: Sarvajit Bhattacharjee [1959] Company Secretary/Director [Indian]

Wester Spirit Co. Ltd
Incorporated: 24 January 2017
Net Worth Deficit: £5,717 Total Assets: £8,331
Registered Office: Unit 2, 8 Meadow Road, Glasgow, G11 6HX
Shareholders: Alexander Aonghas Gregor MacGregor; Allan James Nairn
Officers: Alexander Aonghas Gregor MacGregor [1991] Director; Allan James Nairn [1993] Director

Westgarth Wines Limited
Incorporated: 9 April 2013 Employees: 1
Net Worth Deficit: £1,037 Total Assets: £68,275
Registered Office: Brook Farm, Braintree Road, Wethersfield, Braintree, Essex, CM7 4BX
Major Shareholder: Alexander Westgarth
Officers: Alexander Westgarth [1982] Director/Wine Merchant; Hilary Westgarth [1955] Director

Westvine International Ltd
Incorporated: 17 February 2017 Employees: 1
Net Worth: £6,245 Total Assets: £40,563
Registered Office: 7 Ballygelagh Village, Portstewart, Co Londonderry, BT55 7WA
Officers: James Lyttle [1992] Director/Self Employed

Westworld Impex Limited
Incorporated: 23 April 2018
Registered Office: 0-2, 59 Mannering Court, Glasgow, G41 3QH
Major Shareholder: Arun Goyal
Officers: Arun Goyal [1981] Director [Indian]

Wetherby Brew Co Limited
Incorporated: 26 July 2017
Registered Office: Wetherby Brew Co, York Road Estate, York Road, Wetherby, W Yorks, LS22 7SU
Shareholders: John David Frgusson; Richard Ivan Roberts
Officers: John David Fergusson [1971] Director; Richard Ivan Roberts [1957] Director; Thomas Gwilym Roberts [1990] Director

Whigham Fergusson Limited
Incorporated: 17 April 1980
Registered Office: 4th Floor, Saltire Court, 20 Castle Terrace, Edinburgh, EH1 2EN
Parent: John E Fells & Sons Ltd
Officers: Louise Catherine Rimes, Secretary; Stephen Antony Moody [1960] Managing Director

The Whiskey and Bourbon Club Ltd
Incorporated: 14 December 2018
Registered Office: 41 Acacia Avenue, Verwood, Dorset, BH31 6XF
Major Shareholder: Oliver Lewis Irwin
Officers: Oliver Lewis Irwin [1996] Director

Whiskies from Scotland Limited
Incorporated: 18 October 2010
Registered Office: 136 Nithsdale Road, Glasgow, G41 5RB
Major Shareholder: Henry Allan Cunningham
Officers: Henry Allan Cunningham [1955] Director

Whisky 78 Ltd
Incorporated: 4 January 2017 Employees: 1
Net Worth Deficit: £12,154 Total Assets: £17,832
Registered Office: 606 Delta Office Park, Welton Road, Swindon, Wilts, SN5 7XF
Major Shareholder: Matthew Richard Sloane
Officers: Matthew Richard Sloane [1968] Director

The Whisky Baron Ltd.
Incorporated: 29 January 2018
Registered Office: April House, 6 Springfield Meadows, Weybridge, Surrey, KT13 8AJ
Major Shareholder: Jake Jacob Patrick Sharpe
Officers: Jake Jacob Patrick Sharpe [1994] Director/Founder [Irish]

Whisky Biz Glasgow Ltd
Incorporated: 4 November 2016
Registered Office: c/o Robb Ferguson, Regent Court, 70 West Regent Street, Glasgow, G2 2QZ
Major Shareholder: Patricia Dillon
Officers: Patricia Dillon [1968] Director

Whisky Galore Limited
Incorporated: 15 January 2001
Registered Office: 28 Albyn Place, Aberdeen, AB10 1YL
Major Shareholder: Euan Coutts Shand
Officers: Euan Coutts Shand [1956] Director

Whisky Global Ltd
Incorporated: 24 August 2011
Net Worth Deficit: £13,644 *Total Assets:* £6,154
Registered Office: Pilgrim House, Oxford Place, Plymouth, PL1 5AJ
Major Shareholder: David John Cogley
Officers: David John Cogley [1964] Director

Whisky Merchants Trading Limited
Incorporated: 19 April 2018
Registered Office: 6 St Colme Street, Edinburgh, EH3 6AD
Major Shareholder: Edward Coutts Davidson
Officers: Patrick Henry Costello [1991] Director [New Zealander]; Edward Coutts Davidson [1970] Director

The Whisky Palate Limited
Incorporated: 8 December 2016
Net Worth: £15,194 *Total Assets:* £76,051
Registered Office: First Floor, Winston House, 349 Regents Park Road, London, N3 1DH
Major Shareholder: Daniel Smolowitz
Officers: Daniel Smolowitz [1976] Director/Rabbi

Whisky Point Limited
Incorporated: 8 January 2018
Registered Office: Birchwood House, Woldingham Road, Woldingham, Surrey, CR3 7LR
Major Shareholder: Yinghui Chen
Officers: Yinghui Chen [1970] Director [Chinese]

Whisky Rebellion Limited
Incorporated: 5 April 2018
Registered Office: Montpelier Professional (Galloway) Ltd, 1 Dashwood Square, Newton Stewart, Dumfries & Galloway, DG8 6EQ
Major Shareholder: Rose Higginson
Officers: Rose Higginson [1993] Director; James Murray [1992] Director

The Whisky Seller Limited
Incorporated: 13 May 2016
Registered Office: 21 Knockagony Avenue, Belfast, BT4 2PY
Officers: Shona Winter Gladwin [1962] Director

The Whisky Trading Company Limited
Incorporated: 7 September 2012
Registered Office: 4th Floor, Reading Bridge House, George Street, Reading, Berks, RG1 8LS
Officers: Sukhjinder Singh Atwal [1971] Director/Banker; Lindon Wilson Neil [1962] Director/Banker; David Graham Robertson [1968] Director/Whisky Consultant; Susan Jane Robertson [1965] Director/Finance Officer; Nuno Tome [1973] Director [Portuguese]

Whisky Work Play Ltd
Incorporated: 9 January 2019
Registered Office: 17 Glade Walk, London, E20 1DL
Shareholders: Joseph Liam Boxall; Alessandro Bartelli
Officers: Alessandro Bartelli [1986] Director/Bars Manager [Italian]; Joseph Liam Boxall [1985] Director/Bars Manager

Whiskybroker Limited
Incorporated: 1 October 2013 *Employees:* 14
Net Worth: £500,817 *Total Assets:* £1,463,636
Registered Office: Barholm Works, Creeton, Newton Stewart, Dumfries & Galloway, DG8 7EN
Shareholder: Jane Armstrong
Officers: Jane Armstrong, Secretary; Jane Armstrong [1987] Director; Raymond Martin Armstrong [1987] Director

H.T.White & Company,Limited
Incorporated: 13 January 1927 *Employees:* 103
Net Worth: £5,921,272 *Total Assets:* £8,944,191
Registered Office: Unit 3 Stainburn Road, Manchester, M11 2DN
Parent: LWC Drinks Limited
Officers: Robin MacEwan Gray [1951] Director; Ebrahim Kassam Mukadam [1957] Director

The White Lion Gin Company Limited
Incorporated: 1 October 2018
Registered Office: 135 High Street North, Dunstable, Beds, LU6 1JN
Major Shareholder: Steven Paul Kirby
Officers: Steven Paul Kirby [1966] Director

White Pearl Ltd
Incorporated: 8 April 2008
Net Worth: £144 *Total Assets:* £105,756
Registered Office: Unit 12 Nechells Place, Boultbee Business Units, Birmingham, B7 5AR
Major Shareholder: Piotr Loba
Officers: Piotr Loba [1983] Director [Polish]

White Willows Beers, Wines and Spirits Limited
Incorporated: 8 March 2007
Net Worth Deficit: £25,321 *Total Assets:* £657
Registered Office: 32 Bank End Road, Worsbrough Dale, Barnsley, S Yorks, S70 4AF
Major Shareholder: Adrian Stuart Willis
Officers: Adrian Stuart Willis, Secretary; Adrian Stuart Willis, Secretary/Director/Trader; Adrian Stuart Willis [1960] Director/Trader

White Wolf Brewery Ltd
Incorporated: 14 September 2017
Registered Office: 36 Stocker Way, Eynesbury Manor, St Neots, Cambs, PE19 2HA
Major Shareholder: Gregory Daren Peddell-Grant
Officers: Gregory Daren Peddell-Grant, Secretary; Gregory Daren Peddell-Grant [1970] Director/Facilities Delivery Manager

White's Cellar Supplies (UK) Limited
Incorporated: 5 March 2007
Net Worth: £216,254 *Total Assets:* £236,451
Registered Office: Unit B, Berkeley Court, Earl Russell Way, Lawrence Hill, Bristol, BS5 0BX
Shareholder: Wayne Jewell
Officers: Wayne Terence Francis Jewell [1970] Director/Manager

Whitebridge Wines Limited
Incorporated: 5 July 1983 *Employees:* 7
Net Worth: £205,500 *Total Assets:* £564,395
Registered Office: Unit 21 Whitebridge Industrial Estate, Stone, Staffs, ST15 8LQ
Shareholders: Felicity Bridget Emma Peel; Imogen Peel
Officers: Kathy Howcroft, Secretary; Kathleen Florence Howcroft [1951] Director/Manager; Francis Edward Guy Peel [1959] Director/Wine Merchant; Patricia Jane Peel [1964] Director/Wine Shipper

Whiteleys of Halifax Limited
Incorporated: 13 January 1995 *Employees:* 2
Net Worth: £202 *Total Assets:* £17,691
Registered Office: 5-6 Bank End, Upper Greetland, Halifax, W Yorks, HX4 8PR
Shareholder: Robin William Whiteley
Officers: Carolyn Whiteley, Secretary; Carolyn Whiteley [1957] Company Secretary/Director; Robin William Whiteley [1957] Director

Whitetail Spirits Limited
Incorporated: 5 September 2016
Net Worth Deficit: £4,439 *Total Assets:* £42,150
Registered Office: Tiroran House, Tiroran, Isle of Mull, PA69 6ES
Officers: Katherine Louise MacKay [1962] Director/Hotelier; Laurence MacKay [1957] Director/Hotelier; Jamie Munro [1989] Director/Hotelier

Whitley Neill Limited
Incorporated: 6 May 2004 *Employees:* 1
Net Worth Deficit: £434,893 *Total Assets:* £11,612
Registered Office: The Gables, High Street, Chieveley, Newbury, Berks, RG20 8TE
Major Shareholder: John James Whitley Neill
Officers: Nicola Ann Neill, Secretary; John James Whitley Neill [1972] Director/Spirits Wholesaler

Whitmore and White Limited
Incorporated: 26 November 2013 *Employees:* 15
Net Worth Deficit: £156,368 *Total Assets:* £172,988
Registered Office: Unit 3 St Ives Way, Sandycroft, Chester, CH5 2QS
Shareholders: Joseph William Whittick; James Kingsley Andrew Godber-Ford Moore
Officers: James Kingsley Andrew Godber-Ford Moore [1979] Director; Laura Owen [1978] Director; Joseph William Whittick [1981] Director

Whittaker Wines Limited
Incorporated: 7 February 1986 *Employees:* 1
Net Worth: £126,590 *Total Assets:* £206,756
Registered Office: Bakestonedale Farm, Bakestonedale Road, Pott Shrigley, Macclesfield, Cheshire, SK10 5RU
Major Shareholder: Judith Whittaker
Officers: Judith Whittaker [1961] Director

Whittalls Wines Limited
Incorporated: 20 August 1997 *Employees:* 4
Net Worth: £413,219 *Total Assets:* £418,278
Registered Office: European House, Darlaston Road, Walsall, W Midlands, WS2 9SQ
Parent: EFB Holdings Ltd
Officers: Ayodele Akintola [1967] Director; Balbir Singh Chatha [1963] Director

Wholesale Beer Supplies Ltd
Incorporated: 13 April 2011 *Employees:* 4
Net Worth: £807 *Total Assets:* £108,286
Registered Office: Edward House, North Mersey Business Centre, Woodward Road, Knowsley, Merseyside, L33 7UY
Major Shareholder: Gary Jones
Officers: Gary Jones [1966] Director

Wholly Grape Limited
Incorporated: 26 March 2013
Net Worth: £440,170 *Total Assets:* £444,273
Registered Office: Camburgh House, 27 New Dover Road, Canterbury, Kent, CT1 3DN
Major Shareholder: Adam Digby Knight
Officers: Adam Digby Knight [1974] Director

Wickedsoup Ltd.
Incorporated: 26 January 2004 *Employees:* 4
Net Worth: £86,753 *Total Assets:* £199,057
Registered Office: Unit 7 Annfield Row, Dundee, DD1 5JH
Major Shareholder: Patrick Rohde
Officers: Patrick Rohde, Secretary; Patrick Rohde [1969] Director/Wine Merchant

Wickersley Fine Wines Ltd
Incorporated: 15 August 2017
Registered Office: 15 Kingsley Drive, Ravenfield, Rotherham, S Yorks, S65 4GY
Officers: Michael Burns [1983] Director; Darren Burton [1971] Director

Wigan Beer Company Limited
Incorporated: 5 July 1994 *Employees:* 25
Net Worth: £1,015,077 *Total Assets:* £2,080,144
Registered Office: Units 13-14 Victoria Trading Estate, Miry Lane, Wigan, Lancs, WN3 4BW
Officers: Angela Ann Jones, Secretary; Adam Clarke Jones [1987] Director; Angela Ann Jones [1955] Director/CS; Harold Jones [1955] Director; Kieran Jones [1991] Director

Wight & Wessex Wines Limited
Incorporated: 21 September 2018
Registered Office: The Barn, Niton Manor Farm, Blackgang Road, Niton, Isle of Wight, PO38 2BW
Shareholders: Matthew Rogers; Michael Shorrock
Officers: Matthew Rogers [1975] Director; Michael Shorrock [1981] Director

Wiland Wines Limited
Incorporated: 15 January 1999 *Employees:* 3
Net Worth: £12,586 *Total Assets:* £62,519
Registered Office: 4 Ellis Street, Anstey, Leicester, LE7 7FG
Shareholders: Mark Egerton Little-Jones; Roseleen Little-Jones
Officers: Mark Egerton Little-Jones, Secretary/Director; Mark Egerton Little-Jones [1951] Director; Rosaleen Little-Jones [1952] Director

Wild Foragin Ltd
Incorporated: 22 October 2018
Registered Office: Knapp Cottage, Bredwardine, Hereford, HR3 6BZ
Shareholders: Natalie Louise Evans; Jonathan Richard Evans
Officers: Jonathan Richard Evans [1979] Director; Natalie Louise Evans [1981] Director

Wild Life Botanicals Ltd
Incorporated: 28 February 2019
Registered Office: 20-22 Wenlock Road, London, N1 7GU
Major Shareholder: Jonathan Paul Steadman Archer
Officers: Jonathan Paul Steadman Archer [1966] Director

Wildflower Wines Limited
Incorporated: 21 August 2002 *Employees:* 4
Net Worth Deficit: £19,311 *Total Assets:* £163,233
Registered Office: Unit 8 Mill Road Industrial Estate, Linlithgow Bridge, Linlithgow, W Lothian, EH49 7SF
Shareholder: David Knox Moore
Officers: Robert Alan Chapman, Secretary; Robert Alan Chapman [1964] Director; David Moore [1961] Director

Wilkies International Ltd
Incorporated: 28 June 2018
Registered Office: Suite 11, West Africa House, Ashbourne Road, London, W5 3QP
Major Shareholder: Gurmeet Kishore Singh
Officers: Gurmeet Kishore Singh [1965] Director [Singaporean]

Wilkinson Vintners Limited
Incorporated: 23 January 1992 *Employees:* 9
Net Worth: £10,180,608 *Total Assets:* £13,420,092
Registered Office: 38 Chagford Street, London, NW1 6EB
Major Shareholder: Patrick Luke Wilkinson
Officers: Patrick Luke Wilkinson, Secretary; Paul Henry Bowker [1962] Director; Fiona Jane Wilkinson [1962] Director; Patrick Luke Wilkinson [1961] Director/Wine Merchant

Wilks & Company Wine Merchants Limited
Incorporated: 10 September 2002 *Employees:* 3
Net Worth: £534,970 *Total Assets:* £783,659
Registered Office: Unit 1a Concord Farm, School Road, Rayne, Braintree, Essex, CM77 6SP
Major Shareholder: Brian David Wilks
Officers: Brian David Wilks [1958] Director/Wine Merchant

William of Orange Brands Limited
Incorporated: 23 March 2018
Registered Office: G01 Charrington Tower, 11 Biscayne Avenue, London, E14 9AY
Major Shareholder: Matthew Joseph Maslin
Officers: Matthew Joseph Maslin [1974] Director

Willoughbys Limited
Incorporated: 4 July 1967
Total Assets: £14,821
Registered Office: Greengate Brewery, Middleton Junction, Middleton, Manchester, M24 2AX
Parent: JW Lees & Co (Brewers) Limited
Officers: Simon Cross, Secretary; William Richard Lees Jones [1933] Director; Christopher Peter Lees-Jones [1936] Director

Andrew R. Wilson Limited
Incorporated: 20 September 1984
Net Worth: £100 *Total Assets:* £100
Registered Office: The Steading, New Cample Farm, Thornhill, Dumfries & Galloway, DG3 5EY
Shareholders: Ben Reynolds; Rebecca Lloyd
Officers: Clare Alison Lloyd [1961] Director/Administration; Rebecca Lloyd [1987] Director/Sales & Marketing; Steven Michael Lloyd [1951] Director/Whisky Broker; Ben Reynolds [1980] Director/Sales and Marketing; Georgine Reynolds [1990] Director/Sales & Marketing

Wiltshire Liqueur Company Limited
Incorporated: 10 August 1994
Net Worth: £3,569 *Total Assets:* £74,776
Registered Office: Henley Lodge, Henley, Marlborough, Wilts, SN8 3RJ
Shareholders: Tiffinie Jane Pride; Christopher Edward Robinson
Officers: Tiffinie Jane Pride [1967] Director/Liqueur Merchant; Christopher Edward Robinson [1955] Director/Tour Operator

Wimbledon Wine Cellar Limited
Incorporated: 27 September 1991
Net Worth: £79,769 *Total Assets:* £901,411
Registered Office: 3rd Floor, Vyman House, 104 College Road, Harrow, Middlesex, HA1 1BQ
Major Shareholder: Andrew Nicholas Pavli
Officers: Peter Emmi, Secretary; Andrew Nicholas Pavli [1964] Director/Wine Merchant

Wincarnis Limited
Incorporated: 9 September 1998
Registered Office: Russell House, Dunnet Way, Broxburn, W Lothian, EH52 5BU
Parent: Ian MacLeod Distillers Limited
Officers: Michael James Younger, Secretary; Leonard Stuart Russell [1961] Marketing Director

Windermere Wine Stores Limited
Incorporated: 13 May 1980 *Employees:* 10
Net Worth: £85,006 *Total Assets:* £177,601
Registered Office: 11 Crescent Road, Windermere, Cumbria, LA23 1EA
Major Shareholder: Joanne Harris
Officers: Elaine Ann Ratcliffe, Secretary; Joanne Harris [1972] Director

Windfall Logistics Limited
Incorporated: 20 March 2007 *Employees:* 7
Net Worth: £163,940 *Total Assets:* £877,970
Registered Office: Windfall House, D1, The Courtyard, Alban Park, St Albans, Herts, AL4 0LA
Major Shareholder: Angelos Panayiotou
Officers: Angelos Panayiotou, Secretary; Angelos Panayiotou [1975] Director/Accountant; Michael Sears [1956] Director

Windrush Holdings Ltd
Incorporated: 14 September 1988
Registered Office: Castlett Farm Cottage, Guiting Power, Cheltenham, Glos, GL54 5UZ
Officers: Annabel Mary Savage, Secretary; Annabel Mary Savage [1951] Director/Housewife; Mark Savage [1949] Director/Master of Wine

Windward Trading Company Ltd
Incorporated: 3 February 2011
Net Worth Deficit: £15,929 *Total Assets:* £10,507
Registered Office: 304 High Road, Benfleet, Essex, SS7 5HB
Major Shareholder: Cynthia Yvonne Thomas
Officers: Cynthia Yvonne Thomas [1954] Director; Richard Henry Thomas [1954] Director

Wine & People Limited
Incorporated: 24 January 2019
Registered Office: 189 Applegarth House, Nelson Square, London, SE1 0PZ
Major Shareholder: Omar Ahmed Salah
Officers: Omar Ahmed Salah [1995] Director [Italian]

Wine & Spirit International Limited
Incorporated: 8 January 1980 *Employees:* 3
Net Worth: £186,093 *Total Assets:* £551,883
Registered Office: 272 Regents Park Road, Finchley, London, N3 3HN
Major Shareholder: Dale Laurence Sklar
Officers: Daliah Rebecca Sklar, Secretary/Director; Dale Laurence Howard Sklar [1951] Managing Director; Daliah Rebecca Sklar [1978] Director; Gina Tamara Sklar [1980] Director; Karen Sklar [1961] Director/Solicitor; Tanya Sara Sklar [1983] Director

Wine & Spirits Club SA Ltd
Incorporated: 2 August 2018
Registered Office: 20-22 Wenlock Road, London, N1 7GU
Major Shareholder: Alexandra Bourjac
Officers: Alexandra Bourjac [1979] Director [French]

Wine Affairs Limited
Incorporated: 15 June 2018
Registered Office: 10 Western Road, Romford, Essex, RM1 3JT
Shareholders: Laura Jane Burridge; Marcus Venverloo
Officers: Laura Jane Burridge [1970] Director/Producer; Marcus Venverloo [1966] Director [Dutch]

The Wine Agency Ltd
Incorporated: 18 March 2011 *Employees:* 1
Net Worth: £35,077 *Total Assets:* £39,880
Registered Office: 7 Cholmondeley Road, West Kirby, Merseyside, CH48 7HB
Major Shareholder: David Gordon Large

Wine Art Company Limited
Incorporated: 5 September 2017
Registered Office: Unit 22 Roxwell Trading Park, Argall Avenue, London, E10 7QY
Major Shareholder: Ahmet Turgay Simsek
Officers: Ahmet Turgay Simsek [1962] Director

Wine Associates Limited
Incorporated: 17 October 2012
Net Worth Deficit: £6,677 *Total Assets:* £4,361
Registered Office: 76 Victoria Park Road, Bournemouth, BH9 2RH
Major Shareholder: Alex Richard Palmer
Officers: Alex Richard Palmer [1976] Sales Director

The Wine Barn Limited
Incorporated: 3 August 1998 *Employees:* 1
Net Worth: £120,173 *Total Assets:* £351,738
Registered Office: 16 Taylors Yard, Sutton Scotney, Winchester, Hants, SO21 3XX
Major Shareholder: Iris Ellmann
Officers: Iris Ellmann [1969] Director [German]

Wine Bliss Ltd
Incorporated: 6 September 2018
Registered Office: 20-22 Wenlock Road, London, N1 7GU
Shareholders: Cristin Bezede; Vladimir Margarint
Officers: Vladimir Margarint [1969] Director [Romanian]

The Wine Butler Limited
Incorporated: 2 April 2014
Net Worth Deficit: £42,337 *Total Assets:* £6,000
Registered Office: 28 Jewry Street, Winchester, Hants, SO23 8FE
Officers: Josephine Latouf, Secretary; Kevin John Latouf [1985] Director [Irish]

The Wine Byre Limited
Incorporated: 2 April 2013
Registered Office: 189 Irish Green Street, Limavady, Co Londonderry, BT49 9AR
Shareholders: Laura Doyle; Julie Lapsley
Officers: Laura Doyle [1980] Director/Chartered Accountant; Julie Lapsley [1985] Director/Entrepreneur

The Wine Carafe Limited
Incorporated: 21 December 2010 *Employees:* 6
Net Worth: £1 *Total Assets:* £22,122
Registered Office: 3rd Floor, Dudley House, Stone Street, Dudley, W Midlands, DY1 1NS
Major Shareholder: Sumerjit Kaur Sanghera
Officers: Sumerjit Kaur Sanghera [1966] Director

Wine Castle Ltd
Incorporated: 5 June 2018
Registered Office: 97 Palmyra Road, Gosport, Hants, PO12 4EE
Major Shareholder: Nilaan Puvirajasingam
Officers: Nilaan Puvirajasingam [1993] Director/Manager

The Wine Cellar Midlands Limited
Incorporated: 26 June 2012
Net Worth: £2,586 *Total Assets:* £59,721
Registered Office: 26 Binswood Street, Leamington Spa, Warwicks, CV32 5RN
Shareholder: Kamalprit Singh Punia
Officers: Gina Kaur Heer [1974] Director; Kamalprit Singh Punia [1972] Director

Wine City Limited
Incorporated: 4 April 2018
Registered Office: c/o The Store Room, P O Box 7, Unit 7 Foxholes Road, Leicester, LE3 1TH
Shareholders: Basil Enok; Wilson Enwerem
Officers: Basil Enok [1975] Director; Wilson Enwerem [1975] Director

Wine Consultants Limited
Incorporated: 11 November 2004
Net Worth Deficit: £9,876 *Total Assets:* £39,437
Registered Office: 45 Queen Street, Deal, Kent, CT14 6EY
Shareholders: Guy Ralph Boursot; Sophie Elizabeth Ann Branson
Officers: Guy Ralph Philip Boursot [1954] Director/Wine Trader

The Wine Cru Limited
Incorporated: 28 November 2018
Registered Office: 103 Cannon Workshops, Cannon Drive, London, E14 4AS
Major Shareholder: Dale Agar
Officers: Dale Agar [1975] Managing Director

Wine de Vine Ltd
Incorporated: 24 January 2013 *Employees:* 5
Net Worth: £57,578 *Total Assets:* £355,235
Registered Office: 7 Sackville Road, Southchurch, Southend on Sea, Essex, SS2 4UQ
Major Shareholder: Wendy Marian Lee
Officers: Wendy Marian Lee [1959] Director/Wine Merchant

Wine Divine Ltd
Incorporated: 20 March 2005 *Employees:* 3
Previous: Wines of Excellence Limited
Net Worth: £9,035 *Total Assets:* £70,521
Registered Office: 56 Chippers Road, Worthing, W Sussex, BN13 1DG
Major Shareholder: Gilles Dubourg
Officers: Gilles Roger Charles Dubourg [1968] Director/Wine Importer [French]

The Wine Enterprise Investment Scheme Limited
Incorporated: 4 November 2011
Net Worth: £3,866,181 *Total Assets:* £4,181,794
Registered Office: 15 Clifford Street, London, W1S 4JY
Officers: Rodney Birrell [1952] Director [Canadian]; Andrew Eugene Nicholas Della Casa [1956] Director

The Wine Explorer Limited
Incorporated: 4 July 2002
Net Worth Deficit: £68,876 *Total Assets:* £77,764
Registered Office: Norfolk House, 75 Bartholomew Street, Newbury, Berks, RG14 5DU
Shareholders: Graham Christopher Mitchell; Nicola Mitchell
Officers: Graham Mitchell, Secretary; Graham Christopher Mitchell [1964] Director/Wine Merchant; Nicola Mitchell [1968] Director/Secretary

Wine Express Ltd
Incorporated: 11 June 2018
Registered Office: 5 Dukeminster Road, Dunstable, Beds, LU5 4FF
Major Shareholder: Francis Iwuchukwu Madubuike
Officers: Francine Lithy Madubuike, Secretary; Francis Iwuchukwu Madubuike [1989] Director

Wine for Drinking Limited
Incorporated: 29 November 2011
Registered Office: 2 Hampstead Heights, London, N2 0PX
Major Shareholder: Alan Marc Judes
Officers: Ruth Judes, Secretary; Alan Marc Judes [1953] Director/Wine Merchant

Wine Freedom Limited
Incorporated: 22 August 2018
Registered Office: Electric House, Ninian Way, Wilnecote, Tamworth, Staffs, B77 5DE
Shareholders: Lucy Jayne Foster; Samuel Lister Olive
Officers: Dr Lucy Jayne Foster [1981] Director; Samuel Lister Olive [1981] Director

The Wine Fusion Limited
Incorporated: 14 January 2008 *Employees:* 4
Net Worth Deficit: £92,039 *Total Assets:* £1,592,013
Registered Office: Unit 2 Greencroft Estates, Tower Road, Annfield Plain, Stanley, Co Durham, DH9 7XP
Parent: Lanchester Wine Cellars Limited
Officers: Adam Richard Black [1968] Director; Anthony Austin Cleary [1952] Director; Veronica Anne Cleary [1954] Director; Andrew George Porton [1974] Director/Wine Merchant; Mark Anthony Satchwell [1964] Director

Wine Group Ltd
Incorporated: 1 June 2018
Registered Office: 59 Devons Road, London, E3 3DW
Major Shareholder: Alina Nedelcu
Officers: Alina Nedelcu [1983] Director [Romanian]

The Wine House Warwick Limited
Incorporated: 16 January 2018
Registered Office: 34 Smith Street, Warwick, CV34 4HS
Major Shareholder: Sezai Aslan
Officers: Sezai Aslan [1956] Director/Manager

Wine Importers (Edinburgh) Limited
Incorporated: 12 March 1975
Net Worth: £1,092,763 *Total Assets:* £1,966,941
Registered Office: 26 Charlotte Square, Edinburgh, EH2 4ET
Parent: Chardon Wines Limited
Officers: William Joseph Bell Birse-Stewart [1951] Director/Wine Merchant; Sir David Edward Murray [1951] Director; Keith Andrew Murray [1975] Director; Neil Macpherson Renton [1965] Director/Wine Merchant; Gordon Thomas White [1956] Director/Wine Merchant

Wine in Cornwall Limited
Incorporated: 19 October 2001
Registered Office: 3 Chapel Street, Redruth, Cornwall, TR15 2BY
Parent: Keltek Cornish Brewery Ltd
Officers: Helen Maguire, Secretary; Nigel Stuart Logan [1953] Director/Restaurateur; Michael Anthony Maguire [1954] Director/Restaurateur; Henry Edward Shaw [1952] Director

Wine IT Limited
Incorporated: 8 May 2015
Net Worth Deficit: £16,387 *Total Assets:* £8,423
Registered Office: 1st Floor, 85 Great Portland Street, London, W1W 7LT
Major Shareholder: Claudio Povero
Officers: Claudio Povero [1978] Director/Accounts Manager [Italian]

The Wine Keg Company Limited
Incorporated: 26 June 2014
Net Worth Deficit: £6,608 *Total Assets:* £13,335
Registered Office: Bank House, Southwick Square, Southwick, W Sussex, BN42 4FN
Shareholder: Louise Oliver
Officers: Scott Barry Daniels [1975] Director; Louise Oliver [1974] Director/Wine Importer; Andrew James Pottinger [1981] Director

The Wine Library Limited
Incorporated: 9 September 1999 *Employees:* 4
Net Worth: £10,508 *Total Assets:* £77,615
Registered Office: BCL House, 2 Pavilion Business Park, Royds Hall Road, Leeds, LS12 6AJ
Shareholder: Peter James Wendell Prescott
Officers: Lucy Deborah Prescott, Secretary; Henry John Krzymuski [1964] Director; Peter James Wendell Prescott [1960] Director/Wine Merchant

Wine Marketings Europe Ltd
Incorporated: 27 March 2015 *Employees:* 1
Net Worth: £688 *Total Assets:* £7,894
Registered Office: 61 Plodder Lane, Farnworth, Bolton, Lancs, BL4 0BX
Major Shareholder: Peter Timothy Scott
Officers: Peter Timothy Scott [1958] Director

UK Wholesalers of Beers, Wines and Spirits   dellam

The Wine Merchant Ltd
Incorporated: 22 November 2017
Registered Office: Bowdens Farm, Hambridge, Langport, Somerset, TA10 0BP
Major Shareholder: George Anthony Edward Lang
Officers: George Anthony Edward Lang [1993] Director/Wholesaler

Wine Online Ltd
Incorporated: 18 December 2018
Registered Office: Block B, OCC Estate, 105 Eade Road, London, N4 1TJ
Major Shareholder: Morris Herzog
Officers: Morris Rothbart [1973] Director

Wine Outlet Ltd.
Incorporated: 27 March 2015
Registered Office: 4 Devonshire Street, London, W1W 5DT
Major Shareholder: Gianfranco Spallarossa
Officers: Gianfranco Spallarossa [1980] Director/Business Consultant [Italian]

Wine Pantry (Wholesale) Limited
Incorporated: 24 October 2016
Net Worth: £1 Total Assets: £1
Registered Office: 10 Beaumont Avenue, Richmond, Surrey, TW9 2HE
Parent: Wine Pantry Limited
Officers: Julia Claire Stafford [1982] Director

Wine Pantry Limited
Incorporated: 3 March 2011
Registered Office: 10 Beaumont Avenue, Richmond, Surrey, TW9 2HE
Shareholders: Julia Claire Stafford; Samuel Tempest Brooks
Officers: Julia Claire Stafford [1982] Director

Wine People Europe Ltd
Incorporated: 19 November 2009
Registered Office: 29-30 Fitzroy Square, London, W1T 6LQ
Officers: Carel Sebastiaan Botha, Secretary; David Eduan Steynberg [1966] Director/Accountant [South African]

The Wine Place Limited
Incorporated: 27 November 2018
Registered Office: 106 Carlton Road, Reigate, Surrey, RH2 0JF
Major Shareholder: Bruno Cernecca
Officers: Bruno Cernecca [1971] Director [Italian]

Wine Poole Limited
Incorporated: 11 December 2012 Employees: 2
Net Worth: £11,485 Total Assets: £169,965
Registered Office: Fulford House, Newbold Terrace, Leamington Spa, Warwicks, CV32 4EA
Shareholders: Barry Kenneth Clive Poole; Lindsay Jane Poole
Officers: Barry Kenneth Clive Poole [1948] Director; Lindsay Jane Poole [1957] Director

The Wine Portfolio UK Limited
Incorporated: 19 March 2009
Previous: Morton Estate Wines UK Limited
Net Worth Deficit: £65,833 Total Assets: £190,148
Registered Office: Windsor House, 26 Mostyn Avenue, Craig-Y-Don, Llandudno, Conwy, LL30 1YY
Major Shareholder: John Mark Coney
Officers: John Mark Coney [1947] Director

The Wine Prophets Limited
Incorporated: 17 March 2017
Net Worth Deficit: £24,636 Total Assets: £33,557
Registered Office: 85 Lauderdale Road, Maida Vale, London, W9 1LX
Major Shareholder: Kyle Paskett
Officers: Kyle Paskett [1983] Strategy Director [Australian]

Wine Raiders Limited
Incorporated: 5 September 2017
Registered Office: 56 Government Row, Enfield, Middlesex, EN3 6JN
Major Shareholder: Les Lancaster
Officers: Leslie Lancaster [1967] Director

Wine Rascals Yorkshire Limited
Incorporated: 2 March 2006 Employees: 1
Previous: Barry Groves Limited
Net Worth Deficit: £35,053 Total Assets: £1,532
Registered Office: Suite 9, Parkhill Business Centre, Walton Road, Wetherby, W Yorks, LS22 5DZ
Major Shareholder: Barry Nigel Groves
Officers: Barry Groves, Secretary; Barry Nigel Groves [1956] Director/Consultant

Wine Research Limited
Incorporated: 13 December 2013
Registered Office: 4 Amwell Place, Hertford Heath, Hertford, SG13 7SE
Shareholders: Viktor Otkidych; Leonid Kovalchuk
Officers: Richard Parry, Secretary; Kristina Otkidych [1986] Director [Kazakh]

The Wine Shop Limited
Incorporated: 19 December 2018
Registered Office: Bern Cottage, Pennar Lane, Pentwynmawr, Newbridge, Newport, NP11 4GY
Officers: Owain Andrew Davies [1981] Director

Wine Story Limited
Incorporated: 27 October 2004
Net Worth: £64,817 Total Assets: £109,905
Registered Office: 47 Church Street, Great Baddow, Chelmsford, Essex, CM2 7JA
Major Shareholder: Thibault Marcel Lavergne
Officers: Thibault Marcel Lavergne [1972] Managing Director [French]

Wine Tasting Angels Ltd
Incorporated: 14 September 2018
Registered Office: The Shacks House, Roils Head, Halifax, W Yorks, HX2 0SX
Shareholders: Ovidiu Emilian Draghici; Octavian Alexandru Vasilescu
Officers: Ovidiu Emilian Draghici [1975] Director/Manager; Octavian Alexandru Vasilescu [1977] Director/Manager

The Wine Treasury Limited
Incorporated: 21 December 2001 Employees: 7
Net Worth Deficit: £180,557 Total Assets: £723,456
Registered Office: 10 Orange Street, Haymarket, London, WC2H 7DQ
Officers: Julian Patrick Ashley Greene, Secretary; Rory Peter Cochrane Benham [1973] Director; James Anthony Doidge [1971] Director; Julian Patrick Ashley Greene [1951] Director; Leslie Edward Small [1942] Director [Irish]

Wine UK Direct Limited
Incorporated: 17 November 2014
Registered Office: 12 Balfour Grove, London, N20 0SJ
Major Shareholder: Victoria Nestor
Officers: Viktorija Nestor [1966] Director/Import-Export

Wine World Producers Limited
Incorporated: 30 August 2006
Net Worth: £2,288,969 Total Assets: £2,516,579
Registered Office: The Old Police Station, Whitburn Street, Bridgnorth, Salop, WV16 4QP
Officers: Davide Zondini, Secretary; Harry Rollo Gabb [1972] Director; Alfeo Martini [1968] Director [Italian]

Wine-Invest Ltd
Incorporated: 26 February 2008 Employees: 5
Net Worth: £757,261 Total Assets: £3,189,529
Registered Office: 10 Barley Mow Passage, London, W4 4PH
Officers: Marie-Caroline Guerin, Secretary; Marie-Caroline Guerin [1978] Director/Operations Manager [French]; Nicolas Guerin [1978] Director/Wine Merchant [French]

Wine2trade Limited
Incorporated: 19 July 2013 Employees: 3
Previous: D:Fine Wines Limited
Net Worth Deficit: £11,044 Total Assets: £126,735
Registered Office: Monometer House, Rectory Grove, Leigh on Sea, Essex, SS9 2HN
Shareholders: Paul Stephen Frederick Dowling; James William Preston Dowling
Officers: James William Preston Dowling [1979] Director; Paul Stephen Frederick Dowling [1951] Director

Wineaux Ltd
Incorporated: 15 July 2005
Net Worth Deficit: £12,897 Total Assets: £5,934
Registered Office: 23a Craven Terrace, London, W2 3QH
Major Shareholder: Barry McCaughley
Officers: Natalie Joanne McCaughley, Secretary; Barry McCaughley [1973] Director

Winecall Limited
Incorporated: 10 May 1983
Registered Office: 7 Weybridge Park, Weybridge, Surrey, KT13 8SJ
Major Shareholder: Benedict Scott Greaves
Officers: Benedict Scott Greaves [1976] Director/Purchasing

Wineclub Online Limited
Incorporated: 23 March 2018
Registered Office: 21 Greenacres, Bath, BA1 4NR
Major Shareholder: Oliver Rayner
Officers: Oliver Rayner [1989] Director

Winecorp Limited
Incorporated: 7 December 2007 Employees: 1
Net Worth: £15,786 Total Assets: £49,438
Registered Office: First Floor, Woburn Court, 2 Railton Road, Woburn Road Industrial Estate, Kempston, Bedford, MK42 7PN
Shareholders: Devinder Singh Chahal; Reddil Properties Limited
Officers: Devinder Singh Chahal, Secretary; Devinder Singh Chahal [1969] Director; Bhupinder Singh Lidder [1966] Director

Winecraft Ltd
Incorporated: 1 February 2016
Net Worth Deficit: £2,793 Total Assets: £7,578
Registered Office: Unit 5 The Yard, Yorkton Street, London, E2 8NH
Shareholders: Julien Olivier Manrique; Sebastian Ludwig Bayer
Officers: Sebastian Ludwig Bayer [1976] Director/Account Manager [German]; Julien Olivier Manrique [1976] Director/Wine Buyer [French]

Wined Ltd
Incorporated: 21 August 2017
Registered Office: 183 Scott Ellis Gardens, London, NW8 9RS
Officers: Andrea Tettamanti [1986] Director/Self Employed [Italian]

Winefantastic Limited
Incorporated: 21 July 2003
Net Worth: £49,831 Total Assets: £387,084
Registered Office: Warrens Farm, Brook Road, Great Tey, Colchester, Essex, CO6 1JG
Major Shareholder: John Roland Greenwold
Officers: Katharine Esther Prestwich, Secretary; John Roland Greenwold [1967] Director; John Peter Williams [1964] Director

Winegrowers Direct Limited
Incorporated: 30 October 2001
Net Worth: £115,545 Total Assets: £305,624
Registered Office: 2 Station Road, Swavesey, Cambridge, CB24 4QJ
Major Shareholder: Jonathan Kinns
Officers: Elizabeth Kinns, Secretary; Elizabeth Kinns [1953] Director/Admin Assistant; Jonathan Kinns [1951] Director

Wineguise Limited
Incorporated: 16 November 2011
Net Worth Deficit: £22,554 Total Assets: £16,154
Registered Office: 9 St Keyna Avenue, Hove, E Sussex, BN3 4PN
Major Shareholder: Christopher Andrew Orr
Officers: Christopher Andrew Orr [1968] Director/Wine Consultancy

Winehood Ltd
Incorporated: 23 November 2018
Registered Office: 40b Napier Road, London, NW10 5XJ
Shareholders: Francesca Anna Darby; Emma Louise Alicia Collyear
Officers: Emma Louise Alicia Collyear [1985] Director/Co-Founder; Francesca Anna Darby [1990] Director/Co-Founder

Winehunters Ltd
Incorporated: 14 April 2008
Registered Office: The Vineyards, Doddenham, Broadwas, Worcester, WR6 5NZ
Major Shareholder: Alan Stephen Hunter
Officers: Alan Stephen Hunter, Secretary/Wine Importer; Alan Stephen Hunter [1950] Director/Wine Importer

Winelink Limited
Incorporated: 13 September 1983
Registered Office: Link House, 51, Stanley Road, Carshalton, Surrey, SM5 4LE
Shareholders: Jacqueline Toulmin; Nigel Victor Toulmin
Officers: Jacqueline Toulmin [1961] Director/Bookkeeper

Winelistphobia Ltd
Incorporated: 30 May 2018
Registered Office: 27 Corner Fielde, London, SW2 4TH
Major Shareholder: Vincenzo Modugno
Officers: Vincenzo Modugno [1991] Director [Italian]

The Winemakers Club 2000 Limited
Incorporated: 18 April 2000 Employees: 13
Net Worth Deficit: £359,724 Total Assets: £518,368
Registered Office: 41a Farringdon Street, London, EC4A 4AN
Shareholders: Robin Frederick Baum; John Haddon Baum
Officers: John Haddon Baum, Secretary; John Haddon Baum [1980] Director/Wine Merchant; Robin Frederick Baum [1945] Director

The Wineman (UK) Ltd
Incorporated: 1 February 2012
Net Worth Deficit: £1,841 Total Assets: £45,825
Registered Office: The Stable Yard, Vicarage Road, Stony Stratford, Milton Keynes, Bucks, MK11 1BN
Major Shareholder: Kevin John O'Rourke
Officers: Kevin John O'Rourke [1969] Director/Wine Merchant

The Wineman Limited
Incorporated: 26 March 1999 Employees: 3
Net Worth: £15,360 Total Assets: £142,958
Registered Office: Cottesmore, Rectory Road, Streatley, Reading, Berks, RG8 9QA
Shareholders: Ian Hewson; Paula Hewson
Officers: Ian Hewson, Secretary/Wine Merchant; Ian Hewson [1962] Director; Paula Hewson [1964] Director

Wineologia Ltd
Incorporated: 30 May 2018
Registered Office: 808 Frobisher House, Dolphin Square, London, SW1V 3LW
Major Shareholder: Roberto Sanchez Hernandez
Officers: Roberto Sanchez Hernandez [1989] Director/Sommelier [Spanish]

Winepro Limited
Incorporated: 21 July 2010
Net Worth: £257,161 Total Assets: £312,193
Registered Office: 2 Spur Gate, 24 Spur Hill Avenue, Poole, Dorset, BH14 9PH
Shareholders: Anne Barbara Butler; Robert John Pond Butler
Officers: Anne Barbara Butler [1946] Director; Robert John Pond Butler [1944] Director

Winery Classic Limited
Incorporated: 23 November 1994 Employees: 3
Net Worth: £13,915 Total Assets: £82,842
Registered Office: 6 Genesis Business Centre, Redkiln Way, Horsham, W Sussex, RH13 5QH
Major Shareholder: Gennaro D'Angelo
Officers: Gennaro D'Angelo, Secretary/Wine Dealer [Italian]; Gennaro D'Angelo [1960] Director/Wine Dealer [Italian]; Marco Fantinel [1970] Director/Wine Dealer [Italian]

Winery Jakubik UK Ltd
Incorporated: 6 November 2018
Registered Office: 143 Beech Avenue, Northampton, NN3 2LE
Shareholders: Jiri Hasmanda; Martina Hasmandova
Officers: Jiri Hasmanda [1978] Director [Czech]; Martina Hasmandova [1979] Director [Czech]

Wines Around Mediterranean Limited
Incorporated: 5 March 2018
Registered Office: 105 Seven Sisters Road, London, N7 7QR
Shareholders: Yiannakis Ioannou; Stella Peppa
Officers: Yiannakis Ioannou [1967] Director; Stella Peppa [1990] Director [Greek]

Wines of The Americas Limited
Incorporated: 18 May 2016 Employees: 3
Net Worth Deficit: £9,614 Total Assets: £45,502
Registered Office: Gaskyns, Lyons Road, Slinfold, Horsham, W Sussex, RH13 0QT
Shareholder: Eric Mariani
Officers: Eric Mariani [1964] Director [French]

Wineservice Limited
Incorporated: 22 August 2007 Employees: 5
Net Worth: £1,492,967 Total Assets: £1,668,640
Registered Office: 206 Upper Richmond Road West, East Sheen, London, SW14 8AH
Shareholders: Colleen Hillman; Nicholas Hillman
Officers: Colleen Eileen Hillman, Secretary; Colleen Eileen Hillman [1951] Director; Nicholas Hillman [1956] Director/Wine Merchant

The Winesider UK Ltd
Incorporated: 20 July 2009
Previous: Tuamoto Limited
Net Worth Deficit: £1,721,067 Total Assets: £1,261
Registered Office: 15 Northfields Prospect, Northfields, London, SW18 1PE
Officers: Marco Acquistapace [1958] Director/Manager

WinesOnline Ltd
Incorporated: 3 November 2014 Employees: 3
Net Worth: £9,005 Total Assets: £112,107
Registered Office: Louis Pearlman Centre, Unit 51 Goulton Street, Hull, HU3 4DL
Major Shareholder: James Gordon Mason
Officers: Calvin Robert Allan Innes [1983] Director

Winetage Ltd
Incorporated: 12 November 2018
Registered Office: Flat 6, The Wickets, 150 Windsor Road, Slough, SL1 2JB
Major Shareholder: Federico Ignacio Arango Abello
Officers: Federico Ignacio Arango Abello [1986] Director [Italian]

Winetraders (UK) Limited
Incorporated: 6 July 1998 Employees: 4
Net Worth: £202,518 Total Assets: £643,969
Registered Office: 5 Bankside, Hanborough Business Park, Long Hanborough, Witney, Oxon, OX29 8LJ
Major Shareholder: Michael Ian Norman Palij
Officers: Michael Ian Norman Palij [1966] Director/Wine Merchant & Consultant; Marija Simovic [1970] Director/Consultant

Wineways (Harrogate) Limited
Incorporated: 20 January 2010
Net Worth Deficit: £291,050 Total Assets: £357,956
Registered Office: 32 Leeds Road, Harrogate, N Yorks, HG2 8BQ
Major Shareholder: Martin Jeffery
Officers: Tara Fay Stagman, Secretary; Edward Stuart Ake [1964] Director; Martin Robert Jeffery [1966] Director/Wine Merchant; Tara Fay Stagman [1975] Director/Finance Manager

Wineworld Exchange UK Limited
Incorporated: 26 January 2017
Registered Office: 66 Shaftesbury Avenue, London, W1D 6LX
Major Shareholder: Shuk Yi Mariana Lam
Officers: Shuk Yi Mariana Lam [1975] Director/Business Executive [Chinese]

Wingwalker Vodka Limited
Incorporated: 20 February 2019
Registered Office: Strathmashie Distillery, Laggan, Newtonmore, Highland, PH20 1BU
Major Shareholder: Chris Paul Molyneaux
Officers: Chris Paul Molyneaux [1977] Managing Director

Winicious Limited
Incorporated: 29 September 2015
Registered Office: The Old Bakery, Green Street, Lytham St Annes, Lancs, FY8 5LG
Officers: Rossella di Tuoro [1984] Director [Italian]; Alberto Pagni [1983] Director [Italian]

Winkleigh Cider Company Limited
Incorporated: 11 February 2011 *Employees:* 5
Net Worth: £40,443 *Total Assets:* £220,834
Registered Office: 69 High Street, Bideford, Devon, EX39 2AT
Shareholders: David Austin Bridgman; Kylie Jane Beardon; Christopher John Beardon
Officers: Kylie Jane Beardon, Secretary; Christopher John Beardon [1986] Director; Kylie Jane Beardon [1988] Director; David Austin Bridgman [1951] Director

Winnack and Hart Industries Ltd
Incorporated: 19 December 2018
Registered Office: 155a Queens Road, Leicester, LE2 3FN
Shareholders: Jack Andrei Geoffrey Winnack; Samuel Lewis Hart
Officers: Samuel Lewis Hart [1993] Director/Consultant; Jack Andrei Geoffrey Winnack [1990] Director/Management Accountant

Winning Invest & Trade Ltd
Incorporated: 7 April 2010 *Employees:* 1
Net Worth Deficit: £170,759 *Total Assets:* £3,470,543
Registered Office: 78 York Street, London, W1H 1DP
Major Shareholder: Eliahu (Eli) Robinovich
Officers: Arthur Joseph Grice [1942] Director/Consultant in Oil Industry

Wintrad Ltd
Incorporated: 5 July 1996
Previous: M & D Wine Merchants Limited
Net Worth: £28,948 *Total Assets:* £48,892
Registered Office: 60-61 Windmill Street, Gravesend, Kent, DA12 1BB
Officers: Kuljit Kaur Dosanjh - Cheema [1978] Director/Manager

Winz International UK Ltd
Incorporated: 30 March 2017
Registered Office: 3rd Floor, 207 Regent Street, London, W1B 3HH
Officers: Huarong Zhang [1955] Director [Chinese]

Wisca Beverages Limited
Incorporated: 13 February 2018
Registered Office: Manuka Heights, Victory Parade, London, E20 1GH
Major Shareholder: Alpesh Bijlani
Officers: Alpesh Bijlani, Secretary; Alpesh Bijlani [1994] Director/Entrepreneur [Indian]

Wisdom Whisky & Wine (Scotland) Ltd
Incorporated: 17 January 2017
Registered Office: Strathleven House, Vale of Leven Industrial Estate, Dumbarton, G82 3PD
Shareholders: Timothy Paul Ashley; Benjamin Edward Lancaster
Officers: Timothy Paul Ashley [1982] Director; Benjamin Edward Lancaster [1983] Director/Member

Wisdom Whisky & Wine Limited
Incorporated: 24 November 2016
Registered Office: Bridge House, 4 Borough High Street, London Bridge, London, SE1 9QR
Shareholders: Timothy Paul Ashley; Benjamin Edward Lancaster
Officers: Benjamin Edward Lancaster [1983] Director/Member

Wise Imports Limited
Incorporated: 1 February 2017
Net Worth Deficit: £3,395 *Total Assets:* £284
Registered Office: Jarrow Business Centre, Viking Business Park, Jarrow, Tyne & Wear, NE32 3DT
Officers: Joan Targas Marcilla [1983] Director [Spanish]

Wise Trading Limited
Incorporated: 13 December 1988 *Employees:* 15
Net Worth: £8,364,867 *Total Assets:* £16,904,696
Registered Office: Long Drive, Station Approach, South Ruislip, Middlesex, HA4 0HN
Officers: Iqbal Singh Johal, Secretary; Balkar Singh Johal [1946] Director; Balraj Singh Johal [1948] Director; Iqbal Singh Johal [1954] Director; Jasbir Singh Johal [1953] Director; Sarnpal Singh Johal [1957] Director

Witek Spirits Ltd
Incorporated: 4 June 2018
Registered Office: 9 Church Street, Woodbridge, Suffolk, IP12 1DS
Shareholders: James Peter Anthony Gwizdala; Alina Dorota Gwizdala; Jozef Stefan Christopher Gwizdala
Officers: James Peter Anthony Gwizdala [1960] Director

Withers Agencies Limited
Incorporated: 2 April 1990
Net Worth: £16,671 *Total Assets:* £113,726
Registered Office: Dene Cottage, North Street, Alfriston, Polegate, E Sussex, BN26 5UQ
Major Shareholder: David John Withers
Officers: David John Withers [1948] Director/Wine Broker

Witney Wine Limited
Incorporated: 25 February 2016
Net Worth: £100 *Total Assets:* £104
Registered Office: 39 St James's Street, London, SW1A 1JD
Officers: John Michael Botros [1948] Director/Barrister

WLG Limited
Incorporated: 24 February 2000
Net Worth: £400,030 *Total Assets:* £1,649,945
Registered Office: Unit L/T, Westwood Industrial Estate, Arkwright Street, Oldham, Lancs, OL9 9LZ
Officers: Steven Peter Wild, Secretary/Director; Andrew Paul Wild [1962] Director; Steven Peter Wild [1960] Director

WLL Wholesale Ltd
Incorporated: 26 April 2018
Registered Office: c/o Trustax Services Limited, Unit V15 Howitt Building, Lenton Boulevard, Nottingham, NG7 2BY
Shareholders: Kapil Lathia; Zepeng Wen
Officers: Kapil Lathia [1982] Director; Zepeng Wen [1988] Director [Chinese]

Woburn Wine Company Limited
Incorporated: 28 February 2011
Net Worth Deficit: £26,762 *Total Assets:* £34,697
Registered Office: Manor House, Farm Beckerings Park, Lidlington, Bedford, MK43 0RA
Officers: George Evelyn Atkinson-Clark [1960] Director/Wine Merchant; Sarah Anne Atkinson-Clark [1962] Director/Psychotherapist

UK Wholesalers of Beers, Wines and Spirits   dellam

Wokka Spirits Limited
Incorporated: 30 June 2000
Net Worth: £4,618 Total Assets: £5,231
Registered Office: Timber Mill Way, Gauden Road, London, SW4 6LY
Shareholders: A E Chapman & Son Limited; James Michael Eden
Officers: Andre Eugene Chapman [1964] Director; Karon Louise Chaproniere [1965] Director; James Michael Eden [1975] Director; Wellwood George Charles Maxwell [1952] Director/Distiller

Wold Toppers Limited
Incorporated: 17 April 2000 Employees: 18
Net Worth: £407,383 Total Assets: £1,794,538
Registered Office: Hunmanby Grange, Wold Newton, Driffield, E Yorks, YO25 3HS
Shareholders: Thomas Leslie Mellor; Gillian Mary Mellor
Officers: Thomas Leslie Mellor, Secretary; Alexander David Balchin [1988] Director/Operations Manager; Katherine Emma Balchin [1987] Director/Accounts Manager; Gillian Mary Mellor [1960] Director/Farmer; Thomas Leslie Mellor [1959] Director/Farmer

Wolf Leisure Limited
Incorporated: 19 September 2007
Registered Office: 90 Brixton Hill, London, SW2 1QN
Shareholder: Tary Osman Mustafa
Officers: Mustafa Osman Tary, Secretary; Mustafa Osman Tary [1968] Director; Yusuf Osman Tary [1970] Director/Wholesaler

Wolf Wine Limited
Incorporated: 19 September 2018
Registered Office: Wolf Wine, Green Park Station, Bath, BA1 1JB
Major Shareholder: Samuel James Shaw
Officers: Samuel James Shaw [1991] Director

Woodland Wine Store Limited
Incorporated: 7 August 2012
Net Worth: £5,356 Total Assets: £25,614
Registered Office: Maria House, 35 Millers Road, Brighton, BN1 5NP
Shareholders: Nilkanth Patel; Jyoti Patel
Officers: Nilkanth Patel [1957] Director

Woodwinters Agencies Limited
Incorporated: 11 May 2017
Net Worth: £10,041 Total Assets: £40,392
Registered Office: Unit 4, 15 Borrowmeadow Road, Stirling, FK7 7FB
Officers: Andrew Johnson [1971] Director; Douglas Alan Wood [1975] Director

Woody Nook Wines (UK) Limited
Incorporated: 13 March 2006 Employees: 2
Net Worth Deficit: £1,504,307 Total Assets: £55,008
Registered Office: Edwin Smith Chartered Accountants, 32 Queen's Road, Reading, Berks, RG1 4AU
Shareholders: Peter John Bailey; Jane Bailey
Officers: Jane Bailey, Secretary; Jane Bailey [1947] Director; Peter John Bailey [1945] Director

Michael Woolley Limited
Incorporated: 9 September 1949
Net Worth: £281,232 Total Assets: £308,670
Registered Office: Mayfield House, Mayfield Flat, Cross in Hand, Heathfield, E Sussex, TN21 0TU
Shareholders: Adrian Cromar Walker; Michele Susan Walker
Officers: Adrian Cromar Walker, Secretary; Adrian Cromar Walker [1955] Director

Woori Trade Ltd
Incorporated: 24 September 2015
Net Worth Deficit: £45,608 Total Assets: £22,853
Registered Office: Unit 2, 5 & 6, Second Floor, 39-41 High Street, New Malden, Surrey, KT3 4BY
Major Shareholder: Mi Kyung Han
Officers: Mi Kyung Han [1973] Director [South Korean]

Workshy Brewing Ltd
Incorporated: 9 October 2017
Registered Office: 1 Glendale House, Cardigan Road, London, TW10 6BW
Shareholders: Tom Paunic; Louis Salem
Officers: Tom Paunic [1979] Director; Louis Salem [1976] Director [Australian]

World Beers Limited
Incorporated: 5 September 2011
Net Worth: £13,073 Total Assets: £242,761
Registered Office: Suite S17, Allen House, The Maltings, Station Road, Sawbridgeworth, Herts, CM21 9JX
Major Shareholder: Peter Robert Anthony Karsten
Officers: Peter Robert Anthony Karsten, Secretary; Peter Robert Anthony Karsten [1952] Director

World Brands Duty Free Limited
Incorporated: 6 October 1992 Employees: 90
Net Worth: £31,163,000 Total Assets: £82,534,000
Registered Office: Building 12, Chiswick Park, 566 Chiswick High Road, London, W4 5AN
Parent: Chivas Brothers (Holdings) Limited
Officers: Timiko Cranwell, Secretary; Nathalie Boeuf [1972] Director [French]; Antonio Duva [1968] Director/General Sales Manager [Italian]; Olivier Gasperin [1966] Director/Vice President, Finance [French]; Mohit Lal [1964] Managing Director [Indian]; Franck Michel Jean Lapeyre [1967] Director/Chief Operating Officer [French]; Charles Anthony Raciti [1960] Sales Director [American]

World Cider Box Limited
Incorporated: 15 September 2016
Net Worth Deficit: £33,776 Total Assets: £11,461
Registered Office: 71-75 Shelton Street, Covent Garden, London, WC2H 9JQ
Major Shareholder: Brian Wild
Officers: Brian Wild [1979] Director/Founder

World of Drams Ltd
Incorporated: 11 October 2018
Registered Office: Spring Grove Barn, Spring Grove, Laneshawbridge, Colne, Lancs, BB8 7HQ
Major Shareholder: Mark Ashworth
Officers: Mark Ashworth [1967] Director

World of Drinks Limited
Incorporated: 5 March 2018
Registered Office: Hope House, Barton Road, Bramley, Guildford, Surrey, GU5 0EA
Major Shareholder: Aaron Marcus Hibbert
Officers: Aaron Marcus Hibbert [1981] Director/Businessman

World of Patria International Limited
Incorporated: 21 October 2005
Net Worth: £63,872 Total Assets: £4,085,428
Registered Office: Suite 2a, 1st Floor, Warren Court, Park Road, Crowborough, E Sussex, TN6 2QX
Parent: World of Patria International Holdings Ltd
Officers: Andrew Michael Kerr [1969] Managing Director; Robert Ian Nichols [1968] Director; Steve William Smith [1961] Director

World Sake Imports UK Ltd
Incorporated: 28 July 2008
Net Worth: £72,855 Total Assets: £125,186
Registered Office: Office A, Hoste House, Whiting Street, Bury St Edmunds, Suffolk, IP33 1NR
Parent: World Sake Inc
Officers: Chris Pearce [1949] Director [American]

World Traveller Wines Limited
Incorporated: 7 April 2014
Registered Office: 78 Wharfdale Road, Birmingham, B11 2DE
Major Shareholder: Budge Dhariwal
Officers: Budge Dhariwal [1961] Director/MD

World Wide Wines Limited
Incorporated: 5 April 1988
Registered Office: 2 Lavender Lane, Rowledge, Farnham, Surrey, GU10 4AY
Major Shareholder: Salvatore Castiglione
Officers: Lorraine Castiglione [1957] Director/Customer Care; Salvatore Castiglione [1947] Director/Retired

World Wine Imports Limited
Incorporated: 2 May 2018
Registered Office: London Level 1, 184 Shepherds Bush Road, London, W6 7NL
Major Shareholder: Timothy David Clarke
Officers: Timothy David Clarke [1969] Managing Director [Australian]

Worldewide Limited
Incorporated: 12 April 1999
Net Worth: £416,784 Total Assets: £1,188,543
Registered Office: Doshi Accountants Ltd, 6th Floor, Amp House, Dingwall Road, Croydon, Surrey, CR0 2LX
Shareholders: Stuart Tarrant; Darren Andrew Wheeler
Officers: Jennifer Tarrant, Secretary; Stuart Tarrant [1968] Director; Darren Andrew Wheeler [1968] Director/Manager

Worldwide Drinks Limited
Incorporated: 10 January 2006 Employees: 2
Net Worth: £5,032 Total Assets: £356,987
Registered Office: 79 Eastgate, Cowbridge, S Glamorgan, CF71 7AA
Shareholders: John Martin Howkins; Catrin Rachel Howkins
Officers: Catrin Rachel Howkins [1969] Director; John Martin Howkins [1968] Director

Worldwine UK Ltd
Incorporated: 13 March 2015
Net Worth: £9,422 Total Assets: £1,121,270
Registered Office: 5 Elstree Gate, Elstree Way, Borehamwood, Herts, WD6 1JD
Major Shareholder: Islam Magkometov
Officers: Islam Magkometov [1976] Director [Greek]

Worsley Gin Ltd
Incorporated: 22 May 2017
Registered Office: 7 Brindley House, 1 Waters Way, Worsley, Manchester, M28 2AG
Major Shareholder: Andrew Niedzwiecki
Officers: Andrew Niedzwiecki [1980] Director/Chief Executive Officer

Worsley Wines Limited
Incorporated: 28 April 2011 Employees: 4
Net Worth: £149,748 Total Assets: £228,447
Registered Office: 30 Leigh Cliff Road, Leigh on Sea, Essex, SS9 1DJ
Shareholders: Philip John Worsley; Peter Thomas
Officers: Philip John Worsley [1953] Director/Business Consultant

Worthington Wine and Spirits UK Limited
Incorporated: 16 May 2013
Net Worth: £40,770 Total Assets: £45,061
Registered Office: Bank House, 81 St Judes Road, Englefield Green, Surrey, TW20 0DF
Major Shareholder: John Vernon Hooper
Officers: John Vernon Hooper [1972] Director/Wine and Spirit Merchant [South African]

The Wright Wine Company Limited
Incorporated: 16 October 2000 Employees: 12
Net Worth: £1,204,604 Total Assets: £1,964,576
Registered Office: The Old Smithy, Raikes Road, Skipton, N Yorks, BD23 1NP
Major Shareholder: Julian Jepson Kaye
Officers: Julian Jepson Kaye [1972] Director/Wine and Spirit Merchant

Wrights Lion Brewery Limited
Incorporated: 2 October 2015 Employees: 8
Net Worth Deficit: £48,361 Total Assets: £264,481
Registered Office: The Little House, 88a West Street, Farnham, Surrey, GU9 7EN
Shareholder: Richard Stacey Wright
Officers: Margaret Anne Wright [1948] Director; Richard Stacey Wright [1946] Director/Retailer; Sally Eileen Wright [1979] Director

WSB Investment and Consultancy Ltd
Incorporated: 8 February 2018
Registered Office: 20-22 Wenlock Road, London, N1 7GU
Major Shareholder: Chris Denman
Officers: Chris Denman [1988] Director

Wycombe Wine Company Limited
Incorporated: 17 February 1982
Net Worth Deficit: £169,064 Total Assets: £5,927
Registered Office: Mead Court, 10 Mead Business Centre, 176-178 Berkhampstead Road, Chesham, Bucks, HP5 3EE
Officers: Simon Andrew Harwood, Secretary; Simon Andrew Harwood [1971] Director/Manager

Wyfold Vineyard Limited
Incorporated: 9 January 2014
Net Worth Deficit: £97,327 Total Assets: £160,521
Registered Office: The Chalet, Peppard Common, Henley on Thames, Oxon, RG9 5EH
Shareholders: Barbara Laithwaite; Henry John Hugh Laithwaite; Cherry Thompson; Ben Postlethwaite
Officers: Barbara Anne Laithwaite [1946] Director/Company Chairman; Henry John Hugh Laithwaite [1980] Director/Wine Grower; Ben Thomas Postlethwaite [1980] Director/Motorsport Executive; Cherry Ruth Stuart Thompson [1944] Director/Retired

Wyld Rose Ltd
Incorporated: 20 March 2017
Net Worth: £53,247 Total Assets: £78,176
Registered Office: Bear Cottage, Nettleton Shrub, Chippenham, Wilts, SN14 7NN
Major Shareholder: Rose Catherine Unwin
Officers: Rose Catherine Unwin [1988] Director/Sales Professional

Xardins Wines and Cava Ltd
Incorporated: 14 May 2018
Registered Office: 92b Trafalgar Street, Brighton, BN1 4ER
Officers: Julia Harding [1968] Director

Xeco Wines Limited
Incorporated: 6 December 2016 Employees: 1
Net Worth Deficit: £121,550 Total Assets: £95,740
Registered Office: Galla House, 695 High Road, North Finchley, London, N12 0BT
Shareholder: Caroline Geraedts-Espey
Officers: Polly Belinda Aylwin-Foster [1986] Director; Caroline Geraedts-Espey [1982] Director; Alexa Jane Keymer [1984] Director

Xenon Wines & Spirits Limited
Incorporated: 2 February 2016
Registered Office: 1 Warner House, Harrovian Business Village, Bessborough Road, Harrow, Middlesex, HA1 3EX
Major Shareholder: Ranjeeta Bizlall
Officers: Ranjeeta Bizlall [1981] Director; Atul Khosla [1990] Director [Indian]; Ram Kumar Khosla [1980] Director [Indian]

Xi-Spain Ltd
Incorporated: 23 January 2019
Registered Office: 68 Windsor Drive, Orpington, Kent, BR6 6HD
Major Shareholder: Juan Fernandez Alameda
Officers: Juan Fernandez Alameda [1979] Director/Consultant [Spanish]

Xisto Wines Limited
Incorporated: 30 April 2014
Net Worth Deficit: £32,162 Total Assets: £41,343
Registered Office: 34 Maple Road, Bristol, BS7 8RQ
Officers: Anthony Michael Mann [1963] Director/Wine Merchant; Lela McTernan-Mann [1964] Director/Wine Merchant

Xorta Global Management Limited
Incorporated: 4 May 2016
Net Worth: £1,101 Total Assets: £2,801
Registered Office: c/o Lohur & Co, 35 New England Road, Brighton, BN1 4GG
Major Shareholder: Amanda Denise Miranda
Officers: Amanda Denise Miranda, Secretary; Amanda Denise Miranda [1967] Director

Xpress Bootleg Limited
Incorporated: 9 May 2017
Net Worth: £13,562 Total Assets: £13,562
Registered Office: 34a Western Avenue, London, W3 7TZ
Officers: Samuel Livingstone Aird Aird [1985] Director

Xpress Drinks Ltd
Incorporated: 11 May 2017
Registered Office: 143 Sandy Lane, Darwen, Lancs, BB3 0PL
Shareholder: James Mason Tipping
Officers: Michael Ross [1986] Director; James Mason Tipping [1993] Director

Xpress Resolution Ltd
Incorporated: 14 November 2018
Registered Office: 248 Brixton Road, London, SW9 6AQ
Major Shareholder: Green Acharaike
Officers: Green Acharaike [1972] Managing Director

Xtraflow Limited
Incorporated: 7 May 2013
Net Worth Deficit: £6,190 Total Assets: £3,007
Registered Office: Flat 12, Mounts Court, Mounts Road, Greenhithe, Kent, DA9 9LX
Major Shareholder: Jacek Wolfart
Officers: Joanna Kostepski [1984] Director/Housewife [Polish]; Jacek Wolfart [1983] Director/Service Engineer [Polish]

Xuyang International Ltd
Incorporated: 26 February 2009
Net Worth: £102 Total Assets: £672,420
Registered Office: 40 Founes Drive, Chafford Hundred, Grays, Essex, RM16 6DU
Shareholders: Zixia Zheng; Danyang Wang
Officers: Danyang Wang [1974] Director [Chinese]

Yaad Rum Ltd
Incorporated: 23 May 2017
Net Worth: £79,112 Total Assets: £89,509
Registered Office: First Floor, 15 Young Street, London, W8 5EH
Shareholder: Rodolphe Frerejean Taittinger
Officers: Jonathan Almonte Felix [1984] Sales Director [Spanish]; Guillaume Pierre Marie Eric Frerejean Taittinger [1978] Director [French]; Rodolphe Jean Marie Humbert Guy Frerejean Taittinger [1986] Director/Businessman [French]; Florestan Frederic Marie Loriot de Rouvray [1990] Director [French]; Rakesh Madhub [1972] Director

Yapp Brothers Limited
Incorporated: 20 February 1985 Employees: 16
Net Worth: £1,263,214 Total Assets: £1,948,024
Registered Office: The Old Brewery, Mere, Wilts, BA12 6DY
Major Shareholder: Carl Reh
Officers: Thomas Rowland Ashworth, Secretary; Thomas Rowland Ashworth [1970] Director; Giles William Charles Dessain [1948] Director/Chartered Accountant; Richard Nicholas Jones [1957] Director; Alexander Rittlinger [1973] Director [German]; Jason Christopher Yapp [1967] Sales Director

Yarm Gin Ltd
Incorporated: 29 August 2017
Registered Office: Gin Without Borders Ltd, The Manor House (1707), West End, Sedgefield, Co Durham, TS21 2BW
Major Shareholder: Matthew Philip Wilson
Officers: Matthew Philip Wilson [1986] Director/Owner

The Yarm Spirits Company Ltd
Incorporated: 29 August 2017
Registered Office: Gin Without Borders Ltd, The Manor House (1707), West End, Sedgefield, Co Durham, TS21 2BW
Major Shareholder: Matthew Philip Wilson
Officers: Matthew Philip Wilson [1986] Director/Owner

Yates Iow Brewery Limited
Incorporated: 4 April 2005 Employees: 8
Net Worth: £206,726 Total Assets: £545,559
Registered Office: Unit 4 Langbridge Business Centre, Newchurch, Sandown, Isle of Wight, PO36 0NP
Shareholders: David Robert Yates; David Robert Yates
Officers: David Robert Yates [1973] Director/Wholesaler; David Stanley Yates [1942] Director/Brewer

Yaved Ltd
Incorporated: 30 April 2015 Employees: 2
Net Worth: £33,291 Total Assets: £48,884
Registered Office: SKN Business Centre, 1 Guildford Street, Birmingham, B19 2HN
Major Shareholder: Mohammed Yaved
Officers: Mohammed Yaved [1968] Director

YC Wines Limited
Incorporated: 2 December 2010
Net Worth Deficit: £11,881 Total Assets: £2,220
Registered Office: Flat 1, 17 Castle Hill Avenue, Folkestone, Kent, CT20 2TD
Major Shareholder: Yann Chauvin
Officers: Yann Chauvin [1973] Director/Wine Agent [French]

Yeast To West Ltd
Incorporated: 3 May 2018
Registered Office: 4 Warren Road, Twickenham, Middlesex, TW2 7DL
Major Shareholder: Attila Schmidt
Officers: Attila Schmidt [1988] Director [Hungarian]

Yeastie Boys UK Ltd
Incorporated: 19 May 2015
Net Worth Deficit: £123,778 Total Assets: £319,667
Registered Office: 21 Lambarde Drive, Sevenoaks, Kent, TN13 3HX
Shareholders: Stuart Ian McKinlay; Samuel Ian Possenniskie
Officers: Stuart Ian McKinlay [1975] Director; Samuel Ian Possenniskie [1976] Director [New Zealander]

Yoka Family Limited
Incorporated: 2 November 2018
Registered Office: 11 Rochford Way, Croydon, Surrey, CR0 3AG
Major Shareholder: Shanthini Sothinarayasamy
Officers: Shanthini Sothinarayasamy [1965] Company Secretary/Director [Sri Lankan]

Yorke Vines Ltd
Incorporated: 24 March 2016 Employees: 5
Net Worth: £8,490 Total Assets: £223,394
Registered Office: Greenhill Farm, Pound Road, Thornford, Sherborne, Dorset, DT9 6QD
Shareholders: Simon Yorke; Jane Yorke
Officers: Jane Louise Yorke [1970] Director; Simon Anketel Hamilton Yorke [1967] Director

Yorkshire Beers Limited
Incorporated: 14 August 2008
Net Worth: £42,255 Total Assets: £185,037
Registered Office: 20 Owl Lane, Dewsbury, W Yorks, WF12 7RQ
Major Shareholder: Paul Neil Fahey
Officers: Paul Neil Fahey [1963] Director/Property Developer

Yorkshire Vino Ltd
Incorporated: 14 April 2014
Net Worth: £41,102 Total Assets: £72,066
Registered Office: Unit C9 & C10, New Pudsey Square, Stanningley, Pudsey, Leeds, LS28 6PX
Officers: Mandeep Singh Sidhu [1987] Director/Shop Manager

Yorkshire Vintners Limited
Incorporated: 21 May 2010
Net Worth: £998 Total Assets: £725,154
Registered Office: Unit 2 Ripon Business Park, Charter Road, Ripon, N Yorks, HG4 1AJ
Major Shareholder: Simon Edwin Jackson
Officers: Simon Edwin Jackson [1977] Director

Young in Spirit Ltd
Incorporated: 24 June 2016
Net Worth: £1,800 Total Assets: £46,004
Registered Office: c/o Archer Associates, Churchill House, 120 Bunns Lane, London, NW7 2AS
Shareholders: Elizabeth Jennifer Ashworth; Camilla Brown
Officers: Elizabeth Jennifer Ashworth [1987] Director/Alcoholic Drinks Company; Camilla Brown [1986] Director/Alcoholic Drinks Company

Young Malt Company Ltd
Incorporated: 13 November 2018
Registered Office: 23 Melville Street, Edinburgh, EH3 7PE
Shareholders: John Ferguson; Alexander James Harrison
Officers: John Ferguson [1988] Director; Alexander James Harrison [1990] Director

Young's Beers Wines & Spirits Ltd
Incorporated: 19 November 2009 Employees: 21
Net Worth: £370,960 Total Assets: £1,238,026
Registered Office: Unit 20 Churchill Way, Lomeshaye Industrial Estate, Nelson, Lancs, BB9 6RT
Officers: John James Stephenson [1962] Director; Albert Roger Young [1965] Director

Zachicado Ltd
Incorporated: 26 April 2017
Registered Office: 35 The Reddings, London, NW7 4JN
Officers: Wilfred Machicado [1981] Director/Project Manager; Kate Zadah [1981] Director

Zarb Distribution Ltd
Incorporated: 12 February 2018
Registered Office: 12 Compton Park Road, Mannamead, Plymouth, PL3 5BU
Major Shareholder: Rodney Dennis Alexander Jordan
Officers: Rodney Dennis Alexander Jordan [1943] Director

Zefino Family Limited
Incorporated: 13 April 2016 Employees: 1
Net Worth Deficit: £22,039 Total Assets: £21,233
Registered Office: 13 Chime Square, St Albans, Herts, AL3 5JZ
Major Shareholder: Ferenc Zelenak
Officers: Ferenc Zelenak [1979] Director/Manager [Hungarian]

Zetas Ventures Ltd
Incorporated: 12 December 2017
Registered Office: 18 Spedan Close, London, NW3 7XF
Major Shareholder: Paolo Zanelli
Officers: Natalia Krupina [1983] Director/VP [Russian]; Paolo Zanelli [1983] Director [Italian]

Zinea Global Services Limited
Incorporated: 15 November 2016
Net Worth: £339 Total Assets: £7,704
Registered Office: 324 Burnt Oak Lane, Sidcup, Kent, DA15 8LW
Major Shareholder: Moses Oseyaede Azilomhen
Officers: Moses Oseyaede Azilomhen [1975] Director/Businessman [French]

Zing Vodk Limited
Incorporated: 5 February 2013 Employees: 2
Previous: Vodk Ltd
Net Worth Deficit: £191,448 Total Assets: £23,873
Registered Office: 32 Church Road, Hove, E Sussex, BN3 2FN
Shareholder: Michael Peter Mills
Officers: Jenny Mills [1965] Director; Michael Peter Mills [1948] Director

Zinstream Wine Limited
Incorporated: 11 February 2011
Net Worth Deficit: £1,366 *Total Assets:* £6,356
Registered Office: 9 Westwood Close, Sheffield, S6 1UQ
Shareholders: Mark Christopher Haddrell; Olivia Kathryn Haddrell
Officers: Mark Christopher Haddrell, Secretary; Mark Christopher Haddrell [1979] Director/Project Manager; Olivia Kathryn Haddrell [1980] Director/Project Manager

Ziv & Zivka Ltd
Incorporated: 4 June 2018
Registered Office: Van Brugh, Gate Lodge, Greenwich Park, London, SE10 8XH
Major Shareholder: Marija Trachtenberg
Officers: Marija Trachtenberg [1990] Director [American]

ZLCSolutions Ltd
Incorporated: 5 January 2018
Registered Office: 3 Dulnan Close, Reading, Berks, RG30 4YN
Shareholder: Beryl Okeyo
Officers: Zachary Osano Okeyo [1970] Director/Sales Advisor

Zonin UK Limited
Incorporated: 16 June 2003 *Employees:* 16
Net Worth: £2,388,265 *Total Assets:* £4,857,743
Registered Office: 16 Great Queen Street, Covent Garden, London, WC2B 5AH
Officers: Francesco Zonin, Secretary; Gianluca Antonini [1968] Finance & Operations Director [Italian]; Massimo Tuzzi [1973] Director/Manager [Italian]; Francesco Zonin [1974] Director [Italian]

This page is intentionally left blank

Index of Directorships

Ababio, Biggy
Ababio Express Limited

Abad Acosta, Enrique
Dillon Bass Limited

Abbas, Muhammad
Babuji Ltd

Abbot, Christopher Charles
The Rock and Roll Spirit Co Ltd

Abbot, Timothy Stuart
The Rock and Roll Spirit Co Ltd

Abbott, Graham David
Easier Sales Limited

Abdullah, Idris
Kamros Cash and Carry Limited

Abela, Marlon Ralph Pietro
Marc Fine Wines Limited

Aben, Denise Natalie
Aben Wines Limited

Aben, Maurice Joseph
Aben Wines Limited

Abert, Mel
MA Wine and Spirit Imports Ltd
Novel Spirits Collection Ltd
Novel Spirits Limited

Abraham, Jacob Sunny
Allied Wholesale Ltd

Abraham, Malcolm Joseph
Citrosoft Drinks Limited

Abraham, Neville Victor
Liberty Wines Limited

Abraham, Patricia Anne
Citrosoft Drinks Limited

Acharaike, Green
Xpress Resolution Ltd

Achim, Florentin Alexandru
Full Logistic Ltd

Acodrinesei, Silviu Sorin
Acod S & C Ltd

Acquistapace, Marco
Birrificio Del Ducato London Ltd
The Winesider UK Ltd

Adaka, Christopher Sosomadina
Adaka Group Ltd

Adam, Jean-Charles
The French Wine Project Ltd

Adam, Laszlo
Copricom Ltd

Adam, Piers Benedict
Quaich Whisky Investments Ltd

Adams, Edward Charles William
Bonfire Hill Limited

Adams, Mike Peter
Oak Group One P.L.C.

Adams, Paul
TPDirect Ltd

Adams, Warren Charles
Bablake Wines Limited

Adamson, Samuel James
Distant Lands Ltd

Addis, Leonardo
Eurowines Limited

Addison, Richard
Valley Vineyards Limited

Addison-Scott, Alexandra Katherine
Champagne Cellar Limited

Adedeji, Olutimilehin Adedayo
GDD Chapuy Limited

Adegbite, Moses Adedoyin
Bellwether Impex (UK) Limited

Ademola, Adekunle Akanji
Topmost Foods Distribution Ltd.

Adenuga, Mike Babajide
Champsonthego.co.uk Ltd

Adepoju, Adedolapo
Infinitygroup1 Limited

Adeyemi, Babajide Adelekan
Obadec Enterprises Limited

Adeyemi, Titilope
Obadec Enterprises Limited

Adjei-Ampofo, Prince Michael Waddy
M & M Community Development Initiatives

Adjovi, Michael
Mina Collection Ltd

Adnams, Jonathan
Adnams PLC

Adu-Gyamfi, Princess Serwah
Botan Grey Ltd

Adwick, Andrew
River Widow Brewery Ltd

Afasy-Brown, Benson
OAB Ventures Limited

Aftinescu, Alexandru
Alegri Trade Ltd.

Agar, Dale
The Wine Cru Limited

Agate, Michael
Bargate Drinks Limited

Agbeyo, Tolulope Ayomide
Burble Foods and Beverages Ltd
Cornfield Foods and Beverages Ltd

Aghajanzadeh-Langaroody, Gholam Reza
American Fizz (UK) Limited

Agrawal, Nileshkumar
Thames Cash & Carry (Birmingham) Ltd

Aguilar Cabrera, Enrique Eduardo
Peruvian Enterprises Limited

Aguilar, Manuel Jimenez
Gonzalez Byass UK Limited

Agutter, Charles Brodie
UK Vintners (of London) PLC

Ah-Ton, Karine
La Peira Limited

Ahmad-Vellani, Nina
Global Foods Limited

Ahmed Salah, Omar
Relais La Torre UK Ltd
Wine & People Limited

Ahmed, Iftikhar
Aims & Co Ltd

Ahmed, Ishtiaq
Ocean Wines Limited

Ahmed, Mamun
Deshi Bazar Ltd

Ahmed, Salmon
Eurochoice Limited

Ahmed, Umair
A & S Drinks Ltd

Aidan, Amrik Singh
B & W Distributors Limited

Aikman, Michael
Cross Brew Ltd

Ainsworth, Sammy-Jo
SMCA Enterprises Ltd.

Ainsworth, Timothy Stewart
SMCA Enterprises Ltd.

Aird, Samuel Livingstone
Club Belmont Ltd

Aird, Samuel Livingstone Aird
Xpress Bootleg Limited

Aje, Benson
B & F Enterprise UK Ltd
BF Wines UK Ltd

Akande, Adeoluwa Joel
Afrogrocers Ltd

Akande, Hannah Adejumoke
Afrogrocers Ltd

Ake, Edward Stuart
Wineways (Harrogate) Limited

Akers, Anthony Charles
Beer Gonzo Ltd

Akgul, Deniz
Vintage 1947 Limited

Akintola, Ayodele
Whittalls Wines Limited

UK Wholesalers of Beers, Wines and Spirits   dellam

Akker, Brett Jamie
The Liquid Market Limited

Aksakal, Serkan
Choise Group Ltd

Alap Madhusudan Bhausar, Alap Madhusudan
Darlaston Drink Shop Limited

Albacete Fernandez, David Nicolas
Afco Traders Ltd

Albacete, Arturo Felipe
Afco Traders Ltd

Albacete, Hipolito Felipe
Afco Traders Ltd

Albanese, Giovanni
Amore G.N.A. Limited

Albanese, Nicola
Amore G.N.A. Limited

Aldaco, Gonzalo
ASG Wines Limited

Aleksic, Dragan
Aleksic & Mortimer Ltd

Alexander, Anne-Marie Marie
The Queen of The Moorlands Whisky Co Ltd

Alexander, Fraser Douglas
Alexander Wines Ltd.

Alexander, Gavin John
Just Miniatures Limited

Alexander-Johnson, Cerise
The HSE of Drinks Ltd

Alexanian, Karine
Noy Brothers Enterprises Ltd

Alexanian, Navasard
Noy Brothers Enterprises Ltd

Alfano, Gaetano
Annessa Imports Limited
Alfie Fiandaca Limited

Alford, James Congdon
Platinum Gin Ltd

Ali, Liaqat
Orion Cash & Carry Limited

Ali, Mousin
Kingdom Foods & Drinks Limited

Ali, Mubarik
Global Foods Limited

Ali, Shan
Delivery Offlicence Ltd

Ali, Yasar Razwan
Orion Cash & Carry Limited

Ali, Zahid Rana
UK Foods & Drinks Ltd

Ali-Zade, Alikhan
Agrosale UK Limited

Aljija, Sazan
Swinging Vine Ltd

Alken, Anthony
BL011 Limited

Alken, Gregory
BL011 Limited

Allcorn, David John
Vats Wine Co. Limited

Allen, David Melvyn
Pigs Ears Beers Limited

Allen, James
Shelsley Brewing Co Ltd

Allen, Nicholas
Hic-Cup Wines Limited

Allen, Nigel Geoffrey
Everards Brewery Limited

Allen, Samuel Louis
Beer Seller Ltd

Allingham, William Charles Baden
Steamin' Billy (Property) Ltd

Allison, Craig
Bullards Spirits Limited

Allison, Scott Michael
MegaTradingLtd Limited

Allott, Ian David
Chequers Distribution Ltd

Almeida, Carlos Manuel Ferreira Duarte
Nielsen McKinsey Global Tourism & Hospitality Consulting

Almond, Amanda Claire
Bacardi-Martini Limited

Almonte Felix, Jonathan
Yaad Rum Ltd

Altaf Bibi, Muhammad Tahir
Meridale Store Ltd

Alves Da Silva Toscano, Catarina Maria
Edrington-Beam Suntory UK Distribution

Alvis of Lee, Querida
Sir Richard Blake & Associates Ltd

Amadi, Edoardo
Trywines Expertise Limited

Amadi, Helen
Trywines Expertise Limited

Amado, Lindorf Nicholas
Nick Drinks Limited

Amber, Shahid
Leo's Cash & Carry Ltd

Ambler, David Paul
Expressmode Limited

Ambler, Richard Charles Quintin
Broad Street Brands Limited

Amery, Phillip
Albion Fine Wines Ltd
Albion Wine Shippers Limited

Amici, Andrea
Bibere Ltd.

Amin, Daniel James
Balkan Wines Ltd

Amin, Rohit Dhirajlal
Tikka Beer Limited

Amirante, Esteban
Amirante Empire Limited

Amlot, Dylan James
Amlot Morgan Fine Wines Ltd

Amlot, Peter Lloyd
Amlot Morgan Fine Wines Ltd

Amodio, Pier-Francesco
Staibano Ltd

Amodu, Doris Idowu
Ebony Drinks Limited

Amorim, Rui
Mayfair Delivers Limited

An, Guinan
Paradigm Red Limited

An, Qi
Morecambe Bay Wines Limited

An, Xiangshou
Paradigm Red Limited

Anand, Jaspreet
Jassim Limited
Roohop Ltd

Anandan, Christopher Jeremy Leopold
Capsule Wine Ltd

Anbouche, Amir William
4 Acre Brewing Co. Ltd
Jackrabbit Brewing Co. Ltd

Andersen, Kasper Moos
Edrington European Travel Retail Ltd

Anderson, Billy
Carpet Bagger Limited

Anderson, Caitlin Sian
Anderson Beverages Ltd

Anderson, Chloe Dawn
Anderson Beverages Ltd

Anderson, Donald Andrew James
Native Oracle Limited

Anderson, Garreth William
DGB Europe Limited

Anderson, Gary
Edinburgh Cocktail Week Ltd

Anderson, John Frederick
Chelsea Vintners London Ltd

Anderson, Laura Kirstin
RR Whisky Ltd

Anderson, Marc John
The 19th Beer Co Ltd

Anderson, Nana Natalie Dokua
Cacheflow Ltd

Anderson, Nicholas James
NJA Marketing Ltd

Anderson, Ron
Italicus Ltd

Anderson, Simon George
Big Mouth Wine Limited

Anderson, Stephen
Carpet Bagger Limited

Andrea, Andrew Andonis
Marston's Acquisitions Limited

Andrea, Dercole
Italy Abroad Network Limited

Andreev, Andrey Ivanov
Andreev Services Ltd

Andres, Pedro de Los Bueis
SW Group Spanish Wine Ltd

Andretta, Guido
Agro Investment Ltd

Andrew, James
J & M Whisky Limited

Andrew, Mark Peter
Keeling Andrew & Co Limited

Andrews, Grahame Francis
The Bosun's Brewery Tap Ltd

Andrews, Kevin Lewis
Cantium Spirit Ltd

Andrews, Zoe Elizabeth
Bosco-UK Limited
La Delizia UK Limited

Angeles, Clariephine Almoguerra
UK McLouis Liquor Co Ltd

Angelkov, Christopher Anthony
Lost and Found Taprooms Ltd

Anglesey, Susan Blanche Louise, Lady
De Paolis Limited

Angove, John Carlyon
Angove's (Europe) Limited

Ani, Joshua Solomon
Luxury Alcohols Limited

Ani, Solomon
Luxury Alcohols Limited

Anikejenko, Aleksandr
Inconcept Ltd

Annely, Karen Elizabeth
Beer Paradise (York) Limited

Annessa, Domenico
Annessa Imports Limited
Alfie Fiandaca Limited

Annessa, Gianni Enrico
Annessa Imports Limited

Annessa, Maria Giovanna
Annessa Imports Limited

Anolue, Ogonna Solomon
Jascera UK Ltd

Anoufa, Sacha
Kosher Wines Limited

Ansah, Olivia Ama
Rum Runna Ltd

Ansah, Yasmin Bluette
Rum Runna Ltd

Ansell, Clare Marie
Coss Wines Ltd.

Anstee, John
Glamorgan Brewing Co Ltd

Anstee, Rhys Thomas
Glamorgan Brewing Co Ltd

Anstee, Richard Morgan
Glamorgan Brewing Co Ltd

Antar, Pablo
Icomex London Limited

Anthony, Neil
Head Thirst Ltd

Antollini, Isabella
Simply Drinks Distribution Ltd

Antonini, Alberto
Natural Bay Limited

Antonini, Gianluca
Zonin UK Limited

Antrobus, Ian
Antrobus Brothers Limited

Antrobus, Neil
Antrobus Brothers Limited

Ap Breian, Steffan
Grwp Silwriad Cyf

Appleton-Davies, Sean
Ffarm Vintners Limited

Apthorp, Justin James
Majestic Wine PLC

Aramesh, Danial
Pure Techno Ltd

Arango Abello, Federico Ignacio
Winetage Ltd

Arano Nacif, Carlos Nelson
Evok3 Ltd

Arbery, Christopher John
Skyfall Distribution Limited

Arbery, David Stephen
Skyfall Distribution Limited

Arcaini, Jonathan
Falcon Vintners Limited

Arcari, Fabio Vittorio
Arcari & Sons Ltd.

Archer, Caron Patricia
Padstow Brewing Company (2013) Ltd

Archer, Desmond John
Padstow Brewing Company (2013) Ltd

Archer, Jonathan Paul Steadman
Wild Life Botanicals Ltd

Archibald, David George
House of Townend Limited

Arcin, Florent Remi
Artizen Raw Ltd

Arethedathu, Omprakash Damodaran
The Compasses Gomshall Ltd

Argeband, Daniel Baron
Espir Baron & Solomon Limited

Argyrou, Christos
Leomar Limited

Argyrou, Leonidas
Leomar Limited

Ariu, Cristiano
Desideria Ltd

Arkell, Alexander Thomas
Arkell's Brewery Limited

Arkell, George James
Arkell's Brewery Limited

Arkell, James Rixon
Arkell's Brewery Limited
Donnington Brewery Limited

Arkell, Nicholas Henry
Arkell's Brewery Limited

Arkley, Alistair Grant
S.A.Brain & Co Ltd

Armstrong Carey, Patrick Guy
All English Distribution Ltd.

Armstrong, Craig Christian
Eythrope Wine Limited

Armstrong, Florence Elizabeth
Classic Malts Limited

Armstrong, Jane
Whiskybroker Limited

Armstrong, Michael
W.J.Armstrong Limited

Armstrong, Nigel Anthony
W.J.Armstrong Limited

Armstrong, Nigel James
Richmond Distillers (Zurich) Ltd

Armstrong, Paul Jeremy
Cellartrade Ltd

Armstrong, Philip Michael
W.J.Armstrong Limited

Armstrong, Raymond
Classic Malts Limited

Armstrong, Raymond Martin
Whiskybroker Limited

Armstrong, Tim
Tims Tuga Ltd

Arnhold, Joerg Gottlob Paul-Heinz
Lorelei Fine Wines Limited

Arnold, Dohne
Oldschool Wines Limited

Arnold, John Charles
A & B Vintners Limited
Triage Wines Limited

Arnott, Robert Graeme
New Wave (Scotland) Limited

Aron, Simon Michael
Cask Trade Ltd

Arrigoni, Christopher
More or Less Drinks Co Ltd

Arthur, Carmel Charmain
Pure Organic Drinks Limited

Asare, Nana Ama Werehemaa
Sundown Vino & Liquor Ltd

Ascani, Maurizia
Giovanni Food & Wine Limited

Asciamprener, Andrea Bruno
Fourteen Drops Ltd

Ascroft, Samuel James William
Taste Italia Limited

Ashbridge-Thomlinson, Claire
East London Brewing Co Ltd

Ashley, Nigel George
Marlborough International (UK) Ltd

Ashley, Timothy Paul
Wisdom Whisky & Wine (Scotland) Ltd

Ashraf, Sajjad
Saj Holdings Ltd

Ashton, Grant William Sandiford
PMWine Trade Limited
St James's Fine Wine Limited

Ashton, Stephen Robert
Middleton Associates Limited

Ashworth, Elizabeth Jennifer
Young in Spirit Ltd

Ashworth, Mark
World of Drams Ltd

Ashworth, Thomas Rowland
Yapp Brothers Limited

Askew, William Paul
The Art of Wine Ltd

Aslam, Harris Shahzad
Greens Wholesale Ltd

Aslan, Sezai
The Wine House Warwick Limited

Aspinall, William
Staid London Limited

Assemian, N'dolykhan Franck Elvis Thierry
De Christ Wines Ltd

Assi, Nadim
Thomas Lowndes & Co. Limited

Athanasiadou, Sofia
VDK Import Export Limited

Atherton, Lisa
Lisaavo Ltd

Atherton, Paul
Chiltern Trading Ltd

Athey, Martin Vivian
Waud Wines Limited

Atkin, Jonathan
Noahs Estate Ltd

Atkings, John David
Ellismuir Limited
The Highland Scotch Whisky Co Ltd

Atkins, David John
Glamorgan Brewing Co Ltd

Atkins, Thomas Hector
The Diss Honest Brewing Co Ltd

Atkinson, Leon
Atkinson's Gin Ltd

Atkinson, Nigel John Bewley
Wadworth and Co Ltd

Atkinson-Clark, George Evelyn
Woburn Wine Co Ltd

Atkinson-Clark, Sarah Anne
Woburn Wine Co Ltd

Attias, Jehu
Colombier Vins Fins Limited

Attias, Micheline
Colombier Vins Fins Limited

Atwal, Sukhjinder Singh
The Whisky Trading Co Ltd

Aubry Sharratt, Margaux
Unfiltered Wines Limited

Aucutt, David
East West Ales Limited

Audo, Yves
Row & Co Ltd

Austin, Frances Marie
J. Chandler & Company, Limited

Austin, Leigh
Cremant Inc Ltd

Austin, Matt John
V & A Jobs UK Ltd

Austin, William
Union Brands Ltd

Avellaneda, Monica
Anglocolombian Ltd

Avellano, Mark
Highly Spirited Ltd
Jam Consultants Global Limited

Avery, Zak
Beer Paradise (York) Limited

Awin, Elliot James Michael
London Wine Shippers Limited

Awin, Michael Hugh
London Wine Shippers Limited

Aydin, Yemilhan
Anna Wine & Food Ltd

Aykroyd, James Alexander Frederic, Sir
Alexander Muir & Son Limited

Aylas Aliaga, Waldyr Wildo
Perscot Ltd

Ayling, Jacqui
Tom's Tap and Brewhouse Ltd

Ayling, Sean Edward
Tom's Tap and Brewhouse Ltd

Aylwin-Foster, Polly Belinda
Xeco Wines Limited

Azilomhen, Moses Oseyaede
Zinea Global Services Limited

Aziz, Qaiser
Global Foods Limited

Babiciu, Delia
Vino Unico Limited

Babiec, Joseph Raymond
Belfast Distillery Co Ltd

Bacha, Yogendranath
Green Island (UK) Limited

Bache, Justin
Little Horse Wines Limited

Bacon, Daniel Joseph
Loxwood Meadworks Ltd

Bacon, Richard Alan Kenneth
London Wine Shippers Limited

Badar, Waqas
United Wholesale Grocers Ltd

Badea, Florin
Florin Wholesaler Ltd

Badenoch, Patrick Robert
Vintage 1947 Limited

Baeza-Wigzell, Jack Luis Pablo
Bwinfusions Ltd

Bagchi, Abhishek
Glenreidh Liquor Co Ltd

Bagley, Douglas John
William Grant & Sons Brands Ltd

Bagley, Thomas
Momento Vivere Holdings Ltd

Bagnall, Brian
Hydes' Brewery Limited

Bagnall, Roland Henry
Gordano Wines Limited

Bagnall, Rupert
Wadworth and Co Ltd

Bagot, Robert William
Buon Vino Ltd
The Natural Wine Co Ltd

Bahra, Balvinder Singh
Balman Import & Export Limited

Baig, Nabeela
Tops Food and Wine Limited

Baijot, Philippe
Lanson International UK Ltd

Bailey, Christopher Edward
Clapham Wine Co Ltd

Bailey, Claire Rosalie
Occidental & Oriental Cellars Ltd
Vinum Fine Wines Limited

Bailey, James
Tipsy Tea Limited

Bailey, Jane
Woody Nook Wines (UK) Limited

Bailey, Jessica Lucy
Bad Joke Brew Co Ltd

Bailey, Karnis Kate
Tipsy Tea Limited

Bailey, Peter John
Woody Nook Wines (UK) Limited

Bailey, Thomas Matthew
Tipsy Tea Limited

Bain, Michael
Burnobennie Distillery Limited

Baines, John Charles
Today's Wholesale Services Ltd

Bains, Ranjeet
Appleton Estate Wines Ltd

Bajaj, Kamaljit Singh
Liquor World Venture Ltd

Bak, Mickel Johan Frederik
Bak Family Wines Limited

Bak, Moritz Walter
Pull The Cork Limited

Baker, Alexis Ross
Lusus Wines Ltd

Baker, Claire Louise
Lusus Wines Ltd

Baker, Edmund Anthony
Bottle Green Limited

Baker, Ellenor Joy
The Poshmakers Ltd

Baker, Matthew William James
At The Group Ltd

Baker, Michael Oliver
Peachy Glow Limited

Balasko, Szabolcs
Corvinus Beverages International Ltd

Balchin, Alexander David
Wold Toppers Limited

Balchin, Katherine Emma
Wold Toppers Limited

Baldwin, David John
Australian Wine Services Ltd
Passion Wine International Ltd

Baldwin, Paul
Castle Eden Beer Co Ltd

Balivada, Ashwin
3ABC Ltd
Glen Monarch Distillery Ltd
Jocks and Peers Brewing Co Ltd

Balivada, Mohan Krishna, Dr
Glen Monarch Distillery Ltd

Balkaya, Mahfuz
Truk Limited

Ball, Gareth
Sherwood Outlaws Brewing Co Ltd

Ball, John Richard
Southern England Wines (UK) Ltd

Ball, Phillip
Solitude Wines Limited

Ballance, Michael Peter
The Ballance Group Limited
Ital Sardo Limited

Ballantyne, Karina Lianne Jayne
Tipo Loco Drinks Co. Limited

Ballantyne, Michael Alexander
Tipo Loco Drinks Co. Limited

Ballard, Thomas Edward
Anglocolombian Ltd

Ballard, Timothy Edward
Anglocolombian Ltd

Balloch, Walter Geoge
Jub Club Top Bar Ltd

Balogh, Csaba
ACK Trading Ltd

Bambani, Kalin
Evergreen Foods Limited

Bangert, Sara Elizabeth
General Wine and Liquor Co Ltd

Banham, Anthony
Webdrinks Ltd

Banham, Mark Stephen
Morrish & Banham Ltd

Banjo, Babatunde
Taabs Investment UK Limited

Bankole, Adenrele
Flava Foods Ltd

Banks, Andrew William
Banks & Company (Vintners) Ltd.

Banks, Richard John
Richard Banks & Co Ltd

Bannino, Celine
Kal Wine Source UK Ltd

Banton, Ryan
Punchline Ltd

Banus, Borja
Casa Cocktails Limited

Barac, Miro
Natural Marketing Ltd

Barbier, Georges Fernand
Georges Barbier of London Ltd

Barbier, Mary Lynn
Georges Barbier of London Ltd

Barbulata, Jekaterina
Champagne House Ltd

Barclay, Colin Shields
J. & G. Barclay and Co Ltd
J.G. Distillers Limited

Barclay, David Ellis
J. & G. Barclay and Co Ltd

Barclay, Fiona Adair
J. & G. Barclay and Co Ltd

Barclay, Fraser
Loughborough Student Services Ltd

Barclay, Michael Shields
J. & G. Barclay and Co Ltd

Barczynski, Tomasz
Rafti Ltd.

Barette, Martin John
The Society of Vintners Ltd

Bargeton, Gregory Justin
William Grant & Sons Brands Ltd

Bari, Hawa
ERE Igga Ltd

Barics, Steven John Anthony
Barokes Limited

UK Wholesalers of Beers, Wines and Spirits dellam

Barker, James Michael
Premium Beverage Refreshments Ltd

Barker, Neil Peter
William Grant & Sons UK Ltd

Barlow, Paul Jonathan
Loughborough Student Services Ltd

Barnard, Teresa
Champagne Warehouse Ltd

Barnes, George Harold Abbott
Shepherd Neame Limited

Barnes, Gerard Hugh
St.Austell Brewery Co Ltd

Barnes, Jane
Mothership Beer Ltd

Barnes, John Henry
Simply 1st Wine Co Ltd

Barnes, Paul
Waverley Drinks Limited

Barnes, Roger Paul
Spirits International Management Ltd

Barnett, Rachel Jane
Corktalk Limited

Barnett, Simon Campbell
Rawson Trading (Doncaster) Ltd

Barodawalla, Zainab Juzer
Basket Press Wines Ltd

Baroutsis, Aristotelis
Edrington European Travel Retail Ltd
Edrington-Beam Suntory UK Distribution
Highland Distillers Limited

Barozzi, Franco James
Giovanni Food & Wine Limited

Barrett, Damian Paul
Cellar Twelve Limited

Barrie, Lee
Aussie Rules Ltd

Barrie, Michelle Lisa
Aussie Rules Ltd

Barron, Emma
Seb and Emma Ltd

Barsottini, Andrea
Hoops and Champagne Ltd

Bartelli, Alessandro
Whisky Work Play Ltd

Bartholdi, Clare Miquette
David Berryman Holdings Ltd

Bartholomew, Charles John Eric
Wadworth & Company (Burford) Ltd
Wadworth and Co Ltd

Bartholomew, Edward
E J Bartholomew Limited

Bartholomew, Jack
E J Bartholomew Limited

Bartley, Daniel
Cross Brew Ltd

Barton, Christian Peter
Chilli Brands (New Zealand) Ltd
Chilli Brands Limited
Chilli Marketing Brand Management Ltd

Barton, David Reginald
Harvey's Wholesale Limited

Barton, John Thomas
T. & J.T. Barton (Bottlers) Ltd

Barton, Kieron
Chilli Brands (New Zealand) Ltd

Barton, Kieron Mark
Chilli Brands Limited
Chilli Marketing Brand Management Ltd
Chilli Marketing Promotions Ltd

Bartosova, Barbora
Vinovitaj Ltd

Bascau, Nicu Bogdan
Stockwell Beverages Ltd

Bashforth, Edward Michael
Innspired Taverns Limited

Bashutskyy, Oleh
Novarto Drinks Ltd

Basi, Navdeep
Native Oracle Limited

Bassi, Amit Singh
Grape Merchants Ltd

Bassi, Jaspal
Teqbev Ltd

Bassi, Parminder Singh
PSB Trading Limited

Bassi, Sukhjinder Singh
Finedon Convenience Store Ltd

Bassra, Paramdeep Singh
Bassrap Ltd

Batavia, Rajesh
Always Available Ltd

Bates, Colin Ripley
Real Ales AT Limited

Bates, Nina Diane
Flying Firkin Distribution Ltd

Bates, Richard Alexander
Cornucopia Wines Limited

Bathia, Amal
Kegs R Us Ltd

Bathia, Paresh Govindji
Kegs R Us (Leicester) Ltd
Kegs R Us Ltd

Batistatou, Evridiki
Infotonomy Ltd

Batliwala, Peri
Oeno Limited

Battistel, Nello
Eurowines Limited

Batty, David William
Battys Discount Drinks Store Ltd

Batty, Michelle
Battys Discount Drinks Store Ltd

Baum, John Haddon
The Winemakers Club 2000 Ltd

Baum, Robin Frederick
RBW Fine Wines Limited
The Winemakers Club 2000 Ltd

Bawa, Manpreet
Teqbev Ltd

Bawden, Peter Timothy
Samphire Drinks Ltd

Bawi, Amir Eisa
Glenroy Spirits Limited

Baxendale, Marcus James
Hindsight Collective Ltd

Baxendale, Paul
Flagship Brands Ltd

Bay, Clive
Grace Tilly Limited

Bayer, Sebastian Ludwig
Winecraft Ltd

Baykara, Deniz Metehan
Bournemouth Food Ltd

Bayley, Timothy James
Noetic Wine Limited

Bayram, Mesut
Knights Catering Impex Ltd

Bazan Martinez, Jon
Evok3 Ltd

Beach, Bryn
Elixir Wine Ltd

Beach, Danielle
Elixir Wine Ltd

Beach, Gary
Elixir Wine Ltd

Beagley, Gary Robert
Libra Drinks Wholesale Limited

Beagrie, Nicholas James
Inn Control Management Services Ltd

Beaman, Annabelle
Bridgnorth Brewing Co Ltd

Beamish, Michael Frank
The Three Stills Co Ltd

Bear, Jonathan
New World Trading Europe Ltd.

Bearcroft, Michael
Land's End Gin Limited

Beard, John Edward
Wadworth and Co Ltd

Beardon, Christopher John
Winkleigh Cider Co Ltd

Beardon, Kylie Jane
Winkleigh Cider Co Ltd

Beashel, Caroline Natasha
Paisajes Trading Ltd

Beattie, Colin MacLean
Bekel Limited

Beattie, Thomas Ian James
Beattie & Roberts Imports Ltd

Beaumont, Generald Xavier Jose Generald
AOC Distribution Ltd

Beaumont, Sarah-Jane
AOC Distribution Ltd

Beaumont, Sophie
Beaumont Beverages Ltd.

Beavis, Paul Edward
Lanson International UK Ltd

Beck, Paul
Midhurst Wine Shippers Limited

Beckett, Victoria Ruth
Alexander Wines Ltd.

Beckford-Miller, Laurenzay
Firewater Merchants Ltd

Bedawi, Jill
Ginkhana Limited

Bedesha, Gurmit Singh
Beer Barrels & Minerals (Wales) Ltd
Cold Black Label Limited
Wellsh Brewers Cardiff Ltd

Bedesha, Rachel
Cold Black Label Limited

Bedford, David Charles John
Gunners Cocktails Limited

Bedford, Paul Nicholas
T.M.B Wine Trading Ltd

Bedini, Marco Carlo
Fine & Rare Wines Limited

Bee, Gareth Richard
Pomona Island Brew Co Ltd

Beedell, Lloyd
Chesters Wine Merchants Ltd

Bees, Matthew Jason
Buckingham Fine Wine Ltd

Beeslaar, Gabriel Jacobus
Dragon Wines Limited

Beeson, William
Headline Wines Ltd

Beeston, Joanna Elizabeth
Hayward Bros (Wines) Limited

Beetham, Angela Mary
Grassington Spirit Co Ltd

Beever, Graham William
GWB Associates Limited

Beevers, Matthew
Maison du Vin Ltd

Bekker, Danielle
Good Living Brew Co Limited

Belcher, Paul
DSC Imports Limited

Belizaire, Aidan Ross
Belizaire Drinks Ltd

Bell, Nicholas James
Majestic Wine Warehouses Ltd

Bell, Peter
C.O.D. Beers Limited

Bell, Thomas Neale
Skinny Booze Limited

Bella, Jessica
Vitena Wines Ltd

Bella, Marco
Laurito Ltd

Belli, Louisa Kate Arabella
Davenport Vineyards Limited

Bello, Gbola Daud
Gabby & Bello Enterprises Ltd

Bellwood, Graham
Now This Is It Ltd

Belsole, Andrea
Sol Regem Ltd.

Belt, Lyndon Bernard
Templeton Beer Wine & Spirit Co Ltd

Benat, Geoffray
Be My Wine Ltd.

Benato, Stefano
Astrum Wine Cellars Limited

Beneforti, Antonio
Strongwells Limited

Benenson, Uri
Barcode Traders Limited

Benham, Rory Peter Cochrane
The Wine Treasury Limited

Benito, Felix
C & D Wines Limited

Benito, Jennifer Christine
C & D Wines Limited

Benito-Barnett, David Charles
C & D Wines Limited

Benjamin, Paul Andrew
Benjamin & Blum Limited

Benjamin, Richard Marc
Manchester Drinks Co Ltd

Benlamkadem, Meriem
Medusa Wines Ltd

Benner, Michael Peter
Flying Firkin Distribution Ltd

Bennett, Graham Charles
Gleneagles Distillery Limited

Bennett, Rodane Anthony
Bottles on Demand Limited

Bennett, Victoria Margaret Anne
Piaff Trading UK Limited

Benson, Nicholas John
Source 360 Ltd

Bentley, Dene
Fcuk Ltd

Bentley, James
Stour Valley Events Limited

Beran, Julia Helena
The Vintner London Ltd

Berardi, Gianluca
Superba London Wines Ltd

Berecic-Hall, Mirjana
Aizia Ltd

Berg, Carl Eric
Cider of Sweden Ltd

Berkmann, Ewa Smolinska
Berkmann Family Holdings Ltd

Berkmann, Joseph
Berkmann Family Holdings Ltd
Berkmann Wine Cellars Limited

Berkmann, Rupert Anthony
Berkmann Family Holdings Ltd
Berkmann Wine Cellars Limited
Churchill Vintners Limited
T.M. Robertson & Son Limited
Spirit Cartel Limited

Berliand, David Michael
London Wine Agencies Limited

Bermudez de La Puente Sanchez-Aguilera, Del Pino, Madame
Thomas Lowndes & Co. Limited

Bernard, Fabrice
Millesima Limited

Bernard, Jean
Millesima Limited

Bernardello, Giulio
I'll Ask The Boys Ltd

Bernasconi, Carlo
Chacalli-De Decker Ltd.

Bernie, Patrick Bernard
Redevined Wines Limited

Bernotavicius, Evaldas
Monolith (UK) Ltd

Bernstein, Olivier
Burgundys Collection Limited

Berry, Colin George
The Saucy Drinks Co Ltd

Berry, Elizabeth Jane Rosemary
La Vigneronne Fine Wines Ltd

Berry, Fernando
Otros Vinos Limited

Berry, Michael William
La Vigneronne Fine Wines Ltd

Berry, Richard
Burton Rd Brewing Co Limited

Berry, Samuel Rupert
The Good Life Gin Co Ltd

Berryman, David Alec
David Berryman Holdings Ltd
David Berryman Limited

Berryman, Tom David
David Berryman Holdings Ltd

Bertellotti, Carla Antonella
Vinos Latinos Ltd

Bertheleme, Sylvain Roger
Les Vins de Sylvain Ltd

Bertone, Gabriele
Ultravino Limited

Bertoni, Fabrizio
Goodeataly Ltd

Besa, Bruno
Astrum Wine Cellars Limited

Besenyi, Janos Peter
Second Eger Ltd

Best, William Trevorian Stuart
Bloody Drinks Limited

Bestel, Frederic Joseph Nicholas
Litchquor UK Ltd

Bethell, Nicholas Alexander
Snobby's Ltd

Betts, Matthew James
Premia Brands Trading Limited

Bevan, Georgie
Nexus Wine Trading Ltd

Bewes, Andrew Nicholas
Hallgarten Wines,Limited

Beydon, Alain
Maisons Marques et Domaines Ltd

Bhandal, Hardeep Singh
Indra Beverages Limited

Bhandari, Kalpit
Golden Everest Limited

Bhandari, Paritosh
Tipple Brands Ltd

Bharania, Bharat Mohanlal
Inter Trading Leicester Ltd

Bharania, Dilip
Inter Trading Leicester Ltd

Bharj, Malkit Singh
AI Liver Management Limited

Bharwani, Joanne
Horizons Enterprise Ltd
RDV Spirits Ltd

Bhatia, Deepak
Signature Wines Ltd

Bhatoa, Kultar Singh
Six Rivers Limited

Bhattachan, Bhim
New Claire Wine Ltd

Bhattacharjee, Sarvajit
Westend Cash and Carry Ltd

Bhatti, Amardip Singh
Blue Momentum Limited

Bhebhe, Lovemore
BLSN Limited

Bholah, Deepraj
3R'SB Limited

Bianchi, Mattia
Dirt. Ltd

Bickley, Brian
Henderik & Co Limited

Biddiss, Gary Alan
Goldcrest Drinks Limited

Bienvenu, Philippe Eric Jean Claude
Cattier UK Limited

Biernikowicz, Anna Maria
A-Holding Ltd

Bihal, Jasmohinder
MSB Wholesale Services Limited

Bihal, Priya
Empire Drinks Ltd
PT Drinks Ltd

Bihal, Shamir
Landmark Wholesale Limited

Bihal, Tia
PT Drinks Ltd

Bijlani, Alpesh
Wisca Beverages Limited

Bilev, Kostadin Vasilev
Russian Investment II Limited

Bilimoria, Karan Faridoon, Lord
Cobra Beer Partnership Limited
General Bilimoria Wines Ltd

Bilimoria, Lady Lynne Heather
Faridoon Wines Ltd

Bilimoria, Lord Karan
Faridoon Wines Ltd

Billett, Richard Edward
Maisons Marques et Domaines Ltd

Billingsley, Peter John
North West Spirits Limited

Billington, Julien Robert
Prosecco 1754 Limited

Bilsland, Ross Tomas
Bacardi-Martini Limited

Binder, Ylva
Rhuby Limited

Binning, Amrik Singh
Barrel Booze Limited
Cellarvino Limited

Binning, Nirmal Jeet Singh
Binning Trading Co Ltd

Birch Throckmorton, Imogen Clare
Nothing But The Grape Limited

Birch, Barry Desmond
Durrants Fine Wines Limited

Birch, Karen Fiona
Nothing But The Grape Limited

Birch, Magnus Courtenay
Nothing But The Grape Limited

Birch, Matthew St John
Durrants Fine Wines Limited

Birch, Rupert Sylvester
Nothing But The Grape Limited

Birch, Timothy James
Durrants Fine Wines Limited

Bird, Ryan James
The Beverage Boutique Ltd

Bird, Sara Jean
The Beverage Boutique Ltd

Birk, Rajinder Singh
Drinks Factory Limited

Birkitt, Joanne Claire
The Nolo Drinks Co Ltd

Birrell, Rodney
The Wine Enterprise Investment Scheme

Birse-Stewart, William Joseph Bell
Wine Importers (Edinburgh) Ltd

Bisan-Etame Mayer, Dionisio
Guinexport Trade and Services Ltd

Biscaldi, Pietro
Ty Nant Spring Water Limited

Bishop, James Andrew
Speymalt Whisky Distributors Ltd

Bishop, Steven Garry
The Grape Variety Ltd

Bishop, Trevor James
Aurora Ales Limited

Bisset, Alexander Melville
Douglas Laing & Co Ltd.

Bittles, Ciaran
Bittles Irish Whiskey Co Ltd

Bittles, Fergal
Bittles Irish Whiskey Co Ltd

Bittles, John
Bittles Irish Whiskey Co Ltd

Bivol, Iurie
Ocavia Wine & Spirits Ltd

Bizlall, Ranjeeta
Xenon Wines & Spirits Limited

Bizot, Etienne
Mentzendorff & Co Ltd

Bizouard de Montille, Louis Bertrand Marie Henri
NYSA International Ltd

Bizouard de Montille, Ludovic Luc Marie Lazare
NYSA International Ltd

Black, Adam Richard
Lanchester Wine Cellars Ltd
The Wine Fusion Limited

Black, Raymond
Bigg Market Beer Co Ltd
Bigg Market Brewery Co Ltd

Blackburn, Andrew Stewart
Northern Hospitality (MCR) Ltd

Blackman, Ian Nicholas
N20winery Ltd

Blackman, Robert James
Franc Wine Ltd

Blackwood, David
Daves Drinks Ltd

Blackwood, Thomas Joseph
The Near Beer Brewing Co. Ltd

Blain, Mathew Nicholas Sonny
Pot Still Drinks Ltd.

Blake, Patrick Declan
Blakes Fine Wine Ltd

Blakemore, Peter Francis
Capper & Co Ltd

Blanco, Jose Rodriguez-Ameijeiras
The Poshmakers Ltd

Blandford-Newson, Christopher John
Distell International Holdings Ltd

Blaney, Judith
Molendinar Spirits Limited

Blattler, Daniel
Neatly London Limited

Blennerhassett, Jamie
Clos Vintners Limited

Blesson, Gregory Francis
Red Squirrel Brewery Limited

Blewitt, Mark
Dragon Drinks Limited

Blij, Antoon Cornelis Jan
Toorank UK Limited

Block, Timothy Michael
Hatton & Edwards Fine Wine Merchants

Bloom, Mark
Vektor Vodka UK Ltd

Blues, Alan
Greater London Beer Exports Ltd

Blumsom, Jack Alexander
Other World Wines Limited

Bocking, Colin John
Crouch Vale Brewery Limited

Bocking, Fiona Michelle
Crouch Vale Brewery Limited

Bodart, Michele
The Drinks Agency Ltd

Boeuf, Nathalie
World Brands Duty Free Limited

Bogaert, Gilles Pierre Francis
Pernod Ricard UK Limited

Bolitho, Oliver Robert Morgan
Goedhuis & Co Ltd

Bolt, Benjamin James
Blue Tree Limited

Bolton, James Stacey
Da Vinci Traders Ltd

Bolton, Philip
PNJ Bolton International Ltd

Bonadies, Lucia
Dago Wines Ltd

Bond, Stuart Andrew
Slurp Wine Co Ltd

Bondar, Kathleen Julia
Personalised Care Solutions Ltd

Bonner, James Eugene
Mundus Wines Limited

Bonner, Matthew William
The Portuguese Fine Wine Co Ltd

Bonnie, Chris
Bonvoy Limited

Boobbyer, David Martin
Reid Wines (1992) Limited

Boogert, Alastair Stewart
Regent Wines Limited

Booker, Andrew Mark
Lytham Brewery Limited

Booker, James Anthony
Lytham Brewery Limited

Booker, Julie Louise
Lytham Brewery Limited

Bookman, Jordan Ashley
Russian Doll Vodka Limited

Boom, Gary James
BI Wines and Spirits Limited
Barrique Vintners Limited
Andrew Bruce Fine Wines Ltd
Watermark Fine Wine Limited

Boote, Richard Edward Michael
New Generation Wines Limited

Booth, Andrew Michael
Grassington Spirit Co Ltd

Booth, James Arthur
New Generation Wines Limited
Spirit Generation Limited

Booth, Phillip John
Panache Natural Flavour Infusions

Boothe, Amari
Punchline Ltd

Booty, William Howard
Reid Wines (1992) Limited

Borer, Peter Henry
Vitesse Vintners Limited

Borin, Alberto
Lafferty & Sons Ltd

Borley, Christopher
North East Hold Limited

Bosisio, Marco Alessandro
Heronsgate 7 Limited

Bosman, Jan Christoffel
BFV International Limited

Bosman, Petrus Wilhelmus Jacobus
BFV International Limited
Bosman Wines UK Ltd

Botros, John Michael
Global Wine Distributors Ltd
Witney Wine Limited

Bott, Tom
Signature Brew Ltd

Bottomley, Andrew Peter
Fine & Rare Wines Limited

Bottomley, Elizabeth Mary
Titanic Wines Limited

Bou Antoun, Michael Hani
Astir Cigars & Wine Ltd

Bou Antoun, Nauf
Astir Cigars & Wine Ltd

Bouglet, Emma Louise
Fidra Fine Spirits Limited

Boulger, Graham David
Battlefield Brewery Limited

Boulger, Susan Sharon
Battlefield Brewery Limited

Bourjac, Alexandra
Wine & Spirits Club SA Ltd

Boursot, Guy Ralph Philip
Wine Consultants Limited

Bouteiller, Christian
Alliance Wine Co Ltd

Boutflower, Robert Charles
Tanners Wines Limited

Bowcock, David
Russbrit Ltd

Bowden, Julia Priscilla
Cameron Cavendish Fine Wines Ltd

Bowden, Julian Cameron
Cameron Cavendish Fine Wines Ltd

Bowden, Matthew David
M & P Diffusion Limited

Bowe, Anne
Fair Fayre Food & Wines Ltd

Bowe, Paul
Fair Fayre Food & Wines Ltd

Bowen, Christopher Peter
Babco UK Ltd.
Main Sail Trading Co Ltd

Bowen, Christopher Stephen
Southbrew Co Ltd

Bowen, Derek Clive
The Ironbridge Gorge Gin Co Ltd

Bowen-Thomas, Berin Chesney
The Near Beer Brewing Co. Ltd

Bower, Hugh Francis
Ghost Drinks Ltd

Bowers, Daniel
Punchy Drinks Limited

Bowers, Kevin James
Marta Vine Limited

Bowers, Trevor
Hills Prospect Holdings Ltd
Hills Prospect PLC

Bowker, Paul Henry
Wilkinson Vintners Limited

Bowler, Emily Louise
Classic Cask Limited

Bowles, Jack Frederick
Profile Wines Limited

Bowman-Hood, Lisa June
Frederick's Wine Co Ltd
Openwine Limited

Bowman-Hood, Stuart Gregory
Frederick's Wine Co Ltd
Openwine Limited

Bowyer, Peter
The Cognac Growers' Collective Ltd
Marlborough International (UK) Ltd

Boxall, Joseph Liam
Whisky Work Play Ltd

Boyd, Jonathan Robert
Made To Measure Ltd

Boyer, Paul Henri
Viniguide Limited

Boyes, Nathan
Padlock Brewery Ltd.

Brace, Stephen Anthony
Sunderland Gin Limited

Bracher, Maxwell Charles
Templar Wines Ltd

Bradbeer, Nicola Elizabeth
For The Love of Wine Limited

Bradbury, John Andrew
The Cornish Rum Co Ltd

Bradbury, Tod Luke
Prestige Whisky Worldwide Ltd

Bradford, James
Bigg Market Beer Co Ltd
Bigg Market Brewery Co Ltd

Bradley, Christopher Joseph Ross
Spirit of Glasgow Ltd

Bradshaw, Eleanor Annette
Drinkologie Limited

Bradshaw, Thomas Edward
Abercrombie Fine Wines Limited

Brady, Arlo
Hurricane Rum Co Ltd

Brady, Elaine
The Perth Distillery Co Ltd

Braham-Everett, Jonathan Joseph
J.Braham Everett Imports Ltd

Braham-Everett, Lorraine Mandy
J.Braham Everett Imports Ltd

Braileanu, Aliona
Novus BH Magister Ltd

Brain, Charles Nicholas
S.A.Brain & Co Ltd

Braithwaite, Mark
Momentum Wines Limited

Brambilla, Ettore
Tec-Sol Limited

Bramwell, Joel Anthony Southby
Dragon Wines Limited

Brannigan, Laurence Stephen
My Gin My Way Ltd

Bratten, Andrew Douglas
Agave Union Limited
Indie Brands Ltd.
Indie Spirits Limited
Neat Drinks Limited

Brauer, Matthew Campbell
Beeble Liquor Limited

Bravo, Giuseppe Franco
G. Bravo & Son Limited

Brazza, Michele
D D S Food Imports Ltd

Brearley, John Richard
Northern Hospitality (MCR) Ltd

Bremner, David John
Leinburn Limited

Bremner, Stephen McKerron
Moonshine Traders Ltd

Brennan, Liam Aaron
Trinity Drinks Limited

Breslin, Graeme
Corkers Wine Limited

Bret, Harald Eric
The Bath Gin Co Ltd

Brett, Daphne
Asta Barista Baby Ltd

Brett, William John
Shepherd Neame Limited

Brett-Smith, Adam de La Falaise Brett
Corney and Barrow Group Ltd
Corney and Barrow Limited

Breunig, Timo Alexander
The German Beer Co Limited

Brewer, Gary William
William Grant & Sons Brands Ltd

Brewis, Christopher
Brewis Beer Co Ltd

Brewis, Maxine
Brewis Beer Co Ltd

Bridge, Adrian William Michael
Mentzendorff & Co Ltd

Bridge, Andrew Daniel
Abyss Brewing Ltd

Bridge, Jonathan
S.A.Brain & Co Ltd

Bridge, Laura
Roydon Flavours Ltd

Bridge-Collyns, David John
Drinkscraft Limited

Bridgeman, Stephen Dennis
Alivini (North) Limited
Alivini Co Ltd
Franciacorta Limited

Bridgman, David Austin
Winkleigh Cider Co Ltd

Brierley, Clifford
Deckers Restaurants Limited

Brierly, Maxwell James
Deckers Restaurants Limited

Briers Louw, Christoffel Jacobus
Saam Wine Co Ltd

Briggs, Daniel Patrick
Billings & Briggs Ltd

Briggs, Darren Charles
Ascona Retail (Leases) Limited

Briggs, Martin
Loopland Brewing Co Ltd

Briggs, Sarah Penelope
Made To Measure Ltd

Brigham, Emma Louise
Walnut Tree Distillery Ltd

Brind, David Leonard
Churnet Valley Drinks Limited
H.B.Clark & Co.(Successors) Ltd
Kitwave Limited
M.& M.Value Limited
Thorne Licence Wholesale Ltd

Briot, Jean-Baptiste
Dillon Bass Limited

Brisset, Hugues
Epicure Wines Ltd

Broad, Simon Andrew
Terra Toda Ltd.

Brobson, Lee Aaron
The Traditional Italian Wine Co Ltd

Brocklehurst, Caroline Cordelia Ridley
Sixpenny Wines Limited

Brockwell, Simon
Art Beer Co Ltd

Brodie, Zoe
Honkytonk Wine Library Limited

Brogan, David Andrew
Colorado Craft Spirits Ltd

Brogan, Liam
Ireland Craft Beers Ltd

Brogan, Stephen Michael
Drinks21 Ltd
Ooberstock Limited

Brogden, Darren Joseph
Vincisive Wines Limited

Brokemper, Andreas, Dr
Freixenet Copestick Limited

Bromley, Daniel
Brew Boxes Ltd

Bronsman, Peter
Cider of Sweden Ltd

Brook, Giles Thomas Turner
All Market Europe Limited

Brook, Michael Jonathan
Triple Point Brewing Ltd

Brooke, Joan
Greenfield Bacon Limited

Brookes, Catherine Lucy
Vine Trail Limited

Brookes, James Nicholas William
Vine Trail Limited

Brookes, Philip James
Barcalima Wines Limited

Brooks, Andrew Crawford
The Gower Gin Co Ltd

Brooks, Deborah
Vinandar Wines Limited

Brooks, Sam
Brooks & Whitaker Limited

Brooks, Sian Margaret
The Gower Gin Co Ltd

Brooksbank, Jack
Jack Brooksbank Limited

Brosseau, Barthelemy Timothee Lawrence Edvard
Greenwood Distillers Limited
Greenwood Spirits Limited

Brotherton, Helen Christine
Fine Wine Works Limited

Broussard, Kent
The Last Drop Distillers Ltd

Browett, Ben David Hulton
Browett & Fair Ltd

Browett, Stephen John
Farr Vintners Limited

Brown, Andrew Percival
Ratcliffe & Brown Wines and Spirits

Brown, Antony Malcolm
Boutinot Limited

Brown, Brian Michael
Dillon Bass Limited

Brown, Camilla
Young in Spirit Ltd

Brown, Charlotte Emma
Vino Vero Ltd

Brown, Colin William
Belvoir Brewery Limited

Brown, David Stewart
Global Beer Co Ltd

Brown, Derek Charles
Michel Roux Limited

Brown, Donald Stuart
Largesse Corporate Gifts (2007) Ltd

Brown, Elizabeth Jane
Calduero Wine Importers Ltd

Brown, Jacqui
KB Agencies Ltd

Brown, James Francis McKenzie
Source 360 Ltd

Brown, James Ronald
Beer52 Limited

Brown, Kenneth
KB Agencies Ltd

Brown, Lee
B & P Beverages Ltd

Brown, Matthew Alexander Richard
Calduero Wine Importers Ltd

Brown, Megan Elizabeth
Eastlin Alba Limited

Brown, Melanie
The Australian Cellar Ltd

Brown, Melanie Paula
Specialist Cellars Ltd

Brown, Michael Christopher
Chateau Miao Ltd

Brown, Nigel Wooldridge
Thorman Hunt & Co Limited

Brown, Peter Maclin
Forest Road Brewing Co Ltd

Brown, Peter Richard
Calduero Wine Importers Ltd

Brown, Richard
The Way Outback Brewery Ltd

Brown, Sam Dixon
Vino Vero Ltd

Brown, Stephen
Hopper House Brew Farm Ltd

Brown, Stephen Frederick
VDS UK Limited

Brown, Stephen Joseph
Drinks Inc. Ltd

Brown, Susan
Calduero Wine Importers Ltd

Browne, Kiera
Seafire Brewing Co. Ltd

Browne, Martyn Victor
The Drinks Guild Ltd

Browne, Nicholas Ainger
J & W Nicholson & Co Ltd

Brownstein, Marc
Brockmans Gin Limited

Bruce, Craig
Rosemount Pub Co. Limited

Brudenell-Bruce, Andrew Robert Joel
BI Wines and Spirits Limited

Brugues, Elise
Special Cases Limited

Brumana, Giovanni
Orsa Major Ltd

Bruneau, Aymeric Valere Raymond
Groupe Prestige Ltd

Brunt, Joanna Mary
Le Petit Wine Cellar Ltd

Brunt, Nina Maria Emily
Broadoak Cider Co Ltd

Brunt, Peter William
Le Petit Wine Cellar Ltd

Brunt, Steven Lee
Broadoak Cider Co Ltd

Bruschetta, Federico
Pandemonio Limited

Bryan, John
Bellwether Wines Ltd

Bryant, Felix Kelvin
Adonko Bitters (UK) Ltd

Bryden, Alfred Lockhart
The Highland Malt Whisky Co Ltd

Brydie, Alison Joanne
Fidra Fine Spirits Limited

Bu, Haibao
Asia-Pacific 11230699 Vitamin Beverage Co.,

Buchanan, Martin Thomas
Buchanan Wines Ltd.

Buchanan, Martin Thomas
Ourglass & Partners Ltd

Buchanan, Peter Henry McKinnon
Buchanan Wines Ltd.

Buckland, Daniel
Drum and Black Rum Co Ltd

Buckland, William Thomas George
T.M.B Wine Trading Ltd

Buckley, Jane Elizabeth
Noble Green Wines Limited

Buckley, Peter Ralph
Noble Green Wines Limited

Buckley, Stephen David
Expressmode Limited

Bucknall, William
Kicking Horse Ltd.

Buckwell, Alan Arthur
Rimpex-UK Limited

Budibent, Giles Willson
Barton, Brownsdon & Sadler Ltd

Budibent, John Barry
Barton, Brownsdon & Sadler Ltd

Budibent, Nicholas John
Barton, Brownsdon & Sadler Ltd

Buer, Kamil
Preston Wines Ltd

Bulimwengu, Anthony
Nephtis Limited

Bull, Mary Christine
Baton Rouge Limited

Bull, Ross Douglas
Baton Rouge Limited

Buller, Alexander
Anthony James Beverages Ltd

Bulloch, Alexander
ABA Eaglesham Ltd
GSWD Catrine Ltd
William Morton Limited
Portavadie Distillery Limited

Bulloch, Carol Anne
GCBW Catrine Ltd
If Eaglesham Ltd

Bungay, Dean Apollo
Duchy Beverages Ltd

Bunting, Nigel James
Davy & Co Ltd
Shepherd Neame Limited

Burckhard, Patrick, Dr
Bacchus-Les-Vignobles de France Ltd

Burden, Archibald Robert
Doctor Bird Rum Ltd

Burdett, Carl Stuart
Burdett Wines Ltd

Burdett, Lorraine
Burdett Wines Ltd

Burdon, Andrew
The Indian Runner Drinks Co Ltd

Burghard, Lucy
Perscot Ltd

Burke, John Michael
The Bombay Spirits Co Ltd

Burkowski, Arkadiusz
Logistic Park Ltd

Burkowski, Dariusz Waldemar
Logistic Park Ltd

Burn, Jon
Stableyard Wines Limited

Burnett, Steven
Corkhaus Ltd

Burnham, Paul Simon
PSR Distribution Limited

Burns, Judith Elaines
Pacta Connect UK Limited

Burns, Michael
Wickersley Fine Wines Ltd

Burns, Samuel James
Pago Wines Limited

Burr, Christopher
Csburrwine Ltd

Burridge, Edward Nicholas
Oliver Burridge & Co Ltd
Burridges of Arlington St Ltd

Burridge, Laura Jane
Wine Affairs Limited

Burridge, Teresa Maria
Oliver Burridge & Co Ltd
Burridges of Arlington St Ltd

Burrow, Benjamin Robert
Signature Wine Gifts Ltd

Burrows, Andrew William
Broad Street Brands Limited

Burrows, Barry
Terrae Vinariae Limited

Burrows, Darius
Trilogy Beverage Brands Ltd

Burrows, Kerry James
Hitchin Distillery Limited

Burrows, Michael James
Terrae Vinariae Limited

Burston, Nicola Jane
Thru The Glass Limited

Burt, Callum Donaldson
Moonshine Traders Ltd

Burt, Charles Jack Jeffrey
Bankside Brewing Limited

Burton, Darren
Wickersley Fine Wines Ltd

Burton, Stephen Charles
Green Room Ales Limited

Bussey, Edmund
River Widow Brewery Ltd

Bussi, Michele
Diwine Piemonte Limited

Butcher III, George William
Port City Brewing UK Limited

Butler, Anne Barbara
Winepro Limited

Butler, Craig
The Baijiu Beer Co Ltd
Baijiu Evolution Ltd
The Spirit Beer Co Ltd

Butler, Katie
Black Dog Wine Agency Limited

Butler, Richard John Ellery
UWD Limited

Butler, Robert John Pond
Winepro Limited

Butterwick, Antony Guy
Claret-E Limited

Butterworth, Richard
Craftmaster Social Ltd

Butucel, Igor
Lux Ex Dignitas Limited

Buxton, Joseph
Three Shires Distillery Ltd

Buxton, Richard
Cheshire Gin Co Ltd

Buxton, Richard Anthony
Three Shires Distillery Ltd

Buxton, Shelly Frances
Three Shires Distillery Ltd

Buxton, Sophie
Three Shires Distillery Ltd

Bvuure-Gaynor, Sheila
Sheila's Rum Punch Ltd

Byrne, Anthony Edward
Anthony Byrne Fine Wines Ltd

Byrne, John
Hofmeister Enterprises Ltd

Byrne, Rae
Anthony Byrne Fine Wines Ltd

Byrne, Thomas
The Totally Awesome Wine Co Ltd

Bytyqi, Zenel
M & B Distributions (UK) Ltd

Cacicovschi, Vitalie
VIP Services Scotland Ltd

Cadestin, Etienne Jose
Cadestin International Wines Ltd

Cadwell, Alison Jane
Beacon Wines Limited

Cadzow, Thomas Richard
Momento Vivere Holdings Ltd

Cahill, Daniel James
Divergent Drinks Ltd

Caillol, Alexandre Claude Lucien
Groupe Prestige Ltd

Cain, Edward Richard, Reverend
Associated Church Clubs Ltd

Caine, Peter Edward
Celtic Wines Limited

Cairnie, Alexander Small
McNicoll and Cairnie Limited

Cairo, Aboh Roger Albert
Vitis-Terra Limited

Calabria, William
Calabria Family Wines (Europe) Ltd

Calder, Lisa Paige
Creative Juices Bar Limited

Caldicott, Fiona, Dame
Waters (1802) Limited

Caldicott, Robert Gordon Woodruff
Waters (1802) Limited

Cali, Matteo
Trebbiano Wines Ltd

Callaghan, Christopher Paul
India Gold Limited

Callaghan, Nicholas
Hills Prospect Holdings Ltd
Hills Prospect PLC

Calme-Magnan, Stephane
Provence Impex Limited

Calver, Jonathan Charles
Branded Drinks Ltd

Calvet, Benoit Patrice Marie Alain
Garmence Limited

Calvet, Charlotte Catherine Marie
Garmence Limited

Calvet, Valerie Sophie Marie
Garmence Limited

Camacho, Lauren May
Nice Brewing Co Ltd

Cameron, Ewen Irving
Digby Fine English Ltd
Digby Wine Ltd
Forth Wines Limited
The Great Wine Group Limited

Cameron, Jason
Ausavenues Limited

Camille, Janine
Camii Punch Ltd

Campana, Andrew
The Haycock's Drinks Co Ltd

Campana, James Joseph
Haycock's No.9 UK Ltd

Campari, Giovanni
Birrificio Del Ducato London Ltd

Campbell, Alan Robert
John E.Fells & Sons Limited

Campbell, Hugo Argyll
E I Wines Limited

Campbell, Iindeya Shabay
Desirable Drinks Ltd

Campbell, John Leitch
Campbell Inns Limited

Campbell, Jonathan Nathaniel
Joseph Keegan & Sons Limited

Campbell, Kieron Andre-Evans
Rum Runna Ltd

Campbell, Lilian Cunningham
William Cadenhead Limited
Springbank Distillers Limited

Campbell, Michael Robert Blake
Parasol Wines Ltd

Campbell, Peter Francis
Joseph Keegan & Sons Limited

Campling, Kerry Alicia
Time & Tide Brewing Limited

Camplisson, Catherine
Drinks Inc. Ltd

Camplisson, Paul Martin
Drinks Inc. Ltd
Original Liqueur Co Ltd
Uisce Ard Ltd

Campos Lopes, Guilherme
Crazy Brew UK Limited

Can, Mert
Dega Trading Ltd

Canard, Michel
Berkmann Wine Cellars Limited

Canbolat, Ali
Grape Drinks (UK) Limited

Cancea, Mark
Vine Street Wine Co Ltd

Cane, Angelo
Vinum Limited

Cann, James Edward
Library Design Studio Ltd.

Canon, Christopher
Booze 2 U Ltd

Canon, Elizabeth Anne
Axiom Brands Limited

Cant, Andrew John
Drinksbot Limited

Cant, Ekua
Drinksbot Limited

Caputo, Michael William
Cantina Caputo Limited

Caputo, Paul Michael
Cantina Caputo Limited

Caracoi, Alexandro
Gente Di Mare Ltd

Carboni, Margaret, Dr
Glam Drinks Ltd

Carden, Anna Patricia
Manchester Merchant Wines Ltd

Carden, Simon Dennis
Manchester Merchant Wines Ltd

Care, Ritchie Lee
Aztec Spirits Ltd

Carfagnini, Benjamin Robert
Friarwood Fine Wines Limited

Carfagnini, Jay Anthony
Friarwood Fine Wines Limited

Carlaw, Victoria
Kold Group Limited

Carlisle, Eric
Rutherglen Scotch Whisky Co Ltd

Carnevale, Carmine
Belloni Limited
C Carnevale Limited

Carnevale, Luigi
Carson & Carnevale Limited

Carnio, Daniel
Daniel Carnio Ltd

Carnio, Daniel Eros
Oenofuture Limited

Carpenito, Noemio Bruno
Italia Wine and Food Ltd

Carpinelli, Denise
TFC Wholesale Ltd

Carpinelli, Francesco
TFC Wholesale Ltd

Carpinelli, Trentino
TFC Wholesale Ltd

Carr, Michael
Trusty Services Ltd

Carr, Richard John
Premier Cru Fine Wine Ltd.

Carrasco, Emma
Toast Ale Ltd

Carreras Oliva, Monica Violeta
Andina Trade Ltd

Carroll, Charlotte Trudy
Clock Tower Distilleries Ltd

Carroll, Stephen James
Kanlaon Limited

Carson, Christopher
Carson & Carnevale Limited
Carson Wines Ltd

Carson, Jonathan
Carson & Carnevale Limited
Carson Wines Ltd

Carsons, Christopher Timothy
North West Spirits Limited

Carstoiu, Gabriel
LM Spirits Ltd

Carter, Allan
Carter Importing Ltd

Carter, Elizabeth Katherine
Plonq Wines Ltd

Carter, Ian James
Jascots Wine Merchants Limited

Carter, John Vernon
Englishman Supplies Limited

Carter, Phillip
Carter Importing Ltd

Carter, Tamoy
Impression Beverages Ltd

Carter, Teresa
Carter Importing Ltd

Carton, Timothy Ado
Borders Distillers Limited
Borders Distilling Limited
The Three Stills Co Ltd

Cartwright, David
Cartwright Brothers Vintners Ltd

Cartwright, David Antony
Seckford Agencies Limited

Cartwright, Linda Mary
Midhurst Wine Shippers Limited

Cartwright, Martin
Cartwright Brothers Vintners Ltd

Cartwright, Richard Charles
Cartwright Brothers Vintners Ltd

Carver, Michael Joseph
Lacons Brewery Limited

Casas Rodriguez, Santiago
Garumbas Ltd

Caseberry, Gillian
St.Austell Brewery Co Ltd

Casella, Giovanni Marcello
Casella Family Brands (Europe) Ltd

Cashmore Thorley, John James
RDF Paper Ltd

Cassels, Alasdair Lorne
Cassels and Sons Brewing Europe Ltd

Casserley, Lewis Paul
Vektor Vodka UK Ltd

Cassidy, Peter George
Cellar Supplies Cheltenham Ltd
Cellar Supplies Limited

Castello Escriva, Jose Javier
Cascriva Ltd

Castiglione, Lorraine
World Wide Wines Limited

Castiglione, Salvatore
World Wide Wines Limited

Castle, Erica Jane
Bouquet Limited

Castle, Peter Ronald
Bouquet Limited

Caswell, Andrew Michael
European Beer Exports Limited

Caswell, Dennis Geoffrey
Cambridge Champagne Co Ltd

Catchpole, Adam
Gather 77 Limited

Catherall, Paul Gareth
Healthier Products Limited

Cattier, Jean-Jacques Daniel
Cattier UK Limited

Cavanagh, Fiona Jane
Thameside Wines Limited

Cavanagh-Butler, Patrick Charles Arthur
Punchy Drinks Limited

Cayard, Jean Pierre
Glen Turner Co Ltd

Celadnik, Filip, Dr
Czech Beer Alliance Limited

Celegrat, Christopher
Healthy Wines Ltd

Cennerazzo, Gary
Bellissimo Vino Edinburgh Ltd

Cernecca, Bruno
B Wines Limited
The Wine Place Limited

Cersosimo, Antonio
Varmont Ltd

Cetinich, Franko
Franko's Food Ltd

Chacin-Lorenzo, Carlos Luis
Italimport (Wessex) Limited

Chadha, Arshdeep Singh
ASCO Foods Limited

Chadha, Ravneet Singh
ASCO Foods Limited

Chadha, Sundeep Singh
ASCO Foods Limited

Chahal, Devinder Singh
Winecorp Limited

Chahal, Ranjit Singh
Beviqua Ltd
Drayman Drinks Ltd

Chalaris, Georgios
Retaliate Limited

Chalmers, Helen
Highland Liquor Co Ltd

Chaloner, Remy
Freight Brewing Co. Ltd

Chalov, Dmitry Yurievich
The New Muscovy Co Ltd

Chamberlain, Mark
Vincisive Wines Limited

Chamberlain, Philip Anthony
County Catering (Midlands) Ltd

Chamberlain, Richard William David
The Craft Drink Co Ltd

Chamberlen, Caroline
JC Wine Events Ltd

Chamberlen, Julian Seymour
JC Wine Events Ltd

Chambers, Spencer
Hofmeister Enterprises Ltd

Chambers, Tracy
Cow West Yorkshire Limited

Chambi, Stavros
Vinemporium Limited

Chan, Christopher Lian Hock
Attitude Spirits Ltd

Chan, Chun Yip Andy
Master of Sake Ltd

Chand, Avtar
Cubed A Ltd

Chandaria, Jaysri Chix
Hix & Buck Ltd

Chang, Mingxiang
Al & Lu (UK) Ltd

Chang, Yung Sheng
Speyside Bonding Co Ltd
Speyside Distillers Co Ltd

Changela, Dinesh
Berkmann Wine Cellars Limited

Channa, Amrik Singh
Gold Max Distribution Limited

Chapelou, Xavier Rene
Isake International Limited

Chaplin, Jeremy McDowell
Edrington European Travel Retail Ltd
Edrington-Beam Suntory UK Distribution
Highland Distillers Limited
Row & Co Ltd

Chapman, Alison Clare
Union Drinks Ltd

Chapman, Andre Eugene
Wokka Spirits Limited

Chapman, Anthony Edward
Thames Distillers Limited

Chapman, Ian Michael
Speymalt Whisky Distributors Ltd

Chapman, Jonathan Mark
Union Drinks Ltd

Chapman, Mark Jonathan
E I Wines Limited

Chapman, Martin Robert
Peter Osborne Fine Wines Ltd

Chapman, Robert Alan
Wildflower Wines Limited

Chapoulaud-Floquet, Valerie Marie Anne, Madame
Remy Cointreau UK Distribution Ltd

Chappell, Marcus Simon George
Bristol Cider Co Ltd

Chaproniere, Karon Louise
Wokka Spirits Limited

Charalambous, Antony Ring Davis
London Barrelhouse Limited

Charalambous, Peter
London Barrelhouse Limited

Charles, Eldrun
Feewcha Services Ltd

Charles, Jonathan David Gwyther
The Dorset Wine Co Ltd

Charles, Melanie Jane Lister
The Dorset Wine Co Ltd

Charlton, Gareth Howard
Oracle Fine Wines Ltd.

Charnock, John Simon
Jascots Wine Merchants Limited

Chatel, Muriel Hughette
Expression du Terroir Limited

Chater, Max Roberto Derek
V Beverages Limited

Chatfield, Benjamin Paul
Vins Ltd

Chatha, Balbir Singh
Whittalls Wines Limited

Chaturvedi, Samir
Legacy Wines & Beverages UK Ltd

Chatwani, Vimal
IGW Brokers Limited

Chaudhary, Lekhika
Cubed A Ltd

Chaudhry, Sarah
Triumph Foodservice Limited

Chauhan, Arun Kumar, Dr
Anya Global Limited

Chauhan, Jateen Kumar
Beverage Boys Ltd

Chauhan, Sudesh
Urban Wholesalers Limited

Chauvin, Jean-Pierre
The French Sommelier with a Wee Dog Ltd

Chauvin, Yann
YC Wines Limited

Chawla, Ajit Singh
All Drinks Cash & Carry Ltd

Chawla, Babina Kaur
RC Brands Ltd

Chawla, Davinder Pal Singh
PS Drinks Ltd

Chawla, Poonam
PS Drinks Ltd

Chawla, Ramneek
PS Drinks Ltd

Chebotarev, Dmitry
The New Muscovy Co Ltd

Checkley, Simon John
Lost and Found Taprooms Ltd

Cheeseman, Richard Antony
Blue Thorn Gin Limited

Cheeseman, Richard Henry
Blue Thorn Gin Limited

Cheesman, Andrew John
Brighton Soft Drinks Limited

Cheesman, Janet
East West Ales Limited

Chen, Feng
T Warriors Brewery UK Limited

Chen, Yinghui
Whisky Point Limited

Chermont, David John
Monopole Wine Portfolio Management Ltd

Chester, John
Hops and Dots Brewing Co Ltd

Chetiyawardana, Ryan
Cheti & Co Holdings Limited
Cheti & Co Limited

Chiappi, Sarah Jane
Creative Juices Brewing Co Ltd

Chidgey, Craig Stewart
Rara Drinks Co Ltd

Chidiac, Pierre
Lebanese Fine Wines Limited

Chierchia, Giuseppe
Giuseppe's Wines Limited

Chierchia, Maria Anne
Giuseppe's Wines Limited

Child, Antonio
T & S Sales Limited

Chin, Ming-Chi
JW Corporation Ltd

Chirila-Filip, Octavian-Gabriel
Moa Group Ltd

Chirila-Filip, Vasilica-Andreea
Moa Group Ltd

Chitoraga, Nicolae
Be Organiq Limited

Chitsaz Esfahani, Houman
Vitam Dare Limited

Chokshi, Sachin Kanaiyalal
Mantra Trading Limited

Chopra, Aman
Skull X Ltd

Chopra, Dipansh
DC Wine Merchant Ltd

Chopra, Kuldip
Green Leaf Liquids Limited

Chorbov, Angel
United Wines Ltd

Chorlton, Alan Paul, Dr
Alchemist Brewery Limited

Choudhry, Safdar Ali
Huddersfield Cash and Carry Ltd

Chouhan, Rohan
The Vine and Malt Ltd

Chouhan, Sukhraj Singh
The Drink Store Wholesale Ltd

Choy, Ming Keong
Oxford Beer House Limited

Chriqui, Isaac
Glow Glow Ltd.

Christensen, Troy
Coe of Ilford Limited
Enotria Winecellars Limited
Great Western Wine Co Ltd

Christie, Alexander Tomas
The Glenlatterach Whisky Co Ltd

Christie, Roderick George
North of Scotland Distilling Co Ltd

Christison, Colin Eric
Laurence Smith & Son (Edinburgh) Ltd

Christoforou, Pantelis
Aotearoa Distribution Ltd
The Madison Drinks Co Ltd
Venus Wine & Spirit Merchants PLC

Christopher, John Martin
Rock Beverages Limited

Christopherson, Anna Elisabeth Lagervist
MCAL Merchant Limited

Christopherson, Mike Olov
MCAL Merchant Limited
MCAL Sweet Retail Limited

Chrysostomou, Pantelis
Eurovenus Limited

Chudley, Andrew
Davy & Co Ltd

Chukwudi, Victor Nwamaziogbu
Paloma & Pablo Import & Export Ltd

Churchill, Gabriel Llandin
Vegan Wine Company London Ltd

Churchouse, Margaret Mary Bernadette
Beyond The Ale (GB) Limited

Churchouse, Stephen Ronald
Beyond The Ale (GB) Limited

Churchward, Alice Joy
The Real Al Co Ltd

Chymera, Ewhen
Pyvo UK Ltd

Chymera, Martyn Zenovij, Doctor
Pyvo UK Ltd

Chymera-Holloway, Chrystyna
Pyvo UK Ltd

Cianti, Gianfranco
Forward Moving Limited

Ciccarelli, Eugenio
Dago Wines Ltd

Ciccariello, Alessandro
Keep Control Ltd

Ciemniewicz, Michal Adam
Taste of Alcohol Ltd

Ciesiolka, Leszek
The Eastern Pantry Ltd

Cilliers, Patric Michael
Fines Master Spirit Co Ltd

Cinque, Francesco
AFC Direct Ltd

Ciobanu, Ionel
Mercurion Ltd

Ciobanu, Stanislav
Maiden Wines Limited

Cirelli, Francesco
La Collina Biologica Ltd

Claessens, Michael Joseph Francis
Abbey Brands Limited
Pioneering Spirits Limited

Clamens, Thomas Daniel Michel
Martin Miller's Gin Limited

Clapperton, Neil
William Cadenhead Limited
Springbank Distillers Limited

Clark, Annette Emily
Copper and Rye Limited

Clark, Charlie James
Hard Back Rum Limited

Clark, Isabelle Anne
Clark Foyster Wines Limited

Clark, John Martin Brodie
The Taunton Cider Co Ltd

Clark, Peter James
Campania Cucina Ltd

Clark, Philip
Beverage Brothers Limited

Clarke, Alex David Victor
Babicka Vodka (International) Ltd

Clarke, Andrew Terence
Famille Clarke Limited

Clarke, Brian Peter
B & D Clarke Limited

Clarke, Clare Alev
Famille Clarke Limited

Clarke, Damian Michael
Freixenet Copestick Limited
Freixenet UK Ltd

Clarke, David Brian
Thorn-Clarke Wines (UK) Ltd

Clarke, Dawn Mary
B & D Clarke Limited

Clarke, Declan Gerard
Clarke Wholesale Limited

Clarke, Gary
Samuels Brewing Co Ltd

Clarke, Magnus Sean
Bihl Ltd

Clarke, Paul Reece
Sell My Wine Ltd

Clarke, Samuel Balfour
Flint Wines Limited

Clarke, Samuel David
Thorn-Clarke Wines (UK) Ltd

Clarke, Sean
Samuels Brewing Co Ltd

Clarke, Sinead Eileen
Clarke Wholesale Limited

Clarke, Timothy
Hall & Woodhouse Limited

Clarke, Timothy David
World Wine Imports Limited

Clarke, Tracy
Hoppy Days Inn Ltd

Clarkson, Anthony Miles
Inverglen Scotch Whisky Co. Ltd

Clavijo Barrio, Jose Ignacio
Selectia Wine Ltd
Spainorama Ltd

Clavijo Tejero, Jose Ignacio
Spainorama Ltd

Clay, Ian James
Broom House Investments Ltd

Clay, James Anthony
Broom House Investments Ltd

Clay, Timothy James
Asahi UK Ltd

Cleary, Alexandra Louise
Greencroft Bottling Co Ltd

Cleary, Anthony Austin
Greencroft Bottling Co Ltd
Lanchester Wine Cellars Ltd
Lanchester Wine Sales Limited
Merchant Vintners Co Ltd
Parverre Marketing Limited
Universal Wines & Spirits Ltd
The Wine Fusion Limited

Cleary, Benjamin William Andrew
Greencroft Bottling Co Ltd

Cleary, Caroline Robyn
Greencroft Bottling Co Ltd

Cleary, Veronica Anne
Greencroft Bottling Co Ltd
Lanchester Wine Cellars Ltd
Lanchester Wine Sales Limited
Universal Wines & Spirits Ltd
The Wine Fusion Limited

Clement, Roy
MBW Traders Ltd

Clements, George Frederick Tearlach
Clements Harrison Limited

Clements, Oliver Murray
Dirty Drinks Ltd

Clevely, John Davis
Louis Latour Limited

Clevely, Rupert John
Crackerjack Wines Limited

Clewlow, Scott
Babyboyempire. Ltd

Clifford, Edward George
Cabal Estates Limited

Clift, Alan
Simply 1st Wine Co Ltd
Splendid Corks Limited

Clift, Hugh William Paul
Premier Wines & Spirits Ltd

Cloke, Michael Neil John
Ojo de Dios Ltd

Clough, Trevor Todd
Digby Fine English Ltd
Digby Wine Ltd

Clowes, George Mark Somerset
Fine Wine Trading Limited

Coakley, Brendan Dermot
Bedford Continental Wholesale Ltd

Coates, Patricia Etiennette Yveline Annick
Ewer Limited

Cobb, Freddie
Project Urban Wines Ltd

Cobino, Antonio
Minarda General Trade Ltd

Cocelli, Cihan
Atlas Food Wholesale Ltd

Cochrane, Ashley
The Clutha Distillery Co Ltd

Cochrane, Richard
Felix Solis Avantis UK Ltd

Cockburn, Michael
Co.Bru Limited

Cockeram, James Alexander Neil
Moet Hennessy U.K. Limited

Cockerill, Liam
Phoenix Spirits Ltd

Codeghini, Giorgio
Santa Code Limited

Codeghini, Giselle Almeida
Santa Code Limited

Codling, James Robert
Carmelita Limited

Codling, Nicola Katherine
Carmelita Limited

Cody, Shane
The Boutique Spirit Co Ltd

Coe, John Maitland
International Diplomatic Supplies
Mangrove Global Limited

Cogley, David John
Whisky Global Ltd

Cohen, Dan
Be My Wine Ltd.

Coipell, Anna Nina Jessica
Caribswede Ltd

Coipell, Oliver Patrick
Caribswede Ltd

Cokayne, Christopher
See Squared Ltd

Cole, Jason Newton Garwood
Hop To The Vine Limited

Cole, Stuart
Maisons Marques et Domaines Ltd

Coleman, David John
Colemans ABC Ltd

Coleman, Jasmine Elaine
Montann Limited

Coleman, Paul Michael
Nitrogenics Ltd

Coleman, Teresa Ann
Colemans ABC Ltd

Coles, Timothy Richard
Coles Trading Limited

Coles, Trevor John
TJC Corporate Events Limited

Collier, Dominic Edwin
The Fine Wine Trading Company (UK)

Collighan, Giles Thomas
The Rum Club Ltd

Collings, Deborah Leanne
The Firkin Whisky Co Ltd

Collings, Michael George Spencer
Spencer Collings & Co Limited
The Firkin Whisky Co Ltd

Collins, Christopher Douglas
Collins Wines Limited

Collins, Rachel Joy
David Berryman Holdings Ltd
David Berryman Limited

Collins, Scott
Hobo Beer & Co Ltd

Collins, Susanne
Collins Wines Limited

Collis, Linda Heather
Bucks Spirits Ltd

Collyear, Emma Louise Alicia
Winehood Ltd

Colton, Alan [1945]
Rexon Group Festivals Limited

Colton, Alan [1981]
Ballers Brands Ltd

Comfort III, William Twyman
Robin Navrozov Consulting Ltd

Comfort, William Twyman Iii
Fine & Rare Wines Limited

Comyn, Evelyn Belle
Vinexcel Limited

Comyn, John Spencer
Vinexcel Limited

Coney, John Mark
The Wine Portfolio UK Limited

Conigliaro, Antonio Michele
Goldy Gin Limited

Conisbee, Rachael
Shorty's Gins Ltd

Connolly, Barry Thomas
Cider of Sweden Ltd

Connolly, Christopher Michael
Connolly's (Wine Merchants) Ltd

Connolly, Gary Anthony
Connolly Wines Ltd
Connollys' Liquor Wholesale Ltd

Connolly, James William
Drinksman Limited

Connolly, Jamie Francis
Helluva... Limited

Connolly, Mairead
Connollys' Liquor Wholesale Ltd

Connolly, Noleen
Connolly Wines Ltd

Connolly, Tania Elizabeth
Connolly's (Wine Merchants) Ltd

Connon, Emmet Patrick
Red Bay Brewing Co Ltd

Connor, David Alexander James
Sporting Benefits Limited

Connor, Linda Gertrude
Sporting Benefits Limited

Conroy, Generaldine
Conroy-Hood Limited

Conway, Anthony Thomas
Droylsden Craft Limited

Conzimu, Guy Laurant
Vino Italiano Ltd

Conzinu, Guy Laurant
Ital Sardo Limited

Cook, Grant MacDonald
Beer Traders UK Limited

Cook, Irma
Organic Country Drinks Ltd

Cook, Michael
Beer and Spirit Agencies International

Cook, Sally Anne
The Little Vine Co Ltd

Cook, Sarah-Jayne
Craftyard Events Limited

Cook, Vicki Alison
Somborne Valley Vineyard Ltd

Cook, William Roy
Organic Country Drinks Ltd

Cooke, Giles
Alliance Wine Co Ltd

Cooke, Harry
Pale Fox Wines Limited

Cooke, Hugo
O'Donnell Moonshine Limited

Cooke, Martin Alexander
BB & R Spirits Limited
Edrington International Brands Ltd
Glenturret Limited
Matthew Gloag & Son Limited
Marshall McGregor Limited

Coombs, Ralph Edmund
Test Tube Products Limited

Cooper, Andrew [1956]
Barmaster (Independant Wholesalers)
Blue Star Inns Limited
Cooper Hill Brewery Ltd

Cooper, Andrew [1979]
Horizon Soft Drinks Limited

Cooper, Gregory Gary
Beer & Co Distribution and Sales Ltd

Cooper, Rachel Marie Jane
Beer & Co Distribution and Sales Ltd

Copestick, Robin Peto
Freixenet Copestick Limited
Slurp Wine Co Ltd

Copp, Lisa Maria
Fabulous Gin Ltd

Copplestone, Adrian James
DSC Imports Limited

Cordier, Leopold Ernst-Gunther
LC Wine Brokers Limited

Cordoni, Dalila
Cloud Wine Ltd

Corfe, Nicholas Charles Roderick
Go Brazil Wines & Spirits (UK) Ltd

Corish, Miles
Legacy Wines & Beverages UK Ltd

Corless, Terence
Vertigo Beers Limited

Cornell, David Joseph
Keeps Lager Co Ltd

Cornish, Charles Samuel
Charles Samuel Imports & Exports Ltd

Coronini Cronberg, Alexia
Conti Coronini Ltd

Corre, Gilles Pierre Yves
CS Wines Limited

Corstorphine, Shane Alexander
Brewgooder Limited

Corteen, Jake
The Double Hard Whiskey Co Ltd

Cortes Garcia, Adrian
El Toro Wines Limited

Cosentino, Yves
Algebra Drinks Ltd

Cosgrave, Alexandra Theresa
The Belgian Life Limited

Coskun, Ersin
Buke Limited

Coss, Dale Michael
Coss Wines Ltd.

Cossart, David
Cossart,Gordon and Co.Limited

Costa Zaccarelli, Daniele
Ora Brewing Co Ltd

Costello, Jonah
Oak Cask Distribution Ltd

Costello, Patrick Henry
Whisky Merchants Trading Ltd

Costley, Janon Ajene
Human Brands PLC

Cottee, Simon Anthony Robert
Liv-Ex Limited

Cotterill, Andrew Bradley Seton
Simply Drinks Distribution Ltd

Cotton, Charles Edward Hugh
CMT (Wines) Limited

Cotton, Graham
Drum and Black Rum Co Ltd

Coulson, Benjamin James
Two Pal's Co Ltd

Coulson, Joseph Fredrick
Leyland Home Brew Limited

Coulson, Teresa Leokadia
Leyland Home Brew Limited

Coumarakichenane, Daniel
Europebro Wholesalers Ltd

Coupe, Paul Andrew
Holcombe Gin Ltd

Courtauld, Toby Augustine
Liv-Ex Limited

Courtney, Christopher
Weiser Taverns Beers & Minerals Ltd

Couvreur, Marthe Georgette Andree
Michel Couvreur (Scotch Whiskies) Ltd

Coventry, Jake
Londinio Liqueurs Ltd.

Cowan, Douglas
Jenuine Jamaican Products Ltd

Cowan, Rory
Diageo Northern Ireland Ltd

Cowling, Anthony Charles
Cotswolds Wine Co Ltd

Cox, Christopher
Murray Brother's Whisky Ltd

Cox, Ekaterine
Taste of Georgia Limited

Cox, Graham Keith
Signatory Vintage Scotch Whisky Co Ltd

Cox, Richard
Taste of Georgia Limited

Cox, Simon John
Cobra Beer Partnership Limited

Cox, Victoria
Indigo Drinks Limited

Cozzi, Deborah Patricia
Discover Wine Limited

Cozzi, Jason Francis
Discover Wine Limited

Crabtree, Margaret Ruth
Crabtrees Craft Pubs and Bottle Merchants

Cragg, Colin
The Jiggers Whistle Limited

Craig, Andrew John
Reva Drinks Ltd

Craig, Priscilla Joyce
North of Scotland Distilling Co Ltd

Craig, Richard Dudley
Dudley Craig Wines Limited

Craig, Rodger Shiak Burns
Loyalty Wines Limited

Crameri, Peter-Francis
Jiangsu Wine Trading Co Ltd

Craven, Thomas
Vinnaturo Ltd

Crawford, James
Lay & Wheeler Limited
Majestic Wine PLC
Majestic Wine Warehouses Ltd
Naked Fine Wine Bonds PLC
Naked Wines Prepayments Trustee Co Ltd

Crawley, Georgina Lucy
Goedhuis & Co Ltd

Crean, Sean Patrick Diarmaid
Pioneer Gin Limited

Creaney, Ann
L.A. Drinks Co Ltd
Little Rock Wine Co Ltd

Creaney, Laurence
L.A. Drinks Co Ltd
Little Rock Wine Co Ltd

Crecan, Elena
Ana Express Ltd

Criado Perez Trefault, Carlos Maria
Las Bodegas Limited

Criado-Perez, Jose Luis
Las Bodegas Limited

Crick, Samuel Paul
West Spirits MCR Ltd

Crickmore, Gavin Paul
Diageo Great Britain Limited
Justerini & Brooks, Limited

Crljenak, Neven
Spalathos Ltd.

Crockett, Iain James
Foxstead Limited

Croft, David John
Manchester Merchant Wines Ltd

Croft, Elaine
Manchester Merchant Wines Ltd

Croft, Jon
Manchester Merchant Wines Ltd

Crombie, Andrew Ross
Hunter Douglas Scotch Whisky Ltd
Andrew Laing & Co Ltd
The Shieling Scotch Whisky Co Ltd

Crompton, Helen Jane
Montann Limited

Crook, Andrew Brian
The Vintage Malt Whisky Co Ltd

Crook, Caroline Crawford
The Vintage Malt Whisky Co Ltd

Crook, Harry Brian
Highlands & Islands Scotch Whisky Co Ltd
The Vintage Malt Whisky Co Ltd

Crook, John Paul
Grace Wines (UK) Limited

Cropley, Colin Richard
The Porterage Co Ltd

Crosland, Stephen David
Tanners Wines Limited

Cross de Chavannes, Benjamine John
The Alternative Rum Co Ltd

Cross, Barry
Lost Rivers Beer Co Ltd

Cross, Elizabeth Anne
Champagne Imports Limited

Cross, James Phillip
Bad Joke Brew Co Ltd

Cross, Loic Jordan
The Funky Beer Co Ltd
More Beer Wholesale Limited

Cross, Peter Michael
Morecambe Bay Wines Limited

Crossan, Paul
Bristol Records Limited

Crossen, James
Direct Wine Importers Limited

Crossland, David
Henry Mitchell & Sons Limited

Crossland, Stephen
Henry Mitchell & Sons Limited

Croston, Timothy John
Adrian Mecklenburgh Limited

Croucher, Iain Andrew
North Star Spirits Ltd.

Cruickshank, William
W.& J.Cruickshank and Co Ltd

Crump, Mark Andrew
Charter Brands Limited
Kramjar Limited
Marlico Limited
Ripped Earth Wines Limited

Cruz, Antonio Miguel Garcia Rodrigues Da
Outstanding People Limited

Crymble, Lee Raymond
Occidental & Oriental Cellars Ltd
Vinum Fine Wines Limited

Cuchet, Baudouin Roger Marie
Heritiers Domec Ltd

Cudalb, Vladislav
Albert Altima Trade House Ltd

Cui, He
Snow Beer UK Ltd

Cullen, Karen
JD's Sports Bar Ltd

Cullum, Timothy Edward
7 Day Cellar Limited

Cumming, Alison Carolyn
Jenkins and Beckers Fine Wine Ltd

Cumming, Hester Chloe Mary
Jenkins and Beckers Fine Wine Ltd

Cumming, Ian
Forth Wines Limited

Cumming, Phoebe Alice Elizabeth
Jenkins and Beckers Fine Wine Ltd

Cumming, Robert Alexander
Jenkins and Beckers Fine Wine Ltd

Cummings Nielsen, Peter Kristoffer
Champagnehub Limited

Cummings Nielsen, Pia Helena
Champagnehub Limited

Cummings, Rohan
Asahi Premium Brands Ltd
Asahi UK Ltd

Cunliffe, Anthony John, Dr
Redevined Wines Limited

Cunniff, Danielle Louise
HardyDistillery Ltd

Cunningham, Douglas Brougham
Agave Partners Limited
Cariel Spirits International Ltd
The Funemployed Agency Ltd
The Funemployed Ltd
Indie Brands Ltd.
Indie Spirits Limited
Indie Wines Limited
Seriously Vodka Limited

Cunningham, Grant
Indie Brands Ltd.
Indie Spirits Limited

Cunningham, Guy Maxwell
Ellis of Richmond (Holdings) Ltd
Ellis of Richmond Limited

Cunningham, Henry Allan
Deliverance Dot Com Limited
Delivered Drinks Limited
Distilled Brands Limited
Whiskies from Scotland Limited

Cunningham, Karen
Alliance Wine Co Ltd

Cunningham, Lea
888 Global Trade Ltd

Cunningham, Sean
The Funemployed Agency Ltd
The Funemployed Ltd

Cunningham, Stephen
888 Global Trade Ltd

Curl, Jason Hamilton Whinfield
Prodolce Ltd

Curle, Ian Barrett
Edrington International Brands Ltd
Marshall McGregor Limited

Curotto, Romina Andrea
Strategos Limited

Curran, Hamish
Port Ellen Distillery Co Ltd
Port Ellen Distilling Limited

Curtis, Benjamin
The Single Cask Ltd

Curtis, Daniel William
TBD Tipples Ltd

Curtis, Michael James
Deluxe Wines Limited
Drink Warehouse Events Limited

Curtis, Richard Mark
Pigs Ears Beers Limited

Curtis, Stuart Roger Richard
Pigs Ears Beers Limited

Cutlack, Giles William John
SDC Wine Importers Ltd

Czernia, Bartosz
Quick Whisky Limited

Czerniejewski, Sebastian
Value Focused Solutions Ltd

Czopik, Ryszard
Van Pur UK Ltd

Czubak, Michal
Saints Row Brewing Co Ltd

D'aboville, Thomas Yves Marie
Pernod Ricard UK Limited

D'angelo, Gennaro
Winery Classic Limited

D'audiffret-Pasquier, Xavier
Maison Sassy UK Limited

Da Re, Gabriele
Hay Hampers Limited

Dadral, Aaisha
One Stop East Limited

Dagnall, Terry
Meridian Centre Hospitality Ltd

Dahliwal, Ravinder
Barry Drinks Ltd

Dalek, Tomasz Konstanty
Poltom Limited

Dall'omo, Charles Edward, Dr
San Martino Limited

Dall'omo, Stephanie Claire
San Martino Limited

Dallison, Mark Antony
Beer Rocks Brewery Ltd

Dalton, Jonathan Charles
Bloomsbury Drinks Ltd

Daly, Wesley
Tristan James Ltd

Dalyac, Stephane Branislav Demetre
Laurent-Perrier (UK) Limited

Danahy, Andrew
Mother Kelly's Distribution Ltd

Danby-Knight, Andrew Trevor William
Stag Ales Ltd

Dando, Stephen Peter
Innspired Taverns Limited

Dandy, Shaun
Cellar Supplies Cheltenham Ltd

Danes, Jason Allan
Draught Services Ltd

Daniell, Tracey Anne
Vintage & Fine Wine International

Daniels, Scott
House of Hops Limited

Daniels, Scott Barry
The Wine Keg Co Ltd

Danin, Max
Brighton Brew Co Ltd

Dann, Lee
Othello Food and Wine Limited

Danyal, Tolga Serkan
Danyal Ltd

Darar, Satnam Singh
The Sourceror Ltd

Darby, Alistair William
S.A.Brain & Co Ltd

Darby, Francesca Anna
Winehood Ltd

Darlington, Gavin Leslie Brook
Red Squirrel Wine Ltd.

Darlington, Nicholas James
Red Squirrel Wine Ltd.

Darlison, Elizabeth Amanda
Cana Import Limited

Darlison, Robert Kenneth
Cana Import Limited

Dart, Katherine Emma
Grape and Nectar Ltd

Darton-Bigg, Nicholas Leonard Philip
Hurlingham Wine Merchants Ltd

Darton-Bigg, Victoria Joan
Hurlingham Wine Merchants Ltd

Darwin, Karen Linda
Grassington Spirit Co Ltd

Daryanani, Rakesh Ishwar
Drinks R Us Limited
Drinkslynx Limited
Simply Spirits Limited

Daughtrey, Barbara Ann
A Little Luxury Distillery Ltd
Lincolnshire Gin Ltd

Daughtrey, Laura Elizabeth
A Little Luxury Distillery Ltd

Dauthieu, Paul Dominic
E I Wines Limited

Dauthieu, Peter Dominic
E I Wines Limited

Dauthieu, Peter Joseph Paul
E I Wines Limited

Dave, Anil
Chateau de Sours Estates Ltd

Davenport, Baron Wayne Robert
Empire Star Limited

Davenport, William Talbot John
Davenport Vineyards Limited

Davey, Jonothan Michael
Nekter Wines Ltd

Davey, Kenneth John
Original & Distinctive Limited

Davey, Mark Charles
Epic Beers Limited

Davidson, Brian Townsend
Heroes Drinks Company C.I.C.

Davidson, Edward Coutts
Whisky Merchants Trading Ltd

Davie, Peter Alexander Denis
Tortuga Brands Limited

Davies, Alastair Huw
Chosen Wine Limited
Lush Wines Ltd

Davies, Alexander John
Quality Spirits International Ltd

Davies, Barry
Somerset Craft Distillery Ltd

Davies, Christopher Joseph
Hard To Find Wines Limited

Davies, Craig
Expert Euro Exports Ltd

Davies, Craig Paul
Quick-Keg Limited

Davies, David Anthony
Quick-Keg Limited

Davies, David Owen
Global Foods Limited

Davies, Iain Robert
Boutinot Limited
Moreno Wine Importers Co Ltd

Davies, Jeanne Marie, Lady
Domaine des Jeanne Limited

Davies, Mandy
Somerset Craft Distillery Ltd

Davies, Mark Robert
Hard To Find Wines Limited

Davies, Mathew Ian
Real Ale Direct Limited

Davies, Michael Anthony Trehearne
W.H. Brakspear & Sons Limited

Davies, Nicola
JN Trading Limited

Davies, Nicola Louise
James Nicholson Wine Limited

Davies, Owain Andrew
The Wine Shop Limited

Davies, Paul Glyn
C.P.A.'s Wine Limited

Davies, Rhys Phillip
Briton Ferry Brewing Co Ltd

Davies, Richard Graham
Neptune Rum Ltd

Davies, Simon Christopher
A & B Vintners Limited
Triage Wines Limited

Davies, Simon Neale
Lust Promotions Ltd
T & S Sales Limited

Davies, Thomas Anthony Trehearne
W.H. Brakspear & Sons Limited

Davies, Wayne Stephen
Rosie & Gin Limited

Davis, Barnaby Simon
Bancroft Wines Limited
Mason & Mason Wines Limited

Davis, Elizabeth Anne
DLRF Limited

Davis, Julia
Enny Wines Ltd

Davis, Luke Matthew
Tapp'd Cocktails Ltd

Davis, Richard Alan
DBM Wines Limited

Davis, Robert James
James E. McCabe Limited
Philip Russell Limited

Davis, Robin Paul Francis
Swig Wines Limited

Davis, Stuart Charles
Anglo Drinks Limited

Davison, Andrew Haughton
Watermark Fine Wine Limited

Davison, Brooke
Our Tino Ltd

Davy, James Richard John
Davy & Co Ltd

Davy, John Sydney Victor
Davy & Co Ltd

Dawes, Matthew Leslie
Bump Events U.K Limited

Dawkins, Glen
Steel Coulson Ltd

Dawkins, Mark Robert
Charter Brands Limited
Laurus Brands Limited
Ripped Earth Wines Limited

Dawson, Gary
Team Spirit Beverage Ltd

Dawson, James Fyfe
Humble Group Ltd

Dayman, Christina
The Little Vine Co Ltd

Daysh, Simon Richard
Daysh Beers Wines & Spirits Ltd

Dayton, Troy
Checkmate Premium Brands Ltd

De Almeida, Matheus
Drinkz Ltd

De Boer, Brigitte Katharina
R & B Wines Ltd

De Boer, Henk Rudolf
R & B Wines Ltd

De Bortoli, Victor
North South Wines Limited

De Burgh, Tarquin Rohan
De Burgh Fine Wine Limited

De Chalus, Arthur Guillaume Marie
Spirits of Borough Ltd

De Conciliis, Bruno
Vigneti Tardis UK Ltd

De Faye Perkins, Louisa Jane
Montrachet Limited

De Fries, William Francis
Grants-EU Limited

De Fries, William Francis Alan
Vett Limited

De Haan, Carlos
Brunswick Fine Wines and Spirits Ltd

De Haan, Peter Charles
Bancroft Wines Limited
Mason & Mason Wines Limited

De Kervenoael, Maurice Jouan
Laurent-Perrier (UK) Limited

De Klerk, Robbert Jan Franciscus
Bogart Spirits Limited

De La Giraudiere, Bernard
Laurent-Perrier (UK) Limited

De La Purificacion Blazquez, Rocio
Taste of Alcohol Ltd

De La Rochefoucauld, Amaury Christian Charles
Swanbridge Fine Wines Ltd

De La Rochefoucauld, Stanislas Jean Baudouin
Swanbridge Fine Wines Ltd

De La Rochefoucauld, Xavier Jacques Jean-Paul
Swanbridge Fine Wines Ltd

De La Torre Canaveras, David
I8 MGT Limited

De Laszlo, Damon Patrick
Royal Tokaji Wines of Hungary Ltd

De Laureto, Alessio
Maestrale Group Ltd

De Magneval, Joanne
Hidden Caveau Limited

De Magneval, Thierry
Hidden Caveau Limited

De Martin, Paola
Harmonicande Vintners Ltd

De Palma, Alessandra Anita
Taste Italia Limited

De Paolis, Francesca Amanda
De Paolis Limited

De Run, Hamish
Melius Drinks Ltd.

De Ruosi, Domenico
Bacchus Fine Wine & Food Ltd
Hoversy Technologies Ltd

De SA Pinto, Sheron
Quintessential Decadence Ltd

De Salins, Etienne
Marussia Beverages UK Limited

De Souza, David
Latin Spirits & Beers (UK) Ltd

De Wet, Danie
De Wetshof International Ltd

De Wet, Lesca
De Wetshof International Ltd

De Yong, Trevor
Chelsea Vintners London Ltd

Deane, Henry Bruce
John Greenacre Limited

Deane, Joy Gwyneth
John Greenacre Limited

Deans Cane, Damon
D.C Enterprises (Import/Export) Ltd

Deans, Andrew George
Bath Sixteen Limited

Deans, George
Bath Sixteen Limited

Deans-Cane, Yazmin
D.C Enterprises (Import/Export) Ltd

Decobecq, Sophie Anne Celine
Capacha Limited

Deehan, James
SK Trading (N.I.) Ltd

Deehan, Owen
Allied Ship Supplies (Ireland) Ltd

Deer, Clare
Ruby & Claret Limited

Deer, Mark
Ruby & Claret Limited

Deinega, Dmitry
Dima's Vodka UK Ltd

Delage, Jaime
Delage & Haughton Limited

Delamain, Alan John
Appellations Limited

Delamere, Paul
Shindigger Craft Beer Ltd

Delaney, Michael
First Class Beverages Ltd

Delegat, Jakov Nikola
Delegat Europe Limited

Delemico, Alvin
Caribbean Collective Group Ltd

Delivett, Tina
Blush Gin Distrubutors UK Ltd

Della Casa, Andrew Eugene Nicholas
The Wine Enterprise Investment Scheme

Demaiter, Lysander
Be Hop Ltd

Demarco, Daryl
Frequency Enterprises Limited

Demetriou, Axentis Panayiotou
Regency Event Solutions Ltd

Demetriou, Demetrakis Andrew
Corfu SW Limited

Demetriou, Demetri
European Wine Brokers Limited
Grands Vins de France Limited

Demir, Huseyin
HD Wine & Spirit Ltd

Demirci de La Fuente, Derya
Silenus Limited

Demontis, Raimondo
Eataly Food Distributors Ltd

Dempster, Noel
Ashanti Drinks Limited

Denaro, Giovanna Emmanuela
MDF Wholesale Ltd

Deng, Fuji
DH Global Wine Ltd

Deniz, Mahir
M D (Cash & Carry) Limited

Denman, Chris
WSB Investment and Consultancy Ltd

Dennhofer, Heinz
Dennhofer Wines Limited

Dennhofer, Maire Caithlin
Dennhofer Wines Limited

Dennis, Andrew
Chandos Wines Ltd

Dennis, Joanna Marie
Fishers Gin Ltd

Dennis, Thomas
Forest Hill Brewing Co Ltd

Densem, Margaret
RD Wines Limited

Densem, Simon
Rodney Densem Wines Limited
RD Wines Limited

Denton, Anthony
DN Pacifica Ltd

Denton, Margaryta
DN Pacifica Ltd

Deo, Harvinder Singh
Malvern Ltd

Derbyshire, Mark Wayne
Aurora Ales Limited

Deren, Eric Gerard
France Domaines Limited

Derry, Daniel Ironmonger
Sherwood Outlaws Brewing Co Ltd

Deschamps, Alexandra Marie Elisabeth
Michel Couvreur (Scotch Whiskies) Ltd

Deschamps, Cyril
Michel Couvreur (Scotch Whiskies) Ltd

Despont, Serge
Hillbridge Estates Limited

Dessain, Giles William Charles
Yapp Brothers Limited

Devaney, Gearoid Edmund
Flint Wines Limited

Devereux, Ivo Edmund
Sapling Spirits Ltd

Devi, Nisha
Bhanbore Trading Company PVT Ltd

Devine, Damien
Old Red Lion Theatre Pub Ltd

Devine, Helen
Old Red Lion Theatre Pub Ltd

Dezecot, Benoit
BD Wines Limited

Dezfulli, Dariush
Godin Tepe Limited

Dhaliwal, Jaskaran Singh
Kingdom Distillers Limited

Dhamecha, Khodidas Ratanshi
Dhamecha Foods Limited

Dhamecha, Shantilal Ratanshi
Dhamecha Foods Limited

Dhami, Aaron Rico Singh
Earny Limited

Dhamrait, Satnam Singh
Beermaster Derby Ltd

Dhanoa, Harinder Paul Singh
Magik Drinks Limited

Dharcourt, Pierre
The Three Stills Co Ltd

Dhariwal, Budge
Approved Products Ltd
Budge Brands Ltd
Franco Hetty Limited
Hollandwest Limited
World Traveller Wines Limited

Dhariwal, Raji Kaur
Franco Hetty Limited

Dheensa, Gurmit
Cresco Import Exports Ltd

Dhesi, Gurdawar Singh
Dhesis Wholesale Ltd

Dhesi, Gurmej Singh
Icknield Stores Ltd

Dhillon, Devinder Kaur
H R Drinks (Wholesale) Ltd
Hamptons Wine Ltd

Dhillon, Harbeer
Premium Brands Distribution Ltd

Dhillon, Sukhdeep Singh
Cayenes Ltd

Dhingra, Dev
DNG Group Ltd

Dhingra, Dinesh Kumar
Continental Cash & Carry Ltd

Dhingra, Priya
DNG Trading Ltd

Dhokia, Raj
The Tequila Shop Ltd

Dholliwar, Sonya
Stockwell Beverages Ltd

Di Grigoli, Carmeluccia
Themirtis Limited

Di Maria, Adriano
A Di Maria & Sons Ltd

Di Maria, Antonio
A Di Maria & Sons Ltd

Di Palma, Giuseppe
Villa Sofia Limited

Di Pompo, Daniel
AbruzzoWines Ltd

Di Salvo, Danilo Tysoe
Gvino Limited

Di Tuoro, Rossella
Winicious Limited

Dibbs, Ian
Gemeaux Limited

Dibbs, Karen
Gemeaux Limited

Dickens, Karen
Big Red D Ltd

Dickens, Peter
Big Red D Ltd

Dickie, Martin
The Brewgooder Foundation

Dickins, Betty Alma
F.L. Dickins Limited

Dickson, John Raymond
The Old Man Rum Co Ltd

Diggins, Mary Frances
Lanark House Investments Ltd

Dillon, Gregory
Greatdrams Ventures Limited

Dillon, Kirsty
Greatdrams Ventures Limited

Dillon, Patricia
Whisky Biz Glasgow Ltd

Dimaras, Panagiotis
Panemporium Ltd

Dimbu, Dan
Vinotrans Ltd

Dimitrov, Dimitar
Imperial Capital D & G Ltd

Dimitrov, Simeon Dimitrov
Bulgarsko Pivo Limited

Dimitrova, Gabriela Emilova
Reality Bio Wine Ltd

Dimock, James
Pioneer Spirits Ltd

Dimostrato, Roberto
Grandi Vini Limited

Dincer, Victoria
Eda Quality Foods North UK Ltd

Dinte, Adriana
Molvino Fine Wine & Spirits Co Ltd

Dixon, Curtis
Punchline Ltd

Dixon, Mark
Kingsland Drinks Group Limited
Kingsland Drinks Limited

Dluzak, Marek
Bar Joker Ltd

Dobbin, Christine Jane
The Rebel Wine Club Ltd

Dobbs, Jason
Indigo Drinks Limited

Dobby, Steven Richard
The Ship & Mitre Brewing Co Ltd

Dobson, Mark Stuart
Rico Rico Ltd

Doctor, Gordon John
Ian MacLeod Distillers Limited

Doda, Dritan
Ionica Wine Cellars Ltd

Dodd, Richard Francis
FV Craft Beers Ltd

Dodd, Simon Ray
Nectar Imports Limited

Dodds, Michael Edward
Momento Vivere Holdings Ltd

Dodsworth, James Elliot
Mentzendorff & Co Ltd

Dodwell, Oliver
North West Spirits Limited

Doe, Timothy
Farr Vintners Limited

Dogan, Huseyin
Alice Wholesale Trading Ltd

Dogan, Suayp
Korzinka Taste of Europe Ltd

Doggett, Stephen Frederick
Enjoydrinks Limited

Doherty, Fraser
Beer52 Limited

Doherty, Gary
Team Spirit Beverage Ltd

Doidge, James Anthony
The Wine Treasury Limited

Dolan, Nicholas Joseph
Real Ale (Export) Limited
Real Ale (Retail) Limited
Real Ale (Wholesale) Limited
Real Ale Limited

Dolan, Peter
Real Ale (Export) Limited
Real Ale (Retail) Limited
Real Ale (Wholesale) Limited
Real Ale Limited

Dolder, Ryan
Human Brands PLC

Domange, Francois
Caves de Pierre Limited

Domeyko, Thomas
Concha y Toro UK Limited

Domney, Helen
Charles Mitchell Wines Limited

Domney, Howard Charles
Charles Mitchell Wines Limited

Domokos, Csaba
Nutricont Ltd

Donald, John Andrew
Euro Wines (C & C) Limited

Donald, Robert
Ellismuir Limited

Donaldson, Alyson
Diageo Global Supply IBC Ltd

Donaldson, Craig
Northpole Crush Ltd

Donaldson, Keith William
Donaldson Reeves Limited

Donat, Gerard
Usedsoft Ltd

Dondain, Stephanie
Cabezac Collections Limited

Dong, Lue
Cheng International Co Limited

Donnelly, Eileen
J. & J. Hunter Limited

Donnelly, Heath
GreatWineDirect Limited

Donnelly, James Ivan
J. & J. Hunter Limited

Donnelly, James T
J. & J. Hunter Limited

Donnelly, John Nugent
J. & J. Hunter Limited

Donnelly, Richard
J. & J. Hunter Limited

Donnelly, Rory
Donnelly Wholesale Limited

Donovan, David
Storesrealm Limited

Donovan, John Daniel
Storesrealm Limited

Dooher, Michael Eugene
Continental Beer Services Ltd

Dooley, Lauren Rebecca Elaine
Shy Simba Ltd

Doorley, Thomas Christopher FitzGenerald
Real Irish Whiskey Limited

Doran, Caroline
W. Hall & Son (Holywell) Ltd
Hops and Barley Limited
Pemberton Central Limited

Doran, Georgia Maeve
Doran Family Vintners Limited

Doran, Thomas Kavanagh
Doran Family Vintners Limited

Dorgu, Nanaweikule Steve
Flobegill Wines UK Ltd

Dos Santos, Custudio Jose
Alivini (North) Limited
Alivini Co Ltd
Franciacorta Limited

Dos Santos, Eugene Paulo
Dos Santos Bev Co UK Limited

Dos Santos, Julian Paulo
Dos Santos Bev Co UK Limited

Dosanjh - Cheema, Kuljit Kaur
Wintrad Ltd

Dosanjh, Jaspal
Circle View Business Consultancy Ltd

Dosanjh, Narinder Singh
DC Cash and Carry Ltd

Double, Sophie Elizabeth
N.Double and Co Ltd

Dougall, Kevin Brian Edward
Singolo Vino Limited

Dougan, David Robert
Dr Dougan (Enterprises) Ltd

Dougan, Michael Patrick
Le Petit Wine Cellar Ltd

Dougan, Robert Don Hunter
La Peira Limited

Dougherty, Phillip Martin
Hic-Cup Wines Limited

Douglas, Anthony John, Dr
Heroes Drinks Company C.I.C.

Douglas, Craig
Highland Drinks Ltd

Doutch, Calum
Cocksure Brewing Co Ltd

Dove, John Howard
Apley Hall Wines Limited

Dowling, James William Preston
Wine2trade Limited

Dowling, Paul Stephen Frederick
Wine2trade Limited

Downey, Mark John
Brewbarge Limited

Downham, Gary Edward
Golden Crust & Co Limited

Downing, Geoffrey
Continental Wines Limited

Downing, Josephine
Let There Be Beer Ltd

Downing, Julian Conway
Seckford Wines Limited

Dowridge, Beverley Arlene
Redvulette Ltd

Doyle, Generald Francis
Rasputin Leisure Ltd

Doyle, Jeremy Frank
Simply 1st Wine Co Ltd
Splendid Corks Limited

Doyle, John
Rasputin Leisure Ltd

Doyle, Jolene
Phoenix Premium Drinks Limited

Doyle, Laura
The Wine Byre Limited

Doyle, Patrick Henry
International Diplomatic Supplies

Doyle, Robert James Stanley
Hoptimism Limited

Drage, Geoffrey Philip
Rare Whisky Auctioneers Ltd

Draghici, Ovidiu Emilian
Transylvania Wine Ltd
Wine Tasting Angels Ltd

Draghici, Teodora Mirela, Dr
Transylvania Wine Ltd

Dragneva, Gergana Georgieva
Mamada Ltd

Dragoi, Veronica-Isabela
V I Wholsale Limited

Dragomir, Cristian Gabriel
Corvin Import Export Ltd

Drake, Jonalthan Patrick
Creation Wines UK Limited

Drawbell, Annette Patricia
The Salto Cachaca Co Ltd

Drawbell, Stephen Matthew Wedgwood
The Salto Cachaca Co Ltd

Driver, Lucy Ruth Minshaw
SDC Wine Importers Ltd

Drucquer, Frederick
Brazen Rum Ltd

Drummond, Jason Kingsley
Eight Vodka Limited

Drury, David John
Schnapp Lab Ltd

Drysdale, Colin Jonathon
Allson Sparkle Limited

Drysdale, Nicola
Allson Sparkle Limited

Du Toit, Pieter Gerhardus
Bosman Wines UK Ltd

Dubourg, Gilles Roger Charles
Wine Divine Ltd

Dubro, Neils Alex
Street Wines Limited

Dudd, Gregory James
Sunnyside Incorporated Limited

Dudd, Jonathan Howell
Sunnyside Incorporated Limited

Dudgeon, Daniel Robert
The Gin Dobry Gin Co Ltd

Duff, William Peter
Emporia Brands Limited

Duff-Tytler, Natalie Anne
Cador Limited
The Champagne Company (UK) Ltd
The Drinks Emporium Limited

Duffy, Caroline
N. McLoone & Co. Ltd

Duffy, Ericka
Cross Brew Ltd

Duffy, Karen
Star Value Limited

Duffy, Patrick
N. McLoone & Co. Ltd

Duffy, Simon Joseph
Corney and Barrow Limited

Duffy, Siobhan
Star Value Limited

Duffy, Stephen Joseph
Mayfair Brands Limited

Duffy, William
Star Value Limited

Dufouleur, Lois
Harmony Wines Limited

Duggan, Simon
The Cornish Moonshine Co Ltd

Dugmore, Adam Louis
Ester Wines Limited

Dulieu, Nicola Joy
Adnams PLC

Dumenil, Nicholas George
Dumenil Champagne Limited

Dumenil, Timothy Peter
Dumenil Champagne Limited

Dunbavan, Graham
Epic Beers Limited

Duncan, Mark
The Belgian Life Limited

Duncan, Stuart Beange
De Facto Spirits Limited

Duncan-Anderson, Jason Duncan
Red Squirrel Brewery Limited

Dunham, Jane
Janemac Ltd

Dunn, Julie Frances
Alexander Wines Ltd.

Dunn, Stephen, Mr
Message in a Bottle Ltd.

Dunnett, Paul William
Home Farm Gin Limited

Dunning-Lewis, Thomas
Just Incase Wines Ltd

Duong, Nghia Thanh
Golden Coin Trading Limited

Dupuy, Frances
A. Dewar Rattray Limited

Durance, Simon
Black Dog Gin Co Ltd

Durkin, Gary
W D L Wholesale Limited

Dushko, Peter
Con Gusto Wines Limited

Dusi, Luca
Pandemonio Limited

Duva, Antonio
World Brands Duty Free Limited

Duval, Carol
Champagne Duval-Leroy (UK) Ltd

Dyson, Brad
The Brighton and Hove Wine Co Ltd

Dzelzainis, Marcis Alfred
Destilado London Limited

Dzhandarmov, Petar Dimitrov
SAPM Commercial Ltd

Dziebowski, Krzysztof Piotr
Top Alco Ltd

E Cunha, Nuno Brito
Vinterest Limited

Eagle, Jonathan Ernest
Bottle Green Limited

Earl, Andrew
Fine Wine Direct Limited

Earl, Sam Robin
Fine Wine Direct Limited

Earle, John Roderick
Christopher Piper Wines Ltd

East, Jeffrey PM
Alistair McCoist & Jeff East (Vintners)

East, Oliver Neil
Farr Vintners Limited

Eastwood, Anthony William
Small Beer Limited

Eastwood, Judith Anne
Small Beer Limited

Eastwood, Karen Louise
Small Beer Limited

Eastwood, Robert William
Small Beer Limited

Eaton, Callison
Cask Whisky Ltd

Eaton, Debbie Fernanda
Scarlettes Ltd

Eaton, Matthew Robert
Field Bar Gin Limited

Economides, George
Mastiha World Ltd

Economou, Anastasios
Brockmans Gin Limited

Eddy, Andrew
V Beverages Limited

Ede, Nigel James
Experience Wine Limited

Eden, James Michael
Wokka Spirits Limited

Edgar, Raphael Nathaniel
Rivers Rum (UK) Limited

Edinborough, Adam Michael
Crafty Devil Brewing Ltd

Edmondson, Joy
North South Wines Limited

Edmunds, James Matthew Crayden
Cellarers (Wines) Limited
DEF Investments Limited
Diageo Great Britain Limited
Diageo United Kingdom Limited
Justerini & Brooks,Limited

Edwards, Graham Terrence
Edwards Beers and Wine Supplies Ltd

Edwards, Jasper
Lemongrass and Cardamom Ltd

Edwards, John
Vincisive Wines Limited

Edwards, Mark
Authentic French Wines (Importers)

Edwards, Mark John
Atlas Fine Wines Limited

Edwards, Robert John
TVB Retail Limited

Edwards, Suzanne
Edwards Beers and Minerals Ltd
Edwards Beers and Wine Supplies Ltd
Edwards Beers and Wines (Holdings) Ltd
Edwards Wine Agencies Limited

Edwards, Terence Roy
Edwards Beers and Minerals Ltd
Edwards Beers and Wine Supplies Ltd
Edwards Beers and Wines (Holdings) Ltd
Edwards Wine Agencies Limited

Egan, Damien
J & De Limited
The Mixology Collection Ltd

Egan, Eamonn Peter
Artisan Wine Storage Ltd
Cellar Link Limited

Egan, Shane
Maison Shane et Filles Ltd

Egbo, Peter Kehinde
106 Business Solutions Limited

Ehimuan, Emmanuel Omologbe
The Victoria Island Beverage Co Ltd

Ehimuan, Itua Jude
The Victoria Island Beverage Co Ltd

Ehrenkrona, Carl Jakob Alistair
Reformed Spirits Co Ltd

Ehrenkrona, Jacob
Martin Miller's Gin Limited

Ejsmond-Frey, Toby Julian
Friendship Adventure Ltd.

Ekins, Stuart William
Hobo Beer & Co Ltd

Ekwem, Nnamdi
Nue Innovations Limited

Elangcheliyan, Kayilapillai
Sagitha Ltd

Elangovan, Saravanan
Saravanan Traders (UK) Ltd

Element, Jeremy David Viner
Rum Matters Limited

Elemide, Olufemi Tolulope
Tolmid International Ltd

Elfman, Holly Zagor
Camino Real Limited

Elfman, Zachary Scott
Camino Real Limited

Elghanayan, Shahram David
Magenta Wine Investors Limited

Ellefsen, Benedict James Olaf
Atom Supplies Limited

Elliker, Ruth
Shelsley Brewing Co Ltd

Elliott, Ian
Tayler Beers Limited

Elliott, John William
Spokesuk Ltd

Ellis, Anthony
Andrews Beer & Mineral Co Ltd

Ellis, Arlene Patricia
Jenuine Jamaican Products Ltd

Ellis, Christopher Simon
Crush Wines Ltd

Ellis, David Michael
Ellis Wharton Wines Ltd

Ellis, Denise
Andrews Beer & Mineral Co Ltd

Ellis, Henry James
Ellis of Richmond (Holdings) Ltd
Ellis of Richmond Limited
Richmond Wine Agencies Limited

Ellis, John Robert Henry
Ellis of Richmond (Holdings) Ltd
Ellis of Richmond Limited

Ellis, Jonathan Charles
Andrews Beer & Mineral Co Ltd

Ellis, Julian
Andrews Beer & Mineral Co Ltd

Ellis, Karen Lesley
Armit Holding Limited
Armit Wines Limited

Ellis, William Derek
Ellis of Richmond (Holdings) Ltd
Ellis of Richmond Limited

Ellison, Richard Peter
Wanderlust Wine Limited

Elliston, David Michael
Lanark House Investments Ltd

Elliston, Margaret Ruth
Lanark House Investments Ltd

Ellmann, Iris
The Wine Barn Limited

Ellmann, Tom
Swinging Vine Ltd

Elms, Michael David
Swinkels Snackery and Backery Ltd

Elsden, Clive James
Red Fox Wines Limited

Elsden, John Kirk Saunderson
Above Brand Limited

Elsden, Julian Charles
Red Fox Wines Limited

Elsden, Oliver Jack
Red Fox Wines Limited

Elsom, David
Black Dog Gin Co Ltd

Elswood, Daniel Edward
Vinvm Ltd

Emanuel, Daniel
Dave and Dani Ltd

Emeny, Simon
Nectar Imports Limited

Emmans, Christian Dominic Howard
Birdcage Gin Ltd.

Emmerson, Andrew
Solway Spirits Ltd

Empeslidis, Theodoros, Dr
Cask Trade Ltd

Engelbrecht, Nathan
Pingu & Co Ltd

English, Shaun Michael
Moreno Wine Importers Co Ltd

Engutsamy, Selvin
Drinks 2 You Limited

Enok, Basil
Wine City Limited

Entwistle, Nik Andrew
The Spirit Beer Co Ltd
Tattoo Limited

Enwerem, Wilson
Wine City Limited

Erem, Tugba
Fortunae Limited

Ergin, Hasret
HD Wine & Spirit Ltd

Erhuero, Oresiri
Oris Black Ltd

Erkhagen, Morgan Jan Alial
Bristol Records Limited

Erskine, Robin David
Potocki Spirits (Europe) Ltd

Esayanoor Sridharan, Srihari Haran
Srihari Haran Ltd

Escano, Miguel
Capital Languages Ltd

Esler, Niall Edward Lloyd
Nele Drinks Limited

Espir, Robert Aaron
Espir Baron & Solomon Limited

Eustace, Bee Sarah
Universal Wines & Spirits Ltd

Eustace, James John
Merchant Vintners Co Ltd

Eustace, Robert Andrew
Universal Wines & Spirits Ltd

Evans, Carol Susan
Casa Julia Limited

Evans, Clare Joanne
Bullards Spirits Limited
Lord Nelson Burnham Ltd
The Norfolk Vineyard Ltd

Evans, Gareth Alun
Faking Bad Brewery Limited

Evans, George
J. Chandler & Company, Limited

Evans, Jonathan Richard
Wild Foragin Ltd

Evans, Katherine Hannah
Ephemeris Solutions Ltd

Evans, Laura Anne
Frederick's Wine Co Ltd

Evans, Lee
Condor Wines Ltd

Evans, Maria
Condor Wines Ltd

Evans, Natalie Louise
Wild Foragin Ltd

Evans, Richard Martin
Craddock Cocktails Ltd
Tapp'd Ltd

Evans, Richard Neville Lewis
Dedicated Wines Ltd

Evans, Ross
Holborn Gin Co Ltd

Evans, Russell Barrie
TBpub Ltd

Evans, Scott
Vino Unico Limited

Everard, Julian William Spencer
Everards Brewery Limited

Everard, Richard Anthony Spencer
Everards Brewery Limited

Everett, Rachel Nuria
L'Altre VI Limited

Everett, Ruben Felix Loayza
L'Altre VI Limited

Everett-Lyons, Philip
H.B. Evelyo Ltd.

Everitt, Neil John
Brockmans Gin Limited

Evola, Felice
Di Vine Importers Limited

Evola, Michael Francesco
Di Vine Importers Limited

Ewers, Thomas
Malts of Scotland Ltd

Ewing, Harry
Stay Gold Beer Co Ltd

Ewing, Thomas
Stay Gold Beer Co Ltd

Eyles, Raymond Jonathon
Chelsea Vintners London Ltd

Fabbri, Lucca
Palmer Traders Ltd

Fabre, Jean-Philippe
Fabre Brothers Ltd

Fabris, Massimo Antonio
Row & Co Ltd

Faelens, Sebastien
Innvino Ltd

Fagon-Francis, Maureen
B & M Produce Limited

Fagunwa, Babatunde Opeyemi
Bopfags Services Ltd

Fahey, Paul Neil
Yorkshire Beers Limited

Faini, Oberdan
Sangiovesa Ltd

Fair, Nicholas William
Browett & Fair Ltd

Fairbrother, Adam John
Melius Drinks Ltd.

Faiveley, Erwan
Maisons Marques et Domaines Ltd

Fakhry, Walid
Cask Industries Ltd

Faktor, David Michael
Cropol Luxury Products Ltd

Falconer, Malcolm McLeod
Marta's Vinyard Limited

Falk, Howard Warren
Hallgarten Wines,Limited
International Wine Forwarding Ltd
Pieroth Limited
Vicomte Bernard de Romanet Ltd

Fallon, John
International Procurement and Logistics

Falque, Sandra Marie
Square Wine Ltd

Fan, Lihong
United Phoenix Limited

Fantinel, Marco
Winery Classic Limited

Faraoni, Duccio Matteo
Hoghton Brewery Limited

Faraoni, Elena Susanna Isabella
Hoghton Brewery Limited

Farber, David Zwi William
Monopole Wine Portfolio Management Ltd

Farmer, Thomas Andrew
Tom's Tap and Brewhouse Ltd

Farnham, Henry Robert Spencer
Bloody Drinks Limited

Farquhar, Bruce
Dramfool Ltd

Farquharson, Helen Sheila
Helver Wines Ltd

Farquharson, Oliver Douglas
Helver Wines Ltd

Farr, Charles
Stokes Fine Wines Limited

Farr, Deborah Ann
JSF Services Limited

Farr, Justin Stephen
JSF Services Limited

Farr, Simon Charles
Blends Wine Estates UK Ltd
Oeno Limited

Farrar, Richard William
Ian MacLeod Distillers Limited

Farrell, Christopher Mark
Silence of The Drams Limited

Farrell, Richard
North East Drinks Supplies Ltd

Farrington, Gregory Paul
The Near Beer Brewing Co. Ltd

Fascia, Lee James
Pug Vodka Ltd

Fasey, James Edward
International Procurement and Logistics

Fashhou, David
247 Enterprises UK Ltd

Fashhou, Hani
247 Enterprises UK Ltd

Fast, Jacquelyn
Rebel Pi Limited

Fatoye, Kikelomo
Kikijee Global Services Ltd

Faulkner, Edward Theo
Sapling Spirits Ltd

Faure, Laurent
Bubbles & Wines Limited

Fawcett, Cathryn Mary
Field and Fawcett Wine Merchants and Delicatessen

Fawcett, Peter Edward
Field and Fawcett Wine Merchants and Delicatessen

Fearnley Brown, Jordan
Vektor Vodka UK Ltd

Feasey, Jason Francis
Vintage 1947 Limited

Febvre, Jade Anne-Marie
Unfiltered Wines Limited

Fedrick-Illsley, Thomas Alexander
Theatre of Wine Limited

Fegan, Gerard
Fegan Wholesale Ltd

Fegan, Jacqueline
Fegan Wholesale Ltd

Fein, Miron
Barcode Traders Limited

Feldman, Lukka Abramsky
Barndiva Wine Co Ltd

Fell, Craig Edward
414 Alcohols Limited

Fellowes-Freeman, Lindsey Anne
Prosecco 1754 Limited

Felton, Amanda Clare
Hazelbank Limited

Felton, Lorna Clare
Casa Julia Limited

Feneron, Mark Julian
C C & C Limited

Feng, Huibin, Dr
Best Cask Ltd

Fennessy, Sharon Lynnette
Diageo Great Britain Limited
Justerini & Brooks, Limited

Ferdinand, Daniel
FV Trading Europe Ltd

Ferguson, Andrew Robert
UKAFDS Limited

Ferguson, Callum Alexander
Glugged! Ltd

Ferguson, John
Young Malt Co Ltd

Ferguson, Joshua
Mobay Drinks Ltd

Ferguson, Paul
Cazcabel Drinks Limited
Cazcabel Tequila Limited
Cut Rum Limited
Proof Drinks Limited
Ruffnek Beer Limited

Fergusson, John David
Wetherby Brew Co Limited

Fernandes Da Costa, Artur Sebastiao
The Cashew Apple Co Ltd

Fernandes, Antonio
A & G Management Consultancy Ltd

Fernandes, Gabriel Antonio
A & G Management Consultancy Ltd

Fernandez Alameda, Juan
Xi-Spain Ltd

Ferner, Roseanna Emily
Favourite Beers Limited

Ferreira, Seymour Paul
Cellar Trends Limited

Ferrer, Pedro
Freixenet Copestick Limited
Freixenet UK Ltd

Ferrier, Jolyon Alexander Donald
Beets Incorporated Ltd

Fiamma, Damiano
Tutto Wines Limited

Fiandaca, Alfie
Morosini Mills Limited

Fields, Christopher George
G.W. Fields & Sons (Great Yarmouth)

Fields, Harvey Samuel
Rosemount Pub Co. Limited

Fields, Joshua
Rosemount Pub Co. Limited

Fierobe, Maud
Frenchbubbles Limited

Filsell, Darren John
The Craft Beer Collaborative Ltd

Findlay, Ralph Graham
Marston's Acquisitions Limited

Finn, Angela
Ratherhavecava Ltd

Finni, Tunde
Honeybee Farm Ltd

Fiori, Stefano Bartholomeo Guisseppe
Mondial Wine Limited

Firth, Andrew John
Firth and Co Wine Merchants Ltd

Firth, Edward
Hardywood Park Craft Brewery Ltd.
Lonerider UK Ltd
Point Beer UK Limited
Port City Brewing UK Limited

Firuleasa, Bogdan-Costin
Maxwell's Trading Co Ltd

Fishel, Robert Joseph
Gudfish Limited

Fisher, Andrew Noel
Pigs Ears Beers Limited

Fisher, Christopher
Mercurial Brewing Limited

Fisher, Claire
House of Hops Limited

Fisher, Daniel Arthur
Village Selections Limited

FitzGenerald, Clement David Mark
New Age Wines Ltd

FitzGenerald, Eamon William
Naked Wines Prepayments Trustee Co Ltd

FitzGenerald, Jayne Louise
New Age Wines Ltd

FitzGenerald, Olivia
Majestic Wine Warehouses Ltd

Fitzsimons, Alice Louise
The Crest Cyder Co Ltd

Flack, Lisa Ann
The Peculiar Gin Co Ltd

Flanagan, James Anthony
J.T.Flanagan Trading Co Ltd

Flatt, Sandra Jane
The Imperial Wine Co Ltd

Fleetwood, David Spencer
The Mullwood Wine Co Ltd

Fleetwood, Jonathan Colin
Elicite Ltd

Fleetwood, Karen Elizabeth
The Mullwood Wine Co Ltd

Fleming, Robert
Angus Dundee Distillers PLC

Fletcher, James Grey Oliver
Amphora Portfolio Management Ltd

Fletcher, Timothy Wyndham
Rodney Fletcher Vintners Ltd

Flinn, John Malcolm
Italian Appellations Limited

Flint, Evelyn
Eurovines Limited

Flint, Joanne Ruth
Sandbar German Beer Ltd

Flint, Michael Andrew
Sandbar German Beer Ltd

Flint, Timothy Martin
Eurovines Limited

Flores, Eduardo Flores
Botella Imports Ltd

Floridia, Marco
Separateflow Limited

Flower, David James
Lazy Lizard Beer Co Ltd

Flower, Lynn
Lazy Lizard Beer Co Ltd

Flunder, Robert David
Jetchill Ltd

Flynn, Luciann Siobhan
Liberty Wines Limited

Folli, Massimiliano
Astrum Wine Cellars Limited

Fomethe Momo, Patrick Alexandre
Vitis-Terra Limited

Fontannaz, Yves Bernard Adrien
Origin Wine Limited

Foord, Anthony James
Anthony James Beverages Ltd

Forbes, Kathryn Alexandra
Experience Wine Limited

Forbes, Mark St John Graham
Experience Wine Limited

Ford, James William Lance
Champagne Cellar Limited

Ford, Sereen
This Is Not A Party Limited

Ford, Steven Robert
Popjax Limited

Forde, Michael
Kingsland Drinks Group Limited
Kingsland Drinks Limited

Fordham, David
TCG Winchester Limited

Fordyce, Angus James McKellen
Vinterest Limited

Fordyce, Laurence John
Borders Distillers Limited
Borders Distilling Limited
The Three Stills Co Ltd

Foreman, Jack
Laurito Ltd

Forth, Jake Michael
Little White Dog Limited

Fortune, David William
HG & S Ltd

Foster, Anthony Charles
Algodon Europe Limited
BFA Holdings Limited

Foster, Diana Jillian
BFA Holdings Limited

Foster, John Robert
Black & Yellow Developments Ltd

Foster, Lucy Jayne, Dr
Wine Freedom Limited

Fotheringham, Susan Fiona
Albion Fine Wines Ltd

Fougere, Eric Andre Armand
Louis Latour Limited

Fourie, Marc Ralph
CPT Trading Ltd

Fowkes Bolt, Victoria Katharine
Blue Tree Limited

Fowkes, Robert Andrew
Brockmans Gin Limited

Fowler, Benedick
The Sourceror Ltd

Fowler, Fiona Claire
Il Palagio Ltd

Fowler, Mitchel
Ferovinum Ltd

Fowlie, Derek John
Burgundy Wines Limited

Fox, Daniel Peter
Craft Locals Limited

Fox, Vernon
Lough Neagh Distillers - 1837 Ltd

Foyster, Lance Edmund
Clark Foyster Wines Limited

Frampton, Arthur Josiah
Avalon Wholesale and Brewing Ltd

Frampton, Sandra Jane
Avalon Wholesale and Brewing Ltd

Francis, Matthew Charles
Francis Fine Wines Ltd

Francis, Terri Nicole
Atom Supplies Limited

Frank, Osbourne Victor
Caribbean Trade Ltd

Franklin, Chad James
Booze Cruz Ltd

Frantzen, Jean Arnaud
Michel Couvreur (Scotch Whiskies) Ltd

Franyutti, Susana
Mezcal Reina Limited

Fraser, Jeremy William
Stow Brewery Limited

Frazier, Georgina
Frazier's Wine Merchants Ltd.

Frazier, John Lewis Reginald
Frazier's Wine Merchants Ltd.

Frazier, William Jerome
Frazier's Wine Merchants Ltd.

Freddi, Roberto
La Madeleine Wines Limited

Frederick, Christopher Jon
My Nan's Favourite Ltd

Freeman, Beth Emma
Night Out Entertainments Ltd

Freeman, John Anthony
Delegat Europe Limited

Freeman, Rob
Magic F & F Ltd

French, David Neil
Southwell Trading Ltd

French, Timothy Charles
Thorman Hunt & Co Limited

Frerejean Taittinger, Guillaume Pierre Marie Eric
Old Sport Limited
Yaad Rum Ltd

Frerejean Taittinger, Rodolphe
Old Sport Limited
Sagittarius World Limited

Frerejean Taittinger, Rodolphe Jean Marie Humbert Guy
Yaad Rum Ltd

Freshwater, Timothy George
Corney and Barrow Group Ltd
Corney and Barrow Limited

Friel, Lisa Natalie
Cool Apple Limited

Frigerio, Andrea
Family of Hounds Limited

Frigerio, Stefano
Frenchbubbles Limited

Frish, Howard Jonathan
JH Wine Agencies Ltd

Fritz, Franz Kwame
Tesh Beverages Limited

Frizzell, Alan William
BB & R Spirits Limited

Froggatt, Hugh Francis
Talbot & Barr Limited

Frost, Catherine Jill
DC Imports UK Ltd

Frost, George
The Westbourne Drinks Co Ltd

Frost, Paul
Snowy Taverns Ltd

Frost, Richard Fletcher
GNR Distillery Limited

Fruin, Elina
Roust UK Ltd

Fry, Alison Jane
The Italian Wine Club Ltd

Fry, Richard Paul William, Dr
The Italian Wine Club Ltd

Fryer, Anthony Robert
Charles Wells Brewery Limited
Charles Wells, Limited

Fuchs, Giles Michael Gummer
Gunners Cocktails Limited

Fudali Lara, Natalia
Grape Wines Services Ltd

Fuller, Mark Benton
Belfast Distillery Co Ltd

Fuller, Richard Hamilton Fleetwood
Nectar Imports Limited

Fullerton, Andrew
Beveridge Wines Ltd

Furlong, Max Leon
Incapico Inc Limited

Furnell, Julian Nicholas Candish
Viscount Agencies Limited

Furze, James Robert
New Generation Wines Limited

Furze, Mark Richard James
Two Pal's Co Ltd

Fyfe, Camilla
Kinkell Brewery Ltd

Fyfe, Rory John
Kinkell Brewery Ltd

Fyffe, James
Call-a-Keg (Scotland) Limited
JF Kegs (Scotland) Limited

Gabb, Harry Rollo
Cape Wine Exporters (UK) Ltd
Wine World Producers Limited

Gabriel, Alexander
Identity Drinks Brands Limited

Gaddes, Kelly de Burgh
Personalised Care Solutions Ltd

Gaffney-Dodds, Kristian Michael Thomas
Inception Drinks Limited

Gahagan, Patrick
Bonny Gin Ltd

Gain, Simon
Gain & Coombs Ltd

Gala, Biren
Jelly Bowl Ltd

Galand, Rudolph
More Sake Limited

Galbraith, James Joseph
L'Atypique Ltd

Galez, Christophe
Champagnes and Chateaux Ltd.

Gallacher, Deborah Elizabeth
Gallachers Fine Wines Limited

Gallacher, Douglas Martin
United Supplies Limited

Gallagher, Brendan Michael
Altar Wines Limited

Gallagher, Kevin Patrick
De Wetshof International Ltd

Gallagher, Margaret
T. & J.T. Barton (Bottlers) Ltd

Gallagher, Natalie
NDG (Hartlepool) Limited

Gallenzi, Filippo Giulio
FFM Pasta Co Ltd

Gallery, Neil
Art Entertainment Ltd

Gallice, Stephane
Bacchus Vin Ltd

Gallivan, Declan Emmet Cotterill
Vegan Wine Company London Ltd

Gallo, Ciro
Ambassador Commodities Ltd

Gallo, Giuseppe
Italicus Ltd

Gallon, Christina
The Funemployed Agency Ltd
The Funemployed Ltd

Gamage, Paul Lawrence
Batarak Limited
Cobblers Gin Limited

Gamage, Steven Paul
Cobblers Gin Limited
One Love Rum Co Ltd

Gamberucci, Claudia G Ina
Lafferty & Sons Ltd

Game, Martin
Northgate Wines Limited
Vinfinity Limited

Gammell, Matthew David Malcolm
The Snickering Pig Drinks Co Ltd
Spirits for Good CIC
Summerhall Distillery Asia Ltd

Gammie, Duncan George
The Wee Vinoteca Ltd

Ganatra, Mahek
Ace Incorporation Ltd

Gandhi, Jayantilal Chunilal
Mongoose Brewing Co Ltd

Ganley, Frank
Aran Beers Limited

Gant, Matthew John
New School Wines Limited

Garau, Luciano, Dr
Falugamaro International Ltd

Garcia Fernandez, Ana Maria
El Toro Wines Limited

Garcia, Leon Rodolfo
Lupe's Imports Limited

Garcia, Pascal Claude Jacques
Pascal Garcia Consulting Ltd

Garcia, Tansy Louise
Lupe's Imports Limited

Gard, Anthony Charles
The Drinks Guild Ltd

Gardener, David Squire
Nickolls & Perks Limited

Gardener, Jeremy Christopher
Vinceremos Wines & Spirits Ltd

Gardener, William John
Nickolls & Perks Limited

Gardner, Adam
Refresh 24 Group Limited

Gardner, Julian Paul
Dacastello Limited

Gardner, Norman Peter
City Wine Collection Limited

Gargani, Elena
Cru Prive Ltd

Garibaldo, Bortolo
TPSC Ltd

Garlick, Nigel Malcolm
Left Coast Distribution Ltd

Garner, Benjamin Robert James
The Ship & Mitre Brewing Co Ltd

Garnett, Michael John
Baby Bottles (Wholesale) Ltd

Garstang, Tiffany Fleur
Tilted Penguin Gin Ltd

Garstone, Dorothy Anne
Mieland Limited

Garstone, John, Dr
Mieland Limited

Garwood, Tony James
S & T Wines Limited

Gaskell, Lee Paul
Panache Natural Flavour Infusions

Gaskell, Peter
Cassago Imports Limited

Gasperin, Olivier
World Brands Duty Free Limited

Gasser, Moreno
Maurice Richard Ltd

Gauffre, Jean-Michel Hubert
Land'oc Wines Ltd

Gauffre, Karen
Land'oc Wines Ltd

Gaughan, Felicity Jane
The Atlantic Craft Soda Co Ltd

Gaughan, Gerard Brendan
The Atlantic Craft Soda Co Ltd

Gaughan, Thomas
The Salford Rum Co Ltd

Gaunt, Bradley Alan Dean
Momento Vivere Holdings Ltd

Gaur, Kshtiz Jude
The German Beer Co Limited

Gautam, Lov Bikram
Gurkha Beer Ltd

Gauthier, Christophe Maurice Eric Gabriel
Highlands Whisky Co Ltd

Gay, Charles Edward
Favela Cerveja Ltd

Gay, Frederick John
Favela Cerveja Ltd

Gay, Nicholas Robert
Drinkintime Ltd.

Gaynor, Anthony Vivian
Sheila's Rum Punch Ltd

Gee, Denise Pauline
Hot Corks Limited

Gee, Michael Noble
Hot Corks Limited

Gee, Nicholas Malcolm
Hot Corks Limited

Gee, Philippa
The Dulwich Spirits Co Ltd

Gee, Stephen Trevor
Direct Beers Limited

Gent, Nicholas James
RD Wines Limited

Georgel, Kevin Roger
St.Austell Brewery Co Ltd

Georgiou, Chariton Platon
Amathus Drinks PLC
Bablake Wines Limited

Georgiou, Isabella Ava
Amathus Drinks PLC
Bablake Wines Limited

Geraedts-Espey, Caroline
Xeco Wines Limited

Geraedts-Espey, Caroline May
The Last Drop Distillers Ltd

Germa, Erique Almagro
Blends Wine Estates UK Ltd

Gewanter, Henry Leonard
Natural Marketing Ltd

Ghazarians, Alex
Norvic Ltd

Gheorghe, Cezar Darius
Magazin Romanesc Ltd

Ghikas, Spyridon
Remy Cointreau UK Distribution Ltd

Ghosh, Amrita
Tender Vine Limited

Ghosh, Kaushik Rony
Legacy Wines & Beverages UK Ltd

Ghuman Begum, Azrar Ahmed
A A Suppliers Ltd

Ghuman, Balbir Singh
Euro Wines (C & C) Limited

Gianini, Sandro Richard
Maurice Richard Ltd

Gibbons, Andrew William
Amwell Springs Brewery Co Ltd

Gibbons, David Ernest
Amwell Springs Brewery Co Ltd

Gibbons, Michael David
Amwell Springs Brewery Co Ltd

Gibbs, Hilary
Domaine Direct Limited

Gibbs, Justin Geoffrey
Liv-Ex Limited

Gibney, Daniel James
Ferovinum Ltd

Gibson, Craig
JC Wholsale and Distribution Ltd

Gibson, Paul Fredrick
PFG Marketing Ltd

Gibson, Shirley Helen
PFG Marketing Ltd

Giesen, Alexander
Giesen Wines UK Limited

Giesen, Marcel
Giesen Wines UK Limited

Giesen, Theodor
Giesen Wines UK Limited

Gifkins, Lee Antony Robert
Top Deal Services Ltd

Giguashvili, Tamta
Marani Wines Limited

Gilbert, Klinton
Quamina Quality Drinks Co Ltd

Gilbey, Thomas Edward
The Vintner London Ltd

Gilchrist, Alan Colin
55 Above Ltd

Gilchrist, Iain
Philipshill Retirement Village Ltd
Raer Whisky Co Ltd
Raer Whisky Limited

Gill, Bhupinder Singh
VIP Bottles Ltd

Gill, Daljit Singh
Gill Cash & Carry Limited

Gill, Gurmeet Kaur
Cold Black Label Limited

Gill, Jagdeep
Double Measure Club Ltd

Gill, Keith
JKVK International Import and Export Ltd

Gill, Martin James Edgerton
Edgerton Holdings Limited

Gill, Patrick Anthony
New World Trading Europe Ltd.

Gill, Sandeep Singh
Quest Leisure Limited

Gill, Sohan Singh
Quest Leisure Limited

Gillan, Christopher Thomas
Heroes Drinks Company C.I.C.

Gillespie, Hamish Peregrine Curzon
North South Wines Limited

Gillett, Nicholas James
Mangrove Global Limited
Tortuga Brands Limited

Gilmour, Joseph Michael
Blast Vintners Ltd

Gilroy, Stephen Paul
House of Wine Limited

Ginolfi, Danilo
Pastai di Serino Italian Food and Wine Excellence

Gintrac, Jean-Pierre
Silenus Limited

Giolino, Mario
Decanter Trading Co Ltd

Giordano, Margherita
Tenuta Tremollito Wines Ltd

Giordano, Vincenzo
Tenuta Tremollito Wines Ltd

Giorgio, Nick
Ultra Premium Drinks Limited

Girelli, Stefano
North South Wines Limited

Gittens, Ian Hallam
A Taste of The Caribbean Ltd

Gladman, Philip Andrew
William Grant & Sons Brands Ltd
La Guilde du Cognac Limited

Gladwin, Shona Winter
The Whisky Seller Limited

Gladysz, Karolina
Spalco Ltd

Glancey, Stephen
C & C 2011 (NI) Limited
Tennent Caledonian Breweries UK Ltd
Tennent Caledonian Breweries Wholesale
Wallaces Express Limited

Glavana, Elena
Dallyla Ltd

Gleadowe, Frederick Joseph York, Dr
Shandy Shack Ltd

Gleave, David Charles
Liberty Wines Limited

Gleave, Matthew Sam
BI Wines and Spirits Limited

Glen, John Ronald Kerr
The Three Stills Co Ltd

Glenny, Jonathan William
Bielo Limited

Glover, Jessie Pearl
The Society of Vintners Ltd
V.C. Vintners Limited

Gobert, Julia
Bosco-UK Limited
La Delizia UK Limited

Godber-Ford Moore, James Kingsley Andrew
Whitmore and White Limited

Goddard, Marcus Garry Edward
3 Cities Brewing Co Ltd

Goddard, Michael Derek
Freixenet UK Ltd

Godden, Peter Thomas
Spirito Limited

Godfrey, Hugh Edward
Thomas Ridley and Son,Limited

Godfrey, Jennifer Patricia
Thomas Ridley and Son,Limited

Godfrey, Justin Alexander
Thomas Ridley and Son,Limited

Godwin, Charles
Seckford Wines Limited

Godwin, Laura Jane
Burgundys Collection Limited

Goedhuis, Jonathan Daniel
Goedhuis & Co Ltd
Vintage Capital II PLC

Goh, Jen Yeh
Kan Trading Limited

Goiti, Joseph
La Pata Negra Ltd

Goiti, Thomas
La Pata Negra Ltd

Gokani, Karan Anand
Tiger Vines Ltd

Gokani, Sunaina
Tiger Vines Ltd

Gol Mohammad, Alireza
London Calling Sweden Ltd

Goldenberg, Jehuda
Goldex International Ltd

Goldie, Ian Robert
Slightly Squiffy Limited

Goldie, Neil Robert
House of Townend Limited

Goldney, Darren Paul
Today's Wholesale Services Ltd

Goldsmith, Michelle
R & M Chateau Wines Ltd

Goldsmith, Richard Thomas
R & M Chateau Wines Ltd

Gomes Inacio Pinto, Antonio Jorge
Harama Trading Ltd

Gomes de Barros, Herman Stallone
Marlonn Food & Wine Ltd

Gomez Resendiz, Eduardo
Ojo de Dios Ltd

Gomez, Jorge
Silenus Limited

Gonitel, Roman, Dr
Portuguese Story Ltd

Gonultas, Alper
Preston Wines Ltd

Gonzalez-Gordon Lopez de Carrizosa, Mauricio
Gonzalez Byass UK Limited

Goodall, Julia
Real Ale Direct Limited

Goodhart, James Henry
Bon Coeur Fine Wines Limited

Goodhart, Samantha Jane
Bon Coeur Fine Wines Limited

Goodlad, Magnus James
Eythrope Wine Limited

Goodman, Simeon James
Label Bouchon Limited

Goodwin, Sarah Jane
Verre Anglais Limited

Goose, Duncan Hugh
Global Ethics Liquor Co Ltd

Gordon, Andrew Charles Ramsay
MBM Resource Trading International

Gordon, Frances Ann
Astonburgh Limited

Gordon, Shaun
Added Pressure Ltd

Gorlach, Mario
J & M Whisky Limited

Gormley, Rowan
Lay & Wheeler Limited
Majestic Wine PLC
Majestic Wine Warehouses Ltd
Naked Fine Wine Bonds PLC

Gorna, Barbara Elizabeth
Bad Girls Brew Limited

Gorosabel, Hector
Asahi Premium Brands Ltd
Asahi UK Ltd

Goroszeniuk, Teodor
Attitude Spirits Ltd

Gorrichon, Pierrick
Somm in the Must Ltd

Gors, Jordan
Sativatech Ltd

Gorst, Gina Blythe
Festina Drinks Ltd

Gorst, Robert Eric
Festina Drinks Ltd

Gorton, Robert David
Old St.Andrews Limited

Gosling, Christopher James
HG Wine Limited

Goss, Peter Edward
Mayfly Wine Co Ltd.

Gottardo, Fausto
Circus Enjoy with Us Ltd

Gould, Michael John
Noble Green Wines Limited

Gould, Russell Jonathan
The Fine Wine (Old World) Trading Co Ltd

Gould, Stephen
Everards Brewery Limited

Gouldsmith, James David Tze-Ming
The Original Herbale Brewing Co Ltd

Gourgeon, Frederic
Row & Co Ltd

Gourou, Alain
AGT Professional Services Ltd

Govender, Veneshen
Global Brands Trading Ltd

Govindaraju, Retnakumar
Kallwin Limited
Siris Trading Ltd

Gowing, Kieran
Diageo Northern Ireland Ltd

Goyal, Arun
Westworld Impex Limited

Graham, Alan Ronald
Scot Bottle Limited

Graham, Alasdair Innes Henderson
Malt Whisky Agency Ltd

Graham, Alexander
Malt Whisky Agency Ltd

Graham, Anthony Maxwell
Churchill Graham Limited

Graham, Helen
Malt Whisky Agency Ltd

Graham, Jamie Ambrose Kirke
Brunswick Fine Wines and Spirits Ltd

Graham, Janet Shirley
Scot Bottle Limited

Graham, John Lochiel
Churchill Graham Limited

Graham, Paul Alexander
Alexander Wines Ltd.

Graham, Zoe
The International Spirit Vault Ltd

Grainger, Simon
Grainger Fine Wines Ltd

Gramajo Caballero, Bernabe Augusto
La Aurora Ltd

Gramsch, Michael
Erin Vintners Ltd

Gramza, Lukasz
City Wine Collection Limited

Grant, Claude
Michel Roux Limited

Grant, Colin
C & D Exports Ltd

Grant, George
Shindigger Craft Beer Ltd

Grant, Ryan
Grizzly Endeavours Ltd

Granville, Angela Mary
C'est Nous UK Ltd

Granville, Michael
C'est Nous UK Ltd

Gravouil, Antoine
Ossau Vins & Spiritueux Ltd

Gray, Angela Caroline
Vitkovitch Brothers Limited

Gray, Lucinda Rachel
Hall & Woodhouse Limited

Gray, Pavlina
Crystle Limited

Gray, Peter Alan
Crystle Limited

Gray, Robin MacEwan
LWC Drinks Limited
H.T.White & Co Ltd

Gray, Stephen David
Supermalt UK Limited

Grayshon, Neil
I'll Ask The Boys Ltd

Greaves, Benedict Scott
Winecall Limited

Greaves, James
SSL Leisure Limited

Greaves, Ryan Martin
Tirg Limited

Grebenkin, Iurii
Edrington-Beam Suntory UK Distribution

Greco, Barbara
International Business Solutions Ltd

Green, Harrison Aldrich
Albion Gin Ltd

Green, John Ramon
Bordeaux and Beyond Ltd

Green, Kevin
Jays Trading Ltd

Green, Lewis Geoff
Pug Vodka Ltd

Green, Mark
Rachael Green Limited

Green, Rachael
Rachael Green Limited

Green, Simon
Tudor Drinks Ltd

Green, Stefan Courtney
Stida Beverages Ltd

Greenberg, Riki
Select Whisky Limited

Greene, Julian Patrick Ashley
The Wine Treasury Limited

Greenhalgh, Nicholas Anthony
Pomona Island Brew Co Ltd

Greenhalgh, Paul Robert
L'Atelier Terroir Limited

Greenhalgh, Victoria Vladimirovna
L'Atelier Terroir Limited

Greening, Nicola Megan Jane
Cornish Point Wines UK Ltd

Greening, Nigel
Cornish Point Wines UK Ltd

Greenwold, John Roland
Beerfantastic Ltd
Winefantastic Limited

Greenwood, Rita Marie
William Grant & Sons Brands Ltd
William Grant & Sons UK Ltd

Gregory, Pamela
Hannibal Brown Wine Services Ltd

Gregory, Sean Michael
Lacons Brewery Limited

Grewal, Navindh
Vivir Drinks Ltd

Grewal, Sukhvir Singh
Sarpanch Food & Wine Distributors Ltd

Grice, Arthur Joseph
Winning Invest & Trade Ltd

Griessel, Hendrik Jacobus
First Cape Vineyards Ltd

Grieve, Ian
Hopper House Brew Farm Ltd

Griffin, Jacob, Dr
Up Front Brewing Limited

Griffith, Keri Nichole
Ascott Invest Limited

Griffith, Mark
Eventus Global Ltd

Griffiths, Dean John
Cotswold Wines Ltd

Griffiths, Neil Robert Ceidrych
Starstock Ltd

Griffiths, Paul James
The Select Wine Co Ltd

Griffiths, Simon John
Cotswold Wines Ltd

Grigg, Daniel Stephen
Museum Wines Limited

Grigoras, Nadina
Mina Collection Ltd

Grigoriou, Konstantinos
Ormos Trades Limited

Grigsby, Bernard Candler
Corney and Barrow Group Ltd
Corney and Barrow Limited

Grime, Hugh
Hops and Dots Brewing Co Ltd

Grimes, David
Landmark Wholesale Limited

Grimshaw, Jacob Andrew
JG Sousa Limited

Grimwood, Paul William
Ultracomida Trading Co. Ltd

Grindlay, George Scotland
Scotland Grindlay Limited

Grindlay, Moira Elizabeth
Scotland Grindlay Limited

Grivach, Aleksandre
The Tall Blond UK Ltd

Grkajac, Mirko
Sco & Whisky Limited

Grocott, Philip George
Simply Cask Ltd

Groen, Jasper Rogier
Bubbles for Friends Ltd.

Grogan, Amanda
Pub Pool (711) Limited

Grogan, Terry
Pub Pool (711) Limited

Groinen, Tal Isreael
T.W.S Wines Ltd

Gronow, Glyn David
Crafty Wolf (Drinks) Limited
Crafty Wolf Limited

Grosse Mac Dougall, Jorge Alberto
Gonzalez Byass UK Limited

Grotto, Augusto
Prosit Wines Limited

Groves, Barry Nigel
Fine Drinks Cooperative Ltd
Wine Rascals Yorkshire Limited

Gruenefeld, Fritz
River Drinks Ltd

Gruenefeld, Max Christian Friedrich
River Drinks Ltd

Grundy, Paul Donald
Silvertip Imports Limited

Gu, Haiping
Jiangsu Wine Trading Co Ltd

Guan, Zhuqing
Cheng International Co Limited

Gudmundsson, Thor Hallgrimur
Gudfish Limited

Gueret, Basile Hubert Serge
Under The Bonnet Wines Limited

Guerin, Marie-Caroline
Wine-Invest Ltd

Guerin, Nicolas
Wine-Invest Ltd

Guerra Fagalde, Lorenzo
Martin Miller's Gin Limited

Guest, Kelvyn
Guest Wines & Co. Ltd

Guest, Ruth
Guest Wines & Co. Ltd

Guindi, Alan Claude
Hochfeld International Ltd

Guirao, Josep
Foodiebusters Epic Food Authority Ltd

Gul, Mian
GM Catering Supplies Ltd

Gulati, Kulwant Singh
All Drinks Cash & Carry Ltd

Gulliver, Andrew Grant
Berkeley Cellars Limited
London Wine Eis Limited

Gulliver, Stuart Thomas
Samuel Gulliver & Co. Limited

Gulliver, Trevor
HG Wine Limited

Gulotta, Jean-Claude
Mercanti Imports Limited

Gultekin, Haydar
EFE Store Limited

Gunn, Johanna
Angeli Del Vino Limited

Gunson, Dion John
Gunson Fine Wines Limited

Gunther, Martin Louis Leon
Kol App Ltd

Guo, Yang
Wave Wine Ltd

Gupta, Akshit Raj
3ABC Ltd
Jocks and Peers Brewing Co Ltd

Gurney, Nicholas John
John E.Fells & Sons Limited

Gurrieri, Giovanni Gian Battista
Gianni. B. Limited

Gurrieri, Jonathan
Gianni. B. Limited

Gurung, Ishor Jung
AMK Distribution Ltd

Gusic, Nebojsa
Orbit Wines Limited

Guthrie, Charlene
NM Lesuire Ltd

Gutierrez, Peter
The Idle Hour Spirit Co Ltd

Guy, Adam John
Laurent-Perrier (UK) Limited

Guzman, Ignasi
G & G International BCN Ltd

Gvajaia, Solomon
Spirits Logistics Ltd

Gwizdala, James Peter Anthony
Witek Spirits Ltd

Gyenes, Monika Konstantina
Best of Hungary Ltd

Haag, Steven Joseph
Master Spirits Limited

Habtezghi, Pawlos
Robel Import Trading Ltd

Hackney, Kenton
3Squires Ltd
3Squires Wines Ltd

Haddrell, Mark Christopher
Zinstream Wine Limited

Haddrell, Olivia Kathryn
Zinstream Wine Limited

Haddrell, Roger Paul
S and S Wines Limited

Hadfield, Thomas Nicholas
Applethwaite Wines Ltd

Hadfield-Hyde, Sebastian James Anthony Aiden
Kimbland Distillery Ltd

Hadley, Taylor
Valerieblue Ltd

Haggitt, Helene Rose
The Tasting Barn Ltd

Hague, Daniel
Perfect Pair Wines Ltd

Hague, Staci
Perfect Pair Wines Ltd

Haidacher, Peter
Berkmann Family Holdings Ltd

Haigh, Daniel Joseph
Sell My Wine Ltd

Hainsworth, Stewart Andrew
The Bajan Trading Co Ltd
Barwell & Jones Limited
The Cornish Rum Co Ltd
Chalie Richards & Co Ltd

Haisma, Mark John
Beef and Burgundy Limited

Haite, Brian
Prime Drinks Ltd

Halbach, Bernd Friedrich Kurt
Freixenet UK Ltd

Hald, Nicolai
Alky Limited

Haley, Paul
West Coast Wines & Spirits Ltd.

Hall, Gordon Philip
Bijou Bottles Limited

Hall, Jennifer Mary
The Cocktail Pickers Club Ltd

Hall, Lawrence John
The Little Big Wine Co Ltd

Hall, Lukasz
Banini UK Ltd

Hall, Michael Wellington
MWH Wine Agencies Ltd
MWH Wine Merchants Limited

Hall, Robert Campbell
HM47 Investment Projects Ltd

Hallet, Nicolas
Appellations Limited

Halley, Brian Dundas
Slanj Whisky Ltd

Halley, Craig
Slanj Whisky Ltd

Halliday, Ian Kenneth
Rippingale Promotions Limited

Halliday, Patrick Lovell
Raisin Social Limited

Halliday, Simon George
Raisin Social Limited
Vinafrica Limited

Halpern, Mordecai
Kedem Europe Limited

Halsey, Paul
Purity Brewing Co Ltd

Halstead, Barry Christopher
Ojo de Dios Ltd

Hambleton, Christopher Andrew
Bacchus Wine Auctions Limited

Hambleton, Helen Louise
Bacchus Wine Auctions Limited

Hamblin, Richard
More Wine Ltd
Ragtag Wines Ltd

Hameed, Riaz Mohammad
Hameed Investments Limited

Hames, Peter Andrew
Vins Ltd

Hamilton, Christopher Edward
Neil Morrissey Real Ale Co Ltd

Hamilton, David Lindsay Emerson
Occidental & Oriental Cellars Ltd
Vinum Fine Wines Limited

Hamilton, Iain Lindsay
2I Whiskies Limited
Old Town Blending Co Ltd

Hamilton, Irene McKay
2I Whiskies Limited

Hamilton, Nichola Irene
2I Whiskies Limited

Hamilton, Stuart
Maestral de Provence Ltd.

Hammond, Anthony
TH Nightlife Ltd

Hammond, Charlotte Felicity
Teqcoola Limited

Hammond, Jonathan
Hammonds of Knutsford PLC
Paragon Brands Limited

Hammond, Rejane Elizabeth
G.W. Fields & Sons (Great Yarmouth)

Hammond, Sarah Lucy Hancock
Hammonds of Knutsford PLC

Hammond, Thomas James
Amwell Springs Brewery Co Ltd

Hampden-White, Colin George, Sir
Cask Trade Ltd

Han, Mi Kyung
Woori Trade Ltd

Hancock, Edward
Marston's Acquisitions Limited

Hancock, Paul Geoffrey
La Guilde du Cognac Limited

Hancock, Toby Charles Petre
10 International Limited

Handy, Robert Mark
Konigsberg Seven Bridges Breweries Ltd

Hanjra, Manjit Singh
Punjabi Ltd

Hannah, Gregor
Hannah Whisky Merchant's Ltd

Hannah, Simon John
Brewgooder Limited
J.W. Filshill International Ltd

Hannaway, Christopher John
Infinite Session Ltd

Hannaway, Thomas Eamon
Infinite Session Ltd

Hanys, Sam
Loughborough Student Services Ltd

Hardcastle, Keith
Meridian Centre Hospitality Ltd

Hardcastle, Simon Edwin Peter
Estini Ltd

Harding, Francis Ronald Mark
Blux UK Import Ltd

Harding, Ian Andrew
Majestic Wine PLC

Harding, Julia
Xardins Wines and Cava Ltd

Harding, Keith James
Baby Bottles (Wholesale) Ltd

Harding, Mark Robert
7 Day Cellar Limited

Hardwick, Thomas
Innovative Cocktails Ltd

Hardwicke-Wall, Clare Lynne
Grape and Grain Management Ltd

Hare, Jasdip
Magic Spells Brewery Limited

Harford, Edward Scandrett
Wadworth and Co Ltd

Hariyani, Aashima
Globus Wines (UK) Ltd

Harkus, Oliver
Tinnies Ltd

Harlington, Jerome Alexander
Jerome Harlington Limited
Harlington Wine Limited
Trailblazing Wine Ltd

Harlow, John
Dragon Drinks Limited

Harlow, Stephen David
Dragon Drinks Limited

Harper, James
UK Lesiure Ltd

Harper, Susan
Armit Holding Limited

Harriman, Benjamin Peter
The Bloomsbury Distillery Ltd

Harrington, Christopher
Casa Cocktails Limited

Harris, Charlie
Two Toes Ltd

Harris, Craig Allan
Distillers Direct Ltd
Kater Four (Cash & Carry) Ltd

Harris, Jessica Clair
Appellations Limited

Harris, Joanne
Windermere Wine Stores Limited

Harris, Josh Alan Micheal Paul
Smith & Harris Enterprises Ltd.

Harris, Julie Ann
Harris Filters Limited
R & J Harris Ltd

Harris, Philip Lewis
Davenport Vineyards Limited

Harris, Robert John
Harris Filters Limited
R & J Harris Ltd

Harris, Sam
Teca Wines Limited

Harris, Stephen
Bucklebury Brewers Ltd

Harrison, Alexander James
Young Malt Co Ltd

Harrison, Daniel Robert
Import Brothers Limited

Harrison, Douglas Michael
The Best of America Limited
The Best of California Limited

Harrison, Douglas Michael
The Best of Beaujolais Limited
The Best of Bordeaux Limited
The Best of Burgundy Limited
The Best of Loire Limited

Harrison, Edward Peter Douglas
Clements Harrison Limited

Harrison, Fiona Louise
Spain Link Ltd

Harrison, James
The Salford Rum Co Ltd

Harrison, Lydia
Best of Champagne Limited
Best of France Limited
Best of Italy Limited
Best of Portugal Limited
Best of Spain Limited

Harrison, Michael Anthony
Cape Wines Limited

Harrison, Sara Penelope Ritchie
The Circle Wine Co Ltd

Harrison, Simon Nicholas
Harrisons Fine Wines Limited

Harrison, Steven
HBN Ltd

Harrison, Susan Rose
Harrisons Fine Wines Limited

Harrowell, Graeme Nigel
Deliverance Dot Com Limited

Harrowell, Neill Anthony
Montymac Vintners Ltd

Harrsion, Lydia
Best of New World Limited

Hart, David
CDGH Pub Co Ltd

Hart, Ian Nicholas
Ian Hart Distilling Limited
Sacred Spirits Holdings Ltd

Hart, John Blair
Flying Firkin Distribution Ltd

Hart, Samuel Lewis
Winnack and Hart Industries Ltd

Hartley, Gordon Michael
The Bosun's Brewery Tap Ltd

Hartley, Jill
Ital Sardo Limited

Hartley, Oliver
Corney and Barrow Limited

Hartley, Robert Daniel Fergus
Fair City Spirits Limited

Hartnett, Denis
Vintage Wine Investments Ltd

Harvey, Geoffrey Austin
New Generation Wines Limited

Harvey, John Michael
Quality Spirits International Ltd

Harvey, Richard Neville
Richard Harvey Wines Limited

Harvey, Sara Lorelei
Richard Harvey Wines Limited

Harvey-Jones, Richard William
Seckford Agencies Limited
Seckford Wines Limited

Harwood, Holly
H Harwood Ltd

Harwood, Peter John
Ellis of Richmond Limited

Harwood, Simon Andrew
Wycombe Wine Co Ltd

Haselden, Kathleen Alice
Good Food Wines Limited

Haselden, Kevin William Geoffrey
Good Food Wines Limited

Haseman, Louis
Fah Mai Holdings Limited
Rare Whisky Auctioneers Ltd

Hasmanda, Jiri
Winery Jakubik UK Ltd

Hasmandova, Martina
Winery Jakubik UK Ltd

Hassall, Catherine Ann
European Brand Trading Limited

Hassall, Daniel Michael
J M & D Limited

Hassall, Norman
European Brand Trading Limited

Hassan, Mohammed Saber
Crescent Fine Foods Ltd

Hassan, Salih
Tower International Limited

Hatami, Maryam
Drinks To Go Plus Ltd

Hatfield, Roger
Mayfair Brands Limited

Haughton, Georgina Ruth
Delage & Haughton Limited

Haughton, Thomas Patrick
Delage & Haughton Limited

Haussels, May
C. & O. Wines Limited
Squarewalk Limited

Havenhand, Amy Jayne
Deco Spirits Limited

Hawes, Andrew James
Mentzendorff & Co Ltd

Hawgood, Craig Andrew
Taste Merchants Ltd

Hawgood, Dale Peter
Taste Merchants Ltd

Hawgood, Duncan James
Taste Merchants Ltd

Hawgood, Geoffrey Frank
Taste Merchants Ltd

Hawgood, Neville John
Taste Merchants Ltd

Hawgood, Rosemary Ann
Taste Merchants Ltd

Hawkins, Colin Charles
D'Urberville Vineyard Limited

Hawkins, Daniel
Levin Trading Limited

Hawksworth, James Andrew
Pivovar Ltd

Haworth, David Anthony
Pernod Ricard UK Limited

Haxhijani, Saimir
AGS Vintners Limited

Hay, Jack Justin Whitby
Local Beer Delivered Ltd

Hayes, Ann Margaret
Ann et Vin Limited

Hayes, Fiona Ann
Grape and Nectar Ltd

Hayes, Gary
Black Dog Gin Co Ltd

Hayes, Martin Patrick
Artisan Beer Import Co Ltd

Hayes, Neythan Edward
Kernow Rum Co Ltd

Hayes, Paul
Vivir Drinks Ltd

Hayman, Christopher Frank
Thames Distillers Limited

Haynes, Jason Clive Patrick
Flint Wines Limited

Haynes, Kerryn Louise
Diageo Great Britain Limited

Haynes, Michael
Vitesse Vintners Limited

Haythorne, Lesley Karan
Pant y Foel Gin Ltd

Hayward, Brandon
Hayward Bros (Wines) Limited

Hayward, James
Iron Pier Brewery Limited

Hayward, James Brandon
Hayward Bros (Wines) Limited

Hayward, Robert Brandon
Hayward Bros (Wines) Limited

Hayward, Sarah Jayne
Hayward Bros (Wines) Limited

Hayzelden, Charmaine Louisa
Spirimix Limited

Hazell, Gary Elias Jamali
Brummells Gin Limited

Headlam, Patrick John
Uncharted Wine Co Ltd.

Heald, Andrew Michael Hilliard
Fishers Gin Ltd
Sagittarius Royaume-Uni Ltd
Sagittarius World Limited

Heald, Michael Guy Hilliard
Adnams PLC
Fishers Gin Ltd
Sagittarius Royaume-Uni Ltd

Healey, Jennifer Lisa
Buckingtons Ltd

Healy, Michael Christopher
Brewbarge Limited

Hearnden, Stephen
Taste Buds Wines Limited

Heath, Richard
Heath London Limited

Heath, Richard Stuart
Keltek Cornish Brewery Limited

Heath, Stuart
Keltek Cornish Brewery Limited

Heath, William Generald Charles
Keltek Cornish Brewery Limited

Heer, Gina Kaur
The Wine Cellar Midlands Ltd

Heeran, Carmel
Hidden Gem - Urban Artisan Spirit Ltd

Heerema, Eric Niels
South Downs Real Estate Ltd

Heffernan, Riona
C & C 2011 (NI) Limited

Heginbottom, David
Diageo Great Britain Limited
Justerini & Brooks,Limited

Heidsieck, Frederic
Maisons Marques et Domaines Ltd

Heley, David George
Celebration Drinks Limited

Heley, Michael Thomas
Celebration Drinks Limited

Helliwell, Maxine
Evokesomm Limited

Hempshall, Debra Ann
Philsner Ltd

Hempshall, Emma Louise
Philsner Ltd

Hempshall, Kerry Alissia
Philsner Ltd

Hempshall, Philip Charles
Philsner Ltd

Henderson, Alexander Giles Fergus
HG Wine Limited

Henderson, Crawford
C & R Wines Limited

Henderson, Ewan John
William Grant & Sons Brands Ltd
William Grant & Sons UK Ltd
Quality Spirits International Ltd

Henderson, Richard
C & R Wines Limited

Hennings, Edward Charles
Hennings Wine Merchants Ltd

Hennings, Matthew Edward
Hennings Wine Merchants Ltd

Henry, Deborah
Alcofrolics Ltd

Henry, Delphine
Henry de Vaugency Ltd

Henry, Pascal
Henry de Vaugency Ltd

Henshaw, Ben Jon Michael
Biercraft Ltd
Indigo Wine Limited

Henshaw, Benedict Jon Michael
Triangle Wines Limited

Henshaw, Marvin James
Premium Beverage Refreshments Ltd

Henshaw, Stacey Caroline
Indigo Wine Limited

Hepburn, Anna Mary
J.W.G. PLC

Hepburn, George Garland
J.W.G. PLC
Landmark Wholesale Limited

Hepburn, Kenneth Andrew
Coddington Hepburn Limited

Herbert, Evan
Beer Me Now Ltd

Herbert, Raymond Peter
Bucklebury Brewers Ltd

Herbert, Richard Stanley
Hobo Beer & Co Ltd

Hercules, Ian Joseph
Euro-Trade and Finance Limited

Hernandez, Antonio Hernandez
Atlantis Iberica Ltd

Hernandez, Diego Palacio
SP (DPH) Exports Limited

Hernandez, Roberto Sanchez
Wineologia Ltd

Herrando, Vicente
C & D Wines Limited

Herrero Rodriguez, Armando
H & G Corporation Ltd

Hertzenberg, Wiebke
Alfa Drinks Limited

Herzog, Morris
Kedem Europe Limited
Refined Wine Club Ltd.

Hesketh, Michael David
Laurent-Perrier (UK) Limited

Hesley, Laszlo
Mephisto Wine Merchants Ltd

Hess, Henri Louis
Liberty Wines Limited

Hess, Martin Hugo
Bondi Brands Limited
Bondi Brewery Limited

Hester, Karen
Adnams PLC

Hetherington, Andrew John
C.P.A.'s Wine Limited

Hetherington, Graeme
Angus Wines Limited

Hewings, Mark Edward
Retro Shotz Limited

Hewitson, Mark
Stedman Bros. (Events) Limited

Hewitt, Ian
Spitfire Heritage Distillers Ltd

Hewitt, Sarah Vanessa Jane
Spitfire Heritage Distillers Ltd

Hewitt, Stephen William
Victoria Garry Group Ltd

Hewson, Ian
The Wineman Limited

Hewson, Paula
The Wineman Limited

Hewson, Thomas David
Crundale Wines Limited

Heyes, Penelope Ann
The Great Wine Group Limited

Heywood Lonsdale, Tom Norman
Genesis Wines Limited

Hibberd, Jennifer Mary
Vin D'Oc Limited

Hibberd, Robin Victor Bruce
Vin D'Oc Limited

Hibbert, Aaron Marcus
Kapaka Limited
World of Drinks Limited

Hibbert, Marcus
River Widow Brewery Ltd

Hicks, Robert James
Highland Liquor Co Ltd

Hicks, Sara Louise
Vranken Pommery UK Ltd.

Hickson, James Charles
The Beer Boutique Ltd
Two Heads Beer Co Limited

Hidalgo, Luis Emilio Vargas
Strategos Limited

Higgins, David Graham
Rok Drinks Limited

Higgins, John
Better Buy Ltd

Higgins, Paul Justus
Allum Limited

Higgins, Peter James
Investmentwine Ltd

Higginson, Rose
Whisky Rebellion Limited

Higginson, Thomas William Farnorth
Kicking Horse Ltd.

Higgon, Shane David
Ascona Retail (Leases) Limited

Higham, Stephen
Duple Social Club Sth Shore BPL . Ltd

Hikki, Mohammed
Jezba Ltd

Hilder, Paul William
CSS On-Trade Limited
Compass Supply Solutions Ltd

Hiley, William John Haviland
C N Drinks Limited

Hill Smith, Michael Sidney
Liberty Wines Limited

Hill, Andrew Richard
4 Rabbits Ltd

Hill, Andrew Steven
Geo Hill (Grocers) Limited

Hill, Anthony William
Bordeaux and Beyond Ltd

Hill, Christopher Charles
Latitude Wine Limited

Hill, David
Barmaster (Independant Wholesalers)
Beer Supply Limited
Blue Star Inns Limited
Cooper Hill Brewery Ltd

Hill, Derek
House of Townend Limited

Hill, John
Enny Wines Ltd

Hill, John George
Direct Wine Importers Limited

Hill, Mark Adrian Bryan
The Brewers Wholesale Limited

Hill, Mark Douglas
Pale Fox Wines Limited

Hill, Nicky Lee
Beer Supply Limited
Blue Star Inns Limited

Hill, Oliver Colin Robert
Sybarite Cellars Limited

Hill-Smith, Robert Wyndham
John E.Fells & Sons Limited
Negociants Europe Limited
Negociants UK Limited

Hillier, Adam
My Gin My Way Ltd

Hillman, Aaron Nicholas
Angus Dundee Distillers PLC
The Illicit Spirit Co. Limited

Hillman, Benjamin Daniel
Bodega Uncielo (UK) Limited

Hillman, Colleen Eileen
Wineservice Limited

Hillman, Jean Elizabeth
Angus Dundee Distillers PLC

Hillman, Mark
Red Dragon Brewery Ltd.

Hillman, Nicholas
Merchant Vintners Co Ltd
Wineservice Limited

Hillman, Tania
Angus Dundee Distillers PLC
The Illicit Spirit Co. Limited

Hillman, Terence Michael
Angus Dundee Distillers PLC

Hilmi, Alpay
Tower International Limited

Hilton, Adam James
Hilton & Rowley Ltd

Hilton, Marcus James
Prosecco 1754 Limited

Hilton-Johnson, Oliver Rupert
Tengu Sake Limited

Hinch, Julie
Cathedral Wholesale and Events Ltd

Hincks, Alexandra Lesley
Brockmans Gin Limited

Hine, John William Sampson
Vitesse Vintners Limited

Hinks, Paul
Brand Central (UK) Limited

Hipkin, Richard James
Chateau Wines Ltd.

Hipner, Romuald Jan
Poleczka Limited

Hiraide, Soji
Kanpai (London) Food and Beverage Management Co.,

Hirst, Luke
Vino Pronto UK Ltd

Hirst, Noel
Le Bon Vin Limited

Hirt, Liam Scott, Dr
Psychopomp Ltd

Hitchen, Jessica Anne Frances
Morgan Jupe Limited

Hitchins, Nicholas Charles Vedat
Caspian Black Limited

Ho, Anthony Tinchon
Hobros Limited

Ho, Timothy Tinloch
Hobros Limited

Ho, Yu Hung
Harvies of Edinburgh Limited
Speyside Bonding Co Ltd
Speyside Distillers Co Ltd

Hoare Aranda, Sara
Rico Rico Ltd

Hoare, David Harry Christopher
Hall & Woodhouse Limited

Hobhouse, Charles Howard
Punchy Drinks Limited

Hochar, Gaston
Chateau Musar (U.K.) Limited

Hochar, Ronald
Chateau Musar (U.K.) Limited
Chateau Musar International Ltd

Hockedy, Thomas Elliot
Melius Drinks Ltd.

Hocking, James Rylett
James Hocking Wine Limited

Hocking, Joscelyn Frances
James Hocking Wine Limited

Hodder, Brian Gregory
Majestic Wine PLC

Hodgkinson, Neil
Drop The Anchor Brewery Ltd

Hodgkinson, Nicholas David
The Bottle Bank Limited

Hodgson, Jonathan
The Great Newsome Brewery Ltd

Hodgson, Laurence
The Great Newsome Brewery Ltd

Hodgson, Raef Thomas Le Roy
Gergovie Wines Limited

Hodovanets, Oleh
USSR Limited

Hodson, Matthew
The Great Newsome Brewery Ltd

Hoffmann, Ilse Amlot
Amlot Morgan Fine Wines Ltd

Hofstad, Tore
That Wineshop Limited

Hohnen, David James
Crackerjack Wines Limited

Holden, Amelia Grace
Layered Ltd

Holden, John
Village Cottages (Cornwall) Ltd

Holden, Max Yashar
Village Cottages (Cornwall) Ltd

Holden, Scott Thomas
Layered Cakes Ltd
Layered Ltd

Holdsworth Hunt, Christopher
Vintage Capital II PLC

Holdsworth, Claire Denise
Holdsworth Spirits & Co Ltd

Holdsworth, Jonathan
Pivovar Ltd

Holdsworth, Mark Philip
Holdsworth Spirits & Co Ltd

Holford, Mark Douglas
Red Squirrel Wine Ltd.

Holland, Alison
Kairos Solutions Ltd

Holland, Martin
Kairos Solutions Ltd

Hollas, Lydia
Vintage 1947 Limited

Hollinshead, Dominick Chad
Los Perros Sueltos Brewing Co Ltd

Holloway, Karen Elizabeth
F.L. Dickins Limited

Hollyhead, David
Stanley Marlow & Son Limited

Holmes, Fiona Alison
1879 Brand Ventures Ltd.

Holmes, Martin David
North West Spirits Limited

Holmes, Miriam Roseanna
The Lazy Hare Limited

Holmes, Peter Andrew
1879 Brand Ventures Ltd.

Holstein, Louise
Uncharted Wine Co Ltd.

Holt, Thomas William
Paso-Primero UK Ltd.

Holtam, Oliver Christian Wynn
Occidental & Oriental Cellars Ltd
Vinum Fine Wines Limited

Holzberg, Sophie Marie Martine
Bon Vin Inc. Limited
Sophie's Choice Limited

Hone, George Richard
Manor Park Drinks Ltd.

Hone, Richard John
Manor Park Drinks Ltd.

Honegger, Peter
Newcomer Wines Limited

Honing, Jan
Waterland Trading Limited

Honorez, Christian Pierre
H2vin Limited

Hood, Sarah Louise, Dr
Conroy-Hood Limited

Hooda, Manisha
Trinewine Ltd

Hook, Paul Robert
Bellwether Wines Ltd
Morley Way Limited
Nene Charter Co Ltd

Hooper, John Vernon
Worthington Wine and Spirits UK Ltd

Hooper, Matthew Vernon
Vernon Scott Limited

Hoose, Adrian
A.P. Claxton Ltd

Hoose, Jack Edward
A.P. Claxton Ltd

Hooton, Karen
Hooton Management Limited

Hope, John Frederick
Churnet Valley Drinks Limited
H.B.Clark & Co.(Successors) Ltd
Kitwave Limited
M.& M.Value Limited
Thorne Licence Wholesale Ltd

Hopkins, Ashley
Liv-Ex Limited

Hopkins, Christopher Thomas Howard
Hydes' Brewery Limited

Hopkins, Mark
Tasteturkey Limited

Horn, Anker
Traderhorn Limited

Horn, Sally
Traderhorn Limited

Horney, Laura
Brown Bear Tales Ltd

Hornsby, Neil Alistair
Charente Enterprises Limited

Hornsby, Sheila Ann Mary
Charente Enterprises Limited

Horrigan, Ian Robert
Sefton Beer Co Ltd

Horrocks, David James
QNGC Limited

Horsman, Justin Paul
Samuel Gulliver & Co. Limited

Horton, Anthony Ernest
J & A Drinks Limited

Horton, David Howard
Wm.Addison (Newport) Limited

Horton, Jonathan Michael
J & A Drinks Limited

Horton, Jonathan William Addison
Wm.Addison (Newport) Limited

Horton, Lesley Anne
Wm.Addison (Newport) Limited

Hosking, Keith
K & S Hosking Ltd

Hosking, Shaughan
K & S Hosking Ltd

Hothersall, Michael Henry
Mike Hothersall Wines Limited

Hothersall, Valerie
Mike Hothersall Wines Limited

Hou, Wenqi
Mr. Alba International Trading Co Ltd

Hoult, Michael Charles
House of Wine Limited

Household, Richard Edward
The Brompton Wine Co Ltd

Hovington, Catherine Maria
Friends of Wine Ltd

Hovington, James
Friends of Wine Ltd

Hovington, Peter Anthony
Friends of Wine Ltd

Howard, Derrick
Drink Link Grimsby Limited

Howarth, Barry Peter
Lancaster Wines Limited

Howarth, Fiona Mary
Lancaster Wines Limited

Howcroft, Kathleen Florence
Whitebridge Wines Limited

Howden, Stephen Francis
Apical Breweries UK Ltd

Howe, Andrew Neil
Anglo Drinks Limited

Howes, Catherine Margaret
Modern Vintage Wines Ltd

Howes, Donald Wayne
DCFT Investments Ltd.
Modern Vintage Wines Ltd

Howie, Craig
Molvino Fine Wine & Spirits Co Ltd

Howie, Lawrence Jamieson
Molvino Fine Wine & Spirits Co Ltd

Howkins, Ben Walter
Eythrope Wine Limited

Howkins, Catrin Rachel
Worldwide Drinks Limited

Howkins, John Martin
Worldwide Drinks Limited

Howkins, Peter James
H & W Wines Limited

Hriplivii, Irina
Novus BH Magister Ltd

Hriplivii, Sergiu
Novus BH Magister Ltd

Huang, Yinyin
Summerforever Ltd

Hudson, Frances
Tilted Penguin Gin Ltd

Hudson, Thomas Edward
Farr Vintners Limited

Hugget, Jodi
GBW Subscriptions Ltd

Hughes, Abby
Sopwell Gin Co Ltd

Hughes, Corin Simon
Craftibeer Limited

Hughes, David Matthew
Via Academia Vocatus Ltd

Hughes, Elliot
Liquid Projects International Ltd

Hughes, Gregory
Dark Revolution Ltd

Hughes, Nana Anowa
Think Wine Group Ltd

Hughes, Sean
Bondi Brands Limited

Hughes, Tanya
Dark Revolution Ltd

Hughes, Trevor
Trevor Hughes Wines Limited

Hughes-D'aeth, Paul Andrew
Hatch Mansfield Cellars Ltd

Hull, Richard John
Export and Import Trading Ltd

Human, Steven James
Koa Brewing Limited

Humphrey, Neil
Python Controls Ltd

Humphrey, Sandra Carol
Python Controls Ltd

Humphreys, Daniel
Cullercoats Gin Co Ltd

Humphreys, Michael Hubert
Angus Dundee Distillers PLC

Humphreys, William Grant
Cape Secrets Limited

Humphries, Carol Anne
Spiced Wine Co Ltd

Humphries, Jason John, Dr
Digby Fine English Ltd
Digby Wine Ltd

Humphries, Paul
Spiced Wine Co Ltd

Humphris, Roderick
Trade Wines Ltd

Hunger, Markus
Spirit Still Ltd

Hunstone, James
Jimmy's Beer & Gas (Wirral) Ltd

Hunt, Alexander Julian
Berkmann Wine Cellars Limited

Hunt, Brian Clifford
Tipple Transport Limited

Hunt, Charles
Thorman Hunt & Co Limited

Hunt, James Oliver
James E. McCabe Limited
Philip Russell Limited

Hunt, James Patrick
James E. McCabe Limited
Philip Russell Limited

Hunt, Jeremy John Thorman
Thorman Hunt & Co Limited

Hunt, John Simon
Broughton Ales Limited

Hunt, Patrick Mark Paul
James E. McCabe Limited
Philip Russell Limited

Hunt, Patrick Michael Paul
James E. McCabe Limited
Philip Russell Limited

Hunt, Samuel
Buveur Ltd

Hunt, Simon John
William Grant & Sons Brands Ltd

Hunter, Alan Stephen
Winehunters Ltd

Hunter, Annette
Kwik-Keg Limited
Levenridge Limited

Hunter, Lindsey Elizabeth Ross
Kindman Brewing Ltd

Hurd, Kelvin
Laughing Ass Brewery Ltd

Hurley, Barry Neil
Places Trading (Suppliers) Ltd

Hurmiz, Miran
Hurmiz UK Ltd

Hurst, Anne-Marie
Drinkologie Limited
Drinktonics Limited
The Flower Miners Limited

Hurst, Thomas
Rockstar Spirits Limited

Huse, Stephen
Amayan Terroir Selections Ltd

Hussain Thomson, Amanda
Thomson & Scott Limited

Hussain, Gulzar
SSG Service Ltd

Hussain, Haroon
Gin Fizz Ltd

Hussain, Imran
Absolute Wholesale Limited

Hussain, Malik Aftab
Watson Food & Beverages Ltd

Hussain, Mohammad
New Fairdeal Drinks Limited

Hussain, Mohammed Younis
Narang Wholesalers Limited

Hutchens, Nicky Anne
Artisan Lounge and Cellar Ltd

Hutcheon, Graham Robert
Highland Distillers Limited

Hutchings, Daniel John
India Gold Limited

Hutchinson, Alan
The Three Graces Liverpool Ltd

Hutchinson, Drew
The Three Graces Liverpool Ltd

Hutchinson, Jess James
Hindsight Collective Ltd

Hutchinson, Roriki Dwayne Earl
The Drinks Lover Ltd

Hutchinson, Timothy Randolph
DGB Europe Limited

Hutchison, Grant David
Re:Stalk Ltd

Hutton, Ian George
Liqueurs de France Limited

Hutton, Robert
Hutton & Mitchell Licensed Traders

Huuskonen, Harri
London Long Drink Limited

Hyde, Charles Adam
Hydes' Brewery Limited

Hyde, Matthew John
Hyde & Sons Limited

Hyde, Nicholas Andrew Travers
Vranken Pommery UK Ltd.

Hyde, Patricia Mary
Hyde & Sons Limited

Hyde, Paul Andrew
Edrington International Brands Ltd
Marshall McGregor Limited
Snow Leopard Vodka Limited

Hyde, Timothy Alexander David, Dr
Feni Global Limited

Hydleman, Louis Jules
The Drinks Club Ltd

Hyland, Connor
United Wine Merchants Limited

Hyman, Barry Timothy
Neptune Rum Ltd

Hyman, Howard Jonathan
Vinoveritas (Europe) Limited

Hyman, Samuel Archibald
Vinoveritas (Europe) Limited

Hymas, Eric John
El Brewery Limited

Hytner, Catherine Elizabeth
Bosworthcruises Ltd

I'anson, Thomas Peter
Tom I'Anson Wines Ltd

Iaghanashvili, Diana
Freerun Consulting Limited

Ibbotson, Richard Walter
Hallamshire Wine Shipping Co. Ltd

Ibrahim, Rashid Mohamad
Kukuruz Limited

Idle, Thomas David
Tirg Limited

Idrees, Intikab
London Cash & Carry Ltd

Ifrim, Catalin
A2Z Drinks Limited

Ikenye, Frank
Citrone Limited

Iles, Benjamin Richard
Agave Thieves Ltd

Iles, Matthew John
Quercus Wines Ltd

Ilik, Saso
Natural Marketing Ltd

Illi, Alain Maurice
Maurice Richard Ltd

Illsley, Daniel
Theatre of Wine Limited

Iltaf, Mohammad
Booze Crew Leeds Ltd

Impera, Antonino
Da Vinci Finest Italian Products Ltd

Imrie, Andrew
KWM Supplies Ltd

Ingram, Deane Michael
Lock & Barrel Limited

Ingram, Mark
Molvino Fine Wine & Spirits Co Ltd

Ingram, Tameil
Rapid Fill Ltd

Innes, Calvin Robert Allan
WinesOnline Ltd

Inthirakumar, Thushya
Four Seasons Hastings Ltd

Ioannou, Yiannakis
Wines Around Mediterranean Ltd

Ions, Mark
Gin Corporation Limited

Iordanidis, Georgios
Medagio Limited

Ip, Kym Yune Lewis
Red Dragons Trading Limited

Iqbal, Anum Nadia
Bruist Trading Ltd

Iqbal, Shahid
Global Foods Limited

Irshad, Muhammad
Brian Traders Ltd

Irwin, Oliver Lewis
The Whiskey and Bourbon Club Ltd

Irwin, Richard
Titanic Distillers Belfast Ltd

Irwin, Richard Stephen
Connoisseur Estates Limited
Norlin Distribution Limited
Titanic Distillers Limited

Isaac, Tahir
Euro Link Beverages Ltd

Ishani, Rafik
Kane Republik Ltd
RCI Spirits Ltd

Ishaq, Sajid
Fairway Foods Limited

Isherwood, Derek Barney Sealy
DBS Isherwood Limited
Triberg Limited

Isherwood, Fiona Catherine
DBS Isherwood Limited
Triberg Limited

Islam, Sharful
S & T Wines Limited

Italia, Dynshaw Fareed
Cobra Beer Partnership Limited

Ivanov, Ivan Teodorov
United Wines Ltd

Ivell, Robert Lewis
Charles Wells, Limited

Iwanowski, Jaye
Identity Drinks Brands Limited

Izquierdo Cervantes, Diego
D & F Wines Ltd

Jacimowicz, Iwo
SPP Wine Ltd

Jack, Bruce Stanley
Bonfire Hill Limited

Jackaria, Hishan
Green Island (UK) Limited
The Rum Shop Limited

Jackson, Alan Alfred Webster
Jackson Nugent Vintners Ltd

Jackson, Christopher Samuel
Pot Still Drinks Ltd.

Jackson, Clare Juliet
Vintage & Fine Wine International

Jackson, David
Amphora Portfolio Management Ltd

Jackson, David William
Eebria Limited

Jackson, Iain Kenneth
Marston's Acquisitions Limited

Jackson, Jessica Lily
Lexington Trading Limited

Jackson, Jonathan Charles
Cheti & Co Holdings Limited
Cheti & Co Limited

Jackson, Jonathan Christopher
Theatre of Wine Limited

Jackson, Julia Sian
The Special Cider Co Ltd

Jackson, Julie Frances
Jackson Nugent Vintners Ltd

Jackson, Mark Anthony
Cornucopia Wines Limited

Jackson, Mark Richard
The Special Cider Co Ltd

Jackson, Penelope Margaret
The Cognac Growers' Collective Ltd

Jackson, Rachael Sarah
Eebria Limited

Jackson, Simon Edwin
Yorkshire Vintners Limited

Jackson, Steven
Continental Beer Services Ltd

Jackson, Stuart Paul
Graysons Freight Services Ltd

Jacober, Jerome Jean
Eminent Life Limited
Eminent Wines Limited

Jacobs, John Earle
Earle Wines Ltd.

Jacobs, Patricia Rosemary
Earle Wines Ltd.

Jacques, Richard Patrick
Green Heart Wines Ltd

Jaffer, Masadiq Mohamed
Costadoria Ltd

Jagielko, Carol Anne
ABA Eaglesham Ltd
William Morton Limited

Jagielko, Henry John
ABA Eaglesham Ltd
GCBW Catrine Ltd
GSWD Catrine Ltd
William Morton Limited

Jain, Mukesh
Stockholm Distillers and Vintners

Jakimavicius, Egonas
Lithuanian Beer Limited

Jaksic, Nicholas
Belabon Drinks Ltd
Van Pur UK Ltd

James, Amanda
Valentino & Finch Ltd

James, Caroline Sanderson
The Vintage Malt Whisky Co Ltd

James, Justin Dennis
Camden Drinks Co Ltd
Drink Store Limited
Liquid Brand Marketing Limited

James, Mark
Hall & Woodhouse Limited

James, Richard
Valley Vineyards Limited

James-Odukoya, Adetola Adebukunla
Palms & Liquor Enterprises Ltd

Jamison, Antonia Alexandra
Fishers Gin Ltd

Jamshidi, Hooman
Inkd Limited

Janarthanan, Thamayanthy
Ourlocal Limited

Janaway, Ben
Creative Juices Brewing Co Ltd

Janelt, Pawel
Logistic Park Ltd

Jankovic, Marina
Sfuso Wine Limited

Jansen, Henricus Theodorus Franciscus
Dew Hill Blending Company (Glasgow)

Jansen, Herman Diederik
Dew Hill Blending Company (Glasgow)

Januska, Valentinas
Valentino Platinum Ltd

Jarecki, Radoslaw
Ian MacBarrel & Spirits Ltd

Jarrett, Cavell
CMJ Pub Trade Ltd

Jarvis, Carla
Superyacht Supplies Limited

Jarvis, Helen
Cask and Craft Direct Ltd

Jarvis, Ian
Superyacht Supplies Limited

Jarvis, Leslie Paul
Gang of Five Ltd

Jarzebowicz, Jerzy
PPbeer Ltd.

Jasper, Richard Ian
Gleninver Limited

Jasraj, Rajesh Hargovind
Kramjar Limited
The Offie Limited

Jassal, Sunny
Desi Wines Ltd

Jastrzebski, Andy
Expert Euro Exports Ltd

Javed, Salman
Five Star Cash & Carry Ltd

Javed, Vanessa Heidi
Molotov Brand Limited

Jaworski, Mikolaj
OX Bespoke Logistics Ltd

Jeavons, Alan Stanley
Tolchards Limited

Jefferies, Paul David
Hydes' Brewery Limited

Jefferson, Mark Harold
Mark Jefferson Wines Limited

Jeffery, Martin Robert
Wineways (Harrogate) Limited

Jeffries, Douglas Alan
Brazen Rum Ltd

Jeffries, Lee Thomas
Jeffries Vintage Drinks Ltd

Jefimovs, Andrejs
G Point 7 Ltd
R Spirit Ltd

Jeganmogan, Sharmmila
Hi - Line Wines Limited
Hiline Wines Peterborough Ltd
Landmark Wholesale Limited

Jemetta, Paul Louis
Italy on Tap Ltd

Jenkins, Chloe
Jenkins and Beckers Fine Wine Ltd

Jenkins, Darren
Valentino & Finch Ltd

Jenkins, David Clive
Italian Importers Ltd

Jenkins, Howard John
Warwick Banks and Jenkins Ltd

Jenkins, Michael David
Vin Est... Ltd

Jenkins, Nigel John
Warwick Banks and Jenkins Ltd

Jenkins, Rachel Anne
Vin Est... Ltd

Jenner, Ian David
Grande Marque Food & Beverage Ltd

Jenner, Thomas Edward
Bumble Mead Ltd

Jensen, Christian Errboe
Bermondsey Gin Limited

Jensen, James
Love and Labour Ltd.

Jensen, Lars
Supermalt UK Limited

Jervis, Laura
Jervis Trading Limited
Lazy Drinks Ltd.

Jervis, Peter
Jervis Trading Limited

Jestin, Patrick Jean Marie Gilbert
Dourthe UK Limited

Jethwa, Mukesh
K R Wines & Beers Ltd

Jethwa, Ritesh
K R Wines & Beers Ltd

Jethwani, Diana Rani Sirichand
Anglo-African Trade Limited

Jethwani, Meera Sirichand
Anglo-African Trade Limited

Jethwani, Rajendra Sirichand
Anglo-African Trade Limited

Jethwani, Sirichand Narumal
Anglo-African Trade Limited

Jewell, Wayne Terence Francis
White's Cellar Supplies (UK) Ltd

Jeyaseelan, Antony Suthagaran
Hatton Wholesale Ltd

Jiang, Ruizi
Jia Bo Rui International Trade Ltd

Jibodu, Adegbenga Olusola
Shocabo Ltd

Jibodu, Ombolaji
Shocabo Ltd

Jimenez, David Santos
Thames Wholesale Ltd

Jinadu, Olaide Olubunmi
Tolmid International Ltd

Jobling, Geoffrey Michael
Michael Jobling Wines Ltd

Jogani, Sunita
Sun Exports Limited

Johal, Balkar Singh
Wise Trading Limited

Johal, Balraj Singh
Wise Trading Limited

Johal, Iqbal Singh
Wise Trading Limited

Johal, Jasbir Singh
Wise Trading Limited

Johal, Jatinder Singh
Everyday Wholesale Ltd

Johal, Kuldip Singh
Central Drinks Pub Co Ltd

Johal, Rajan Singh
Champagne One Ltd

Johal, Sarnpal Singh
Wise Trading Limited

Johansson, Bjorn Filip Botvid
Bear Smyth Limited

Johansson, Jan Olof
Regent Wines Limited

John, Natalie Caroline
The Broadway Drinks Co Ltd

John, Nicholas David
ND John Wine Limited
N D John Wine Merchants Ltd

John, Tessa Elizabeth Jayne
Rarewood (London) Limited

Johns, Conor Aston
Mr Kegz Ltd

Johns, Gareth
The Tirion Trading Co Ltd

Johns, Leanne Peta
Sloane Home Ltd

Johnson, Andrew
Woodwinters Agencies Limited

Johnson, Benedict Edward Groves
Ourglass & Partners Ltd

Johnson, Darren Mark
Aquitania Ltd

Johnson, David Richard
BCM Brewing Co Ltd

Johnson, Dominique Nichole
Uncle Nearest Ltd.

Johnson, Keleigh Ann-Marie
Happy Girl Beverage Co Ltd

Johnson, Martin David
Childale Limited

Johnson, Nicholas Dominic Bernard
Spirit of Bermondsey Ltd

Johnson, Peter
Hydes' Brewery Limited

Johnson, Philip Andrew
Grassington Spirit Co Ltd

Johnson, Robert Andrew
Glugged! Ltd

Johnson, Simon Christopher
Bancroft Wines Limited
Mason & Mason Wines Limited

Johnson, Stephen Andrew
Peoplegood Limited

Johnson, Thomas Alexander
The Grape Variety Ltd

Johnston, Iain Robert
J.W.G. PLC

Johnston, Maureen
Neill & Company Wine Importers Ltd

Jolley, Mary Ellen
Brexit Import and Export Co Ltd

Jones, Adam Clarke
Wigan Beer Co Ltd

Jones, Andrew
Pearl Leisure Limited

Jones, Angela Ann
Wigan Beer Co Ltd

Jones, Bethan
Pirate's Grog Rum Ltd

Jones, Bryn
The House of Roo Ltd

Jones, Christopher
Paragon Brands Limited

Jones, Christopher Arthur
Bespoke Fine Wines Limited

Jones, Christopher Julius
Shropshire Beers Limited

Jones, Derrick
L H Cellar Supplies Limited

Jones, Eamonn FitzGenerald
Fox Fitzgerald Whisky Trading Co Ltd

Jones, Elizabeth Mary
Amy's Wine House Limited

Jones, Gary
Wholesale Beer Supplies Ltd

Jones, Harold
Wigan Beer Co Ltd

Jones, Harry Alexander Sircom
S H Jones Wines Ltd

Jones, Helen Victoria
Toast Ale Ltd

Jones, Hilary Susan
Ian Hart Distilling Limited
Sacred Spirits Holdings Ltd

Jones, Howard Edward
Momentum Wines Limited

Jones, Jason Mark Anthony
Greenlink Enterprises Limited

Jones, Joanne Elizabeth
Momentum Wines Limited

Jones, Judith Ann
L H Cellar Supplies Limited

Jones, Katherine Maria
Think Wine Group Ltd

Jones, Kieran
Wigan Beer Co Ltd

Jones, Mark Graham
Rok Drinks Limited

Jones, Michael Robert Edwards
Vitesse Vintners Limited

Jones, Oliver John
Twaites and Jones Limited

Jones, Owen
Aztec Spirits Ltd

Jones, Richard Nicholas
S H Jones Wines Ltd
Slurp Wine Co Ltd
Yapp Brothers Limited

Jones, Samantha Ann
Deco Spirits Limited

Jones, Simon Peter Roger
Capsule Wine Ltd

Jones, Susan
Italian Importers Ltd

Jones, Thomas
Life's A Bottle Limited

Jones, Thomas Owen
Bigg Market Beer Co Ltd
Bigg Market Brewery Co Ltd

Jonsson, Per Anders
Seriously Vodka Limited

Jordan, Jason Paul
Alcohollect Ltd

Jordan, Rodney Dennis Alexander
Zarb Distribution Ltd

Joseph, Anthony
Tump By Aj & Sonz Ltd

Joseph, Nabil
Impala Transportation Ltd

Joshi, Mukesh
S & N Products Ltd

Jouan, Dianne Marie
Le Bon Vin Limited

Jouan, Patrick Yves Victor
Le Bon Vin Limited

Journoux, Ioana
Cuvee Cavalier Limited

Jovasevic, Mladen
The Plum Brandy Co Ltd

Jowett, Jodie
Pulp Craft Cider Limited

Joy, Naomi Joy
Vicar's Gin Ltd

Joyce, Gary Richard
J. Chandler & Company, Limited

Joyce, Jane Carol
J. Chandler & Company, Limited

Judes, Alan Marc
Wine for Drinking Limited

Junaid, Mohammed
Pick N Deliver Ltd

Jurciakova, Petra
Teqcoola Limited

KOfficer, Jean Sylvestre Akouete
Sylvestre Limited

Kabilan, Ganeshamoorthy
Celex Foods Limited

Kabir, A T M Humaun
Deshi Bazar Ltd

Kaeda, Balvinder Singh
Coral Management Limited
Novus Drinks Ltd

Kahlon, Harpreet Singh
LGVA Solutions Limited

Kaiser, Christian James
Klostergut Limited

Kaiser, Jurgen
Klostergut Limited

Kaiser, Marcus Jurgen
Klostergut Limited

Kaiser-Helman, Klaudiusz
Chateau Khornabuji Limited

Kaizer, Aristides
Delecta Limited

Kalfakis, Dimitrios
VDK Import Export Limited

Kalsi, Jagjeet Singh
Narang Wholesalers Limited

Kama, Jone Antonio Rabici
Fiji Store Ltd

Kamani, Suleman Nurez
Manchester Trading Limited

Kambic, Bojan
Bihl Ltd

Kan, Chi Chiu
Kan Trading Limited

Kana, Arjan Maldev
D K International (UK) Limited

Kana, Devshi
Europa Drinks Limited

Kanapathipillai, Dhusyanthan
All Food Supplies Ltd
Bestline Wholesale Ltd

Kandeepan, Nagarajan
Maha Cash & Carry Ltd

Kang, Avtar Singh
Sandhar & Kang (Birmingham) Ltd

Kang, Swarn Singh
Sandhar & Kang (Birmingham) Ltd

Kang, Udham Singh
Sandhar & Kang (Birmingham) Ltd

Kapadia, Mayank
Prima Import & Export Ltd

Kappor, Raman
Comercio Ltd

Kara, Pravin Ratna
Eurorock Trading Limited

Karadag, Erdal
O & E Food Ltd

Karaoglan, Hasan
Utku Emre Ltd

Karapetyan, Vahe
Avazak Ltd

Karecki, Krzysztof
Dionysus Boutique Wine Merchants Ltd

Karim, Paul
Pioneer Spirits Ltd

Karim, Shafiq
Werfa Holdings Ltd

Karjalainen, Kimmo Eerik
Bone Machine Brewing Co Ltd

Karjalainen, Marko Antero
Bone Machine Brewing Co Ltd

Karlova, Veronika
Karla & Co. Spirits Limited

Kars, Emre
Turkish Kitchinn Wholesale Ltd

Karsan, Divyesh Kurji
Golden Harvest Wholesale Ltd

Karsten, Peter Robert Anthony
World Beers Limited

Karunakara Arachchige, Kasun Tharindu Madushanka
Kasgo Limited

Kastoris, Georgios
Mediterranean Farm Finest Ltd

Kataria, Rajni
Temple Wines (Cash & Carry) Ltd

Katende, Uzaifa
Estelon Holdings Limited

Katende, Uzaifa
Polat International Ltd

Kato, Archard Lwihula
Alko Vintages UK Ltd

Katsantonis, Lucy
Eurovenus Limited

Kaur, Anuvinder
Stockwell Wholesalers Limited

Kaur, Bakshish
MSD Wholesale Limited

Kaur, Esha
Kaur's Convenience Store Ltd

Kaur, Jaswinder
Cubed A Ltd

Kaur, Kanta
Pau Drinks Limited

Kaur, Mandeep
Drinks Global Ltd

Kaur, Satwant
Newhampton Wines Ltd

Kavanagh, Gerard
Drink Store Limited

Kawi, Bob Kese
Kese International Ltd

Kayan, Ugur
UKAFDS Limited

Kaye, James Henry Newton
Good Spirits Ltd

Kaye, Jonathan Russell
The Beer Boutique Ltd
Two Heads Beer Co Limited

Kaye, Julian Jepson
The Wright Wine Co Ltd

Kaypee, Ravi Inder Singh
Beer Belly's Ltd

Kazimierski, Cyprian Henryk
Cyprian Services Limited

Kc, Niraj
KC Brothers Ltd

Kean, Jacob
Raer Scotch Whisky Ltd

Kean, James Harkins
Raer Scotch Whisky Ltd

Kearney, Allen Charles Michael
DBS Isherwood Limited

Kearsey, Matthew Richard
Hall & Woodhouse Limited

Kearsley, Roy Nigel
Eastcoast Supplies Ltd.

Keartland, Brett Hugh
Mast-Jaegermeister UK Holding Ltd
Mast-Jaegermeister UK Limited

Keating, Kathryn Dibble Andersen
Lay & Wheeler Limited

Kechagias, Nathanail
Leverre Ltd

Keef, James Patrick Alexander
Slurp Wine Co Ltd

Keeley, Mark Steven
Spar (UK) Limited

Keeling, Daniel Benjamin
Keeling Andrew & Co Limited

Keeling, Matthew George
Gather 77 Limited

Keell, Isabella
Bahamian Enterprise UK Limited

Keell, Oliver
Bahamian Enterprise UK Limited

Keenan, Charlotte Clementine
Red Squirrel Wine Ltd.

Kelaty, Shelley Lucy
Select Whisky Limited

Kelland, James
Cellar & Co Limited

Kelleher, Liam Bede
SPP Wine Ltd

Kelley, Rebecca Louise
Smouse & Marchand Limited

Kelley, Richard Paul
Smouse & Marchand Limited

Kellie, Emma
The First & Last Brewery Ltd

Kellie, Sam
The First & Last Brewery Ltd

Kelly, David Michael
Unique Wine Safaris Limited

Kelly, Helen Janet
Claribes Limited

Kelly, Joel John
Atom Brands Limited
Atom Cask Holdings Limited
Atom Drinks Limited
Atom Group Limited
Atom Scotland Limited
Atom Supplies Limited
Master of Malt Limited
Masters of Malt Limited
Maverick Brands Limited
Maverick Drinks Limited
Maverick Spirits Limited

Kemp, Jonathan Paul
Bristol Cider Co Ltd

Kendrick, Jonathan Mark
Bogart Spirits Limited

Kennedy, Benedict Michael
Rive Gauche Wines (UK) Limited

Kennedy, Islay Joy
Vickery Wines Limited

Kennedy, Matthew James Dominic
For Goodness Sake Ltd

Kennedy, Robert Donald
Little Gems Wine Ltd

Kennett, Charles Jonathan
Alliance Wine Co Ltd

Kent, Darius
Vektor Vodka UK Ltd

Kent, James
TPA Trading Limited

Kent, Nicholas Robin
Languedoc Imports Ltd

Kenworthy, Andrew Mark
Diverse Beers Limited

Keogh, Hayley
Lust Promotions Ltd

Keppel, Robert
Quero Enterprise Ltd

Kerr, Alastair Neil
Hoppl Wines Limited

Kerr, Andrew Gary
Lewes Gin Limited

Kerr, Andrew Michael
Babco UK Ltd.
World of Patria International Ltd

Kerr, Jacqueline Carol
Hoppl Wines Limited

Kerry, Simon
Aspall Cyder Limited
Molson Coors Brewing Co (UK) Ltd
Molson Coors Brewing International

Kettle, Peter Brian
Kudu Food and Wine Ltd

Keturakiene, Vida
Champagne Route Limited

Keuchel, Sebastian Thomas
Base Cachaca Import (UK) Ltd

Kewin, Andrew John
GBW Subscriptions Ltd

Keymer, Alexa Jane
Xeco Wines Limited

Khachidze, Bachana
Bach & Co Solution Limited

Khamar, Jayesh
Noble Merchants Limited

Khamar, Rajendra
Noble Merchants Limited

Khamar, Samir
Noble Merchants Limited

Khan, Feisal Mehmood
Panton Ventures Limited

Khan, Imran
Excess UK Limited

Khan, Mohammed
Manor Wholesale Ltd

Khan, Muhammad Rafq
Eastcoast Supplies Ltd.

Khan, Raees
Drill Wholesale Limited

Khan, Sajid
Domal Trading Limited

Khan, Shah Nawaz
H & W Cash & Carry Ltd

Khan, Victoria
Tewaina Ltd

Khanna, Rajiv
Truekeg UK Ltd

Khera, Amarpal Singh
Warwickshire Cash & Carry Ltd

Khera, Dalbire Singh
Warwickshire Cash & Carry Ltd
Warwickshire Drinks Plus Ltd

Khera, Sukhjit
Central Drinks Pub Co Ltd

Khimasia, Kuleen Piyush
Hingston & Co. Ltd

Khosla, Atul
Khosla Wines Ltd
Xenon Wines & Spirits Limited

Khosla, Dharnpal
D K Beers Ltd.

Khosla, Ram Kumar
Khosla Wines Ltd
Xenon Wines & Spirits Limited

Khurana, Manmohan
Landmark Wholesale Limited

Kidd, Gordon George
Faking Bad Brewery Limited

UK Wholesalers of Beers, Wines and Spirits   dellam

Kidney, Alexander Nicholas
A & B Vintners Limited
Triage Wines Limited

Kidney, Phillip John
Pembrokeshire Drinks Limited

Kilby, Kirsten Emma
Armit Holding Limited
Armit Wines Limited

Kilcoyne, Generald
Uokka Limited

Kilcoyne, Luke Anthony
Uokka Limited

Kilian, Richard
Vino Pronto UK Ltd

Kim, Dohyung
Evernex Ltd

Kimmins, Malcolm Brian Johnston
Laurent-Perrier (UK) Limited

Kinder, Howard
Horsetown Beers Limited
Malton Brewery Limited
Russells and Wrangham Limited

Kinder, Nicholas John
Claribes Limited

King, Angela Marie
AMK Wholesale Ltd

King, Cynthia
The Burnfield Trading Co Ltd

King, David Thomas
Speymalt Whisky Distributors Ltd

King, Emma Jane
Lounge Spirits Ltd

King, Jason Stanley
Lounge Spirits Ltd

King, Judith
Hannibal Brown Wine Services Ltd

King, Nicholas Robert
Clique Wine Limited

King, Stefan Paul
The Burnfield Trading Co Ltd

King, Zephaniah Oury
Real Ale (Export) Limited
Real Ale (Retail) Limited
Real Ale (Wholesale) Limited
Real Ale Limited

Kingerley, Mark
Myella Brands Ltd

Kinkladze, Giorgi
Kinkladze Limited

Kinnersley, Andrew
Spot Wines Limited

Kinney, John FitzGenerald
Today's Wholesale Services Ltd

Kinns, Elizabeth
Winegrowers Direct Limited

Kinns, Jonathan
Winegrowers Direct Limited

Kinsley, Josephine Elizabeth
Slainte Mhath Ltd

Kinton, Emma
Hotham's Spirits Ltd

Kirban, Michael
All Market Europe Limited

Kirby, Steven Paul
The White Lion Gin Co Ltd

Kirit Kumar, Hina
HKK and Sons Ltd

Kirk, Alastair Francis
Crafty Pint Limited

Kirkland, Gillian
Gill's Drams Ltd.

Kirkpatrick, Adam Christian
Ask Drinks Ltd

Kirkpatrick, Simon
Ask Drinks Ltd

Kirwin, Sean, Rev
Associated Church Clubs Ltd

Kishimoto, Taketoshi
Demball Limited

Kiss, Martin Robert Alan
Chosen Wine Limited
Lush Wines Ltd

Klocek, Gavin
Fifty One Forty Limited

Knight, Adam Digby
Wholly Grape Limited

Knight, Jane Elizabeth
Knight Trade (Oakham) Limited

Knight, Keith Andrew
RD Wines Limited

Knight, Matthew John
MK Sales Training Limited

Knight, Stephen
Knight Trade (Oakham) Limited

Knight, Susan Margaret
Hayward Bros (Wines) Limited

Knight, William Richard
The Cuba Trading Co Ltd

Knopfler, Joseph
Melius Drinks Ltd.

Knott, Andrew
Liberty Wines Limited

Knott, David Frederick William
The Knotted Vine Limited

Knowles, Michelle
Oak Wines Limited

Knox, Ryan
Gleeson N.I. Limited

Knox, William
Quartz Group Scotland Ltd

Kochhar, Amit
Eclipse Drinks Limited

Kociolek, Jason Kaz Scott
Australian Vintage (Europe) Ltd

Kocon, Michael
Bourne & Co Solutions Ltd

Kohler, Roman Jakob Bruno
Edrington-Beam Suntory UK Distribution

Kokorashvili, Zura
Georgian Wine Co Ltd

Komara, Juraj
Ariki Limited

Konaszczuk, Patryk Stanislaw
Magnate Drinks Ltd

Kondapalli, Manisha Reddy
The Compasses Gomshall Ltd

Kondratyuk, Tetyana
Premier Beverages Limited

Konrads, Igo
Vinvm Ltd

Konstantinou, Nikolaos
Bertrand Tailor Limited

Koo, Kevin
Koomor Brewing Co Ltd

Kooner, Kiran Kaur
Bottle Butler Limited

Koopmans, Rudolf Jozef
William Riddell & Sons Limited

Kopacsi, Zoltan Laszlo
Best of Hungary Ltd

Kore, Gnaly
Best Bordeaux Wines Ltd

Korkmaz, Onder
Organica Food & Wine Ltd

Kormilcevs, Igors
Globe Logistics Limited

Kostepski, Joanna
Xtraflow Limited

Kotecha, Dhiren Lalit
Canal Cellars Ltd

Kotecha, Hemant Dahyalal
Myliko International (Wines) Ltd.

Kotecha, Jayesh
Jake Mason Ltd

Kotomski, Marcin Rafal
Diamonds & Pearl Trading Ltd

Kotomski, Radoslaw
Diamonds & Pearl Trading Ltd

Kouame, Adjet Jean Claude
Enovino Organic Ltd

Kovacs, Gabor
Cellarers (Wines) Limited
Diageo United Kingdom Limited

Kowal, Robert
Super Brit Bery Ltd

Kowzan, Rafal
JR First Choice Cash & Carry Ltd

Koymen, Tolga
Bacchus London Limited

Kozlowski, Jakub
Majlen Ltd

Kozuba, Jakub
Kozuba & Sons Limited

Kozuba, Maciej
Kozuba & Sons Limited

Kraatz, Klaus-Peter
Usedsoft Ltd

Krajewski, Martin John
Chateau de Sours Estates Ltd

Kratky, Frank
K. Colombier Limited

Kratky, Jaroslava
K. Colombier Limited

Krawczyk-Ciesiolka, Rita Anna
The Eastern Pantry Ltd

Kray, Monika
Interactive Stage Ltd

Kremer, Serge Robert Guy
Toast Ale Ltd

Kress Von Wendland, Felix-Johannes Peter Otto
F & M Cressi Limited
Tasty Kameleon Ltd

Krishnan Sivagnanam, Gobi
Lesont Ltd

Kriss, Sophie Gamela
Global Foods Limited

Krupina, Natalia
Zetas Ventures Ltd

Krzymuski, Henry John
The Wine Library Limited

Krzywda, Marcin
London Drinks and Beers Ltd

Kubaczka, Sebastian Rafal
Top Alco Ltd

Kudhail, Amarjeet Singh
Exivi Limited

Kugaevskikh, Andrey
The Hidgate Ltd

Kulandaisamy, Thirunavukkarasu
Heavenly Grapes Limited

Kular, Avtar
Euro Speed Intl Ltd

Kulis, Karol
Distribev Ltd.

Kumar, Darpun
Central Pubs (UK) Limited

Kumar, Naresh
Central Pubs (UK) Limited

Kumarasamy, Kumarathasan
OM Wines Ltd

Kuriakose Kattakkayam, Dinish
Vineco Inco Ltd

Kurshid, Adil
Late Shop Ltd

Kustro, Andrej
Deer & Badger Ltd

Kusturin, Mirko
MK Wine Art Ltd

Kutty, Zack
Realsa Wines Import & Export Ltd

Kwashie, Michael Sidney
Hazewater Food Services Ltd

Kwon, Gapjoong
Asiana Mart Limited

Kynoch, George Alexander Bryson
Red Squirrel Wine Ltd.

Kyprianou, Steven Stellakis
London Spiced Dry Limited

Kypriotis, Sofoklis
Corfu SW Limited

La Ronde, Julia Antonia
Sisserou Marketing Limited

La, Daniel Roger
LA International Trading Ltd

Lacey, Anna Clare
Country Life Brewery Ltd

Lacey, Helen Naomi
De-Laceys Tipples Limited

Lacey, Robert James
Palinka UK Ltd

Lacey, Simon Roy
Country Life Brewery Ltd

Lacour, Elliot Mark
Oxus Gin Ltd.

Ladicova, Michaela
A2Z Wines & Groceries Ltd

Ladlow, Amanda Joy
Slim Gin Ltd

Lagae, Anouk Sophie
Duvel Moortgat UK Limited

Lagerqvist Christopherson, Anna Elisabeth
MCAL Sweet Retail Limited

Lagonigro, Luigi
Cibus Vitae Ltd.

Lagoumidi, Eirini
The Greek Wineshop Ltd

Lahart, Liam
Liquid Projects International Ltd

Laing, Abdon
Desirable Drinks Ltd

Laing, Andrew William Douglas
Edition Spirits Ltd.

Laing, Caraline Sara
The Laing Whisky Co Ltd

Laing, Frederick Hamilton
Distilled Liquor Co Ltd
Douglas Laing & Co Ltd.
Laing Shipping & Export Agency Ltd.
Douglas McGibbon & Co. Limited

Laing, Hamish Alexander
Coombe Castle Fine Wines Ltd

Laing, Ian Michael
Coombe Castle Fine Wines Ltd

Laing, Stewart Hunter
Douglas Export Agency Limited
Raleigh (Glasgow) Limited

Laird, Andrew Robert John
3 Lids Rum Ltd

Laithwaite, Barbara Anne
Wyfold Vineyard Limited

Laithwaite, Henry John Hugh
Harrow & Hope Limited
Wyfold Vineyard Limited

Laithwaite, Kaye Louise
Harrow & Hope Limited

Lake, Adrian John
Recolte Wines Limited

Lake, Christopher John Neville
Dedicated Wine Importers Ltd

Lakhani, Rishi
Direct Booze Limited
Millennium Cash & Carry Ltd

Lakhani, Vasantkumar Dahyalal
Collective Trading Limited

Lal, Harbans
R B M Leisure Limited

Lal, Mohit
World Brands Duty Free Limited

Lal, Selina
Summerforever Ltd

Lalia, Ravneet Singh
Buzz Drinks Limited
Epiphany Bars Limited

Lam, Shuk Yi Mariana
Wineworld Exchange UK Limited

Lamb, Thomas William Charles
Pure Organic Drinks Limited

Lamba, Aaron Ishan
Lamba Trading Co. Limited

Lamba, Bimla
Lamba Trading Co. Limited

Lamba, Kabir Raj
Lamba Trading Co. Limited

Lamba, Kamal
Lamba Trading Co. Limited

Lamba, Michael
Lamba Trading Co. Limited

Lambert, Daniel Sebastian Jeremy
Daniel Lambert Wines Limited

Lambert, Helen Elizabeth
Daniel Lambert Wines Limited

Lambert, Jean Marc
John Dewar and Sons Limited

Lambert, Jerome Thomas
Bijou Bottles Limited

Lamiroy, Hannah Rory
Tinkture Ltd

Lamiroy, Sam Kwinten
Tinkture Ltd

Lamont, Donald Murray
Ebenezer Leisure Limited

Lamont, Michael
William Grant & Sons Brands Ltd
Quality Spirits International Ltd

Lamont, Steven Adam
Exigo (UK) Limited

Lampe, Peter
Cavoda Limited

Lancaster, Benjamin Edward
Wisdom Whisky & Wine (Scotland) Ltd
Wisdom Whisky & Wine Limited

Lancaster, John Thomas
Cleveland Bar Supplies Limited

Lancaster, Leslie
Wine Raiders Limited

Lancaster, Paul Stuart
Fine Wine Works Limited

Land, Stephen Thomas
Swallow (Soft Drinks, Beer and Cider Wholesalers)
Swallow Dispensed Drinks Solutions

Landry, Herve
Adam & Herv Limited

Lane, Marie Elise
Laneberg Wine Ltd

Lane, Stuart Christopher
Majestic Wine Warehouses Ltd

Lang, George Anthony Edward
The Wine Merchant Ltd

Langella, Dario
I.G.T. Management Ltd

Langstone, Myles Anthony
Langstone Beer Exports Ltd

Lapeyre, Franck Michel Jean
World Brands Duty Free Limited

Lapsley, Julie
The Wine Byre Limited

Laravita, Irina
Laravita Ltd

Larcombe, Ben
Pipehouse Gin Limited

Larcombe, Katherine Louise
Pipehouse Gin Limited

Larkin, Simon
Atlas Fine Wines Limited

Lascelles, Stuart Francis
East London Brewing Co Ltd

Lashbrook, Richard Edward
Thorman Hunt & Co Limited

Lasme, Nathanael
Meless Consortium Ltd

Lathia, Kapil
WLL Wholesale Ltd

Latouf, Kevin John
The Wine Butler Limited

Latour, Louis Fabrice
Louis Latour Limited

Lattuca, Josephine
C. & T. Licata & Son Limited

Lau, Chee Leong
G Sake Co Ltd

Laughland, Andrew Iain Stewart
Drink Free Ltd

Laughton, Howard Seymour
Capion Trading Limited

Laupie, Cyrille
Vranken Pommery UK Ltd.

Laurino, Nicola
Italy Service UK Ltd

Laux, Michael
Finest Wine & Delicatessen Brokers Ltd.

Lavaud White, Cecile Marie
Les Producteurs et Vignerons de France

Lavaud, Denise
Les Producteurs et Vignerons de France

Lavaud, Francois Paul Andre, Monsieur
Les Producteurs et Vignerons de France

Laventure, Marc Joseph
Camden Drinks Co Ltd
Liquid Brand Marketing Limited

Lavergne, Thibault Marcel
Wine Story Limited

Lavery, Peter Martin
Titanic Distillers Belfast Ltd

Law, Andrew James
Paisajes Trading Ltd

Lawal, Olalekan
Burgeon Allied Limited

Lawrence, Carol
Associated Church Clubs Ltd

Lawrence, Graham Roy
Konigsberg Seven Bridges Breweries Ltd

Lawrence, Guy Edward
Mast-Jaegermeister UK Holding Ltd
Mast-Jaegermeister UK Limited

Lawrence, Peter Jessel Levay
Algodon Europe Limited

Lawrence, Tara
Little Horse Wines Limited

Laws, David
Party Drinks Co Ltd

Laws, Marie
Party Drinks Co Ltd

Lawson, Andrew Timothy
Attitude Spirits Ltd

Lawson, David
Ginkhana Limited

Lawson, Leeanne
Ginkhana Limited

Lawton, Stuart
The St Ives Grog Co Ltd

Layton, Philip
Play Limited

Lazaro, David Alexander
Philip von Nell Wines Limited

Le Berre, Frederic
MyNaturalCo Ltd

Le Blond, Carl Vincent
Feni Global Limited

Le Bohec, Erwan
Authentic French Wines (Importers)

Le May, Kenneth George
Glasgow Distillers Limited

Le, Hanh Van
Sotus Limited

Le, Thi Doan Trang
Trang Mai Exports Limited

Lea, Charles Algernon
Lea & Sandeman Group of Companies

Leach, William
The Drink Connect Ltd

Leadley, Jacob
Hillcrest Wines Limited

Leadley, Rebecca Anne
Hillcrest Wines Limited

Leal Da Silva, Domingos Miguel
Casa Leal Ltd

Leape, Martin Stephen Paul
Beer Gonzo Ltd

Leape, Micheal Christopher
Beer Gonzo Ltd

Leary, James Edward
The Antipodean Sommelier Ltd

Leask, Talin
Pink City Cider Ltd

Leather, Christopher Edward
Frank Stainton Wines Limited

Lebedevas, Tomas
Home2.0beer UK Ltd
Kraft Beer UK Ltd

Ledas, Julius
Branda Ltd

Ledwidge, Aoife Emily
The Mixed Case Limited

Ledwidge, Johanna Marie
The Mixed Case Limited

Lee, Michael
Blue Magic Limited

Lee, Philip Craig
The Baijiu Beer Co Ltd
The Beer Company (Exports) Ltd
The Spirit Beer Co Ltd
Tattoo Limited

Lee, Stewart David
Savile Row Gin Limited

Lee, Su Jung
Kindred Spirit Partnership Ltd

Lee, Vanessa
Solow Ltd

Lee, Vanzelo
Blue Magic Limited

Lee, Wendy Marian
Wine de Vine Ltd

Lee, Yen-Kai
Urbeer Ltd

Lees Jones, William Richard
Willoughbys Limited

Lees-Jones, Christopher Peter
Willoughbys Limited

Lefort, Olivia
Cellar Select Ltd

Legg, James
Maiden Wines Limited

Leggat, Caraline Sara
Delicious Drinks Limited
Douglas Laing & Co Ltd.

Leggat, Christopher George
Delicious Drinks Limited
Douglas Laing & Co Ltd.

Leighton, Richard John
Chelsea Vintners London Ltd

Leiper, John Edward
Pearly Queen Beer Co Ltd

Leivers, Hayley
The Jin Bar Ltd

Leivers, James
The Jin Bar Ltd

Lejkowski, Marta Magdalena
Benjamin & Blum Limited

Leka, Bujar
DTdist Ltd

Lemon, Michael William
Soar Valley Bar Supplies Ltd

Lemos, George James Demetrius
Vickbar Limited

Lench, Andew
Grand Vin Wine Merchants Ltd

Lench, Andrew Douglas
Bordeaux Wine Investments Ltd

Lenehan, Patrick
Spirit Valley France Limited

Leon, Oliver Nicholas
Dayboat Limited

Leonard, Alexander David
Apex Dispense Limited

Leonard, Benjamin Keene
Provenance Projects 2016 Ltd

Leonard, Steven Edmund
Rodney Densem Wines Limited
RD Wines Limited

Leppelmann, Flora Maria
Leppelmann & Nie Limited

Leroux, Benjamin
Coombe Castle Fine Wines Ltd

Lesch, Marc-Oliver
Deutschlond Brewery Limited

Leschallas, Anthony Simon
Southern Wines Limited

Leslie, Calum Liam
Peatreekers Limited

Lester, Henry Charles
Gergovie Wines Limited

Letchford, Ashley
Laurence Leisure Limited

Letellier, Michael
Evocative Wines Limited

Leuci, Leonardo
Del Professore Limited

Levente, Aleksander Martin
Brazen Beer Limited

Lever, Richard James
Traditional Beer Co Ltd

Leverett, Neville
Home Farm Gin Limited

Levin, David
Levin Wines Limited

Levin, Lynne Julie
Levin Wines Limited

Levine, Brian Colin
Manchester Drinks Co Ltd

Lewell, Daniel Joseph
Charles Samuel Imports & Exports Ltd

Lewens, Jack James Peter
Vigneti Tardis UK Ltd

Lewis, Benjamin
The Galloping Wine Nose Ltd

Lewis, Christopher William
Spar (UK) Limited

Lewis, Elvet Wynne
J.W.L Wholesale Drinks Ltd

Lewis, Lisa May
Super Cooper Ltd

Lewis, Ryan
W D L Wholesale Limited

Lewis, Sarah Jane
Silence of The Drams Limited

Lewis, William
Singolo Vino Limited

Lewitt, Jeremy William
Invest Inns Limited

Lewsey, Richard John
The Bavarian Beer Co Ltd

Li, Linghua
Panda Oriental Supermarket Ltd

Li, Qian, Dr
Vieuxvino Investment Ltd

Li, Rougang
Mr. Alba International Trading Co Ltd

Li, Wei
Chivalry Trading International Co. Ltd

Li, Xiaye
Japan Gourmet (UK) Limited

Li, Xingrong
DFG Distribution Ltd

Liburd, Susan Patricia
Compasse Limited

Licata, Carmelo
C. & T. Licata & Son Limited

Licata, Stefano
C. & T. Licata & Son Limited

Licata, Teresa
C. & T. Licata & Son Limited

Lichine, Alexis
Planet Wine Trading and Consulting

Lidder, Bhupinder Singh
Winecorp Limited

Liddle, Simon James
Solow Ltd

Liegeard, Sebastien
Seb and Emma Ltd

Lilley, Christopher Stanley Alfred
Lilley's Cider Limited

Lilley, Marc
Lilley's Cider Limited

Limbrey, Chai Lin
D.J. Limbrey Distilling Co. Ltd

Limbrey, Dominic James
D.J. Limbrey Distilling Co. Ltd

Limbrey, Sean
Limbrey's Wine and Spirits Ltd

Limon, Fabrice Pierre Michel
Highball Brands Limited

Lin, Yingming
Remfly Wines UK Limited

Lincoln-Creese, Joshua Benjamin Geoffrey
Majestic Wine Warehouses Ltd

Lindley, Michael Robert
Fine Wine World Ltd

Lindley, Paul John
Toast Ale Ltd

Ling, Colin Austin
Middle Kingdom Ltd

Lingard-Lane, Anthony
Apley Hall Wines Limited

Lingard-Lane, Jane Margaret
Apley Hall Wines Limited

Linter, Graham John
Foxhole Spirits Limited

Linter, Samantha Martha
Foxhole Spirits Limited

Lisowski, Bianca
Bianca Trading Wine Ltd

Lithgow, Alexander George
Corelli Wine Co Ltd

Little-Jones, Mark Egerton
Wiland Wines Limited

Little-Jones, Rosaleen
Wiland Wines Limited

Littlejohn, Joshua Howard
The Brewgooder Foundation
Brewgooder Limited

Littler, Lynne Georgina
GW Wines Limited

Littler, Timothy Arthur
GW Wines Limited

Littlewood, Mark Richard
Kudos Drinks Ltd

Littlewood, Paul
The Ale Trader Ltd

Littman, Geoffrey
Champagne Imports Limited

Livesey, Dean James
Hall & Woodhouse Limited

Llewelyn, Benjamin William Thomas
Carte Blanche Wines Limited

Lloyd, Clare Alison
Andrew R. Wilson Limited

Lloyd, Francisca May Han
Te Kano Estate Wines (UK) Ltd

Lloyd, John Nicholas
Everards Brewery Limited

Lloyd, Mark Rhsk
Da Vinci Finest Italian Products Ltd

Lloyd, Rebecca
Andrew R. Wilson Limited

Lloyd, Simon Godfrey
Lloyds Wines Limited

Lloyd, Simon John
Palmerston Fine Wines Ltd.

Lloyd, Stephen John
Tanners Cymru Limited
Tanners Wines Limited

Lloyd, Steven Michael
Andrew R. Wilson Limited

Lo Bue, Francesco
Los Perros Sueltos Brewing Co Ltd

Lo Coco, Valerio
Native Wines Ltd

Loba, Piotr
White Pearl Ltd

Loba, Rafal
Logistic Park Ltd

Lochhead, Iain MacGregor
The Bombay Spirits Co Ltd
John Dewar and Sons Limited

Lockhart, Paul Robert
BL Drinks Ltd

Lockwood, Gregory Kilborn
Liv-Ex Limited

Lockwood, Ian Victor
The Drinks Guild Ltd
Thames Distillers Limited

Logan, Andrew Kenneith
Atom Supplies Limited

Logan, Nigel Stuart
Wine in Cornwall Limited

Loganathan, Pragash
Ambal Fuel Ltd

Loizidis, Dorina
Dorys Shop Ltd

Lombard, Christel Mireille Jeanne
Du Terroir A La Table Limited
T.C.T.C. Services Ltd

Lombard-Chibnall, Margaret Elizabeth
Lombard Scotch Whisky Limited

Lombard-Chibnall, Richard Anthony
Lombard Scotch Whisky Limited

Lomberg, Ashley
Vino Merchant Limited

Lomberg, Martin Rudolf
Vino Merchant Limited

Lomvardos, Christoforos
Parthenon Import Co Ltd

Long, Cinzia
Englishman Supplies Limited

Long, Mark William
Brindle Distillery Limited

Long, Trevor
Pacta Connect UK Limited

Longerinas, Sebastien
Cabezac Collections Limited

Longhurst, Janice
Rhymney Brewery Western Ltd.

Longhurst, Richard Nicholas
Hofmeister Enterprises Ltd

Longhurst, Stewart
Rhymney Brewery Western Ltd.

Longley, Martin Paul
Ellis of Richmond Limited

Lonie, Craig
Malthub Ltd

Lonneux, Julien
Vranken Pommery UK Ltd.

Lopatinsky, Matvey
Chateau de la Combe Ltd

Lopatynskyy, Yuriy
Chateau de la Combe Ltd

Lorie, Harris Mark
Epicurean Food and Drink Corporation

Lorie, Hilton Anthony
Epicurean Food and Drink Corporation

Loriot de Rouvray, Florestan Frederic Marie
Old Sport Limited
Yaad Rum Ltd

Lorusso, Franco
Etna Food & Wine Ltd

Lott, Stephen Lawrence Parker
Rest Wine Ltd

Loue, Yannick
LVB Limited
Le Vignoble Ltd

Lount, Barry
Steamin' Billy (Property) Ltd

Louw, Matthys Michael
Sauvignon Wines UK Ltd

Louw, Thys
The Project Wines UK Limited

Love, Alison Jane
F.L. Dickins Limited

Low, Eileen
Piaff Trading UK Limited

Low, James Hamilton
Abercrombie Fine Wines Limited
Goedhuis & Co Ltd

Low, Richy
Kanpai (London) Food and Beverage Management Co.,

Lowe, Anna Michelle Olivia
Seven Cellars Ltd.

Lowe, Jamie Marie
Barkin Bars Ltd

Lowe, Nicola Jayne
Boutinot Wines Limited

Lowe, William Peter
Berkmann Wine Cellars Limited

Lowe-Smith, Andrew Charles
Agave Thieves Ltd

Lowrey, Joanne
MSSC (NW) Limited

Lowrey, Norman Lee
MSSC (NW) Limited

Lowthian, Ian Stuart
John Dewar and Sons Limited

Lozano-Quintana, Ana Cristina
TL Step By Step Limited

Lozowski, Marek
MSM Foods Limited
Najpol Ltd

Lucas, Charles James Hastings
Bristol Fine Wine Limited

Lucas, Natasha Ann
BI Wines and Spirits Limited

Luck, Thomas Adam
St.Austell Brewery Co Ltd

Luckman, Mark William
Stanley Marlow & Son Limited

Ludbrook, Darren
Mirfield Brewery Limited

Ludbrook, Hamish William
Oui Vino Limited

Ludlow, Amanda Lynn
The Great Whisky Co Ltd

Ludlow, Edward
The Great Spirit Co Ltd

Luinyte, Greta
Suwalki-UK Ltd

Lunardi, Marta
Marta's Vinyard Limited

Lundie, Alan William
Kirklee Scotch Whisky Limited

Lundie, Anne Marion Young
Kirklee Scotch Whisky Limited

Lunn, George Michael
The Stirling Whisky Co Ltd

Lunn, Jamie
The Stirling Whisky Co Ltd

Lunzer, Anna-Sofia Ulrika
Lunzer Wine Group Limited

Lunzer, Peter Anthony
Barrique Vintners Limited
Lunzer Wine Group Limited

Luongo, Tony
Direct Wine Importers Limited

Lupi, Matteo
Matteo Lupi Wines Ltd

Luque Garcia, Libertad
DTB Distribution Ltd

Lushnikov, Aleksei Vladimirovich
CGAVL Imports Limited

Lushnikov, Alexander Vladimirovich
CGAVL Imports Limited

Luthra, Dhruv
Del Professore Limited

Luto, Adrian Peter Stephen
J.R.G. Investments Limited

Ly, Huy Quang
Qtranly Ltd

Lyall, Sebastian Sheiky
Vinny Labs Ltd

Lyle, Timothy Harold Garnett
Broad Street Brands Limited

Lynas, Angela Maria
Amarri Prosecco Limited

Lynch, Fiona
Lynch Associates Ltd

Lynch, George
R.L.G. Trading Limited

Lynch, Jonathan Richard
Lynch Associates Ltd

Lyttle, James
Westvine International Ltd

Mac-Crohon Ron, Ramon
Goldy Gin Limited

MacDonald, Alasdair
Scrawny Al Ltd

MacDonald, Anna Fay
Scrawny Al Ltd

MacDonald, David Graeme
Cellar Twelve Limited

MacDonald, Ian David
Gleninver Limited

MacDonald, Robbie
Renwick MacDonald Bars Ltd

MacDonald, Scott
Brewgooder Limited

MacDonald-Bennett, Andrew John
Goldfinch Whisky Merchants Ltd

MacDuff, Jane Victoria
Cumbrae Supply Co Ltd

MacFarlane, Scott Robertson
Tom MacFarlane and Co Ltd

MacGregor, Alexander Aonghas Gregor
Wester Spirit Co. Ltd

MacGregor, Paul
VDS UK Limited

MacInnes, Miles Thomas
Jascots Wine Merchants Limited

MacKay, Jay
H.B.Clark & Co.(Successors) Ltd
Kitwave Limited

MacKay, Katherine Louise
Whitetail Spirits Limited

MacKay, Laurence
Whitetail Spirits Limited

MacKenzie, Jacqueline Elizabeth
Spar (UK) Limited

MacKenzie, Lucinda Jane
Nestle James & Co Ltd

MacKenzie, Michael
Celtic Spirits Limited

MacKenzie, Peter Douglas Erland
Labrat Brewing Limited

MacKenzie, Roderick Nestle James
Nestle James & Co Ltd

MacKenzie-Gillanders, Julia
Golden Decanters Limited

MacKinnon, Kevin
Ferintosh Distillery Limited

MacLachlan, Ashley Jane
Mixed & Co By A Limited

MacLean, Iain
Quartz Group Scotland Ltd

MacLellan, Donald Alasdair
Wagner Spirits Ltd

MacLennan, Danny
Douglas Laing & Co Ltd.

MacLeod, Alistair
Bondi Brands Limited
Bondi Brewery Limited

MacLeod, Murdina Anne
Kindred Spirit Partnership Ltd

MacNab, Stuart
100 Pipers (Whisky) Limited
Allt A' Bhainne Distillery Ltd
Beefeater Distillery Limited
CADV Limited
Dalmunach Distillery Limited
Martinez Gassiot & Co Ltd
James Hawker and Co Ltd
Pernod Ricard UK Limited

MacNay, James Bruce
Englishman Supplies Limited

MacNicol, George Ian
Dutch Courage Drinks Consultants Ltd

MacSporran, John
Union XV Gin Co Ltd

Macadam, Karen Ann
Altamira Management Services Ltd

Macadam, Richard Desmond
Altamira Management Services Ltd

Mace, Simon Paul
Simon Mace Wine Broking Ltd

Machado, Goncalo Sousa
Liberty Wines Limited

Machicado, Wilfred
Zachicado Ltd

Machlouzarides, Loucia
Amathus Drinks PLC
Bablake Wines Limited

Mack, Peter Edward
Penryn Spirits Limited

Mackie, Ronald John
Alcohol By Volume Limited

Mackintosh, Ewen Cameron
Gordon & MacPhail Limited
Red Door Gin Co Ltd
Speymalt Whisky Distributors Ltd

Mackwood, Gillian Irene
Moet Hennessy U.K. Limited

Macmillan, James Edward
Exmoor Wines Limited

Macpherson, Alan Gordon Henry, Dr
Glenalan Limited
Scotch Whisky International Ltd

Macwan, Neil
Ultimate Drinks Limited

Madhub, Rakesh
Yaad Rum Ltd

Madigan, Patrick Joseph
Padlock Brewery Ltd.

Madubuike, Francis Iwuchukwu
Wine Express Ltd

Mafi, Katherine Victoria
The Dirty Drinks Collective Ltd

Magill, Patrick Maurice
LHK Fine Wines Limited
Vine Wine Limited

Magill, Sophie Emma Grace
Vine Wine Limited

Magkometov, Islam
Worldwine UK Ltd

Maguire, Floyd Damien
A.F.T. (Liquor Stores) Limited

Maguire, Lorna
RHM Retail Ltd

Maguire, Michael Anthony
Wine in Cornwall Limited

Maguire, Phillip
RHM Retail Ltd

Mahabir, Sham Sundar
Shamboozle Limited

Mahal, Harjinder Singh
Mahal Enterprises Limited

Mahalingam, Vijayakumaran
Maha Wholesale Ltd

Mahar, Aijaz Ahmed
Mahar Associates Ltd

Mahler, Aniko
Justerini & Brooks,Limited

Mahmood, Abid
Amis Trading Limited

Mahmood, Amir
AB Care Connect Limited

Mahmood, Wajid
J W Wines Ltd

Mahmud, Taher
Raeburn Fine Wines Ltd.

Mahon, Alan
The Brewgooder Foundation
Brewgooder Limited
Hope Sisters Limited

Mahoney, Richard
Albion Distillery Ltd

Mai, Thanh Tuan
TST Ventures Limited

Maida, Vincenzo
Enzo's Food and Wine Ltd

Maina, Samwel
Intercontinental Trade Solutions Ltd

Mainon, Richard
Hydes' Brewery Limited

Mair, Christopher Alexander
New Wave (Scotland) Limited

Mair, Derek Joseph
Auld Acquaintance Whisky Co Ltd
Gleann Mor Spirits Co Ltd
Leith Distillery Limited

Mair, Vishal Sagar
Tipple Brands Ltd

Majerik, Jiri
Basket Press Wines Ltd

Majid, Abdul
Bengal Foods Limited

Majid, Usman Goni
Bengal Foods Limited

Major, Francis John
Evil Spirits Ltd

Major, Helen
Evil Spirits Ltd

Major, Kara Elizabeth
Cellarers (Wines) Limited
DEF Investments Limited
Diageo United Kingdom Limited
Justerini & Brooks,Limited

Makenchi, Amer Yousif Hanna
Scozia Grappa Ltd

Makin, Colin
Bier UK Limited
Deutsches Beer Limited
Deutsches Bier Limited
The Original Beer Co Ltd
The Original Bier Co Ltd

Mal, Mohan
Bhanbore Trading Company PVT Ltd
Kohisar Limited

Mal, Pesu
Bhanbore Trading Company PVT Ltd
Kohisar Limited

Malde, Parul Keshavlal
Park Royal Wholesale Limited

Malet, Charles Neville Wyndham
Force Brewery Limited

Maley, Daniel Patrick
MBM Resource Trading International

Malhotra, Deepak Kumar
Liquor-Ish Ltd

Malia Barlow, Andrew
Darley Abbey Wines Limited

Malia Barlow, Nichol
Darley Abbey Wines Limited

Malicet, Maryse Elisabeth
Moet Hennessy U.K. Limited

Malinowska, Malgorzata
Kasgo Limited

Mallinson, Lawrence Stuart
Staibano Ltd

Mallya, Vijay, Doctor
Kingfisher Beer Europe Limited

Mallya, Vijay, Dr
United Breweries International (U.K.)

Mammadaliyev, Latif
Grey Cardinal Limited

Mamukashvili, Nino
Nino and Blue Spruce Ltd

Manak, Gurdip Singh
Drinks2u Ltd

Mandalia, Dipin
Chetan Wholesalers Limited

Mandalia, Kishore
Chetan Wholesalers Limited

Mandalia, Nitin
Chetan Wholesalers Limited

Manderson Mills, Mischa Nara
Spirits International Management Ltd

Manera, Claudio
Boutinot Limited
In Vino Bidco Limited
In Vino Limited

Mangles, Andrew
Quantock Abbey Wine Cellars Ltd

Mann, Anthony Michael
Xisto Wines Limited

Mann, Gillian Michelle
The Jaded Group Limited

Mann, Henry Robert
Colchester Mann Limited

Mann, Jaswinder
JJ Wholesalers Ltd

Mann, Jonathon Timothy
Bon Coeur Fine Wines Limited

Mann, Josephine Rachelle
Colchester Mann Limited

Mann, Lynn
Kato Enterprises Limited

Mann, Thomas James
Appellations Limited
LHK Fine Wines Limited

Manning, James David
Shack Drinks Limited

Manning, Richard
Shack Drinks Limited

Manning, Stephen Edward
Divergent Drinks Ltd

Mannion, Anita Elizabeth
The Leamington Wine Co Ltd

Mannion, Frank
Swipe (Wine) Limited

Manoli, Giuliano
Italy Service UK Ltd

Manrique, Julien Olivier
Winecraft Ltd

Mansa Boateng-Dampte, Moesha
Sober Limited

Mansour Dehghan, Abdol Reza
Harlequin (Stockport) Limited

Manzi, Luigi Francesco
Manzi Developments Limited

Manzo, Antonio
Canapacampana Limited

Maqedonci, Fadil
Koha Distribution Limited

Maramba, Martin Luther Junior
The Tap HQ Ltd

Marangoni, Claudio
Dionysius Importers Ltd

Marayana, Rini
SOS Whisky Limited

Marchant, Jamie
Melchior Limited

Marchant, Tom
Quicksip Ltd

Marcos-Ashworth, Daniel
Octagon Industries Ltd

Marcus, David
Alinari Ltd

Mardell, James Charles
Cascade Drinks Limited
Sedgemoor Drinks Limited
Tolchards Limited

Mardell, Karen Michelle
Tolchards Limited

Mardell, Sean Charles
Cascade Drinks Limited

Mardell, Sean Charles
Tolchards Limited

Mardell, Steven Charles
Sedgemoor Drinks Limited
Tolchards Limited

Margarint, Vladimir
Wine Bliss Ltd

Margree, Peter Richard
Norwich Dry Gin Co Ltd

Maria, Richard
The Global Wine Trading Co Ltd

Maria, Van Der Klugt Hermanus Jacobus
M M General Merchandise Ltd

Mariani, Eric
Wines of The Americas Limited

Marinig, Emilia
Uva Wines Ltd

Marino de Oliveira, Joao Paulo
Novarto Drinks Ltd

Marino, Vito
Ambassador Commodities Ltd

Markes, Louise
Billings & Briggs Ltd

Markland, Charles Thomas
Tribeology Limited

Marks, April Deliah
Regency Wines Limited
The Society of Vintners Ltd

Marks, Ian
Regency Wines Limited

Marongui, Pamela
Best-One Local Ltd

Maroso, Antonia
Belloni Limited
Carson & Carnevale Limited

Marquez, Francisca Isabel
Selectia Wine Ltd

Marr, James Michael
Call-a-Keg Beverages Ltd
Call-a-Keg Limited

Marr, Peter Kenneth
Call-a-Keg Beverages Ltd

Marriott, David Geoffrey
Cellar Trends Limited

Marriott, John Charles
Cellar Trends Limited

Marriott, Victoria Louise
Lilo Beverages Ltd

Marsden, Thomas Richard
Sinners Gin Ltd

Marsden-Smedley, James Philip
Foxhole Spirits Limited

Marsh, Paul Anthony
Clock Tower Distilleries Ltd

Marsh, Sarah Anne
Sarah Marsh Ltd

Marsh, Simon David
Vintage Capital II PLC

Marshall, Charles Edward
Berkmann Wine Cellars Limited

Marshall, Lena
Wenlen UK. Ltd

Marston, Benedict John
Chalk & Charcoal Limited

Marston, Kate
Chalk & Charcoal Limited

Martin, Brad Stewart
S & F Drinks Limited

Martin, Edward William Joseph
Berkmann Wine Cellars Limited

Martin, Fay Alison
S & F Drinks Limited

Martin, Rebecca Lucy
The Last Drop Distillers Ltd
Sazerac UK Limited

Martin, Richard Geoffrey
Azizi Drinks Ltd

Martin, Robert Edward
Sporting Benefits Limited

Martin, Stewart Glanmore
S & F Drinks Limited

Martindale-Dopson, Alex
Beer Journey Ltd

Martinez, Enrico Roberto
Archangel Wines Limited

Martini, Alfeo
Wine World Producers Limited

Marton, Attila
Itedomum (UK) Ltd

Martorelli, Francesca
Above Brand Limited

Marty, Olivier Michel
Les Caves de Camille Ltd

Maruszewski, Krzysztof
Ian MacBarrel & Spirits Ltd

Marwaha, Sunil Kumar
LCW (Glasgow) Ltd

Masella, Angela
Ultravino Limited

Maslin, Matthew Joseph
Gravity Drinks Ltd
William of Orange Brands Ltd

Mason, Anthony Frank
Organic Wine Co Ltd

Mason, Christopher Wesley
William Grant & Sons Brands Ltd
William Grant & Sons UK Ltd

Mason, Nicholas Adam
Mason & Mason Wines Limited

Massaiu, Daniele
Dankan Ltd

Massey, David Andrew
C G Supplies Limited

Masters, Kim
Reservedwines Ltd

Masters, Nicholas James Whishaw
180 East Limited

Masters, Paul Stanton
Corney and Barrow Group Ltd
Corney and Barrow Limited

Masurier, Maxence
Made in Little France Import Ltd

Mata, Jean
Petrelli Ltd

Matas Carnero, Juan Manuel
Gourvid Limited

Matei, Ionut
Mother of Wine Ltd

Mathasing, Rahul
Loughborough Student Services Ltd

Matheson, Angus Iain
Matheson Brewers Ltd

Matheson, Felicia Mary
Prohibition Limited

Mathias, Jon Ashwoode
Quellyn Roberts (Wine Merchants) Ltd

Mathieson, Gregor Alexander Jack
Old Town Blending Co Ltd

Mathieson, John Neil MacLeod
Marussia Beverages UK Limited

Mathole, Ngwako Ernest
Mzansi UK Ltd

Matrone, Vincenzo
Cangiani UK Ltd

Matsell, Steven
Tamarind Drinks Limited

Matsui, Takahiro
Panda Trading International Ltd

Matthews, Colin
Glen Scotia Distillery Co Ltd
The Littlemill Distillery Co Ltd
Loch Lomond Distillers Limited
Loch Lomond Distillery Co Ltd

Matthews, Lewis Elliot
The Bottle Bank Limited

Matticx, Reubin
Premier Distillers Ltd

Mattu, Amareet
Just Miniatures Limited

Matwijczuk, Anna
Malthouse Inns PLC

Matwijczuk, Bohdan
Malthouse Inns PLC

Maudsley, Gary
Just Incase Wines Ltd

Mauragas, Regimantas
Alexandria Partners Limited

Mawtus, Matthew John
MJM Hospitality Ltd

Maxey, Maxwell John
Global Wine & Spirits Ltd

Maxted, Ben
Kitwave Limited

Maxwell, Anthony Terence
Liv-Ex Limited

Maxwell, Wellwood George Charles
Thames Distillers Limited
Wokka Spirits Limited

May, Jeremy John Martyn
Island Drinks Limited

May, Joanne
Graysons Freight Services Ltd

May, Jonathan William
JWM Vintners Limited

Mayers, Adam James
Hydes' Brewery Limited

Mayes, Tom
Edmunds Cocktails Ltd

McAlindon, Kevin Peter
Duncairn Wines Limited

McAlindon, Neal Edward
Duncairn Wines Limited

McAulay, John John
Tolsta Brands Limited

McAuley, Martin Francis
United Wine Merchants Limited

McAully, Michael John
The Norfolk Vineyard Ltd

McAvoy, Michelle
Beer Express Limited

McCall, Jonathan
JC Wholsale and Distribution Ltd

McCall, Julie
The International Spirit Vault Ltd

McCall, Leslie Brian
The International Spirit Vault Ltd

McCall, Richard
The International Spirit Vault Ltd

McCallum, Alistair Neil
Ohsake Ltd

McCance, Nicholas James
Nicholas James Gin Ltd

McCandless, Timothy John
The Global Wine Trading Co Ltd

McCardel, Philip Andrew
Aberdrinks Scotland Limited

McCarney, Stephen Lawrence
Broughton Ales Limited

McCarthy, Shane
Ireland Craft Beers Ltd

McCartney, Alan
Kitwave Limited

McCaughley, Barry
Wineaux Ltd

McCaughley, Barry Martin
L.A. Drinks Co Ltd
Little Rock Wine Co Ltd

McCaughley, Elaine Mary
L.A. Drinks Co Ltd
Little Rock Wine Co Ltd

McCloskey, Stuart William
The Vinorium Limited

McClure, Sarah-Jane Noelle
Original Liqueur Co Ltd

McCoist, Alistair Murdoch
Alistair McCoist & Jeff East (Vintners)

McCoubrey, David Andrew
Dowbridge Distributors Ltd

McCoubrey, Elizabeth
Dowbridge Distributors Ltd

McCranor, Stephen
Brewgooder Limited

McCready, Fiona Marion
Terra Toda Ltd.

McCredie, Duncan
Magnus Wines Ltd

McCroskie, Scott John
Edrington European Travel Retail Ltd
Edrington International Brands Ltd
Highland Distillers Limited
Marshall McGregor Limited

McCully, Ben
Silver Rocket Brewing Ltd

McCusker, Thomas Michael
Gleeson N.I. Limited

McDermott, James
Cazcabel Drinks Limited
Cazcabel Tequila Limited
Cut Rum Limited
Proof Drinks Limited
Ruffnek Beer Limited

McDonald, Angus John Snell
General Wine and Liquor Co Ltd

McDonald, Carl Edward James
A Little Bit of French Ltd

McDonald, Iain James
Nightrep Limited
The Perth Distillery Co Ltd

McDonald, Maureen
Beer Express Limited

McDonough, Joanna
Speyside Trading Co Ltd

McDonough, John
Harvies of Edinburgh Limited
Speyside Bonding Co Ltd
Speyside Distillers Co Ltd
Speyside Trading Co Ltd

McDougall, John Charles Alexander
Lamberton Whisky & Spirits Ltd

McElherron, Daisy
Noreast Beers (N.I.) Ltd

McElherron, David
Noreast Beers (N.I.) Ltd

McElherron, Enda Julia
The Beer Bottle Co Ltd
Noreast Beers (N.I.) Ltd

McErlean, Jolian Robert
Stag Brewery Ltd

McEvedy, Allegra Sarah
La Madeleine Wines Limited

McFarland, Ben Aneurin
Hobo Beer & Co Ltd

McFarlane, Leigh
Tom MacFarlane and Co Ltd

McGaw, Roy
Booze 2 U Ltd

McGinn, Celeste Sara
McGin - The Glasgow Gin Ltd

McGlone, James Joseph
The Keg Company (N.I.) Ltd

McGowan, David Andrew
Broughton Ales Limited

McGrath, Killian
Liquid Solutions Distribution (N.I.)

McGrath, Patrick William
Hatch Mansfield Cellars Ltd

McGregor, Sam Alistair
Signature Brew Ltd

McGrotty, Leigh Helen
Kindred Spirit Partnership Ltd

McGuckian, Patrick Generald
Ishke Brands Ltd

McGuigan, Michael
The Gort Inn Ltd

McGuinness, Thomas Stanley
Atom Supplies Limited

McGuire, Christine
Cow West Yorkshire Limited

McGuire, Matthew Christopher
Silver Rocket Brewing Ltd

McGurran, Anthony
Vineyard Belfast Limited-The

McIntyre, Bridget Fiona
Adnams PLC

McIvor, David
Be Rude Not To Ltd

McKay, Eric Scott
Hardywood Park Craft Brewery Ltd.

McKay, Lorna
The Carob Tree Limited

McKay, Nicholas
The Carob Tree Limited

McKay, Trowbridge George
Destilado London Limited

McKee, Matthew Charles William
Magnetic Brands Limited

McKenzie, Brenda
Crafty Connoisseur Limited

McKenzie, Brenda Jane
Gain Brands International (UK) Ltd

McKenzie, James
McKenzie Fine Wines Limited

McKenzie, Stephen Alexander
Crafty Connoisseur Limited
Gain Brands International (UK) Ltd

McKinlay, Stuart Ian
Yeastie Boys UK Ltd

McKinley, Peter David Brian
Spirit Generation Limited

McKinney, John Alexander
Carousel Wines Limited

McLachlan, Kenneth John
Distinction Armagnac Limited
Inverglen Scotch Whisky Co. Ltd

McLain, Bruce Irving, Dr
Fourteen Drops Ltd

McLain, Fiona Eleanor
Fourteen Drops Ltd

McLain, Sarah
Fourteen Drops Ltd

McLaughlin, Cartan
Titanic Holdings Japan Ltd

McLaughlin, Janette Alison
E.W.G.A. Limited

McLaughlin-Green, Alison Mary
Sommeliers Choice Limited

McLaughlin-Green, Timothy Richard
Sommeliers Choice Limited

McLean, Colin
McLean's Gin Ltd

McLean, Ian
MMC Sales and Marketing Ltd

McLean, Karen
Slopemeister Brewing Co Ltd

McLean, Michelle
MMC Sales and Marketing Ltd

McLeod, Alison Meriel
Different Wines Limited

McLeod, Andrew John
Different Wines Limited

McLeod, Kirsty Alison
Duncan Taylor Scotch Whisky Ltd

McLoughlin, Roderick Neal
Victor Lanson Brands Limited
Opus Cellars Limited

McMahon, Patrick
C & C 2011 (NI) Limited
Gleeson N.I. Limited

McMahon, Ryan Francis
Innovative Cocktails Ltd

McManus, Brian
Bevco Limited

McMillan, Thomas
Alchemy Drinks Ltd.
Alchemy Inns Limited

McMullan, Niall Martin
Phoenix Premium Drinks Limited

McMurtry, James Hugh
Libra Drinks Wholesale Limited

McNabb, David Evans
Thirsty Brands Ltd

McNabb, Hannah Louise
Thirsty Brands Ltd

McNally, Nigel Duncan
Brookfield Beverages Limited
Brookfield Drinks Limited
Kestrel Brewing Co Ltd

McNamee, Kevin Andrew
First Crew Ltd

McNamee, Seamus
Jonesborough Wholesale Ltd

McNamee, Seamus Philip
Jonesborough Wholesale Ltd

McNamee, Siofra
Jonesborough Wholesale Ltd

McNaughton, Alan
AMC Trading Co Ltd

McNeil, Steven
Angus Dundee Distillers PLC

McNicholas, Ciaran Thomas
Nightcap Global Limited

McNicoll, Euan
McNicoll and Cairnie Limited

McNulty, Ciaran
The Beer Warehouse (Maidenhead) Ltd
The Marlow Wine Co Ltd

McQuaid, Conor
Dillon Bass Limited

McQuillan, Alan
The Bloomsbury Distillery Ltd

McRae, Ian
Forest Road Brewing Co Ltd

McShane, Michael Joseph
Alchemy Drinks Ltd.
Alchemy Inns Limited

McSherry, Gerrard
J.G. Distillers Limited

McSweeney, Olivia Katie
Senor Agave Limited

McTernan-Mann, Lela
Xisto Wines Limited

McVeigh, Cathal Peter
The Irish Gin Co Ltd

Mchedlishvili, Henry
Georgian British Co Ltd

Meacock, Peter
The Bath Gin Co Ltd

Meadows, John Eric
Organic French Wines Limited

Mechell, Deborah Iris
ANM Wholesale Limited

Medine, Neil Edward
A-Z Spirits Ltd

Medlock, Ann Kirsty
Golden Decanters Limited
Port Ellen Distillery Co Ltd
Port Ellen Distilling Limited

Meeson, Lesley Edna
BCM Brewing Co Ltd

Megaw, Gareth William John
Drumgaw Holdings Ltd

Megson, Brian John
Angus Dundee Distillers PLC

Mehmet-Salih, Susie Umran
Village Cottages (Cornwall) Ltd

Mehran, Pouria
P & P Distribution Limited

Mehran, Pouya
P & P Distribution Limited

Meier, Joaquin
Andina Trade Ltd

Mekata, Megumu
Kanpai (London) Food and Beverage Management Co.,

Melis, Andrea
Luxury Gourmet Ltd

Mellett, Samuel
Oxus Gin Ltd.

Mello Grosso, Andrea
Crudo Limited

Mellor, Andrew Peter
Abyss Brewing Ltd

Mellor, Gillian Mary
Wold Toppers Limited

Mellor, Russell Lawrence
Russell Mellor and Co Ltd

Mellor, Thomas Leslie
Wold Toppers Limited

Melnychenko, Iurii
Gremi Wine Trading (UK) Ltd

Melton, Alison Rose
Norwich Dry Gin Co Ltd

Melton, Simon
Norwich Dry Gin Co Ltd

Melville, Emma
Imbibe Ltd

Melville, Tom Douglas
Black Tartan Limited

Mendoza Tirado, Michael Ivonne
Orale Ltd.

Mendoza, Jose
Cromfine Limited

Meneux, Stephanie
Laurent-Perrier (UK) Limited

Menguini, Philippe Raymond
Trading Import and Export Co Ltd

Merajuddin, Alaa
The Oak Alliance Ltd.

Mercer, Elizabeth
Library Design Studio Ltd.

Mercer, Samuel Raymond
The Three Graces Liverpool Ltd

Mertia, Vikram Singh
The Riding Wine Co Ltd

Merzouk, Hanna Tegest
Candy Cotton Ltd

Mesu, Moshiur Karim
Suntrack Ltd

Metayer, Agathe
France Domaines Limited

Metcalf, Susan
Fabulous Gin Ltd

Methuen, Piers Harry North Dalrymple
Elliston Fine Wines Limited

Methuen, Rebecca
Elliston Fine Wines Limited

Metta, Jimmy
Magenta Wine Investors Limited

Metta, Roger
Magenta Wine Investors Limited

Metzger, Anne
Lothbury Wine Shippers Limited

Metzger, Geoffrey Hugh
Lothbury Wine Shippers Limited

Meyer, Cornelius Francois
Cape Wines Limited

Meyrick, Charles Valentine Llewellyn Tapps Gervis
Balthazar Limited

Meza, Franco Andres
M & M Romanian Imports Ltd

Mezencio, Renato de Paula
The Primos Group Ltd

Miceli, Antonio
Uva Hitchin Ltd

Michael, Andrew George
Cold Formd Ltd

Michael, Kerry
Aotearoa Distribution Ltd
The Madison Drinks Co Ltd
Regency Event Solutions Ltd
Venus Wine & Spirit Merchants PLC

Michaelides, Lakis
Venus Wine & Spirit Merchants PLC

Michalisko, Milan
MCMCtrans Ltd

Michelmore, William Franck
St.Austell Brewery Co Ltd

Miclaus, Radu Gheorghe
Bihl Ltd

Middleton, Howard Arthur
Sporting Benefits Limited

Middleton, Ranulf Peter
D'Arcy Wine Merchants Limited

Migliuolo, Filippo
Real Wine Cellar Limited

Mihailovic, Jovan
Monteadria (UK) Limited

Mijavec, Igor
Mezzaro Ltd

Miklaucich, Gavin
GNR Distillery Limited

Milburn, Thomas David
Birds of Arcadia Ltd

Miles, Henry James Pearson
Liv-Ex Limited

Miles, Richard
Glen Scotia Distillery Co Ltd
The Littlemill Distillery Co Ltd
Loch Lomond Distillers Limited
Loch Lomond Distillery Co Ltd

Miles, Stephen John
SJ Wines Ltd

Millan, Alvaro Ribalta
Triangle Wines Limited

Millar, Jason David
Theatre of Wine Limited

Millar, Jonathan
Inverroche Ireland Ltd

Millar, Sean Lionel
Pruno Wines Ltd

Millard, Andrew Christopher Glanvile
Sharing The Best Limited

Millard, Eny Cristina
Sharing The Best Limited

Miller, Christopher Stuart
Brewgooder Limited
J.W. Filshill International Ltd

Miller, Leon William
Mill Distributors Limited

Miller, Marcin Adam
Number One Drinks Co Ltd

Miller, Nigel Alexander
Stow Brewery Limited

Miller, Ricahrd John
Hardywood Park Craft Brewery Ltd.

Miller, Zavon
After Eight Alcohol Concierge Ltd
Magna Juice Ltd

Millington, Peter
Docklands Trading Co Ltd

Mills, Gary
Fifty One Forty Limited

Mills, Geoffrey Norman John
Landmark Wholesale Limited

Mills, Graham Paul
Walnut Tree Distillery Ltd

Mills, Jenny
Zing Vodk Limited

Mills, Michael Peter
Zing Vodk Limited

Mills, Paul Francis
Intriguing Brands Limited
JJBrands Limited

Milreu, Raquel Melo
The Primos Group Ltd

Mincheva, Petya Ivanova
Premium Bulgarian Wine Ltd

Minerva, Joseph Richard
Global Village Wines Limited
Vinimpo (U.K.) Limited

Minev, George Todorov
The Highland Scotch Whisky Co Ltd

Minhan, Susan Margaret
Meadow Trading Co Ltd

Minhas, Rashid
The Booze Bolton Limited

Minkin, James Philip
Purity Brewing Co Ltd

Minshull, Stephen Thomas
Island Ales Limited
Isle of Wight Brewery Limited

Minshull, Thomas
Island Ales Limited
Isle of Wight Brewery Limited

Minter, Christina Jocelyn
Liquid Ninja Limited

Mir, Yannick
Swissgrapes Limited

Miranda, Amanda Denise
Xorta Global Management Ltd

Mirtahmasebi, Mohammad
Essex Catering Supplies Ltd

Mirti, Francesco
Themirtis Limited

Miserere, Luca
Luca Wine Limited

Mishra, Harshit
The BV Group UK Limited

Misiunas, Arvydas
Blue Diamond (UK) Ltd

UK Wholesalers of Beers, Wines and Spirits   dellam

Mistry, Naunit
India Gold Limited

Mitchell, Adam
Viktor and Walker Ltd

Mitchell, Anthony Vincent
Cellar 28 Ltd
Russetglow Limited

Mitchell, Graham Christopher
The Wine Explorer Limited

Mitchell, John Dennis
Mitchell's Vintners Limited

Mitchell, Nicola
The Wine Explorer Limited

Mitchell, Peter John Birney
Laytons Wine Merchants Limited
Laytons Wine Services Limited

Mitchell, Rachel Ann
Tractor Shed Brewing Limited

Mitchell, Thomas Graeme
Tractor Shed Brewing Limited

Mitica, Stefan
V & A Jobs UK Ltd

Mitrache, Ionut
M & M Romanian Imports Ltd

Mizen, Paul
The Cracking Little Wine Co Ltd

Modugno, Vincenzo
Winelistphobia Ltd

Mody, Kaushik Amritlal
Azizi Drinks Ltd
Docklands Trading Co Ltd
Gandhi Wine Suppliers Limited
Mongoose Brewing Co Ltd

Moeckell, Adrian Christopher
E.W.G.A. Limited

Mohal, Ranveer Singh
Free Trade Beers and Minerals Ltd

Mohamad, Khorshed
Delbrew Ltd
Delbroo Ltd

Mohamed, Azhar
Blu-Dot Commodities Limited

Mohamed, Zubair
The Bottlers Limited
Raeburn Fine Wines Ltd.

Mohammadi, Saeed
Jaguar Beverage Ltd

Mohammed, Naseem Sultan
Triple AAA Limited

Molla-Diez, David
Divergent Drinks Ltd

Molloy, James Edward
Neptune Rum Ltd

Molyneaux, Chris Paul
Wingwalker Vodka Limited

Molyneux-Roberts, Rodger
23 High Path Ltd
Blackcattaverns Ltd

Molyneux-Roberts, Rowan Elizabeth
Blackcattaverns Ltd

Monaghan, Paul
Monaghan Marketing Limited

Monahan, Catherine
Gigglewater Productions Ltd

Monier Williams, Rupert Henry
Decorum Vintners Limited

Monks, James Peter
Decanter Wines Limited

Monks, Krystyna Bernadette
Decanter Wines Limited

Montague, Andrew Terence John
A.F.T. (Liquor Stores) Limited
Mundus Wines Limited

Monti, Matteo, Dr
Falugamaro International Ltd

Montuori, Angelo
Varmont Ltd

Montuori, Luca
Varmont Ltd

Moody, Glen Michael
The Moody Spirit Co Ltd

Moody, Stephen Antony
Cossart,Gordon and Co.Limited
John E.Fells & Sons Limited
Whigham Fergusson Limited

Moon, Emily Jane
Moonberries Ltd

Mooney, Sam Robert
The Mad Batchers Ltd

Moore, Angela
Waveney Ales and Ciders Ltd

Moore, Brandy
BDDR Enterprises Limited

Moore, Darren
Waveney Ales and Ciders Ltd

Moore, David
Wildflower Wines Limited

Moore, David Neill
J.W. Filshill International Ltd
Spirits for Good CIC

Moore, Derek
BDDR Enterprises Limited

Moore, John Clark
The Stirling Whisky Co Ltd

Moore, Jonathan Alan Oliveira
Werfa Holdings Ltd

Moore, Martin John
Moore's Enterprises Limited

Moore, Michelle
Waveney Ales and Ciders Ltd

Moore, Steven
Waveney Ales and Ciders Ltd

Moortgat, Michel Luc Marie Jozef
Duvel Moortgat UK Limited

Morbin, Alex
Nordic Imports Ltd

Moreau, Viviane
Lionel Export Agency Ltd

Morejon Hernandez, Tomas
Toke Commodity Electro Limited

Moreno Costa, Jose Antonio
Aftersunset Ltd

Moreno, Abbi Nicol
Flora Fine Wines Ltd

Moresi, Antonello
Passion Wine International Ltd

Moretti, Anna Veronica
Vento Marino Ltd

Morgan, Adam Geoffrey
Amlot Morgan Fine Wines Ltd

Morgan, Alan John
Deceptive Wines Limited

Morgan, Charles Elliot
Au Vodka Ltd

Morgan, Damian Patrick
Bielo Limited

Morgan, John Peter
Morgan Classic Wines Limited

Morgan, Joshua William Ellis
Morgan Jupe Limited

Morgan, Lorraine Claire
Deceptive Wines Limited

Morgan, Max Samuel
C & E Transport Ltd

Morgan, Michael
MJLM Limited

Morgan, Robert John
Terry Platt Wine Merchants Ltd
Pulling & Co.Limited
Tanners (Shrewsbury) Limited
Tanners Cymru Limited
Tanners Wines Limited

Morgan, Sophia Louise
Morgan Classic Wines Limited

Morgan, Thomas Drummond
Morgan Classic Wines Limited

Morgan, Timothy James
Deskbeers Limited

Moriarty, Michael Joseph
Boutinot Canada Limited
Boutinot Limited
Boutinot USA Limited
Boutinot Wines Limited
In Vino Bidco Limited
In Vino Limited
Moreno Wine Importers Co Ltd
Rude Mechanicals Limited
Vinandar Wines Limited

Morigeon, Thierry Jacques
Champagnes and Chateaux Ltd.

Morley, David
Oliver & Bird Limited

Morrell, Alistair John
Cider Is Wine Ltd

Morrin, Joshua Michael
Koomor Brewing Co Ltd

Morris, Aimee
ANM Trading Limited

Morris, Christopher David
Cask and Craft Direct Ltd

Morris, Duncan Eric
Ascona Retail (Leases) Limited

Morris, Janet
ANM Trading Limited

Morris, John Edward
No.9 Leisure Limited

Morris, Michael Andrew
MC Drinks Limited

Morris, Naomi
ANM Trading Limited

Morris, Richard
Tayst Ltd

Morris, Scott John
ANM Trading Limited

Morris, Susan Coralie
MC Drinks Limited

Morrish-Banham, Caroline Rachael
Morrish & Banham Ltd

Morrison, Gavin Kenneth
Crafty Warehouse Ltd

Morrison, Jamie Walker Stanley Pringle
KIC Inventories Limited
Radleigh Wines Limited

Morrison, Margaret Edith
A. Dewar Rattray Limited

Morrison, Stanley Andrew
A. Dewar Rattray Limited

Morrison, Stanley Walker
A. Dewar Rattray Limited

Morrissey, Neil Anthony
Neil Morrissey Real Ale Co Ltd

Morrow, Annalee Louise
Ratcliffe & Brown Wines and Spirits

Morrow, Grace Emma Mary
Harry's Road Fine Wine Limited

Morsink, Philip
O'Donnell Moonshine Limited

Mortimer, Jason
Asta Barista Baby Ltd

Mortimer, Jessica Elizabeth
Flawless Spirits Ltd

Mortimer, Kelly
Waistcoat Wines Ltd

Mortimer, Lynn
Levenridge Limited

Mortimer, Samuel John
Flawless Spirits Ltd

Moseley, Joanne Nicola
Da'mos Food & Beverages Ltd

Mosley, Peter
Liquid Projects International Ltd

Moss, Daryl
Premium Beverage Refreshments Ltd

Motojima, Yoshisuke
Demball Limited

Mouche, Philippe Alexandre
Noble Wines (UK) Limited

Moulding, Jamie
Liquid Assets Group Ltd.

Moumchi, Fathali
T & M Food Products Ltd

Mounier, Bernard Emile Marie
BM Wines Limited

Mount, Sam Alexander
Kentish Pip Ltd

Mountain, Dave John
MMGT Limited

Mousley, Christopher
Isle of Wight Brewery Limited

Mousley, Christopher Barnet
Island Ales Limited

Moutsou, Maria, Dr
Southern Wine Roads Limited

Moylan, Denis Morgan
J. Chandler & Company, Limited

Moynagh, Michael
A.F.T. (Liquor Stores) Limited

Moysiadis, Ypatios
My Global Ventures Limited

Mudie, Keith Alexander
Aberdrinks Scotland Limited

Mugnano, Maria
Maestrale Group Ltd

Mugnano, Vincenzo
Maestrale Group Ltd

Muiesan, Marcello
Il Tastevin Ltd

Muirhead, Ben Robinson
Rawson Trading (Doncaster) Ltd

Mukadam, Ebrahim Kassam
LWC Drinks Limited
H.T.White & Co Ltd

Mukaila, Olukun
Stoney Hospitality Limited

Mulchandani, Manoher Ghanshamdas
Imperial Cash & Carry Limited

Mulchandani, Phatachand Ghanshamdas
Imperial Cash & Carry Limited

Mulkeen, Rachel Jane
Sips 'n' Nibbles Ltd

Mullen, David Owen
Spirits for Good CIC

Muller, Jorg
Japan Gourmet (UK) Limited

Muller, Norbert
Crucial Brands Holdings Ltd

Mullin, Gillian
Donatel Freres Limited

Mullin, Malcolm George
Donatel Freres Limited

Mullock, Joshua James Richard
Bespoke Fine Wines Limited

Mundroina, Matthew
Good Wine Limited

Munir, Mahim
Bruist Trading Ltd

Munoz Rubio, Alberto Jose
Felix Solis Avantis UK Ltd

Munro, Jamie
Whitetail Spirits Limited

Munro-Morris, Scott
Capper & Co Ltd

Muradov, Dimitry
G Point 7 Ltd
R Spirit Ltd

Murchan, Bernard
Orchard Wine Co Ltd

Murcott, Robert
Murcotts Ltd.

Murdoch, David
C & D Exports Ltd

Muriu, Dennis
Cenimex Ltd

Murland, Rebecca Luise
Smashing Wines Limited

Murphy, Andrew Gavin
Consolidated Wines Limited

Murphy, Daniel
Innovative Cocktails Ltd

Murphy, John Kieran
Crafty Cask Wholesale Ltd

Murphy, Mark Edward
Murphy & Yeung Brewing Co Ltd

Murphy, Robert
Loopland Brewing Co Ltd

Murphy, Ross Andrew
Ramx Ltd

Murray, Alan Campbell
William Cadenhead Limited
Springbank Distillers Limited

Murray, Alexander Julian
B.D. (S/W) Ltd

Murray, David Douglas
Chardon Wines Limited

Murray, David Edward, Sir
Chardon Wines Limited
Wine Importers (Edinburgh) Ltd

Murray, James
Whisky Rebellion Limited

Murray, Keith Andrew
Chardon Wines Limited
Wine Importers (Edinburgh) Ltd

Murray, Lindsey Dawn
B.D. (S/W) Ltd

Murray, Paul David Alan
Hayloft Ventures Ltd

Murray, Steven Craig
Tulaich Ltd

Murtagh, Steven
Jean Juviniere Limited

Murtaugh, James Patrick
Hardywood Park Craft Brewery Ltd.

Murugesan, Nandhakumar
Nandha Murgesan Ltd

Muscat, Andrew Joseph
New Generation Wines Limited

Mustafa, Syeda Monika
RRK Supplies Limited

Myatt, Paul Anthony
Cape Secrets Limited

Myers, Colin
Jetchill Ltd

Myhill, Alexandra
Fizz Guru Limited

Mytilineos, Nikolaos
Cosmic Services Limited

Nadde, Ferass
Buzz Booze Ltd

Nagra, Deepak
Railway Bar & Grill Ltd

Nagra, Poonam
Stargold Wholesale Ltd

Nagra, Sukhjinder Singh
Crazy Gin Ltd

Naheed, Talat
Orion Cash & Carry Limited

Nairn, Allan James
Wester Spirit Co. Ltd

Nakvi, Sayed Anis
Crown Cash & Carry Ltd

Nandwana, Krushnakumar
Kash & Karry Supplies Ltd

Naples, Kyle James
Kindman Brewing Ltd

Narang, Jasbir Singh
Narang Wholesalers Limited

Narayanan, Mahadevan
United Breweries International (U.K.)

Narioo, Eric Serge
Les Caves de Pyrene Limited
Santat Wines Limited

Naritsuka, Yusuke
Asahi Premium Brands Ltd
Asahi UK Ltd

Narsap, Serhat
Sonvino Ltd.

Nash, Edward Charles John
Fine Cider Limited

Nash, Felix
Fine Cider Limited

Nash, Jacob
Peace Bond Ltd

Nastase, Veronica
Rondel Trading Ltd

Natenadze, Ioseb
8000 Vintages Limited

Nathan, Brenda Venestia
Glenbrynth Limited

Nathan, Brian
Glenbrynth Limited

Nathan, David Generald
W.H. Brakspear & Sons Limited

Nathan, James Douglas
Pull The Cork Limited

Nathan, Michael Darren
Glenbrynth Limited

Nathan, Steven Jeffrey
Distell International Holdings Ltd

Naude, Gybertus Du Toit
New Generation Wines Limited

Naughton, Nuala
The Highland Malt Whisky Co Ltd

Naughton, Philip
Better Buy Ltd

Navaladi, Manoj
Manoj Navaladi Ltd
Navaladi Ltd

Navarro, Olivier Santiago
Delivering Happiness Limited

Navrozov, Robin Lee
Robin Navrozov Consulting Ltd

Nawaz-Khan, Hamid
Cellar & Co Limited

Nayiga, Lina Kulthum
Pop Cake Box Limited

Naylor, Jake Jefferson Ryan
The Portsmouth Gin Co Ltd

Naylor, Rachel
Honeybee Farm Ltd

Nazir, Qaiser
London Creek Limited

Neal, Jonathan Lee
My Gin My Way Ltd

Neame, Jonathan Beale
Shepherd Neame Limited
Todd Vintners Limited

Nebbe-Mornod, Joelle
Nick Dobson Ltd

Nedelcu, Alina
Wine Group Ltd

Needham, Leanda Daphne
Scrumpy Wasp Limited

Needham, Timothy Paul
Scrumpy Wasp Limited

Neil, Lindon Wilson
The Whisky Trading Co Ltd

Neill, John James Whitley
Whitley Neill Limited

Neill, Robert Samuel
Neill & Company Wine Importers Ltd

Nekic, Sasha
Test Tube Products Limited

Nel, Jennifer Catherine
Publik Wine Limited

Nelson, Brian Hubert Hamilton
Harry's Road Fine Wine Limited

Nelson, Richard
The House of Roo Ltd

Neri, Giulio
Natural Bay Limited

Nesterenko, Pavel
Humo International Limited

Nestor, Viktorija
Wine UK Direct Limited

Nethercott, Gareth Rory
Drinks Inc. Ltd
Original Liqueur Co Ltd
Uisce Ard Ltd

Neville- O'Brien, James Vincent
Cazcabel Drinks Limited
Cazcabel Tequila Limited
Proof Drinks Limited
Ruffnek Beer Limited

Newall, Sharon
Arisaig Distillers Ltd
The Pink Gin Co Ltd

Newberry, Deborah Louise
Concordia Wines Ltd

Newcomb, Matthew Jeremy
Panache du Sud Ltd

Newman, Daren Paul
Rockstar Spirits Limited

Newstead, David Stephen
Tamarind Drinks Limited

Newton, Kirstine
CHX Distillers Ltd

Nguyen, Hung Duy
Skyden Spirits Ltd

Nguyen, The
Old and Rare Whisky Limited

Nguyen, Thi Hong Duyen
Sotus Limited

Nguyen, Thi MY Hanh
Do Trading Limited

Niang-Fall, Ely
Ely's Cocktails Ltd

Nibbio, Valeria
Vinum Limited

Nicholls, David Christopher John
Grape Opportunities Ltd
D & M Nicholls Limited

Nicholls, Janice
Vanilla Blue Limited

Nicholls, Thomas Edward
Murray Brother's Whisky Ltd

Nichols, Joe
Lanty Slee Liquor Co Ltd

Nichols, Robert Ian
Babco UK Ltd.
World of Patria International Ltd

Nicholson, David Lawrence
DC Imports UK Ltd

Nicholson, James
JN Trading Limited
James Nicholson Wine Limited

Nickerson, Stuart
The Malt Whisky Co Ltd

Nickerson, Wilma
The Malt Whisky Co Ltd

Nicolet, Pierre Andre Lucien
Kol App Ltd

Nicoll, Stuart Ferguson
My Gin My Way Ltd

Nicolson, Todd Brian
New Zealand Beer Collective Ltd

Nicolson, William Alexander
De Burgh Fine Wine Limited

Nie, Zhonglun
Leppelmann & Nie Limited

Niedbalec, Bogdan Piotr
Beerpol Ltd

Niedzwiecki, Andrew
Worsley Gin Ltd

Nielsen, John
Monopole Wine Portfolio Management Ltd

Nightingale, George Edward
Quick Liquids Limited

Nigris, Candido
Vino Italiano Importers Ltd

Nigudkar, Aditya
3ABC Ltd
Jocks and Peers Brewing Co Ltd

Nimmo, Gary Michael
Sky Wines Limited

Nimmo, Lucinda Vivienne
Sky Wines Limited

Nisar, Ammara
Nisar Traders Ltd

Nisar, Muhammad Usman
Sheikh Super Store Ltd

Nita, Florin Cristian
Rosemille Ltd

Nithiyanandan, Senthuran
Thagam UK Limited

Nixon, Stephanie Louise
Lion-Beer, Spirits & Wine (UK) Ltd

Nkumane, Maqhawe Mcabango
Aqua Vitae Vodka Limited

Noack, Michael Heinz
Australian Vintage (Europe) Ltd

Noble, Gareth
Pirate's Grog Rum Ltd

Noble, James Daniel
SPP Wine Ltd

Noble, Lucilla Charlotte James, Lady
Praban Na Linne Limited

Noble, William Edward Philip
QNGC Limited

Nobles, Victoria Jane
Liberty Wines Limited

Noh, Eunji
EJ Orendale Ltd

Nokes, Amanda
Pierhead Drinks Limited

Nolte, Werner
Angola Beverages Holding Co Ltd
Henry C. Collison and Sons Ltd
Distell Europe Ltd.
Distell International Holdings Ltd
Distell International Limited
Imperial Distillers Co. Ltd

Norchi, Alan Gibson
The Plymouth Rum Co Ltd

Norcott, Christopher John
C N Drinks Limited

Norcott, Nicola May
C N Drinks Limited

Noria, Hoshang Rohinton
Hapusa Spirits UK Ltd

Norrie, Jayne Carmichael
The Gin Room Scotland Ltd

Norrie, Mark Willoughby John
Moke Fine Wines Limited

Norrie, Penelope Jane
Moke Fine Wines Limited

Norris, Elliott James
Tamarind Drinks Limited

Norris, Stephen Hedley
More or Less Drinks Co Ltd

North, Simon Paul
Laughing Ass Brewery Ltd

Northway, Thomas
Big Mouth Wine Limited

Norwood, Leigh Richard
Favourite Beers Limited

Norwood, Nicola Carole
Favourite Beers Limited

Notley, Philip Andrew
Demon Vodka Limited

Nott, William
Meanwhile Drinks Ltd.

Novas Hay, Eusebio
Vinova Export Limited

Noyce, Vincent Robert Amos
The Rum Club Ltd

Ntjortjis, Kyriakos Kikis
Tanner Brodin Limited

Ntjortjis, Lewis Loizos
Tanner Brodin Limited

Nuamah, Eric Antwi
Adonko Bitters (UK) Ltd

Nucci, Elio
Vinitaly Limited

Nucci, Giacomo
Vinitaly Limited

Nucci, Giulia
Vinitaly Limited

Nugent, Marguerite Katherine
Iron & Rose Ltd

Nugent, Robin Owen
Iron & Rose Ltd

Nunn, Richard Anthony
Louis Latour Limited

Nuttall, Derek
Red Rose Drinks Limited

Nuttall, Lee Stuart
Extravision Security Systems Ltd

Nwachukwu, Uchenna Donald
Vanilla Blue Limited

O' Shaughnessy, Caroline
Jackson Nugent Vintners Ltd

O'Brien, Christopher David
Pearl Leisure Limited

O'Callaghan, Leon John
Beerspotters Ltd

O'Connell, Brigitte
O'Vineyards Ltd

O'Connor, John
Tech-Beach UK Limited

O'Connor, Patrick
Fine & Rare Wines Limited

O'Donoghue, Jacqueline Margaret
Marathon Beverages Ltd

O'Donohue, Ian Martin
Harry Bromptons Ltd
Tudor Drinks Ltd

O'Donovan, John
Insignia Spirits Limited

O'Donovan, Robert
Insignia Spirits Limited

O'Flaherty, Michelle
Coca-Cola Amatil (UK) Limited

O'Hara, James
Tapp'd Cocktails Ltd

O'Loughlin, John Francis
Bielo Limited

O'Mahony, Alexander David
23-7 Brewing Ltd

O'Mara, Nigel Francis
In Vino Veritas Ltd

O'Neill, Catherine Elizabeth
Saddleworth Real Ale Ltd

O'Neill, Francis Austin
H & F Export Limited
Terrae Vinariae Limited

O'Neill, Generaldine Veronica
O'Neill Fine Wines Limited

O'Neill, Malcolm Alexander
O'Neill Fine Wines Limited

O'Neill, Mark Joseph
The Beer and Gas Man Limited

O'Neill, Stephen Anthony
Ishke Brands Ltd

O'Reilly, Garrett Peter
Anjo Wines Limited

O'Reilly, Kevin Michael
Anjo Wines Limited

O'Reilly, Patrick
Lightbox Brands Limited

O'Rourke, Kevin John
The Wineman (UK) Ltd

O'Shaughnessy, Caroline
Jackson Nugent Vintners Ltd

O'Shea, Justin Daniel
Goldy Gin Limited
Goldy Limited

O'Sullivan, Callum James
RDM Wines Limited

O'Sullivan, Martin Patrick
Hochfeld International Ltd

O'Sullivan, Nigel
Fine Wines Direct UK Limited
RDM Wines Limited

O'Sullivan, Renata Paula
RDM Wines Limited

Oades, Robert John
Essenza Di Romagna Limited

Oates, Alexander George
Sinners Gin Ltd

Oatley, Charles William
Louis Latour Limited

Oatley, Richard Alexander
The Rum Club Ltd

Obiora, Ihiukwu
Divine Associates Ltd

Obrien, Dennis Michael
Eurotrade Supply Limited

Och, Elisabeth
Hay Hampers Limited

Oconnor, Paul
The Hitchin Wine Co Ltd

Oddy, John Mathew Patrick
Premier Cru Fine Wine Ltd.

Odierno, Susan Mary
Inro Drinks (Abtec) Limited

Odierno, Trevor Paul
Inro Drinks (Abtec) Limited

Odim, Edward
Aceo Limited
Coleburn Distillery Limited

Odonohue, Martin
Harry Bromptons Ltd
Tudor Drinks Ltd

Odudu, Ogheneochuko
Delta Western Distributions Ltd

Oenga, Elkanah Ondieki
Alko Vintages UK Ltd

Offord, Malcolm Ian
The Three Stills Co Ltd

Ogunfeibo, Anthony Olukayode
Black Kola UK Limited

Ogungbola, Kayode Ajibola
Kay Distributions Ltd

Ogunniyi, Victoria Ibidun
The Drinks Bay Limited

Ohta, Kumiko
Isake International Limited

Ojosipe, Raufu Adedamola
O & P Investments Limited

Okeyo, Zachary Osano
ZLCSolutions Ltd

Okolie, Chukwuemeka
Emthea Ltd

Okun, Taiwo Odion, Dr
Aziken Ventures Limited

Olaniyan, Kofo
Firewater Merchants Ltd

Olaopa, Folarin
Deholjob Limited
London Drinks Limited

Oldfield, Richard John
Shepherd Neame Limited

Oldschool, Stephen Richard
Oldschool Wines Limited

Olichwier, Milan
Majlen Ltd

Olive, Samuel Lister
Olive Wines Limited
Wine Freedom Limited

Oliver, Louise
Seven Cellars Ltd.
The Wine Keg Co Ltd

Oliver, Paul Andrew
Oliver's Beer and Wine Limited
Olivers Wine Agency Limited
Revilo Group Limited
Vinfinity Limited

Olley, Frank
Olley (NE) Limited

Olley, James Philip, Dr
Fitlikey Brewery Ltd

Olliver, Gray Bensted
Branded Drinks Ltd

Olsen, Sven Ladefoged
Metropolitan Spirits (U.K.) Ltd

Omonforma, Samuel Pius
Sam-Gel Global Ventures Ltd

Oncica, Constantin
ONCC Import Limited

Onofrei, Sava Ionut
Savafrei Ltd

Onwuka, Nnaemeka Francis
Sageitude Ltd

Onyekwere, Chukwuemeka Victor
Bevimangia Limited

Oosthuizen, Nardus
Burn Stewart (U.S. Holdings) Ltd

Orazu, Kenechukwu Chukwuemeka
Samco Global Foods Ltd

Orazu, Virginia Uju
Samco Global Foods Ltd

Orchard-Lisle, James Comrie
Orchard-Lisle Wines Ltd

Ordor, Churchill
Lizard Management Ltd

Orgyan, Janos
Mephisto Wine Merchants Ltd

Ormandy, Christy Shane
The Mad Batchers Ltd

Orr, Christopher Andrew
Wineguise Limited

Orriols-Gil, Jordi
Vintage 1947 Limited

Orrock, Sam James
Gold Tooth Limited

Orsolini, Daniel
Orso Wine Agencies Limited

Orsolini, Nicola Jane
Orso Wine Agencies Limited

Osben, Daniel James
Favela Cerveja Ltd

Osei-Tutu Bonsu, Edward
Bemco International (UK) Ltd

Osuji Odefa, William
Rando Global Alliance Limited

Osunbor, Stella
By His Grace Food Ltd

Otarashvili, Tamar
S & B Impex Ltd

Otkidych, Kristina
Wine Research Limited

Otkidych, Xeniya
OX Wines Ltd

Oueida, Mohamad Khaled
O.W.Loeb & Co Limited
Marc Fine Wines Limited

Ovenden Ferry, Lisa
Canny Class Ltd

Ovenden, David
Manley Wines UK Limited

Ovenden, Leanne
Canny Class Ltd

Owen, Dax
Beer & Wine (Northern) Limited

Owen, Laura
Whitmore and White Limited

Owen, Michael James
Hall & Woodhouse Limited

Owen, Nigel Henry Patrick
Mother Kelly's Distribution Ltd

Owen, Stanley John
SJO Supplies Limited

Owens, David
The Nightingale Drinks Co Ltd

Owensby, Leslie
Headline Wines Ltd

Oyebanji-Kofoworola, Folake Omoshalewa
Nifol Limited

Oyetunde, Kayode Adeniyi
Bdellium Trading Co Ltd

Oyono Tompson, Maria de Los Angeles
Blue Wine Ltd

Ozarowski, Krzysztof
K & G Spirits Ltd

Ozcali, Umit
Bournemouth Food Ltd

Ozdemir, Ethem
Vinovest Limited

Ozerska, Aleksandra
Humo International Limited

Ozgumus, Cuneyt
Beylerbeyi UK Ltd
MDS International Ltd.

Ozkoc, Erol Mustafa
La Diva Drinks & Food Ltd

Ozkoc, Hasan
La Diva Drinks & Food Ltd

Pabial, Ravinder Paul
Green Leaf Liquids Limited

Pacey, Tracey
Charles Mitchell Wines Limited

Pacheco, Ney
DTB Distribution Ltd

Packer, Julian Simon
Exeter Drinks Ltd

Paddison, Carl Robert
Hitchin Brewery Ltd

Paddle, David
Black Dog Wine Agency Limited

Padgett, Denise Mary
Denby Dale Wines Limited

Padgett, Phillip
Denby Dale Wines Limited

Padia, Ashwin Karsandas
Asante Distributors Limited

Padilla Docampo, Estrella Gabriela
GSYB Ltd

Padilla, Manuel
La Cerveceria Limited

Page, Lawrence Anthony
The Society of Vintners Ltd

Page, Liam Ryder
Steel City Exports Ltd

Page, Trevor Andrew
Loughborough Student Services Ltd

Pagni, Alberto
Winicious Limited

Paine, Russell Mark
Galette Wines Limited

Palij, Michael Ian Norman
Winetraders (UK) Limited

Palit, Shumana
Ultracomida Trading Co. Ltd

Pallithazhe, Bejoy
Tropical Ltd

Pallone, Umberto
D & K Capital Ltd

Palmer, Alex Richard
Wine Associates Limited

Palmer, Colin John
Billecart - Salmon (UK) Ltd

Palmer, Neil
Vintage Roots Limited

Palmer, Nigel James
Maison Liedberg Limited

Palous, Joel
Buzwine Limited

Panait, Ion
Fabijhon Wine Ltd

Panaro, Christopher
Uist Distillery Ltd

Panayiotou, Angelos
Windfall Logistics Limited

Pancolini, Sergio
Global Trade & Consulting Ltd

Pandya, Rajesh
P & P Vino Limited

Panesar, Nirmal
Karma Beverages Ltd

Panizzon, Oscar
PimentoDrinks UK Ltd

Panpurin, Daniil
Volfram Ltd

Paoletti, Diletta
Di.Wine Limited

Paoletti, Flavia
Di.Wine Limited

Papalia, Anthony Jon
Cape Wine Merchants Ltd

Papaloizou, Christos Kyrillos Ioannou
Venus Wine & Spirit Merchants PLC

Papanikolaou, Georgios
The Greek Wineshop Ltd

Papic, Milan
Easy9 Limited

Papworth, David Keith
Broad Street Brands Limited

Papworth, Rebecca Louise
Tomlinson Whisky Merchants Ltd

Paramagurusamy, Mohanaraj
Richway Cash and Carry Ltd

Parameswaran, Kartheepan
Silverlite Cash & Carry Ltd

Park, Nathan James
Instabooze Limited

Park, Roman
EL IP Rights Limited
Ellustria Limited

Parker, Alexander William
London & Scottish International Ltd

Parker, Andrew Nicholas
Valley Wines, Beer & Spirits Ltd

Parker, Celia
Parkers Newsagents Ltd

Parker, Christopher Ronald
London & Scottish Spirits Ltd

Parker, Heather Patricia
London & Scottish International Ltd
London & Scottish Spirits Ltd

Parker, James Ian
3 Big Dogs Limited

Parker, John
JDT Drinks Co Ltd

Parker, Percy
Medoff UK Ltd

Parkin, Simon McDearmid
Copper Still Co Ltd

Parkins, Timothy James
Stokes Fine Wines Limited

Parkinson, Timothy Charles
The Tasting Barn Ltd

Parla, Gio
Cask Hub Limited

Parr, Benjamin Thomas Stephen
Rawson Trading (Doncaster) Ltd

Parrett, Mark
M Wines Limited

Parry, Claire Frances
The Hurns Beer Co. Limited
Hurns Mineral Water Co. Ltd

Parry, Constance Patricia
The Hurns Beer Co. Limited
Hurns Mineral Water Co. Ltd

Parry, George
Samphire Drinks Ltd

Parry, William Thomas
The Hurns Beer Co. Limited
Hurns Mineral Water Co. Ltd

Parsons, Anthony Charles
SJZP Limited

Parsons, Daniel
Pioneer Spirits Ltd

Parsons, Jeremy Winslow
Leomar Limited
Tortuga Brands Limited

Parsons, Lesley Ann
SJZP Limited

Partington, Michelle
Shellys Drinks Limited

Partridge, Fergus Christopher
Made To Measure Ltd

Parum, Danis
G Point 7 Ltd

Parvez, Mohammed Akeel
ANA Distribution Limited

Parvulescu, Constantin
Dunarea Albastra Ltd

Paskett, Kyle
The Wine Prophets Limited

Passmore, John Walter Raymond
Bonfire Hill Limited
Bruce Jack Wines Limited

Pastides, Haralambos Michael
Bric Commerce Ltd

Patch, Gemma Nicole
G M Drinks Limited
G M Drinks of Hampshire Ltd

Patch, Marc
G M Drinks Limited
G M Drinks of Hampshire Ltd

Patchett, Nichola
Italian Wine Buyers Club Ltd

Patel, Akash Sudhirkumar
PatelCashAndCarry Limited

Patel, Bhimji Nanji
William James & Sons Ltd

Patel, Chirag Jeetendra
Sofibel Ltd

Patel, Dhara Bhimji
William James & Sons Ltd

Patel, Dipakkumar Babubhai
D & N Supplies Limited

Patel, Dipum
One Point Supplies Limited

Patel, Hanish
HP Enterprises Limited

Patel, Hina
Diageo Great Britain Limited

Patel, Hiren Kumar
Coral MGT Limited

Patel, Imran
Trade Network Supplies Limited

Patel, Jass
The Boutique Spirit Co Ltd

Patel, Jaymish
Unicodrinks ESP Ltd

Patel, Jitendra
Dhamecha Foods Limited

Patel, Kaushikkumar Rambhai
Raks Suppliers Limited

Patel, Kilesh
Champers (Wholesale) Limited

Patel, Kunal Bhimji
William James & Sons Ltd

Patel, Kunal Kumar
HP Enterprises Limited

Patel, Kunver Bhimji
William James & Sons Ltd

Patel, Maheshkumar Ramanlal
Rarus Ltd

Patel, Maulikkumar Ashokbhai
Deeti Wholesale Limited

Patel, Mayur
Most Popular Limited

Patel, Meetal
Pearly Queen Beer Co Ltd

Patel, Nainaben Maheshkumar
Rarus Ltd

Patel, Nalinaben Dipakkumar
D & N Supplies Limited

Patel, Narendra Chhotubhai
Barn Direct Limited

Patel, Nikesh Sushil
8 Barrels Club Ltd

Patel, Nilkanth
Woodland Wine Store Limited

Patel, Pareshkumar Vinubhai
Champers Wines Limited
KSS Drinks Limited

Patel, Praful
Harp Wines & Spirits Ltd

Patel, Rajesh Arvind
Farr Vintners Limited

Patel, Rikul
8 Drinks Ltd
Kristal Spirits UK Limited

Patel, Sandip Navnitbhai
NCE Trading KFT Ltd

Patel, Suneet Chirag
Iberian Wine Shippers Limited

Patel, Tejaswir Jagdishbhai
M & T Wholesale Ltd

Patel, Ushaben Narendra
Barn Direct Limited

Patel, Viral
Unicodrinks ESP Ltd

Pateras, Mary Elizabeth
The Kitchen Table Wine Co. Ltd

Pateras, Polychronis
The Kitchen Table Wine Co. Ltd

Paterson, Andrew
Halifax Wine Co Ltd

Paterson, Isobel
W.G. Paterson & Son Limited

Paterson, Karen
Halifax Wine Co Ltd

Pathak, Manish
Sai Soft Drinks Ltd

Pathak, Vikram
Jivana Spirits Ltd.

Pathmasri, Jeyaratnam
Family Choice Wholesale Ltd

Patidar, Sandip Praful Chandra
Black Forest Beers Limited

Paton, Graeme David
Global Wine Distributors Ltd

Patterson, Adrian James
Tanners Wines Limited

Patterson, Larry Dinell
The Beverage Provider Limited

Pattison, Steven Clark
Bowsaw Bourbon Limited
Drinksology Limited
Mayday Island Limited
McGrath's Brewing Limited
Red Bonny Rum Limited
Sailortown Brewing Limited

Patton, Nigel
Bang The Elephant Brewing Co Ltd

Pau, Amit Jayantilal
Pau Drinks Limited

Paudel, Kul Bahadur
New Claire Wine Ltd

Paunic, Tom
Workshy Brewing Ltd

Paver, Ian Kinloch
IKP Trading Limited

Pavitt, Darren Rudkin
Amwell Springs Brewery Co Ltd

Pavli, Andrew Nicholas
Burgundy Tuscany Piedmont Ltd
Wimbledon Wine Cellar Limited

Pavli, Prodromos
The Last Word Drinks Co Ltd

Pavlovski, Zak
Tikves London Ltd

Pawelek, Tomasz
The Drinks Orchard Ltd
Top Spirits Ltd

Payne, Salomon
Team Yebo Ltd

Peachey, Edward Martin
Justerini & Brooks,Limited

Pearce, Alexander Stephen James
Original Wooden Case Limited

Pearce, Chris
World Sake Imports UK Ltd

Pearce, Christine
Cribbar Limited

Pearce, Gareth David
Goedhuis & Co Ltd

Pearce, Michael
Cribbar Limited

Pearman, Georgina Elizabeth
Bobby Beer Co Ltd

Pears, Rory
Loughborough Student Services Ltd

Pearson, Richard Mark
Burbage Wines Limited

Peddell-Grant, Gregory Daren
White Wolf Brewery Ltd

Pedrick, Peter William
The Champagne Collection Ltd

Peek, David Joel
Forty Acres Ltd
Hayloft Ventures Ltd

Peel, Daniel
Vino Pronto UK Ltd

Peel, Francis Edward Guy
Whitebridge Wines Limited

Peel, Patricia Jane
Whitebridge Wines Limited

Peirce, Michael Alexander
Mayfair Brands Limited

Pellegrino, Marco
Pellegrino Wine and Food Distribution

Penev, Ivailo Penchev
Tiny Vessel Brewing Co Ltd

Penine, Didier
Say It With Champers Ltd

Pennell, Huw Charlton
Edrington-Beam Suntory UK Distribution

Pennington, Thomas B L
Liquid Lounge Drinks Co. Ltd

Penny, Edward
Colton Fox Trading Limited

Pennycook, Liam John
Burnobennie Distillery Limited

Penrith, Victor
St George's Beer Co. of St Austell Ltd

Pepin, Bruno Nicolas
Louis Latour Limited

Peposhi, Sadije
S.X Prosecco Party Limited

Peposhi, Xhemile
S.X Prosecco Party Limited

Peppa, Stella
Wines Around Mediterranean Ltd

Pepper, Andrew John
Bondi Brands Limited
Bondi Brewery Limited

Pepper, Jon
Enotria Winecellars Limited

Percy, Alexander
The Modest Merchant Limited

Pereira, Conceicao
Eden Garden Trading Limited

Perera, Dillon Ladislaus
Vendange (European) Limited

Peres, Sandro
Quintessential Decadence Ltd

Pereyre, Alexandra
Laurent-Perrier (UK) Limited

Perisic, Alexandar
Sco & Whisky Limited

Perisin, Alan Sasa
Vino & Spirits Limited

Periyasamy Manoharan, Ragul
Ragul Ltd

Perkins, Matthew
Perkins Independent Wine Traders Ltd

Perkins, Matthew Rex
Thameside Rum Co Ltd

Perkins, Vanessa Estelle
Perkins Independent Wine Traders Ltd

Perna, Mark
Astrum Wine Cellars Limited

Perret, Aymeric
Maison Sassy UK Limited

Perrin, Marc-Olivier Pierre Jacques Francois
Premium Vineyard Company UK Ltd

Perrin, Matthieu Pierre Marcel Joseph
Premium Vineyard Company UK Ltd

Perry, Bruce
Marussia Beverages UK Limited

Perry, Elizabeth Stefka
Dromedary Trading & Resources Ltd

Perry, Neil Adrian
Balcony Wines Ltd
Drink Artisan Ltd

Perry, Richard Julian
Drink Artisan Ltd

Pert, Janine Mary
Discover Wine (UK) Ltd
Tipsy Events Ltd

Perticati, Andrea
Vine & Cork Limited

Pescod, Henry John Magoveny
Pongolo Ltd

Pestell, Joseph
The Wessex Wine Co Ltd

Peters, Demi Leigh
UK Lesiure Ltd

Peterson, Paul
B & P Beverages Ltd

Petkov, Petko Yordanov
Invino Vitalis Ltd

Petkus, Irmantas
Trading Irmis Ltd

Petrenko, Gleb
Other World Wines Limited

Petrova, Marina
Vineus Limited

Petszaft, Justin Toby
Atom Supplies Limited

Pettifer, Steven Russell
Cadogan Wines Limited

Pettit, Brian Robert, Dr
Childale Limited

Pham, James
JPHA Ltd

Philipon, Jerome Henri
Mentzendorff & Co Ltd

Philippon, Sylvain Jehan Marie Arthur
Square Wine Ltd

Philips, John Donald
The Great Wine Group Limited

Phillimore, William Andrew Justin
Charles Wells Brewery Limited
Charles Wells,Limited

Phillips Bryant, Colin David, Dr
Saam Wine Co Ltd

Phillips, Emma Sally
The Cotswold Port Co. Ltd

Phillips, Fiona Ann
Boxford Wine Co Ltd

Phillips, Hugh Nigel
Boxford Wine Co Ltd

Phillips, Julia Elizabeth
Just Perfect Wines Ltd

Phillips, Kiron Thomas
RK Vodka Limited

Phillips, Matthew James
The Bombay Spirits Co Ltd
John Dewar and Sons Limited

Phillips, Richard Bakewell
Monkey Shed Estate Brewing Co Ltd

Phillips, Robert Kenneth Lewis
Tolchards Limited

Phillips, Sam Merton
Phil Cellars Ltd

Phillips, Zanesh Joseph
RK Vodka Limited

Piagno, Silmara
Direct2door Food & Beverage Ltd.

Picard, Michel Bernard
Spirits Development & Management Company (SDMC)

Picca, Eugenio
Viniexport Limited

Piccoli, Manuel
Birrificio Del Ducato London Ltd

Pickard, David James
Avant Garde Drinks Ltd

Pickard, Robert
Avant Garde Drinks Ltd

Pickard, Stephen Martin
Pesodeocho Wines Ltd

Pickering, Marcus George
The Snickering Pig Drinks Co Ltd
Spirits for Good CIC
Summerhall Distillery Asia Ltd

Pierlot, Clement Albert
Pinglestone Estate Limited

Pierron, Nicolas
Somm in the Must Ltd

Pietrini, Hugues Michel
Cellar Trends Limited

Pigott, Lance
Vintage Roots Limited

Pilar, Beatriz
Europvin UK Limited

Pile, Charlotte Elizabeth
Fairytale Gin Limited

Pile, Mark
Fairytale Gin Limited

Piler, Julian David
Bohemian Brands Limited
JDS Trading Limited

Pilla, Francesca
Ricordo Ltd

Pilla, Giovanni
Ricordo Ltd

Pillai, Vivekanand Raman
Cochin Heritage Ltd

Pillar, Balazs
North West Industries Ltd

Pillhofer, Daniela
Newcomer Wines Limited

Pinckney, Charles William
Pinckneys Gin Limited

Piorecki, Lukasz
Alcos Trade Limited

Piovesana, Valeria
Italicus Ltd

Piper, Christopher Charles Neville
Christopher Piper Wines Ltd

Pires, Jose de Nobrega
Alivini (North) Limited
Alivini Co Ltd
Franciacorta Limited

Pirozzi, Antonio
Alivini (North) Limited
Alivini Co Ltd
Franciacorta Limited

Pisk, Matija Davor Keyworth
Dirty Drinks Ltd

Pitamber, Vinodlal Samji
Espana Imports Ltd

Pitcher, John
Battlefield Beers Limited

Planella Ferrer, Maria Eugenia
Ambessa Goods Ltd

Plant, David Andrew
Present Tense Limited

Plath, Carl Michael
Morgenrot Group PLC

Plath, Rudi Michael
Morgenrot Group PLC

Plath, Valerie Mary
Morgenrot Group PLC

Platt, Jeremy
Ffarm Vintners Limited
Great Orme Drinks Co. Ltd

Platt, Thomas Matthew Fairley
Liberty Wines Limited

Platts, Alan
Presidente Wines Limited

Platts, Hayley Fiona
Presidente Wines Limited

Plattt, Carolyn Sylvia
Great Orme Drinks Co. Ltd

Plazewski, Dariusz
Fortunella Spirits Ltd

Pluznik, Berthold
Richmond Distillers (Zurich) Ltd

Podda, Jean Baptiste
Connecting Italian Food UK Ltd

Pokorny, Jiri
Russian Investment II Limited

Poletti, Emanuele Antonio
Ora Brewing Co Ltd

Polini, Simone
Glenforest Limited

Pollen, Michael Ian
The Opendoor Gin Co Ltd

Pollen, Suzanne Gail
The Opendoor Gin Co Ltd

Polleux, Philippe Sylvian Christian
Dago Wines Ltd

Pollock, Martyn
Kibo Wines Ltd

Pollock, Ross
Copper and Rye Leisure Ltd

Pollock, Sarah
Infinity Wines Limited

Poole, Barry Kenneth Clive
Wine Poole Limited

Poole, Lindsay Jane
Wine Poole Limited

Pope, Jeffrey
Blackstorm Rum Ltd

Pople, Thomas Edward Hugh
The Bath Gin Co Ltd

Portal, Anthony
Portal Dingwall & Norris Ltd

Portal, Jane Marcella
Portal Dingwall & Norris Ltd

Portal, Philip Jeremy
Portal Dingwall & Norris Ltd

Porte, Olivier
Authentic French Wines (Importers)

Porter, Adam James
Jascots Wine Merchants Limited

Porter, David Victor
Quintrox Limited

Porter, Jonathan Paul
Europlus Trading Limited

Porter, Rosalyn
BCM Brewing Co Ltd

Porter, Simon
Itasca Wines Limited

Porter, Stephen John
BCM Brewing Co Ltd

Porton, Andrew George
The Wine Fusion Limited

Posnett, Maurice Adrian
Bellwether Wines Ltd

Possenniskie, Samuel Ian
Yeastie Boys UK Ltd

Postlethwaite, Ben Thomas
Wyfold Vineyard Limited

Potocki, Jan Roman
Potocki Spirits (Europe) Ltd

Pottinger, Andrew James
The Wine Keg Co Ltd

Poulain, Frederic Francois
Mathieu Poulain Limited

Poulain, Mathieu Alex
Mathieu Poulain Limited

Poulter, Roger Alan
A and R Fine Wines Limited

Poulter, Stephen John
Poulter Group UK Limited

Poulton, Thomas Anthony
Cuestion Tequila EMEA Ltd
Cuestion Tequila Limited

Poulton, Tracey Ruth
Cuestion Tequila EMEA Ltd
Cuestion Tequila Limited

Povero, Claudio
Wine IT Limited

Povey, Joseph Alan
Beerco Limited

Powar, Anandpreet Singh
Drinks 4 Less (UK) Limited

Powell, Babara
Vito International Ltd

Powell, Brian Andrew
Castillon International Ltd
Vito International Ltd

Power, Lee
Lpower Ltd

Power, Victoria
Bridge Wine Limited

Pownall, Simon
Hotham's Spirits Ltd

Pownall, Stephen Michael
The Langwith Brewing Co Ltd

Pozzi, Andrea
Bibendum PLB Group Limited
Bibendum Wine Limited
Chalk Farm Wines Ltd
Matthew Clark (Scotland) Ltd
Matthew Clark Bibendum Limited
Matthew Clark Limited
Matthew Clark Wholesale Bond Ltd
Matthew Clark and Sons Limited
Tennent Caledonian Breweries UK Ltd
Tennent Caledonian Breweries Wholesale
Walker & Wodehouse Wines Ltd
Wallaces Express Limited

Prabaharan, Thirunavukarasu
Belgrave Distribution Ltd

Prabhakaran, Virutthasalam
HNB Trade Ltd

Pradines, Veronica
Il Palagio Ltd

Prady, James Edward
Canal Cellars Ltd

Prager, Charles Emanuel
Planet Wine Trading and Consulting

Prasad, Rahul
Prasad Trading Co Ltd

Prasad, Umesh
Vitosha Wine Ltd

Prashanth, Nellutla
N & M Wholesale Ltd

Prat, Aurelia Yveline
Georges de la Chapelle Limited

Prats Perez, Alicia
GSYB Ltd

Praulitis, Andris
Andris Holdings Limited
Vinvm Ltd

Prescott, Peter James Wendell
The Wine Library Limited

Preston, Brett
Neon Brew Co Limited

Preston, Elizabeth Louise
Cubic Brands Limited

Preston, Robert Lee
Cubic Brands Limited

Preston, Simon
Alfa Drinks Limited

Previero, Filippo
Mercury Spirits Ltd

Price, Alec John
Melange Drinks Ltd

Price, Ann Elizabeth
Les Vignerons de Saint Georges Ltd

Price, Caroline Jane
Frontier Trading International Ltd
Frontier Trading Limited

Price, Charlotte Louise
Norman Price Wines Limited

Price, David John
DLRF Limited

Price, Gerard Vincent
Les Vignerons de Saint Georges Ltd

Price, James Brian
Professional Wine Services Ltd

Price, Martin Traquair
Park Place Drinks Limited

Price, Natalie
The Lucky Strike Pub Co Ltd

Price, Richard James
Frontier Trading International Ltd
Frontier Trading Limited

Price, Stephen Kenneth
The Azzurri Kitchen Ltd

Price, Susan Jane
Park Place Drinks Limited

Price, Thomas
Northwest Drinks Ltd

Price, Timothy Charles Rose
Norman Price Wines Limited

Pride, Tiffinie Jane
Wiltshire Liqueur Co Ltd

Priestley, Emma Clare
Pipehouse Gin Limited

Priestley, Samuel Francis
Pipehouse Gin Limited

Priestly-Bingham, Georgina
The Articulate Drinks Co Ltd

Priestly-Bingham, Sarah
The Articulate Drinks Co Ltd

Prioteasa, Anamaria
Sarpe L & C Ltd

Pritchard, Tom
TP Retail Ltd

Probert, Anthony Grigori Tonu
Freight Brewing Co. Ltd

Procter, Cole Peter
Just Incase Wines Ltd

Prosser, Gary
The Fightback Brewing Co Ltd

Prowse, James Edward
Good Spirits Ltd

Prudhomme, Pascal Lucien Emile
CRVC UK Limited

Prymaka, Alexandra Mary Dain
Bugle and Co Ltd

Prymaka, Charles Dominic Owen
Bugle and Co Ltd

Pugh, Stephen Crommelin
Adnams PLC

Puiu, Maxim
Maxim & Co Limited

Pun, Siddanta
Low-Key Essentials Ltd

Puni, Balraj
Magma Liquid Ltd

Punia, Kamalprit Singh
The Wine Cellar Midlands Ltd

Punter, Mark Richard
Portugal Winelist Ltd

Punzano, Laura Bowman
Tipple Spirits Co Ltd

Purcaru, Ruxanda Rodica
Dracula Wine House Ltd

Purcell, Gaynor
Fabulous Gin Ltd

Purcell, Joanne Michelle
Farr Vintners Limited

Purdie, Caroline Amy
J.G. Distillers Limited

Purewal, Jaspal Liam Singh
3 Tigers Limited

Puri, Ajay Krishan
Cascade Trade Services Ltd

Putanu, Mircea Ion
Brown Bear Tales Ltd

Puvirajasingam, Nilaan
Wine Castle Ltd

Qamarauli, Berdia
Cenimex Ltd

Qi, Xiaofei
Redoor Limited

Quadri, Mohd Arsadul
Prime Cash & Carry Limited

Quaglia, Carlo
Del Professore Limited

Quamina, Jamil
Quamina Quality Drinks Co Ltd

Queiros Mota, Pedro Miguel
Ops Wines Ltd

Quellyn Roberts, Paul
Quellyn Roberts (Wine Merchants) Ltd

Quiceno Cardona, Juan Camilo
Chic Fruit Ltd

Quinlan, Catherine Suzanne Genevieve
A and R Fine Wines Limited

Quinn, Anne
The Keg Company (N.I.) Ltd

Quinn, Jackson Aaron
Au Vodka Ltd

Quinn, Julia Fiona
Popaball Limited

Quinney, Gavin Charles Chavasse
Far Out Wines Limited

Qureshi, Haseeb
The Beer People Limited

Qureshi, Latif Ahmed
Viking Enterprises Limited

Ra, Jee Young
London Ale UK Ltd

Raciti, Charles Anthony
World Brands Duty Free Limited

Rackham, Jack Arthur
Emporia Brands Limited
Rackham Investments Limited

Rackham, James Arthur
Emporia Brands Limited
G Life Limited
Mayfield Distilling Co Ltd
Rackham Investments Limited
A.H.Rackham Limited

Radaelli, Elizabeth Eleanor
Ewer Limited

Radaelli, Ernesto Remo
Ewer Limited

Radev, Georgi Dinkov
London Spiced Dry Limited

Radley, John
Intertrade Wholesale Limited

Raffety, Adam
Rafine Limited

Raffety, Michael Charles
Rafine Limited

Raffety, Sarah Wendy
Rafine Limited

Raffy, Guillaume
Bodega Raffy UK Ltd

Rai, Pardeep Singh
Jupiter Wholesale Limited

Rai, Rajinder Singh
Pan Euro Foods Limited

Raia, Agostino
Prestige Wine & Food (UK) Ltd

Railton, Martyn Adam
Euroboozer Limited

Raja, Harshad Kumar
Miracle Drinks Limited

Rajamanickam, Pradeep
Pradeeprjm Limited

Rajenthiram, Sinnathurai
Junga Ltd

Ramade, Natalia
Uropa Group Ltd

Ramade, Rodrigo
Uropa Group Ltd

Ramage, Emma
Quantock Abbey Wine Cellars Ltd

Ramakrishnalal, Athavan
SASC Enterprise Limited

Ramakrishnan, Sonya
Lora Trading (Europe) Ltd

Ramamurthy, Shekar
Kingfisher Beer Europe Limited

Ramirez Gaytan, Isis Elizabeth
Casa Ambar Limited

Ramos, Felix Jose Solis
Felix Solis Avantis UK Ltd

Ramos, Rui Manuel Alves
79North Limited

Ramsay, Claire
Free Spirits Group Ltd

Ramsay, Tristan
Free Spirits Group Ltd

Ramsden, Noel
Davy & Co Ltd

Ramzan, Amaan
Landmark Wholesale Limited
United Wholesale Grocers Ltd

Ramzan, Mohammad
United Wholesale Grocers Ltd

Ramzan, Nabeel
United Wholesale Grocers Ltd

Rana, Bilal, Dr
Alliance Foods Limited

Rance, Paul
Craft Wines Ltd

Randall, Justin
Goedhuis & Co Ltd

Randall, Stuart Graham
The Drinks Club Ltd
Libertine Spirits Ltd

Randhawa, Jothappar Singh
Leo Global Limited

Randhawa, Ravinder
Kingfisher Beer Ltd

Randles, Michael Richard
Asahi UK Ltd

Raninqueo, Carlos Emilio
Eight Brothers Corporation Ltd

Rankin, Andrew William
Greenwood Distillers Limited
Greenwood Spirits Limited

Rankin, Bryan John
A Taste of The Caribbean Ltd

Rankin, Stephen Alexander Masson
Speymalt Whisky Distributors Ltd

Rankine, Adam
Fine Wine Co Ltd

Rankine, Laura Agnes Anne
Ian MacLeod Distillers Limited

Rankine, Patrick Andrew
Symposia Wine Limited

Ransom, William Robert
Highfern Limited

Rao, Vinod
DEF Investments Limited

Rapeneau, Vincent
Champagne G.H. Martel & Co. (U.K.) Ltd

Rashid, Tariq
Bluetec Trading Services Ltd
TBrands Distributor Ltd

Rashkov, Atanas
Atanas Distributors Ltd

Rassu, Dionigi
Earth Elements Ltd

Rasul, Mahmud Ur
Square Wholesale Ltd

Ratasaf, Athaf
Drinkss Cash and Carry Limited

Ratcliffe, Robert John [1957]
Liberty Wines Limited
North South Wines Limited

Ratcliffe, Robert John [1962]
The Bottle Drinks Co Ltd

Ratemo, Paulo Nyambane
Premier Beverages Limited

Rathmnavelu, Jeyalakshmi
Lordsworth Limited

Rathna, Sateesh
Tata Trading Limited

Rathnavelu, Jeyalakshmi
BJ Drinks Ltd

Rathoar, Ansuya Devi
S.A.R.D.V.M Ltd

Ravenscroft, John Kenneth
Beerscellars (UK) Limited
Cosmopolitan Drinks Limited
Global Drinks (UK) Limited
W. Hall & Son (Holywell) Ltd
Hops and Barley (Group) Ltd
Hops and Barley (UK) Limited
Hops and Barley Limited
Pemberton Central Limited

Raventos, Ramon
Codorniu UK Limited

Rawlins, Nelson
Bosco-UK Limited
La Delizia UK Limited

Rawlinson, Jonathan Richard
The Southsea Gin Co Ltd

Rawlinson, Katharine Jane
The Southsea Gin Co Ltd

Rawlinson, Paul Stephen
Charles Wells,Limited

Rawlinson, Peter Andrew
Sheffield Brewers Collective

Raworth, Philip John
The Can Man Ltd

Rawson, Gemma Lucy
Prosecco 1754 Limited

Rawson, Kim Patrick
Asante Distributors Limited

Ray, Joseph Scott
Applecart Drinks Limited

Ray, Rinkal Shivam
Lobins Limited

Rayani, Mahmoud Jiva
Asante Distributors Limited

Raymond, Howard Wyndham
West End Brands Ltd
West End Drinks Limited

Raymond, Issac George
Aqua Vitae Vodka Limited

Rayne, Edwin
Express Drinks Ltd

Rayner, Oliver
Wineclub Online Limited

Razak, Imran
Burton Drinks Limited
Midlands Drinks Limited

Read, Edward Anthony
Distant Lands Ltd

Read, James Graham
James Fine Wines Limited

Rebelo de Oliveira, Claudia
UWD Limited

Rebuelta Del Pedredo Gonzalez, Pedro Andres
Gonzalez Byass UK Limited

Reckley, Anthony Christian
Swimming Pigs Ltd.

Record, Anthony
New Generation Wines Limited

Redfern, Paul William Lawrence
49 Wines Limited

Redpath, George Christopher, Mr
William Cadenhead Limited
Springbank Distillers Limited

Reed, Archie Patrick Finton
Arundo Limited

Reed, Jane Marie
N R Wines Limited

Reed, Martin Stuart
S.A.Brain & Co Ltd

Reed, Nicholas Howard
N R Wines Limited

Reed, Nicola Jane
Beeble Liquor Limited

Rees-Williams, Tudor David
Ambessa Goods Ltd

Reeve, Carol Ann
Manzi Developments Limited

Regan, Amanda
Mymexico Global Ltd

Regan, Kathryn
Plant Relief Ltd

Regan, Nicholas
Plant Relief Ltd

Rehal, Varinder
International Procurement and Logistics

Rehman, Raza
Greens Wholesale Ltd

Reid, Barry
Reids Gold Brewing Co Ltd

Reid, Carl
Batch Cider Ltd

Reid, Kyle Lewis
KLR & RCR Distribution Ltd

Reid, Natalie Anne
The Gin Cooperative Ltd

Reid, Ronald Chisholm
KLR & RCR Distribution Ltd

Reihill, Jane Maria
A.F.T. (Liquor Stores) Limited

Reitz, Thomas
Neu Brandenburger Beer Co Ltd
United Wine Estates Limited

Rekhi, Guneal Singh
Rekhi Wholesale Ltd

Rendle, Christopher Edgcumbe
Highly Spirited Ltd

Rendon, Rodrigo
Dion Wines & Food Limited

Rene, Fred
Oakmount Group Limited

Rennie, Andrew Grant
Grandor Limited

Rennie, Danielle Rose
Grandor Limited

Renny, Bruce William
Bogart Spirits Limited
Rok Drinks Limited

Renton, Neil Macpherson
Wine Importers (Edinburgh) Ltd

Renty, Denis Jean
F & B Premium Brands Limited

Renwick, Brian Hamilton
The Jaded Group Limited

Renwick, Martin
Renwick MacDonald Bars Ltd

Resta, Carlo
Cibusrex Ltd

Restoy Cabrera, Emilio
Martin Miller's Gin Limited

Retsas, John
New School Wines Limited

Reuben, Jonathan
Bohemian Brands Limited

Reuben, Martin Jack
Bohemian Brands Limited

Reuter, Tim
Kane Republik Ltd

Reuter, Tim David
RCI Spirits Ltd

Revell, Joe
Delivering Happiness Limited

Reynolds, Alexander
GCBW Catrine Ltd

Reynolds, Alison
Rendog Gin Ltd

Reynolds, Ben
Andrew R. Wilson Limited

Reynolds, Georgine
Andrew R. Wilson Limited

Reynolds, Martin John Hunter
Raymond Reynolds Limited

Reynolds, Raymond Martin Hunter
Raymond Reynolds Limited

Reynolds, Shaun
Blackedge Brewing Co Ltd

Rhoades-Brown, Matthew Generald
MB Whisky Limited

Rhodes, Michael Kenworthy
Fines Master Spirit Co Ltd

Rhys, George Dafydd
Southwick Court Fine Wines (2012) Ltd

Rhys, John Frederick William
S.A.Brain & Co Ltd

Ribaric, Noemi
Dmomentum Ltd

Ribeiro, Manuel
In Wine & Spirit Solutions, Ltd

Ribeiro, Victor
Lisbon Wines Limited

Rice, Allan Edward
Atom Brewing Co Limited

Rice, Particia Ada
Churnet Valley Drinks Limited

Rice, Patricia Ada
M.& M.Value Limited

Rice, Patricia Ada
H.B.Clark & Co.(Successors) Ltd
Thorne Licence Wholesale Ltd

Rich, Peter Charles
Laytons Wine Merchants Limited
Laytons Wine Services Limited

Richard, Bruno
Berkmann Wine Cellars Limited

Richards, Craig Johnatan
The Beer Belly Company Incorporated
Veda UK Limited

Richards, James Shirley Hart
Vin Neuf Limited

Richards, Joshua Matthew
Mount Fetti Ltd

Richards, Lisa
Hills Prospect PLC

Richards, Serena Anne
Everards Brewery Limited

Richardson, Stephen Michael
Mellasat Wines Limited

Richbell, Keith Robert
Richdells Wine Merchants Holdings

Richell, Alan Charles
The Curious Wine Cellar Ltd

Richell, Andrea Jane
The Curious Wine Cellar Ltd

Richman, Susan
The Norfolk Rum Co Ltd

Richmond, Eleanor Jane
Profile Wines Limited

Richtor, David
Neon Brew Co Limited

Rick, Benjamin
Vintage 1947 Limited

Rider, Mark John
Shepherd Neame Limited
Todd Vintners Limited

Riedemann, Bernd
Riedango Limited

Riera-Duocastella, Joan Marc
Ribox Quality Goods Ltd

Ries, Joachim
Finest Wine & Delicatessen Brokers Ltd.

Rieser, Thilo
Slurp Wine Co Ltd

Riga, Alessandro
Mondial Wine Limited

Rigby, Carl
Bondi Brands Limited
Bondi Brewery Limited

Rijk, Paul Christiaan Jozef
Rip Mountain Brewery Ltd.

Riley, David Francis Riley
Boondales Limited

Riley, Francis Joseph
Boondales Limited

Riley, Mark
Edrington-Beam Suntory UK Distribution

Riley, William
Boondales Limited

Riley-Hicken, Kieren Lee
Hips Drinks Ltd

Rimmer, Allan Douglas
Isle of Bute Gin Co Ltd
Phil Macan Limited

Rinaldi, Fabio
La Vigna Vini Ltd

Ringwood, Joseph Henry Herbie
Brazen Beer Limited

Risby, Christine
Choice Drinks Limited

Risby, John Francis
Choice Drinks Limited

Ristanovic, Zoran
City Wine Collection Limited

Ristanovic-Santrac, Olivera
Sanwin Ltd

Ritchie, Christopher Douglas
Hi-Spirits Ltd
The Last Drop Distillers Ltd
Sazerac UK Limited

Rittlinger, Alexander
Yapp Brothers Limited

Riva, Hilary Susan
Shepherd Neame Limited

Riviere, Alain
Veravinea Ltd

Riviere, Antoine Herve Marie
Chez Antoine Ltd

Rivolta, Jason
Glugit Limited

Rizzelli, Antonio Lloyd
Kanj Wholesale Ltd

Roane, Dayle Ivan
Molotov Brand Limited

Robb, Charles John Edward
Robb Brothers Wine Merchants Ltd

Robb, Denver
Robb Trading Ltd

Robb, Philip Norman James
Robb Brothers Wine Merchants Ltd

Roberson, Clifford John
RWM Holdings Limited
Roberson Wine Merchant Limited

Roberson, Talya
RWM Holdings Limited

Roberts, Anthony Brian
Borders Distillers Limited
Borders Distilling Limited
The Three Stills Co Ltd

Roberts, David William
Goedhuis & Co Ltd

Roberts, Francis Alexander
Beattie & Roberts Imports Ltd

Roberts, Mark
Croatian Fine Wines Limited

Roberts, Mark James Lloyd
Decorum Vintners Limited

Roberts, Marvin Julian Calvin
Paramount Vintners Ltd

Roberts, Michael David
Nottage Bar Supplier Limited

Roberts, Paul Norman
Paul Roberts Wines Limited

Roberts, Peter John
Sheffield Brewers Collective

Roberts, Reginald Roy
Celtic Wines Limited

Roberts, Richard Ivan
Wetherby Brew Co Limited

Roberts, Suzanne Louise
Majestic Wine Warehouses Ltd

Roberts, Thomas Gwilym
Wetherby Brew Co Limited

Roberts, Vicky Louise
High Jinks Limited

Robertson, Andrew John
Schuler Wine St. Jakob's Cellars Ltd

Robertson, Brian Douglas
Forth Wines Limited
Inverarity Vaults Limited
J A Glass Limited

Robertson, Craig
Roblex Ltd

Robertson, David Graham
The Whisky Trading Co Ltd

Robertson, Ewan James
Bibendum PLB Group Limited
Bibendum Wine Limited
Chalk Farm Wines Ltd
Matthew Clark (Scotland) Ltd
Matthew Clark Bibendum Limited
Matthew Clark Limited
Matthew Clark Wholesale Bond Ltd
Matthew Clark and Sons Limited
Tennent Caledonian Breweries UK Ltd
Tennent Caledonian Breweries Wholesale
Walker & Wodehouse Wines Ltd
Wallaces Express Limited

Robertson, Fiona
Roblex Ltd

Robertson, James
Bacana Sangria UK Limited

Robertson, Kenneth Robert
Port Ellen Distillery Co Ltd
Port Ellen Distilling Limited

Robertson, Louise
Rara Drinks Co Ltd

Robertson, Mark
Lupton Wine Limited

Robertson, Paul Michael
Southbrew Co Ltd

Robertson, Rachael
Bacana Sangria UK Limited

Robertson, Sebastian
Highland Vintners Ltd

Robertson, Susan Jane
The Whisky Trading Co Ltd

Robicquet, Jean-Sebastien
La Guilde du Cognac Limited

Robins, Michael Victor Andrew
Laytons Wine Merchants Limited

Robinson, Alan William
The Bajan Trading Co Ltd
Barwell & Jones Limited
The Cornish Rum Co Ltd
Chalie Richards & Co Ltd

Robinson, Christopher Edward
Wiltshire Liqueur Co Ltd

Robinson, Christopher John
BB & R Limited

Robinson, Clifford
AB & R Import and Export Ltd

Robinson, Deborah Mary
Spar (UK) Limited

Robinson, Ian Booth
Lindisfarne Limited

Robinson, Ian Edward
Empire Star Limited

Robinson, James
Feni Global Limited

Robinson, Mark Alan
Trendbev Ltd.

Robinson, Nicholas Kent
Kilo Wines Ltd

Robinson, Paul
Grafham Brewing Co Ltd

Robson, Alexandra Georgina
West End Brands Ltd
West End Drinks Limited

Robson, James Wesley
Vinature Ltd

Robson, Peter
Devine Distillates Group Ltd

Robson, Samuel Benzie
London Spiced Dry Limited

Rocca, Gianpiero, Dr
Vine & Cork Limited

Roche, Ashley
The Double Hard Whiskey Co Ltd

Roche, Sean
Loaded Spirits Ltd

Rochford, Paul Henry
William Grant & Sons Brands Ltd
William Grant & Sons UK Ltd

Rockett, Jeremy
Laurus Brands Limited

Rockley, Terry Albert
Vintage Wines Limited

Rocos, Cleo
Tequilas of Mexico Limited

Rodgers, Gus Frederick Augustus
JF Tobias Limited

Rodgers, Nicholas
Identity Drinks Brands Limited

Rodgerson, Christopher
CRC Delta Ltd

Rodica, Ales
Rodica Wine and Spirits Ltd

Rodrigues Ramos, Vera Isabel
Viserra Limited

Rodriguez Alonso, Carlos
El Toro Wines Limited

Roe, Harvey
Truly Spirited Ltd

Rogers, Adam
Deskbeers Limited

Rogers, Matthew
Wight & Wessex Wines Limited

Rogers, Nicholas Ian
Blue Marble Consultants Ltd

Rohde, Ludwig Martin
Wein Forum - Fine Wines Ltd

Rohde, Patrick
Wickedsoup Ltd.

Rojas Buitrago, Sergio
Grape Merchants Ltd

Roland-Billcart, Mathieu
Billecart - Salmon (UK) Ltd

Rolfe, Simon William
10 International Limited

Rolfe, William Generald
10 International Limited

Rolland, Didier
La Guilde du Cognac Limited

Rolls, Robert Jonathan
London Wine Agencies Limited
Robert Rolls & Co. Limited

Romano, Davide
Valinch & Mallet Limited

Rompante, Norma Patricia
Robb Brothers Wine Merchants Ltd

Ronaldson, Simon Bryan Shaw
Beacon Wines Limited

Roos, Athila
Athila Roos Ltd

Roper, Rowena Rose
Blackedge Brewing Co Ltd

Roper, Wayne
Blackedge Brewing Co Ltd

Ropiak, Katarzyna
Lioness Paw UK Limited

Rosciglione, Sergio, Dr
Ubicumque International Ltd

Rose, Hugo David
Cellar & Co Limited

Rose, Kenneth James
LDC Scotland Limited

Rose, Nicholas
Glen Scotia Distillery Co Ltd
The Littlemill Distillery Co Ltd
Loch Lomond Distillers Limited
Loch Lomond Distillery Co Ltd

Rose, Stephen John
A1 Resources Limited

Rosellini, Valerio
Grapebee Ltd

Rosen, Jacob Hamilton
I'll Ask The Boys Ltd

Rosin, Patrick Nicolas
ADP Wines Ltd

Ross, Caroline
Spirit O' Clyde Drinks Co Ltd

Ross, David George
Oso Brew Co Ltd

Ross, John D'Ell
D & V Wines Ltd

Ross, Mark Richard
Farr Vintners Limited

Ross, Michael
Xpress Drinks Ltd

Ross, Moira Allan
Oxford Brewery Limited
The Oxford Brewing Co Ltd

Ross, Neville Douglas
Edrington-Beam Suntory UK Distribution

Ross, Norman
Speymalt Whisky Distributors Ltd

Ross, Simon
Spirit O' Clyde Drinks Co Ltd

Rossborough, Peter Daniel
Saltrock Brewing Co Ltd

Rossi, Paul
Ayr Brewing Co Ltd

Rotaru, Lilian
Old Wine House Ltd

Rothbart, Morris
Wine Online Ltd

Rothwell, John
The Bitter End Limited

Roughley, Claudia
Underground Spirits Limited

Roux, Alain Albert
Michel Roux Limited

Rouzaud, Frederick
Maisons Marques et Domaines Ltd

Rowan, James Columba
Alexander Wines Ltd.
The Society of Vintners Ltd

Rowe, Sebastian Elliot
BI Wines and Spirits Limited

Rowley, George William
Bohemia Beer House Limited

Rowley, Mark Christopher
Hilton & Rowley Ltd

Rowley, Stewart
Kolson Energy Limited

Royden, Warwick James
Tan Dowr Limited

Royes, Daniel
Ineffable LDN Limited

Rubbianesi, Pietro
Ora Brewing Co Ltd

Rudd, Elizabeth Margaret
BB & R Limited

Rummer, Andrew John
Sipping Liquor Ltd

Rusby, Robert Charles
Hallamshire Wine Shipping Co. Ltd

Rushforth, James Joseph
Hop Drop Limited

Rushton, Frederick Johnthomas
Hamer & Perks Limited

Rushton, William Paul
Scimedex Limited

Russell, Angela Mary
Ian MacLeod Distillers Limited
Ian MacLeod and Co Ltd

Russell, Anthony
Quantum Vintners Limited

Russell, Barry John
Arkell's Brewery Limited

Russell, David Michael
GDK Drinks Ltd

Russell, David William Hodder
Ian MacLeod Distillers Limited
Ian MacLeod and Co Ltd
Wm Maxwell (Scotch Whisky) Ltd

Russell, Edith Stuart
Ian MacLeod Distillers Limited
Ian MacLeod and Co Ltd

Russell, Gordon Iain
New Wave (Scotland) Limited

Russell, James William Oxley
Landmark Wholesale Limited

Russell, Leonard Stuart
Hedges & Butler Limited
Lang Brothers Limited
Ian MacLeod Distillers Limited
Ian MacLeod and Co Ltd
Wm Maxwell (Scotch Whisky) Ltd
Peter J Russell & Co Ltd.
Wincarnis Limited

Russell, Lucinda
Peter J Russell & Co Ltd.

Russell, Patricia
GDK Drinks Ltd

Russell, Peter James Sidney
Ian MacLeod Distillers Limited
Ian MacLeod and Co Ltd
Wm Maxwell (Scotch Whisky) Ltd

Russell, Philip
GDK Drinks Ltd

Russell, Sandra Glenys
Ales. R. Russ Limited

Russell, Stephen Gerard
Forth Wines Limited
Inverarity Vaults Limited
J A Glass Limited
William Morton Limited

Russell, Stephen John
Ales. R. Russ Limited

Russell, Stuart Stephen
Ales. R. Russ Limited

Russell-Davis, Generald
KRD Distribution Co Ltd

Russell-Davis, Kassandra
KRD Distribution Co Ltd

Russo, Felice
Cibus Vitae Ltd.

Ruston, Alexander Joseph William
Fifty One Forty Limited

Rusu, Octavian
Green Cash & Carry Ltd

Rutherford, Philip
Molson Coors Brewing International

Rutland, Alan Charles
Barokes Limited

Ryan, Christopher Edward
Pure Organic Drinks Limited

Ryan, Eugene, Dr
Ishka Wines and Spirits UK Ltd

Ryan, Eunan Joseph
Original Liqueur Co Ltd

Ryan, Kenneth Roy
Town Centre Inns Limited

Ryan, Patrick
Ishka Wines and Spirits UK Ltd

Ryan, Richard
Bowsaw Bourbon Limited
Drinksology Limited
Kirker & Greer Whiskey Limited
Mayday Island Limited
McGrath's Brewing Limited
Red Bonny Rum Limited
Sailortown Brewing Limited

Ryan, Wayne Adam
Phone A Fix Ltd

Rybak, Marcin Miroslaw
MM Drinks Ltd

Rybarczyk, Marta Katarzyna
MM Drinks Ltd

Rycroft, Stephen
M.& M.Value Limited

Ryder, Paul Richard
Southbourne Brewing Limited

Ryland, Charles Norman
The Two Essentials Ltd.

Ryman, Nicolas David
Maison Liedberg Limited

Rys, Lukasz Marcin
Ftspot Limited

Sabatini, Franco
Consulting & Food Ltd

Sabharwal, Sachin
Liquor-Ish Ltd

Sabourin, Eric
Falcon Vintners Limited

Sachdeva, Nirmal Singh
Bacchus Merchantry Limited

Safadi, Sami
Oyster Import Export Limited

Safavand, Ali
Ali Booze Co Ltd

Sagar, Andrew Jonathan
Bottle Green Limited
Kingsland Drinks Group Limited
Kingsland Drinks Limited
Stratford's Wine Shippers and Merchants

Sager, Michael
Destilado London Limited

Sahin, Ali
The Liquor Box Ltd

Sahni, Saravpreet
Impulse Global Ltd

Sahota, Rajvir Singh
Lordsworth Limited

Sai Mui, Cheung
Always 20 Limited

Sain, Harry Benjamin
Melange Drinks Ltd

Saini, Harpreet
Delicatezze Siciliane Limited

Saini, Karamjit Singh
KD Wholesale Ltd

Salah, Sheena
Grace Wines (UK) Limited

Salamini, Cristian
Goodeataly Ltd

Saleh, Hani Omar
The Hop Shed Limited

Saleh, Sarah Louise
The Hop Shed Limited

Salem, Louis
Workshy Brewing Ltd

Saletti, Adam
Adam & Herv Limited

Salevourakis, Diana Aphrodite
More Sake Limited

Salih, Hakan
Universal Drinks Ltd

Sallesio, Gaetano
Enopoli Limited

Salpietro, Salvatore
Cloud Wine Ltd

Salter, Clay
Mojito Bar Ltd

Salter, Gruffald Benjamin
Provenance Marketing Ltd

Salter, Martin John
Imprint Wine Limited

Saly, Arthur
Beercall Ltd

Sam, Pearman
Bobby Beer Co Ltd

Samba, Momodou Adama
GDD Chapuy Limited

Sambhi, Manjit Singh
Kallwin Limited

Samokhvalov, Vladimir
Lucky Spirits Ltd

Sampene, Henrietta
Exul Limited

Sample, Andrew
Sunset Wines Limited

Sample, Carl
Sunset Wines Limited

Sample, Matthew Paul
Sunset Wines Limited

Sampson, Phoebe Elizabeth
Maverick Ventures UK Ltd

Samuel, David Huw
Pieroth Limited
Vicomte Bernard de Romanet Ltd

Samuel, Frank
Legends of Drinks Ltd

Samuels, Joshua
Rich & Bad Ltd

San, Myat Min
Delta World Trading Limited

Sanadze, Vladimer
G Point 7 Ltd

Sandbach, Henry Alistair Samuel
Ledbury Wine Limited

Sandesara, Diptiben Chetankumar
Sterling Wine Agencies Limited

Sandham, Helga
Sandham Wine Merchants Ltd

Sandham, Jeremy John William
Sandham Wine Merchants Ltd

Sandham, Thomas Edward Horan
Hobo Beer & Co Ltd

Sandhu, Arvinder Singh
Sandhu Wholesale & Events Ltd

Sandhu, Gursharn Singh
Big D'Z Convenience and Winery Ltd

Sandhu, Parmjit Singh
Sandhu IT Services Ltd

Sandhu, Rizwan Azmat
Urban Warehousing Limited

Sandhu, Taranjeet Singh
Grape Merchants Ltd

Sands, Mark
Chillwines Limited

Sangha, Rajvinder Singh
Prostimo Ltd

Sanghera, Rajinder Singh
Euro Beer Distribution Ltd

Sanghera, Shivcharan Singh
Harrydev Limited

Sanghera, Sumerjit Kaur
The Wine Carafe Limited

Sanghera, Tajinder Singh
Sanghera Rum Co Ltd

Sanguineti, Antonio Giorgio
Terrae Vinariae Limited

Sankey, Gordon Ian
Airways Bonded Warehouse Ltd

Sanne, Emily
Mead Ho! Limited

Sant, Peter John
Remy Cointreau UK Distribution Ltd

Santillan Giles, David Celso Eduardo
Agua Piedra Mezcal & Co Ltd

Santomauro, Gerardo
G & G Gallo Enterprises Ltd

Santomauro, Giuseppina
G & G Gallo Enterprises Ltd

Santomauro, Julia Adelaide
Casa Julia Limited

Santomauro, Nicola Elizabeth
Casa Julia Limited

Santomauro, Pasquale Luca
G & G Gallo Enterprises Ltd

Santomauro, Paula Ann
Casa Julia Limited

Santoro, Alfonso
Alf Vini Limited

Santoro, Paul John Evangelista
Vinissimo Limited

Santos-Pires, Maria Vitoria
Alivini (North) Limited
Alivini Co Ltd
Franciacorta Limited

Santrac, Miroslav
Sanwin Ltd

Sapkota, Som Nath
Euro Asia Distriubtion Limited

Saracino, Antonio
D & K Capital Ltd

Saraf, Suneil Steven Paul
The Near Beer Brewing Co. Ltd

Sarais, Joshua Richard
Cru Classe Limited

Sardinheiro, Mauro Azoia
L'Atelier Terroir Limited

Sargsjan, Hratschja
Global World Wide Beer Limited

Sarguns, Marcis
Twilight Drinks Ltd

Sarikhani, Nima Habibollah
Monopole Wine Portfolio Management Ltd

Sarwar, Waseem
Rajpoot Traders Ltd

Satchwell, Mark Anthony
Greencroft Bottling Co Ltd
Lanchester Wine Cellars Ltd
Lanchester Wine Sales Limited
The Wine Fusion Limited

Sathiyaseelan, Theerththiga
J K Wholesales Ltd

Sattar, Abdul
SmsZee Limited

Sattar, Sahar
SmsZee Limited

Sattar, Sana
SmsZee Limited

Sattar, Waheeda Tasleem
SmsZee Limited

Saturno, Leon Erman
Longview Wines Ltd

Sauerbrey, Michael Stefan Alwin
Master Spirits Limited

Savage, Annabel Mary
The Curious Wine Cellar Ltd
Savage Selection Limited
Windrush Holdings Ltd

Savage, Duncan Alexander
The Project Wines UK Limited
Savage Wines UK Limited

Savage, Malcolm John
Morecambe Bay Wines Limited

Savage, Mark
The Curious Wine Cellar Ltd
Savage Selection Limited
Windrush Holdings Ltd

Savage, Nigel Steven
Private Wine Shippers Ltd

Savage, Patricia Bridget
The Glenallachie Distillers Co Ltd

Savage, Roger Anthony John
Nice Brewing Co Ltd

Savage, Sophie
Late Night Liquor Ltd

Savani, Jagdish Parbat
Jays Beverages Limited

Savic, Kristijan
Foxbusiness Tobacco Ltd

Savile, Mark William
Raven Hill Brewery Limited

Savonije, Johannes Fredericus Christiaan Maria
Supermalt UK Limited

Savvopoulos, Anastasios
CRA Ltd
Infotonomy Ltd

Sawhney, Rajbir Singh
Speciality Brands Ltd
Speciality Drinks Limited

Sawhney, Sukhinder Singh
Speciality Brands Ltd
Speciality Drinks Limited

Sawlani, Hotchand
Safeway Distribution Limited

Sawlani, Hotchard
Safeway Distribution Limited

Sawyer, Alison
AKS Brands Limited

Saxlund, Preben Jensen
House of Sparkling Ltd

Sayania, Surag Narpatsinh
Shree Sai Trading Ltd

Scacchi, Glenna
Colosseum Wines Limited

Scacchi, Massimiliano
Colosseum Wines Limited

Scaife, Antony Paul
Event Wine Solutions Limited

Scaife, Debra Jane
Event Wine Solutions Limited

Scandellari, Filippo
Asahi Premium Brands Ltd

Scanlon, John
Supermarket Solutions Limited

Scaramelli, Riccardo
Alinari Ltd

Scaramucci, Olivier
Boutique Brands Limited

Scarlett, Eleanor Hepta
Orchard-Lisle Wines Ltd

Scarlett, Thomas Guy
3Squires Ltd
3Squires Wines Ltd

Scarratt, Jessica Louise
Brix & Porter Ltd.

Scavelli, Vito
Scavelli's Limited

Schaafsma, Paul Michael
Benchmark Drinks Ltd

Schendel, Anthony
Hayward Bros (Wines) Limited

Schenkelberg, Gian Philipp
Shop Wine Limited

Schmidt, Attila
Yeast To West Ltd

Schmidt, Ramona
Global D & F Ltd

Schofield, Andrew Mark
Lilo Beverages Ltd

Schofield, John
National Drink Distributors Ltd
Today's Wholesale Services Ltd

Schofield, Patricia Ann
The Beer People Limited

Schonenberger, Luke Von
11:11 Gin Ltd

Schonlaub, Thomas
Schoenlaub Limited

Schroder, Benjamin
Meanwhile Drinks Ltd.

Schroeder, Peter James
CKW (Europe) Limited
CKW Trading Limited

Schuler, Jakob
Schuler Wine St. Jakob's Cellars Ltd

Schuringa, Mark Andries
Ditton Wine Traders Ltd

Schuurman, Maarten
United Wine Merchants Limited

Schwartz, Yosef
Walking Back The Cat Limited

Scopes, Andrew James
Cru Classe Limited

Scorer, Claire
Jean Juviniere Limited

Scorer, Julia
Jean Juviniere Limited

Scorer, Ronald
Jean Juviniere Limited

Scott, Alexander Douglas
Gelston Castle Fine Wines Ltd

Scott, Ashley
Added Pressure Ltd

Scott, Douglas George William
Best Cask Ltd

Scott, James Martin
Hall & Woodhouse Limited

Scott, Jason
Cross Brew Ltd

Scott, Jonathan James
Jascots Wine Merchants Limited

Scott, Katie
Love and Labour Ltd.

Scott, Michael Leslie
Boot Liquor Wholesale Limited

Scott, Paul John
V.C. Vintners Limited

Scott, Peter Timothy
Wine Marketings Europe Ltd

Scott, Stephen Robert
Scott's of Quorn (Wine Bar & Vintners)

Scott, Thomas
Loaded Spirits Ltd

Scott, Warren Michael
Quintessential Brands Premium Brands
Quintessential Brands Spirit Solutions
Quintessential Brands UK Ltd
Quintessential Spirits Holdings Ltd
Quintessential Spirits Limited
Quintessential Spirits UK Ltd
Quintessential Wines Holdings Ltd
Quintessential Wines Limited

Scott-Larsen, Audrey Jane
ABA Eaglesham Ltd

Scoynes, Arthur William John
The Keg & Bottle Ltd

Scoynes, Linda Margaret
The Keg & Bottle Ltd

Scriven, Timothy John Adam
Chalgrove Wines Limited

Scrivener, Wayne Alan
Satellite Brands Limited

Seabrook, Julian Graham
Seabrook Wines Limited

Seale, Chris
Speciality Brands Ltd

Seaman, Steven
A. S. D. Wholesale Limited

Sears, Michael
The Free from Beer Co Ltd
Windfall Logistics Limited

Sears, Thomas Paul
The Free from Beer Co Ltd

Sebaratnam, Sebajeevan
Ellismuir Limited

Sebestyen, Csilla
Grapes of Hungary Ltd

Seddon, Robert James
Jackson & Seddon Ltd

Seden, Andrew William
Hillcrest Wines Limited

Seden, Marilyn Elizabeth
Hillcrest Wines Limited

Seden, William Edward
Hillcrest Wines Limited

Sefton, Amanda Jane
Sip Sip Wine Limited

Segatta, Gianni
Alivini (North) Limited
Alivini Co Ltd
Franciacorta Limited

Selezneva, Elena, Dr
Gem Wines Ltd

Sellers, Brenda Rose
Franchiserv Limited

Sellers, Paul Thomas Garfield
Franchiserv Limited

Selvaraj, Vijay
Glennlay & Co Ltd

Selvarasa, Karthigesu
Church Road Mini Market Ltd

Selvi, Duran
UKAFDS Limited

Semancik, Radoslav
R Spirit Ltd

Senechko, Oleh
PPbeer Ltd.

Seneviratne, Rachitha
Jivana Spirits Ltd.

Senior, Monique
Mo Madness Drinks Limited

Senkul, Osman
Melen London Ltd.

Sequeira, Gaylord Carlos Aurelien
Pinglestone Estate Limited

Seraly, Moez
The Perfect Cellar Ltd

Sergi, Lorenzo
Dmomentum Ltd

Sergio, Roberta
100cl Limited

Sergiu-Vladut, Zoltan
Drink247 Ltd

Serobyan, Zaruhi
Ginvino Ltd

Servant, Charlotte Laurence Marie
Lavinia UK Limited

Seth Smith, John David Vaughan
Imported Brands International Ltd

Seth, Arjun
Seth Ventures Limited

Seth, Yvan Jack
Jolly Good Beer Ltd

Seth-Smith, William Jonathan Cory
Imported Brands International Ltd

Sethi, Harash Pal
Tiger Vines Ltd

Sevani, Mitesh
The Indian Ice Gola Co Ltd
The Street Food & Beverages Co Ltd

Seymour, Gordon Lewis
Gordons (Bolton) Limited

Seymour, Gordon Richard
Gordons (Bolton) Limited

Seymour, Jane Deborah
Meadrising Limited

Seymour, Marjorie
Gordons (Bolton) Limited

Seymour, Natalie Victoria
Gordons (Bolton) Limited

Seymour, Nicola Rachel
Gordons (Bolton) Limited

Shabani, Pleuat
Konik's Tail Limited
United Spirit Brands Limited

Shackleton, Ian Alexander
Ian MacLeod Distillers Limited

Shah, Anis Sobhag
Swara Trading International Ltd

Shah, Babulal
Ray Jules Limited

Shah, Binny
City Beer Limited

Shah, Dipak Lalji
Beatville Limited
Fortmount Trading Limited

Shah, Himanshu
Premier UK Trading Limited

Shah, Kavit
City Beer Limited

Shah, Ketan
City Beer Limited

Shah, Kirtan
The Gala Drinks Co Ltd

Shah, Minal Anis
Swara Trading International Ltd

Shah, Nirav
The Gala Drinks Co Ltd

Shah, Rasiklal Devshi
Orsa Major Ltd

Shah, Richard Sanat
Diamond Stag Importers Ltd.

Shah, Sharan Shashikant
Mezzaro Ltd

Shah, Swapnil Niranjan
Beverages Distribution Limited
Booze Village Limited

Shah, Zawar Hussain
Up Drinks Ltd

Shaia, Johny Habib Karromi
JD Group Enterprises Ltd

Shakeshaft, Peter Robert
Provenance Fine Wines Ltd
Vin-X Enterprise Investment Scheme Ltd

Shakoor, Abdul
Euroworld Foods Limited

Shakouri, Paloma Paradis
Birdcage Gin Ltd.

Shand, Euan Coutts
Single Malts Limited
Duncan Taylor Scotch Whisky Ltd
Whisky Galore Limited

Shapiro, Alan Michael
Highly Spirited Ltd

Shapiro, Joseph
Mead Ho! Limited

Shareef, Jafar
Fourteen Twelve Trading Ltd

Sharma, Ajay
Jaitly Trading Co Ltd

Sharma, Ashok Kumar
Ragarfield International Ltd

Sharma, Neelu
Ragarfield International Ltd

Sharman, Mark Richard William
Sharpham Wine Limited

Sharp, Jacqueline
Evokesomm Limited

Sharp, Jonathan William
J. Chandler & Company, Limited

Sharp, Michael
Hobnobber Ltd

Sharp, Steven Michael, Dr
Adnams PLC

Sharpe, Jake Jacob Patrick
The Whisky Baron Ltd.

Sharples, Edward Hartland
TFWF Ltd

Sharrocks, Cheryl Anne
Stockport Gin Ltd

Sharrocks, Paul John
Stockport Gin Ltd

Shaw, Gregory Norman
S H Jones Wines Ltd
New Fine Wines Ltd

Shaw, Henry Edward
Wine in Cornwall Limited

Shaw, Mark Glenn Bridgman
Opus Wines Limited

Shaw, Samuel James
Wolf Wine Limited

Shaw, Sarah Elizabeth
Penzance Gin Ltd

Shearer, James Christian
Aspall Cyder Limited
Cobra Beer Partnership Limited
Molson Coors Brewing Co (UK) Ltd

Sheepshanks, Andrew Charles
Nowselect Limited

Sheikh, Rizwan
Sladecs247 Ltd

Sheikh, Shahbaz Ali Amjad
London Wholesale Ltd

Shekel, Dan
Line Point Global UK Limited

Shendgay, Kishore
KT Global Ltd

Shepherd, Michael
Brayston Leisure Ltd.

Sheppard, Susannah George Fullerton
Blue Island Limited

Shestakov, Egor
Russbrit Ltd

Shields, Thomas McGregor
Staibano Ltd

Shimitra, Sotera
Marathon Food Limited

Shimoi, Hisanori
Peoplegood Limited

Shinde, Sandeep
Flavour Foods & Drinks Ltd

Shipman, Michael
Bang The Elephant Brewing Co Ltd

Shirlaw, Campbell
J & G Stewart Scotch Whisky Ltd

Shirlaw, Iain Clunes
RSD Whisky International Ltd

Shirlaw, Robert Campbell
Rutherford, Shirlaw and Denholm Ltd

Shore, Gillian
Northwest Drinks Ltd

Shore, Michael John
Key Brands International Ltd

Shore, Zoe Rachel
Key Brands International Ltd

Shorrock, Michael
Wight & Wessex Wines Limited

Short, Iain David
William Grant & Sons UK Ltd

Short, Terence Reginald
Ravensbourne Wine Co Ltd

Shotton, Robert Alan
David Berryman Holdings Ltd
David Berryman Limited

Showering, Samuel Francis
Melius Drinks Ltd.

Shrestha, Deepak Kumar
Best Price Retail and Wholesale Ltd

Shrestha, Sachin
Gurkha Beer Ltd

Shuttleworth, Nicholas John
European Beer Exports Limited

Sibley, Damian Theobald Oliver
Corney and Barrow Group Ltd
Corney and Barrow Limited

Sidhu, Mandeep Singh
Yorkshire Vino Ltd

Sidhu, Surinderjit
Sin Shots (U.K.) Ltd.

Sigaut, Clement
Smashing Wines Limited

Signorelli, Alessandro
Signorellis Deli Ltd
Simavin Limited

Sikka, Sankalp Rajen
Iturn Global Ltd

Silvestre, Mikael Sammy
R. St Barth Limited

Silvestre, Severine Laetitia
R. St Barth Limited

Sim, Alison Jane
Raven Spirits Limited

Sim, Callum Downie
Raven Spirits Limited

Sim, Peter Robert
Raven Spirits Limited

Simmonds, Carl Antony
Old Brenin Distillery Ltd

Simmons, Adrian Generald
South Eastern Beers & Minerals Ltd

Simovic, Marija
Winetraders (UK) Limited

Simpson, Alison Louise
The Taunton Cider Co Ltd

Simpson, Charles William
Simpsons Wine Imports Limited

Simpson, Martyn
Cask Industries Ltd

Simpson, Robert Andrew
Import Brothers Limited

Simpson, Ruth Elizabeth
Simpsons Wine Imports Limited

Simpson-Daniel, Charlie
Champions Cider Ltd

Simsek, Ahmet Turgay
Wine Art Co Ltd

Sina, Xhulio
The Broadway Drinks Co Ltd

Sinclair, Alastair Robert Frazer
Scotia Blending Co Ltd

Sinclair, Alistair Robert Fraser
George Sinclair & Sons Limited

Sinclair, Edith May
George Sinclair & Sons Limited

Singer, Harry Munro
Dram-a-Drinks Ltd.

Singh Johal, Balvinder
Venus 14 Limited

Singh Johal, Harpreet
Superior Import/Export Limited

Singh, Ajminder
Pulse Products Limited

Singh, Amardeep
Intelligent Trade Limited

Singh, Amritraj
Knightrate Wines Ltd

Singh, Annabelle
Goldy's Corner Shop Ltd

Singh, Ashmeet
Pristine Trades Ltd

Singh, Balwant
Spirit Traders Ltd

Singh, Bikram
KB Suppliers Ltd

Singh, Dalbir
Mille Gusti Limited

Singh, Dalil
Barry Drinks Ltd
Middlesex Wines Limited

Singh, Daljit [1964]
AK Cash & Carry Ltd
Sindherfoods Limited

Singh, Daljit [1982]
Soltano Wines Ltd

Singh, Daljit [1970]
Smartprice (NE) Ltd

Singh, Gurmail
Laki & G Ltd

Singh, Gurmeet Kishore
Wilkies International Ltd

Singh, Gurmukh
Icknield Stores Ltd

Singh, Gurnam [1968]
Star Beers Ltd

Singh, Gurnam [1971]
Himalaya Wines Limited

Singh, Hardev
West Country Wines Limited

Singh, Harjinder
R & B Drinks Ltd

Singh, Harpinder
Quint-Essential JQ Ltd

Singh, Himat
Drinks Direct Limited

Singh, Ivneet
Bargain Food and Booze Limited

Singh, Jagjit Singh
Acacia Drinks Ltd

Singh, Jagmohan
Edward James Limited

Singh, Jaideep
Kuchh Hai Limited

Singh, Jasdeep
Pivo Beverages Ltd

Singh, Jasvinder
N G K Wholesale Limited

Singh, Jasvinder Pal
Maharaja & Sons Ltd

Singh, Jaswinder
Tenby Drinks (UK) Limited

Singh, Jatinder
Drinks Depot Ltd
Drinks Direct Limited

Singh, Kamaljit
Parmar Drinks & Wines Ltd

Singh, Kanwar Gurmohan
Ryder Partners Limited

Singh, Kulwinder
Simply Beers Limited

Singh, Makhan
Goldbeach Trading Limited

Singh, Mandeep
Pivo Beverages Ltd

Singh, Mandip
Euro Beer Distribution Ltd

Singh, Manjinder
Clarkes Drinks Direct Limited

Singh, Manpreet
Urban Wholesalers Limited

Singh, Marcus
Landmark Wholesale Limited

Singh, Ranjeev
Kaleboard Limited

Singh, Ranjit
Ramstrad Trading Ltd

Singh, Ravneet
RS Wholesale Limited

Singh, Sandeep
One Source Global Limited

Singh, Satnam [1988]
Goldy's Corner Shop Ltd

Singh, Satnam [1972]
Lucky Drinks 4 U Ltd

Singh, Satvinder
Smart Save Distribution Ltd

Singh, Satwant
Free Trade Beers and Minerals Ltd

Singh, Satwinder
Rurkee Trading Co Ltd

Singh, Shalinder
Shonty Group Ltd

Singh, Shamsher
JBD Booze Ltd
Agencia Ltd

Singh, Sudesh
IBL Wines Ltd
Iceaction Limited

Singh, Sukhwinder
G B Consortium Wholesale Ltd

Singh, Sukvinder
W S B C Limited

Singh, Sunil
Diamond Aces Limited

Singh, Surinder [1974]
East and West Foods Cash and Carry

Singh, Surinder [1952]
Central Pubs (UK) Limited

Singla, Arun Aditya
Kristal Spirits UK Limited

Singleton, Catherine
Brindle Distillery Limited

Singleton, Gerard Edmund John
Brindle Distillery Limited

Singleton, Josef Ben
Disley Gin Ltd

Sinkovicz, Abel
Hoops and Champagne Ltd

Sitarek, Tomasz
A-Z Spirits Ltd

Siudaj, Marcin Tadeusz
Marcin & Son Ltd

Sivills, Ross
From Cask To Bottle Limited

Skedd, Alison Jane
Wadworth and Co Ltd

Skene, Andrew George Campbell
Black Tartan Limited

Skinger, Christopher Robin
Hi-Spirits Ltd
The Last Drop Distillers Ltd
Sazerac UK Limited

Skinner, Antonia
Pigs Ears Beers Limited

Skinner, Michelle
Kegs of Camberley Limited

Skinner, Steve
Kegs of Camberley Limited

Sklar, Dale Laurence Howard
Wine & Spirit International Ltd

Sklar, Daliah Rebecca
Wine & Spirit International Ltd

Sklar, Gina Tamara
Wine & Spirit International Ltd

Sklar, Karen
Wine & Spirit International Ltd

Sklar, Tanya Sara
Wine & Spirit International Ltd

Skorupa, Robert Artur
Hydraun Limited

Skott, Jacqueline
The Danish Snaps Co Ltd

Skott, Kell
The Danish Snaps Co Ltd

Sky, Jordan
Jordan Sky Ltd

Slater, Alexander
Panache du Sud Ltd

Slater, Benjamin John
Pollen Cider Ltd

Slatter, Des
Sopwell Gin Co Ltd

Slattery, Michael Joseph
Drinkrite Limited

Slingsby, Richard
Neil Morrissey Real Ale Co Ltd

Sloane, Matthew Richard
Whisky 78 Ltd

Slocombe, Philip Anthony
Fine Wine House Ltd

Sloots, Martin Alexander
David Alexander Wine Merchants Maidenhead
Martin Enterprises Limited

Sloper, Thomas Hendrie
Slopemeister Brewing Co Ltd

Slusarczyk, Sebastian
K & A Eagle Limited

Small, Leslie Edward
The Wine Treasury Limited

Smallbone, Robin Christopher
Rockin Robin Brewery Ltd

Smallrdge, Theres
Prestige Vintners Limited

Smart, Darren
Hills Prospect PLC

Smatt, Ashley John
The Great Smattsby Limited

Smedley, Robert
Andes Trading Limited

Smedley, Robert Bryan
Andes Trading Limited

Smeralda, David
Rome de Bellegarde Wines Ltd

Smillie, Peter James
PJ's Virtual Brewing Co Ltd

Smith Hilliard, Max Sandiford
International Procurement and Logistics

Smith Walker, Giles Iain
The Independent Vintner Ltd

Smith, Aidan Stuart
Fox Fitzgerald Whisky Trading Co Ltd

Smith, Andrew John
Mentzendorff & Co Ltd

Smith, Benjamin
Smith & Humpston Ltd

Smith, David
HG & S Ltd

Smith, David John
The Salmon Lady Limited
Swinkels Snackery and Backery Ltd

Smith, Duncan Ross
Laurence Smith & Son (Edinburgh) Ltd

Smith, Edward Nicholas Russell
Russell Smith F & B Limited

Smith, Gail Irene Allan
ABA Eaglesham Ltd
Inverarity Vaults Limited
William Morton Limited

Smith, Gavin Robert Morgan
The Bespoke London Wine Co Ltd

Smith, Geoffrey Lilley
Ralph's Wines Ltd

Smith, George Richard
Il Tipico Italiano Ltd

Smith, George Robert Peter
Bruce Burlington and Co Ltd

Smith, Guy Christopher
Frederick's Wine Co Ltd

Smith, Henry Oliver
International Wine Emporium Ltd.

Smith, Ian William
Main Rum Co Ltd

Smith, Jack David
Alky Limited

Smith, Laurence Rognvald
Laurence Smith & Son (Edinburgh) Ltd

Smith, Lee Martell
Rumbaclaat Ltd

Smith, Liane Margaret, Dr
Fairview Vineyard Ltd

Smith, Mark Edward Charles
Hardywood Park Craft Brewery Ltd.
Lonerider UK Ltd
Point Beer UK Limited
Port City Brewing UK Limited

Smith, Martin Peter
Spokesuk Ltd

Smith, Mathew David Stanley
Smith & Harris Enterprises Ltd.

Smith, Michael Norman
Southern England Wines (UK) Ltd

Smith, Neville Mark
Ran Ales Ltd

Smith, Nicholas Roy
Bruce Burlington and Co Ltd

Smith, Nigel Generall Lind
Malpas Stallard Limited

Smith, Paul Colin Warren
La Madeleine Wines Limited

Smith, Peter Andrew
East Street Wine Co Ltd

Smith, Peter Overett
Bruce Burlington and Co Ltd

Smith, Ralph Timothy
Ralph's Wines Ltd

Smith, Richard James Murray
The Fightback Brewing Co Ltd

Smith, Robert
Fairview Vineyard Ltd

Smith, Rosalind Jean Carlyon
Malpas Stallard Limited

Smith, Shelagh Lesley
The Bespoke London Wine Co Ltd

Smith, Steve William
Babco UK Ltd.
World of Patria International Ltd

Smith, Steven Alexander
Ghost Laboratories Limited

Smith, Suzy
Matthew Gloag & Son Limited

Smith, Thomas
Bringmevino (UK) Limited

Smith, Tye
Pryzm Cocktails Limited

Smith, William
Fairview Vineyard Ltd

Smolowitz, Daniel
The Whisky Palate Limited

Smyth, David
Pinewood Vyntners Limited

Smyth, Gerard Anthony
Bear Smyth Limited

Smyth, Richard Andrew
Konigsberg Seven Bridges Breweries Ltd

Sneddon, Derek Downie
Team Spirit Beverage Ltd

Snell, Michael John Bland
International Procurement and Logistics

Snelling, Alan John
Ufton Travel Retail Limited

Snelling, Margaret Helena Anne
Ufton Travel Retail Limited

Snelling, Mark
Ufton Travel Retail Limited

Snook, Ryan James
Fyre Festival UK Ltd

Snow, Daniel Edward
Cocksure Brewing Co Ltd

Snudden, Alan David
General Wine and Liquor Co Ltd

Soden, Graham Barry
Invest Inns Limited

Soguksu, Cagdas
The Liquor Box Ltd

Sohal, Bhupinder Singh
Pallet Price Wholesale Ltd

Sohal, Charanjit Singh
Hunny Pot Pub Co. Limited

Sohal, Jagdeep Singh
Hunny Pot Pub Co. Limited

Sohal, Soraya
The Little Grape Co Ltd

Soiledis, Panagiotis
Hellenic Agora Limited

Sokoli, Qazim
Vranac Stonecastle Limited

Solar, Osvaldo
Concha y Toro UK Limited

Solesbury, Jonathan
Bibendum PLB Group Limited
Bibendum Wine Limited
Chalk Farm Wines Ltd
Matthew Clark (Scotland) Ltd
Matthew Clark Bibendum Limited
Matthew Clark Limited
Matthew Clark Wholesale Bond Ltd
Matthew Clark and Sons Limited
Walker & Wodehouse Wines Ltd

Soliman, Mohamed
Greatvine Ltd

Soliman, Sherril
Greatvine Ltd

Solle, Peter Anthony
UK Vintners (of London) PLC

Somasutharam, Rajan
Raks Suppliers Limited

Somel, Sukhbir Singh
Dragonwood Limited

Somoza, Diego Munoz
Iberiandrinks UK Ltd

Soni, Krishan
R S Wines Limited

Soni, Krishi Kiritkumar
Tipton Wines Limited

Soni, Rajan
49 Wines Limited
R S Wines Limited

Sood, Subhash Chander
Bayede Wines UK Ltd

Soofi, Sajjad
Penny Prize Limited

Sorenson, Casey
Hingston & Co. Ltd

Sory, Jean-Baptiste
JB Champagne & Co Ltd

Sosnierz, Janusz Wojciech
Orale Ltd.

Sostok, Jan
Cider Centrum Ltd

Sothinarayasamy, Shanthini
Yoka Family Limited

Sotiri, Klitos
Soho Wine Supply Limited

Sotiri, Kyriacos
Soho Wine Supply Limited

Sotiri, Panayiotis
Soho Wine Supply Limited

Sotiropoulos, Nick
Kold Group Limited

Sottou, Franck
Franc Wine Ltd

Soudah, Kay Madeline
Grape Passions Limited

Soudah, Mark Nicholas
Grape Passions Limited

Souliotis, Konstantinos
Impexpo Ltd

Soussi, Imane
Amis Trading Limited

Southall, Joseph Matthew
Glacon Limited

Southon, Ben
Chesters Wine Merchants Ltd

Southwell-Sander, Duncan Piers
Sky Wines Limited

Sowinska-Turatti, Jowita
Europemarca Limited

Sowter, Michael Howard
Bridge Vintners Limited

Soyan, Gurvade
V G International Trading Ltd

Spac, Grigore
Alegri Trade Ltd.

Spallarossa, Gianfranco
Wine Outlet Ltd.

Sparrow, Stephen Roger
Snow Leopard Vodka Limited

Speakman, Edward Joseph
Morgan Edwards Limited

Spence, Michelle Jayne
Citrosoft Drinks Limited

Spencer, Christopher James
The Baijiu Beer Co Ltd
Baijiu Evolution Ltd
The Spirit Beer Co Ltd
Tattoo Limited

Spencer, Daniel
East Street Wine Co Ltd

Spencer, Fitzroy Joseph
Honkytonk Wine Library Limited

Spencer, Jack William
Rum Fellows Limited

Spencer, Michael Alan
BI Wines and Spirits Limited

Spencer, Oliver Morley James
Reva Drinks Ltd

Spencer-Smith, Angelo Michael
Maverick Ventures UK Ltd

Spiers, Miriam
Alliance Wine Co Ltd

Spiliadis, George
Cava Spiliadis UK Limited

Spiliopoulos, Eleftherios
Holy Grape Ltd

Spinath, Daniel
Frizzenti Limited

Spitzer, Abraham
Drumstick Products Co Ltd

Spitzer, Esther
Drumstick Products Co Ltd

Spitzer, Neil
Drumstick Products Co Ltd

Spitzer, Richard
Drumstick Products Co Ltd

Spitzer, Samuel
Drumstick Products Co Ltd

Spooner, Ian John
Global Ethics Liquor Co Ltd

Sporborg, William Henry
Vintage Capital II PLC

Spowart, Kathleen Ross
Spowart Wines Limited

Springett, Roderick Francis
Essenza Di Romagna Limited

Spurrell, Simon John
Cheshire Gin Co Ltd

Squibb, Gary
Emporium Import Ltd

Squibb, John Gary
Emporium Import Ltd

Squires, Edward John Heskett
Dedicated Wines Ltd

Sriskantharajah, Luxan
J & D Wholesalers Ltd

St Aubyn, Davina Katharine
Rebel Wine Ltd.

St Aubyn, Rupert
Rebel Wine Ltd.

St John, Jefferson Luther King Campbell
Tasmanian Liquor Distributors Ltd

St. Aubyn, Rupert
Southern Wines Limited

St.John, Markku
Nordic Imports Ltd

Stacey, Jamie
Chaps Group Limited

Stacey, Martin
Hoppy Days Inn Ltd

Stafford, Julia Claire
Wine Pantry (Wholesale) Ltd
Wine Pantry Limited

Stafford, Nicholas Rowland
Flying Firkin Distribution Ltd

Stafin, Lukasz
Fortunella Spirits Ltd

Stagman, Tara Fay
Wineways (Harrogate) Limited

Stahmer, Andreas Benno Frederik
ASA Ventures Limited

Stahmer, Axel Frederik Stephan
ASA Ventures Limited

Stainton, Frank Evan
Frank Stainton Wines Limited

Stainton, Jennifer
Frank Stainton Wines Limited

Stamp, Robert John
C G Supplies Limited

Stan, Catalin Ionut
Cotrade Ltd

Stanickzi, Gulzar
GS Wholesalers Ltd

Staniland, Christopher
Quantock Abbey Wine Cellars Ltd

Staniland, Philippa
Quantock Abbey Wine Cellars Ltd

Stankevicius, Rimvydas
Sky9 Ltd

Stanley, Aleksandra
Interlink UK Exports Limited

Stanley, Darren
Webdrinks Ltd

Stanley, Paul
Guilty Libations Limited

Stanley, Robert Neil
Explore British Drinks Limited

Stapleton, Edward
Shandy Shack Ltd

Stassi, Luca
Azienda Vitivinicola Stassi Ltd

Staughton, Simon James
Drinklink Limited
Walter Hicks Limited
St.Austell Brewery Co Ltd

Stead, David Anthony
Majestic Wine PLC

Stedman, Christopher Barry
Stedman Bros. (Events) Limited

Steel, Andrew
Connoisseur Estates Limited
St Pierre Partners Limited
The Tasting Barn Ltd

Steel, Robert James Douglas
For The Love of Wine Limited

Steevenson, Charles Patrick Carson
Steevenson Wines Limited

Steevenson, Liam James
Red & White Wines Limited

Steevenson, Moira Ann
Steevenson Wines Limited

Stegierski, Pawel Andrzej
Spalco Ltd

Steip, Bertrand
Dillon Bass Limited
Moet Hennessy U.K. Limited

Stencel, Arkadiusz
Fast Moving Goods Ltd

Stenhouse, Nicola Claire
Wadworth and Co Ltd

Stepanov, Nikita
Modern Botanicals Limited

Stephens, Andrew Neil
Sheffield Brewers Collective

Stephens, Daryl William
DWS Wholesale Limited

Stephens, Lloyd John
Wadworth and Co Ltd

Stephens, Nicholas
Bordeaux Undiscovered Limited
I I Wine Limited

Stephenson, Benjamin Edward Francis
Hanging Ditch Wine Merchants Ltd

Stephenson, Carl Louis
Elements Eight Rum Co Ltd

Stephenson, David
Tayler Beers Limited

Stephenson, John James
Young's Beers Wines & Spirits Ltd

Stephenson, Keith Caville
Lindisfarne Limited

Stephenson, Patrick Julian
Liberty Liquors Ltd

Stephenson, Roger
Hanging Ditch Wine Merchants Ltd

Stephenson, William Richard
Blind Monkey Limited

Steri, Riccardo
Desideria Ltd

Stern, Benjamin
Kedem Europe Limited

Steuart, Mike
Amphora Portfolio Management Ltd

Steven, Pattison
Kirker & Greer Whiskey Limited

Stevens, Barry John
Horizon Soft Drinks Limited

Stevens, David Barry
Horizon Soft Drinks Limited

Stevens, Jonathan
Dago Wines Ltd

Stevens, Thomas Peter, Dr
Shandy Shack Ltd

Stevenson, Alistair James Graham
The Glenallachie Distillers Co Ltd

Stewart, Johnathan Charles
Bearded Lion Drinks Co Ltd

Stewart, Karen Margaret
Wemyss Vintage Malts Limited

Stewart, Kenneth
Brunswick Fine Wines and Spirits Ltd

Stewart, Lucilda
Stewart Hill Walker UK Limited

Stewart, Paul Michael
Aberdrinks Scotland Limited

Stewart, Richard Andrew
Stewart Wines Limited

Steynberg, David Eduan
Wine People Europe Ltd

Stidwill, Emily Sarah
Little White Dog Limited

Stillwell, Victoria Jane
Mysomm.Com Ltd

Stimpson, Edward John
Liptons Food & Wine Limited

Stimpson, Kim Joanna
Liptons Food & Wine Limited

Stimpson, Sarah
Clara Wines Limited

Stirk, David James Millard
The Creative Whisky Co Ltd

Stirk, Dawn
The Creative Whisky Co Ltd

Stirling, Alistair Frederick
Abloc UK Ltd

Stock, Keith
Global24-7 (UK) Ltd
Nat Trade SRL Ltd
Urban Beers and Wines Ltd

Stocker, James
The Bajan Trading Co Ltd

Stockley, William Henry
The Responsible Trading Co Ltd

Stockton, Alexander Frederick William
Big Fish Brewing Co Ltd

Stones, Antony
Champagne Warehouse Ltd
Fine Drinks Cooperative Ltd

Stones, Helen Louise
Champagne Warehouse Ltd

Stopford Sackville, Thomas Nigel
Goedhuis & Co Ltd

Storey, Christopher
Copper and Rye Leisure Ltd

Storey, Jane
Jam Consultants Global Limited

Storey, Michael Charles
Savage Selection Limited

Storey, Peter Frank
PFS Business Services Limited

Stow, Sarah
Portavadie Distillery Limited

Stoyanov, Ivan Stoyanov
MPS 64 Ltd

Stoyanov, Stoyan Ivanov
The Old Cellar Ltd

Stoye, Anne Christine
Enmore Wine Limited

Stoykov, Mariyan Stoykov
D.Rock Champagne Ltd

Strachan, Ian Watt
United Supplies Limited

Strahan, Eric Edward
Main Rum Co Ltd

Strahan, Pauline
The Alternative Rum Co Ltd

Strang, David
Estini Ltd

Stratford, Angela Louise
Old Butcher's Wine Cellar Ltd

Stratford, Paul Victor
Old Butcher's Wine Cellar Ltd

Stratton, Colin John
St.Austell Brewery Co Ltd

Street, Michael Anthony
Hall & Woodhouse Limited

Street, Roland
Maidenhead Wine Co Ltd

Strickland, Thomas James
Milk Vin Ltd

Stringer, Mark David
Metropolitan Spirits (U.K.) Ltd

Stronati, Simone
Markets It Ltd.

Strong, Harry
HS13 Trading Ltd

Stroud, Caroline Jane
Iron Pier Brewery Limited

Strutt, James Edward
Goedhuis & Co Ltd

Stuart, Tristram James Avondale
Toast Ale Ltd

Stuart-Gammie, James Angus
Milk Money Limited

Sturges, Hugh Francis Dering
Laytons Wine Merchants Limited
Laytons Wine Services Limited

Subanney, Brandon Robert
Apical Breweries UK Ltd

Subanney, Robert Owen
Apical Breweries UK Ltd

Suddes, Chloe Danielle
Caps Off Ltd.

Sudera, Rajan
The Naked Spirit Co Ltd

Sudre, Guillaume
Ely's Cocktails Ltd

Sugden, Jacqueline Carol
Grassington Spirit Co Ltd

Sujanthan, Lazarus Cruz
STM Traders & Services Ltd

Sulimierski, Daniel Maksymilian
Top Alco Ltd

Sulkhanishvili, Giorgi
Freerun Consulting Limited

Sullivan, John
Jack Sullivan (Properties) Ltd
Jack Sullivan Limited

Sullivan, Michael
Jack Sullivan (Properties) Ltd
Jack Sullivan Limited

Sumeray, Graham Paul
The Great Wine Group Limited

Summers, Martin Nicholas
Clarence Spirits Limited

Sumner, Anita Marie
Il Palagio Ltd

Sumra, Ana Magdalena
Brewed 4 U Ltd

Sun, Jian
Panda Trading International Ltd

Sun, Yu
Sunny Group Limited

Sundar, Sampath Sudesh
Greenlink Enterprises Limited

Sundin, Adrian John
Maison Maurice Limited

Sundin, Jonathan Mark
Maison Maurice Limited

Sunner, Harvinder Singh
Bull Trading Worldwide Ltd

Suppiah, Ulaganathan
Frenchvines Limited

Surana, Gurjinder Singh
K & G Spirits Ltd

Suri, Preet Singh
Barrys Discount Ltd.

Susana, Alessandra
KBB Components Ltd

Suterwalla, Jehangir
Landmark Wholesale Limited

Suttie, Ian Alexander
First Whisky Limited

Sutton, Mark
Fine Food & Wine Limited

Swaine, Jonathon David
Nectar Imports Limited

Swann, James Oliver
Brocour Ltd.

Swann, Louis
Le Venue Wine Warehouse Ltd

Swarbrick, Damon William Thornton
KBE Drinks Enterprises Limited
Kingfisher Beer Europe Limited
UBI Drinks Enterprises Limited

Swayamprakasam, Kirubanandam
Richway Cash and Carry Ltd

Sweaney, Emma
Pulp Craft Cider Limited

Sweeney, Matthew
Boar Wine Ltd

Swindells, David William Harold
Richdells Wine Merchants Holdings

Swindells, Harry Robert John
Richdells Wine Merchants Holdings

Swindells, Jack David
Richdells Wine Merchants Holdings

Swinfen, Matthew James
SO & T Consulting Limited

Swinney, Paul
The Bitter End Limited

Symeonides, Simon
UK Wine & Food Supplies Ltd

Symeou, Andrew
AKM Trading Services Ltd

Symeou, Constantine
AKM Trading Services Ltd

Symington, Andrew William
Inverheath Limited
Prestonfield Whisky Co Ltd
Signatory Vintage Scotch Whisky Co Ltd

Symington, John Andrew Douglas
John E.Fells & Sons Limited

Symington, Paul Douglas
John E.Fells & Sons Limited

Symington, Stephen Brian
Connoisseur Estates Limited
Norlin Distribution Limited
Titanic Distillers Limited

Symonds, Melanie
Quiqui Mezcal Ltd

Symonowicz, Anna Monika
Carter Importing Ltd

Szasz, Jozsef
Azurapada Worldwide Ltd

Szczesny, Sebastian Remigiusz
MSM Foods Limited
Najpol Ltd

Szekely, Borbala
Diwine London Ltd

Szelbracikowski, Krzysztof Robert
101 Reykjavik UK Ltd

Szente, Zsolt
Vinolex Ltd

Szicsek, Aniko
Szicsek Palinka Ltd

Szilagyi, Laszlo
Interseel Ltd

Szimeiszter, Roland
Roland Wines Ltd

Szmajdzinski, Lukasz Piotr
Polskie Wodki Ltd

Szymanowski, Jakub
Brewland Ltd

Tadych, Magdalena Ewa
Hi-Spirits Ltd
Sazerac UK Limited

Tagoe, Ben
Origin Drinks Limited

Tait, Ronald Thomas
Lindisfarne Limited

Takhar, Gary Gurjinder Singh
Eden Fine Wines Limited

Talat-Kelpsa, Andrius
Beer Land Ltd

Taleghani, Ash
The Drink Driver Ltd

Talwar, Davinder
Rondel Trading Ltd

Tam, Sam
Appletree Cider Limited

Tamilazhagan, Sambathkumar
Sambath Trading Limited
Sambatha Ltd

Tan, Aby Juan Poo
Occidental & Oriental Cellars Ltd

Tan, Chinghung
Eastlin Alba Limited

Tanaka, Katsuhiko
Kingsbury Wine & Spirits Co Ltd

Tanc, Barbaros
Melen London Ltd.

Tang, Beibei
Smiley Rhyme Limited

Tank, Anil
Mega Kegs Limited

Tank, Bimla Kumari
Mega Kegs Limited
St.James Winery Ltd

Tanner, Betty
Cuvee Cavalier Limited

Tanner, James Jonathan
Merchant Vintners Co Ltd
Terry Platt Wine Merchants Ltd
Pulling & Co.Limited
Tanners (Shrewsbury) Limited
Tanners Cymru Limited
Tanners Wines Limited

Tanner, Katherine Elizabeth Anne
Tanners (Shrewsbury) Limited

Tanoh-Koutoua, Frederic
Surprising Wines Ltd

Tapper, Matthew John Purcell
Lion-Beer, Spirits & Wine (UK) Ltd

Taraf Kojok, Sofia
Artizen Raw Ltd

Tarakci, Serkan
Dionysus Premium Drinks Ltd

Tardivel, Simon
Isle of Bute Gin Co Ltd

Targas Marcilla, Joan
Wise Imports Limited

Tarrant, Stuart
Worldewide Limited

Tary, Mustafa Osman
Wolf Leisure Limited

Tary, Yusuf Osman
Oliver's Beer and Wine Limited
Wolf Leisure Limited

Tate-Smith, Catherine Louise
Tate-Smith Limited

Tate-Smith, Constance Maria
Tate-Smith Limited

Tate-Smith, Paul Thomas
The Society of Vintners Ltd
Tate-Smith Limited

Tatham, Edward Jeremy
Edward Tatham Champagne Ltd

Taukoor, Baboo Oomeshwarsingh
Dodotraders UK Limited

Tawadey, Rohan
Toff Wine Ltd

Tawari, Eniye Blessing
Palms & Liquor Enterprises Ltd

Taylor, Andrew
Pioneer Spirits Ltd

Taylor, Caroline Elizabeth
Slightly Squiffy Limited

Taylor, Charles Edward
Montrachet Limited
Charles Taylor Wines Limited

Taylor, David Edward
Independent Drinks Supplies Ltd

Taylor, David Kennedy
Fine Products Exporters Ltd

Taylor, Helen Frances
Blue Marble Consultants Ltd

Taylor, Hugh
Slurp Wine Co Ltd

Taylor, Ian David
Spar (UK) Limited

UK Wholesalers of Beers, Wines and Spirits dellam

Taylor, James Geoffrey Bethune
180 East Limited

Taylor, James John
DT1 Ltd
Diabolus Limited

Taylor, Joanne
The Beer Company (Exports) Ltd
The Beer Company Consolidations Ltd
The Beer Co Ltd
Sherwood Outlaws Brewing Co Ltd

Taylor, Louisa Jane
Charles Taylor Wines Limited

Taylor, Peter
The Little Big Wine Co Ltd

Taylor, Peter John
Hanwood Limited

Taylor, Philip Francis
Fine Products Exporters Ltd

Taylor, Rupert James
Uncharted Wine Co Ltd.

Taylor, Ryan Jack
Gin Fizz Ltd

Tchuente, Elody Kodelne
Kolden Ltd

Teasdale, Lesley Ann
Rippingale Promotions Limited

Teilhard de Chardin, Nathalie Anne Alberte
Bourgognes Only Limited

Teilhard de Chardin, Philippe Henri Urbain
Bourgognes Only Limited

Teixeira, Rui Cesar
Stallion Spirits Limited

Tektas, Serwan
Lioness Paw UK Limited

Telser, Marcel
Telser & Pauli Ltd

Temperley, Humphrey Peter Neville
Temperley Wines Limited

Temperley, Susan Elizabeth
Temperley Wines Limited

Templeman, Miles Howard
Shepherd Neame Limited

Terry, Alan
Liquid Indulgence Ltd

Terry, John Frederick
Evolution Drinks Ltd

Tersigni, Danilo
Mercury Spirits Ltd

Tesfa, Wassihun Yimenu
Limalimo UK Ltd

Tester, Simon Ransom
Cador Limited
The Champagne Company (UK) Ltd
The Drinks Emporium Limited

Tettamanti, Andrea
Wined Ltd

Tezgor, Tolga
Mamajuana UK Ltd

Th'ng, Natalie
Majestic Wine Warehouses Ltd

Thackray, Christopher James
Craftwater Brewing Co Ltd

Thackray, Sarah, Dr
Atom Brewing Co Limited

Thakkar, Amish
Amish Wholesalers Limited
Cobev Limited

Thakker, Jesal
The Riding Wine Co Ltd

Thakrar, Jalpesh Dinsukhrai
88 Connect Ltd

Thakrar, Kapil Mahendra
Star Direct Hospitality Ltd

Thakrar, Prakash
HT Drinks Ltd

Thakrar, Sagar
Champers (Wholesale) Limited
HT Drinks Ltd

Thakrar, Sanjay
Champers (Wholesale) Limited
HT Drinks Ltd

Thakrar, Shohil
Gift Creation and Design Ltd

Thambiah, Indira
Silly Point Wines Limited

Thaniotis, Nikos James
The Portuguese Winery Limited

Thannikkatt, Sujith Sudevan
Legacy Wines & Beverages UK Ltd

Thapa, Om
Best Price Retail and Wholesale Ltd

Tharmaraja, Kuberan
NTKS Ltd

Thavarajah, Yostinappu Philip
UK Beer & Soft Drinks Ltd

Thayananthan, Bhavani
ABR Restaurant Group Ltd
Abra Export UK Limited

Thayananthan, Thuraichamy
ABR Restaurant Group Ltd
Abra Export UK Limited

Theobalds, Estelle
Canopy Beer Co Ltd

Theobalds, Matthew James
Canopy Beer Co Ltd

Thewlis, Andrew Mark
Landmark Wholesale Limited

Thienot, Stanislas
Champagnes and Chateaux Ltd.

Thirumaran, Thiruchittampalam
STM Traders & Services Ltd

Thiyagarajan, Karthikeyan
Thiyagu Ltd

Thomas, Alan
Booze 2 U Ltd

Thomas, Cerith James
NineTailsDistillery Ltd

Thomas, Clive
The Drinks Link International Ltd

Thomas, Cynthia Yvonne
Windward Trading Co Ltd

Thomas, David Michael
BI Wines and Spirits Limited

Thomas, Denzil Philip
The Fightback Brewing Co Ltd

Thomas, James Barry
Premier Pubco Limited

Thomas, James Christopher Macpherson
Tiger Vines Ltd

Thomas, Jonathan
Wadworth and Co Ltd

Thomas, Jonathan David
The Proper Wine Co Ltd

Thomas, Kevin
Silver Fox Wines Ltd

Thomas, Kuravakalyil Thomas
Anglo-African Trade Limited

Thomas, Leah Katherine Alice
Pellegrino Wine and Food Distribution

Thomas, Lesley
Silver Fox Wines Ltd

Thomas, Nicholas David
Fifty One Forty Limited

Thomas, Richard Henry
Windward Trading Co Ltd

Thomas, Siobhan
Bond Bar Ltd

Thomas, Susan
Premier Pubco Limited

Thompson, Alexander James
Uncharted Wine Co Ltd.

Thompson, Cherry Ruth Stuart
Wyfold Vineyard Limited

Thompson, Frazer Douglas
London and East India Drinks Co Ltd

Thompson, Marco
Just Incase Wines Ltd

Thompson, Michael Anthony, Reverend
Associated Church Clubs Ltd

Thompson, Piers Michael
St.Austell Brewery Co Ltd

Thompson, Ryan
Pomona Island Brew Co Ltd

Thompson, Stephen Paul
Spencers (Bromsgrove) Limited

Thomson, Duncan William Harold
Abercrombie Fine Wines Limited

Thomson, George Preston
Craft Distillers Scotland Ltd
Siderea Consulting Limited
Small Batch Bottlers Scotland Ltd

Thomson, Ian Arthur McAinsh
Thomson & Scott Limited

Thomson, John Alexander
414 Alcohols Limited

Thomson, Neil Michael
Tipple Spirits Co Ltd

Thomson, Simon David
Talking Wines Limited

Thorne, George Edward
Thorne Wines Limited

Thorne, James Harry
Thorne Wines Limited

Thorne, John William
Polaris Wines Ltd

Thorne, Malcolm Roger
Thorne Wines Limited

Thorne, Sarah Ann
Thorne Wines Limited

Thornton, Edward Jared MacLeod
John E.Fells & Sons Limited

Thornton, Fraser John
The Bunnahabhain Distillery Co Ltd
Burn Stewart (U.S. Holdings) Ltd
Henry C. Collison and Sons Ltd
Distell Europe Ltd.
Distell International Holdings Ltd
Distell International Limited
Gordon Graham & Co Ltd
Imperial Distillers Co. Ltd

Thornton, Howard
First Bar Supplies Limited

Thornton, Jolyon Kenneth
Moet Hennessy U.K. Limited

Thornton, Vondeira
First Bar Supplies Limited

Thorold, Marcus Guy Francis
Freshfield Fine Wines Limited

Thorp, Stephen
The Idle Hour Spirit Co Ltd

Thorpe, Simon William Michael
John E.Fells & Sons Limited

Thranum, Dominic
DT Wine Importers Ltd

Tian, Yajun
Voubearst Limited

Tianle, Ma
St. Max Wine Limited

Tienta, Franck Cedric
Vitis-Terra Limited

Tiffin, Hershey
Allum Limited

Tilling, William James Charles
Firth and Co Wine Merchants Ltd

Tillston, Robert William
Trendbev Ltd.

Tilt, Nicholas Jonathan Lloyd
The Firkin Whisky Co Ltd

Timblo, Anna
Feni Global Limited

Tingay, Jennifer Alison
Southbourne Brewing Limited

Tipping, James Mason
Xpress Drinks Ltd

Tipping, Stephen
West Lancs Drinks Ltd

Tiskaya, Donus
Kayzar Ltd

Titley, Marcus Millward
Seckford Wines Limited

Tob-Ogu, James
3 Barrel Co Ltd

Todd, Hardip
Premier Inc. Ltd

Todd, Sukhwinder
Premier Inc. Ltd

Todd, William Jackson
The Rebel Wine Club Ltd

Togut, James Andrew
Shamboozle Limited

Toichieva, Gulnida
Calibre Brands Limited

Tolan, Claire
Dillon Bass Limited

Tolomei, Hugo
IMC Business Group Limited

Toma, Ioan
John Toma TDE Ltd

Toma, Oscar Lawrence
Shake's Ink Limited

Tomasin, Thierry
Monopole Wine Portfolio Management Ltd

Tomaszewicz, Grzegorz Jerzy
Dita Grappolo Ltd

Tomcanyi, Viliam
Pandemonium Wines Ltd

Tome, Nuno
The Whisky Trading Co Ltd

Tomekovic, Mario
Deer & Badger Ltd

Tomlinson, Lee John
Cask Trade Ltd
Tomlinson Whisky Merchants Ltd

Tompkin, Rodney Arthur
Rodney Tompkin Fine Wines Ltd

Tonbul, Fatma
Arda Rohat Limited

Toner, Regan
Distillery 96 Limited

Toogood, George Alec John
Prime Wines Limited
Unique Wine Safaris Limited

Toro Figueroa, Juan Diego
Toro Industries Ltd

Torre, Massimiliano
4 Star (Leicester) Limited

Torres Maczassek, Miguel
John E.Fells & Sons Limited

Torroella, Monica
Mezcal Reina Limited

Toth, Ana Maria
Carpe Vinum Ltd

Toth, Csaba
Tokaj Merchants Ltd

Toth, Sandor
Carpe Vinum Ltd

Tott, Adam
Draft Link Limited

Tough, Michael Stuart
Galldachd Na H-Alba Brewing Ltd

Toulmin, Jacqueline
Winelink Limited

Tovmasian, Gkor
Bassen Ltd
Noah Brothers Ltd

Town, Tracey
Cumberland Bargin Booze Ltd

Townend, Alexandra Louise
House of Townend Limited

Townend, Jennifer Ann
House of Townend Limited

UK Wholesalers of Beers, Wines and Spirits dellam

Townend, John Charles
House of Townend Limited
Merchant Vintners Co Ltd

Townsend Green, Colin David
Absolutely Organic Limited

Townsend Green, Rachel Ellen
Absolutely Organic Limited

Toyinbo, Kayode Sunday
Kato Enterprises Limited

Tracey, Daniel Marcus
Dragon Wines Limited

Trachtenberg, Marija
Ziv & Zivka Ltd

Tran, Alex
Chevalier de Mentaubert Ltd

Tran, Hung
Tulaich Ltd

Travers, David
Castle Eden Brewery Ltd
DTA Drinks Ltd

Travers, Stewart
The Proper Wine Co Ltd

Travers, Stuart
DTA Drinks Ltd

Travis, Neil Thomas
Clubinn Together Limited
Creswick Inns & Leisure Ltd

Treacy, Aidan Denis
Atlas Fine Wines Limited

Trease, Alan William
Weavers (Nottingham) Limited

Trease, Diana Kay
Weavers (Nottingham) Limited

Trease, Mary Elizabeth
Merchant Vintners Co Ltd
Weavers (Nottingham) Limited

Trease, Philip Geoffrey
Weavers (Nottingham) Limited

Tredre, Grace Elizabeth Georgia
TheTipsyTransit Ltd

Trela, Dariusz Krzysztof
Greenmount Holdings Limited

Trenciansky, Stanislav
R Spirit Ltd

Tresnan, Guy
London and East India Drinks Co Ltd

Trevena, John Morgan
Pimlico Cellars (Agencies) Ltd
Pimlico Dozen Limited

Trevor, Simon Richard
Original Wooden Case Limited

Tricio, Luis Javier
Paragon Wines Limited

Triefus, Graham Peter
Ellis of Richmond (Holdings) Ltd
Ellis of Richmond Limited

Trivedi, Hiren Vinodchandra
Hayk Corporation Ltd

Trotter, John Justin
Blush Gin Distrubutors UK Ltd

Trounce, Dominic Graham
The Plymouth Rum Co Ltd

Trow, Steven Thomas
Brew Boxes Ltd

Trower, Nicholas James
Biercraft Ltd

Trudgill, Andrew Peter
Avant Garde Drinks Ltd

Truman, Robert Paul
Truman's Drink Solutions Ltd

Tsai, Yiyang
Relaxandrinks Limited

Tskouaseli, Simon
Real Grapes Ltd

Tu, Chun-Kuang
Angel Wine & Spirit Group Co., Ltd.

Tucci, Paolo Camillo
John Dewar and Sons Limited

Tucek, Hannah Eveline
Blackadder International Ltd

Tucek, Robin Michael
Blackadder International Ltd

Tuck, Patrick Lloyd
Oso Brew Co Ltd

Tucker, Carl
Shocabo Ltd

Tucker, Jody Scott
Vernon Scott Limited

Tuffour-Kensah, Dennis Paul
Bubra Drinks Ltd

Tuite, Danielle Lisa
D & F Inns Ltd

Tuite, Finbarr Andrew
D & F Inns Ltd

Tunnicliffe-Squirrell, Lucinda Jane
Life's A Bottle Limited

Tunnicliffe-Squirrell, Martin Andrew
Life's A Bottle Limited

Turano, Antonio
Etna Food & Wine Ltd

Turatti, Pierluigi
Europemarca Limited

Turgut, Leyla
Thrace Premium Drinks Ltd

Turnage, William
180 East Limited

Turnbull, Benjamin Howard
Iridium Supplies Limited

Turnbull, James Douglas
William Morton Limited

Turnbull, John Neilson
Scotia Blending Co Ltd

Turnbull, Steven Francis
Italian Appellations Limited

Turner, Aidan
Lyndon Drinks Limited

Turner, Brett Alexander Charles
Cambridge Wine Merchants Ltd

Turner, Christopher Paul
Halton Turner Brewing Co Ltd

Turner, David Allen
Epic Beers Limited

Turner, Eric Charles
Marussia Beverages UK Limited

Turner, Grenville
Empress Ale Ltd

Turner, John Edward
Vyce Ltd

Turner, Louisa Caroline
Peter Graham Wines Limited

Turner, Peter Graham
Mumbles Brewery Ltd

Turner, Robert Stephen
Mumbles Brewery Ltd

Turpin, Vincent
100 Pipers (Whisky) Limited
Allt A' Bhainne Distillery Ltd
Beefeater Distillery Limited
CADV Limited
Dalmunach Distillery Limited
Martinez Gassiot & Co Ltd
James Hawker and Co Ltd

Turton, Maxeen Ann
Schnapp Lab Ltd

Turton, Robert Peter
I I Wine Limited

Tut, Seref
Solent Off-License Ltd

Tutisani, Tapiwa
Magna Juice Ltd

Tuzzi, Massimo
Zonin UK Limited

Twaites, Christopher Matthew
Twaites and Jones Limited

Twiss, David John
Life Science Limited

Tyler-Street, Rubina
Soul Spirits Ltd

Tyler-Street, William Gannel
Soul Spirits Ltd

Tynan, Fergal
Alliance Wine Co Ltd

Tzechilidis, Efthymios
Salonica Limited

Ubsdell, Mark
The Cuba Trading Co Ltd

Ucar, Dogan
DLG Wholesale Ltd

Ucur, Ercan
Eda Quality Foods North UK Ltd

Ucur, Sercihan Yusuf
Ever-Tree Wholesale & Retail Ltd

Uddin, Jijan
Triumph Foodservice Limited

Ukachukwu, Chukwuebuka
Fameface Import Limited

Ulcay, Ali
London Drinks Supplier Ltd

Ullah, Javed Farhat
Beatville Limited
Fortmount Trading Limited

Ullrich, August
O'Donnell Moonshine Limited

Ulph, Samuel Maximillian
Starstock Ltd

Umar, Fadhilat Sope Fabiola
Candy Cotton Ltd

Unaka, Afamdi Maduabuchi
Mail-a-Wine Limited

Underwood, Nicholas John Cockburn
County Catering (Midlands) Ltd

Underwood, Timothy Morris
County Catering (Midlands) Ltd

Underwood, Toby James
The Wedding Wine Shop Ltd

Unimke, Jonathan Ashvin
Ark Inta Ltd

Unwin, Rose Catherine
Wyld Rose Ltd

Uppal, Avtar Singh
VIP Bottles Ltd

Uppal, Harbinder Singh
Empire Star Limited

Uraon, Francis
Maximus Wholesale Limited

Urquhart, Neil Edward
Speymalt Whisky Distributors Ltd

Urquhart, Stuart David
Speymalt Whisky Distributors Ltd

Ustuner, Ali
Ustuner Ltd

Uzukauskas, Robertas
Bent Distribution Ltd

Vadher, Ratilal
Belloni Limited

Vadoliya, Nilesh Kanjibhai
Welford Retail Limited

Vaduva, Beniamin
V B Cash & Carry Ltd

Vahvaselkae, Paavo Ollipekka
Oak Group One P.L.C.

Vainella, Anna
Belloni Limited

Valenta, Christoffer
Valenta Wine Limited

Valenti, Anthony
Ayr Brewing Co Ltd

Valentine, Matthew John
Mode de Vie (Carbon) Limited

Valentino, Lee
The Rustic Tap Limited

Van Den Oort, Cornelis Fredericus Matheus
Beautiful Beers East Anglia (UK) Ltd

Van Der Venter, Craig Martin William
Talbot & Barr Limited

Van Der Vliet, Bart Laurens
Ditton Wine Traders Ltd

Van Der Vyver, Willem Jacobus
First Cape Vineyards Ltd

Van Der Watt, James Andrew Thomas
Jabru Bevco Ltd

Van Horne, Frank
Focus Beverages Ltd

Van T Hof, Carole Anne
R. St Barth Limited

Van Zyl, Johan
Distell International Limited

Van de Meutter, Ben Frieda Emiel
Hoops and Champagne Ltd

Varatharaj, Komathi
Valvai Cash & Carry Ltd
Valvai Ltd

Varatharaj, Kumareswararaja
Valvai Cash & Carry Ltd
Valvai Ltd

Varchetta, Enrico
Varmont Ltd

Varian, David
Diageo Global Supply IBC Ltd

Varma, Anil
Just A Splash Limited

Varma, Pia
Just A Splash Limited

Varma, Ranjeet
Nine Reigns Limited

Varroquier, Anne-Louise
Pernod Ricard UK Limited

Varsani, Chetan Shivji
The Indian Ice Gola Co Ltd

Vasile, Razvan Tiberiu
Buffet Restaurant Northampton Ltd

Vasilescu, Octavian Alexandru
Wine Tasting Angels Ltd

Vassiljev, Maksim
Ryder Partners Limited

Vasudevan, Shinoj
Lord Krishna Trade Ltd
Realsa Wines Import & Export Ltd

Vazquez, Iago
Foodiebusters Epic Food Authority Ltd

Vazquez, Marco Antonio Marco Antonio
Mexican Spirits Carmen Del Rio Ltd

Veale, Timothy Alexander
Fishers Gin Ltd

Vedhara, Ashish
3F Leisure Limited

Vedi, Gaurav
OM Beers & Minerals Ltd

Vedi, Rahul [1957]
Keg Delivery Service Ltd

Vedi, Rahul [1987]
Miraj Beers & Wines Limited

Vedi, Rajiv
Keg Delivery Service Ltd
Miraj Beers & Wines Limited

Veenstra, Jaap Christiaan
Bubbles for Friends Ltd.

Veglio, Annamaria
Sammartini Ltd

Velasco-Carrillo, Miguel
Atlasaim International Limited

Velge, Bertrand Roger
Graftyset Limited

Velinor, Tyrone
Kylemore Trading Ltd

Velliangattur Senniappan, Saravanan
Heavenly Grapes Limited

Velo-Rego, Jose
C & D Wines Limited

Venables, Max
MV Distribution Ltd

Venguswamy, Kannuswamy
Tioluxe Europe Limited

Veniat, Michael
Louis Latour Limited

Venner, Charles Malcolm
Iron Pier Brewery Limited

Venter, Brett Jason
Good Living Brew Co Limited

Venverloo, Marcus
Wine Affairs Limited

Verhoye, Nicolas Gael
More Sake Limited

Verlet, Marc
The Beer Boutique Ltd

Verlet, Marc Johan Robert
Two Heads Beer Co Limited

Verma, Vikram
Trust in Global Food Ltd

Vernau, David Alan
The Red Bottle Co Ltd

Verney, Andrew Christopher
Carpe Vinum Ltd

Verney, Katharine Mary
Carpe Vinum Ltd

Verrillo, Lynsey Abernethy
The Verrillo Partnership Ltd

Verrillo, Sergio Milan
The Verrillo Partnership Ltd

Versteegh, Andreas Mikael
Martin Miller's Gin Limited

Veselaj, Sokol
Drinkable Ltd

Vesey, Damian, The Hon
Laurito Ltd

Vestey, Samuel George Armstrong, Lord
Coombe Farm Wines Limited

Viader, Gilbert
Viader Vintners Limited

Vibhakar, Dipesh
Group93 Ltd

Vibhakar, Sudhir
Group93 Ltd

Vickers, Clive Martin Charles
GBW Subscriptions Ltd

Vickers, Lisa Christine
GBW Subscriptions Ltd

Villar, John Gaspard
John Villar Wines Limited

Villiers, Christopher Chris
Cellar & Co Limited

Vimala-Raj, Nitkuna Raj
Berkmann Wine Cellars Limited

Vinall, Ian Michael
Vines Wines Limited

Vinall, Rachel Louisa
Vines Wines Limited

Vinals, Rolando
Vinals Wine & Food Limited

Vintner, Katalin Eva
Palinka UK Ltd

Vipond, Christopher
Now This Is It Ltd

Virk, Surjeeven
Empress Ale Ltd

Visone, Vincenzo
Quintessential Brands Premium Brands
Quintessential Brands Spirit Solutions
Quintessential Brands UK Ltd
Quintessential Spirits Holdings Ltd
Quintessential Spirits Limited
Quintessential Spirits UK Ltd
Quintessential Wines Holdings Ltd
Quintessential Wines Limited

Viswanathan, Prabhaharan
DEF Investments Limited

Vitas, Romana
RJR Fort Ltd

Vitega, Dragos
Rovial Trans Ltd

Vitellino, Antonia
Diffusion Food By Pina Co Ltd

Viva Rol, Alberto
Garumbas Ltd

Vleugels, Lodewijk
Anglium Ltd

Vlierboom, Carsten Erik
Main Rum Co Ltd

Voisin, Christine Eve
FVFC Limited

Voisin, Fabien
FVFC Limited

Vojvodic, Nino Vang
Milae Vodka Limited

Volf, Michael Joseph
The Gibraltar Gin Co Ltd

Volschenk, Leonard Jacobus
Distell International Holdings Ltd

Von Wendland, Marcelle Michelle Georgina Maria
F & M Cressi Limited
Tasty Kameleon Ltd

Vonka, Jaromir
FV Trading Europe Ltd

Vowles, Charlotte Ione
Everards Brewery Limited

Vranken, Nathalie Jeanne Marie Odile
Vranken Pommery UK Ltd.

Vranken, Paul Francois Edouard Joseph
Vranken Pommery UK Ltd.

Vranken, Paul-Francois Edouard Joseph
Pinglestone Estate Limited

Waddingham, Paul Anthony
Shires Wine Services Limited

Waddingham, Tina
Shires Wine Services Limited

Wade, Barrie
The Laughing Pug Ltd

Wadsworth, Emily Louise
T J Wines Ltd

Wadsworth, Oliver James
T J Wines Ltd

Wadsworth, Steven
T J Wines Ltd

Wadsworth, Tracey Jane
T J Wines Ltd

Wahi, Jyotika
Morosini Mills Limited

Wahid, Abdul
Global Foods Limited

Waite, Philip
F8t B8dgers Ltd

Wakelin, Paul James
LJW Wholesale Limited

Walcott, Jacob David
Spokesuk Ltd

Waldman, Mordecai Leib
Sibell Trading Limited

Walfall, Natasha Chantel
Late Night Liquor Ltd

Walford, Douglas
Afterthought Spirits Co Ltd

Walford, James Anthony
Regent Wines Limited

Walford, Mark George Hedley
Le Soula Limited

Walkden, David
Glug Limited

Walker, Adrian Cromar
Michael Woolley Limited

Walker, Alistair Craig
Alistair Walker Whisky Co Ltd

Walker, Andrew George
Solaris Wines Ltd

Walker, Cliff
Castle Eden Brewery Ltd

Walker, Daniel Lee
Psychopomp Ltd

Walker, James
Highfern Limited

Walker, Jean Frances
Highfern Limited

Walker, John Robert William
JH Wine Agencies Ltd

Walker, Kathryn
Liquid Brand Exports Limited

Walker, Linda Elizabeth
HardyDistillery Ltd

Walker, Malcolm Thomas
Itasca Wines Limited

Walker, Mark
Newchesters Ltd

Walker, Natalie Jane
Spain Link Ltd

Walker, Peter
Alcohology Ltd

Walker, Simon Antony Frederick
London Wine Eis Limited

Walker, William James
The Glenallachie Distillers Co Ltd

Wall, Andrew Thomas
Neptune Rum Ltd

Wall, Benjamin
Wall2wall Wines Limited

Wall, Graham Meredith
Grape and Grain Management Ltd

Wall, Jonathan Hugh
Wall2wall Wines Limited

Wallace, Alistair Luke
Keepr's Ltd

Wallace, Clare Emma
Gusto Wines Ltd

Wallace, Simon Peter
Gusto Wines Ltd

Wallace, Stephen Keith
The Bajan Trading Co Ltd

Wallace, Stuart
Creative Juices Brewing Co Ltd

Wallbank, Alexander James
Paradigm Red Limited

Waller, Andrew
Deckers Restaurants Limited

Wallington, Jonathan Christopher Gerrard
Southover Drinks Limited

Wallis, Barnaby George
Wallis Ventures Ltd

Wallis, Robert
Buveur Ltd

Wallis-Jones, Shem
Franklyn Road Brewing Ltd

Walmsley, John
Lanty Slee Liquor Co Ltd

Walmsley, Thomas
TW Wine Solutions Ltd

Walsh, Adrian James
A J Walsh Consultant Limited

Walsh, Brendan
Heroes Drinks Company C.I.C.

Walsh, Cathy
Bakewell Road Brewery Ltd

Walsh, David Stuart
Bakewell Road Brewery Ltd

Walsh, Neil
St Davids Gin Limited

Walsh, Ruth Louise
St Davids Gin Limited

Walsh, Steven
The Can Man Ltd

Walters, Ryan Lee
It's A Gin Thing Ltd

Walton, Kieran Richard
KRW Leisure Limited

Walton, Mark Corin
Bloomsbury Drinks Ltd

Walton, Stuart Lester
The Grape Escape Limited

Walwyn, Nicola
KRD Distribution Co Ltd

Walwyn-James, Christopher Darryl
Lindisfarne Limited

Wambaki, King'ori
Muratina Limited

Wan, Kwok Manager
London SCC Group Ltd

Wang, Danyang
Xuyang International Ltd

Wang, Hongxiao
Ross Earl Wine Co., Ltd.

Wang, Xiuyun
UK Blue Ribbon Group Beer Co., Ltd

Wang, Zhiliang
UK McCullenvis Wine Group Ltd

Ward, Anthony Richard Bangor
Southern Wines Limited

Ward, Morgan
Morgan Edwards Limited

Ward, Neil Robert
Neilward Ltd

Ward, Steve Charles
Myella Brands Ltd

Ward, Thomas
The Busted Cow Ltd

Warden, John Anthony Leslie
Iron Pier Brewery Limited

Warder, Kevin James
The Compasses Gomshall Ltd

Ware, David John
Greens Beers Limited

Warner, Lucy Margaret Faraday
Bosman Wines UK Ltd
The Project Wines UK Limited
Sauvignon Wines UK Ltd
Warner Family Wines Limited

Warren, Alex John
Cassels and Sons Brewing Europe Ltd

Warren, Andrew Philip
A.I.M.S. (Refreshments) Ltd

Warren, Luke Anthony
Bitter Lemons Gin Ltd

Warren, Philip
Union Brands Ltd

Warwick Banks, Oliver Graham
Warwick Banks and Jenkins Ltd

Warwick, David John
Vicarage Spirit Limited

Warwick, Janet Anne
Vicarage Spirit Limited

Waterman, Nicholas Burns
Negociants Europe Limited
Negociants UK Limited

Waters, Calum Jonathan Martin
Blue Thorn Gin Limited

Waters, David
Blue Thorn Gin Limited

Waterston, Clifford James
North East Drinks Supplies Ltd

Wates, Neil Edward
Friendship Adventure Ltd.

Watkin, John
Lincoln West End Limited

Watkins, Anthony Graham
Celtavini.Com Limited

Watkins, Rhys David
Crafty Devil Brewing Ltd

Watmough, George
Adventure Brands Ltd

Watmough, Jayne Margaret
Adventure Brands Ltd

Watson, Alan John
Raisin Social Limited

Watson, Andrew
Outlander Brands Limited

Watson, Elizabeth
Domaine Watson Ltd

Watson, Gillian Anne McGregor
Speymalt Whisky Distributors Ltd

Watson, Michael Wilmer
Finebatch Limited

Watson, Paul
Kermis Bier Ltd

Watson, Peter Wilmer
Finebatch Limited

Watson, Ronald George
Half Cut Wines Limited

Watson, Scott McMurray
Crucial Brands Holdings Ltd
Crucial Drinks US Holdings Ltd
LDC Scotland Limited
The Lost Distillery Co Ltd
Old Tullymet Whisky Co Ltd

Watson-Burge, Alison Jayne
Law and Disorder Brew Co Ltd

Watson-Burge, Simon David
Law and Disorder Brew Co Ltd

Watt, Alan MacDonald
Alpha Whisky Ltd

Watt, David James Sinclair
David J. Watt (Fine Wines) Ltd

Watt, Frances Elizabeth Mary
David J. Watt (Fine Wines) Ltd

Watt, Gordon Robert
Old Town Blending Co Ltd

Watt, James Bruce
The Brewgooder Foundation

Wattie, Robert John
CBD Drinks Co Ltd
Fairview Wines Limited
Functional Drinks Co Limited

Watts, Deborah Irene
Cincin Wines Ltd

Watts, Geoffrey Fraser
Cellar Trends Limited

Watts, Lynne
Lothbury Wine Shippers Limited

Watts, Martin Fraser
Cellar Trends Limited

Watts, Michael John
Cincin Wines Ltd

Watts, Peter
Lothbury Wine Shippers Limited

Waud, Jeremy Charles
Waud Wines Limited

Weatherall, Edward Percy Keswick
Corney and Barrow Group Ltd
Corney and Barrow Limited

Weaver, Fawn
Uncle Nearest Ltd.

Webb, Katie Elizabeth
Angeli Del Vino Limited

Webb, Kevin Ivan
Blux UK Import Ltd

Webb, Lee Trevor
Blux UK Import Ltd

Webb, Nicole Marie
NMWLeisure Ltd

Webster, Laurence William
Las Bodegas Limited

Webster, Mark Timothy
Tinkture Ltd

Webster, Richard Joseph
Tennent Caledonian Breweries UK Ltd
Tennent Caledonian Breweries Wholesale

Weddell, Karl Patrick
Beer and Spirit Agencies International

Wedgbury, Sarah Louise
Wedgbury Connections Ltd

Wei, Bo
Co Stars London Ltd

Wei, Xiangyu
H & F Export Limited

Weijers, Pascal
Focus Beverages Ltd

Welby, Dominic John Earle
Medoc Wines Limited

Welch, Darren
BL Drinks Ltd

Welch, David Peter
The 19th Beer Co Ltd

Welch, Thomas Peter James
Falcon Wholesaler Limited

Welch, Timothy Emerson
CHX Distillers Ltd

Welham, Christopher
Wadworth and Co Ltd

Weller, Sam
Conscious Collaborative Ltd

Wellings, Antony David
The Antipodean Sommelier Ltd

Wellings, Philip Scott
Veini Wine Co Ltd

Wells, Christopher Gerard
London Wine Shippers Limited

Wells, Geoffrey Charles Vaughan
Charles Wells,Limited

Wells, Liam
97 Catering Ltd

Wells, Paul Richard
Charles Wells Brewery Limited
Charles Wells,Limited

Wells, Peter John
Charles Wells,Limited

Welsh, Santino
Northern Supplies (NE) Ltd

Wemyss, Isabella Alethea
Wemyss Vintage Malts Limited
Wemyss Wines and Spirits Ltd

Wemyss, John
Kegspertise Ltd

Wemyss, William John
Wemyss Vintage Malts Limited
Wemyss Wines and Spirits Ltd

Wen, Zepeng
WLL Wholesale Ltd

Wentworth, Geoffrey
Let There Be Beer Ltd

Werner, Willoughby Oliver
Penryn Spirits Limited

Werstyn, Anna Mikalina
Distillers Direct Ltd
Kater Four (Cash & Carry) Ltd

Wescott, Stephen Robert
Airways Bonded Warehouse Ltd

Wessely, Oliver Sebastian
Benchmark Drinks Ltd

West, Anthony Frederick
Wadworth & Company (Burford) Ltd

West, Atherton John
Emporia Brands Limited

West, Colin Thomas
BI Wines and Spirits Limited
Bordeaux Index Limited

West, George William Arthur
Southbourne Brewing Limited

Westcott, Tom Wiilliam
Burton Rd Brewing Co Limited

Westgarth, Alexander
Westgarth Wines Limited

Westgarth, Hilary
Westgarth Wines Limited

Westmacott, Mark
The Spiritory Ltd

Weston, Adrian Robert
Everards Brewery Limited

Wetzel, Petra Margareta
Heidi Beers Limited

Wharton, Barnaby James
CHX Distillers Ltd

Wharton, Charles Edward Clegg
Ellis Wharton Wines Ltd

Wharton, Dale
Bablake Wines Limited

Whatley, Steve Dennis
Webdrinks Ltd

Wheater, Dylan
Barge & Barrell Inns Ltd

Wheatley, Douglas Gordon George
Isle of Bute Gin Co Ltd

Wheatley, Lewis Scott
Phil Macan Limited

Wheeler, Darren Andrew
Worldewide Limited

Wheeler, Fergus Oliver
Red Bay Brewing Co Ltd

Wheeler, Timothy Albert William
Ramx Ltd

Whelan, Karen Elizabeth
Compasse Limited

Whenham-Bossy, Patrick
Terra Wines Limited

Whiley, Matthew Jefrey Allen
Gold Tooth Limited

White, Christopher
Parched Drinks Ltd

White, Gordon Thomas
Wine Importers (Edinburgh) Ltd

White, Nicholas John
A. Dewar Rattray Limited

White, Phillip David
Conscious Collaborative Ltd

White, Thomas Edward
Unwined Limited

Whitehead, Alan John
House of Townend Limited

Whitehead, Angus Joseph
House of Townend Limited

Whitehead, Nicola Elizabeth
Mythop Gardens Limited

Whitehead, Peter John
Mythop Gardens Limited

Whitehead, Philip Mark
Aspall Cyder Limited
Cobra Beer Partnership Limited
Molson Coors Brewing Co (UK) Ltd
Molson Coors Brewing International

Whiteley, Carolyn
Whiteleys of Halifax Limited

Whiteley, Dennis
Boutinot Canada Limited
Boutinot Limited
Boutinot USA Limited
Boutinot Wines Limited
In Vino Bidco Limited
In Vino Limited
Moreno Wine Importers Co Ltd
Rude Mechanicals Limited
Vinandar Wines Limited

Whiteley, Matthew
Rude Mechanicals Limited

Whiteley, Robin William
Whiteleys of Halifax Limited

Whiteley, Simon William Henry
Campania Cucina Ltd

Whiteley, Thomas
Rude Mechanicals Limited

Whitfield, Damilola
Quamina Quality Drinks Co Ltd

Whiting, Andrew George
Crafted Beverages Limited

Whiting, Emma
Crafted Beverages Limited

Whittaker, David
LDW Wines Limited

Whittaker, Judith
Whittaker Wines Limited

Whittaker, Lucy Elizabeth
LDW Wines Limited

Whittaker, William
Marston's Acquisitions Limited

Whittick, Joseph William
Whitmore and White Limited

Whittington, Jake Arthur James
My Cocktail Club Limited

Whittington-Bowers, Collette
Hills Prospect PLC

Whittle, Gareth Andrew
Chilli Brands (New Zealand) Ltd
Chilli Brands Limited
Chilli Marketing Brand Management Ltd
Chilli Marketing Promotions Ltd

Whyte, Alexander William
Tutto Wines Limited

Wickman, Paul Nigel
The Bloomsbury Distillery Ltd

Wickramage, Kemasiri
Stack United Limited

Widlarz, Marek
MGW World Ltd

Wiechmann, Jim
Point Beer UK Limited

Wigginton, Gordon Roy
Hic-Cup Wines Limited

Wight, Zoe
North Star Spirits Ltd.

Wightman, Jamie
New Wave (Scotland) Limited

Wilcock, Ben Mark
Lant Street Wine Co Ltd

Wilcock, David Roy
Lant Street Wine Co Ltd

Wilcox, William Christopher
Landmark Wholesale Limited

Wild, Alastair
Caps Off Ltd.

Wild, Andrew Paul
The Society of Vintners Ltd
WLG Limited

Wild, Brian
World Cider Box Limited

Wild, Steven Peter
WLG Limited

Wilding, Katharine
Angel Feathers Limited

Wilding, Mark Steven
Angel Feathers Limited

Wildman, Glen
Lancashire Beer Co Ltd

Wilkie, Alexander Stewart
The Salt Rock Liquor Co Ltd

Wilkin, Matthew Robert
H2vin Limited

Wilkinson, Fiona Jane
Wilkinson Vintners Limited

Wilkinson, Gail
Amlot Morgan Fine Wines Ltd

Wilkinson, John Anthony
Kerry Wines Limited

Wilkinson, Julia
Europvin UK Limited

Wilkinson, Leigh Simon
Intercellar Distribution Ltd

Wilkinson, Patrick Luke
Wilkinson Vintners Limited

Wilkinson, Samantha Jayne
Drink Kind Ltd

Wilks, Brian David
Wilks & Company Wine Merchants Ltd

Willan, John Anthony
Thorman Hunt & Co Limited

Willatt, Jenny
J & De Limited
The Mixology Collection Ltd

Willetts, James William
Birdcage Gin Ltd.

Williams, Ade
Jade General Merchants Ltd

Williams, Christopher Henry
South WLC Limited

Williams, Craig
Official Box Office UK Ltd

Williams, Daniel
Bespoke Wines Ltd
The Bottle Shop (Penarth) Ltd

Williams, Elizabeth Grace
Tour de Force Wines Limited

Williams, Emma
Paso-Primero UK Ltd.

Williams, Gregory Thomas
Fine Wines Direct UK Limited
RDM Wines Limited

Williams, Jack Julius
Reva Drinks Ltd

Williams, John Peter
Beerfantastic Ltd
Winefantastic Limited

Williams, John Richard
Rossendale Brew Co Ltd

Williams, Joseph Thomas
Beer Journey Ltd

Williams, Marion
Sloshed Puppy Ltd

Williams, Michael [1943]
Keepr's Ltd

Williams, Michael [1960]
Liquid Measure Limited

Williams, Rosie Anna
Rosie & Gin Limited

Williams, Stephen [1957]
The Antique Wine Co (Holdings) Ltd

Williams, Stephen [1982]
Gergovie Wines Limited

Williams, Stephen John
Ravensbourne Wine Co Ltd

Williams, Stuart Anthony
Grape Wines Services Ltd

Williams, Thomas Francis
TTO Limited

Williams, Vaughan
Amore G.N.A. Limited

Williamson, Jared Matthew
Provino Limited

Williamson, Leon
Jeffries Vintage Drinks Ltd

Williamson, Robert Brian, Sir
Liv-Ex Limited

Willis, Adrian Stuart
White Willows Beers, Wines and Spirits

Willmott, Kevin Nash Knight
Fronsacdirect Limited
Fronsacwines Limited

Wills, Joshua William
Drinkz Ltd

Wilson, Alexander John Adamson
Myrlex Southend Limited

Wilson, Alison
Fizz Guru Limited

Wilson, Aston
Glo-Rum Enterprise Limited

Wilson, Bianca Bailey, Dr
Glo-Rum Enterprise Limited

Wilson, Cathryn Mary
The Langwith Brewing Co Ltd

Wilson, Christine Ann
Inside Trax Limited

Wilson, David
The Langwith Brewing Co Ltd

Wilson, David John
Inside Trax Limited

Wilson, Desmond Barry
Champagne Charlie (Midlands) Ltd

Wilson, Diane
Medicare Health & Energy Drinks Ltd

Wilson, Eleanar
EW Bars Limited

Wilson, Graham
Mountcharge Limited

Wilson, Joyce Elizabeth
Mountcharge Limited

Wilson, Karen
Kingsland Drinks Group Limited
Kingsland Drinks Limited

Wilson, Kim Jane
North South Wines Limited

Wilson, Linda Jayne
M.& M.Value Limited

Wilson, Mark Anthony
Mickey Finn's Liquor Co Ltd.

Wilson, Matthew James
Brix & Porter Ltd.

Wilson, Matthew Philip
Botanicals and Hops Limited
Hierarchy Brewing Co Ltd
Yarm Gin Ltd
The Yarm Spirits Co Ltd

Wilson, Nicholas Henry
Heath Trading Limited

Wilson, Peter John
S.A.Brain & Co Ltd

Wilson, Richard Clive
Ciderfex Limited

Wilson, Robert
Harp & Crown Cider Co Ltd
I Caesar Limited
Lamson Wine Co Ltd
Union International Drinks Corporation

Wilson, Robert John Niven
Toast Ale Ltd

Wilson, Timothy Hal Quentin
Cambridge Wine Merchants Ltd

Wilson, Victoria Elizabeth
The Drinks Network Ltd

Wilton, Michael Anthony
Maw Berwick Ltd

Wilton, Robert Lawrence
Delegat Europe Limited

Wiltshire, Simon Joseph
Capper & Co Ltd

Winckley, Peter Frederick
J. Chandler & Company, Limited

Winfield, Timothy
The Quarter Cafe Bar Limited

Wing, Daniel Andrew
DW Brands Ltd

Wingate Gray, Julia Rosemary
Hop Hideout Limited

Winnack, Jack Andrei Geoffrey
Winnack and Hart Industries Ltd

Winning, Arthur Hamilton Brown
James MacArthur & Co Limited

Winslow, Ronald Basil
J.R.G. Investments Limited

Winstanley, James
Trilogy Beverage Brands Ltd

Winton, Allan
Oliver's Beer and Wine Limited

Winton, Susanne Patricia
Urban Wine Co. Ltd

Wiseman, Andrew Reginald
Route des Vins Limited
Sheridan Cooper's Limited

Wiseman, Sheridan Phyllis
Sheridan Wines Limited

Witham, Sara
The Peculiar Gin Co Ltd

Withers, David John
Withers Agencies Limited

Wodehouse, Robin Nigel
Walker & Wodehouse Wines Ltd

Wodke, Maciej
Almaster Limited
Liquid Vision Enterprise Ltd

Wodke, Monika
Almaster Limited

Wolens, Roger
Land's End Gin Limited

Wolfart, Jacek
Xtraflow Limited

Wolfson, Andrew Daniel
Fine & Rare Wines Limited

Wolpert, Alexander Michael
Destilado London Limited

Wolstenholme, Jacqueline
Somborne Valley Vineyard Ltd

Wolstenholme, Nigel Timothy
Somborne Valley Vineyard Ltd

Wolton, Andrew John
Beerfantastic Ltd

Wood, Alan
Dowbridge Distributors Ltd

Wood, Andrew Charles
Adnams PLC

Wood, Anita Pauline
Dowbridge Distributors Ltd

Wood, Camilla Jane
Imprint Wine Limited

Wood, Christopher James Dinsdale
Chelsea Vintners London Ltd

Wood, David Jonathan
CSS On-Trade Limited
Compass Supply Solutions Ltd

Wood, Douglas Alan
Woodwinters Agencies Limited

Wood, Edmund
The Cartmel Spirit Co Ltd

Wood, Jean
B & B Drinks Ltd

Wood, Matthew
Conscious Collaborative Ltd

Woodhouse, Anthony Ashton
Premium Beverage Refreshments Ltd

Woodhouse, Anthony William
Hall & Woodhouse Limited

Woodhouse, Mark John Michael
Hall & Woodhouse Limited

Woodhouse, Richard Alexander Bruce
London and East India Drinks Co Ltd

Woods, Alexander Michael
Pongolo Ltd

Woods, Brian David
Crucial Brands Holdings Ltd
Crucial Drinks US Holdings Ltd
LDC Scotland Limited
The Lost Distillery Co Ltd
Old Tullymet Whisky Co Ltd

Woods, Daniel Martin
Fieldscot Ltd

Woods, James Michael
FD Gin Co Ltd

Woods, Philippa Jane
Seckford Agencies Limited
Sunbird Wines UK Ltd

Woolf, Sebastian Joseph
Artful Dodger Whisky Ltd

Woolnough, Paul
Manteo Trading Co Ltd

Woolwich, Diane
Colne Confectionery Ltd

Workman, George Edward
Frizzenti Limited

Wormleighton, James
Waistcoat Wines Ltd

Woroniecki, Jan Felix Michael
Okowita Vodka Limited

Worontschak, John Robert
Litmus Wine Agencies Limited

Worrall, Stephen John
St.Austell Brewery Co Ltd

Worsley, Jonathan David
Bancroft Wines Limited
Mason & Mason Wines Limited

Worsley, Philip John
Worsley Wines Limited

Wouhra, Gurdashan Singh
Landmark Wholesale Limited

Wozniak, Bartosz Wiktor
Ttow Ltd

Wratten, Danette
Bedminster Beer Co Ltd

Wratten, Kathryn Margaret Mary
Black Cat Brewery Limited

Wratten, Paul [1964]
Black Cat Brewery Limited

Wratten, Paul [1985]
Bedminster Beer Co Ltd

Wright, Andrew Glyn
Baby Bottles (Wholesale) Ltd

Wright, Brian Michael
Primo Drinks (Lancashire) Ltd
Primo Drinks (Merseyside) Ltd
Primo Drinks (North East) Ltd
Primo Drinks (Staffordshire) Ltd
Primo Drinks (Yorkshire) Ltd
Primo Drinks Ltd
Same Day Beers Group Ltd

Wright, David Franklin Thomas
David Alexander Wine Merchants
Maidenhead

Wright, Gavin
Primo Drinks (Lancashire) Ltd
Primo Drinks (Staffordshire) Ltd
Primo Drinks (Yorkshire) Ltd
Primo Drinks Ltd

Wright, Gavin Michael
Primo Drinks (Merseyside) Ltd
Primo Drinks (North East) Ltd
Same Day Beers Group Ltd

Wright, Gordon Henry
Kingsbury Wine & Spirits Co Ltd

Wright, Kieron
Mexcal Ltd

Wright, Lucy Katherine
Island Drinks Limited

Wright, Margaret Anne
Wrights Lion Brewery Limited

Wright, Mary
Newchesters Ltd

Wright, Philippa Jane Graeme
Goedhuis & Co Ltd

Wright, Richard Stacey
Wrights Lion Brewery Limited

Wright, Sally Eileen
Wrights Lion Brewery Limited

Wu, Daomeng
Summerforever Ltd

Wu, Ming Wah
Cathay Importers (London) Ltd

Wyatt, Gary Paul
Liberty Wines Limited

Wyatt, Hugh Geoffrey Robert
Rum Fellows Limited

Wylie, Andrew Robertson
Cellar Capital Limited

Wynn, Michael William
Three Swallows Ltd

Wynter, Anthony Timothy
Thirstee Business Limited

Wynter, Sally
Biotanica Ltd

Xu, Thomas Yucheng
Chivalry Trading International Co. Ltd

Xu, Xu Dong
CPC Business Limited

Xu, Yanzhong, Dr
Imperial 21 Joya Ltd

Xuereb, Emmanuel Antoine
Les Vins de Latour Limited

Yadav, Yashpal Singh
Anya Global Limited

Yadirgi, Ozan
O & E Food Ltd

Yanagida, Maki
G Sake Co Ltd

Yanez, Felix Solis
Felix Solis Avantis UK Ltd

Yapp, Jason Christopher
Yapp Brothers Limited

Yaqub, Mohammed
Global Foods Limited

Yarbrough, Victor
Victory Global Ltd

Yates, David Robert
Yates low Brewery Limited

Yates, David Stanley
Yates low Brewery Limited

Yates, Nicholas
Adrian Mecklenburgh Limited

Yaved, Mohammed
Yaved Ltd

Yenugula, Pavan Kumar
The Compasses Gomshall Ltd

Yeomans, Stanley
Ozpax Limited

Yeter, Ferhat
Premium Bottles Limited

Yeung, Tak Wai
Murphy & Yeung Brewing Co Ltd

Yiangou, Avgerinos
Haslemere Wine Merchants Ltd

Yiangou, Deborah Michelle
Haslemere Wine Merchants Ltd

Yildirim, Sebahattin
Alexandria Partners Limited

Yildiz, Hassan
European Beverages Ltd

Yiminyi, Paul Kevin
Ineffable LDN Limited

Yip, Kim Fung
Chevalier de Mentaubert Ltd

Yolay, Ismail
Deniz & Ada Limited

Yolland, David Terrence
Kitwave Limited

Yolland, Richard Charles
Vice Enterprises Limited

Yoong, Ann
Lamjen Limited

Yoong, Chih Pin
Lamjen Limited

Yorke, Jane Louise
Yorke Vines Ltd

Yorke, Simon Anketel Hamilton
Yorke Vines Ltd

Young, Albert Roger
Young's Beers Wines & Spirits Ltd

Young, Danielle
C C and C London Ltd

Young, Hamish Gavin
New Generation Wines Limited

Young, Michael
Kitwave Limited

Young, Nicholas
The Natural Beer Co Ltd

Young, Paul Sinclair
Imbibros Ltd

Young, Paul Victor
Churnet Valley Drinks Limited
H.B.Clark & Co.(Successors) Ltd
Kitwave Limited
M.& M.Value Limited
Thorne Licence Wholesale Ltd

Young, Sharon Denise
Hobo Beer & Co Ltd

Young, Sheldon Ashley
Southbourne Brewing Limited

Young, Stuart
Four Corners Wine Co Ltd

Younger, Michael James
Ian MacLeod Distillers Limited

Yu, Qiao
Seawoods Wine Ltd

Yuan, Fuqing
Camis International Trading Co., Ltd.

Yusen, Jonathan Mark
William Grant & Sons Brands Ltd

Zadah, Kate
Zachicado Ltd

Zagorowski, Tomasz Jan
Gargara Limited

Zaidi Kahtoon, Syed Javed
The Booze Bolton Limited

Zaidova, Gunel
Bazaar Store Ltd

Zajaczkowski, Marcin
A-Z Spirits Ltd

Zakharov, Anton Yurievich
The New Muscovy Co Ltd

Zaman, Shan Roheel
Northern Supplies (NE) Ltd

Zamani, Said
Cocktail Express Ltd

Zambianchi, Alberto
Provino Limited

Zampieron, Vilmar
Stallion Spirits Limited

Zanelli, Paolo
Zetas Ventures Ltd

Zarach, Barrington Philip
Les Vignerons de Saint Georges Ltd

Zarate Avila, Maria Lorena
Amirante Empire Limited

Zaum, Dan Lawrence
Greenwood Distillers Limited
Greenwood Spirits Limited

Zawodny, Jaroslaw Marek
JR First Choice Cash & Carry Ltd

Zdrojek, Michal
Bosworthcruises Ltd

Zeisler, Gabor
Diageo Great Britain Limited

Zelenak, Ferenc
Zefino Family Limited

Zeloof, Jason
Ely & Sidney Limited

Zhang, Hongchun
Chivalry Trading International Co. Ltd

Zhang, Huarong
Winz International UK Ltd

Zhang, Lian
Guest Wines & Co. Ltd

Zhang, Weicheng
Digby Fine English Ltd
Digby Wine Ltd

Zhang, Yechuan
The Fine Wine (Old World) Trading Co Ltd

Zhang, Zhenzhen
Golden Whisky Limited

Zhao, Jing
Redoor Limited

Zheng, Fei Lun
Euroofar Trading Limited

Zhong, Hua
Seawoods Wine Ltd

Zhu, Tong
Oriental Drinks Limited

Ziane, Wahab
Mywinelabel Limited

Zintu, Roberto
Sardinia Wine Ltd

Zonin, Francesco
Zonin UK Limited

Zonneveld, Catharina Margaretha
J. & G. Barclay and Co Ltd

Zsebok, Zsigmond
Hungarian Wine Ltd

This page is intentionally left blank

Standard Industrial Classification
excluding
Wholesale of wine, beer, spirits and other alcoholic beverages

01210 Growing of grapes
Colchester Mann Limited
Crundale Wines Limited
Fairview Vineyard Ltd
Pinglestone Estate Limited
Relais La Torre UK Ltd
Southern England Wines (UK) Ltd
Tewaina Ltd
Wyfold Vineyard Limited

01240 Growing of pome fruits and stone fruits
South Downs Real Estate Ltd

01270 Growing of beverage crops
Fairview Vineyard Ltd

01500 Mixed farming
Brindle Distillery Limited
Everards Brewery Limited

01610 Support activities for crop production
Python Controls Ltd

01629 Support activities for animal production (other than farm animal boarding)
Python Controls Ltd

02100 Silviculture and other forestry activities
Martin Enterprises Limited

02200 Logging
Trusty Services Ltd

02400 Support services to forestry
Trusty Services Ltd

10120 Processing and preserving of poultry meat
Alliance Foods Limited

10130 Production of meat and poultry meat products
Deckers Restaurants Limited

10390 Other processing and preserving of fruit and vegetables
A Little Luxury Distillery Ltd
Brown Bear Tales Ltd
Lincolnshire Gin Ltd
Ramx Ltd

10512 Butter and cheese production
C Carnevale Limited

10710 Manufacture of bread; manufacture of fresh pastry goods and cakes
Layered Ltd

10720 Manufacture of rusks and biscuits; manufacture of preserved pastry goods and cakes
Layered Cakes Ltd
Layered Ltd

10831 Tea processing
Benjamin & Blum Limited

10832 Production of coffee and coffee substitutes
Burble Foods and Beverages Ltd
Cornfield Foods and Beverages Ltd
Crabtrees Craft Pubs and Bottle Merchants

10890 Manufacture of other food products n.e.c.
Ashanti Drinks Limited
Burble Foods and Beverages Ltd
Cornfield Foods and Beverages Ltd
Tasty Kameleon Ltd

11010 Distilling, rectifying and blending of spirits [179]
180 East Limited
3 Lids Rum Ltd
55 Above Ltd
A Little Luxury Distillery Ltd
Adnams PLC
Adventure Brands Ltd
Afterthought Spirits Co Ltd
Alko Vintages UK Ltd
Angola Beverages Holding Co Ltd
Arisaig Distillers Ltd
Arundo Limited
Atom Brands Limited
Atom Cask Holdings Limited
Atom Drinks Limited
Atom Group Limited
Atom Scotland Limited
Atom Supplies Limited
Aztec Spirits Ltd
Be Rude Not To Ltd
Bearded Lion Drinks Co Ltd
Beeble Liquor Limited
Beets Incorporated Ltd
Benjamin & Blum Limited
Bitter Lemons Gin Ltd
Black Cat Brewery Limited
Bloomsbury Distillery Ltd
Bombay Spirits Co Ltd
Bonny Gin Ltd
Borders Distillers Limited
Borders Distilling Limited
Botan Grey Ltd
Brindle Distillery Limited
Broad Street Brands Limited
Brockmans Gin Limited
Broughton Ales Limited
Bunnahabhain Distillery Co Ltd
Burn Stewart (U.S. Holdings) Ltd
Chalk & Charcoal Limited
Clock Tower Distilleries Ltd
Cognac Growers' Collective Ltd
Coleburn Distillery Limited
Spencer Collings & Co Limited
Conscious Collaborative Ltd
Michel Couvreur (Scotch Whiskies)
Crafted Beverages Limited
Cuba Trading Co Ltd
De Facto Spirits Limited
Deco Spirits Limited
Delicious Drinks Limited
Demball Limited
Demon Vodka Limited
John Dewar and Sons Limited
Diageo Great Britain Limited
Dirty Drinks Collective Ltd
Distell International Holdings Ltd
Distell International Limited
Distillery 96 Limited
Doctor Bird Rum Ltd
Droylsden Craft Limited
Duchy Beverages Ltd
Edmunds Cocktails Ltd
Eight Vodka Limited
Ely's Cocktails Ltd
H.B. Evelyo Ltd.
Family of Hounds Limited
Foxhole Spirits Limited
GNR Distillery Limited
Galldachd Na H-Alba Brewing Ltd
Gibraltar Gin Co Ltd
Gin Dobry Gin Co Ltd
Ginkhana Limited
Glen Monarch Distillery Ltd
Glen Scotia Distillery Co Ltd
Glenallachie Distillers Co Ltd
Gleneagles Distillery Limited
Glenturret Limited
Matthew Gloag & Son Limited
Goldy Gin Limited
Good Life Gin Co Ltd
Good Spirits Ltd
Gordon & MacPhail Limited
Gordon Graham & Co Ltd
Greenwood Spirits Limited
Guilty Libations Limited
Halton Turner Brewing Co Ltd
Ian Hart Distilling Limited
Hidden Gem - Urban Artisan Spirit Ltd
Highland Distillers Limited
Hunter Douglas Scotch Whisky Ltd
Hurricane Rum Co Ltd
Irish Gin Co Ltd
Ironbridge Gorge Gin Co Ltd
Isle of Bute Gin Co Ltd
Jervis Trading Limited
Jivana Spirits Ltd.
Justerini & Brooks,Limited
Kimbland Distillery Ltd
Kirklee Scotch Whisky Limited
Kozuba & Sons Limited
LDC Scotland Limited
Andrew Laing & Co Ltd
Lamson Wine Co Ltd
Lang Brothers Limited
Lanty Slee Liquor Co Ltd
Lazy Drinks Ltd.
Lincolnshire Gin Ltd
Liquid Lounge Drinks Co. Ltd
Liquid Vision Enterprise Ltd
Littlemill Distillery Co Ltd
Loaded Spirits Ltd
Loch Lomond Distillers Limited
Loch Lomond Distillery Co Ltd
Lombard Scotch Whisky Limited
Londinio Liqueurs Ltd.
London Spiced Dry Limited
Lough Neagh Distillers - 1837 Ltd
Ian MacLeod Distillers Ltd
Ian MacLeod and Co Ltd

UK Wholesalers of Beers, Wines and Spirits   dellam

Master of Malt Limited
Masters of Malt Limited
Maverick Brands Limited
Maverick Drinks Limited
Maverick Spirits Limited
Wm Maxwell (Scotch Whisky) Ltd
Mayfield Distilling Co Ltd
McLean's Gin Ltd
Mezcal Reina Limited
Modern Botanicals Limited
Molotov Brand Limited
Mr Kegz Ltd
My Nan's Favourite Ltd
Nele Drinks Limited
Nightrep Limited
NineTailsDistillery Ltd
Norfolk Rum Co Ltd
Old Brenin Distillery Ltd
Pant y Foel Gin Ltd
Perth Distillery Co Ltd
Pink Gin Co Ltd
Portavadie Distillery Limited
Portsmouth Gin Co Ltd
Pryzm Cocktails Limited
Psychopomp Ltd
Raer Scotch Whisky Ltd
Raven Spirits Limited
Red Door Gin Co Ltd
Maurice Richard Ltd
William Riddell & Sons Ltd
Row & Co Ltd
Rum Club Ltd
Peter J Russell & Co Ltd.
Russian Doll Vodka Limited
Sacred Spirits Holdings Ltd
Shieling Scotch Whisky Co Ltd
Solway Spirits Ltd
Somerset Craft Distillery Ltd
Speymalt Whisky Distributors Ltd
Speyside Distillers Co Ltd
Spirit of Glasgow Ltd
Spirits Development & Management Company (SDMC)
St Davids Gin Limited
Stockholm Distillers and Vintners
Stockport Gin Ltd
Sunderland Gin Limited
TBD Tipples Ltd
Telser & Pauli Ltd
Thames Distillers Limited
Three Stills Co Ltd
Tipo Loco Drinks Co. Limited
Titanic Distillers Limited
UK McLouis Liquor Co Ltd
Uncle Nearest Ltd.
West Spirits MCR Ltd
Whisky Galore Limited
Whitetail Spirits Limited
Whitley Neill Limited
Wild Foragin Ltd
Yarm Gin Ltd
Yarm Spirits Co Ltd

11020 Manufacture of wine from grape [46]
Alko Vintages UK Ltd
Amwell Springs Brewery Co Ltd
B & F Enterprise UK Ltd
BF Wines UK Ltd
Bach & Co Solution Limited
Brighton and Hove Wine Co Ltd
Michel Couvreur (Scotch Whiskies)
Crundale Wines Limited

D'Urberville Vineyard Limited
Davenport Vineyards Limited
Digby Fine English Ltd
Digby Wine Ltd
Direct Wine Factory Ltd
Drinktonics Limited
Duncairn Wines Limited
Flower Miners Limited
General Bilimoria Wines Ltd
Globus Wines (UK) Ltd
Guinexport Trade and Services Ltd
Harrow & Hope Limited
Itasca Wines Limited
Laneberg Wine Ltd
Lindisfarne Limited
Little Horse Wines Limited
Magnus Wines Ltd
Alistair McCoist & Jeff East (Vintners)
Noahs Estate Ltd
Oui Vino Limited
Pinglestone Estate Limited
Realsa Wines Import & Export Ltd
Rebel Pi Limited
Ross Earl Wine Co., Ltd.
Schoenlaub Limited
Selectia Wine Ltd
Sharpham Wine Limited
Simpsons Wine Imports Limited
Somborne Valley Vineyard Ltd
Somm in the Must Ltd
Southern England Wines (UK) Ltd
Spirits Development & Management Company (SDMC)
Tewaina Ltd
Verrillo Partnership Limited
Vitosha Wine Ltd
Wild Life Botanicals Ltd
Wine Fusion Limited
Winehood Ltd

11030 Manufacture of cider and other fruit wines [22]
A Little Luxury Distillery Ltd
Angola Beverages Holding Co Ltd
BF Wines UK Ltd
Batch Cider Ltd
Branded Drinks Ltd
Broadoak Cider Co Ltd
Broughton Ales Limited
Bumble Mead Ltd
Craftwater Brewing Co Ltd
Distell International Holdings Ltd
Flower Miners Limited
L'Atypique Ltd
Lamson Wine Co Ltd
Laughing Ass Brewery Ltd
Lilley's Cider Limited
Monkey Shed Estate Brewing Co Ltd
Noahs Estate Ltd
Organic Country Drinks Ltd
Scrumpy Wasp Limited
Sharpham Wine Limited
Solway Spirits Ltd
Wild Life Botanicals Ltd

11040 Manufacture of other non-distilled fermented beverages [15]
Amwell Springs Brewery Co Ltd
Angola Beverages Holding Co Ltd
Dirty Drinks Collective Ltd
Distell International Holdings Ltd

Ellismuir Limited
First Cape Vineyards Ltd
Good Living Brew Co Limited
Ineffable LDN Limited
Mobay Drinks Ltd
Norfolk Rum Co Ltd
Rum Club Ltd
Shy Simba Ltd
Sober Limited
Thames Distillers Limited
Two Pal's Co Ltd

11050 Manufacture of beer [145]
23-7 Brewing Ltd
3 Cities Brewing Co Ltd
3ABC Ltd
4 Acre Brewing Co. Ltd
888 Global Trade Ltd
Abyss Brewing Ltd
Adnams PLC
Amwell Springs Brewery Co Ltd
Arkell's Brewery Limited
Atlantic Craft Soda Co Ltd
Atom Brewing Co Limited
Aurora Ales Limited
BCM Brewing Co Ltd
BL Drinks Ltd
Bad Girls Brew Limited
Bad Joke Brew Co Ltd
Bakewell Road Brewery Ltd
Bang The Elephant Brewing Co Ltd
Belvoir Brewery Limited
Black Cat Brewery Limited
Blackedge Brewing Co Ltd
Bobby Beer Co Ltd
Bone Machine Brewing Co Ltd
S.A.Brain & Co Ltd
Branded Drinks Ltd
Brewis Beer Co Ltd
Bridgnorth Brewing Co Ltd
Broughton Ales Limited
Bucklebury Brewers Ltd
Canopy Beer Co Ltd
H.B.Clark & Co.(Successors) Ltd
Cobra Beer Partnership Limited
Cold Formd Ltd
Craftwater Brewing Co Ltd
Creative Juices Brewing Co Ltd
Crouch Vale Brewery Limited
Dark Revolution Ltd
Deutschlond Brewery Limited
Donnington Brewery Limited
Droylsden Craft Limited
Drumgaw Holdings Ltd
East London Brewing Co Ltd
Ellismuir Limited
Epic Beers Limited
Everards Brewery Limited
Faking Bad Brewery Limited
Force Brewery Limited
Forest Hill Brewing Co Ltd
Galldachd Na H-Alba Brewing Ltd
Gleneagles Distillery Limited
Good Living Brew Co Limited
Grafham Brewing Co Ltd
Great Newsome Brewery Limited
Hall & Woodhouse Limited
Halton Turner Brewing Co Ltd
Head Thirst Ltd
Hindsight Collective Ltd
Hitchin Brewery Ltd
Hopper House Brew Farm Ltd

Hops and Dots Brewing Co Ltd
Hydes' Brewery Limited
Incapico Inc Limited
Infinite Session Ltd
Jabru Bevco Ltd
Jackrabbit Brewing Co. Ltd
Jocks and Peers Brewing Co Ltd
Kairos Solutions Ltd
Keltek Cornish Brewery Limited
Kimbland Distillery Ltd
Kinkell Brewery Ltd
Konigsberg Seven Bridges Breweries Ltd
Koomor Brewing Co Ltd
Laughing Ass Brewery Ltd
Laughing Pug Ltd
Law and Disorder Brew Co Ltd
Lion-Beer, Spirits & Wine (UK) Ltd
London Ale UK Ltd
Loopland Brewing Co Ltd
Los Perros Sueltos Brewing Co Ltd
Lough Neagh Distillers - 1837 Ltd
Marston's Acquisitions Limited
Matheson Brewers Ltd
McGrath's Brewing Limited
Molson Coors Brewing Co (UK) Ltd
Monkey Shed Estate Brewing Co Ltd
Morecambe Bay Wines Limited
Mumbles Brewery Ltd
Myrlex Southend Limited
Near Beer Brewing Co. Ltd
Oxford Brewery Limited
Oxford Brewing Co Ltd
Padlock Brewery Ltd.
Padstow Brewing Company (2013) Ltd
Pivo Beverages Ltd
Play Limited
Pomona Island Brew Co Ltd
Pongolo Ltd
Punjabi Ltd
Purity Brewing Co Ltd
Raven Hill Brewery Limited
Red Bay Brewing Co Ltd
Red Squirrel Brewery Limited
Reids Gold Brewing Co Ltd
River Widow Brewery Ltd
Rockin Robin Brewery Ltd
Rossendale Brew Co Ltd
Rude Mechanicals Limited
Saints Row Brewing Co Ltd
Saltrock Brewing Co Ltd
Samuels Brewing Co Ltd
Seafire Brewing Co. Ltd
Shandy Shack Ltd
Sheffield Brewers Collective
Shelsley Brewing Co Ltd
Shepherd Neame Limited
Shropshire Beers Limited
Signature Brew Ltd
Silver Rocket Brewing Ltd
Sloane Home Ltd
Slopemeister Brewing Co Ltd
Solway Spirits Ltd
Southbourne Brewing Limited
Southbrew Co Ltd
St.Austell Brewery Co Ltd
Stag Ales Ltd
Stag Brewery Ltd
Stay Gold Beer Co Ltd
Steel Coulson Ltd
Time & Tide Brewing Limited
Tiny Vessel Brewing Co Ltd
Tom's Tap and Brewhouse Ltd

Triple Point Brewing Ltd
Urbeer Ltd
Van Pur UK Ltd
Via Academia Vocatus Ltd
Vitosha Wine Ltd
Wadworth and Co Ltd
Charles Wells Brewery Limited
Charles Wells,Limited
Wetherby Brew Co Limited
White Wolf Brewery Ltd
Wold Toppers Limited
Workshy Brewing Ltd
Xtraflow Limited
Yates low Brewery Limited

11060 Manufacture of malt
Glen Monarch Distillery Ltd
Justerini & Brooks,Limited

11070 Manufacture of soft drinks; production of mineral waters and other bottled waters [26]
Alko Vintages UK Ltd
Allson Sparkle Limited
Bad Girls Brew Limited
Bloody Drinks Limited
Burble Foods and Beverages Ltd
Citrosoft Drinks Limited
Cornfield Foods and Beverages Ltd
W.& J.Cruickshank and Co Ltd
Diageo Great Britain Limited
Gibraltar Gin Co Ltd
Green Leaf Liquids Limited
Infinite Session Ltd
Life Science Limited
Lough Neagh Distillers - 1837 Ltd
Mobay Drinks Ltd
Nele Drinks Limited
Portavadie Distillery Limited
Punchline Ltd
Seafire Brewing Co. Ltd
Shandy Shack Ltd
Bertrand Tailor Limited
Tasty Kameleon Ltd
Ty Nant Spring Water Limited
UK Blue Ribbon Group Beer Co., Ltd
Vitosha Wine Ltd
Wild Life Botanicals Ltd

13960 Manufacture of other technical and industrial textiles
Python Controls Ltd

20420 Manufacture of perfumes and toilet preparations
Sloane Home Ltd

25910 Manufacture of steel drums and similar containers
Truekeg UK Ltd

27110 Manufacture of electric motors, generators and transformers
Voubearst Limited

28990 Manufacture of other special-purpose machinery n.e.c.
Jetchill Ltd

29320 Manufacture of other parts and accessories for motor vehicles
Voubearst Limited

32120 Manufacture of jewellery and related articles
Oris Black Ltd

32300 Manufacture of sports goods
New Age Wines Ltd

32401 Manufacture of professional and arcade games and toys
Spokesuk Ltd

32990 Other manufacturing n.e.c.
Crescent Fine Foods Ltd
Kingsland Drinks Group Limited
Kingsland Drinks Limited
Loxwood Meadworks Ltd
Truly Spirited Ltd
Whisky Galore Limited

33140 Repair of electrical equipment
Hayk Corporation Ltd

33200 Installation of industrial machinery and equipment
Hayk Corporation Ltd

41100 Development of building projects
BV Group UK Limited
Carpet Bagger Limited
Hameed Investments Limited
Quest Leisure Limited
Raer Scotch Whisky Ltd

41202 Construction of domestic buildings
Lux Ex Dignitas Limited

43210 Electrical installation
Bopfags Services Ltd
Hayk Corporation Ltd

43220 Plumbing, heat and air-conditioning installation
Bopfags Services Ltd

43290 Other construction installation
Carpet Bagger Limited
Lux Ex Dignitas Limited
V & A Jobs UK Ltd

43341 Painting
Interseel Ltd

43390 Other building completion and finishing
V & A Jobs UK Ltd

43999 Other specialised construction activities n.e.c.
Inconcept Ltd
Prostimo Ltd
Scrumpy Wasp Limited

45111 Sale of new cars and light motor vehicles
DN Pacifica Ltd
Dunarea Albastra Ltd

45112 Sale of used cars and light motor vehicles [10]
Chivalry Trading International Co. Ltd
Dunarea Albastra Ltd
Ftspot Limited
Infinitygroup1 Limited
Panton Ventures Limited
Rovial Trans Ltd
Taabs Investment UK Limited
Tata Trading Limited
UK Lesiure Ltd
Werfa Holdings Ltd

45310 Wholesale trade of motor vehicle parts and accessories
Imperial Capital D & G Ltd
Nino and Blue Spruce Ltd
Voubearst Limited

45320 Retail trade of motor vehicle parts and accessories
Cyprian Services Limited

46110 Agents selling agricultural raw materials, livestock, textile raw materials and semi-finished goods
Mina Collection Ltd
Pure Techno Ltd
Tata Trading Limited

46120 Agents involved in the sale of fuels, ores, metals and industrial chemicals
AKM Trading Services Ltd
Albert Altima Trade House Ltd
Mahar Associates Ltd
Top Deal Services Ltd

46130 Agents involved in the sale of timber and building materials
Agencia Ltd
V I Wholsale Limited

46140 Agents involved in the sale of machinery, industrial equipment, ships and aircraft
Tata Trading Limited
Westworld Impex Limited

46150 Agents involved in the sale of furniture, household goods, hardware and ironmongery
Intercontinental Trade Solutions Ltd
KBB Components Ltd
Kikijee Global Services Ltd
Nielsen McKinsey Global Tourism & Hospitality Consulting
Rovial Trans Ltd

46160 Agents involved in the sale of textiles, clothing, fur, footwear and leather goods
AbruzzoWines Ltd
Comercio Ltd
KBB Components Ltd

46170 Agents involved in the sale of food, beverages and tobacco [150]
3F Leisure Limited
ANM Trading Limited
AbruzzoWines Ltd
Afco Traders Ltd
Alice Wholesale Trading Ltd
Art Entertainment Ltd
Asiana Mart Limited
Asta Barista Baby Ltd
Azienda Vitivinicola Stassi Ltd
B & M Produce Limited
BLSN Limited
Bacchus Merchantry Limited
Bahamian Enterprise UK Limited
Beerpol Ltd
Big D'Z Convenience and Winery Ltd
PNJ Bolton International Ltd
Branded Drinks Ltd
Buke Limited
CDGH Pub Co Ltd
Caribbean Collective Group Ltd
Caribswede Ltd
C Carnevale Limited
Cask Trade Ltd
Chateau de la Combe Ltd
Chetan Wholesalers Limited
Cheti & Co Holdings Limited
Cheti & Co Limited
Clara Wines Limited
Clubinn Together Limited
Comercio Ltd
Copricom Ltd
Craft Beer Collaborative Ltd
F & M Cressi Limited
Csburrwine Ltd
D.C Enterprises (Import/Export) Ltd
Darlaston Drink Shop Limited
Direct Wine Factory Ltd
Distell Europe Ltd.
Distilled Brands Limited
Dmomentum Ltd
Drunk Maitre D Limited
Earny Limited
Eastern Pantry Ltd
Edrington-Beam Suntory UK Distribution
El Toro Wines Limited
Enmore Wine Limited
Euroworld Foods Limited
F8t B8dgers Ltd
Finedon Convenience Store Ltd
Florin Wholesaler Ltd
Fox Fitzgerald Whisky Trading Co Ltd
Franklyn Road Brewing Ltd
From Cask To Bottle Limited
Gin Corporation Limited
Go Brazil Wines & Spirits (UK) Ltd
Golden Whisky Limited
Gravity Drinks Ltd
Greatdrams Ventures Limited
Healthier Products Limited
Highland Drinks Ltd
Hobros Limited
Huddersfield Cash and Carry Ltd
I.G.T. Management Ltd
Ian MacBarrel & Spirits Ltd
Impexpo Ltd
Intriguing Brands Limited
Ishka Wines and Spirits UK Ltd
Italy Service UK Ltd
Jenuine Jamaican Products Ltd
Jervis Trading Limited

Kairos Solutions Ltd
Kan Trading Limited
Kindred Spirit Partnership Ltd
Konigsberg Seven Bridges Breweries Ltd
Landmark Wholesale Limited
Languedoc Imports Ltd
Lazy Drinks Ltd.
Line Point Global UK Limited
Liquid Brand Exports Limited
Liquid Market Limited
Luxury Gourmet Ltd
Magic F & F Ltd
Magik Drinks Limited
Manoj Navaladi Ltd
Meridian Centre Hospitality Ltd
Monolith (UK) Ltd
Most Popular Limited
MyNaturalCo Ltd
N R Wines Limited
Nine Reigns Limited
Oakmount Group Limited
Official Box Office UK Ltd
Ohsake Ltd
Ooberstock Limited
Outlander Brands Limited
Outstanding People Limited
PMWine Trade Limited
Palmerston Fine Wines Ltd.
Palms & Liquor Enterprises Ltd
Panda Oriental Supermarket Ltd
Panda Trading International Ltd
Panemporium Ltd
Peace Bond Ltd
Perfect Pair Wines Ltd
Portuguese Winery Limited
Quarter Cafe Bar Limited
Quintessential Decadence Ltd
R B M Leisure Limited
R. St Barth Limited
Ragul Ltd
Rajpoot Traders Ltd
Ray Jules Limited
Refresh 24 Group Limited
Rico Rico Ltd
Riedango Limited
Rutherford, Shirlaw and Denholm Ltd
SSG Service Ltd
Sam-Gel Global Ventures Ltd
Sanwin Ltd
Sativatech Ltd
Scotia Blending Co Ltd
Sharing The Best Limited
Silenus Limited
Smart Save Distribution Ltd
Spirits International Management Ltd
St Ives Grog Co Ltd
Swara Trading International Ltd
TH Nightlife Ltd
TP Retail Ltd
Taabs Investment UK Limited
Tequilas of Mexico Limited
Think Wine Group Ltd
Thiyagu Ltd
Tipple Transport Limited
Tipton Wines Limited
Today's Wholesale Services Ltd
Toro Industries Ltd
Trang Mai Exports Limited
Ubicumque International Ltd
Uropa Group Ltd
Valentino & Finch Ltd
Veini Wine Co Ltd

Vine & Cork Limited
Vineyard Belfast Limited
Vino & Spirits Limited
Vinova Export Limited
Westworld Impex Limited
Withers Agencies Limited
World Cider Box Limited
Xi-Spain Ltd

46180 Agents specialised in the sale of other particular products
Bemco International (UK) Ltd
Emthea Ltd
Malt Whisky Agency Ltd
Stallion Spirits Limited
Valentino & Finch Ltd

46190 Agents involved in the sale of a variety of goods [48]
888 Global Trade Ltd
Albert Altima Trade House Ltd
Always 20 Limited
Asiana Mart Limited
B & M Produce Limited
BLSN Limited
Bevimangia Limited
Brexit Import and Export Co Ltd
Chaps Group Limited
Deliverance Dot Com Limited
Dunarea Albastra Ltd
Evernex Ltd
F & B Premium Brands Limited
Foodiebusters Epic Food Authority Ltd
Glennlay & Co Ltd
Gold Max Distribution Limited
Hellenic Agora Limited
IKP Trading Limited
Icomex London Limited
Impexpo Ltd
Intercontinental Trade Solutions Ltd
JKVK International Import and Export Ltd
Jade General Merchants Ltd
LA International Trading Ltd
Laravita Ltd
Largesse Corporate Gifts (2007) Ltd
Magik Drinks Limited
Most Popular Limited
Oakmount Group Limited
Orale Ltd.
Outlander Brands Limited
Perscot Ltd
Poleczka Limited
Poltom Limited
Quintessential Decadence Ltd
R B M Leisure Limited
Ray Jules Limited
Rovial Trans Ltd
SSG Service Ltd
Shonty Group Ltd
Silenus Limited
Sun Exports Limited
Tiny Vessel Brewing Co Ltd
Tioluxe Europe Limited
Ubicumque International Ltd
Ultra Premium Drinks Limited
Vanilla Blue Limited
Wenlen UK. Ltd

46210 Wholesale of grain, unmanufactured tobacco, seeds and animal feeds
Eight Brothers Corporation Ltd

46220 Wholesale of flowers and plants
Asante Distributors Limited

46310 Wholesale of fruit and vegetables [38]
ASCO Foods Limited
Agrosale UK Limited
Banini UK Ltd
Brian Traders Ltd
Caribbean Trade Ltd
Cascriva Ltd
Chic Fruit Ltd
Colne Confectionery Ltd
DTdist Ltd
Dega Trading Ltd
Dmomentum Ltd
Dorys Shop Ltd
Dracula Wine House Ltd
Estelon Holdings Limited
Ever-Tree Wholesale & Retail Ltd
Feewcha Services Ltd
Hazewater Food Services Ltd
Hochfeld International Ltd
International Procurement and Logistics
Iturn Global Ltd
Kukuruz Limited
Manoj Navaladi Ltd
Manteo Trading Co Ltd
Moa Group Ltd
Molvino Fine Wine & Spirits Co Ltd
Myella Brands Ltd
NCE Trading KFT Ltd
O & E Food Ltd
Organica Food & Wine Ltd
Othello Food and Wine Limited
Polat International Ltd
Pradeeprjm Limited
Ragul Ltd
S & N Products Ltd
Samco Global Foods Ltd
Thiyagu Ltd
Usedsoft Ltd
Winz International UK Ltd

46320 Wholesale of meat and meat products [44]
Afrogrocers Ltd
Agrosale UK Limited
Alivini (North) Limited
Alivini Co Ltd
Alliance Foods Limited
Atlas Food Wholesale Ltd
Bazaar Store Ltd
Choise Group Ltd
Crescent Fine Foods Ltd
Dracula Wine House Ltd
East and West Foods Cash and Carry
Eastcoast Supplies Ltd.
Eda Quality Foods North UK Ltd
G.W. Fields & Sons (Great Yarmouth)
Franciacorta Limited
GM Catering Supplies Ltd
Harlequin (Stockport) Limited
Hazewater Food Services Ltd
Hidden Caveau Limited
Jade General Merchants Ltd
Jays Trading Ltd
Jezba Ltd
Jia Bo Rui International Trade Ltd
Kaleboard Limited

Kanpai (London) Food and Beverage Management Co.,
Landmark Wholesale Limited
MBW Traders Ltd
MSM Foods Limited
Najpol Ltd
Nutricont Ltd
O & E Food Ltd
Othello Food and Wine Limited
Our Tino Ltd
Seb and Emma Ltd
Superyacht Supplies Limited
T & M Food Products Ltd
Thiyagu Ltd
Today's Wholesale Services Ltd
Triumph Foodservice Limited
Ultracomida Trading Co. Ltd
Usedsoft Ltd
Vinova Export Limited
W D L Wholesale Limited
Whiskey and Bourbon Club Ltd

46330 Wholesale of dairy products, eggs and edible oils and fats [33]
Ace Incorporation Ltd
Alivini Co Ltd
Always 20 Limited
Atlas Food Wholesale Ltd
Comercio Ltd
Crescent Fine Foods Ltd
Dmomentum Ltd
Eda Quality Foods North UK Ltd
Eight Brothers Corporation Ltd
GM Catering Supplies Ltd
Green Leaf Liquids Limited
H & G Corporation Ltd
Harlequin (Stockport) Limited
Hatton Wholesale Ltd
Hidden Caveau Limited
Kukuruz Limited
Manoj Navaladi Ltd
Navaladi Ltd
Ormos Trades Limited
Othello Food and Wine Limited
Our Tino Ltd
Panemporium Ltd
Pradeeprjm Limited
Ragul Ltd
Rico Rico Ltd
Seb and Emma Ltd
Sheikh Super Store Ltd
Superyacht Supplies Limited
Themirtis Limited
Topmost Foods Distribution Ltd.
Ultracomida Trading Co. Ltd
Viserra Limited
W D L Wholesale Limited

46341 Wholesale of fruit and vegetable juices, mineral water and soft drinks [164]
A A Suppliers Ltd
AKM Trading Services Ltd
Ace Incorporation Ltd
After Eight Alcohol Concierge Ltd
Agencia Ltd
Albert Altima Trade House Ltd
Alivini (North) Limited
Alivini Co Ltd
All English Distribution Ltd.
Ana Express Ltd
Anderson Beverages Ltd

UK Wholesalers of Beers, Wines and Spirits　　　　　　　　　　　　　　　　　　　　　　　dellam

Anya Global Limited
Apna Distribution Ltd
Asta Barista Baby Ltd
Ayr Brewing Co Ltd
BV Group UK Limited
Bassen Ltd
Bazaar Store Ltd
Bellwether Impex (UK) Limited
Beverage Brothers Limited
Bibere Ltd.
Bloomsbury Drinks Ltd
Brewed 4 U Ltd
Brighton Brew Co Ltd
Browett & Fair Ltd
Bubra Drinks Ltd
Camii Punch Ltd
Caribbean Trade Ltd
Caspian Black Limited
Cellar Twelve Limited
Cheti & Co Holdings Limited
Cheti & Co Limited
Choise Group Ltd
City Beer Limited
Colemans ABC Ltd
D D S Food Imports Ltd
DLG Wholesale Ltd
DNG Group Ltd
DNG Trading Ltd
Deeti Wholesale Limited
Direct2door Food & Beverage Ltd.
Dodotraders UK Limited
Drink Free Ltd
Drinkable Ltd
Drinks Bay Limited
Drinks R Us Limited
Drinks2u Ltd
Drinkslynx Limited
ERE Igga Ltd
East and West Foods Cash and Carry
Eda Quality Foods North UK Ltd
Ely & Sidney Limited
Estelon Holdings Limited
Eurotrade Supply Limited
Ever-Tree Wholesale & Retail Ltd
Export and Import Trading Ltd
Firewater Merchants Ltd
Five Star Cash & Carry Ltd
Flavour Foods & Drinks Ltd
Forward Moving Limited
GM Catering Supplies Ltd
GWB Associates Limited
Gabby & Bello Enterprises Ltd
Georgian Wine Co Ltd
Gibraltar Gin Co Ltd
Giovanni Food & Wine Limited
Green Cash & Carry Ltd
H & F Export Limited
Hamer & Perks Limited
Harp & Crown Cider Co Ltd
Hatton Wholesale Ltd
Hellenic Agora Limited
Hoversy Technologies Ltd
Infinite Session Ltd
Intercontinental Trade Solutions Ltd
Interseel Ltd
Iturn Global Ltd
J & D Wholesalers Ltd
J M & D Limited
Jaguar Beverage Ltd
Jascera UK Ltd
Jays Trading Ltd
Kaleboard Limited

Kasgo Limited
Knights Catering Impex Ltd
Liquid Brand Exports Limited
Lithuanian Beer Limited
London Drinks Supplier Ltd
London Wholesale Ltd
Lora Trading (Europe) Ltd
Loughborough Student Services Ltd
MBW Traders Ltd
MSM Foods Limited
Magna Juice Ltd
Manchester Drinks Co Ltd
Manor Wholesale Ltd
Manteo Trading Co Ltd
Marathon Food Limited
Marcin & Son Ltd
Adrian Mecklenburgh Limited
Meless Group Limited
Henry Mitchell & Sons Limited
Montann Limited
More or Less Drinks Co Ltd
NCE Trading KFT Ltd
Najpol Ltd
Noah Brothers Ltd
O & E Food Ltd
Ooberstock Limited
PSB Trading Limited
Pallet Price Wholesale Ltd
Panton Ventures Limited
Paradigm Red Limited
Pick N Deliver Ltd
Polat International Ltd
Premier Pubco Limited
Punchy Drinks Limited
Pure Organic Drinks Limited
Rarewood (London) Limited
Ravensbourne Wine Co Ltd
Rimpex-UK Limited
Samco Global Foods Ltd
Saravanan Traders (UK) Ltd
Sativatech Ltd
Seafire Brewing Co. Ltd
Shack Drinks Limited
Sheikh Super Store Ltd
Shree Sai Trading Ltd
Simply Spirits Limited
SmsZee Limited
Source 360 Ltd
Stack United Limited
Star Direct Hospitality Ltd
Stockwell Beverages Ltd
Stockwell Wholesalers Limited
Storesrealm Limited
Suntrack Ltd
Supermalt UK Limited
Superyacht Supplies Limited
Swallow Dispensed Drinks Solutions
TFC Wholesale Ltd
Talbot & Barr Limited
Taste Merchants Ltd
Tate-Smith Limited
Temple Wines (Cash & Carry) Ltd
Thames Wholesale Ltd
Thirstee Business Limited
Tolmid International Ltd
Topmost Foods Distribution Ltd.
Triumph Foodservice Limited
Trust in Global Food Ltd
Turkish Kitchinn Wholesale Ltd
UK Beer & Soft Drinks Ltd
Usedsoft Ltd
Utku Emre Ltd

Viserra Limited
W D L Wholesale Limited
WLL Wholesale Ltd
Whiskey and Bourbon Club Ltd
Windfall Logistics Limited
Wine City Limited
Winnack and Hart Industries Ltd
Winz International UK Ltd
Xorta Global Management Ltd

46350 Wholesale of tobacco products [35]
A.F.T. (Liquor Stores) Limited
Ace Incorporation Ltd
Alky Limited
W.J.Armstrong Limited
Barn Direct Limited
Bhanbore Trading Company PVT Ltd
Brexit Import and Export Co Ltd
Colne Confectionery Ltd
D & N Supplies Limited
Florin Wholesaler Ltd
Foxbusiness Tobacco Ltd
Gold Max Distribution Limited
Icknield Stores Ltd
Imperial Capital D & G Ltd
J & D Wholesalers Ltd
Kitwave Limited
Kohisar Limited
M.& M.Value Limited
Magik Drinks Limited
Henry Mitchell & Sons Limited
NTKS Ltd
Nandha Murgesan Ltd
Navaladi Ltd
Philip Russell Limited
Safeway Distribution Limited
Sambatha Ltd
Saravanan Traders (UK) Ltd
Sheikh Super Store Ltd
Square Wholesale Ltd
Srihari Haran Ltd
TP Retail Ltd
Thames Wholesale Ltd
Tipton Wines Limited
United Supplies Limited
United Wholesale Grocers Ltd

46360 Wholesale of sugar and chocolate and sugar confectionery [30]
A A Suppliers Ltd
Andreev Services Ltd
Apna Distribution Ltd
Bellwether Impex (UK) Limited
Bibere Ltd.
Cayenes Ltd
Drumstick Products Co Ltd
Evergreen Foods Limited
JJBrands Limited
Kasgo Limited
Kitwave Limited
Knights Catering Impex Ltd
Leomar Limited
M.& M.Value Limited
More or Less Drinks Co Ltd
Navaladi Ltd
Ooberstock Limited
Paradigm Red Limited
PatelCashAndCarry Limited
Plant Relief Ltd
Popaball Limited
S & N Products Ltd

SmsZee Limited
Spalathos Ltd.
Sun Exports Limited
TP Retail Ltd
Taste Merchants Ltd
Topmost Foods Distribution Ltd.
Viserra Limited
Waterland Trading Limited

46370 Wholesale of coffee, tea, cocoa and spices [42]
106 Business Solutions Limited
AB & R Import and Export Ltd
Amirante Empire Limited
Ana Express Ltd
Anya Global Limited
Apna Distribution Ltd
Bassen Ltd
Best of Hungary Ltd
Blu-Dot Commodities Limited
Botan Grey Ltd
Camis International Trading Co., Ltd.
Cayenes Ltd
Connecting Italian Food UK Ltd
Direct2door Food & Beverage Ltd.
Evergreen Foods Limited
Evernex Ltd
Gift Creation and Design Ltd
Helluva... Limited
Hoversy Technologies Ltd
Hurmiz UK Ltd
Jaguar Beverage Ltd
Jordan Sky Ltd
Lazy Hare Limited
Leomar Limited
Maha Wholesale Ltd
Adrian Mecklenburgh Limited
Orale Ltd.
Outstanding People Limited
Perscot Ltd
Plant Relief Ltd
Popaball Limited
Prasad Trading Co Ltd
Prestige Wine & Food (UK) Ltd
Ribox Quality Goods Ltd
S & N Products Ltd
S.A.R.D.V.M Ltd
Scarlettes Ltd
Stack United Limited
Taste Merchants Ltd
Winz International UK Ltd
Woori Trade Ltd
ZLCSolutions Ltd

46380 Wholesale of other food, including fish, crustaceans and molluscs [39]
A Di Maria & Sons Ltd
Agrosale UK Limited
Alivini (North) Limited
Bacchus Fine Wine & Food Ltd
Bengal Foods Limited
Bibere Ltd.
Bournemouth Food Ltd
Connecting Italian Food UK Ltd
Cropol Luxury Products Ltd
Delecta Limited
Diffusion Food By Pina Co Ltd
Dorys Shop Ltd
ERE Igga Ltd
Etna Food & Wine Ltd
Fiji Store Ltd

Flava Foods Ltd
Intriguing Brands Limited
Italia Wine and Food Ltd
Italy Service UK Ltd
Jia Bo Rui International Trade Ltd
Knights Catering Impex Ltd
London Wholesale Ltd
MSM Foods Limited
Maharaja & Sons Ltd
Marathon Food Limited
Meless Consortium Ltd
Moet Hennessy U.K. Limited
Najpol Ltd
Nue Innovations Limited
OAB Ventures Limited
Prestige Wine & Food (UK) Ltd
SP (DPH) Exports Limited
Seb and Emma Ltd
Stoney Hospitality Limited
Triumph Foodservice Limited
Vine & Cork Limited
Vinova Export Limited
Wenlen UK. Ltd
Wold Toppers Limited

46390 Non-specialised wholesale of food, beverages and tobacco [139]
3R'SB Limited
ASCO Foods Limited
AbruzzoWines Ltd
Absolute Wholesale Limited
Afrogrocers Ltd
Aims & Co Ltd
Alliance Foods Limited
Allson Sparkle Limited
Amish Wholesalers Limited
Annessa Imports Limited
Arkell's Brewery Limited
Ascona Retail (Leases) Limited
Atlas Food Wholesale Ltd
Azienda Vitivinicola Stassi Ltd
Aziken Ventures Limited
BJ Drinks Ltd
Bacchus London Limited
Bacchus Merchantry Limited
Bassen Ltd
Bazaar Store Ltd
Bedford Continental Wholesale Ltd
Bhanbore Trading Company PVT Ltd
Brexit Import and Export Co Ltd
Brown Bear Tales Ltd
C C & C Limited
Camis International Trading Co., Ltd.
Campania Cucina Ltd
Canapacampana Limited
Capper & Co Ltd
Casa Julia Limited
Cascade Drinks Limited
Choice Drinks Limited
Choise Group Ltd
Cobev Limited
Coles Trading Limited
Colne Confectionery Ltd
Corvin Import Export Ltd
Cotrade Ltd
Crafted Beverages Limited
W.& J.Cruickshank and Co Ltd
DNG Trading Ltd
Da'mos Food & Beverages Ltd
Deeti Wholesale Limited
Dega Trading Ltd
Dhamecha Foods Limited

Direct2door Food & Beverage Ltd.
Distillers Direct Ltd
ERE Igga Ltd
Earth Elements Ltd
Eastern Pantry Ltd
Eataly Food Distributors Ltd
Espana Imports Ltd
European Brand Trading Limited
Excess UK Limited
Export and Import Trading Ltd
Family Choice Wholesale Ltd
G.W. Fields & Sons (Great Yarmouth)
Fieldscot Ltd
Franko's Food Ltd
Ftspot Limited
Functional Drinks Co Limited
Global D & F Ltd
Goldy's Corner Shop Ltd
Goodeataly Ltd
Green Cash & Carry Ltd
Greenfield Bacon Limited
Greens Wholesale Ltd
HT Drinks Ltd
Harlequin (Stockport) Limited
Hatton Wholesale Ltd
Hay Hampers Limited
Hayloft Ventures Ltd
Hi - Line Wines Limited
Highland Vintners Ltd
Imperial Capital D & G Ltd
Italy Service UK Ltd
J & D Wholesalers Ltd
J.W.G. PLC
JR First Choice Cash & Carry Ltd
Jenuine Jamaican Products Ltd
Jezba Ltd
KD Wholesale Ltd
Kasgo Limited
Kater Four (Cash & Carry) Ltd
Keep Control Ltd
Key Brands International Ltd
Kohisar Limited
Lamba Trading Co. Limited
Late Shop Ltd
Laurus Brands Limited
Lindisfarne Limited
Luxury Gourmet Ltd
MDF Wholesale Ltd
Markets It Ltd.
Adrian Mecklenburgh Limited
Mediterranean Farm Finest Ltd
Mojito Bar Ltd
Monolith (UK) Ltd
Noble Merchants Limited
Ops Wines Ltd
Pallet Price Wholesale Ltd
Panemporium Ltd
Park Royal Wholesale Limited
Pastai di Serino Italian Food and Wine Excellence
Plant Relief Ltd
Prasad Trading Co Ltd
Premier UK Trading Limited
Prestige Wine & Food (UK) Ltd
R B M Leisure Limited
RRK Supplies Limited
Relais La Torre UK Ltd
Richway Cash and Carry Ltd
Thomas Ridley and Son, Limited
Ripped Earth Wines Limited
Sai Soft Drinks Ltd
Sandhar & Kang (Birmingham) Ltd

Sarpanch Food & Wine Distributors Ltd
Shree Sai Trading Ltd
Six Rivers Limited
SmsZee Limited
Sofibel Ltd
Spalathos Ltd.
Square Wholesale Ltd
Srihari Haran Ltd
Stack United Limited
Stockwell Beverages Ltd
Stockwell Wholesalers Limited
Sun Exports Limited
Supermarket Solutions Limited
T & M Food Products Ltd
Taabs Investment UK Limited
Tanner Brodin Limited
Trang Mai Exports Limited
USSR Limited
United Wholesale Grocers Ltd
VDS UK Limited
Wedgbury Connections Ltd
World Cider Box Limited
Xorta Global Management Ltd

46410 Wholesale of textiles
Above Brand Limited
Jezba Ltd
Narang Wholesalers Limited
Sambath Trading Limited
Thames Wholesale Ltd
Whiteleys of Halifax Limited

46420 Wholesale of clothing and footwear [16]
3R'SB Limited
Anya Global Limited
Azurapada Worldwide Ltd
Barcode Traders Limited
DTdist Ltd
KC Brothers Ltd
Kanj Wholesale Ltd
Manteo Trading Co Ltd
Orale Ltd.
Oris Black Ltd
Rich & Bad Ltd
Maurice Richard Ltd
S.A.R.D.V.M Ltd
Sotus Limited
Southwell Trading Ltd
Spainorama Ltd

46431 Wholesale of audio tapes, records, CDs and video tapes and the equipment on which these are played
Europebro Wholesalers Ltd

46440 Wholesale of china and glassware and cleaning materials
Cheti & Co Holdings Limited
Cheti & Co Limited
Ely & Sidney Limited
Leomar Limited

46450 Wholesale of perfume and cosmetics [11]
Always 20 Limited
Ark Inta Ltd
Asante Distributors Limited
Europebro Wholesalers Ltd
Jia Bo Rui International Trade Ltd
Kanj Wholesale Ltd
Santa Code Limited
Sloane Home Ltd
Square Wholesale Ltd
Tioluxe Europe Limited
Vett Limited

46460 Wholesale of pharmaceutical goods
Nino and Blue Spruce Ltd
Wilkies International Ltd

46470 Wholesale of furniture, carpets and lighting equipment
Brian Traders Ltd
Chivalry Trading International Co. Ltd
Delta Western Distributions Ltd
KBB Components Ltd

46480 Wholesale of watches and jewellery
Barcode Traders Limited
Chivalry Trading International Co. Ltd
KC Brothers Ltd
Oakmount Group Limited
Oris Black Ltd
Tioluxe Europe Limited

46499 Wholesale of household goods (other than musical instruments) n.e.c
Barn Direct Limited
I8 MGT Limited
London Wholesale Ltd
Noble Merchants Limited
Saj Holdings Ltd

46510 Wholesale of computers, computer peripheral equipment and software
Delta Western Distributions Ltd
Palmer Traders Ltd

46520 Wholesale of electronic and telecommunications equipment and parts
Ark Inta Ltd
Minarda General Trade Ltd
Shonty Group Ltd

46650 Wholesale of office furniture
Sotus Limited

46660 Wholesale of other office machinery and equipment
Global Trade & Consulting Ltd

46719 Wholesale of other fuels and related products
Top Deal Services Ltd

46720 Wholesale of metals and metal ores
Meless Group Limited
Murcotts Ltd.

46730 Wholesale of wood, construction materials and sanitary equipment
Glow Glow Ltd.
Maximus Wholesale Limited
Palmer Traders Ltd
Pristine Trades Ltd

46740 Wholesale of hardware, plumbing and heating equipment and supplies
Narang Wholesalers Limited

46750 Wholesale of chemical products
Novus BH Magister Ltd

46770 Wholesale of waste and scrap
Copricom Ltd

46900 Non-specialised wholesale trade [57]
3R'SB Limited
888 Global Trade Ltd
97 Catering Ltd
AB & R Import and Export Ltd
Afco Traders Ltd
Agencia Ltd
Banini UK Ltd
Bellwether Impex (UK) Limited
Blue Diamond (UK) Ltd
Bruist Trading Ltd
Buke Limited
Copricom Ltd
Dirty Drinks Collective Ltd
Dr Dougan (Enterprises) Ltd
Dromedary Trading & Resources Ltd
Ebony Drinks Limited
Eight Brothers Corporation Ltd
Eurotrade Supply Limited
Export and Import Trading Ltd
Finebatch Limited
Glennlay & Co Ltd
Global Trade & Consulting Ltd
Glow Glow Ltd.
Gremi Wine Trading (UK) Ltd
HNB Trade Ltd
Hazewater Food Services Ltd
Highland Vintners Ltd
Jays Trading Ltd
Jervis Trading Limited
Kaleboard Limited
Kanj Wholesale Ltd
Kedem Europe Limited
Key Brands International Ltd
Landmark Wholesale Limited
Maximus Wholesale Limited
Mercurion Ltd
Novus BH Magister Ltd
Outlander Brands Limited
Oyster Import Export Limited
Palmer Traders Ltd
Panda Trading International Ltd
Pristine Trades Ltd
Maurice Richard Ltd
Saj Holdings Ltd
Silenus Limited
Sofibel Ltd
Spainorama Ltd
Swara Trading International Ltd
Tiny Vessel Brewing Co Ltd
Today's Wholesale Services Ltd
Trang Mai Exports Limited

United Supplies Limited
V I Wholsale Limited
Vineco Inco Ltd
Vino & Spirits Limited
Waterland Trading Limited
Xuyang International Ltd

47110 Retail sale in non-specialised stores with food, beverages or tobacco predominating [77]
3F Leisure Limited
ANM Trading Limited
Above Brand Limited
Ale Trader Ltd
Azurapada Worldwide Ltd
Bacchus London Limited
Bargain Food and Booze Limited
Bassrap Ltd
Bhanbore Trading Company PVT Ltd
Big D'Z Convenience and Winery Ltd
Birdcage Gin Ltd.
Bruist Trading Ltd
Burdett Wines Ltd
CHX Distillers Ltd
Chateau Wines Ltd.
Church Road Mini Market Ltd
Cognac Growers' Collective Ltd
Henry C. Collison and Sons Ltd
Csburrwine Ltd
DTB Distribution Ltd
Darlaston Drink Shop Limited
Drum and Black Rum Co Ltd
EFE Store Limited
Earth Elements Ltd
Empress Ale Ltd
Evil Spirits Ltd
Fairview Vineyard Ltd
Falugamaro International Ltd
Finedon Convenience Store Ltd
Four Seasons Hastings Ltd
Fourteen Twelve Trading Ltd
Greenfield Bacon Limited
I Caesar Limited
I'll Ask The Boys Ltd
Icomex London Limited
Ineffable LDN Limited
Intriguing Brands Limited
Italian Appellations Limited
Keeling Andrew & Co Limited
Kohisar Limited
Kudu Food and Wine Ltd
Late Shop Ltd
Lobins Limited
Mahar Associates Ltd
Monolith (UK) Ltd
Mzansi UK Ltd
NTKS Ltd
North West Industries Ltd
Ourlocal Limited
Parkers Newsagents Ltd
Play Limited
Premier UK Trading Limited
Prostimo Ltd
Real Ales AT Limited
Refresh 24 Group Limited
Roblex Ltd
Rosemille Ltd
Rum Club Ltd
Sarpe L & C Ltd
Sativatech Ltd
Sindherfoods Limited
Six Rivers Limited

Snow Beer UK Ltd
Sunset Wines Limited
Suwalki-UK Ltd
TBD Tipples Ltd
Templar Wines Ltd
Thameside Rum Co Ltd
Tinkture Ltd
Tipton Wines Limited
Titanic Holdings Japan Ltd
Ubicumque International Ltd
Venus 14 Limited
Wine Bliss Ltd
Wine City Limited
Wintrad Ltd
Yoka Family Limited

47190 Other retail sale in non-specialised stores [25]
97 Catering Ltd
Afrogrocers Ltd
Attitude Spirits Ltd
Barrys Discount Ltd.
Beer Gonzo Ltd
Big D'Z Convenience and Winery Ltd
Champagnehub Limited
Darlaston Drink Shop Limited
Emthea Ltd
Finedon Convenience Store Ltd
Hidden Gem - Urban Artisan Spirit Ltd
Ian MacBarrel & Spirits Ltd
Interseel Ltd
LM Spirits Ltd
London Drinks Supplier Ltd
Low-Key Essentials Ltd
Medusa Wines Ltd
Nutricont Ltd
STM Traders & Services Ltd
Sambath Trading Limited
Sambatha Ltd
Snow Beer UK Ltd
UK Lesiure Ltd
Wine Cellar Midlands Limited
Wine City Limited

47210 Retail sale of fruit and vegetables in specialised stores
Iturn Global Ltd
London Drinks Supplier Ltd
Panda Oriental Supermarket Ltd
Spar (UK) Limited

47220 Retail sale of meat and meat products in specialised stores
Kanpai (London) Food and Beverage Management Co.,

47240 Retail sale of bread, cakes, flour confectionery and sugar confectionery in specialised stores
Daysh Beers Wines & Spirits Ltd
Field and Fawcett Wine Merchants and Delicatessen
Magazin Romanesc Ltd
Mahar Associates Ltd
Mzansi UK Ltd
Pop Cake Box Limited
Wine Bliss Ltd

47250 Retail sale of beverages in specialised stores [253]
3 Barrel Co Ltd
8000 Vintages Limited
A & B Vintners Limited
A-Z Spirits Ltd
ASA Ventures Limited
Ababio Express Limited
Adnams PLC
Amathus Drinks PLC
Ann et Vin Limited
Arda Rohat Limited
W.J.Armstrong Limited
Atom Brands Limited
Atom Cask Holdings Limited
Atom Drinks Limited
Atom Group Limited
Atom Scotland Limited
Atom Supplies Limited
BB & R Limited
BB & R Spirits Limited
Bacchus London Limited
Bankside Brewing Limited
T. & J.T. Barton (Bottlers) Ltd
Bassrap Ltd
Bath Gin Co Ltd
Beautiful Beers East Anglia (UK) Ltd
Beer Boutique Ltd
Beer Gonzo Ltd
Beer Land Ltd
Bespoke Wines Ltd
Best Cask Ltd
Beyond The Ale (GB) Limited
Birdcage Gin Ltd.
Bonny Gin Ltd
Bottle Shop (Penarth) Limited
Bourne & Co Solutions Ltd
Brewbarge Limited
Brix & Porter Ltd.
Broadway Drinks Co Ltd
Busted Cow Ltd
CMT (Wines) Limited
William Cadenhead Limited
Cador Limited
Cambridge Wine Merchants Ltd
Celtavini.Com Limited
Champagne Cellar Limited
Champagne Warehouse Ltd
Cheng International Co Limited
Chesters Wine Merchants Ltd
Cocktail Pickers Club Ltd
Spencer Collings & Co Limited
Connolly's (Wine Merchants) Ltd
Cotswold Wines Ltd
Craft Drink Co Ltd
Craft Locals Limited
Crafty Pint Limited
Crafty Warehouse Ltd
Creative Juices Brewing Co Ltd
Cribbar Limited
Crouch Vale Brewery Limited
DTB Distribution Ltd
Dago Wines Ltd
Danish Snaps Co Ltd
Davenport Vineyards Limited
Davy & Co Ltd
De Facto Spirits Limited
Deco Spirits Limited
Denby Dale Wines Limited
Rodney Densem Wines Limited
A. Dewar Rattray Limited
Diageo United Kingdom Limited

Different Wines Limited
Direct Wine Factory Ltd
Discover Wine Limited
Nick Dobson Ltd
Drinkologie Limited
Drinks Emporium Limited
Drinktonics Limited
Drum and Black Rum Co Ltd
Duncairn Wines Limited
Edgerton Holdings Limited
Englishman Supplies Limited
Essenza Di Romagna Limited
Evil Spirits Ltd
Expression du Terroir Limited
Falugamaro International Ltd
Far Out Wines Limited
Field and Fawcett Wine Merchants and Delicatessen
Flora Fine Wines Ltd
Fourteen Drops Ltd
Frazier's Wine Merchants Ltd.
G Sake Co Ltd
GNR Distillery Limited
General Wine and Liquor Co Ltd
Gin Dobry Gin Co Ltd
Golden Coin Trading Limited
Good Spirits Ltd
Goodeataly Ltd
Gordon & MacPhail Limited
Gordons (Bolton) Limited
Grainger Fine Wines Ltd
Grants-EU Limited
Great Newsome Brewery Limited
Great Wine Group Limited
Greek Wineshop Ltd
Greens Beers Limited
H R Drinks (Wholesale) Ltd
Hamptons Wine Ltd
Hanging Ditch Wine Merchants Ltd
Harrisons Fine Wines Limited
H Harwood Ltd
Hennings Wine Merchants Ltd
Geo Hill (Grocers) Limited
Hix & Buck Ltd
Honkytonk Wine Library Limited
Hop Hideout Limited
House of Hops Limited
House of Townend Limited
Hunter Douglas Scotch Whisky Ltd
I Caesar Limited
Imperial Wine Co Ltd
In Wine & Spirit Solutions, Ltd
Iridium Supplies Limited
Iron & Rose Ltd
Ishka Wines and Spirits UK Ltd
JN Trading Limited
Jaded Group Limited
Nicholas James Gin Ltd
S H Jones Wines Ltd
KWM Supplies Ltd
Kinkell Brewery Ltd
Knotted Vine Limited
LDW Wines Limited
Andrew Laing & Co Ltd
Laki & G Ltd
Lamson Wine Co Ltd
Lancaster Wines Limited
Laneberg Wine Ltd
Languedoc Imports Ltd
Latitude Wine Limited
Lavinia UK Limited
Laytons Wine Merchants Limited

Le Bon Vin Limited
Les Vignerons de Saint Georges Ltd
Library Design Studio Ltd.
Lion-Beer, Spirits & Wine (UK) Ltd
Liqueurs de France Limited
London Spiced Dry Limited
Lordsworth Limited
Love and Labour Ltd.
Made in Little France Import Ltd
Marston's Acquisitions Limited
Master of Malt Limited
Masters of Malt Limited
Maverick Brands Limited
Maverick Drinks Limited
Maverick Spirits Limited
Alistair McCoist & Jeff East (Vintners)
Medicare Health & Energy Drinks Ltd
Moet Hennessy U.K. Limited
NTKS Ltd
New Fine Wines Ltd
James Nicholson Wine Limited
Nino and Blue Spruce Ltd
No.9 Leisure Limited
Noble Green Wines Limited
Northern Hospitality (MCR) Ltd
Ohsake Ltd
Old Butcher's Wine Cellar Ltd
Organic Country Drinks Ltd
Orsa Major Ltd
Oxford Brewery Limited
PS Drinks Ltd
Perfect Cellar Ltd
Pioneer Spirits Ltd
Christopher Piper Wines Ltd
Terry Platt Wine Merchants Ltd
Play Limited
Plonq Wines Ltd
Portal Dingwall & Norris Ltd
Profile Wines Limited
Quarter Cafe Bar Limited
Quercus Wines Ltd
R & B Wines Ltd
RD Wines Limited
Readywine UK Ltd
Real Ale Limited
Red Door Gin Co Ltd
Rockin Robin Brewery Ltd
Rum Matters Limited
Philip Russell Limited
Sacred Spirits Holdings Ltd
Sfuso Wine Limited
Sharpham Wine Limited
Sheffield Brewers Collective
Shieling Scotch Whisky Co Ltd
Shy Simba Ltd
Single Cask Ltd
Single Malts Limited
Slanj Whisky Ltd
Slurp Wine Co Ltd
Small Beer Limited
Snow Beer UK Ltd
Soho Wine Supply Limited
Solow Ltd
Somerset Craft Distillery Ltd
South Downs Real Estate Ltd
Southbourne Brewing Limited
Speymalt Whisky Distributors Ltd
Spirit of Glasgow Ltd
Spirits of Borough Ltd
Frank Stainton Wines Limited
Symposia Wine Limited
TBD Tipples Ltd

Tanners (Shrewsbury) Limited
Tanners Wines Limited
Tasmanian Liquor Distributors Ltd
Thameside Rum Co Ltd
Theatre of Wine Limited
Toast Ale Ltd
Town Centre Inns Limited
Trinewine Ltd
Two Heads Beer Co Limited
Union International Drinks Corporation
Unwined Limited
VIP Bottles Ltd
Valentino Platinum Ltd
Varmont Ltd
Vett Limited
Village Cottages (Cornwall) Ltd
Vin Est... Ltd
Vino Vero Ltd
Vintage Wines Limited
Vintner London Ltd
Wester Spirit Co. Ltd
Wetherby Brew Co Limited
Whisky Baron Ltd.
Whitetail Spirits Limited
Windermere Wine Stores Limited
Wine Bliss Ltd
Wine Byre Limited
Wine Castle Ltd
Wine Library Limited
Wine Marketings Europe Ltd
Wine Pantry Limited
Wine Place Limited
Wineways (Harrogate) Limited
Wold Toppers Limited
Wolf Wine Limited
World Cider Box Limited
Worsley Gin Ltd
Wrights Lion Brewery Limited
Yapp Brothers Limited
Zachicado Ltd

47260 Retail sale of tobacco products in specialised stores
W.J.Armstrong Limited
Daysh Beers Wines & Spirits Ltd
Frazier's Wine Merchants Ltd.
Late Shop Ltd
Philip Russell Limited
SSG Service Ltd
STM Traders & Services Ltd
Spar (UK) Limited

47290 Other retail sale of food in specialised stores [18]
Beer Land Ltd
Blue Wine Ltd
Dallyla Ltd
Earth Elements Ltd
Englishman Supplies Limited
Evergreen Foods Limited
G Sake Co Ltd
Goodeataly Ltd
Guinexport Trade and Services Ltd
Hobros Limited
Honkytonk Wine Library Limited
Jade General Merchants Ltd
Moet Hennessy U.K. Limited
Relais La Torre UK Ltd
Samco Global Foods Ltd
Spar (UK) Limited
TL Step By Step Limited
Whitmore and White Limited

47300 Retail sale of automotive fuel in specialised stores
STM Traders & Services Ltd

47410 Retail sale of computers, peripheral units and software in specialised stores
N.Double and Co Ltd

47421 Retail sale of mobile telephones
BLSN Limited

47520 Retail sale of hardware, paints and glass in specialised stores
Lindisfarne Limited

47530 Retail sale of carpets, rugs, wall and floor coverings in specialised stores
Carpet Bagger Limited

47599 Retail of furniture, lighting, and similar (not musical instruments or scores) in specialised store
AMC Trading Co Ltd

47620 Retail sale of newspapers and stationery in specialised stores
Most Popular Limited
Mzansi UK Ltd

47630 Retail sale of music and video recordings in specialised stores
Bristol Records Limited

47640 Retail sale of sports goods, fishing gear, camping goods, boats and bicycles
AMC Trading Co Ltd

47650 Retail sale of games and toys in specialised stores
AMC Trading Co Ltd

47710 Retail sale of clothing in specialised stores
Bristol Records Limited
Bump Events U.K Limited
Domal Trading Limited
Low-Key Essentials Ltd
Rich & Bad Ltd

47750 Retail sale of cosmetic and toilet articles in specialised stores
Ababio Express Limited
Do Trading Limited
Low-Key Essentials Ltd
Vett Limited

47770 Retail sale of watches and jewellery in specialised stores
Anglocolombian Ltd
Emthea Ltd

47781 Retail sale in commercial art galleries
Camis International Trading Co., Ltd.

47791 Retail sale of antiques including antique books in stores
Do Trading Limited

47799 Retail sale of other second-hand goods in stores (not incl. antiques)
Bacchus Wine Auctions Limited

47810 Retail sale via stalls and markets of food, beverages and tobacco products [59]
11:11 Gin Ltd
8000 Vintages Limited
Angel Feathers Limited
Bath Gin Co Ltd
Be Hop Ltd
Beacon Wines Limited
Beverage Boutique Ltd
Blush Gin Distrubutors UK Ltd
Bobby Beer Co Ltd
Brewland Ltd
Caps Off Ltd.
Cartwright Brothers Vintners Ltd
Cashew Apple Co Ltd
Corfu SW Limited
Creative Juices Bar Limited
Creative Juices Brewing Co Ltd
DTB Distribution Ltd
Deco Spirits Limited
Deer & Badger Ltd
Drum and Black Rum Co Ltd
Eastern Pantry Ltd
Empress Ale Ltd
Evolution Drinks Ltd
Forest Hill Brewing Co Ltd
Ginvino Ltd
Glennlay & Co Ltd
Good Spirits Ltd
H Harwood Ltd
Hobros Limited
Ineffable LDN Limited
Nicholas James Gin Ltd
Lincolnshire Gin Ltd
Little Grape Co Ltd
Little White Dog Limited
London Spiced Dry Limited
Love and Labour Ltd.
Mamada Ltd
Medicare Health & Energy Drinks Ltd
Modern Botanicals Limited
North West Industries Ltd
Ohsake Ltd
Perth Distillery Co Ltd
Pipehouse Gin Limited
Premier UK Trading Limited
Rexon Group Festivals Limited
Saltrock Brewing Co Ltd
Sheffield Brewers Collective
Shellys Drinks Limited
Shy Simba Ltd
Swimming Pigs Ltd.
Thameside Rum Co Ltd
Tipple Spirits Co Ltd
Veini Wine Co Ltd
Vinolex Ltd
Wallis Ventures Ltd
Wetherby Brew Co Limited
Winecraft Ltd
Worsley Gin Ltd
Wyld Rose Ltd

47820 Retail sale via stalls and markets of textiles, clothing and footwear
Above Brand Limited

47890 Retail sale via stalls and markets of other goods
Best of Hungary Ltd
Famille Clarke Limited
KC Brothers Ltd
Official Box Office UK Ltd
Shellys Drinks Limited

47910 Retail sale via mail order houses or via Internet [113]
101 Reykjavik UK Ltd
11:11 Gin Ltd
3 Barrel Co Ltd
3 Big Dogs Limited
8 Barrels Club Ltd
Alegri Trade Ltd.
Alky Limited
Allum Limited
Balcony Wines Ltd
Bath Gin Co Ltd
Be Hop Ltd
Be My Wine Ltd.
Best of Hungary Ltd
Bihl Ltd
Birds of Arcadia Ltd
Bourne & Co Solutions Ltd
Brix & Porter Ltd.
Brown Bear Tales Ltd
CMT (Wines) Limited
William Cadenhead Limited
Cador Limited
Caps Off Ltd.
Cashew Apple Co Ltd
Champagne Company (UK) Limited
Co Stars London Ltd
Colorado Craft Spirits Ltd
Dudley Craig Wines Limited
F & M Cressi Limited
Cromfine Limited
Deliverance Dot Com Limited
Delivered Drinks Limited
Delivering Happiness Limited
Dionysius Importers Ltd
Drinks Depot Ltd
Drinks Direct Limited
Drinks Emporium Limited
Drinks21 Ltd
Eebria Limited
Empress Ale Ltd
Famille Clarke Limited
Fiji Store Ltd
Fine Wine World Ltd
GS Wines Ltd
GSYB Ltd
Georges de la Chapelle Limited
Ginvino Ltd
Glacon Limited
Gleneagles Distillery Limited
Goldy Gin Limited
H Harwood Ltd
Helluva... Limited
Hop Hideout Limited
Humo International Limited
Hunter Douglas Scotch Whisky Ltd
Il Tastevin Ltd
Invino Vitalis Ltd
Jaded Group Limited

Nicholas James Gin Ltd
Just Miniatures Limited
Andrew Laing & Co Ltd
Late Night Liquor Ltd
Little Grape Co Ltd
Little White Dog Limited
Maiden Wines Limited
Medusa Wines Ltd
Minarda General Trade Ltd
Novus BH Magister Ltd
Nutricont Ltd
Old Cellar Ltd
Ourglass & Partners Ltd
Oxford Beer House Limited
Padstow Brewing Company (2013) Ltd
Panda Trading International Ltd
Parthenon Import Co Ltd
Pastai di Serino Italian Food and Wine Excellence
Perth Distillery Co Ltd
Piaff Trading UK Limited
Pipehouse Gin Limited
Christopher Piper Wines Ltd
Portavadie Distillery Limited
Prosit Wines Limited
Quicksip Ltd
Quintessential Decadence Ltd
Raven Spirits Limited
Reids Gold Brewing Co Ltd
Scrawny Al Ltd
Seth Ventures Limited
Shieling Scotch Whisky Co Ltd
Signature Wine Gifts Ltd
Six Rivers Limited
Sourceror Ltd
Speciality Drinks Limited
Stag Brewery Ltd
Super Brit Bery Ltd
Swimming Pigs Ltd.
Swissgrapes Limited
Symposia Wine Limited
Tengu Sake Limited
Tipple Spirits Co Ltd
Tokaj Merchants Ltd
VIP Bottles Ltd
Vinolex Ltd
Vinorium Limited
Vinos Latinos Ltd
Wedgbury Connections Ltd
Whiskies from Scotland Limited
Whisky 78 Ltd
Wine Prophets Limited
Wineman (UK) Ltd
WinesOnline Ltd
Worsley Gin Ltd
Yapp Brothers Limited
Zetas Ventures Ltd

47990 Other retail sale not in stores, stalls or markets [34]
8000 Vintages Limited
Angel Feathers Limited
Ascott Invest Limited
Attitude Spirits Ltd
Barrique Vintners Limited
Beverage Boutique Ltd
Birds of Arcadia Ltd
Buchanan Wines Ltd.
Chillwines Limited
Co.Bru Limited
Crafty Pint Limited
DT1 Ltd

Drunk Maitre D Limited
Famille Clarke Limited
Fine Wine World Ltd
Finebatch Limited
GS Wines Ltd
Galloping Wine Nose Limited
Gelston Castle Fine Wines Ltd
Gill's Drams Ltd.
Late Night Liquor Ltd
Liquid Market Limited
MK Wine Art Ltd
Meless Group Limited
Minarda General Trade Ltd
Quantum Vintners Limited
Red Squirrel Wine Ltd.
Signature Wine Gifts Ltd
Tipsy Tea Limited
UK Beer & Soft Drinks Ltd
Vin-X Enterprise Investment Scheme Ltd
David J. Watt (Fine Wines) Ltd
Wine Enterprise Investment Scheme
Zachicado Ltd

49410 Freight transport by road
C & E Transport Ltd
Expert Euro Exports Ltd
Full Logistic Ltd
OX Bespoke Logistics Ltd
Polskie Wodki Ltd
Tipple Transport Limited
John Toma TDE Ltd

49420 Removal services
Dracula Wine House Ltd

50200 Sea and coastal freight water transport
J.Braham Everett Imports Ltd
Jascera UK Ltd
ZLCSolutions Ltd

50300 Inland passenger water transport
Bosworthcruises Ltd

52102 Operation of warehousing and storage facilities for air transport activities
106 Business Solutions Limited

52103 Operation of warehousing and storage facilities for land transport activities [18]
Atom Brands Limited
Atom Cask Holdings Limited
Atom Drinks Limited
Atom Group Limited
Atom Scotland Limited
Bridge Vintners Limited
Coleburn Distillery Limited
Dr Dougan (Enterprises) Ltd
Glow Glow Ltd.
Lanchester Wine Cellars Ltd
Logistic Park Ltd
Master of Malt Limited
Masters of Malt Limited
Maverick Brands Limited
Maverick Drinks Limited
Maverick Spirits Limited
OX Bespoke Logistics Ltd
United Supplies Limited

52243 Cargo handling for land transport activities
Expert Euro Exports Ltd

52290 Other transportation support activities
Alinari Ltd
Amore G.N.A. Limited
Beverage Boutique Ltd
Caribswede Ltd
Graysons Freight Services Ltd
International Wine Emporium Ltd.
OX Bespoke Logistics Ltd

55100 Hotels and similar accommodation
S.A.Brain & Co Ltd
Chateau Khornabuji Limited
Circus Enjoy with Us Ltd
Morgan Jupe Limited
Shepherd Neame Limited

56101 Licenced restaurants [34]
At The Group Ltd
Be My Wine Ltd.
Be Rude Not To Ltd
Beacon Wines Limited
Broadway Drinks Co Ltd
Buffet Restaurant Northampton Ltd
Chateau Khornabuji Limited
Circus Enjoy with Us Ltd
Cochin Heritage Ltd
Connecting Italian Food UK Ltd
Copper and Rye Leisure Ltd
Dallyla Ltd
Davy & Co Ltd
FFM Pasta Co Ltd
Foodiebusters Epic Food Authority Ltd
Fourteen Drops Ltd
Hall & Woodhouse Limited
Humble Group Ltd
I'll Ask The Boys Ltd
Kanpai (London) Food and Beverage Management Co.,
Lavinia UK Limited
London Calling Sweden Ltd
London SCC Group Ltd
Love and Labour Ltd.
MCAL Merchant Limited
MJM Hospitality Ltd
Mina Collection Ltd
Ryder Partners Limited
Single Cask Ltd
Smith & Harris Enterprises Ltd.
Vinature Ltd
Whiskey and Bourbon Club Ltd
Whisky Work Play Ltd
Wine Prophets Limited

56102 Unlicenced restaurants and cafes
Amirante Empire Limited
Artizen Raw Ltd
Bassrap Ltd
Bristol Records Limited
Chateau Khornabuji Limited
Eastcoast Supplies Ltd.
London Ale UK Ltd
London Calling Sweden Ltd

56103 Take-away food shops and mobile food stands [12]
Artizen Raw Ltd
Bournemouth Food Ltd
Brian Traders Ltd
Dallyla Ltd
FFM Pasta Co Ltd
Kapaka Limited
Lazy Hare Limited
London Calling Sweden Ltd
Mad Batchers Ltd
Mamada Ltd
North West Industries Ltd
Smith & Harris Enterprises Ltd.

56210 Event catering activities [42]
3F Leisure Limited
97 Catering Ltd
After Eight Alcohol Concierge Ltd
Apex Dispense Limited
Bang The Elephant Brewing Co Ltd
Be Hop Ltd
Cold Formd Ltd
Crabtrees Craft Pubs and Bottle Merchants
Deer & Badger Ltd
Dionysius Importers Ltd
Draught Services Ltd
Firewater Merchants Ltd
Frizzenti Limited
Fyre Festival UK Ltd
Glo-Rum Enterprise Limited
Glugged! Ltd
I'll Ask The Boys Ltd
Indian Ice Gola Co Ltd
Jin Bar Ltd
Kolden Ltd
Modern Botanicals Limited
N20winery Ltd
Near Beer Brewing Co. Ltd
Nielsen McKinsey Global Tourism & Hospitality Consulting
Nordic Imports Ltd
Obadec Enterprises Limited
Old Empire Events Ltd
Popaball Limited
Portuguese Winery Limited
Pure Techno Ltd
Sober Limited
Spiritory Ltd
St James's Fine Wine Limited
Street Food & Beverages Co Ltd
Swinging Vine Ltd
Themirtis Limited
Titanic Holdings Japan Ltd
Ultimate Drinks Limited
Uncharted Wine Co Ltd.
Vinolex Ltd
Werfa Holdings Ltd
Wine Pantry (Wholesale) Ltd

56290 Other food services [42]
AK Cash & Carry Ltd
ANM Trading Limited
Alky Limited
Ana Express Ltd
Asia-Pacific 11230699 Vitamin Beverage Co., Azurapada Worldwide Ltd
Best Price Retail and Wholesale Ltd
Buffet Restaurant Northampton Ltd
C & D Wines Limited
Casa Cocktails Limited
Cascriva Ltd
Chez Antoine Ltd
Concordia Wines Ltd
Consulting & Food Ltd
Cyprian Services Limited
Deer & Badger Ltd
Diffusion Food By Pina Co Ltd
Eastcoast Supplies Ltd.
Essex Catering Supplies Ltd
FFM Pasta Co Ltd
Foodiebusters Epic Food Authority Ltd
Fyre Festival UK Ltd
Gordons (Bolton) Limited
Hellenic Agora Limited
Indian Ice Gola Co Ltd
Kolden Ltd
Laurito Ltd
Mamada Ltd
McKenzie Fine Wines Limited
Moa Group Ltd
Panda Oriental Supermarket Ltd
Portuguese Winery Limited
RRK Supplies Limited
Relaxandrinks Limited
Separateflow Limited
Sips 'n' Nibbles Ltd
Street Food & Beverages Co Ltd
Tolmid International Ltd
Tops Food and Wine Limited
Uncle Nearest Ltd.
Vinnaturo Ltd
WSB Investment and Consultancy Ltd

56301 Licenced clubs
Beets Incorporated Ltd

56302 Public houses and bars [71]
23 High Path Ltd
Apex Dispense Limited
Arkell's Brewery Limited
B Wines Limited
Bang The Elephant Brewing Co Ltd
Be Rude Not To Ltd
Beacon Wines Limited
Beer Seller Ltd
Belvoir Brewery Limited
Bihl Ltd
Blackcattaverns Ltd
S.A.Brain & Co Ltd
Brewland Ltd
Brindle Distillery Limited
Broadway Drinks Co Ltd
Buzz Drinks Limited
Caps Off Ltd.
Chaps Group Limited
Circus Enjoy with Us Ltd
Crabtrees Craft Pubs and Bottle Merchants
Craft Beer Collaborative Ltd
Craft Locals Limited
Crafty Pint Limited
Davy & Co Ltd
Donnington Brewery Limited
EJ Orendale Ltd
Epiphany Bars Limited
Everards Brewery Limited
Fabijhon Wine Ltd
Fizz Guru Limited
Fyre Festival UK Ltd
Gergovie Wines Limited
Gort Inn Ltd
Hall & Woodhouse Limited
Halton Turner Brewing Co Ltd
Hop To The Vine Limited
Hopper House Brew Farm Ltd
House of Hops Limited
Hydes' Brewery Limited
Jin Bar Ltd
Jub Club Top Bar Ltd
KRW Leisure Limited
Kinkell Brewery Ltd
LVB Limited
Laughing Pug Ltd
Le Vignoble Ltd
London Ale UK Ltd
London SCC Group Ltd
MCAL Merchant Limited
MCAL Sweet Retail Limited
Magic F & F Ltd
Malthouse Inns PLC
Neilward Ltd
Olivers Wine Agency Limited
Publik Wine Limited
Renwick MacDonald Bars Ltd
Riding Wine Co Ltd
Shandy Shack Ltd
Shepherd Neame Limited
Single Cask Ltd
Snobby's Ltd
St.Austell Brewery Co Ltd
Steel Coulson Ltd
Tom's Tap and Brewhouse Ltd
Triple Point Brewing Ltd
Uva Hitchin Ltd
Wadworth and Co Ltd
Wee Vinoteca Ltd
Charles Wells,Limited
Whisky Work Play Ltd
Wine House Warwick Limited

58142 Publishing of consumer and business journals and periodicals
Kindred Spirit Partnership Ltd

58190 Other publishing activities
Invino Vitalis Ltd
Largesse Corporate Gifts (2007) Ltd
Sarah Marsh Ltd

59111 Motion picture production activities
Cuba Trading Co Ltd
Swipe (Wine) Limited

59113 Television programme production activities
Cuba Trading Co Ltd
Swipe (Wine) Limited

59120 Motion picture, video and television programme post-production activities
Domal Trading Limited

59133 Television programme distribution activities
Swipe (Wine) Limited

59200 Sound recording and music publishing activities
Bump Events U.K Limited

61100 Wired telecommunications activities
Andreev Services Ltd

61200 Wireless telecommunications activities
Domal Trading Limited

62012 Business and domestic software development
Ascott Invest Limited
Drinksbot Limited
John Greenacre Limited

62020 Information technology consultancy activities [14]
Ascott Invest Limited
BDDR Enterprises Limited
CPC Business Limited
CRC Delta Ltd
Ephemeris Solutions Ltd
Georges de la Chapelle Limited
John Greenacre Limited
JSF Services Limited
Leo Global Limited
Present Tense Limited
Sandhu IT Services Ltd
Scrawny Al Ltd
Vinny Labs Ltd
Xi-Spain Ltd

62090 Other information technology service activities
TPDirect Ltd

63120 Web portals
Afco Traders Ltd
BDDR Enterprises Limited
Champagnehub Limited
Riedango Limited

63990 Other information service activities n.e.c.
Asiana Mart Limited

64205 Activities of financial services holding companies
S.A.R.D.V.M Ltd

64209 Activities of other holding companies n.e.c.
Angel Wine & Spirit Group Co., Ltd.
Cornish Rum Co Ltd

64991 Security dealing on own account
Graftyset Limited

64999 Financial intermediation not elsewhere classified
Caribswede Ltd

68100 Buying and selling of own real estate
Buzwine Limited
Cosmic Services Limited
Gordons (Bolton) Limited
Itedomum (UK) Ltd
Lamba Trading Co. Limited
N.Double and Co Ltd
Quartz Group Scotland Ltd

68201 Renting and operating of Housing Association real estate
J. & J. Hunter Limited
Innspired Taverns Limited
Itedomum (UK) Ltd

68209 Other letting and operating of own or leased real estate [22]
W.H. Brakspear & Sons Limited
Cacheflow Ltd
Cromfine Limited
Empire Star Limited
Hameed Investments Limited
Hydes' Brewery Limited
IKP Trading Limited
Lamba Trading Co. Limited
Lanark House Investments Ltd
Loughborough Student Services Ltd
Manzi Developments Limited
Mieland Limited
Morgan Jupe Limited
N.Double and Co Ltd
Nickolls & Perks Limited
Orsa Major Ltd
Quartz Group Scotland Ltd
Redoor Limited
Squarewalk Limited
Tewaina Ltd
UK Lesiure Ltd
Waters (1802) Limited

68310 Real estate agencies
Buzwine Limited
Impexpo Ltd
Itedomum (UK) Ltd
Lizard Management Ltd

68320 Management of real estate on a fee or contract basis
Buzwine Limited
Hameed Investments Limited
Morley Way Limited
Nene Charter Co Ltd
Prostimo Ltd
South Downs Real Estate Ltd

69109 Activities of patent and copyright agents; other legal activities n.e.c.
Glenforest Limited

69201 Accounting and auditing activities
PFS Business Services Limited

69202 Bookkeeping activities
106 Business Solutions Limited

69203 Tax consultancy
Ephemeris Solutions Ltd

70100 Activities of head offices
David Berryman Holdings Ltd
Buchanan Wines Ltd.
Burn Stewart (U.S. Holdings) Ltd
Diageo Great Britain Limited
General Bilimoria Wines Ltd
Tanners (Shrewsbury) Limited
Vickbar Limited
Wein Forum - Fine Wines Ltd

70210 Public relations and communications activities
Cascade Trade Services Ltd
F & B Premium Brands Limited
Titanic Wines Limited

70221 Financial management
Blue Marble Consultants Ltd
Ephemeris Solutions Ltd
Fine Wine Works Limited
Hayloft Ventures Ltd

70229 Management consultancy activities other than financial management [58]
A & G Management Consultancy Ltd
A-Holding Ltd
Belabon Drinks Ltd
Broadoak Cider Co Ltd
Cacheflow Ltd
Cascade Trade Services Ltd
Circle View Business Consultancy Ltd
Colchester Mann Limited
Consulting & Food Ltd
Craft Locals Limited
F & B Premium Brands Limited
Fine Wine Works Limited
Finebatch Limited
Franchiserv Limited
Freerun Consulting Limited
Freixenet Copestick Limited
Glenforest Limited
Global Trade & Consulting Ltd
Graftyset Limited
Grape Wines Services Ltd
Hayloft Ventures Ltd
I8 MGT Limited
IKP Trading Limited
Imbibros Ltd
In Wine & Spirit Solutions, Ltd
Inside Trax Limited
International Wine Emporium Ltd.
Knight Trade (Oakham) Limited
Laurence Leisure Limited
Laurus Brands Limited
MMC Sales and Marketing Ltd
MMGT Limited
Markets It Ltd.
Martin Enterprises Limited
Maverick Ventures UK Ltd
Moa Group Ltd
Morley Way Limited
Nene Charter Co Ltd
Nielsen McKinsey Global Tourism & Hospitality Consulting
Nightrep Limited
Orsa Major Ltd
PFG Marketing Ltd
Perfect Pair Wines Ltd
Personalised Care Solutions Ltd
Ripped Earth Wines Limited
Shamboozle Limited
Smiley Rhyme Limited
T.W.S Wines Ltd
Tech-Beach UK Limited
Titanic Wines Limited
Uropa Group Ltd
VDK Import Export Limited
Valinch & Mallet Limited
Vickbar Limited
Vin Est... Ltd
WSB Investment and Consultancy Ltd

Wine Rascals Yorkshire Limited
Zetas Ventures Ltd

71121 Engineering design activities for industrial process and production
Bone Machine Brewing Co Ltd

71122 Engineering related scientific and technical consulting activities
Drumgaw Holdings Ltd
Nightrep Limited

71129 Other engineering activities
Bulgarsko Pivo Limited
Second Eger Ltd

71200 Technical testing and analysis
Lynch Associates Ltd

72190 Other research and experimental development on natural sciences and engineering
Bulgarsko Pivo Limited

73110 Advertising agencies
11:11 Gin Ltd
Aizia Ltd
Inconcept Ltd
NJA Marketing Ltd
Present Tense Limited
Russian Investment II Limited
Ultra Premium Drinks Limited
Wine Group Ltd

73120 Media representation services
Gin Cooperative Ltd

73200 Market research and public opinion polling
Ftspot Limited
Uropa Group Ltd
Xi-Spain Ltd

74100 Specialised design activities [11]
Bowsaw Bourbon Limited
Chalk & Charcoal Limited
Drinksology Limited
Kirker & Greer Whiskey Limited
Library Design Studio Ltd.
Made To Measure Ltd
Mayday Island Limited
McGrath's Brewing Limited
Red Bonny Rum Limited
Sailortown Brewing Limited
Spalathos Ltd.

74202 Other specialist photography
Mojito Bar Ltd

74209 Photographic activities not elsewhere classified
Mojito Bar Ltd

74300 Translation and interpretation activities
Interlink UK Exports Limited

74909 Other professional, scientific and technical activities n.e.c.
Malt Whisky Co Ltd

74990 Non-trading company
Bunnahabhain Distillery Co Ltd
Distell Europe Ltd.
Gordon Graham & Co Ltd
If Eaglesham Ltd
Imperial Distillers Co. Ltd
Smith & Humpston Ltd

77110 Renting and leasing of cars and light motor vehicles
Cacheflow Ltd

77291 Renting and leasing of media entertainment equipment
Quartz Group Scotland Ltd

77390 Renting and leasing of other machinery, equipment and tangible goods n.e.c.
Apex Dispense Limited
Draught Services Ltd

77400 Leasing of intellectual property and similar products, except copyright works
Haycock's Drinks Co Ltd

78109 Other activities of employment placement agencies
K & A Eagle Limited

78200 Temporary employment agency activities
Lux Ex Dignitas Limited

78300 Human resources provision and management of human resources functions
Outstanding People Limited

79110 Travel agency activities
Easy9 Limited
VDK Import Export Limited

79120 Tour operator activities
Caribbean Trade Ltd
Golden Whisky Limited
Morgan Jupe Limited
Mr. Alba International Trading Co Ltd
Spainorama Ltd

79901 Activities of tourist guides
Perscot Ltd

79909 Other reservation service activities n.e.c.
Golden Whisky Limited
Riedango Limited

80100 Private security activities
Bopfags Services Ltd
MPS 64 Ltd
Natural Marketing Ltd

80200 Security systems service activities
B & F Enterprise UK Ltd
Extravision Security Systems Ltd

80300 Investigation activities
B & F Enterprise UK Ltd

81210 General cleaning of buildings
New Age Wines Ltd

81299 Other cleaning services
Cyprian Services Limited

81300 Landscape service activities
Michel Couvreur (Scotch Whiskies)
V & A Jobs UK Ltd

82110 Combined office administrative service activities
Best of Beaujolais Limited
Best of Loire Limited
Lesont Ltd

82200 Activities of call centres
Ark Inta Ltd

82301 Activities of exhibition and fair organisers
Invino Vitalis Ltd
Lizard Management Ltd
MMC Sales and Marketing Ltd
Sotus Limited

82920 Packaging activities
Deliverance Dot Com Limited
Delivering Happiness Limited
Distell International Limited
Fill Macan Limited
Greencroft Bottling Co Ltd
MBW Traders Ltd
Phil Macan Limited

82990 Other business support service activities n.e.c. [22]
Beer Company Consolidations Ltd
Bombay Spirits Co Ltd
Carob Tree Limited
Cascade Trade Services Ltd
Coles Trading Limited
Collins Wines Limited
F & M Cressi Limited
Crudo Limited
D.C Enterprises (Import/Export) Ltd
Dourthe UK Limited
Draught Services Ltd
Laravita Ltd
MMC Sales and Marketing Ltd
Prasad Trading Co Ltd
Schuler Wine St. Jakob's Cellars Ltd
Superba London Wines Ltd
Swallow (Soft Drinks, Beer and Cider Wholesalers)
Bertrand Tailor Limited
V G International Trading Ltd
West End Brands Ltd
West End Drinks Limited
Wyld Rose Ltd

84300 Compulsory social security activities
Dorys Shop Ltd

85510 Sports and recreation education
Artizen Raw Ltd

85520 Cultural education
Drinks Emporium Limited
Fine Wine Works Limited
Jaded Group Limited

85590 Other education n.e.c.
AB Care Connect Limited
Drunk Maitre D Limited
Heronsgate 7 Limited
Kindred Spirit Partnership Ltd
Symposia Wine Limited
Woburn Wine Co Ltd

85600 Educational support services
Redoor Limited
Smiley Rhyme Limited

86210 General medical practice activities
Aziken Ventures Limited

86900 Other human health activities
Easy9 Limited

88910 Child day-care activities
Loughborough Student Services Ltd

90010 Performing arts
Old Red Lion Theatre Pub Ltd

90020 Support activities to performing arts
Beets Incorporated Ltd

93110 Operation of sports facilities
West End Brands Ltd

93199 Other sports activities
Bihl Ltd

93290 Other amusement and recreation activities n.e.c.
Bump Events U.K Limited
Official Box Office UK Ltd
Park Royal Wholesale Limited

94110 Activities of business and employers membership organisations
Alinari Ltd

94910 Activities of religious organisations
Kairos Solutions Ltd

94990 Activities of other membership organisations n.e.c.
Alinari Ltd

96020 Hairdressing and other beauty treatment
Do Trading Limited
Sam-Gel Global Ventures Ltd

96090 Other service activities n.e.c. [15]
A & G Management Consultancy Ltd
Alternative Rum Co Ltd
Bar Joker Ltd
Cask Trade Ltd
Ely & Sidney Limited
Ian MacBarrel & Spirits Ltd
Lisaavo Ltd
Main Rum Co Ltd
PPbeer Ltd.
R. St Barth Limited
Refresh 24 Group Limited
Schoenlaub Limited
Tolmid International Ltd
Whisky Galore Limited
ZLCSolutions Ltd

98000 Residents property management
Bulgarsko Pivo Limited
Laravita Ltd
Lizard Management Ltd

99999 Dormant company
Bedford Continental Wholesale Ltd
Coleburn Distillery Limited
Curious Wine Cellar Limited
Hidden Gem - Urban Artisan Spirit Ltd
Thorn-Clarke Wines (UK) Ltd
Traditional Italian Wine Co Ltd

This page is intentionally left blank

Printed in 8pt Nimbus Sans L

Designed by URW++ Design and Development GmbH

Dellam Publishing Limited

2 Heath Drive, Sutton, Surrey, SM2 5RP

Fax: 020 8770 7478   email: enquiries@dellam.com

SAN: 0177881   EAN/GLN: 5030670177882